高等院校双语教学适用教材

工商管理

Research Methods for Business Students

Seventh Edition

Mark Saunders Philip Lewis Adrian Thornhill

（第7版）

研究方法

为商科学生量身定制

［英］马克·桑德斯　菲利普·刘易斯　阿德里安·桑希尔　著

张宜霞　余宇莹　译注

东北财经大学出版社
Dongbei University of Finance & Economics Press
大连

辽宁省版权局著作权合同登记号:图字06-2017-144号

图书在版编目（CIP）数据

研究方法：为商科学生量身定制：第七版 / （英）马克·桑德斯（Mark Saunders）等著；张宜霞，余宇莹译注. —影印版. —大连：东北财经大学出版社，2018.5
（高等院校双语教学适用教材·工商管理）
ISBN 978-7-5654-3117-3

Ⅰ．研… Ⅱ．①马… ②张… ③余… Ⅲ．经济管理-研究方法-双语教学-高等学校-教材 Ⅳ．F2-3

中国版本图书馆CIP数据核字（2018）第048917号

东北财经大学出版社出版发行
　　大连市黑石礁尖山街217号　邮政编码　116025
　　网　　　址：http://www.dufep.cn
　　读者信箱：dufep@dufe.edu.cn
大连图腾彩色印刷有限公司印刷

幅面尺寸：185mm×260mm　字数：1200千字　印张：44　插页：1
2018年5月第1版　　　　2018年5月第1次印刷
责任编辑：刘东威　　　　责任校对：清　灵
封面设计：冀贵收　　　　版式设计：钟福建
定价：96.00元

教学支持　售后服务　　联系电话：（0411）84710309
版权所有　侵权必究　　举报电话：（0411）84710523
如有印装质量问题，请联系营销部：（0411）84710711

简要目录

目 录

Brief contents

Contents

Contents

Supporting resources

Visit **www.pearsoned.co.uk/saunders** to find valuable online resources:

Companion Website for students

- Multiple-choice questions to test your learning
- Tutorials and datasets for Excel, NVivo and SPSS
- Updated research datasets to practise with
- Updated additional case studies with accompanying questions
- Smarter Online Searching Guide – how to make the most of the Internet in your research
- Online glossary

For instructors

- Complete, downloadable Instructor's Manual
- PowerPoint slides that can be downloaded and used for presentations

Also: The regularly maintained Companion Website provides the following features:

- Search tool to help locate specific items of content
- Email results and profile tools to send results of quizzes to instructors
- Online help and support to assist with website usage and troubleshooting

For more information please contact your local Pearson Education sales representative or visit www.pearsoned.co.uk/saunders.

Research Methods for Business Students

How to use this book

This book is written with a progressive logic, which means that terms and concepts are defined when they are first introduced. One implication of this is that it is sensible for you to start at the beginning and to work your way through the text, various boxes, self-check questions, review and discussion questions, case studies and case study questions. You can do this in a variety of ways depending on your reasons for using this book. However, this approach may not necessarily be suitable for your purposes, and you may wish to read the chapters in a different order or just dip into particular sections of the book. If this is true for you then you will probably need to use the glossary to check that you understand some of the terms and concepts used in the chapters you read. Suggestions for three of the more common ways in which you might wish to use this book follow.

As part of a research methods course or for self-study for your research project

If you are using this book as part of a research methods course the order in which you read the chapters is likely to be prescribed by your tutors and dependent upon their perceptions of your needs. Conversely, if you are pursuing a course of self-study for your research project, dissertation or consultancy report, the order in which you read the chapters is your own choice. However, whichever of these you are, we would argue that the order in which you read the chapters is dependent upon your recent academic experience.

For many students, such as those taking an undergraduate degree in business or management, the research methods course and associated project, dissertation or consultancy report comes in either the second or the final year of study. In such situations it is probable that you will follow the chapter order quite closely (see Figure P.1). Groups of chapters within which we believe you can switch the order without affecting the logic of the flow too much are shown on the same level in this diagram and are:

- those associated with data collection (Chapters 8, 9, 10 and 11);
- those associated with data analysis (Chapters 12 and 13).

Within the book we emphasise the importance of beginning to write early on in the research process as a way of clarifying your thoughts. In Chapter 1 we encourage you to keep a reflective diary, notebook or journal throughout the research process so it is helpful to read this chapter early on. We recommend you also read the sections in Chapter 14 on writing prior to starting to draft your critical review of the literature (Chapter 3).

Alternatively, you may be returning to academic study after a gap of some years, to take a full-time or part-time course such as a Master of Business Administration, a Master of Arts or a Master of Science with a Business and Management focus. Many students in such situations need to refresh their study skills early in their programme, particularly those associated with critical reading of academic literature and academic writing. If you

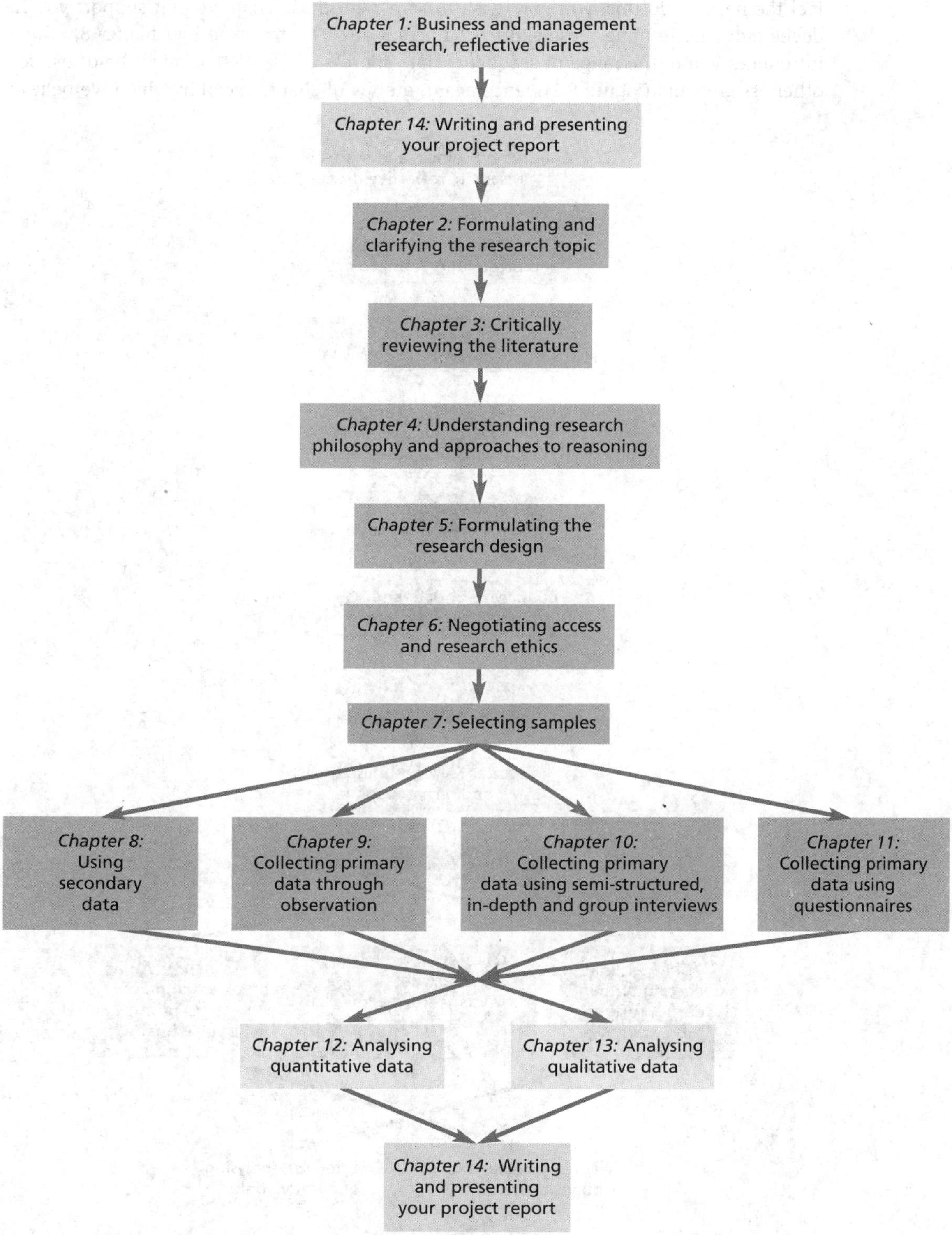

Chapter 1: Business and management
research, reflective diaries

Chapter 14: Writing and presenting
your project report

Chapter 2: Formulating and
clarifying the research topic

Chapter 3: Critically
reviewing the literature

Chapter 4: Understanding research
philosophy and approaches to reasoning

Chapter 5: Formulating the
research design

Chapter 6: Negotiating access
and research ethics

Chapter 7: Selecting samples

Chapter 8:
Using
secondary
data

Chapter 9:
Collecting primary
data through
observation

Chapter 10:
Collecting primary
data using semi-structured,
in-depth and group interviews

Chapter 11:
Collecting primary
data using
questionnaires

Chapter 12: Analysing
quantitative data

Chapter 13: Analysing
qualitative data

Chapter 14: Writing
and presenting
your project report

Figure P.1 Using this book in your final year of study

feel the need to do this, you may wish to start with those chapters that support you in developing and refining these skills (Chapters 3 and 14), followed by Chapter 8, which introduces you to the range of secondary data sources available that might be of use for other assignments (Figure P.2). Once again, groups of chapters within which we believe

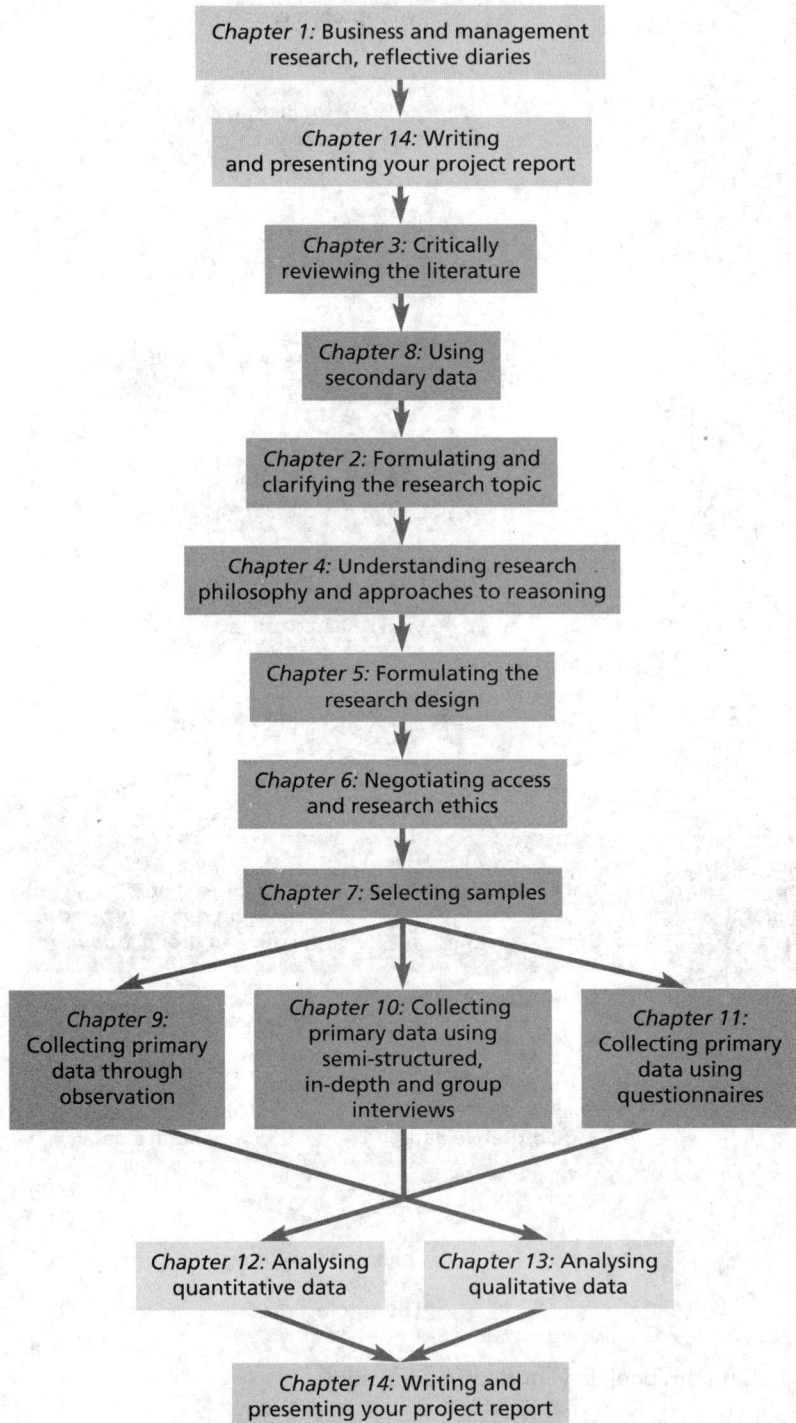

```
┌─────────────────────────────────────┐
│ Chapter 1: Business and management   │
│     research, reflective diaries     │
└─────────────────────────────────────┘
                   ↓
┌─────────────────────────────────────┐
│       Chapter 14: Writing            │
│ and presenting your project report   │
└─────────────────────────────────────┘
                   ↓
┌─────────────────────────────────────┐
│       Chapter 3: Critically          │
│      reviewing the literature        │
└─────────────────────────────────────┘
                   ↓
┌─────────────────────────────────────┐
│        Chapter 8: Using              │
│          secondary data              │
└─────────────────────────────────────┘
                   ↓
┌─────────────────────────────────────┐
│  Chapter 2: Formulating and          │
│ clarifying the research topic        │
└─────────────────────────────────────┘
                   ↓
┌─────────────────────────────────────┐
│ Chapter 4: Understanding research    │
│ philosophy and approaches to reasoning│
└─────────────────────────────────────┘
                   ↓
┌─────────────────────────────────────┐
│    Chapter 5: Formulating the        │
│        research design               │
└─────────────────────────────────────┘
                   ↓
┌─────────────────────────────────────┐
│  Chapter 6: Negotiating access       │
│     and research ethics              │
└─────────────────────────────────────┘
                   ↓
┌─────────────────────────────────────┐
│    Chapter 7: Selecting samples      │
└─────────────────────────────────────┘
```

Chapter 9: Collecting primary data through observation

Chapter 10: Collecting primary data using semi-structured, in-depth and group interviews

Chapter 11: Collecting primary data using questionnaires

Chapter 12: Analysing quantitative data

Chapter 13: Analysing qualitative data

Chapter 14: Writing and presenting your project report

Figure P.2 Using this book as a new returner to academic study

you can switch the order without affecting the logic of the flow too much are shown on the same level in the diagram and are:

- those chapters associated with primary data collection (Chapters 9, 10 and 11);
- those associated with data analysis (Chapters 12 and 13).

In addition, we would recommend that you re-read Chapter 14 prior to starting to write your project report, dissertation or consultancy report, or if you need to undertake a presentation.

Whichever order you choose to read the chapters, we would recommend that you attempt all the self-check questions, review and discussion questions and those questions associated with the case studies. Your answers to the self-check questions can be self-assessed using the answers at the end of each chapter. However, we hope that you will actually attempt each question prior to reading the answer! If you need further information on an idea or a technique, then first look at the references in the further reading section.

At the end of each chapter, the section headed 'Progressing your research project' lists a number of tasks. Such tasks might involve you in just planning a research project or, alternatively, designing and administering a questionnaire of your own. They all include making an entry in your reflective diary or notebook. When completed, these tasks will provide a useful aide-mémoire for assessed work (including a reflective essay or learning log) and can be used as the basis for the first draft of your project report. It is worth pointing out here that many consultancy reports for organisations do not require you to include a review of the academic literature.

As a guide through the research process

If you are intending to use this book to guide you through the research process for a research project you are undertaking, such as your dissertation, we recommend that you read the entire book quickly before starting your research. In that way you will have a good overview of the entire process, including the range of techniques available, and will be better able to plan your work.

After you have read the book once, we suggest that you re-read Section 1.5 on keeping a reflective diary or notebook and Sections 14.2–14.6 on writing first. Then work your way through the book again following the chapter order. This time you should attempt the self-check questions, review and discussion questions and those questions associated with each case study to ensure that you have understood the material contained in each chapter prior to applying it to your own research project. Your responses to self-check questions can be assessed using the answers at the end of each chapter.

If you are still unsure as to whether particular techniques, procedures or ideas are relevant, then pay special attention to the 'focus on student research', 'focus on management research' and 'focus on research in the news' boxes. 'Focus on student research' boxes are based on actual students' experiences and illustrate how an issue has been addressed or a technique or procedure used in a student's research project. 'Focus on management research' boxes discuss recent research articles in established refereed academic journals, allowing you to see how research is undertaken successfully. These articles are easily accessible via the main online business and management databases. 'Focus on research in the news' boxes provide topical news stories of how particular research techniques, procedures and ideas are used in the business world. You can also look in the 'further reading' for other examples of research where these have been used. If you need further information on an idea, technique or procedure then, again, start with the references in the further reading section.

Material in some of the chapters is likely to prove less relevant to some research topics than others. However, you should beware of choosing techniques because you are happy with them, if they are inappropriate. Completion of the tasks in the section headed 'Progressing your research project' at the end of Chapters 2–13 will enable you to generate all the material that you will need to include in your research project, dissertation or consultancy report. This will also help you to focus on the techniques and ideas that are most appropriate to your research. When you have completed these tasks for Chapter 14 you will have written your research project, dissertation or consultancy report.

As a reference source

It may be that you wish to use this book now or subsequently as a reference source. If this is the case, an extensive index will point you to the appropriate page or pages. Often you will find a 'checklist' box within these pages. 'Checklist' boxes are designed to provide you with further guidance on the particular topic. You will also find the contents pages and the glossary useful reference sources, the latter defining some 600 research terms. In addition, we have tried to help you to use the book in this way by including cross-references between sections in chapters as appropriate. Do follow these up as necessary. If you need further information on an idea or a technique then begin by consulting the references in the further reading section. Wherever possible we have tried to reference books that are in print and readily available in university libraries and journal articles that are in the major business and management online databases.

Preface

In writing the seventh edition of *Research Methods for Business Students* we have responded to the many comments we have received regarding previous editions. In particular, this has led us to fully revise Chapter 4 to incorporate a new section on the philosophical underpinnings of management research, a discussion of postmodernism and a new reflexive tool (HARP) to help readers heighten their awareness of research philosophies when progressing their research project; Chapter 9 to include new sections on Internet-mediated observation and observation using videography; Chapter 11 to more fully reflect the use of online survey tools; Chapter 13 including restructuring and including a new section on content analysis; Chapter 14 including a new section on writing a reflective essay or section; and to develop further the Glossary, which now includes some 600 research-related terms. New case studies at the end of each chapter have been developed with colleagues, providing up-to-date scenarios through which to illustrate issues associated with undertaking research. Alongside this we have also taken the opportunity to also update examples and revise the tables of Internet addresses.

As in previous editions, we have taken a predominantly non-software-specific approach in our discussion of methods. By doing this, we have been able to focus on the general principles needed to utilise a range of analysis software and the Internet effectively for research. However, recognising that many students have access to sophisticated data-analysis software and may need help in developing these skills, we continue to provide access to up-to-date 'teach yourself' guides to IBM SPSS Statistics™, Excel™, NVivo™ and Internet searching via the book's website (**www.pearsoned.co.uk/saunders**). Where appropriate, these guides are provided with data sets. In the preparation of the seventh edition we were fortunate to receive considerable feedback from colleagues in universities throughout the world. We are extremely grateful to all the reviewers who gave their time and shared their ideas.

Inevitably, the body of knowledge of research methods has developed further since 2012, and we have revised all chapters accordingly. Our experiences of teaching and supervising students and working through the methods in classes have suggested alternative approaches and the need to provide alternative material. Consequently, we have taken the opportunity to update and refine existing worked examples, remove those that were becoming dated, and develop new ones where appropriate. However, the basic structure remains much the same as the previous six editions.

Other minor changes and updating have been made throughout. Needless to say, any errors of omission and commission continue to remain our responsibility.

As with previous editions, much of our updating has been guided by comments from students and colleagues, to whom we are most grateful. We should like particularly to thank students from University of Surrey, Prague University of Economics, and on the Research Methods Summer Schools and Doctoral Symposiums for their comments on all of the chapters. Colleagues in both our own and other universities have continued to provide helpful comments and advice. We are particularly grateful to Andrew

Armitage (Anglia Ruskin University), Murray Clark (Sheffield Hallam University), Sandra Corlett (Northumbria University), Graham Dietz (Durham University), Trevor Morrow (University of Ulster), Alexandros Paraskevas (University of West London), Richard Slack (Durham University), Paul Tosey (Surrey University) and Keith Townsend (Griffith University). Colleagues and friends again deserve thanks for their assistance in providing examples of research across the spectrum of business and management, co-authoring chapters, writing case studies and in reviewing parts of this book: Marie Ashwin (Ecole de Management de Normandie), Frank Bezzina (University of Malta), Alexandra Bristow (University of Surrey), Vincent Cassar (University of Malta), Catherine Cassell (University of Leeds), Gail Clarkson (University of Leeds), Rosanna Cole (Roehampton University), David Denyer (Cranfield University), Alan Hirst (Assumption University), Amanda Lee (Coventry University), Bill Lee (University of Sheffield), Jenny Ma (University of Worcester), Sophie Mills (Coventry University), Miriam Muethel (WHU – Otto Beisheim School of Management), Susann Power (University of Surrey), Noelia-Sarah Reynolds (University of Essex), Céline Rojon (Edinburgh University), Catherine Wang (Royal Holloway, University of London).

The contributions of Lynette Bailey, Darren Bolton and Martin Jenkins to Chapters 3 and 8 and of Andrew Guppy to Chapter 12 in early editions of this book are gratefully acknowledged.

We would also like to thank all of the staff at Pearson (both past and present) who supported us through the process of writing the seventh edition. Our thanks go, in particular, to Tom Hill, our present commissioning editor, and David Harrison, our previous commissioning editor for their support and enthusiasm throughout the process. We would also like to express our thanks to Andrew Muller as desk editor and Annette Abel as copy-editor.

MNKS
PL
AT
May 2015

Contributors

Mark N.K. Saunders, BA, MSc, PGCE, PhD, Chartered FCIPD, is Professor of Business Research Methods in the Birmingham Business School, University of Birmingham. He is a Fellow of the British Academy of Management and member of the Fellows' College. He currently holds visiting professorships at the University of Malta and the University of Worcester. Mark teaches research methods to master's and doctoral students as well as supervising master's dissertations and research degrees. He has published articles on research methods and human resource aspects of the management of change, including trust and organisational learning, in a range of journals such as *Human Relations*, *Journal of Personnel Psychology*, *Journal of Small Business Management*, *Management Learning* and *Social Science and Medicine*. Mark is book series editor of the *Handbooks of Research Methods* (Edward Elgar) and co-series book editor of *Understanding Research Methods for Business and Management Students* (Sage). He is co-author with Phil and Adrian of three further books, all published by Pearson. He is lead editor of *Organizational Trust: A Cultural Perspective* (Cambridge University Press) and co-editor of the *Handbook of Research Methods on Human Resource Development* and the *Handbook of Research Methods on Trust*. Mark has also written two books on business statistics, the most recent being *Statistics: What You Need to Know* (Open University Press), co-authored with Reva Berman-Brown. He continues to undertake consultancy in the public, private and not-for-profit sectors. Prior to becoming an academic, he had a variety of research jobs in the public sector. Mark also enjoys dinghy sailing, hill walking and riding his motorbike.

Philip Lewis, BA, PhD, MSc, Chartered MCIPD, PGDipM, Cert Ed, began his career in HR as a training adviser with the Distributive Industry Training Board. He then taught HRM and research methods in three UK universities. He studied part-time for degrees with the Open University and the University of Bath, from which he gained an MSc in industrial relations and a PhD for his research on performance pay in retail financial services. He is co-author with Adrian and Mark of *Employee Relations: Understanding the Employment Relationship* and with Mark, Adrian, Mike Millmore and Trevor Morrow of *Strategic Human Resource Management* and with Adrian, Mark and Mike Millmore of *Managing Change: A Human Resource Strategy Approach*, all published by Pearson. He has undertaken consultancy in both public and private sectors.

Adrian Thornhill, BA, PhD, PGCE, Chartered FCIPD. Prior to his career as a university lecturer and Head of Department, he worked as an industrial relations researcher and in training and vocational education. He has also undertaken consultancy and training for a range of private- and public-sector organisations. He has taught a range of subjects, including HRM, the management of change and research methods, to undergraduate, postgraduate and professional students. He has experience of supervising undergraduate and postgraduate dissertations, professional management projects and research degrees.

Adrian has published a number of articles principally associated with employee and justice perspectives related to managing change and the management of organisational downsizing and redundancy. He is co-author with Phil and Mark of *Employee Relations: Understanding the Employment Relationship*, with Phil, Mark, Mike Millmore and Trevor Morrow of *Strategic Human Resource Management* and with Phil, Mark and Mike Millmore of *Managing Change: A Human Resource Strategy Approach*, all published by Pearson. He has also co-authored a book on downsizing and redundancy.

Professor Marie Ashwin is Professor of Marketing and Management at the Ecole de Management de Normandie, France.

Dr Frank Bezzina is a Senior Lecturer in Applied Business Statistics and Deputy Dean of the Faculty of Economics, Management and Accountancy, University of Malta.

Dr Alexandra Bristow is a Lecturer in Organisational Behaviour at the University of Surrey.

Dr Gail Clarkson is Lecturer and Subject Group Leader in Organisational Behaviour, Leeds University Business School.

Rosanna Cole is a Lecturer in Business Management at the University of Roehampton Business School.

Dr Vincent Cassar is a Senior Lecturer in Organisational Behaviour in the Department of Management at the University of Malta.

Professor Catherine Cassell is Deputy Dean of Leeds University Business School and Professor of Organisational Psychology.

Professor David Denyer is Professor of Organisational Change and Director of Research at Cranfield School of Management.

Dr Alan Hirst is Visiting Professor of International Business at Assumption University, Bangkok, Thailand.

Amanda Lee is a Senior Lecturer in Human Resource Management at Coventry Business School, Coventry University.

Professor Bill Lee is Professor of Accounting and Head of Accounting and Financial Management Division at The Management School University of Sheffield.

Dr Jenny W. Ma is a Senior Lecturer in Marketing at Worcester Business School, University of Worcester.

Sophie Mills is a Senior Lecturer in Human Resource Management at Coventry Business School, Coventry University.

Professor Dr Miriam Muethel is a Full Professor at WHU – Otto Beisheim School of Management, where she holds the Chair of Organisational Behavior.

Dr Susann Power is a Lecturer in Business Ethics in the School of Hospitality and Tourism Management, University of Surrey.

Dr Noelia-Sarah Reynolds (née Schnurr) is a Lecturer in Strategic Management at Essex Business School, The University of Essex.

Dr Céline Rojon is a Lecturer in Human Resource Management at the University of Edinburgh Business School.

Professor Catherine L. Wang is Professor of Strategy and Entrepreneurship at the School of Management, Royal Holloway, University of London.

Publisher's acknowledgements

We are grateful to the following for permission to reproduce copyright material:

Figures

Figure on page 256 from iTunes silhouette poster; Figure on page 437 from Morrison Bowmore Distillers Ltd; Figures on page 455, page 460 from This question was generated using Qualtrics software, Version 595160.546s of the Qualtrics Research Suite. Copyright © 2014 Qualtrics. Qualtrics and all other Qualtrics product or service names are registered trademarks or trademarks of Qualtrics, Provo, UT, USA. http://www.qualtrics.com. The authors are not affiliated to Qualtrics; Figure on page 477 from Question layout created by SurveyMonkey Europe and its affiliates (2014) Palo Alto, California. Reproduced with permission; Figure 11.2 adapted from *Constructing Questions for Interviews and Questionnaires*, Cambridge University Press (Foddy, W. 1994) Fig. 5.1, p.53; Figure on page 518 adapted from Chart that tells a story - tax summaries, *Financial Times* 06/11/2014 (Palin, A.), © The Financial Times Limited. All Rights Reserved; Figures 12.2, 12.3 from Eurostat (2014) Environment and Energy Statistics, © European Union, 1995-2014; Figure 13.3 adapted from *Discourse and Social Change*, Polity Press (Fairclough, N. 1992) p.73

Screenshots

Screenshot on page 59 from Microsoft Outlook's 'Tasks', Microsoft product screenshot(s) reprinted with permission from Microsoft Corporation; Screenshot on page 71 from 2014 Home Retail Group. Reproduced with permission; Screenshot on page 99 from EBSCO Host; Screenshot on page 103 from Saunders et al. (2014). Copyright © 2014 Emerald Group Publishing (http://www.emeraldinsight.com/journals.htm?issn = 2046-9012&volume = 38& issue = 1&articleid = 17103591&show = html). Reproduced by permission of the publisher; Screenshot on page 337 from Facebook - Morgan Motor Company, 2014; Screenshots on page 340, page 341 from Eurostat (2014) Copyright European Communities, 2014. Reproduced with permission., © European Union, 1995-2014; Screenshot on page 443 from Screenshot created by SurveyMonkey Europe and its affiliates (2014) Palo Alto, Reproduced with permission; Screenshot on page 461 from Question layout created by SurveyMonkey Europe and its affiliates (2014) Palo Alto, California. Reproduced with permission.; Screenshots on page 502, page 504, page 507, page 521, page 522, page 522, page 540, page 549, page 540, page 546, page 550, page 555 from Reprint Courtesy of International Business Machines Corporation, © SPSS, Inc, screenshots reprinted courtesy of International Business Machines Corporation, © SPSS Inc., an IBM Company. SPSS was acquired by IBM in October, 2009. IBM, the IBM logo, ibm.com, and SPSS are trademarks of International Business Machines Corp., registered in many jurisdictions worldwide. Other product and service names might be trademarks of IBM or other companies. A current list of IBM trademarks is available on the Web at "IBM Copyright and trademark information" at www.ibm.com/legal/copytrade.shtml.;

Tables

Text

from Plagiarism storm forces Merkel minister to resign, *Financial Times*, 11/02/2013 (Peel, Q.), © The Financial Times Limited. All Rights Reserved; Box 4.2 adapted from Glastonbury festival, Worthy Farm, Somerset. Review, *Financial Times*, 29/06/2014 (Ludovic Hunter-Tilney), © The Financial Times Limited. All Rights Reserved; Box 5.1 adapted from Middle-aged Britons are so downbeat about money, *Financial Times*, 02/11/2013 (Cohen, N.), © The Financial Times Limited. All Rights Reserved; Box 7.1 from The Art Market: Hopes pitched too high for comfort, *Financial Times*, 08/11/2013 (Adam, G.), © The Financial Times Limited. All Rights Reserved; Box 8.4 adapted from 'The evidence is growing: there really is a business case for diversity, *Financial Times*, 14/05/2014 (Smedley, T.), © The Financial Times Limited. All Rights Reserved; Box 8.10 after Authors' experience; Blumberg et al. (2008); Dale et al. (1988); Dochartaigh (2007); Kervin (1999); Smith (2006); Stewart and Kamins (1993); Box 9.2 after BUSINESS LIFE - WORKING LIVES - Close observers of consumers, *Financial Times*, 20/09/2013 (Jacobs, E.), © The Financial Times Limited. All Rights Reserved; Box 10.16 adapted from The avatar will see you now: interviewers go virtual, *Financial Times*, 23/02/2014 (Bounds, A.), © The Financial Times Limited. All Rights Reserved; Extract on page 348 from Morrison Bowmore Distillers Ltd; Newspaper Headline on page 456 from Masthead, Daily Mail; Newspaper Headline on page 456 from Masthead, Daily Mirror; Newspaper Headline on page 456 from Masthead, Daily Star and Daily Express; Newspaper Headline on page 456 from Masthead, Financial Times, © The Financial Times Limited. All Rights Reserved.; Newspaper Headline on page 456 from Masthead, Daily Telegraph, copyright © Telegraph Media Group Limited; Newspaper Headline on page 456 from Masthead, The Guardian; Newspaper Headline on page 456 from Masthead, The Independent; Newspaper Headline on page 456 from Masthead, The Times & The Sun; Box 11.5 after Piety gives way to secularism and heavy metal worship, *Financial Times*, 15/12/2012 (Engel, M.), © The Financial Times Limited. All Rights Reserved.; Box 11.9 adapted from Salmond's wording on vote for Scotland rejected', Kiran Stacey and Mure Dickie, 31 Jan 2013 *Financial Times*, 31/01/2013 (Stacey, K. & Dickie, M.), © The Financial Times Limited. All Rights Reserved.; Box 12.21 after Global Review - US Advance continues as German data and M&A buoy sentiment, *Financial Times*, 25/11/2014 (Shellock, D.), © The Financial Times Limited. All Rights Reserved; Box 13.6 adapted from The active worker: Compliance and autonomy at the workplace, *Journal of Contemporary Ethnography*, Vol.20(1), pp.47-48 (Hodson, R. 1991), Copyright © 1991 by Sage Publications, Inc. Reprinted by permission; Box 13.14 adapted from Health reform fails to lift private patient income, *Financial Times*, 04/08/2014 (Neville, S.), © The Financial Times Limited. All Rights Reserved; Box 14.4 adapted from Emerald Group Publishing (2014) 'How to.. write an abstract'. From The Emerald website, www.emeraldgrouppublishing.com/authors/guides/write/abstracts.htm; Box 14.5 from Trust and distrust: polar opposites, or independent but co-existing?, *Human Relations*, Vol.67(6), p.639 (Saunders, M.N.K. Dietz, G. and Thornhill, A. 2014); Box 14.8 adapted from High pay does not equal high quality, *Financial Times*, 30/05/2013 (Sullivan, R.), © The Financial Times Limited. All Rights Reserved

Photographs

Alamy Images: 67photo (p. 355); Fotolia.com: burnstuff2003 (p. 117), corepics (p. 221), RioPatuca Images (p. 317), terex (p. 46); Getty Images: Lloyd Bishop (p. 389); Pearson Education Ltd: Gareth Dewar (p. 183), Geo Martinez (p. 670), Konstantin Chagin (p. 431); Shutterstock.com: Bartlomiej Magierowski (p. 64), Gustavo Frazao (p. 123), Monkey Business Images (p. 384), Poznyakov (p. 623), Tupungato (p. 497), wavebreakmedia (p. 559)

All other images © Pearson Education

In some instances we have been unable to trace the owners of copyright material, and we would appreciate any information that would enable us to do so. We would be pleased to insert the appropriate acknowledgement in any subsequent edition of this publication.

Chapter 1

Business and management research, reflective diaries and the purpose of this book 工商管理研究、反思日记及本书的目的

Learning outcomes 学习目标

By the end of this chapter you should:

- be able to outline the purpose and distinct focus of business and management research;
- be able to place your research project on a basic–applied research continuum according to its purpose and context;
- understand the utility and importance of keeping a reflective diary;
- understand the stages you will need to complete (and revisit) as part of your research process;
- have an overview of this book's purpose, structure and features;
- be aware of some of the ways you can use this book.

1.1 Introduction 引 言

This book is designed to help you to undertake your research project, whether you are an undergraduate or postgraduate student of business and management or a manager. It provides a clear guide on how to undertake research as well as highlighting the realities of undertaking research, including the more common pitfalls. The book is written to provide you with a guide to the research process and with the necessary knowledge and skills to undertake a piece of research from first thoughts about a research topic to writing your project report. As such, you will find it useful as a manual or handbook on how to tackle your research project.

After reading the book you will have been introduced to research philosophies and approaches to reasoning, and explored a range of strategies, techniques and procedures with which you could tackle your research project. Of equal importance, you will know that there is no one best way for undertaking all research. Rather you will be aware of the choices you will have to make and how these will impact upon what you can find out. This means you will be able to make a series of informed choices including your research philosophy, approaches to reasoning, strategies, techniques and procedures that are most suitable to your own research project and be able to justify them. In reading the book you will have been introduced to the wealth of data that can be obtained via the Internet, techniques for collecting your own data and procedures for analysing different types of data, have had a chance to practise them, and be able to select and justify which to use. When selecting and using these techniques and procedures you will be aware of the contribution that the appropriate use of information technology can make to your research.

The Post-it® note is one of the best-known and most widely used office products in the world. Yet, despite the discovery of the repositionable adhesive that made the Post-it® note possible in 1968, it was not until 1980 that the product was introduced to the market (Post-it 2014). In the 1960s 3M research scientist Spencer Silver was looking for ways to improve the adhesive used in tapes. However, he discovered something quite different from what he was looking for, an adhesive that did not stick strongly when coated onto the back of tapes! What was unclear was how it might be used. Over the next five years he demonstrated and talked about his new adhesive to people working within the company.

Post-it® notes in use
Source: © Mark Saunders 2015

Most people working for 3M know the story of what happened next and how the Post-it® note concept came about. A new product development researcher working for 3M, Art Fry, was frustrated by how the scraps of paper he used as bookmarks kept falling out of his church choir hymn book. He realised that Silver's adhesive would mean his bookmarks would not fall out. Soon afterwards the Post-it® note concept was developed and market research undertaken. This was extremely difficult as the product was revolutionary and was, in effect, designed to replace pieces of torn scrap paper! However, despite some initial scepticism within the company, Post-it® notes were launched in 1980. One year after their launch, they were named 3M's outstanding new product.

While your research project will be within the business and management discipline rather than natural science (such as developing a new adhesive), our introductory example still offers a number of insights into the nature of research and in particular the business and management research you will be undertaking. In particular, it highlights that when undertaking research we should be open to finding the unexpected and how sometimes the applicability of our research findings may not be immediately obvious. It also emphasises the importance of discussing your ideas with other people.

However, a word of caution before you continue. In your study, you will inevitably read a wide range of books and articles. In many of these the terms 'research method' and 'research methodology' will be used interchangeably, perhaps just using methodology as a more verbose way of saying method. In this book we have been more precise in our use of these terms. Throughout the book we use the term **methods** to refer to techniques and procedures used to obtain and analyse data. This, therefore, includes questionnaires, observation and interviews as well as both quantitative (statistical) and qualitative (non-statistical) analysis techniques and, as you have probably gathered from the title, is the main focus of this book. In contrast, the term **methodology** refers to the theory of how research should be undertaken. We believe it is important that you have some understanding of this so that you can make informed choices about your research. For this reason, we also discuss a range of philosophical assumptions upon which research can be based and the implications of these for the method or methods adopted.

1.2   The nature of research   研究的特性

When listening to the radio, watching the television or reading a daily newspaper it is difficult to avoid the term 'research'. The results of 'research' are all around us. A debate about the findings of a recent poll of people's opinions inevitably includes a discussion of 'research', normally referring to the way in which the data were collected. Politicians often justify their policy decisions on the basis of 'research'. Newspapers report the findings of academics' research (Box 1.1). Documentary programmes tell us about 'research findings', and advertisers may highlight the 'results of research'

◉ Box 1.1 Focus on research in the news

Businesses need 'patient' funding

By Jonathan Moules

Most owners of small and medium-sized enterprises (SMEs) use just one source of finance to start up, according to research by academics at the University of Surrey.

The study of 1,000 businesses found that 58 per cent use just one funding means to initiate their business, while 42 per cent rely on only one source to sustain their business. Most of those interviewed borrowed from family or friends or reinvested retained profits, while banks came a poor third in terms of finance sources.

David Gray, who led the study, said SMEs needed "patient" capital, which could finance growth over the longer term. "This is the only way to stimulate and sustain high growth businesses," he added.

The findings of the research, commissioned by chartered accountancy firm Kingston Smith, come just weeks after government proposals were announced to launch a British business bank to help SMEs and support economic growth. More details are expected in the Autumn Statement on December 5.

FT *Source:* Article by Jonathan Moules, *FT.com*, 15 October 2012. Copyright © 2012 The Financial Times.

to encourage you to buy a particular product or brand. However, we believe that what these examples really emphasise is the wide range of meanings given to the term 'research' in everyday speech.

Walliman (2011) argues that many of these everyday uses of the term 'research' are not research in the true meaning of the word. As part of this, he highlights ways in which the term is used wrongly:

- just collecting facts or information with no clear purpose;
- reassembling and reordering facts or information without interpretation;
- as an esoteric activity with no or little relevance to everyday life;
- as a term to get your product or idea noticed and respected.

The first of these highlights the fact that, although research often involves the collection of information, it is more than just reading a few books or articles, talking to a few people or asking people questions. While collecting data may be part of the research process, if it is not undertaken in a systematic way, on its own and, in particular, without a clear purpose, it will not be seen as research. The second of these is commonplace in many reports. Data are collected, perhaps from a variety of different sources, and then assembled in a single document with the sources of these data listed. However, there is no interpretation of the data collected. Again, while the assembly of data from a variety of sources may be part of the process of research, without interpretation it is not research. The third emphasises how despite research often appearing abstract, it influences our daily lives and creates our understanding of the world. Finally, the term 'research' can be used to get an idea or product noticed by people and to suggest that people should have confidence in it. In such instances, when you ask for details of the research process, these are either unclear or not forthcoming.

Based upon this brief discussion we can already see that research has a number of characteristics:

- Data are collected systematically.
- Data are interpreted systematically.
- There is a clear purpose: to find things out.

We can therefore define **research** as a process that people undertake in a systematic way in order to find out things, thereby increasing their knowledge. Two phrases are important in this definition: 'systematic way' and 'to find out things'. 'Systematic' suggests that research is based on logical relationships and not just beliefs (Ghauri and Grønhaug 2010). As part of this, your research will involve an explanation of the method or methods used to collect the data, will argue why the results obtained are meaningful and will explain any limitations that are associated with them. 'To find out things' suggests there are a multiplicity of possible purposes for your research. It is therefore an activity, which means it has to be finished at some time to be of use. This will undoubtedly be true for your research project, which will have a specific deadline. Purposes may include describing, explaining, understanding, criticising and analysing (Ghauri and Grønhaug 2010). However, it also suggests that you have a clear purpose or set of 'things' that you want to find out, such as the answer to a question or number of questions.

1.3 Business and management research 工商管理研究

Using our earlier definition of research we can define business and management research as undertaking systematic research to find out things about business and management.

Easterby-Smith et al. (2012) argue that three features combine to make business and management a distinctive focus for research:

- The eclectic nature of management and management research, drawing upon knowledge developed in different disciplines such as sociology, geography, psychology, economics and statistics, which have different underlying assumptions.
- The high levels of education of both managers and employees. Most now have undergraduate or master's degrees and, as such, tend often to be as well educated as those conducting research about them.
- The expectation for research to have some practical consequence and to lead directly to action. This means it either needs to contain the potential for taking some form of action or needs to take account of the practical consequences of the findings. It also means that managers are unlikely to allow research access unless they can see an advantage for their organisation or themselves.

Ongoing debate within journals has explored the nature and purpose of business and management research, its relevance and utility, as well as the purpose and future status of business schools where much of this research is located (Cassell and Lee 2011b). One feature, which has gained considerable support, is the transdisciplinary nature of such research. While this has similarities to Easterby-Smith et al.'s (2012) point regarding the use of knowledge from other disciplines, it also emphasises that the research 'cannot be reduced to any sum of parts framed in terms of contributions to associated disciplines' (Tranfield and Starkey 1998: 352). In other words, using knowledge from a range of disciplines enables management research to gain new insights that cannot be obtained through all of these disciplines separately. Another feature of management research highlighted in the debate is a belief that it should be able to develop ideas and relate them to practice. In particular, that research should complete a virtuous circle of theory and practice (Tranfield and Starkey 1998) through which research on managerial practice informs practically derived theory. This in turn becomes a blueprint for managerial practice, thereby increasing the stock of relevant and practical management knowledge. Thus, business and management research needs to engage with both the world of theory and the world of practice. Consequently, the problems addressed should grow out of interaction between these two worlds rather than either on their own.

An article by Hodgkinson et al. (2001) offers a useful four-fold taxonomy for considering rigour and relevance in relation to managerial knowledge. Using the dimensions of theoretical and methodological rigour and of practical relevance they identify four quadrants (see Table 1.1). Hodgkinson et al. argue that pedantic science is characterised by a focus on increasing methodological rigour at the expense of results that are relevant. This can sometimes be found in refereed academic journals. In contrast, popularist

Table 1.1 A taxonomy for considering the 'relevance gap' in relation to managerial knowledge

Theoretical and methodological rigour	Practical relevance	Quadrant
Higher	Lower	Pedantic science
Lower	Higher	Popularist science
Lower	Lower	Puerile science
Higher	Higher	Pragmatic science

Source: Developed from Hodgkinson et al. (2001)

science is characterised by a focus on relevance and usefulness while neglecting theoretical and methodological rigour, examples being found in some books targeted at practising managers. Consequently, while findings might be useful to managers, the research upon which they are based is unlikely to be valid or reliable. Puerile science both lacks methodological rigour and is of limited practical relevance and, although unlikely to be found in refereed academic journals, can be found in other media. Finally, pragmatic science is both theoretically and methodologically rigorous and relevant.

In the past two decades debate about the nature of management research has focused on how it can meet the double hurdle of being both theoretically and methodologically rigorous, while at the same time embracing the world of practice and being of practical relevance (Hodgkinson et al. 2001; Wensley 2011); the latter being reframed more recently as socially useful (Hodgkinson and Starkey 2011). Much of this debate has centred around the work by Gibbons et al. (1994) on the production of knowledge and, in particular, the concepts of Mode 1 and Mode 2 knowledge creation. **Mode 1** knowledge creation emphasises research in which the questions are set and solved by academic interests, emphasising a fundamental rather than applied nature, where there is little, if any, focus on utilisation of the research by practitioners. In contrast, **Mode 2** emphasises a context for research governed by the world of practice, highlighting the importance of collaboration both with and between practitioners (Starkey and Madan 2001) and the need for the production of practical relevant knowledge. Based upon this, Starkey and Madan (2001) observe that research within the Mode 2 approach offers a way of bringing the supply side of knowledge represented by universities together with the demand side represented by businesses and overcoming the double hurdle. Bresnen and Burrell (2012: 25) suggest a further alternative, which they consider is a 'more insidious' form of knowledge production. This form, termed **Mode 0** knowledge creation, they argue has been around since the seventeenth century. It refers to knowledge production based on power and patronage, being particularly visible in the close relationships between sponsor and researcher, for example pharmaceutical industry sponsorship of medical research.

Drawing upon these debates, it could be argued that business and management research not only needs to provide findings that advance knowledge and understanding, it also needs to address business issues and practical managerial problems. However, this would negate the observation that Mode 2 practices develop from Mode 1. It might also result in business and management research that did not have obvious commercial benefit not being pursued. This, Huff and Huff (2001) argue, could jeopardise future knowledge creation, as research that is currently not valued commercially might have value in the future. Building upon these ideas, Huff and Huff, rather like Fukami (2007) who found a third road in addition to the two academic career roads of research and teaching, highlight a further form of knowledge production: Mode 3. **Mode 3** knowledge production focuses on an appreciation of the human condition as it is and as it might become, its purpose being to 'assure survival and promote the common good at various levels of social aggregation' (Huff and Huff 2001: 53). This emphasises the importance of broader issues of human relevance of research and, we consider, links to the idea of research being socially useful. Consequently, in addition to research that satisfies your intellectual curiosity for its own sake, the findings of business and management research might also contain practical implications, and these findings may have societal consequences far broader and complex than perhaps envisaged by Mode 2.

Tranfield and Denyer (2004) draw attention to concerns resulting from the separation of knowledge producers from knowledge users. This has introduced a schism, or what Starkey and Madan (2001) call the 'relevance gap', which has been the subject of considerable debate for more than a decade. Rousseau (2006) has drawn attention to ways of closing what she terms the prevailing 'research–practice gap' – the failure of organisations and managers to base practices on the best available evidence. She extols the virtues of 'evidence-based management', which derives principles from research evidence and translates them into practices that solve organisational problems. Research findings do not appear to have transferred well to the workplace. Instead of a scientific understanding of human behaviour and organisations, managers, including those with MBAs, continue to rely largely on personal experience, to the exclusion of more systematic knowledge. This has been discussed in articles and entire special issues of journals, including the *Journal of Management Studies* (2009, volume 46, number 3) and the *British Journal of Management* (2010, volume 21, supplement), as well as in volumes such as Cassell and Lee's (2011a) *Challenges and Controversies in Management Research*. Within these debates some maintain that the gap between rigour and relevance is fundamentally unbridgeable because management researchers and the researched inhabit different worlds, are engaged in different activities and have different research orientations, while others disagree. Hodgkinson and Rousseau (2009), for example, argue that the research–practice gap is due to more than differences in style and language, and that management researchers can generate knowledge that is both socially useful and academically rigorous.

Not surprisingly, many managers and academics perceive the gap between research undertaken by academics and the practice of management as a problem. Saunders (2011) categorises these as differences between academics' and practitioners' orientations in relation to their foci of interest, methodological imperatives, the key outcomes and how each views the other. These we summarise in Table 1.2, the contrasting orientations indicating where tensions may occur.

However, perhaps the most telling comment on the so-called 'relevance gap' is from Tranfield and Denyer (2004: 13), who assert that ignoring such a gap would be 'unthinkable in other professional fields, such as medicine or engineering, where a national scandal would ensue if science base and practice were not inextricably and necessarily interlinked'. This relates to the idea of conceptualising management as a

Table 1.2 Practitioner and management researcher orientations

Management researcher		Practitioner
Basic understanding	**Focus of interest**	Usable knowledge
General enlightenment		Instrumental
Theoretical explanation		Practical problem solutions
'Why' knowledge		'How to' knowledge
Substantive theory building		Local theory-in-use
Theoretical and methodological rigour	**Methodological imperative**	Timeliness
Academic publication	**Key outcome**	Actionable results with practice impact
Disdain of practitioner	**Views of other**	Deprecate or ignore
Desire to make a difference to practice		Belief research can provide relevant (socially useful) fresh insights to managers' problems

Source: Developed from Saunders (2011)

design science rather than a social science. From the design science perspective, the main purpose of academic management research is therefore only to develop valid knowledge to support organisational problem solving. While many researchers would probably agree that the mission of management research, like other social sciences, is description, explanation and prediction, taking a design science mission therefore focuses upon solution-orientated research to develop valid knowledge which supports practitioners in solving business problems (Van Aken 2005). The counter argument proposes that management practice is characterised by a wide variety of organisational phenomena that are often ambiguous, and may not be suited to rule-like explanations offered by design science, and that there needs to be a balance between explanation and application (Pandza and Thorpe 2010).

Within the boundaries of advancing knowledge, addressing business issues, solving managerial problems and promoting the common good, the purpose and the context of your research project can differ considerably. For some research projects your purpose may be to understand and explain the impact of something, such as a particular policy. You may undertake this research within an individual organisation and suggest appropriate action on the basis of your findings. For other research projects you may wish to explore the ways in which various organisations do things differently. In such projects your purpose may be to discover and understand better the underlying processes in a wider context, thereby providing greater understanding for practitioners. For yet other research projects you may wish to place an in-depth investigation of an organisation within the context of a wider understanding of the processes that are operating.

Despite this variety, we believe that all business and management research projects can be placed on a continuum (Figure 1.1) according to their purpose and context. At

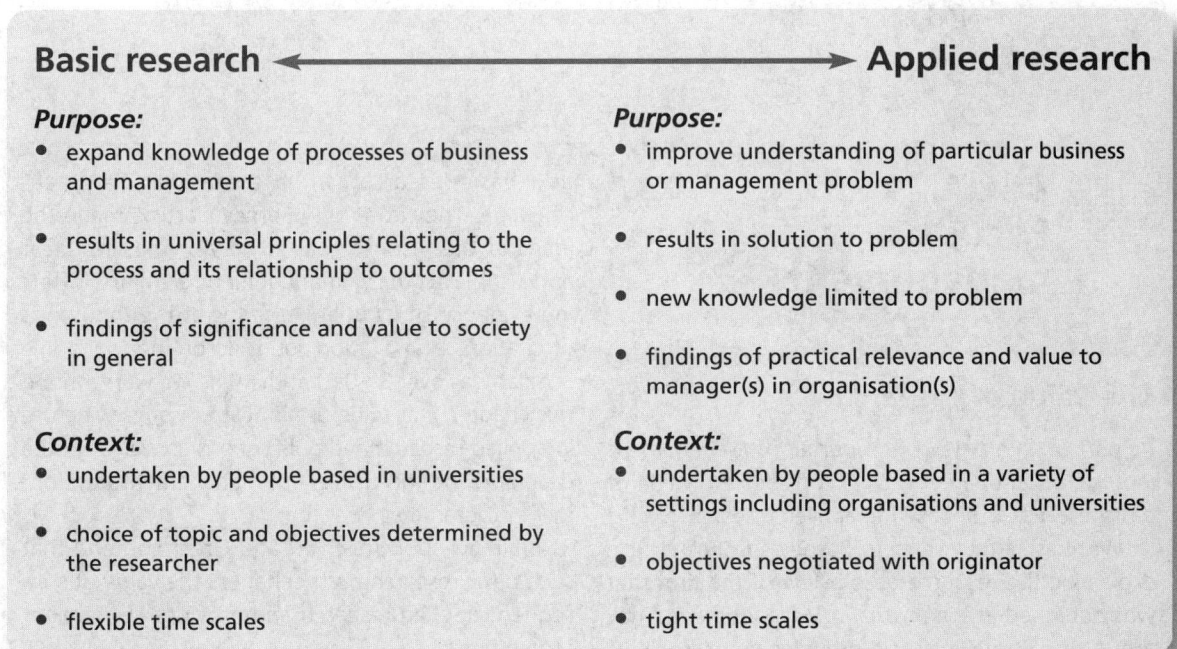

Basic research ←――――――――――――――――――――――→ **Applied research**

Purpose:
- expand knowledge of processes of business and management

- results in universal principles relating to the process and its relationship to outcomes

- findings of significance and value to society in general

Context:
- undertaken by people based in universities

- choice of topic and objectives determined by the researcher

- flexible time scales

Purpose:
- improve understanding of particular business or management problem

- results in solution to problem

- new knowledge limited to problem

- findings of practical relevance and value to manager(s) in organisation(s)

Context:
- undertaken by people based in a variety of settings including organisations and universities

- objectives negotiated with originator

- tight time scales

Figure 1.1 Basic and applied research
Source: Authors' experience; Easterby-Smith et al. (2012); Hedrick et al. (1993)

one extreme of the continuum is research that is undertaken purely to understand the processes of business and management and their outcomes. Such research is undertaken largely in universities and largely as the result of an academic agenda. Its key consumer is the academic community, with relatively little attention being given to its practical applications. This is often termed **basic**, **fundamental** or **pure research** and, although the focus may not have been on practical or commercial value, as illustrated in Box 1.2, the resultant model may be of considerable utility. Given our earlier discussion, it is unlikely that Mode 2 and Mode 3 business and management research would fulfil the criterion of being undertaken 'purely to understand' due to at least some consideration being given to the practical consequences of what has been found out. Through considering the practical consequences, the research would start to move towards the other end of the continuum (Figure 1.1). At this end is research that is of direct and immediate use to managers, addresses issues that they see as important, and is presented in ways that they understand and can act on. This is termed **applied research**. In our view applied research can be very similar to consultancy, particularly when the latter is conducted in a thorough manner.

Wherever your research project lies on this basic–applied continuum, and for each of the orientations in Table 1.2, we believe that you should undertake your research with rigour. To do this you will need to pay careful attention to the entire research process.

Inevitably, your own beliefs and feelings will impact upon your research. Although you might feel that your research will be value neutral (we will discuss this in greater detail later, particularly in Chapter 4), it is unlikely that you will stop your own beliefs and feelings influencing your research. Your choice of what to research is also likely to be influenced by topics that excite you, the way you collect and analyse your data and by the skills you have or are able to develop. (Similarly, as hinted by 'timeliness' in Table 1.2, in Chapter 2 we discuss practical considerations such as access to data and the time and resources you have available, which will also impact upon your research process.)

Box 1.2
Focus on management research

The value of research

As part of an article in the *Journal of Management Inquiry* Hitt and Greer (2012) consider the value of basic research as opposed to applied research.

Within this they refer to Barney's (1991) article explaining the resource-based view of the firm that was published in the *Journal of Management*. They argue that Barney's article provides an example of how basic research can have considerable practical value. They note how Barney's article made the ideas of the resource-based view of the firm clear and usable to many management scholars; offering evidence of its utility in terms of the thousands of citations (the citation count according to Google Scholar was over 37,000 at the time we were writing this chapter!), its wide use in textbooks, its wide use in applied research and publications as well as in the development and delivery of management development programmes.

Building upon this, Hitt and Greer contend that such basic research both enhances the value of subsequent applied research and provides content for programmes.

1.4   The research process   研究过程

Most research textbooks represent research as a multi-stage process that you must follow in order to undertake and complete your research project. The precise number of stages varies, but they usually include formulating and clarifying a topic, reviewing the literature, designing the research, collecting data, analysing data and writing up. In the majority of these the research process, although presented with rationalised examples, is described as a series of stages through which you must pass. Articles you have read may also suggest that the research process is rational and straightforward. Unfortunately this is very rarely true, and the reality is considerably messier, with what initially appear as great ideas sometimes having little or no relevance. While research is often depicted as moving through each of the stages just outlined, one after the other, this is unlikely to be the case. In reality some stages will overlap and you will probably revisit each stage more than once. Each time you revisit a stage you will need to reflect on the associated issues and refine your ideas. In addition, as highlighted by some textbooks, you will need to consider ethical and access issues during the process.

This textbook also presents the research process as a series of linked stages and gives the appearance of being organised in a linear manner. However, as you use the book you will see that we have recognised the concurrent and iterative nature of the research process you will follow in the examples of research by well-known academic researchers, student research, how research is reported in the news and case studies as well as our extensive use of cross-referencing. As part of this process, we believe it is vital that you spend time formulating and clarifying your research topic. This we believe should be expressed as one or more research questions that your research must answer, accompanied by a set of objectives that your research must address. However, we would also stress the need to reflect on your ideas continually and revise both these and the way in which you intend to progress your research.

We believe that writing is an intrinsic part of developing your ideas and understanding your research. Indeed we, and our students, have found that it is not until we write our ideas that we discover where our arguments need further clarification. Often this will involve revisiting stages (including research question(s) and objectives) and working through them again. There is also a need to plan ahead, thereby ensuring that the necessary preliminary work for later stages has been undertaken. This is emphasised by Figure 1.2, which also provides a schematic index to the remaining chapters of the book. Within this flow chart (Figure 1.2) the stages you will need to complete as part of your research project are emphasised in the centre of the chart. However, be warned: the process is far messier than a brief glance at Figure 1.2 suggests!

1.5   Keeping a reflective diary or research notebook   写反思日记或研究笔记

You will notice in Figure 1.2 on page 12 that we include a series of arrows labelled 'reflection and revision'. During your research project you will find it helpful to keep a separate **reflective diary** in which you note down what has happened and the lessons you have learnt both from things that have gone well and things that have not gone so well during the research process. Some researchers incorporate their reflective diary into a **research notebook** in which they record chronologically other aspects of their research

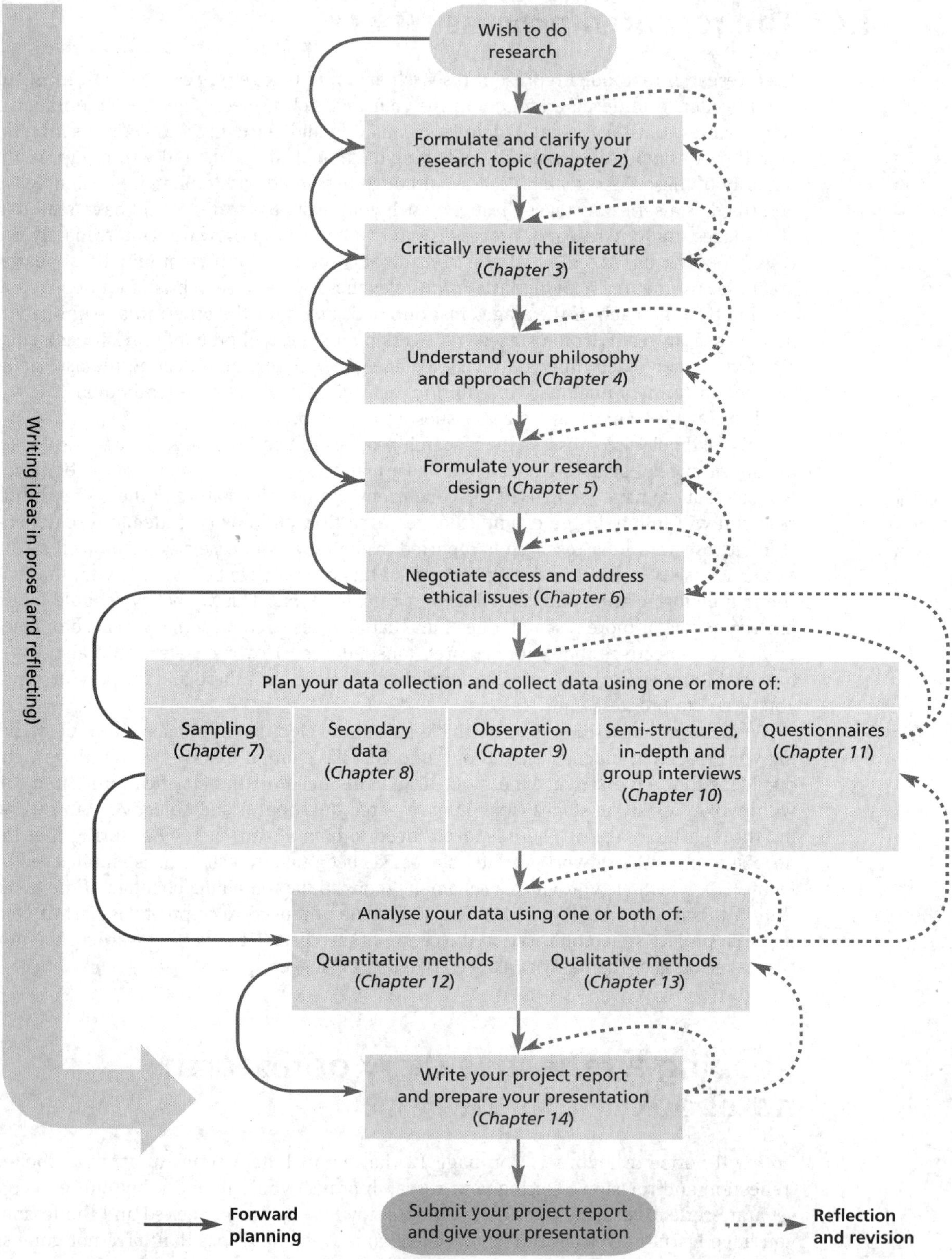

Figure 1.2 The research process

Source: © Mark Saunders, Philip Lewis and Adrian Thornhill 2015

project such as useful articles they have read, notes of discussions with their project supervisor and other interesting conversations alongside their emergent thoughts about all aspects of their research. We have also found this helpful. The process of observing your own research practice and examining the way you do things is termed **reflection**. However, there is a more complex process incorporating interpretation as well as reflection and involving you in thinking about your experiences and questioning the way you have done things. This process, known as **reflexivity**, involves you in thinking about and interpreting your role in the research and the way in which this is influenced by the object of the research; and acknowledging the way you affect both the processes of the research and the outcomes (Haynes 2012; Box 1.3). (This is discussed further in Section 13.5.)

You will almost certainly remember from your earlier studies the work of Kolb and of Honey and Mumford on the learning cycle (Marchington and Wilkinson 2012). This views the learning process as going through a four-stage cycle of:

1 concrete experience;
2 observation and reflection in relation to the experience;
3 forming abstract concepts and generalisations from these observations and reflections;
4 testing these concepts and generalisations in new situations.

The learning cycle emphasises that for learning to happen you need to pass through the complete cycle, as without reflection there will be no learning from experience. Such reflection is the process of stopping and thinking about a concrete experience that has happened or is happening, and the subsequent forming of concepts and generalisations, so you can apply what you have learnt from your experiences to new situations.

Box 1.3
Focus on student research

Keeping a reflective diary as part of a research notebook

As part of her master's research project Amanda's project tutor had encouraged her to incorporate her reflective diary into a research notebook. Over time she began to realise that her diary entries were providing her with a useful way of not only recording her experiences, but also questioning her research practice. An extract from her reflective diary follows:

Monday 6th April 7:30 P.M.

I did my first observation today in shop, watching and recording what people did when they came in, browsed the shoes and then, perhaps, made a purchase and left. Following what the textbook had told me, I sat as unobtrusively as possible in the corner on one of the sofas and used my tablet to make notes about the customer's and the sales assistant's behaviours. I'd prepared a checklist of what I was looking for. It all seemed to go well and, using the checklist, I made some interesting observations about the sorts of interactions customers were having with the sales assistants when they purchased shoes. Also I feel my position was unobtrusive and I was not really noticed. What went less well was the fact I could not hear precisely what was being said. I was too far away from the sales assistant and the customer. I need to make adjustments and be closer next time, while still being unobtrusive.

10:00 P.M.

I have just watched a television documentary on retail shopping and the changing nature of such shops. I'm feeling worried that I might not have really observed all of what was happening. The programme makers had filmed the same purchase in a shop from three different views, presumably using different cameras. One camera filmed the purchase from low down and appeared to be quite a distance

---

Box 1.3
Focus on student research (*continued*)

Keeping a reflective diary as part of a research notebook

from the purchase. It seemed as if the camera operator was sitting on a sofa, rather like my observation. Another had filmed it more closely from behind the sales assistant so you could see the expressions on the customer's face and easily hear the conversation. The final camera had filmed from behind the customer and this time you could see the sales assistant's face; she looked really disinterested. I had never really thought about the impact of my position in the shop on what I would see and the data I would be able to collect until I saw that programme. I definitely need to think this through.

Tuesday 7th April, 7:30 A.M.

On reflection I really need to think more carefully about where would be the best place from which to observe and collect my data. I have already thought about the data I need, but given my emphasis on the interaction with customers, I think I was not in the right place to collect it for my first observation. I need to be able to see both the customer and the sales assistant and to hear what is being said and the tones of the voices. But, at the same time, I need to be unobtrusive as well so my presence does not influence the interaction. Also, there is also only one of me, so I cannot be in three places at once! However, if I remember correctly, there was a place to sit and try on shoes next to the sales desk. Perhaps that would be a better place to observe. I cannot use videography to record what is happening as, if I ask for permission to do this, it will completely change the way the people react with each other. However, I could note down what I saw and heard immediately afterwards. I'll talk to my project tutor.

Given the benefits to learning, it is not surprising that many universities require students to write a reflective essay or a reflective practice statement as part of the assessment for their research project. In order to do this well, and more importantly to enhance your learning during the research process, we recommend that you keep a reflective diary or notebook (sometimes called a learning log or learning journal) in which you make entries at regular intervals regarding what has gone well, what has gone less well, what you have learnt from each experience and how you will apply this learning in the future. Indeed, as you read on you will find that we ask you to do this at the end of each chapter in the section 'Progressing your research project'! Questions our students have found helpful to guide them when making their diary entries are listed as a checklist in Box 1.4.

Box 1.4
Checklist of questions to ask yourself when making reflective diary entries

✔ What has gone well in relation to each experience?
  • Why has it gone well?

✔ What has not gone so well in relation to each experience?
  • Why has it not gone so well?
✔ What adjustments will/did I make to my ongoing research following my reflection?
  • Why will/did I make these adjustments?
✔ (Looking back) how could I have improved on these adjustments?
  • Why?
✔ What have I learnt in relation to each experience?
✔ How will I apply what I have learnt from each experience to new situations?

Be warned, many students forget to make entries in their reflective diaries regularly; this makes writing a good reflective essay difficult as much of the learning will have been forgotten!

1.6   The purpose and structure of this book

本书的目的和框架

The purpose

As we stated earlier (Section 1.1), the overriding purpose of this book is to help you to undertake research. This means that early on in your research project you will need to be clear about what you are doing, why you are doing it and the associated implications of what you are seeking to do. You will also need to ensure that you can show how your ideas relate to research that has already been undertaken in your topic area and that you have a clear research design and have thought about how you will collect and analyse your data. As part of this you will need to consider the validity and reliability (or credibility and dependability) of the data you intend to use, along with associated ethical and access issues. The appropriateness and suitability of the analytical techniques you choose to use will be of equal importance. Finally, you will need to write and present your research project report as clearly and precisely as possible, making sure you meet your university's assessment criteria.

The structure of each chapter

Each of the subsequent chapters deals with part of the research process outlined in Figure 1.2. The ideas, methods and techniques are discussed using appropriate terms, but as little jargon as possible. Where appropriate you will find summaries of these, using tables, checklists or diagrams. When new terms are introduced for the first time they are shown in **bold**, and a definition or explanation follows shortly afterwards. They are also listed with a brief definition in the glossary. The use of appropriate information technology is considered in most instances as an integral part of the text. Discussion of information technology is not software specific but is concerned with general principles. However, we recognise that you may wish to find out more about how to use data analysis software packages and so have included tutorials for the quantitative data analysis software IBM SPSS Statistics, the spreadsheet Excel™ and the qualitative data analysis software NVivo™ (with practice data sets) on this book's companion website. These will enable you to utilise whatever software you have available most effectively. We have also included the Smarter Online Searching Guide to help you with your Internet searches. Chapters have been cross-referenced as appropriate, and an index is provided to help you to find your way around the book.

Included within the text of each chapter are one or more boxes, which are called *Focus on student research*. These, like Box 1.3, reflect actual research projects, undertaken by students, in which points made in the text are illustrated. In many instances these examples illustrate possible pitfalls you may come across while undertaking your research. Further illustrations are provided by *Focus on management research* and *Focus on research in the news* boxes. *Focus on management research* boxes (such as Box 1.2) discuss recent research in business and management. These are normally derived from refereed academic journal articles and you are likely to be able to download the actual articles from online databases at your university. *Focus on research in the news* boxes, one of which you will have already read (Box 1.1), provide topical newspaper articles that illustrate pertinent research-related issues. All these will help you to understand the technique or idea and to assess its suitability or appropriateness for your research. Where a pitfall has been illustrated, it will, it is hoped, help you to avoid making the same mistake. There is also a series of boxed *Checklists* (such as Box 1.4) to provide you with further focused guidance for your own research. At the end of each chapter there is a *Summary* of key points, which you may look at before and after reading the chapter to ensure that you have digested the main points.

To enable you to check that you have understood the chapter a series of *Self-check questions* is included at the end. These can be answered without recourse to other (external) resources. *Answers* are provided to all these self-check questions at the end of each chapter. Self-check questions are followed by *Review and discussion questions.* These suggest a variety of activities you can undertake to help you further develop your knowledge and understanding of the material in the chapter, often involving discussion with a friend. Self-test multiple choice questions are available on this book's companion website. Each chapter also includes a section towards the end headed *Progressing your research project.* This contains a series of questions that will help you to consider the implications of the material covered by the chapter for your research project. Answering the questions in the section *Progressing your research project* for each chapter will enable you to generate all the material that you will need to include in your project report and, where required, your reflective statement. Each chapter's questions involve you in undertaking activities that are more complex than self-check questions, such as a library-based literature search or designing and piloting a questionnaire. They are designed to help you to focus on the techniques that are most appropriate to your research. However, as emphasised by Figure 1.2, you will almost certainly need to revisit and revise your answers as your research progresses.

Each chapter is also accompanied by *References, Further reading* and a *Case study.* Further reading is included for two distinct reasons:

- to direct you to other work on the ideas and concepts contained within the chapter;
- to direct you to further examples of research where the ideas contained in the chapter have been used.

The main reasons for our choice of further reading are therefore indicated.

The new case studies towards the end of every chapter are drawn from a variety of business and management research scenarios and have been based on the case study's authors' and students' experiences when undertaking a research project. All case studies have been written to highlight real issues that occur when undertaking business and management research. To help to focus your thoughts or discussion on some of the pertinent issues, each case is followed by evaluative questions. Further case studies relating to each chapter are available from the book's companion website. This provides hyperlinks to over 60 additional case studies.

An outline of the chapters

The book is organised in the following way.

Chapter 2 is written to assist you in the generation of ideas, which will help you to choose a suitable research topic, and offers advice on what makes a good research topic. If you have already been given a research topic, perhaps by an organisation or tutor, you will need to refine it into one that is feasible, and should still therefore read this chapter. After your idea has been generated and refined, the chapter discusses how to turn this idea into a clear research question(s), aim and objectives. (Research questions and objectives are referred to throughout the book.) Finally, the chapter provides advice on how to write your research proposal.

The importance of the critical literature review to your research is discussed in Chapter 3. This chapter outlines what a critical review needs to include and the range of secondary and primary (the latter also known as Grey) literature sources available. The chapter explains the purpose of reviewing the literature, discusses a range of search strategies and contains advice on how to plan and undertake your search and to write your review. The processes of identifying key words and searching using online databases and search engines are outlined. It also offers advice on how to record (reference) items and to evaluate their relevance.

Chapter 4 addresses the issue of understanding different research philosophies, including positivism, critical realism, interpretivism, post modernism and pragmatism. Within this the functionalist, interpretive, radical humanist and radical structuralist paradigms are discussed. Deductive, inductive and abductive approaches to theory development are also considered. In this chapter we challenge you to think about your own values and beliefs reflexively and the impact this will have on the way you undertake your research.

These ideas are developed further in Chapter 5, which explores formulating your research design. As part of this, the methodological choice of quantitative, qualitative or mixed methods is considered. A variety of research strategies are explored and longitudinal and cross-sectional time horizons discussed. Consideration is given to the implications of research design for the credibility of your research findings and conclusions.

Chapter 6 explores issues related to gaining access and to research ethics. It offers advice on how to gain access both to organisations and to individuals using both traditional and Internet-mediated strategies. Potential ethical issues are discussed in relation to each stage of the research process and different data collection methods. Issues of data protection are also introduced.

A range of the probability and non-probability sampling techniques available for use in your research is explained in Chapter 7. The chapter considers why sampling is necessary, and looks at issues of sample size and likely response rates for both probability and non-probability samples. Advice on how to relate your choice of sampling techniques to your research topic is given, and techniques for assessing the representativeness of those who respond are discussed.

Chapters 8, 9, 10 and 11 are concerned with different methods of obtaining data. The use of secondary data is discussed in Chapter 8. This chapter introduces the variety of data that are likely to be available, and suggests ways in which they can be used. Advantages and disadvantages of secondary data are discussed, and a range of techniques for locating these data is suggested. Chapter 8 provides an indication of the myriad of sources available via the Internet and also offers advice on how to evaluate the suitability of secondary data for your research.

In contrast, Chapter 9 is concerned with collecting primary data through observation. The chapter examines four types of observation: participant observation, structured observation, Internet-mediated observation and observation using videography. Practical advice on using each is offered, and particular attention is given to ensuring that the data you obtain are both reliable and valid.

Chapter 10 is also concerned with collecting primary data, this time using semi-structured, in-depth and group interviews. The appropriateness of using these interviews in relation to your research strategy is discussed. Advice on how to undertake interviews is offered, including the conduct of focus groups, Internet-mediated (including online) and telephone interviews. Particular attention is given to ensuring that the data collected are both reliable and valid.

Chapter 11 is the final chapter concerned with collecting data. It introduces you to the use of both self-completed and interviewer-completed questionnaires, and explores their advantages and disadvantages. Practical advice is offered on the process of designing, piloting and delivering Internet, postal, delivery and collection, telephone and face-to-face questionnaires to enhance their response rates. Particular attention is again given to ensuring that the data collected are both reliable and valid.

Analysis of data is covered in Chapters 12 and 13. Chapter 12 outlines and illustrates the main issues that you need to consider when preparing and analysing data quantitatively by computer. Different types of data are defined and advice is given on how to create a data matrix and to code data. Practical advice is also offered on the analysis of these data using computer-based analysis software. The most appropriate diagrams to explore and illustrate data are discussed and suggestions are made about the most appropriate statistics to use to describe data, to explore relationships and to examine trends.

Chapter 13 outlines and discusses the main approaches available to you to analyse data qualitatively both manually and using computer-aided qualitative data analysis software (**CAQDAS**). The nature of qualitative data and issues associated with transcription are discussed. The use of deductively based and inductively based analytical approaches is discussed and different types of procedures are outlined to analyse your qualitative data. A number of aids that will help you to analyse these data and record your ideas about progressing your research are also discussed.

Chapter 14 helps you with the structure, content and style of your final project report and any associated oral and poster presentations. Above all, and as illustrated by Figure 1.2, it encourages you to see writing as an intrinsic part of the research process that should not be left until everything else is completed.

Appendices and glossary

This book contains four appendices designed to support you at different stages of your research project. In the early stages, as you begin to read, you will need to keep a reference of what you have read using a recognised system, the most frequently used of which are detailed in Appendix 1. When selecting your sample you may need to calculate the minimum sample size required and use random sampling numbers (Appendices 2 and 3). Finally, when designing your data collection tools and writing your project report you will need to ensure that the language you use is non-discriminatory. Guidelines for these are given in Appendix 4. A separate glossary of some 600 research-methods-related terms is also included for quick reference.

1.7 **Summary** 小 结

- This book is designed to help you to undertake a research project whether you are an undergraduate or postgraduate student of business and management or a manager. It is designed as an introductory text and will guide you through the entire research process.
- Business and management research involves undertaking systematic research to find out things. It is transdisciplinary, and engages with both theory and practice.

- All business and management research projects can be placed on a basic–applied continuum according to their purpose and context.
- Wherever your research project lies on this continuum, you should undertake your research with rigour. To do this you will need to pay careful attention to the entire research process.
- In order to enhance your learning during your research we recommend you keep a reflective diary or notebook.
- In this book, research is represented as a multi-stage process; however, this process is rarely straightforward and will involve both reflecting on and revising stages already undertaken and forward planning.
- The text of each chapter is supported through a series of boxed examples. These include focus on student research, focus on management research and focus on research in the news. In addition, there are checklists, self-check questions and review and discussion questions, an assignment and a case study with questions. Answers to all self-check questions are at the end of the appropriate chapter.
- Answering the questions in the section 'Progressing your research project' for Chapters 2–13 will enable you to generate all the material that you will need to include in your project report and reflect on what you have learnt. When you have also answered the questions in this section for Chapter 14, you will have written your research report.

Self-check questions 自测题

Help with these questions is available at the end of the chapter.

1.1 Outline the features that can make business and management research distinctive from research in other disciplines.

1.2 What are the key differences between basic and applied research (and consultancy)?

1.3 Examine Figure 1.2. What does this suggest about the need to plan and to reflect on and revise your ideas?

Review and discussion questions 复习与讨论题

1.4 Agree with a friend to each read a different quality newspaper. Make a note of at least 10 articles in your newspaper that mention the word 'research'. Now examine the articles one at a time. As you examine each article, does the reference to research:
- refer to the collection of facts or information with no clear purpose?
- refer to the reassembling and reordering of facts or information without interpretation?
- provide a means of getting the reader to respect what is being written?
- refer to the systematic collection and interpretation of data with a clear purpose? Discuss your answers with your friend.

1.5 Revisit Table 1.2 and look at the differences in management researcher and practitioner orientations for foci of interest, methodological imperatives, key outcomes and how each views the other. For each of the continua implied by this table, where would you place yourself? To what extent do you believe that business and management research should meet the practitioner requirements? Give reasons for your answer.

Progressing your research project
改进研究项目
Starting your reflective diary or notebook 开始记反思日记或笔记

- Find out if your university requires you to write a reflective practice statement, learning journal or keep a reflective diary or research notebook as part of your research project or research methods module.
- If the answer is 'yes', look carefully at what is required by the assessment criteria and ensure that your reflective diary or research notebook entries will enable you to meet fully the assessment criteria. In particular be sure to ascertain whether you are expected to be reflective or reflexive.
- When doing this, amend the questions in Box 1.4 to guide your diary or notebook entries as necessary.
- If the answer is 'no', we still believe it will be beneficial to your learning for your research project or research methods module if you keep a reflective diary or research notebook on a regular basis. Please use the questions in Box 1.4 to guide your reflective entries at the end of each chapter.

Self-check answers 自测题答案

1.1 The features you outline are likely to include:

- the transdisciplinary nature of business and management research;
- the development of ideas that are related to practice and in particular the requirement for the research to have some practical consequence;
- the need for research to complete the virtuous circle of theory and practice;
- addressing problems that grow out of the interaction between the worlds of theory and practice.

1.2 The key differences between basic and applied research relate to both the purpose and the context in which it is undertaken. They are summarised in Figure 1.1.

1.3 Figure 1.2 emphasises the importance of planning during your research project. Forward planning needs to occur at all stages up to submission. In addition, you will need to reflect on and to revise your work throughout the life of the research project. This reflection needs to have a wide focus. You should both consider the stage you have reached and revisit earlier stages and work through them again. Reflection may also lead you to amend your research plan. This should be expected, although large amendments in the later stages of your research project are unlikely.

Get ahead using resources on the companion website at: **www.pearsoned.co.uk/saunders**.

- Improve your IBM SPSS Statistics and NVivo research analysis with practice tutorials.
- Save time researching on the Internet with the Smarter Online Searching Guide.
- Test your progress using self-assessment questions.
- Follow live links to useful websites.

Chapter 2

Formulating and clarifying the research topic 提出和阐述研究主题

Learning outcomes 学习目标

By the end of this chapter you should be able to:

- identify the attributes of a good research topic;
- generate and refine research ideas to choose a suitable research topic;
- turn your research idea into a research project that has a clear research question(s), aim and objectives;
- understand the relationship between a research question(s), a research aim and research objectives;
- recognise the role of theory in developing a research question(s), a research aim and research objectives;
- draft a research proposal that outlines your proposed research project.

2.1 Introduction 引 言

Many students think that choosing their research topic is the most exciting part of their course. After all, this is something that they get to decide for themselves rather than having to complete a task decided by their tutors. We will stress in this chapter that it is important to choose something that will sustain your interest throughout the months that you will need to complete it. You may even decide to do some research on something that forms part of your leisure activities!

Before you start your research you need to have at least some idea of what you want to do. This is probably the most difficult, and yet the most important, part of your research project. Up until now most of your studies have been concerned with answering questions that other people have set. This chapter is concerned with how to formulate and clarify your research topic, research question and related aim and objectives. If you are not clear about what you are going to research, it is difficult to plan how you are going to research it. This reminds us

of a favourite quote in *Alice's Adventures in Wonderland*. This is part of Alice's conversation with the Cheshire Cat. In this Alice asks the Cat (Carroll 1989: 63–4):

'Would you tell me, please, which way I ought to walk from here?'
'That depends a good deal on where you want to get to', said the Cat.
'I don't much care where', said Alice.
'Then it doesn't matter which way you walk', said the Cat.

Formulating and clarifying the research topic is the starting point of your research project. Once you are clear about this, you will be able to choose the most appropriate research strategy and data collection and analysis techniques. The formulating and clarifying process is time consuming and will probably take you up blind alleys (Saunders and Lewis 1997). However, without spending time on this stage you are far less likely to achieve a successful project.

Choosing your research topic is a developmental exercise – not just in terms of refining a research idea and turning it into a research project, but also in terms of self-development and personal learning. Research will involve you in engaging in personal reflectivity and reflexivity. In Section 1.5 we referred to the experiential learning cycle, where personal reflection is vital to learning from experience. Choosing and formulating your research topic will involve you in a period of intense intellectual activity that will provide you with the opportunity to learn from this experience. You will be able to make a number of entries in your reflective diary or learning journal to record the stages of choosing your research topic and the learning points that emerge for you from this process. Related to this will be personal reflexivity.

Lincoln et al. (2011: 124) define **reflexivity** as 'the process of reflecting critically on the self as researcher'. As we say elsewhere in this book, research is like going on a journey. It is a journey that involves you making a number of decisions. Being reflexive will ensure you reflect on why you choose a research topic, why you prefer one research strategy over another, how you engage with those whom you wish to take part in your research, how you use the data they reveal to you, how you deal with any problems that confront you during your project and so on. It will allow you to surface any preconceived ideas that you may have about your topic and what you expect to find, and help you to be aware of your own biases. Through doing this you will recognise your role or 'self' within the process of the research, remaining critically reflective and being open to new learning. This chapter is intended to encourage a reflective and reflexive approach and we would encourage you to retain these qualities as your research progresses.

In the initial stages of the formulating and clarifying process you will be generating and refining research ideas (Section 2.3). It may be that you have already been given a research idea, perhaps by an organisation or tutor. Even if this has happened you will still need to refine the idea into one that is feasible. Once you have done this you will need to turn the idea into a research question(s), aim and objectives (Section 2.4) and to write the research proposal for your project (Section 2.5).

However, before you start the formulating and clarifying process we believe that you need to understand what makes a good research topic. For this reason we begin this chapter with a discussion of the attributes required for a good research topic.

Research starts with ideas. An article in the *Wall Street Journal* (Shellenbarger 2013) looks at recent work to encourage creativity and the generation of ideas. It provides comfort for those of us who don't find it easy to generate ideas, whether for research or some other purpose.

While preparation is needed to start the process of generating ideas, sometimes people need to step back from their hard work to enjoy an 'aha moment', the article reports. This might be as simple as allowing yourself a little time in your work schedule to daydream, look out of a window, or do something else to relax, such as go for a walk or a run.

South Devon
© Jan Thornhill 2015

The article discusses research that found the colour green may encourage creativity, helping people to generate ideas. Seeing or thinking about a pleasant, green environment may provide precious moments of relaxation and help to produce a positive mood that allows the brain to generate an idea when you least expect it. Other research found that seeing blue may also be linked to the encouragement of creativity. It seems that it may be the vivacity and brightness of these colours that may encourage creativity. Imagine, then, walking in a space surrounded by greenery, such as trees, plants or grass, with water nearby.

Such 'time out' allows the brain to make sense of a person's preparatory work, while being relaxed and in a positive mood may also help to encourage creativity and the generation of ideas. A positive mood and creativity may also be helped by socialising or watching something that makes you laugh such as a comedy show.

2.2 Attributes of a good research topic 好研究主题的特征

The attributes of a business and management research topic do not vary a great deal between universities, although there will be differences in the emphasis placed on these attributes. If you are undertaking your research project as part of a course of study then the most important attribute will be that it meets the examining body's requirements and, in particular, that it is at the correct level. This means that you must choose your topic with care. For example, some universities require students to collect their own data as part of their research project, whereas others allow them to base their project on data that have already been collected. Alternatively, some ask you to undertake an organisation-based piece of applied research, while others simply say that it must be within the subject matter of your course or programme. You therefore need to check the assessment criteria for your project and ensure that your choice of topic will enable you to meet these criteria. If you are unsure, you should discuss any uncertainties with your project tutor.

In addition, your research topic must be something you are capable of undertaking and one that excites your imagination. Capability can be considered in a variety of ways. At the personal level you need to feel comfortable that you have, or can develop, the skills that will be required to research the topic. We hope that you will develop your research skills as part of undertaking your project. However, some skills, for example learning a new foreign language, may be impossible to acquire in the time you have available. As well as having the necessary skills we believe that you also need to have a genuine interest in the topic. Most research projects are undertaken over at least a four-month period. A topic in which you are only vaguely interested at the start is likely to become a topic in which you have no interest and with which you will fail to produce your best work.

Your ability to find the financial and time resources to undertake research on the topic will also affect your capability. This relates to the concept of feasibility (which we also discuss in Chapter 6 (Section 6.2)). Some topics are unlikely to be possible to complete in the time allowed by your course of study. This may be because they require you to measure the impact of an intervention over a long time period (Box 2.1). Similarly, topics that are likely to require you to travel widely or need expensive equipment should also be disregarded unless financial resources permit.

Capability also means you must be reasonably certain of gaining access to any data you might need to collect. Many people start with ideas where access to data will prove difficult. Certain, more sensitive topics, such as financial performance or decision making by senior managers, are potentially fascinating. However, they may present considerable access problems. You should, therefore, discuss this with your project tutor after reading Chapter 6.

It is important that the issues within your research are capable of being linked to academic theory. Initially, theory may be based just on the reading you have undertaken as part of your study to date. However, as part of your assessment criteria you are almost certain to be asked to set your topic in context (Sections 2.4 and 3.2). As a consequence you will need to have knowledge of the literature and to undertake further reading as part of defining your research question(s), aim and objectives (Section 2.4).

Box 2.1
Focus on student research

Turning ideas into a viable project

Zaynab was not short of ideas for her research. But she was much less sure about how to turn her topic of interest into a question that could be answered for her research project. Her tutors emphasised that thinking of topics was relatively easy compared to turning them into viable research projects.

Having explored various websites and looked at relevant publications in the library, she drew up a plan of action which she was sure would give her the material necessary to write her research proposal.

Charting ideas

At the start of her project, Zaynab got a huge sheet of paper to make a mind map of all of her ideas, questions, associations, sources and leads. She marked her most compelling thoughts in red. Then she marked the main links to those ideas in red too. She was careful not to discard her weaker or isolated thoughts. She felt this mind map would help her sort through all her thoughts. She thought that she could make another mind map later in the project if she felt there was too much information.

Recording questions

Next Zaynab recorded the authors who had originally asked a potential research question and left a space by each to record possible answers or places to look for answers. She then highlighted the questions that she found most exciting; the ones that really grabbed her attention. She thought that recording all of these questions would encourage her to develop her own ideas. She also recorded her own thoughts as a further set of questions that were designed as prompts to help her to be clear about what she needed to do to progress her research ideas.

Box 2.1
Focus on student research (*continued*)

Turning ideas into a viable project

Blogging it

Zaynab was a keen blogger so she posted summaries of her ideas and questions on a blog. She asked site visitors to suggest further reading, new research methods or for possible answers to her questions. She received 20 posts which she used to help turn her favourite idea into a question that could be answered for her research project.

Thinking about applying findings

Zaynab knew that she would be expected to comment on the practical implications of her findings when writing up her research. Therefore, an important part of her action plan was to ask herself what would be the implications for practice for the various outcomes that might be expected.

Most project tutors will argue that one of the attributes of a good topic is a clearly defined research question(s), aim and objectives (Section 2.4). These will, along with a good knowledge of the literature, enable you to assess the extent to which your research is likely to provide new insights into the topic. Many students believe this is going to be difficult. Fortunately there are numerous ways in which such insight can be defined as new (Sections 2.3 and 2.4).

If you have already been given a research idea (perhaps by an organisation) you will need to ensure that your question(s), aim and objectives relate clearly to the idea. It is also important that your topic will have **symmetry of potential outcomes**: that is, your results will be of similar value whatever you find out (Gill and Johnson 2010). Without this symmetry you may spend a considerable amount of time researching your topic, only to find an answer of little importance. Whatever the outcome, you need to ensure you have the scope to write an interesting project report.

Finally, it may be important to consider your future aspirations. If you wish to obtain employment or pursue a career in a particular subject area, it is sensible to use this opportunity to start to develop some expertise in it.

It is almost inevitable that the extent to which these attributes apply to your research topic will depend on your topic and the reasons why you are undertaking the research. However, most will apply. For this reason it is important that you check and continue to check any potential research topic against the summary checklist contained in Box 2.2.

Box 2.2
Checklist

Attributes of a good research topic

Capability: is it feasible?

✔ Is the topic something with which you are really fascinated?

✔ Do you have, or can you develop within the project time frame, the necessary research skills to undertake the topic?

✔ Is the research topic achievable within the available time?

✔ Will the topic still be current when you finish your project?

✔ Is the topic achievable within the financial resources that are likely to be available?

✔ Are you reasonably certain of being able to gain access to data you are likely to require for this topic?

Appropriateness: is it worthwhile?

✔ Does the topic fit the specifications and meet the standards set by the examining institution?

✔ Does your topic contain issues that have a clear link to theory?

✔ Are you able to state your research question(s), aim and objectives clearly?

✔ Will your proposed research be able to provide fresh insights into this topic?

✔ Does your topic relate clearly to the idea you have been given (perhaps by an organisation)?

✔ Are the findings for this topic likely to be symmetrical: that is, of similar value whatever the outcome?

✔ Does the topic match your career goals?

提出和提炼研究想法

2.3   Generating and refining research ideas

Some business and management students are expected both to generate and to refine their own research ideas. Others, particularly those on professional and post-experience courses, are provided with a research idea by an organisation or their university. In the initial stages of their research they are expected to refine this to a clear and feasible idea that meets the requirements of the examining organisation. If you have already been given a research idea we believe you will still find it useful to read the next sub-section, which deals with generating research ideas. Many of the techniques which can be used for generating research ideas can also be used for the refining process.

Generating research ideas

If you have not been given an initial **research idea** there is a range of techniques that can be used to find and select a topic that you would like to research. They can be thought of as those that are predominantly **rational thinking** and those that involve more **creative thinking** (Table 2.1).

The precise techniques that you choose to use and the order in which you use them are entirely up to you. However, we believe you should choose those that you believe are going to be of most use to you and which you will enjoy using. By using one or more creative techniques you are more likely to ensure that your heart as well as your head is in your research project. In our experience, it is usually better to use both rational and creative techniques. In order to do this you will need to have some understanding of the techniques and the ways in which they work. We therefore outline the techniques

Table 2.1 More frequently used techniques for generating and refining research ideas

Rational thinking	Creative thinking
Examining your own strengths and interests	Keeping a notebook of your ideas
Examining staff research interests	Exploring personal preferences using past projects
Looking at past project titles	
Discussion	Exploring relevance to business using the literature
Searching existing literature	Relevance trees
Scanning the media	Brainstorming

in Table 2.1 and subsequently discuss possible ways they might be used to generate research ideas. These techniques will generate one of two outcomes:

- one or more possible project ideas that you might undertake;
- few ideas that relate to your interests. In this case you may want to revise the area in which you are interested, either by choosing another area or by refining and perhaps narrowing or widening your original area of interest.

In either instance we suggest that you make some notes and arrange to talk to your project tutor.

Examining your own strengths and interests

It is important that you choose a topic in which you are likely to do well and, if possible, already have some academic knowledge. One way of doing this is to look at those assignments for which you have received good grades. For most of these assignments they are also likely to be the topics in which you were interested (Box 2.1). They will provide you with an area in which to search and find a research idea. In addition, you may, as part of your reading, be able to focus more precisely on the sort of ideas about which you wish to conduct your research.

As noted in Section 2.1, there is the need to think about your future. If you plan to work in financial management it would be sensible to choose a research project in the financial management field. One part of your course that will inevitably be discussed at any job interview is your research project. A project in the same field will provide you with the opportunity to display clearly your depth of knowledge and your enthusiasm.

Examining staff research interests

You may follow the links within your institution's website to the profile pages of academic staff. These pages are likely to display information about their teaching and research interests. You may be able to use this as a funnel to help you to explore and generate research ideas in which you would be interested for your own project. In very many cases, these pages will provide you with the overall subject area taught by each member of staff (e.g. accounting, international management, marketing, strategic management). These pages are also likely to list the particular research interests of each member of staff within her or his subject area (e.g. regulation of accounting standards, transnational management, pricing and price promotions, organisational learning). In many cases, a member of staff will offer a short commentary on her or his research interests which will provide more specific details. Lists of publications and conference papers with hyperlinks to online copies may be included. These will provide even more detail about the exact nature of the research interests of a member of staff. Working through this information may allow you to generate ideas for your own research and guide you to some initial reading to test this interest.

Looking at past project titles

Many of our students have found looking at past projects a useful way of generating research ideas. For undergraduate and taught master's degrees these are often called **dissertations**. For research degrees they are termed **theses**. A common way of doing this is to scan your university's list of past project titles for anything that captures your imagination. Titles that look interesting or which grab your attention should be noted down, as should any thoughts you have about the title in relation to your own research idea. In this process the fact that the title is poorly worded or the project report received a low mark is immaterial. What matters is the fact that you have found a topic that interests you. Based on this you can think of new ideas in the same general area that will enable you to provide fresh insights.

Scanning actual research projects may also produce research ideas. However, you need to beware. The fact that a project is in your library is no guarantee of the quality of the arguments and observations it contains. In many universities all projects are placed in the library whether they are bare passes or distinctions.

Discussion

Colleagues, friends and university tutors are all potentially good sources of possible research ideas. Often project tutors will have ideas for possible student projects, which they will be pleased to discuss with you.

Ideas can also be obtained by talking to people who work in or have direct experience of the topic area in which you are interested to develop a research idea. People who have experience of a topic area may include managers and other practitioners such as accountants, business analysts, marketing executives, human resource administrators, purchasing or sales staff as well as many others. Self-employed people and small business owners may be useful to talk to depending on your proposed topic area. Members of professional groups or workplace representatives may also provide you with insights that help to generate research ideas. Your contact with such people at this early stage may be fortuitous, relying on being able to talk to someone you already know such as those in an organisation in which you have undertaken a work placement. If such people are willing to spare some time to talk to you, it may be worthwhile to help you towards generating a research idea. It is important that as well as discussing possible ideas you also make a note of them. What seemed like a good idea in the coffee shop may not be remembered quite so clearly after the following lecture!

Searching existing literature

As part of your discussions, relevant literature may also be suggested. There are various types of literature that are of particular use for generating research ideas. These include:

- articles in academic journals;
- articles in professional journals;
- reports;
- books.

Academic journal articles are intended to produce a theoretical contribution and will therefore contain a section that reviews literature relevant to the article's topic area. Given the nature of published research, journal articles are generally highly specialised, focusing on a particular aspect of a management subject. You will need to be prepared to undertake an extensive search lasting some hours (or even days) to find articles that might be helpful in generating research ideas related to your broader topic of interest. Of particular use, where you can find suitable ones, are academic **review articles**. Some journals focus on publishing review articles – so look out for these! These articles contain a considered review of the state of knowledge in a particular topic area and are therefore likely to contain a wealth of ideas about that area (Box 2.3). These ideas will act as pointers towards aspects where further research needs to be undertaken. In addition,

Box 2.3
Focus on management research

Evaluating the scope for strategic human resource management

A series of review articles was published in an issue of the *Academy of Management Perspectives* in 2012 focusing on literature about strategic human resource management. This is a complex area of study that seeks to understand the relationship between human resource management practices and organisational performance. The idea of strategic human resource management has become particularly important in the context of the globalisation of production and increased global competition. However, given its theoretical nature, questions are raised in the literature about its applicability in practice and across national boundaries.

An introductory review article in this issue (Marler 2012) introduces succinctly the subject of strategic human resource management and outlines the development of theoretical perspectives used to define and identify it. Further review articles examine and evaluate the literature on the evidence and scope for strategic human resource management in the United States (Kaufman 2012), Germany (Festing 2012) and China (Liang et al. 2012). Together these articles provide a very useful review of the academic literature as well as numerous further references to follow up.

you can browse recent publications online, in particular journals, for possible research ideas (Section 3.5).

For many subject areas your project tutor will be able to suggest recent review articles, or articles that contain recommendations for further research. Reports may also be of use. The most recently published are usually up to date and, again, often contain recommendations that may form the basis of your research idea. Books by contrast may be less up to date than other written sources. They often, however, contain a good overview of research that has been undertaken, which may suggest ideas to you.

Alvesson and Sandberg (2011) report that articles published in academic management journals are predominantly based on research that finds new ways to investigate around existing theoretical perspectives. They call this approach 'gap spotting', suggesting it results in incremental changes in theory. They identify a more critical and reflexive but rarer approach to research that challenges the assumptions underpinning existing theoretical perspectives and which has the potential to lead to more interesting and high-impact theories. Given the difficulties associated with designing an assumption-challenging study, it is much more likely that you will adopt the first approach. We discuss this further when we consider the importance of theory in writing research questions and objectives in Section 2.4.

Searching for publications is only possible when you have at least some idea of the area in which you wish to undertake your research. One way of obtaining this is to re-examine your lecture notes and course textbooks and to note those subjects that appear most interesting (discussed earlier in this section) and the names of relevant authors. This will give you a basis on which to undertake a **preliminary search** (using techniques outlined in Sections 3.4 and 3.5). When the articles, reports and other items have been obtained it is often helpful to look for unfounded assertions and statements on the absence of research, as these are likely to contain ideas that will enable you to provide fresh insights.

Scanning the media

Keeping up to date with items in the news can be a very rich source of ideas. The stories which occur every day in the 'broadsheet' or 'compact' newspapers, in both online and traditional print versions, may provide ideas which relate directly to the item (e.g. the extent to which items sold by supermarkets contravene the principles of 'green consumerism' by involving excessive 'food miles' in order to import them). Please note, however, that some of these online media are only available by subscription. The stories in these media may also suggest other ideas which flow from the central story (e.g. the degree to which a company uses its claimed environmental credentials as part of its marketing campaign).

Keeping a notebook of your ideas

One of the more creative techniques that we all use is to keep a **notebook of ideas**. This involves simply noting down any interesting research ideas as you think of them and, of equal importance, what sparked off your thought. You can then pursue the idea using more rational thinking techniques later. Mark keeps a notebook by his bed so he can jot down any flashes of inspiration that occur to him in the middle of the night!

Exploring personal preferences using past projects

One way to generate and evaluate possible project ideas is to explore your personal preferences by reading through a number of past project reports from your university. To get started you need to search through these and select a number that you like and a number that you do not like.

For each project that you like, note down your first thoughts in response to each of the following questions:

1 What do you like in general about the project?
2 Why do you like the project?
3 Which ideas in the project appeal to you?

For each project that you do not like, note down your first thoughts in response to each of the following questions:

1 What do you dislike in general about the project?
2 Why do you dislike the project?
3 Which ideas in the project do not appeal to you?

When you have completed this task, you may find it helpful to spend some time reflecting on each set of notes – for the projects you like and those you do not. By reflecting on and thinking about each list you should begin to understand those project characteristics that are important to you and with which you feel comfortable. Of equal importance, you will have identified those with which you are uncomfortable and should avoid.

This process has two benefits. Firstly, it may help you to generate possible research ideas. Secondly, you may use the project characteristics that emerge from exploring your personal preferences as parameters against which to evaluate possible research ideas.

Exploring relevance to business using the literature

There is an enormous amount of research published in business and management journals. The nature of these journals varies considerably, ranging from those with a more applied focus to those that are more esoteric. As a result, there will be many ways in which you may explore the relevance to business of ideas published in the literature. The relevance to business practice of academic business research and education remains a key issue (Box 2.4). Even more esoteric journal articles contain a wealth of ideas that may be explored for their relevance to business. Such articles may contain ideas that you may be able to translate, make operational and test in practice in a given setting, such as a particular organisation, albeit using a simpler methodology

Box 2.4 Focus on research in the news

A degree of relevance for the 21st century?

By Emma Boyde

If business schools cannot tailor the education they offer to suit the new demands of the workplace they risk being sidelined, writes *Emma Boyde*

Business degrees account for a vast section of the undergraduate and postgraduate higher education market. In its Business School Data Trends 2013 the AACSB International, the US-based accrediting body, estimates that as of last February there were 15,673 institutions worldwide offering business degrees at all levels.

In the US, the gold standard MBA degree is thought to account for two-thirds of all graduate business degrees conferred in the US.

The UK's Association of Business Schools has estimated that one in seven UK undergraduates are studying business and management, and expects the number studying at both undergraduate and graduate level to rise as students seek subjects with clear links to employability.

David Gann, vice-president of Imperial College and founding head of its Innovation and Entrepreneurship Group, thinks that some basic changes in the mindset of some business educators could help.

"I would say in general there's a big question about some of the relevance of business schools and how they operate," he says. These issues are being addressed particularly in North America and Europe, he adds,

Prof Gann believes that part of the problem is the disconnect between research and the role of business schools in preparing students for their future positions in the business world.

"The world has moved on, the question is: have business schools moved on and I think the answer to that is: not yet.

Prof Gann believes that business education should model itself a little more closely on disciplines such as engineering or medicine.

"You need practical application, not just research." Although he stresses: "It's not either/or, you need both."

FT *Source of extract:* Boyde, E. (2013) 'A degree of relevance for the 21st century?', *Financial Times*, 15 July. Copyright The Financial Times Limited.

than that in the published study. The 'Discussion' section in many business and management journals routinely includes an 'Implications for practice' sub-section, which may guide you towards developing a research idea to explore the relevance of the theory in the article to a particular business setting, such as your employing organisation.

Articles based on empirical studies may also provide you with research ideas. A published empirical study may have been undertaken as a case study. It may have been based in a particular sector or industry, and it may have been based in a particular organisation or type of organisation. Reading it may lead you to think that you could undertake a similar study, albeit possibly scaled down, in a different type of organisation, in a different industry or sector.

There may be scope for you to undertake a case study that seeks to apply the findings from a large sample statistical study to a particular organisational context or type of organisation. This will allow you to test the applicability of these previous findings and to convert them into a relevant and accessible form for a particular context.

Creatively approaching the literature to convert existing work into a relevant and specifically applied study, in the ways we have described, may provide you with a rich and valuable research idea.

Relevance trees

Relevance trees may also prove useful in generating research topics. In this instance, their use is similar to that of mind mapping (Buzan 2011) in which you start with a broad concept from which you generate further (usually more specific) topics. Each of these topics forms a separate branch from which you can generate further, more detailed sub-branches. As you proceed down the sub-branches more ideas are generated and recorded. These can then be examined and a number selected and combined to provide a research idea. This technique is discussed in more detail in Section 3.4 (and illustrated in Box 3.8).

Brainstorming

The technique of **brainstorming** (Box 2.5), taught as a problem-solving technique on many business and management courses, can also be used to generate and refine research ideas. It is best undertaken with a group of people, although you can brainstorm on your own. Brainstorming involves a number of stages:

1 *Defining the problem*. This will focus on the sorts of ideas you are interested in – as precisely as possible. In the early stages of formulating a topic this may be as vague as, 'I am interested in marketing but don't know what to do for my research topic'.
2 *Asking for suggestions*. These will relate to the problem.
3 *Recording suggestions*. As you record these you will need to observe the following rules:
   • No suggestion should be criticised or evaluated in any way before all ideas have been considered.
   • All suggestions, however wild, should be recorded and considered.
   • As many suggestions as possible should be recorded.
4 *Reviewing suggestions*. You will seek to explore what is meant by each as you review these.
5 *Analysing suggestions*. Work through the list of ideas and decide which appeal to you most as research ideas and why.

Box 2.5
Focus on student research

Brainstorming

George's main interest was football. In his university city he worked part-time in the retail store of the local football club and thought he would like to carry out his research project in this setting.

When he finished university he wanted to work in marketing, preferably for a sports goods manufacturer. He had examined his own strengths and discovered that his best marks were in marketing. He wanted to do his research project on some aspect of marketing, preferably linked to the football club, but had no real research idea. He asked three friends, all taking business management degrees, to help him brainstorm the problem.

George began by explaining the problem in some detail. At first the suggestions emerged slowly. He noted them down on some flipchart sheets. Soon a number of sheets of paper were covered with suggestions and pinned up around the room. George counted these and discovered there were over 100.

Reviewing individual suggestions produced nothing that any of the group felt to be of sufficient merit for a research project. However, George recalled an article they had been asked to read based on a case study of an English Premier League football club (Ogbonna and Harris 2014). He had found this interesting because of its subject. He recalled that it was about organisational culture being perpetuated within organisations that have a long history of success, and stakeholder groups such as football fans who have a strong sense of identity.

George's recollections of this article encouraged the group to discuss their suggestions further. Combining a number of suggestions from the flipchart sheets with their discussion about organisational cultural perpetuation, George noted a possible research idea as: 'the impact of factors that perpetuate organisational culture on the development of marketing strategies – help or hindrance?'

George thought this idea could be based on his local football club.

George arranged to see his project tutor to discuss how to refine the idea they had just generated.

Refining research ideas

The Delphi technique

An approach that our students have found useful to refine their research ideas is the **Delphi technique** (Box 2.6). One approach to this, known as 'Policy Delphi', encourages the identification of refinements or alternatives to an initial research idea. It involves using an informal group of people, such as some of your classmates or colleagues who are interested in the initial idea, to generate related ideas, evaluate these and perhaps to arrive at a consensus around a specific research idea (Paraskevas and Saunders 2012). To use this technique you need:

1 to brief the members of the group about the initial research idea (they can make notes if they wish);
2 to, at the end of the briefing, encourage group members to seek clarification and more information as appropriate;
3 to ask each member of the group, including the originator of the research idea, to generate independently up to three alternative research ideas based on the initial idea (they can also be asked to provide a justification for their specific ideas);
4 to collect the research ideas in an unedited and non-attributable form and to distribute them to all members of the group to reflect on;

Box 2.6
Focus on student research

Using a Delphi Group

Tim explained to the group that his research idea was concerned with understanding the decision-making processes associated with mortgage applications and loan advances. His briefing to the three other group members, and the questions that they asked him, considered aspects such as:

- the particular situation of potential first-time house buyers;
- the way in which the nature of contact between potential borrowers and financial institutions might influence decision making.

The group then moved on to generate a number of more specific research ideas, among which were the following:

- the effect of being a first-time house purchaser on mortgage application decision making;
- the effect of websites and mobile apps that facilitate property searching and links to mortgage specialists on decision making;
- the effect of interpersonal contact on mortgage decisions;
- the attributes that potential applicants look for in financial institutions operating in the mortgage market.

These ideas were considered and commented on by all the group members. At the end of the second cycle Tim had, with the other students' agreement, refined his research idea to:

- an evaluation of the factors that influence potential first-time buyers' choice of lending institution.

Tim now needed to pursue this idea by undertaking a preliminary search of the literature.

---

5 to encourage group members to comment on each research idea, including giving reasons for their opinions;

6 a second cycle of steps 2 to 5 to encourage further refinements or new options in light of what others have said during the first cycle;

7 subsequent cycles of the process until an outcome is reached. This may be a consensus around a particular research idea. It may occur when saturation occurs – no further ideas are forthcoming. It may also occur when participants become tired and less productive. In practice, three cycles of this technique are likely to produce an effective outcome.

This process works well, not least because people enjoy trying to help one another. In addition, it is very useful in forming cohesive groups.

The preliminary inquiry

It is often necessary to refine your research idea in order to turn it into a research question and then into your research project. This may involve a **preliminary inquiry** or initial inquiry. This is likely to involve searching for and evaluating relevant literature and other related sources (Box 2.7 provides a rare reported example of this in the literature). This may lead to the first iteration of your critical literature review, or help to inform it (Figure 3.1).

For some researchers this process may also include informal discussions with people who have personal experience of and knowledge about your research ideas. It may also involve **shadowing** employees who are likely to be important in your research and who may therefore be able to provide some initial insights. If you are planning on undertaking

Box 2.7
Focus on management research

The rare case of a reported preliminary inquiry

There are few reports in journal articles of the preliminary inquiries that researchers undertake. Generally the 'methods' section of a journal article only describes the research methodology and techniques used in the actual study. This is probably due to word limits and the presentation of research as an unproblematic process. However, in many studies there may not be a well-defined theoretical base from which to commence the research. There may instead be several possible theoretical strands that might be useful for the proposed study, which need to be explored first. Researchers may need to search for and familiarise themselves with theoretical strands that were previously unknown to them. These possibilities are likely to be the case where the proposed research seeks to explore a new area.

Elsbach et al. (2010) describe how a group of researchers undertook a preliminary inquiry to help establish the need for a substantive research study. Their research, published in *Human Relations*, examines 'how passive "face time" (i.e. the amount of time one is passively observed without interaction) affects how one is perceived at work' (Elsbach et al. 2010: 735). For example, it is likely to be important for new employees to create an impression of being a diligent worker, without the observer knowing exactly what the person being observed is actually doing. Being seen is what Elsbach and colleagues call 'expected face time'. Positive impressions may be created by being seen in the right places (e.g. at one's desk, in meetings, taking part in events) rather than being based on actual performance. There is also 'extracurricular face time', where the impression an employee creates is also shaped by his or her involvement outside work.

Elsbach et al. identified this as a research idea that had not been investigated previously. They thought that this was surprising because of the increasing numbers of employees who spend much time working away from their work base, as well as the existence of anecdotal evidence indicating that remote workers may feel anxious about their lack of face time.

They conducted a preliminary inquiry that commenced with the collection of anecdotal evidence which suggested that passive face time was linked to the creation of positive impressions of employees in professional jobs. This anecdotal evidence was gleaned from newspaper articles, business magazines and books. In order to understand this relationship further they located two strands of theoretical literature which offered them 'clues' about 'how and why passive face time affects perceptions of employees who display it' (Elsbach et al. 2010: 739). These two strands of literature related to research on organisational citizenship behaviour and research on trait inferences. While these strands of literature had not been designed to focus on passive face time, they lent some support to the idea that being seen in the workplace was likely to lead observers to infer positive attributes about those being observed.

This preliminary inquiry led Elsbach and colleagues to identify that this was an area worth researching to close the gap in our understanding of this phenomenon. They devised a research question – 'How do observers perceive displayers of passive face time in professional work contexts?' (Elsbach et al. 2010: 742) – as a result of their preliminary inquiry, which led to a substantive research project composed of two stages. The first of these, called 'Study 1', involved an exploratory stage that used semi-structured interviews which were analysed inductively using the principles of Grounded Theory (Chapter 5). The second of these, called 'Study 2', involved an experimental design (Chapter 5) to test the 'proposed effects of passive face time' (Elsbach et al. 2010: 748).

your research within an organisation, it is also important to gain a good understanding of your host organisation (McDonald 2005). However, whatever techniques you use, the underlying purpose is to gain a greater understanding so that your research question can be refined, perhaps by also revisiting some of the techniques we discussed earlier in this section.

At this stage you will need to test your research ideas against the checklist in Box 2.2 and where necessary change them. It may be that after a preliminary inquiry, or discussing your ideas with colleagues, you decide that the research idea is no longer feasible in the form in which you first envisaged it. If this is the case, do not be too downhearted. It is far better to revise your research ideas at this stage than to have to do it later, when you have undertaken far more work.

Integrating ideas

The integration of ideas from these techniques is essential if your research is to have a clear direction and not contain a mismatch between objectives and your final project report. Jankowicz (2005: 34–6) suggests an integrative process that our students have found most useful. This he terms 'working up and narrowing down'. It involves classifying each research idea first into its area, then its field, and finally the precise aspect in which you are interested. These represent an increasingly detailed description of the research idea. Thus your initial area, based on examining your coursework, might be accountancy. After browsing some recent journals and discussion with colleagues this becomes more focused on the field of financial accounting methods. With further reading, the use of a Delphi technique and discussion with your project tutor you decide to focus on the aspect of activity-based costing.

You will know when the process of generating and refining ideas is complete as you will be able to say, 'I'd like to do some research on ...'. Obviously there will still be a big gap between this and the point when you are ready to start serious work on your research. Sections 2.4 and 2.5 will ensure that you are ready to bridge that gap.

Refining topics given by your employing organisation

As a part-time student, your manager may provide you with a research topic. This may be something that affects your work and in which you have an interest. You may have discussed this with your manager and relish the opportunity to tackle this topic.

It may, however, be a topic in which you are not particularly interested. In this case you will have to weigh the advantage of doing something useful to the organisation against the disadvantage of a potential lack of personal motivation. You therefore need to achieve a balance. Often the research project your manager wishes you to undertake is larger than is appropriate for your course. In such cases, it may be possible to complete both by isolating an element of the larger organisational project that you find interesting and treating this as the project for your course.

One of our students was asked to do a preliminary investigation of the strengths and weaknesses of her organisation's pay system and then to recommend consultants to design and implement a new system. She was not particularly interested in this project. However, she was considering becoming a freelance personnel consultant. Therefore, for her research project she decided to study the decision-making process in relation to the appointment of personnel consultants. Her organisation's decision on which consultant to appoint, and why this decision was taken, proved to be a useful case study against which to compare management decision-making theory.

In this event you would write a larger report for your organisation and a part of it for your project report. Section 14.4 offers some guidance on writing two separate reports for different audiences.

Other problems may involve your political relationships in the organisation. For example, there will be those keen to commission a project which justifies their particular policy position and see you as a useful pawn in advancing their political interests. It is important to have a clear stance with regard to what you want to do, and your personal objectives, and to stick to this.

A further potential problem may be one of your own making: to promise to deliver research outcomes to your employer and not do so.

Conducting research in your own organisation is also likely to be problematic because of your role as an internal researcher (Tietze 2012). We return to discuss a range of issues related to this role in Section 5.9.

将研究想法转化为研究项目

2.4   Turning research ideas into research projects

Writing research questions

It will be important for you to turn your research idea into a clearly defined **research question** before commencing the research process. As a student, you are likely to be required to include a research question in your written research proposal (Section 2.5). The importance of creating a clearly defined research question cannot be overemphasised. A research question will allow you to say what the issue or problem is that you wish to study and what your research project will seek to find out, explain and answer. One of the key criteria of your research success will be whether you have developed a set of clear conclusions from the data you have collected. The extent to which you can do that will be determined largely by the clarity with which you have posed your research question (Box 2.8).

This research question will be at the centre of your research project. It will influence your choice of literature to review, your research design, the access you need to negotiate, your approach to sampling, your choice of data collection and analysis methods, and help to shape the way in which you write your project report. This overarching research question is sometimes referred to as a 'general research question', 'general focus research question' or 'central research question'. It will also be used to generate a set of more detailed research objectives or investigative questions to guide your research, discussed later.

However, it is also important to recognise that some research approaches and research strategies start off in a more exploratory and emergent direction (Chapter 5). For a researcher undertaking this type of research, her or his finalised research question may only emerge during the process of data collection and analysis as she or he discovers the exact focus of her or his research project and refines its direction. Such an approach is open ended and time consuming and is unlikely to be practical where you are undertaking a time-limited research project. Despite this, some of the mainly qualitative strategies (discussed in Chapter 5), including Ethnographic Studies and Grounded Theory, are exploratory and emergent and will often lead you, where you use one of these, to refine your initial research question and project as you progress. Most tutors will say in such

Box 2.8
Focus on student research

Defining the research question

Imran was studying for a BSc in Business Management and undertaking his placement year in an advanced consumer electronics company. When he first joined the company he was surprised to note that the company's business strategy, which was announced in the company newsletter, seemed to be inconsistent with what Imran knew of the product market.

Imran had become particularly interested in corporate strategy in his degree. He was familiar with some of the literature which suggested that corporate strategy should be linked to the general external environment in which the organisation operated. He wanted to do some research on corporate strategy in his organisation for his degree dissertation.

After talking this over with his project tutor, Imran decided on the following research question: 'Why does [organisation's name]'s corporate strategy not seem to reflect the major factors in the external operating environment?'

cases that it is part of the process to refine your original research question as your project progresses to reflect the direction of your emerging research. It is always advisable to discuss such developments with your project tutor! The key point is that if you use such a research approach it is still important to define a clear research question at the outset of your project to focus your research, even if you then refine your research question accordingly.

Defining research questions, rather like generating research ideas (Section 2.3), is not a straightforward matter. It is important that the question is sufficiently involved to generate the sort of project that is consistent with the standards expected of you (Box 2.2). A question that only prompts a descriptive answer – for example, 'What is the proportion of graduates entering the civil service who attended the pre-1992 UK universities?' – is far easier to answer than: 'Why are graduates from pre-1992 UK universities more likely to enter the civil service than graduates from other universities?' However, answering the first question is unlikely to satisfy your examining body's requirements as it only needs description.

Questions may be divided into ones that are exploratory, descriptive, explanatory or evaluative (Section 5.4). Any research question you ask is likely to begin with or include either 'What', 'When', 'Where', 'Who', 'Why', or 'How'. Each of these will lead to an answer that is partly descriptive and sometimes entirely descriptive, such as: 'How much did the marketing campaign for the new range of products cost?' Exploratory questions are likely to begin with 'How' or 'What'. For example, 'How has the corporate rebranding strategy affected consumer attitudes?' Questions that seek explanations will either commence with 'Why' or contain this word within the question. For example, a question may ask customers what they think about a new product and why they like or dislike it. Questions that are evaluative are also likely to begin with 'How' or 'What' but unlike the 'How much...?' or 'How has...?' questions, an evaluative question might ask, 'How effective was the marketing campaign for the new range of products?' Another way of wording this type of question might be, 'To what extent was the marketing campaign effective and why?' We discuss further the relationship between 'How', 'What' and 'Why' questions later in this section.

While some questions may be too simple, it is perhaps more likely that you might fall into the trap of asking research questions that are too difficult. The question cited earlier, 'Why are graduates from pre-1992 UK universities more likely to enter the civil service than graduates from other universities?', is a case in point. It would probably be very difficult to gain sufficient access to the inner portals of the civil service to get a good grasp of the subtle 'unofficial' processes that go on at staff selection which may favour one type of candidate over another. Over-reaching yourself in the definition of research questions is a danger.

Clough and Nutbrown (2012) use what they call the '**Goldilocks test**' to decide if research questions are either 'too big', 'too small', 'too hot' or 'just right'. Those that are too big probably need significant research funding because they demand too many resources. Questions that are too small are likely to be of insufficient substance, while those that are too 'hot' may be so because of sensitivities that might be aroused as a result of doing the research. This may be because of the timing of the research or the many other reasons that could upset key people who have a role to play, either directly or indirectly, in the research context. Research questions that have been written to take into account the researcher's status and the availability of resources, including time and the research setting, are more likely to be about right.

The pitfall you must avoid at all costs is asking a research question that will not generate new insights (Box 2.2). This raises the question of the extent to which you have consulted the relevant literature. It is perfectly legitimate to replicate research because you have a genuine concern about its applicability to your research setting (for example, your organisation). However, it certainly is not legitimate to display your ignorance of the literature.

In order to clarify a research question, Clough and Nutbrown (2012) talk of the Russian doll principle. This means refining a draft research question until it reflects the essence of your research idea without including any unnecessary words or intentions. By stripping away any unnecessary layers (the larger outer dolls), the clearly defined research question (the smallest doll) that you reveal should provide you with an appropriately focused starting point for your research project.

Writing your research questions will be, in most cases, your task but it is useful to get other people to help. An obvious source of guidance is your project tutor. Consulting your project tutor will avoid the pitfalls of the questions that are too easy or too difficult or have been answered before. Discussing your area of interest with your project tutor will lead to your research questions becoming much clearer.

Prior to discussion with your project tutor you may wish to conduct a brainstorming session with your peers or use the Delphi technique (Section 2.3). Your research questions may flow from your initial examination of the relevant literature. As outlined in Section 2.3, journal articles reporting primary research will often end with a conclusion that includes the consideration by the author of the implications for future research of the work in the article. This may be phrased in the form of research questions. However, even if it is not, it may suggest possible research questions to you.

Table 2.2 provides some examples of general focus research questions.

Writing a research aim and set of research objectives

As well as your research question, you may also be required to formulate a **research aim**. A research aim is a brief statement of the purpose of the research project. It is often written as a sentence stating what you intend to achieve through your research. To illustrate this, the examples of research questions in Table 2.2 have been matched to their

Table 2.2 Examples of research ideas and resulting general focus research questions

Research idea	Research question
Media campaign following product recalls	How effective is a media campaign designed to increase consumer trust in [company name] following a series of product recalls?
Graduate recruitment via the Internet	To what extent and in what type of context is Internet-based recruitment and selection of graduates effective and why?
Supermarket coupons as a promotional device	In what ways do the issue of coupons at supermarket checkouts affect buyer behaviour?
Challenger banks and small businesses	How has the emergence of challenger banks impacted upon small businesses' financing and why?

research aims in Table 2.3. You will see the close relationship between these – one stated as a question, the other as an aim.

Your research question and research aim are complementary ways of saying what your research is about. However, neither gives sufficient detail about the steps you will need to take to answer your question and achieve your aim.

To do this you will need to devise a set of investigative questions or research objectives. Your research question may be used to generate more detailed investigative questions, or you may use it as a base from which to write a set of **research objectives**. Objectives are more generally acceptable to the research community as evidence of the researcher's clear sense of purpose and direction. Once you have devised your research question and research aim, we believe that research objectives are likely to lead to greater specificity than using investigative questions. It may be that either is satisfactory. Do check whether your examining body has a preference.

Table 2.3 Examples of research questions and related research aims

Research question	Research aim
How effective is a media campaign designed to increase consumer trust in [company name] following a series of product recalls?	The aim of this research is to assess the effectiveness of a media campaign by [company name] designed to increase consumer trust following a series of recalls of its products
In which situations and to what extent is Internet-based recruitment and selection of graduates effective and why?	The aim of this research is to understand situations within which Internet-based recruitment and selection of graduates is effective and why
In what ways do the issue of coupons at supermarket checkouts affect buyer behaviour?	The aim of this research is to explore how the issue of coupons at supermarket checkouts affects buyer behaviour
How has the emergence of challenger banks impacted upon small businesses' financing and why?	The aim of this research is to explore how the emergence of challenger banks has impacted upon small businesses' financing and why

Table 2.4 Criteria to devise useful research objectives

Criterion	Purpose
Transparency (What does it mean?)	The meaning of the research objective is clear and unambiguous
Specificity (What I am going to do?)	The purpose of the research objective is clear and easily understood, as are the actions required to fulfil it
Relevance (Why I am going to do this?)	The research objective's link to the research question and wider research project is clear
Interconnectivity (How will it help to complete the research project?)	Taken together as a set, the research objectives illustrate the steps in the research process from its start to its conclusion, without leaving any gaps. In this way, the research objectives form a coherent whole
Answerability (Will this be possible?) (Where shall I obtain data?)	The intended outcome of the research objective is achievable. Where this relates to data, the nature of the data required will be clear or at least implied
Measurability (When will it be done?)	The intended product of the research objective will be evident when it has been achieved

Research objectives allow you to **operationalise** your question – that is, to state the steps you intend to take to answer it. A similar way of thinking about the difference between questions, aims and objectives is related to 'what' and 'how'. Research questions and aims express 'what' your research is about. Research objectives express 'how' you intend to structure the research process to answer your question and achieve your aim. In this way, research objectives can be seen to complement a research question and aim, through providing the means to operationalise them. They provide a key step to transform your research question and aim into your research project.

Writing useful research objectives requires you to fulfil a number of fit-for-purpose criteria. Table 2.4 sets out criteria to help you devise research objectives to operationalise your research question and aim. Each of these criteria is also rephrased as a short question, which you can use as a checklist to evaluate your own draft research objectives.

Box 2.9 provides an example set of objectives at the stage when a student's research question and aim were developed into a sequence of research objectives.

Box 2.9
Focus on student research

Writing a set of research objectives

Tom was a part-time student who worked for a large power and gas company employing several thousand employees across many different sites. Tom had been undertaking an employment-related project on employee engagement and had decided to focus his

university research project on employee communication. His employing organisation had been increasingly focusing its employee communication towards Internet- and intranet-based channels. Tom had noted the following comment in the CIPD Factsheet on employee communication (2012: 5): 'A communication process needs to be reviewed regularly, to see if it is meeting the needs of both the organisation and the employee. In measuring communication it is important to assess … if appropriate methods of communication are being used.'

Following a process of generating and refining ideas for research Tom decided that he would like to explore the effectiveness of employee communication developments in his employing organisation. This idea had been approved by the internal communication management team and he was informed that his request for access to managers would be supported.

Tom refined his research question until he was satisfied with it: 'How effective are Internet and intranet channels as a means to communicate with employees in [company name]?' He also turned this into a research aim: 'The aim of this research is to evaluate the effectiveness of Internet and intranet channels as a means to communicate with employees in [company name]'. He and his project tutor felt that the scope of this research question and related aim was 'just about right'. They felt it was 'doable' and that it focused on an issue that was important and relevant for the business.

Tom's project tutor asked Tom to draw up a set of interconnected research objectives that would operationalise his research and provide a set of evaluation criteria to enable him to address his 'how effective ...' type of question. Tom came up with the following set of research objectives. Objective 2 allowed Tom to identify the company's objectives for each channel

and objectives 3–6 allowed Tom to measure and then compare channels in order to draw conclusions about 'how effective' they were.

1 To identify each Internet and intranet channel of employee communication used in the company;

2 To describe the company's objectives for each channel (e.g. conveying news about the business, facilitating communication across the company, announcing results and targets, bringing about behavioural change);

3 To identify and explore specific examples of how each channel has been beneficial or influential;

4 To identify and explore specific examples where each channel has not been beneficial or influential;

5 To determine a measure of effectiveness for each channel that shows whether and how the channel had met, exceeded or failed to meet the objectives set for it;

6 To compare measures of effectiveness across channels related to different organisational objectives;

7 To make recommendations about each channel's future use and fitness for purpose.

The importance of theory in writing research questions and objectives

Section 4.4 outlines the role of theory in helping you to decide your approach to research design. However, your consideration of theory should begin earlier than this. It should inform your research questions and research objectives.

To help you to think about this, we ask four questions that relate to the role of theory. What is theory? Why is theory important? How is theory developed? What types of theoretical contribution might be made? These questions lead into the discussion in Section 4.4.

What is theory?

To address the question 'what is theory?' we use the influential work of Whetten (1989). Whetten identified that theory is composed of four elements, related to 'what', 'how', 'why' and a fourth group of 'who', 'where' and 'when'. The first of these may be summarised as: what are the variables or concepts that the theory examines? For example, in Box 2.9, the variables in Tom's research question are communication channels and employees (their awareness and behaviours).

The second element may be summarised as: how are these variables or concepts related? Tom's research question was designed to examine the relationship between communication channels and employees. A key aspect here is **causality**. Theory is concerned with cause and effect. In Tom's research, Tom was interested to explore how each communication channel influenced employees' levels of awareness and behaviour. In other words, does the use of a particular channel have an effect on employees' levels of awareness and behaviour.

The third element may be summarised as: why are these variables or concepts related? This is the critical element in a theory because it explains the nature of the relationship between the variables or concepts. According to Whetten, 'what' and 'how' are descriptive; it is 'why' that explains the relationship. This point is worth developing, as you may be asking, 'what is the difference between "how" and "why" in this context?' In the case of Tom's research, Tom found that his data suggested some channels were better at communicating news from the senior management team, whereas other channels were better at facilitating communication between employees. His data helped him to recognise relationships that he could describe. However, Tom needed to analyse his data further (and where necessary to extend its collection) to answer the question, 'why do these relationships exist in my data?'

To summarise so far, good theory must not only include 'what' and 'how' elements to identify underpinning variables and describe the nature of their relationship (cause and effect); it must also use **logical reasoning** to explain why the relationship exists. 'Logical' because you will be looking for good reasons to explain 'why' and 'reasoning' because your use of logic will be based on what you already know, related to the 'what' and 'how'. Once a valid explanation has been developed, the theory may be used not only to explain why the relationship exists but also to make predictions about new outcomes if the variables on which the theory is based are manipulated (or changed). In the case of Tom's research, his theory may be used to predict that increasing investment in an effective communication channel will lead to improvements in employee awareness. Conversely, it may be used to predict that withdrawing investment in this channel will be a false cost saving.

While good theory has the power to explain and predict, it may also be subject to limitations. The scope of many theories will be limited by one or more constraints. The fourth group of elements that Whetten identified may therefore be summarised as: who does this theory apply to; where does this theory apply; when does this theory apply? In the case of Tom's research, Tom recognised that some of his theoretical conclusions applied to engineering staff but not to administrative staff. Other conclusions applied to head office employees but not to regional employees. He also recognised that as new communication channels were introduced by the company, the application of his conclusions to these would need to be re-evaluated in the future.

In this way, the explanations of the cause-and-effect relationships between variables in a theory may be contextual and time limited, indicating constraints to their generalisability. Another important contribution that addresses the question 'what is theory?' starts from the opposite perspective by discussing 'What theory is not' (Sutton and Staw 1995). This is a helpful contribution to our understanding and provides a complementary approach to that of Whetten (1989) (Box 2.10).

Box 2.10
Focus on management research

Clarifying what theory is not

Sutton and Staw (1995) make a helpful contribution to the question 'What is theory?' by defining what it is not. In their view theory is not:

1 *References.* Listing references to existing theories and mentioning the names of such theories may look impressive. However, alluding to the theory developed by other researchers may only provide a smokescreen. Instead researchers need to identify the concepts, causal relationships and logical explanations that they are using from previous theoretical work in relation to their own work.

2 *Data.* Data are important to be able to confirm, revise or overturn existing theory and to be able to develop new theory. However, data are used to describe the relationships or patterns that are revealed from their collection and analysis. Description by itself does not equal theory. Theory also requires logical explanations to discuss why such relationships or patterns were revealed, or

why they might be expected to be revealed when testing existing theory (Section 4.3).

3 *Lists of variables.* Variables are important in the process of theory development but simply presenting or listing these by themselves does not represent a theory.

4 *Diagrams.* Diagrams are often helpful to show observed or expected causal relationships and how different relationships are related or how they are expected to be related. However, by themselves diagrams or figures are not theory. Sutton and Staw (1995: 376) state: 'Good theory is often representational and verbal.' They say that clear explanations can be represented graphically but that, to be able to develop a rich theoretical understanding, these will also require written discussion to explain why these relationships exist.

5 *Hypotheses or predictions.* In a similar manner to point 3, hypotheses are an important part of the process of developing and testing theory in particular theoretical approaches (Experiment in Section 5.5), but they do not constitute a theory by themselves.

You are likely to use research questions rather than hypotheses in your research design and we would add to point 5 that the propositions or concepts that inform your research questions are also not theory by themselves.

Why is theory important?

There is probably no word that is more misused and misunderstood in education than the word 'theory'. It is thought that material included in textbooks is 'theory', whereas what is happening in the 'real world' is practice. Students who saw earlier editions of this book remarked that they were pleased that the book was not too 'theoretical'. What they meant was that the book concentrated on giving lots of practical advice. Yet the book is full of theory. Advising you to carry out research in a particular way (variable A) is based on the theory that this will yield effective results (variable B). This is the cause-and-effect relationship referred to in the definition of theory developed earlier and is very much the view of Kelly (1955). Kelly argues that the individual who attempts to solve the daily problems which we all face goes about this activity in much the same way as the scientist. Both continuously make and test hypotheses and revise their concepts accordingly. Both organise their results into what are called schemata and then into a system of broader schemata which are called theories. Kelly asserts that we need such schemata and theories in order to make sense of the complexity of the world in which we live. Without these organising frameworks we would be overwhelmed by the unconnected detail we would have to recall.

Implicitly each of us uses theory in our lives and in the jobs that we undertake. For example, the marketing manager believes that the use of loyalty cards in the supermarket chain for which he or she works makes customers less likely to shop regularly at a competitor supermarket. This is a theory even though the marketing manager would probably not recognise it as such. He or she is less likely to refer to it as a theory, particularly in the company of fellow managers. Many managers are very dismissive of any talk that smacks of 'theory'. It is thought of as something that is all very well to learn about at business school but which bears little relation to what goes on in everyday organisational life. Yet the loyalty card example shows that it has everything to do with what goes on in everyday organisational life. By introducing loyalty cards (variable A), the retailing company is attempting to influence the behaviour of customers (variable B). As every supermarket chain introduces their own loyalty card, the marketing manager's personal theory that this encourages loyalty may begin to seem inadequate when confronted by a range of other complementary and innovative strategies to encourage customers to switch where they shop.

The use of a loyalty card may become just one variable among many as supermarkets compete by offering extra loyalty card bonus points on particular goods, double or treble points if customers spend over a certain amount, the opportunity to redeem the value from accumulated bonus points against a range of discounted offers and so on. In this case, research will provide the marketing manager with a much greater understanding of the effectiveness of the strategies used within her or his supermarket chain. The data collected will allow theoretical explanations to be developed, based on causal relationships that may then be used to predict which of these strategies is more effective. It may also indicate that different strategies will be effective in different locations and perhaps that specific strategies are more effective at particular times of the year, or that specific strategies should be targeted at particular socioeconomic groups. The ability to make these predictions potentially allows the supermarket chain to compete more effectively against its rivals. Valid theoretical explanations may lead to predictions that offer the supermarket chain increased opportunities for influence and control and the possibility of increasing market share.

If theory is so rooted in our everyday lives, it is something that we need not be apprehensive about. If it is implicit in all of our decisions and actions then recognising its importance means making it explicit. In research, the importance of theory must be recognised: therefore it must be made explicit.

How is theory developed and how does theory inform your research question and research objectives?

So far we have defined the elements of theory and discussed the need to recognise it in your research, even as you start to plan this. At this point, you may be asking, 'why is it important for me to recognise theory at this early stage, when writing my research question and research objectives?' Apart from its capacity to inform your research ideas (discussed earlier), the answer to this relates to the ways in which theory may also inform your research question and how theory is developed.

Theory published in the literature may inform your proposed research question in several ways. It will help you to formulate a research question that should lead to a theoretical explanation, rather than just a descriptive answer. It will allow you to find out whether others have asked similar questions to the question you propose. Where you find that a similar research question to yours has been addressed in the literature, you will be able to learn about the context within which it was explored and how the research was conducted. This may help to focus your question to provide you with a set of variables to test, or concepts to explore, to determine whether, how and why they are related in the context of your own research project (Box 2.11).

Using relevant theory to inform your research question will also sensitise you to the nature and level of importance of the research topic surrounding your question. You may find that a considerable body of relevant work exists, either in business and management or in another subject domain, for example in psychology, economics or sociology. Discovering this may help you to focus your research question so that later on you can firmly connect your findings and conclusions to this existing theory. It is unlikely that you will fail to find any literature that relates to your proposed question, although where you find that you are working in a more specialised topic area, this discovery may also help to focus your research question to relate to the theory that you locate. It will be important to discuss how the results of your research relate to theory, to be able to assess that theory in the context of your work and to demonstrate the theoretical contribution, no matter how limited, of your research.

Where you simply find it difficult to formulate a research question from your research idea, using existing theory may also help you to achieve this.

How theory is developed also provides a crucial reason for recognising relevant theory when writing your research question and objectives. Your research project will be designed to test a theory or to develop a theory. Where you wish to adopt a clear theoretical position that you will test through the collection of data, your research project will be theory driven and you will be using a **deductive approach**. Where you wish to explore a topic and develop a theoretical explanation as the data are collected and analysed, your research project will be data driven and you will be adopting an **inductive approach**.

Box 2.11
Focus on student research

Writing a research question based on theory

Justine was a final-year marketing undergraduate who was interested in the theory of cognitive dissonance (Festinger 1957). She wanted to apply this to consumer purchasing decision making in the snack foods industry (e.g. buying potato crisps) in the light of the adverse publicity that the consumption of such foods has as a result of 'healthy eating' campaigns.

Justine applied Festinger's theory by arguing in her research project proposal that a consumer who learns that eating too many snacks is bad for her health will experience dissonance, because the knowledge that eating too much snack food is bad for her health will

be dissonant with the cognition that she continues to eat too many snacks. She can reduce the dissonance by changing her behaviour, i.e. she could stop eating so many snacks. (This would be consonant with the cognition that eating too many snacks is bad for her health.) Alternatively, she could reduce dissonance by changing her cognition about the effect of snack overeating on health and persuade herself that it does not have a harmful effect on health. She would look for positive effects of eating snacks, for example by believing that it is an important source of enjoyment which outweighs any harmful effects. Alternatively, she might persuade herself that the risk to health from snack overeating is negligible compared with the danger of car accidents (reducing the importance of the dissonant cognition).

Justine's research question was, 'To what extent does adverse "healthy eating" campaign publicity affect the consumer's decision to purchase snack foods and why?'

We discuss theory development in much greater detail (in Section 4.4), but it is useful to introduce this fundamental difference in the way theory is developed to be able to show why you need to think about this when drafting your research question and research objectives. A deductive approach will require you to identify a clear theoretical position when you draft the research question that you will then test. This is the approach we outlined earlier (Box 2.11).

An inductive approach does not rely on identifying an existing theoretical position but it is likely that if you adopt this approach you will still need to familiarise yourself with theory in your chosen subject area before you draft your research question. Using an inductive approach does not mean disregarding theory as you formulate your research question and objectives. An inductive approach is intended to allow meanings to emerge from data as you collect them in order to identify patterns and relationships to build a theory, but it does not prevent you from using existing theory to formulate your research question and even to identify concepts that you wish to explore in the research process (Section 4.4). In this way, all researchers are likely to commence their research with knowledge of relevant literature and the theory it contains.

There is a further relationship between theory and your research question that is important to recognise when drafting your research question. In our discussion of theory we recognised that it is crucial to be able to explain how variables or concepts are related and why they are related. Research questions may therefore play a crucial role in encouraging research that is designed to produce theoretical explanations, no matter how limited these explanations might be (see the following sub-section). A question that only encourages a descriptive outcome will not lead to a theoretical explanation. For example, compare the following questions. 'How satisfied are employees with recent changes in the department's business strategy?' 'What are the implications of recent changes in the department's business strategy for employee satisfaction and why?' The first question is written to produce a descriptive outcome. The second question has the potential to explore and test relationships and to arrive at theoretical explanations to explain why these might exist.

What types of theoretical contribution might be made?

This discussion of theory has probably left you asking, 'what does this mean for me?' While you will be expected to produce a theoretical explanation, you will not be expected to develop a momentous theory that leads to a new way of thinking about management! Not all theoretical contributions are the same and it is reassuring to look at the threefold typology of theories shown in Figure 2.1.

'Grand theories' are usually thought to be the province of the natural scientists (e.g. Newton's theory of gravity, Darwin's theory of evolution or Einstein's theory of relativity).

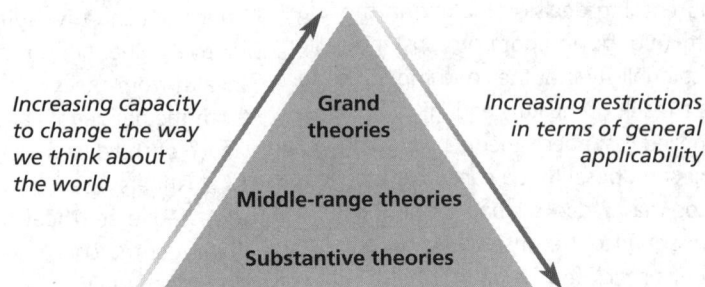

Increasing capacity to change the way we think about the world

Grand theories

Increasing restrictions in terms of general applicability

Middle-range theories

Substantive theories

Figure 2.1 Grand, middle-range and substantive theories

Box 2.12
Focus on management research

What makes a theoretical contribution?

Corley and Gioia's (2011) study found that the theoretical contribution of management research can be measured along two dimensions. One of these relates to what they call the 'originality' of the contribution. This they divide into a contribution that is either 'incremental' or 'revelatory'. An incremental theoretical contribution is one that adds to or builds on a theory, perhaps by applying it in a new context. A revelatory theoretical contribution is more profound, offering a new theory to make sense of a problem or explain a phenomenon. The other dimension relates to what they call the 'utility' or 'usefulness' of a contribution. This they divide into a contribution that has 'scientific usefulness' or 'practical usefulness'. A scientifically useful contribution is one that emphasises methodological rigour and usefulness to an academic audience. A practically useful contribution emphasises organisational application and usefulness to organisational practitioners.

However, while theoretical contributions on the first dimension are likely to be exclusively either 'incremental' or 'revelatory' (it's unlikely that a contribution could be both!), this does not have to be the case on the second dimension. Corley and Gioia focus much of their article on discussing how to achieve research that is capable of being both academically and practically useful. They refer to designing research that has scope to be theoretically relevant to both academics and organisational practitioners. They consider ways in which this type of theoretical contribution may be achieved. This includes a continuing emphasis on examining the links between theoretical abstractions and practice implications. In interpreting their results, researchers also need to go beyond narrow generalisations and look for insights that can inform organisational practice. In a similar way, when developing theory, researchers need to look not only at the validity of their theories but also their usefulness and applicability. Researchers also need to exercise some foresight when choosing their research topics so they pursue research that has and will have relevance to the problems and issues faced by organisations and organisational practitioners.

These may be contrasted with 'middle-range theories', which lack the capacity to change the way in which we think about the world but are nonetheless of significance. Some of the theories of human motivation well known to managers would be in this category. However, most of us are concerned with 'substantive theories' that are restricted to a particular time, research setting, group or population or problem.

For example, studying the implications of a cost-saving strategy in a particular organisation would be an example of a substantive theory. Although they may be restricted, a host of 'substantive theories' that present similar propositions may lead to 'middle-range theories'. By developing 'substantive theories', however modest, we are doing our bit as researchers to enhance our understanding of the world about us. A grand claim, but a valid one!

Another way to examine the theoretical contributions of research into business and management is to assess its practical usefulness for organisations and those who work in them (Box 2.12).

2.5 Writing your research proposal 撰写研究提案

The **research proposal**, occasionally referred to as a protocol or outline, is a structured plan of your proposed research project. In this section we discuss why it is necessary and how it may be structured, but it is important to recognise that a competent research proposal needs to draw on material discussed in subsequent chapters. Before you can write your research proposal you will need to be aware of available literature and appropriate theory (Section 2.4 and Chapter 3), the research philosophy and approach that you wish to use (Chapter 4), your research design including methodological choice, research strategy and time frame (Chapter 5), access and ethical issues (Chapter 6), sample selection (Chapter 7), data collection methods and data analysis techniques (Chapters 8–13).

Why is a research proposal necessary?

Creating a clear specification to guide your research project

Your research project is likely to be a large element in your course. It is also yours! You will be responsible for conceiving, conducting and concluding this project and creating the report, dissertation or thesis. Apart from applying your research methods training and the advice you receive from your project tutor, it will be your piece of work. From this perspective, developing a research proposal offers you the opportunity to think carefully about your research project (Box 2.13).

We do not suggest that you use these questions to provide headings under which you write responses, but we feel that they should be helpful as a guide and as a checklist against which to evaluate your research proposal before submitting it to your tutor. A well-thought-out and well-written research proposal has the potential to provide you with a clear specification of the what, why, how, when and where of your research project.

Producing a research proposal is demanding: thinking through what you wish to do and why, identifying and synthesising literature and then envisaging all of the stages of your research will be time consuming, as will the necessary revisions to create a coherent and clearly written proposal. However, the effort is likely to prove to be very worthwhile. As you juggle several activities during the period of your research project, there may be occasions when you pick up your research proposal and feel glad that you spent so much time producing a clear specification to guide your project through its various stages.

Box 2.13
Checklist to guide and evaluate your research proposal

✔ Have I explained what am I going to do?
✔ Have I explained why I am doing this?
✔ Have I said why it is worth doing?
✔ Have I explained how it relates to what has been done before in my subject area?
✔ Have I stated which theory or theories will inform what I am doing and how I will use it or them?
✔ Have I stated my research question(s), research aim and my research objectives?
✔ Have I outlined how I will conduct my research?
✔ Have I outlined my research design?
✔ Have I outlined what data I need?
✔ Have I stated who and where my intended participants are?
✔ Have I explained how I will select my participants?
✔ Have I explained how I will gain access?
✔ Have I outlined how I will collect my data?
✔ Have I outlined how I will analyse my data and use this to develop theoretical explanations?
✔ Have I outlined what data quality issues I might encounter?
✔ Have I outlined how I will seek to overcome these data quality issues?
✔ Have I considered the ethical issues I might encounter at each stage of my research?
✔ Have I outlined how I will address these?

Meeting the requirements of those who approve and assess your project

It is likely that your research proposal will be assessed before you are allowed to carry on with your research project. A proportion of the overall marks available for your project report may be given for the research proposal. Alternatively, a research proposal may be subject to approval before you are permitted to proceed with your research project. In either case, it will be necessary to reach a certain standard before being allowed to progress. There are potentially a number of different criteria that may be used to assess a research proposal. These may include criteria that are specific to each of the components of the proposal, which we describe later in this section. Part of the assessment and approval process may also centre on criteria that focus on more general concerns. We first consider three such criteria that are likely to be used to assess your research proposal: coherence, ethical clearance and feasibility.

Coherence

A research project is a complex and time-consuming activity. As we indicated earlier, you are likely to benefit from creating a clear specification to guide your research project. Your project tutor and any other assessor will be looking for evidence of coherence and lucidity in the way you have written your research proposal, to demonstrate that it will be fit for purpose and able to direct your research activity.

Ethical clearance

Part of the approval process for your research proposal may involve it being considered and approved by a research ethics committee. Your university's code of ethical practice is likely to require all research involving human participants to be considered and approved, especially where research involves young or vulnerable participants. It may also be necessary to state how data will be stored, whether they will be kept subsequently and under what conditions, in order to ensure the continuing anonymity of the participants and confidentiality of their data. Section 6.5 discusses ethical issues related to the design stage of a research project. You will need to be aware of and abide by the ethical requirements of your institution. These requirements will add to the time that you will need to allow for the planning stage of your research project. As a professional student you may also need to be aware of and abide by the ethical requirements of your professional institute.

Feasibility

You may have devised a coherent and well-structured research proposal that would create much interest but it may not be possible to achieve, or sensible to contemplate. Feasibility is a multifaceted criterion that your assessors will be concerned about. Your proposal may not be possible to achieve in the time available to undertake the research project and produce your dissertation or management report. It may be that data collection would not be possible because you would not be able to gain access to participants, or it might not be practical and your tutor will tell you so! The proposal may require resources that are not available, finance commitments that are unaffordable or skills that you have not developed and would not be able to acquire in the timescale of the project.

It is always helpful to discuss your research proposal with a tutor. Where there are concerns about any of the issues just considered, it will be possible to discuss these to work out how the proposed research may be amended. For example, in relation to feasibility something more modest in scope may be discussed. Your task will then be to amend initial ideas and convince your tutor that the proposed research is achievable within the time and other resources available.

Ensuring that your research project isn't based on preconceived ideas

Your research project offers a valuable way to learn the skills involved in this activity. These skills are transferable to many other situations, including the world of work. It is about process as well as outcome. Concerns about feasibility (related to overenthusiasm) lie at one end of a continuum, at other end of which lies a very occasional concern about sincerity. Do not be like the student who came to Phil to talk over a research proposal and said, 'Of course, I know what the answer will be'. When asked to explain the purpose of doing the research if he already knew the answer, he became rather defensive and eventually looked for another supervisor and, probably, another topic.

Approval of your research proposal implies that it is satisfactory. While this is no guarantee of subsequent success, it will reassure you to know that you have started your research journey with an appropriate destination and journey plan. It will be for you to ensure that you do not get lost!

How may your research project be structured?

Perhaps the first comment to make is that there are potentially different ways to structure your research proposal. Different research traditions (Chapter 5) may lead to different ways of structuring your proposal and, later on, your project report (Chapter 14). We describe what may be thought of as the standard approach to structuring your research proposal. You will need to make yourself aware if there is any variation to this in your institution's or faculty's requirements. Whichever structure you are required to adopt, this will be driven by and focused on your research question, aim and research objectives, and you will need to ensure that you produce a coherent proposal.

Title

The title should simply and concisely summarise the research question. It should avoid unnecessary phrases such as, 'A study to explore …' Instead it should reflect the concepts or variables in your research (Box 2.14). If your research question changes, this will naturally lead to a change to your title.

Box 2.14
Focus on student research

Devising research proposal titles

Imran (Box 2.8) reworded his research question into the following title for his research proposal:

'Reasons for mismatch between corporate strategy and the external environment.'

Tom (Box 2.9) devised this title for his research proposal:

'The effectiveness of Internet and intranet channels for employee communication.'

Justine (Box 2.11) used her research question to develop this title for her proposal:

'The effect of "healthy eating" publicity on snack foods purchasing decisions.'

Background

This section has a number of related functions. It needs to introduce the reader to the research issue or problem. This addresses the question, 'what am I going to do?' You also need to provide a rationale for your proposed research and to justify this. This may be composed of two elements, one relating to you and the other relating to the value of the work. Your reader will be looking for some evidence that this is a topic in which you have sufficient interest to sustain the effort that will be required from you over the period of the research project. This may relate to the need to tackle a problem, to your intellectual curiosity, or to your intended career direction. It relates to the question, 'why am I going to do this?' The rationale will also need to address the question, 'why is it worth doing?' This will relate to one of the following types of justification: the application of a theory to a particular context (such as within an organisation); the development of a theory within a research setting; testing a theory within a given context. Your research may propose other such justifications depending on its nature.

This leads to another function of this section: to demonstrate 'how my research relates to what has been done before in this subject area'. In achieving this you will show your knowledge of relevant literature and clarify where your proposal fits into the debate in this literature (Section 3.2). You will also be able to begin to show 'which theory or theories will inform what I am doing and how I will use it or them'. The intention will be not to write a detailed review of the literature but rather to provide an overview of key literature sources from which you will draw and the theory or theories within them. This will not be the same as the critical literature review (Section 3.2) that you will present in your final project report but the start of the process that leads to it.

Research questions, aim and objectives

The Background section should lead logically into a statement of your research question, aim and research objectives. These should leave the reader in no doubt about what your research seeks to achieve. Be careful here to ensure that your objectives are precisely written and will lead to observable outcomes (Box 2.9).

Method

The Background and Method will be the longest sections of your proposal. The Method is designed to answer the question, 'how shall I conduct my research?' The Method may be divided into sub-sections that deal with research design, participants, techniques and procedures and ethical considerations. This final element may need to be dealt with in a discrete section of your research proposal.

Research design is discussed in Chapter 5. It involves you making a number of decisions about, 'what is my research design?' You will need to make a methodological choice between a quantitative, qualitative or multiple methods design. You will also need to select one or more research strategies (e.g. an experiment, a case study, a survey, a Grounded Theory strategy) and determine an appropriate time frame for your project depending on the nature of your research. You will need to describe each of these and justify your choice by the way these elements fit together to form a coherent whole.

How you design your research will affect the type of data you require, where you intend to locate them and from whom you will collect them. Your data may be collected from human participants, or they may be secondary data (Chapter 8) such as from archival research (Section 5.5) or a combination of these. You will therefore need to address the question, 'what type of data do I need?' If you are using secondary data you will need to explain what these are, where they are located, any issues related to access and justify this choice. If you intend to collect data from human participants, you will need to answer, 'who and where are my intended participants?' You may be intending to conduct research in a single organisation or across a number of organisations. You will need to explain and justify the nature of the organisation or organisations and possibly the sector or sectors within which it operates (or they operate). Your intended participants may be located within a specific part of an organisation or be drawn from across it. You will need to explain and justify this.

You will also need to explain the nature of your research population and why you chose it. For example, they may be entrepreneurs, managerial employees, non-managerial employees, a particular occupational group, trade union officials or some combination of these. Where you need to select a sample from within a research population you will need to address the question, 'how shall I select them?' Chapter 7 discusses types of probability and non-probability sampling and you will need to describe and justify your sampling technique and sample size.

You will also need to describe the data collection and analysis techniques you intend to use by answering the questions, 'how will I collect my data?' and 'how will I analyse it and use this to develop theoretical explanations?' Data collection techniques include examination of secondary data, questionnaires, interviews and observation (Chapters 8–11). You will not need to explain the precise details of the technique you intend to use, such as including a copy of your questionnaire, interview questions or the content of an observation schedule but you will need to describe how you will use it. For example, if you are using interviews, what type will you use, how many will you conduct, with what type of participant, their intended duration, how will you record the data (e.g. note taking and/or audio-recording). You will also need to describe, albeit briefly, how you intend to analyse each type of data that you collect.

It will also be important to discuss ethical considerations so that you anticipate these and demonstrate to your tutor and ethics committee that your research design and proposal has been formulated to minimise ethical concerns and avoid unethical practice. This will be essential where you are dealing with human participants, and sometimes even if using secondary data already collected from human participants. There may be a reduced need for some of you undertaking certain types of research (e.g. where this is based on macro-level, completely anonymised data) but in nearly all cases this requirement is very likely to mean that you need to be sensitive to ethical concerns.

Timescale

This will help you and your reader to decide on the viability of your research proposal. It will be helpful if you divide your research plan into stages. This will give you a clear idea as to what is possible in the given timescale. Experience has shown that however well the researcher's time is organised, the whole process seems to take longer than anticipated (Box 2.15).

As part of this section of their proposal, many researchers find it useful to produce a schedule for their research using a Gantt chart. Developed by Henry Gantt in 1917, this provides a simple visual representation of the tasks or activities that make up your research project, each being plotted against a timeline. The time we estimate each task will take is represented by the length of an associated horizontal bar, while the task's start and finish times are represented by its position on the timeline. Case 2 at the end of this chapter includes a Gantt chart for a student's research project. As we can see from the first bar on this chart, the student has decided to schedule in two weeks of holiday. The first of these occurs over the Christmas and New Year period, and the second occurs while her tutor is reading a draft copy of the completed project in April. We can also see

Box 2.15
Focus on student research

Louisa's research timescale

As part of the final year of her undergraduate business studies degree, Louisa had to undertake an 8000–10,000-word research project. In order to assist her with her time management, she discussed the following 'To-Do List', developed using Microsoft Outlook's project planning tool 'Tasks', with her tutor.

from the second and fourth bar that, like many of our students, she intends to begin to draft her literature review while she is still reading new articles and books. However, she has also recognised that some activities must be undertaken sequentially. For example, bars 9 and 10 highlight that before she can administer her questionnaire (bar 10) she must complete all the revisions highlighted as necessary by the pilot testing (bar 9). Finally this student has noted that her project assessment criteria include a reflective essay and has decided to keep a reflective diary throughout the research project (bar 20).

Resources

This is another facet of feasibility (Box 2.2 and also our earlier discussion in this section). Including this discussion in your research proposal will allow you and your tutor to assess whether what you are proposing can be resourced. Resource considerations may be categorised as finance, data access and equipment.

Conducting research costs money. This may include for example: travel, subsistence, help with data entry or transcription, or postage for questionnaires. Think through the expenses involved and ensure that you can meet them.

Assessors of your proposal will need to be convinced that you have access to the data you need to conduct your research (Sections 6.2 and 6.3). This may be unproblematic if you are carrying out research in your own organisation. Many academic committees wish to see written approval from host organisations in which researchers are planning to conduct research. You will also need to convince your reader of the likely response rate to any questionnaire that you send.

It is surprising how many research proposals have ambitious plans for large-scale data collection with no thought given to how the data will be analysed. It is important that you convince the reader of your proposal that you have access to the necessary computer software to analyse your data. Moreover, it will be necessary for you to demonstrate that you have either the necessary skills to perform the analysis or can learn the skills in an appropriate time, or you have access to help.

References

It is not necessary to try to impress your proposal reader with an enormous list of references. A few key literature sources to which you have referred in the background section and which relate to the previous work and theory that directly informs your own proposal, as well as references to the methods literature, should be all that is necessary.

Case 2 at the end of this chapter provides an example of a student research proposal.

2.6 Summary 小 结

- The process of formulating and clarifying your research topic is a key part of your research project.
- Attributes of a good research topic do not vary a great deal between universities. The most important of these is that your research topic will meet the requirements of the examining body.
- Generating and refining research ideas makes use of a variety of techniques. It is important that you use a variety of techniques, including those involving rational thinking and those involving creative thinking.
- Further refinement of research ideas may be achieved through using a Delphi technique, conducting a preliminary inquiry and integrating ideas by working these up and narrowing them down.
- A clearly defined research question expresses what your research is about and will become the focal point of your research project.
- A research aim is a brief statement of the purpose of the research project. It is often written as a sentence stating what you intend to achieve through your research.
- Well-formulated research objectives operationalise how you intend to conduct your research by providing a set of coherent and connected steps to answer your research question.
- It will be important to use academic theory to inform your research topic irrespective of the approach you will use to conduct your research project.
- A research proposal is a structured plan of your proposed research project.
- A well-thought-out and well-written research proposal has the potential to provide you with a clear specification of the what, why, how, when and where of your research project.

Self-check questions 自测题

Help with these questions is available at the end of the chapter.

2.1 For the workplace project for her professional course, Karen had decided to undertake a study of the effectiveness of the joint consultative committee in her NHS Trust. Her title was 'An evaluation of the effectiveness of the Joint Consultative Committee in Anyshire's Hospitals NHS Foundation Trust'. Draft some objectives which Karen may adopt to complement her title.

2.2 You have decided to search the literature to 'try to come up with some research ideas in the area of operations management'. How will you go about this?

2.3 A colleague of yours wishes to generate a research idea in the area of accounting. He has examined his own strengths and interests on the basis of his assignments and has read some review articles, but has failed to find an idea about which he is excited. He comes and asks you for advice. Suggest two techniques that your colleague could use, and justify your choices.

2.4 You are interested in doing some research on the interface between business organisations and schools. Write three research questions that may be appropriate.

2.5 How may the formulation of an initial substantive theory help in the development of a research proposal?

2.6 How would you demonstrate the influence of relevant theory in your research proposal?

Review and discussion questions 复习与讨论题

2.7 Together with a few colleagues discuss the extent to which a number of research ideas would each constitute a 'good research topic' using the checklist in Box 2.2. The set of ideas you use may be past ones obtained from your tutor that relate to your course. Alternatively, they may be those which have been written by you and your colleagues as preparation for your project(s).

2.8 Look through several of the academic journals that relate to your subject area. Choose an article which is based upon primary research. Assuming that the research question and objectives are not made explicit, infer from the content of the article what the research question and objectives may have been.

2.9 Watch the news on television or access a news website. Look for a news item based on research which has been carried out to report a current issue related to business. Spend some time investigating other news websites (e.g. http://www.news.google.com) to learn more about the research which relates to this business news story. Study the story carefully and decide what further questions the report raises. Use this as the basis to draft an outline proposal to seek answers to one (or more) of these questions.

Progressing your research project 改进研究项目

From research ideas to a research proposal 从研究想法到研究提案

- If you have not been given a research idea, consider the techniques available for generating and refining research ideas. Choose a selection of those with which you feel most comfortable, making sure to include both rational and creative thinking techniques. Use these to try to generate a research idea or ideas. Once you have got some research ideas, or if you have been unable to find an idea, talk to your project tutor.

- Evaluate your research ideas against the checklist of attributes of a good research project (Box 2.2).

- Refine your research ideas using a selection of the techniques available for generating and refining research ideas. Re-evaluate your research ideas against the checklist of attributes of a good research project (Box 2.2). Remember that it is better to revise (and in some situations to discard) ideas that do not appear to be feasible at this stage. Integrate your ideas using the process of working up and narrowing down to form one research idea.

- Use your research idea to write a research question. Where possible this should be a 'how?' or a 'why?' rather than a 'what?' question.

> ## Progressing your research project (*continued*) 改进研究项目（续）
>
> ### From research ideas to a research proposal 从研究想法到研究提案
>
> - Use this research question to write a research aim and a set of connected research objectives.
> - Write your research proposal making sure it includes a clear title and sections on:
>
> - the background to your research;
> - your research questions, aim and research objectives;
> - the method you intend to use including research design, participants (data), techniques and procedures and ethical considerations;
> - the timescale for your research;
> - the resources you require;
> - references to any literature to which you have referred.
>
> - Use the questions in Box 1.4 to guide your reflective diary entry.

Self-check answers 自测题答案

2.1 These may include:
- To identify the management and trade union objectives for the Joint Consultative Committee and use this to establish suitable effectiveness criteria.
- To review key literature on the use of joint consultative committees.
- To carry out primary research in the organisation to measure the effectiveness of the Joint Consultative Committee.
- To identify the strengths and weaknesses of the Joint Consultative Committee.
- To make recommendations for action to ensure the effective function of the Joint Consultative Committee.

2.2 One starting point would be to ask your project tutor for suggestions of possible recent review articles or articles containing recommendations for further work that he or she has read. Another would be to browse recent editions of operations management journals such as the *International Journal of Operations and Production Management* for possible research ideas. These would include both statements of the absence of research and unfounded assertions. Recent reports held in your library or on the Internet may also be of use here. You could also scan one or two recently published operations management textbooks for overviews of research that has been undertaken.

2.3 From the description given, it would appear that your colleague has considered only rational thinking techniques. It would therefore seem sensible to suggest two creative thinking techniques, as these would hopefully generate an idea that would appeal to him. One technique that you could suggest is brainstorming, perhaps emphasising the need to do it with other colleagues. Exploring past projects in the accountancy area would be another possibility. You might also suggest that he keeps a notebook of ideas.

2.4 Your answer will probably differ from the points that follow. However, the sorts of things you could be considering include:

- How do business organisations benefit from their liaison with schools?
- Why do business organisations undertake school liaison activities?
- To what extent do business organisations receive value for money in their school liaison activities?

2.5 Let us go back to the example used in the chapter of the supermarket marketing manager who theorises that the introduction of a loyalty card will mean that regular customers are less likely to shop at competitor supermarkets. This could be the research proposal's starting point, i.e. a hypothesis that the introduction of a loyalty card will mean that regular customers are less likely to shop at competitor supermarkets. This prompts thoughts about the possible use of literature in the proposal and the research project itself. This literature could have at least two strands. First, a practical strand which looks at the research evidence which lends credence to the hypothesis. Second, a more abstract strand that studies human consumer behaviour and looks at the cognitive processes which affect consumer purchasing decisions.

 This ensures that the proposal and resultant research project are both theory driven and also ensures that relevant theory is covered in the literature.

2.6 Try including a sub-section in the background section that is headed 'How the previous published research has informed my research question, aim and objectives'. Then show how, say, a gap in the previous research that is there because nobody has pursued a particular approach before has led to you to fill that gap.

Get ahead using resources on the companion website at: **www.pearsoned .co.uk/saunders.**

- Improve your IBM SPSS Statistics and NVivo research analysis with practice tutorials.
- Save time researching on the Internet with the Smarter Online Searching Guide.
- Test your progress using self-assessment questions.
- Follow live links to useful websites.

Chapter 3

Critically reviewing the literature 文献综述

Learning outcomes 学习目标

By the end of this chapter you should:

- understand the importance and purpose of the critical literature review to your research project;
- be able to adopt a critical perspective in your reading;
- know what you need to include when writing your critical review;
- be able to identify search terms and to undertake online literature searches;
- be able to evaluate the relevance, value and sufficiency of the literature found;
- be able to reference the literature found accurately;
- understand what is meant by plagiarism;
- be able to apply the knowledge, skills and understanding gained to your own research project.

3.1 Introduction 引 言

As part of your studies, you have almost certainly been asked by your tutors to 'review the literature', 'write a literature review' or 'critically review the literature' on a given topic. You may be like many students and have grown to fear the literature review, not because of the associated reading but because of the requirement both to make reasoned judgements about the value of each piece of work and to organise ideas and findings of value into a review. It is these two processes in particular that many find both difficult and time consuming.

There are three ways in which you are likely to use literature in your research project (Creswell 2012). The first, for the preliminary search that helps you to generate and refine your research ideas and draft your research proposal, has already been discussed in Sections 2.3 and 2.5. The second, often referred to as the **critical review** or **critical literature review**, provides the context and theoretical framework for your research and is the focus of this chapter. The third is to place your research findings within the wider body of knowledge and forms part of your discussion chapter. We discuss this in Section 14.3. Most research textbooks, as well as your project tutor, will argue that the critical review of the literature is necessary. Although you may feel that you already have a reasonable knowledge of your research area, we believe that reviewing the literature critically is essential. Project assessment criteria usually require you to demonstrate awareness of the current state of knowledge in your subject, its limitations and how your research fits in this wider context (Gill and Johnson 2010). As Colquitt (2013: 1211) reiterates, you need to connect your work with what has already been said and acknowledge

Recently, we were discussing the difficulties students have when writing their literature reviews for their research projects. Mark summarised what he felt we and fellow project tutors were saying:

So what happens sometimes is . . . a student comes to see their project tutor having obviously done a great deal of work. The student presents the tutor with what they say is the finished critical literature review. Yet the purpose of their review is unclear. It is little more than a summary of the articles and books read, each article or book being given one paragraph. Some students have arranged these paragraphs alphabetically in author order, others have arranged them in chronological order. None have linked or juxtaposed the ideas.

Their literature reviews look more like an online retailer's web pages than a critical review. Just like the items on these pages, each article or book has some similarities in terms of subject matter and so are grouped together. However, unlike the retailer's web pages, the reasons for these groupings are not made explicit. In addition, while it makes sense to provide similar length summary descriptions of items on the retailer's web pages to help

Screenshot from Argos.co.uk
Source: © 2014 Home Retail Group. Reproduced with permission.

the prospective purchaser come to a decision about whether or not to purchase, this is not the case in a literature review. For each article or book in a literature review, the amount written should reflect its value to the student's research project.

Mark concluded: 'While such an approach obviously makes good sense for retailers and prospective purchasers, it does not work for the critical review of the literature. We obviously need to explain better what we mean by a critical review of the literature to our students.'

your 'intellectual indebtedness'. This means you have to discuss what has been published and is relevant to your research topic critically.

The significance of your research and what you find out will inevitably be judged in relation to other people's research and their findings. You therefore need to show you understand your field and its key theories, concepts and ideas, as well as the major issues and debates about your topic (Denyer and Tranfield 2009). In doing this you are establishing what research has been published in your chosen area and, if possible, identifying any other research that might currently be in progress. Although the literature you read will enhance your subject knowledge and help you to clarify your research question(s) further, only those that are relevant to your research will be included in your review. This process is called 'critically reviewing the literature'.

For most research projects, your literature search will be an early activity. Despite this early start, it is usually necessary to continue searching throughout your project's life. The process can be likened to an upward spiral, culminating in the final draft of your written critical literature review (Figure 3.1). Traditionally, in the initial stage of your literature review you will start to define the parameters to your research and the review (Section 3.4). After generating search terms and conducting your first search (Section 3.5), you will have a list of references to authors who have published on these subjects. Once the associated documents have been obtained, you can evaluate them (Section 3.6), record the ideas (Section 3.7) and start drafting your review, fully acknowledging the sources.

After the initial search, you will be able to revise your parameters and undertake further searches, keeping in mind your research question(s) and objectives. As your thoughts develop, each later search will be focused more precisely on material that is likely to be relevant. You will probably also refine your research question(s) and objectives in the light of your reading (Section 2.4).

Alternatively, you may decide that rather than undertaking a traditional literature review, your review will be a self-contained project to explore a clearly defined research question. In such situations, particularly where questions are derived from organisational practice or policy problems, business and management researchers are increasingly adopting the Systematic Review methodology to critically review the literature. We discuss this in more detail in Section 3.8.

Unlike some academic disciplines, business and management research makes use of a wide range of literature. While your review is likely to include specific business disciplines such as finance, strategy, marketing and human resource management, it is also likely to include other disciplines. Those most frequently consulted by our students include economics, psychology, sociology and geography. Given this, and the importance of the review to your research, it is vital for you to be aware of what a critical literature review is and the range of literature available before you start the reviewing process. We therefore start this chapter by outlining the purpose and types of critical review of the literature, its content and what we mean by 'critical' (Section 3.2) and then outlining the literature resources available (Section 3.3). Subsequently we explore how to plan and conduct your literature search (Sections 3.4 and 3.5), obtain, evaluate and record the literature (Sections 3.6 and 3.7) and discuss both Systematic Review (Section 3.8) and plagiarism (Section 3.9).

3.2   The critical review   批判性综述

Your critical literature review should be a constructively critical analysis that develops a clear argument about what the published literature indicates is known and not known about your research question (Wallace and Wray 2011). This means your literature

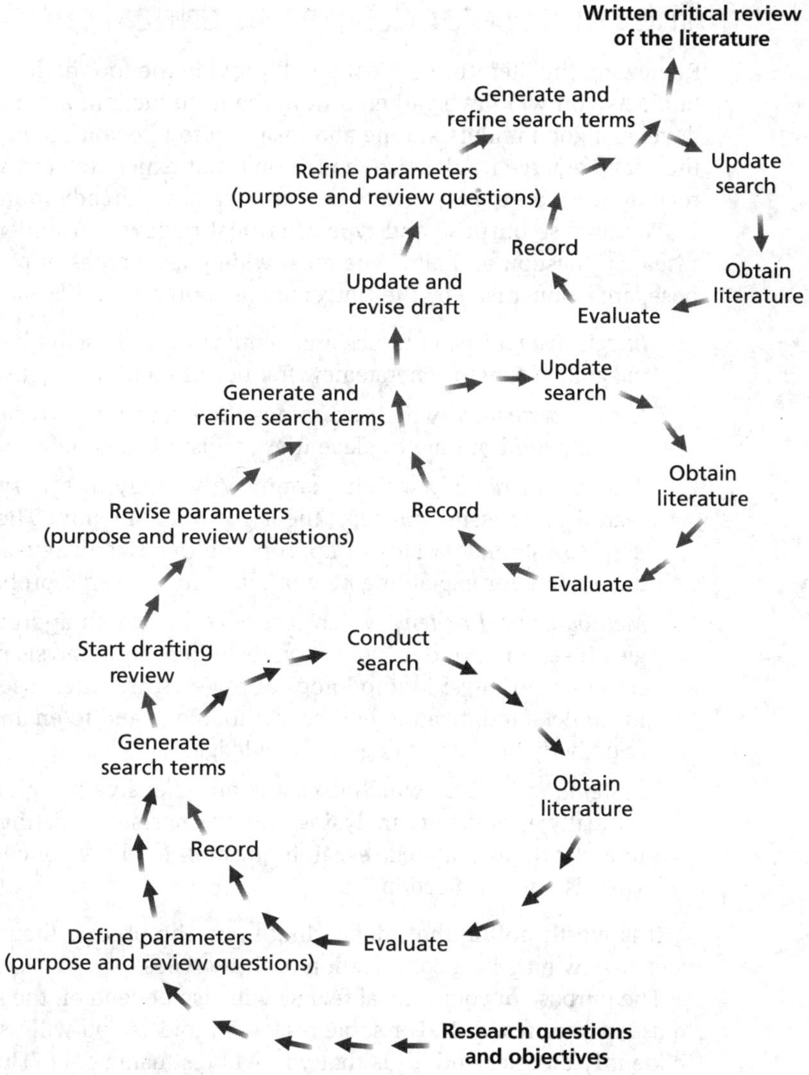

Written critical review of the literature
Generate and refine search terms
Update search
Refine parameters (purpose and review questions)
Record
Obtain literature
Update and revise draft
Evaluate
Update search
Generate and refine search terms
Obtain literature
Revise parameters (purpose and review questions)
Record
Evaluate
Start drafting review
Conduct search
Obtain literature
Generate search terms
Record
Evaluate
Define parameters (purpose and review questions)
Research questions and objectives

Figure 3.1 The literature review process

review is not just a series of book and journal article reviews describing and summarising what each is about. Rather, you will need to assess what is significant to your research and, on this basis, decide whether or not to include it. If you think the concepts, theories, arguments or empirical research findings reported and discussed in an article are unclear, biased or inconsistent with other work and need to be researched further, you will need to justify why. This is not easy and requires careful thought. However, by doing this you will be able to provide a reasonably detailed, constructively critical analysis of the key literature that relates to your research question. Within this you will need to include both theoretical research and empirical research that supports and opposes your ideas.

The purpose and types of critical review

Reviewing the literature critically will provide the foundation on which your research is built. As you will have gathered from the introduction, a critical review will help you to develop a good understanding and insight into relevant previous research and the trends that have emerged. Likewise, you should not expect to start your research without first reading what other researchers in your area have already found out.

The precise purpose and type of critical review you undertake will depend on your research question and aim. The most widely used types of review, along with their purpose, are summarised by the University of Southern California (2014) and include the:

Integrative review, critiques and synthesises representative literature on a topic in an integrative way to generate new frameworks and perspectives on a topic.

Historical review, which examines the evolution of research on a particular topic over a period of time to place it in an historical context.

Theoretical review, which examines the body of theory that has accumulated in regard to an issue, concept, theory or phenomenon. Theoretical reviews are often used to establish a lack of appropriate theories or reveal that current theories are inadequate for explaining new or emerging research problems.

Methodological review, which focuses on research approaches (Section 4.3), strategies (Section 5.5), data collection techniques or analysis procedures, rather than the research findings. Methodological reviews are often used to provide a framework for understanding a method or methodology and to enable researchers to draw on a wide body of methodological knowledge.

Systematic Review, which uses a comprehensive pre-planned strategy for locating, critically appraising, analysing and synthesising existing research that is pertinent to a clearly formulated research question to allow conclusions to be reached about what is known (Section 3.8).

It is worth noting that, depending upon the precise focus of your research project, your review may be a combination of these types.

The purpose of your critical review will also depend on the approach you are intending to use in your research. For some research projects you will use the literature to help you to identify theories and ideas that you will test using data. This is known as a **deductive approach** (Section 4.3) in which you develop a theoretical or conceptual framework which you subsequently test using data. For other research projects you will be planning to explore your data and to develop theories from them that you will subsequently relate to the literature in subsequent discussion. This is known as an **inductive approach** (Section 4.3) and, although your research still has a clearly defined purpose with research question(s) and objectives, you do not start with any predetermined theories or conceptual frameworks. We believe such an approach cannot be taken without a competent knowledge of the literature in your subject area.

It is impossible to review every single piece of the literature before collecting your data. Consequently, your literature review will review the most relevant and significant research on your topic. If your review is effective, new findings and theories will emerge that neither you nor anyone else has thought about (Corbin and Strauss 2008). Despite this, when you write your critical review you will need to show how your findings and the theories you have developed, or are using, relate to the research that has gone before. This will help you demonstrate that you are familiar with what is already known about your research topic.

Adopting a critical perspective in your reading

Harvard College Library (2013) provides its students with a useful checklist of skills to be practised for effective reading. These skills include:

Previewing: which is considering the precise purpose of the text before you start reading in order to establish it may inform your literature search.

Annotating: that is, conducting a dialogue with yourself, the author and the issues and ideas at stake (Box 3.1).

Summarising: the best way to determine that you've really got the point is to be able to state it in your own words. Outlining the argument of a text is a version of annotating, and can be done quite informally in the margins of the text.

Comparing and contrasting: ask yourself how your thinking has been altered by this reading or how it has affected your response to the issues and themes in your research.

The Harvard College Library advice suggests that you should get into the habit of hearing yourself ask questions of your reading. Wallace and Wray (2011) recommend the use of **review questions**. These are specific questions you ask of the reading, which will be linked either directly or indirectly to your research question. So you may, for example, address a piece of reading with the view to it answering the question: 'What does research suggest are the main reasons why customers are likely to change car insurance provider?'

Box 3.1
Checklist

Annotating your critical reading. Advice on how to read in a 'thinking-intensive' way

✔ First of all, throw away the highlighter in favour of a pen or pencil. Highlighting can actually distract from the business of learning and dilute your comprehension. It only seems like an active reading strategy; in actual fact, it can lull you into a dangerous passivity.

✔ Mark up the margins of your text with words: ideas that occur to you, notes about things that seem important to you, reminders of how issues in a text may connect with your research questions and objectives. If you are reading a PDF copy on screen, use the 'sticky notes' feature of Adobe Reader®. This kind of interaction keeps you conscious of the reason you are reading. Throughout your research these annotations will be useful memory triggers.

✔ Develop your own symbol system: asterisk a key idea, for example, or use an exclamation point for the surprising, absurd, bizarre etc. Like your margin words, your hieroglyphs can help you reconstruct the important observations that you made at an earlier time. And they will be indispensable when you return to a text later in the term, in search of a particular passage that you may want to include in your project report.

✔ Get in the habit of hearing yourself ask questions – 'what does this mean?'; 'why is he or she drawing that conclusion?' Write the questions down (in your margins, at the beginning or end of the reading, in a notebook, or elsewhere). They are reminders of the unfinished business you still have with a text: to come to terms with on your own, once you've had a chance to digest the material further, or have done further reading.

The word 'critical' has appeared in this chapter a number of times so far. It is vital in your reading of the literature that a critical stance should be taken. So what is meant by critical reading? Wallace and Wray (2011: 9) sum this up rather succinctly by saying that 'the lengthy list of critical skills (required for critical reading) boil down to just two: the capacity to evaluate what you read and the capacity to relate what you read to other information'.

More specifically, Wallace and Wray (2011) advocate the use of five critical questions to employ in critical reading. These are:

1 Why am I reading this? (The authors argue that this is where the review question is particularly valuable. It acts as a focusing device and ensures that you stick to the purpose of the reading and do not get sidetracked too much by the author's agenda.)

2 What is the author trying to do in writing this? (The answer to this may assist you in deciding how valuable the writing may be for your purposes.)

3 What is the writer saying that is relevant to what I want to find out?

4 How convincing is what the author is saying? (In particular, is the argument based on a conclusion which is justified by the evidence?)

5 What use can I make of the reading?

The content of the critical review

As you begin to find, read and evaluate the literature, you will need to think how to combine the academic theories and ideas about which you are reading to form the critical review that will appear in your project report. Your review will need to evaluate the research that has already been undertaken in the area of your research project, show and explain the relationships between published research findings and reference the literature in which they were reported (Appendix 1). It will draw out the key points and trends (recognising any omissions and bias) and present them in a logical way which also shows the relationship to your own research. In doing this you will provide readers of your project report with the necessary background knowledge to your research question(s) and objectives and establish the boundaries of your own research. Your review will also enable the readers to see your ideas against the background of previous published research in the area. This does not necessarily mean that your ideas must extend, follow or approve those set out in the literature. You may be highly critical of the earlier research reported in the literature and seek to question or revise it through your own research. However, if you wish to do this you must still review this literature, explain clearly why you consider it may require revision and justify your own ideas through clear argument and with reference to the literature.

In considering the content of your critical review, you will therefore need:

• to include the key academic theories within your chosen area of research that are pertinent to or contextualise your research question;
• to demonstrate that your knowledge of your chosen area is up to date;
• to enable those reading your project report to find the original publications which you cite through clear complete referencing.

The content of your critical review can be evaluated using the checklist in Box 3.2.

Box 3.2
Checklist

Evaluating the content of your critical literature review

✔ Have you ensured that the literature covered relates clearly to your research question and objectives?

✔ Have you covered the most relevant and significant theories of recognised experts in the area?

✔ Have you covered the most relevant and significant literature or at least a representative sample?

✔ Have you included up-to-date relevant literature?

✔ Have you referenced all the literature used in the format prescribed in the assessment criteria?

What is really meant by being 'critical' about the content

Within the context of your course you have probably already been asked to take a critical approach for previous assignments. However, it is worth considering what we mean by critical within the context of your literature review. Mingers (2000: 225–6) argues that there are four aspects of a critical approach that should be fostered by management education:

- critique of rhetoric;
- critique of tradition;
- critique of authority;
- critique of objectivity.

The first of these, the 'critique of rhetoric', means appraising or evaluating a problem with effective use of language. In the context of your critical literature review, this emphasises the need for you, as the reviewer, to use your skills to make reasoned judgements and to argue effectively in writing. The other three aspects Mingers identifies also have implications for being critical when reading and writing about the work of others. This includes using other literature sources to question, where justification exists to do so, the conventional wisdom, the 'critique of tradition' and the dominant view portrayed in the literature you are reading, the 'critique of authority'. Finally, it is likely also to include recognising in your review that the knowledge and information you are discussing are not value-free, the 'critique of objectivity'.

Being critical in reviewing the literature is, therefore, a combination of your skills and the attitude with which you read. In critically reviewing the literature, you need to read the literature about your research topic with some scepticism and be willing to question what you read. This means you need to be constantly considering and justifying your own critical stance with clear arguments and references to the literature rather than just giving your own opinion. You will have to read widely on your research topic and have a good understanding of the literature. Critically reviewing the literature for your research project, therefore, requires you to have gained topic-based background knowledge, understanding, the ability to reflect upon and to analyse the literature and, based on this, to make reasoned judgements that are argued effectively. When you use these skills to review the literature, the term 'critical' refers to the judgement you exercise. It therefore describes the process of providing a detailed and justified analysis of, and commentary on, the merits and faults of the key literature within your chosen area. This means that, for your review to be critical, you will need to have shown critical judgement.

Part of this judgement will inevitably mean being able to identify the most relevant and significant theories and recognised experts highlighted in Box 3.3. For some research topics there will be a pre-existing, clearly developed theoretical base. For others you will need to integrate a number of different theoretical strands to develop your understanding. Dees (2003) suggests that this means you should:

- refer to and assess research by recognised experts in your chosen area accurately;
- consider and discuss research that supports and research that opposes your ideas;
- make reasoned judgements regarding the value of others' research, showing clearly how it relates to your research and acknowledging key work;
- justify your arguments with valid evidence in a logical manner;
- distinguish clearly between fact and opinion;
- ensure your references are completely accurate.

Box 3.3 Focus on research in the news

Perils of placing faith in a thin theory – a critique of tradition and authority

By Wolfgang Münchau

In April 2013 research by a graduate student and his professors (later published as Herndon et al. 2013) convincingly demonstrated that Reinhart and Rogoff's (2010) paper 'Growth in a time of debt' had inaccurately represented the relationship between public debt and gross domestic product. This was important, as Reinhart and Rogoff's finding that countries with public debt that exceed 90 per cent of annual economic output grew more slowly was used widely by governments to justify austerity policies. Herndon et al.'s critique of tradition and authority was reported on FT.com by Wolfgang Münchau on 21 April 2013:

> Since the publication in 2011 of their bestselling book, *This Time Is Different*, and their subsequent research on the relationship between debt and growth, Reinhart and Rogoff have left no doubt that they believe the data show there is a 90 per cent threshold of debt to gross domestic product beyond which economic growth declines rapidly. Many policy makers have interpreted this rule as a call to reduce debt to below that level for the sake of growth. Profs Reinhart and Rogoff have thus become the intellectual godmother and godfather of austerity.
>
> The Reinhart and Rogoff thesis, as it is understood by policy makers, incorporates two separate myths. The first is the existence of the 90 per cent threshold. The second is about causality.

> The first was debunked last week by Thomas Herndon, Michael Ash and Robert Pollin, researchers from the University of Massachusetts Amherst. Their corrected figures show a rather smooth negative relationship between growth and debt. Economists will always squabble about statistical issues – whether to use the median or the mean, and the like. But no matter how you twist and turn this, there is no structural break at a 90 per cent threshold. There is no structural break anywhere.
>
> For the policy discussion, this point is hugely important. It pulls apart the notion of 90 per cent as some magic number – which European policy makers now obsess about, just as they used to about annual budget deficits not exceeding 3 per cent of GDP, for which there was no theoretical basis.
>
> The reduction of everything to a single number was followed by an exaggeration of the impact. Causation could go from high debt to low growth, as the authors suggest; or the other way round; or in both directions. Or the relation might be spurious. Or something altogether different might cause both. If causality is the other way round, the story is much less exciting for someone who peddles economic policies. You might as well say: people are poor because they have no money. If your growth is negative, your debt ratio rises for the simple reason that it is expressed in terms of nominal GDP.

Box 3.4 Checklist

Evaluating whether your literature review is critical

✔ Have you contextualised your own research showing how your research question relates to previous research reviewed, acknowledging seminal work?

✔ Have you assessed the strengths and weaknesses of the previous research reviewed?

✔ Have you been objective in your discussion and assessment of other people's research?

✔ Have you included references to research that is counter to, as well as supports, your own opinions?

✔ Have you distinguished clearly between facts and opinions?

✔ Have you made reasoned judgements about the value and relevance of others' research to your own?

✔ Have you justified clearly your own ideas?

✔ Have you highlighted those areas where new research (yours!) is needed to provide fresh insights and taken these into account in your arguments? In particular:

- where there are inconsistencies in current knowledge and understanding?
- where there are omissions or bias in published research?
- where research findings need to be tested further?
- where evidence is lacking, inconclusive, contradictory or limited?

✔ Have you justified your arguments by accurately referencing published research?

These points are developed in Box 3.4, which contains a checklist to evaluate the extent to which your literature review is critical. The more questions to which you can answer 'yes', the more likely your review will be critical!

Structuring and drafting the critical review

The **literature review** that you write for your project report should be a description and critical analysis of what other authors have written. When drafting your review you therefore need to focus on your research question(s) and objectives. One way of helping you to focus is to think of your literature review as discussing how far existing published research goes in answering your research question(s). The shortfall in the literature will be addressed, at least partially, in the remainder of your project report – unless your entire research project is a literature review! Another way of helping you to focus is to ask yourself how your review relates to your objectives. If it does not, or does so only partially, there is a need for a clearer focus on your objectives. The precise structure of the critical review is usually your choice, although you should check, as it may be specified in the assessment criteria. Three common structures are:

- a single chapter;
- a series of chapters (for example in a larger research project);
- occurring throughout the project report as you tackle various issues (for example where your research project is conducted inductively).

In all project reports, you should return to the key issues you raise in your literature review in your discussion and conclusions (Section 14.3).

In drafting your critical review, you will need to juxtapose different authors' ideas and form your own opinions and conclusions based on these. Although you will not be able to start writing until you have undertaken some reading, we recommend that you start drafting your review early (Figure 3.1). What you write can then be updated and revised as you read more.

A common mistake with critical literature reviews, highlighted at the start of this chapter, is that they become uncritical listings of previous research. Often they are little more than annotated bibliographies (Hart 1998), individual items being selected on the subjective findings and conclusions of the researcher (Tranfield et al. 2003). This is problematic as it is crucial that you show discernment in your literature review by including earlier key research of relevance to your own work, representing this work correctly and referencing it accurately (Colquitt 2013). In the introduction we highlighted a common problem with literature reviews: they just describe what each author has written, one author after another (vertical arrows in Figure 3.2). It is much easier to be critical (and more interesting to read) if you take a thematic approach comparing and, where necessary, contrasting the authors who discuss each theme (horizontal arrows in Figure 3.2). Although there is no single structure that your critical review should take, our students have found it useful to think of the review as a funnel in which you:

1 start at a more general level before narrowing down to your specific research question(s) and objectives;
2 provide a brief overview of key ideas and themes;
3 summarise, compare and contrast the research of the key authors;
4 narrow down to highlight previous research work most relevant to your own research;
5 provide a detailed account of the findings of this research and show how they are related;
6 highlight those aspects where your own research will provide fresh insights;
7 lead the reader into subsequent sections of your project report, which explore these issues.

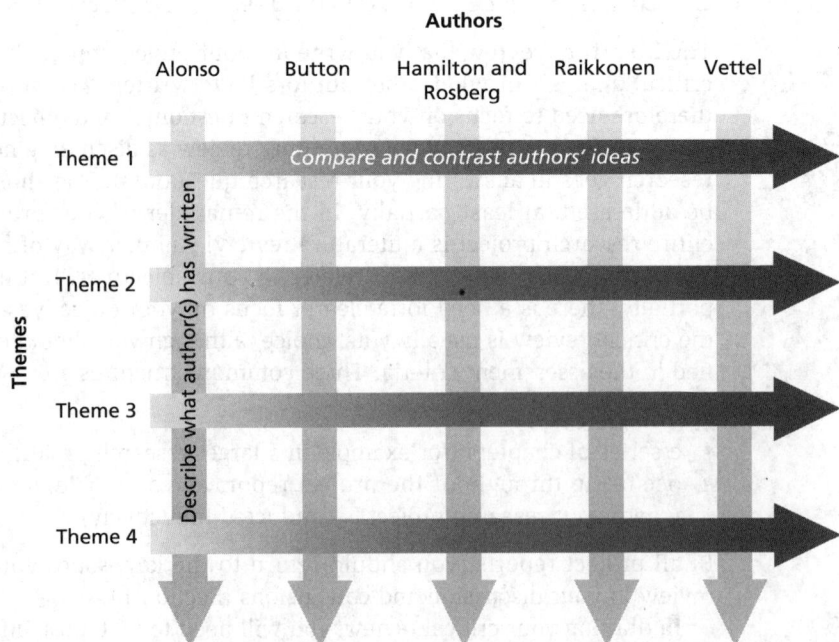

Figure 3.2 Literature review structure

Box 3.5
Checklist

Evaluating the structure of your literature review

✔ Does your literature review have a clear title, which describes the focus of your research rather than just saying 'literature review'?

✔ Have you explained precisely how you searched the literature, and the criteria used to select those studies included?

✔ Does your review start at a more general level before narrowing down?

✔ Is your literature review organised thematically around the ideas contained in the research being reviewed rather than the researchers?

✔ Are your arguments coherent and cohesive – do your ideas link in a way that will be logical to your reader?

✔ Have you used subheadings within the literature review to help guide your reader?

✔ Does the way you have structured your literature review draw your reader's attention to those issues that are the focus of your research, in particular your objectives?

✔ Does your literature review lead your reader into subsequent sections of your project report?

In order to improve the transparency of your review process, you should explain precisely how you selected the literature you have included in your review, outlining your choice of search terms and of databases used (Tranfield et al. 2003). This is essential if you are using the Systematic Review methodology (Section 3.8). Within the 'funnel' we have just proposed, this can be thought of as 'step 0'! This is discussed in more detail in Sections 3.4 and 3.5.

Whichever way you structure your review, you must demonstrate that you have read, understood and evaluated the items you have located and know those which are key to your own research. The key to writing a critical literature review is therefore to link the different ideas you find in the literature to form a coherent and cohesive argument, which sets in context and justifies your research. Obviously, it should relate to your research question and objectives. It should show a clear link from these as well as a clear link to the empirical work that will follow. Box 3.5 provides a checklist to help you ensure that the structure of your literature review supports this. Subsequent parts of your project report (Section 14.3) must follow on from this. Box 3.6 provides an extract from the literature review in a recently published paper.

Box 3.6
Focus on management research

Structure of the literature review

A refereed academic journal article by Mark Saunders, Graham Dietz and Adrian Thornhill, published in *Human Relations* (Saunders et al. 2014), includes

a review of the literature on trust and distrust. The following are extracts taken from their article; your review will be longer than these extracts. The first extract (pp. 640–1) illustrates:

- an overall structure which starts at a more general level (the second extract illustrates a narrowing down);
- provision of a brief overview of the key ideas referenced to their authors (in this extract Lewicki et al. 1998; Mayer et al. 1995; and Rousseau et al. 1998);

Box 3.6
Focus on management research (*continued*)

- linking of different researchers' ideas (in the extract these relate to definitions of trust and distrust);
- a clear justification leading to the research aim or question (in this extract two questions).

General agreement has now emerged regarding the definition of trust. Outlined in similar terms by scholars such as Lewicki et al. (1998), Mayer et al. (1995), and Rousseau et al. (1998), trust is depicted as occurring under conditions of risk which require the trusting party (the 'trustor') to develop favourable expectations of the intentions and behaviour of the other party ('trustee'), sufficient to prompt a willingness to become vulnerable to the trustee's future conduct. In Mayer et al.'s (1995) widely cited model, for example, the trustor's assessment of the trustee covers the latter's ability (technical competence to carry out a given task), benevolence (their motives toward the trustor) and integrity (their adherence to commonly held principles, such as fairness and honesty). These beliefs inform a subsequent "willingness to render oneself vulnerable" (Rousseau et al., 1998: 395), and this 'trust' is demonstrated with a risk-taking act.

Far less agreement exists on how distrust, sometimes termed mistrust, should be conceptualised. Most researchers conceptualise trust and distrust as "antithetical" (Bigley and Pearce, 1998: 407), at mutually exclusive ends of a single continuous construct. 'Low trust' is seen as equivalent to 'high distrust' and vice versa (Bigley and Pearce, 1998), i.e. it is an 'either/or' relationship. Summarising this view, Schoorman et al. (2007: 350) declare, "We can find no credible evidence that a concept of distrust that is conceptually different from trust is theoretically or empirically viable."

Others disagree, notably Lewicki et al. (1998). They conceptualise trust and distrust as separate, "independent" constructs with their own distinct antecedents and consequences, but which are nevertheless linked, and can therefore "co-exist" in the same relationship. In their words: "just as it is possible . . . to like and dislike, and to love and hate, it may be possible to trust and distrust others" (1998: 449) – a 'both/and' relationship. McKnight and Chervany (2001: 29) argue that one might believe in another party (i.e. trust them), but still have a back-up in the form of distrust. Additionally, one may trust the other party on the basis of the presence of (distrusting?) controls (see Poppo and Zenger, 2002; Strätling et al., 2011). Thus, the split in the academic debate has centred upon two inter-related questions. First, are trust and distrust judgements symmetrical (Schoorman et al., 2007) or might they occur simultaneously (Lewicki et al., 1998)? Second, do trust and distrust judgements entail the same or conceptually different expectations, as revealed in expressions and anticipated manifestations (Lewicki et al., 1998)? . . .

In this article, Saunders et al. focus subsequently on the expressions and manifestations of trust and distrust before introducing their empirical research conducted in the UK's public sector. The second extract (pp. 641–2) illustrates:

- a narrowing down to highlight that work which is explicitly relevant to the research reported (in this extract the contrasting of researchers' views as to whether or not trust and distrust are opposites or independent but linked constructs).

. . . In the depiction of distrust as simply the opposite of trust (Mayer et al., 1995; Bigley and Pearce, 1998), the trustor either trusts or distrusts the trustee; the two conditions are "mutually exclusive" (Bigley and Pearce, 1998: 414). A state of mind consisting of one precludes the presence of its counter-position: "a complete lack of trust and distrust are the *same thing"* (Schoorman et al., 2007: 350 – emphasis added).

Lewicki et al. (1998) and McKnight and Chervany (2001) argue instead that this bipolar view does not reflect the reality of contemporary "multiplex" relationships. Invoking an analogy from physics, Lewicki et al. (1998: 444) depict modern working relationships as being in a state of "quasi-stationary equilibrium", in which actors in their dealings with each other seek a balance and/or reconciliation between the two positions. They argue that trust and distrust are better approached as separate, independent but linked constructs, in which "low distrust is *not the same thing* as high trust, and high distrust is not the same thing as low trust" (emphasis added). Moreover, both conditions can co-exist, each

resting on their own combinations of expectations (beneficial or otherwise), and revealed in particular expressions and manifest actions. Consequently, it is possible for an individual within a given relationship to experience one of four prototypical relationship conditions (Lewicki et al., 1998):

Low Trust/Low Distrust is a position of arms-length, casual indifference regarding trust/distrust judgements (neither a willingness nor a reluctance about becoming vulnerable to the trustee). An individual's perceptions of the other party provide no firm reasons to expect favourable or unfavourable treatment . . .

Source: Saunders, M.N.K., Dietz, D. and Thornhill, A. (2014). Copyright ©SAGE Reproduced by permission of the publisher

3.3 Literature sources 文献来源

The amount of literature available to help you to develop a good understanding of, and insight into, previous research is expanding rapidly as new resources are developed and made available online. The literature sources you are likely to make most use of are often referred to as:

- **secondary literature** sources, these being formally published items such as journals and books;
- **grey** (or **primary**) **literature** sources, these being items produced by all levels of government, academics, business and industry in print and electronic formats, but which are not controlled by commercial publishers; including materials such as reports and conference proceedings.

Your university's librarians are likely to be aware of a wide range of business and management literature sources that can be accessed, principally from your library's web pages, and will keep themselves up to date with new resources. In addition you may wish to visit your country's national library or your local public library.

The main secondary and primary literature sources that you are likely to use are outlined in Table 3.1. The most important when placing your ideas in the context of earlier research are refereed academic journals. Books (many of which will be available as e-books) are, however, likely to be more important than professional and trade journals in this context.

Journals

Journals are also known as 'periodicals', 'serials' and 'magazines', and are published on a regular basis. While many are still produced in printed form, virtually all can now be accessed using full-text online databases, through your university. Journals are a vital literature source for any research. The articles are easily accessible, although online

Table 3.1 Main literature sources

Source	Content	Use for the literature review	Coverage by online databases	Likely availability
Refereed (peer-reviewed) academic journal	Detailed reports of research. Written by experts and evaluated by other experts to assess quality and suitability for publication. Rigorous attention paid to detail and verification	Most useful of all	Well covered. In addition, content pages often available for searching via publishers' websites	Majority accessible online through various subscription services. Increasingly available via institutional repositories, national 'access to research' initiatives or social networking sites. Those not available can usually be obtained using inter-library loans
Non-refereed academic journal	May contain detailed reports of research. Selected by editor or editorial board with subject knowledge	Varies considerably Beware of bias	Reasonably well covered. In addition, content pages often available for searching via publishers' websites	Majority accessible online through various subscription services. Increasingly available via institutional repositories, national 'access to research' initiatives or social networking sites. Those not available can usually be obtained using inter-library loans
Professional journals	Mix of news items and practical detailed accounts. Sometimes include summaries of research	Insights into practice but use with caution	Reasonably well covered by online databases. In addition, content pages often available for searching via professional associations' websites	Majority accessible online through various subscription services. Those not available can usually be obtained using inter-library loans. Professional associations may also provide access to their journals via their own web pages

Source	Content	Use for the literature review	Coverage by online databases	Likely availability
Trade journals/ magazines	Mix of news items and practical detailed accounts	Insights into practice but use with caution	Content pages often available for searching via professional associations' websites	Not as widely available in university libraries as academic and refereed journals. Most trade associations will have an associated website
Books and e-books	Written for specific audiences. Usually in an ordered and relatively accessible format. Often draw on wide range of sources	Particularly useful for an overview and to find recognised experts	Well covered by abstracts and indexes. Searches can be undertaken on remote university OPACs* via the Internet	Widely available. Those not available locally can be obtained using inter-library loans
Newspapers	Written for a particular market segment. Filtered dependent on events. May be written from particular viewpoint	Good for topical developments. Beware of possible bias in reporting and coverage	National newspapers reasonably well covered by specialised databases	Recent paper copies of home nation 'quality' newspapers kept as reference in most university libraries. Online access to stories, often with additional information on the websites, for most national and international 'quality' newspapers via subscription services
Conference proceedings	Selected papers presented at a conference	Can be very useful if on same theme as research	Depends on conference, although often limited. Specialist indexes sometimes available, such as 'Index to conference proceedings'	Not widely held by university libraries. Can be difficult to find unless online
Reports	Topic specific. Written by academics and organisation. Those from established organisations often of high quality	Very useful, when matches your topic	Poor, although some specialised indexes exist	Not widely held by university libraries. Often available online. May be possible to obtain others using inter-library loans

(continued)

Table 3.1 (*Continued*)

Source	Content	Use for the literature review	Coverage by online databases	Likely availability
Theses	Often most up-to-date research but very specific	Good for PhD and MPhil research degrees, otherwise less useful	Covered by indices of theses	Still usually obtained using inter-library loans, although increasingly available online. May still only be one hard (paper) copy

*OPAC, Online Public Access Catalogue.

Source: © Mark Saunders, Philip Lewis and Adrian Thornhill 2015

access is usually restricted to members of the university (Table 3.1). Fortunately, a growing number of national governments, including the UK, are implementing 'access to research' initiatives to provide free, walk-in access to academic articles and research in public libraries (Access to Research 2014). Trade and some professional journals may be covered only partially by online databases (Table 3.2). You therefore need to browse these journals regularly to be sure of finding useful items. Although these are increasingly available online, they are often only available to subscribers. For many academic journals you can receive email 'alerts' of the table of contents (TOC). TOCs can also be browsed online and downloaded through tertiary literature sources such as JournalTOCs and the British Library's ZETOC database (Table 3.2 and Section 3.5).

Articles in **refereed academic journals** (such as the *Journal of Management Studies* and the *Academy of Management Review*) are evaluated by academic peers prior to publication to assess their quality and suitability. They are usually written by recognised experts in the field. There will usually be detailed footnotes; an extensive list of references; rigorous attention to detail and verification of information. Such articles are written for a narrower audience of scholars with a particular interest in the field. The language used may be technical or highly specialised as a prior knowledge of the topic will be assumed. Prior to being accepted for publication, articles usually undergo several serious revisions, based on the referees' comments, before they are published.

These are usually the most useful for research projects as they will contain detailed reviews of relevant earlier research. Not all academic journals are refereed. Most *non-refereed academic journals* will have an editor and possibly an editorial board with subject knowledge to select articles. The relevance and usefulness of such journals varies considerably, and occasionally you may need to be wary of possible bias (Section 3.6).

Professional journals (such as *People Management*) are produced for their members by organisations such as the Chartered Institute of Personnel and Development (CIPD), the Association of Chartered Certified Accountants (ACCA) and the American Marketing Association (AMA). They contain a mix of news-related items and articles that are more detailed. However, you need to exercise caution, as articles can be biased towards their author's or the organisation's views. Articles are often of a more practical nature and more closely related to professional needs than those in academic journals. Some organisations will also produce newsletters or current awareness publications that you may find useful for up-to-date information. Some professional organisations now give access to selected articles in their journals via their web pages, although these may be only accessible to members (see Table 8.2 and Section 3.5). **Trade journals** fulfil a similar function to professional journals. They are published by trade organisations or aimed at particular industries or trades such as catering or mining. Often they focus on new products or services and news items. They rarely contain articles based on empirical research, although some provide summaries of research. You should therefore use these with considerable caution for your research project.

Books

Books and monographs are written for specific audiences. Some are aimed at the academic market, with a theoretical slant. Others, aimed at practising professionals, may be more applied in their content. The material in books is usually presented in a more ordered and accessible manner than in journals, pulling together a wider range of topics. They are, therefore, particularly useful as introductory sources to help clarify your research question(s) and objectives or the research methods you intend to use. Most academic textbooks, like this one, are supported by web pages providing additional information. However, books may contain out-of-date material even by the time they are published.

Newspapers

Newspapers are a good source of topical events, developments within business and government, as well as recent statistical information such as share prices. They also sometimes review recent research reports (Box 3.3). Back copies starting in the early 1990s are available online via a full-text subscription service, such as *Nexis* (Table 3.2). Current editions of newspapers are available in print form and online, although there is often a charge for full online access. Items in earlier issues are more difficult to access and often only include text. An exception is the *Times Digital Archive 1785–1985* (Table 3.2) of *The Times* newspaper. You need to be careful, as newspapers may contain bias in their coverage, be it political, geographical or personal. Reporting can also be inaccurate, and you may not pick up any subsequent amendments. In addition, the news presented is filtered depending on events at the time, with priority given to more headline-grabbing stories (Stewart and Kamins 1993).

Reports

Reports include market research reports such as those produced by Mintel and Key Note, government reports and academic reports. Even if you are able to locate these, you may find it difficult to gain access to them because they are often not available free of charge (Section 8.4). Reports are not well indexed in the databases, and you will need to rely on specific search tools such as the *British Library Integrated Catalogue* (see Table 3.2).

Freedom of information legislation by many governments now means a vast number of reports are now available online, for example through the European Union's EUROPA website and the Commission's Statistics website Eurostat. These and other governmental websites are listed in Table 8.2.

Conference proceedings

Conference proceedings, sometimes referred to as symposia, are often published as unique titles within journals or as books. Most conferences will have a theme that is

Table 3.2 Online databases, portals and their coverage

Name	Coverage
Access to Research	Online database giving free access to over 1.5 million research articles (including Business and Management) in participating UK public libraries
Blackwell Reference Online	Blackwell Encyclopedia of Management, Blackwell 'handbooks' and 'Companions' in Management
British National Bibliography (BNB)	Bibliographic information for books and serials (journals) deposited at the British Library by UK and Irish publishers since 1950
British Library Integrated Catalogue	Online catalogue of print and electronic resources held by the British Library. Includes reference collections and document supply collections
British Library Management and Business Studies Portal	Online interface to digital full-text research reports, summaries, working papers, videos and articles as well as details of journal articles, sound recordings video and other resources relevant to business and management
British Newspapers 1600–1900	Cross-searchable interface to full-text British Newspapers
Business Source Complete (also referred to as EBSCO)	Database including full-text articles from over 2900 management, business, economics and information technology journals, mainly since 1990s. Contains a wide range of trade and professional titles. Gives access to *Datamonitor*
Conference Index	British Library database containing proceedings of all significant conferences held worldwide (over 400,000 at time of writing)
Emerald Management eJournals (also known as Emerald Insight)	Database providing access to over 160 full-text journals and reviews from 300 management journals
Hospitality and Tourism Index	Bibliographic database covering English language hospitality and tourism journals and trade magazines. Some full-text links. Coverage since early 1960s
Index to Theses	A comprehensive listing of theses with abstracts accepted for higher degrees by universities in Great Britain and Ireland since 1716
IngentaConnect	Details of articles from over 28,000 publications, some of which are available on subscription. Pay-per-view access available. Updated daily
ISI Web of Knowledge	Includes access to a wide range of services, including citation indexes for social sciences and for arts and humanities
JournalTOCs	Tables of contents (TOCs) for over 12,500 journals. Can specify journals for which wish to receive future TOCs
JSTOR	Database containing full-text journals, most going back to first issue (in some cases going back to the eighteenth or nineteenth century). Covers sciences, social sciences and arts and humanities. Most recent years usually not available

Name	Coverage
Key Note	Database containing over 1600 market reports covering a range of sectors
Mintel Reports	Database containing detailed market research reports on wide range of sectors
Nexis	Database of full text of UK national and regional newspapers. Some international coverage and company data
Orbis	Information on companies from around the world
ProQuest (formerly ABI/INFORM)	Database covering over 5400 journals, covering key business disciplines over 80 per cent in full text. Includes wide range of trade and professional titles. Covers additional subjects such as engineering, law and medicine
Regional Business News	Database of full text of 75 US business journals, newspapers and newswires. Updated daily
Sage Premier	Database of full text of over 480 Sage journals including business, humanities, social sciences and research methods since 1999
Science Direct	Database of full text of over 1600 Elsevier journals including social sciences
Social Science Citation Index	Access to current and retrospective bibliographic information, author abstracts, and cited references found in over 1700 social sciences journals covering more than 50 disciplines. Also covers items from approximately 3300 of the world's leading science and technology journals
Times Digital Archive 1785–1985	Database containing complete digital editions (including photographs, illustrations and advertisements) from *The Times* national newspaper (UK)
Web of Knowledge	Single access point to Web of Science, Journal Citation Reports, Current Contents and many others
Wiley Online	Database of 1100 full-text journals including business and law
ZETOC	British Library's index of journals and conference proceedings tables of contents (TOCs). Allows setting up of email alerts of selected journal contents pages

very specific, but some have a wide-ranging overview. Proceedings are not well indexed by tertiary literature, so, as with reports, you may have to rely on specific search tools such as the *Index to Conference Proceedings* and the *British Library Integrated Catalogue* (Table 3.2) as well as general search engines. If you do locate and are able to obtain the proceedings for a conference on the theme of your research, you will have a wealth of relevant information. Many conferences have associated web pages providing abstracts and occasionally the full papers presented at the conference.

Theses

Theses are unique and so for a major research project can be a good source of detailed information; they will also be a good source of further references. Unfortunately, they can be difficult to locate and, when found, difficult to access as there may be only one copy at the awarding institution. Specific search tools are available, such as *Index to Theses* (see Table 3.2). Only research degrees such as PhD and MPhil are covered well by these tertiary resources. Research undertaken as part of a taught master's degree (usually called a dissertation) is not covered as systematically.

规划文献检索策略

3.4   Planning your literature search strategy

It is important that you plan this search carefully to ensure that you locate relevant and up-to-date literature. This will enable you to establish what research has previously been published in your area and to relate your own research to it. All our students have found their literature search a time-consuming process, which takes far longer than expected. Fortunately, time spent planning will be repaid in time saved when searching for relevant literature. As you start to plan your search, you need to beware of information overload! One of the easiest ways to avoid this is to start the main search for your critical review with clearly defined research question(s), objectives and outline proposal (Sections 2.4 and 2.5). Before commencing your literature search, we suggest that you undertake further planning by writing down your search strategy and, if possible, discussing it with your project tutor. This should include:

- the parameters of your search;
- the search terms and phrases you intend to use;
- the online databases and search engines you intend to use;
- the criteria you intend to use to select the relevant and useful studies from all the items you find.

While it is inevitable that your search strategy will be refined as your literature search progresses, we believe that such a planned approach is important as it forces you to think carefully about your research strategy and justify, at least to yourself, why you are doing what you are doing.

Defining the parameters of your search

For most research questions and objectives you will have a good idea of which subject matter is going to be relevant. You will, however, be less clear about the parameters within which you need to search. In particular, you need to be clear about the following (derived from Bell and Waters 2014):

- language of publication (e.g. English);
- subject area (e.g. accountancy);
- business sector (e.g. manufacturing);
- geographical area (e.g. Europe);
- publication period (e.g. the last 10 years);
- literature type (e.g. refereed journals and books).

One way of starting to firm up these parameters is to re-examine your lecture notes and course textbooks in the area of your research question. While re-examining these, we suggest you make a note of subjects that appear most pertinent to your research question and the names of relevant authors. These will be helpful when generating possible search terms and phrases later.

For example, if your research was on the benefits of cause-related marketing to charities you might identify the subject area as marketing and charities. Implicit in this is the need to think broadly. A frequent comment we hear from students who have attempted a literature search is 'there's nothing written on my research topic'. This is usually because they have identified one or more of their parameters too narrowly (or chosen their search terms poorly, Section 3.5). We therefore recommend that if you encounter this problem you broaden one or more of your parameters to include material that your narrower search would not have located (Box 3.9).

Generating your search terms

It is important at this stage to read both articles by key authors and recent review articles in the area of your research. This will help you to define your subject matter and to suggest appropriate search terms and phrases. Recent review articles in your research area are often helpful here as they discuss the current state of research for a particular topic and can help you to refine your search terms. In addition, they will probably contain references to other work that is pertinent to your research question(s) and objectives (Box 3.7). If you are unsure about review articles, your project tutor should be able to point you in the right direction. Another potentially useful source of references is dissertations and theses in your university's library.

After re-reading your lecture notes and textbooks and undertaking this limited reading, you will have a list of subjects that appear relevant to your research project. You now need to define precisely what is relevant to your research in terms of search terms.

The identification of search terms is the most important part of planning your search for relevant literature (Bell and Waters 2014). **Search terms** are the basic terms that describe your research question(s) and objectives, and will be used to search the tertiary literature. Search terms (which can include authors' family names identified in the

---

Box 3.7
Focus on student research

Generating search terms

Han's research question was, 'How do the actual management requirements of a school pupil record administration system differ from those suggested by the literature?' She brainstormed this question with her peer group, all of whom were teachers in Hong Kong of china. The resulting list included the following search terms and phrases:

- schools, pupil records, administration, user requirements, computer, management information system, access, legislation, information, database, security, UK, Hong Kong of china, theories

The group evaluated these and others. As a result, the following search terms (and phrases) were selected:

- pupil records, management information system, computer, database, user requirement

Online dictionaries and encyclopaedias were used subsequently to add to the choice of search terms:

- student record, MIS, security

Han made a note of these prior to using them in combination to search the tertiary literature sources.

examination of your lecture notes and course textbooks) can be identified using one or a number of different techniques in combination. Those found most useful by our students include:

Discussion

We believe you should be taking every opportunity to discuss your research. In discussing your work with others, whether face-to-face, by Facebook or by email, you will be sharing your ideas, getting feedback and obtaining new ideas and approaches. This process will help you to refine and clarify your topic.

Initial reading, dictionaries, encyclopaedias, handbooks and thesauruses

To produce the most relevant search terms you may need to build on your brainstorming session with support materials such as dictionaries, encyclopaedias, handbooks and thesauruses, both general and subject specific. These are also good starting points for new topics with which you may be unfamiliar and for related subject areas. Initial reading, particularly of recent review articles, may also be of help here. Project tutors, colleagues and librarians can also be useful sources of ideas.

It is also possible to obtain definitions via the Internet. The online search engine Google offers a 'define' search option (by typing 'Define:[enter term]') that provides links to websites providing definitions. Definitions are also offered in free online encyclopaedias such as Wikipedia. These are often available in multiple languages and, although anyone is allowed to edit the entries, inappropriate changes are usually removed quickly. While articles tend to become more comprehensive and balanced as contributors add to and revise them, recent articles in particular may contain misinformation or unencyclopaedic content (Wikipedia 2014). However, while these websites may be useful for a quick reference or in helping to define keywords, your university will almost certainly expect you to justify the definitions in your research project using refereed journal articles or textbooks.

Brainstorming

Brainstorming has already been outlined as a technique for helping you to develop your research question (Section 2.3). However, it is also helpful for generating search terms. Either individually or as part of a group, you write down all the words and short phrases that come to mind on your research topic (Box 3.7). These are then evaluated and search terms (and phrases) selected.

Relevance trees

Relevance trees provide a useful method of bringing some form of structure to your literature search and of guiding your search process (Sharp et al. 2002). They look similar to an organisation chart and are a hierarchical 'graph-like' arrangement of headings and subheadings (Box 3.8). These headings and subheadings describe your research question(s) and objectives and may be terms (including authors' names) with which you can search. Relevance trees are often constructed after brainstorming. They enable you to decide, either with help or on your own (Jankowicz 2005):

- which search terms are directly relevant to your research question(s) and objectives;
- which areas you will search first and which your search will use later;
- which areas are more important – these tend to have more branches.

Box 3.8
Focus on student research

Using a relevance tree

Sadie's research question was 'Is there a link between benchmarking and Total Quality Management?' After brainstorming her question, she decided to construct a relevance tree on her tablet using the search terms and phrases that had been generated.

Using her relevance tree Sadie identified those areas that she needed to search immediately (in blue) and those that she particularly needed to focus on (starred*).

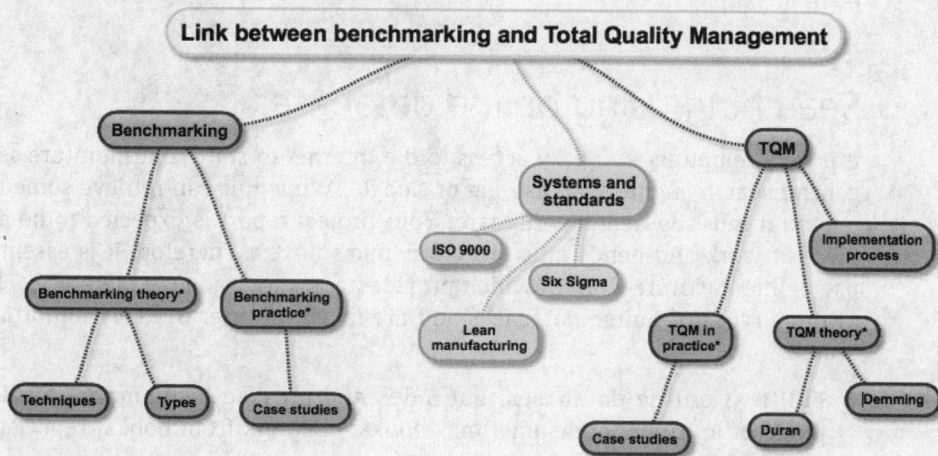

```
             Link between benchmarking and Total Quality Management

  Benchmarking                                                          TQM

                                    Systems and
                                     standards
                                                                          Implementation
                            ISO 9000                                         process

  Benchmarking theory*   Benchmarking              Six Sigma
                          practice*
                                         Lean              TQM in      TQM theory*
                                      manufacturing       practice*

  Techniques    Types    Case studies                                              Demming

                                                      Case studies    Duran
```

To construct a relevance tree:

1 Start with your research question or an objective at the top level.
2 Identify two or more subject areas that you think are important.
3 Further subdivide each major subject area into sub-areas that you think are of relevance.
4 Further divide the sub-areas into more precise sub-areas that you think are of relevance.
5 Identify those areas that you need to search immediately and those that you particularly need to focus on. Your project tutor will be of particular help here.
6 As your reading and reviewing progress, add new areas to your relevance tree.

Apps such as SimpleMind (2014) and software such as Webspiration (2014) and MindGenius (2014) can be used to help generate relevance trees. Many apps or software also allow you to attach notes to your relevance tree and can help generate an initial structure for your literature review.

3.5 Conducting your literature search 文献检索

Your literature search will probably be conducted using a variety of approaches:

- searching using online databases;
- obtaining relevant literature (Section 3.6) referenced in books and journal articles you have already read;

- scanning and browsing secondary literature in your library;
- general online searching.

Eventually it is likely you will be using a variety of these in combination. However, we suggest that you start your search by obtaining relevant literature that has been referenced in books and articles you have already read. Although books are unlikely to give adequate up-to-date coverage of your research question, they provide a useful starting point and usually contain some references to further reading. Reading these will enable you to refine your research question(s), objectives and the associated search terms prior to searching using tertiary literature sources. It will also help you to see more clearly how your research relates to previous research, and will provide fresh insights.

Searching using online databases

It is very tempting with easy access to the Internet to start your literature search with a general search engine such as Bing or Google. While this can retrieve some useful information it must be treated with care. Your project report is expected to be an academic piece of work and hence must use academic sources. Therefore it is essential that you use online literature sources which provide access to academic literature. These consist of three types of online databases and are listed in order of likely importance to your search:

1 **Full-text online databases** that index and provide a summary of articles from a range of journals (and sometimes books, chapters from books, reports, theses and conferences), as well as the full text of articles.
2 **Abstracts** that only include an index and a summary of articles from a range of journals (and sometimes books, chapters from books, reports, theses and conferences), hence the name abstract.
3 **Indexes** that, as the name suggest, only index articles from a range of journals (and sometimes books, chapters from books, reports, theses and conferences).

Within all of these, the information provided will be sufficient to locate the item – for example, for journal articles:

- author or authors of the article;
- date of publication;
- title of the article;
- title of the journal;
- volume and part number of the journal issue;
- page numbers of the article.

Most searches will be undertaken to find articles using key words, often selected from a pre-specified list, or the author's name. Occasionally you may wish to search by finding those authors who have referenced (cited) an article after it has been published. A citation index enables you to do this as it lists by author the other authors who have cited that author's works subsequent to their publication. In contrast, the abstract can be useful in helping you to assess the content and relevance of an article to your research before obtaining a copy. You should beware of using abstracts, as a substitute for the full article, as a source of information for your research. They contain only a summary of the article and are likely to exclude much of relevance. Full-text databases usually allow both the searching and retrieval of the full text, principally of journal articles; the articles being retrieved in portable document file (PDF) format. These are read using software such as Adobe Reader, which can be downloaded free of charge.

Your access to the majority of online databases will be paid for by a subscription from your university (Table 3.2). There are, however, some pay-as-you-use online databases, where the cost of the search is passed on to the user. Online databases provide a wealth of information. While many online databases are intuitive to use, it is still advisable to obtain a librarian's help or to attend a training session prior to your search to find out about the specific features available. It is also vital that you plan and prepare your search in advance so your time is not wasted. For virtually all online databases, password-protected access is now possible anywhere there is an Internet connection.

Virtually all university library OPACs (online public access catalogues) are accessible online. These provide a very useful means of locating resources. If you identify useful collections of books and journals, it is possible to make use of other university libraries in the vacations. Within the UK, the SCONUL Vacation Access Scheme gives details of access policies of the libraries in UK higher education institutions.[1] Over 70 research libraries in the UK and Ireland (including the British Library, Oxford and Cambridge Universities and the National Libraries of Scotland and Wales) have also made their catalogues available online. These can be accessed through COPAC, the National Academic and Specialist Library Catalogue.[2]

To ensure maximum coverage in your search, you need to use all appropriate online databases. One mistake many people make is to restrict their searches to one or two business and management online databases rather than use a variety. The coverage of each online database differs both geographically and in type of journal. In addition, a database may state that it indexes a particular journal yet may do so only selectively. This emphasises the importance of using a range of databases to ensure a wide coverage of available literature. Some of those more frequently used are outlined in Table 3.2. However, new databases and portals are being developed all the time, so it is worth asking a librarian for advice.

Searching

Once your search terms have been identified, searching using online databases is a relatively straightforward process. You need to:

1 make a list of the search terms that describe your research question(s) and objectives;
2 search appropriate online databases;
3 note precise details, including the search strings used, of the actual searches you have undertaken for each database;
4 note the full reference of each item found; this can normally be done by importing the references into software for managing bibliographies, such as Endnote™ or Reference Manager™ or research tools such as 'Mendeley' or 'Zotero'.
5 Wherever possible import the article into your bibliography or research tool or, alternatively, download it in PDF format and save it on your USB mass storage device using the author, date and a brief description as a filename. This will help you locate it later. For example, an article by Mark on the use of web questionnaires might be saved using the filename: Saunders[2012]web_questionnaire.pdf.

---

[1]Details of these can be found at: http://www.sconul.ac.uk/page/vacation-access-to-other-higher-education-libraries

[2]The Internet address for COPAC is http://copac.ac.uk/

Box 3.9
Checklist

Minimising problems with your online database or portal search

✔ Is the spelling incorrect? Behaviour is spelt with a 'u' in the UK but without in the USA.
✔ Is the language incorrect? Chemists in the UK but drug stores in the USA.
✔ Are you using incorrect terminology? In recent years some terms have been replaced by others, such as 'redundancy' being replaced by 'downsizing'.

✔ Are you using recognised acronyms and abbreviations? For example, UK for United Kingdom or BA instead of British Airways.
✔ Are you avoiding jargon and using accepted terminology? For example, downsizing rather than redundancy.
✔ Are you using words that are in the controlled index language?
✔ Are you searching over a sensible publication period? For example, the last 15 years rather than the last 5 years.
✔ Are you searching the most suitable type of literature for your research project? For example, peer-reviewed (refereed) journal articles rather than all articles.

Tranfield et al. (2003) emphasise the importance of reporting your literature search strategy in sufficient detail to ensure that your search could be replicated (see Box 3.10). Your review will be based on the subset of those items found which you consider are relevant.

Most online databases and portals now allow full-text searches using natural language where you decide on the word or phrase combinations for search terms. This means, for example, you can search the complete text of an article using your search terms. However, some rely on or also offer the option to search using a **controlled index language** of pre-selected terms and phrases or 'descriptors'. These can include specified subject words, author names and journal titles. If your search terms do not match those in the controlled index language, your search will be unsuccessful. In such a situation, you therefore need to check your search terms with the 'index' or 'browse' option prior to searching. This is especially useful to establish how an author is indexed or whether hyphens should be used when entering specific terms. Despite using these tools, your searches may still be unsuccessful. The most frequent causes of failure are summarised in Box 3.9 as a checklist.

Searches normally use a combination of search terms linked using **Boolean logic**. These are known as **search strings** and enable you to combine, limit or widen the variety of items found using 'link terms' (Table 3.3). Boolean logic can also be used to construct search strings using dates, journal titles and names of organisations or people. Initially it may be useful to limit your search to peer-reviewed journal articles for which the full text is available. It may also be valuable to narrow your search to specific years, especially if you are finding a wealth of items and need to concentrate on the most up to date. By contrast, searching by author allows you to broaden your search to find other work by known researchers in your area.

There are, however, problems with searching the full text. In particular, the context of a search term may be inappropriate, leading to retrieval of numerous irrelevant articles and information overload. Fortunately, you can also search one or more specified fields in the database such as the abstract, author or title. Usually searching the abstract results in fewer irrelevant articles although, inevitably, you may not find some relevant ones either! Specifying other fields, for example the abstract, will be useful if you wish to find articles by a key author in your subject area.

Box 3.10
Focus on management research

Identifying evidence gaps, conflicting research findings and a starting point for future research

In a recent article in the *International Journal of Management Reviews*, Nijmeijer et al. (2014) synthesised 126 peer-reviewed empirical journal articles on the factors that make franchising work, integrating these into a framework. Their review article shows the outcomes of franchising are determined by five distinct clusters of factors.

The process used to search the literature followed the Systematic Review methodology (see also Section 3.8). This involved:

1 Defining clearly the focus of the research: the relationship between the outcomes of franchising and the franchise design or process; and the precise meaning of terms such as 'outcomes', 'design' and 'process'.

2 Identifying eight online databases which would be searched for articles. These included *ABI/Inform* and *EBSCO* within which English Language articles were searched using the term franchis* combined using the connector AND with terms such as effect*, efficiency, impact,

innovation*, outcome*, perform and quality. The online database *Emerald* was also searched, although this did not allow the use of truncated terms signified by the asterisk. References of all the included articles were also checked to identify additional relevant articles.

3 Evaluating the abstracts of the 2079 articles retrieved against clear inclusion/exclusion criteria to establish their suitability, resulting in 189 potentially relevant articles.

4 Evaluating and summarising the full text of the 189 articles against inclusion/exclusion criteria, resulting in 107 relevant articles.

5 Using the reference lists from these articles to identify a further 19 relevant studies.

The subsequent review of these articles explored the relationship between studies with different foci, theories and methodologies thematically revealing five major clusters of factors, each with multiple sub-factors. These are: ownership structure, business format, contract design, behaviour of and interaction between franchisor and franchisee, and the age and size of the franchise system and franchise firm.

Based on their review Nijmeijer et al. offer clear guidance regarding what franchisors and franchisees need to do in order to be successful. They also highlight clear gaps in knowledge, such as which franchise designs are valued by customers, and conclude that these suggest promising avenues for further research.

Table 3.3 Search connectors and characters

Connector or characters	Purpose	Example	Outcome
AND	Narrows search	Recruitment AND interviewing AND skills	Only articles containing all three search terms selected
OR	Widens search	Recruitment OR selection	Articles with at least one search term selected
NOT	Excludes terms from search	Recruitment NOT selection	Selects articles containing the search term 'recruitment' that do not contain the search term 'selection'
*(truncation)	Uses word stems to pick up different word forms	Motivat*	Selects articles with: motivate, motivation, motivating
? (wild card)	Picks up different spellings	behavio?r	Selects articles with: behavior, behaviour

Browsing and scanning

Any search will find only some of the relevant literature. You will therefore also need to browse and scan the literature. New publications such as journals are unlikely to be indexed immediately in online databases, so you will need to browse these publications to gain an idea of their content. In contrast, scanning will involve you going through individual items such as a journal article to pick out points and references to additional relevant articles, which you have not found elsewhere (Box 3.10). It is particularly important that you browse and scan trade and professional journals, as these are less likely to be covered by the online databases.

To make browsing and scanning easier you should:

- identify when those journals that are the most relevant are published and, where possible, ensure you receive email 'alerts' of their tables of contents (TOCs);
- identify those professional journals that are most relevant and regularly browse them;
- browse new book displays in libraries;
- scan new book reviews in journals and newspapers;
- scan publishers' new book catalogues where available;
- discuss your research with your project tutor and librarians, who may be aware of other relevant literature.

Websites of bookshops such as Amazon, Blackwell and the Internet Book Shop provide access to catalogues of books in print. These can usually be searched by author, title and subject, and may have reviews attached. Some bookseller websites (and Google Books) have a facility whereby you can view selected pages from the book. However, as when using electronic indexes and abstracts, it is important that you keep full details of the literature you have scanned and browsed (Box 3.11). As well as enabling you to outline the method you used for your literature review, it will also help prevent you repeating searches you have already undertaken.

General online searching

When searching online, we recommend you keep full details of the searches you have undertaken, making a note of:

- the search tool used;
- the precise search undertaken;
- the date when the search was undertaken;
- the total number of items retrieved.

Search tools

Search tools, often referred to as **search engines**, are probably the most important method of online searching for your literature review as they will enable you to locate most current and up-to-date items. Although normally accessed through home pages, each search tool will have its own address (Table 3.4). Search tools can be divided into four distinct categories (Table 3.4):

- general search engines;
- metasearch engines;
- specialised search engines and information gateways;
- subject directories.

Box 3.11
Focus on student research

Searching using online databases

Matthew described his research project using the search terms 'entrepreneur' and 'finance'. Unfortunately, he encountered problems when carrying out his search using one of the online databases of full text and abstracts for business, management and economics journals to which his university subscribed.

When he entered the search term 'entrepreneur', he retrieved references to over 81,000 items, many of which were in trade magazines. Entering the term 'finance' on its own retrieved even more references, over 1,484,000! He was unsure how to combine his search terms into search strings to make his search more specific. Full-text versions were not available for many of the most recent items retrieved.

After discussing the problem, the librarian showed Matthew how to use the advanced search option of the online database. Using this, Matthew first searched using the terms 'entrepreneur' AND 'finance' combined as a search string. This still resulted in over 8600 items being highlighted. He then refined his search further by limiting it to the collection of scholarly (peer-reviewed) journals. This resulted in over 2600 items being retrieved. He therefore decided to limit his search to the abstract field rather than the full text. This resulted in 333 items being retrieved.

He then copied the references for these items (articles) onto his MP3 player. As Matthew scrolled through these, he noted that some of them had direct links to copies of the full text stored as a PDF file. For many of the others, the librarian informed him that he could access the full text using different online databases. However, he still needed to assess each article's relevance to his research before obtaining full copies.

Matthew made a note of the details of his search:

Database:	Business Source Complete
Collection:	Scholarly (peer-reviewed) journals
Dates:	1934 to 2014
Search:	entrepreneur AND finance
Fields searched:	Abstract
Date of search:	6 April 2014
Total items retrieved	333

Table 3.4 Selected online search tools and their coverage

Name	Internet address	Comment
General search engines		
Bing	www.bing.com	Access to billions of web pages, can link to Facebook
Google	www.google.com	Access to billions of web pages
Google UK	www.google.co.uk	Country-based Google – optimised to show country results
Specialised search engines		
Google Scholar	www.scholar.google.com	Searches scholarly literature allowing you to locate the complete document
UK government	www.gov.uk	Searches central and local government websites and government agencies
Information gateways		
Biz/Ed	www.bized.co.uk	Information service, links economics and business students and teachers and information providers
Publishers' catalogues homepage	www.lights.ca/publisher/	Searchable links to major publishers' websites, listed alphabetically by country
Subject directories		
About.com	www.about.com	Organised by subjects, offers numerous guides
ipl2	www.ipl.org	High-quality site only providing 'information you can trust'
Yahoo!	http://dir.yahoo.com/	Organised by subject, particularly useful for popular and commercial topics

Most search engines index every separate document. In contrast, subject directories index only the 'most important' online documents. Therefore, if you are using a clear term to search for an unknown vaguely described document, use a search engine. If you are looking for a document about a particular topic, use a subject directory.

General search engines such as Google and Bing normally use search terms and Boolean logic (Table 3.3) or a phrase. Each search engine indexes and searches automatically, usually finding a very large number of sites (Box 3.12). As people have not evaluated these sites, many are inappropriate or unreliable. As no two general search engines search in precisely the same way, it is advisable (and often necessary) to use more than one. In contrast, meta-search engines allow you to search using a selection of search engines at the same time, using the same interface. This makes searching easier, and the search can be faster. Unfortunately, it is less easy to control the sites that are retrieved. Consequently, metasearch engines often generate more inappropriate or unreliable sites than general search engines.

Specialised search engines cater for specific subject areas. For example, Google Scholar searches scholarly literature across many disciplines using sources such as

Box 3.12
Focus on student research

Undertaking an online search using a general search engine

Zeineb's research question was reasonably defined, if somewhat broad. She wanted to look at dark tourism and the impact of place on visitors to sites of genocide. As part of her search strategy she decided, alongside the academic databases of business and management journals, to search the Internet using a general search engine. Her first search term 'dark tourism' revealed that there were over 80,300,000 sites and displayed the first 10. Of these, the second appeared to be potentially useful as it related to an institute for dark tourism research.

Zeineb clicked on this link, which took her to the website of the Institute of Dark Tourism Research based at the University of Central Lancashire. Clicking through a series of links from the home page for the Institute took her to a page that listed the research publications of people associated with the Institute. As many could be downloaded as PDF files, she downloaded, and saved those publications that seemed relevant on her MP3 player. Zeineb then made a note of the authors listed on the page, so she could search for them, using her university's online databases.

articles, theses, books and abstracts from academic publishers, professional bodies, universities and websites, allowing you to locate the complete document. Documents are subsequently ranked on a combination of factors including how often it has been cited, where it was published and by whom it was written. Of particular use is the direct link to open access articles stored on institutional repositories and on social networking sites (discussed next). To use specialised search engines it is necessary to define your general subject area prior to your search. Information gateways also require you to define your subject area. Information gateways are often compiled by staff from departments in academic institutions. Although the number of websites obtained is fewer, they can be far more relevant, as each site is evaluated prior to being added to the gateway.

Subject directories are searchable catalogues of sites collected and organised by humans. The sites are categorised into subject areas, and are useful for searching for broad topics. As people normally compile them, their content has been partly censored and evaluated. Consequently, the number of sites retrieved is fewer but they usually provide material that is more appropriate (Table 3.4).

Search tools are becoming more sophisticated all the time. Be careful, their use can be extremely time consuming. Your search will probably locate a mass of resources, many of which will be irrelevant to you. It is also easy to become sidetracked to more interesting and glossy websites not relevant to your research needs! There are an increasing number of web-based tutorials to help you learn to search the web. One of these, Marketing Insights' *Smarter Online Searching Guide*, is available via this book's web page. This highlights using search tools, including Advanced search in Google and online e-business resources.

Institutional repositories and social networking sites

Many universities now expect their academics to deposit digital full-text copies of their publications, particularly journal articles, in an **institutional repository**. This is an open access collection of the university's research outputs from which full-text items can be downloaded. Increasingly academics (including Mark!) are also uploading copies of their publications to social networking sites such as academia.edu and ResearchGate. Providing you know the author and their university, you can often access their publications through these resources free of charge. Such institutional repositories and social networking sites are useful if your university does not subscribe to the online database of full-text articles in which their publications are stored, particularly as uploaded copies can often be found using specialised search engines such as Google Scholar (Table 3.4).

3.6 Obtaining and evaluating the literature
获取文献和评价文献

Obtaining the literature

As we discussed in the previous section, searches using online databases (Table 3.2) and search tools (Table 3.4) will provide you with details of what literature is available and where to locate it, in many cases providing a hyperlink to an electronic copy. We emphasise again, you should, whenever possible, download the electronic copy in PDF format and save it on your USB mass storage device. However, where there is no hyperlink, the next stage (Figure 3.1) is to obtain the remaining items. To do this you need to:

1 Check your library online catalogue to find out whether your library holds the appropriate publications.
2 For those publications that are held by your library or available online, note their location and:
   i find the publication and scan it to discover whether it is likely to be worth reading thoroughly – for articles it is often possible to make a reasonable assessment of their utility using the abstract (Box 3.13); or
   ii browse other books and journals with similar classmarks to see whether they may also be of use.

Box 3.13
Focus on student research

Assessing the utility of an article using the abstract

Jana's research project was about how small- and medium-sized enterprises' (SMEs) use of formal and informal learning differed between Eastern and Western European countries. In a search using the Emerald Insight online database she had found a peer-reviewed article in the *European Journal of Training and Development* by Saunders, Gray and Goregaokar (2014) that she considered might be useful. She decided to read the abstract online to check:

The abstract confirmed that the **Purpose** of the article was to explore how SMEs learn and innovate using both formal and informal learning. More details regarding this were given in the **findings** section of the abstract. The **design/methodology/approach** indicated that the research had been undertaken with over 1000 SMEs, data being collected using both questionnaires and focus groups. The **research limitations/implications** section indicated the need for further research to understand the interrelationships between informal learning, crisis events and SME innovation. Jana wondered if this might be a good aspect to focus on in her research.

Based on this information, Jana decided the article was likely to be useful for her research project, so she downloaded it and saved an electronic copy in PDF format.

SME innovation and learning: the role of networks and crisis events

Document Information:

Title:	SME innovation and learning: the role of networks and crisis events
Author(s):	Mark N.K. Saunders, (Surrey Business School, University of Surrey, Guildford, UK), David E. Gray, (Greenwich Business School, University of Greenwich, London, UK), Harshita Goregaokar, (Surrey Business School, University of Surrey, Guildford, UK)
Citation:	Mark N.K. Saunders, David E. Gray, Harshita Goregaokar, (2014) "SME innovation and learning: the role of networks and crisis events", European Journal of Training and Development, Vol. 38 Iss: 1/2, pp.136 - 149
Keywords:	Crisis event, Entrepreneur, Innovation, Learning, Mixed method, Network, SME
Article type:	Research paper
DOI:	10.1108/EJTD-07-2013-0073 (Permanent URL)
Publisher:	Emerald Group Publishing Limited
Acknowledgements:	The authors would like to thank Kingston Smith LLP for financing this research project, the many businesses and individuals who took part, and the many organisations such as Chambers of Commerce that promoted the research survey amongst their membership.

Abstract:

Purpose – The purpose of this paper is to contribute to the literature on innovation and entrepreneurial learning by exploring how SMEs learn and innovate, how they use both formal and informal learning and in particular the role of networks and crisis events within their learning experience.

Design/methodology/approach – Mixed method study, comprising 13 focus groups, over 1,000 questionnaire responses from SME managers, and 20 case studies derived from semi-structured interviews.

Findings – SMEs have a strong commitment to learning, and a shared vision. Much of this learning is informal through network events, mentoring or coaching. SMEs that are innovative are significantly more committed to learning than those which are less innovative, seeing employee learning as an investment. Innovative SMEs are more likely to have a shared vision, be open-minded and to learn from crises, being able to reflect on their experiences.

Research limitations/implications – There is a need for further process driven qualitative research to understand the interrelationship between, particularly informal, learning, crisis events and SME innovation.

Practical implications – SME owners need opportunities and time for reflection as a means of stimulating personal learning – particularly the opportunity to learn from crisis events. Access to mentors (often outside the business) can be important here, as are informal networks.

Originality/value – This is one of the first mixed method large scale studies to explore the relationship between SME innovation and learning, highlighting the importance of informal learning to innovation and the need for SME leaders to foster this learning as part of a shared organisational vision.

✓ Document Options:

Content access

View HTML

View PDF (106kb)

References

References (38)

Citations

Further reading

Related Content
Search our articles for similar content

Marked list

Add to marked list:
Session — Go

Bookmark & share

Reprints & permissions

Reprints & Permissions

---

3 For those items not held by your library either as paper copies or via online subscriptions, it may still be possible to obtain them online, either through institutional repositories or, for books which are no longer copyright, through Google Books.

4 Alternatively you may be able:

   i   to borrow the item from another library using the **inter-library loan** service. This is not a free service so make sure you really need it first. Our students have found that, in general, it is only worthwhile to use inter-library loans for articles from refereed journals and books; or

   ii visit a library where they are held as 'reference only' copies. The British Library in London, for example, has one of the most extensive collection of books, journals, market research reports, trade literature, company annual reports, research reports, doctoral theses and conference proceedings in the world.[3]

Evaluating the literature

Although the Internet has revolutionised searching for literature, you should beware as the quantity of material is enormous and the quality highly variable. Not surprisingly, a question frequently asked by our students is, 'How do I know what I'm reading is relevant?' Two further questions often asked by our students are, 'How do I assess the value of what I read?' and 'How do I know when I've read enough?' All of these are concerned with the process of evaluation. They involve defining the scope of your review and assessing the value of the items that you have obtained in helping you to answer your research question(s) and meet your objectives. Although there are no set ways of approaching these questions, our students have found the following advice helpful.

Assessing relevance

Assessing the relevance of the literature you have collected to your research depends on your research question(s) and objectives. Remember that you are looking for relevance, not critically assessing the ideas contained within. When doing this, it helps to have thought about and made a note of the criteria for inclusion and exclusion prior to assessing each item of literature. Box 3.13 provides some help here.

You should, of course, try to read all the literature that is most closely related to your research question(s) and objectives. The literature that is most likely to cause problems is that which is less closely related (Gall et al. 2006). For some research questions, particularly for new research areas, there is unlikely to be much closely related literature and so you will have to review more broadly. For research questions where research has been going on for some years, you may be able to focus on more closely related literature.

Remember to make notes about the relevance (and value) of each item as you read it and the reasons why you came to your conclusion. You may need to include your evaluation as part of your critical review.

Assessing value

Assessing the value of the literature you have collected is concerned with the quality of the research that has been undertaken. As such it is concerned with issues such as methodological rigour, theory robustness and the quality of the reasoning or arguments. For example, you need to beware of managerial autobiographies, where a successful entrepreneur's or managing director's work experiences are presented as the way to achieve business

---

[3]Further details of the business and management collection can be found at www.bl.uk/managementbusiness.

success (Fisher 2010), and articles in trade magazines. The knowledge presented in such books and articles may well be subjective rather than based upon systematic research.

For refereed journal articles (and some book chapters), the review process means that peers have assessed the quality of research and suggested amendments before they are published. This means the research is likely to have been undertaken with methodological rigour, have used theory appropriately and been argued cogently. However, it is still important to assess the value yourself in terms of possible bias, methodological omissions and precision (Box 3.14).

It is worth noting that, within business and management and other subjects, lists exist that rank peer-reviewed journals according to their quality; higher rankings indicating better quality journals. The fortunes of academics and their business schools depend on publishing in such highly ranked journals. Harzing (2014) provides a regularly updated Journal Quality List for business and management, which includes lists from over 20 different sources. While there is little doubt that journals ranked highly on lists are quality journals and are more likely to contain quality articles, this does not mean that every single paper within them will be of the same high quality. It also does not mean that articles in lower ranked journals are of little value. As pointed out by MacDonald and Kam (2007), there is a circularity in the argument that quality journals contain quality papers which are known to be quality papers because they appear in quality journals!

Box 3.14
Checklist

Evaluating the relevance, value and sufficiency of literature to your research

Relevance

✔ How recent is the item?
✔ Is the item likely to have been superseded?
✔ Are the research questions or objectives sufficiently close to your own to make it relevant to your own research (in other words, does the item meet your relevance criteria for inclusion)?
✔ Is the context sufficiently different to make it marginal to your research question(s) and objectives (in other words, is the item excluded by your relevance criteria)?
✔ Have you seen references to this item (or its author) in other items that were useful?
✔ Does the item support or contradict your arguments? For either it will probably be worth reading!

Value

✔ Has the item been subject to a reviewing process prior to publication?

✔ Does the item appear to be biased? For example, does it use an illogical argument, emotionally toned words or appear to choose only those cases that support the point being made? Even if it is, it may still be relevant to your critical review!
✔ What are the methodological omissions within the work (e.g. sample selection, data collection, data analysis)? Even if there are many it still may be of relevance!
✔ Is the precision sufficient? Even if it is imprecise it may be the only item you can find and so still of relevance!
✔ Does the item provide guidance for future research?

Sufficiency

✔ As I read new items, do I recognise the authors and the ideas from other items I have already read?
✔ Have I read the work by those acknowledged by others as key researchers in my research area?
✔ Can I critically discuss the academic context of my research with confidence?
✔ Have I read sufficient items to satisfy the assessment criteria for my project report?

Sources: Authors' experience; Bell and Waters (2014); Colquitt (2013); Fisher (2010); Jankowicz (2005); McNeill (2005)

Consequently, although journal ranking lists can provide a broad indicator of the quality of research, they are not a substitute for reading the article and making your own assessment. You should not just rely on these lists but should make your own assessment of the quality of the research in relation to your research question(s) and objectives. The checklist in Box 3.14 will help in this assessment.

Assessing sufficiency

Your assessment of whether you have read a sufficient amount is even more complex. It is impossible to read everything, as you would never start to write your critical review, let alone your project report. Yet you need to be sure that your critical review discusses what research has already been undertaken and that you have positioned your research project in the wider context, citing the main writers in the field (Section 3.2). One clue that you have achieved this is when further searches provide mainly references to items you have already read (Box 3.14). You also need to check what constitutes an acceptable amount of reading, in terms of both quality and quantity, with your project tutor.

3.7 Recording the literature   记录文献

The literature search, as you will now be aware, is a vital part of your research project, in which you will invest a great deal of time and effort. As you read each item, you need to ask yourself how it contributes to your research question(s) and objectives and to make notes with this focus (Bell and Waters 2014). When doing this, many students download and save copies of articles or photocopy or scan pages from books to ensure that they have all the material. We believe that, even if you save, print or photocopy, you still need to make notes.

The process of note making will help you to think through the ideas in the literature in relation to your research. When making your notes, make sure you always use quotation marks and note the page number if you are copying the text exactly. This will ensure you know it is a direct quotation when you begin to write your project report and so help you avoid committing plagiarism (Section 3.9).

In addition to making notes, Sharp et al. (2002) identify three sets of information you need to record. These are:

- bibliographic details;
- brief summary of content;
- supplementary information.

Bibliographic software such as Reference Manager™, EndNote™ or research tools such as 'Mendeley' or 'Zotero' provide a powerful and flexible method for recording the literature and automatically generating references in the required style. In addition there are online bibliography generators such as or 'Cite This For Me' which can help you create a bibliography or reference list in the prescribed format. Many search engines, such as Google Scholar, allow references (and in some case full text) to be exported directly into such software and tools. Where this is not the case, recording can seem very tedious, but it must be done. We have seen many students frantically repeating searches for items that are crucial to their research because they failed to record all the necessary details in their database of references.

Bibliographic details

For some project reports you will be required to include a **bibliography**. Convention dictates that this should include all the relevant items you consulted for your project, including those not directly referred to in the text. For the majority, you will be asked to include only a list of **references** for those items referred to directly in the text. The **bibliographic details** contained in both need to be sufficient to enable readers to find the original items. These details are summarised in Table 3.5.

If you located the item online, you need to record the full Internet address of the resource and the date you accessed the information (Appendix 1). This address is the URL, the unique resource location or universal/uniform resource locator. For a journal article accessed online, and some other electronic documents, it is becoming more usual to also include that document's **digital object identifier** (DOI). The DOI provides a permanent and unique two-part identifier for the electronic document.

Most universities have a preferred referencing style that you must use in your project report. This will normally be prescribed in your assessment criteria. Three of the most common styles are the Harvard system (a version of which we have used in this book), the American Psychological Association (APA) system and the Vancouver or footnotes system. Guidelines on using each of these are given in Appendix 1.

Brief summary of content

A brief summary of the content of each item in your reference database will help you to locate the relevant items and facilitate reference to your notes and photocopies. This can be done by annotating each record with the search terms used, to help locate the item and the abstract. It will also help you to maintain consistency in your searches.

Supplementary information

As well as recording the details discussed earlier, other information may also be worth recording. These items can be anything you feel will be of value. In Table 3.6 we outline those that we have found most useful.

Table 3.5 Bibliographic details required

Journal	Book	Chapter in an edited book
• Author(s) – family name, first name, initials	• Author(s) – family name, first name initials	• Author(s) – family name, first name initials
• Year of publication (in parentheses)	• Year of publication (in parentheses)	• Year of publication (in parentheses)
• Title of article	• Title and subtitle of book (italicised)	• Title of chapter
• Title of journal (italicised)	• Edition (unless first)	• Author(s) of book – family name, first name initials
• Volume	• Place of publication	• Title and subtitle of book (italicised)
• Part/issue	• Publisher	• Edition (unless first)
• Page numbers (preceded by 'p'. for page or 'pp'. for pages)		• Place of publication
		• Publisher
		• Page numbers of chapter (preceded by 'pp'. for pages)

Table 3.6 Supplementary information

Information	Reason
ISBN	The identifier for any book, and useful if the book has to be requested on inter-library loan
DOI	The digital object identifier is both permanent and unique, meaning an electronic document can be found more easily
Class number (e.g. Dewey decimal)	Useful to locate books in your university's library and as a pointer to finding other books on the same subject
Quotations	Always note useful quotations in full and with the page number of the quote; if possible also take a photocopy or save entire document as a PDF file
Where it was found	Noting where you found the item is useful, especially if it is not in your university library and you could only take notes
The search engine, database, encyclopaedia, bibliography or other resource used to locate it	Useful to help identify possible resources for follow-up searches
Evaluative comments	Your personal notes on the value of the item to your research in relation to your relevance and value criteria
When the item was consulted	Especially important for items found via the Internet as these may disappear without trace
Filename	Useful if you have saved the document as a PDF file

3.8   Using Systematic Review   使用系统化综述

Systematic Review is a process for reviewing the literature using a comprehensive pre-planned strategy to locate existing literature, evaluate the contribution, analyse and synthe-sise the findings and report the evidence to allow conclusions to be reached about what is known and, also, what is not known (Denyer and Tranfield 2009). Originating in the medical sciences, Systematic Review has been used widely to evaluate specific medical treatments; in the past two decades its importance has been recognised in other disciplines. Within busi-ness and management Denyer and Tranfield (2009) have adapted the medical sciences guid-ance, ensuring that the process is transparent, inclusive, explanatory and enables learning. Systematic Reviews usually, although not exclusively, focus on policy or practice questions such as the effectiveness of a particular intervention and the associated mechanisms with an emphasis on informing action. It is therefore not surprising that Petticrew and Roberts (2006) argue that Systematic Review is only suitable for some research projects (Box 3.15), emphasising that it is time-consuming and the need to involve others in the process.

Prior to conducting your Systematic Review, most writers suggest you undertake an exploratory **scoping study** to assess whether or not other Systematic Reviews have already been published and determine the focus of the literature search. Subsequent to this, a five-step process in which the each stage is noted precisely is suggested (Denyer and Tranfield 2009):

1 Formulate the review question(s), for example 'What are marketing professionals' understanding and definition of viral marketing?', involving a broad range of expert stakeholders such as potential academic and practitioner users of the review as an advisory group. Resulting review questions can be developed using the CIMO

**Box 3.15
Checklist**

**Establishing whether a project may
be suitable for Systematic Review**

✔ Is there uncertainty about the effectiveness of the
policy/service/intervention?

✔ Is there a need for evidence about the likely
effects of a policy/service/intervention?

✔ Despite a large amount of research on the topic,
do key questions remain unanswered?

✔ Is there a need for a general overall picture of the
research evidence on the topic to direct future
research?

✔ Is an accurate picture of past research and
associated methods needed to help develop new
methods?

(If the answer to one or more of these is 'yes'
then the project may be suitable for Systematic
Review.)

Source: Developed from Petticrew and Roberts (2006)

acronym. This emphasises the need to include review questions which relate the context, the **i**ntervention, the **m**echanisms of interest (how does the intervention within
the context result in the outcome?), and the **o**utcome of the intervention.

2 Locate and generate a comprehensive list of potentially relevant research studies using online database searches, specialist bibliographies, tables of contents and other
sources and attempt to track down unpublished research (Section 3.3).

3 Select and evaluate relevant research studies using predetermined explicit inclusion
and exclusion (selection) checklists of criteria to assess the relevance of each in relation to the review question(s). These checklists can be developed by undertaking a
small number of pilot searches and making a list for reasons for inclusion or exclusion of each article or adapting checklists developed for previous Systematic Reviews,
by journals to assess general quality of research or to assess issues of relevance and
value (Box 3.15). Common criteria include adequate methods, clear data analysis and
conclusions derived from findings. Selection and evaluation are usually undertaken:
a Initially by title and abstract;
b For those not excluded by title and abstract, by reading the full text.

4 Analyse and synthesise the relevant research studies by:
a Breaking down each study into its constituent parts and recording the key points
(research question/aim; study context – country, industry sector, organisational
setting etc.; method(s) of data collection; sample size, frame and demographics;
key findings; relevance to review questions) on a data extraction form;
b Using the data extraction forms to explore and integrate the studies and answer the
specific review questions.

5 Report the results providing:
a an introductory section that states the problem and review questions;
b a methodology section that provides precise details of how the review was conducted (search strategy, selection criteria, key points used for the analysis and synthesis) (Sections 3.3 and 3.4);
c findings and discussion sections that review all the studies (Section 3.2), specifying
precisely what is known and what is not known in relation to the review questions.

Many researchers who use Systematic Review are adopting the PRISMA (Preferred
Reporting Items for Systematic Reviews and Meta Analyses) checklist (Moher et al. 2009)
and flow diagram for reporting and presenting their Systematic Reviews. Using their
checklist when presenting your Systematic Review will help ensure the report of your

| 2. Location of studies | Number of studies identified searching online databases | Number of studies identified through other sources |

Number of studies after duplicates excluded ——→ Number excluded

| 3. Selection and evaluation | Number of studies after screening by title and abstract | ——→ Number excluded |

Number of studies evaluated by full text ——→ Number excluded

| 4. Analysis and synthesis | Number of studies included in analysis and synthesis |

Figure 3.3 Flow diagram for reporting Systematic Review
Source: Developed from Moher et al. 2009

review is clear, allowing others to assess the strengths and weaknesses of the studies you have reviewed. Using a flow diagram (Figure 3.3) allows the number of studies reviewed in stages two and three in the Systematic Review process to be reported clearly.

3.9   Plagiarism   剽 窃

There is no doubt that plagiarism has become an enormous concern in academic institutions in recent years, largely as a result of the ease with which material can be copied from the Internet and passed off as the work of the individual student. It is a serious topic because the consequences of being found guilty of plagiarism can be severe, as the example in Box 3.16 from the *Financial Times* shows.

Neville (2010) argues that plagiarism is an issue that runs parallel to a debate with recurring questions about the purpose of higher education in the twenty-first century. He notes that, on the one hand, there is the argument that an insistence on 'correct' referencing is supporting a system and a process of learning that is a legacy of a different time and society. This argument holds that universities are enforcing upon you an arcane practice of referencing that you will probably never use again outside higher education. On the other hand, there is the argument that plagiarism is an attack upon values of ethical, proper, decent behaviour – values consistent with a respect for others. These are ageless societal values that universities should try to maintain.

So what precisely is plagiarism? Quite simply, it is presenting work or ideas as if they are your own when in reality they are the work or ideas of someone else, and failing to acknowledge the original source. Park (2003) lists four common forms of plagiarism which are commonly found in universities. These are:

1 Stealing material from another source and passing it off as your own, for example:
   • buying a paper from a research service, essay bank or term-paper mill (either specially written for the individual or pre-written);
   • copying a whole paper from a source text without proper acknowledgement;
   • submitting another student's work with or without that student's knowledge (e.g. by copying a file);

2 submitting a paper written by someone else (e.g. a peer or relative) and passing it off as your own;

3 copying sections of material from one or more source texts, supplying proper documentation (including the full reference) but leaving out quotation marks, thus giving the impression that the material has been paraphrased rather than directly quoted;

4 paraphrasing material from one or more source texts without supplying appropriate documentation.

It is tempting to think that all cases of plagiarism are a consequence of students either being too idle to pursue their research and writing diligently, or wishing to appear cleverer that they really are. But the fact is that plagiarism is an extremely complex issue and the reasons for it may owe as much to student confusion as wilful negligence. That said, there is little excuse for confusion. All universities have ample guidance for students on the topic of plagiarism and will emphasise that it is the responsibility of the individual student to become aware of the university's regulations surrounding its conduct. In addition, an increasing number of universities ask students to check their own work using plagiarism detection software and submit an electronic copy of their work.

Box 3.16 Focus on research in the news

Plagiarism storm forces Merkel minister to resign

By Q Peel

Angela Merkel, the German chancellor, faces a new challenge to the credibility of her centre-right coalition government following the resignation of her education minister, Annette Schavan, over accusations of plagiarism in her doctoral thesis. Ms Schavan, one of Ms Merkel's closest friends and confidantes, leaves the government title more than seven months before a general election.

The chancellor said on Saturday she had accepted the move "with a very heavy heart", as she also announced the appointment of Johanna Wanka, hitherto education minister in the state of Lower Saxony, to the cabinet job. Pressure on Ms Schavan surged four days earlier when the Düsseldorf university ruled that her PhD thesis in 1980 contained unattributed quotations that amounted to "deliberate deception through plagiarism".

It also stripped her of her title of doctor of philosophy. Ms Schavan said she had neither copied material nor cheated but added: "If a research minister sues a university, it could cause damage to my office, the ministry, the federal government and the CDU [Christian Democratic Union].That is exactly what I want to avoid."

FT *Source:* Peel, Q. (2013). Plagiarism storm forces Merkel minister to resign', *Financial Times*, 11 February. Available at: http://www.ftsyndication.com/preview.php?id=201302111446FT_____ NEWS_____4342f2ee-73b9-11e2-9e92-00144fe_6670.1 [Accessed 6 April 2014], Copyright © 2014 The Financial Times Limited

3.10   Summary   小 结

- A critical review of the literature is necessary to help you to develop a thorough understanding of, and insight into, previous work that relates to your research question(s) and objectives. Your review will set your research in context by critically discussing and referencing work that has already been undertaken, drawing out key points and presenting them in a logically argued way, and highlighting those areas where you will provide fresh insights. It will lead the reader into subsequent sections of your project report.
- There is no one correct structure for a critical review, although it is helpful to think of it as a funnel in which you start at a more general level prior to narrowing down to your specific research question(s) and objectives.
- You are most likely to make use of formally published items (secondary literature) and those not controlled by commercial publishers (grey literature). Your use of these resources will depend on your research question(s) and objectives. Some may use only secondary literature. For others, you may need to locate grey literature as well.
- When planning your literature search you need to:
  - have a clearly defined research question(s) and research objectives;
  - define the parameters of your search;
  - generate search terms and phrases;
  - discuss your ideas as widely as possible.
- Techniques to help you in this include brainstorming and relevance trees.
- Your literature search is likely to be undertaken using a variety of approaches in tandem. These will include:
  - searching using online databases and search engines;
  - following up references in articles you have already read;
  - scanning and browsing books and journals in your university library.
- Don't forget to make precise notes of the search processes you have used and their results.
- Once obtained, the literature must be evaluated for its relevance and value to your research question(s) and objectives. Each item must be read and noted. Bibliographic details, a brief description of the content and appropriate supplementary information should also be recorded.
- For literature reviews focusing on policy or practice questions in particular, you may decide to a use a Systematic Review.
- Care should be taken when writing your literature review not to plagiarise the work of others.

Self-check questions   自测题

Help with these questions is available at the end of the chapter.

3.1   The following extract and associated references are taken from the first draft of a critical literature review. The research project was concerned with the impact of changes to UK legal aid legislation on motor insurance pricing policies.

List the problems with this extract in terms of its:

a content;

b structure.

The primary function of motor insurance is to provide financial protection against damage to vehicles and bodies resulting from traffic conditions and the liabilities that can arise (Wikipedia 2014). O'Brian (2014) suggests that motor insurers have been too eager to reap the benefits of legal aid. Papra-Servano (2013) notes that the average car insurance premium has reduced since changes in legislation brought about by the UK Legal Aid, Sentencing and Punishment of Offenders Act. This act prohibits the payment and receipt of referral fees in relation to personal injury claims by solicitors, claims companies and other authorised persons (Norton Ross Fulbright 2012). Motor insurance is particularly price sensitive because of its compulsory nature and its perception by many to have no real 'value' to themselves.

O'Brien, S. (2013). 'Motor insurance: Jumping the gun'. *Post*. 29 October. Available at: http://www.postonline.co.uk/post/analysis/2301953/motor-insurance-jumping-the-gun. [Accessed 7 April 2014]

Norton Ross Fulbright. (2012). *The regulation of the motor industry.* Available at: http://www.nortonrosefulbright.com/knowledge/publications/63780/the-regulation-of-the-motor-insurance-industry [Accessed 7 April 2014].

Papra-Servano, C. (2013). 'Rates drop as motor insurers anticipate legal reform windfall'. *Post*. 17 July. Available at: http://www.postonline.co.uk/post/news/2282883/rates-drop-as-motor-insurers-anticipate-legal-reform-windfall [Accessed 7 April 2014]

Wikipedia (2014) *Vehicle Insurance.* Available at: http://en.wikipedia.org/wiki/Vehicle_insurance. [Accessed 7 April 2014].

3.2 Outline the advice you would give a colleague on:

   a how to plan her search;

   b which literature to search first.

3.3 Brainstorm at least one of the following research questions, either on your own or with a colleague, and list the search terms that you have generated.

   a How effective are share options as a motivator?

   b How do the opportunities available to a first-time house buyer through interpersonal discussion influence the process of selecting a financial institution for the purposes of applying for a house purchase loan?

   c To what extent do new methods of direct selling of financial services pose a threat to existing providers?

3.4 You are having considerable problems with finding relevant material for your research when searching online databases. Suggest possible reasons why this might be so.

3.5 Rewrite the following passage as part of a critical literature review using the Harvard system of referencing:

Past research indicates important gender differences in the use of networks[1], and suggests that male SME owners are more likely to successfully network and benefit from networks-driven performance in contrast to female SME owners[2]. In particular, as many women come to self-employment from domestic or non-management background[3], and thus are likely to have previously engaged in the relatively isolating domestic and childrearing work or lower-status support work, they can be expected to possess fewer, more personal, less formal and less powerful contacts, as well as less time for networking[1,4,5,6,7]. However, recent empirical

---

[1]Hanson, S. and Blake, M. (2009) 'Gender and entrepreneurial networks', *Regional Studies*, Vol. 43, pp. 135–49.

[2]Watson, J. (2012) 'Networking: Gender differences and the association with firm performance', *International Small Business Journal*, Vol. 30, pp. 536–58.

[3]Cromie, S. and Birley, S. (1992) 'Networking by female business owners in Northern Ireland', *Journal of Business Venturing*, Vol. 7, pp. 237–51.

[4]Ardrich, H. (1989) 'Networking among women entrepreneurs', in O. Hagan, C.S. Rivchun and D. Sexton (eds) *Women-Owned Businesses*. New York: Praeger, pp. 103–32.

[5]Moore, G. (1990) 'Structural determinants of men's and women's personal networks', *American Sociological Review*, Vol. 55, pp. 726–35.

[6]Munch A., McPherson J.M. and Smith-Lovin L. (1997) 'Gender, children, and social contact: The effects of childrearing for men and women', *American Sociological Review*, Vol. 62, pp. 509–20.

[7]Orhan, M. (2001) 'Women business owners in France: The issue of financing discrimination', *Journal of Small Business Management*, Vol. 39, pp. 95–102.

studies of SME owners challenge such expectations. For example, according to a 2012 survey of 2919 male- and 181 female-controlled SMEs, there is little gender difference, after controlling for education, experience, industry, age and size, in the SME owners' use of networking and its impact on business performance – in other words, SMEs owned by women and men enjoy similar performance benefits of networking [2].

Review and discussion questions 复习与讨论题

3.6   Go to the website of the general search engine Google (www.google.com). Use the specialised search services such as 'Google Scholar' and 'Google Finance' to search for articles on a topic which you are currently studying as part of your course.

   a Make notes regarding the types of items that each of these services finds.

   b How do these services differ?

   c Which service do you think is likely to prove most useful to your research project?

3.7   Agree with a friend to each review the same article from a refereed academic journal which contains a clear literature review section. Evaluate independently the literature review in your chosen article with regard to its content, critical nature and structure using the checklists in Boxes 3.2 and 3.4 respectively. Do not forget to make notes regarding your answers to each of the points raised in the checklists. Discuss your answers with your friend.

3.8   Visit an online database or your university library and obtain a copy of an article that you think will be of use to an assignment you are both currently working on. Use the checklist in Box 3.14 to assess the relevance and value of the article to your assignment.

Progressing your research project
改进研究项目
Critically reviewing the literature
文献综述

- Consider your research question(s) and objectives. Use your lecture notes, course textbooks and relevant review articles to define both narrow and broader parameters of your literature search, considering language, subject area, business sector, geographical area, publication period and literature type.

- Generate search terms using one or a variety of techniques such as reading, brainstorming and relevance trees. Discuss your ideas widely, including with your project tutor and colleagues.

- Start your search using online databases, available via your university library's web pages, to identify relevant secondary literature. Begin with those online databases that abstract and index academic journal articles and books. At the same time, obtain relevant literature that has been referenced in articles you have already read. Do not forget to record your searches systematically and in detail.

- Expand your search using online search engines and by browsing and scanning articles and books.

- Obtain copies of items, evaluate them systematically and make notes. Remember also to record bibliographic details, a brief description of the content and supplementary information in your bibliographic software.

- Start drafting your critical review as early as possible, keeping in mind its purpose and taking care to reference properly and avoid plagiarism.

- Continue to search the literature throughout your research project to ensure that your review remains up to date.

- Use the questions in Box 1.4 to guide your reflective diary entry.

Self-check answers 自测题答案

3.1   There are numerous problems with the content and structure of this extract. Some of the more obvious include:

- The content consists of Wikipedia, a company website and an online trade magazine, *Post*, and there are no references of academic substance.
- You would not expect to see Wikipedia referenced in a research project for reasons outlined earlier in this chapter.
- Some of the references to individual authors have discrepancies: for example, was the article by O'Brien (or is it O'Brian?) published in 2014 or 2013?
- The UK Government Act is not referenced directly (it should be!) and you would expect the actual Act to be referred to rather than a company's (Norton Ross Fulbright 2012) comments on the preceding draft bill.
- There is no real structure or argument in the extract. The extract is a list of what people have written, with no attempt to critically evaluate or juxtapose the ideas.

3.2   This is a difficult one without knowing her research question! However, you could still advise her on the general principles. Your advice will probably include:

- Define the parameters of the research, considering language, subject area, business sector, geographical area, publication period and literature type. Generate search terms using one or a variety of techniques such as reading, brainstorming or relevance trees. Discuss her ideas as widely as possible, including with her tutor, librarians and you.
- Start the search using online databases in the university library to identify relevant literature. She should commence with those online databases that abstract and index academic journal articles. At the same time she should obtain relevant literature that has been referenced in articles that she has already read.

3.3   There are no incorrect answers with brainstorming! However, you might like to check your search terms for suitability prior to using them to search an appropriate database. We suggest that you follow the approach outlined in Section 3.5 under 'searching using online databases'.

3.4   There are a variety of possible reasons, including:

- One or more of the parameters of your search are defined too narrowly.
- The keywords you have chosen do not appear in the controlled index language.
- Your spelling of the search term is incorrect.
- The terminology you are using is incorrect.
- The acronyms you have chosen are not used by databases.
- You are using jargon rather than accepted terminology.

3.5   There are two parts to this answer: rewriting the text and using the Harvard system of referencing. Your text will inevitably differ from the answer given below owing to your personal writing style. Don't worry about this too much as it is discussed in far more detail in Section 14.6. The references should follow the same format.

Past research indicates important gender differences in the use of networks (Hanson and Blake 2009), and suggests that male SME owners are more likely to successfully network and benefit from networks-driven performance in contrast to female SME owners (Watson 2012). In particular, as many women come to self-employment from domestic or non-management background (Cromie and Birley 1992), and thus are likely to have previously engaged in the relatively isolating domestic and childrearing work or lower-status support work, they can be expected to possess fewer, more personal, less formal and less powerful contacts, as well as less time for networking (Ardrich 1989; Hanson and Blake 2009;

Moore 1990; Munch et al. 1997; Orhan 2001). However, recent empirical studies of SME owners challenge such expectations. For example, according to Watson's (2012) survey of 2919 male- and 181 female-controlled SMEs, there is little gender difference, after controlling for education, experience, industry, age and size, in the SME owners' use of networking and its impact on business performance – in other words, SMEs owned by women and men enjoy similar performance benefits of networking.

Ardrich, H. (1989) 'Networking among women entrepreneurs', in O. Hagan, C.S. Rivchun and D. Sexton (eds) *Women-Owned Businesses.* New York: Praeger, pp. 103–32.

Cromie, S. and Birley, S. (1992) 'Networking by female business owners in Northern Ireland', *Journal of Business Venturing*, Vol. 7, pp. 237–51.

Hanson, S. and Blake, M. (2009) 'Gender and entrepreneurial networks', *Regional Studies*, Vol. 43, pp. 135–49.

Moore, G. (1990) 'Structural determinants of men's and women's personal networks', *American Sociological Review*, Vol. 55, pp. 726–35.

Munch, A., McPherson, J.M. and Smith-Lovin, L. (1997) 'Gender, children, and social contact: The effects of childrearing for men and women', *American Sociological Review*, Vol. 62, pp. 509–20.

Orhan, M. (2001) 'Women business owners in France: The issue of financing discrimination', *Journal of Small Business Management*, Vol. 39, pp. 95–102.

Watson, J. (2012) 'Networking: Gender differences and the association with firm performance', *International Small Business Journal*, Vol. 30, pp. 536–58.

Get ahead using resources on the Companion Website at: **www.pearsoned .co.uk/saunders**.

- Improve your SPSS and NVivo research analysis with practice tutorials.
- Save time researching on the Internet with the Smarter Online Searching Guide.
- Test your progress using self-assessment questions.
- Follow live links to useful websites.

Chapter 4

Understanding research philosophy and approaches to theory development
理解研究哲学和理论发展的方法

Learning outcomes   学习目标

By the end of this chapter you should be able to:

- define ontology, epistemology and axiology, and explain their relevance to business research;
- reflect on your own epistemological, ontological and axiological stance;
- understand the main research paradigms that are significant for business research;
- explain the relevance for business research of philosophical positions such as positivism, critical realism, interpretivism, postmodernism and pragmatism;
- reflect on and articulate your own philosophical position in relation to your research;
- distinguish between deductive, inductive, and abductive approaches to theory development.

4.1 Introduction 引 言

Much of this book is concerned with the way in which you collect data to answer your research question(s). Most people plan their research in relation to a question that needs to be answered or a problem that needs to be solved. They then think about what data they need and the techniques they use to collect them. You are not therefore unusual if early on in your research you consider whether you should, for example, use a questionnaire or undertake interviews. However, how you collect your data belongs in the centre of the research 'onion', the diagram we use to depict the issues underlying the choice of data collection techniques and analysis procedures in Figure 4.1. In coming to this central point you need to explain why you made the choice you did so that others can see that your research should be taken seriously (Crotty 1998). Consequently there are important outer layers of the onion that you need to understand and explain rather than just peel and throw away!

This chapter is concerned principally with the outer two of the onion's layers: philosophy (Sections 4.2 and 4.3) and approach to theory development (Section 4.4). In Chapter 5 we examine the layers we call methodological choice, strategy and time horizon. The sixth layer (data collection and analysis) is dealt with in Chapters 7–13.

Our own beliefs and assumptions about what is important affected all of us in the decisions we made about what we wished to study and at which university, and the research we undertook in order to make that decision. Like us, every year hundreds of thousands of people each make the personal decision about what and where to study. Not only is the variety of possible undergraduate and master's programmes extremely diverse, ranging from the natural sciences to the arts and humanities, as well as including vocational subjects such as business and management, but there are also, potentially, thousands of universities to choose from.

Each individual applicant's personal decision about the programme they wish to study and at which university is based, at least in part, on what motivates them to study, the information they find useful in making decisions, alongside a wide variety of other influencing factors. Recent research undertaken for the Higher Education Funding Council England (Dye 2013; Mellors-Bourne et al. 2014) on the decisions made about taught master's degree programmes acknowledges that applicants are a diverse and complex group. Not surprisingly, the researchers conclude that these people approach their decision making in different ways. Drawing on their findings, they offer clear recommendations about the nature of information prospective students require. They highlight how prospective students' information needs upon which they can base their decisions differ markedly across a variety of dimensions. These include whether or not prospective applicants are students continuing directly from an undergraduate degree or returning to study after a period in employment, and whether or not they are overseas or UK-based applicants.

Just as our beliefs and assumptions affected our decisions about what to study and at which university, they can also have an important impact on the research we decide to pursue and the methodology and methods we use.

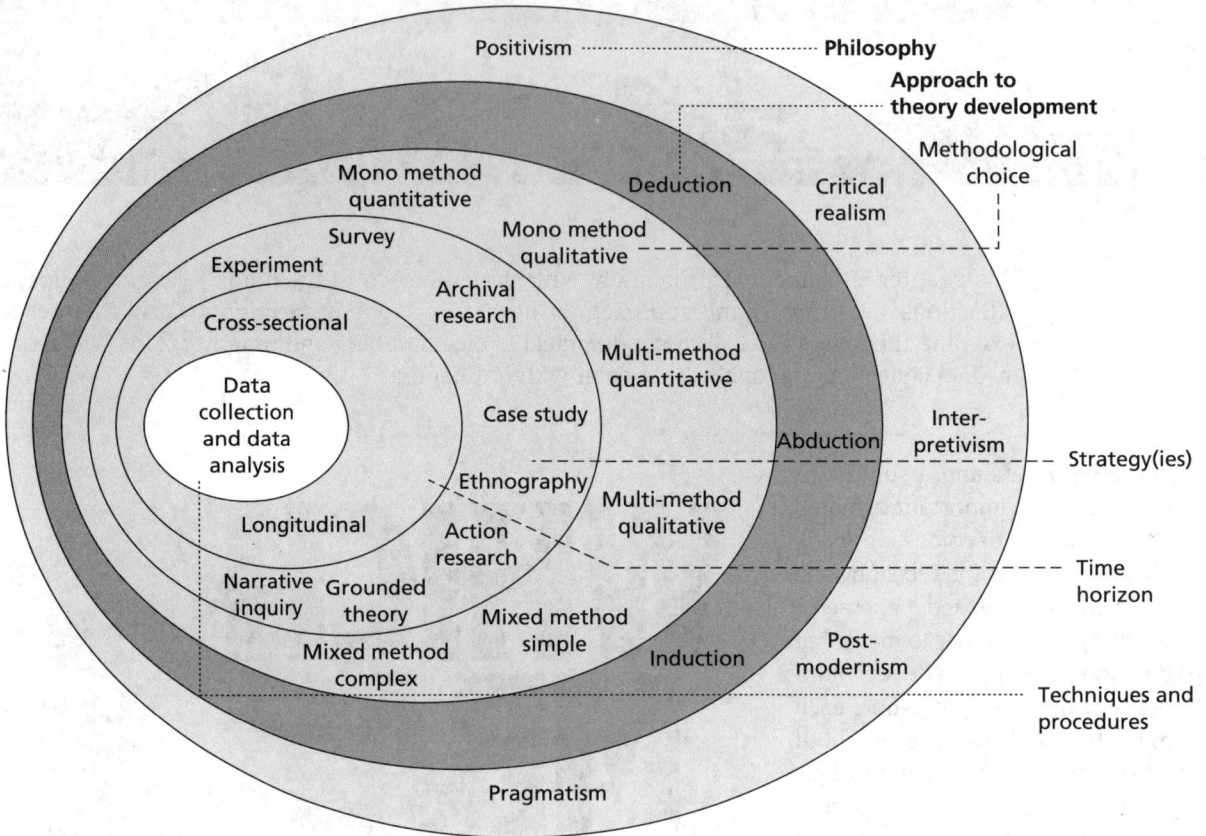

Figure 4.1 The research 'onion'
Source: © 2015 Mark Saunders, Philip Lewis and Adrian Thornhill

4.2 The philosophical underpinnings of business and management 工商管理的哲学基础

What is research philosophy?

The term **research philosophy** refers to a system of beliefs and assumptions about the development of knowledge. Although this sounds rather profound, it is precisely what you are doing when embarking on research: developing knowledge in a particular field. The knowledge development you are embarking upon may not be as dramatic as a new theory of human motivation, but even answering a specific problem in a particular organisation you are, nonetheless, developing new knowledge.

Whether you are consciously aware of them or not, at every stage in your research you will make a number of types of assumption (Burrell and Morgan 1979). These include assumptions about human knowledge (epistemological assumptions), about the realities you encounter in your research (ontological assumptions) and the extent and ways your own values influence your research process (axiological assumptions). These assumptions inevitably shape how you understand your research questions, the methods you use and how you interpret your findings (Crotty 1998). A well-thought-out and consistent set of assumptions will constitute a credible research philosophy, which will underpin your methodological choice, research strategy and data collection techniques and analysis procedures. This will allow you to design a coherent research project, in which all elements of research fit together. Johnson and Clark (2006) note that, as business and management researchers, we need to be aware of the philosophical commitments we make through our choice of research strategy, since this will have a significant impact on what we do and how we understand what it is we are investigating.

Prior to undertaking a research methods module, few of our students have thought about their own beliefs about the nature of the world around them, what constitutes acceptable and desirable knowledge, or the extent to which they believe it necessary to remain detached from their research data. The process of exploring and understanding your own research philosophy requires you to hone the skill of reflexivity, that is, to question your own thinking and actions, and learn to examine your own beliefs with the same scrutiny as you would apply to the beliefs of others (Gouldner 1970). This may sound daunting, but we all do this in our day-to-day lives when we learn from our mistakes. As a researcher, you need to develop your reflexivity, to become aware of and actively shape the relationship between your philosophical position and how you undertake your research (Alvesson and Sköldberg 2000).

You may be wondering about the best way to start this reflexive process. In part, your exploration of your philosophical position and how to translate it into a coherent research practice will be influenced by practical considerations, such as the time and finances available for your research project, and the access you can negotiate to data. However, there are two things that you can do to start making a more active and informed philosophical choice:

- begin asking yourself questions about your research beliefs and assumptions;
- familiarise yourself with major research philosophies within business and management.

This section introduces you to the philosophical underpinnings of business and management, and Section 4.3 to the five research philosophies most commonly adopted by its researchers. We will encourage you to reflect on your own beliefs and assumptions in relation to these five philosophies and the research design you will use to undertake your research (Figure 4.2). The chapter will also help you to outline your philosophical choices and justify them in relation to the alternatives you could have adopted (Johnson and Clark 2006). Through this you will be better equipped to explain and justify your methodological choice, research strategy and data collection procedures and analysis techniques.

At the end of the chapter in the section 'Progressing your research project', you will find a reflexive tool (HARP) designed by Bristow and Saunders to help you think about your values and beliefs in relation to research. This will help you to make your values and assumptions more explicit, explain them using the language of research philosophy, and consider the potential fit between your own beliefs and those of the five major philosophies used in business and management research.

Is there a best philosophy for business and management research?

You may be wondering at this stage whether you could take a shortcut, and simply adopt 'the best' philosophy for business and management research. One problem with such a shortcut would be the possibility of discovering a clash between 'the best' philosophy and your own beliefs and assumptions. Another problem would be that

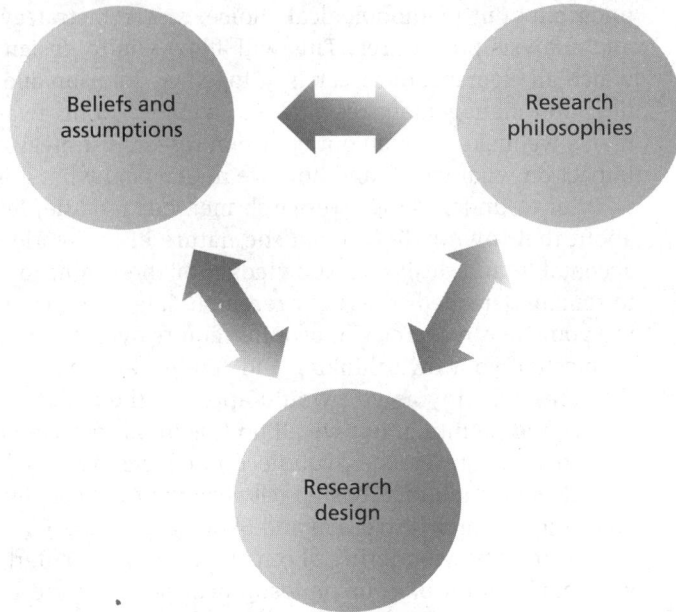

Figure 4.2 Developing your research philosophy: a reflexive process
Source: © Alexandra Bristow and Mark Saunders 2015

business and management researchers do not agree about one best philosophy (Tsoukas and Knudsen 2003). In terms of developing your own philosophy and designing your research project, it is important to recognise that philosophical disagreements are an intrinsic part of business and management research. When business and management emerged as an academic discipline in the twentieth century, it drew its theoretical base from a mixture of disciplines in the social sciences (e.g. sociology, psychology, economics), natural sciences (e.g. chemistry, biology), applied sciences (e.g. engineering, statistics), humanities (e.g. literary theory, linguistics, history, philosophy) and the domain of organisational practice (Starbuck 2003). In drawing on these disciplines it absorbed the various associated philosophies dividing and defining them, resulting in the coexistence of multiple research philosophies, paradigms and approaches and methodologies we see today.

Business and management scholars have spent long decades debating whether this multiplicity of research philosophies, paradigms and methodologies is desirable, and have reached no agreement. Instead, two opposing perspectives have emerged: pluralism and unificationism. Unificationists see business and management as fragmented, and argue that this fragmentation prevents it from becoming more like a true scientific discipline. They advocate unification of management research under one strong research philosophy, paradigm and methodology. Pluralists see the diversity of the field as helpful, arguing it enriches business and management (Knudsen 2003).

In this chapter, we take a pluralist approach and suggest that each research philosophy and paradigm contributes something unique and valuable to business and management research, representing a different and distinctive 'way of seeing' organisational realities (Morgan 1986). However, we believe that you need to be aware of the depth of difference and disagreements between these distinct philosophies. This will help you to both outline and justify your own philosophical choices in relation to your chosen research method.

Ontological, epistemological and axiological assumptions

Before we discuss individual research philosophies in Section 4.3, we need to be able to distinguish between them. We do this by considering the differences in the assumptions each makes. We look at three types of research assumptions to distinguish research philosophies: ontology, epistemology and axiology.

Ontology refers to assumptions about the nature of reality. Although this may seem abstract and far removed from your intended research project, your ontological assumptions shape the way in which you see and study your research objects. In business and management these objects include organisations, management, individuals' working lives and organisational events and artefacts. Your ontology therefore determines how you see the world of business and management and, therefore, your choice of what to research for your research project.

Imagine you wanted to research resistance to organisational change. For a long time, business and management scholars made the ontological assumption that resistance to change was highly damaging to organisations. They argued it was a kind of organisational misbehaviour, and happened when change programmes went wrong. Consequently they focused their research on how this phenomenon could be eliminated, looking for types of employee that were most likely to resist change and the management actions that could prevent or stop resistance. More recently, some researchers have started to view the concept of resistance to change differently, resulting in a new strand of research. These researchers see resistance as a phenomenon that happens all the time whenever organisational change takes place, and that benefits organisations by addressing problematic aspects of change programmes. Their different ontological assumptions mean that they focus on how resistance to change can best be harnessed to benefit organisations, rather than looking for ways to eliminate resistance (Thomas and Hardy 2011).

Epistemology concerns assumptions about knowledge, what constitutes acceptable, valid and legitimate knowledge, and how we can communicate knowledge to others (Burrell and Morgan 1979). Whereas ontology may initially seem rather abstract, the relevance of epistemology is more obvious. The multidisciplinary context of business and management means that different types of knowledge – ranging from numerical data to textual and visual data, from facts to interpretations, and including narratives, stories and even fictional accounts – can all be considered legitimate. Consequently different business and management researchers adopt different epistemologies in their research, including projects based on archival research and autobiographical accounts (Martí and Fernández 2013), narratives (Gabriel et al. 2013) and fictional literature (De Cock and Land 2006).

This variety of acceptable epistemologies gives you a much greater choice of methods than you would have in many other academic disciplines. However, it is important to understand the implications of different epistemological assumptions in relation to your choice of method(s) and the strengths and limitations of subsequent research findings. For example, the (positivist) assumption that objective facts offer the best scientific evidence is likely to result in the choice of quantitative research methods. Within this the subsequent research findings are likely to be considered objective and generalisable. However, they will also be less likely to offer a rich and complex view of organisational realities, account for the differences in individual contexts and experiences or, perhaps, propose a radically new understanding of the world than if you based your research on a different view of knowledge. In other words, despite this diversity, it is your own epistemological assumptions that will govern what you consider legitimate for your research.

Axiology refers to the role of values and ethics within the research process. This incorporates questions about how we, as researchers, deal with both our own values and those of our research participants. As we saw in the opening vignette, the role that your own values play in all stages of the research process is of great importance if research results are to be credible. Heron (1996) argues that our values are the guiding reason for all human action. He further argues that researchers demonstrate axiological skill by being able to articulate their values as a basis for making judgements about what research they are conducting and how they go about doing it. Choosing one topic rather than another suggests that you think one of the topics is more important. Your choice of philosophy is a reflection of your values, as is your choice of data collection techniques. For example, conducting a study where you place great importance on data collected through interview work suggests that you value personal interaction with your respondents more highly than their views expressed through an anonymous questionnaire.

Some of our students have found it helpful to write their own statement of personal values in relation to the topic they are studying. For example, for the topic of career development, your personal values may dictate that you believe developing their career is an individual's responsibility. In finance, a researcher may believe (hold the value) that as much information as possible should be available to as many stakeholders as possible. Writing a statement of personal values can help heighten your awareness of value judgements you are making in drawing conclusions from your data. Being clear about your own value position can also help you in deciding what is appropriate ethically and explaining this in the event of queries about decisions you have made (Sections 6.5–6.7).

Objectivism and subjectivism

Now you are familiar with the types of assumptions that research philosophies make, you need to be able to distinguish between them. Earlier in this chapter we discussed the emergence of business and management as a discipline and how it absorbed a range of philosophies from natural sciences, social sciences and arts and humanities. Although this offers philosophical and methodological choice, it also means that business and management research philosophies are scattered along a multidimensional set of continua (Niglas 2010) between two opposing extremes. Table 4.1 summarises the continua and their objectivist and subjectivist extremes in relation to the three types of philosophical assumption that we have just discussed.

Objectivism incorporates the assumptions of the natural sciences, arguing that the social reality that we research is external to us and others (referred to as social actors) (Table 4.1). This means that, ontologically, objectivism embraces **realism**, which, in its most extreme form, considers social entities to be like physical entities of the natural world, in so far as they exist independently of how we think of them, label them, or even of our awareness of them. Because the interpretations and experiences of social actors do not influence the existence of the social world, an objectivist in the most extreme form believes that there is only one true social reality experienced by all social actors. This social world is made up of solid, granular and relatively unchanging 'things', including major social structures into which individuals are born (Burrell and Morgan 1979).

From an objectivist view point, social and physical phenomena exist independently, being universal and enduring in character. Consequently, it makes sense to study them in the same way as a natural scientist would study nature. Epistemologically, objectivists seek to discover the truth about the social world, through the medium of observable, measurable facts, from which law-like generalisations can be drawn about the universal social reality. Axiologically, since the social entities and social actors exist independently of each other, objectivists seek to keep their research free of values, which they believe

Table 4.1 Philosophical assumptions as a multidimensional set of continua

Assumption type	Questions	Continua with two sets of extremes		
		Objectivism	⇔	**Subjectivism**
Ontology	• What is the nature of reality?	Real	⇔	Nominal/decided by convention
	• What is the world like?	External	⇔	Socially constructed
	• For example:	One true reality (universalism)	⇔	Multiple realities (relativism)
	– What are organisations like?	Granular (things)	⇔	Flowing (processes)
	– What is it like being in organisations?	Order	⇔	Chaos
	– What is it like being a manager or being managed?			
Epistemology	• How can we know what we know?	Adopt assumptions of the natural scientist	⇔	Adopt the assumptions of the arts and humanities
	• What is considered acceptable knowledge?	Facts	⇔	Opinions
	• What constitutes good-quality data?	Numbers	⇔	Narratives
	• What kinds of contribution to knowledge can be made?	Observable phenomena	⇔	Attributed meanings
		Law-like generalisations	⇔	Individuals and contexts, specifics
Axiology	• What is the role of values in research? How should we treat our own values when we do research?	Value-free	⇔	Value-bound
		Detachment	⇔	Integral and reflexive
	• How should we deal with the values of research participants?			

could bias their findings. They therefore also try to remain detached from their own values and beliefs throughout the research process.

The social phenomenon of management can be researched in an objectivist way (Box 4.1). You may argue that management is an objective entity and decide to adopt an objectivist stance to the study of particular aspects of management in a specific organisation. In order to justify this you would say that the managers in your organisation have job descriptions which prescribe their duties, there are operating procedures to which they are supposed to adhere, they are part of a formal structure which locates them in a hierarchy with people reporting to them and they in turn report to more senior managers. This view emphasises the structural aspects of management and assumes that management is similar in all organisations. Aspects of the structure in which management operates may differ but the essence of the function is very much the same in all organisations. If you took this ontological stance, the aim of your research would be to discover the laws that govern management behaviour to predict how management would act in the future. You would also attempt to lay aside any beliefs you may have developed from interacting with individual managers in the past, in order to avoid these experiences colouring your conclusions about management in general.

Box 4.1
Focus on student research

A management exodus at ChemCo

As part of a major organisational change, all the managers in the marketing department of the chemical manufacturer ChemCo left the organisation. They were replaced by new managers who were thought to be more in tune with the more commercially aggressive new culture that the organisation was trying to create. The new managers entering the organisation filled the roles of the managers who had left and had essentially the same job duties and procedures as their predecessors.

John wanted to study the role of management in ChemCo and in particular the way in which managers liaised with external stakeholders. He decided to use the new managers in the marketing department as his research 'subjects'.

In his research proposal he outlined briefly his research philosophy. He defined his ontological position as that of the objectivist. His reasoning was that management in ChemCo had a reality that was separate from the managers who inhabit that reality. He pointed to the fact that the formal management structure at ChemCo was largely unchanged from that which was practised by the managers who had left the organisation. The process of management would continue in largely the same way in spite of the change in personnel.

Alternatively, you may prefer to consider the objective aspects of management as less important than the way in which managers attach their own individual meanings to their jobs and the way they think that those jobs should be performed. This approach would be very much more akin to the subjectivist view.

Subjectivism incorporates assumptions of the arts and humanities (Table 4.1), asserting that social reality is made from the perceptions and consequent actions of social actors (people). Ontologically, subjectivism embraces nominalism (also sometimes called conventionalism). **Nominalism**, in its most extreme form, considers that the order and structures of social phenomena we study (and the phenomena themselves) are created by us as researchers and by other social actors through use of language, conceptual categories, perceptions and consequent actions. For nominalists, there is no underlying reality to the social world beyond what people (social actors) attribute to it, and, because each person experiences and perceives reality differently, it makes more sense to talk about multiple realities rather than a single reality that is the same for everyone (Burrell and Morgan 1979). A less extreme version of this is **social constructionism**, which puts forward that reality is constructed through social interaction in which social actors create partially shared meanings and realities.

As social interactions between actors are a continual process, social phenomena are in a constant state of flux and revision. This means it is necessary as a researcher to study a situation in detail, including historical, geographical and socio-cultural contexts in order to understand what is happening or how realities are being experienced. Unlike an objectivist researcher who seeks to discover universal facts and laws governing social behaviour, the subjectivist researcher is interested in different opinions and narratives that can help to account for different social realities of different social actors. Subjectivists believe that as they actively use these data they cannot detach themselves from their own values. They therefore openly acknowledge and actively reflect on and question their own values (Cunliffe (2003) calls this 'radical reflexivity') and incorporate these within their research.

Let us suppose that you have decided to research customer motives and behaviour. Customers, like other social actors, may interpret the situations in which they find themselves differently as a consequence of their own view of the world. Their different interpretations are likely to affect their actions and the nature of their social interaction with others. From a subjectivist view, the customers you are studying both interact with their environment and seek to make sense of it through their interpretation of events and the meanings that they draw from these events. Consequently their actions may be seen by others as being meaningful in the context of these socially constructed interpretations and meanings.

As a subjectivist researcher, it is your role to seek to understand the different realities of the customers in order to be able to make sense of and understand their motives, actions and intentions in a way that is meaningful (Box 4.2). All this is some way from the objectivist position that customer service in an organisation has a reality that is separate from the customers who perceive that reality. The subjectivist view is that customer service is produced through the social interactions between service providers and customers and is continually being revised as a result of this. In other words, at no

Box 4.2 Focus on research in the news

Glastonbury Festival, Worthy Farm, Somerset – review

By Ludovic Hunter-Tilney

"Welcome to Glaston-mud," announced the bus driver on the way from the train station to the festival. "A few days ago we were getting sunburnt." At least the humour is always dry in the West Country. But in the event the rain that swept over Glastonbury when its stages opened on Friday turned out not to be too bad. The mud was bearable. Passages of sunshine provided respite. The real threat of a damp squib lay elsewhere.

On paper the three-day line up didn't lack star power. In Lana Del Rey and Ed Sheeran it had the current holders of the number one album in the US and the UK respectively.

Elsewhere was the usual amazing profusion of acts, hundreds of them. On the main Pyramid Stage, Robert Plant looked over the tens of thousands of people in front of him and recalled how, many riffs ago, Led Zeppelin played the 1970 Bath Festival of Blues and Progressive Music, Glastonbury's forerunner. "Quite a trip," the relic sighed.

The variety was immense, from queen of country Dolly Parton to fratboy favourite DJ Skrillex. Yet a crucial element was missing: the "wow" factor, as provided by the Rolling Stones last year and Beyoncé in 2011. Prince would have fitted the bill, but the festival fumbled negotiations with him to appear: according to festival organiser Michael Eavis, the publicity shy singer pulled out when news of the possible booking leaked. So instead we got two headliners drawn from Glastonbury's indie-rock comfort zone – Arcade Fire on the first night, Kasabian on the last – flanking an oddity: Metallica, the first heavy metal headliner in the festival's history. That was a curveball, true – but more "really?" than "wow!".

The stage was thus set for Saturday's headliners, Metallica. An introductory film showed the thrash metal veterans shooting fox hunters, a comic peace offering to critics who felt that singer James Hetfield's enthusiasm for slaughtering big game was somehow contrary to the Glastonbury spirit. Their set was equally eager to please, a powerful and focused tour through their biggest hits.

A conceptual leap was required to link Hetfield in Glasto hippy mode ("Hands up all those who want to make the world a better place") with the bulging-veined roarer of songs such as "Cyanide" and "Creeping Death", but the band's bulldozing force won out, sending revellers off into the night chanting the pulverising riff from "Seek & Destroy". Only the absence of new material led one to suspect that Glastonbury's first heavy metal headliner would have been even more remarkable 30 years ago when they were in their pomp.

time is there a definitive entity called 'customer service'. Different versions of customer service are experienced by different individuals, and as an aggregate it is constantly changing.

Research paradigms

Another dimension that can help you to differentiate between research philosophies relates to the political or ideological orientation of researchers towards the social world they investigate. Like the objectivism–subjectivism dimension, this ideological dimension has two opposing poles or extremes. Burrell and Morgan (1979) call these extremes 'sociology of regulation' (for short, regulation) and 'sociology of radical change' (simply, radical change).

Researchers working within the **regulation perspective** are concerned primarily with the need for the regulation of societies and human behaviour. They assume an underlying unity and cohesiveness of societal systems and structures. Much of business and management research can be classed as regulation research that seeks to suggest how organisational affairs may be improved within the framework of how things are done at present rather than radically challenging the current position. However, you may wish to do research precisely because you want to fundamentally question the way things are done in organisations, and, through your research, offer insights that would help to change the organisational and social worlds. In this case, you would be researching within the **radical change perspective**. Radical change research approaches organisational problems from the viewpoint of overturning the existing state of affairs (Box 4.3). Such research is often visionary and utopian, being concerned with what is possible and alternatives to the accepted current position (Burrell and Morgan 1979). Table 4.2 summarises the differences between the regulation and radical change perspectives.

In their book *Sociological Paradigms and Organisational Analysis* (1979) Burrell and Morgan combine the objectivist–subjectivist continuum with a regulation–radical change continuum to create a 2 × 2 matrix of four distinct and rival 'paradigms' of organisational analysis (Figure 4.3). In their interpretation (and also as we use the term here) a **paradigm** is a set of basic and taken-for-granted assumptions which underwrite the frame of reference, mode of theorising and ways of working in which a group operates. The matrix's four paradigms represent four different ways of viewing the social and organisational world.

In the bottom right corner of the matrix is the **functionalist paradigm**. This is located on the objectivist and regulation dimensions, and is the paradigm within which most business and management research operates. Research in this paradigm is concerned with rational explanations and developing sets of recommendations within the current structures. Functionalist theories and models of management, such as business process re-engineering,

Table 4.2 The regulation–radical change dimension

The regulation perspective . . .	⇔	The radical change perspective . . .
. . . advocates the status quo	⇔	. . . advocates radical change
. . . looks for order	⇔	. . . looks for conflict
. . . looks for consensus	⇔	. . . questions domination
. . . looks for integration and cohesion	⇔	. . . looks for contradiction
. . . seeks solidarity	⇔	. . . seeks emancipation
. . . sees the satisfaction of needs	⇔	. . . sees deprivation
. . . sees the actual	⇔	. . . sees the potential

Source: developed from Burrell and Morgan (1979)

Radical change

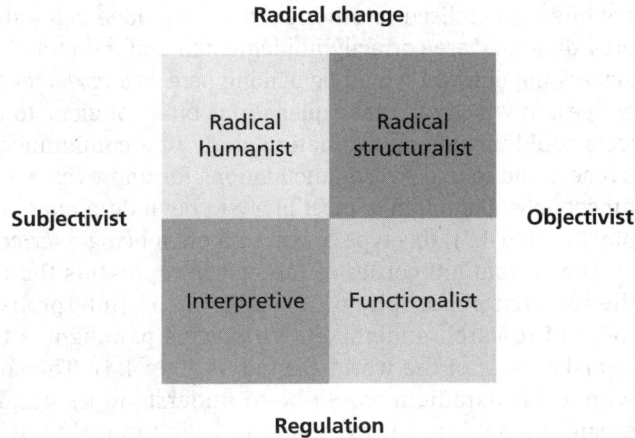

Subjectivist   Objectivist

Radical humanist	Radical structuralist
Interpretive	Functionalist

Regulation

Figure 4.3 Four paradigms for organisational analysis
Source: Developed from Burrell and Morgan (1982) *Social Paradigms and Organisational Analysis.*
Reproduced with permission of Ashgate Publishing Company

Box 4.3 Focus on management research

Critical Management Studies: questioning management

Much of business and management research undertaken from within the radical change perspective would fall within the area of management known as Critical Management Studies (CMS). CMS researchers question not only the behaviour of individual managers but also the very societal systems within which that behaviour is situated. CMS research aims to challenge their taken-for-granted acceptance as 'the best' or 'the only available' ways of organising societies (Fournier and Grey 2000). It therefore attempts to expose the problems and weaknesses, as well as the damaging effects, of these dominant ideas and practices.

CMS researchers also challenge dominant organisational ideas and practices, including 'management' itself. In his book *Against Management: Organization in the Age of Managerialism*, Martin Parker (2002: 1–2) challenges the acceptance of management.

Parker starts by acknowledging just how difficult and almost unthinkable is it to be against something

like management, which shapes so completely our everyday lives in today's world. It is one thing, he writes, to question some aspects of management, or some of its effects, so that we can learn how to do management better. It is a completely different and much harder thing to be against management itself, as a whole and categorically – it is a bit like opposing buildings, society or air. Nevertheless, Parker insists, it is the latter, radical questioning of management that is the purpose of his book. Just because management is everywhere, he writes, does not mean that management is necessary or good, or that it is not worthwhile being against it.

Parker builds his radical critique by questioning three key assumptions typically made about management:

- Management is part of scientific thought that allows human beings increasing control over their environment;
- Management increases control over people;
- Management is the best way to control people.

Questioning these assumptions might suggest that management is damaging to organisations and societies. For example, does the environment benefit from being controlled by people? Alternatively, is controlling employees necessarily good for organisations?

are often generalised to other contexts, the idea being that they can be used universally providing they are correctly implemented and monitored (Kelemen and Rumens 2008). A key assumption you would be making here as a researcher is that organisations are rational entities, in which rational explanations offer solutions to rational problems. Research projects could include an evaluation study of a communication strategy to assess its effectiveness and to make recommendations for improvement. Research carried out within the functionalist paradigm is most likely to be underpinned by the positivist research philosophy (Section 4.3), this type of research often being referred to as 'positivist-functionalist'.

The bottom left corner of the matrix represents the **interpretive paradigm**. As with the research philosophy of the same name (interpretivism, Section 4.3), the primary focus of research undertaken within this paradigm is the way we as humans attempt to make sense of the world around us (Box 4.4). The concern you would have working within this paradigm would be to understand the fundamental meanings attached to organisational life. Far from emphasising rationality, it may be that the principal focus you have here is discovering irrationalities. Concern with studying an organisation's communication strategy may focus on understanding the ways in which it fails due to unseen reasons, maybe reasons which are not apparent even to those involved with the strategy. This is likely to take you into the realm of the organisation's politics and the way in which power is used. Your concern here would be to become involved in the organisation's everyday activities in order to understand and explain what is going on, rather than change things (Kelemen and Rumens 2008).

Box 4.4
Focus on student research

Researching the emotional effect of psychological contract violation

Working within an interpretive paradigm, Robyn believed that reality is socially constructed, subjective and could be perceived in different ways by different people. While reading for her master's programme she had been surprised by how many of the research papers she read on the psychological contract, an individual's belief regarding the terms and conditions of a reciprocal agreement between themselves and another, focused on aggregate findings rather than the details of situations. She considered that these researchers often ignored the individualistic and subjective aspects of contracts as well as individuals' emotional responses. Robyn therefore decided her research would be concerned with the emotional effect that employers' psychological contract violation had on employees, and how these emotions impacted upon their attitudes and behaviours. Based on a thorough review of the literature she developed three objectives:

- to establish how individuals decided their psychological contracts were being violated and their emotions in response to this violation;
- to ascertain the extent to which individuals' attitudes towards their employer changed as a result of these emotions;
- to explore attitudinal and behavioural consequences of this violation.

Robyn argued in her methodology chapter that, as a subjectivist, she was concerned with understanding what her research participants perceived to be the reality of their psychological contract violation as they constructed it. She stated her assumption that every action and reaction was based in a context that was interpreted by the participant as she or he made sense of what had happened. It was her participants' perceptions and their emotional reactions to these perceptions that would then inform their actions. Robyn also made clear in the methodology chapter that her research was concerned primarily with finding the meaning and emotions that each participant attached to their psychological contract violation and their reactions rather than changing what happened in organisations. This she equated with the regulatory perspective.

In the top right corner of the matrix, combining objectivist and radical change, is the **radical structuralist paradigm**. Here your concern would be to approach your research with a view to achieving fundamental change based upon an analysis of organisational phenomena such as structural power relationships and patterns of conflict. You would be involved in understanding structural patterns within work organisations such as hierarchies and reporting relationships and the extent to which these may produce structural domination and oppression. You would adopt an objectivist perspective due to your concern with objective entities. Research undertaken within the radical structuralist paradigm is often underpinned by a critical realist philosophy (Section 4.3), although such researchers differentiate themselves from extreme objectivists.

Finally, the **radical humanist paradigm** is located within the subjectivist and radical change dimensions. As we noted earlier, the radical change dimension adopts a critical perspective on organisational life. It emphasises both its political nature and the consequences that one's words and deeds have upon others (Kelemen and Rumens 2008). Working within this paradigm you would be concerned with changing the status quo. As with the radical structuralist paradigm, your primary focus would concern the issues of power and politics, domination and oppression. However, you would approach these concerns from within a subjectivist ontology, which would lead you to emphasise the importance of social construction, language, processes, and instability of structures and meanings in organisational realities.

Burrell and Morgan's (1979) book, although contentious, has been highly influential in terms of how organisational scholarship is seen. One of the most strongly disputed aspects of their work is the idea of **incommensurability**: the assertion that the four paradigms contain mutually incompatible assumptions and therefore cannot be combined. This debate is often referred to as 'paradigm wars'. Whether or not you think that different research paradigms can be combined will depend to some extent on your own research philosophy and, going back to our discussion of philosophies as a set of assumptions, the extremity of your views on these continua (Table 4.1) and within paradigms (Figure 4.3). You will see later (Section 4.3) that pragmatists seek to overcome dichotomies such as objectivism–subjectivism in their research, and as such are quite likely to engage in multi-paradigmatic research. Critical realists, who are less objectivist than positivists, embrace 'epistemological relativism', which may include more subjectivist as well as objectivist research, ranging from radical structuralism to radical humanism. The connections between paradigms and research philosophies therefore need to be seen in terms of philosophical affinity rather than equivocality, and should be treated with some caution and reflexivity. You will find such reflexivity easier as you become familiar with individual research philosophies.

4.3 Five major philosophies 五种主要的哲学

In this section, we discuss five major philosophies in business and management: positivism, critical realism, interpretivism, postmodernism and pragmatism (Figure 4.1).

Positivism

We introduced the research philosophy of positivism briefly in the discussion of objectivism and functionalism earlier in this chapter. **Positivism** relates to the philosophical stance of the natural scientist and entails working with an observable social reality to produce law-like generalisations. It promises unambiguous and accurate knowledge and originates in the works of Francis Bacon, Auguste Comte and the early twentieth-century group of philosophers and scientists known as the Vienna Circle. The label positivism refers to the importance of what is 'posited' – i.e. 'given'. This emphasises the positivist focus on strictly scientific empiricist method designed to yield pure data and facts uninfluenced by human interpretation or bias (Table 4.3). Today there is a 'bewildering array of positivisms', some counting as many as 12 varieties (Crotty 1998).

If you were to adopt an extreme positivist position, you would see organisations and other social entities as real in the same way as physical objects and natural phenomena are real. Epistemologically you would focus on discovering observable and measurable facts and regularities, and only phenomena that you can observe and measure would lead to the production of credible and meaningful data (Crotty 1998). You would look for causal relationships in your data to create law-like generalisations like those produced by scientists (Gill and Johnson 2010). You would use these universal rules and laws to help you to explain and predict behaviour and events in organisations.

Table 4.3 Comparison of five research philosophies in business and management research

Ontology (nature of reality or being)	Epistemology (what constitutes acceptable knowledge)	Axiology (role of values)	Typical methods
Positivism			
Real, external, independent	Scientific method	Value-free research	Typically deductive, highly structured, large samples, measurement, typically quantitative methods of analysis, but a range of data can be analysed
One true reality (universalism)	Observable and measurable facts	Researcher is detached, neutral and independent of what is researched	
Granular (things)	Law-like generalisations		
Ordered	Numbers	Researcher maintains objective stance	
	Causal explanation and prediction as contribution		
Critical realism			
Stratified/layered (the empirical, the actual and the real)	Epistemological relativism	Value-laden research	Retroductive, in-depth historically situated analysis of pre-existing structures and emerging agency. Range of methods and data types to fit subject matter
External, independent Intransient	Knowledge historically situated and transient	Researcher acknowledges bias by world views, cultural experience and upbringing	
Objective structures	Facts are social constructions	Researcher tries to minimise bias and errors	
Causal mechanisms	Historical causal explanation as contribution	Researcher is as objective as possible	
Interpretivism			
Complex, rich	Theories and concepts too simplistic	Value-bound research	Typically inductive. Small samples, in-depth investigations, qualitative methods of analysis, but a range of data can be interpreted
Socially constructed through culture and language	Focus on narratives, stories, perceptions and interpretations	Researchers are part of what is researched, subjective	
Multiple meanings, interpretations, realities	New understandings and worldviews as contribution	Researcher interpretations key to contribution	
Flux of processes, experiences, practices		Researcher reflexive	

Ontology (nature of reality or being)	Epistemology (what constitutes acceptable knowledge)	Axiology (role of values)	Typical methods
Postmodernism			
Nominal Complex, rich Socially constructed through power relations Some meanings, interpretations, realities are dominated and silenced by others Flux of processes, experiences, practices	What counts as 'truth' and 'knowledge' is decided by dominant ideologies Focus on absences, silences and oppressed/repressed meanings, interpretations and voices Exposure of power relations and challenge of dominant views as contribution	Value-constituted research Researcher and research embedded in power relations Some research narratives are repressed and silenced at the expense of others Researcher radically reflexive	Typically deconstructive – reading texts and realities against themselves In-depth investigations of anomalies, silences and absences Range of data types, typically qualitative methods of analysis
Pragmatism			
Complex, rich, external 'Reality' is the practical consequences of ideas Flux of processes, experiences and practices	Practical meaning of knowledge in specific contexts 'True' theories and knowledge are those that enable successful action Focus on problems, practices and relevance Problem solving and informed future practice as contribution	Value-driven research Research initiated and sustained by researcher's doubts and beliefs Researcher reflexive	Following research problem and research question Range of methods: mixed, multiple, qualitative, quantitative, action research Emphasis on practical solutions and outcomes

As a positivist researcher you might use existing theory to develop hypotheses. These hypotheses would be tested and confirmed, in whole or part, or refuted, leading to the further development of theory which then may be tested by further research. However, this does not mean that, as a positivist, you necessarily have to start with existing theory. All natural sciences have developed from an engagement with the world in which data were collected and observations made prior to hypotheses being formulated and tested. The hypotheses developed, as in Box 4.5, would lead to the gathering of facts (rather than impressions) that would provide the basis for subsequent hypothesis testing.

As a positivist you would also try to remain neutral and detached from your research and data in order to avoid influencing your findings (Crotty 1998). This means that you would undertake research, as far as possible, in a value-free way. For positivists, this is a plausible position, because of the measurable, quantifiable data that they collect. They claim to be external to the process of data collection as there is little that can be done to alter the substance of the data collected. Consider, for example, the differences between data collected using an Internet questionnaire (Chapter 11) in which the respondent self-selects from responses predetermined by the researcher, and in-depth interviews (Chapter 10). In the Internet questionnaire, the researcher determines the list of possible responses as part of the design process. Subsequent to this she or he

Box 4.5
Focus on student research

The development of hypotheses

Brett was conducting a piece of research for his project on the economic benefits of working from home for software developers. He studied the literature on home working and read two dissertations in his university's library that dealt with the same phenomenon, albeit that they did not relate specifically to software developers. As a result of his reading, Brett developed a number of theoretical propositions, each of which contained specific hypotheses. One of his propositions related to the potential increased costs associated with home working.

THEORETICAL PROPOSITION: Increased costs may negate the productivity gains from home working. From this he developed four SPECIFIC HYPOTHESES:

1 Increased costs for computer hardware, software and telecommunications equipment will negate the productivity gains from home working.
2 Home workers will require additional support from on-site employees, for example technicians, which will negate the productivity gains from home working.
3 Work displaced to other employees and/or increased supervisory requirements will negate the productivity gains from home working.
4 Reduced face-to-face access by home workers to colleagues will result in lost opportunities to increase efficiencies, which will negate the productivity gains from home working.

can claim that her or his values do not influence the answers given by the respondent. In contrast, an in-depth interview necessitates the researcher framing the questions in relation to each participant and interpreting their answers. Unlike in a questionnaire, these questions are unlikely to be asked in exactly the same way. Rather the interviewer exercises her or his judgement in what to ask to collect participant-led accounts that are as rich as possible.

You may believe that excluding our own values as researchers is impossible. Even a researcher adopting a positivist stance exercises choice in the issue to study, the research objectives to pursue and the data to collect. Indeed, it could be argued that the decision to try to adopt a value-free perspective suggests the existence of a certain value position!

Positivist researchers are likely to use a highly structured methodology in order to facilitate replication (Gill and Johnson 2010). Furthermore, the emphasis will be on quantifiable observations that lend themselves to statistical analysis (Box 4.5). However, as you will read in later chapters, sometimes positivist research extends itself to other data collection methods and seeks to quantify qualitative data, for example by applying hypothesis testing to data originally collected in in-depth interviews.

Critical realism

It is important not to confuse the philosophy of critical realism with the more extreme form of realism underpinning the positivist philosophy. The latter, sometimes known as **direct realism** (or naïve empirical scientific realism), says that what you see is what you get: what we experience through our senses portrays the world accurately. By contrast, the philosophy of **critical realism** focuses on explaining what we see and experience, in terms of the underlying structures of reality that shape the observable events.

Critical realism originated in the late twentieth century in the work of Roy Bhaskar, as a response to both positivist direct realism and postmodernist nominalism (discussed later), and occupies a middle ground between these two positions (Reed 2005).

For critical realists, reality is the most important philosophical consideration, a structured and layered ontology being crucial (Fleetwood 2005). Critical realists see reality as external and independent, but not directly accessible through our observation and knowledge of it (Table 4.3). Rather, what we experience is 'the empirical', in other words sensations, which are some of the manifestations of the things in the real world, rather than the actual things. Critical realists highlight how often our senses deceive us. When you next watch a cricket or rugby match on television you are likely to see an advertisement for the sponsor on the actual playing surface. This advertisement appears to be standing upright on the pitch. However, this is an illusion. It is, in fact, painted on the grass. So what we see are sensations, which are representations of what is real.

Critical realism claims there are two steps to understanding the world. First, there are the sensations and events we experience. Second, there is the mental processing that goes on sometime after the experience, when we 'reason backwards' from our experiences to the underlying reality that might have caused them (this reasoning backwards is known as 'retroduction') (Reed 2005). Direct realism says that the first step is enough. To pursue our cricket (or rugby) example, the umpire who is a direct realist would say about her or his umpiring decisions: 'I give them as they are!' The umpire who is a critical realist would say: 'I give them as I see them!' Critical realists would point out that what the umpire has observed (the 'Empirical') is only a small part of everything that he or she could have seen; a small fraction of the sum total of the 'Actual' events that are occurring at any one point in time (Figure 4.4). A player may, perhaps, have obscured the umpire's view of another player committing a foul. Critical realists would emphasise that what the umpire has not seen are the underlying causes (the 'Real') of a situation (Figure 4.4). For example, was a head-butt a real, intentional foul, or an accident? The umpire cannot experience the real significance of the situation directly. Rather, she or he has to use his/her sensory data of the 'Empirical' as observed and use reasoning to work it out.

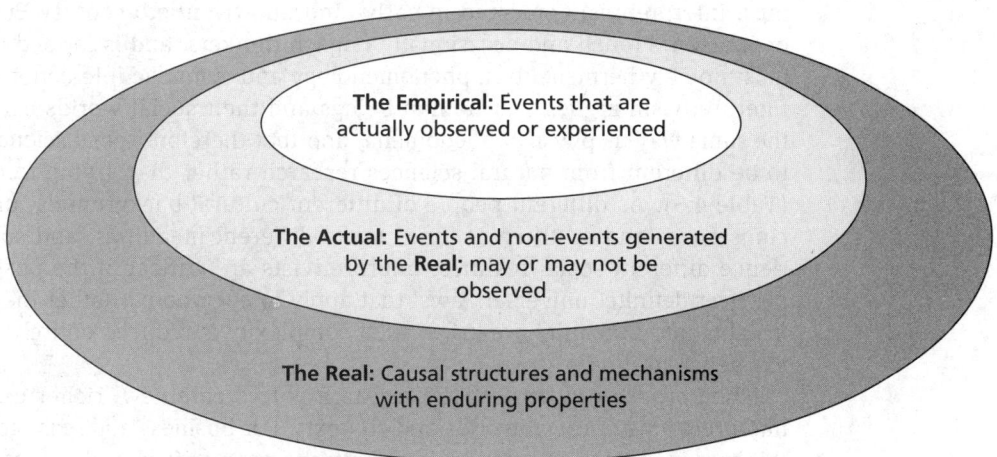

The Empirical: Events that are actually observed or experienced

The Actual: Events and non-events generated by the Real; may or may not be observed

The Real: Causal structures and mechanisms with enduring properties

Figure 4.4 Critical realist stratified ontology
Source: Developed from Bhaskar (1978)

If you believe that, as researchers, we need to look for the bigger picture of which we see only a small part, you may be leaning towards the critical realist philosophy. Bhaskar (1989) argues that we will only be able to understand what is going on in the social world if we understand the social structures that have given rise to the phenomena that we are trying to understand. He writes that we can identify what we do not see through the practical and theoretical processes of the social sciences. Critical realist research therefore focuses on providing an explanation for observable organisational events by looking for the underlying causes and mechanisms through which deep social structures shape everyday organisational life. Due to this focus, much of critical realist research takes the form of in-depth historical analysis of social and organisational structures, and how they have changed over time (Reed 2005).

Within their focus on the historical analysis of structures, critical realists embrace epistemological relativism (Reed 2005), a (mildly) subjectivist approach to knowledge. **Epistemological relativism** recognises that knowledge is historically situated (in other words, it is a product of its time and is specific to it), and that social facts are social constructions agreed on by people rather than existing independently (Bhaskar 1989). This implies that critical realist notions of causality cannot be reduced to statistical correlations and quantitative methods, and that a range of methods is acceptable (Reed 2005). A critical realist's axiological position follows from the recognition that our knowledge of reality is a result of social conditioning (e.g. we know that if the rugby player runs into an advertisement that is actually standing up he or she will fall over!) and cannot be understood independently of the social actors involved. This means that, as a critical realist researcher, you would strive to be aware of the ways in which your socio-cultural background and experiences might influence your research, and would seek to minimise such biases and be as objective as possible.

Interpretivism

Interpretivism, like critical realism, developed as a critique of positivism but from a subjectivist perspective. **Interpretivism** emphasises that humans are different from physical phenomena because they create meanings. Interpretivists study these meanings. Interpretivism emerged in early- and mid-twentieth-century Europe, in the work of German, French and occasionally English thinkers, and is formed of several strands, most notably hermeneutics, phenomenology and symbolic interactionism (Crotty 1998). Interpretivism argues that human beings and their social worlds cannot be studied in the same way as physical phenomena, and that therefore social sciences research needs to be different from natural sciences research rather than trying to emulate the latter (Table 4.3). As different people of different cultural backgrounds, under different circumstances and at different times make different meanings, and so create and experience different social realities, interpretivists are critical of the positivist attempts to discover definite, universal 'laws' that apply to everybody. Rather they believe that rich insights into humanity are lost if such complexity is reduced entirely to a series of law-like generalisations.

The purpose of interpretivist research is to create new, richer understandings and interpretations of social worlds and contexts. For business and management researchers, this means looking at organisations from the perspectives of different groups of people. They would argue, for example, that the ways in which the CEO, board directors, managers, shop assistants, cleaners and customers see and experience a large retail company are different, so much so that they could arguably be seen as experiencing different workplace realities. If research focuses on the experiences that are common to all at all times, much of the richness of the differences between them and their individual circumstances will be lost, and the understanding of the organisation that the research delivers will reflect this. Furthermore, differences that make organisations complex are not simply contained to different organisational roles. Male or female employees or customers, or those from different ethnic/cultural backgrounds, may experience workplaces, services or events in different ways. Interpretations of what on the surface appears to be the same thing (such as a luxury product) can differ between historical or geographical contexts.

Interpretivist researchers try to take account of this complexity by collecting what is meaningful to their research participants. Different strands of interpretivism place slightly different emphasis on how to do this in practice, so **phenomenologists**, who study existence, focus on participants' lived experience; that is, the participants' recollections and interpretations of those experiences. **Hermeneuticists** focus on the study of cultural artefacts such as texts, symbols, stories, images. **Symbolic interactionists**, whose tradition derives from pragmatist thinking (discussed later in this section) and who see meaning as something that emerges out of interactions between people, focus on the observation and analysis of social interaction such as conversations, meetings, teamwork. In general, interpretivists emphasise the importance of language, culture and history (Crotty 1998) in the shaping of our interpretations and experiences of organisational and social worlds.

With its focus on complexity, richness, multiple interpretations and meaning-making, interpretivism is explicitly subjectivist. An axiological implication of this is that interpretivists recognise that their interpretation of research materials and data, and thus their own values and beliefs, play an important role in the research process. Crucial to the interpretivist philosophy is that the researcher has to adopt an empathetic stance. The challenge for the interpretivist is to enter the social world of the research participants and understand that world from their point of view. Some would argue the interpretivist perspective is highly appropriate in the case of business and management research. Not only are business situations complex, they are often unique, at least in terms of context. They reflect a particular set of circumstances and interactions involving individuals coming together at a specific time.

Postmodernism

Postmodernism emphasises the role of language and of power relations, seeking to question accepted ways of thinking and give voice to alternative marginalised views (Table 4.3). It emerged in the late twentieth century and has been most closely associated with the work of French philosophers Jean-François Lyotard, Jacques Derrida, Michel Foucault, Gilles Deleuze, Félix Guattari and Jean Baudrillard. Postmodernism is historically entangled with the intellectual movement of poststructuralism. As the differences in focus between postmodernism and poststructuralism are subtle and have become less discernible over time, in this chapter for the sake of simplicity we will focus on one label, postmodernism.

Postmodernists go even further than interpretivists in their critique of positivism and objectivism, attributing even more importance to the role of language (Table 4.3). They reject the modern objectivist, realist ontology of things, and instead emphasise the chaotic primacy of flux, movement, fluidity and change. They believe that any sense of order is provisional and foundationless, and can only be brought about through our language with its categories and classifications (Chia 2003). At the same time they recognise that language is always partial and inadequate. In particular, it always marginalises, suppresses and excludes aspects of what it claims to describe, while privileging and emphasising other aspects. As there is no order to the social world beyond that which we give to it through language, there is no abstract way of determining the 'right' or the 'true' way to describe the world. Instead, what is generally considered to be 'right' and 'true' is decided collectively. These collective 'choices', in turn, are shaped by the power relations and by the ideologies that dominate particular contexts (Foucault 1991). This does not mean that the dominant ways of thinking are necessarily the 'best' – only that they are seen as such at a particular point in time by particular groups of people. Other perspectives that are suppressed are potentially just as valuable and have the power to create alternative worlds and truths.

Postmodernist researchers seek to expose and question the power relations that sustain dominant realities (Calás and Smircich 1997). This takes the form of 'deconstructing' (taking apart) these realities, as if they were texts, to search for instabilities within their widely accepted truths, and for what has not been discussed – absences and silences created in the shadow of such truths (Derrida 1976). Postmodernists strive to make what has been left out or excluded more visible by the deconstruction of what counts as 'reality' into ideologies and power relations that underpin it, as you would dismantle an old building into the bricks and mortar that make it up. The goal of postmodern research is therefore to radically challenge the established ways of thinking and knowing (Kilduff and Mehra 1997) and to give voice and legitimacy to the suppressed and marginalised ways of seeing and knowing that have been previously excluded (Chia 2003).

As a postmodernist researcher, you would, instead of approaching the organisational world as constituted by things and entities such as 'management', 'performance' and 'resources', focus on the ongoing processes of organising, managing and ordering that constitute such entities. You would challenge organisational concepts and theories, and seek to demonstrate what perspectives and realities they exclude and leave silent and whose interests they serve. For example, you might wish to follow the work of Barbara Townley (1994), and explore the ways in which the label 'human resources' (HR) privileges particular ways of seeing and dealing with human beings in organisations and show what other alternatives it suppresses. You might explore how the HR label makes acceptable and legitimate a whole range of ideas and practices that we know as 'human resource management', thus serving the interests of managers rather than those of their subordinates (Townley 1994).

As a postmodernist, you would be open to the deconstruction of any forms of data – texts, images, conversations, voices and numbers. Like interpretivists, you would be undertaking in-depth investigations of phenomena. Fundamental to postmodernist research is the recognition that power relations between the researcher and research subjects shape the knowledge created as part of the research process. As power relations cannot be avoided, it is crucial for researchers to be open about their moral and ethical positions (Calás and Smircich 1997), and thus you would strive to be radically reflexive about your own thinking and writing (Cunliffe 2003).

Pragmatism

By now you may be thinking: do these differences in assumptions really matter? The proponents of the philosophies discussed above would say that they do, as they delineate fundamentally different ways of seeing the world and carrying out research. However, you may be feeling differently. If you are becoming impatient with the battle of ontological, epistemological and axiological assumptions between the different philosophies, if you are questioning their relevance, and if you would rather get on with research that would focus on making a difference to organisational practice, you may be leaning towards the philosophy of pragmatism. However, you need to be sure that you are not treating pragmatism as an escape route from the challenge of understanding other philosophies!

Pragmatism asserts that concepts are only relevant where they support action (Kelemen and Rumens 2008). Pragmatism originated in the late-nineteenth–early-twentieth-century USA in the work of philosophers Charles Pierce, William James and John Dewey. It strives to reconcile both objectivism and subjectivism, facts and values, accurate and rigorous knowledge and different contextualised experiences (Table 4.3). It does this by considering theories, concepts, ideas, hypotheses and research findings not in an abstract form, but in terms of the roles they play as instruments of thought and action, and in terms of their practical consequences in specific contexts (Table 4.3; Box 4.6). Reality matters to pragmatists as practical effects of ideas, and knowledge is valued for enabling actions to be carried out successfully.

For a pragmatist, research starts with a problem, and aims to contribute practical solutions that inform future practice. Researcher values drive the reflexive process of inquiry, which is initiated by doubt and a sense that something is wrong or out of place, and which re-creates belief when the problem has been resolved (Elkjaer and Simpson 2011). As pragmatists are more interested in practical outcomes than abstract distinctions, their research may have considerable variation in terms of how 'objectivist' or 'subjectivist' it turns out to be. If you were to undertake pragmatist research, this would mean that the most important determinant for your research design and strategy would be the research problem that you would try to address, and your research question. Your research question, in turn, would be likely to incorporate the pragmatist emphasis of practical outcomes.

If a research problem does not suggest unambiguously that one particular type of knowledge or method should be adopted, this only confirms the pragmatist's view that it is perfectly possible to work with different types of knowledge and methods. This reflects a theme which recurs in this book – that multiple methods are

Box 4.6
Focus on management research

Investigating the realities of how things work in organisations

In an article in the *Journal of Management Studies*, Watson (2011) discusses the rationale for undertaking good ethnographic research when investigating the realities of how things work in organisations. Within this he argues that pragmatist realist principles of truth, reality and relevance to practice provide a powerful rationale for focusing on investigating the realities of how things work in organisations using ethnography.

In his article Watson highlights how he has always believed that it is not possible to learn a great deal about what actually happens or how things work in organisations without undertaking intensive research that involves observation or the researcher participating, both of which are essential to ethnography. In developing this argument, Watson (2011: 204) emphasises the importance of the 'relevance to practice' principle of pragmatism, stating: 'I felt that there was no real alternative to this if I wanted to contribute in a worthwhile way to the social scientific understanding of how managers manage, how organisational change comes about, how micro politics operate, and how employment relationships are shaped and maintained.'

often possible, and possibly highly appropriate, within one study (see Section 5.3). Pragmatists recognise that there are many different ways of interpreting the world and undertaking research, that no single point of view can ever give the entire picture and that there may be multiple realities. This does not mean that pragmatists always use multiple methods; rather they use the method or methods that enable credible, well-founded, reliable and relevant data to be collected that advance the research (Kelemen and Rumens 2008).

4.4 Approaches to theory development 理论发展的方法

We emphasised that your research project will involve the use of theory (Chapter 2). That theory may or may not be made explicit in the design of the research (Chapter 5), although it will usually be made explicit in your presentation of the findings and conclusions. The extent to which you are clear about the theory at the beginning of your research raises an important question concerning the design of your research project. This is often portrayed as two contrasting approaches to the reasoning you adopt: deductive or inductive. Deductive reasoning occurs when the conclusion is derived logically from a set of premises, the conclusion being true when all the premises are true (Ketokivi and Mantere 2010). For example, our research may concern likely online retail sales of a soon-to-be-launched new games console. We form three premises:

- that online retailers have been allocated limited stock of the new games consoles by the manufacturer;
- that customers' demand for the consoles exceeds supply;
- that online retailers allow customers to pre-order the consoles.

If these premises are true we can deduce that the conclusion that online retailers will have 'sold' their entire allocation of the new games consoles by the release day will also be true.

In contrast, in inductive reasoning there is a gap in the logic argument between the conclusion and the premises observed, the conclusion being 'judged' to be supported by the observations made (Ketokivi and Mantere 2010). Returning to our example of the likely online retail sales of a soon-to-be-launched new games console, we would start with observations about the forthcoming launch. Our observed premises would be:

- that news media are reporting that online retailers are complaining about only being allocated limited stock of the new games consoles by manufacturers;
- that news media are reporting that demand for the consoles will exceed supply;
- that online retailers are allowing customers to pre-order the consoles.

Based on these observations, we have good reason to believe online retailers will have 'sold' their entire allocation of the new games consoles by the release day. However, although our conclusion is supported by our observations, it is not guaranteed. In the past, manufacturers have launched new games consoles which have been commercial failures (Zigterman 2013).

There is also a third approach to theory development that is just as common in research, abductive reasoning, which begins with a 'surprising fact' being observed (Ketokivi and Mantere 2010). This surprising fact is the conclusion rather than a premise. Based on this conclusion, a set of possible premises is determined that is considered sufficient or nearly sufficient to explain the conclusion. It is reasoned that, if this set of premises was true, then the conclusion would be true as a matter of course. Because the set of premises is sufficient (or nearly sufficient) to generate the conclusion, this provides reason to believe that it is also true. Returning once again to our example of the likely online retail sales of a soon-to-be-launched new games console, a surprising fact (conclusion) might be that online retailers are reported in the news media as stating they will have no remaining stock of the new games console for sale on the day of its release. However, if the online retailers are allowing customers to pre-order the console prior to its release then it would not be surprising if these retailers had already sold their allocation of consoles. Therefore, using abductive reasoning, the possibility that online retailers have no remaining stock on the day of release is reasonable.

Building on these three approaches to theory development (Figure 4.1), if your research starts with theory, often developed from your reading of the academic literature, and you design a research strategy to test the theory, you are using a **deductive approach** (Table 4.4). Conversely, if your research starts by collecting data to explore a phenomenon and you generate or build theory (often in the form of a conceptual framework), then you are using an **inductive approach** (Table 4.4). Where you are collecting data to explore a phenomenon, identify themes and explain patterns, to generate a new or modify an existing theory which you subsequently test through additional data collection, you are using an **abductive approach** (Table 4.4).

The next three sub-sections explore the differences and similarities between these three approaches and their implications for your research.

Table 4.4 Deduction, induction and abduction: from reason to research

	Deduction	Induction	Abduction
Logic	In a deductive inference, when the premises are true, the conclusion must also be true	In an inductive inference, known premises are used to generate untested conclusions	In an abductive inference, known premises are used to generate testable conclusions
Generalisability	Generalising from the general to the specific	Generalising from the specific to the general	Generalising from the interactions between the specific and the general
Use of data	Data collection is used to evaluate propositions or hypotheses related to an existing theory	Data collection is used to explore a phenomenon, identify themes and patterns and create a conceptual framework	Data collection is used to explore a phenomenon, identify themes and patterns, locate these in a conceptual framework and test this through subsequent data collection and so forth
Theory	Theory falsification or verification	Theory generation and building	Theory generation or modification; incorporating existing theory where appropriate, to build new theory or modify existing theory

Deduction

As noted earlier, deduction owes much to what we would think of as scientific research. It involves the development of a theory that is then subjected to a rigorous test through a series of propositions. As such, it is the dominant research approach in the natural sciences, where laws present the basis of explanation, allow the anticipation of phenomena, predict their occurrence and therefore permit them to be controlled.

Blaikie (2010) lists six sequential steps through which a deductive approach will progress:

1 Put forward a tentative idea, a premise, a hypothesis (a testable proposition about the relationship between two or more concepts or variables) or set of hypotheses to form a theory.
2 By using existing literature, or by specifying the conditions under which the theory is expected to hold, deduce a testable proposition or number of propositions.
3 Examine the premises and the logic of the argument that produced them, comparing this argument with existing theories to see if it offers an advance in understanding. If it does, then continue.
4 Test the premises by collecting appropriate data to measure the concepts or variables and analysing them.
5 If the results of the analysis are not consistent with the premises (the tests fail!), the theory is false and must either be rejected or modified and the process restarted.
6 If the results of the analysis are consistent with the premises then the theory is corroborated.

Deduction possesses several important characteristics. First, there is the search to explain causal relationships between concepts and variables. It may be that you wish to establish the reasons for high employee absenteeism in a retail store. After reading about absence patterns in the academic literature you develop a theory that there is a relationship between absence, the age of workers and length of service. Consequently, you develop a number of hypotheses, including one which states that absenteeism is significantly more likely to be prevalent among younger workers and another which states that absenteeism is significantly more likely to be prevalent among workers who have been employed by the organisation for a relatively short period of time. To test this proposition you collect quantitative data. (This is not to say that a deductive approach may not use qualitative data.) It may be that there are important differences in the way work is arranged in different stores: therefore you would need to specify precisely the conditions under which your theory is likely to hold and collect appropriate data within these conditions. By doing this you would help to ensure that any change in absenteeism was a function of worker age and length of service rather than any other aspect of the store, for example the way in which people were managed. Your research would use a highly **structured methodology** to facilitate replication, an important issue to ensure reliability, as we shall emphasise in Section 5.8.

An additional important characteristic of deduction is that concepts need to be **operationalised** in a way that enables facts to be measured, often quantitatively. In our example, one variable that needs to be measured is absenteeism. Just what constitutes absenteeism would have to be strictly defined: an absence for a complete day would probably count, but what about absence for two hours? In addition, what would constitute a 'short period of employment' and 'younger' employees? What is happening here is that the principle of **reductionism** is being followed. This holds that problems as a whole are better understood if they are reduced to the simplest possible elements.

The final characteristic of deduction is **generalisation.** In order to be able to generalise it is necessary to select our sample carefully and for it to be of sufficient size (Sections 7.2 and 7.3). In our example above, research at a particular store would allow us only to make inferences about that store; it would be dangerous to predict that worker youth and short length of service lead to absenteeism in all cases. This is discussed in more detail in Section 5.8.

Induction

An alternative approach to developing theory on retail store employee absenteeism would be to start by interviewing a sample of the employees and their supervisors about the experience of working at the store. The purpose here would be to get a feel of what was going on, so as to understand better the nature of the problem. Your task then would be to make sense of the interview data you collected through your analysis. The result of this analysis would be the formulation of a theory, often expressed as a conceptual framework. This may be that there is a relationship between absence and the length of time a person has worked for the retail store. Alternatively, you may discover that there are other competing reasons for absence that may or may not be related to worker age or length of service. You may end up with the same theory, but your reasoning to produce that theory is using an inductive approach: theory follows data rather than vice versa, as with deduction.

We noted earlier that deduction has its origins in research in the natural sciences. However, the emergence of the social sciences in the twentieth century led social science researchers to be wary of deduction. They were critical of a reasoning approach that enabled a cause–effect link to be made between particular variables without an understanding of the way in which humans interpreted their social world. Developing such an understanding is, of course, the strength of an inductive approach. In our absenteeism example, if you were adopting an inductive approach you would argue that it is more realistic to treat workers as humans whose attendance behaviour is a consequence of the way in which they perceive their work experience, rather than as if they were unthinking research objects who respond in a mechanistic way to certain circumstances.

Followers of induction would also criticise deduction because of its tendency to construct a rigid methodology that does not permit alternative explanations of what is going on. In that sense, there is an air of finality about the choice of theory and definition of the hypothesis. Alternative theories may be suggested by deduction. However, these would be within the limits set by the highly structured research design. In this respect, a significant characteristic of the absenteeism research design noted above is that of the operationalisation of concepts. As we saw in the absenteeism example, age was precisely defined. However, a less structured approach might reveal alternative explanations of the absenteeism–age relationship denied by a stricter definition of age.

Research using an inductive approach to reasoning is likely to be particularly concerned with the context in which such events take place (Box 4.7). Therefore, the study of a small sample of subjects might be more appropriate than a large number as with the deductive approach. Researchers in this tradition are more likely to work with qualitative data and to use a variety of methods to collect these data in order to establish different views of phenomena (as will be seen in Chapter 10).

Box 4.7
Focus on management research

Developing theory inductively

In their paper titled 'Sustainable entrepreneurship, is entrepreneurial will enough?' Spence et al. (2011) analyse 44 cases from Canada, Tunisia and Cameroon to determine the fundamentals of sustainable entrepreneurship in small- and medium-sized enterprises (SMEs). The overall objective of their research was to analyse and explain SMEs' practices by comparing and contrasting levels of sustainable entrepreneurship in these three countries. They argue that, because the concept of sustainable entrepreneurship was not well defined among SMEs in emerging and developing countries, an inductive approach would be most appropriate.

Data were collected using interviews, organisational documents provided by the owner-manager and by examining the SMEs' websites where available. Interviews lasted between one and two hours and were undertaken using a guide comprising of open questions designed to enable an understanding of each SME's level of sustainable entrepreneurship, as well as their business objectives. The questions allowed the interviewer to pursue topics such as the owner-manager's knowledge of sustainability issues, their personal beliefs and a detailed account of their firm's involvement in sustainability.

These data were used subsequently to induce qualitative indicators and develop a typology of sustainable development.

Abduction

Instead of moving from theory to data (as in deduction) or data to theory (as in induction), an abductive approach moves back and forth, in effect combining deduction and induction (Suddaby 2006). This, as we have noted earlier, matches what many business and management researchers actually do. Abduction begins with the observation of a 'surprising fact'; it then works out a plausible theory of how this could have occurred. Van Maanen et al. (2007) note that some plausible theories can account for what is observed better than others and it is these theories that will help uncover more 'surprising facts'. These surprises, they argue, can occur at any stage in the research process, including when writing your project report! Van Maanen et al. also stress that deduction and induction complement abduction as logics for testing plausible theories.

Applying an abductive approach to our research on the reasons for high employee absenteeism in a retail store would mean obtaining data that were sufficiently detailed and rich to allow us to explore the phenomenon and identify and explain themes and patterns regarding employee absenteeism. We would then try to integrate these explanations in an overall conceptual framework, thereby building up a theory of employee absenteeism in a retail store. This we would test using evidence provided by existing data and new data and revise as necessary.

At this stage you may be asking yourself: So what? Why is the choice that I make about my approach to theory development so important? Easterby-Smith et al. (2012) suggest three reasons. First, it enables you to take a more informed decision about your research design (Chapter 5), which is more than just the techniques by which data are collected and procedures by which they are analysed. It is the overall configuration of a piece of research involving questions about what kind of evidence is gathered and from where, and how such evidence is interpreted in order to provide good answers to your initial research question.

Second, it will help you to think about those research strategies and methodological choice that will work for you and, crucially, those that will not. For example, if you are particularly interested in understanding why something is happening, rather than being able to describe what is happening, it may be more appropriate to undertake your research inductively rather than deductively.

Third, Easterby-Smith et al. (2012) argue that knowledge of the different research traditions enables you to adapt your research design to cater for constraints. These may be practical, involving, say, limited access to data, or they may arise from a lack of prior knowledge of the subject. You simply may not be in a position to frame a hypothesis because you have insufficient understanding of the topic to do this.

Using approaches in combination

So far, when discussing induction and deduction we have conveyed the impression that there are rigid divisions between deduction and induction. This would be misleading. As we have seen in our discussion of abduction, is it possible to combine deduction and induction within the same piece of research. It is also, in our experience, often advantageous to do so, although often one approach or another is dominant.

At this point you may be wondering whether your reasoning will be predominantly deductive, inductive or abductive. The honest answer is, 'it depends'. In particular, it depends on the emphasis of the research (Box 4.8) and the nature of the research topic. A topic on which there is a wealth of literature from which you can define a theoretical framework and a hypothesis lends itself more readily to deduction. With research into a topic that is new, is exciting much debate and on which there is little existing literature, it may be more appropriate to work inductively by generating data and analysing and reflecting upon what theoretical themes the data are suggesting. Alternatively, a topic about which there is a wealth of information in one context but far less in the context in which you are researching may lend itself to an abductive approach enabling you to modify an existing theory.

The time you have available will be an issue. Deductive research can be quicker to complete, albeit that time must be devoted to setting up the study prior to data collection and analysis. Data collection is often based on 'one take'. It is normally possible to predict the time schedules accurately. On the other hand, abductive and, particularly, inductive research can be much more protracted. Often the ideas, based on a much longer period of data collection and analysis, have to emerge gradually. This leads to another important consideration, the extent to which you are prepared to indulge in risk. Deduction can be a lower-risk strategy, although there are risks, such as the non-return of questionnaires. With induction and abduction you have to live with the fear that no useful data patterns and theory will emerge. Finally, there is the question of audience. In our experience, most managers are familiar with deduction and much more likely to put faith in the conclusions emanating from this approach. You may also wish to consider the preferences of the person marking your research report. We all have our preferences about the approach to adopt.

This last point suggests that not all your decisions about the approach to reasoning should always be practically based. Hakim (2000) uses an architectural metaphor

Box 4.8
Focus on student research

Deductive, inductive and abductive research

Sadie decided to conduct a research project on violence at work and its effects on the stress levels of staff. She considered the different ways she would approach the work were she to adopt:

- the deductive approach;
- the inductive approach;
- the abductive approach.

If she adopted a deductive approach to her reasoning, she would have to:

1 start with the hypothesis that staff working directly with the public are more likely to experience the threat or reality of violence and resultant stress;
2 decide to research a population in which she would have expected to find evidence of violence, for example, a sizeable social security office;
3 administer a questionnaire to a large sample of staff in order to establish the extent of violence (either actually experienced or threatened) and the levels of stress experienced by them;
4 be particularly careful about how she defined violence;
5 standardise the stress responses of the staff, for example, days off sick or sessions with a counsellor.

If she adopted an inductive approach then she might have decided to interview some staff who had been subjected to violence at work. She might have been interested in their feelings about the events that they had experienced, how they coped with the problems they experienced and their views about the possible causes of the violence.

If she adopted an abductive approach, she might have developed a conceptual model on the basis of her interview. She might then have used this model to develop a series of hypotheses and designed a questionnaire to collect data with which to test these hypotheses. Based on analyses of these data she might then have refined her conceptual model.

All approaches would have yielded valuable data about this problem (indeed, within this abductive approach, both inductive and deductive approaches were used at different stages). No approach should be thought of as better than the others. They are better at different things. It depends where her research emphasis lies.

to illustrate this. She introduces the notion of the researcher's preferred style, which, rather like the architect's, may reflect 'the architect's own preferences and ideas . . . and the stylistic preferences of those who pay for the work and have to live with the final result' (Hakim 2000: 1). This echoes the feelings of Buchanan et al. (2013: 59), who argue that 'needs, interests and preferences (of the researcher) . . . are typically overlooked but are central to the progress of fieldwork'. However, a note of caution: it is important that your preferences do not lead to you changing the essence of the research question, particularly if it has been given to you by an organisation as a consultancy project.

4.5 Summary 小 结

- The term 'research philosophies' refers to systems of beliefs and assumptions about the development of knowledge. This means that your research philosophy contains important assumptions about the way in which you view the world. These assumptions shape all aspects of your research projects.

- To understand your research philosophy, you need to develop the skill of reflexivity, which means asking yourself questions about your beliefs and assumptions, and treating these with the same scrutiny as you would apply to the beliefs of others.
- There is no single 'best' business and management research philosophy. Each philosophy contributes a unique and valuable way of seeing the organisational world.
- All research philosophies make three major types of assumption: ontological, epistemological and axiological. We can distinguish different philosophies by the differences and similarities in their ontological, epistemological and axiological assumptions.
  - Ontology concerns researchers' assumptions about the nature of the world and reality. Ontological assumptions you make determine what research objects and phenomena you focus on, and how you see and approach them.
  - Epistemology concerns assumptions about knowledge – how we know what we say we know, what constitutes acceptable, valid and legitimate knowledge, and how we can communicate knowledge to fellow human beings. Epistemological assumptions you make determines what sort of contribution to knowledge you can make as a result of your research.
  - Axiology refers to the role of values and ethics within the research process, which incorporates questions about how we, as researchers, deal with our own values and also with those of our research participants.
- Research philosophies can be differentiated in terms of where their assumptions fall on the objectivism–subjectivism continua.
  - Objectivism incorporates assumptions of the natural sciences. It entails realist ontology (which holds that social entities exist in reality external to and independent from social actors), epistemology focused on the discovery of truth by means of observable, measurable facts, and claims to have a value-free, detached axiology.
  - Subjectivism incorporates assumptions of the arts and humanities. It entails nominalist ontology (which holds that social phenomena are created through the language, perceptions and consequent actions of social actors), epistemology focused on the social actors' opinions, narratives, interpretations, perceptions that convey these social realities, and claims to have a value-bound, reflexive axiology.
- Management and business research can be understood in terms of four social research paradigms: functionalist, interpretive, radical structuralist and radical humanist. These paradigms add the dimension of the political rationale for research to the objectivism–subjectivism continua.
- Management and business research comprises five main philosophies: positivism, critical realism, interpretivism, postmodernism and pragmatism.
  - Positivism relates to the philosophical stance of the natural scientist. This entails working with an observable social reality and the end product can be law-like generalisations similar to those in the physical and natural sciences.
  - Critical realism focuses on explaining what we see and experience in terms of the underlying structures of reality that shape the observable events. Critical realists tend to undertake historical analyses of changing or enduring societal and organisational structures, using a variety of methods.
  - Interpretivism is a subjectivist philosophy, which emphasises that human beings are different from physical phenomena because they create meanings. Interpretivists study meanings to create new, richer understandings of organisational realities. Empirically, interpretivists focus on individuals' lived experiences and cultural artefacts, and seek to include their participants' as well as their own interpretations into their research.

- Postmodernism emphasises the world-making role of language and power relations. Postmodernists seek to question the accepted ways of thinking and give voice to alternative worldviews that have been marginalised and silenced by dominant perspectives. Postmodernists deconstruct data to expose the instabilities and absences within them. Postmodernist axiology is radically reflexive.
- Pragmatist ontology, epistemology and axiology are focused on improving practice. Pragmatists adopt a wide range of research strategies, the choice of which is driven by the specific nature of their research problems.
- There are three main approaches to theory development: deduction, induction and abduction.
  - With deduction, a theory and hypothesis (or hypotheses) are developed and a research strategy designed to test the hypothesis.
  - With induction, data are collected and a theory developed as a result of the data analysis.
  - With abduction, data are used to explore a phenomenon, identify themes and explain patterns, to generate a new or modify an existing theory which is subsequently tested, often through additional data collection.

Self-check questions   自测题

Help with these questions is available at the end of the chapter.

4.1   You have decided to undertake a project and have defined the main research question as 'What are the opinions of consumers on a 10 per cent reduction in weight, with the price remaining the same, of "Snackers" chocolate bars?' Write a hypothesis that you could test in your project.

4.2   Why may it be argued that the concept of the manager is socially constructed rather than 'real'?

4.3   Why are the radical paradigms relevant in business and management research given that most managers would say that the purpose of organisational investigation is to develop recommendations for action to solve problems without radical change?

4.4   You have chosen to undertake your research project following a deductive approach. What factors may cause you to work inductively, although working deductively is your preferred choice?

Review and discussion questions   复习与讨论题

4.5   Visit an online database or your university library and obtain a copy of a research-based refereed journal article that you think will be of use to an assignment you are currently working on. Read this article carefully. From which philosophical perspective do you think this article is written? Use Section 4.2 to help you develop a clear justification for your answer.

4.6   Think about the last assignment you undertook for your course. In undertaking this assignment, were you predominantly inductive or deductive? Discuss your thoughts with a friend who also undertook this assignment.

4.7   Agree with a friend to watch the same television documentary.
   a To what extent is the documentary inductive, deductive or abductive in its use of data?
   b Is the documentary based on positivist, critical realist, interpretivist or pragmatist assumptions?
   c Do not forget to make notes regarding your reasons for your answers to each of these questions and to discuss your answers with your friend.

改进研究项目

Progressing your research project

提高你的研究哲学意识

Heightening your Awareness of your Research Philosophy (HARP)*

HARP is a reflexive tool that has been designed by Bristow and Saunders to help you explore your research philosophy. It is just a starting point for enabling you to ask yourself more refined questions about how you see research. It will not provide you with a definitive answer to the question 'What is my research philosophy?' Rather it will give you an indication as to where your views are similar to and different from those of five major philosophical traditions discussed in this chapter. Do not be surprised if your views are similar to more than one tradition. Such potential tensions are an ideal opportunity to inquire into and examine your beliefs further.

HARP consists of six sections each comprising five statements (a total of 30 statements). Each section considers one aspect of philosophical beliefs (ontology, epistemology, axiology, purpose of research, meaningfulness of data and structure/agency). Each statement epitomises a particular research philosophy's position in relation to that particular aspect. By indicating your agreement or disagreement with each statement you can discover your similarities and differences with different aspects of each research philosophy. Following the completion of HARP, refer to the scoring key to calculate your score and interpret your answer.

HARP Statements	Strongly Agree	Agree	Slightly Agree	Slightly Disagree	Disagree	Strongly Disagree
Please indicate your agreement or disagreement with the statements below. There are no wrong answers.						
Your views on the nature of reality (ontology)						
1 Organisations are real, just like physical objects.	☐	☐	☐	☐	☐	☐
2 Events in organisations are caused by deeper, underlying mechanisms.	☐	☐	☐	☐	☐	☐
3 The social world we inhabit is a world of multiple meanings, interpretations and realities.	☐	☐	☐	☐	☐	☐
4 'Organisation' is not a solid and static thing but a flux of collective processes and practices.	☐	☐	☐	☐	☐	☐
5 'Real' aspects of organisations are those that impact on organisational practices.	☐	☐	☐	☐	☐	☐
Your views on knowledge and what constitutes acceptable knowledge (epistemology)						
6 Organisational research should provide scientific, objective, accurate and valid explanations of how the organisational world really works.	☐	☐	☐	☐	☐	☐
7 Theories and concepts never offer completely certain knowledge, but researchers can use rational thought to decide which theories and concepts are better than others.	☐	☐	☐	☐	☐	☐
8 Concepts and theories are too simplistic to capture the full richness of the world.	☐	☐	☐	☐	☐	☐

*HARP and all materials relating to HARP are copyright © 2014 A. Bristow and M.N.K. Saunders.

Progressing your research project (continued)

Heightening your Awareness of your Research Philosophy (HARP)

HARP Statements	Strongly Agree	Agree	Slightly Agree	Slightly Disagree	Disagree	Strongly Disagree
Please indicate your agreement or disagreement with the statements below. There are no wrong answers.						
9 What generally counts as 'real', 'true' and 'valid' is determined by politically dominant points of view.	❏	❏	❏	❏	❏	❏
10 Acceptable knowledge is that which enables things to be done successfully.	❏	❏	❏	❏	❏	❏
Your views on the role of values in research (axiology)						
11 Researchers' values and beliefs must be excluded from the research.	❏	❏	❏	❏	❏	❏
12 Researchers must try to be as objective and realistic as they can.	❏	❏	❏	❏	❏	❏
13 Researchers' values and beliefs are key to their interpretations of the social world.	❏	❏	❏	❏	❏	❏
14 Researchers should openly and critically discuss their own values and beliefs.	❏	❏	❏	❏	❏	❏
15 Research shapes and is shaped by what the researcher believes and doubts.	❏	❏	❏	❏	❏	❏
Your views on the purpose of research						
16 The purpose of research is to discover facts and regularities, and predict future events.	❏	❏	❏	❏	❏	❏
17 The purpose of organisational research is to offer an explanation of how and why organisations and societies are structured.	❏	❏	❏	❏	❏	❏
18 The purpose of research is to create new understandings that allow people to see the world in new ways.	❏	❏	❏	❏	❏	❏
19 The purpose of research is to examine and question the power relations that sustain conventional thinking and practices.	❏	❏	❏	❏	❏	❏
20 The purpose of research is to solve problems and improve future practice.	❏	❏	❏	❏	❏	❏
Your views on what constitutes meaningful data						
21 Things that cannot be measured have no meaning for the purposes of research.	❏	❏	❏	❏	❏	❏
22 Organisational theories and findings should be evaluated in terms of their explanatory power of the causes of organisational behaviour.	❏	❏	❏	❏	❏	❏

HARP Statements								
		Strongly Agree	Agree	Slightly Agree	Slightly Disagree	Disagree	Strongly Disagree
Please indicate your agreement or disagreement with the statements below. There are no wrong answers.							
23	To be meaningful, research must include participants' own interpretations of their experiences, as well as researchers' interpretations.	❑	❑	❑	❑	❑	❑
24	Absences and silences in the world around us are at least as important as what is prominent and obvious.	❑	❑	❑	❑	❑	❑
25	Meaning emerges out of our practical, experimental and critical engagement with the world.	❑	❑	❑	❑	❑	❑
Your views on the nature of structure and agency							
26	Human behaviour is determined by natural forces.	❑	❑	❑	❑	❑	❑
27	People's choices and actions are always limited by the social norms, rules and traditions in which they are located.	❑	❑	❑	❑	❑	❑
28	Individuals' meaning-making is always specific to their experiences, culture and history.	❑	❑	❑	❑	❑	❑
29	Structure, order and form are human constructions.	❑	❑	❑	❑	❑	❑
30	People can use routines and customs creatively to instigate innovation and change.	❑	❑	❑	❑	❑	❑

Now please complete the scoring key below.

Your answer scores

Give yourself the points as indicated above for each answer within each philosophical tradition. The different philosophies are represented by specific questions in the HARP as indicated below. Fill each philosophy table with your answer scores, then total up the numbers for each philosophy. (For your reference, in the tables below the letters in brackets indicate whether the question tests your agreement with the ontological, epistemological, axiological, purpose of research, meaningfulness of data and structure and agency aspects of research philosophy.)

Each answer you gave is given a number of points as shown in the table below:

Strongly agree	Agree	Slightly agree	Slightly disagree	Disagree	Strongly disagree
3	2	1	−1	−2	−3

Progressing your research project (continued)

Heightening your Awareness of your Research Philosophy (HARP)

Positivism: Questions 1, 6, 11, 16, 21, 26

Question	1 (ontology)	6 (epistemology)	11 (axiology)	16 (purpose)	21 (data)	26 (structure/agency)	Total
Answer score							

Critical Realism: Questions 2, 7, 12, 17, 22, 27

Question	2 (ontology)	7 (epistemology)	12 (axiology)	17 (purpose)	22 (data)	27 (structure/agency)	Total
Answer score							

Interpretivism: Questions 3, 8, 13, 18, 23, 28

Question	3 (ontology)	8 (epistemology)	13 (axiology)	18 (purpose)	23 (data)	28 (structure/agency)	Total
Answer score							

Poststructuralism/postmodernism: Questions 4, 9, 14, 19, 24, 29

Question	4 (ontology)	9 (epistemology)	14 (axiology)	19 (purpose)	24 (data)	29 (structure/agency)	Total
Answer score							

Pragmatism: Questions 5, 10, 15, 20, 25, 30

Question	5 (ontology)	10 (epistemology)	15 (axiology)	20 (purpose)	25 (data)	30 (structure/agency)	Total
Answer score							

Reflection

Now, for the first of what will almost certainly be many philosophical reflections, consider the following questions regarding how you scored yourself.

1 Do you have an outright philosophical winner? Or do you have a close contention between two or more philosophies?
2 Why do you think this is?
3 Which philosophy do you disagree with the most?
4 Why do you think this is?

Self-check answers   自测题答案

4.1   Probably the most realistic hypothesis here would be 'consumers of "Snackers" chocolate bars did not notice the difference between the current bar and its reduced weight successor'. Doubtless that is what the Snackers' manufacturer would want confirmed!

4.2   Although you can see and touch a manager, you are only seeing and touching another human being. The point is that the role of the manager is a socially constructed concept. What a manager is will differ between different national and organisational cultures and will differ over time. Indeed, the concept of the manager as we generally understand it is a relatively recent human invention, arriving at the same time as the formal organisation in the past couple of hundred years.

4.3   The researcher working in the radical humanist or structuralist paradigms may argue that it is predictable that managers would say that the purpose of organisational investigation is to develop recommendations for action to solve problems without radical change because radical change may involve changing managers! Radicalism implies root-and-branch investigation and possible change, and most of us prefer 'fine-tuning' within the framework of what exists already, particularly if change threatens our vested interests.

4.4   The question implies an either/or choice. But as you work through this chapter (and, in particular, the next on deciding your research design), you will see that life is rarely so clear-cut! Perhaps the main factor that would cause you to review the appropriateness of the deductive approach would be that the data you collected might suggest an important hypothesis, which you did not envisage when you framed your research objectives and hypotheses. This may entail going further with the data collection, perhaps by engaging in some qualitative work, which would yield further data to answer the new hypothesis.

Get ahead using resources on the companion website at:**www.pearsoned .co.uk/saunders**.

- Improve your IBM SPSS Statistics and NVivo research analysis with practice tutorials.
- Save time researching on the Internet with the Smarter Online Searching Guide.
- Test your progress using self-assessment questions.
- Follow live links to useful websites.

Chapter 5

Formulating the research design
制定研究设计

Learning outcomes   学习目标

By the end of this chapter you should be able to:

- understand the importance of your decisions when designing research and the need to achieve methodological coherence throughout your research design;
- explain the differences between quantitative, qualitative and mixed methods research designs and choose between these;
- explain the differences between exploratory, descriptive, explanatory and evaluative research;
- identify the main research strategies and choose from among these to achieve coherence throughout your research design;
- consider the implications of the time frames required for different research designs;
- consider some of the main ethical issues implied by your research design;
- understand criteria to evaluate research quality and consider these when designing your research;
- consider the constraints of your role as researcher when designing your research.

5.1 Introduction 引言

In Chapter 4 we introduced the research onion as a way of depicting the issues underlying your choice of data collection method or methods and peeled away the outer two layers – research philosophy and approach to theory development. In this chapter we uncover the next three layers: methodological choice, research strategy or strategies and choosing the time horizon for your research. As we saw in Chapter 4, the way you answer your research question will be influenced by your research philosophy and approach to theory development. Your research philosophy and approach to theory development, whether this is deliberate or by default, will subsequently influence your selections shown in the next three layers of the research onion

(Figure 5.1). These three layers can be thought of as focusing on the process of research design, which is the way you turn your research question into a research project. The key to these selections will be to achieve coherence all the way through your research design.

研究设计的选择和一致性

5.2 Choice and coherence in research design

Your **research design** is the general plan of how you will go about answering your research question(s) (the importance of clearly defining the research question cannot be overemphasised). It will contain clear objectives derived from your research question(s), specify the sources from which you intend to collect data, how you propose to collect and analyse these, and discuss

The cover photographs of recent editions of this book have indicated that the research process is like a journey – a journey along a road with you as the driver of the vehicle. Like many such journeys, there is generally a choice of roads to travel along. When you are thinking about setting out on a new journey of some distance, you will probably find a road map and look at the options to get to your destination. A number of factors may influence your decision about which route to take, including speed, time, cost and your preference between taking the shortest route or staying on the motorway network and main roads. The route you plan is likely to be as coherent as you can work out from the map in front of you given your travel criteria. As you actually undertake your journey you will find yourself interacting with the reality of your planned route. Some parts of the journey will go according to plan; other parts may not and you may need to alter your route. You may change your route because a better option presents itself as you

Travelling downriver
Source: © Jan Thornhill 2015

travel along. In many ways, designing research is like planning a journey. Formulating the most appropriate way to address your research question is similar to planning the route to your destination, your research objectives are a little like your planning criteria, the need for coherence is the same in each situation and the journey itself, like the research process, will necessarily prove to be an interactive experience.

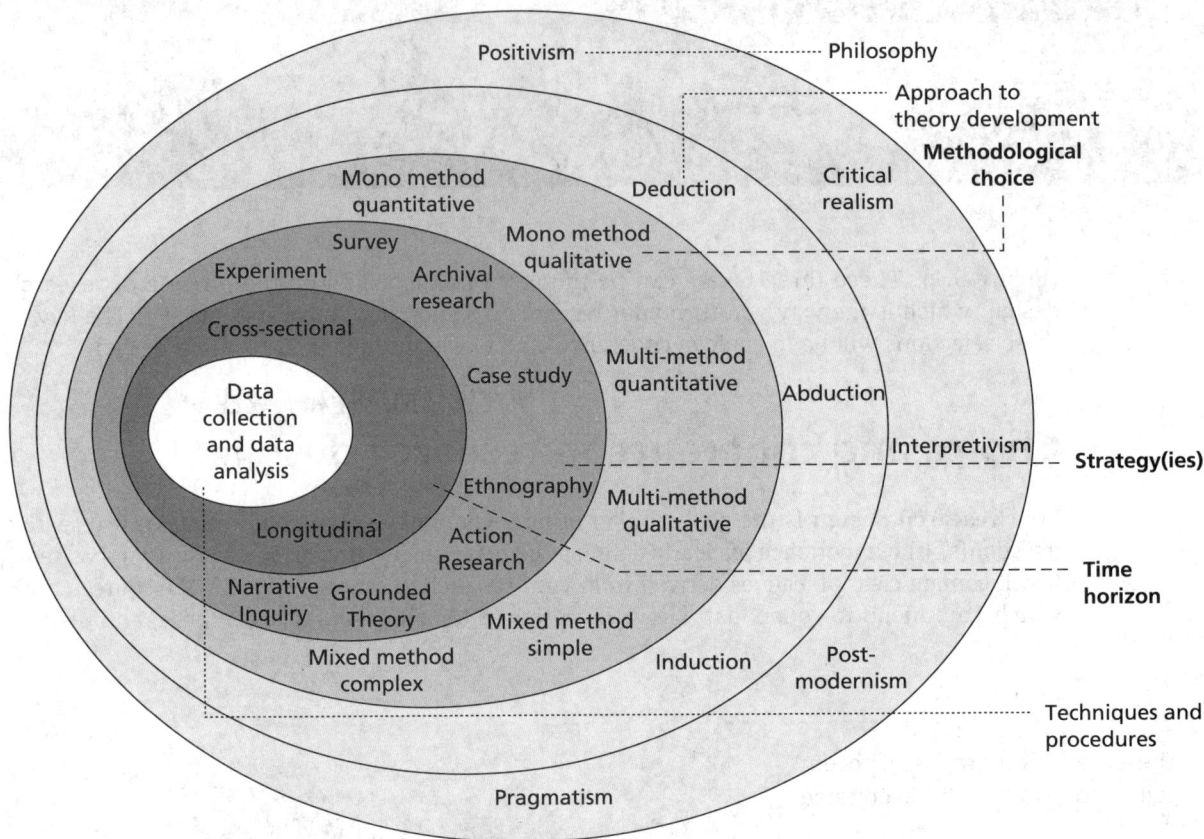

Figure 5.1 The research onion
Source: © 2015 Mark Saunders, Philip Lewis and Adrian Thornhill

ethical issues and the constraints you will inevitably encounter (e.g. access to data, time, location and money). Crucially, it should demonstrate that you have thought through the elements of your particular research design.

The first methodological choice is whether you follow a quantitative, qualitative or mixed methods research design. Each of these options is likely to call for a different mix of elements to achieve coherence in your research design. We return to consider what this involves in Section 5.3. The nature of your research project will also be either exploratory, descriptive, explanatory, evaluative or a combination of these, and we discuss the role of these in your research design in Section 5.4. Within your research design you will need to use one or more research strategies, to ensure coherence within your research project. We discuss research strategies, their fit to research philosophy and to quantitative, qualitative or mixed methods methodological choices in Section 5.5. Your methodological choice and related strategies will also influence the selection of an appropriate time horizon, and we consider this in Section 5.6. Each research design will lead to potential ethical concerns and it will be important to consider these, in order to minimise or overcome them. We briefly consider ethical issues related to research designs in Section 5.7, before discussing these in greater detail in Sections 6.5 and 6.6. It is also important to establish the quality of your research design, and we discuss the ways in which this may be considered in Section 5.8. Finally, we recognise that practical constraints will affect research design, especially the nature of your own role as researcher, and briefly consider this in Section 5.9.

These aspects of your research design are vital to understand what you wish to achieve and how you intend to do so, even if your design changes subsequently. You are likely to be assessed at this stage of your research project by your university or examining institution and your research design will need to achieve a pass standard before you are allowed to proceed. You therefore need to have a clear design with valid reasons for each of your research design decisions. Your justification for each element should be based on the nature of your research question(s) and objectives, show consistency with your research philosophy and demonstrate coherence across your research design.

It is useful at this point to recognise a distinction between design and tactics. Design is concerned with the overall plan for your research project; tactics are about the finer details of data collection and analysis – the centre of the research onion. Decisions about tactics will involve you being clear about the different quantitative and qualitative data collection techniques (e.g. questionnaires, interviews, focus groups and secondary data) and subsequent quantitative and qualitative data analysis procedures, which are discussed in later chapters.

We first outline the nature of quantitative, qualitative and mixed methods research and how these may be combined to help you to choose and design your research.

5.3 Methodological choice: the use of a quantitative, qualitative or mixed methods research design 方法选择：定量、定性或混合方法研究设计的应用

One way of differentiating quantitative research from qualitative research is to distinguish between numeric data (numbers) and non-numeric data (words, images, video clips and other similar material). In this way, 'quantitative' is often used as a synonym for any data collection technique (such as a questionnaire) or data analysis procedure (such as graphs or statistics) that generates or uses numerical data. In contrast, 'qualitative' is often used as a synonym for any data collection technique (such as an interview) or data analysis procedure (such as categorising data) that generates or uses non-numerical data. This is an important way to differentiate this methodological choice; however, this distinction is both problematic and narrow.

It is problematic because, in reality, many business and management research designs are likely to combine quantitative and qualitative elements. This may be for a number of reasons. For example, a research design may use a questionnaire but it may be necessary to ask respondents to answer some 'open' questions in their own words rather than ticking the appropriate box, or it may be necessary to conduct follow-up interviews to seek to explain findings from the questionnaire. Equally, some qualitative research data may be analysed quantitatively, or be used to inform the design of a subsequent questionnaire. In this way, quantitative and qualitative research may be viewed as two ends of a continuum, which in practice are often mixed. A research design may therefore mix methods in a number of ways, which we discuss later.

The distinction drawn earlier between quantitative research and qualitative research is also narrow. The purpose of Chapter 4 was to ask you to consider your research question through a philosophical lens. Given the way in which your philosophical assumptions inform your methodological choice, the initial distinction drawn earlier between numeric and non-numeric data appears insufficient for the purpose of designing research. From this broader perspective, we can reinterpret quantitative and qualitative methodologies through their associations to philosophical assumptions and also to research approaches and strategies. This will help you to decide how you might use these in a coherent way to address your research question. We now briefly outline some of these key associations.

Quantitative research design

Research philosophy

Quantitative research is generally associated with positivism, especially when used with predetermined and highly structured data collection techniques. However, a distinction needs to be drawn between data about the attributes of people, organisations or other things and data based on opinions, sometimes referred to as 'qualitative' numbers (Box 5.1). In this way, some survey research, while conducted quantitatively, may be seen to fit partly within an interpretivist philosophy. Quantitative research may also be used within the realist and pragmatist philosophies (see 'Mixed methods research design' later).

Approach to theory development

Quantitative research is usually associated with a deductive approach, where the focus is on using data to test theory. However, it may also incorporate an inductive approach, where data are used to develop theory.

Characteristics

Quantitative research examines relationships between variables, which are measured numerically and analysed using a range of statistical and graphical techniques. It often incorporates controls to ensure the validity of data, as in an experimental design. Because data are collected in a standard manner, it is important to ensure that questions are expressed clearly so they are understood in the same way by each participant. This methodology often uses probability sampling techniques to ensure generalisability (Section 7.2). The researcher is seen as independent from those being researched, who are usually called respondents.

A quantitative research design may use a single data collection technique, such as a questionnaire, and corresponding quantitative analytical procedure. This is known as a **mono method quantitative study** (Figures 5.1 and 5.2). A quantitative research design may also use more than one quantitative data collection technique and corresponding analytical procedure. This is known as a **multi-method quantitative study** (Figures 5.1 and 5.2). You might, for example, decide to collect quantitative data using both questionnaires and structured observation, analysing these data using statistical (quantitative) procedures. **Multi-method** is the branch of **multiple methods** research that uses more than one quantitative or qualitative method but does not mix the two (Figure 5.2).

Use of multiple methods has been advocated within business and management research (Bryman 2006) because it is likely to overcome weaknesses associated with using only a single or mono method, as well as providing scope for a richer approach to data collection, analysis and interpretation.

Box 5.1 Research in the news

Middle-aged are so downbeat about money

By Norma Cohen

The 45 to 54-year-old cohort have high but increasingly unrealistic expectations and struggle to make sense of their financial futures, reports *Norma Cohen*.

Early middle age, it seems, is the new winter of our discontent.

According to a new study from fund managers Black-Rock, people aged 45 to 54 are the most negative about their financial future and the least confident about their ability to control their finances, pay for their children's education or make the right decisions about investments.

That is not what you might expect. The young, embarking on their careers while saddled with heavy debts, and facing a struggle to get on the housing ladder, are more optimistic and in some ways better prepared. Those closest to retirement are content with their lot. But the group who appear to have the best odds of managing their way out of tough times and into a reasonable retirement are thoroughly miserable – in the UK and in other countries.

A close look at data from Britain's Office for National Statistics backs up the hunch that this group is doing fine. On average, wealth is highest among the 45 to 64-year-old age group, remains relatively high among the 65-plus age group, but is lower for households with adults aged 25 to 44 in which children or young adults live, the ONS says in its latest report on household wealth. Roughly a quarter of 45 to 54-year-olds have total household wealth of between £500,000 and £1m – and a further fifth have wealth of more than £1m. That is much higher than younger age groups – and not much lower than for over-65s.

Neither has this group suffered from unemployment; the unemployment rate for those aged 35 to 49 and those aged 50 to 64 has straddled 5 per cent against a national average of 7.7–8.0 per cent. And of the younger group, 92 per cent are participating in work. But this group is much less satisfied with its income than those aged 60 and over, although marginally happier with it than are younger groups. The ONS found they are much more likely to describe their financial situation as "quite or very difficult" than those aged over 55.

Greg Davies, head of behavioural finance at Barclays Wealth, says that the reason the 45 to 54-year-old age group might feel miserable and gloomy may not be because objectively, its finances are deteriorating. Rather, it is just a tough age to be generally.

"This is a pattern we see globally," Mr Davies says, noting that this age group appears glum in happiness surveys in many countries (as it did in the BlackRock one). "There is a U-shaped curve in happiness. It may have nothing to do with their finances."

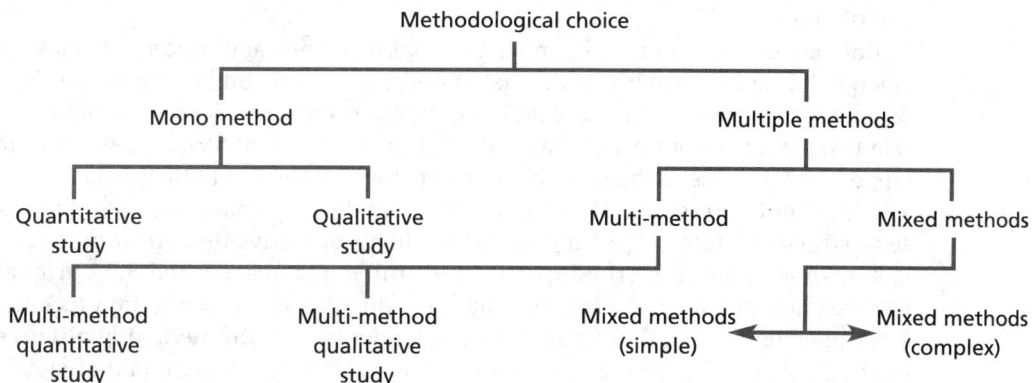

Figure 5.2 Methodological choice

Research strategies

Quantitative research is principally associated with experimental and survey research strategies, which we discuss in Section 5.5. In quantitative research, a survey research strategy is normally conducted through the use of questionnaires or structured interviews or, possibly, structured observation. Techniques associated with the use of these particular methods are considered in Chapters 9, 11 and 12.

Qualitative research design

Research philosophy

Qualitative research is often associated with an interpretive philosophy (Denzin and Lincoln 2011). It is interpretive because researchers need to make sense of the subjective and socially constructed meanings expressed about the phenomenon being studied. Such research is sometimes referred to as naturalistic since researchers need to operate within a natural setting, or research context, in order to establish trust, participation, access to meanings and in-depth understanding. Like quantitative research, qualitative research may also be used within realist and pragmatist philosophies (see 'Mixed methods research design' later).

Approach to theory development

Many varieties of qualitative research commence with an inductive approach to theory development, where a naturalistic and emergent research design is used to build theory or to develop a richer theoretical perspective than already exists in the literature. However, some qualitative research strategies start with a deductive approach, to test an existing theory using qualitative procedures (Yin 2014). In practice, much qualitative research uses an abductive approach to theory development where inductive inferences are developed and deductive ones are tested iteratively throughout the research (Section 4.4).

Characteristics

Qualitative research studies participants' meanings and the relationships between them, using a variety of data collection techniques and analytical procedures, to develop a conceptual framework and theoretical contribution. Bansal and Corley (2011) point out that while qualitative research is characterised by methodological variations, it remains vital irrespective of the method used to demonstrate methodological rigour and theoretical contribution.

Data collection is non-standardised so that questions and procedures may alter and emerge during a research process that is both naturalistic and interactive. It is likely to use non-probability sampling techniques (Section 7.2). The success of the researcher's role is dependent not only on gaining physical access to participants but also building rapport and demonstrating sensitivity to gain cognitive access to their data.

A qualitative research design may use a single data collection technique, such as semi-structured interviews, and corresponding qualitative analytical procedure. This is known as a **mono method qualitative study** (Figures 5.1 and 5.2). A qualitative research design may also use more than one qualitative data collection technique and corresponding analytical procedure. This is known as a **multi-method qualitative study** (Figures 5.1 and 5.2). You might, for example, decide to collect qualitative data using in-depth interviews and diary accounts, analysing these data using qualitative procedures. Box 5.2 provides an example of a multi-method qualitative study.

Box 5.2
Focus on student research

Multi-method qualitative study

Harry wanted to establish how new supervisors learned to do their job. In order to do this he thought it essential that he should have the clearest possible grasp of what the supervisor's job entailed.

This involved him in:

- shadowing a new supervisor for a week (qualitative data);

- interviewing a day and a night shift supervisor to establish any differences in approach (qualitative data);
- interviewing the managers to whom these two supervisors reported (qualitative data).

This gave Harry a much better grasp of the content of the supervisor's job. It also did much to enhance his credibility in the eyes of the supervisors. He was then able to draw on the valuable data he had collected to complete his main research task: interviewing new supervisors to discover how they learned to do the job. This provided further qualitative data.

Research strategies

Qualitative research is associated with a variety of strategies. While these share ontological and epistemological roots and common characteristics, each strategy has a specific emphasis and scope as well as a particular set of procedures. Some of the principal strategies used with qualitative research are: action research, case study research, ethnography, Grounded Theory and narrative research. These are discussed in Section 5.5. Some of these strategies can also be used in a quantitative research design such as a case study strategy, or used in a mixed methods research design as we now discuss. Techniques associated with the use of particular methods are considered in Chapters 9, 10 and 13.

Mixed methods research design

Research philosophy

We consider two philosophical positions that often lead to mixed methods research designs. **Mixed methods** research is the branch of multiple methods research that combines the use of quantitative and qualitative data collection techniques and analytical procedures (Figure 5.2).

In Sections 4.2 and 4.3 we discussed the philosophical position of realism and in particular that of the critical realists. They believe that while there is an external, objective reality to the world in which we live, the way in which each of us interprets and understands it will be affected by our particular social conditioning. To accommodate this realist ontology and interpretivist epistemology (Tashakkori and Teddlie 2010), researchers may, for example, use quantitative analysis of officially published data followed by qualitative research methods to explore perceptions.

Pragmatism may also be likely to influence a mixed methods research design. Pragmatists view the exclusive adoption of one philosophical position as unhelpful and choose instead to see these as either end of a continuum, allowing a choice of whichever position or mixture of positions will help them to undertake their research (Tashakkori and Teddlie 2010). For pragmatists, the nature of the research question, the research context and likely research consequences are driving forces determining the most appropriate methodological choice (Nastasi et al. 2010). Both quantitative and qualitative research are valued by pragmatists and the exact choice will be contingent on the particular nature of the research.

Approach to theory development

A mixed methods research design may use a deductive, inductive or abductive approach to theory development. For example, quantitative or qualitative research may be used to test a theoretical proposition or propositions, followed by further quantitative or qualitative research to develop a richer theoretical understanding. Theory may also be used to provide direction for the research. In this way a particular theory may be used to provide a focus for the research and to limit its scope (Tashakkori and Teddlie 2010).

Characteristics

In mixed methods research quantitative and qualitative techniques are combined in a variety of ways that range from simple, concurrent forms to more complex and sequential forms (Figure 5.2). The ways in which quantitative and qualitative research may be combined, as well as the extent to which this may occur, have led to the identification of a number of variations of mixed methods research (Creswell and Plano Clark 2011; Nastasi et al. 2010). We now briefly consider these.

Concurrent mixed methods research involves the separate use of quantitative and qualitative methods within a single phase of data collection and analysis (a **single-phase research design**) (Figure 5.3). This allows both sets of results to be interpreted together to provide a richer and more comprehensive response to the research question in comparison to the use of a mono method design. Where you collect qualitative and quantitative data in the same phase of research in order to compare how these data sets support one another, you will be using a **concurrent triangulation design**.

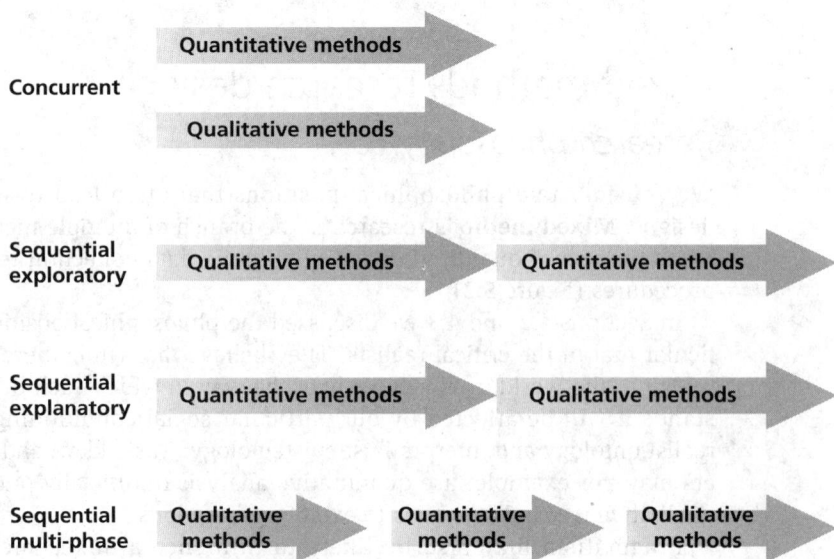

Figure 5.3 Mixed methods research designs

Using a concurrent mixed methods design should provide richer data than a mono method design and be shorter in timescale as well as more practical to undertake than a sequential mixed methods design.

Sequential mixed methods research involves more than one phase of data collection and analysis (Figure 5.3). In this design, the researcher will follow the use of one method with another in order to expand or elaborate on the initial set of findings. In a **double-phase research design** this leads to two alternative mixed methods research strategies, either a **sequential exploratory research design** (qualitative followed by quantitative) or a **sequential explanatory research design** (quantitative followed by qualitative). In a more complex, sequential, **multi-phase design**, mixed methods research will involve multiple phases of data collection and analysis (e.g. qualitative followed by quantitative, then by a further phase of qualitative) (Box 5.3).

Using a double-phase or multi-phase research design suggests a dynamic approach to the research process which recognises that mixed methods research is both interactive and iterative, where one phase subsequently informs and directs the next phase of data collection and analysis. The exact nature of this interaction and iteration in a particular research project may shape the way in which qualitative and quantitative methods are chosen and integrated at each phase of the research (Greene 2007; Nastasi et al. 2010; Ridenour and Newman 2008; Teddlie and Tashakkori 2009).

Where you mix quantitative and qualitative methods at every stage of your research (design, data collection and analysis, interpretation and presentation of the research), you will be using a **fully integrated mixed methods research** design. Where you use

Box 5.3
Focus on student research

Mixed methods research

Andreas conducted research into organisational change in an IT company, using a mixed methods research design. This was designed as a sequential mixed methods research project and consisted of four stages:

1 *Initial exploratory discussions* were held with key senior managers, which combined the purpose of helping to negotiate access, agree the scope of the project and gain essential contextual data. These data were analysed qualitatively in order to get a picture of important internal and external organisational issues.
2 *Individual in-depth interviews* were held with 28 directly employed staff (excluding contractor staff), who formed a sample representing the organisation across its departments and

throughout its grade structure. These data were also analysed qualitatively. This was to establish the issues that were important to staff, to help to inform the content of the questionnaire.
3 *A questionnaire* was designed, pilot-tested, amended and then administered to a representative sample of directly employed staff, producing a 42 per cent response rate. The quantitative data produced were analysed statistically to allow the views of employee groups to be compared for differences by age, gender, length of service, occupation and grade. The subsequent production of summary data based on these findings was particularly important to the IT company.
4 A fourth stage consisted of *presentations to groups of employees*. This allowed employees' questions to be answered with care, while continuing to ensure anonymity. It also allowed discussion to occur to clarify the content of some of the questionnaire results. Notes from these presentations were analysed quantitatively.

quantitative and qualitative methods at only one stage or particular stages of your research, you will be using a **partially integrated mixed methods research** approach (Nastasi et al. 2010; Teddlie and Tashakkori 2009, 2011).

Quantitative and qualitative methods may also be 'merged' so that qualitative data are '**quantitised**' (e.g. specific events in the data are counted as frequencies and numerically coded for statistical analysis) and quantitative data are '**qualitised**' (e.g. frequencies are turned into text, although this is extremely rare in practice). Both types of data may also be presented together on a matrix, qualitative data may be presented diagrammatically (Box 13.15) and quantitative data presented using categorisation. This approach to mixing methods may be risky, since there is a danger that the respective value of each form of data may be diluted; for example, excessively 'quantitising' qualitative data may lead to loss of its exploratory or explanatory richness.

Mixed methods research may use quantitative research and qualitative research equally or unequally (Creswell and Plano Clark 2011). In this way, the priority or weight given to either quantitative or qualitative research may vary, so that one methodology has a dominant role, while the other plays a supporting role, depending on the purpose of the research project. This prioritisation may also reflect the preferences of the researcher or the expectations of those who commission the research (such as your project tutor or the managers in an organisation).

The purpose of the research may emphasise the initial use and prioritisation of qualitative research (as in an exploratory study, where qualitative precedes quantitative) or the initial use and prioritisation of quantitative research (as in a descriptive study, before the possible of supporting qualitative research to explain particular findings further). The overall purpose of the research may also emphasise the dominance of either quantitative or qualitative research (e.g. as in a sequential project which commences with a qualitative, exploratory phase, followed by a quantitative, descriptive phase and which is completed by a further qualitative, explanatory phase). The purpose of other research projects may lead to the more equal use of quantitative and qualitative research methods. The research approach may also lead to the relative prioritisation of either quantitative or qualitative methods. In this way, an inductive approach designed to generate theoretical concepts and to build theory may lead to a greater emphasis on the use of qualitative methods.

Embedded mixed methods research is the term given to the situation where one methodology supports the other (Creswell and Plano Clark 2011). During data collection, this may occur in a number of ways. One methodology may be embedded within the other during a single means to collect data (e.g. some quantitative questions are included in an interview schedule, or some questions within a questionnaire require a qualitative response). This is known as a **concurrent embedded design**. Alternatively, a single-phase research design may use both quantitative and qualitative methods concurrently but collect these separately, one of which will be analysed to support the other. Within a double-phase, sequential research design, both quantitative and qualitative methods will be collected and analysed, one after the other, with one being used in a supporting role.

The characteristics that help to define mixed methods research highlight how quantitative and qualitative methods may be combined in a number of ways to provide you with better opportunities to answer your research question (Tashakkori and Teddlie 2010). Table 5.1 outlines a number of reasons for and advantages of using a mixed methods design. The specific nature of your mixed methods design will be related to particular reasons and advantages.

Box 5.4 summarises how mixed methods have been used in management research.

Table 5.1 Reasons for using a mixed methods design

Reason	Explanation
Initiation	Initial use of a qualitative or quantitative methodology may be used to define the nature and scope of sequential quantitative or qualitative research. May also be used to provide contextual background and to better understand the research problem (e.g. Box 5.3). May also help in the formulation or redrafting of research questions, interview questions and questionnaire items and the selection of samples, cases and participants
Facilitation	During the course of the research, one method may lead to the discovery of new insights which inform and are followed up through the use of the other method
Complementarity	Use of mixed methods may allow meanings and findings to be elaborated, enhanced, clarified, confirmed, illustrated or linked
Interpretation	One method (e.g. qualitative) may be used to help to explain relationships between variables emerging from the other (e.g. quantitative)
Generalisability	Use of mixed methods may help to establish the generalisability of a study or its relative importance. In a similar way the use of mixed methods may help to establish the credibility of a study or to produce more complete knowledge (Section 5.8)
Diversity	Use of mixed methods may allow for a greater diversity of views to inform and be reflected in the study
Problem solving	Use of an alternative method may help when the initial method reveals unexplainable results or insufficient data
Focus	One method may be used to focus on one attribute (e.g. quantitative on macro aspects), while the other method may be used to focus on another attribute (e.g. qualitative on micro aspects)
Triangulation	Mixed methods may be used in order to combine data to ascertain if the findings from one method mutually corroborate the findings from the other method (Section 5.8)
Confidence	Findings may be affected by the method used. Use of a single method will make it impossible to ascertain the nature of that effect. To seek to cancel out this 'method effect', it is advisable to use mixed methods. This should lead to greater confidence in your conclusions

Source: Developed from Bryman (2006), Greene et al. (1989), Molina-Azorin (2011) and authors' experience

Research design

As we have just discussed, different combinations of mixed methods research characteristics lead to various research designs. The principal mixed methods research designs summarised earlier in this section are: concurrent triangulation design, concurrent embedded design, sequential exploratory design, sequential explanatory design (Creswell 2009; Creswell and Plano Clark 2011) and sequential, multi-phase design. Quantitative

> ### Box 5.4
> ### Focus on management research
>
> #### Use of mixed methods in strategic management research
>
> It is interesting to note the findings of Molina-Azorin (2012), who analysed the methodologies used in articles published in the *Strategic Management Journal* from 1980 to 2006. Out of 1086 empirical articles published in this journal during this period, 165 used a mixed methods approach (15.2%). Of these, one method was used in a dominant role in just over 80 per cent (134) of these mixed methods-based articles. Quantitative methods dominated in 129 of these 134
>
> cases. A sequential research design also dominated over the use of a concurrent research design, used in 150 of these 165 articles (90%). It is interesting to speculate how the use of mixed methods research may vary in other business and management subject areas.
>
> Molina-Azorin (2012) also found that these mixed methods articles attracted more citations in subsequent publications than a comparison group of mono method-based articles. He believes this may be explained by the enhanced value of mixed methods research. The use of qualitative as well as quantitative methods may enhance theory development, allow the research context to be better understood, permit case-specific variables to be better identified and encourage the research process to produce analytical outcomes to a greater extent than might be the case with a mono method design (Molina-Azorin 2012).

data collection techniques and analysis procedures that may be used as part of mixed methods research are considered in Chapters 9, 11 and 12 and qualitative techniques and procedures that may be used as part of mixed methods research are considered in Chapters 9, 10 and 13.

5.4 Recognising the purpose of your research design 确定研究设计的目的

In Section 5.3 we referred to your research following an exploratory or explanatory purpose. Research can be designed to fulfil either an exploratory, descriptive, explanatory or evaluative purpose, or some combination of these. In Chapter 2 we encouraged you to think about your research project in terms of the question you wish to answer and your research objectives. The way in which you ask your research question will inevitably involve you in exploratory, descriptive, explanatory or evaluative research. The purpose of your research may also change over time.

In this section we discuss each purpose in more detail to help you to choose which of these is appropriate to the nature of your research project.

Exploratory studies

An **exploratory study** is a valuable means to ask open questions to discover what is happening and gain insights about a topic of interest. As we noted in Section 2.4, research questions that are exploratory are likely to begin with 'What' or 'How'. Questions that you ask during data collection to explore an issue, problem or phenomenon will also be likely to start with 'What' or 'How' (Chapter 10). An exploratory study is particularly useful if you wish to clarify your understanding of an issue, problem or phenomenon, such as if you are unsure of its precise nature. It may be that time is well spent on exploratory research, as it might show that the research is not worth pursuing!

There are a number of ways to conduct exploratory research. These include a search of the literature; interviewing 'experts' in the subject; conducting in-depth individual interviews or conducting focus group interviews. Because of their exploratory nature, these interviews are likely to be relatively unstructured and to rely on the quality of the contributions from those who participate to help guide the subsequent stage of your research (Section 10.2).

Exploratory research has the advantage that it is flexible and adaptable to change. If you are conducting exploratory research you must be willing to change your direction as a result of new data that appear and new insights that occur to you. A quotation from the travel writer V.S. Naipaul (1989: 222) illustrates this point beautifully:

> I had been concerned, at the start of my own journey, to establish some lines of enquiry, to define a theme. The approach had its difficulties. At the back of my mind was always a worry that I would come to a place and all contacts would break down . . . If you travel on a theme the theme has to develop with the travel. At the beginning your interests can be broad and scattered. But then they must be more focused; the different stages of a journey cannot simply be versions of one another. And . . . this kind of travel depended on luck. It depended on the people you met, the little illuminations you had. As with the next day's issue of fast-moving daily newspapers, the shape of the character in hand was continually being changed by accidents along the way.

Exploratory research may commence with a broad focus but this will become narrower as the research progresses.

Descriptive studies

The purpose of **descriptive research** is to gain an accurate profile of events, persons or situations. As we noted in Section 2.4, research questions that are descriptive are likely to begin with, or include, either 'Who', 'What', 'Where', 'When' or 'How'. Questions that you ask during data collection to gain a description of events, persons or situations will also be likely to start with, or include, 'Who', 'What', 'Where', 'When' or 'How' (Chapters 10 and 11). Descriptive research may be an extension of a piece of exploratory research or a forerunner to a piece of explanatory research. It is necessary to have a clear picture of the phenomenon on which you wish to collect data prior to the collection of the data. One of the earliest well-known examples of a descriptive survey is the *Domesday Book*, which described the population of England in 1085.

Often project tutors are rather wary of work that is too descriptive. There is a danger of their saying 'That's very interesting . . . but so what?' They will want you to go further and draw conclusions from the data you are describing. They will encourage you to develop the skills of evaluating data and synthesising ideas. These are higher-order skills than those of accurate description. Description in business and management research has a very clear place. However, it should be thought of as a means to an end rather than an end in itself. This means that if your research project utilises description it is likely to be a precursor to explanation. Such studies are known as **descripto-explanatory** studies.

Explanatory studies

Studies that establish causal relationships between variables may be termed **explanatory research**. As we noted in Section 2.4, research questions that seek explanatory answers are likely to begin with, or include, 'Why' or 'How'. Questions that you ask during data collection to gain an explanatory response will also be likely to start with, or include, 'Why' or 'How' (Chapters 10 and 11).

The emphasis in explanatory research is to study a situation or a problem in order to explain the relationships between variables. You may find, for example, that a cursory analysis of quantitative data on manufacturing scrap rates shows a relationship between scrap rates and the age of the machine being operated. You could go ahead and subject the data to statistical tests such as correlation (discussed in Section 12.5) in order to get a clearer view of the relationship. As an alternative example, you might collect qualitative data to explain the reasons why customers of your company rarely pay their bills according to the prescribed payment terms.

Evaluative studies

The purpose of **evaluative research** is to find out how well something works. As we noted in Section 2.4, research questions that seek to evaluate answers are likely to begin with 'How', or include 'What', in the form of 'To what extent'. Evaluative research in business and management is likely to be concerned with assessing the effectiveness of an organisational or business strategy, policy, programme, initiative or process. This may relate to any area of the organisation or business: for example, evaluating a marketing campaign, a personnel policy, a costing strategy, the delivery of a support service.

Questions that you ask during data collection to seek an evaluative understanding will be likely to start with, or include, 'What', 'How' or 'Why'. As part of your evaluative study you may also be interested to make comparisons between events, situations, groups, places or periods, so that you are interested to ask questions that include 'Which', 'When', 'Who' or 'Where' (Chapters 10 and 11). Asking such questions would help you to compare the effectiveness of, say, an advertising campaign in different locations or between different groups of consumers. In this way, evaluative research allows you assess performance and to compare this. An evaluative study may produce a theoretical contribution where emphasis is placed on understanding not only 'how effective' something is, but also 'why', and then comparing this explanation to existing theory.

Combined studies

A research study may combine more than one purpose in its design. This may be achieved by the use of mixed methods in the research design (Section 5.3), to facilitate some combination of exploratory, descriptive, explanatory or evaluative research. Alternatively a single method research design may be used in a way that provides scope to facilitate more than one purpose. Box 5.5 describes a qualitative study that used relatively unstructured interviews to facilitate collection of data that were exploratory, descriptive and explanatory.

Box 5.5
Focus on management research

Demonstrating an exploratory, descriptive and explanatory purpose in a study about workplace bullying

Jenkins and colleagues (2012) undertook an unusual study into workplace bullying which focused on the perspective of those accused of this behaviour. Their study published in the *British Journal of Management* is based on an analysis of interviews conducted with 24 managers accused of workplace bullying. They describe how many of these accused managers reported that their places of work were highly stressful, and marked by staff shortages, unclear roles, conflict and wide-ranging improper workplace behaviours.

Jenkins et al. (2012: 491) commenced their research with a stated aim and two research questions. Their research aim was 'to elicit the views, perceptions and attributions of the alleged perpetrator, helping to bridge the gap between perpetrator- and target-orientated approaches to examining workplace bullying'. Their research questions were: '(1) What behaviours have the accused bullies been accused of? Do these behaviours fit the recognised definitions of workplace bullying? (2) How do the accused bullies describe the complainants' behaviour?' They describe

their study as being exploratory, in order to seek to understand the perceptions and experiences of those accused of workplace bullying. However, the article demonstrates that the scope of their research project was not only exploratory but also descriptive and explanatory. To understand this phenomenon they used semi-structured interviews that allowed (from the perspective of an alleged perpetrator) behaviours to be described and workplace factors to be discussed. These led to explanation building for some aspects of these behaviours during the analysis of the data collected.

Jenkins et al. describe how they used an analytical approach that identified themes in their data and then examined how these related to existing theory in relevant literature. In this way, the results from their study confirmed the importance of organisational climate and workplace pressures as contributory, if not causal, factors in the incidence of workplace bullying – a relationship also identified from research on workplace bullying that focuses on the perspective of those being bullied. However, Jenkins et al. report that the results of their study may raise doubts about some accepted relationships about workplace bullying: notably that workplace bullying is necessarily downward (they report descriptions of upward bullying) and that the demarcation between being a perpetrator and a target of bullying may in some cases be ill defined.

The study demonstrates how a combination of exploratory, descriptive and explanatory research helps to generate a theoretical contribution.

选择一种研究策略或多种策略

5.5   Choosing a research strategy or strategies

The different research strategies

In this section we turn our attention to your choice of **research strategy** (Figure 5.1). In general terms, a strategy is a plan of action to achieve a goal. A research strategy may therefore be defined as a plan of how a researcher will go about answering her or his research question. It is the methodological link between your philosophy and subsequent choice of methods to collect and analyse data (Denzin and Lincoln 2011).

Different research traditions have led to a number of possible research strategies, as we outlined earlier. In Section 5.3 we outlined the research strategies that are principally linked with quantitative, qualitative and mixed methods research designs, respectively. Particular research strategies may be associated with one of the philosophies discussed in Chapter 4 and also a deductive or inductive approach; however, we also recognised in Section 5.3 that there are often open boundaries between research philosophies, research approaches and research strategies. In a similar way, a particular research strategy should not be seen as inherently superior or inferior to any other. Consequently, we believe that what is most important is not attaching labels for their own sake, or linking research elements to try to be methodologically aloof. For us, the key to your choice of research strategy or strategies is that you achieve a reasonable level of coherence throughout your research design which will enable you to answer your particular research question(s) and meet your objectives. Your choice of research strategy will therefore be guided by your research question(s) and objectives, the coherence with which these link to your philosophy, research approach and purpose, and also to more pragmatic concerns including the extent of existing knowledge, the amount of time and other resources you have available and access to potential participants and to other sources of data. Finally, it must be remembered that these strategies should not be thought of as being mutually exclusive. For example, it is quite possible to use the survey strategy within a case study, or combine a number of different strategies within mixed methods.

The first two research strategies in the list below that we consider in this section are principally or exclusively linked to a quantitative research design. The next two may involve quantitative or qualitative research, or a mixed design combining both. The final four strategies are principally or exclusively linked to a qualitative research design.

In our experience it is the choice between qualitative research strategies that is likely to cause the greatest confusion. Such confusion is often justified given the diversity of qualitative strategies (many more than those we consider), with their conflicting tensions and 'blurred genres' (Denzin and Lincoln 2011: 3). In our discussion we draw out the distinctions between these strategies to allow you to make an informed choice between qualitative strategies (as between or across quantitative and qualitative strategies). This is intended to help you avoid the vague assertion that you are 'doing qualitative research', without any further qualification! The strategies we discuss are:

- Experiment;
- Survey;
- Archival and Documentary Research;
- Case Study;
- Ethnography;
- Action Research;
- Grounded Theory;
- Narrative Inquiry.

Experiment

We start with discussion of the experiment strategy because its roots in natural science, laboratory-based research and the precision required to conduct it mean that the 'experiment' is often seen as the 'gold standard' against which the rigour of other strategies is assessed. **Experiment** is a form of research that owes much to the natural sciences, although it features strongly in psychological and social science research. The purpose of an experiment is to study the probability of a change in an **independent variable** causing a change in another, **dependent variable**. Table 5.2 provides a description of types of variable. An experiment uses predictions, known as hypotheses, rather than research questions. This is because the researcher anticipates whether or not a relationship will exist between

Table 5.2 Types of variable

Variable	Meaning
Independent (IV)	Variable that is being manipulated or changed to measure its impact on a dependent variable
Dependent (DV)	Variable that may change in response to changes in other variables; observed outcome or result from manipulation of another variable
Mediating (MV)	A variable located between the independent and dependent variables, which explains the relationship between them (IV → MV → DV)
Moderator	A new variable that is introduced which will affect the nature of the relationship between the IV and DV
Control	Additional observable and measurable variables that need to be kept constant to avoid them influencing the effect of the IV on the DV
Confounding	Extraneous but difficult to observe or measure variables that can potentially undermine the inferences drawn between the IV and DV. Need to be considered when discussing results, to avoid spurious conclusions

the variables. Two types of (opposing) hypothesis are formulated in a standard experiment: the **null hypothesis** and the **alternative hypothesis** (often referred to as the **hypothesis**). The null hypothesis predicts that there will not be a significant difference or relationship between the variables. An example of a null hypothesis might be that:

customer services training of IT telephone support staff will not lead to a significant improvement in users' satisfaction feedback.

The alternative hypothesis predicts that there may be a significant difference or relationship between the variables. An example of a (directional) alternative hypothesis might be that:

customer services training of IT telephone support staff will lead to a significant improvement in users' satisfaction feedback.

In an experiment, it is the null hypothesis that is tested statistically. Where the probability of there being no statistical difference is greater than a prescribed value (usually 0.05), the null hypothesis is accepted and the alternative hypothesis is rejected. Where the probability is less than or equal to the prescribed value (usually 0.05), this indicates that the alternative hypothesis is likely to be true. The simplest experiments are concerned with whether there is a link between two variables. More complex experiments also consider the size of the change and the relative importance of two or more independent variables. Experiments therefore tend to be used in exploratory and explanatory research to answer 'what', 'how' and 'why' questions.

Different experimental designs may be used, each with different advantages and disadvantages, particularly in relation to **control variables** and **confounding variables** (Table 5.2). Experimental designs include classical experiments, quasi-experiments and within-subject designs. In a **classical experiment**, a sample of participants is selected and then randomly assigned to either an experimental group or to the control group. In the **experimental group**, some form of planned intervention or manipulation will be tested. In the **control group**, no such intervention is made. Random assignment means each group should be similar in all aspects relevant to the research other than whether or not they are exposed to the planned intervention or manipulation. In assigning the members to the control and experimental groups at random and using a control group, you try to control (that is, remove) the possible effects of an alternative explanation to the planned intervention (manipulation) and eliminate threats to internal validity. This is because the control group is subject to exactly the same external influences as the experimental group other than the planned intervention and, consequently, this intervention is the only explanation for any changes to the dependent variable.

A **quasi-experiment** will still use an experimental group(s) and a control group, but the researcher will not randomly assign participants to each group, perhaps because participants are only available in pre-formed groups (e.g. existing work groups). Differences in participants between groups may be minimised by the use of matched pairs. **Matched pair analysis** leads to a participant in an experimental group being paired with a participant in the control group based on matching factors such as age, gender, occupation, length of service, grade etc., to try to minimise the effect of extraneous variables on the experiment's outcomes. Those factors relevant to the nature of the experiment will need to be matched.

The basic experimental procedure in classical and quasi-experiments is the same (Figure 5.4), with the exception of random assignment, and we illustrate this procedure with an example related to the introduction of a sales promotion. The dependent variable in this example, purchasing behaviour, is measured for members of both the experimental group and control group before any intervention occurs. This provides a **pre-test** measure of purchasing behaviour. A planned intervention is then made to members of the experimental group in the form of a 'buy two, get one free' promotion. In the control group, no such intervention is made. The dependent variable, purchasing behaviour, is measured after the manipulation of the independent variable (the use of the 'buy two, get one free' promotion) for both the experimental group and the control group, so that a pre-test and **post-test** comparison can be made. On the basis of this comparison, any difference between the experimental and control groups for the dependent variable (purchasing behaviour) is attributed to the intervention of the 'buy two, get one free' promotion. This experimental approach is known as a **between-subjects design**, where participants belong to either the experimental group or control group but not both. In a between-subjects design, if more than one intervention or manipulation is to be tested, a separate experimental group will be required for each test (known as **independent measures**). For example, if the experiment was designed to compare two separate interventions, such as a 'buy one, get one free' as well as the 'buy two, get one free' manipulation, two experimental groups would be required alongside the control group.

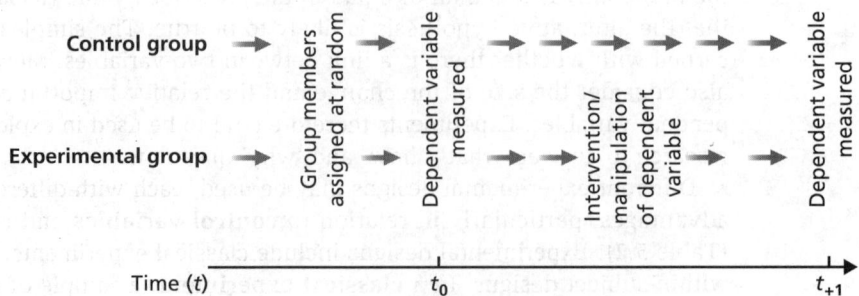

Figure 5.4 A Classical experiment strategy

In a **within-subjects design**, or within-group design, there will be only a single group, rather than a separation into an experimental group and a control group. In this approach every participant is exposed to the planned intervention or series of interventions. For this reason, this approach is known as **repeated measures**. The procedure involves a pre-intervention observation or measurement, to establish a baseline (or control for the dependent variable). This is followed by a planned intervention (independent variable) and subsequent observation and measurement (related to the dependent variable). Following the withdrawal of the intervention and a period of 'reversal', to allow a return to the baseline, a further planned intervention may be attempted followed by subsequent observation and measurement. A within-subject design may be more practical than a between-subjects design because it requires fewer participants, but it may lead to carryover effects where familiarity or fatigue with the process distorts the validity of the findings. This may lead to a counterbalanced design, where some of the participants undertake tasks in a different order to see if familiarity or fatigue affects the outcomes.

Often experiments, including those in disciplines closely associated with business and management such as organisational psychology, are conducted in laboratories rather than in the field. This means that you have greater control over aspects of the research process such as sample selection and the context within which the experiment occurs. However, while this improves the **internal validity** of the experiment, that is, the extent to which the findings can be attributed to the interventions rather than any flaws in your research design, **external validity** is likely to be more difficult to establish (we discuss issues of validity in Section 5.8). Laboratory settings, by their very nature, are unlikely to be related to the real world of organisations. As a consequence, the extent to which the findings from a laboratory experiment are able to be generalised to all organisations is likely to be lower than for a field-(organisation-) based experiment.

The feasibility of using an experimental strategy will depend on the nature of your research question. As we noted, an experiment uses predictive hypotheses rather than open research questions. It may be appropriate to turn your question into hypotheses where you wish to test for expected relationships between variables. However, most business and management research questions will be designed to inquire into the relationships between variables, rather than to test a predicted relationship. This indicates the difference between experiments and other research strategies. Within quantitative research designs, it highlights a key difference between an experimental strategy and a survey strategy.

Survey

The **survey** strategy is usually associated with a deductive research approach. It is a popular and common strategy in business and management research and is most frequently used to answer 'what', 'who', 'where', 'how much' and 'how many' questions. It therefore tends to be used for exploratory and descriptive research. Survey strategies using questionnaires are popular as they allow the collection of standardised data from a sizeable population in a highly economical way, allowing easy comparison. In addition, the survey strategy is perceived as authoritative by people in general and is comparatively easy both to explain and to understand. Every day a news bulletin, news website or newspaper reports the results of a new survey that is designed to find out how a population thinks or behaves in relation to a particular issue (Box 5.6).

Box 5.6 Focus on research in the news

Shoppers turn to web for deals

By Scheherazade Daneshkhu

Consumers with Internet access in developing countries are just as likely to search for money-saving grocery deals to beat food price inflation as those in the developed world, according to a new report.

The online survey of 29,000 shoppers in 58 countries conducted by Nielsen, the global information company, showed many similarities in behaviour no matter where the consumer lives – but also striking differences.

In the US, half of those who responded said they would stock up on sale items as a way of beating inflation compared to one-third in the Asia-Pacific region, possibly reflecting space and transport differences.

But social media plays a bigger role in developing countries. In South Africa and South Korea, 43 per cent said they would use social media to find online deals compared to 20 per cent in the US and 24 per cent in Canada.

Overall, 32 per cent of shoppers in developing countries said they would turn to the internet as a tool to beat food price inflation, only fractionally below the 33 per cent in developed economies.

Since the survey was based on respondents with online access, Nielsen said the results indicated that "consumers in developing regions actually outperformed those in developed markets for their intention to use online sources to search for deals".

FT *Source of extract:* Daneshkhu, S. and Consumer Industries Editor (2013) 'Emerging markets shoppers turn to web for deals', *Financial Times*, 13 October. Copyright The Financial Times Limited

The survey strategy allows you to collect quantitative data which you can analyse quantitatively using descriptive and inferential statistics (Sections 12.4 and 12.5). In addition, data collected using a survey strategy can be used to suggest possible reasons for particular relationships between variables and to produce models of these relationships. Using a survey strategy should give you more control over the research process and, when probability sampling is used, it is possible to generate findings that are statistically representative of the whole population at a lower cost than collecting the data for the whole population (Section 7.2). You will need to spend time ensuring that your sample is representative, designing and piloting your data collection instrument and trying to ensure a good response rate. Preparing and analysing the data will also be time consuming, even with readily available analysis software. However, it will be your time and, once you have collected your data, you will be independent. Many researchers complain that their progress is delayed by their dependence on others for information.

The data collected using a survey strategy is unlikely to be as wide ranging as those collected by other research strategies. For example, there is a limit to the number of questions that any questionnaire can contain if the goodwill of the respondent is not to be presumed on too much. Despite this, perhaps the biggest drawback with using a questionnaire as part of a survey strategy is (as emphasised in Section 11.2) the capacity to do it badly!

The questionnaire, however, is not the only data collection technique that belongs to the survey strategy. Structured observation, of the type most frequently associated with organisation and methods (O&M) research, and structured interviews, where standard-ised questions are asked of all interviewees, also often fall into this strategy. Structured observation techniques are discussed in Section 9.3 and structured interviews in Section 11.2.

Archival and documentary research

The digitalisation of data and the creation of online archives have increased the scope for you to use an archival or documentary research strategy. Because of the Internet and the digitalisation of university-based, governmental, organisational and media docu-ments and other data, it is now possible to access such sources from around the world. This potentially provides you with considerable scope to design a research project that capitalises on a wide range of available data sources. There are limitations in attempting to use this strategy and we briefly consider these after outlining types of documentary sources and discussing their attributes.

It is difficult to describe adequately the range of archival and documentary sources potentially available. Lee (2012: 391) suggests that 'a document is a durable repository for textual, visual and audio representations'. This illustrates the wide range of sources encompassed by this definition. Categories of textual documents include:

- communications between individuals or within groups such as email, letters, social media and blog postings;
- individual records such as diaries, electronic calendars and notes;
- organisational sources such as administrative records, agendas and minutes of meet-ings, agreements, contracts, memos, personnel records, plans, policy statements, press releases, reports and strategy documents;
- government sources such as publications, reports and national statistics;
- media sources including printed and online articles and other data.

Visual and audio sources include advertising posters, artefacts, audio recordings, audio-visual corporate communications, digital recordings, DVDs, films, photographs, products, promotional advertisements and recordings, television and radio programmes and web images.

Many types of archival and documentary sources may be accessed online. Section 8.2 and in particular Table 8.1 provide examples of online data archives and gateways to governmental websites. Organisations' websites may provide access to certain types of documentary sources such as annual reports, company results, financial highlights, press releases and regulatory news. Media websites also provide facilities to search for articles about organisations and business and management topics. As we discuss in Sections 6.2 to 6.4, other internal organisational documents are less likely to be available online and you would need to contact an organisation to seek access, providing these were not considered to be commercially sensitive. Some documents created by individuals may be accessible through data archives (e.g. a collection of papers of a notable business person) but use of recently created materials will probably require you to contact a potential participant to negotiate access, where these are not considered to be private or commercially sensitive (Sections 6.2–6.4).

Documents used for research are considered secondary sources because they were originally created for a different purpose (see the earlier bullet-point list). Research-ers using an archival or documentary research strategy therefore need to be sensitive to the fact that the documents they use were not originally created for a research purpose. We discuss the advantages and disadvantages of using secondary source material in Section 8.4. However, we would like to stress the difference between a secondary data analysis that re-analyses data originally collected for a research purpose and using secondary sources in an archival or documentary research strategy. Where original research data are re-analysed for a different purpose in a secondary data analysis, you should assess the quality of the original research data – i.e. were these data drawn from a representative sample; was the original research designed to overcome threats to reliability and validity (Section 5.9). In contrast, where documents are used as secondary sources in an archival or documentary research strategy, their original purpose had nothing to do with research and so as a researcher using this strategy, you will need to be sensitive to the nature and original purpose of the documents you select, the way in which you analyse them and the generalisations that you can draw (Hakim 2000).

While great care needs to be taken when using documents for research purposes, they potentially offer a rich source of data for you to analyse. The data they provide may be quantitative, qualitative or both. Using qualitative documents may allow you to generate a rich or 'thick' description of key events, the context within which these events occurred, the roles of the actors involved, the influence of external influences such as economic or commercial pressures, as well as outcomes. Your scope to achieve such an outcome will of course depend on the nature of your research question and whether you find suitable documents. Documents may, for example, allow you to analyse critical incidents or decision-making processes, or evaluate different policy positions or strategies. Using quantitative data in documents such as annual or financial reports will provide you with access to actual data that may, for example, facilitate comparisons between organisations or across reporting periods. Prior (2007) points out that documents can also be analysed to reveal:

- not only what they contain but what is omitted;
- which facts are used and why these might be emphasised while others are not used;
- how they are used in an organisation and how they are circulated and to whom.

Archival or documentary research may be an effective and efficient strategy to use but this will depend on its appropriateness to your research question and being able to gain access to sufficient numbers of suitable documents. You may be refused access to use documents, or find that some data are restricted for confidentiality reasons. You may also find that the documents you locate vary in quality, especially where they come from different sources. Some data may be missing or not presented in a consistent way, making comparison difficult or potentially leaving gaps in your analysis. Using an archival research strategy may therefore necessitate you establishing what documents are available and designing your research to make the most of these. This may mean combining this research strategy with another. This could be undertaken in a number of ways, so that, for example, you conduct documentary research alongside a Grounded Theory strategy based on qualitative interviews and use a similar procedure to analyse both sets of data. Another example could involve using documentary research within a case study strategy.

Case study

A **case study** is an in-depth inquiry into a topic or phenomenon within its real-life setting (Yin 2014). The 'case' in case study research may refer to a person (e.g. a manager), a group (e.g. a work team), an organisation (e.g. a business), an association (e.g. a joint venture), a change process (e.g. restructuring a company), an event (e.g. an annual general meeting) as well as many other types of case subject. Choosing the case to be studied and determining the boundaries of the study is a key factor in defining a case study (Flyvberg 2011). Once defined, case study research sets out to understand the dynamics of the topic being studied within its setting or context (Eisenhardt 1989; Eisenhardt and Graebner 2007). 'Understanding the dynamics of the topic' refers to the interactions between the subject of the case and its context.

The study of a case within its real-life setting or context helps to distinguish this research strategy from others. In an experimental strategy, outlined earlier, contextual variables are highly controlled as they are seen as a potential threat to the validity of the results. In a survey strategy, research is undertaken in a real-life setting, but the ability to understand the impact of this context is limited by the number of variables for which data can be collected. In contrast, case study research is often used when the boundaries between the phenomenon being studied and the context within which it is being studied are not always apparent (Yin 2014). Understanding context is fundamental to case study research.

A case study strategy has the capacity to generate insights from intensive and in-depth research into the study of a phenomenon in its real-life context, leading to rich, empirical descriptions and the development of theory (Dubois and Gadde 2002; Eisenhardt 1989; Eisenhardt and Graebner 2007; Ridder et al. 2014; Yin 2014). Dubois and Gadde (2002: 554) make the point that, 'the interaction between a phenomenon and its context is best understood through in-depth case studies'. An in-depth inquiry can be designed to identify what is happening and why, and perhaps to understand the effects of the situation and implications for action. To achieve such insights, case study research draws on quantitative or qualitative research and frequently uses a mixed methods approach, to understand fully the dynamics of the case.

Flyvberg (2011) refers to the paradox of case study research: case studies have been widely used over a long period, including in business and management, but have been criticised by some as a research strategy because of 'misunderstandings' about their ability to produce generalisable, reliable and theoretical contributions to knowledge. This is largely based on positivist criticisms of using small samples and more generally about using interpretive, qualitative research. This type of criticism has been countered in many works (e.g. Buchanan 2012; Flyvberg 2011) and is generally losing favour as the value of qualitative and mixed methods research is being recognised much more widely (e.g. Bansal and Corley 2011; Denzin and Lincoln 2011). We return to consider how the quality of both quantitative and qualitative research may be recognised in Section 5.8.

The long and widespread use of case studies has resulted in them being designed in different ways and for different purposes. They have been used by 'positivist' as well as 'interpretivist' researchers; deductively as well as inductively; and for descriptive, exploratory or explanatory purposes. Some positivist researchers have advocated using case studies inductively to build theory and develop theoretical hypotheses, which can be tested subsequently. In this way, the use of the case study is advocated in the early, exploratory stage of research as a complement to deductive research (Eisenhardt 1989; Eisenhardt and Graebner 2007). This approach has been called 'indicative case study research', designed to reveal 'specific attributes' rather than rich description (Ridder et al. 2014: 374). Yin (2014) recognises that case studies may be used not only for exploratory but also descriptive and explanatory purposes. An explanatory case study is likely to use a deductive approach, using theoretical propositions to test their applicability in the case study, to build and verify an explanation (Chapter 13). Interpretivist researchers are more interested, at least initially, to develop richly detailed and nuanced descriptions of their case study research (Ridder et al. 2014). For some interpretivists, making comparisons with existing theory is unnecessary. Stake (2005) says that many interpretivist researchers prefer to describe their case study in ample detail, allowing readers to make their own links to existing theory. Other interpretivist researchers will work inductively, analysing their data, identifying themes and patterns in these data, and at some point locating this in existing literature in order to refine, extend or generate theory (Ridder et al. 2014; Chapter 13). Where you work as an interpretivist, it is highly likely that you will need to follow this second route and provide a clear link to theory!

The existence of these various approaches to case study research potentially provides you with opportunities to use this strategy, as well as challenges when using it. Where you are considering using a case study strategy, you may be able to find earlier work in the social sciences if not specifically in business and management, which provides guidance in an approach that logically fits your research idea and question (deductive or inductive, exploratory or explanatory etc.). To achieve an in-depth inquiry and a rich, detailed flow of analytical data, a case study strategy can offer you the opportunity to use a mixed methods research design (although case studies may rely on a mono or multi-method choice). Case study research may beneficially use some combination of archival records and documentation (discussed earlier and in Chapter 8), different forms of observation (Chapter 9), ethnography (discussed later in this section), interviews and focus groups (Chapter 10), questionnaires (Chapter 11), reflection and the use of research diaries and other research aids (Chapters 1 and 13). Case study research is likely to prove to be challenging because of its intensive and in-depth nature and your need to be able to identify, define and gain access to a case study setting.

You will also need to identify the nature of your case study strategy and we conclude our discussion of this by considering ways in which your case study research may be structured. Yin (2014) distinguishes between four case study strategies based upon two discrete dimensions:

- single case versus multiple cases;
- holistic case versus embedded case.

A single case is often used where it represents a critical case or, alternatively, an extreme or unique case. Conversely, a single case may be selected purposively because it is typical or because it provides you with an opportunity to observe and analyse a phenomenon that few have considered before (Section 7.3). Inevitably, an important aspect of using a single case is defining the actual case. For many part-time students this is the organisation for which they work (Box 5.7). The key here will be to ensure that this approach is suitable for the nature of your research question and objectives.

Box 5.7
Focus on student research

Using a single organisation as a case study

Simon was interested in discovering how colleagues within his organisation were using a recently introduced financial costing model in their day-to-day work. In discussion with his project tutor, he highlighted that he was interested in finding out how it was actually being used in his organisation as a whole, as well as seeing if the use of the financial costing model differed between senior managers, departmental managers and front-line operatives. Simon's project tutor suggested that he adopt a case study strategy, using his organisation as a single case within which the senior managers', departmental managers' and front-line operatives' groups were embedded cases. He also highlighted that, given the different numbers of people in each of the embedded cases, Simon would be likely to need to use different data collection techniques with each.

A case study strategy can also incorporate multiple cases, that is, more than one case. The rationale for using multiple cases focuses on whether findings can be replicated across cases. Cases will be carefully chosen on the basis that similar results are predicted to be produced from each one. Where this is realised, Yin (2014) terms this **literal replication**. Another set of cases may be chosen where a contextual factor is deliberately different. The impact of this difference on the anticipated findings is predicted by the researcher. Where this predicted variation is realised, Yin terms this a **theoretical replication**. Yin (2014) proposes that a multiple case study strategy may combine a small number of cases chosen to predict literal replication and a second small number chosen to predict theoretical replication. Where all of the findings from these cases are as predicted, this would clearly produce very strong support for the theoretical propositions on which these predictions were based. This particular approach to case study strategy therefore commences deductively, based on theoretical propositions and theory testing, before possibly incorporating an inductive or abductive approach (Section 4.4). Where the findings are in some way contrary to the predictions in the theoretical propositions being tested, it would be necessary to reframe these propositions and choose another set of cases to test them.

Yin's second dimension, holistic versus embedded, refers to the unit of analysis. For example, you may have chosen to use an organisation in which you have been employed or are currently employed as your case. If your research is concerned only with the organisation as a whole then you are treating the organisation as a holistic case study. Conversely, even if you are only researching within a single organisation, you may wish to examine a number of logical sub-units within the organisation, such as departments or work groups. Your case will inevitably involve more than one unit of analysis and, whichever way you select these units, would be called an embedded case study (Box 5.7).

As a student you are likely to find a single case study strategy to be more manageable. Alternatively, you may be able to develop a research design based on two to three cases, where you seek to achieve a literal replication. However, as we have indicated earlier, choosing between a single or multiple case study is not simply related to producing more evidence. While a multiple case study is likely to produce more evidence, the purpose of each approach is different. A single case study approach is chosen because of the nature of the case (i.e. because it is a critical, unique or typical case etc.). A multiple case study approach is chosen to allow replication. Where you are interested in using this strategy, you will therefore need to ensure that the approach chosen is suitable for the nature of your research question and objectives.

Ethnography

Ethnography is used to study the culture or social world of a group. Ethnography literally means a written account of a people or ethnic group. It is the earliest qualitative research strategy, with its origins in colonial anthropology. From the 1700s to the early 1900s, ethnography was developed to study cultures in so-called 'primitive' societies that had been brought under the rule of a colonial power, to facilitate imperialist control and administration. Early anthropologists treated those among whom they lived and conducted their fieldwork as subjects and approached their ethnography in a detached way, believing that they were using a scientific approach, reminiscent of a positivism, to produce monographs that were meant to be accurate and timeless accounts of different cultures (Denzin and Lincoln 2005; Tedlock 2005). From the 1920s the use of ethnography changed through the work of the Chicago School (University of Chicago), which used ethnographic methods to study social and urban problems within cultural groups in the

USA. A seminal example of this work is Whyte's 'Street Corner Society' published in 1943, which examined the lives of street gangs in Boston. This approach to ethnography involved researchers living among those whom they studied, to observe and talk to them in order to produce detailed cultural accounts of their shared beliefs, behaviours, interactions, language, rituals and the events that shaped their lives (Cunliffe 2010). This use of ethnography adopted a more interpretive and naturalistic focus by using the language of those being studied in writing up cultural accounts. However, the researcher remained the arbiter of how to tell the story and what to include, leading many to question how the socialisation and values of this person might affect the account being written (Geertz 1988).

This problem of 'representation' (Denzin and Lincoln 2011) meant that ethnography, as well as qualitative research more generally, was still in a fluid developmental state. Researchers developed a 'bewildering array' (Cunliffe 2010: 230) of qualitative research strategies in the second half of the twentieth century, associated with a great deal of 'blurring' across these strategies (Denzin and Lincoln 2011). We go on to discuss some of these new strategies (action research, grounded theory and narrative inquiry) in this section. As we shall see, these other strategies were designed for a different research focus to that of ethnography. Ethnographers study people in groups, who interact with one another and share the same space, whether this is at street level, within a work group, in an organisation or within a society. Conflict about how best to achieve this focus led to a range of ethnographic strategies of which Cunliffe (2010) outlines three: Realist Ethnography, Impressionist or Interpretive Ethnography and Critical Ethnography.

Realist Ethnography is the closest to the ethnographic strategy described earlier. The realist ethnographer believes in objectivity, factual reporting and identifying 'true' meanings. She or he will report the situation observed through facts or data about structures and processes, practices and customs, routines and norms, artefacts and symbols. Such reporting is likely to use standardised categories that produce quantitative data from observations. The realist ethnographer will write up her or his account in the third person, portraying their role as the impersonal reporter of facts. This account will present a detailed contextual background and the nature of the cultural interactions observed, and identify patterns of behaviour and social processes. It will use edited quotations in a dispassionate way without personal bias or seeking to act as an agent for change. The realist ethnographer's final written account is his or her representation of what he or she has observed and heard.

In contrast, **Interpretive Ethnography** places much greater stress on subjective impressions than on objectivity. The interpretive ethnographer believes in the likelihood of multiple meanings rather than being able to identify a single, true meaning. Multiple meanings will be located in the socially constructed interpretations of the different participants. This suggests a more pluralistic approach, in which the interpretive ethnographer focuses on understanding meanings, with those being observed treated as participants rather than subjects. This requires an ethnographic researcher to engage in continuous reflexivity to try to ensure reliability and validity in this research process (Delamont 2007). The research report will reflect the participation of both the ethnographer (writing in the first person, editing herself into the text, rather than out of it) and those being observed, through devices such as personalisation, use of dialogue and quotations, dramatisation and presentation of different perspectives as well as contextualisation, orderly and progressive description, factual reporting, analysis and evaluation.

Critical Ethnography has a radical purpose, designed to explore and explain the impact of power, privilege and authority on those who are subject to these influences or marginalised by them. You may therefore ask if it can have any appeal to business and management research that is dependent on achieving organisational access. Critical ethnographers often adopt an advocacy role in their work to try to bring about change. You may adopt a constrained or bounded version of Critical Ethnography to explore the impact of a problematic issue within an organisation or work group with a view to advocating internal or external change. Such an issue might be concerned with strategy, decision-making procedures, regulation, governance, organisational treatment, reward and promotion, communication and involvement and so forth.

We have partly presented our discussion of ethnography as a developmental account because it would be misleading to suggest that ideas about this strategy are unified. While ethnography is a demanding strategy to use because you would need to develop some grounding in this approach and because of the time scale and intensity involved, it may be relevant to you. If you are currently working in an organisation, there may be scope to undertake participant observation of your workgroup or another group in the organisation (Chapter 9). Alternatively, where you have recently undertaken a work placement, you will be familiar with the context and complexity of this workplace and you may be able to negotiate access based on your credibility to undertake an ethnographic study related to a work group.

Ethnography is relevant for modern organisations. For example, in market research ethnography is a useful technique when companies wish to gain an in-depth understanding of their markets and the experiences of their consumers (Cayla and Arnould 2013; IJMR 2007) (Box 5.8). If you are interested in undertaking your research in the field of marketing, the use of an ethnographic research strategy may be relevant to you. Likewise, use of this research strategy may well be relevant in other business and management subject areas.

Being successful with this strategy is likely to include making sure that the scale or scope of your proposed ethnographic research project is achievable. This will relate to your research question and objectives, which you should discuss with your project tutor. When undertaking 'fieldwork' you will need to make detailed notes of everything you observe and spend as much time as you can reflecting on what you have observed. You will also need to make additional notes to elaborate on these and supplement the process of observation by conducting informal discussions and interviews to explore what you have observed, and collect any documentation that supports your data collection (Delamont 2007). This should help you to collect a sufficient set of data to analyse to answer your research question and fulfil your objectives.

Where an ethnographic strategy is appropriate to you and proves to be feasible (Sections 6.2–6.4), you will need to consider which ethnographic approach relates to the nature of your research question. You should then be in position to build trust and commence fieldwork to be able to undertake this approach successfully.

Action Research

Lewin first used the term **Action Research** in 1946. It has been interpreted subsequently by management researchers in a variety of ways, but a number of common and related themes have been identified within the literature. In essence, Action Research is an emergent and iterative process of inquiry that is designed to develop solutions to real organisational problems through a participative and collaborative approach, which uses different forms of knowledge, and which will have implications for participants and the organisation beyond the research project (Coghlan 2011; Coghlan and Brannick 2014). Our definition identifies five themes, which we briefly consider in the following order: purpose, process, participation, knowledge and implications.

Box 5.8
Focus on management research

How companies use ethnographic stories in their market research and market learning

Cayla and Arnould (2013) explore how companies use a combination of ethnographic investigation and narrative presentation in their market research, in an article published in the *Journal of Marketing*.

Cayla and Arnould conducted semi-structured interviews with 35 participants. These participants worked either as managers in companies who commissioned ethnographic market research, or as corporate ethnographers providing this service. Some of these ethnographic researchers were directly employed by a commissioning company whereas others were external consultants. The aim of Cayla and Arnould's research was to understand how companies use ethnography in strategic marketing decision making. They developed four research questions and interview themes. (1) How do companies use ethnography in marketing decision making? (2) What is the scope of ethnography's application? (3) What are the benefits of using ethnography? (4) What are the challenges of using ethnography, including ethical ones?

While quantitative research and analysis generates broad generalisations, the use of corporate ethnography was found to be effective in understanding the detailed nature and complexity of human behaviour in relation to perceptions about products, purchasing decisions, use of products and so forth. Ethnographic research involves corporate ethnographers getting to know consumers by spending time with them in their homes and in their cars, talking and listening to them,

and noting their conversations, stories and reflections to understand how they feel about and use the product(s) being researched. The ethnographers who participated in Cayla and Arnould's study undertook ethnographic investigations into a range of products including alcoholic drinks, consumer goods, mobile phones, electronic devices, cars, banking services and health products. Cayla and Arnould found that visually recording these observations was a critical part of the corporate ethnographic research process. The use of video-recording allows corporate ethnographers to record and edit their observations of consumers into stories that provide a powerful way of presenting a coherent and insightful account of consumer experiences. Cayla and Arnould refer to these accounts as ethnographic stories, helping corporate ethnographers make sense of reality and construct meaning.

They discuss a number of advantages of using a narrative form to present the key points from corporate ethnographic research. Creating a story from the pre-edited observations of a consumer allows that consumer's experiences to be sequenced and structured around a revelatory incident that incorporates sufficient detail and emotional content to make the resulting account meaningful for the company managers who commissioned the research. Cayla and Arnould emphasise how using this narrative approach has the potential to allow strategic marketing decision-makers to better understand their company's product market; better understand their company's consumers and how they relate to the company's products; and to revise and develop their marketing strategies.

Cayla and Arnould's article demonstrates how combining ethnographic investigation and narrative presentation forms a powerful strategy to stimulate managerial action. Ethnographic stories facilitate market learning because of the way they illuminate consumer behaviour and provide memorable accounts of their experiences that point to the potential for managerial action.

The purpose of an Action Research strategy is to promote organisational learning to produce practical outcomes through identifying issues, planning action, taking action and evaluating action. Coghlan and Brannick (2014: 4) state that Action Research is about 'research in action rather than research about action'. This is because Action Research focuses on 'addressing worthwhile practical purposes' (Reason 2006: 188) and resolving real organisational issues (Shani and Pasmore 1985).

The process of Action Research is both emergent and iterative. An Action Research strategy commences within a specific context and with a research question but because it works through several stages or iterations the focus of the question may change as the research develops. Each stage of the research involves a process of diagnosing or constructing issues, planning action, taking action and evaluating action (Figure 5.5). Diagnosing or constructing issues, sometimes referred to as fact finding and analysis, is undertaken to enable action planning and a decision about the actions to be taken. These are then taken and the actions evaluated (cycle 1). This evaluation provides a direction and focus for the next stage of diagnosing or constructing issues, planning action, taking action and evaluating action (cycle 2), demonstrating the iterative nature of the process. Subsequent cycles (cycle 3 and possibly beyond) involve further diagnosing or constructing of issues, taking into account previous evaluations, planning further actions, taking these actions and evaluating them. In this way, Action Research differs from other research strategies because of its explicit focus on action related to multiple stages, to explore and evaluate solutions to organisational issues and to promote change within the organisation.

Participation is a critical component of Action Research. Greenwood and Levin (2007) emphasise that Action Research is a social process in which an action researcher works with members in an organisation, as a facilitator and teacher, to

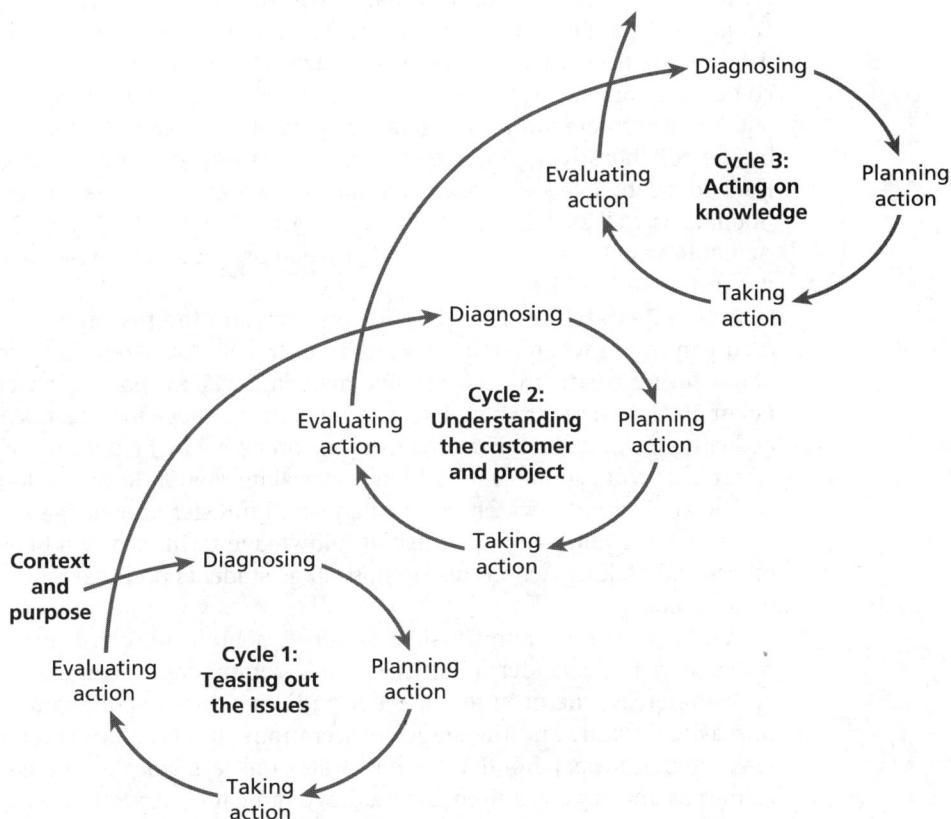

Figure 5.5 The three cycles of the Action Research spiral

improve the situation for these participants and their organisation. For Greenwood and Levin, a process can only be called Action Research if research, action and participation are all present. Participation by organisational members may take a number of forms. Firstly, organisational members need to cooperate with the researcher to allow their existing work practices to be studied. The process of Action Research then requires participation in the form of collaboration through its iterative cycles (as we described earlier) to facilitate the improvement of organisational practices. Collaboration means building a democratic approach to communication and decision making when constructing, planning, taking and evaluating each Action Research stage or cycle. The researcher passes on her or his skills and capabilities to participants so that they effectively become co-researchers in the Action Research process. Without such participation, this approach simply would not be viable, although creating such participation is likely to be difficult in practice and to meet with resistance at various levels (Reason 2006).

How then may this form of participation be developed? Eden and Huxham (1996: 75) argue that the participation of organisational members results from their involvement in 'a matter which is of genuine concern to them'. Schein (1999) emphasises that members of an organisation are more likely to implement change they have helped to create. Once the members of an organisation have identified a need for change and have widely shared this need, it becomes difficult to ignore, and the pressure for change comes from within the organisation. In this way, an Action Research strategy combines both data gathering and the facilitation of change.

The nature of Action Research means that it will also be able to incorporate different forms of knowledge. Action Research will not only be informed by abstract theoretical knowledge, known as propositional knowledge, but also by participants' everyday lived experiences (their experiential knowledge) and knowing-in-action (knowledge that comes from practical application) (Reason 2006). These forms of knowledge will inform and be incorporated into each stage or cycle of the Action Research process, encouraged by the collaborative approach that underpins this strategy. Incorporating these forms leads to 'actionable knowledge' that has the potential to be useful to organisational practitioners as well as being academically robust (Coghlan 2011: 79). Coghlan believes that Action Research not only affects 'what we know' but emphasises understanding of 'how we know'.

Action Research also has implications beyond the research project. Participants in an organisation where action research takes place are likely to have their expectations about future treatment and involvement in decision making raised (Greenwood and Levin 2007). There are also likely to be consequences for organisational development and culture change. Implications from the process may be used to inform other contexts. Academics will use the results from undertaking Action Research to develop theory that can be applied more widely. Consultants will transfer knowledge gained to inform their work in other contexts. Such use of knowledge to inform, we believe, also applies to others undertaking Action Research, such as students undertaking research in their own organisations.

Where you think about using Action Research there will be a number of practical concerns to consider. Identifying an accommodating context, the emergent nature of this strategy, the need to engender participation and collaboration, the researcher's role as facilitator, and the stages or iterations involved are some of the reasons that make Action Research a demanding strategy in terms of the intensity involved and the resources and time required. As we have indicated, Action Research can be suited to part-time students who undertake research in their own organisation. The longitudinal nature of this strategy means that it is more appropriate for medium- or long-term research projects rather than short-term ones. There is the related issue of deciding how many Action Research cycles are sufficient. Where these practical as well as political concerns have been properly anticipated and evaluated in terms of a feasible design, Action Research has the potential to offer a worthwhile and rich experience for those involved.

Grounded Theory

'**Grounded theory**' can be used to refer to a methodological approach, a method of inquiry and the result of a research process (Bryant and Charmaz 2007; Charmaz 2011; Corbin and Strauss 2008). 'Grounded theory methodology' refers to the researcher's choice of this strategy as a way to conduct research. '**Grounded theory method**' refers to the data collection techniques and analytic procedures that it uses (discussed in Chapter 13). 'Grounded theory' may be used loosely to incorporate methodology and method but more specifically it refers to a theory that is grounded in or developed inductively from a set of data. In this section we refer to 'Grounded Theory' (i.e. as a proper noun), to indicate its use as a research strategy and to distinguish this from 'a grounded theory' (no capital letters).

Grounded Theory was developed by Glaser and Strauss (1967) as a response to the 'extreme positivism' of much social research at that time (Suddaby 2006: 633). They disputed the view that social research should use a paradigm based on a premise that theory will reveal a pre-existing reality. In positivism, reality is seen as existing independently and externally (to human cognition). While positivism is suited to research in the natural sciences, they believed that social research should use a different philosophy. By adopting interpretivism in social research, 'reality' is seen as being socially constructed through the meanings that social actors ascribe to their experiences. Grounded Theory was therefore developed as a process to analyse, interpret and explain the meanings that social actors construct to make sense of their everyday experiences in specific situations (Charmaz 2006; Glaser and Strauss 1967; Suddaby 2006).

Grounded Theory is used to develop theoretical explanations of social interactions and processes in a wide range of contexts, including business and management. As much of business and management is about people's behaviours, for example consumers' or employees', a Grounded Theory strategy can be used to explore a wide range of business and management issues. As the title of Glaser and Strauss's (1967) book *The Discovery of Grounded Theory* indicates, the aim is to 'discover' or generate theory grounded in the data produced from the accounts of social actors.

We now briefly outline the key elements of Grounded Theory to enable you to assess whether it may be appropriate for the nature of your proposed research project, before evaluating its use in practice. Grounded Theory provides a systematic approach to collect and analyse qualitative data. Its use is often well suited to the nature of qualitative research. Whereas in quantitative research it is usual to collect a complete set of data and then analyse these, in qualitative data it is often useful to analyse data as you collect them (e.g. you conduct an interview and analyse it before conducting the next one). Grounded Theory is designed to allow you to achieve this. In this way, Grounded Theory provides you with a systematic and emergent strategy to undertake qualitative research.

Grounded Theory is usually referred to as taking an inductive approach, although, as we discuss later, it may be more appropriate to think of it as abductive, moving between induction and deduction (Charmaz 2011; Strauss and Corbin 1998; Suddaby 2006). The researcher collects and analyses data simultaneously, developing analytical codes as these emerge from the data in order to reorganise (fragment) these data into categories. In the Grounded Theory strategy of Strauss and Corbin (1998) there are three coding stages: the reorganisation of data into categories is called **open coding**, the process of recognising relationships between categories is referred to as **axial coding** and the integration of categories to produce a theory is labelled **selective coding**. Charmaz (2006) simplifies this to two principal stages: **initial coding** and **focused coding**, supported by sufficient stages of sampling (Section 13.7). More recently, Corbin has altered the approach in Corbin and Strauss (2008), with axial coding being combined within open coding and selective coding simply becoming 'integration'. We expand on analytical coding in some detail in Section 13.9; needless to say here that coding is a key element of Grounded Theory.

Underpinning coding is the process of **constant comparison**. Each item of data collected is compared with others, as well as against the codes being used to categorise data. This is to check for similarities and differences, to promote consistency when coding data and to aid the process of analysis. Where appropriate, new codes are created and existing codes reanalysed as new data are collected. Constant comparison promotes the higher levels of analytical coding we referred to earlier because it involves moving between inductive and deductive thinking. As the researcher codes data into categories, a relationship may begin to suggest itself between specific codes (here, the researcher is using inductive thinking because she or he will be linking specific codes to form a general proposition). This emerging interpretation will need to be 'tested' through collecting data from new cases (here, the researcher will use deductive thinking to 'test' this abstract generalisation back to a new set of specific cases, to see if it stands up as an explanatory relationship to form a higher-level code) (Strauss and Corbin 1998). The process of gaining insights to create new conceptual possibilities which are then examined is termed abduction (Charmaz 2011; Reichertz 2007; Suddaby 2006) (Section 4.4).

Another key element that aids the development of grounded theory is **memo writing** (Section 13.5). Memos are created throughout a research project to define or make notes about:

- the codes being used;
- how codes change through the research process;
- how codes might be related, leading to the identification of theoretical relationships and the emergence of higher-level codes and categories;
- any other ideas that occur to the researcher that help her or him to develop the research process and analyse the data.

Where you use a Grounded Theory strategy, your collection of self-memos will provide you with a chronological record of the development of your ideas and your project, and show how you arrived at your grounded theory.

When using Grounded Theory you will also need to decide how to select cases for your research. As you analyse data, the categories being developed will indicate the type of new cases (e.g. new participants) to select for further data collection. The purpose of sampling is therefore to pursue theoretical lines of enquiry rather than to achieve population representativeness. As you identify a core theme, relationship or process around which to focus the research, a particular focus will be provided from which to select new cases to collect and analyse further data. This approach is a special form of purposive sampling, known as **theoretical sampling** (Section 7.3), which continues until **theoretical saturation** is reached. This occurs when data collection ceases to reveal any new properties that are relevant to a category, where categories have become well developed and understood and relationships between categories have been verified (Strauss and Corbin 1998). This is also referred to as achieving conceptual density (Glaser 1992) or conceptual saturation (Strauss and Corbin 2008). Using these elements of Grounded Theory means that the process of data collection and analysis becomes increasingly focused, leading to the generation of a contextually based theoretical explanation (Bryant and Charmaz 2007).

Grounded Theory is a useful and widely recognised research strategy and yet it has been the subject of much evaluation, criticism and even misunderstanding (Box 5.9). This is partly due to the development of different approaches to grounded theory method. Glaser and Strauss, who developed Grounded Theory, each went on to develop different approaches to its use. Strauss has become associated with the development of a particularly prescriptive approach to grounded theory method (e.g. Corbin and Strauss 2008; Strauss and Corbin 1998).

A further difference has been revealed by Charmaz (2006: 130–31), who makes a distinction between 'objectivist grounded theory' and 'constructivist grounded theory'. Charmaz views the approach of Glaser, Strauss and Corbin to grounded theory as being 'objectivist', which assumes that data have an external reality, just waiting to be 'discovered'. She considers that, 'objectivist grounded theory resides in the positivist tradition' (Charmaz 2006: 131). According to this view, it is only 'constructivist' grounded theory that is truly based on an interpretive approach (Section 5.3), because it recognises that the researcher's role in interpreting the data will affect the development of a grounded theory. In this approach, grounded theories are 'constructed', not discovered. This might seem a rather abstract difference, but because Charmaz advocates a 'constructivist' approach she also promotes a more flexible approach to grounded theory method (Section 13.9).

Adopting a Grounded Theory strategy leads to other issues and implications. These concern the collection of data; the use of existing theory; identifying a core category or categories around which to focus the research; the emergence of theory; and the time required to undertake this strategy. We briefly consider each of these.

In Grounded Theory, data collection may start as soon as the research idea has been developed and the initial research participants have agreed to take part (or the first set of documents have been identified). Using this strategy places an obligation on you to make sure you are interested in and committed to your research idea.

There is sometimes confusion about the role of published theory in a Grounded Theory research project. Grounded Theorists may use published theory before and during their research project (Box 5.9). The idea for such a research project may come from existing theory and your understanding of the theoretical background to your research topic may help to inform the project in general terms. Where existing theory should not be allowed to influence the conduct of your Grounded Theory project is in relation to the way you code your data, decide on new cases and conduct your analysis, as we have discussed in this section. Grounded Theory is an emergent strategy and researchers wish to be guided by concepts emerging from the data they collect rather than being sensitised by concepts in existing theory. Using this strategy will mean you should avoid being overly sensitised to pre-existing theoretical concepts, to allow yourself to make sense of participants' meanings in the data to guide your research. This is known as **theoretical sensitivity**, where you focus on interpreting meanings by using *in vivo* and researcher generated rather than *a priori* codes (explained in Section 13.6) to analyse your data and construct a grounded theory (Glaser 1978). Theoretical sensitivity means that you must be sensitive to meanings in your data and orientated towards generating a grounded theory from these data. You will, however, need to allow yourself sufficient time later on to link your grounded theory to published theories as you write your research report!

Box 5.9
Focus on management research

Using Grounded Theory, or not!

Bryant and Charmaz (2007) in *The Sage Handbook of Grounded Theory* report that this strategy has, for the last couple of decades, been the qualitative research method used most widely across a range of subjects. They cite Titscher et al. (2000), who reported that out of 4134 citations for all types of research methods in the Social Science Citation Index between 1991 and 1998, Grounded Theory accounted for 2622 of these. However, Titscher et al. (2000, cited in Bryant and Charmaz 2007) question whether the ascendancy of Grounded Theory is as dominant as these data appear to suggest. Bryant and Charmaz (2007: 2) reflect back to Lee and Fielding (1996) in concluding that 'the discrepancy between claiming use of [Grounded Theory] and actual evidence of this continues today'. Lee and Fielding (1996:3.1) had stated in their *Sociological Research Online comment* that, 'When qualitative researchers are challenged to describe their approach, reference to "grounded theory" has the highest recognition value. But the very looseness and variety of researchers' schooling in the approach means that the tag may well mean something different to each researcher. A detailed examination of work claiming the label may deviate sharply from what Glaser and Strauss had in mind'.

More recently, O'Reilly et al. (2012) report a search using Business Source Premier to find out how Grounded Theory was being used in practice. This search revealed 126 journal articles that used 'grounded theory' in their titles over a recent 5-year period, of which 46 reported using Grounded Theory Method. However, of these just 16 reported using more than one element of Grounded Theory, with the considerable majority only reporting the use of its coding procedures.

Suddaby (2006) published an excellent article in the *Academy of Management Journal* based on reviewing pre-publication management research manuscripts claiming to use Grounded Theory. He identifies six common misconceptions about Grounded Theory. We briefly summarise these, but where you are thinking about using Grounded Theory we would advise you to read Suddaby's article as we believe that it will help you to understand this approach and avoid these common misunderstandings:

1 Ignoring literature until late in the research project. It is a mistake to ignore existing literature before and during undertaking Grounded Theory.
2 Presenting raw data. Grounded Theory should never present unanalysed data. This is to ignore the essence of Grounded Theory, which is a conceptual process to develop a theory from the data.
3 Using inappropriate philosophical assumptions and testing theory rather than developing theory. Avoid methodological confusions or 'slurring' such as starting with positivist assumptions or commencing with interpretive assumptions but then proceeding to use objectivist rather than Grounded Theory methods.
4 Mechanically following Grounded Theory procedures without sufficient creative insight. The use of Grounded Theory procedures and techniques needs to be accompanied by creative insights and theoretical sensitivity to infer meanings in the data, to progress the research and in writing it up.
5 Following Grounded Theory procedures rigidly. In practice Grounded Theory procedures are 'messy' and require researchers to develop a tacit feel for their research to make judgements about issues such as deciding when theoretical saturation is achieved.
6 Grounded Theory is methodologically simple. Instead, it requires practice, dedication, creativity and sometimes good luck. Using it is also not an excuse to avoid developing a clear methodology based on the core principles and procedures of coding, constant comparison, theoretical sensitivity, theoretical sampling and theoretical saturation.

Because Grounded Theory is emergent, you will need at some point to identify a core category or categories around which to focus your research and develop a grounded theory to explain the relationships you identify. This will require rigorous use of coding, constant comparison, theoretical sampling, theoretical saturation and theoretical sensitivity to develop a theoretical explanation. Use of this strategy is also associated with a concern that either little of significance will emerge at the end of the research process, or that what emerges is simply descriptive.

Using Grounded Theory is time consuming, intensive and reflective. Before committing yourself to this strategy, you need to consider the time that you have to conduct your research, the level of competence you will need, your access to data, and the logistical implications of immersing yourself in an intensive approach to research. Kenealy (2012) advises novice Grounded Theory researchers to identify one approach to grounded theory method and follow it without too much adaptation. He also advises researchers to focus on identifying 'ideas that fit and work' from their data to develop a grounded theory (Kenealy 2012: 423). Kenealy recognises that using Grounded Theory requires experience but says that the only way to build this is to practise the use of grounded theory method!

In summary, while some Grounded Theory authors produce prescriptive accounts of grounded theory method and others offer more flexible accounts, all appear to be agreed on the key elements we discussed earlier:

- Early commencement of data collection;
- Concurrent collection and analysis of data;
- Developing codes and categories from the data as these are collected and analysed;
- Use of constant comparison and writing of self-memos to develop conceptualisation and build a theory;
- Use of theoretical sampling and theoretical saturation aimed at building theory rather than achieving (population) representativeness;
- Use of an abductive approach that seeks to gain insights to create new conceptual possibilities which are then examined;
- Initial use of literature as a complementary source to the categories and concepts emerging in the data, rather than as the source to categorise these data. Later use to review the place of the grounded theory in relation to existing, published theories;
- Development of a theory that is grounded in the data.

Narrative Inquiry

A narrative is a story; a personal account which interprets an event or sequence of events (Box 5.8). Using the term 'narrative' requires a distinction to be drawn between its general meaning and the specific meaning used here. A qualitative research interview inevitably involves a participant in storytelling. In this way, the term 'narrative' can be applied generally to describe the nature or outcome of a qualitative interview. As a research strategy, however, **Narrative Inquiry** has a more specific meaning and purpose. There will be research contexts where the researcher believes that the experiences of her or his participants can best be accessed by collecting and analysing these as complete stories, rather than collecting them as bits of data that flow from specific interview questions and which are then fragmented during data analysis. Chase (2011) distinguishes between asking participants to generalise when answering questions in more structured types of qualitative research and being invited to provide a complete narrative of their experience. This contrasts with the approach to Grounded Theory which we discussed earlier.

Narrative Inquiry seeks to preserve chronological connections and the sequencing of events as told by the narrator (participant) to enrich understanding and aid analysis. Chase (2011: 421) refers to this strategy as providing the opportunity to connect events, actions and their consequences over time into a 'meaningful whole'. Through storytelling the narrator will also provide his or her interpretation of these events, allowing the narrative researcher to analyse the meanings which the narrator places on events. Where there is more than one participant providing a personal account of a given context, the narrative researcher will also be able to compare and to triangulate or contrast these narratives.

The depth of this process is also likely to produce 'thick descriptions' of contextual detail and social relations. Gabriel and Griffiths (2004: 114) believe that using this strategy may allow researchers to 'gain access to deeper organisational realities, closely linked to their members' experiences'. A **narrative** may therefore be defined as an account of an experience that is told in a sequenced way, indicating a flow of related events that, taken together, are significant for the narrator and which convey meaning to the researcher (Coffey and Atkinson 1996).

In Narrative Inquiry, the participant is the narrator, with the researcher adopting the role of a listener facilitating the process of narration (Box 5.10). The narrative provided may be a short story about a specific event; a more extended story (for example, about a work project, managing or setting up a business, or an organisational change programme); or a complete life history (e.g. Chase 2011; Maitlis 2012). While in-depth interviews are the primary method to collect stories, other methods may be used by the narrative researcher to record stories as they occur naturally, such as participant observation in the research setting (Coffey and Atkinson 1996; Gabriel and Griffiths 2004). Other sources of narratives include autobiographies, authored biographies, diaries, documentation (see our earlier discussion of this strategy) and informal discussions (Chase 2011; Maitlis 2012). This raises the issue of the Narrative Researcher adopting the role of narrator in particular circumstances, which we will consider further later. It is also important to note that Narrative Inquiry may be used as the sole research strategy, or it may be used in conjunction with another strategy as a complementary approach (Musson 2004).

Narrative Inquiry may be used in different ways. It may be used with a very small number of participants (one, two or three), where these are selected because they are judged as being typical of a much larger culture-sharing population (Chase 2011). As an example, you may decide to interview a small number of accountants or marketing managers who are typical of their occupational population (Box 5.10). It may also be used with a very small sample because those selected are judged as being critical cases or extreme cases, from whom much may be learnt. In this context, in-depth narrative interviews with a small sample of company founders or entrepreneurs may prove to be valuable (Musson 2004). Narrative Inquiry may also be used with slightly larger samples, where, for example, narrative interviews are conducted with, or observations made of, participants from across an organisation, to be able to analyse how narratives are constructed around an event or series of events and to be able to compare how accounts differ, such as between departments, occupational groups, genders and/or grades.

This strategy is generally associated with small, purposive samples (Section 7.3) because of its intensive and time-consuming nature. It is likely to generate large amounts of data in the form of interview transcripts or observational notes. The narratives that emerge may not do so in an easy-to-use structural and coherent form (Gabriel and

Box 5.10
Focus on student research

Using narrative inquiry to explore a marketing strategy

Kasia was undertaking a marketing degree and, because of her longstanding interest in fashion and textiles, she hoped to find a job in that sector. Kasia's interests led her to focus her research project on factors that affected the success of marketing strategies in a small sample of fashion companies. After considering her choice of research strategy and discussing this with her project tutor, she decided to use a narrative inquiry strategy, using in-depth interviews with senior managers in a sample of carefully selected companies. She negotiated access to conduct interviews with the marketing directors or managers of three medium-sized fashion companies. Kasia realised that the outcome of her research would very much depend on the quality of these three in-depth interviews and the ways in which her interviewees responded to her request to participate in this narrative approach. She decided to send each of these three managers a letter very briefly outlining this approach and a list of the structural elements of narrative inquiry she had read about.

She was nervous going to the first interview and realised that her participant, Hetal, sensed this. Hetal had read Kasia's letter and knew a little about narrative inquiry from her own degree studies. Hetal provided Kasia with a full and useful narrative of the factors affecting the outcomes of her employer's marketing strategy over the past year. However, after the interview Kasia realised that she had interrupted Hetal unnecessarily with interview questions on several occasions, interrupting the flow of Hetal's narrative account. Kasia wrote and thanked Hetal for her very useful narrative account and resolved to read more about conducting this type of in-depth interview before conducting the second one. She read Czarniawska's (1997) book, *Narrating the Organization*, and learnt that she would need to move from the interviewer's standard role of asking questions and instead allow her interviewees to act as narrators, using their own voices to tell their stories.

Kasia contacted her next participant and went to the interview with a list of elements and themes in which she was interested but resolved that her second participant, Jorg, should be allowed to use his own voice. Jorg provided Kasia with another full and useful narrative, with Kasia acting as listener rather than traditional interviewer, only seeking clarification occasionally, after explaining the nature and purpose of the process as they started. Kasia left this second interview feeling very pleased, and looked forward to the next one.

Griffiths 2004). Coffey and Atkinson (1996) recognise this, drawing on previous research to outline the structural elements that are useful to facilitate analysis of narratives:

- What is the story about?
- What happened, to whom, whereabouts and why?
- What consequences arose from this?
- What is the significance of these events?
- What was the final outcome?

To achieve such analytical coherence in a narrative account may involve the narrative researcher in (re)constructing the story from the strands that emerge from conducting a number of in-depth interviews with one participant or with different participants (Box 5.8). As we recognised earlier, this action places the narrative researcher in a central role in telling the story. Decisions will need to be taken about what to include and what to leave out, and how to connect parts of the account. We consider issues of narrative analysis further in Section 13.10.

Where your research question and objectives suggest the use of an interpretive and qualitative strategy, Narrative Inquiry may be suitable for you to use. Narrative Inquiry will allow you to analyse the linkages, relationships and socially constructed explanations that occur naturally within narrative accounts in order 'to understand the complex processes which people use in making sense of their organisational realities' (Musson 2004: 42). The purpose of Narrative Inquiry is to derive theoretical explanations from narrative accounts while maintaining their integrity. While analysis in Narrative Inquiry does not use the analytical fragmentation of Grounded Theory, neither does it offer a well-developed set of analytical procedures comparable to those used by grounded theorists. Despite this, analytical rigour is still important in order to derive constructs and concepts to develop theoretical explanations. While narrative researchers may believe that predefined analytical procedures are neither advisable nor desirable, this may make the task of analysis more demanding for you. We return in Section 13.10 to consider some of the approaches that narrative researchers have used to analyse their data.

5.6 Choosing a time horizon 选择时间跨度

An important question to be asked in designing your research is, 'Do I want my research to be a "snapshot" taken at a particular time or do I want it to be more akin to a diary or a series of snapshots and be a representation of events over a given period?' This will, of course, depend on your research question. The 'snapshot' time horizon we call **cross-sectional**, while the 'diary' perspective we call **longitudinal**.

Cross-sectional studies

It is probable that your research will be cross-sectional, involving the study of a particular phenomenon (or phenomena) at a particular time. We say this because we recognise that most research projects undertaken for academic courses are necessarily time constrained. However, the time horizons on many courses do allow sufficient time for a longitudinal study, provided, of course, that you start your research early!

Cross-sectional studies often employ the survey strategy. They may be seeking to describe the incidence of a phenomenon (for example, the IT skills possessed by managers in one organisation at a given point in time) or to explain how factors are related in different organisations (e.g. the relationship between expenditure on customer care training for sales assistants and sales revenue). However, they may also use qualitative or mixed methods research strategies. For example, many case studies are based on interviews conducted over a short period of time.

Longitudinal studies

The main strength of longitudinal research is its capacity to study change and development. This type of study may also provide you with a measure of control over some of the variables being studied. One of the best-known examples of this type of research comes from outside the world of business. It is the long-running UK television series, 'Seven Up'. This has charted the progress of a cohort of people every seven years of their life. Not only is this fascinating television, it has also provided the social scientist with a rich source of data on which to test and develop theories of human development.

Even with time constraints it is possible to introduce a longitudinal element to your research. There is a massive amount of published data collected over time just waiting to be reanalysed (as Section 8.2 indicates)! An example is the Workplace Employment Relations Study, conducted in 1980, 1984, 1990, 1998, 2004 and 2011 (Department for Business, Innovation and Skills 2013). From these surveys you would be able to gain valuable secondary data, which would give you a powerful insight into developments in human resource management and employee relations over a period of wide-ranging change.

确定研究设计的道德规范

5.7 Establishing the ethics of the research design

Research ethics are a critical part of formulating your research design. This is discussed in detail in Chapter 6, which focuses on issues associated with negotiating access and research ethics. In particular, Section 6.5 defines research ethics and discusses why it is crucial to act ethically, and Section 6.6 highlights ethical issues at specific stages, including when designing research and gaining access. Here we introduce two ethical issues that you need to consider when starting to design your research.

Your choice of topic will be governed by ethical considerations. You may be particularly interested to study the consumer decision to buy flower bouquets. Although this may provide some interesting data collection challenges (who buys, for whom and why), there are not the same ethical difficulties as will be involved in studying, say, the funeral purchasing decision. Your research design in this case may have to concentrate on data collection from the undertaker and, possibly, the purchaser at a time as close to the death as delicacy permits. The ideal population, of course, may be the purchaser at a time as near as possible to the death. It is a matter of judgement as to whether the strategy and data collection method(s) suggested by ethical considerations will yield data that are valid. The general ethical issue here is that the research design should not subject those you are researching to the risk of embarrassment, pain, harm or any other material disadvantage.

Your research design may need to consider whether you should collect data if those you are researching are unaware they are the subject of research and so have not consented. There was a dispute between solicitors and the Consumers' Association (CA). Telephone enquiries were conducted by the CA with a sample of solicitors for the purpose of assessing the accuracy of legal advice given and the cost of specified work. The calls were, allegedly, made without the CA's identity or the purpose of the research being disclosed (Gibb 1995). Although it is for you to decide whether a similar covert research design for your project would be ethical, it is worth emphasising that many university research ethics procedures preclude the use of covert research. Circumstances related to the use of covert observation and issues related to privacy are considered further in Chapters 6 and 9.

确定研究设计的质量

5.8 Establishing the quality of the research design

Underpinning our discussion of research design is the issue of the quality of the research and its findings. This is neatly expressed by Raimond (1993: 55) when he subjects findings to the 'how do I know?' test, 'Will the evidence and my conclusions stand up to the closest scrutiny?' For example, how do you know that the advertising campaign for a new product has resulted in enhanced sales? How do you know that manual employees in an electronics factory have more negative feelings towards their employer than their clerical counterparts? The answer, of course, is that, in the literal sense of the question, you cannot know. All you can do is reduce the possibility of getting the answer wrong. This is why good research design is important. This is aptly summarised by Rogers (1961; cited by Raimond 1993: 55): 'scientific methodology needs to be seen for what it truly is, a way of preventing me from deceiving myself in regard to my creatively formed subjective hunches which have developed out of the relationship between me and my material'.

A split often occurs at this point between positivist and interpretivist researchers. The former will use the 'canons of scientific inquiry' related to reliability and validity to assess the quality of their research or, perhaps more pertinently, that of others. The latter either seek to adapt these terms to assess their research, or reject them as inappropriate to interpretivist studies (Guba and Lincoln 1989, 2005; Lincoln and Guba 1985; Lincoln et al. 2011). We briefly discuss each of these approaches to establish and assess research quality.

Scientific canons of inquiry: reliability and validity

Reliability and validity are central to judgements about the quality of research in the natural sciences and quantitative research in the social sciences. Their role in relation to qualitative research is contested, as we discuss later. **Reliability** refers to replication and consistency. If a researcher is able to replicate an earlier research design and achieve the same findings, then that research would be seen as being reliable. In essence, **validity** refers to the appropriateness of the measures used, accuracy of the analysis of the results and generalisability of the findings:

1 Do the measures being used in the research to assess the phenomenon being studied actually measure what they are intended to – are they appropriate for their intended purpose?
2 Are the analysis of the results and the relationships being advanced accurate?
3 What do the research findings represent: does the claim about how generalisable they are stand up?

This first aspect of validity is sometimes termed **measurement validity** and is associated with different types of validity designed to assess this intention. These include face validity, construct validity, content validity and predictive validity (which are discussed in Section 11.4). The second aspect of validity refers to internal validity and the third aspect to external validity, both discussed later in this section.

When considering reliability, sometimes a distinction is made between internal reliability and external reliability. Internal reliability refers to ensuring consistency during a research project. This may be achieved, where possible, by using more than one researcher within a research project to conduct interviews or observations and to analyse data to be able to evaluate the extent to which they agree about the data and its analysis. You may seek to ensure consistency through the stages of your research project by writing memos to promote stability in the way you code your data, and analyse and interpret it. External reliability refers to whether your data collection techniques and analytic procedures would produce consistent findings if they were repeated by you on another occasion or if they were replicated by a different researcher. Ensuring reliability is not necessarily easy and a number of threats to reliability are described in Table 5.3. Research that is unreliable will also prove to be invalid since any error or bias will affect

Table 5.3 Threats to reliability

Threat	Definition and explanation
Participant error	Any factor which adversely alters the way in which a participant performs. For example, asking a participant to complete a questionnaire just before a lunch break may affect the way they respond compared to choosing a less sensitive time (i.e. they may not take care and hurry to complete it)
Participant bias	Any factor which induces a false response. For example, conducting an interview in an open space may lead participants to provide falsely positive answers where they fear they are being overheard, rather than retaining their anonymity
Researcher error	Any factor which alters the researcher's interpretation. For example, a researcher may be tired or not sufficiently prepared and misunderstand some of the more subtle meanings of his or her interviewees
Researcher bias	Any factor which induces bias in the researcher's recording of responses. For example, a researcher may allow her or his own subjective view or disposition to get in the way of fairly and accurately recording and interpreting participants' responses

the results and subsequent interpretation, and possibly cast doubt on the means to measure the phenomenon being studied.

These threats imply that you will need to be methodologically rigorous in the way you devise and carry out your research to seek to avoid threatening the reliability of your findings and conclusions. More specific advice appears in other chapters but one key aspect is to ensure that your research process is clearly thought through and evaluated and does not contain 'logic leaps and false assumptions'. You will need to report each part of your work in a fully transparent way to allow others to judge for themselves and to replicate your study if they wished to do so.

Reliability is a key characteristic of research quality; however, while it is necessary, it is not sufficient by itself to ensure good-quality research. As indicated earlier, the quality of research depends not only on its reliability but also its validity. Forms of measurement validity are discussed in Section 11.4. **Internal validity** is established when your research accurately demonstrates a **causal relationship** between two variables. For example, in an experiment internal validity would be established where an intervention can be shown statistically to lead to an outcome. In a questionnaire-based survey, internal validity would be established where a set of questions can be shown statistically to be associated with an analytical factor or outcome (Chapter 11). This concept is associated with positivist and quantitative research: it can be applied to causal or explanatory studies, but not to exploratory or purely descriptive studies.

Your research findings would be seen as invalid when a finding has been arrived at falsely or when a reported relationship is inaccurate. There are a number of reasons that might threaten the internal validity of your research (Cook and Campbell 1979). We offer definitions and examples of the most frequent in Table 5.4. Research that produces invalid results and conclusions will also adversely affect its reliability since it will be highly unlikely for a subsequent study to find the same false results and statistical relationships.

Table 5.4 Threats to internal validity

Threat	Definition and explanation
Past or recent events	An event which changes participants' perceptions. For example, a vehicle maker recalling its cars for safety modifications may affect its customers' views about product quality and have an unforeseen effect on a planned study (unless the objective of the research is to find out about post-product recall opinions)
Testing	The impact of testing on participants' views or actions. For example, informing participants about a research project may alter their work behaviour or responses during the research if they believe it might lead to future consequences for them
Instrumentation	The impact of a change in a research instrument between different stages of a research project affecting the comparability of results. For example, in structured observational research on call centre operations, the definitions of behaviours being observed may be changed between stages of the research, making comparison difficult
Mortality	The impact of participants withdrawing from studies. Often participants leave their job or gain a promotion during a study
Maturation	The impact of a change in participants outside of the influence of the study that affects their attitudes or behaviours etc. For example, management training may make participants revise their responses during a subsequent research stage
Ambiguity about causal direction	Lack of clarity about cause and effect. For example, during a study, it was difficult to say if poor performance ratings were caused by negative attitudes to appraisal or if negative attitudes to appraisal were caused by poor performance ratings

External validity is concerned with the question: can a study's research findings be generalised to other relevant settings or groups? For example, a corporate manager may ask, 'Can the findings from the research study in one organisation in our corporation also be used to inform policy and practice in other organisations in the group?' The chief executive of a county council may ask, 'Are the findings from the survey in the Finance and Resources Department applicable to other departments in the Council?' Just as researchers take great care when selecting a sample from within a population to make sure that it represents that population, researchers and their clients are often concerned to establish the generalisability of their findings to other contexts. Even in such cases, however, it will be necessary to replicate the study in that other context, or contexts, to be able to establish such statistical generalisability.

Alternative criteria to assess the quality of research inquiry

All researchers take issues of research quality seriously if they wish others to accept their research as credible. However, while types of measurement validity (Section 11.4) are appropriate to assess quantitative research based on positivist assumptions, they are often considered as philosophically and technically inappropriate in relation to qualitative research based on interpretive assumptions, where reality is regarded as being socially constructed and multifaceted. If good-quality research is judged against the criteria of reliability and validity, but these concepts are applied in a rigid way that is inappropriate to qualitative research, it becomes difficult for qualitative researchers to demonstrate that their research is of high quality and credible.

Three types of response to this are evident. Firstly, there are those who continue to use the concepts of reliability and validity, adapting them to qualitative research. Those who adopt this response generally believe that since all research needs to be reliable and valid, using these terms is important to be able to demonstrate the quality and comparable status of qualitative research. As we recognise in Section 10.4, qualitative research is not necessarily intended to be replicated because it will reflect the socially constructed interpretations of participants in a particular setting at the time it is conducted. However, rigorous description of the research design, context and methods may help others to replicate similar studies. Where possible, use of more than one interviewer, observer and data analyst will also improve the quality of the research, referred to as its internal reliability. As we note in Section 10.4, the adaptation of the concept of internal validity to qualitative research is generally not seen as a problem since the in-depth nature of qualitative methods means that the theoretical relationships that are proposed can be shown to be well grounded in a rich collection of data. The adaptation of external validity to qualitative research has been questioned because small samples limit the generalisability of such studies. However, qualitative researchers have pointed to other forms of generalisability that demonstrate the quality and value of qualitative research. For example, findings from one qualitative research setting may lead to generalisations across other settings, where, for example, characteristics of the research setting are similar, or where learning from the research setting can be applied in other settings (Buchanan 2012).

Secondly, there are those who have developed parallel versions of reliability, internal validity and external validity, with distinct names, that recognise the nature of qualitative research. In this regard, Lincoln and Guba (1985) formulated 'dependability' for 'reliability', 'credibility' for 'internal validity' and 'transferability' for 'external validity' (Table 5.5). Thirdly, there are those who have moved further away from the concepts of reliability and validity and have sought to develop new concepts through which to ensure and judge the quality of qualitative research. In this regard, Guba and Lincoln (1989, 2005; Lincoln et al. 2011) have developed 'authenticity criteria' as an alternative to validity (Table 5.5).

A key concern in designing your research will be to familiarise yourself with the criteria to be used to assess your research project. These assessment criteria might state that your research design and report has to consider issues of reliability/dependability and validity/credibility/authenticity. Other assessment criteria will be generic, related to analytical and evaluative abilities, only implicitly recognising the need for reliable/dependable and valid/credible/authentic research in assessing your research design and outcomes. Familiarising yourself with the assessment criteria to be used will help you to decide how you should approach the way you describe and discuss the quality of your research.

Validation

In our discussion about assessing quality and alternative criteria to evaluate it (i.e. reliability/dependability and validity/credibility/authenticity) we have already referred to techniques of validation (e.g. measurement validity, checking data with participants),

Table 5.5 Alternative quality criteria

Criterion	Definition and techniques to achieve each criterion
Dependability	This is the parallel criterion to reliability. In interpretivist research, the research focus is likely to be modified as the research progresses. Dependability in this context means recording all of the changes to produce a reliable/dependable account of the emerging research focus that may be understood and evaluated by others
Credibility	This is the parallel criterion to internal validity. Emphasis is placed on ensuring that the representations of the research participants' socially constructed realities actually match what the participants intended. A range of techniques to ensure this match include: • lengthy research involvement to build trust and rapport and to collect sufficient data; • use of reflection using a different person to discuss ideas and test out findings etc.; • developing a thorough analysis that accounts for negative cases by refining the analysis in order to produce the best possible explanation of the phenomenon being studied; • checking data, analysis and interpretations with participants; • making sure that the researchers' preconceived expectations about what the research will reveal are not privileged over the social constructions of the participant by regularly recording these and challenging them during analysis of the data
Transferability	This is the parallel criterion to external validity or generalisability. By providing a full description of the research questions, design, context, findings and interpretations, the researcher provides the reader with the opportunity to judge the transferability of the study to another setting in which the reader is interested to research
Authenticity criteria	These were not conceived as parallel criteria but as criteria that are specifically designed for the nature of constructivist/interpretivist research. Guba and Lincoln (1989) devised 'fairness', 'ontological', 'educative', 'catalytic' and 'tactical' authenticity criteria. These are designed to promote fairness by representing all views in the research; raise awareness and generate learning; and bring about change

Sources: Developed from Guba and Lincoln 1989; Lincoln and Guba 1985; Lincoln et al. 2011

without using this term. **Validation** is the process of verifying research data, analysis and interpretation to establish their validity/credibility/authenticity. We now discuss two validation techniques which may help you to establish the quality of your research:

• triangulation;
• participant or member validation.

Triangulation involves using more than one source of data and method of collection to confirm the validity/credibility/authenticity of research data, analysis and interpretation. This will necessitate you using a multi-method quantitative study, multi-method qualitative study or a mixed methods study (Section 5.3). The purpose is to use two or more independent sources of data and methods of collection within one study to ensure that the data are telling you what you think they are telling you. In a research study based on positivist assumptions, this will help to reveal the 'reality' in the data. Interpretivist researchers challenge this outcome as they consider that in relation to studies involving people's beliefs, attitudes and interpretations, 'reality' is socially constructed and multifaceted. For interpretivists, the value of using triangulation is that it adds depth, breadth, complexity and richness to their research (Denzin 2012; Denzin and Lincoln 2011).

Participant or **member validation** involves taking or sending research data back to participants to allow them to confirm its accuracy, by permitting them to comment on and correct it to validate it. This may take the form of showing them interview transcripts, observation or other notes, storied accounts as well as researcher interpretations of participants' data (e.g. Cayla and Arnould 2013). Participant collaboration is essential in some qualitative research strategies such as Action Research, while forms of collaboration such as member validation will be important in other qualitative research strategies and in mixed methods research. While the nature of quantitative data may preclude member validation, where you use a survey strategy you may still find it useful to discuss the results from your quantitative analysis with a sample of your respondents to help you to explain and interpret these data. Member validation may be problematic when a participant wishes to withdraw some of the data shared with you. You will need to differentiate between cases where participants correct your interpretation of the data they shared with you and cases where they simply change their attitude. The latter scenario may relate to an ethical concern and you will need to reflect on the extent to which you should alter the original data (Sections 6.5 and 6.6).

Logic leaps and false assumptions

So far in this chapter we have shown that there are a host of research design decisions to be made in order that your research project can yield sufficient good-quality data. These decisions will necessitate careful thought. Your research design will need to be logical and, along with any assumptions you make, to stand up to careful scrutiny. Raimond (1993: 128) advises you to 'stand back from your research [design] and take a critical, objective view of it, as though you were a detached observer'. This will allow you to see your design as others might, so that you can examine the logic of the research steps you propose to take to see if they will stand up to rigorous scrutiny.

考虑你作为研究者的角色

5.9 **Taking into account your role as researcher**

This chapter has discussed the decisions you will need to take to formulate your research design. You need to choose between quantitative, qualitative or mixed methods; between research strategies; and between time frames. Each decision will have implications for the nature of your design (between an exploratory, descriptive, explanatory or evaluative purpose, or some combination of these). Each decision also has implications for the ways in which you seek to establish a quality research design that is ethical. As you have read through this chapter, you have probably been evaluating each of these decisions in relation to practical constraints as well as personal preferences. We have alluded to practical constraints in a number of places in the chapter in terms of the way they may affect each choice. An important practical consideration in deciding how to formulate a research design is related to your role as researcher.

The role of the external researcher

If you are a full-time student you are likely to adopt the role of an **external researcher**, as you need to identify an organisation within which to conduct your research. In such cases you will need to negotiate access to the organisation and to those from whom you would like to collect data. Having achieved this you will need to gain their trust so that they will participate meaningfully to allow you to collect these data. You will need to take these practical factors into account when formulating your research question and your research design. Sections 6.2 to 6.4 provide more detail about issues of access that you need to take into account as an external researcher before finalising your research design.

The role of the internal researcher or practitioner researcher

If you are currently working in an organisation, you may choose to undertake your research project within that organisation, adopting the role of an **internal researcher** or **practitioner researcher**. As a part-time student, you will be surrounded by numerous opportunities to pursue business and management research. You are unlikely to encounter one of the most difficult hurdles that an external researcher has to overcome: that of negotiating research access. Indeed, like many people in such a position, you may be asked to research a particular problem by your employer.

As an internal researcher, another advantage for you will be your knowledge of the organisation and all this implies about understanding the complexity of what goes on in that organisation. It will not be necessary to spend a great deal of time 'learning the context' in the same way as an external researcher will need to do. However, this advantage carries with it a significant disadvantage. You must be very conscious of the assumptions and preconceptions that you carry around with you. This is an inevitable consequence of knowing the organisation well and can prevent you from exploring issues that would enrich the research.

Familiarity may create other problems for the internal researcher. When we were doing case study work in a manufacturing company, we found it very useful to ask 'basic' questions revealing our ignorance about the industry and the organisation. These 'basic' questions are ones that as a practitioner researcher you would be less likely to ask because you, and your respondents, would feel that you should know the answers already. There is also the problem of status. If you are a junior employee you may feel that working with more senior colleagues inhibits your interactions as researcher practitioner. The same may be true if you are more senior than your colleagues.

A more practical problem is that of time. Combining two roles at work is obviously very demanding, particularly as it may involve you in much data recording 'after hours'. This activity is hidden from those who determine your workload. They may not appreciate the demands that your researcher role is making on you. For this reason, practitioner researchers may need to negotiate a proportion of their 'work time' to devote to their research. There are no easy answers to these problems. All you can do is be aware of the possible impact on your research of being too close to your research setting.

Tietze (2012) offers some guidance for internal researchers. These include reflecting on your role as internal researcher so that you may recognise how this affects the way you design and conduct your research (where you have scope to influence what you are going to research). The research you undertake and the report you produce of it may have implications for those you work with and you will therefore need to consider the implications of how you research and what you report (Section 6.6). You will need to consider your emotions and to manage these during this process of being an internal researcher. The process of analysing, interpreting and theorising about the research data you collect may have the effect of making 'strange the all-too-familiar' (Tietze 2012: 68) and you will need to cope with the degree of detachment that this may produce as you re-evaluate the way in which you view the organisation.

5.10 Summary 小 结

- Research design is the way a research question and objectives are operationalised into a research project. The research design process involves a series of decisions that need to combine into a coherent research project.
- Research design will be informed by your research philosophy.
- A choice has to be made to use quantitative or qualitative methods, or both, to create a mono method, multi-method or mixed methods research design.
- The focus of your research will be exploratory, descriptive, explanatory, evaluative or a combination of these.
- A decision will be made to use one or more research strategies, related to the nature of the research question and objectives and to ensure coherence with the other elements of your research design.
- Possible research strategies include: Experiment; Survey; Archival and Documentary Research; Case Study; Ethnography; Action Research; Grounded Theory and Narrative Inquiry.
- Choice of research strategy or strategies will be related to use of an appropriate time horizon.
- Research ethics play a critical part in formulating a research design.
- Establishing the quality of research is also a critical part of formulating a research design. Researchers from different research traditions have developed different criteria to judge and ensure the quality of research.
- Practical considerations will also affect research design, including the role of the researcher.

Self-check questions 自测题

Answers to these questions are available at the end of the chapter.

5.1 You wish to study the reasons why car owners join manufacturer-sponsored owners' clubs. You choose to use a qualitative methodology and narrative inquiry research strategy involving unstructured 'discussions' with some members of these owners' clubs. You are asked by a small group of marketing managers to explain why your chosen research design is as valid as a quantitative methodology, survey strategy that uses a questionnaire. What would be your answer?

5.2   You are working in an organisation that has branches throughout the country. The managing director is mindful of the fact that managers of the branches need to talk over common problems on a regular basis. That is why there have always been monthly meetings. However, she is becoming increasingly concerned that these meetings are not cost-effective. Too many managers see them as an unwelcome intrusion. They feel that their time would be better spent pursuing their principal job objectives. Other managers see it as a 'day off': an opportunity to recharge the batteries.

She has asked you to carry out some research on the cost effectiveness of the monthly meetings. You have defined the research question you are seeking to answer as 'What are the managers' opinions of the value of their monthly meetings?'

Your principal research strategy will be a survey using a questionnaire to all managers who attend the monthly meetings. However, you are keen to triangulate your findings. How might you do this?

5.3   You have started conducting interviews in a university with the non-academic employees (such as administrative and other support staff). The research objective is to establish the extent to which those employees feel a sense of 'belonging' to the university. You have negotiated access to your interviewees through the head of each of the appropriate departments. In each case you have been presented with a list of interviewees.

It soon becomes apparent to you that you are getting a rather rosier picture than you expected. The interviewees are all very positive about their jobs, their managers and the university. This makes you suspicious. Are all the non-academic staff as positive as this? Are you being given only the employees who can be relied on to tell the 'good news'? Have they been 'got at' by their manager?

There is a great risk that your results will not be valid. What can you do?

5.4   You are about to embark on a year-long study of customer service training for sales assistants in two national supermarket companies. The purpose of the research is to compare the way in which the training develops and its effectiveness. What measures would you need to take in the research design stage to ensure that your results were valid?

Review and discussion questions 复习与讨论题

5.5   Agree with a friend to watch the same television documentary.

a Does the documentary use a quantitative, qualitative or mixed methods research methodology?

b To what extent is the nature of the documentary exploratory, descriptive, explanatory, evaluative or a combination of these?

c What other observations can you make about the research strategy or strategies the documentary makers have used in their programme?

Do not forget to make notes regarding your reasons for your answers to each of these questions and to discuss these answers with your friend.

5.6   Use the search facilities of an online database to search for scholarly (peer-reviewed) articles which have used firstly a case study, secondly Action Research and thirdly experiment research strategy in an area of interest to you. Download a copy of each article. What reasons do the articles' authors give for the choice of strategy?

5.7   Visit the online gateway to the European Union website (http://europa.eu/) and click on the link in your own language. Discuss with a friend how you might use the data available via links from this web page in archival research. In particular, you should concentrate on the research questions you might be able to answer using these data to represent part of the reality you would be researching.

改进研究项目
Progressing your research project
研究设计的决策
Deciding on your research design

- Review your research question and objectives. Make notes on your philosophy and how it will impact on your research (which philosophy and the likely impact).

- Do your research question and objectives and philosophy support using mono method quantitative or qualitative, multi-method quantitative or qualitative, or mixed methods research design? Make notes for and against using each methodological choice. Decide which one is most appropriate.

- Based on the decisions you have made so far, create a shortlist of research strategies which may be appropriate to conduct your research, together with the advantages and disadvantages of each. Set this shortlist aside. Search for studies in the literature that are similar to your own. Use these to note which strategies have been used.

What explanations do the researchers give for their choice of strategy? Evaluate your shortlist against the notes from your search of studies in the literature. Use this evaluation to decide which strategy or combination of strategies would be most appropriate for your own research.

- Decide on the time frame to conduct your proposed research.

- Ask yourself, 'What are the practical constraints on my proposed design?' Use this question to review your decisions above and if necessary make changes. Repeat this step until you are satisfied your proposals are practical.

- Use your draft research design to list (1) potential threats to research quality and (2) ethical issues in your design and make notes about how you propose to deal with each. Where necessary, make further changes to the decisions in the steps above until you are satisfied with your research design.

- You should now be ready to discuss your proposed research design with your project tutor.

- Use the questions in Box 1.4 to guide your reflective diary entry.

Self-check answers   自测题答案

5.1   You would need to stress here that your principal interest would be in getting a deep understanding of why car owners join manufacturer-sponsored owners' clubs. You would discover why the owners joined these clubs and what they thought of them. In other words, you would establish what you set out to establish and, no doubt, a good deal besides. There is no reason why your discussions with owners should not be as valid as a survey questionnaire. Your initial briefing should be skilful enough to elicit rich responses from your interviewees (Chapter 10) and you may also use prompts to focus on themes that emerge in the narratives of your participants.

Of course, you may alleviate any fears about 'validity' by using a mixed methods research methodology and delivering a questionnaire as well, so that your findings may be triangulated!

5.2   The questionnaire will undoubtedly perform a valuable function in obtaining a comprehensive amount of data that can be compared easily, say, by district or age and gender. However, you would add to the understanding of the problem if you observed managers' meetings. Who does most of the talking? What are the non-verbal behaviour patterns displayed by managers? Who turns up late, or does not turn up at all? You could also consider talking to managers in groups or individually. Your decision here would be whether to talk to them before or after the questionnaire, or both. In addition, you could study the minutes of the meetings to discover who contributed the most. Who initiated the most discussions? What were the attendance patterns?

5.3   There is no easy answer to this question! You have to remember that access to organisations to research is an act of goodwill on the part of managers, and they do like to retain
a certain amount of control. Selecting whom researchers may interview is a classic way
of managers doing this. If this is the motive of the managers concerned then they are
unlikely to let you have free access to their employees.

What you could do is ask to see all the employees in a particular department rather
than a sample of employees. Alternatively, you could explain that your research was still
uncovering new patterns of information and more interviews were necessary. This way
you would penetrate deeper into the core of the employee group and might start seeing
those who were rather less positive. All this assumes that you have the time to do this!

You could also be perfectly honest with the managers and confess your concern. If you
did a sound job at the start of the research in convincing them that you are purely interested in academic research, and that all data will be anonymous, then you may have less
of a problem.

Of course, there is always the possibility that the employees generally are positive and
feel as if they really do 'belong'!

5.4   This would be a longitudinal study. Therefore, the potential of some of the threats to
internal validity explained in Section 5.8 is greater simply because they have longer to
develop. You would need to make sure that most of these threats were controlled as
much as possible. For example, you would need to:

- account for the possibility of a major event during the period of the research (wide-
  scale redundancies, which might affect employee attitudes) in one of the companies
  but not the other;
- ensure that you used the same data collection devices in both companies;
- be aware of the 'mortality' problem. Some of the sales assistants will leave. You
  would be advised to replace them with assistants with similar characteristics, as far as
  possible.

Get ahead using resources on the companion website at: **www.pearsoned
.co.uk/saunders**.

- Improve your IBM SPSS for Windows and NVivo research analysis with practice
  tutorials.
- Save time researching on the Internet with the Smarter Online Searching Guide.
- Test your progress using self-assessment questions.
- Follow live links to useful websites.

Chapter 6

Negotiating access and research ethics
协商访问与研究道德规范

Learning outcomes 学习目标

By the end of this chapter you should be:

- aware of issues associated with gaining traditional and Internet-mediated access;
- able to evaluate a range of strategies to help you to gain access to organisations and to individual participants;
- aware of the importance of research ethics and the need to act ethically;
- able to anticipate ethical issues at each stage of your research and in relation to particular techniques, and aware of approaches to help you deal with these;
- aware of the principles of data protection and data management.

6.1 Introduction 引 言

Many students want to start their research as soon as they have identified a topic area, forgetting that access and ethics are critical aspects for the success of any research project. Such considerations are equally important whether you are using secondary data (Chapter 8), or collecting primary data through person-to-person, Internet-mediated or questionnaire-based methods. Over the past decade, concerns about the ethics of research practice have grown substantially. Consequently, you need to think carefully about how you will gain access to undertake your research and about possible ethical concerns that could arise throughout the conduct of your research project. Without paying careful attention to how you are going to gain access to the data you require and acting ethically, what seem like good ideas for research may flounder and prove impractical or problematic once you attempt to undertake them.

Business and management research almost inevitably involves human participants. Ethical concerns are greatest where research involves human participants, irrespective of whether the research is conducted person-to-person. In thinking about undertaking business and management research you need to be aware that most universities, as well as an increasing number of organisations, require researchers to obtain formal Research Ethics Committee approval (or a favourable ethical opinion) for their proposed research prior to granting permission to commence a project. Universities and other organisations help to facilitate the process of

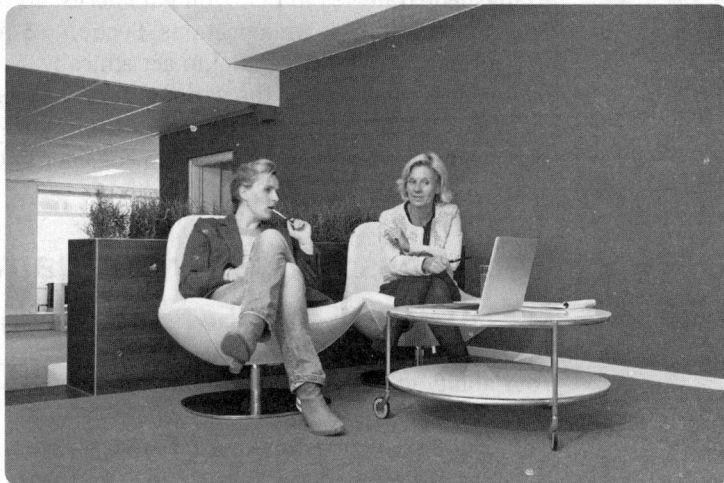

Ethical concerns pervade every aspect of life. Palmer (2013) writing in the *California Management Review* says that for organisations, unethical behaviour or wrongdoing can be costly in a number of ways. People will be offended by such behaviour and may act by taking their custom elsewhere. This will have adverse consequences for the organisation, perhaps leading to a public relations campaign to retain customer loyalty and win back trust. It may also have adverse consequences for individuals in the organisation who are implicated in unethical behaviour.

Palmer says the dominant view of unethical behaviour in organisations is that it is atypical. He cites four commonly held reasons for this view. Firstly, most observers view unethical behaviour as being infrequent. Secondly, unethical behaviour is generally judged as being uncharacteristic and anomalous to normal, acceptable behaviours. Thirdly, unethical behaviour is detestable, carried out by overbearing individuals serving their own ends over those of their employing organisation. Fourthly, such behaviour is encouraged by poorly designed structures, systems or incentive schemes that are out of line with corporate objectives.

However, Palmer reviews new research that believes unethical behaviour in organisations may be more common and normal than we might think. He outlines four reasons for this emerging view. Firstly, unethical behaviour is more frequent than has been thought. Secondly, rather than being seen as abnormal, it may be difficult in some instances to differentiate clearly between unethical and ethical behaviours, especially where cultural norms vary between societies. Thirdly, those who engage in unethical behaviour may in many aspects of their life be moral individuals, rather than wholly deviant and amoral. Fourthly, it is not just poorly designed structures, systems and policies that facilitate unethical behaviour, but the inherent pressures within all organisational structures and systems combined with human limitations that may encourage such behaviour.

Palmer outlines a number of implications for managers to discourage and deal with the occurrence of unethical behaviours in organisations. The prevalence of unethical behaviours that Palmer discusses also has implications for researchers. The pressures and constraints on researchers mean that they need to reflect carefully on their practices to ensure that the principles of ethical research are upheld, including maintaining integrity, respecting others, avoiding harm, not pressuring participants, adhering to informed consent, ensuring confidentially and anonymity, and practising responsibility in analysing data and reporting findings.

ethical scrutiny and approval by developing ethical guidelines for researchers to use in developing their research projects. We consider ethical guidelines later but it is worth noting that ethical concerns remain an ongoing source of concern, requiring continuous reflection and evaluation, as our opening vignette illustrates.

In this chapter we start by considering types and levels of traditional access and the issues associated with these (Section 6.2). In this section we also explore issues of feasibility and sufficiency in relation to gaining access and the impact of these on the nature and content of your research question and objectives. Section 6.3 examines Internet-mediated access and the issues associated with this. Section 6.4 discusses a number of established strategies to help you gain access to organisations and to your intended participants within these organisations. Section 6.5 provides an overview of research ethics and outlines why it is essential to act ethically. Section 6.6 anticipates the scope for ethical issues to occur during the various stages of your research project and in relation to the use of particular techniques. Section 6.7 introduces principles of data protection and data management, which you will need to consider in order to manage your data ethically.

6.2   Issues associated with gaining traditional access   与获取传统访问相关的问题

Your ability to obtain either primary or secondary data will depend on gaining access to an appropriate source, or sources where there is a choice. The appropriateness of a source will, of course, depend on your research question, related objectives and research design (Chapter 5). In this discussion we refer to levels and **types of access**. It is useful to offer a definition of each at this point. The first type is **traditional access**, which involves face-to-face interactions (to conduct experiments, interviews, focus groups, observations or to deliver questionnaires), telephone conversations (for telephone interviews), correspondence (for postal questionnaires) or visiting data archives (such as record offices or organisational archives, where data are not available online). The second type is **Internet-mediated access**, which involves the use of different computing technologies (e.g. the Web, email, instant messaging, webcams), to gain virtual access to deliver questionnaires, conduct archival research, discussions, experiments or interviews, or to gather secondary data. A variant of this is **intranet-mediated access**, where you seek to gain virtual access as an employee or worker in an organisation using its intranet. Even where you attempt to gain Internet- or intranet-mediated access it is likely that you will still need to use an element or some elements of traditional access. We therefore define a further type, **hybrid access**, which combines traditional and Internet-mediated approaches. We focus on traditional access in this section and on Internet, intranet and hybrid types of access in Section 6.3.

Levels of access vary depending on the nature and depth of the access that you achieve. We discuss three levels of access: physical, continuing and cognitive. Even where you seek to use the Internet or an intranet to gain virtual access, you may first need to achieve physical access and, subsequently, to negotiate your access on a continuing basis. You will certainly need to achieve cognitive access where your research involves human participants. As a result, the discussion in this section is likely to be relevant to you irrespective of the type of access that you intend to use.

The first level of access is **physical access** or entry (Gummesson 2000). The Internet has undoubtedly made accessing some secondary data easier. However, for much secondary as well as primary data gaining physical access can be difficult. First, organisations, groups or individuals may not be prepared to engage in additional, voluntary activities because of the time and resources required. Many organisations receive frequent student requests for access and cooperation and would find it impossible to agree to all or even some of these. Second, the request for access and cooperation may fail to interest the **gatekeeper** or **broker** who receives it, and who makes the final decision whether or not to allow the researcher to undertake the research. This may be for a number of reasons, related to:

- a lack of perceived value in relation to the work of the organisation, group or the individual;
- the nature of the topic because of its potential sensitivity, or because of concerns about the confidentiality of the information that would be required;
- perceptions about your credibility and doubts about your competence.

Third, the organisation or group may find itself in a difficult situation owing to external events totally unrelated to any perceptions about the nature of the request or the person making it, so that they have no choice but to refuse access. There may be other reasons for refusing access, known to the organisation, group or individuals concerned. Even when someone is prepared to offer access this may be overruled at a higher level in the organisation. This may result in a 'false start' and an associated feeling of disappointment (Johnson 1975). Where you are unable to gain this type of access, you will need to find another organisation or group, or to modify your research question and objectives.

However, even when you are able to negotiate entry there are other levels of access that you will need to consider and plan for if your research strategy is to be realised. Many writers see access as a **continuing** process and not just an initial or single event (Gummesson 2000; Marshall and Rossman 2011; Okumus et al. 2007). This may take two forms. First, access may be an iterative and incremental process, so that you gain entry to carry out the initial part of your research and then seek further access in order to conduct another part (see Box 6.1).

Second, those from whom you wish to collect data may be a different set of people to those who agreed to your request for access. Physical access to an organisation will be granted formally through its management. Because of this it will also be necessary for you to gain the acceptance and trust of, as well as consent from, intended participants within the organisation or group in order to gain actual access to the data that they are able to provide. This type of access is referred to as **cognitive access**. Where you achieve this, you will have gained access to the data that you need your intended participants to share with you in order to be able to address your research question and objectives. Simply obtaining physical access to an organisation is likely to be inadequate unless you are also able to negotiate yourself into a position where you can collect data that reveal the reality of what is occurring in relation to your research question and objectives.

Box 6.1
Focus on student research

Negotiating incremental access

Luc wished to undertake a series of interviews in the departments and sections of a data management company. He initially managed to negotiate access to commence his research in the management systems support department, where he was granted access to interview a sample of information systems support workers. As a result of conducting these interviews, he was then granted access within the same department to interview a sample of staff in the information technology section. Following the conduct of these interviews, the department's management team agreed to support his attempt to negotiate further access to interview staff in the company's accounting, human resources, marketing and sales departments.

Box 6.2
Focus on student research

Gaining access to a suitable sample

Maria wished to discover how component suppliers viewed the just-in-time delivery requirements of large manufacturing organisations that they supplied. Two large manufacturing organisations agreed to introduce her to a sample of their component suppliers, whom Maria could then interview. While undertaking the interviews Maria noted that all of the interviewees' responses were extremely positive about the just-in-time delivery requirements of both large manufacturing organisations. As both manufacturing organisations had selected who would be interviewed, Maria wondered whether these extremely positive responses were typical of all the component suppliers used by these organisations, or whether they were providing an unreliable and untypical picture.

The nature of the access you manage to negotiate may impact upon your ability to select a suitable sample of participants, or of secondary data, affecting your attempt to produce reliable and valid data to fulfil your objectives and answer your research question in an unbiased way (Box 6.2). In order to select a suitable sample of, for example, customers, clients or employees you will require access to organisational data, either directly or indirectly, through a request that outlines precisely how you require the sample to be selected (see Chapter 7 for a full discussion of sampling techniques). Where you wish to undertake a longitudinal study using primary data, you will require access to the organisation and your research participants on more than one occasion. The difficulty of obtaining access in relation to these more **intrusive methods** and approaches has been recognised many times in the literature (e.g. Buchanan et al. 2013; Johnson 1975).

Negotiating access is therefore likely to be important to gain **personal entry** to an organisation (or, in the case of Internet-mediated research, virtual access) and develop cognitive access to allow you to collect the necessary data. In this context, there are two general concepts that you may consider, which will help you to evaluate the nature of the access that you will require. These concepts are feasibility and sufficiency. **Feasibility** is concerned with whether it is practicable to negotiate access for your proposed research project. A research proposal may be grand and elegant, but if it is not possible to gain access to data then it will be necessary to revise what is being proposed. Once you have a proposal that you believe will be feasible in general terms, the next point to consider is whether you will be able to gain sufficient access to fulfil all of your research objectives. **Sufficiency** is therefore concerned with the extent to which the access you negotiate will enable your proposed research project to be achieved. You do not want to have to say, 'I could achieve objectives a, b and c but not x, y and z!' Or, perhaps more likely, 'I can achieve objectives a, b, y and z, but now I think about this carefully, I'm going to find it difficult to collect much data for c and x!' You therefore need to consider fully the nature of the access that you will require and whether you will able to gain sufficient access in practice to fulfil all of your objectives, to answer your research question. These issues of feasibility and sufficiency will be related in practice but it is useful to consider them separately as you formulate your research proposal. Your clarity of thought, which should result from having considered the nature and extent of the access that you require, may also be helpful in persuading organisations or groups to grant entry since they are more likely to be convinced about your credibility and competence.

The issues of feasibility and sufficiency will determine the construction or refinement of your research question and objectives, and may sometimes lead to a clash with the hallmarks of good research (e.g. Marshall and Rossman 2011; Sekaran and Bougie 2013). The ways in which these issues may clash with the hallmarks of good research and also affect the practice of research has been recognised by Buchanan et al. (2013: 53–4):

> Fieldwork is permeated with the conflict between what is theoretically desirable on the one hand and what is practically possible on the other. It is desirable to ensure representativeness in the sample, uniformity of interview procedures, adequate data collection across the range of topics to be explored, and so on. But the members of organisations block access to information, constrain the time allowed for interviews, lose your questionnaires, go on holiday, and join other organisations in the middle of your unfinished study. In the conflict between the desirable and the possible, the possible always wins.

This quotation highlights how, even when you consider feasibility and sufficiency carefully, you may still meet problems in practice. However, it should not be read as a justification for not considering these issues carefully. By considering these issues you will be more able to anticipate and overcome problems that occur in practice. The extent to which a careful consideration of feasibility will affect the approach that you adopt is made clear by Johnson (1975). He recognises that the reality of undertaking a research project may be to consider where you are likely to be able to gain access and to develop a topic to fit the nature of that access.

Problems of access may also vary in relation to your status as either a full-time or part-time student. We therefore consider further your role as either an external researcher or as an internal researcher. This latter role may involve you adopting the role of participant researcher.

Access issues as an external researcher

As a full-time student, approaching an organisation or group where you have little or no prior contact, you will be seeking to act as an **external researcher**. You will need to negotiate access at each level discussed earlier (physical, continuing and cognitive). Operating as an external researcher is likely to pose problems, although it may have some benefits. Your lack of status in relation to an organisation or group in which you wish to conduct research will mean not only that gaining physical access is a major issue to overcome but also that this concern will remain in relation to negotiating continued and cognitive access (Box 6.3). Goodwill on the part of the organisation or group and its members is something that external researchers have to rely on at each level of access. In this role, you need to remain sensitive to the issue of goodwill and seek to foster it at each level. Your ability to demonstrate clearly your research competence and integrity, and in particular your ability to explain your research project clearly and concisely, will also be critical at each level of access. These are key issues of access faced by all external researchers.

Where you are able to demonstrate competence (see Chapters 9 to 11) and integrity, your role as an external researcher may prove to be beneficial. This is because participants are usually willing to accept you as being objective and without a covert, often organisationally focused agenda. Your gatekeeper can also play an important role by creating awareness of your research, adding credibility by her or his intervention, and introducing you and your research project to the relevant people.

Box 6.3
Focus on student research

The impact of a researcher's organisational status

David recalls a case of mistaken identity. His research involved gaining access to several employers' and trade union organisations. Having gained access to the regional office of one such organisation, David read and noted various organisational documents kept there over a period of a few days. During the first day David was located in a large, comfortable room and frequently brought refreshments by the caretaker of the building. This appeared to David to be very kind treatment. However, David did not know that a rumour had spread among some staff that he was from 'head office' and was there to 'monitor' in some way the work of the office. On attending the second day, David was met by the caretaker and taken to a small, plain room and no more refreshments appeared for the duration of the research visit. The rumour had been corrected!

Of course this example of the effect of the researcher's (lack of) organisational status is most unfair on the large number of people who treat those who undertake research within their organisation very well in full knowledge of their status. However, it illustrates the way in which some people may react to perceptions about status.

Access issues as an internal researcher or participant researcher

As an organisational employee or group member operating in the role of an **internal researcher** or a **participant researcher**, you are still likely to face problems of access to data, although these may differ compared to those faced by external researchers. As an internal researcher you may still face the problems associated with negotiating physical or continuing access, and may still need to obtain formal approval to undertake research in your organisation or group. In addition, your status in the organisation or group may pose particular problems in relation to cognitive access. This may be related to suspicions about why you are undertaking your research project and the use that will be made of the data, perceptions about the part of the organisation for which you work and your status in relation to those whom you wish to be your research participants. Any such problems may be exacerbated if you are given a project to research, perhaps by your line manager or mentor, where others are aware that this is an issue about which management would like to implement change. This is particularly likely to be the case where resulting change is perceived as being harmful to those whom you would wish to be your research participants. This will not only provide a problem for you in terms of gaining cognitive access but may also suggest ethical concerns as well (which we discuss in Section 6.5). As an internal researcher, you will need to consider these issues and, where appropriate, discuss them with those who provide you with the research project.

6.3 Issues associated with Internet-mediated access 与互联网访问相关的问题

The Internet enables access to research data and to research participants in a variety of ways, although its use also raises a number of data quality and ethical issues. We outline these ways before considering data quality and ethical issues later. Quantitative and qualitative data collection techniques are increasingly used via the Internet. Questionnaires may be delivered as a hyperlink within an email, completed and returned online. Certain types of experiment may be conducted via the Internet (Birnbaum 2004). Interviews or discussion groups may take place online. For example, Stieger and Goritz (2006) explored the use of instant messaging and social networking, such as MSN Messenger and Facebook, to conduct Internet-based interviews. Interviews may also be conducted by email. They may also be conducted using a webcam, helping to overcome the impersonal nature of a text-based Internet interview. We discuss Internet-mediated research strategies and data collection methods, including the use of online documents, observation, interviewing and questionnaires, in Sections 5.3, 9.2, 10.9 and 11.5.

Online communities have generated extremely large amounts of qualitative material, some of which has been accessed by researchers. As these communities organise around an interest or a particular product, service, place or lifestyle, bulletin boards can be used to post messages and create a discussion over time among members. Email lists also allow groups to converse around a subject or subjects of mutual interest. Linked web pages provide online community resources organised by interest, such as for consumer-to-consumer discussion. **Blogs** (web logs) and limited character blogs or tweets are also popular. As a form of online journal or diary, where an individual provides for public consumption a narrative about his or her everyday life, or some aspect of it, blogs provide a commentary on events at a group, organisational or societal level. For example, numerous bloggers comment on political events, often from the perspective of their political beliefs. Others comment on their shopping experiences and offer consumer advice, or on their employment (Schoneboom 2011). Many blogs are organised through content management systems, and can also be accessed through specialised blog search engines as well as Internet search engines (Hookway 2008; Kozinets 2006).

These Internet-mediated methods are subject to the same issues that affect traditional methods to gain research access. In some circumstances, issues associated with access may even be exacerbated using Internet-based methods. While the Internet, and more specifically the use of email, social networking or a webcam, may facilitate communication between you and your participants, it will first be necessary to determine the most suitable way to negotiate access and conduct your research. This will, of course, depend on the nature of your research question and research objectives. Where your research is designed to be conducted through an organisation, it may be more appropriate to negotiate traditional access to collect data. This is because you will need to obtain the permission of a broker or gatekeeper to gain access to organisational members. Where you wish to negotiate access on a continuing basis (Box 6.1) your chance of success is likely to be enhanced where you meet with participants and organisational managers to develop rapport, demonstrate your competence and establish trust. Finally, where you are using more intrusive forms of data collection, such as an in-depth interview, a personal approach may provide you with richer research data. This indicates circumstances where traditional access will continue to be the most effective way to conduct research (Box 6.4).

Where you subsequently consider using Internet-mediated techniques, there may be circumstances where it would still be advantageous to negotiate initial access on a personal basis. This will remain the case where you require access to an organisation and need to obtain the permission of a broker or gatekeeper to gain access to a sample of organisational members. Where you are able to negotiate this, you may then be able to get the organisation to allow you to advertise your research by email, and provide a hyperlink to your questionnaire (Section 11.5). This highlights how access to organisations, intended participants and data may involve a **hybrid access strategy**, where access combines traditional and Internet-mediated approaches to achieve this.

Box 6.4
Focus on student research

Where sensitivity and context determined type of access

Sab had a keen interest in IT and thought that he would conduct his research using Internet-mediated access and data collection methods. His research focused on the ways in which senior managers influence board-level strategic decision making. His interest in this topic had developed after a fortuitous conversation with a senior personnel policy manager who worked for a large organisation, who had explained how in some cases strategy formation was influenced by promoting incremental changes rather than trying to bring about a radical change in one movement. This idea interested Sab and he formulated a research project to explore it in a range of organisational contexts. However, the more he thought about it and discussed it with his project tutor the more he realised that he would have to research it using traditional methods.

After negotiating physical access to interview six senior managers who worked in different functional areas in different organisations, he conducted an in-depth, exploratory interview with each one. While conducting these interviews he realised that the value and depth of the data he collected would have been much less if he had tried to conduct these using the Internet. His questioning was shaped by the data each participant shared with him during the interview. Because of the sensitive nature of the topic most of the interviews took the form of discussions, allowing Sab to clarify points and ask for illustrative examples. As each interview progressed, he found that some of his participants were willing to show him quite sensitive documents in the privacy of the interview room (which was the manager's own office). He found that rapport and trust were vital to the conduct of each interview. He also found that conducting an interview at the organisation helped to focus his mind and enhance his understanding of the organisational context. This in turn helped him to make sense of the data his participants shared with him.

Sab concluded that first negotiating physical access and then cognitive access on a person-to-person basis had been the most appropriate strategy to adopt and also the most effective. However, as he had met with each participant and established some rapport and trust, he asked each one if he would be able to email any further questions for clarification. Some agreed but others said that they would prefer to undertake this either by telephone or another face-to-face discussion.

Where you plan to conduct your research with a number of individuals it may be beneficial to identify an appropriate sample directly and then to negotiate **virtual access** (the equivalent of physical access) and cognitive access to your intended participants. The ability to identify your sample will be a key determinant of the feasibility of this approach. The choice of this access strategy will also depend on the nature of your research question and research objectives (Box 6.5).

6.4 Strategies to gain access 获取访问的策略

This section considers strategies that may help you to obtain physical, virtual, continuing and cognitive access to appropriate data. The applicability of the strategies discussed here to gain access will depend on the nature of your research design and research strategy (Chapter 5). It will also depend on your data collection methods (Chapters 8–11) and your use of traditional or Internet-mediated means to gain access. However, where you wish to gain access to an organisation, irrespective of whether you intend to use traditional or Internet-mediated means, or where your research involves human participants,

Box 6.5
Focus on student research

Where topic and strategy determined type of access

Elina's research focused on consumers' purchasing decisions. She was interested in assessing the relative importance of information obtained from online shopping sites and from high street shops in informing purchasing decisions for different product categories. These categories covered all of the products purchased by her age group, such as people on her marketing course.

Elina had formulated a mixed methods research design. She had designed a Web questionnaire that asked respondents to identify actual recent purchasing decisions related to the categories in which she was interested. For each of these, where applicable, she asked questions about the product, the sources of information used to inform the purchase decision and the way in which these sources determined the purchasing decision. Following ethical approval from her university, an email was sent to each person on

her course asking for their help and containing a hyperlink to the questionnaire. The questionnaire included a question asking each respondent if they were willing to help further by completing an electronic diary. Those who answered yes were asked to provide their email address so Elina could send them the diary.

Elina emailed the template of the electronic diary to all those willing to help further. She had designed this to allow respondents to record purchasing decisions related to her list of product categories, the sources of information used to inform these purchases and the way in which these sources determined the decision. Respondents returned the diary as an email attachment.

Elina was aware that her request to maintain an electronic diary of influences on purchasing decisions would sensitise respondents to their use of different information sources, so had distributed the questionnaire first. This she felt would help her judge the extent the participant had been sensitised as well as about the relative impact of these different sources.

Her use of an Internet-mediated access strategy proved successful in gaining access to both questionnaire respondents and a group of people who would keep a diary.

irrespective of whether you wish to observe them or ask them to complete a postal or Internet questionnaire, the strategies discussed here should be applicable. In addition, some of the points that follow will apply to the way in which you construct the pre-survey contact and the written request to complete the questionnaire (Sections 11.4 and 11.5). The applicability of these strategies will also vary in relation to your status as either an internal researcher or an external researcher. Table 6.1 presents the list of strategies that may help you to gain access.

Table 6.1 Strategies that may help you to gain access

- Ensuring you are familiar with the organisation or group before making contact
- Allowing yourself sufficient time
- Using existing contacts and developing new ones
- Providing a clear account of the purpose of your research and the type of access required
- Overcoming organisational concerns about granting access
- Identifying possible benefits to the organisation of granting you access
- Using suitable language
- Facilitating replies when requesting access
- Developing access incrementally
- Establishing your credibility

Ensuring familiarity with the organisation or group

Before attempting to gain physical access it is essential that you familiarise yourself fully with the characteristics of the organisation or group. The knowledge you gain will enable you to signal to the gatekeeper that you have thought carefully about your research, as you will be able to provide a credible case to justify your request to grant access to the organisation or group.

Allowing yourself sufficient time

Physical access may take weeks or even months to arrange, and in many cases the time invested will not result in access being granted (Buchanan et al. 2013). An approach to an organisation or group will result in either a reply or no response at all. A politely worded but clearly reasoned refusal at least informs you that access will not be granted. The non-reply situation means that if you wish to pursue the possibility of gaining access you will need to allow sufficient time before sending further correspondence, emailing or making a follow-up telephone call. Great care must be taken in relation to this type of activity so that no grounds for offence are given. Seeking access to a large, complex organisation, where you do not have existing contacts, may also necessitate several telephone calls to contact the most appropriate person to consider your request for access, or to establish who this will be. You may also consider using email as a way of making contact, although great care needs to be taken given the ease with which emails may sent 'in all directions'. Care also needs to taken in the composition of any email, as with any phone call or letter. As highlighted in Box 6.6, the process of gaining access to those who take part in your research may also involve several stages, for which you need to allow sufficient time.

Box 6.6 Focus on management research

Process to gain access

In a paper in *Gender, Work and Organization*, Kumra and Vinnicombe outline the process of gaining access to conduct research within a large, international consulting company. This research focused on conducting qualitative interviews with 19 female and 15 male consultants, 'to elicit their understanding of the conditions necessary to advance in their firm' related to the theory of social capital accumulation (Kumra and Vinnicombe 2010: 529).

The initial stage of this research project necessitated gaining access to the organisation. The next stage involved identifying a sample 'from the overall population to reflect a broad range of views on this topic' (Kumra and Vinnicombe 2010: 529). This first involved presenting the aims of the research project to representatives from the company's various Human Resource (HR) departments in the UK. The researchers then discussed and agreed with these HR representatives the criteria to be used to select potential participants. A list of potential participants was drawn up which was given to an administrator who wrote to each person with details about the purpose of the study and an invitation to take part. Following responses from those agreeing to participate, dates and times for interviews were then arranged and agreed.

At the stage of gaining face-to-face access to each participant the researcher opened the interview using an interview guide (Section 10.5; Box 10.6). This had a number of functions. It very briefly outlined the purpose of the study and the objectives for the interview. It assured participants about data confidentiality. It also listed 12 questions to guide the conduct of the interview. Data collection was then able to begin.

If you can contact a participant directly, such as a manager, an exchange of correspondence may be sufficient to gain access. Here you should clearly set out what you require from this person and persuade them of the value of your work and your credibility. Even so, you will still need to allow time for your request to be received and considered and an interview meeting to be arranged at a convenient time for your research participant. This may take a number of weeks, and you may have to wait for longer to schedule the actual interview.

Where you are seeking access to conduct a number of interviews, to undertake a questionnaire, to engage in observation or to use secondary data, your request may be passed 'up' the organisation or group for approval and is likely be considered by a number of people. Where you are able to use a known contact in the organisation or group this may help, especially where they are willing to act as a sponsor for your research. Even so, you will still need to allow for this process to take weeks rather than days. Where the organisation or group is prepared to consider granting access, it is likely that you will be asked to attend a meeting to discuss your research. There may also be a period of delay after this stage while the case that you have made for access is evaluated in terms of its implications for the organisation or group, and it may be necessary to make a number of telephone calls or emails to pursue your request politely.

In the situation where your intended participants or respondents are not the same people who grant you physical access, you will need to allow further time to gain their acceptance. This may involve you making **pre-survey contact** by telephoning these people (Section 11.5), engaging in correspondence or holding an explanatory meeting with them (discussed later). You may well need to allow a couple of weeks or more to establish contact and to secure cooperation, especially given any operational constraints that restrict individuals' availability.

Once you have gained physical access to the organisation or group and to your participants or respondents, you will be concerned with gaining cognitive access. Whichever method you are using to gather data will involve you in a time-consuming process, although some methods will require that more of your time be spent within the organisation or group to understand what is happening. The use of a questionnaire will mean less time spent in the organisation compared with the use of non-standardised interviews, whereas the use of some observation techniques can result in even more time being spent gathering data (Chapter 9). Where you are involved in a situation of continuing access, as outlined in this section, there will also be an issue related to the time that is required to negotiate, or renegotiate, access at each stage. You will need to consider how careful planning may help to minimise the possibility of any 'stop–go' approach to your research activity.

Using existing contacts and developing new ones

Most management and organisational researchers suggest that you are more likely to gain access where you are able to use **existing contacts** (Buchanan et al. 2013; Johnson 1975). Buchanan et al. (2013: 56) say that, 'we have been most successful where we have a friend, relative or student working in the organisation'. We have also found this to be the case. In order to request access we have approached colleagues, present or past students, course advisors, LinkedIn connections or those who are otherwise known to us through our networks. Their knowledge of us means that they can trust our stated intentions and the assurances we give about the use of any data provided. It can also be useful to start a research project by utilising these existing contacts in order to establish a track record that you can refer to in approaches you make to other organisations or groups where you do not have such contacts. This should help your credibility with these new contacts.

Use of known contacts will depend largely on your choice of research strategy, approach to selecting a sample, research question and objectives. It is likely to be easier to use this approach where you are using a case study, Action Research or ethnographic research strategy (Section 5.5). This will certainly be likely where you undertake an in-depth study that focuses on a small, purposively selected sample (Section 7.3). However, it may well be that you have a large number of connections through your professional and online networks and could adopt a survey strategy. There will clearly be a high level of convenience in terms of gaining access through contacts that are familiar; however, these contacts may also be cases in other non-probability samples (Section 7.3).

In many instances it may be possible for you to use your work placement organisation as the context for your research project. Where you have enjoyed a successful work placement, you will undoubtedly have made a number of contacts who may be able to be very helpful in terms of cooperating with you and granting access. You may have become interested in a particular topic because of the time that you spent in your placement organisation. Where this is so, you can spend time reading theoretical work that may be relevant to this topic, then identify a research question and objectives, and plan a research project to pursue your interest within the context of your placement organisation. The combination of genuine interest in the topic and relatively easy access to organisational participants should help towards the production of a good-quality and useful piece of work.

Where you need to develop **new contacts**, there may be several ways of finding these, depending on your research topic. You may consider asking the local branch of an appropriate professional association for the names and business addresses of key employees to contact in organisations where it would be suitable for you to conduct research. You could also contact this professional association at national level, where this is more appropriate to your research question and objectives. It might also be appropriate to contact either an employers' association for a particular industry, or a trade union, at local or national level. Alternatively, it might be appropriate for you to contact one or more chambers of commerce, skills training organisations or other employers' network. However, you need to be mindful that such associations and organisations are likely to receive literally hundreds of requests from students every year and so may have insufficient time or resources to respond.

You may also consider making a direct approach to an organisation or group in an attempt to identify the appropriate person to contact in relation to a particular research project. This has the advantage of potentially providing access to organisations or groups that you would like to include in your research project; however, great care needs to be exercised at each stage of the process (Box 6.7).

Using the approach outlined in Box 6.7 may result in you obtaining the business email addresses of possible organisational 'leads'. In this case you will need to send an email request to each person (Box 6.8). Where you consider this to be appropriate you will, of course, still need to follow the standards of care that you should use in drafting and sending a letter. The ease of using email may tempt some to use a lower level of care about the way their written communication is constructed. It may also lead to a temptation to send repeated messages. Use of email is considered later in our discussion about 'netiquette'. From a practical point of view using this means to make contact may result in a greater danger that the recipient of your email request simply deletes the message!

Box 6.7
Focus on student research

Identifying possible contacts through whom to request access

Andrew identified a number of specific organisations that matched the criteria established for the types of business he wished to include in his research project. Many of these were organisations where he did not have an appropriate contact, or indeed any contact at all. The different types of organisational structure in these organisations added to his difficulties in tracking down the most appropriate employee to contact in order to request access.

Organisations' websites were used to identify the corporate headquarters of each organisation, which was then contacted by telephone. When talking to each organisation, Andrew explained that he was a student and gave the title of his course and the name of his university. He also gave a very brief explanation of his research to the person who answered the telephone. This resulted in him being provided with a telephone number or email address for that part of the organisation the person who answered the telephone thought was appropriate, or being connected directly. Andrew always ended this initial telephone conversation by thanking the person for the help that they had provided.

At the next stage, Andrew again explained that he was a student and gave the title of his course and the name of his university. The purpose of the research was also explained briefly to the personal assistant who inevitably answered the telephone. Andrew asked for the name and business address of the person whom the personal assistant thought would be the most appropriate person to write to, or to email. In most cases the people to whom he spoke at this stage were helpful and provided some excellent leads.

Sometimes, particularly in relation to complex organisations, Andrew found that he was not talking to someone in the appropriate part of the organisation. He therefore asked the person to help by transferring the telephone call. Sometimes this led to a series of calls to identify the right person. Andrew always remained polite, thanking the person to whom he spoke for her or his help. He always gave his name and that of his university to reduce the risk of appearing to be threatening in any way. It was most important to create a positive attitude in what could be perceived as a tiresome enquiry.

Andrew chose to ask for the name and business address of a hoped-for organisational 'lead'. Using this he could send a written request to this person, which could be considered when it was convenient, rather than attempt to talk to them then, when it might well have not been a good time to make such a request. This process resulted in many successes, and Andrew added a number of good contacts to his previous list. However, the key point to note is the great care that was exercised when using this approach.

People who receive large numbers of email may cope by deleting any that are not essential. Sending a letter to a potential gatekeeper may result in that person considering your request more carefully!

Using the type of contact outlined in Box 6.7 may result in identifying the person whom you wish to participate in your research. Alternatively, your reason for making contact with this person may be to ask them to grant you access to others in the organisation or group whom you wish to be your participants, or to secondary data. This type of contact may be the functional manager or director of those staff to whom you would like access. Having identified a gatekeeper you will have to persuade that person about your credibility, overcome any issues that exist about the sensitivity of your research project and demonstrate the potential value of this for the organisation.

Box 6.8
Focus on student research

Email requesting access

Annette was undertaking her research project on the use of lean production systems. Having made telephone contact with the Production Controller's personal assistant, she was asked to send an email requesting access (see below).

Unfortunately, Annette relied on her email software's spellcheck to proofread her email. This resulted in the Production Controller receiving an email containing four mistakes:

- the addition of the word 'I' at the end of the first paragraph;
- the phrase 'between 30 minutes and half an hour' instead of 'between 30 minutes and an hour' at the end of the second paragraph;
- two digits being transposed in the mobile telephone number at the end of the last paragraph, resulting in it being incorrect;
- the second sentence of the final paragraph being poorly worded.

Not surprisingly, Annette was denied access.

Research Project: The Use of Lean Production Systems   Draft saved at (

B *I* U Aa A⁺ A ✎ ☰ ☷ ⇥ ⇤ ☰ ☰ ☰ ∞ ☺

Dear Mr Kolowski

Further to my telephone conversation with your personal assistant, Tom Penny, I would like to meet with you and discuss the use of lean production systems at Manufac PLC. The interview is part of a series I am arranging with a carefully selected sample of production managers for my degree in Business Management at the University of Anytown. I

An outline of my proposed interview structure is attached, although it is not my intention to follow it slavishly. I am hoping to conduct these interviews in January and February and envisage that they will last between 30 minutes and half an hour.

I am fully aware of the need to treat the data you give me with the utmost confidentiality. No source, individual or organisational, will be identified or comment attributed without written permission of the originator.

One of my intended outputs will be a report summarising the findings and I will be sending a copy of this to each of the participants in the study.

I hope that you are able to help me and would be extremely grateful if you could let me know by replying to this email. As discussed with Tom Penny, I can then contact them to arrange a suitable time and venue at your convenience. If you prefer to talk to me to agree a suitable time and venue, please telephone me on 07987-6543210. If you require further information, please do not hesitate to get in touch.

Yours sincerely,

Providing a clear account of the purpose and type of access required

Providing a clear account of your requirements will allow your intended participants to be aware of what will be required from them. Asking for access and cooperation without being specific about your requirements will probably lead to a cautious attitude on their part since the amount of time that could be required might prove to be disruptive. It is also likely to be considered unethical (Section 6.5). Even where the initial contact or request for access involves a telephone call, it is still probably advisable to send a letter or email that outlines your proposed research and requirements (Box 6.8).

Your **introductory letter** requesting access should outline in brief the purpose of your research, how the person being contacted might be able to help, and what is likely to be involved in participating. The success of this letter will be helped by the use of short and clear sentences. Its tone should be polite, and it should seek to generate interest on the part of intended respondents.

Establishing your credibility will be vital in order to gain access. The use of known contacts will mean that you can seek to trade on your existing level of credibility. However, when you are making contact with a potential participant for the first time, the nature of your approach will be highly significant in terms of beginning to establish credibility – or not doing so! Any telephone call, introductory letter or email will need to be well presented, and demonstrate your clarity of thought and purpose. Any lack of preparation at this stage will be apparent and is likely to reduce the possibility of gaining access. These issues are discussed in more detail in Section 10.4.

Overcoming organisational concerns about granting access

Organisational concerns may be placed into one of three categories. First, concerns about the amount of time or resources that will be involved in the request for access. Your request for access is more likely to be accepted if the amount of time and resources you ask for are kept to a minimum. As a complementary point, Healey (1991) reports earlier work which found that introductory letters (or emails) containing multiple requests are also less likely to be successful. However, while the achievement of access may be more likely to be realised where your demands are kept to a minimum, there is still a need to maintain honesty. For example, where you wish to conduct an interview you may be more likely to gain access if the time requested is kept within reason. Remember, stating falsely that it will last for only a short time and then deliberately exceeding this is very likely to upset your participant and may prevent you gaining further access.

The second area of concern is related to **sensitivity** about the topic. We have found that organisations are less likely to cooperate where the topic of the research has negative implications. Organisations do not normally wish to present themselves as not performing well in any aspect of their business. If this is likely to be the case you will need to consider carefully the way in which your proposed research topic may be perceived by those whom you ask to grant access. In such cases you may be able to highlight a positive approach to the issue by, for example, emphasising that your work will be designed to identify individual and organisational learning in relation to the topic (a positive inference). You should avoid sending any request that appears to concentrate on aspects associated with non-achievement or failure if you are to gain access. Your request for access is therefore more likely to be favourably considered where you are able to outline a research topic that does not appear to be sensitive to the organisation.

The third area of concern is related to the **confidentiality** of the data that would have to be provided and the **anonymity** of the organisation or individual participants. To overcome this concern, you will need to provide clear assurances about these aspects (Box 6.8). When offering these you must be sure that you will be able to keep to your agreement. Strictly, if you have promised confidentiality you should not share your raw data with anyone, not even your project tutor, or present this as it may be recognised or identified. Data remain confidential and you will need to present the analysed results at a sufficient level of generalisation so that identification is not possible. Anonymity ensures that no one will know who participated in your research and that no one is able to identify the source of any response. One advantage of using an introductory letter is to give this guarantee in writing at the time of making the request for access, when this issue may be uppermost in the minds of those who will consider your approach. Once initial access has been granted you will need to repeat any assurances about anonymity and confidentiality to your participants as you seek their consent (Section 6.6). You will also need to consider how to maintain these assurances when you write up your work in situations where particular participants could be indirectly identified (Section 14.6). Illustrations of how not to do this are provided in Box 6.18.

Possible benefits to the organisation of granting access

Apart from any general interest that is generated by the subject of your proposed research, you may find that it will be useful to the jobs undertaken by those whom you approach for access. Practitioners often wrestle with the same subjects as researchers and may therefore welcome the opportunity to discuss their own analysis and course of action related to an issue, in a non-threatening, non-judgemental environment. A discussion may allow them to think through an issue and to reflect on the action that they have adopted to manage it. For this reason, in our own interviews with practitioners we are pleased when told that the discussion has been of value to them.

For those who work in organisations where they are perhaps the only subject practitioner, this may be the first time they have had this type of opportunity. You therefore need to consider whether your proposed research topic may provide some advantage to those from whom you wish to gain access, although this does not mean that you should attempt to 'buy' your way in based on some promise about the potential value of your work. Where it is unlikely that your proposed research may assist those whose cooperation you seek, you will need to consider what alternative course of action to take.

It may help to offer a summary report of your findings to those who grant access. The intention here would be to provide something of value and to fulfil any expectations about exchange between the provider and receiver of the research data, thereby prompting some of those whom you approach to grant access (Johnson 1975). We believe it is essential that this summary report is designed specifically to be of use to those who granted access rather than, say, a copy of the research report you need to submit to your university. It is also possible that feedback from the organisation about this summary report may help you further with your research.

Where access is granted in return for supplying a report of your findings it may be important to devise a simple 'contract' to make clear what has been agreed. This should state the broad form of the report and the nature and depth of the analysis that you agree to include in it, and how you intend to deal with issues of confidentiality and anonymity. This may vary from a summary report of key findings to a much more in-depth analysis. For this reason it will be important to determine what will be realistic to supply to those who grant you access.

Using suitable language

Some researchers advise against using certain research terms when making an approach to an organisation for access, because these may be perceived as threatening or not interesting to the potential participant. Buchanan et al. (2013: 57) suggest using the phrase 'learn from your experience' in place of research, 'conversation' instead of interview and 'write an account' rather than publish.

Use of language will depend largely on the nature of the people you are contacting. Your language should be appropriate to the person being contacted, without any hint of being patronising, threatening or just boring. Given the vital role of initial telephone conversations, introductory letters or emails, we would suggest allowing adequate time to consider and draft these and using someone to check through your message. (You may find Section 11.4, and in particular Box 11.15, helpful in this process.) Do not forget that you need to engender interest in your research project, and the initial point of contact needs to convey this.

Facilitating replies when requesting access

We have found that the inclusion of a number of different contact methods (telephone, mobile phone, email) in our written requests for access helps to ensure a reply. These may not be suitable in all cases, and should be selected to fit the data collection technique you intend to use. Inclusion of a stamped or postage pre-paid (freepost) addressed envelope may also facilitate a reply.

Developing access incrementally

We have already referred to the strategy of achieving access by stages, as a means of overcoming organisational concerns about time-consuming, multiple requests. Johnson (1975) provides an example of developing access on an incremental basis. He used a three-stage strategy to achieve his desired depth of access. The first stage involved a request to conduct interviews. This was the minimum requirement in order to commence his research. The next stage involved negotiating access to undertake observation. The final stage was in effect an extension to the second stage and involved gaining permission to audio-record the interactions being observed.

There are potentially a number of advantages related to the use of this strategy. As suggested earlier, a request to an organisation for multiple access may be sufficient to cause them to decline entry. Using an incremental strategy at least gains you access to a certain level of data. This strategy will also allow you the opportunity to develop a positive relationship with those who are prepared to grant initial access of a restricted nature. As you establish your credibility, you can develop the possibility of achieving a fuller level of access. A further advantage may follow from the opportunity that you have to design your request for further access specifically to the situation and in relation to opportunities that may become apparent from your initial level of access. On the other hand, this incremental process will be time consuming, and you need to consider the amount of time that you will have for your research project before embarking on such a strategy. In addition, it can be argued that it is unethical not to explain your access requirements fully.

Establishing your credibility

In Section 6.2 we differentiated between physical and cognitive access. Just because you have been granted entry into an organisation you will not be able to assume that those whom you wish to interview, observe or answer a questionnaire will be prepared to provide their cooperation. Indeed, assuming that this is going to happen raises an ethical issue that is considered in the next section. Gaining cooperation from intended participants is a matter of developing relationships. This will mean repeating much of the process that you will have used to gain entry into the organisation. You will need to share with them the purpose of your research project, state how you believe that they will be able to help your study and provide assurances about confidentiality and anonymity. This may involve writing to your intended participants or talking to them individually or in a group. Which of these means you use will depend on your opportunity to make contact with participants, the number of potential participants involved, the nature of the setting and your intended data collection techniques. However, your credibility and the probability of individuals' participation are likely to be enhanced if the request for participation is made jointly with a senior person from the organisation (Box 6.9). Where your intended data collection technique may be considered intrusive, you may need to exercise even greater care and take longer to gain acceptance. This might be the case, for example, where you wish to undertake observation (Chapter 9). The extent to which you succeed in gaining cognitive access will depend on this effort.

The strategies that we have outlined to help you to gain access to organisations and to those whom you wish to participate in your research project are summarised as a checklist in Box 6.10.

Box 6.9
Focus on student research

Email request to participate in a focus group

Sara's research project involved her in undertaking a communication audit for an organisation near her university. As part of her research design she had chosen to use mixed method research using focus groups followed by a questionnaire. Those selected to attend the focus groups were invited by individual emails sent jointly from herself and a senior manager within the organisation.

Invitation to Join an Employee Discussion Group   Draft saved at 18

B *I* U̲ Aa A⁺ A̲ ∠ ⅓≡ ≔ ≑ ∗≑ ≡ ≡ ≡ ⊖ ☺

Dear <forename> <family name>

As you have read in the latest edition of *Staff News*, we are undertaking a communications audit. This work is being undertaken on our behalf by Sara Smith from the University of Anytown Business School. In order to explore attitudes held by members of staff we will be holding a series of five discussion groups. Your views are important in order for us to be able to build up a clear picture of employee attitudes about internal communication. The attitudes revealed at these discussion groups will be used to help design a questionnaire emailed to all members of staff.

Each discussion group should last no longer than one hour. Comments made during the discussion group will not be attributable to nay individual or that group and will only be used to help designing the questionnaire. The discussion group will be chaired by Sara Smith from the University. On completion of the audit, key results will be communicated to all members of staff in *Staff News*.

The discussion group to which you have been invited will be held on <day> <date> of <month> at <time> in room <number>. Whilst you are under no obligation to attend, we hope you will. If you are unable to attend, please can you click on the reply button. Alternatively you can contact Sara at the University on 01234-567891. This will allow us to invite an appropriate alternative person in your place.

We very much hope that you can attend. If you have any queries or are unable to attend, please let Sara or myself know.

Yours sincerely

Michaela Munroe   Sara Smith
Director of Personnel   University of Anytown
Ext. 12345   01234-567891

Box 6.10
Checklist

To help to gain access

✔ Have you allowed yourself plenty of time for the entire process?

✔ Are you clear about the purpose of your research project?

✔ Are you clear about your requirements when requesting access (at least your initial requirements)?

✔ Can you use existing contacts, at least at the start of your research project, in order to gain access and gather data?

✔ (If you have been on a work placement) Is your work placement organisation an appropriate setting for your research project?

✔ Have you approached appropriate local and/or national employer, or employee, professional or trade bodies to see if they can suggest contacts through whom you might gain access?

✔ Have you considered making a direct approach to an organisation to identify the most appropriate person to contact for access?

✔ Have you identified the most appropriate person and been willing to keep on trying to make contact?

✔ Have you drafted a list of the points you wish to make, including your thanks to those to whom you speak?

✔ Have you considered and thought through how you will address likely organisational concerns such as:

- the amount of time or resources that would be involved on the part of the organisation;
- the sensitivity of your research topic;
- the need for confidentiality and anonymity?

✔ Have you considered the possible benefits for the organisation should access be granted to you, and the offer of a report summarising your findings to enhance your chance of achieving access?

✔ Are you willing to attend a meeting to present and discuss your request for access?

✔ Where your initial request for access involves a telephone conversation, have you followed this with an introductory letter to confirm your requirements?

✔ Is the construction, tone and presentation of your introductory letter likely to support your request to gain access?

✔ Have you ensured that your use of language is appropriate to the person who receives it without any hint of being patronising, threatening or boring?

✔ Have you considered including a range of contact methods for recipients to use to reply?

✔ Are you prepared to work through organisational gatekeepers in order to gain access to intended participants?

✔ Have you allowed sufficient time to contact intended participants and gain their acceptance once physical access has been granted?

✔ Have you allowed sufficient time within your data collection to gain 'cognitive access' to data?

6.5 Research ethics and why you should act ethically 研究道德规范以及为什么行为应符合道德规范

Defining research ethics

Ethical concerns will emerge as you design and plan your research, seek access to organisations and to individuals, collect, analyse, manage and report your data. In the context of research, **ethics** refer to the standards of behaviour that guide your conduct in relation to the rights of those who become the subject of your work, or are affected by it. Standards of behaviour will be guided by a number of influences. The appropriateness or acceptability of a researcher's conduct will be influenced by broader social norms of behaviour. A **social norm** indicates the type of behaviour that a person ought to adopt in a particular situation; however, the norms of behaviour that prevail will in reality allow for a range of ethical positions.

The philosophical foundations of research ethics also illustrate that a researcher's conduct may be open to competing and conflicting ethical positions (Berry 2004; Thomas 1996). Two dominant and conflicting philosophical positions have been identified: deontological and teleological. A **deontological view** is based on following rules to guide researchers' conduct. According to this view, acting outside the rules can never be justified. Where the rules are inadequate or contested, it would be necessary to reappraise and if required amend them. In contrast, the **teleological view** argues that deciding whether an act of conduct is justified or not should be determined by its consequences, not by a set of predetermined rules. This would involve deciding whether the benefits of undertaking an act outweigh the negative consequences from this action. However, it is unlikely that a simple comparison between the benefits to one group and costs to another would provide you with a clear answer to such an ethical dilemma.

Attempts to overcome ethical dilemmas arising from different social norms and conflicting philosophical approaches have resulted in the widespread development of **codes of ethics**. These generally contain a list of principles outlining the nature of ethical research and a statement of ethical standards to accompany these principles that are intended to guide your research conduct. As a member of a university (and where appropriate a professional association) you are likely to be required to abide by such an ethical code or adhere to its ethical guidelines for research. Codes of ethics (Table 6.2) explicitly or implicitly recognise that ethical dilemmas exist and that it will often be necessary to exercise some choice about conduct. For example, the Statement of Ethical Practice produced by British Sociological Association expressly recognises that it is not possible to produce 'a set of recipes' to deal with all ethical dilemmas but that researchers need to exercise choice based on ethical principles and standards (British Sociological Association 2002: 1). The key point is that by producing such ethical principles and standards, researchers and ethical reviewers (discussed shortly) have an ethical basis against which to anticipate issues and risk, and exercise choice to avoid conflict and harm.

The conduct of your research is therefore likely to be guided by your university's code of ethics or ethical guidelines, highlighting what is and what is not considered ethical. This will be helpful and, where followed, should ensure that you do not transgress the behavioural norms established by your university or professional association. However, as Bell and Bryman (2007) point out, such codes tend to be written in abstract terms and are designed to prevent misconduct. This means you will need to interpret the principles and standards contained in the code of ethics with care and apply them to the context of your own proposed research project. Table 6.2 provides Internet addresses for a selection of codes of ethics and ethical guidelines, which may be potentially useful for your research.

You should expect to submit your research proposal for ethical review. All students' research will be expected to comply with a university's code of ethics or ethical guidelines and the principles and standards that it contains. The nature of ethical review will depend on the nature of the research being proposed. Ethical review may be conducted by your project tutor or by two or more academic staff using an ethics protocol. You may also be asked to complete an ethical review form. This 'light touch' or 'fast track' review, overseen by your school or faculty ethics committee, is likely to allow non-controversial research proposals that pose minimal risk to participants and others to be considered without too much delay. A fuller ethical review conducted by your school or faculty ethics committee may be required where proposals raise ethical concerns or are considered

Table 6.2 Internet addresses for ethical codes, guidelines and statements of research practice

Name	Internet address
Academy of Management's Code of Ethics	http://www.aomonline.org/governanceandethics/aomrevisedcodeofethics.pdf
Academy of Social Sciences' Generic Ethical Principles	https://acss.org.uk/developing-generic-ethics-principles-social-science/
American Psychological Association's Ethical Principles of Psychologists and Code of Conduct	http://www.apa.org/ethics/code/principles.pdf
Association of Business Schools' Ethics Guide	http://www.associationofbusinessschools.org/sites/default/files/2010_ethics_guide_agm_version.pdf
British Academy of Management's Code of Ethics and Best Practice	https://www.bam.ac.uk/sites/bam.ac.uk/files/The%20British%20Academy%20of%20Management%27s%20Code%20of%20Ethics%20and%20Best%20Practice%20for%20Members.pdf
British Psychological Society's Code of Ethics and Conduct	http://www.bps.org.uk/system/files/documents/code_of_ethics_and_conduct.pdf
British Sociological Association's Statement of Ethical Practice	http://www.britsoc.co.uk/media/27107/StatementofEthicalPractice.pdf
Economic and Social Research Council's (ESRC) Framework for Research Ethics (FRE)	http://www.esrc.ac.uk/_images/framework-for-research-ethics-09-12_tcm8-4586.pdf
European Union's Respect Code of Practice for Socio-Economic Research (The Respect Project)	http://www.respectproject.org/code/respect_code.pdf
European Science Foundation's The European Code of Conduct for Research Integrity	http://www.esf.org/fileadmin/Public_documents/Publications/Code_Conduct_ResearchIntegrity.pdf
Market Research Society's Code of Conduct	http://www.mrs.org.uk/pdf/code_of_conduct.pdf
Researcher Development Initiative's Research Ethics Guidebook	www.ethicsguidebook.ac.uk
Social Research Association's Ethical Guidelines	http://the-sra.org.uk/wp-content/uploads/ethics03.pdf
UK Department for Innovation, Universities and Skills' Universal Ethical Code for Scientists	http://www.bis.gov.uk/assets/goscience/docs/u/universal-ethical-code-scientists.pdf
UK Research Integrity Office's Code of Practice for Research	http://www.ukrio.org/publications/code-of-practice-for-research/
Universities UK's The Concordat to Support Research Integrity	http://www.universitiesuk.ac.uk/highereducation/Pages/Theconcordattosupportresearchintegrity.aspx#.UzFfB854B0p

to have higher levels of risk. You will need to be aware of potential ethical concerns and risks to those involved as you design your research proposal so that you can seek to avoid them. You should not assume that using particular techniques will reduce the possibility of ethical concerns or risk. While the use of observation or interviews may appear to be more intrusive than designing a questionnaire, it is possible that the latter may raise ethical concerns and risk to participants. It is the nature of the questions that you wish to ask and the nature of your intended participants that may raise ethical concerns rather than the research method that you intend to use.

Research ethics committees fulfil a number of objectives. These may include a proactive role, such as developing an ethical code, and an educational one, such as disseminating advice about conducting research ethically. The primary role of a research ethics committee will be to review all research conducted by those in the institution that involves human participants and personal data. The research ethics committee will be responsible for examining aspects of research quality that relate to ethics; protecting the rights, dignity and welfare of those who participate in this research as well as others who may be affected by it; and considering the safety of researchers. A research ethics committee is therefore responsible for all aspects of ethical review and approval. It is likely to be composed of experienced researchers from a variety of backgrounds, who are able to draw on their range of experience and knowledge of different ethical perspectives to provide advice. It will be expected to act in an impartial and independent way and its independence is likely to be supported by the inclusion of at least one external member, who otherwise has no connection to the institution.

In some cases you may also have to satisfy the requirements of an ethics committee established in your host organisation as well as your university. This may apply where your research is based in the health service. For example, many of our students undertaking research within the UK's National Health Service (NHS) have had to meet the requirements established by their local NHS Trust's ethics committee (Box 6.11). Such a requirement is often time consuming to meet.

Approval of your research proposal should not be interpreted as the end of your consideration of ethical issues (McAreavey and Muir 2011). Consideration of ethical issues should remain at the forefront of your thinking throughout the course of your research project and even beyond it. In Section 6.6 we consider ethical issues that arise at specific stages in the research process. In preparation for this consideration we firstly consider a range of general ethical issues that permeate research and which therefore form the focus of codes of ethical conduct. We also consider a range of general issues that are associated with Internet-mediated research.

General categories of ethical issues and the formulation of principles to recognise and overcome or minimise these

General categories of ethical issues are recognised in codes of ethics. These are ethical issues that occur across many approaches to research. Rather than write highly detailed and prescriptive regulations to anticipate and deal with these for each research approach, codes of ethics instead contain a set of principles that allow researchers to apply these principles to the context of their own research and to that of others. We now consider a number of principles that have been developed to recognise ethical issues that occur across many different approaches to research. These are outlined in Table 6.3.

Box 6.11
Focus on student research

Establishing whether research warrants mandated ethical review

Rachel worked for a local hospital. At her first meeting with her project tutor, he had reminded her to check with the hospital and establish if she would need to submit her research project to the hospital's research ethics committee for review. Subsequently, she discussed this with her line manager who suggested she check with the UK National Health Service's National Research Ethics Service. Using the Google search engine, Rachel found the Service's website and downloaded their leaflet, *Defining Research* (Health Research Authority 2013).

The *Defining Research* leaflet highlighted that, although research normally requires a Research Ethics Committee review, it was not mandatory for either audit or service evaluation. This did not mean there were no ethical issues associated with audit or service evaluation,

only that there was not a mandatory requirement for a Research Ethics Committee review. The leaflet also provided clear definitions of what was meant by the terms 'research', 'audit' and 'service evaluation':

Research is 'the attempt to derive generalisable new knowledge including studies that aim to generate hypotheses, as well as studies that aim to test them'.

Audit is 'designed and conducted to produce information to inform delivery of best care'.

Service evaluation is 'designed and conducted solely to define or judge current care'.

Based on these definitions and the other information in the leaflet, Rachel felt that her research project was 'service evaluation' rather than research. She discussed this with her line manager who agreed, but suggested that she also confirm with the Chair of the Research Ethics Committee that her project was a 'service evaluation'. The Committee Chair agreed with Rachel and her line manager.

Table 6.3 Ethical principles and the ethical rationale for and development of each principle

Ethical principle	Ethical rationale for and development of this principle
Integrity and objectivity of the researcher	The quality of research depends in part on the integrity and objectivity of the researcher. This means acting openly, being truthful and promoting accuracy. Conversely it also means avoiding deception, dishonesty, misrepresentation (of data and findings etc.), partiality, reckless commitments or disingenuous promises. Where appropriate, any conflict of interest or commercial association should be declared
Respect for others	A researcher's position is based on the development of trust and respect. The conduct of research entails social responsibility and obligations to those who participate in or are affected by it. The rights of all persons should be recognised and their dignity respected
Avoidance of harm (non-maleficence)	Any harm to participants must be avoided. Harm may occur through risks to emotional well-being, mental or physical health, or social or group cohesion. It may take a number of forms including embarrassment, stress, discomfort, pain or conflict. It may be caused by using a research method in an intrusive or zealous way that involves mental or social pressure causing anxiety or stress. It may also be caused by violating assurances about confidentiality and anonymity, or through harassment or discrimination

(continued)

Table 6.3 (*Continued*)

Ethical principle	Ethical rationale for and development of this principle
Privacy of those taking part	Privacy is a key principle that links to or underpins several other principles considered here. Respect for others, the avoidance of harm, the voluntary nature of participation, informed consent, ensuring confidentiality and maintaining anonymity, responsibility in the analysis of data and reporting of findings, and compliance in the management of data are all linked to or motivated by the principle of ensuring the privacy of those taking part
Voluntary nature of participation and right to withdraw	The right not to participate in a research project is unchallengeable. This is accompanied by the right not to be harassed to participate. It is also unacceptable to attempt to extend the scope of participation beyond that freely given. Those taking part continue to exercise the right to determine how they will participate in the data collection process, including rights: not to answer any question, or set of questions; not to provide any data requested; to modify the nature of their consent; to withdraw from participation and possibly to withdraw data they have provided
Informed consent of those taking part	The principle of informed consent involves researchers providing sufficient information and assurances about taking part to allow individuals to understand the implications of participation and to reach a fully informed, considered and freely given decision about whether or not to do so, without the exercise of any pressure or coercion. This leads to the right of those taking part to expect the researcher to abide by the extent of the consent given and not to find that the researcher wishes to prolong the duration of an interview or observation, or to widen the scope of the research without first seeking and obtaining permission, or to commit any subsequent breach of the consent given
Ensuring confidentiality of data and maintenance of anonymity of those taking part	Research is designed to answer 'who', 'what', 'when', 'where', 'how' and 'why' questions, not to focus on those who provide the data to answer these. Individuals and organisations should therefore remain anonymous and the data they provide should be processed to make it non-attributable, unless there is an explicit agreement to attribute comments. Harm may result from unauthorised attribution or identification. Reliability of data is also likely to be enhanced where confidentiality and anonymity are assured. This principle leads to the right to expect assurances about anonymity and confidentiality to be observed strictly
Responsibility in the analysis of data and reporting of findings	Assurances about privacy, anonymity and confidentiality must be upheld when analysing and reporting data. Primary data should not be made up or altered and results should not be falsified. Findings should be reported fully and accurately, irrespective of whether they contradict expected outcomes. The same conditions apply to secondary data, the source or sources of which should also be clearly acknowledged. Analyses and the interpretations that follow from these should be checked carefully and corrections made to ensure the accuracy of the research report and any other outcome

Ethical principle	Ethical rationale for and development of this principle
Compliance in the management of data	Research is likely to involve the collection of personal data. Many governments have passed legislation to regulate the processing of personal data. There is therefore a statutory requirement to comply with such legislation. In the European Union, European Directive 95/46/CE has led member states to pass data protection legislation. Other laws may exist in particular countries relating to the processing, security and possible sharing of data. It will therefore be essential for researchers to understand and comply with the legal restrictions and regulations that relate to the management of research data within the country or countries within which they conduct research
Ensuring the safety of the researcher	The safety of researchers is a very important consideration when planning and conducting a research project. The Social Research Association's Code of Practice for the Safety of Social Researchers identifies possible risks from social interactions including 'risk of physical threat or abuse; risk of psychological trauma . . . ; risk of being in a compromising situation . . . ; increased exposure to risks of everyday life' (Social Research Association 2001: 1). Research design therefore needs to consider risks to researchers as well as to participants

Notes and Sources: The ethical codes and guidelines listed in Table 6.2 were helpful in informing the contents of this table. Table 6.3 seeks to synthesise key points from many different approaches to writing ethical principles. It should not be interpreted as providing completely comprehensive guidance. You are advised to consult the code of ethics defined as being appropriate for your research project. References to legislation in Table 6.3 and elsewhere provide only general indications and should not be interpreted as providing legal advice, or the existence of such types of law in all countries.

Codes of ethics are intended to avoid poor practice, malpractice and harm (**non-maleficence**) as well as to promote ethical practice and private or public good (**beneficence**). To avoid harm, or at the very least to minimise it, it is necessary to evaluate risk. Evaluating risk involves thinking about the likelihood of harm occurring and the extent or severity of the harm that would be caused. As we indicated in Table 6.3, harm may take a number of forms and lead to a range of consequences. Estimating risk is not straightforward and it may be affected by a number of contextual or cultural factors. However, it is important to anticipate risk in each research situation to attempt to avoid the likelihood of causing harm. Box 6.12 suggests a number of questions that you may ask to seek to assess risk, although others may suggest themselves related to the research context within which you are operating (Section 6.6).

Research may result in benefits for the researcher, research participants, the group or organisation being researched, or for the community or society within which it occurs. As we discussed in Section 6.4, it is important and ethical to be realistic about the benefits you claim for your research project and to honour any promises made about sharing findings, such as promising to send a summary report to an organisation that provides access to host your research. Adopting ethical behaviour means more than just using a code of ethics as a way to get your research proposal approved. Acting ethically means thinking about each aspect and each stage of your research from an ethical perspective. Where you do this, you will have internalised the values of acting ethically and this should help you to anticipate concerns at each stage of your research.

Box 6.12
Checklist

Assessing risk in research

✔ Is your proposed research likely to harm the well-being of those participating?

✔ Will others be harmed by the process or outcomes of your proposed research?

✔ How may this harm occur and what characteristics may make this more likely?

✔ How likely it is that harm might result?

✔ How severe would be any resulting harm?

✔ Which features or what aspects of your research may cause harm?

✔ How intrusive is your proposed research method or methods?

✔ How sensitive are your proposed questions, observations, searches or requests for data?

✔ Can you justify your choice of research method or methods and tactics; in particular, can you explain why alternatives that involve fewer potential risks cannot be used?

✔ Where anticipated risk cannot be reduced any further during the design of the research

and ethical review is favourable, how will the implementation of your research seek to avoid the occurrence of risk in practice, or at the very least to seek to minimise it?

✔ Does the information you provided to intended participants to facilitate informed consent also allow them to contact you to discuss potential concerns? How have you facilitated this while maintaining your own privacy (e.g. using a university email address, not your personal email or home address)?

✔ How will you commence a data collection activity to allow potential concerns to be raised first? How will you make yourself aware of themes that may be sensitive for particular participants?

✔ How will you reinforce the voluntary nature of participation to allow participants not to answer a particular question, set of questions, or to decline any request for data?

✔ Other potential risks are likely to be evident within the context of your particular research project. What might these be and how will you manage them?

General ethical issues associated with Internet-mediated research

While the Internet may help to facilitate access to some categories of participants and certain types of data, its use raises a number of issues and even dilemmas about the applicability of the ethical principles referred to in Table 6.3 to Internet-mediated research. The ethical issues and dilemmas raised by the use of blogs, bulletin boards, chat rooms, discussion groups, email lists, social networking and web pages include the following points:

• *Scope for deception.* Researchers joining online communities with the intention of collecting data rather than participating and seeking consent (known as 'passive analysis' or 'lurking') may be seen as committing a form of deception. Declaring your real intention after a period of 'lurking' is seen by many moderators of online groups as unethical and may increase the chance of you, as a researcher, being asked to leave (Madge 2010).

• *Lacking respect and causing harm.* 'Harvesting' data from online communities without the knowledge and permission of those who create it may also be seen as disrespectful and opposed to the principle of gaining trust (e.g. Bakardjieva and Feenberg 2000; Berry 2004). Deception and the development of mistrust may cause damage to online communities and to their members (Eysenbach and Till 2001).

- *Respecting privacy.* While it may be technically possible to access online communities because they operate in a publicly accessible virtual space, it may be argued that content on these websites should be treated as private conversations, albeit 'publicly private' ones (e.g. Bakardjieva and Feenberg 2000; Waskul and Douglass 1996).
- *Nature of participation and scope to withdraw.* 'Harvesting' data may be seen as violating the principle of the voluntary nature of participation. Lack of consent while using accessible material also negates the right to limit the nature of data used or to withdraw.
- *Informed consent.* Is it ethical to waive the need to obtain consent because material is seen as being in the public domain and because it may be difficult to achieve this (e.g. Eysenbach and Till 2001; Hookway 2008)? Informed consent in a virtual setting may be obtained by contacting an online community's moderator or administrator; or by specifically asking participants in the case of a web questionnaire or online interview, for example. Informed consent for online research may include agreed limits about the scope of participation. It may also include procedures to allow concerns to be raised or for withdrawal to take place. Such procedures will be important in Internet-mediated research because the issue of distance and lack of face-to-face contact makes it difficult to anticipate participants' concerns and attitudes (British Psychological Society 2013). Signed consent may be facilitated by issuing a consent form by email or online using electronic checkboxes.
- *Confidentiality of data and anonymity of participants.* Even though members of an online community may produce discussions that are publicly accessible and which create a permanent record, they may do this in the belief that no one will be 'harvesting' or analysing this material, or using it subsequently. Bakardjieva and Feenberg (2000) found that members of an online community expected to be asked for consent before access was achieved in practice; and that access was then only granted for subsequently generated online discussions, not to archived discussions that took place before community members knew they were to be the subject of research. This approach enables members of online communities to control data that is available to researchers. Bakardjieva and Feenberg (2000) provide an example of how members of an online community went further to exercise control and to protect the confidentiality of their discussions and their anonymity. The researchers were not permitted to save these online discussions or to use quotations from them. Instead they were allowed to read these discussions and then ask members questions about what they had read. The researchers were allowed to use these answers and to take suitably anonymised quotations from them for their research. This effectively separated the private nature of members' online discussions from public access to research data, enabling members of the online community to control their participation and to ensure the confidentiality of their discussions as well as maintaining their anonymity.
- *Analysis of data and reporting of findings.* Issues of confidentiality, anonymity, privacy and copyright are raised when Internet data are analysed and reported. Where data are 'harvested' the researcher is confronted with the dilemma of whether to use these data openly or anonymously. Since 'harvesting' occurs without obtaining consent, at least initially, should the researcher use pseudonyms and other changes to disguise the identities of those who created the material? Where the researcher wishes to quote from this material, there is the possibility that others could use Internet search engines to identify the author of a quotation (Eysenbach and Till 2001). This raises issues about the confidentiality of the data and researchers should avoid using quotations that would be traceable without first obtaining consent, particularly where harm may result (British Psychological Society 2013). These issues are compounded by copyright. Blogs are protected by copyright laws and those who create them have exclusive rights in relation to

their reproduction (Hookway 2008). Web pages and content on social network sites are also protected by copyright laws (British Psychological Society 2013). Those who author or create web materials may wish their work to be properly attributed; conversely they may wish to protect its use, or for any permitted use to be anonymised (Eysenbach and Till 2001). Seeking informed consent should help to overcome the dilemmas associated with using materials from the Internet as data.

- *Management of data*. Data protection legislation has (or is likely to have, depending on country) implications for Internet-mediated research, including in the UK the need for notification and consent if personal data are to be processed. Researchers using the Internet need to comply with current data protection legislation as well as with any other legal requirements. A further set of issues concerns the potential insecurity of data transmission and storage. This may be because of errors. For example, emails containing personal data may be sent to the wrong address. Questionnaire software may contain errors. Insecurity may also occur because others have access to a website and are able to alter data or to copy and direct it elsewhere. As researchers do not control websites or networks, risks associated with data transmission and storage need to be recognised and participants told about these in relation to confidentiality, anonymity and possible 'data hacking' or misuse as part of seeking informed consent (e.g. British Psychological Society 2013; Madge 2010).

- *Safety of the researcher*. The researcher may help to ensure her or his safety when conducting Internet-mediated research by using a university email address, not a personal one. Researchers also need to be diligent when setting up access rights to their own personal information on social network sites to protect their privacy.

This review has highlighted some of the issues and dilemmas associated with the use of Internet-mediated research, although several more exist in practice. In addition, many more details associated with these issues need to be considered before using this approach to research. Table 6.4 refers to sets of guidelines for Internet-mediated research. Internet-mediated research is still in a formative stage and it is noticeable how opinions and guidance about its use vary across sources. There is scope for a greater consensus about its ethical use but achieving this may not be an easy matter. You will therefore need to refer very carefully to your university's guidelines about Internet-mediated research (or those that they recommend you to use), where you consider the possibility of using this approach.

A further aspect of Internet use concerns **netiquette**, which refers to user standards to encourage courtesy. The principal focus of netiquette is the use of email and

Table 6.4 Internet addresses for ethical guidelines for the conduct of online research

Name	Internet address
Association of Internet Researchers Ess, C. and AoIR ethics working committee (2002)	http://aoir.org/reports/ethics.pdf
Markham. A., Buchanan, E. and AoIR Ethics Working Committee (2012) Ethical Decision-Making and Internet Research	http://aoir.org/reports/ethics2.pdf
British Psychological Society Ethics Guidelines for Internet-mediated Research	http://www.bps.org.uk/publications/policy-and-guidelines/research-guidelines-policy-documents/research-guidelines-poli

messaging. The ease of creating these may lead to issues that impair your attempt to use Internet-mediated research. Emails and messages may be poorly worded (Box 6.8), and they may appear unfriendly or unclear so that they fail to interest those whom you approach. Emails and messages need to be worded appropriately for their intended audience and to be clearly structured, relevant and succinct. The ease of sending emails and messages may lead to 'spamming' potential and actual participants. 'Spamming' involves sending large numbers of unwanted mail and should be avoided. Another netiquette custom involves respecting the intentions of other users, so that private messages should not subsequently be made public. We consider netiquette further in Sections 6.6, 10.9 (Internet-mediated interviews) and 11.5 (Internet questionnaires).

6.6 Ethical issues at specific stages of the research process 研究过程中特定阶段的道德规范问题

As can be seen in Figure 6.1, ethical issues are likely to be of importance throughout your research. This will require ethical integrity from you in relation to your role as the researcher, any organisational gatekeeper(s) involved and, where appropriate, your research sponsor. Where you are undertaking research for an organisation you will need to find the middle ground between the organisation's expectation of useful research and your right not to be coerced into researching a topic in which you are not interested or that does not satisfy the assessment requirements of your university.

Ethical issues during design and gaining access

Most ethical issues can be anticipated and dealt with during the design stage of any research project. This should be attempted by planning to conduct the research project in line with the ethical principle of not causing harm (discussed earlier) and by adapting your research strategy or choice of methods where appropriate. Evidence that ethical issues have been considered and evaluated at this stage is likely to be one of the criteria against which your research proposal is judged.

One of the key stages at which you need to consider the potential for ethical issues to arise is when you seek access. As noted earlier, you should not attempt to apply any pressure on intended participants to grant access. This is unlikely to be the case where you are approaching a member of an organisation's management to request access. However, where you are undertaking a research project as an internal researcher within your employing organisation (Section 6.2), in relation to a part-time qualification, there may be a temptation to apply pressure on others (colleagues or subordinates) to cooperate. Individuals have a right to privacy and should not feel pressurised or coerced into participating. By not respecting this, you may well be causing harm.

Consequently, you will have to accept any refusal to take part. Box 6.13 contains a short checklist to help you ensure that you are not putting pressure on individuals to participate. You may also cause harm by the nature and timing of any approach that you make to intended participants – perhaps by telephoning at 'unsociable' times, or, if possible, by 'confronting' those from whom you would like to collect data. Access to secondary data may also raise ethical issues in relation to harm. Where you happen to obtain access to personal data about individuals who have not consented to let you have

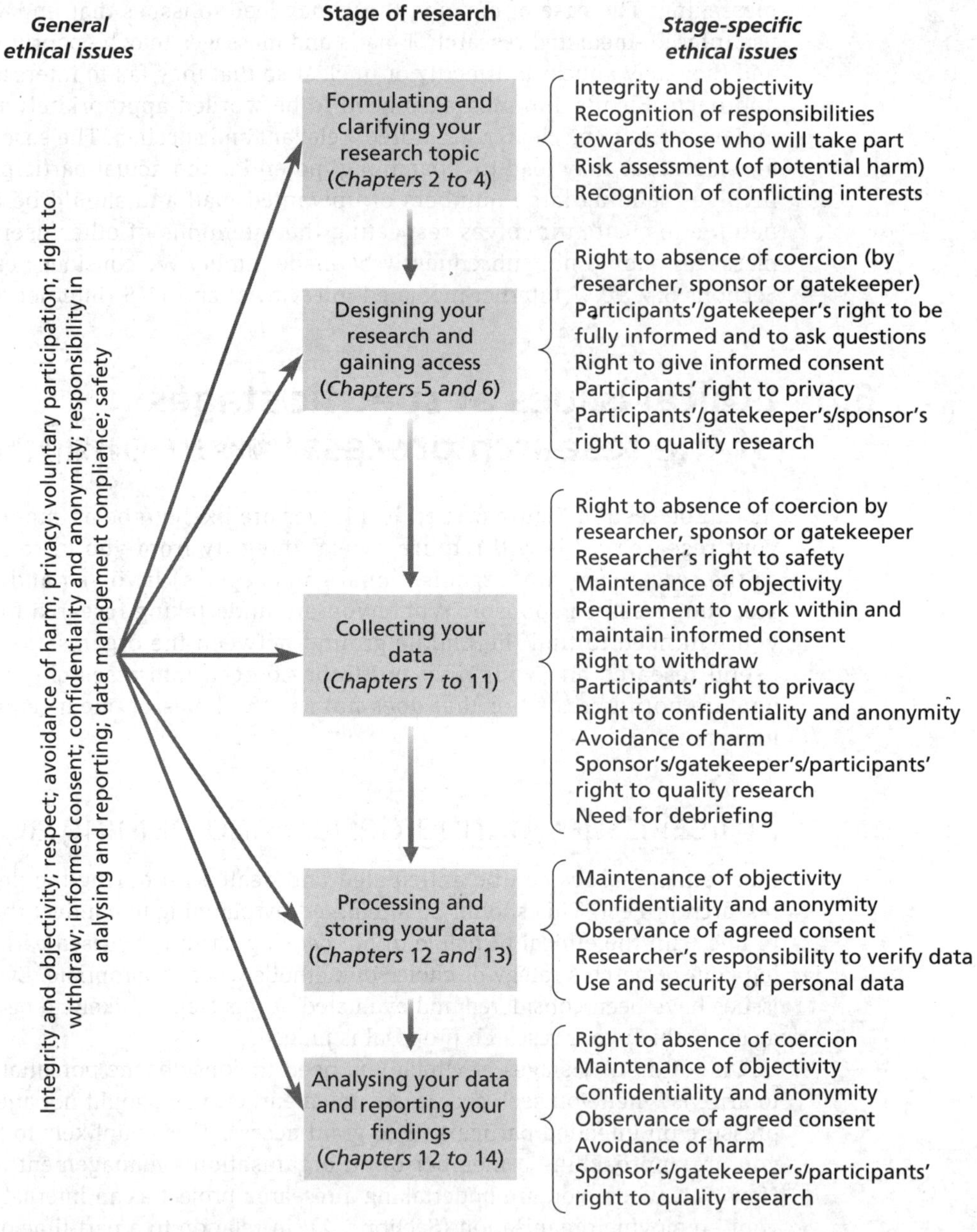

Figure 6.1 Ethical issues at different stages of research

this (through personnel or client records), you will be obliged to anonymise these or to seek informed consent from those involved.

Consent to participate in a research project is not a straightforward matter (Box 6.14). In general terms, an approach to a potential participant or respondent is an attempt to gain consent. However, this raises a question about the scope of any consent given. Where someone agrees to participate in a particular data collection method, this does not necessarily imply consent about the way in which the data provided may be used. Clearly, any assurances that you provide about anonymity or confidentiality will help to

Box 6.13
Checklist

Assessing your research in relation to not pressurising individuals to participate

✔ Have you ensured that participants have not been coerced into participating?

✔ Have you made sure that no inducements (e.g. financial payments), other than reimbursement for travel expenses or in some cases time, are offered?

✔ Have you checked that the risks involved in participation are likely to be acceptable to those participating?

✔ Are participants free to withdraw from your study at any time and have you informed them of this?

develop an understanding of the nature of the consent being entered into, but even these may be inadequate in terms of clarifying the nature of that consent.

This suggests a continuum that ranges from a lack of consent, involving some form of deception, through **inferred consent**, where agreement to take part leads the researcher to assume that data may be analysed, used, stored and reported as he or she wishes without clarifying this with the participant, to informed consent. **Informed consent** involves ensuring those involved in the research are given sufficient information (discussed next), the opportunity to ask questions, and time to consider without any pressure or coercion, to be able to reach a fully informed, considered and freely given decision about whether or not to take part (see Table 6.3). This continuum is shown in Figure 6.2.

Three points are outlined in Figure 6.2, although in reality this is likely to operate as a continuum because a multitude of positions are possible around the points described. For example, research that is conducted with those who have agreed to participate can still involve an attempt to deceive them in some way. This **deception** may be related to deceit over the real purpose of the research, or in relation to some undeclared sponsorship, or related to an association with another organisation that will use any data gained

Box 6.14
Focus on management research

The problematic nature of informed consent

Plankey-Videla (2012) draws on her experiences of conducting an ethnographic study in an organisation to discuss the problematic nature of gaining informed consent from those she worked alongside, in an article published in *Qualitative Sociology*.

It was necessary for senior management to approve initial access to the organisation to undertake the study but this had the effect of making many employees wary of her presence, believing that she may have been an agent of the management rather than an impartial researcher. The dynamics of the organisation's situation then had the effect of altering the focus of her research, but this raised a further issue in terms of whom she required consent from in order to be able to conduct her research.

This led her to conclude that obtaining informed consent can be complex and problematic in such a research strategy. The intention to gain informed consent may be affected by pressures to progress research, requiring researchers to adopt a proactive and reflexive stance to deal with the complexity inherent in such a demanding situation.

Lack of consent	Inferred consent	Informed consent
• Person involved lacks knowledge • Researcher uses deception to collect data	• Person involved does not fully understand her or his rights • Researcher infers consent about use of data from fact of access or return of questionnaire	• Person involved gives consent freely based on full information about participation rights and use of data

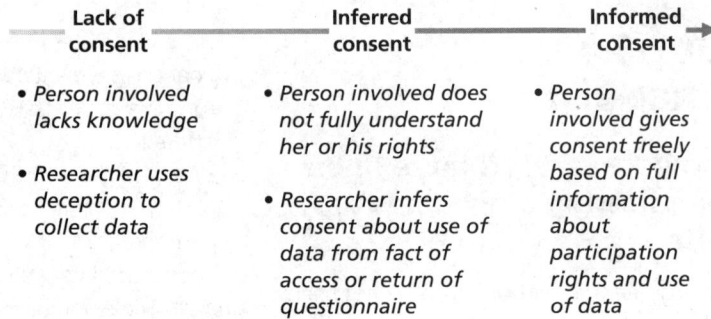

Figure 6.2 The nature of consent

for commercial advantage. Where this is the case, it could cause embarrassment or harm to those who promote your request for access within their employing organisation, as well as to yourself.

The information that is required for prospective participants or respondents to reach a fully informed decision about whether or not to participate should be produced formally as a **participant information sheet** or **information sheet**. This may be given or sent to intended participants or respondents, or emailed or made available online in the case of Internet-mediated research. It should include information about the nature of the research, the requirements and implications of taking part, participants' or respondents' rights, how their data will be analysed, reported and stored and whom to contact in the case of concerns. These points are developed in Box 6.15, where they are presented as a checklist.

The nature of information required for informed consent may vary according to your research strategy, as will the way in which you seek to establish consent. If you are intending to use a questionnaire where personal data are not collected or where data are completely anonymised, the return of a completed questionnaire by a respondent is often taken to grant consent. However, this will require you to include an information sheet detailing how these data will be analysed and reported, for what purpose, and what will then happen to them, as well as your identity (UK Data Archive 2011). If you are intending to interview a senior manager, correspondence may be exchanged, such as that discussed in Section 6.4, to establish informed consent. When interviewing individuals, informed consent should be supplemented by a more detailed written agreement, such as a **consent form** (Box 6.16), which is signed by both parties. Use of a written consent form helps to clarify the boundaries of consent and should help you to comply with data protection legislation where your research involves the collection of confidential, personal or sensitive personal data (see Section 6.7) (UK Data Archive 2011). Depending on the nature of your research project you may also seek consent to photograph or video-record data. Where the nature of the data make this a possibility, it would be necessary to gain a participant's consent to do this before the event, given potential reluctance or sensitivity about using these types of recording media. Your consent form should be amended to record such consent formally.

You will also need to operate on the basis that informed consent is a continuing requirement for your research. This, of course, will be particularly significant where you seek to gain access on an incremental basis (Section 6.4). Although you may have established informed consent through prior written correspondence, it is still worthwhile to reinforce this at the point of collecting data. (An example of this is provided

Box 6.15
Checklist

Requirements for an information sheet

Organisational 'gatekeepers' (discussed earlier in Section 6.4) and intended participants need to be informed about the following aspects of the research. This information can be drawn together in a participant information sheet.

About the nature of the research
- ✔ What is its purpose?
- ✔ Who is or will be undertaking it?
- ✔ Is it being funded or sponsored – if so, by whom and why?
- ✔ Who is being asked to participate – i.e. broad details about the sampling frame, sample determination and size?
- ✔ How far has the research project progressed?

About the requirements of taking part
- ✔ What type of data will be required from those who agree to take part?
- ✔ How will these data be collected (e.g. interview, observation or questionnaire)?
- ✔ How much time will be required, and on how many occasions?
- ✔ What are the target dates to undertake the research and for participation?

About the implications of taking part and the rights of those taking part
- ✔ Recognition that participation is voluntary.
- ✔ Recognition that those taking part have the right to decline to answer a question or set of questions; or to be observed in particular circumstances.
- ✔ Recognition that those taking part have control over the right to record any of their responses where a voice recorder is used.
- ✔ Recognition that those taking part may withdraw at any time.
- ✔ What will be the consequences of participating – possible risks, depending on the nature of the approach and purpose and expected benefits?
- ✔ What assurances will be provided about anonymity and data confidentiality?

About the use of the data collected and the way in which it will be reported
- ✔ Who will have access to the data collected?
- ✔ How will the results of the research project be disseminated?
- ✔ How will assurances about anonymity and confidentiality be observed at this stage?
- ✔ What will happen to the data collected after the project is completed?
- ✔ Where data are to be destroyed, what is the date by which this will happen?
- ✔ Where data are to be preserved, where and how will these be stored securely, who might be given access to them, and what safeguards will be established to ensure the continuing future confidentiality of these data and anonymity of those taking part?

Whom to contact to raise any concerns and questions about the research
- ✔ Have you established how you will provide those taking part with a person to contact about the research, including name, work address, email and contact phone number?

in Box 10.9, which contains a worked example about opening a semi-structured interview.) You will also need to gain informed consent from those whom you wish to be your intended participants as well as those who act as organisational gatekeepers, granting you access.

Earlier (Section 6.4) we discussed possible strategies to help you to gain access. One of these was related to possible benefits to an organisation of granting you access. You should be realistic about this. Where you are anxious to gain access, you may be

Box 6.16
Focus on student research

Consent form

Anna's research involved interviewing a number of franchisees who had expanded their franchises to run multiple outlets, to understand the competence required to achieve this expansion successfully and how they had developed this. Prior to commencing each interview, Anna gave each participant an information sheet that summarised her research project, including the possible benefits and disadvantages of taking part. After carefully explaining her research, the reasons why (with the participant's permission) she wished to audio-record the interview and emphasising that individuals were not obliged to participate unless they wished, Anna asked them if they wished to participate. Those who did were asked to complete and sign the following consent form:

Anytown Business School

U*of*A

CONSENT FORM

Title of research project:
Competence for multiple franchising

Name and position of researcher:
Anna Janssen, Final year student, Anytown Business School, University of Anytown

please initial box

1. I confirm that I have read and understand the information sheet for the above study and have had the opportunity to ask questions.

2. I understand that my participation is voluntary and that I am free to withdraw at any time without giving reason.

3. I agree to take part in the study.

please tick box

	Yes	No
4. I agree to the interview being audio recorded.		
5. I agree to the use of anonymised quotes in publications.		

Name of participant: Date: Signature:

Anna Janssen (researcher)   Date: Signature:

---

tempted to offer more than is feasible. Alternatively, you may offer to supply information arising from your work without intending to do this. Such behaviour would be unethical and, to make this worse, the effect of such action (or inaction) may result in a refusal to grant access to others who come after you.

Ethical issues during data collection

As highlighted in Figure 6.1, the data collection stage is associated with a range of ethical issues. Some of these are general issues that will apply to whichever technique is being used to collect data. Other issues are more specifically related to a particular data collection technique. Finally, and of paramount importance, there are issues associated with ensuring your own safety while collecting your data.

Irrespective of data collection technique, there are a number of ethical principles to which you need to adhere. In the previous subsection we referred to the importance of not causing harm or intruding on privacy. This was in relation to the right not to take part. Once individuals or organisations have consented to take part in your research, they still maintain their rights. This means that they have the right to withdraw, and that they may decline to take part in a particular aspect of your research. You should not ask them to participate in anything that will cause harm or intrude on their privacy, where this goes beyond the scope of the access agreed. We have also referred to rights in relation to deceit. Once access has been granted, you should keep to the aims of your research project that you agreed. To do otherwise, without raising this with those taking part and renegotiating access, would be, in effect, another type of deceit. This would be likely to cause upset, and could result in the premature termination of your data collection. There are perhaps some situations where deception may be accepted in relation to 'covert' research, and we shall discuss this later in this subsection.

Another general ethical principle is related to the maintenance of your objectivity. During the data collection stage this means making sure that you collect your data accurately and fully – that you avoid exercising subjective selectivity in what you record. The importance of this action also relates to the validity and reliability of your work, which is discussed in Chapters 5 and 7 to 11. Without objectively collected data, your ability to analyse and report your work accurately will be impaired. We return to this as an ethical issue in the next subsection. Obviously, falsification (distorting) and fabrication (inventing) of any data are also totally unacceptable and unethical courses of action.

Confidentiality and anonymity may be important in gaining access to organisations and individuals (Section 6.4). Once such promises have been given, it is essential to make sure that these are maintained. Where confidentiality has been promised you must ensure the data collected remain confidential. This is particularly important in relation to personal and sensitive personal data (see Section 6.7). Ways of ensuring anonymity are inevitably research-method specific. While the main concern is likely to be individuals or organisations being able to be identified, it is worth recognising that permission may be given for data to be attributed directly to them.

Anonymising quantitative data by aggregating or removing key variables is relatively straightforward. However, where qualitative data are being reported it may be less straightforward. New points of significance will emerge as the research progresses which you will wish to explore with others. Your key concern is to ensure that you do not cause harm. For example, within interviews, participants can often infer what earlier interviewees might have said from the questions being asked. This may lead to participants indirectly identifying which person was responsible for making the earlier point that you now wish to explore with them, with repercussions for the person whose openness allowed you to identify this point for exploration. Where you wish to get others to discuss a potentially sensitive point you may attempt to steer the discussion to see if they will raise it without in any way making clear that one of the other participants has already referred to it.

Use of the Internet and email during data collection will lead to the possibility of serious ethical and netiquette issues, related to confidentiality and anonymity. For example, it would be technically possible to forward the email (or interview notes) of one research participant to another participant in order to ask this second person to comment on the issues being raised. Such an action would infringe the right to confidentiality and anonymity, perhaps causing harm. It should definitely be avoided. It may also lead to data protection issues related to the use of personal data (discussed in Section 6.7).

The ability to explore data or to seek explanations through interview-based techniques means that there will be greater scope for ethical and other issues to arise in relation to this approach to research. The resulting personal contact, scope to use non-standardised questions or to observe on a 'face-to-face' basis, and capacity to develop your knowledge on an incremental basis, mean that you will be able to exercise a greater level of control (Chapter 10). This contrasts with the use of a quantitative approach based on structured interviews or self-completed questionnaires (Chapter 11).

The relatively greater level of research control associated with interview-based techniques should be exercised with care so that your behaviour remains within appropriate and acceptable parameters. In face-to-face interviews, you should avoid overzealous questioning and pressing your participant for a response. Doing so may make the situation stressful for your participant. You should also make clear to your interview participants that they have the right to decline to respond to any question. The nature of questions to be asked also requires consideration. For example, you should avoid asking questions that are in any way demeaning to your participant (Sections 10.5, 10.6, 10.8 and 10.9 provide a fuller consideration of related issues). In face-to-face interviews it will clearly be necessary to arrange a time that is convenient for your participant; however, where you wish to conduct an interview by telephone (Sections 10.9, 11.2 and 11.5) you should not attempt to do this at an unreasonable time of the day. In interviews, whether face-to-face or using a telephone, it would also be unethical to attempt to prolong the discussion when it is apparent that your participant has other commitments.

The use of observation techniques raises its own ethical concerns (Chapter 9). The boundaries of what is permissible to observe need to be drawn clearly. Without this type of agreement those being observed may feel that their actions are constrained. You should also avoid attempting to observe behaviour related to private life, such as personal telephone calls and so forth. Without this, the relationship between observer and observed will break down, with the latter finding the process to be an intrusion on their right to privacy. There is, however, a second problem related to the use of this method. This is the issue of '**reactivity**' – the reaction on the part of those being investigated to the researcher and their research instruments (Bryman 1988: 112). This issue applies to a number of strategies and methods but is clearly a particular problem in observation.

One solution to this problem could be to undertake a **covert** study so that those being observed are not aware of this fact. In a situation of likely 'reactivity' to the presence of an observer you might use this approach in a deceitful yet benign way, since to declare your purpose at the outset of your work might lead to non-participation or to problems related to validity and reliability if those being observed altered their behaviour. The rationale for this choice of approach would thus be related to a question of whether 'the ends justify the means', provided that other ethical aspects are considered (Wells 1994: 284). However, the ethical concern with deceiving those being observed may prevail over any pragmatic view. Indeed, the problem of reactivity may be a diminishing one where those being observed adapt to your presence as declared observer. Their adaptation is known as **habituation** (Section 9.2).

Where access is denied after being requested you may consider that you have no other choice but to carry out covert observation – where this would be practical. We strongly advise against this. Covert observation after access has been denied will prove to be a considerable source of irritation. Indeed, many universities' ethical codes prohibit any form of research being carried out if access has been denied. In such situations, you will need to re-evaluate your research where any denial of access is critical to your intended project.

One group of students who sometimes consider using a covert approach are internal researchers or practitioner–researchers. There are recognised advantages and disadvantages associated with being an internal researcher (see Sections 6.2 and 9.3). One of the possible disadvantages is related to your relationship with those from whom you will need to gain cooperation in order to acquire cognitive access to their data. This may be related to the fact that your status is relatively junior to these colleagues, or that you are more senior to them. Any status difference can impact negatively on your intended data collection. One solution would therefore be to adopt a covert approach in order to seek to gain data. You may therefore decide to interview subordinate colleagues, organise focus groups through your managerial status or observe interactions during meetings without declaring your research interest. The key question to consider is: will this approach be more likely to yield trustworthy data than declaring your real purpose and acting overtly? The answer will depend on a number of factors:

- the existing nature of your relationships with those whom you wish to be your participants;
- the prevailing managerial style within the organisation or that part of it where these people work;
- the time and opportunity that you have to attempt to develop the trust and confidence of these intended participants in order to gain their cooperation.

Irrespective of the reason why a deception occurred, it is widely accepted that after the observation has taken place you should inform those affected about what has occurred and why. This process is known as **debriefing**. Debriefing also occurs after agreed participation in strategies such as a research experiment. The purpose of debriefing is to inform participants about the nature of the research, its outcomes and to ascertain if there have been any adverse consequences from taking part; if so, to talk to the participant affected and arrange for assistance as required (British Psychological Society 2009).

Absolute assurances about the use of the data collected may also be critical to gain trust, and the time you invest in achieving this may be very worthwhile. You will also need to consider the impact on yourself of adopting a covert approach when others learn of it.

In comparison with the issues discussed in the preceding paragraphs, Dale et al. (1988) believe that the ethical problems associated with questionnaires and other research using the survey strategy are likely to be less onerous. This is due to the nature of structured questions, which are rarely designed to explore responses, and the avoidance of the in-depth interview situation, where the ability to use probing questions can lead to more revealing information. However, where questionnaires are designed to ask questions of a personal or sensitive nature, respondents may be reluctant to answer these or to participate in the research. One method to overcome this issue is the use of computer-assisted self-interviewing. This involves the interviewer handing a laptop or tablet to respondents for them to enter their own responses to questions, thereby ensuring confidentiality. Using this method may lead to data quality and data processing advantages, but is likely to be suitable only for a large-scale survey and where the researcher has access to specialist software and programming expertise.

When thinking about avoiding harm, many researchers forget about themselves! The possibility of harm to you as the researcher is an important ethical issue that you should not ignore. You should not reveal personal information about yourself such as your home address or telephone number. Careful consideration needs to be given to a range of risk factors including the nature of the research, the location and timing of data collection activities, and health and safety considerations. Researchers need to consider risks to their safety and to seek to avoid these through strategies such as meeting participants in safe spaces, conducting data collection during the daytime and letting other people know your arrangements, including where you will be.

In discussing the safety of researchers with our students, we have found the guidance sheets provided by the Suzy Lamplugh Trust (http://www.suzylamplugh.org/) to be extremely helpful. As the Trust's guidance sheets emphasise, you should never allow your working practices (research design) to put your own safety in danger. The Social Research Association (2001) has also published 'A Code of Practice for the Safety of Social Researchers', which contains very helpful advice for research managers and researchers, including a range of strategies to promote safety (Box 6.17).

These points are suggestions only and should not be regarded as comprehensive advice. You need to take into account the nature of your research, your participants, data collection methods and the locations to collect data to assess potential risks associated with undertaking this activity. We advise you to consult the 'Code of Practice for the Safety of Social Researchers' (Social Research Association 2001) and guidance leaflets on working alone and dealing with aggression available from the Suzy Lamplugh Trust (http://www.suzylamplugh.org/), as these may contain other items of advice that are relevant to the context of your research.

Box 6.17
Checklist

Personal safety when collecting primary data

✔ Plan your meeting with a person in a busy public place or office where other people work nearby if at all possible

✔ Carefully consider the location you are travelling to and your travel plans: what risks might you encounter; note your route and carry a map; consider whether you will use public transport, a reputable taxi firm or a private car (if you use a private car is there a safe place to leave it)

✔ Carry sufficient money to cover your expenses and any unexpected ones; in some cities where you have a local transport travel card make sure it has sufficient credit

✔ Carry a mobile phone and make sure it is switched on

✔ Make a mental note of a safe way to leave the building or place where you meet

✔ Make a telephone call to a friend before a particular meeting to tell them who you are meeting, where and how long you expect the meeting to last; call them again to tell them you have left and about your subsequent meeting plans and/or travel arrangements

✔ Set up a system where you contact someone each day with a full list of whom you are meeting, where and at what times;

✔ In a meeting be aware of the use of body language, appearance, cultural norms, social distance and the gender dynamics of interactions

✔ The considerable majority of meetings are helpful and non-threatening but in very rare cases someone may become aggressive or angry: be aware of any changes in behaviour; consider what questions you are asking and how you are asking them; remain calm; where necessary be assertive but not aggressive; if necessary end the meeting politely and leave quickly

✔ Carry a screech alarm in case of an emergency

✔ Be careful not to tell anyone if you are alone in a workplace

✔ Always consider your safety and any risks to yourself, and avoid situations that might be difficult or dangerous

Ethical issues related to analysis and reporting

The maintenance of your research objectivity will be vital during the analysis stage to make sure that you do not misrepresent the data collected. This will include not being selective about which data to report or, where appropriate, misrepresenting its statistical accuracy. A great deal of trust is placed in each researcher's integrity, and it would clearly be a major ethical issue were this to be open to question. This duty to represent your data honestly extends to the analysis and reporting stage of your research. Lack of objectivity at this stage will clearly distort your conclusions and any associated recommendations.

The ethical issues of confidentiality and anonymity also come to the fore during the reporting stage of your research. Wells (1994) recognises that it may be difficult to maintain the assurances that have been given. However, allowing a participating organisation to be identified by those who can 'piece together' the characteristics that you reveal may result in embarrassment and also in access being refused to those who seek this after you. Great care therefore needs to be exercised to avoid this situation. You also have the option of requesting permission from the organisation to use their name. To gain this permission you will almost certainly need to let them read your work to understand the context within which they would be named.

This level of care also needs to be exercised in making sure that the anonymity of individuals is maintained (Box 6.18). Embarrassment and even harm could result from reporting data that are clearly attributable to a particular individual. Care therefore needs to be taken to protect those who participate in your research. Do not collect data that identify individuals where it is not necessary to do so, e.g. full names where you do not need this type of data. Always seek to anonymise the identities of those who take part by using a level of generalisation which ensures that others are not able to identify them. For example, do not refer to specific ages, dates, locations, names of countries, real names, actual organisational names or job positions and so forth that will make it easy to

---

Box 6.18
Focus on student research

Inadvertently revealing participants' identities

Over the years we have been fortunate to read a large number of student research projects. The following examples, drawn from some of these, highlight how easy it is to inadvertently reveal the identities of research participants when presenting your findings:

- reporting a comment made by a female accounts manager when in fact there is only one such person;
- referring to a comment made by a member of the sales team, when only one salesperson would

have had access to the information referred to in the comment;
- reporting data and comments related to a small section of staff, where you state the name or job title of the one person interviewed from that section elsewhere in your research report;
- referring to an 'anonymous' organisation by name on the copy of the questionnaire placed in an appendix;
- attributing comments to named employees;
- thanking those who participated in the research by name;
- using pseudonyms where the initials of the pseudonym are the same as those of the actual person interviewed, or where the name is similar, e.g. using Tim Jennings for Tom Jenkins;
- including a photograph of the interview site or interviewee in your project report.

identify participants or respondents, participating organisations, groups or communities (UK Data Archive 2014), unless there is express permission to identify any of these.

A further ethical concern stems from the use made by others of the conclusions that you reach and any course of action that is explicitly referred to or implicitly suggested, based on your research data. How ethical would it be to use the data collected from a group of people effectively to disadvantage them because of the decisions that are then made in the light of your research? On the other hand, there is a view which says that while the identity of those taking part should not be revealed, they cannot be exempt from the way in which research conclusions are then used to make decisions. This is clearly an ethical issue, requiring very careful evaluation.

Where you are aware that your findings may be used to make a decision that could adversely affect the collective interests of those who took part, it would be ethical to refer to this possibility even if it reduces the level of access you achieve. An alternative position is to construct your research question and objectives to avoid this possibility, or so that decisions taken as a result of your research should have only positive consequences for the collective interests of those who participate. You may find that this alternative is not open to you, perhaps because you are a part-time student in employment and your employing organisation directs your choice of research topic. If so, it will be more honest to concede to your participants that you are in effect acting as an internal consultant rather than in a (dispassionate) researcher's role.

This discussion about the impact of research on the collective interests of those who participate brings us back to the reference made earlier to the particular ethical issues that arise in relation to the analysis of secondary data derived from questionnaires. Dale et al. (1988) point out that where questionnaire data are subsequently used as secondary data the original assurances provided to those who participated in the research may be set aside, with the result that the collective interests of participants may be disadvantaged through this use of data. The use of data for secondary purposes therefore also leads to ethical concerns of potentially significant proportions, and you will need to consider these in the way in which you make use of this type of data.

A final checklist to help you anticipate and deal with ethical issues is given in Box 6.19.

Box 6.19 Checklist

To help anticipate and deal with ethical issues

✔ Attempt to recognise potential ethical issues that will affect your proposed research.
✔ Utilise your university's code on research ethics to guide the design and conduct of your research.
✔ Anticipate ethical issues at the design stage of your research and discuss how you will seek to control these in your research proposal.
✔ Seek informed consent through the use of openness and honesty, rather than using deception.

✔ Do not exaggerate the likely benefits of your research for participating organisations or individuals.
✔ Respect others' rights to privacy at all stages of your research project.
✔ Maintain integrity and quality in relation to the processes you use to collect data.
✔ Recognise that more intrusive approaches to research will be associated with greater scope for ethical issues to arise, and seek to avoid the particular problems related to interviews and observation.
✔ Avoid referring to data gained from a particular participant when talking to others, where this would allow the individual to be identified with potentially harmful consequences to that person.

- ✔ Only consider covert research where reactivity is likely to be a significant issue and a covert presence is practical. However, other ethical aspects of your research should still be respected when using this approach and where possible debriefing should occur after the collection of data.
- ✔ Maintain your objectivity during the stages of analysing and reporting your research.
- ✔ Maintain the assurances that you gave to participating organisations with regard to confidentiality of the data obtained and their organisational anonymity.
- ✔ Recognise that use of the Internet may raise particular ethical issues and dilemmas. Anticipate these in relation to your project to determine how you will conduct your Internet-mediated research ethically. You should be able to justify your approach to those who review and assess it.
- ✔ Where you use Internet-mediated research, seek informed consent and agreement from those taking part; maintain confidentiality of data and anonymity of participants, unless they expressly wish to be acknowledged; consider issues related to copyright of Internet sources.

- ✔ Avoid using the Internet or email to share data with others taking part.
- ✔ Protect those involved by taking great care to ensure their anonymity in relation to anything that you refer to in your project report unless you have their explicit permission to do otherwise.
- ✔ Consider how the collective interests of those involved may be adversely affected by the nature of the data that you are proposing to collect, and alter the nature of your research question and objectives where this possibility is likely. Alternatively, declare this possibility to those whom you wish to participate in your proposed research.
- ✔ Consider how you will use secondary data in order to protect the identities of those who contributed to its collection or who are named within it.
- ✔ Unless necessary, base your research on genuinely anonymised data. Where it is necessary to process personal data, ensure that you comply carefully with all current data protection legal requirements.

数据保护和数据原则简介

6.7 An introduction to the principles of data protection and data management

This section outlines the principles of data protection and data management, which you will need to consider in order to manage your data ethically and even lawfully. Within the European Union, issues of data protection have assumed an even greater importance since the implementation of Directive 95/46/EC. This provides protection for individuals in relation to the processing, storing and movement of personal data. Data protection legislation is likely to exist in countries outside the European Union, and you will need to be familiar with legislative requirements where you undertake your research project.

Article 1 of Directive 95/46/EC requires member states to protect individuals' rights and freedoms, including their right to privacy, with regard to the processing of personal data. Article 2 provides a number of definitions related to the purpose of the Directive. **Personal data** are defined as data that relate to a living person which allow that individual to be identified, perhaps in combination with other information known to the controller of the data. Where you control and process this type of data your research will become subject to the provisions of the data protection legislation of the country in which you live. In the context of UK legislation, this refers to the provisions of the

Data Protection Act 1998 (Stationery Office 1998). This Act, in following the Articles of the Directive, outlines the principles with which anyone processing personal data must comply. Although the following list provides a summary of these principles, you are strongly advised to familiarise yourself with the definitive legal version and to determine its implications for your research project and approach to collecting, processing, storing and use of data.

Personal data must be:

1 processed fairly and lawfully;
2 obtained for specified, explicit and lawful purposes and not processed further in a manner incompatible with those purposes;
3 adequate, relevant and not excessive in relation to the purpose for which they are processed;
4 accurate and, where necessary, kept up to date;
5 kept (in a form that allows identification of data subjects) for no longer than is necessary;
6 processed in accordance with the rights granted to data subjects by the Act;
7 kept securely;
8 not transferred to a country outside the European Economic Area unless it ensures an adequate level of protection in relation to the rights of data subjects.

These principles have implications for all research projects that involve the processing of personal data. There are certain, limited exemptions to the second, fifth and seventh data principles (and to Section 7 of the 1998 Act) related to the processing and use of personal data for research purposes. These are contained in Section 33 of the Data Protection Act 1998. Where data are not processed to support measures or decisions with respect to particular individuals and are not processed in a way that will cause substantial damage or distress to a data subject:

• personal data may be processed further for a research purpose, although it may be necessary to inform data subjects about this new purpose and who controls these data;
• personal data, where processed only for research purposes, may be kept indefinitely;
• personal data that are processed only for research will be exempt from Section 7, which provides data subjects with rights to request information, where the results of the research, including any statistics, are not made available in a form that identifies any data subject.

In addition, there is a further category of personal data, known as **sensitive personal data**, which covers information held about a data subject's racial or ethnic origin, political opinions, religious or other similar beliefs, trade union membership, physical or mental health or condition, sexual life, commission or alleged commission of any offence, or any proceedings or sentence related to an (alleged) offence. This type of data may be processed only if at least one of the conditions in Schedule 3 of the 1998 Act is met. The first of these conditions refers to the data subject providing their explicit consent to the processing of such data. Effective explicit consent is likely to mean clear and unambiguous written consent in this context.

Our brief summary of this legislation should be treated as providing only a general outline and not as providing advice. You should instead seek advice that is appropriate to the particular circumstances of your research project where this involves the collection, processing, storage or use of personal data.

These legally based data protection concerns have hopefully focused your mind on the question of keeping personal data and also on whether the use of these data allows any participant to be identified. Unless there is a clear reason for processing these types of data, the best course of action is likely to be to ensure that your data are completely and genuinely anonymised and that any 'key' to identify data subjects is not retained by those who control these data.

Files containing confidential or personal data will also need to be properly labelled and securely kept. This refers not only to your original notes or recordings, but also to any subsequent drafts, transcriptions, re-recordings, backup and anonymised versions. Original notes or recordings will be likely to include personal identifiers such as names, job titles, workplace locations and so forth that clearly identify the person being interviewed or observed. Personal identifiers may also exist on completed questionnaire forms. Anonymised versions of data will have used tactics such as aggregating data, pseudonyms and higher levels of generalisation to remove personal identifiers. Nevertheless, where these personal identifiers still exist in another document, there remains the possibility that they may be used to reveal the identities of participants or respondents. Original and anonymised data therefore need to be stored securely to protect these from unauthorised access. Particular care needs to be exercised when storing original versions of data that include personal identifiers, or when storing personal identifiers that relate to anonymised versions of data where these identifiers hold the key to revealing the identities of individuals in these anonymised versions. Data that contain personal identifiers therefore need to be held securely but separately to anonymised versions of data to which they relate (UK Data Archive 2011).

Security will take a number of forms. Paper copies of interview or observation notes, signed consent forms, structured observation forms, questionnaires, transcriptions and other documents that contain confidential or personal data need to be held in a restricted, secure and safe place. Data held on external hard disc drives, compact discs and other audio-recordings will also need to be held under the same conditions. Data held on a computer hard drive will need to be protected through the use of a password as well as by firewall and network protection software. Online file sharing and storage services will also allow you to keep an online copy of your data files, although it is advisable not to store confidential or sensitive data in a cloud service without first using additional security. This may involve you storing your data in an encrypted vault. You should consult your university's guidance about using cloud storage.

When data are to be destroyed this needs to be carried out with due care so that paper documents are shredded, not just placed in a bin, and computer files and other digital material are permanently deleted (UK Data Archive 2011). The management of your data in these ways illustrates how ethical concerns are likely to remain beyond the end of your research project in order to continue to maintain the confidentiality of the data that was collected, the anonymity of participants, their privacy and to ensure that harm is not caused to those who helped you.

6.8 Summary 小 结

- Access and ethics are critical aspects for the conduct of research.
- Different types of access exist: traditional access, Internet-mediated access, intranet-mediated access and hybrid access. Each of these types of access is associated with issues that may affect your ability to collect suitable, high-quality data.
- Different levels of access have been identified: physical access, continuing access and cognitive access.
- Feasibility and sufficiency are important determinants of what you choose to research and how you will conduct it.

- Issues related to gaining access will depend to some extent on your role as either an external researcher or a participant researcher.
- Your approach to research may combine traditional access with Internet- or intranet-mediated access leading to the use of a hybrid access strategy.
- There are a range of strategies to help you to gain access to organisations and to intended participants or respondents within them.
- Research ethics refers to the standards of behaviour that guide your conduct in relation to the rights of those who become the subject of your work, or are affected by it.
- Potential ethical issues should be recognised and considered from the outset of your research and are one of the criteria against which your research is judged. Issues may be anticipated by using codes of ethics, ethical guidelines and ethical principles.
- The Internet has facilitated access for particular types of research strategy; however, its use is associated with a range of ethical concerns and even dilemmas in certain types of research, notably related to respecting rights of privacy and copyright.
- Ethical concerns can occur at all stages of your research project: when seeking access, during data collection, as you analyse data and when you report your findings.
- Qualitative research is likely to lead to a greater range of ethical concerns in comparison with quantitative research, although all research methods have specific ethical issues associated with them.
- Ethical concerns are also associated with the 'power relationship' between the researcher and those who grant access, and the researcher's role (as external researcher, internal researcher or internal consultant).
- Researchers also need to consider their own safety very carefully when planning and conducting research.
- Further ethical and legal concerns are associated with data protection and data management, affecting the collection, processing, storage and use of personal and confidential data. Researchers need to comply carefully with data protection legislation when using personal data, to protect the privacy of their data subjects and to avoid the risk of any harm occurring.

Self-check questions   自测题

Help with these questions is available at the end of the chapter.

6.1   How can you differentiate between types of access, and why is it important to do this?

6.2   What do you understand by the use of the terms 'feasibility' and 'sufficiency' when applied to the question of access?

6.3   Which strategies to help to gain access are likely to apply to the following scenarios:

   a an 'external' researcher seeking direct access to managers who will be the research participants;

   b an 'external' researcher seeking access through an organisational gatekeeper/broker to their intended participants or respondents;

   c an internal researcher planning to undertake a research project within their employing organisation?

6.4   What are the principal ethical issues you will need to consider irrespective of the particular research methods that you use?

6.5   What problems might you encounter in attempting to protect the interests of participating organisations and individuals despite the assurances that you provide?

Review and discussion questions 复习与讨论题

6.6 In relation to your proposed research project, evaluate your scope to use:
   a a traditional approach;
   b an Internet- or intranet-mediated approach;
   c a hybrid access strategy
   to gain access to those you wish to take part. Make notes about the advantages and disadvantages of each access strategy.

6.7 With a friend, discuss the outcomes of the evaluation you carried out for Question 6.6. From this, discuss how you intend to gain access to the data you need for your research project. In your discussion make a list of possible barriers to your gaining access and how these might be overcome. Make sure that the ways you consider for overcoming these barriers are ethical!

6.8 Agree with a friend to each obtain a copy of your university's or your own professional association's ethical code. Each of you should make a set of notes regarding those aspects in the ethical code that you feel are relevant to your own research proposal and a second set of notes of those aspects you feel are relevant to your friend's research proposal. Discuss your findings.

6.9 Visit the Suzy Lamplugh Trust website at http://www.suzylamplugh.org and the Social Research Association at http://the-sra.org.uk/sra_resources/safety-code/. Browse the guidance leaflets/web pages and safety code located at these websites. Make a list of the actions you should take to help ensure your own personal safety when undertaking your research project. Make sure you actually put these into practice.

6.10 Visit the Research Ethics Guidebook at www.ethicsguidebook.ac.uk and browse through the sections of this guide. In relation to the context of your proposed research project, make a note of points that provide additional guidance to help you to anticipate and deal with potential ethical concerns.

改进研究项目

Progressing your research project

Negotiating access and addressing ethical issues 协商访问及道德规范问题

Consider the following aspects:

- Which types of data will you require in order to be able to answer your proposed research question and address your research objectives sufficiently?
- Which research methods will you attempt to use to yield these data (including secondary data as appropriate)?
- What type(s) of access will you require in order to be able to collect data?
- What problems are you likely to encounter in gaining access?
- Which strategies to gain access will be useful to help you to overcome these problems?
- Depending on the type of access envisaged and your research status (i.e. as an external researcher or internal/practitioner researcher), produce appropriate requests for organisational access and/or requests to individuals for their cooperation along with associated information sheets.
- Describe the ethical issues that are likely to affect your proposed research project, including your own personal safety. Discuss how you will seek to overcome or control these. This should be undertaken in relation to the various stages of your research project.
- Note down your answers. Use the questions in Box 1.4 to guide your reflective diary entry.

Self-check answers 自测题答案

6.1 The initial types of access we referred to in this chapter are traditional, Internet- and intranet-mediated and hybrid. Traditional access is divided into a number of levels. These are: physical entry or initial access to an organisational setting; continuing access, which recognises that researchers often need to develop their access on an incremental basis; and cognitive access, where you will be concerned to gain the cooperation of individuals once you have achieved access to the organisation in which they work. We also referred to personal access, which allows you to consider whether you actually need to meet with participants in order to carry out an aspect of your research as opposed to corresponding with them or sending them a self-completed, postal questionnaire. Internet- and intranet-mediated access involves using one or more computing technologies to gain access to participants. Hybrid access involves using a combination of traditional and Internet-mediated forms of access. Access is strategically related to the success of your research project and needs to be carefully planned. In relation to many research designs, it will need to be thought of as a multifaceted aspect and not a single event.

6.2 Gaining access can be problematic for researchers for a number of reasons. The concept of feasibility recognises this and suggests that in order to be able to conduct your research it will be necessary to design it with access clearly in mind. Sufficiency refers to another issue related to access. There are two aspects to the issue of sufficiency. The first of these relates to whether you have sufficiently considered and therefore fully realised the extent and nature of the access that you will require in order to be able to answer your research question and objectives. The second aspect relates to whether you are able to gain sufficient access in practice in order to be able to answer your research question and objectives.

6.3 We may consider the three particular scenarios outlined in the question in Table 6.5.

Table 6.5 Considering access

	Scenario A	Scenario B	Scenario C
Allowing yourself sufficient time to gain access	Universally true in all cases. The practitioner–researcher will be going through a very similar process to those who wish to gain access from the outside in terms of contacting individuals and organisations, meeting with them to explain the research, providing assurances, etc. The only exception will be related to a covert approach, although sufficient time for planning, etc. will of course still be required		
Using any existing contacts	Where possible		Yes
Developing new contacts	Probably necessary		This may still apply within large, complex organisations, depending on the nature of the research
Providing a clear account of the purpose of your research and what type of access you require, with the intention of establishing your credibility	Definitely necessary		Still necessary although easier to achieve (verbally or internal memo) with familiar colleagues. Less easy with unfamiliar colleagues, which suggests just as much care as for external researchers
Overcoming organisational concerns in relation to the granting of access	Definitely necessary	Absolutely necessary. This may be the major problem to overcome since you are asking for access to a range of employees	Should not be a problem unless you propose to undertake a topic that is highly sensitive to the organisation! We know of students whose proposal has been refused within their organisation
Outlining possible benefits of granting access to you and any tangible outcome from doing so	Probably useful		Work-based research projects contain material of value to the organisation, although they may largely be theoretically based
Using suitable language	Definitely necessary		Still necessary at the level of individuals in the organisation
Facilitating ease of reply when requesting access	Definitely useful		Might be useful to consider in relation to certain internal individuals
Developing your access on an incremental basis	Should not be necessary, although you may wish to undertake subsequent work	Definitely worth considering	Might be a useful strategy depending on the nature of the research and the work setting

	Scenario A	Scenario B	Scenario C
Establishing your credibility	Access is not being sought at 'lower' levels within the organisation: however, there is still a need to achieve credibility in relation to those to whom you are applying directly	Definitely necessary	May still be necessary with unfamiliar individuals in the organisation

6.4 The principal ethical issues you will need to consider irrespective of which research method you use are:

- maintaining your integrity and objectivity during the data collection, analysis and reporting stages;
- avoiding deception about why you are undertaking the research, its purpose and how the data collected will be used;
- respecting rights to privacy and not to be exposed to the risk of harm;
- emphasising that participation is voluntary and that participants retain the right not to answer any questions that they do not wish to, or to provide any data requested. Those involved also retain the right to withdraw;
- achieving consent that is fully informed, considered and freely given. Research without prior fully informed consent should only be acceptable in very specific and previously approved circumstances;
- respecting assurances provided to organisations about the confidentiality of data and their anonymity;
- respecting assurances given to individuals about the confidentiality of the data they provide and their anonymity;
- considering the collective interests of individuals and organisations in the way you analyse, use and report the data which they provide;
- complying with legislation and other legal requirements relating to the processing and management of personal and confidential data;
- considering your own personal safety and that of other researchers.

6.5 A number of ethical problems might emerge. These are considered in turn. You may wish to explore a point made by one of your participants but to do so might lead to harmful consequences for this person where the point was attributed to him or her. It may be possible for some people who read your work to identify a participating organisation, although you do not actually name it. This may cause embarrassment to the organisation. Individual participants may also be identified by the nature of the comments that you report, again leading to harmful consequences for them. Your report may also lead to action being taken within an organisation that adversely affects those who were kind enough to take part in your research. Finally, others may seek to reuse any survey data that you collect, and this might be used to disadvantage those who provided the data by responding to your questionnaire or other data collection method. You may have thought of other problems that might also emerge.

Get ahead using resources on the companion website at: **www.pearsoned .co.uk/saunders**.

- Improve your IBM SPSS Statistics and NVivo research analysis with practice tutorials.
- Save time researching on the Internet with the Smarter Online Searching Guide.
- Test your progress using self-assessment questions.

Chapter 7

Selecting samples 选取样本

7.1 Introduction 引 言

Whatever your research question(s) and objectives, you will need to consider whether you need to use sampling. Occasionally, it may be possible to collect and analyse data from every possible case or group member; this is termed a **census**. However, for many research questions and objectives it will be impossible for you either to collect or to analyse all the potential data available to you, owing to restrictions of time, money and often access. In the opening vignette you will see that it was not possible to use a list of all outdoor advertising posters from all times, or to obtain opinions of the entire 'general public'. Sampling techniques enable you to reduce the amount of data you need to collect by considering only data from a sub-group rather than all possible cases or **elements**. Some research questions will require sample data to generalise statistically about all the cases from which your **sample** has been selected. For example, if you asked a sample of consumers what they thought of a new healthy snack and 75 per cent said that they thought it was too expensive, you might infer that 75 per cent of

all consumers felt that way. Other research questions may not involve such generalisations. To gain an understanding of how people manage their careers, you may select a sample of company chief executives. For such research your sample selection would be based on the premise that, as these people have reached executive level and have been successful in managing their own careers, they are most likely to be able to offer insights from which you can build understanding. Even if you are adopting a case study strategy using one large organisation and collecting your data using unstructured interviews, you will still need to select your case study (sample) organisation and a group (sample) of employees and managers to interview. For example, in the opening vignette, a report of findings in some UK media inferred they were based on a statistically representative public vote. Consequently, whatever your research question, an understanding of techniques for selecting samples is likely to be very important.

In selecting a sample to study, it should represent the full set of cases in a way that is meaningful and which we can justify (Becker 1998). In the opening vignette, the Outdoor Media Centre provides information regarding how its sample of 228 advertising posters was selected. This allows us to assess whether this was meaningful with regard to establishing the 100 best advertising posters of all time. It also outlines briefly how the people who voted

In February 2011 the UK's Outdoor Media Centre launched its 'Hall of Fame' competition to identify the 100 best advertising posters of all time. Working with the History of Advertising Trust, they generated a list of 500 advertising campaigns. This was reduced to a shortlist of 228 campaigns by a committee of media and creative experts together with the editor of the weekly magazine for the advertising media and communications industry – *Campaign*. These were displayed on a dedicated website, www.outdoorhalloffame.co.uk.

Creative agencies, media planners, advertisers, media owners and the general public were invited in an article in *Campaign* to go to the website, view the advertising campaigns and cast their votes for what they considered to be the best outdoor posters (Bidlake 2011). Each person was able to cast a total of 10 votes, the best advertisements being chosen after more than 10,000 reader votes had been cast (Farey-Jones 2011).

On 31 March 2011 the results were announced, being reported widely in the UK media. TBWA's 1995 'Hello Boys' billboard poster advertising Wonderbra was voted the best poster ever created. In second place was Saatchi & Saatchi's 'Labour Isn't Working' poster created for the Conservative Party in the late 1970s. The 1914 UK First World War army recruiting poster 'Lord Kitchener Wants You' by Caxton Advertising took third place. The highest ranking outdoor poster from the last decade was TBWA's 2002/3 iTunes silhouette poster for Apple.

iTunes silhouette poster for Apple
Source: **© Apple Inc. Used with permission. All rights reserved. Apple® and the Apple logo are registered trademarks of Apple Inc.**

(creative agencies, media planners, advertisers, media owners and the general public) were selected, providing an indication of who the sample was: predominantly people employed in media industries. This allows us to assess whether the claim that those receiving the most votes were the 100 best advertising posters of all time is justifiable.

The full set of cases or elements from which a sample is taken is called the **population**. In sampling, the term 'population' is not used in its normal sense, as the full set of cases need not necessarily be people. For research to discover the level of service at Indian restaurants throughout a country, the population from which you would select your sample would be all Indian restaurants in that country. Alternatively, you might need to establish the normal 'range' in miles that can be travelled by electric cars in everyday use produced by a particular manufacturer. Here the population would be all the electric cars in everyday use produced by that manufacturer.

The need to sample

For some research questions it is possible to collect data from an entire population as it is of a manageable size. However, you should not assume that a census would necessarily provide more useful results than collecting data from a sample that represents the entire population. Sampling provides a valid alternative to a census when:

• it would be impracticable for you to survey the entire population;
• your budget constraints prevent you from surveying the entire population;
• your time constraints prevent you from surveying the entire population.

For all research questions where it would be impracticable for you to collect data from the entire population, you need to select a sample. This is equally important whether you are planning to use interviews, questionnaires, observation or some other data collection technique. You might be able to obtain permission to collect data from only two or three organisations. Alternatively, testing an entire population of products to destruction, such as to establish the actual duration of long-life batteries, would be impractical for any manufacturer.

With other research questions it might be theoretically possible for you to collect data from the entire population but the overall cost would prevent it. It is obviously cheaper for you to collect, prepare for analysis and check data from 250 customers than from 2500, even though the cost per case for your study (in this example, customer) is likely to be higher than with a census. Your costs will be made up of new costs such as sample selection, and the fact that overhead costs such as the questionnaire, interview or observation schedule design and general preparation of data for analysis are spread over a smaller number of cases. Sampling also saves time, an important consideration when you have tight deadlines. The organisation of data collection is more manageable as fewer people are involved. As you have fewer data to prepare for analysis and then to analyse, the results will be available more quickly.

Many researchers, for example Barnett (2002), argue that using sampling makes possible a higher overall accuracy than a census. The smaller number of cases for which you need to collect data means that more time can be spent designing and piloting the means of collecting these data. Collecting data from fewer cases also means that you can collect information that is more detailed. If you are employing people to collect the data (perhaps as interviewers) you can afford higher-quality staff. You can also devote more time to trying to obtain data from more difficult to reach cases. Once your data have been collected, proportionally more time can be devoted to checking and testing the data for accuracy prior to analysis. However, one point remains crucial when selecting a sample: it must enable you to answer your research question!

The importance of defining the research population clearly

The sample selected is related to the population that is highlighted in the research question and objectives. This means that if a research question is about all owners of a particular brand of laptop, then the population is all owners of a particular brand of tablet computer, and the sample selected should be a subset of all those owners. This sample, providing it is selected carefully, will allow conclusions to be drawn about all owners of that brand of tablet. However, such a population may be difficult to research as not all elements or cases may be known to the researcher or easy to access. Consequently the researcher may redefine the population as something more manageable. This is often a subset of the population and is called the **target population** (Figure 7.1). This name indicates it is this population that is the actual focus or target of the research inquiry (Kervin 1999). For example, rather than defining your population as all owners of a particular brand of tablet computers, you may redefine your target population as all owners of a particular brand of tablet who are studying for a business and management degree at one university. However, business and management students at one university are unlikely to be same as all tablet owners and even students from other universities may differ! Consequently, using a sample drawn from this target population of students to find out about all owners of a brand of tablet may result in biased or incorrect conclusions if the research is about all owners. In selecting your sample from this target population, you have narrowed the focus of your research to business and management students at a particular university who own that brand of tablet computer. We discuss this further in Sections 7.2 and 7.3.

An overview of sampling techniques

Sampling techniques available to you can be divided into two types:

- probability or representative sampling;
- non-probability sampling.

Those discussed in this chapter are highlighted in Figure 7.2. With **probability samples** the chance, or probability, of each case being selected from the target population is known and is usually equal for all cases. This means it is possible to answer research questions

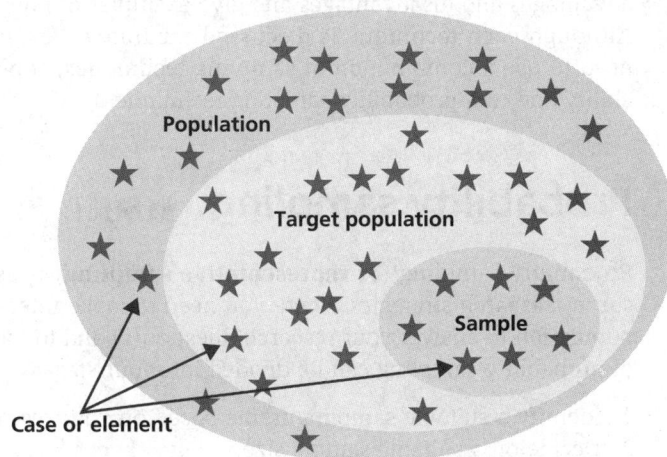

Figure 7.1 Population, target population, sample and individual cases

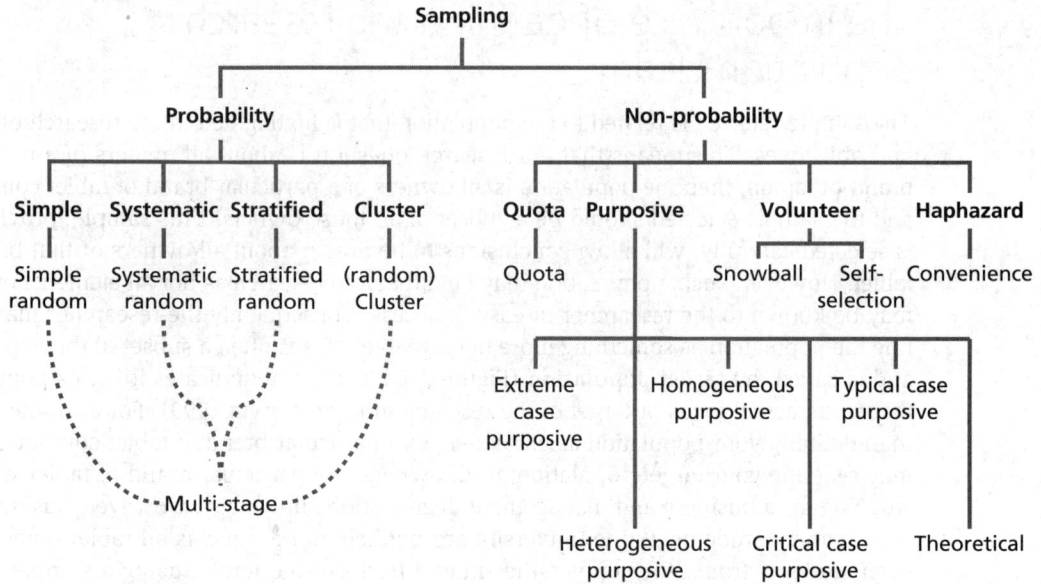

Figure 7.2 Sampling techniques

and to achieve objectives that require you to estimate statistically the characteristics of the target population from the sample. Consequently, probability sampling is often associated with survey and experiment research strategies (Section 5.5). For **non-probability samples**, the probability of each case being selected from the target population is not known and it is impossible to answer research questions or to address objectives that require you to make statistical inferences about the characteristics of the population. You may still be able to generalise from non-probability samples about the target population, but not on statistical grounds. However, with both types of sample you can answer other forms of research question, such as 'What job attributes attract people to jobs?' or 'How are financial services institutions adapting their services in response to the post-2009 crash liquidity rules?'

Subsequent sections of this chapter outline the most frequently used probability (Section 7.2) and non-probability (Section 7.3) sampling techniques, discuss their advantages and disadvantages and give examples of how and when you might use them. Although each technique is discussed separately, for many research projects you will need to use a combination of sampling techniques, some projects involving both probability and non-probability sampling techniques.

7.2 Probability sampling 概率抽样

Probability sampling (or **representative sampling**) is associated most commonly with survey research strategies where you need to make inferences from your sample about a population to answer your research question(s) and to meet your objectives. The process of probability sampling can be divided into four stages:

1 Identify a suitable sampling frame based on your research question(s) and objectives.
2 Decide on a suitable sample size.
3 Select the most appropriate sampling technique and select the sample.
4 Check that the sample is representative of the target population.

Each of these stages will be considered in turn. However, for target populations of fewer than 50 cases Henry (1990) advises against probability sampling. He argues that you should collect data on the entire target population, as the influence of a single extreme case on subsequent statistical analyses is more pronounced than for larger samples.

Identifying a suitable sampling frame and the implications for generalisability

The **sampling frame** for any probability sample is a complete list of all the cases in the target population from which your sample will be drawn. Without a sampling frame, you will not be able to select a probability sample and so will have to consider using non-probability sampling. If your research question or objective is concerned with members of a student society, your sampling frame will be the complete membership list for that society. If your research question or objective is concerned with registered child-minders in a local area, your sampling frame will be the directory of all registered child-minders in this area. Alternatively, if your research question is concerned with organisations in a particular sector, you may be thinking of creating a sampling frame from an existing database of companies available at your university, such as Fame or Amadeus. You then select your sample from your list.

Obtaining a sampling frame is therefore essential if you are going to use probability sampling. However, as highlighted in research by Edwards et al. (2007), you need to be aware of the possible problems of using existing databases for your sampling frame. In their work on multinationals in Britain, they found that:

- individual databases are often incomplete;
- the information held about organisations in databases is sometimes inaccurate;
- the information held in databases soon becomes out of date.

This emphasises the importance of ensuring your sampling frame is as complete, accurate and up to date as possible. An incomplete or inaccurate list means that some cases will have been excluded and so it will be impossible for every case in the target population to have a chance of selection. If this is the case you need to state it clearly (Box 7.1).

Where no suitable list exists, and you wish to use probability sampling, you will have to compile your own sampling frame (perhaps drawing upon existing lists). It is important to ensure that your sampling frame is valid. You might decide to use a business directory as the sampling frame from which to select a sample of typical businesses. However, the business directory covers only subscribers who pay to be listed, often in one geographical area. Your sample will therefore be biased towards businesses that have chosen to subscribe. Because the directory is only updated annually, the sampling frame will be out of date ('non-current'). As some businesses choose not to subscribe, it will not be a valid representation as it does not include these businesses. This means that you will be selecting a sample of businesses that choose to subscribe at the date the directory was compiled by a particular company!

The way you define your sampling frame also has implications regarding the extent to which you can generalise from your sample. As we have already discussed, sampling is used when it is impracticable or unnecessary to collect data from the entire population. Within probability sampling, by defining the sampling frame you are defining the target population about which you want to generalise. This means that if your sampling frame is a list of all customers of an organisation, strictly speaking you can only generalise, that is apply the findings based upon your sample, to that target population. Similarly, if your sampling frame is all employees of an organisation (the list being the organisation's payroll) you can only generalise to employees of that organisation. This can create

Box 7.1 Focus on research in the news

The Art Market: Hopes pitched too high for comfort

By Georgina Adam

There is nothing new in seeing art as an asset class but a recent report by three professors of finance claims that returns have been significantly overestimated, and the risk underestimated. "Investors would be wise to be wary," they say.

The authors of the Social Science Research Network paper (available at ssrn.com/abstract=2280099) question the returns that until now have been reported as 10 percent on average annually, over the past four decades, based on the RSR (repeat sales) index. They say that the index does not take into account selection bias, and after studying the repeat sales of more than 20,500 works of art between 1972 and 2010, they conclude that the annual return on art was nearer 6.5 percent.

Selection bias means that a work of art that goes up the most in value tends to be resold more frequently, just as in the real estate market rapidly appreciating properties are traded more often. So only the most desirable works of art resell, and using their good performance to assign a value to others, via the RSR index, is misleading, say the authors, whose conclusion is severe. "When we compared the investment returns and risk of all the styles of art to a portfolio of pure stocks, we found that art investments would not substantially improve the risk/return profile of a portfolio diversified among traditional asset classes, such as stocks and bonds."

Philip Hoffman, chief executive of the Fine Art Fund, rather naturally rejects the findings of the report, as least as far as funds are concerned. "The data is highly inaccurate," he says.

"The sample is far too small. And as far as our fund is concerned, since we buy 95 percent of our works privately, this data isn't relevant." His first fund is due to be wound up at the end of 2015, and he expects its return will be between 6 and 10 percent, "which was always our aim". However, he admits the research gives "insight into what the market does overall".

FT *Source:* Extract from Adam G (2013) 'The Art Market: Hopes pitched too high for comfort', FT.com, 8 November. Available at http://www.ft.com/cms/s/2/ab0ff19a-47a0-11e3-9398-00144feabdc0.html [Accessed 10 Mar. 2015] Copyright © 2013 The Financial Times

problems, as often we hope that our findings have wider applicability than the target population from which our sample was selected. However, even if your probability sample has been selected from one large multinational organisation, you should not claim that what you have found would also occur in similar organisations. In other words, you should not generalise beyond your sampling frame. Despite this, researchers often do make such claims, rather than placing clear limits on the generalisability of the findings.

An increasing number of organisations specialise in selling electronic lists of names, addresses and email addresses. These lists include a wide range of people such as company directors, chief executives, marketing managers, production managers and human resource managers, for public, private and non-profit-making organisations, and can be merged into standard letters such as those included with questionnaires (Section 11.4). Some organisations also specialise in delivering your questionnaire to an online 'survey panel' of potential respondents, guaranteeing you obtain a specified number of completed questionnaires for a sample tailored to your specific requirements. Because you pay for the list or completed questionnaire by the case (named individual), the organisations that provide them usually select your sample. It is therefore important to establish precisely how they will select your sample as well as obtaining an indication of the organisation database's completeness, accuracy and currency. For example, when obtaining a list of email addresses don't forget that some people change their Internet service provider and their email address regularly. This means the sampling frame is likely to under-represent this group. Usage patterns of the Internet both in organisations and at home are changing rapidly; you therefore need to ensure your intended sampling frame is relevant to your target population. If you are intending to use an online survey panel you need to establish whether or not the organisation offers panel members an incentive to encourage response and the likely implications of this for the characteristics of respondents and consequently their responses (Section 11.2). Box 7.2 provides a checklist against which to check your sampling frame.

Deciding on a suitable sample size

Generalisations about target populations from data collected using any probability samples are based on statistical probability. The larger your sample's size the lower the likely error in generalising to the target population. Probability sampling is therefore a compromise between the accuracy of your findings and the amount of time and money you invest in collecting, checking and analysing the data. Your choice of sample size within this compromise is governed by:

- the confidence you need to have in your data – that is, the level of certainty that the characteristics of the data collected will represent the characteristics of the target population;
- the margin of error that you can tolerate – that is, the accuracy you require for any estimates made from your sample;
- the types of analyses you are going to undertake – in particular, the number of categories into which you wish to subdivide your data, as many statistical techniques have a minimum threshold of data cases for each cell (e.g. chi square, Section 12.5); and, to a lesser extent,
- the size of the target population from which your sample is being drawn.

Given these competing influences, it is not surprising that the final sample size is almost always a matter of judgement as well as of calculation. However, as we discuss in Section 12.5, if your sample is extremely large you may find that while relationships are statistically significant, the practical implications (effect size) of this difference are small (Lenth 2001). For many research questions and objectives, your need to undertake

---

Box 7.2
Checklist

Selecting your sampling frame

✔ Are cases listed in the sampling frame relevant to your research topic, in other words does your target population enable you to answer your research question and meet your objectives?

✔ How recently was the sampling frame compiled, in particular is it up to date?

✔ Does the sampling frame include all cases in the target population, in other words is it complete?

✔ Does the sampling frame contain the correct information, in other words is it accurate?

✔ Does the sampling frame exclude irrelevant cases, in other words is it precise?

✔ (For purchased lists and online panels) Can you establish and control precisely how the sample will be selected?

✔ (For an online panel) Can you establish whether incentives will be used to enhance the likely response and provide an assessment of the impact of this on respondent characteristics and consequently responses?

particular statistical analyses (Section 12.5) will determine the threshold sample size for individual categories. In particular, an examination of virtually any statistics textbook (or Sections 12.3 and 12.5 of this book) will highlight that, in order to ensure spurious results do not occur, the data analysed must be normally distributed. While the normal distribution is discussed in Chapter 12, its implications for sample size need to be considered here. Statisticians have proved that the larger the absolute size of a sample, the closer its distribution will be to the normal distribution and thus the more robust it will be. This relationship, known as the **central limit theorem**, occurs even if the population from which the sample is drawn is not normally distributed. Statisticians have also shown that a sample size of 30 or more will usually result in a sampling distribution for the mean that is very close to a normal distribution. For this reason, Tennent's (2013) advice of a minimum number of 30 for statistical analyses provides a useful rule of thumb for the smallest number in each category within your overall sample. Where the population in the category is less than 30, and you wish to undertake your analysis at this level of detail, you should normally collect data from all cases in that category. Alternatively, you may have access to an expert system such as Ex-Sample™. This software calculates the minimum sample size required for different statistical analyses as well as the maximum possible sample size given resources such as time, money and response rates. In addition, it provides a report justifying the sample size calculated (Idea Works 2012).

It is likely that, if you are undertaking statistical analyses on your sample, you will be drawing conclusions from these analyses about the target population from which your sample was selected. This process of coming up with conclusions about a population on the basis of data describing the sample is called **statistical inference** and allows you to calculate how probable it is that your result, given your sample size, could have been obtained by chance. Such probabilities are usually calculated automatically by statistical analysis software. However, it is worth remembering that, providing they are not biased, samples of larger absolute size are more likely to be representative of the target population from which they are drawn than smaller samples and, in particular, the mean (average) calculated for the sample is more likely to equal the mean for the target population. This is known as the **law of large numbers**.

Researchers normally work to a 95 per cent level of certainty. This means that if your sample was selected 100 times, at least 95 of these samples would be certain to represent the characteristics of the target population. The confidence level states the precision of your estimates of the target population as the percentage that is within a certain range or margin of error. Table 7.1 provides a rough guide to the different minimum sample sizes required from different sizes of target population given a 95 per cent confidence level for different margins of error. It assumes that data are collected from all cases in the sample (full details of the calculation for minimum sample size and adjusted minimum sample size are given in Appendix 2). For most business and management research, researchers are content to estimate the target population's characteristics at 95 per cent certainty to within plus or minus 3 to 5 per cent of its true values. This means that if 45 per cent of your sample are in a particular category then you will be 95 per cent certain that your estimate for the target population within the same category will be 45 per cent plus or minus the margin of error – somewhere between 42 and 48 per cent for a 3 per cent margin of error.

As you can see from Table 7.1, the smaller the absolute size of the sample and, to a far lesser extent, the smaller the relative proportion of the target population sampled, the greater the margin of error. Within this, the impact of absolute sample size on the margin of error decreases for larger sample sizes. De Vaus (2014) argues that it is for this reason that many market research companies limit their samples' sizes to approximately 2000. Unfortunately, from many samples, a 100 per cent response rate is unlikely and so your sample will need to be larger to ensure sufficient responses for the margin of error you require.

Table 7.1 Sample sizes for different sizes of target population at a 95 per cent confidence level (assuming data are collected from all cases in the sample)

Target population	Margin of error			
	5%	3%	2%	1%
50	44	48	49	50
100	79	91	96	99
150	108	132	141	148
200	132	168	185	196
250	151	203	226	244
300	168	234	267	291
400	196	291	343	384
500	217	340	414	475
750	254	440	571	696
1 000	278	516	706	906
2 000	322	696	1091	1655
5 000	357	879	1622	3288
10 000	370	964	1936	4899
100 000	383	1056	2345	8762
1 000 000	384	1066	2395	9513
10 000 000	384	1067	2400	9595

The importance of a high response rate

The most important aspect of a probability sample is that it represents the target population. A perfect **representative sample** is one that exactly represents the target population from which it is taken. If 60 per cent of your sample were small service sector companies then, provided the sample was representative, you would expect 60 per cent of the target population to be small service sector companies. You therefore need to obtain as high a response rate as possible to reduce the risk of non-response bias and ensure your sample is representative (Groves and Peytcheva 2008). This is not to say that a low response rate will necessarily result in your sample being biased, just that it is more likely!

In reality, you are likely to have non-responses. Non-respondents are different from the rest of the target population because they have refused to be involved in your research for whatever reason. Consequently, your respondents will not be representative of the target population, and the data you collect may be biased. In addition, each non-response will necessitate an extra respondent being found to reach the required sample size, increasing the cost of your data collection.

You should therefore collect data on refusals to respond to both individual questions and entire questionnaires or interview schedules to check for bias (Section 12.2) and report this briefly in your project report. For returned questionnaires or structured interviews, the American Association for Public Opinion Research (2011) defines four levels of non-response that can be reported for questionnaires and structured interviews:

- **complete refusal**: none of the questions answered;
- **break-off**: less than 50 per cent of all questions answered other than by a refusal or no answer (this therefore includes complete refusal);

- **partial response**: 50 per cent to 80 per cent of all questions answered other than by a refusal or no answer;
- **complete response**: over 80 per cent of all questions answered other than by a refusal or no answer.

Non-response is due to four interrelated problems:

- refusal to respond;
- ineligibility to respond;
- inability to locate respondent;
- respondent located but unable to make contact.

The most common reason for non-response is that your respondent refuses to answer all the questions or be involved in your research, but does not give a reason. Such non-response can be minimised by paying careful attention to the methods used to collect your data (Chapters 9, 10 and 11). Alternatively, some of your selected respondents may not meet your research requirements and so will be **ineligible** to respond. Non-location and non-contact create further problems; the fact that these respondents are **unreachable** means they will not be represented in the data you collect.

As part of your research report, you will need to include your **response rate**. Neuman (2014) suggests that when you calculate this you should include all eligible respondents:

$$\text{total response rate} = \frac{\text{total number of responses}}{\text{total number in sample} - \text{ineligible}}$$

This he calls the **total response rate**. A more common way of doing this excludes ineligible respondents and those who, despite repeated attempts (Sections 10.3 and 11.5), were unreachable. This is known as the **active response rate**:

$$\text{active response rate} = \frac{\text{total number of responses}}{\text{total number in sample} - (\text{ineligible} + \text{unreachable})}$$

An example of the calculation of both the total response rate and the active response rate is given in Box 7.3.

Even after ineligible and unreachable respondents have been excluded, it is probable that you will still have some non-responses. You therefore need to be able to assess how

Box 7.3
Focus on student research

Calculation of total and active response rates

Ming had decided to administer a telephone questionnaire to people who had left his company's employment over the past five years. He obtained a list of the 1034 people who had left over this period (the total population) and selected a 50 per cent sample.

Unfortunately, he could obtain current telephone numbers for only 311 of the 517 ex-employees who made up his total sample. Of these 311 people who were potentially reachable, he obtained a response from 147. In addition, his list of people who had left his company was inaccurate, and nine of those he contacted were ineligible to respond, having left the company over five years earlier.

$$\text{His total response rate} = \frac{147}{517 - 9} = \frac{147}{508} = 28.9\%$$

$$\text{His active response rate} = \frac{147}{311 - 9} = \frac{147}{302} = 48.7\%$$

representative your data are and to allow for the impact of non-response in your calculations of sample size. These issues are explored in subsequent sections.

Estimating response rates and actual sample size required

With all probability samples, it is important that your sample size is large enough to provide you with the necessary confidence in your data. The margin of error must be within acceptable limits, and you must ensure that you will be able to undertake your analysis at the level of detail required. You therefore need to estimate the likely response rate – that is, the proportion of cases from your sample who will respond or from which data will be collected – and increase the sample size accordingly. Once you have an estimate of the likely response rate and the minimum or the adjusted minimum sample size, the actual sample size you require can be calculated using the following formula:

$$n^a = \frac{n \times 100}{re\%}$$

where n^a is the actual sample size required,
n is the minimum (or adjusted minimum) sample size (see Table 7.1 or Appendix 2),
$re\%$ is the estimated response rate expressed as a percentage.

This calculation is shown in Box 7.4.

If you are collecting your sample data from a secondary source (Section 8.2) within an organisation that has already granted you access, for example a database recording customer complaints, your response rate should be virtually 100 per cent. Your actual sample size will therefore be the same as your minimum sample size.

In contrast, estimating the likely response rate from a sample to which you will be sending a questionnaire or interviewing is more difficult. One way of obtaining this estimate is to consider the response rates achieved for similar surveys that have already been undertaken and base your estimate on these. Alternatively, you can err on the side

Box 7.4
Focus on student research

Calculation of actual sample size

Jan was a part-time student employed by a large manufacturing company. He had decided to send a questionnaire to the company's customers and calculated that an adjusted minimum sample size of 439 was required. From previous questionnaires that his company had used to collect data from customers, Jan knew the likely response rate would be

approximately 30 per cent. Using these data he could calculate his actual sample size:

$$n^a = \frac{439 \times 100}{30}$$

$$= \frac{43900}{30}$$

$$= 1463$$

Jan's actual sample, therefore, needed to be 1463 customers. The likelihood of 70 per cent non-response meant that Jan needed to include a means of checking that his sample was representative when he designed his questionnaire.

of caution. For most academic studies involving individuals or organisations' representatives, response rates of approximately 50 per cent and 35 to 40 per cent respectively are reasonable (Baruch and Holtom 2008).

However, beware: response rates can vary considerably when collecting primary data. Neuman (2014) suggests response rates of between 10 and 50 per cent for postal questionnaire surveys and up to 90 per cent for face-to-face interviews. The former rate concurs with a questionnaire survey we undertook for a multinational organisation that had an overall response rate of 52 per cent. In our survey, response rates for individual sites varied from 41 to 100 per cent, again emphasising variability. Our examination of response rates to recent business surveys reveals rates as low as 10–20 per cent for Web and postal questionnaires, an implication being that respondents' questionnaire fatigue was a contributory factor! With regard to telephone questionnaires, response rates have fallen from 36 per cent to less than 9 per cent, due in part to people using answering services to screen calls (Dillman et al. 2014). Fortunately a number of different techniques, depending on your data collection method, can be used to enhance your response rate. These are discussed with the data collection method in the appropriate sections (Sections 10.3 and 11.5).

Selecting the most appropriate sampling technique and the sample

Having chosen a suitable sampling frame and establishing the actual sample size required, you need to select the most appropriate sampling technique to obtain a representative sample. Five main techniques can be used to select a probability sample (Figure 7.3):

• simple random;
• systematic random;
• stratified random;
• cluster;
• multi-stage.

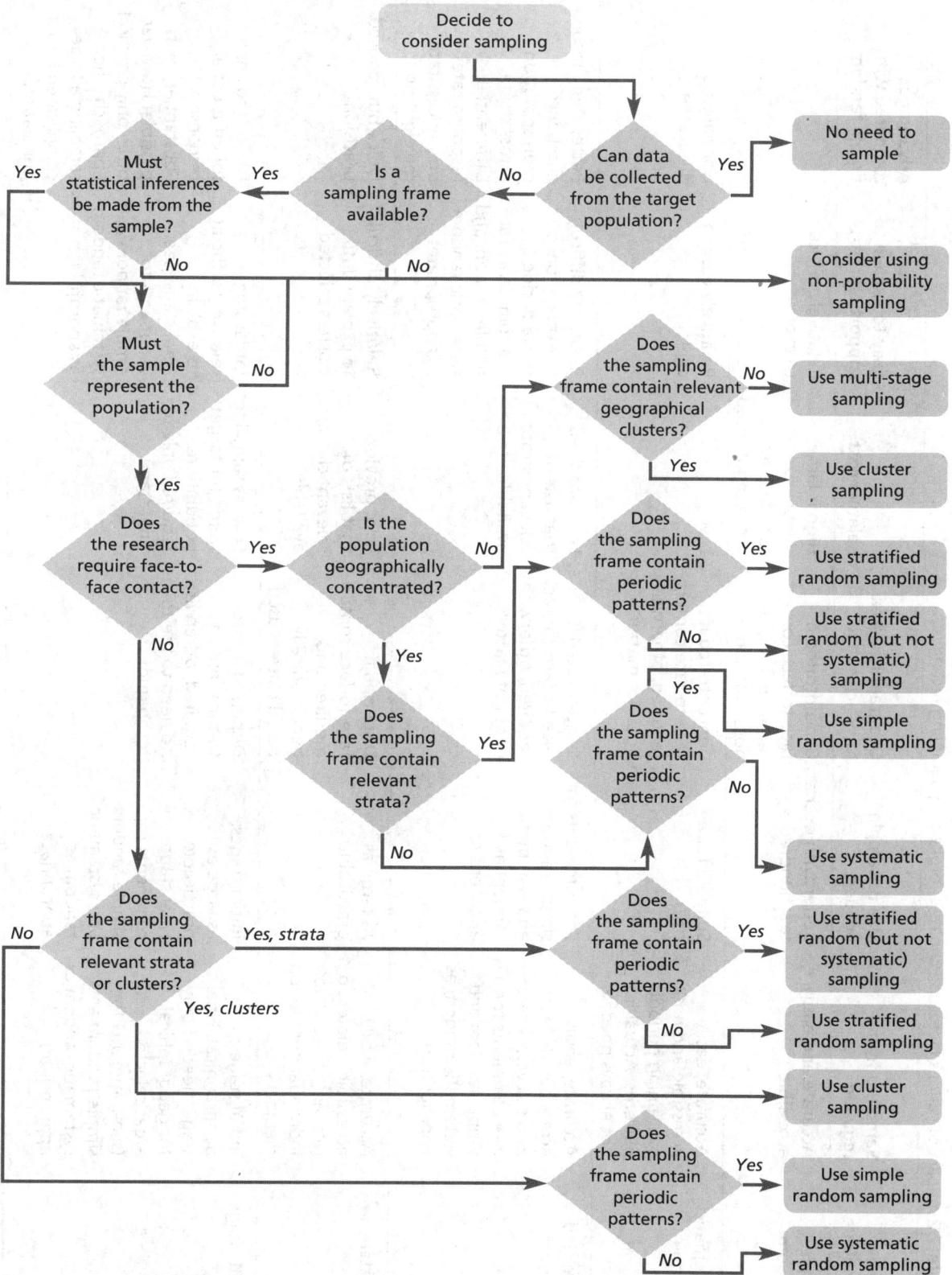

Figure 7.3 Choosing a probability sampling technique
Note: Simple random sampling ideally requires a sample size of over a few hundred

Table 7.2 Impact of various factors on choice of probability sampling techniques

Sample technique	Sampling frame required	Size of sample needed	Geographical area to which suited	Relative cost	Easy to explain to support workers?	Advantages compared with simple random
Simple random	Accurate and easily accessible	Better with over a few hundred	Concentrated if face-to-face contact required, otherwise does not matter	High if large sample size or sampling frame not computerised	Relatively difficult to explain	
Systematic random	Accurate, easily accessible and not containing periodic patterns. Actual list not always needed	Suitable for all sizes	Concentrated if face-to-face contact required, otherwise does not matter	Low	Relatively easy to explain	Normally no difference
Stratified random	Accurate, easily accessible, divisible into relevant strata (see comments for simple random and systematic random as appropriate)	See comments for simple random and systematic random as appropriate	Concentrated if face-to-face contact required, otherwise does not matter	Low, provided that lists of relevant strata available	Relatively difficult to explain (once strata decided, see comments for simple random and systematic random as appropriate)	Better comparison and hence representation across strata. Differential response rates may necessitate reweighting
Cluster	Accurate, easily accessible, relates to relevant clusters, not individual population members	As large as practicable	Dispersed if face-to-face contact required and geographically based clusters used	Low, provided that lists of relevant clusters available	Relatively difficult to explain until clusters selected	Quick but reduced precision
Multi-stage	Initial stages: geographical. Final stage: needed only for geographical areas selected (see comments for simple random and systematic random as appropriate)	Initial stages: as large as practicable. Final stage: see comments for simple random and systematic random as appropriate	Dispersed if face-to-face contact required, otherwise no need to use this technique!	Low, as sampling frame for target population required only for final stage	Initial stages: relatively difficult to explain. Final stage: see comments for simple random and systematic random as appropriate	Difficult to adjust for differential response rates. Substantial errors possible! However, often only practical approach when sampling a large complicated target population

Source: © Mark Saunders, Philip Lewis and Adrian Thornhill 2015

Your choice of probability sampling technique depends on your research question(s) and your objectives. Subsequently, your need for face-to-face contact with respondents, and the geographical area over which the population is spread, further influence your choice of probability sampling technique (Figure 7.3). The structure of the sampling frame, the size of sample you need and, if you are using support workers, the ease with which the technique may be explained will also influence your decision. The impact of each of these is summarised in Table 7.2.

Simple random sampling

Simple random sampling (sometimes called just **random sampling**) involves you selecting the sample at random from the sampling frame using either a computer or random number tables (Appendix 3). To do this you:

1 Number each of the cases in your sampling frame with a unique number. The first case is numbered 0, the second 1 and so on.
2 Select cases using random numbers (e.g. Table 7.3, Appendix 3) until your actual sample size is reached.

If using random number tables you must select your first random number at random (closing your eyes and pointing with your finger is one way!) as this ensures that the set of random numbers obtained for different samples is unlikely to be the same. If you do not, you will obtain sets of numbers that are random but identical.

Starting with this number, you read off the random numbers (and select the cases or elements) in a regular and systematic manner until your sample size is reached. If the same number is read off a second time it must be disregarded as you need different cases. This means that you are not putting each case's number back into the sampling frame after it has been selected and is termed 'sampling without replacement'. If a number is selected that is outside the range of those in your sampling frame, you simply ignore it and continue reading off numbers until your sample size is reached (Box 7.6).

If you are using an online random number generator or spreadsheet to generate random numbers, you must ensure that the numbers generated are within your range and that if a number is repeated it is ignored and replaced. If details of your sampling frame are stored on the computer it is possible to generate a sample of randomly selected cases. For telephone interviews, many market research companies now use computer-aided telephone interviewing (CATI) software to select and dial telephone numbers at random from an existing database or random digit dialling and to contact each respondent in turn.

Table 7.3 Extract from random number tables

78	41	11	62	72	18	66	69	58	71	31	90	51	36	78	09	41	00
70	50	58	19	68	26	75	69	04	00	25	29	16	72	35	73	55	85
32	78	14	47	01	55	10	91	83	21	13	32	59	53	03	38	79	32
71	60	20	53	86	78	50	57	42	30	73	48	68	09	16	35	21	87
35	30	15	57	99	96	33	25	56	43	65	67	51	45	37	99	54	89
09	08	05	41	66	54	01	49	97	34	38	85	85	23	34	62	60	58
02	59	34	51	98	71	31	54	28	85	23	84	49	07	33	71	17	88
20	13	44	15	22	95												

Source: Appendix 3

Box 7.6
Focus on student research

Simple random sampling

Jemma was undertaking her work placement at a large supermarket, where 5011 of the supermarket's customers used the supermarket's Internet purchase and delivery scheme. She was asked to interview customers and find out why they used this scheme. As there was insufficient time to interview all of them she decided to interview a sample using the telephone. Her calculations revealed that to obtain acceptable levels of confidence and accuracy she needed an actual sample size of approximately 360 customers. She decided to select them using simple random sampling.

Having obtained a list of Internet customers and their telephone numbers, Jemma gave each of the cases (customers) in this sampling frame a unique number. In order that each number was made up in exactly the same way she used 5011 four-digit numbers starting with 0000 through to 5010. So customer 677 was given the number 0676.

The first random number she selected was 01 (shown in bold and shaded in Table 7.3). Starting with this number she read off the two-digit random numbers in a regular and systematic manner (in this example continuing along the line):

01 55 10 91 83 21 13 32 59 53 03 38
79 32 71 60 20 . . .

Jemma combined the first two-digit random number (01) with the second (55) to get her first four-digit random number 0155. She continued combining random numbers in this manner until 360 different cases had been selected. These formed her random sample. Numbers selected that were outside the range of those in her sampling frame (such as 8321, 5953 and 7932) were simply ignored.

Random numbers allow you to select your sample without bias. The sample selected, therefore, can be said to be representative of the target population. However, it is not a perfect miniature replica of this population, since it still possesses sampling error. In addition, the selection that simple random sampling provides is more evenly dispersed throughout the target population for samples of more than a few hundred cases. The first few hundred cases selected using simple random sampling normally consist of groups of cases whose numbers are close together followed by a gap and then a further grouping. For more than a few hundred cases, this pattern occurs far less frequently. Because of the technique's random nature it is possible that a chance occurrence of such patterns will result in certain parts of a population being over- or under-represented.

Simple random sampling is best used when you have an accurate and easily accessible sampling frame that lists the target population, preferably in electronic format. While you can often obtain these for employees within organisations or members of clubs or societies, adequate lists are less likely to be available for organisations. If your population covers a large geographical area, random selection means that selected cases are likely to be dispersed throughout the area. Consequently, this form of sampling is not suitable if collecting data over a large geographical area using a method that requires face-to-face contact, owing to the associated high travel costs. Simple random sampling would still be suitable for a geographically dispersed area if you used an alternative technique of collecting data such as web or postal questionnaires or telephone interviewing (Chapter 11).

Sampling frames used for telephone interviewing have been replaced increasingly by random digital dialling. By selecting particular within-country area dialling codes this provides a chance to reach any household within that area represented by that code which has a telephone, regardless of whether or not the number is ex-directory. However, care must be taken as, increasingly, households have more than one telephone number. Consequently there is a higher probability of people in such households being selected as part of the sample. In addition, such a sample would exclude people who use only mobile telephones as their dialling codes are telephone network operator rather than geographical area specific (Tucker and Lepkowski 2008).

Systematic random sampling

Systematic random sampling (often called just **systematic sampling**) involves you selecting the sample at regular intervals from the sampling frame. To do this you:

1 Number each of the cases in your sampling frame with a unique number. The first case is numbered 0, the second 1 and so on.
2 Select the first case using a random number.
3 Calculate the sampling fraction.
4 Select subsequent cases systematically using the sampling fraction to determine the frequency of selection.

To calculate the **sampling fraction** – that is, the proportion of the target population that you need to select – you use the formula:

$$\text{Sampling fraction} = \frac{\text{actual sample size}}{\text{total population}}$$

If your sampling fraction is 1/3 you need to select one in every three cases – that is, every third case from the sampling frame. Unfortunately, your calculation will usually result in a more complicated fraction. In these instances it is normally acceptable to round your population down to the nearest 10 (or 100) and to increase your minimum sample size until a simpler sampling fraction can be calculated.

On its own, selecting one in every three would not be random as every third case would be bound to be selected, whereas those between would have no chance of selection. To overcome this, a random number is used to decide where to start on the sampling frame. If your sampling fraction is 1/3 the starting point must be one of the first three cases. You therefore select a random number (in this example a one-digit random number between 0 and 2) as described earlier and use this as the starting point. Once you have selected your first case at random you then select, in this example, every third case until you have gone right through your sampling frame (Box 7.7).

In some instances it is not necessary to actually construct a list for your sampling frame. For Internet questionnaires, such as pop-up questionnaires that appear in a window on the computer screen, there is no need to create an actual list if an invitation to participate is triggered at random. For systematic random sampling, a random selection could be triggered by a mechanism such as every tenth visitor to the website over a specified time period (Bradley 1999).

Despite the advantages, you must be careful when using existing lists as sampling frames. You need to ensure that the lists do not contain periodic patterns. Let us assume a high street bank needs you to administer a questionnaire to a sample of individual customers with joint bank accounts. A sampling fraction of 1/2 means that you will need to select every second customer on the list. The names on the customer lists, which you intend to use as the sampling frame, are arranged alphabetically by joint account, with predominantly males followed by females (Table 7.4). If you start with a male customer, the majority of those in your sample will be male. Conversely, if you start with a female customer, the majority of those in your sample will be female. Consequently your sample will be biased (Table 7.4). Systematic random sampling is therefore not suitable without reordering or stratifying the sampling frame (discussed later).

Box 7.7
Focus on student research

Systematic random sampling

Stefan worked as a receptionist in a dental surgery with approximately 1500 patients. He wished to find out their attitudes to the new automated appointments scheme. As there was insufficient time and money to collect data from all patients using a questionnaire he decided to send the questionnaire to a sample. The calculation of sample size revealed that to obtain acceptable levels of confidence and accuracy he needed an actual sample size of approximately 300 patients. Having obtained ethical approval he used the patient files kept in the filing cabinet as a sampling frame, and decided to select his sample systematically.

First he calculated the sampling fraction:

$$\frac{300}{1500} = \frac{1}{5}$$

This meant that he needed to select every fifth patient from the sampling frame. Next he used a random number to decide where to start on his sampling frame. As the sampling fraction was 1/5, the starting point had to be one of the first five patients. He therefore selected a one-digit random number between 0 and 4.

Once he had selected his first patient at random he continued to select every fifth patient until he had gone right through his sampling frame (the filing cabinet). If the random number Stefan had selected was 2, then he would have selected the following patient numbers:

2 7 12 17 22 27 32 37

and so on until 300 patients had been selected.

Unlike simple random sampling, systematic random sampling works equally well with a small or large number of cases. However, if your target population covers a large geographical area, the random selection means that the sample cases are likely to be dispersed throughout the area. Consequently, systematic random sampling is suitable for geographically dispersed cases only if you do not require face-to-face contact when collecting your data.

Stratified random sampling

Stratified random sampling is a modification of random sampling in which you divide the target population into two or more relevant and significant strata based on one or a number of attributes. In effect, your sampling frame is divided into a number of subsets. A random sample (simple or systematic) is then drawn from each of the strata. Consequently, stratified random sampling shares many of the advantages and disadvantages of simple random or systematic random sampling.

Table 7.4 The impact of periodic patterns on systematic random sampling

Number	Customer	Sample	Number	Customer	Sample
000	Mr L. Baker	✓	006	Mr A. Saunders	✓
001	Mrs B. Baker	*	007	Mrs C. Saunders	*
002	Mr P. Knight	✓	008	Mr J. Smith	✓
003	Ms J. Farnsworth	*	009	Mrs K. Smith	*
004	Mr J. Lewis	✓	010	Mr R. Dwight	✓
005	Mrs P. Lewis	*	011	Mr D. Furness	*

✓Sample selected if you start with 000. * Sample selected if you start with 001.

Dividing the population into a series of relevant strata means that the sample is more likely to be representative, as you can ensure that each of the strata is represented proportionally within your sample. However, it is only possible to do this if you are aware of, and can easily distinguish, significant strata in your sampling frame. In addition, the extra stage in the sampling procedure means that it is likely to take longer, to be more expensive, and to be more difficult to explain than simple random or systematic random sampling.

In some instances, as pointed out by De Vaus (2014), your sampling frame will already be divided into strata. A sampling frame of employee names that is in alphabetical order will automatically ensure that, if systematic random sampling is used (discussed earlier), employees will be sampled in the correct proportion to the letter with which their name begins. Similarly, membership lists that are ordered by date of joining will automatically result in stratification by length of membership if systematic random sampling is used. However, if you are using simple random sampling or your sampling frame contains periodic patterns, you will need to stratify it. To do this you:

1 Choose the stratification variable or variables.
2 Divide the sampling frame into the discrete strata.
3 Number each of the cases within each stratum with a unique number, as discussed earlier.
4 Select your sample using either simple random or systematic random sampling, as discussed earlier.

The stratification variable (or variables) chosen should represent the discrete characteristic (or characteristics) for which you want to ensure correct representation within the sample (Box 7.8).

Samples can be stratified using more than one characteristic. You may wish to stratify a sample of an organisation's employees by both department and salary grade. To do this you would:

1 Divide the sampling frame into the discrete departments.
2 Within each department divide the sampling frame into discrete salary grades.
3 Number each of the cases within each salary grade within each department with a unique number, as discussed earlier.
4 Select your sample using either simple random or systematic random sampling, as discussed earlier.

In some instances the relative sizes of different strata mean that, in order to have sufficient data for analysis, you need to select larger samples from the strata with smaller target populations. Here the different sample sizes must be taken into account when aggregating data from each of the strata to obtain an overall picture. More sophisticated statistical analysis software packages enable you to do this by differentially weighting the responses for each stratum (Section 12.2).

Cluster sampling

Cluster sampling (sometimes known as **one-stage cluster sampling**) is, on the surface, similar to stratified random sampling as you need to divide the target population into discrete groups prior to sampling (Barnett 2002). The groups are termed clusters in this form of sampling and can be based on any naturally occurring grouping. For example, you could group your data by type of manufacturing firm or geographical area (Box 7.9).

For cluster sampling, your sampling frame is the complete list of clusters rather than a complete list of individual cases within the population. You then select a few clusters,

Box 7.8
Focus on student research

Stratified random sampling

Dilek worked for a major supplier of office supplies to public and private organisations. As part of her research into her organisation's customers, she needed to ensure that both public- and private-sector organisations were represented correctly. An important stratum was, therefore, the sector of the organisation. Her sampling frame was therefore divided into two discrete strata: public sector and private sector. Within each stratum, the individual cases were then numbered (see below).

She decided to select a systematic random sample. A sampling fraction of 1/4 meant that she needed to select every fourth customer on the list. As indicated by the ticks (✓), random numbers were used to select the first case in the public sector (001) and private sector (003) strata. Subsequently, every fourth customer in each stratum was selected.

Public sector stratum			Private sector stratum		
Number	Customer	Selected	Number	Customer	Selected
000	Anyshire County Council		000	ABC Automotive manufacturer	
001	Anyshire Hospital Trust	✓	001	Anytown printers and bookbinders	
002	Newshire Army Training Barracks		002	Benjamin Toy Company	
003	Newshire Police Force		003	Jane's Internet Flower shop	✓
004	Newshire Housing		004	Multimedia productions	
005	St Peter's Secondary School	✓	005	Roger's Consulting	
006	University of Anytown		006	The Paperless Office	
007	West Anyshire Council		007	U-need-us Ltd	✓

Box 7.9
Focus on student research

Cluster sampling

Ceri needed to select a sample of firms to undertake an interview-based survey about the use of large multi-purpose digital printer copiers. As she had limited resources with which to pay for travel and other associated data collection costs, she decided to interview firms in four geographical areas selected from a cluster grouping of local administrative areas. A list of all local administrative areas formed her sampling frame. Each of the local administrative areas (clusters) was given a unique number, the first being 0, the second 1 and so on. The four sample clusters were selected from this sampling frame of local administrative areas using simple random sampling.

Ceri's sample was all firms within the selected clusters. She decided that the appropriate directories could probably provide a suitable list of all firms in each cluster.

normally using simple random sampling. Data are then collected from every case within the selected clusters. The technique has three main stages:

1 Choose the cluster grouping for your sampling frame.
2 Number each of the clusters with a unique number. The first cluster is numbered 0, the second 1 and so on.
3 Select your sample of clusters using some form of random sampling, as discussed earlier.

Selecting clusters randomly makes cluster sampling a probability sampling technique. Despite this, the technique normally results in a sample that represents the target population less accurately than stratified random sampling. Restricting the sample to a few relatively compact geographical sub-areas (clusters) maximises the amount of data you can collect using face-to-face methods within the resources available. However, it may also reduce the representativeness of your sample. For this reason you need to maximise the number of sub-areas to allow for variations in the target population within the available resources. Your choice is between a large sample from a few discrete subgroups and a smaller sample distributed over the whole group. It is a trade-off between the amount of precision lost by using a few subgroups and the amount gained from a larger sample size.

Multi-stage sampling

Multi-stage sampling, sometimes called *multi-stage cluster sampling,* is a development of cluster sampling. It is normally used to overcome problems associated with a geographically dispersed population when face-to-face contact is needed or where it is expensive and time consuming to construct a sampling frame for a large geographical area. However, like cluster

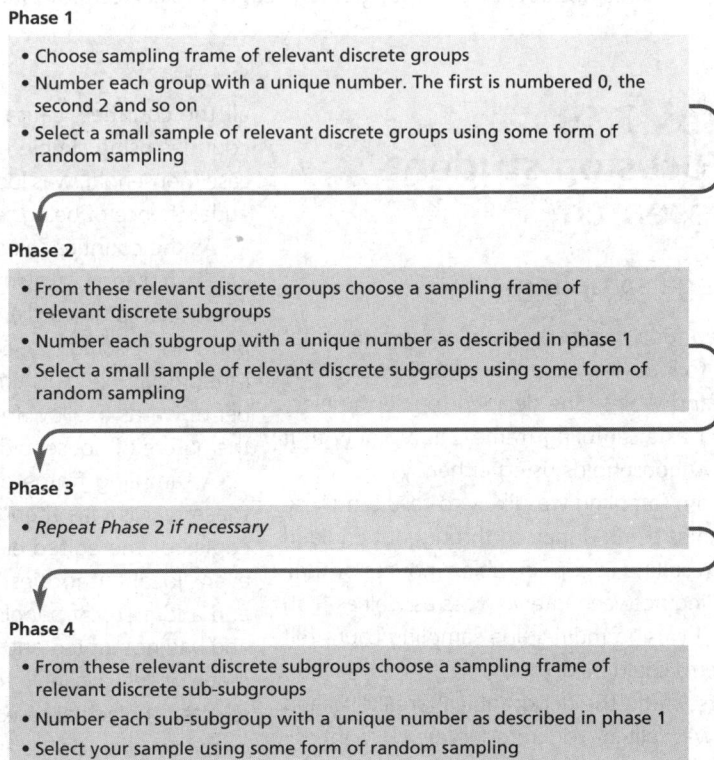

Phase 1
- Choose sampling frame of relevant discrete groups
- Number each group with a unique number. The first is numbered 0, the second 2 and so on
- Select a small sample of relevant discrete groups using some form of random sampling

Phase 2
- From these relevant discrete groups choose a sampling frame of relevant discrete subgroups
- Number each subgroup with a unique number as described in phase 1
- Select a small sample of relevant discrete subgroups using some form of random sampling

Phase 3
- *Repeat Phase 2 if necessary*

Phase 4
- From these relevant discrete subgroups choose a sampling frame of relevant discrete sub-subgroups
- Number each sub-subgroup with a unique number as described in phase 1
- Select your sample using some form of random sampling

Figure 7.4 Phases of multi-stage sampling

sampling, you can use it for any discrete groups, including those that are not geographically based. The technique involves modifying a cluster sample by adding at least one more stage of sampling that also involves some form of random sampling. This aspect is represented by the dotted lines in Figure 7.2, the drawing of these samples being termed sub-sampling. Multi-stage sampling can be divided into four phases. These are outlined in Figure 7.4.

Because multi-stage sampling relies on a series of different sampling frames, you need to ensure that they are all appropriate and available. In order to minimise the impact of selecting smaller and smaller subgroups on the representativeness of your sample, you can apply stratified random sampling techniques (discussed earlier). This technique can be further refined to take account of the relative size of the subgroups by adjusting the sample size for each subgroup. As you have selected your sub-areas using different sampling frames, you only need a sampling frame that lists all the members of the population for those subgroups you finally select (Box 7.10). This provides considerable savings in time and money.

Checking that the sample is representative

Often it is possible to compare data you collect from your sample with data from another source for the population, such as data contained in an 'archival' database. For example, you can compare data on the age and socioeconomic characteristics of respondents in a marketing survey with these characteristics for the population in that country as recorded by the latest national census of population. If there is no statistically significant difference, then the sample is representative with respect to these characteristics.

When working within an organisation, comparisons can also be made. In a questionnaire Mark sent to a sample of employees in a large UK organisation, he asked closed questions about salary grade, gender, length of service and place of work. Possible responses

Box 7.10
Focus on student research

Multi-stage sampling

Laura worked for a market research organisation that needed her to interview a sample of 400 households in England and Wales. She decided to use the electoral register as a sampling frame. Laura knew that selecting 400 households using either systematic or simple random sampling was likely to result in these 400 households being dispersed throughout England and Wales, resulting in considerable amounts of time spent travelling between interviewees as well as high travel costs. By using multi-stage sampling Laura felt these problems could be overcome.

In her first stage the geographical area (England and Wales) was split into discrete sub-areas (counties). These formed her sampling frame. After numbering all the counties, Laura selected a small number of counties using simple random sampling. Since each case (household) was located in a county, each had an equal chance of being selected for the final sample.

As the counties selected were still too large, each was subdivided into smaller geographically discrete areas (electoral wards). These formed the next sampling frame (stage 2). Laura selected another simple random sample. This time she selected a larger number of wards to allow for likely important variations in the nature of households between wards.

A sampling frame of the households in each of these wards was then generated. Laura purchased copies of the edited electoral register from the relevant local authorities. These contained the names and addresses of people who had registered to vote and had not 'opted out' of allowing their details to be made widely available for others to use. Laura finally selected the actual cases (households) that she would interview using systematic random sampling.

to each question were designed to provide sufficient detail to compare the characteristics of the sample with the characteristics of the entire population of employees as recorded by the organisation's personnel database. At the same time he kept the categories sufficiently broad to preserve, and to be seen to preserve, the confidentiality of individual respondents. The two questions on length of service and salary grade from a questionnaire he developed illustrate this:

97 How long have you worked for **organisation's name?**

less than 1 year   ❏   1 year to less than 3 years   ❏   3 or more years ❏

98 Which one of the following best describes your job?

Clerical (grades 1–3)	❏	Management (grades 9–11)	❏
Supervisory (grades 4–5)	❏	Senior management (grades 12–14)	❏
Professional (grades 6–8)	❏	Other (please say)	❏

Using the Kolmogorov test (Section 12.5), Mark found there was no statistically significant difference between the proportions of respondents in each of the length of service groups and the data obtained from the organisation's personnel database for all employees. This meant that the sample of respondents was representative of all employees with respect to length of service. However, those responding were (statistically) significantly more likely to be in professional and managerial grades than in technical, administrative or supervisory grades. He therefore added a note of caution about the representativeness of his findings.

You can also assess the representativeness of samples in a variety of other ways (Rogelberg and Stanton 2007). Those our students have used most often, in order of quality of assessment of possible bias, include:

- replicating your findings using a new sample selected using different sampling techniques, referred to as 'demonstrate generalisability';
- resurveying non-respondents, the 'follow-up approach';
- analysing whether non-response was due to refusal, ineligibility or some other reason through interviews with non-respondents, known as 'active non-response analysis';
- comparing late respondents' responses with those from early respondents, known as 'wave analysis'.

In relation to this list, the quality of the assessment of bias provided by archival analysis, as outlined earlier, is similar to that provided by the follow-up approach and active non-response analysis.

7.3 Non-probability sampling 非概率抽样

The techniques for selecting samples discussed earlier have all been based on the assumption that your sample will be chosen at random from a sampling frame. Consequently, it is possible to specify the probability that any case will be included in the sample. However, within business research, such as market surveys and case study research, this may either not be possible (as you do not have a sampling frame) or not be appropriate to answering your research question. This means your sample must be selected some other way. Non-probability sampling (or **non-random sampling**) provides a range of alternative techniques to select samples, the majority of which include an element of subjective judgement. In the exploratory stages of some research projects, such as a pilot testing a questionnaire, a non-probability sample may be the most practical, although it will not allow the extent of the problem to be determined. Subsequent to this, probability

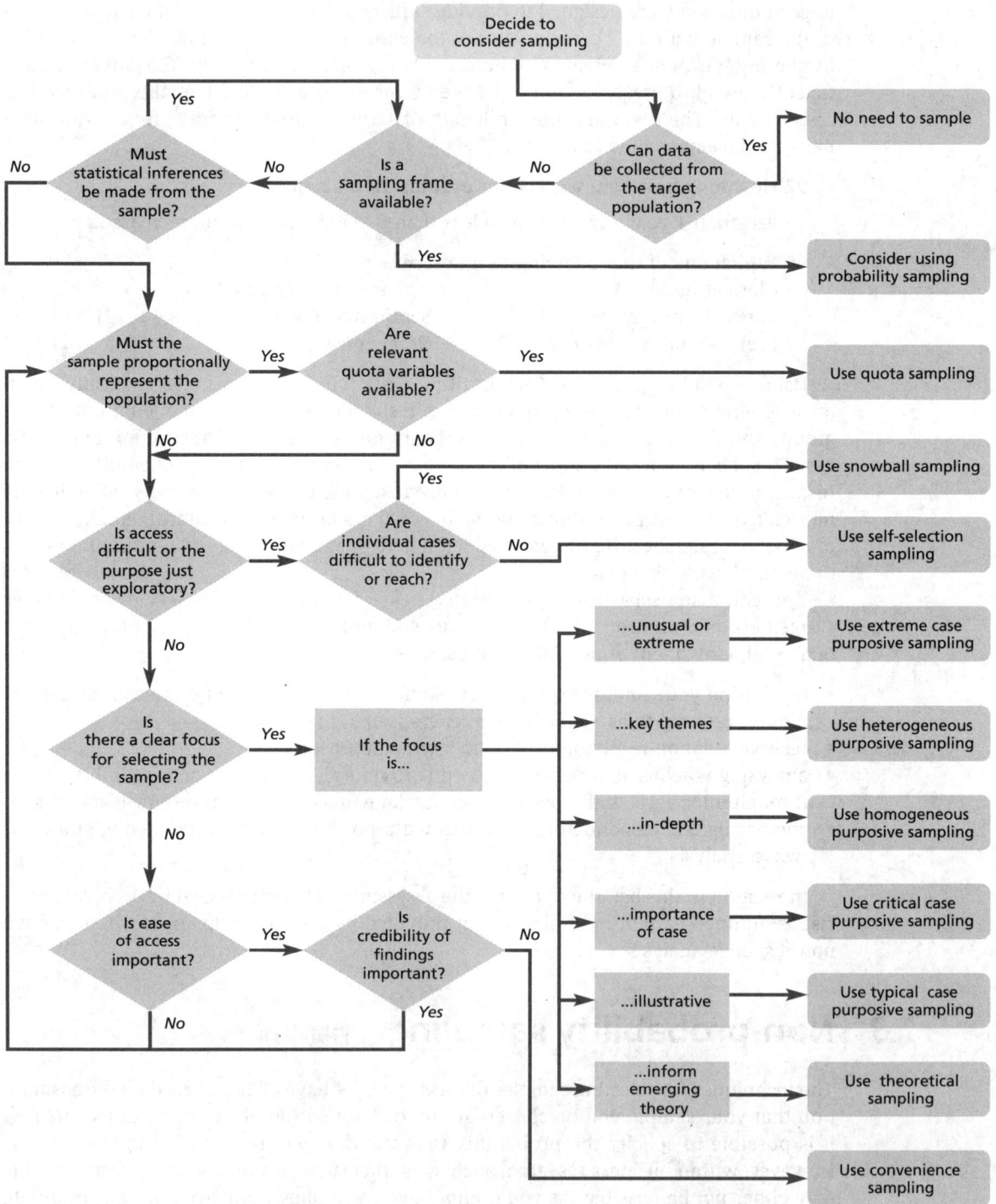

Figure 7.5 Choosing a non-probability sampling technique

sampling techniques may be used. For other business and management research projects your research question(s), objectives and choice of research strategy (Sections 2.4 and 5.5) may dictate non-probability sampling. To answer your research question(s) and to meet your objectives you may need to undertake an in-depth study that focuses on a small number of cases, perhaps one, selected for a particular purpose. This sample would provide you with an information-rich case study in which you explore your research question and gain theoretical insights.

Deciding on a suitable sample size

For all non-probability sampling techniques, other than for quota samples (which we discuss later), the issue of sample size is ambiguous and, unlike probability sampling, there are no rules. Rather the logical relationship between your sample selection technique and the purpose and focus of your research is important (Figure 7.5), generalisations being made to theory rather than about a population. Consequently, your sample size is dependent on your research question(s) and objectives – in particular, what you need to find out, what will be useful, what will have credibility and what can be done within your available resources (Patton 2002). This is particularly so where you are intending to collect qualitative data using semi-structured or unstructured interviews (Chapter 10). Although the validity, understanding and insights that you will gain from your data will be more to do with your data collection and analysis skills than with the size of your sample (Patton 2002), it is possible to offer guidance as to the sample size to ensure you have conducted sufficient interviews or undertaken sufficient observations.

In addressing this issue, many research textbooks simply recommend continuing to collect qualitative data, such as by conducting additional interviews, until **data saturation** is reached: in other words until the additional data collected provide little, if any, new information or suggest new themes. While this is helpful, it does not answer the question of how many participants you are likely to need in your sample. Fortunately, Saunders (2012) summarises the limited guidance available for different types of study (Table 7.5). For research where your aim is to understand commonalities within a fairly homogenous group, 12 in-depth interviews should suffice (Guest et al. 2006). However, Guest et al. also note that 12 interviews are unlikely to be sufficient where the sample is drawn from a heterogeneous population or the focus of the research question is wide ranging. Given this, we would suggest that, for a general study, you should expect to undertake between 5 and 30 interviews (Creswell 2013). Additionally, where your research requires comparison between distinct groups, the sample size will need to be larger, treating each group as a separate homogeneous population.

Table 7.5 Minimum non-probability sample size

Nature of study	Minimum sample size
Semi-structured/In-depth interviews	5–25
Ethnographic	35–36
Grounded Theory	20–35
Considering a homogeneous population	4–12
Considering a heterogeneous population	12–30

Source: Developed from Saunders (2012)

Selecting the most appropriate sampling technique and the sample

Having decided the likely suitable sample size, you need to select the most appropriate sampling technique to enable you to answer your research question from the range of non-probability sampling techniques available (Figure 7.2). At one end of this range is quota sampling, which, like probability samples, tries to represent the total population. At the other end of this range is haphazard sampling, based on the need to obtain a sample as quickly as possible. With this technique you have virtually no control over the cases that will be included in your sample. Purposive sampling and volunteer sampling techniques lie between these extremes (Table 7.6).

Table 7.6 Impact of various factors on choice of non-probability sampling techniques

Group	Technique	Likelihood of sample being representative	Types of research in which useful	Relative costs	Control over sample contents
Quota	Quota	Reasonable to high, although dependent on selection of quota variables	Where costs constrained or data needed very quickly so an alternative to probability sampling needed	Moderately high to reasonable	Specifies quota selection criteria
Purposive	Extreme case	Low	Unusual or special	Reasonable	Specifies selection criteria
	Heterogeneous	Low, although dependent on researcher's choices	Reveal/illuminate key themes	Reasonable	Specifies selection criteria
	Homogeneous	Low	In-depth focus	Reasonable	Specifies selection criteria
	Critical case	Low	Importance	Reasonable	Specifies selection criteria
	Typical case	Low, although dependent on researcher's choices	Illustrative	Reasonable	Specifies selection criteria
	Theoretical	Low	Inform emerging theory	Reasonable	Specifies selection criteria
Volunteer	Snowball	Low, but cases likely to have characteristics desired	Where cases difficult to identify	Reasonable	Selects initial participant
	Self-selection	Low, as cases self-selected	Where access difficult, research exploratory	Reasonable	Offers only general invitation
Haphazard	Convenience	Very low (often lacks credibility)	Ease of access	Low	Haphazard

Sources: Developed from Kervin (1999); Patton (2002); Saunders (2012)

Quota sampling

Quota sampling is entirely non-random and is often used for structured interviews as part of a survey strategy. It is based on the premise that your sample will represent the target population as the variability in your sample for various quota variables is the same as that in the target population. Quota sampling is therefore a type of stratified sample in which selection of cases within strata is entirely non-random (Barnett 2002). Quota sampling has similar requirements for sample size as probabilistic sampling techniques (Section 7.2). To select a quota sample you:

1 Divide the population into specific groups.
2 Calculate a quota for each group based on relevant and available data.
3 Give each interviewer an 'assignment', which states the number of cases in each quota from which they must collect data.
4 Combine the data collected by interviewers to provide the full sample.

Quota sampling has a number of advantages over the probability sampling techniques. In particular, it is less costly and can be set up very quickly. If, as with television audience research surveys, your data collection needs to be undertaken very quickly then quota sampling may be the only possibility. In addition, it does not require a sampling frame and therefore may be the only technique you can use if one is not available. Quota sampling is normally used for large target populations. Decisions on sample size are governed by the need to have sufficient responses in each quota to enable subsequent statistical analyses to be undertaken. This often necessitates a sample size of between 2000 and 5000.

Calculations of quotas are based on relevant and available data and are usually relative to the proportions in which they occur in the population (Box 7.11). Without sensible and relevant quotas, data collected may be biased. For many market research projects, quotas are derived from census data. Your choice of quota is dependent on two main factors:

- usefulness as a means of stratifying the data;
- ability to overcome likely variations between groups in their availability for interview.

Box 7.11
Focus on student research

Devising a quota sample

Paolo was undertaking the data collection for his dissertation as part of his full-time employment. For his research he needed to interview a sample of people representing those aged 16–74 who were either economically active or inactive. No sampling frame was available. Once the data had been collected, he was going to disaggregate his findings into subgroups dependent on gender and whether they were economically active or economically inactive. Previous research had suggested that whether or not people were retired would also have an impact on responses and so he needed to make

sure that those interviewed in each group also reflected these people. Fortunately, his country's national census of population contained a breakdown of the number of people who were economically active and inactive, their employment status and gender. These formed the basis of the categories for his quotas:

Gender ×	economic activity ×	employment status
male,	active, inactive	part-time employee,
female		full-time employee,
		self-employed,
		unemployed,
		full-time student,
		retired, student,
		looking after home
		or family, long-term
		sick or disabled,
		other

Box 7.11
Focus on student research (*continued*)

As he was going to analyse the data for economic activity and gender, it was important that each of these four groups (male and economically active, male and economically inactive, female and economically active, female and economically inactive) had sufficient respondents (at least 30) to enable meaningful statistical analyses. Paolo calculated that a 0.00001 per cent quota (1 in 100,000) would provide sufficient numbers in each of these four groups. This gave him the following quotas:

Gender	Economic activity	Employment status	Population	Quota
Male	Active	Part-time employee	1 175 518	12
		Full-time employee	9 013 615	90
		Self-employed	2 670 662	27
		Unemployed	1 015 551	10
		Full-time student	619 267	6
	Inactive	Retired	2 270 916	22
		Student	1 148 356	11
		Looking after home or family	156 757	2
		Long-term sick or disabled	823 553	8
		Other	385 357	4
Female	Active	Part-time employee	4 158 750	42
		Full-time employee	6 002 949	60
		Self-employed	1 122 970	11
		Unemployed	687 296	7
		Full-time student	717 556	7
	Inactive	Retired	3 049 775	30
		Student	1 107 475	11
		Looking after home or family	1 538 377	15
		Long-term sick or disabled	750 581	8
		Other	467 093	5
Total			38 882 374	388

These were then divided into assignments of between 40 and 50 people for each interviewer.

Where people who are retired are likely to have different opinions from those in work, a quota that does not ensure that these differences are captured may result in the data being biased as it would probably be easier to collect the data from those people who are retired. Quotas used in market research surveys and political opinion polls usually include measures of age, gender and economic activity or social class. These may be supplemented by additional quotas, dictated by the research question(s) and objectives (Box 7.11).

Once you have given each interviewer their particular assignment, they decide whom to interview until they have completed their quota. You then combine the data from this assignment with those collected by other interviewers to provide the full sample. Because the interviewer can choose within quota boundaries whom they interview, your quota sample may be subject to bias. Interviewers tend to choose respondents who are easily accessible and who appear willing to answer the questions. Clear controls may therefore be needed. In addition, it has been known for interviewers to fill in quotas incorrectly. This is not to say that your quota sample will not produce good results; they can and often do! However, you cannot measure the level of certainty or margins of error as the sample is not probability based.

Purposive sampling

With **purposive sampling** you need to use your judgement to select cases that will best enable you to answer your research question(s) and to meet your objectives. For this reason it is sometimes known as **judgemental sampling**. You therefore need to think carefully about the impact of your decision to include or exclude cases on the research when selecting a sample in this way. Purposive sampling is often used when working with very small samples such as in case study research and when you wish to select cases that are particularly informative (Neuman 2005). A particular form of purposive sampling, theoretical sampling, is used by researchers adopting the Grounded Theory strategy (Section 13.8).

Purposive samples cannot be considered to be statistically representative of the target population. The logic on which you base your strategy for selecting cases for a purposive sample should be dependent on your research question(s) and objectives (Box 7.12). Patton (2002) emphasises this point by contrasting the need to select information-rich cases in purposive sampling with the need to be statistically representative in probability sampling. The more common purposive sampling strategies were outlined in Figure 7.2.

Extreme case or **deviant sampling** focuses on unusual or special cases on the basis that the data collected about these unusual or extreme outcomes will enable you to learn the most and to answer your research question(s) and meet your objectives most effectively (Box 7.12). This is often based on the premise that findings from extreme cases will be relevant in understanding or explaining more typical cases (Patton 2002).

Heterogeneous or **maximum variation sampling** uses your judgement to choose participants with sufficiently diverse characteristics to provide the maximum variation possible in the data collected. It enables you to collect data to describe and explain the key themes that can be observed. Although this might appear a contradiction, as a small sample may contain cases that are completely different, Patton (2002) argues that this is in fact a strength. Any patterns that do emerge are likely to be of particular interest and value and represent the key themes. In addition, the data collected should enable you to document uniqueness. To ensure maximum variation within a sample, Patton (2002) suggests you identify your diverse characteristics (sample selection criteria) prior to selecting your sample.

Box 7.12
Focus on management research

Extreme case sampling

In their 2014 *Academy of Management Journal* article 'It's not easy being green: The role of self evaluations in explaining the support of environmental issues', Sonenshein, DeCelles and Dutton outline their mixed methods approach comprising an initial inductive qualitative study followed by an quantitative observational study. In the first study they develop theory regarding how environmental supporters evaluate themselves both positively and negatively and how these evaluations are shaped on an ongoing basis by work, home and other contexts. In the second study, using observational data, they derive three distinct profiles of environmental supporters and relate these profiles to environmental issue supportive behaviours.

The sample for the first qualitative study was drawn from a degree programme at a North American university called the 'Environment and Business Program'. This programme was designed to develop sustainability-orientated leaders who could also act as change agents. Sonnenshein et al. (2014) argue that although these people were clearly different from the population, this sample was important for developing theory as it allowed the researchers to learn from a non-typical group of people who had taken steps to learn about how to address climate change.

Using contact details provided by the degree programme for 25 current and 25 past students selected at random, individuals specifically interested in climate change were asked if they would be willing to take part in the research. Twenty-nine (14 current students and 15 past students) agreed to participate, identifying themselves as climate change issue supporters. Each of these people were interviewed for approximately an hour, each interview being transcribed in full.

Following analysis of data from the qualitative study, the second quantitative study collected data from two independent samples of environmental issues supporters in a large North American city. Participants were recruited by contacting the leaders of 21 groups that described themselves as active in environmental issues. Nineteen of these groups' leaders agreed to forward information about the research to their members with a link to a secure website through which they could sign up to take part in the research. In all, 91 people who were active members of environmental groups agreed to take part, comprising a second extreme case sample.

In direct contrast to heterogeneous sampling, **homogeneous sampling** focuses on one particular subgroup in which all the sample members are similar, such as a particular occupation or level in an organisation's hierarchy. Characteristics of the selected participants are similar, allowing them to be explored in greater depth and minor differences to be more apparent.

Critical case sampling selects critical cases on the basis that they can make a point dramatically or because they are important. The focus of data collection is to understand what is happening in each critical case so that logical generalisations can be made. Patton (2002) outlines a number of clues that suggest critical cases. These can be summarised by the questions such as:

- If it happens there, will it happen everywhere?
- If they are having problems, can you be sure that everyone will have problems?
- If they cannot understand the process, is it likely that no one will be able to understand the process?

In contrast, **typical case sampling** is usually used as part of a research project to provide an illustrative profile using a representative case. Such a sample enables you to provide an illustration of what is 'typical' to those who will be reading your research report and may be unfamiliar with the subject matter. It is not intended to be definitive.

Theoretical sampling is a special case of purposive sampling, being particularly associated with Grounded Theory and analytic induction (Sections 13.9 and 13.8). Initially you need to have some idea of where to sample, although not necessarily what to sample for, participants being chosen as they are needed. Subsequent sample selection is dictated by the needs of the emerging theory and the evolving storyline, your participants being chosen purposively to inform this. A theoretical sample is therefore cumulatively chosen according to developing categories and emerging theory based upon your simultaneous collecting, coding and analysis of the data.

Volunteer sampling

Snowball sampling is the first of two techniques we look at where participants are volunteered to be part of the research rather than being chosen. It is used commonly when it is difficult to identify members of the desired population, for example people who are working while claiming unemployment benefit. You, therefore, need to:

1 Make contact with one or two cases in the population.
2 Ask these cases to identify further cases.
3 Ask these new cases to identify further new cases (and so on).
4 Stop when either no new cases are given or the sample is as large as is manageable.

The main problem is making initial contact. Once you have done this, these cases identify further members of the population, who then identify further members, and so the sample snowballs (Box 7.13). For such samples the problems of bias are huge, as respondents are most likely to identify other potential respondents who are similar to themselves, resulting in a homogeneous sample (Lee 2000). The next problem is to find these new cases. However, for populations that are difficult to identify, snowball sampling may provide the only possibility.

Self-selection sampling is the second of the volunteer sampling techniques we look at. It occurs when you allow each case, usually individuals, to identify their desire to take part in the research. You therefore:

1 Publicise your need for cases, either by advertising through appropriate media or by asking them to take part.
2 Collect data from those who respond.

Publicity for convenience samples can take many forms. These include articles and advertisements in magazines that the population are likely to read, postings on appropriate online newsgroups and discussion groups, hyperlinks from other websites as well as letters, emails or tweets of invitation to colleagues and friends (Box 7.13). Cases that self-select often do so because of their strong feelings or opinions about the research

Box 7.13
Focus on student research

Self-selection sampling

Siân's research was concerned with the impact of student loans on studying habits. She had decided to distribute her questionnaire using the Internet. She publicised her research on Facebook in a number of groups' pages, using the associated description to invite people to self-select and click on the link to the questionnaire. Those who self-selected by clicking on the hyperlink were automatically taken to the Web questionnaire she had developed using the SurveyMethods.com online survey software.

question(s) or stated objectives. In some instances, this is exactly what the researcher requires to answer her or his research question and meet the objectives.

Haphazard sampling

Haphazard sampling occurs when sample cases are selected without any obvious principles of organisation in relation to your research question, the most common form being **convenience sampling** (also known as **availability sampling**). This involves selecting cases haphazardly only because they are easily available (or most convenient) to obtain for your sample, such as the person interviewed at random in a shopping centre for a television programme 'vox pop'. Although convenience sampling is used widely (for example, Facebook polls or questions), it is prone to bias and influences that are beyond your control. Cases appear in the sample only because of the ease of obtaining them; consequently all you can do is make some statement about the people who felt strongly enough about the subject of your question to answer it (and were using Facebook) during the period your poll was available! Not surprisingly, as emphasised in Figure 7.5, findings from convenience samples are often given very little credibility. Despite this, Saunders (2012) points out that samples ostensibly chosen for convenience often meet purposive sample selection criteria that are relevant to the research aim. It may be that an organisation you intend to use as a case study is 'convenient' because you have been able to negotiate access through existing contacts. Where this organisation also represents a 'typical' case, it can also offer an appropriate illustrative scenario, providing justification regarding its purpose when addressing the research aim. Alternatively, whilst a sample of operatives in another division of an organisation for which you work might be easy to obtain and consequently 'convenient', the fact that such participants allow you to address a research aim necessitating an in-depth focus on a particular homogenous group is more crucial.

Where the reasons for using a convenience sample have little, if any, relevance to the research aim, participants appear in the sample only because of the ease of obtaining them. Whilst this may not be problematic if there is little variation in the target population, where the target population is more varied it can result in participants that are of limited use in relation to the research question. Often a sample is intended to represent more than the target population, for example managers taking a part-time MBA course as a surrogate for all managers. In such instances the selection of individual cases may introduce bias to the sample, meaning that subsequent interpretations must be treated with caution.

7.4 Summary 小 结

- Your choice of sampling techniques is dependent on the feasibility and sensibility of collecting data to answer your research question(s) and to address your objectives from the target population. For target populations of fewer than 50 it is usually more sensible to collect data from the entire population where you are considering using probability sampling.
- Choice of sampling technique or techniques is dependent on your research question(s) and objectives:
  - Research question(s) and objectives that need you to estimate statistically the characteristics of the target population from a sample require probability samples.
  - Research question(s) and objectives that do not require such generalisations can, alternatively, make use of non-probability sampling techniques.
- Probability sampling techniques all necessitate some form of sampling frame, so they are often more time consuming than non-probability techniques.

- Where it is not possible to construct a sampling frame you will need to use non-probability sampling techniques.
- Factors such as the confidence that is needed in the findings, accuracy required and likely categories for analyses will affect the size of the sample that needs to be collected:
  - Statistical analyses usually require a minimum sample size of 30.
  - Research question(s) and objectives that do not require statistical estimation may need far smaller samples.
- Sample size and the technique used are also influenced by the availability of resources, in particular financial support and time available to select the sample and to collect, input and analyse the data.
- Non-probability sampling techniques also provide you with the opportunity to select your sample purposively and to reach difficult-to-identify members of the target population.
- For many research projects you will need to use a combination of different sampling techniques.
- All your choices will be dependent on your ability to gain access to organisations. The considerations summarised earlier must therefore be tempered with an understanding of what is practically possible.

Self-check questions 自测题

Help with these questions is available at the end of the chapter.

7.1 Identify a suitable sampling frame for each of the following research questions.
   a How do company directors of manufacturing firms of over 500 employees think a specified piece of legislation will affect their companies?
   b Which factors are important in accountants' decisions regarding working in mainland Europe?
   c How do employees at Cheltenham Gardens Ltd think the proposed introduction of compulsory Sunday working will affect their working lives?
7.2 Lisa has emailed her tutor with the following query regarding sampling and dealing with non-response. Imagine you are Lisa's tutor. Draft a reply to answer her query.

Help!!! Sampling non response

Draft saved at 09:39

B *I* U Aa A° A ∠ ⋮≡ ≔ ⋲⁺ ⋲⁺ ≡ ≡ ≡ ⊖ ☺

Hi

I interviewed someone yesterday and I (almost) failed to get him to say anything useful for my research project. This was strange as he had what appeared to be an extremely useful background. I was unable to get him to reflect on the issue of inhibitors of spin out companies in the *light of his own experiences* or *provide actual examples*. He clearly wanted to follow a format he had decided upon prior to the interview 😊. This was that there was a right and a wrong answer and he was guessing at what inhibited people rather than giving me the actual examples I asked for. This did not allow for feedback loops or linkages or ideas, which as you know, is what my research is about. It was a very linear model of innovation. My attempts to get the conversation onto my research were gently, but firmly, put aside. *He had his format on paper when I arrived.*

My question is: Can I just exclude this interview from my sample? He was a super guy and I enjoyed meeting him. But, because I could not get him to answer my questions the interview did not yield any insights. What should I do?

Yours

Lisa

7.3   You have been asked to select a sample of manufacturing firms using the sampling frame below. This also lists the value of their annual output in tens of thousands of pounds over the past year. To help you in selecting your sample the firms have been numbered from 0 to 99.

   a Select two simple random samples, each of 20 firms, and mark those firms selected for each sample on the sampling frame.

   b Describe and compare the pattern on the sampling frame of each of the samples selected.

   c Calculate the average (mean) annual output in tens of thousands of pounds over the past year for each of the samples selected.

   d Given that the true average annual output is £6,608,900, is there any bias in either of the samples selected?

	Output		Output		Output		Output		Output
0	1163	20	1072	40	1257	60	1300	80	1034
1	10	21	7	41	29	61	39	81	55
2	57	22	92	42	84	62	73	82	66
3	149	23	105	43	97	63	161	83	165
4	205	24	157	44	265	64	275	84	301
5	163	25	214	45	187	65	170	85	161
6	1359	26	1440	46	1872	66	1598	86	1341
7	330	27	390	47	454	67	378	87	431
8	2097	28	1935	48	1822	68	1634	88	1756
9	1059	29	998	49	1091	69	1101	89	907
10	1037	30	1298	50	1251	70	1070	90	1158
11	59	31	10	51	9	71	37	91	27
12	68	32	70	52	93	72	88	92	66
13	166	33	159	53	103	73	102	93	147
14	302	34	276	54	264	74	157	94	203
15	161	35	215	55	189	75	168	95	163
16	1298	36	1450	56	1862	76	1602	96	1339
17	329	37	387	57	449	77	381	97	429
18	2103	38	1934	58	1799	78	1598	98	1760
19	1061	39	1000	59	1089	79	1099	99	898

7.4   You have been asked to select a 10 per cent sample of firms from the sampling frame used for self-check question 7.3.

   a Select a 10 per cent systematic random sample and mark those firms selected for the sample on the sampling frame.

   b Calculate the average (mean) annual output in tens of thousands of pounds over the past year for your sample.

   c Given that the true average annual output is £6,608,900, why does systematic random provide such a poor estimate of the annual output in this case?

7.5   You need to undertake a series of face-to-face interviews with managing directors of small- to medium-sized organisations. From the data you collect you need to be able to generalise about the attitude of such managing directors to recent changes in government policy towards these firms. Your generalisations need to be accurate to within plus or minus 5 per cent. Unfortunately, you have limited resources to pay for interviewers, travelling and other associated costs.

a How many managing directors will you need to interview?

b You have been given the choice between cluster and multi-stage sampling. Which technique would you choose for this research? You should give reasons for your choice.

7.6 You have been asked to undertake face-to-face interviews with local residents to discover their opinions regarding the siting of a new supermarket in an inner city sub-urb (estimated catchment population 111,376 at the last census). The age and gender distribution of the catchment population at the last census is listed below.

	Age group							
Gender	**0–4**	**5–15**	**16–19**	**20–29**	**30–44**	**45–59 /64***	**60/65#–74**	**75+**
Males	3498	7106	4884	7656	9812	12892	4972	2684
Females	3461	6923	6952	9460	8152	9152	9284	4488

*59 females, 64 males; #60 females, 65 males.

a Devise a quota for a quota sample using these data.

b What other data would you like to include to overcome likely variations between groups in their availability for interview and replicate the target population more precisely? Give reasons for your answer.

c What problems might you encounter in using interviewers?

7.7 For each of the following research questions it has not been possible for you to obtain a sampling frame. Suggest the most suitable non-probability sampling technique to obtain the necessary data, giving reasons for your choice.

a What support do people sleeping rough believe they require from social services?

b Which television advertisements do people remember watching last weekend?

c How do employers' opinions vary regarding the impact of European Union legislation on age discrimination?

d How are manufacturing companies planning to respond to the introduction of road tolls?

e Would users of the squash club be prepared to pay a 10 per cent increase in subscriptions to help fund two extra courts (answer needed by tomorrow morning!)?

Review and discussion questions 复习与讨论题

7.8 With a friend or colleague choose one of the following research questions (or one of your own) in which you are interested.

• What attributes attract people to jobs?

• How are financial institutions adapting the services they provide to meet recent legislation?

Use the flow charts for both probability sampling (Figure 7.3) and non-probability sampling (Figure 7.5) to decide how you could use each type of sampling independently to answer the research question.

7.9 Agree with a colleague to watch a particular documentary or consumer rights programme on the television. If possible, choose a documentary with a business or management focus. During the documentary, pay special attention to the samples from which the data for the documentary are drawn. Where possible, note down details of the sample such as who were interviewed, or who responded to questionnaires, and the reasons why these people were chosen. Where this is not possible, make a note of the information you would have liked to have been given. Discuss your findings with your colleague and come to a conclusion regarding the nature of the sample used, its representativeness and the extent to which it was possible for the programme maker to generalise from that sample.

7.10 Obtain or access online a copy of a quality daily newspaper and, within the newspaper, find an article that discusses a 'survey' or 'poll'. Share the article with a friend. Make notes of the process used to select the sample for the 'survey' or 'poll'. As you make your notes, note down any areas where you feel there is insufficient information to fully understand the sampling process. Aspects for which information may be lacking include the target population, size of sample, how the sample was selected, representativeness and so on. Discuss your findings with your friend.

改进研究项目

Progressing your research project

Using sampling as part of your research 使用抽样作为你研究的一部分

- Consider your research question(s) and objectives. You need to decide whether you will be able to collect data on the entire population or will need to collect data from a sample.
- If you decide that you need to sample, you must establish whether your research question(s) and objectives require probability sampling. If they do, make sure that a suitable sampling frame is available or can be devised, and calculate the actual sample size required, taking into account likely response rates. If your research question(s)

and objectives do not require probability sampling, or you are unable to obtain a suitable sampling frame, you will need to use non-probability sampling.

- Select the most appropriate sampling technique or techniques after considering the advantages and disadvantages of all suitable techniques and undertaking further reading as necessary.
- Select your sample or samples following the technique or techniques as outlined in this chapter.
- Remember to note down the reasons for your choices when you make them, as you will need to justify your choices when you write about your research method.
- Use the questions in Box 1.4 to guide your reflective diary entry.

Self-check answers 自测题答案

7.1 **a** A complete list of all directors of large manufacturing firms could be purchased from an organisation that specialised in selling such lists to use as the sampling frame. Alternatively, a list that contained only those selected for the sample could be purchased to reduce costs. These electronic data could be merged into standard letters such as those included with questionnaires.

b A complete list of accountants, or one that contained only those selected for the sample, could be purchased from an organisation that specialised in selling such lists. Care would need to be taken regarding the precise composition of the list to ensure that it included those in private practice as well as those working for organisations. Alternatively, if the research was interested only in qualified accountants then the professional accountancy bodies' yearbooks, which list all their members and their addresses, could be used as the sampling frame.

c Subject to ethical approval, the personnel records or payroll of Cheltenham Gardens Ltd could be used. Either would provide an up-to-date list of all employees with their addresses.

7.2   Your draft of Lisa's tutor's reply is unlikely to be worded the same way as the one below. However, it should contain the same key points:

"tutor's name" <lisas.tutor@anytown.ac.uk>

To: <lisa@anytown.ac.uk>

Sent: today's date 7:06

Subject: Re: Help!!! Sampling non-response?

Hi Lisa

Many thanks for the email. This is not in the least unusual. I reckon to get about 1 in 20 interviews which go this way and you just have to say 'c'est la vie'. This is not a problem from a methods perspective as, in sampling terms, it can be treated as a non-response due to the person refusing to respond to your questions. This would mean you could not use the material. However, if he answered some other questions then you should treat this respondent as a partial non-response and just not use those answers.
Hope this helps.

'Tutor's name'

7.3   a   Your answer will depend on the random numbers you selected. However, the process you follow to select the samples is likely to be similar to that outlined. Starting at randomly selected points, two sets of 20 two-digit random numbers are read from the random number tables (Appendix 3). If a number is selected twice it is disregarded. Two possible sets are:

Sample 1: 38 41 14 59 53 03 52 86 21 88 55 87 85 90 74 18 89 40 84 71
Sample 2: 28 00 06 70 81 76 36 65 30 27 92 73 20 87 58 15 69 22 77 31

These are then marked on the sampling frame (sample 1 is shaded in blue, sample 2 is shaded in orange) as shown below:

0	1163	20	1072	40	1257	60	1300	80	1034
1	10	21	7	41	29	61	39	81	55
2	57	22	92	42	84	62	73	82	66
3	149	23	105	43	97	63	161	83	165
4	205	24	157	44	265	64	275	84	301
5	163	25	214	45	187	65	170	85	161
6	1359	26	1440	46	1872	66	1598	86	1341
7	330	27	390	47	454	67	378	87	431
8	2097	28	1935	48	1822	68	1634	88	1756
9	1059	29	998	49	1091	69	1101	89	907
10	1037	30	1298	50	1251	70	1070	90	1158
11	59	31	10	51	9	71	37	91	27
12	68	32	70	52	93	72	88	92	66
13	166	33	159	53	103	73	102	93	147
14	302	34	276	54	264	74	157	94	203
15	161	35	215	55	189	75	168	95	163
16	1298	36	1450	56	1862	76	1602	96	1339
17	329	37	387	57	449	77	381	97	429
18	2103	38	1934	58	1799	78	1598	98	1760
19	1061	39	1000	59	1089	79	1099	99	898

b Your samples will probably produce patterns that cluster around certain numbers in the sampling frame, although the amount of clustering may differ, as illustrated by samples 1 and 2 above.

c The average (mean) annual output in tens of thousands of pounds will depend entirely upon your sample. For the two samples selected the averages are:

Sample 1 (enclosed by a box): £6,752,000
Sample 2 (shaded): £7,853,500

d There is no bias in either of the samples, as both have been selected at random. However, the average annual output calculated from sample 1 represents the target population more closely than that calculated from sample 2, although this has occurred entirely at random.

7.4 a Your answer will depend on the random number you select as the starting point for your systematic sample. However, the process you followed to select your sample is likely to be similar to that outlined. As a 10 per cent sample has been requested, the sampling fraction is 1/10. Your starting point is selected using a random number between 0 and 9, in this case 2. Once the firm numbered 2 has been selected, every tenth firm is selected:

2 12 22 32 42 52 62 72 82 92

These are marked with orange shading on the sampling frame and will result in a regular pattern whatever the starting point:

0	1163	20	1072	40	1257	60	1300	80	1034
1	10	21	7	41	29	61	39	81	55
2	57	22	92	42	84	62	73	82	66
3	149	23	105	43	97	63	161	83	165
4	205	24	157	44	265	64	275	84	301
5	163	25	214	45	187	65	170	85	161
6	1359	26	1440	46	1872	66	1598	86	1341
7	330	27	390	47	454	67	378	87	431
8	2097	28	1935	48	1822	68	1634	88	1756
9	1059	29	998	49	1091	69	1101	89	907
10	1037	30	1298	50	1251	70	1070	90	1158
11	59	31	10	51	9	71	37	91	27
12	68	32	70	52	93	72	88	92	66
13	166	33	159	53	103	73	102	93	147
14	302	34	276	54	264	74	157	94	203
15	161	35	215	55	189	75	168	95	163
16	1298	36	1450	56	1862	76	1602	96	1339
17	329	37	387	57	449	77	381	97	429
18	2103	38	1934	58	1799	78	1598	98	1760
19	1061	39	1000	59	1089	79	1099	99	898

b The average (mean) annual output of firms for your sample will depend upon where you started your systematic sample. For the sample selected above it is £757,000.

c Systematic sampling has provided a poor estimate of the annual output because there is an underlying pattern in the data, which has resulted in firms with similar levels of output being selected.

7.5 a If you assume that there are at least 100,000 managing directors of small- to medium-sized organisations from which to select your sample, you will need to interview approximately 380 to make generalisations that are accurate to within plus or minus 5 per cent (Table 7.1).

b Either cluster or multi-stage sampling could be suitable; what is important is the reasoning behind your choice. This choice between cluster and multi-stage sampling is dependent on the amount of limited resources and time you have available. Using multi-stage sampling will take longer than cluster sampling as more sampling stages will need to be undertaken. However, the results are more likely to be representative of the target population owing to the possibility of stratifying the samples from the sub-areas.

7.6 a Prior to deciding on your quota you will need to consider the possible inclusion of residents who are aged under 16 in your quota. Often in such research projects residents aged under 5 (and those aged 5–15) are excluded. You would need a quota of between 2000 and 5000 residents to obtain a reasonable accuracy. These should be divided proportionally between the groupings as illustrated in the possible quota below:

	Age group					
Gender	16–19	20–29	30–44	45–59/64	60/65–74	75+
Males	108	169	217	285	110	59
Females	154	209	180	203	205	99

b Data on social class, employment status, socioeconomic status or car ownership could also be used as further quotas. These data are often available from your national Census and are likely to affect shopping habits.

c Interviewers might choose respondents who were easily accessible or appeared willing to answer the questions. In addition, they might fill in their quota incorrectly or make up the data.

7.7 a Either snowball sampling as it would be difficult to identify members of the target population or, possibly, convenience sampling because of initial difficulties in finding members of the target population.

b Quota sampling to ensure that the variability in the target population as a whole is represented.

c Purposive sampling to ensure that the full variety of responses are obtained from a range of respondents from the target population.

d Self-selection sampling as it requires people who are interested in the topic.

e Convenience sampling owing to the very short timescales available and the need to have at least some idea of members' opinions.

Get ahead using resources on the companion website at: **www.pearsoned .co.uk/saunders**.

- Improve your IBM SPSS Statistics and NVivo research analysis with practice tutorials.
- Save time researching on the Internet with the Smarter Online Searching Guide.
- Test your progress using self-assessment questions.
- Follow live links to useful websites.

Chapter 8

Using secondary data 使用二手数据

Learning outcomes 学习目标

By the end of this chapter you should be able to:

- identify the full variety of secondary data that are available;
- appreciate ways in which secondary data can be utilised to help to answer your research question(s) and to meet your objectives;
- understand the advantages and disadvantages of using secondary data in research projects;
- use a range of techniques to search for secondary data;
- evaluate the suitability of secondary data for answering your research question(s) and meeting your objectives in terms of measurement validity, coverage, reliability, validity, measurement bias, costs and benefits;
- apply the knowledge, skills and understanding gained to your own research project.

8.1 Introduction 引言

When thinking about how to obtain data to answer their research question(s) or meet their objectives, students are increasingly expected to consider undertaking further analyses of data that were collected initially for some other purpose. Such data are known as **secondary data** and include both raw data and published summaries. Once obtained, these data can be further analysed to provide additional or different knowledge, interpretations or conclusions (Bulmer et al. 2009). Despite this, many students automatically think in terms of collecting new (**primary**) **data** specifically for that purpose. Yet, unlike national governments, non-governmental agencies and other organisations, they do not have the time, money or access to collect detailed large data sets themselves. Fortunately, over the past decade the numbers of sources of potential secondary data have, alongside the ease of gaining access, grown rapidly. Such secondary data may enable you to answer, or partially answer, your research question(s).

Most organisations collect and store a wide variety and large volume of data to support their day-to-day operations: for example, payroll details, copies of letters, minutes of meetings and business transactions such as sales queries and purchases. Quality daily newspapers contain a wealth of data, including reports about takeover bids and companies' share prices. Government departments undertake surveys and publish official statistics covering social, demographic and economic topics. Consumer research organisations collect data that are used subsequently by different clients. Trade organisations collect data from their members on topics such as sales that are subsequently aggregated and published. Search engines such as Google collect data on the billions of searches undertaken daily, and social networking sites (such as Facebook) host web pages for particular interest groups, including those set up by organisations, storing them alongside other data group members' posts and photographs.

Big data are everywhere in business, with organisations using powerful computational techniques to analyse large volumes of data to create and capture value for businesses (Manyika et al. 2011). Such big data are generated from a wide variety of sources, ranging from Internet searches and social media posts to transactions such as supermarket purchases, and, although often collected for an immediate purpose (for example, stock control and tenable payment), are also combined with official statistics and archival sources and reanalysed to unveil new insights into trends and patterns.

One such example of the use of big data is Google Flu Trends (Google 2014), a flu tracking system that has been used to predict how many people have an influenza-like illness. Google has found a close relationship between how many people search for flu-related topics and how many people actually have flu symptoms (Ginsberg et al. 2009). Although full details of the data and analysis procedures are not provided, Google argues that, by counting how often a range of such search queries are used, it can estimate how much flu is circulating in different countries and regions of the world (Google 2014).

Yet, according to researchers at Harvard and Northwestern universities (Lazer et al. 2014), Google Flu Trends consistently overestimated the number of influenza cases in the United States for 100 of 108 weeks. This, they argue, offers critical lessons for the use of big data. Among these are: firstly, the importance of transparency, including providing sufficient information about the precise source(s) of the data used to allow replication by others; and, secondly, the need to recognise that, although big data offers enormous possibilities for new insights, traditional collection methods can often provide information that is not containable in big data.

Some of these data, in particular documents such as company minutes, are available only from the organisations that produce them, and so access will need to be negotiated (Sections 6.2 to 6.4). Others, such as web pages on social networking sites, can range from being 'open' for everyone using the site to view to being completely 'restricted' other than to group members. Governments' survey data, such as censuses of population, are widely available to download in aggregated form via the Internet as governments allow open access to data they have collected. Such survey data are also often deposited in, and available from, data archives. Online computer databases containing company information, such as Amadeus and Datamonitor, can often be accessed via your university library web pages (Table 8.2). In addition, companies and professional organisations usually have their own websites, which may contain data that are useful to your research project.

For certain types of research project, such as those requiring national or international comparisons or data from a large number of people, secondary data will probably provide the main source to answer your research question(s) and to address your objectives. However, if you are undertaking your research project as part of a course of study, we recommend that you check the assessment regulations before deciding whether you are going to use primary or secondary or a combination of both types of data. Some universities explicitly require students to collect primary data for their research projects. Most research questions are answered using some combination of secondary and primary data. Invariably where limited appropriate secondary data are available, you will have to rely mainly on data you collect yourself.

In this chapter we examine the different types of secondary data that are likely to be available to help you to answer your research question(s) and meet your objectives, how you might use them (Section 8.2) and a range of methods for locating these data (Section 8.3). We then consider the advantages and disadvantages of using secondary data (Section 8.4) and discuss ways of evaluating their validity and reliability (Section 8.5). We do not attempt to provide a comprehensive list of secondary data sources because as these are expanding rapidly it would be an impossible task.

二手数据类型及在研究中的使用
8.2   Types of secondary data and uses in research

Secondary data include both quantitative (numeric) and qualitative (non-numeric) data (Section 5.3), and are used principally in both descriptive and explanatory research. The secondary data you analyse further may be **raw data**, where there has been little if any processing, or **compiled data** that have received some form of selection or summarising. Many secondary data sets currently available were primary data sets that have been re-combined with other data sets to create larger data sets. Where data sets are massive, complex, and difficult to process using traditional computational analyses techniques (as in our opening vignette), they are referred to as **big data**. Within business and management research projects secondary data are used most frequently as part of a case study or survey research strategy. However, there is no reason not to include secondary data in other research strategies, including Archival Research, Action Research and Experimental Research.

Different researchers (e.g. Bryman 1989; Dale et al. 1988; Hakim 1982, 2000) have generated a variety of classifications for secondary data. These classifications do not, however, capture the full variety of data. We have therefore built on their ideas to create three main subgroups of secondary data: document based, survey based and those compiled from multiple sources (Figure 8.1).

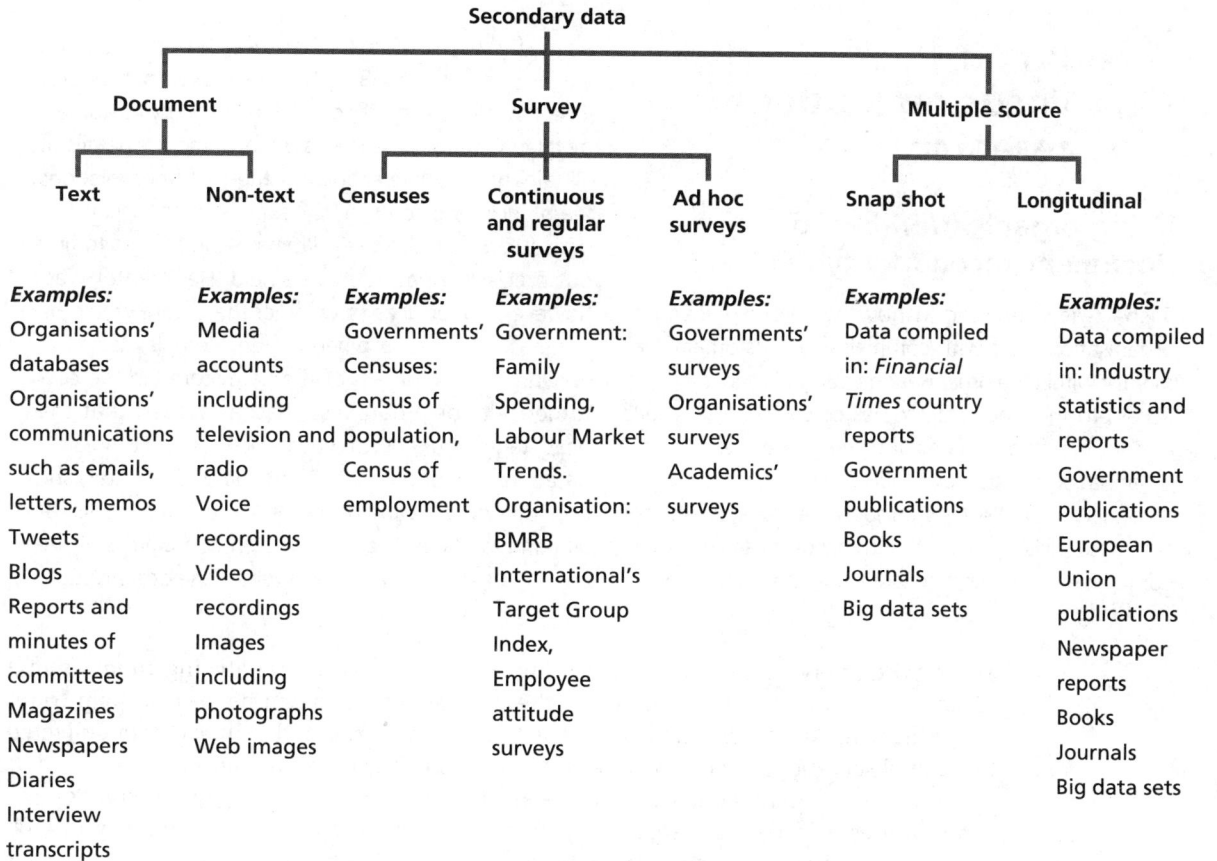

Figure 8.1 Types of secondary data
Source: © Mark Saunders, Philip Lewis and Adrian Thornhill 2015

Document secondary data

Document secondary data are often used in research projects that also collect primary data. However, you can also use them on their own or with other sources of secondary data, for example for business history research within an Archival Research strategy. **Document secondary data** are defined as data that, unlike the spoken word, endure physically (including digitally) as evidence, allowing data to be transposed across both time and space and reanalysed for a purpose different to that for which they were originally collected (Lee 2012). Increasingly available online, they include both text materials and non-text materials. Text materials include notices, correspondence (including emails), minutes of meetings, reports to shareholders, diaries, transcripts of speeches and conversations, administrative and public records as well as text of web pages (Box 8.1). Text can also include books, journal and magazine articles and newspapers. Although books, articles, journals and reports are a common storage medium for compiled secondary data, the text can be important raw secondary data in its own right. You could analyse the text of companies' annual reports to establish the espoused attitude of companies in different sectors to environmental issues. Using Content Analysis (Section 13.12) such text secondary data could also be used to generate statistical measures such as the frequency with which environmental issues are mentioned.

Secondary data also include non-text materials (Figure 8.1), such as voice- and video-recordings, pictures, drawings, films and television programmes (Lee 2012) as well as the non-text content of web pages. These data can be analysed both quantitatively

Box 8.1
Focus on student research

Using organisation-based document secondary data

Sasha was interested in how her work placement organisation dealt with complaints by customers. Her mentor within the organisation arranged for her to have access to the electronic copies of customers' emails and letters of complaint and the replies sent by the organisation's customer relations team (text document secondary data). Reading through these customers' letters, Sasha soon realised that many of these customers complained in writing because they had not received

a satisfactory response when they had complained earlier by telephone. She therefore asked her mentor if records were kept of complaints made by customers by telephone. Her mentor said that summary details of all telephone conversations by the customer relations team, including complaints (text document secondary data), were stored in their database and offered to find out precisely what data were held. Her mentor was, however, doubtful as to whether these data would be as detailed as the customers' written complaints.

On receiving details of the data stored in the customer relations' database, Sasha realised that the next stage would be to match the written complaints data with telephone complaints data. The latter, she hoped, would enable her to obtain a complete list of all complaints and set the written complaints in the context of all complaints received by the organisation.

and qualitatively, including transcribing spoken words and analysing them as text (Sections 13.10 to 13.13). In addition, these secondary data can be used to help triangulate findings based on other data, such as text material and primary data collected through observation, interviews or questionnaires (Chapters 9, 10 and 11).

Increasingly researchers are making use of web-based materials generated by online communities as document secondary data. While data stored in the majority of web pages, such as blogs and those set up by social networking sites' user groups, were never intended to be used in this way, they can still provide secondary data for research projects. There are, however, a number of issues related to using such data, including locating it, evaluating its usefulness in relation to your research question and objectives and associated ethical issues (Sections 6.5, 6.6 and 9.4).

Records stored in public, private and not-for-profit organisations' databases as part of their day-to-day business operations are another form of document that, when reanalysed for a different purpose, are secondary data. These include details of employees, members and customers and their interactions, such as customer transactions, mobile telephone calls and, as illustrated by the opening vignette, Internet search terms used by millions of users of a search engine. Providing you are able to gain access and satisfy ethical concerns, it may be possible to reanalyse such records using normal analysis software (Chapter 12). Where such data have been collected and stored on a very large scale, they are increasingly referred to as **big data**. For such secondary data, the massive size of the data set means patterns and trends can only be unveiled by powerful computer techniques (George et al. 2014). Consequently, although new insights can be gleaned from the reanalysis of big data and their combining as multiple-source secondary data sets, this is unlikely to be practicable for most undergraduate and master's research projects.

For your research project, the document sources you have available can depend on whether you have been granted access to an organisation's records as well as on your success in locating data archives, and other Internet, commercial and library sources (Section 8.3). Access to an organisation's data will be dependent on gatekeepers within that organisation (Sections 6.2–6.4). In our experience, those research projects that make use of document secondary data often do so as part of a within-company Action Research project or a case study of a particular organisation (Box 8.1).

Box 8.2
Focus on student research

When are the reports in newspapers and on YouTube secondary data?

Jana's research question was 'to what extent is the media's reporting of government policies on pension reform biased?' She had downloaded and read journal articles about the case for pension reform as well as a number of government documents on the subject. The latter included an information pack about the Pensions Act 2014 from the UK government's Department of Work and Pensions website, which she used to establish the government's stated reasons for pension reform. She had also obtained copies of newspaper reports about pension reform for the past two years and found YouTube clips of television news reports uploaded by television companies such as the BBC, Sky News and Independent Television News.

As she began to write the method chapter of her research project Jana became confused. She knew that the journal articles about the case for pension reform were literature rather than secondary data. However, she was unclear whether the government's information pack, the newspaper reports and the YouTube clips were secondary data. She emailed her tutor who responded:

Insert ∨   Save draft   Options ∨   Cancel   Mark Saunders

RE: When are newspaper reports and YouTube videos s: Draft saved at

B *I* U Aa A˙ **A** ∠ ≔ ≔ ⇥ ⇤ ≡ ≡ ≡ ⊖ ☺

Hi Jana

Thanks for your email. The answer to your question depends on how you are using these 'documents' in your research project. From you research question it seems that the newspaper reports will be the actual subjects of your analysis. By this I mean that you are using these reports as your data and analyzing them to establish whether or not their reporting of the government's pension reforms is biased.

However, you are using YouTube as a place to find secondary data, that is the television news reports that were originally broadcast by the television companies. Consequently YouTube is simply the place these secondary data, the news reports, are stored. However, if instead you used these news reports as the place to find secondary data such as a record of the number of people who had taken strike action in protest about pension reforms, then they would not be secondary data. Your secondary data (and the subject of your analysis) would be the number of people who had taken strike action, not the news report.

I hope this clarifies things.

Mark

P.S. You can treat the Government's information pack as secondary data as you are using it to establish their espoused view and reasoning behind the policy.

When you analyse text and non-text materials, such as a web page, a television news report or a newspaper article directly as part of your research, you are using those materials as secondary data. However, often such materials are just the source of your secondary data, rather than the actual secondary data you are analysing (Box 8.2).

Survey-based secondary data

Survey-based secondary data refers to existing data originally collected for some other purpose using a survey strategy, usually questionnaires (Chapter 11). Such data normally refer to organisations, people or households. They are made available as compiled data tables or, increasingly frequently, as a downloadable matrix of raw data (Section 12.2, Box 8.9) for secondary analysis.

Survey-based secondary data will have been collected through one of three distinct subtypes of survey strategy: censuses, continuous/regular surveys or ad hoc surveys (Figure 8.1). Censuses are usually carried out by governments and are unique because, unlike surveys, participation is obligatory. Consequently, they provide very good coverage of the population surveyed. They include censuses of populations, which have been carried out in many countries since the eighteenth century and in the UK since 1801 (Office for National Statistics 2014a). Published tabulations are available via the Internet for more recent UK censuses, and the raw data 100 years after the census was conducted can also be accessed via the Internet. The data from censuses conducted by many governments are intended to meet the needs of government departments as well as of local government. As a consequence they are usually clearly defined, well documented and of a high quality. Such data are easily accessible in compiled form, and are widely used by other organisations and individual researchers.

Continuous and regular surveys are those, excluding censuses, which are repeated over time (Hakim 1982). They include surveys where data are collected throughout the year, such as the UK's General Lifestyle Survey (Office for National Statistics 2013), and those repeated at regular intervals. The latter include the EU Labour Force Survey, which since 1998 has been undertaken quarterly using a core set of questions by member states throughout the European Union. This means that some comparative data are available for member states, although access to these data is limited by European and individual countries' legislation (European Commission 2015). Non-governmental bodies also carry out regular surveys. These include general-purpose market research surveys such as Kantar Media's Target Group Index. Because of the commercial nature of such market research surveys, the data are likely to be costly to obtain. Many large organisations also undertake regular surveys, a common example being the employee attitude survey. However, because of the sensitive nature of such information, it is often difficult to gain access to such survey data, especially in its raw form.

Census and continuous and regular survey data provide a useful resource with which to compare or set in context your own research findings from primary data. Aggregate data are usually available via the Internet (Section 8.3), in particular for government surveys. When using these data you need to check when they were collected, as there can be over a year between collection and publication! If you are undertaking research in one UK organisation, you could use these data to place your case study organisation within the context of its industry group or division using the Annual Employment Survey. Aggregated results of the Annual Employment Survey can be found via the UK government's statistics information gateway, the *Office for National Statistics* (Table 8.1). Alternatively, you might explore issues already highlighted by undertaking further analysis of data provided by an earlier organisation survey through in-depth interviews.

Survey secondary data may be available in sufficient detail to provide the main data set from which to answer your research question(s) and to meet your objectives. They may be the only way in which you can obtain the required data. If your research question is concerned with national variations in consumer spending it is unlikely that you will be able to collect sufficient data of your own. You will therefore need to rely on secondary data such as those contained in the report *Family Spending* (Office for National Statistics 2014b). For some research questions and objectives suitable data will be available in published form. For others, you may need more disaggregated data. This is most likely to be available via the Internet, often from

Table 8.1 Selected Internet secondary data gateways and archives

Name	Internet address	Comment
General focus		
RBA Business Information Sources	www.rba.co.uk/sources/	Gateway with links to business, statistical, government and country sites
UK Data Archive	www.data-archive.ac.uk/	Archive of UK digital data in the social science and humanities fields. Links to data archives worldwide
UK Data Service (UKDS)	ukdataservice.ac.uk/	Gateway to and support for economic and social data, both quantitative and qualitative for both the UK and other countries
Euromonitor International	www.euromonitor.com/	Business intelligence on countries, companies, markets and consumers
Hemscott	www.hemscott.com/	Financial information, guide to companies and investment trusts, report service and market activity analysis
MIMAS	www.mimas.ac.uk/	National data centre for UK higher education institutions providing gateway to key data such as UK census. NB: for some data sets you will need to register through your university
Country focus		
Australia: Australian Social Science Data Archive	www.assda.edu.au/	Archive of Australian social science data sets including census. Includes data from other Asia-Pacific countries. Links to other secondary data sites
Canada: Statistics Canada	www.statcan.gc.ca/start-debut-eng.html	Gateway to statistics on economy, culture, society and culture (including census) of Canada
China: Universities Service Centre Databank for China Studies	www.usc.cuhk.edu.hk/Eng/Default.aspx	Archive of social science data about People's Republic of China
Czech Republic: Czech Social Science Data Archive	archiv.soc.cas.cz/en	Archive of social science data about the Czech Republic.
European Union: Europa	europa.eu/	Gateway to information (including press releases, legislation, fact sheets) published by the European Union. Links include Eurostat statistics information gateway

(continued)

Table 8.1 (*Continued*)

Name	Internet address	Comment
France: National Institute for Statistics	www.insee.fr/en/default.asp	France's National Institute for Statistics gateway for both statistics and government publications. Much of this website is available in English
Germany: Federal Statistics Office	www.destatis.de/EN/Homepage.html	Germany's Federal Statistical Office providing a gateway to data. Much of this website is available in English
Ireland (Eire): Central Statistics Office	www.cso.ie/	Irish Central Statistical Office (CSO), the government body providing a gateway to Irish official statistics
Japan: Social Science Japan Data Archive	ssjda.iss.u-tokyo.ac.jp/en/	Archive of social science datasets available providing details in both Japanese and English. Datasets in Japanese only
Korea: Korean Social Science Data Archive	www.kossda.or.kr/eng/w05_05a.asp	Archive of social science statistical data including census available in Korean, English and Japanese
The Netherlands: Statistics Netherlands	www.cbs.nl/en-GB/menu/home/default.htm	Site of the Netherlands' Central Bureau of Statistics (CBS). Much of this website is available in English. Provides gateway to StatLine, which contains statistical data that can be downloaded free of charge
Norway: Norwegian Social Science Data Services	www.nsd.uib.no/nsd/english/index.html	Archive of social science data on Norway
South Africa: South African Data Archive	sada.nrf.ac.za/	Archive of social science data such as the census on South Africa
United Kingdom: GOV.UK	www.gov.uk/	UK government information service providing a gateway to government departments, official statistics, etc.
United Kingdom: Office for National Statistics	www.ons.gov.uk/ons/index.html	The official UK statistics gateway containing official UK statistics and information about statistics, which can be accessed and downloaded free of charge

data archives (Section 8.3). We have found that for most business and management research requiring secondary data you are unlikely to find all the data you require from one source. Rather, your research project is likely to involve detective work in which you build your own multiple-source data set using different data items from a variety of secondary data sources (Box 8.3). Like all detective work, finding data that help to answer a research question or meet an objective is immensely satisfying but also time consuming.

Box 8.3 Focus on management research

Corporate diversification, information asymmetry and insider trading

Academic literature in general suggests that corporate diversification destroys firm value, arguing that this is due to managers pursuing diversification strategies to benefit themselves rather than to increase the firm's value. Yet, research by Ali Ataullah and colleagues (Ataullah et al. 2014) provides evidence that this may not be the case. Using secondary data on the market's reaction to insider trading, they answer two questions:

1 Do corporate insiders pursue diversification strategies primarily to benefit themselves?

2 Do outside investors believe that managers diversify solely to benefit themselves?

Their data consists of measures of:

- Insider trading – drawing on the number and value of shares purchased and shares traded by directors of each firm;

- Corporate industrial diversification – drawing on the segment-level accounting data reported by each firm;
- Other factors affecting insider trading such as firm size (total book value of assets) and analyst following (number of financial analysts following each firm).

Data on firm directors' trading (as insiders) were obtained from Hemmington Scott (Financial Information Publishers), this containing details of over 100,000 open market trades. Firms' annual reports were used to provide data on stock-based incentives such as executive options and shares. Other accounting and financial data were obtained from Datastream.

Based on analysis of these data, Ataullah and colleagues argued that corporate insiders consider diversification strategies to be of sufficient value to justify purchasing more of their own firms' shares on the open market. They also note that outside investors react to these purchases more favourably when corporate diversification is high, suggesting a belief by these investors that managers do not diversify solely to benefit themselves.

Ad hoc surveys are usually one-off surveys and are far more specific in their subject matter. They include data from questionnaires that have been undertaken by independent researchers as well as interviews undertaken by organisations and governments. Because of their ad hoc nature, you will probably find it more difficult to discover relevant surveys. However, it may be that an organisation in which you are undertaking research has conducted its own questionnaire or interview-based survey on an issue related to your research. Some organisations will provide you with a report containing aggregated data; others may be willing to let you undertake further analyses using the raw data from this ad hoc survey. Alternatively, you may be able to gain access to and use raw data from an ad hoc survey that has been deposited in a data archive (Section 8.3).

Multiple-source secondary data

Multiple-source secondary data can be compiled entirely from document or survey secondary data, or can be an amalgam of the two. The key factor is that different data sets have been combined to form another data set prior to your accessing the data. One of the more common types of multiple-source data that you are likely to come across are online compilations of company information stored in databases such as *Amadeus* (Table 8.2). This contains comparable financial data about over 18 million public and private European companies. Other multiple-source secondary data include the various share price listings for different stock markets reported in the financial pages of quality newspapers. While newspapers are usually available online, there may be a charge to view their web pages. Fortunately university libraries usually have recent paper copies, while national and regional newspapers can also be accessed using online databases such as *Nexis* and, for older newspapers, *British Newspapers 1600–1900* (Table 8.2).

The way in which a multiple-source data set has been compiled will dictate the sorts of research question(s) or objectives for which you can use it. One method of compilation is to extract and combine selected comparable variables from a number of surveys or from the same survey that has been repeated a number of times to provide **longitudinal** data. For many undergraduate and taught master's courses' research projects, this is one of the few ways in which you will be able to obtain data over a long period. Other ways of obtaining time-series data are to use a series of company documents, such as appointment letters or public and administrative records, as sources from which to create your own longitudinal secondary data set. Examples of such data sets include the UK Employment Department's stoppages at work data held by the UK Data Archive (Table 8.1) and those derived by researchers from nineteenth- and early twentieth-century population census returns, the raw data for which can often be accessed through national governments' information gateways such as the UK's Office for National Statistics (Table 8.1).

Table 8.2 Selected online databases with potential secondary data

Name	Secondary data
Amadeus	Financial, descriptive and ownership information for 250,000 companies in Europe
British Newspapers 1600–1900	Full text of British newspapers
Datamonitor	Company profiles for world's 10,000 largest companies, industry profiles for various industries
Datastream	Company, financial and economic information
Euromonitor International	Global market information database searchable by industry, product, country etc.
Key Note Reports	1600 market reports covering a range of sectors
Mintel Reports	Market research reports on wide range of sectors
Nexis	Full text of UK national and regional newspapers. Some international coverage and company data
QIN	Company accounts, ratios and activities for over 300,000 companies in mainland China
Regional Business News	Full text of US business journals, newspapers and newswires. Updated daily
Times Digital Archive 1785–1985	Digital editions (including photographs, illustrations and advertisements) from *The Times* national newspaper (UK)

Data can also be compiled for the same population over time using a series of 'snapshots' to form **cohort studies**. Such studies are relatively rare, owing to the difficulty of maintaining contact with members of the cohort from year to year. An example is the UK television series 'Seven Up', which has followed a cohort since they were schoolchildren at seven-year intervals since 1964.

Secondary data from different sources can also be combined, if they have the same geographical basis, to form area-based data sets (Hakim 2000). Such data sets usually draw together quantifiable information and statistics. They are commonly compiled by national governments for their country and their component standard economic planning regions and by regional and local administrations for their own region. Such area-based multiple-source data sets are increasingly only available online through national governments' information gateways, regional administration's information gateways or data archives (Table 8.1). Widely used European examples include the European Union's annually published *Europe in Figures: Eurostat Yearbook* (Eurostat 2014) and collections such as Eurostat's (2015) statistical data for member countries (Box 8.9).

8.3 Searching for secondary data 检索二手数据

Unless you are approaching your research project with the intention of analysing one specific secondary data set that you already know well, your first step will be to ascertain whether the data you need are available. Your research question(s), objectives and the literature you have already reviewed will guide this. For many research projects you are likely to be unsure as to whether the data you require are available as secondary data. Fortunately, there are a number of clues to the sorts of data that are likely to be available.

The breadth of data discussed in the previous section serves only to emphasise that, despite the increasing importance of the Internet, potential secondary data may be stored in a variety of locations. Finding relevant secondary data requires detective work, which has two interlinked stages:

1 establishing whether the sort of data you require are likely to be available as secondary data;
2 locating the precise data you require.

Establishing the likely availability of secondary data

There are a number of clues to whether the secondary data you require are likely to be available. As part of your literature review you will have already read journal articles and books on your chosen topic. Where these have made use of secondary data (as in Box 8.3), they will provide you with an idea of the sort of data that are available. In addition, these articles and books should contain full references to the sources of the data. Where these refer to published secondary data such as those stored in online databases or multiple-source or survey reports, it is usually relatively easy to find the original source. Your university library will have subscriptions to a number of these online databases (Table 8.2) and is well worth browsing to establish the secondary data that are available. Quality national newspapers are also often a good source as they often report summary findings of recent reports (Box 8.4) and can be searched online. Your tutors have probably already suggested that you read a quality national newspaper on a regular basis, advice we would fully endorse as it is an excellent way of keeping up to date with recent events in the business world. In addition, there are many online news services, although some charge a subscription.

The evidence is growing – there really is a business case for diversity

By Tim Smedley

The business case for diversity seems intuitive. Teams of mixed gender, ethnicity, physical ability, age and sexual orientation are more representative of customers. They offer a variety of viewpoints and a wider range of experience, which improves decision-making and problem solving. Most business leaders seem to agree with this assertion.

Research by recruiter Korn/Ferry in November 2013 found that almost all the global executives it polled believe diversity and inclusion can boost results. But what evidence is there that they are right? First, a little debunking is needed. The research most often cited as evidence is provided by separate studies by consultants Catalyst and McKinsey published in 2007. Both compared the financial performance of large organisations according to the gender diversity at senior levels, and both found that high returns on equity correlated with greater diversity. Rather than irrefutable proof, however, neither study was able to show causation.

Research last year by the New York-based Center for Talent Innovation (CTI), however, began to take us a step closer.

Involving more than 40 case studies and 1,800 employee surveys, it looked at what it termed "two dimensional diversity", namely "inherent diversity" – such as gender and race – combined with "acquired diversity" – such as global experience and language skills.

It found that publicly traded companies with two-dimensional diversity were 45 per cent more likely than those without to have expanded market share in the past year and 70 per cent more likely to have captured a new market. When teams had one or more members who represented a target end-user, the entire team was as much as 158 per cent more likely to understand that target end-user and innovate accordingly.

A 2012 research report from Deloitte, "Waiter, is that inclusion in my soup?" edges us further towards causation. It is based on the experiences of 1,550 employees in three large Australian businesses. It identified an 80 per cent improvement in business performance when levels of diversity and inclusion were high.

An American Sociological Association study supports this, finding that for every 1 per cent rise in the rate of gender diversity and ethnic diversity in a workforce there is a 3 and 9 per cent rise in sales revenue, respectively . . .

. . . There is a twist in this evidential tale, however. Almost all the research on workplace diversity is unanimous on one thing: it can go wrong. Organisations without proper managerial or cultural understanding of diversity can end up with heightened conflict and reduced productivity.

As Deloitte's "Only skin deep?" 2011 report says, "it is not enough to create a corporate version of Noah's Ark bringing in 'two of each kind' . . . There is a clear argument for actively managing diversity rather than assuming we will naturally derive the benefits".

A McKinsey 2012 report found that, "though CEOs made gender diversity a priority in more than 80 per cent of our 60 participating companies, only about half of employees surveyed from the same companies agreed that the CEO is committed to it". The business case for diversity may now be proven, but it seems that action is lagging behind words.

Minority markets: Women and LGBT consumers reward company diversity

Businesses without a varied mix of employees can miss out on the spending power of minority markets.

. . . With annual listings of top gay-friendly employers becoming more prevalent, it takes only a quick internet search to see which companies are well positioned to capitalise on diversity and which remain firmly in the closet.

References for unpublished and document secondary data are often less specific, referring to 'unpublished survey results' or an 'in-house company survey'. Although these may be insufficient to locate or access the actual secondary data, they still provide useful clues about the sort of data that might be found within organisations and which might prove useful. Subject-specific textbooks such as Bradley's (2013) *Marketing Research: Tools and Techniques* can provide a clear indication of secondary data sources available in your research area, in this instance marketing. Other textbooks, such as Kavanagh et al.'s (2012) *Human Resource Information Systems: Basics, Applications and Future Directions*, can provide you with valuable clues about the sort of documentary secondary data that are likely to exist within organisations' management information systems.

Establishing the availability of relevant web-based materials generated by online communities which can be used as secondary data such as blogs and pages set up by social networking sites' user groups can be even more difficult. With the number of blogs growing rapidly and over 200 billion blogs in existence, there are almost certainly going to be blogs about your research topic. However, as we discuss later in this section, actually finding them is more difficult! In contrast, although estimates suggest similar rapid growth for organisation web pages, with more than 128 million .com and .net domain names in existence (VeriSign Inc. 2014), finding these organisations or their Facebook pages is far easier.

Tertiary literature such as indexes and catalogues can also help you to locate secondary data (Sections 3.3–3.5). Online searchable data archive catalogues, such as for the UK Data Archive, may prove a useful source of the sorts of secondary data available (Table 8.1). This archive holds the UK's largest collection of qualitative and quantitative digital social science and humanities data sets for use by the research community (UK Data Archive 2014). These data have been acquired from academic, commercial and government sources, and relate mainly to post-war Britain. However, it should be remembered that the supply of data and documentation for all of the UK Data Archive's data sets is charged at cost, and there may be additional administrative and royalty charges.

Online indexes and catalogues often contain direct linkages to downloadable files, often in spreadsheet format. Government websites (Table 8.1) such as the UK government's *Direct.gov* and the European Union's *Europa* provide useful gateways to a wide range of reports, legislative documents and statistical data as well as links to other sites. However, although data from such government sources are usually of good quality, those from other sources may be neither valid nor reliable. It is important, therefore, that you evaluate the suitability of such secondary data for your research (Section 8.5).

Finally, informal discussions are also often a useful source. Acknowledged experts, colleagues, librarians or your project tutor may well have knowledge of the sorts of data that might be available.

Locating secondary data

Once you have ascertained that secondary data are likely to exist, you need to find their precise location. For secondary data held in online databases to which your university subscribes, published by governments or held by data archives this will be relatively easy, especially where other researchers have made use of them and a full reference exists! All you will need to do is search the appropriate online database (Table 8.2) data archive or gateway (Table 8.1), find and download your data. Locating published secondary data held by specialist libraries is also relatively straightforward. Within the UK, specialist libraries with specific subject collections can usually be located using the most recent Chartered Institute of Library and Information Professional's (2014) publication *Libraries and Information Services in the United Kingdom and Republic of Ireland*.

If you are unsure where to start, confess your ignorance and ask a librarian. This will usually result in a great deal of helpful advice, as well as saving you time. Once the appropriate abstracting tool or catalogue has been located and its use demonstrated, it can be searched using similar techniques to those employed in your literature search (Section 3.5).

Data that are held by organisations are more difficult to locate. For within-organisation data we have found that the information or data manager within the appropriate department is most likely to know the precise secondary data that are held. This is the person who will also help or hinder your eventual access to the data and can be thought of as the gatekeeper to the information (Section 6.2).

One way to locate relevant web-based materials generated by online communities is to use Blog Content Management Systems such as Blogster and Blogit, which contain their own search engines, to identify potentially relevant blogs. Another is to use a general search engine such as Google or Bing. However, as highlighted by Hookway (2008), who spent four months working through some 200 blogs composed of an indeterminate number of postings only to locate 11 that were useful, this can be extremely time consuming! You may find it easier to set up your own blog and collect primary data (Section 10.9). In contrast, home and Facebook pages of organisations can be located easily using a general search engine or, in the case of UK-based companies, the links provided by the Yell UK business search engine. However, you will still need to assess their relevance.

Data sets on the Internet can also be located using archives such as the UK Data Archive (Table 8.1), or search engines where you search for all possible locations that match search terms associated with your research question(s) or objectives (Section 3.5). In some cases data will be stored at sites hosted by companies and professional organisations or trade associations and other than for aggregated data there is likely to be a charge. Additional guidance regarding how to use general search engines such as Google is given in Marketing Insights' *Smarter Internet Searching Guide*, which is available via this book's web page. However, searching for relevant data is often very time consuming. Although the amount of data on the Internet is increasing rapidly, much of it is, in our experience, of dubious quality. Consequently the evaluation of secondary data sources is crucial (Section 8.5).

Once you have located a possible secondary data set, you need to be certain that it will meet your needs. For most forms of secondary data the easiest way is to obtain and evaluate a sample copy of the data and a detailed description of how they were collected. For survey-derived data this may involve some cost. One alternative is to download and evaluate detailed definitions for the data set variables (which include how they are coded; Section 12.2) and the documentation that describes how the data were collected. This evaluation process is discussed in Section 8.5.

8.4 Advantages and disadvantages of secondary data 二手数据的优缺点

Advantages

May have fewer resource requirements

For many research questions and objectives the main advantage of using secondary data is the enormous saving in resources, in particular your time and money (Vartanian 2011). In general, it is much less expensive and time consuming to use secondary data than to collect the data yourself, especially where the data can be downloaded as a file that is compatible with your analysis software. You will also have more time to think about theoretical aims and substantive issues, and subsequently you will be able to spend more time and effort analysing and interpreting the data. If you need your data quickly, secondary data may be the only viable alternative. In addition, they are often higher-quality data than could be obtained by collecting your own (Smith 2006).

Unobtrusive

Using secondary data within organisations may also have the advantage that, because they have already been collected, they provide an unobtrusive measure. Cowton (1998) refers to this advantage as eavesdropping, emphasising its benefits for sensitive situations.

Longitudinal studies may be feasible

For many research projects time constraints mean that secondary data provide the only possibility of undertaking longitudinal studies. This is possible either by creating your own or by using an existing multiple-source data set (Section 8.2). Comparative research may also be possible if comparable data are available. You may find this to be of particular use for research questions and objectives that require regional or international comparisons. However, you need to ensure that the data you are comparing were collected and recorded using methods that are comparable. Comparisons relying on unpublished data or data that are currently unavailable in that format, such as the creation of new tables from existing census data, are likely to be expensive, as such tabulations will have to be specially prepared. Although your research is dependent on access being granted by the owners of the data, principally governments, many countries are enshrining increased rights of access to information held by public authorities through freedom of information legislation such as the UK's Freedom of Information Act 2005. This gives a general right to access to recorded information held by public authorities, although a charge may be payable. However, this is dependent upon your request not being contrary to relevant data protection legislation or agreements (Section 6.7).

Can provide comparative and contextual data

Often it can be useful to compare data that you have collected with secondary data. This means that you can place your own findings within a more general context (Box 8.5) or, alternatively, triangulate your findings (Section 5.3). If you have used a questionnaire, perhaps to collect data from a sample of potential customers, secondary data such as a national census can be used to assess the generalisability of findings, in other words how representative these data are of the total population (Section 7.2).

Can result in unforeseen discoveries

Reanalysing secondary data can also lead to unforeseen or unexpected new discoveries. Dale et al. (1988) cite establishing the link between smoking and lung cancer as an example of such a serendipitous discovery. In this example the link was established through secondary analysis of medical records that had not been collected with the intention of exploring any such relationship.

Permanence of data

Unlike data that you collect yourself, secondary data generally provide a source of data that is often permanent and available in a form that may be checked relatively easily by others (Denscombe 2007). This means that the data and your research findings are more open to public scrutiny.

Box 8.5
Focus on management research

Using secondary data to provide contextual information

In their 2014 *Human Relations* paper Saunders and colleagues use secondary data to provide contextual information about the two public-sector organisations from which their primary data were collected. These two organisations were selected on the basis of their relative performance and differing recent experiences of organisational change.

Using secondary data from the UK government's Audit Commission Saunders et al. (2014) were able to provide independent contextual information about the two organisations' performance. The performance of the first of these organisations (Newcounty), they noted, had been assessed by the Audit Commission as 'excellent' since 2005. They also referred a more recent Audit Commission report, which had praised Newcounty's management and 'outstanding cultural change'. In contrast, the second organisation (District) had been rated by the Audit Commission as 'performing well' since 2005; they had also commented that improvement was 'below average' and staff sickness levels were 'high'.

Unusually, Saunders et al. (2014) do not include these Audit Commission reports in their list of references. Rather, they note in their article that full references to County's Corporate Assessment Report and District's Annual Audit Report are not included to preserve anonymity. They do, however, provide a web link to the Audit Commission's reports for all English Local Authorities, stating that these are available at http://www.audit-commission.gov.uk/audit/Pages/Default.aspx.

Disadvantages

May be collected for a purpose that does not match your need

Data that you collect yourself will be collected with a specific purpose in mind: to answer your research question(s) and to meet your objectives. Unfortunately, secondary data will have been collected for a specific purpose that differs from your research question(s) or objectives (Denscombe 2007). Consequently, the data you are considering may be inappropriate to your research question. If this is the case then you need to find an alternative source, or collect the data yourself! More probably, you will be able to answer your research question(s) or address your objectives only partially. Common reasons for this include the data being collected a few years earlier and so not being current, or the methods of collection differing between the original data sources which have been amalgamated subsequently to form the secondary data set you intend to use (Box 8.6). For example, the 2011 UK National Census question on marital status asked 'What is your legal marital or same-sex civil partnership status?' while the 2001 question on marital status asked 'What is your marital status?' (Office for National Statistics 2014c), reflecting changes in social norms and legislation. Where the data are non-current and you have access to primary data, such as in a research project that is examining an issue within an organisation, you are likely to have to combine secondary and primary data. Alternatively, the secondary data you rely on may 'leave things out because the people whose information we are using don't think it's important, even if we do' (Becker 1998: 101).

Box 8.6
Focus on student research

The pitfalls of secondary data

Alison Wolf is the Sir Roy Griffiths Professor of Public Sector Management at King's College, London. In a 2007 article in *The Times Higher Education Supplement* (Wolf 2007), she issues some warnings to students using secondary data in their research, particularly in an era when such data are readily available on the Internet. Her main concern is the lack of questioning that many of us adopt when approaching secondary data. In her view, many of us 'have a tendency to assume that quantitative data must be out there waiting to be found: on the Web, organised and collated. How the figures get there and who collected the data and analysed them are not questions they seem to ask. Nor do they probe definitions (let alone response rates) – or not unless and until they start trying to locate, manipulate and integrate a variety of data on a specific subject' (Wolf 2007).

According to Wolf, some of the major pitfalls are assuming that samples are representative; and that the people who filled in questionnaires all did so in such a way that we can put faith in the results. They may not have been truthful in their responses,

have taken the questions seriously or, indeed, have understood the questions fully. Moreover, Wolf notes that it should not be assumed that whoever coded and entered the data knew what they were doing; and that it was clear what all the observations meant.

Wolf gives the example of one of her recent students who wanted to track how many history graduates from a given university enter teaching over a 20-year period. She points out that 'teaching' as a recorded student destination sometimes includes further education as well as schools, sometimes includes higher education as well, and sometimes neither. Also, what counts as a 'history' graduate may not be clear.

Wolf sounds other warnings, using the example of official UK government statistics. First, statistics that were routinely calculated can suddenly disappear. She gives the example of the decision, by the Office for National Statistics, suddenly to stop calculating average non-manual earnings. This caused major problems for one of her students. In addition, and more frequently, definitions change constantly in ways that seem to be dictated by changing government priorities. This makes it difficult to track changes over time. Wolf cites the example of education, where statistics are reported in terms of performance targets that keep changing. She concludes that this is a serious matter as good statistics are at the heart of governmental accountability, as well as good policymaking.

Access may be difficult or costly

Where data have been collected for commercial reasons, gaining access may be difficult or costly. Market research reports, such as those produced by Mintel or Key Note (Table 8.1), may cost a great deal if the report(s) that you require are not available online via your university's library.

Aggregations and definitions may be unsuitable

The fact that secondary data were collected for a different purpose may result in other, including ethical (Section 6.6), problems. Much of the secondary data you use is likely to be in published reports. As part of the compilation process, data will have been aggregated in some way. These aggregations, while meeting the requirements of the original research, may not be quite so suitable for your research. The definitions of data variables may not be the most appropriate for your research question(s) or objectives. In addition, where you are intending to combine data sets, definitions may differ markedly or have been revised over time (Box 8.7). Alternatively, the documents you are using may represent the interpretations of those who produced them, rather than offer an objective picture of reality.

Box 8.7
Focus on student research

Changing definitions

As part of his research, Jeremy wished to use longitudinal data on the numbers of males and females disaggregated by some form of social grouping. Using the UK Office for National Statistics website (Table 8.1), he quickly found and downloaded data which classified males and females using the National Statistics Socio-economic Classification (NS-SEC). However, this classification appeared to have been used only from 2001. Prior to this date, two separate classifications had been used: social class (SC) and socio-economic group (SEG), for which much longer time series of data were available. Before arranging an appointment with his project tutor to discuss this potential problem, Jeremy made a note of the two classifications:

NS-SEC		SC	
1	Higher managerial and professional occupations	I	Professional
2	Lower managerial and professional occupations	II	Managerial and technical
3	Intermediate occupations	IIIa	Skilled non-manual
4	Small employers and own account workers	IIIb	Skilled manual
5	Lower supervisory and technical occupations	IV	Semi-skilled
6	Semi-routine occupations	V	Unskilled
7	Routine occupations		

During their meeting later that week, Jeremy's tutor referred him to research on the NS-SEC which compared this with the old measures of SC and SEG and made suggestions regarding the continuity of the measures. Jeremy noted down the reference: Heath, A., Martin, J. and Beerten, R. (2003) 'Old and new social class measures – a comparison', in D. Rose and D.J. Pevalin (eds) *A Researcher's Guide to the National Statistics Socio-economic Classification*. London: Sage, pp. 226–42.

No real control over data quality

Although many of the secondary data sets available from governments and data archives are likely to be of a higher quality than you could ever collect yourself, there is still a need to assess the quality of these data. Wernicke (2014) notes that although many national statistical agencies are obliged by national law to provide data of high quality, this may not be the case. Looking at official economic data he argues that these are distorted, by the informal economy, hidden money and false and non-responses. For this reason care must be taken and all data sources must be evaluated carefully, as outlined in Section 8.5.

Initial purpose may affect how data are presented

When using data that are presented as part of a report you also need to be aware of the purpose of that report and the impact that this will have on the way the data are presented. This is especially so for internal organisational documents and external documents such as published company reports and newspaper reports. Reichman (1962; cited by Stewart and Kamins 1993) emphasises this point referring to newspapers, although the sentiments apply to many documents. He argues that newspapers select what they consider to be the most significant points and emphasise these at the expense of supporting data. This, Reichman states, is not a criticism as the purpose of the reporting is to bring these points to the attention of readers rather than to provide a full and detailed account. However, if we generalise from these ideas, we can see that the culture, predispositions and ideals of those who originally collected and collated the secondary data will have influenced the nature of these data at least to some extent. For these reasons you must evaluate carefully any secondary data you intend to use. Possible ways of doing this are discussed in the next section.

8.5 Evaluating secondary data sources 评估二手数据来源

Secondary data must be viewed with the same caution as any primary data that you collect. You need to be sure that:

- they will enable you to answer your research question(s) and to meet your objectives;
- the benefits associated with their use will be greater than the costs;
- you will be allowed access to the data (Sections 6.2–6.4).

Secondary sources that appear relevant at first may not on closer examination be appropriate to your research question(s) or objectives. It is therefore important to evaluate the suitability of secondary data sources for your research. Invariably, as highlighted in the chapter's opening vignette, this can be problematic where insufficient information is provided by the data source to allow this.

Stewart and Kamins (1993) argue that, if you are using secondary data, you are at an advantage compared with researchers using primary data. Because the data already exist you can evaluate them prior to use. The time you spend evaluating any potential secondary data source is time well spent, as rejecting unsuitable data earlier can save much wasted time later! Such investigations are even more important when you have a number of possible secondary data sources you could use. Most authors suggest a range of validity and reliability (Section 5.8) criteria against which you can evaluate potential secondary data. These, we believe, can be incorporated into a three-stage process (Figure 8.2). However, this is not always a straightforward process, as sources of the secondary data do not always contain all the information you require to undertake your evaluation.

Alongside this process you need also to consider the accessibility of the secondary data. For some secondary data sources, in particular those available via the Internet or in your university library, this will not be a problem. It may, however, still necessitate long hours working in the library if the sources are paper based and 'for reference only'. For other data sources, such as those within organisations, you need to obtain permission prior to gaining access and may well also need to consider potential ethical implications where personal data are involved. This will be necessary even if you are working for the organisation. These issues are discussed in Chapter 6, so we can now consider the evaluation process in more detail.

Overall suitability

Measurement validity

One of the most important criteria for the suitability of any data set is **measurement validity**. Secondary data that fail to provide you with the information that you need to answer your research question(s) or meet your objectives will result in invalid answers

Overall suitability of data to research question(s) and objectives
Measurement validity
Coverage including unmeasured variables
(If not suitable, then do not proceed)

Precise suitability of data for analysis
Reliability and validity
Measurement bias
(If not suitable, then do not proceed)

**Assessment of costs
and benefits**
(If costs outweigh benefits,
do not proceed)

Figure 8.2 Evaluating potential secondary data sources

(Smith 2006). Often when you are using secondary survey data you will find that the measures used do not quite match those that you need. For example, a manufacturing organisation may record monthly sales whereas you are interested in monthly orders, hence the measure is invalid.

This may cause you a problem when you undertake your analyses believing that you have found a relationship with sales whereas in fact your relationship is with the number of orders. Alternatively, you may be using minutes of company meetings as a proxy for what actually happened in those meetings. These are likely to reflect a particular interpretation of what happened, the events being recorded from a particular viewpoint, often the chairperson's. You therefore need to be cautious before accepting such records at face value (Denscombe 2007).

Unfortunately, there are no clear solutions to problems of measurement invalidity. All you can do is try to evaluate the extent of the data's validity and make your own decision (Box 8.8). A common way of doing this is to examine how other researchers have coped with this problem for a similar secondary data set in a similar context. If they found that the measures, while not exact, were suitable, then you can be more certain that they will be suitable for your research question(s) and objectives. If they had problems, then you may be able to incorporate their suggestions as to how to overcome them. Your literature search (Sections 3.4 and 3.5) will probably have identified other such studies already.

Coverage and unmeasured variables

The other important overall suitability criterion is **coverage**. You need to be sure that the secondary data cover the population about which you need data, for the time period you need, and contain data variables that will enable you to answer your research question(s) and to meet your objectives. For all secondary data sets coverage will be concerned with two issues:

- ensuring that unwanted data are or can be excluded;
- ensuring that sufficient data remain for analyses to be undertaken once unwanted data have been excluded (Hakim 2000).

When analysing secondary survey data, you will need to exclude those data that are not relevant to your research question(s) or objectives. Service companies, for example,

Box 8.8
Focus on student research

Using a social networking site as a source of secondary data

Mike's research project was concerned with the impact of social media on brand awareness and brand loyalty. He was particularly interested in how small automobile manufacturers used social networking sites in their marketing. His research question was: 'How effectively do small automotive manufacturers use social networking sites in their marketing?'

Mike was aware from the academic (Choudhury and Harrigan 2014) and trade (DeMers 2014) literature that social media was of major importance in marketing and could influence various aspects of consumer behaviour, such as product awareness, information acquisition and purchase behaviour. Based on the academic literature on branding and social media, Mike argued that, to use social media most effectively, organisations needed to follow a three-stage process of providing material of interest, engaging people and using them as advocates for their products.

Mike was also aware from Internet searches and his own interest in cars that automotive manufacturers had each created their own Facebook presence, providing content, and using their pages to interact with their fans (customers). Mike was already a fan of the Morgan Motor Company's Facebook page which was 'liked' by over 36,000 Facebook members. Morgan's wall contained company posts about their products and comments and other posts from fans. Although the data in these posts were not originally intended to answer Mike's research question, after careful evaluation he considered that further analysis of the posts and comments would enable him to do this.

Because Morgan's Facebook page was open to everyone, Mike considered that the information was in the public domain and so he could use it for his research project without seeking consent. He now needed to analyse the posts (data) available on Morgan's Facebook wall to establish the extent to which this form of social media was being used by the organisation to provide consumers with material of interest, engage them and allow them to become advocates for the product.

Source: ©Morgan Motor Company, 2014. Reproduced with permission

need to be excluded if you are concerned only with manufacturing companies. However, in doing this it may be that insufficient data remain for you to undertake the quantitative analyses you require (Sections 12.4 and 12.5). For documentary sources, you will need to ensure that the data contained in them relate to the population identified in your research. For example, check that the social media content on an organisation's social media pages actually relate to the organisation. Where you are intending to undertake a longitudinal study, you also need to ensure that the data are available for the entire period in which you are interested.

Some secondary data sets, in particular those collected using a survey strategy, may not include variables you have identified as necessary for your analysis. These are termed unmeasured variables. Their absence may not be particularly important if you are undertaking descriptive research. However, it could drastically affect the outcome of explanatory research as a potentially important variable has been excluded.

Precise suitability

Reliability and validity

The reliability and validity (Section 5.8) you ascribe to secondary data are functions of the method by which the data were collected and the source. You can make a quick assessment of these by looking at the source of the data. Dochartaigh (2007) and others refer to this as assessing the authority or reputation of the source. Survey data from large, well-known organisations such as those found in Mintel and Key Note market research reports (Table 8.2) are likely to be reliable and trustworthy. The continued existence of such organisations is dependent on the credibility of their data. Consequently, their procedures for collecting and compiling the data are likely to be well thought through and accurate. Survey data from government organisations are also likely to be reliable, although they may not always be perceived as such. However, you will probably find the validity of documentary data such as organisations' records more difficult to assess. While organisations may argue that their records are reliable, there are often inconsistencies and inaccuracies. You therefore need also to examine the method by which the data were collected and try to ascertain the precision needed by the original (primary) user.

Dochartaigh (2007) suggests a number of areas for initial assessment of the authority of documents available via the Internet. These, we believe, can be adapted to assess the authority of all types of secondary data. First, as suggested in the previous paragraph, it is important to discover the person or organisation responsible for the data and to be able to obtain additional information through which you can assess the reliability of the source. For data in printed publications this is usually reasonably straightforward (Section 3.6).

However, for secondary data obtained via the Internet it may be more difficult. Although organisation names, such as the 'Center for Research into . . .' or 'Institute for the Study of . . .', may appear initially to be credible, publication via the Internet is not controlled, and such names are sometimes used to suggest pseudo-academic credibility. Dochartaigh (2007) therefore suggests that you look also for a copyright statement and the existence of published documents relating to the data to help validation. The former of these, when it exists, can provide an indication of who is responsible for the data. The latter, he argues, reinforces the data's authority, as printed publications are regarded as more reliable. In addition, Internet sources often contain an email address or other means of contacting the author for comments and questions about the Internet site and its contents. However, beware of applying these criteria too rigidly as sometimes the most authoritative web pages do not include the information outlined above. Dochartaigh (2007) suggests that this is because those with most authority often feel the least need to proclaim it!

For all secondary data, a detailed assessment of the validity and reliability will involve you in an assessment of the method or methods used to collect the data (Dale et al. 1988). These may be provided as hyperlinks for Internet-based data sets, although they may not be sufficiently detailed to enable you to make a full assessment. Alternatively, they may be discussed in the methodology section of an associated report. Your assessment will involve looking at who were responsible for collecting or recording the information and examining the context in which the data were collected. From this you should gain some feeling regarding the likelihood of potential errors or biases. In addition, you need to look at the process by which the data were selected and collected or recorded. Where sampling has been used to select cases (usually as part of a survey strategy), the sampling procedure adopted and the associated sampling error and response rates (Section 7.2) will give clues to validity. Secondary data collected using a questionnaire with a high response rate are also likely to be more reliable than those from one with a low response rate. However, commercial providers of high-quality, reliable data sets may be unwilling to disclose details about how data were collected. This is particularly the case where these organisations see the methodology as important to their competitive advantage.

For some documentary sources, such as blogs, social media pages and transcripts of interviews or meetings, it is unlikely that there will be a formal methodology describing how the data were collected. The reliability of these data will therefore be difficult to assess, although you may be able to discover the context in which the data were collected. For example, blogs, emails and memos contain no formal obligation for the writer to give a full and accurate portrayal of events. Rather they are written from a personal point of view and expect the recipient to be aware of the context (Hookway 2008). This means that these data are more likely to be useful as a source of the writer's perceptions and views than as an objective account of reality. The fact that you did not collect and were not present when these data were collected will also affect your analyses. Dale et al. (1988) argue that full analyses of in-depth interview data require an understanding derived from participating in social interactions that cannot be fully captured by audio-recording or transcript.

The validity and reliability of collection methods for survey data will be easier to assess where you have a clear explanation of the techniques used to collect the data (Box 8.9). This needs to include a clear explanation of any sampling techniques used and response rates (discussed earlier) as well as a copy of the data collection instrument, which is usually a questionnaire. By examining the questions by which data were collected, you will gain a further indication of the validity.

Where data have been compiled, as in a report, you need to pay careful attention to how these data were analysed and how the results are reported. Where percentages (or proportions) are used without actually giving the totals on which these figures are based, you need to examine the data very carefully. For example, a 50 per cent increase in the number of clients from two to three for a small company may be of less relevance than the 20 per cent increase in the number of clients from 1000 to 1200 for a larger company in the same market! Similarly, where quotations appear to be used selectively without other supporting evidence you should beware, as the data may be unreliable.

Box 8.9
Focus on student research

Assessing the suitability of online multiple-source longitudinal data

As part of her research project on changing consumer spending patterns in Europe, Jocelyn wished to establish how the cost of living had altered in the European Union since the accession of the 10 new member states in 2004. Other research that she had read as part of her literature review had utilised the European Union's Harmonized Index of Consumer Prices (HICPs). She therefore decided to see whether this information was available via the Internet from the European Union's *Europa* information gateway. She clicked on the link to the *Eurostat Official EU Statistics* home page and searched for 'Harmonized Indices of Consumer Prices'. This revealed that there were publications, monthly data and indices data of consumer prices.

Jocelyn then clicked on the link to the Harmonized Indices of Consumer Prices (HCIP) Metadata and read the data description. As the data were relevant to her research she clicked on and viewed the content revealed by a number of different links, eventually finding the one that enabled her to specify the dataset she wanted: 'HICP all items – annual average indices'.

Source: Eurostat (2014) Copyright European Communities, 2014. Reproduced with permission

She clicked on this link and looked briefly at the data table. It appeared to be suitable in terms of coverage for her research so she downloaded and saved it as an Excel spreadsheet on her MP3 player.

Jocelyn was happy with the data's overall suitability and the credibility of the source, the data having been compiled for the European Union using data collected each year by each of the member

Source: Eurostat (2014) Copyright European Communities, 2014. Reproduced with permission

states. She also discovered that the actual data collected were governed by a series of European Union regulations.

In order to be certain about the precise suitability of the HICP, Jocelyn needed to find out exactly how the index had been calculated and how the data on which it was based had been collected. Hyperlinks from the data description web page provided an overview of how the index was calculated, summarising the nature of goods and services that were included. The data for the HICP were collected in each member state using a combination of visits to local retailers and service providers and central collection (via mail, telephone, email and the Internet), over 1 million price observations being used each month! One potential

problem was also highlighted: there was no uniform basket of goods and services applying to all member states. Rather, the precise nature of some goods and services included in the HICP varied from country to country, reflecting the reality of expenditure in each of the countries. Jocelyn decided that this would not present too great a problem as she was going to use these data only to contextualise her research.

The Eurostat web pages emphasised that the HICP was a price rather than a cost of living index. However, it also emphasised that, despite conceptual differences between price and the cost of living, there were unlikely to be substantial differences in practice. Jocelyn therefore decided to use the HICP as a surrogate for the cost of living.

Measurement bias

Measurement bias can occur for three reasons (Hair et al. 2011):

- deliberate distortion of data;
- changes in the way data are collected;
- when the data collection technique did not truly measure the topic of interest.

Deliberate distortion occurs when data are recorded inaccurately on purpose, and is most common for secondary data sources such as organisational records. Managers may deliberately fail to record minor accidents to improve safety reports for their departments. Data that have been collected to further a particular cause or the interests of a particular group are more likely to be suspect as the purpose of the study may be to reach a predetermined conclusion (Smith 2006). Reports of consumer satisfaction surveys may deliberately play down negative comments to make the service appear better to their target audience of senior managers and shareholders, and graphs may deliberately be distorted to show an organisation in a more favourable light.

Other distortions may be deliberate but not intended for any advantage. Employees keeping time diaries might record only the approximate time spent on their main duties rather than accounting precisely for every minute. People responding to a structured interview (questionnaire) might adjust their responses to please the interviewer (Section 11.2).

Unfortunately, measurement bias resulting from deliberate distortion is difficult to detect. While we believe that you should adopt a neutral stance about the possibility of bias, you still need to look for pressures on the original source that might have biased the data. For written documents such as minutes, reports and memos the intended target audience may suggest possible bias, as indicated earlier in this section. Therefore, where possible you will need to triangulate the findings with other independent data sources. Where data from two or more independent sources suggest similar conclusions, you can have more confidence that the data on which they are based are not distorted. Conversely, where data suggest different conclusions you need to be more wary of the results.

Changes in the way in which data were collected can also introduce changes in measurement bias. Provided that the method of collecting data remains constant in terms of the people collecting it and the procedures used, the measurement biases should remain constant. Once the method is altered, perhaps through a new procedure for taking minutes or a new data collection form, then the bias also changes. This is very important for longitudinal data sets where you are interested in trends rather than actual numbers. Your detection of biases is dependent on discovering that the way data are recorded has changed. Within-company sources are less likely to have documented these changes than government-sponsored sources.

Measurement bias also occurs where the data collected does not truly represent the topic of interest. For example, minimum income standards need to take account of what people need for a minimum acceptable standard of living, something that both differs between countries and has altered over time. In establishing their 2014 minimum income standard for the UK, the Joseph Rowntree Foundation (Davis et al., 2014) included in the basket of minimum requirements the necessity for pensioner households to have a computer and the Internet, something that would not be normal in all countries.

Costs and benefits

Hair et al. (2011) argue an assessment of secondary data also needs to consider the costs of acquiring them with the benefits they will bring. Costs include both time and financial resources that you will need to devote to locating and obtaining the data. Some data will be available online at no charge (Box 8.9). Other data will require lengthy negotiations to gain access, the outcome of which may be a polite 'no' (Sections 6.2–6.4). Data from market research companies or special tabulations from government surveys will have to be ordered specially and will normally be charged for: consequently, these will be relatively costly.

Benefits from data can be assessed in terms of the extent to which they will enable you to answer your research question(s) and meet your objectives. You will be able to form a judgement on the benefits from your assessment of the data set's overall and precise suitability (discussed earlier in this section). This assessment is summarised as a checklist of questions in Box 8.10. An important additional benefit is the form in which you receive the data. If the data are already in spreadsheet readable

Box 8.10 Checklist

Evaluating your secondary data sources

Overall suitability

✔ Does the data set contain the information you require to answer your research question(s) and meet your objectives?

✔ Do the measures used match those you require?

✔ Is the data set a proxy for the data you really need?

✔ Does the data set cover the population that is the subject of your research?

✔ Does the data set cover the geographical area that is the subject of your research?

✔ Can data about the population that is the subject of your research be separated from unwanted data?

✔ Are the data for the right time period or sufficiently up to date?

✔ Are data available for all the variables you require to answer your research question(s) and meet your objectives?

✔ Are the variables defined clearly?

Precise suitability

✔ How reliable is the data set you are thinking of using?

✔ How credible is the data source?

✔ Is it clear what the source of the data is?

✔ Do the credentials of the source of the data (author, institution or organisation sponsoring the data) suggest it is likely to be reliable?

✔ Do the data have an associated copyright statement?

✔ Do associated published documents exist?

✔ Does the source contain contact details for obtaining further information about the data?

✔ Is the method described clearly?

✔ If sampling was used, what was the procedure and what were the associated sampling errors and response rates?

✔ Who was responsible for collecting or recording the data?

✔ (For surveys) Is a copy of the questionnaire or interview checklist included?

✔ (For compiled data) Are you clear how the data were analysed and compiled?

✔ Are the data likely to contain measurement bias?

✔ What was the original purpose for which the data were collected?

✔ Who was the target audience and what was its relationship to the data collector or compiler (were there any vested interests)?

✔ Have there been any documented changes in the way the data are measured or recorded including definition changes?

✔ How consistent are the data obtained from this source when compared with data from other sources?

✔ Have the data been recorded accurately?

✔ Are there any ethical concerns with using the data?

Costs and benefits

✔ What are the financial and time costs of obtaining these data?

✔ Can the data be downloaded into a spreadsheet, statistical analysis software or word processor?

✔ Do the overall benefits of using these secondary data sources outweigh the associated costs?

And finally

✔ Is permission required to use these data and, if 'yes', can you obtain it?

Source: Authors' experience; Dale *et al.* (1988); Dochartaigh (2007); Hair et al. (2011); Smith (2006); Stewart and Kamins (1993); Vartanian (2011)

format (often referred to as csv, comma separated values), this will save you considerable time as you will not need to re-enter the data prior to analysis (Sections 12.2 and 13.3). However, when assessing the costs and benefits you must remember that data that are not completely reliable and contain some bias are better than no data at all, if they enable you to start to answer your research question(s) and achieve your objectives.

8.6   Summary   小 结

- Secondary data are data that you analyse which were originally collected for some other purpose, perhaps processed and subsequently stored. There are three main types of secondary data: document, survey and multiple source.
- Most research projects require some combination of secondary and primary data to answer your research question(s) and to meet your objectives. You can use secondary data in a variety of ways. These include:
  - to provide your main data set;
  - to provide longitudinal (time-series) data;
  - to provide area-based data;
  - to compare with, or set in context, your own research findings.
- Any secondary data you use will have been collected for a specific purpose. This purpose may not match that of your research. Secondary data are often less current than any data you collect yourself.
- Finding the secondary data you require is a matter of detective work. This will involve you in:
  - establishing whether the sort of data that you require are likely to be available;
  - searching for and locating the precise data.
- Once located, you must assess secondary data sources to ensure their overall suitability for your research question(s) and objectives. In particular, you need to pay attention to the measurement validity and coverage of the data.
- You must also evaluate the precise suitability of the secondary data. Your evaluation should include reliability and any likely measurement bias. You can then make a judgement on the basis of the costs and benefits of using the data in comparison with alternative sources.
- When assessing costs and benefits, you need to be mindful that secondary data that are not completely reliable and contain some bias are better than no data at all if they enable you partially to answer your research question(s) and to meet your objectives.

Self-check questions   自测题

Help with these questions is available at the end of the chapter.

8.1   Give three examples of different situations where you might use secondary data as part of your research.

8.2   You are undertaking a research project as part of your course. Your initial research question is 'How has the UK's import and export trade with other countries altered since its entry into the European Union?' List the arguments that you would use to convince someone of the suitability of using secondary data to answer this research question.

8.3   Suggest possible secondary data that would help you answer the following research questions. How would you locate these secondary data?
  a   To what extent do organisations' employee relocation policies meet the needs of employees?
  b   How have consumer spending patterns in your home country changed in the last 10 years?
  c   How have governments' attitudes to the public sector altered in the twenty-first century?

8.4   As part of case study research based in a manufacturing company with over 500 customers, you have been given access to an internal market research report. This was undertaken by the company's marketing department. The report presents the results of a recent customer survey as percentages. The section in the report that describes how the data were collected and analysed is reproduced below:

> Data were collected from a sample of current customers selected from our customer database. The data were collected using an Internet questionnaire designed and administered via the online software tool Qualtrics™. Twenty-five customers responded, resulting in a 12.5 per cent response rate. These data were analysed using IBM SPSS Statistics. Additional qualitative data based on in-depth interviews with customers were also included.

a Do you consider these data are likely to be reliable?

b Give reasons for your answer.

Review and discussion questions 复习与讨论题

8.5 With a friend revisit Figure 8.1, types of secondary data, and re-read the accompanying text in Section 8.2. Agree to find and, where possible, make copies (either electronic or photocopy) of at least two examples of secondary data for each of the seven subheadings:

a text materials;

b non-text materials;

c snapshot;

d longitudinal;

e censuses;

f continuous and regular surveys;

g ad hoc surveys.

Compare and contrast the different examples of secondary data you have found.

8.6 Choose an appropriate information gateway from Table 8.1 to search the Internet for secondary data on a topic which you are currently studying as part of your course.

a 'Add to favourites' (bookmark) those sites which you think appear most relevant.

b Make notes regarding any secondary data that are likely to prove useful to either seminars for which you have to prepare or coursework you have still to undertake.

8.7 Agree with a friend to each evaluate the same secondary data set obtained via the Internet. This could be one of the data sets you found when undertaking Question 8.6. Evaluate independently your secondary data set with regard to its overall and precise suitability using the checklist in Box 8.10. Do not forget to make notes regarding your answers to each of the points raised in the checklist. Discuss your answers with your friend.

改进研究项目

Progressing your research project

Assessing the suitability of secondary data for your research
评估二手数据对你研究的适用性

- Consider your research question(s) and objectives. Decide whether you need to use secondary data or a combination of primary and secondary data to answer your research question. (If you decide that you need only use secondary data and you are undertaking this research as part of a course of study, check your course's assessment regulations to ensure that this is permissible.)

- If you decide that you need to use secondary data, make sure that you are clear why and how you intend to use these data.

改进研究项目（续）

Progressing your research project (*continued*)

- Locate the secondary data that you require and make sure that, where necessary, permission for them to be used for your research is likely to be granted. Evaluate the suitability of the data for answering your research question(s) and make your judgement based on assessment of its suitability, other benefits and the associated costs.
- Note down the reasons for your choice(s), including the possibilities and limitations of the data. You will need to justify your choice(s) when you write about your research methods.
- Use the questions in Box 1.4 to guide your reflective diary entry.

Self-check answers   自测题答案

8.1   Although it would be impossible to list all possible situations, the key features that should appear in your examples are listed below:

- to compare findings from your primary data;
- to place findings from your primary data in a wider context;
- to triangulate findings from other data sources;
- to provide the main data set where you wish to undertake research over a long period, to undertake historical research or to undertake comparative research on a national or international scale with limited resources.

8.2   The arguments you have listed should focus on the following issues:

- The study suggested by the research question requires historical data so that changes that have already happened can be explored. These data will, by definition, have already been collected.
- The timescale of the research (if part of a course) will be relatively short. One solution for longitudinal studies in a short time frame is to use secondary data.
- The research question suggests an international comparative study. Given your likely limited resources, secondary data will provide the only feasible data sources.

8.3   a   The secondary data required for this research question relate to organisations' employee relocation policies. The research question assumes that these sorts of data are likely to be available from organisations. Textbooks, research papers and informal discussions would enable you to confirm that these data were likely to be available. Informal discussions with individuals responsible for the personnel function in organisations would also confirm the existence and availability for research of such data.

   b   The secondary data required for this research question relate to consumer spending patterns in your home country. As these appear to be the sort of data in which the government would be interested, they may well be available via the Internet or in published form. For the UK, examination of the Office for National Statistics and gov.uk information gateways (Table 8.1) would reveal that these data were collected by the annual Expenditure and Food Survey providing hyperlinks to a series of reports including *Family Spending: 2014 Edition* (Office for National Statistics 2014b). Summary data could also be downloaded. In addition, reports could be borrowed either from your university library or by using inter-library loan.

c The secondary data required for this research question are less clear. What you require is some source from which you can infer past and present government attitudes. Relative changes in spending data, such as appears in quality newspapers, might be useful; although this would need to be examined within each department budget. Transcripts of ministers' speeches and newspaper reports might prove useful. However, to establish suitable secondary sources for this research question you would need to pay careful attention to those used by other researchers. These would be outlined in research papers and textbooks. Informal discussions could also prove useful.

8.4 a The data are unlikely to be reliable.

b Your judgement should be based on a combination of the following reasons:

- Initial examination of the report reveals that it is an internally conducted survey. As this has been undertaken by the marketing department of a large manufacturing company, you might assume that those undertaking the research had considerable expertise. Consequently, you might conclude the report contains credible data. However:
- The methodology is not clearly described. In particular:
  - The sampling procedure and associated sampling errors are not given.
  - It does not appear to contain a copy of the questionnaire. This means that it is impossible to check for bias in the way that questions were worded.
  - The methodology for the qualitative in-depth interviews is not described.
  - In addition, the information provided in the methodology suggests that the data may be unreliable:
    - The reported response rate of 12.5 per cent is very low for a telephone survey (Section 7.2).
    - Responses from 25 people means that all tables and statistical analyses in the report are based on a maximum of 25 people. This may be too few for reliable results (Sections 7.2 and 12.5).

Get ahead using resources on the companion website at: **www.pearsoned.co .uk/saunders**.

- Improve your IBM SPSS Statistics and NVivo research analysis with practice tutorials.
- Save time researching on the Internet with the Smarter Online Searching Guide.
- Test your progress using self-assessment questions.
- Follow live links to useful websites.

Chapter 9

Collecting primary data through observation 通过观察收集原始数据

Learning outcomes 学习目标

By the end of this chapter you should:

- appreciate the role of observation as a data collection method;
- be able to differentiate between participant observation, structured observation, Internet-mediated observation and observation using videography, and understand their differing applications;
- be aware of approaches to data collection for each type of observation;
- be able to identify issues related to data quality from each type of observation and appreciate how to reduce these.

9.1 Introduction 引 言

Observation has been a somewhat neglected method for business and management research. Yet it can be rewarding and enlightening to pursue and, what is more, add considerably to the richness of your research data. Technological changes mean that observation may become a more popular research method, as the opening vignette suggests. If your research question(s) and objectives are concerned with what people do, an obvious way in which to discover this is to watch them do it. This is essentially what **observation** involves: the systematic viewing, recording, description, analysis and interpretation of people's behaviour.

Four approaches to observation are examined in this chapter: two traditional approaches and two technology-mediated approaches. Traditionally, observation involves using participant observation (Section 9.2) or structured observation (Section 9.3). **Participant observation** is qualitative and derives from the work of social anthropology early in the twentieth century. Its emphasis is on discovering the meanings that people attach to their actions. In contrast, **structured observation** is quantitative and is more concerned with the frequency of actions (what rather than why). Technology facilitates new ways to conduct observation. These are Internet-mediated observation (Section 9.4) and observation using videography (Section 9.5). **Internet-mediated observation** involves the collection of data from online communities. This approach adapts traditional observation by changing its mode of observing from oral/visual/near to textual/digital/virtual to allow researchers purely to

observe or to participate with members of an online community to collect data. Observation using **videography** involves recording moving images onto electronic media to collect observational data.

It is interesting to note that these technology-mediated forms of observation affect the nature of data collection. Participant observation and structured observation have traditionally involved researchers collecting primary data. Internet and video technologies make it possible for researchers to apply observational techniques to secondary data as well as to collect primary data. This is reflected in the discussion in Sections 9.4 and 9.5.

Technology and observation appear to be converging through the advent of the body-worn camera. These are small or even tiny cameras that are worn on top of clothing or attached to a pair of spectacles, hat or helmet. They can also be fixed into items of clothing or handheld bags. They allow the wearer to record his or her interactions with others or to record an event from the wearer's point of view. Body-worn cameras may be used for different purposes. They are increasingly being used by police officers as they carry out their duties on the street. They can also be used by insurance investigators, lone workers, mystery shoppers, private detectives, undercover reporters, security employees and many other groups of workers. Once the camera is switched on, filming is recorded onto internal flash storage and can be downloaded into a computer, mobile phone or recorder for use.

Body-worn cameras allow interactions or events to be recorded covertly or overtly. Mystery shoppers, private detectives or undercover reporters using these cameras will be interested to conceal their real purpose and to film covertly. Others will want their use of a body-worn camera to be known by those with whom they are interacting, so that filming is carried out overtly.

Body-worn cameras are increasingly being trialled or adopted by police forces in different countries. Use of body-worn cameras by police officers to observe and record interactions may lead to particular benefits but are also associated with some ethical concerns. Filming interactions provides direct evidence of a situation, where those involved may otherwise recall different versions of the same event. Behaviour is likely to be more polite where those involved know that a situation is being filmed, and complaints about behaviour are likely to be reduced where those involved know that a recording of the event exists. The existence of concrete evidence may also assist prosecutions of wrongdoers. However, there may be a danger of over-relying on recorded evidence in some situations. Camera recording may also prove to be inappropriate in some sensitive contexts. Concerns also exist about the security of recordings and when they should be deleted.

In other approaches to research, those who take part are called either respondents or participants. Those who complete a questionnaire are usually called respondents. Those who agree to take part in most forms of qualitative research are usually called participants. These labels don't work for observation since it is the researcher who is participating in the environment of other people, responding to the ways in which they carry out their usual activities. In observational research, those who agree to be observed are usually called **informants** (Monahan and Fisher 2010). This is the term that we will use throughout this chapter.

A common theme in this book is our effort to discourage you from thinking of the various research methods as the sole means you should employ in your study. This is equally true of observation methods. It may meet the demands of your research question(s) and objectives to use observation in your study as either the main method of data collection or to supplement other methods.

9.2   Participant observation   参与观察

What is participant observation?

In participant observation, the researcher enters into the social world of those to be observed and attempts to participate in their activities by becoming a member of their workgroup, organisation or community. The extent of participation varies according to the type of participant observation (discussed later), from pure observation to full participation. For example, Plankey-Videla (2012) became a garment worker in a clothing factory for several months. Brannan (Brannan and Oultram 2012) became an employee in a call centre for a year. Through this process of immersion, the researcher learns by directly experiencing the social situation or research setting. It has been used extensively in disciplines such as social anthropology and industrial sociology to attempt to get to the root of 'what is going on' in a wide range of social settings.

Participant observation has its roots in social anthropology, but it was the Chicago School (at the University of Chicago) that changed its focus by using ethnographic methods to study social and urban problems within cultural groups in the USA. A seminal example of this work is Whyte's (1943) *Street Corner Society*, which examined the lives of street gangs in Boston. This approach involved researchers living among those whom they studied, to observe and talk to them to produce detailed cultural accounts of their shared beliefs, behaviours, interactions, language, rituals and the events that shaped their lives (Cunliffe 2010). Participant observation is a key data collection technique used within an ethnographic study, although the two concepts should not be used interchangeable as ethnography refers to a research strategy and to a particular type of research output (Section 5.3).

The high level of immersion achieved by the researcher in the research setting is a key strength of using participant observation, especially when compared with other data collection techniques. Brannan (Brannan and Oultram 2012) reports that when he returned to interview his former call centre co-workers some four to six months after working alongside them, their willingness to share their thoughts with him had diminished. The resulting interviews were more formal than expected and his informants were reluctant for their answers to his questions to be audio-recorded.

Because the researcher becomes a member of the group within which participant observation is conducted, she or he comes to understand the symbolic world of the informants and their perceptions about their social situation. This allows the participant observer to develop a deep and nuanced understanding of the meanings of informants' interactions, and how they respond to their social situation and changes to it. This is quite different from using a questionnaire to collect data, where ability to understand individual interactions and relationship to social context is likely to be less. Brannan's reflections on returning to interview his former co-workers illustrates that even using interviews may not reveal the same level of depth in comparison to engaging in participant observation to understand informants' symbolic world.

The symbolic frame of reference is located within the school of sociology known as **symbolic interactionism**. In symbolic interactionism the individual derives a sense of identity from interaction and communication with others. Through this process of interaction and communication the individual responds to others and adjusts his or her understandings and behaviour as a shared sense of order and reality is 'negotiated' with others. Central to this process is the notion that people continually change in the light of the social circumstances in which they find themselves. The transition from full-time student to career employee is one example of this. (How often have you heard people say, 'she's so different since she's worked at that new place'?) The individual's sense of identity is constantly being constructed and reconstructed as he or she moves through differing social contexts and encounters different situations and different people.

Where your research question is intended to explore the dynamics of a social situation, this may point you to the use of participant observation where this technique is practical (Box 9.1).

Box 9.1
Focus on student research

Managers and their use of power: a cross-cultural approach

Mong was a young Chinese business graduate who had recently been working in a Chinese/German joint venture in the automobile industry. She was located in the supply chain department. Mong was completing the latter stages of her MBA and had to submit a research project on a management topic of her choice.

Mong was fascinated by the international management component of her course that dealt with cross-cultural matters. This was particularly significant in her case as she worked at a company site that comprised both Chinese and German managers.

Mong felt that a body of theory, which she could profitably link to the issue of cross-cultural integration, was that of power. With help from her project tutor she developed a research question that allowed her to explore the way in which Chinese and German managers used power to 'negotiate' their relationships in a situation which was unfamiliar to both sets of managers. Mong's question was: 'What strategies are used by different groups of national managers collaborating in an international joint venture to negotiate their transnational relationships and how effective are these?'

Mong was fortunate that one of her duties was to take minutes at the twice-weekly management meetings in the department. She obtained permission to observe these meetings to collect her data. She developed an observation schedule, which related to her research objectives, and used this during each meeting.

Data collection was not easy for Mong as she had to take minutes in addition to noting the type and frequency of responses of managers. However, as time progressed she became very skilled at fulfilling both her minute-taking and data collection roles. She also obtained permission to audio-record the meetings. At the end of four months, when she had attended over 30 meetings, she had collected a wealth of data and was in a good position to analyse them and draw some fascinating conclusions.

Mong's observation role raised ethical questions as she did not reveal her researcher role to the meeting delegates. She discussed these questions with her senior manager in the company and project tutor and completed the necessary university ethics committee documentation. It was agreed by all concerned that Mong's research objectives justified the data collection approach chosen and that the university's ethical code had not been breached.

Different types of participant observation

There are four types of participant observation. These four types are distinguished by two separate dimensions (Figure 9.1). One dimension relates to whether the researcher's identity is revealed (overt observation) or concealed (covert observation). In overt observation, the researcher is open about the fact that she or he is conducting research; in covert observation, the researcher conceals what he or she is doing. The other dimension relates to the extent to which the researcher participates in the activities of the organisation, group or community that she or he is observing.

These four types of observation lead to roles that are labelled (Figure 9.1):

- complete participant;
- complete observer;
- observer-as-participant;
- participant-as-observer.

Complete participant

The **complete participant** role sees you as the researcher attempting to become a member of the group in which you are researching. You do not reveal your true purpose to the group members. You may be able to justify this role on pure research grounds in the light of your research questions and objectives. For example, you may be interested to know the extent of lunchtime drinking in a particular work setting. You would probably be keen to discover which groups of employees drink at lunchtimes, what they drink, how much they drink and how they explain their drinking. Were you to explain your research objectives to the group you wished to study, it is rather unlikely that they would cooperate since employers would usually discourage lunchtime drinking. In addition, they might see your research activity as prying.

This example raises questions of ethics. You would be in a position where you were 'spying' on people who have probably become your friends as well as colleagues. They may have learnt to trust you with information that they would not share were they to know your true purpose. This example suggests the researcher should not adopt this role where the focus of the research may cause harm to individuals (Section 6.5). However, there may be other foci where you might consider adopting the role of complete participant,

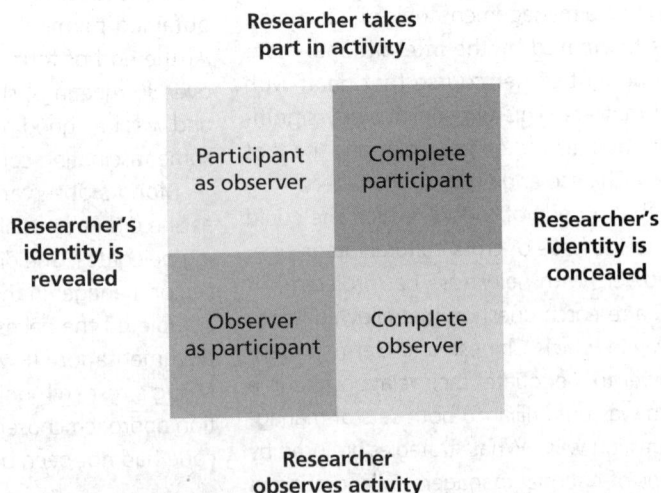

Figure 9.1 Typology of participant observation researcher roles

where there would not be any risks of breaching trust or creating harm. An example might be where you were researching working practices in an organisation, to evaluate the relationship between theory and practice, where it would be possible to maintain the anonymity of both the organisation and informants as you participated as a co-worker.

Complete observer

Here too you would not reveal the purpose of your activity to those you were observing. However, unlike the complete participant role, you would not take part in the activities of the group. For example, the **complete observer** role may be used in studying consumer behaviour in supermarkets. Your research question may concern your wish to observe consumers at the checkout. Which checkouts do they choose? How much interaction is there with fellow shoppers and the cashier? How do they appear to be influenced by the attitude of the cashier? What level of impatience is displayed when delays are experienced? This behaviour may be observed by the researcher being located near the checkout in an unobtrusive way. The patterns of behaviour displayed may be the precursor to research by structured observation (Section 9.3), in which case this would be the exploratory stage of such a research project.

Observer-as-participant

Acting in the role of **observer-as-participant** will primarily involve you in observing, although your purpose will be known to those whom you are studying (Box 9.2). In some cases this role may verge on that of participant-as-observer, where it becomes necessary to have some interaction with informants. For example, adopting the role of

Box 9.2 Focus on research in the news

Close observers of consumers

By Emma Jacobs

John Curran spent weeks shadowing British people going about their daily business. He was there on the school run, he followed them to the supermarket and lurked in cafés while they sipped cappuccinos. Mr Curran is not a private investigator hoping to uncover a dirty secret but an anthropologist – a social scientist who studies human behaviour through systematic observation – working on behalf of a greeting card company. His task? To discover events in need of commemoration.

The "informants", as he calls the people he observed, revealed a need to remember deceased relatives. Many he discovered kept shrines, for example on pianos, and performed rituals on anniversaries, such as lighting candles. Some included cards at such ceremonies but found most greetings cards lacking because they were written in the present tense. Such insights, Mr Curran says, were unlikely to have been discovered using conventional market research methods such as focus groups – especially on the taboo subject of death.

Mr Curran is one of a growing number of anthropologists employed by companies researching new markets or designing products to fit with users' lifestyles. "We take a sledgehammer to [received wisdom] and then piece it all together . . . It's a challenging way of ruffling feathers, and from that opportunities arise."

observer-as-participant in an outward-bound course to assist team building would mean that you were there as a spectator but it may be necessary to interact with informants and take part in some activities to be able to conduct your observation.

As an observer-as-participant, your identity as a researcher would be clear to all concerned and they would know your purpose. This would present the advantage of you being able to focus on your researcher role. For example, you would be able to jot down insights as they occurred to you. You would be able to concentrate on your discussions with the informants. What you would lose, of course, would be the emotional involvement: really knowing what it feels like to be on the receiving end of the experience.

Participant-as-observer

In the role of **participant-as-observer** you would both take part and reveal your purpose as a researcher. This role is potentially a broad one. On the one hand, you may become a fully accredited participant by becoming, for example, an employee in order to undertake your observation study in a particular context (e.g. Brannan and Oultram 2012; Plankey-Videla 2012). As a part-time business or management student you may be able to use your existing employment status to adopt the role of participant-as-observer.

Alternatively, you may participate in a group without taking on all of the attributes of its members. For example, Waddington (2004) describes his experiences of being a participant-as-observer, in which he participated in a strike, spending long hours on the picket line and socialising with those on strike, without being an employee of the company involved. To achieve this, it was necessary to gain the support and trust of those involved. Waddington describes how he immersed himself in this context, how he experienced the emotional involvement of participating in this event and how he experienced the same feelings as the defeated strikers at the end of the strike.

Factors that will determine the choice of participant observer role

The purpose of your research

You should always be guided by the appropriateness of the method for your research question(s) and objectives. A research question that seeks to develop an understanding of a phenomenon about which the research informants would be naturally defensive is one that lends itself to the complete participant role. Discovering what it is like to be a participant on a particular training course is more appropriate to the participant-as-observer role.

Your status

If you work full- or part-time as well as being a student, there may be an opportunity for you to use one of the participant observation roles in your employing organisation as the means to collect data to answer your research question and address your research objectives. Depending on the nature and focus of your research question and objectives you may be able to adopt the role of either complete participant, or participant-as-observer or observer-as-participant. As a part-time student you will be likely to encounter advantages as well some issues where you conduct research as an insider within your employing organisation.

If you do not work for an organisation, you will need to secure access before adopting this approach but may still be able to adopt any of the four roles depending on the nature of your research question and objectives, the time you have to devote to your research and your circumstances.

The time you have to devote to your research

Some of the roles outlined earlier may be very time consuming. If you are to develop a rich and deep understanding of an organisational phenomenon, it will need much careful study. A period of attachment to the organisation will often be necessary. Many full-time courses have placement opportunities that may be used for this purpose. In addition, many full-time students have part-time jobs, which provide wonderful opportunities to understand the 'meanings' that their fellow employees, for whom the work is their main occupation, attach to a variety of organisational processes. What is needed is a creative perspective on what constitutes research and research opportunities. The possibilities are potentially numerous.

The degree to which you feel suited to participant observation

Not everybody feels suited to observational research. Much of it relies on the building of relationships with others. A certain amount of personal flexibility is also needed. As the participant observer you have to be 'all things to all people'. Your own personality must be suppressed to a greater extent. This is not something with which you may feel comfortable.

Organisational access

This may present a problem for some researchers as it is obviously a key issue. More is said about gaining access to organisations for research in Sections 6.2 to 6.4.

Ethical considerations

The degree to which you reveal your identity as the researcher or adopt a covert stance will be dictated by ethical considerations. The topic of ethics in research is dealt with in detail in Sections 6.5 and 6.6.

Data collection

Data from participant observation are emergent and will require you to start analysis as you collect them (Chapter 13). That is, you will be carrying out data collection and analysis simultaneously. Let us say you were acting as the complete participant observer in attempting to establish 'what is going on' in terms of sex discrimination at the workplace in which you were researching. You would observe informal discussion, hear conversations of a discriminatory nature and talk to those who 'approved' and 'disapproved' of the activity. All this would be part of your everyday work. These events would yield data that you would record, as far as possible, right away, or at least note soon afterwards. You would turn these rough notes into something rather more systematic, along the lines of the types of data outlined in Table 9.1 and discussed more fully in Chapter 13. Themes would emerge that you wish to follow up in your continued observation.

Note making and recording data

Note making is very important in observation-based studies. Your notes are likely to be composed of different types of data. These may be categorised as 'primary', 'secondary' and 'experiential' (Table 9.1). In addition, you will find it helpful to record contextual data.

Table 9.1 Types of data generated by participant observation

Data type	Explanation
Primary observations	Those data where you would note what happened or what was said at the time. Keeping a diary is a good way of doing this
Secondary observations	Statements by observers of what happened or was said. This necessarily involves observers' interpretations
Experiential data	Those data on your perceptions and feelings as you experience the process you are researching. Keeping a diary of these perceptions proves a valuable source of data when the time comes to write up your research. This may also include notes on how you feel that your values have intervened, or changed, over the research process
Contextual data	Those data related to the research setting; for example, roles played by key informants and how these may have changed; organisational structures and communication patterns that will help you to interpret other data

Source: Developed from Delbridge and Kirkpatrick (1994)

Progressing data collection

It is likely that your primary data collection will go through various phases, as you first seek to become familiar with the setting in which you are conducting observation before focusing on those aspects that will allow you to answer your research question and meet your objectives. Robson (2011) outlines a process that involves descriptive observation, then creating a narrative account before possibly undertaking a phase of focused observation. In **descriptive observation** you will concentrate on observing and describing the physical setting, the key informants and their activities, particular events and their sequence and the attendant processes and emotions involved. This description may be the basis for you to write a **narrative account**, in much the same way as an investigative journalist would write one. However, Robson (2011) makes the point that the researcher must go much further than the journalist. Your job as researcher is to go on and develop a framework or theory that will help you to understand, and to explain to others, what is going on in the research setting you are studying. To achieve this it may become evident to you that your observation needs to focus on particular events or on the interactions between key informants, which will lead you to undertake a phase of **focused observation**.

What will be clear from the types of data you will collect as participant observer is that formal set-piece interviewing is unlikely to take place at this stage of your research, although you undertake some interviews. Such 'interviewing' as does take place is likely to be informal discussion. It will be part of the overall approach of asking questions that should be adopted in this research method. These questions are of two types (Robson 2011): first, to informants to clarify the situations you have observed and, second, to yourself to clarify the situation and the accounts given of the situation.

How you record your data will depend to a great extent on the role you play as observer. The more 'open' you are the more possible it will be for you to make notes at the time the event is being observed or reported. In any event, there is one golden rule: recording must take place on the same day as the fieldwork in order that you do not forget valuable data. The importance placed on this by one complete participant observer, working in a bakery, is evident from the following quotation:

> Right from the start I found it impossible to keep everything I wanted in my head until the end of the day . . . and had to take rough notes as I was going along. But I was 'stuck on the line', and had nowhere to retire to privately to note things down. Eventually, the wheeze of using innocently provided lavatory cubicles occurred to me. Looking back, all my notes for that third summer were on Bronco toilet paper! Apart from the awkward tendency for pencilled notes to be self-erasing from hard toilet paper . . . my frequent requests for 'time out' after interesting happenings or conversations in the bakehouse and the amount of time that I was spending in the lavatory began to get noticed . . .
>
> Ditton (1977), cited in Bryman (1989: 145)

Issues related to data quality from participant observation

As participant observation involves studying social actors and social phenomena (i.e. informants and their activities) in their natural setting, research findings usually exhibit high **ecological validity** because of their relevance to the situation. However, using participant observation may lead to a number of threats to reliability/dependability and validity/credibility (Section 5.8 and in particular Table 5.5). This is because the setting is unknown to the observer and he or she needs to understand the cultural and interpersonal nuances that characterise it in order to interpret it; or because, as an insider, the observer is so familiar with it that she or he may take some things for granted instead of 'standing back' and analysing these through a more objective, theoretical lens. In relation to participant observation, we discuss three such issues related to observer error, observer bias and observer effect.

Observer error

Your lack of understanding of, or over-familiarity with, the setting in which you are trying to operate as a participant observer may lead you unintentionally to misinterpret what is happening. This would be **observer error**. This error would not be because of any deliberate bias but because you need to understand the setting better before you seek to interpret it. Interpretation arises from understanding and the insights that follow from understanding. This point helps to illustrate that observation is a process that involves immersion in a context in order to produce valid and reliable results.

Related to observer error is the idea of **observer drift**. This occurs when the observer starts to redefine the way in which similar observations are interpreted. This may be caused by increasing familiarity in the research setting, with the result that later interpretations of similar events are not consistent with earlier ones. As data collection and data analysis are part of an ongoing iterative process, observers need to revisit their earlier observations and analysis as they continue to collect and analyse data in order to maintain consistency of interpretation.

Observer bias

Conversely, an observer may not allow herself or himself the time necessary to develop the depth of understanding required in order to interpret the setting objectively. This would lead to **observer bias** where the observer uses her or his own subjective view or disposition to interpret events in the setting being observed. The observer may be unaware that she or he is doing this.

When you are using observation, you will need to be aware that every observation you record may be open to more than one interpretation. This may appear to be a daunting thought! However, it shouldn't be read as such. Instead it should encourage you to give yourself enough time in the setting to begin to understand it and then to develop a rigorous analytical approach to the way you make interpretations.

Your attempts to make objective interpretations will depend on whether you are using covert or overt observation. As a covert researcher, you will not be able to check your interpretations with informants. You will therefore need to think about the possible ways that a particular type of observation may be interpreted and then, as you continue to observe and collect more primary observations (see Table 9.1), you will need to test out which interpretation appears to fit best. This process illustrates the interactive nature of data collection and data analysis.

Where you are using overt observation, you have the possibility of asking your informants to read some of the secondary observations that relate to them. This would provide you with the opportunity to check some of your interpretations with your informants and perhaps to benefit from the insights that they are able to add to your own views (see Box 9.3). This process is known as **informant verification** and is similar to participant or member validation discussed in Section 5.8.

Observer effect

A more tricky threat to the reliability and validity of data collected through observation relates to the presence of the observer. By simply being present, the researcher may affect the behaviour of those being observed, potentially resulting in unreliable and invalid data (LeCompte and Goetz 1982; Spano 2005). This is referred to as the **observer effect**. The implication of this effect is that informants will work harder or act more ethically when

---

Box 9.3
Focus on student research

Informant verification

Susanna undertook participant observation in the customer services call centre of a retail company. Her research focused on the training and quality assurance of call centre staff. One of the aspects of her research project focused on the training needed to be able to deal with complex customer issues. For this aspect of her research project, Susanna negotiated access to spend a period in the call centre, in the role of observer-as-participant. This gave her access to observe call centre staff dealing with complex customer issues, to understand how they used their discretion to deal with customers sensitively while seeking to adhere to their training and to any scripted parts of

their telephone conservations with callers. To achieve cognitive access (Chapter 6), she gained the consent of individual informants to observe each for a day or part of a day. This provided her with the opportunity to observe a number of informants during the period of her agreed access.

Susanna negotiated to meet each informant during part of his or her main rest break on the following day. This provided Susanna with the opportunity to describe and discuss her secondary observations about a particular call that the informant had taken. Most of these informants were interested to help and provided Susanna with their own interpretations and insights, often recalling what they had been thinking as they had dealt with the call being discussed. These additional interpretations, directly from the informants, were very helpful to Susanna as she continued to observe and interpret and later when she wrote up her research project.

they know they are being observed (Monahan and Fisher 2010). Conversely, those being observed may decide to slow their work if they feel that any measurements of this will lead to them being given more demanding targets. Either way, observations will not be reliable.

One solution to this is for the observer to act covertly. This solution assumes that it would be appropriate for the researcher to adopt the role of complete participant or of complete observer (Figure 9.1). However, this may not be appropriate, even if it were ethically acceptable. Another solution to this is for the observer to achieve **minimal interaction**, where the observer tries as much as possible to 'melt into the background' – having as little interaction as possible with informants. This may involve sitting in an unobtrusive position in the room and avoiding eye contact with those being observed. In relation to Figure 9.1, this would mean adopting a purely observing role, rather than a participatory one – acting in the role of observer-as-participant. However, as we discussed earlier, adopting this role may not be appropriate to the nature of the research.

A further solution where the observation is overtly conducted is related to familiarisation. As you operate in the role of participant-as-observer or observer-as-participant your informants will become familiar with you and take less notice of your presence, where they feel they can trust you. This is known as **habituation**, where the informants being observed become familiar with the process of observation so that they take it for granted and behave normally. To achieve habituation it will probably be necessary for you to undertake several observation sessions in the same research setting with the same informants before you begin to achieve reliable and valid data. In fact, it will probably be necessary for you to undertake several sessions in order to begin to understand the dynamics of this setting, so this would be time well spent.

Not all researchers agree that observer effects inevitably lead to unreliable results. In addition, other strategies have been proposed to recognise and manage observer effects (Box 9.4). The advantages and disadvantages of participant observation are summarised in Table 9.2.

Box 9.4 Focus on management research

Observer effects

Monahan and Fisher (2010) in an article in *Qualitative Research* challenge some of the assumptions about observer effects. They argue that all research methods can have researcher effects that may lead to bias. In this way qualitative research including participant observation may be no more prone to bias than quantitative approaches to research, which are often held up as being more objective.

They also cast doubt on the idea that observer effects will always be negative and negate the value of the observer's results. Instead they believe that while the presence of an observer may have an effect on those whom they observe, the result of this effect may actually lead to the collection of valuable data. For them, observer effects may prove to be positive rather than being negative. They refer to the possibilities that informants may either 'stage' a performance for an observer or 'self-censor' their activities.

Monahan and Fisher suggest that staged performances may be welcomed because informants demonstrate an idealised set of behaviours to observers. They show what the informants think the observer ought to know and see. This idealised performance may then be compared to other observations where the performance cannot be staged or managed so easily. This may occur when the observer is watching a more pressured or stressful situation, or perhaps where other organisational participants are involved and the ability to manage a staged performance is not possible. Observations made of other informants in the same or a similar setting may also be compared to those that are being staged. Such situations offer

▶

Box 9.4
Focus on
management
research (*continued*)

Observer effects

the possibility of gaining rich and multi-layered data that would be very valuable to the observer in understanding the setting and when undertaking data analysis and interpretation.

Another way in which informants may try to manage their performance is through self-censorship. This may be designed to hide any behaviour that informants feel would be undesirable for the observer to see. Monahan and Fisher suggest that informants may behave worse when not being observed but are unlikely to behave better. Habituation may result in

such cloaking behaviour being dropped. Apart from habituation, observers may try to check the validity of their observations by looking for inconsistencies in the data they observe and also by identifying differences between informants, to identify any facade of self-censorship.

Monahan and Fisher conclude that irrespective of whether a performance is being staged, or whether self-censorship is occurring, or whether neither of these is affecting what is being observed, the process of observation allows researchers to get close to and interact with informants. This may be seen as providing observation with an advantage over other research methods where distance and separation mean that data cannot be as intricate and rich. Rather than only focusing on observer effects, there is scope to focus on these other attributes of observation in assessing its value as a research method.

9.3 Structured observation 结构化观察

What is structured observation?

In contrast to participant observation, structured observation has a high level of predetermined structure. If you use this data collection method as part of your research strategy you will be adopting a more detached stance. Your concern will be to quantify behaviour. As such, structured observation may form only a part of your data collection approach because its function is to tell you how often things happen rather than why they happen. Once again, we see that all research methods may have a place in an

Table 9.2 Advantages and disadvantages of participant observation

Advantages	Disadvantages
• It is good at explaining 'what is going on' in particular social situations • It heightens the researcher's awareness of significant social processes • It is particularly useful for researchers working within their own organisations • Some participant observation affords the opportunity for the researcher to experience 'for real' the emotions of those who are being researched • Virtually all data collected are useful	• It can be very time consuming • It can pose difficult ethical dilemmas for the researcher • There can be high levels of role conflict for the researcher (e.g. 'colleague' versus researcher) • The closeness of the researcher to the situation being observed can lead to significant observer bias • The participant observer role is a very demanding one, to which not all researchers will be suited • Access to organisations may be difficult • Data recording is often very difficult for the researcher

overall research strategy. What is important is choosing methods that are suitable for your research question and objectives.

Structured observation as a method of collecting and analysing data in business may be more prevalent than we realise. It has a long history that extends into the present, linked to computer technologies. It was used over many decades to analyse how factory workers carried out their tasks and to measure the times that it took to complete these. This is known as a 'time-and-motion' study and was used by employers to increase their control over the way work was conducted. It has been used to 'speed up' work by reducing the time required to undertake different tasks. This approach has been facilitated more recently by computer technologies. Computers may be used to record the work activities of those who work in call centres and on checkouts in shops, for example. Most of us participate in forms of structured observation without really thinking about it or consciously giving our consent. You may have a 'loyalty' card from a retailer that allows them to record what you have purchased when you present the card at the checkout. Using the Internet or phone produces data that may be structured or unstructured – that is, in a form which is ready to be analysed or not. Digital or video-recording adds another layer of observation to monitor those in particular types of workplace as well as within areas covered by CCTV, such as in city and town centres, shopping centres and within retail outlets. We live in a world where in many situations our movements are routinely observed while we go about our daily lives, often without being aware that this is happening. Adrian uses an independent retail outlet which makes light of this situation: at various places in the store there are signs which state, 'Smile, you're on camera!'

The Internet has widened the scope to conduct forms of structured observation. The Internet may be used in 'real time' to make virtual structured observations. These range from simple to more complex structured observations. Every time you 'visit' a website this will be recorded electronically. This allows organisations to count the number of visits to their websites and how much time is spent on each page. Internet behaviour may also be tracked and analysed. Search engine companies such as Google undertake research on the search behaviour of their users. This has been termed 'indirect observation', where traces of users' behaviour are recorded and analysed (Hewson et al. 2003: 46). For example, marketing and advertising companies have invested in ways to obtain more detailed online data that will allow them to observe and analyse the links between online behaviour. Hewson et al. (2003) point out that using the Internet for structured observation offers researchers the advantage of non-intrusiveness and the removal of possible observer bias.

Structured observation by itself may be little more than surveillance or fact finding. It is the ways in which such data are analysed that can transform this activity into valuable research findings. One of the best-known examples of managerial research that used structured observation as part of its data collection approach was the study of the work of senior managers by Mintzberg (1973). This led Mintzberg to cast doubt on the long-held theory that managerial work was a rational process of planning, controlling and directing. Mintzberg studied what five chief executives actually did during one of each of the executives' working weeks. He did this by direct observation and the recording of events on three predetermined coding schedules. This followed a period of 'unstructured' observation in which the categories of activity that formed the basis of the coding schedules he used were developed. In this way Mintzberg 'grounded' his structured observation on data collected in an initial period of participant observation (Grounded Theory is explained in Section 5.5 and in Chapter 13).

Modern uses of structured observation do not have to rely on computer technologies. Structured observation is still used as a tool to assess the way in which workers in modern workplaces carry out their tasks, as Box 9.5 indicates. The advantages and disadvantages of structured observation are summarised in Table 9.3.

Box 9.5
Focus on student research

Observing staff behaviours at Fastfoodchain

Sangeeta worked at Fastfoodchain for her vacation job. She became interested in measuring service quality in her course and decided to do a preliminary study of customer interaction at Fastfoodchain.

Fastfoodchain has restaurants all over the world. Central to its marketing strategy is that the customer experience should be the same in every restaurant in every country of the world. An important part of this strategy is ensuring that customer-facing staff observe the same behavioural standards in every restaurant. This is achieved by defining precise standards of behaviour that customers should experience in every transaction undertaken. These standards are used in the training of staff and assessment of their performance. Reproduced below is part of the section of the standards schedule concerned with dealing with the customer. (There are also sections which deal with the behaviours needed to prepare for work, e.g. till readiness, and general issues, e.g. hygiene.)

The standards schedule is as an observation document used by trainers in order to evaluate the degree to which their training is effective with individual employees. It is also used by managers in their assessment of the performance of employees. Sangeeta was very impressed with the level of precision contained in this schedule and wondered whether it could form the basis of her research project.

Section 2: Delighting the customer

Staff member: ....

Behaviour	Was the behaviour observed?	Comments
Smiles and makes eye contact with the customer		
Greets the customer in a friendly manner		
Gives the customer undivided attention throughout the transaction		
Suggests extra items that have not been ordered by the customer		
Places items on clean tray with tray liner facing customer		
Ensures that customer is told where all relevant extras (e.g. cream, sugar) are located		
Explains to customer reasons for any delays and indicates likely duration of delay		
Neatly double-folds bags containing items with the Fastfoodchain logo facing the customer		
Price of order is stated and customer thanked for payment		
Lays all money notes across till drawer until change is given and clearly states the appropriate amount of change		
Customer is finally thanked for transaction, hope expressed that the meal will be enjoyed, and an invitation to return to the restaurant issued		

Data collection

As noted earlier, structured observation adopts a more detached stance. Using this method would place you in the role of being a pure observer, rather than a participant. In this role, you may be observing the activities of a single person, such as a manager,

Table 9.3 Advantages and disadvantages of structured observation

Advantages	Disadvantages
• It can be used by anyone after suitable training in the use of the measuring instrument. Therefore, you could delegate this extremely time-consuming task. In addition, structured observation may be carried out simultaneously in different locations. This would present the opportunity of comparison between locations • It should yield reliable results by virtue of its replicability. The easier the observation instrument is to use and understand, the more reliable the results will be • Structured observation is capable of more than simply observing the frequency of events. It is also possible to record the relationship between events. For example, does a visit to a website lead to the exploration of related pages and video-recordings; does this lead to a decision to purchase? • The method allows the collection of data at the time they occur in their natural setting. Therefore, there is no need to depend on 'second-hand' accounts of phenomena from participants who put their own interpretation on events • Structured observation secures data that most informants would ignore because to them these are too mundane or irrelevant	• Unless virtual observation is used, the observer must be in the research setting when the phenomena under study are taking place • Behaviours, interactions and events being observed may occur simultaneously or in complex ways, making coding difficult and potentially unreliable (discussed later in 'Issues related to data quality from structured observation') • While structured observation is helpful in recording the incidence of behaviours, interactions or events these observations are limited to overt actions or surface indicators. This may be inadequate to explore the impact or effectiveness of the behaviours, interactions or events being observed, leaving the observer to make inferences • Without the prior specification or development of theory, structured observations will be of only limited value for research. Analysis needs to look for patterns of behaviours, interactions or events to explain the data collected and to understand their impact in the observed situation. Such analysis may show how behaviours are linked, which are effective or ineffective and how they affect outcomes • Not recognising environmental variability within a research setting may invalidate conclusions drawn from structured observation. Behaviours, interactions and events are likely to be contingent on (shaped by) the environment and ignoring this variable is likely to cast doubt on the conclusions. Conversely, controlling for or taking environmental variables into account is likely to enhance the validity of the conclusions drawn • Data may be slow (and expensive) to collect, although this is not always the case

or the interactions between a group of informants or the prevalence of particular events. Structured observation records categories of behaviours, interactions or events that have been predetermined and defined before observation takes place (Box 9.6).

Using coding schedules to collect data

Data collection in structured observation will involve you using a coding schedule. One example of a coding schedule is shown in Box 9.5 and another example is indicated in Box 9.6. A quick look at each of these examples shows how their purpose varies. The example in Box 9.5 records whether a category of behaviour has occurred. It forms a checklist of numerous items that need to be recorded as having been observed or not. The example in Box 9.6 focuses on a smaller number of more general categories that provide a predetermined basis to record the frequencies of each category of behaviour or interaction.

Further variations of coding schedules are possible. For example, behaviours, interactions or events may be recorded as a sequence rather than as frequencies. They may also be recorded by time intervals, such as recording behaviours or interactions evident at the beginning of a meeting, those evident in the middle of a meeting and those at the end of

Box 9.6
Focus on student research

Structured observation schedule of categories and codes

Adam undertook a project examining the effectiveness of team meetings in his employing organisation. As part of this he planned to undertake structured observation of a number of team meetings in different parts of the organisation. He developed a schedule of categories and codes for his structured observation that included the following extract.

Adam produced an observation sheet from the full schedule to record the frequencies of these behaviours at each team meeting he observed. He attended the equivalent meeting held by three different teams and produced a summary sheet of his structured observations from these meetings.

Category	Definition	Observable action	Code
Providing Information	Provision of facts or information to others	Team Leader provides information to team members	TLPI
		Team member provides information to others	TMPI
Seeking Information	Seeking facts or clarification of information from another person	Team Leader seeks information from team members	TLSI
		Team member seeks information from Team Leader	TMSI
Checking understanding of others	Seeking to establish whether earlier facts or information has been understood by others	Team Leader checks understanding of team members	TLCU
		Team member checks understanding of others	TMCU
Offering clarification	Offer of clarification of earlier information to others	Team Leader offers clarification to team members	TLOC
		Team member offers clarification to others	TMOC
Giving viewpoint	Expression of opinions on facts and information provided or on a point of discussion	Team Leader expresses viewpoint to team members	TLGV
		Team member expresses viewpoint to others	TMGV
Summarising	Sum up or go over the main points of earlier information or a recent discussion	Team Leader summarises information for team members	TLSUM
		Team member summarises information for others	TMSUM

Meeting	Summary of structured observations from team meetings in Week 6											
	Providing Information		Seeking Information		Checking Understanding		Offering Clarification		Giving Viewpoint		Summarising	
	TLPI	TMPI	TLSI	TMSI	TLCU	TMCU	TLOC	TMOC	TLGV	TMGV	TLSUM	TMSUM
1	15	2	5	4	4	1	5	0	7	1	5	0
2	11	4	3	7	6	1	6	2	4	5	7	3
3	7	6	4	6	4	4	3	4	3	8	2	4
TOTALS	33	12	12	17	14	6	14	6	14	14	14	7

He arranged to conduct a semi-structured interview with each team leader and with a sample of the members from each team. He also undertook a theoretical review of the literature (Chapter 3) to help to analyse and interpret his data to explain it and to evaluate the effectiveness of team meetings in his employing organisation.

the meeting. You may also be interested to observe the occurrence of particular behaviours. For example, if you were conducting the research project described in Box 9.6, you might focus on recording behaviours that follow from cases of disagreement. In this case, you would wait for disagreement to occur and code the following sequence of behaviour. Structured observation potentially provides you with a number of options to collect data depending on your research question and objectives.

Deciding on a coding schedule to collect data

A key decision you will need to make before undertaking structured observation is whether to use an existing coding schedule or to design your own. We now discuss these options.

Using an existing coding schedule is associated with key disadvantages and advantages. The first task you will face is finding an existing coding schedule, which is suitable to answer your research question and address your objectives, or part of them. This may not prove to be possible. We would go further and say that for most business and management research projects using structured observation you will not find an existing coding schedule that is suitable and available for you to use. For some research projects you may be fortunate and locate previous research that provides you with an existing coding schedule (Box 9.7).

Box 9.7 Focus on management research

Structured observation of entrepreneurs' behaviour

Mueller, Volery and von Siemens (2012) undertook structured observation to examine the behaviour of entrepreneurs. Their study is published in *Entrepreneurship Theory and Practice*. They used a purposive sample composed of six entrepreneurs who were engaged in the start-up stage of their businesses and a further six entrepreneurs whose businesses were in a growth stage. These entrepreneurs had set up businesses in Austria, Germany and Switzerland.

Mueller and colleagues requested access to each entrepreneur for four days, so that one of them could observe that person's non-confidential business-related behaviours during each workday. During periods of confidential activity, the researcher asked the entrepreneur to self-report this using the observation template the researchers developed. They asked entrepreneurs to select four days that would allow observation of representative (rather than unusual) events undertaken by each entrepreneur. The researchers' observations of these entrepreneurs totalled 542 hours of structured observation (just over 11 hours for an average day).

They developed an observation template to record their observations, following from Mintzberg's (1973) research on senior managers (discussed earlier). This template was designed to record the date of the activity being observed, its start time, a brief description of the activity, who was involved in this activity, where it took place, whether it was a planned activity or a spontaneous one and who had initiated the activity. In total they observed 4479 units of activity, which formed the basis of data analysis.

Where you are fortunate to locate an existing coding schedule you will need to evaluate its suitability for your research question and objectives. It will be unlikely that this coding schedule was designed to address the same research question and objectives as yours; but even if it does, you will still need to evaluate if it is designed to address all of the behaviours, interactions or events in which you are interested. If it is designed to address these, you will still need to evaluate whether the observation schedule is well designed to overcome concerns about reliability and validity. Here, you may be asking, 'How can I do this?' Box 9.8 offers advice on evaluating and developing a coding schedule.

Where you manage to locate an existing coding schedule that is suitable for your research question and objectives and which is adequately designed to overcome concerns about its reliability and validity, you will be able to enjoy two important advantages. Firstly, its use will save you the need to develop a new coding schedule. Secondly, it will be tried and tested, which may help to make your results and conclusions more reliable and valid as well as comparable to those from its earlier use.

However, where existing coding schedules are unsuitable for your purposes, or where none exist, you will need to develop your own schedule. Box 9.8 contains a checklist to guide this activity, to help to ensure the reliability and ease of use of the codes you devise. There are a number of sources that may help you to devise categories, definitions and codes for your own coding schedule. Your research question and objectives will help to focus your efforts to devise your own coding schedule as it must be suitable to answer this question and address your research objectives. In addition, your research design may be sequential so that you initially undertake some in-depth or semi-structured interviews, or a period of participant observation, to determine categories for structured observation and develop a coding schedule. You may also identify categories for structured observation from existing research or theories, through reading journal articles and other published literature. Your experience as a participant or inside researcher, or work placement student, may also help you to develop categories for structured observation and a coding schedule. Always evaluate your own coding schedule (Box 9.8) and pilot test it before using it to collect data (Section 11.4).

Another alternative approach may be to incorporate part or parts of an existing schedule into your own coding schedule. Existing coding schedules may be inappropriate for your own research but you may be able to model your own schedule on the design of

Box 9.8
Checklist

To evaluate or develop a coding schedule

✔ Is the coding schedule suitable to answer your research question and address your objectives?
✔ Does the coding schedule cover all of the specific behaviours, interactions or events in which you are interested and exclude others outside the scope of your research?

✔ Are these categories of behaviour, interaction or events clearly defined and written down, observable in action and exclusive (not overlapping)?
✔ Are the categories in the coding schedule flexible enough to be applied across the different settings of your research?
✔ Are the codes being used indicated on the observation sheet, simple to understand and undemanding to apply so that you will not need to memorise or check their meanings?

one used for a different purpose, or to incorporate some part of it into yours. If this is the option that seems most appropriate in the light of your research question(s) and objectives, we recommend that you also use the checklist in Box 9.8 to ensure that your schedule is as valid and reliable as possible and to pilot test it.

Issues related to data quality from structured observation

The main issues for structured observation relate to aspects of reliability (Section 5.8): observer error, informant error, time error and observer effects. We discussed observer error and observer effects earlier, in Section 9.2. Here we consider informant error and time error.

Informant error

Informant error may cause your data to be unreliable. You may be concerned with observing the normal output of sales administrators as measured by the amount of orders they process in a day. Informant error may be evident if you are observing administrators in a work group that was short-staffed owing to illness. This may mean that they were spending more time answering telephones and less time processing orders, as there were fewer people available to handle telephone calls. The message here is clear: select your sample of informants using the sampling technique that best enables you to answer your research question and meet your objectives (Chapter 7).

Time error

Closely related to the issue of informant error is that of **time error**. It is essential that the time at which you conduct an observation does not provide data that are untypical of the total time period in which you are interested. For example, the number of calls taken in a call centre is often higher in the hours surrounding lunchtime in comparison to any other two-hour period. Conversely, it may be lower in the hours just before the lines close than in any other two-hour period. It would therefore be necessary to conduct periods of observation at intervals throughout the day in order to gain a reliable set of data. Of course, electronic monitoring allows a researcher with access to use already collected data to establish which periods were busiest as well as other aspects such as average call times, the number of calls taken by particular members of staff and how many callers were waiting to be answered at particular times of the day!

9.4 Internet-mediated observation 互联网观察

Using Internet-mediated observation to collect data

Researchers using an ethnographic research strategy (Section 5.5) increasingly make use of Internet-mediated observation to collect data. This has led to various terms to describe this research approach. These include netnography, online ethnography, virtual ethnography and webethnography. Traditional ethnography studies people in a physically defined, face-to-face, natural setting, such as in a workgroup or organisation, and perhaps in relation to an issue that affects those who are members of that group or organisation, such as an advertising campaign or a change programme. Online ethnography studies people in online or virtual communities, whose participation is motivated by shared interest (Angrosino and Rosenberg 2011; Prior and Miller 2012). Online communities organise themselves around shared interests; for example in relation to a particular brand, product, service, occupation or lifestyle. These online communities operate through bulletin boards, email lists, Internet forums, linked web pages and social networks (Section 6.3). These communities can provide large amounts of qualitative material, in the form of text and audio-visual material.

Online ethnography shares many attributes of traditional ethnography, although its use affects the way data are collected. Participant observation, informal discussions and interviews are important means to collect data in traditional ethnography. In online ethnography, the nature of observation is altered and the scope for informal discussions and interviews depends on the type of engagement a researcher has with a specific online community. The primary methods that participants in online communities use to communicate with one another are synchronous and asynchronous text. Paechter (2013: 73) refers to online textual exchanges as 'analogous to written speech', to which the researcher 'listens in' in a similar way to the traditional participant observer who listens to oral exchanges before writing these down. Online text provides a complete record of observed exchanges compared to the notes made from observing oral exchanges. While the traditional researcher is able to observe body language, facial expressions and tone of voice to assist in the interpretation of interactions she or he observes, the online researcher may be able to recognise nuances in the text and audio-visual material available to aid interpretation. Online observation may also take place in real time, like traditional observation. In these ways, Internet-mediated observation has the capacity to reveal plentiful amounts of rich data.

Internet-mediated observation also affects the nature of the researcher's participation. In Section 9.2 we outlined four types of participant observation, arranged across two dimensions (Figure 9.1). Depending on accessibility to an online community, it may be possible for a researcher to enter the website as a guest without revealing his or her identity or without participating other than reading or viewing available material. This is a form of lurking (Section 6.5) and is similar to the 'complete observer' role shown in Figure 9.1. A researcher may also become a member of an online community but remain 'silent' as a non-participant and only be interested in reading and observing what others have posted (although her or his presence may be detectable to others when online). This is also a form of lurking and still similar to the 'complete observer' role shown in Figure 9.1 since the researcher is not participating and while his or her presence may be detectable, the researcher's purpose is not revealed. The alternative to lurking is to participate in an online community (by adopting one of the other roles in Figure 9.1).

Paechter (2013) discusses the relative merits of non-participation and participation when collecting data from an online community. She asks whether lurking is sufficient to collect data or whether more active participation is necessary to achieve a richer understanding. Full and open participation, which is similar to the participant-as-observer role shown in Figure 9.1, potentially has a number of advantages. It should help to avoid missing important aspects of the interactions between members of the community, and reduce misunderstanding. Full and open participation allows a researcher to check her or his interpretations (Section 5.8) and to explore these with members. Participation in the interactions of the online community is more likely to provide the deepest level of access to understand it. While non-participation may provide access to data, acting covertly and practising deception is fraught with ethical issues (see our discussion of issues relating to informed consent and privacy among others in Section 6.5) and may lead to researchers being asked to leave when they reveal their activity and request access to undertake research overtly (Madge 2010; Paechter 2013).

Paechter (2013) outlines the process of collecting data that she used when researching an online community. The first issue was to identify material available in the online community which would address the research question and objectives (we return to consider this further in the next sub-section). Having identified the source of data, she decided to use an approach which was analogous to participant observation. The appropriate and available postings in the online forum were treated as observational data (see 'Data Collection' in Section 9.2). She read through each thread in a relevant topic domain and took notes. This allowed her to identify threads on which she wished to focus. Note making also commenced the process of data analysis by coding these data, which can then be sorted into categories (see 'Grounded Theory' in Sections 5.5 and 13.9). She also identified a number of key informants upon whom she wished to focus her data collection and analysis. She was able to track these informants through their community profiles in order to use their posts and blog entries to collect data and analysis these.

Issues related to data quality from Internet-mediated observation

If you decide that Internet-mediated observation is an appropriate method for you to collect data, you will need to think through the issues that will arise from your approach. In evaluating the issues and risks associated with your approach, you will need to explain how you will seek to overcome or at least minimise these and be able to justify your approach in relation to any alternative course of action that might be open to you to adopt. A central issue that we have discussed is about adopting a covert approach rather than an overt one, and the ethical dilemmas that follow from this (Section 6.5).

A further set of issues for you to consider relates to evaluating the quality of the data produced from using Internet-mediated observation. Issues discussed earlier relating to data collected using participant observation and structured observation will be relevant. These include observer error and observer bias, and may include observer effects where you collect data overtly. Prior and Miller (2012) consider other issues related to data quality from using Internet-mediated observation. These are considered under the headings of: the scope of online communities; the nature of data from Internet-mediated observation; the reliability/dependability and validity/credibility/transferability of Internet-mediated observation data.

The scope of online communities

This issue relates to understanding the nature of the sample you have chosen to research. In a traditional ethnographic study, you should be able to observe all of the interactions in the setting to which you have gained access. Where access is denied to some aspect of the setting (e.g. you may be granted access to observe a workgroup but not to observe confidential meetings between the managers of that group), you will be aware of the limitations placed on your observation. Where you base your research on 'observing' an online community, you will need to determine whether the online exchanges you make use of represent all or nearly all of the interactions between its members, or whether those members also interact 'offline', through other forums such as physical meetings or conferences, or perhaps even through other, related Internet forums to discuss the same shared interest. It is likely that where your research is based on using Internet-mediated observation you will focus on using one online community, so you will need to evaluate whether this accounts for the majority of the interactions of the group you are researching.

The nature of data from Internet-mediated observation

Prior and Miller (2012) consider the characteristics of Internet-mediated observation data that affect its representativeness in comparison to traditionally derived observation data. They report that while some members of an online community will consistently post messages over time, others may be active for a period but then become less active or inactive, while many others will only lurk, reading the posts of others and perhaps making the occasional post. They note that these patterns will not be consistent with the 'offline' behaviours of these members. Members of an online community may also adopt an online pseudonym or persona, which can protect their identity but may also be used to project views that they would not voice in face-to-face communication. These characteristics may cast doubt on the representativeness of Internet-mediated observation data in two ways. Firstly, the views of more active members may not represent the opinions of the whole group. Secondly, views expressed may not represent those that are held more widely in the population where this is also composed of others who are not members of an online community.

Prior and Miller argue that because interactions between members in an online community rely on written text, this may mean that the language used does not adequately represent the complexity of the issue being discussed and may lack the type of contextual consideration that would facilitate a fuller evaluation. On the other hand, a range of posts by different members or contributors may produce a range of perspectives that does permit an adequate contextualisation and evaluation.

Where you use Internet-mediated observation you will need to consider the range of contributors to each discussion, the possible impact from using online pseudonyms, and the nature of the language used and contextualisation included in discussion to evaluate the data you collect. Internet-mediated observation may produce a rich and valuable source of data, and represent a range of views on a pertinent topic, which help you to pursue your research, but it may also be of variable quality.

The reliability/dependability and validity/credibility/transferability of Internet-mediated observation data

The scope and nature of data collected from Internet-mediated observation are likely to affect its reliability/dependability as well as the research's internal validity/credibility and generalisability/transferability (Section 5.8 and in particular Table 5.5). Data that only represent the views of some members of an online community may be unreliable or undependable because 'observing' the views of other members may produce data with a different emphasis. Using data that does not adequately represent the views of all members of an online community or their behaviour in real life will also adversely affect the internal validity/credibility and generalisability/transferability of the research (Section 5.8). This does not mean that data collected using Internet-mediated observation are of dubious quality but, rather, you will need to evaluate the suitability of this method in the context of your research project before embarking on its use.

9.5   Observation using videography   运用摄像来观察

Using videography to collect observational data

Videography has two distinct meanings. The first is technical and refers to the process of recording moving images onto electronic media. We use the term 'video' in the text here to refer to this meaning of videography to avoid confusion with the second, related to the ethnographic analysis of recorded sequences (Knoblauch 2012).

Video-recording may be used in several ways to aid the collection of data. A few of these ways relate to methods discussed in other chapters. For example, semi-structured or in-depth interviews may be recorded using video (Chapter 10). But it is in relation to observation that video offers the most ways to aid the collection of data. Some of these involve the researcher collecting or arranging for the collection of primary data while others involve the use of secondary data.

Researchers may collect their own observational data by videoing their informants in a research setting (Box 9.9). The opening vignette in this chapter illustrates how body-worn cameras facilitate observation. A body-worn camera may be used by the researcher to collect data in a research setting or by informants, to allow the researcher to gain observational data from the perspective of the research informant (Starr and Fernandez 2007). Researchers may also ask informants to record video diaries related to the focus of their research. This approach may be particularly useful where considerable distances exist between researcher and informants, making face-to-face observation difficult or impossible to undertake. In such a case, a video diary or blog may be uploaded to the Internet by willing informants and downloaded for analysis by the researcher. Video and Internet technologies mean that an event may be recorded in its entirety and streamed to a different location, so that the researcher may still operate as an observer in the role of either complete observer or observer-as-participant (Figure 9.1). Mobile phones may also be used in observational research to record digital video (Hein et al. 2011; Jarzabkowski et al. 2014).

Video also facilitates the use of secondary data in observational research. Jarzabkowski et al. (2014) report that some organisations are creating video archives

Box 9.9
Focus on management research

Using video to collect observational data in market research

In Box 5.7 we describe a study by Cayla and Arnould (2013) published in the *Journal of Marketing* that explored how companies use a combination of ethnographic inquiry and narrative presentation in their market research. They refer to this fusion as 'ethnographic stories'; hence the title of their article, 'Ethnographic Stories for Market Learning'.

Rather than analyse observational data through fragmentation into bits or chunks (Chapter 13), companies have instead realised the value of developing a storyline from these data to create a compelling narrative of key points that reveals learning about their markets and consumers. Video plays an important role in facilitating this approach.

Cayla and Arnould describe instances of organisational ethnographers using video-recordings to create narrative accounts that sum up consumers' experiences. These edited video stories are capable of influencing the managers who watch them.

The value of using video-recording in the creation of these narratives is evident from the views of organisational ethnographers who participated in the research conducted by Cayla and Arnould. One organisational ethnographer reports that once edited into a story, the video-recordings made during observation were capable of providing a powerful outline of the phenomenon being researched. Another referred to clients' reactions to the use of video to summarise and convey consumer experiences. These included valuing the use of video-based stories over other media such as written reports. Video stories were seen as insightful, engaging (being able to make people cry or laugh) and influential, with organisational clients being able to see how their consumers talk about their experiences and how they engage with the organisation's products. These videos formed a powerful stimulus to encourage and shape managerial action.

that may provide a valuable resource for researchers where access can be negotiated. Recorded material may also be downloaded through the Internet, from media, sharing and social networking websites. Video-blogs may provide suitable sources from which to collect data for research.

A number of advantages from using video have been identified (Basil 2011; Jarzabkowski et al. 2014). Video-recording creates a permanent record, overcoming the transient nature of observation. This allows the researcher to achieve a number of outcomes that would not be possible where observation only involves watching and note taking. Because video provides a record in real time, a recording can be replayed many times to allow the researcher to reflect on the behaviours being shown, informants' interactions and the role of the environment or setting. This should enhance accuracy when coding data and permit verification of observational events.

Observation is demanding to undertake and you may miss important data when using this method which a video-recording would subsequently allow you to notice. Video-recordings may be paused, slowed, rewound, fast forwarded, zoomed, copied and subsequently edited to help you code sequences of this record. Jarzabkowski et al. (2014: 3) point out that this helps to identify 'who did what, when, where and how'. Basil (2011) says that the scope for reflection permitted by video-recording encourages a deeper understanding and allows alternative explanations to be evaluated by replaying this material.

There are also particular advantages related to the use of body-worn cameras and the recording of video diaries for observational research. Starr and Fernandez (2007) believe that the use of a body-worn camera, as used in consumer marketing research, can help to convey the narrative of the research and create a richer understanding of a subject. Use of this recording device facilitates the capture of precise details and exact cognitions, helping to differentiate between perceptions/recollections and reality, and encourages expression of informants' thoughts and feelings about the processes portrayed. In a similar way, a video diary is capable of creating an influential narrative and shared understanding in observational research (Cayla and Arnould 2013).

If the use of video to collect observational data is associated with a number of possible benefits, there are also a number of potential difficulties and disadvantages. We consider these in relation to issues related to data quality from using videography.

Issues related to data quality from using videography

Using video to help you collect observational data is likely to be technically and practically challenging. While it may be relatively easy to use a camera, the act of doing so begins to limit what will be recorded for future analysis. Selecting a frame and focusing a camera therefore has implications for the collection of data. Luff and Heath (2012) discuss some of the technical challenges of using video to record and collect observational data. Recording sound is also likely to be necessary where you decide to use video to record an observation. Recording good-quality sound may be difficult depending on the nature of the research setting and the equipment being used.

The practical difficulties of using audio-visual recording equipment are therefore likely to be much greater than simply being physically present in a research setting, watching what is occurring and using a pad to make notes. One of our colleagues who used video commented that the researcher tends to focus on using the recording equipment and capturing the event rather than trying to make sense of it at the time it occurs. Using video may therefore be problematic where the quality of the recording is poor in some way or where a technical issue occurs during recording. Using more than one researcher when using video to record observational data may help to overcome some of these issues.

Our discussion in this section indicates that the advantages to the researcher of directly using video to collect observational data need to be balanced against these technical and practical issues. On the one hand, good-quality recorded data may help to overcome the likelihood of observer bias discussed in Section 9.2. On the other hand, poor-quality recorded data may make the process of analysis difficult and increase the likelihood of observer error and observer bias occurring.

There are other issues related to recording an observation that may also affect data quality. Recording an observation using video is much more intrusive than simply watching and making notes. This raises a number of ethical issues discussed in Section 6.5, including respect for others, avoidance of harm, informed consent, privacy, confidentiality, use of the data and data management. Negotiating these issues with potential informants may be problematic given the intrusive nature of this means of recording data. However, even where access can be negotiated and agreed, there may be a continuing issue related to the willingness of informants to act as they would without the presence of the video. Informants may be concerned about the way in which the recording may be edited and the use to be made of this and other, raw data. We discussed the process where informants become familiar with being observed, known as habituation, in Section 9.2, so that they accept being observed and behave normally. We noted that to achieve habituation, it will probably be necessary for you to undertake several observation sessions in the same research setting with the same informants before you begin to achieve reliable and valid data. We also noted in Box 9.5 that informants may respond to being observed by using this as an opportunity to 'stage' a performance for the observer or to 'self-censor' their activities. Given the intrusive nature of video-recording observation, it is likely that you would need not only to spend time in the research setting to understand its dynamics but also then to record several observation sessions to develop trust and for informants to behave normally. While this would be time well spent, it will be intensive and very time consuming.

Researchers may ask informants to create video diaries. This approach also has implications for data quality and analysis. Data quality will partly be dependent on the willingness and competence of informants to undertake this task. In addition, while informants' video diaries provide a first-person perspective and encourage expression of informants' thoughts and feelings, a major disadvantage is the loss of external physical clues. Often, when a body-worn camera is used, the researcher will see what the informant sees, hear everything he or she may say and be able to watch much of what he or she does, but the frame of the recording is likely to be forward looking and narrow. The researcher will not be able to see what the informant looks like while she or he is holding the video-recorder or wearing the body-worn camera. In this way, this approach does not capture the informants' facial expressions or body language while they are engaging in the focal activity and may also not record the surrounding, situational context.

If body-worn cameras are used covertly, there will also be serious ethical issues to consider when using this technology (including a number of those discussed in Section 6.5), which will especially need to be considered in relation to non-participants who are inadvertently recorded.

Using secondary video data in observational research may also lead to data quality issues. The key here is suitability. Such material may provide you with a source of data but this will have been collected and edited for a different purpose to that of your research question and objectives and so may be of limited use. In evaluating the possible use of such secondary video data, you will need to consider the original intentions of the video maker and evaluate how editing this material may have affected its properties and purpose (Jarzabkowski et al. 2014).

9.6 Summary 小结

- Participant observation is an approach that allows the researcher to participate in or closely observe the lives and activities of those whom they are studying. It is used to attempt to get to the root of 'what is going on' in a wide range of social settings.
- Four types of participant observation are distinguished by two separate dimensions: whether the researcher's identity is revealed or concealed and the extent to which the researcher participates in the activities being observed.
- If you are not in employment, your choice of one of these types will be influenced by a number of factors including the nature of your research question and objectives, your ability to negotiate access, the time you have to devote to your research and your circumstances.
- If you are in full- or part-time employment and wish to use your organisation, your choice of one of these types will be influenced by factors including the nature of your research question and objectives, your ability to simultaneously undertake your job and manage the demands of participant observation, being able to maintain objectivity and ensuring that your closeness to informants does not lead to conflict.
- Participant observation has high ecological validity but may be affected by observer error, observer drift, observer bias and observer effects. These issues may be minimised or overcome by observer familiarisation, interpretive rigour, informant verification, habituation and the observer using strategies to explore and validate interpretations. Using these strategies can allow the benefits of gaining intricate and rich data to prevail over concerns about unreliable data.
- Structured observation is concerned with the frequency of events. It is characterised by a high level of predetermined structure and quantitative analysis.
- Structured observation will involve the use of a coding schedule, which you will probably need to develop and pilot test before using in your research setting.
- Structured observation may be affected by observer error, informant error, time error and observer effects. These issues may also be minimised or overcome by those strategies discussed in relation to participant observation and by designing a coding schedule that is free from interpretive ambiguity.
- Internet-mediated observation involves the collection of data from online communities, with the researcher purely observing or participating in an online community to collect data.
- Internet-mediated observation may be affected by observer error, observer drift, observer bias and observer effects. The reliability and validity of these data may also be affected by the scope of the online community and the nature of data from Internet-mediated observation.
- Observation using videography involves recording moving images onto electronic media to collect observational data. Video may be used in several ways to aid the collection of observational data.
- The advantages of video-recording observational data need to be evaluated in relation to the technical and practical challenges of using this medium to record these data.
- Observation using videography may also be affected by its intrusive nature, leading to a number of ethical issues and which may affect the reliability of the data in comparison to traditional forms of participant observation.

Self-check questions 自测题

Help with these questions is available at the end of the chapter.

9.1 You are a project manager responsible for the overall management of a large project to introduce your company's technology into the development of a new hospital. Most of the members of your team are from the UK, France and Germany. However, several of the newer engineers are from other EU member states. You notice at project meetings that these engineers tend to be far more reticent than the other team members in volunteering ideas for solving problems.

  This issue has coincided with the arrival on the scene of a management student from the local university who is keen to study a real-life management problem for her final-year undergraduate dissertation. You have asked her to study the assimilation experience of these engineers into your company with a view to recommending any changes that may be necessary to change the programme designed to effect the assimilation process.

  You ask her to start the research by sitting in on the project team meetings and, in particular, observing the behaviour of these newer engineers. What suggestions would you make to your student to help her structure her observation of the meetings?

9.2 You have been asked to give a presentation to a group of managers at the accountancy firm in which you are hoping to negotiate access for research. You wish to pursue the research question: 'What are the informal rules that govern the way in which trainee accountants work, and how do they learn these rules?'

  You realise that talk of 'attempting to learn the trainee accountants' symbolic world' would do little to help your cause with this group of non-research-minded businesspeople. However, you wish to point out some of the benefits to the organisation that your research may yield. Outline what you believe these would be.

9.3 You are a bank branch manager. You feel your staff are too reluctant to generate interest from customers in relation to new accounts that the bank offers. You would like to understand the reasons for their reluctance.

  a As the participant observer, how would you go about this?

  b How would you record your observations?

9.4 You have been granted access to conduct observation in the department of an organisation where you previously undertook a work placement. You are considering seeking permission to video-record some periods of observation. What issues would be raised by this?

Review and discussion questions 复习与讨论题

9.5 Compile a behaviour observation sheet similar to that in Box 9.6 in respect of either your job or that of a friend. Use this to compile a record of the behaviours observed.

9.6 Choose an everyday example of social behaviour, such as the way that motorists park their cars in 'open' (not multi-storey) car parks. Observe this behaviour (for example, the distance from the entrance/exit that they park) and draw general conclusions about observed behaviour patterns.

9.7 Video-record a current affairs (or similar) discussion on TV. Initially watch the programme to identify the main categories of behaviour that occur. It may be appropriate to use some of the categories listed in the schedule in Box 9.7. Having developed a draft coding schedule, watch the programme again to record the interactions evident in the discussion and then assess these interaction patterns.

改进研究项目

Progressing your research project

Deciding on the appropriateness of observation   观察的恰当性决策

- Return to your research question(s) and objectives. Decide how appropriate it would be to use observation as part of your research strategy.
- If you decide that this is appropriate, explain the relationship between your research question(s) and objectives and observation. If you decide that using observation is not appropriate, justify your decision. Respond for each form of observation discussed in this chapter.
- If you decide that one or more of these forms of observation is appropriate, address the following questions for each type of observation that you consider using:
  - What practical problems do you foresee?
  - Which ethical dilemmas will arise (see Chapter 6)?
  - What threats to data quality are you likely to encounter?
  - How will you attempt to overcome these issues?
- If you decide that structured observation is appropriate, attempt to develop a coding schedule that will be suitable for your research, conduct a pilot test if possible at this stage and amend it if appropriate.
- Use the questions in Box 1.4 to guide your reflective diary entry.

Self-check answers   自测题答案

9.1   It may be as well to suggest to her that she start her attendance at meetings with an unstructured approach in order to simply get the 'feel' of what is happening. She should make notes of her general impressions of these newer team members' general participation in meetings. She could then analyse these data and develop an observational instrument which could be used in further meetings she attends. This instrument would be based on a coding schedule that allowed her to record, among other things, the amount of contribution by each person at the meeting and the content of that contribution.

Data collection at the meetings does, of course, raise questions of research ethics. In our view, you, as the project manager, should explain to the team the role that the researcher is playing at the meetings. It would be quite truthful to say that the meeting participation of all team members is being observed with the overall purpose of making the meetings more effective, although it need not be emphasised what gave rise to the project manager's initial concern.

9.2   The research question is very broad. It allows you plenty of scope to discover a host of interesting things about the world of the trainee accountant. Without doubt, one of the things you will emerge with a clear understanding of is what they like about their work and what they do not like. This has practical implications for the sort of people that the firm ought to recruit, and how they should be trained and rewarded. You may learn about some of the short cuts practised by all occupations that may not be in the interest of the client. By the same token you will probably discover aspects of good practice that managers can disseminate to other accountants. The list of practical implications is numerous.

All this assumes, of course, that you will supply the managers with some post-research feedback. This does raise issues of confidentiality, which you must have thought through beforehand.

9.3 This is a difficult one. The question of status may be a factor. However, this would depend on your relationship with the staff. If you are, say, of similar age and have an open, friendly, 'one of the team' relationship with them, then it may not be too difficult. The element of threat that would attend a less open relationship would not be present.

You could set aside a time each day to work on the counter in order really to get to know what life is like for them. Even if you have done their job, you may have forgotten what it is like! It may have changed since your day. Direct conversations about account generation would probably not feature in your research times. However, you would need to have a period of reflection after each 'research session' to think about the implications for your research question of what you have just experienced.

9.4 A number of issues may occur that you would need to consider and seek to overcome. You may have enjoyed your work placement and become an accepted member of your workgroup. However, you may find that you are viewed differently when you return as a researcher. As a member of the workgroup, you became an insider and aware of the views of your co-workers. As a researcher, you would be returning as an outsider, although with recollections of having been an insider. This may mean that your former colleagues are more distant than you might expect.

You now wish to return to observe your former colleagues and also to video-record some periods of observation. This will mean that you will need to explain your intentions to those who would be affected by your research and negotiate access at various levels (Chapter 6) in order to be able to collect reliable observational data. This may not be easy to achieve and will in any case be a time-consuming activity. It may be that your former colleagues are very willing to become informants in your observational research and for their work-related activities and interactions to be video-recorded; however, you would not be wise to expect this to be the case without needing to discuss and negotiate this with them.

Where you are able to negotiate access and gain informed consent, you will still need to remain vigilant of the ethical issues that we referred to earlier in this chapter. Observation is an intrusive research method. While there are many potential benefits to be gained from video-recording observations, the use of this method to collect data means that you would be using a very intrusive approach that may inhibit or alter the behaviours of your intended informants. This effect should not be underestimated. In addition, there are technical and practical challenges to video-recording observation. These challenges would require you to develop a sufficient level of competence before embarking on the use of this method to avoid the risk of ending up with poor-quality recorded data.

Get ahead using resources on the companion website at: **www.pearsoned. co.uk/saunders**.
- Improve your IBM SPSS Statistics and NVivo research analysis with practice tutorials.
- Save time researching on the Internet with the Smarter Online Searching Guide.
- Test your progress using self-assessment questions.
- Follow live links to useful websites.

Chapter **10**

Collecting primary data using semi-structured, in-depth and group interviews
利用半结构化访谈、深度访谈、分组访谈收集原始资料

Learning outcomes 学习目标

By the end of this chapter you should be:

- able to classify research interviews in order to help you to understand the purpose of each type;
- aware of research situations favouring the use of semi-structured and in-depth interviews, and the logical and resource issues that affect their use;
- able to analyse potential data quality issues and evaluate how to overcome these;
- able to consider the development of your competence to undertake semi-structured and in-depth interviews;
- aware of the advantages and disadvantages of using one-to-one and group interviews, including focus groups, in particular contexts;
- aware of the issues and advantages of conducting interviews by telephone and via the Internet.

10.1 Introduction 引 言

The **research interview** is a purposeful conversation between two or more people, requiring the interviewer to establish rapport and ask concise and unambiguous questions, to which the interviewee is willing to respond, and to listen attentively. Essentially it is about asking purposeful questions and carefully listening to the answers to be able to explore these further. The use of interviews can help you to gather valid and reliable data that are relevant to your research question(s) and objectives. Interviews can also be used to help you refine your ideas where you have not yet fully formulated a research question and objectives.

We considered how objective and subjective perspectives inform opposing views about the nature of reality (Section 4.2). This distinction may be applied to approaches to interviewing. An objective approach sees the interview as a method to collect data from interviewees who are treated as witnesses to a reality that exists independently from them. This approach has historical roots in research which used interviews to obtain answers to questions that were largely treated as being factual. In this way, the interview was seen as being fairly unproblematic and an effective means to gather data, providing that access to appropriate respondents could be gained. The problem with this approach is that it only seeks responses rather than trying to understand the views and culture of interviewees, as social actors who interact with,

Interviews are occurring constantly. Every day there is scope to read about, listen to and watch interviews. These include interviews given by business leaders in quality newspapers, those with celebrities on television and radio programmes and those about news events on a range of media. Every time an event happens, those who witness it, those who are involved in it and those who have some expertise associated with it will be interviewed. However, despite the seeming ease with which interviews may be conducted, using the interview to collect research data requires considerable skill.

One profession that relies on good-quality interviewing skills is journalism. The BBC College of Journalism outlines a number of key interviewing skills on its website. Interviewers need to think clearly about the purpose of each interview and to be aware that their first question will set the direction of an interview and establish its style. Think of the interview style of a 'hard' interviewer you have seen or heard and contrast that with the style of a 'friendly, inviting' interviewer! Interviewers also need to be clear in the way they ask questions and not to be obscure or to use jargon. One key way to realise clarity is to achieve simplicity. This means finding ways to ask questions about complex issues that are simple and direct. Interviewers should also ask questions that are appropriate. Open questions invite interviewees to describe or explain, or to develop a previous answer. Closed questions seek straightforward answers, like 'yes' or 'no'. In journalism, this type of question can be used to get to the heart of a particular matter and for this reason it is often called the 'killer' question. Where an interviewee wants to avoid directly answering such a question, its use will expose this reluctance to give a straightforward answer. The use of a 'killer' question isn't likely to be appropriate in business and management research interviewing, but the skills outlined on the BBC College of Journalism website (2014) are likely to be helpful to business and management researchers. This website contains video guides that you can access to watch highly skilled journalists demonstrating a range of interviewing skills.

create and interpret their social world. A subjective approach is linked to the perspective that views about the social world are socially constructed. This approach sees interview data as being socially constructed; co-produced on the one hand by the views and interpretations of the participant and on the other hand by the interviewer, who asks questions, responds to the participant's views and interprets the resulting data during data analysis (Denzin 2001; Heyl 2005). It recognises the central role of the interviewer in the process of constructing meaning and the need for reflexivity, to reflect on and evaluate his or her approach to interviewing. These two approaches to interviewing indicate a distinct contrast in philosophy, purpose and style.

The research interview is a general term for several types of interview. This is important, since the nature of any interview should be consistent with your research question(s) and objectives, the purpose of your research and the research strategy that you have adopted. We provide an overview of types of interview in the next section (Section 10.2) and show how each type is related to a research purpose. Our main focus in this chapter is on semi-structured, in-depth and group interviews, with structured interviews (interviewer-completed questionnaires) being discussed in Chapter 11.

Section 10.3 considers situations favouring the use of semi-structured and in-depth interviews. Section 10.4 identifies data quality issues associated with their use and discusses how to overcome these. Section 10.5 discusses preparing for semi-structured and in-depth interviews and Section 10.6 their conduct. Section 10.7 considers logistical and resource issues and how to manage these. Section 10.8 considers the particular advantages and issues associated with the use of group interviews and focus groups. Finally, Section 10.9 explores the advantages and issues associated with telephone and Internet-mediated (electronic) interviews.

10.2   Types of interview and their link to the purpose of research and research strategy

Types of interview   访谈的类型以及与研究目的和研究策略的联系

Interviews may be highly formalised and structured, using standardised questions for each research participant (Section 11.2), or they may be informal and unstructured conversations. In between there are intermediate positions depending on the level of formality and structure used. For example, an interview may contain some highly structured sections and some unstructured parts, depending on its purpose. One typology that is commonly used relates to these levels of formality and structure, where interviews are categorised as either:

- structured interviews;
- semi-structured interviews;
- unstructured or in-depth interviews.

Another commonly used typology differentiates between:

- standardised interviews;
- non-standardised interviews.

A different typology was suggested by Powney and Watts (1987):

- respondent interviews;
- informant interviews.

There is overlap between these different typologies, although consideration of each typology adds to our overall understanding of the nature of research interviews.

Structured interviews use questionnaires based on a predetermined and 'standardised' or identical set of questions and we refer to them as interviewer-completed questionnaires (Section 11.2). You would read out each question and then record the response on a standardised schedule, usually with pre-coded answers (Sections 11.4 and 12.2). While there is social interaction between you and the respondent, such as the preliminary explanations that you will need to provide, the questions should be asked exactly as written and in the same tone of voice so that you do not indicate any bias. As structured interviews are used to collect quantifiable data they are also referred to as 'quantitative research interviews'.

By comparison, semi-structured and in-depth (unstructured) interviews are 'non-standardised'. These are often referred to as qualitative research interviews. In **semi-structured interviews** the researcher has a list of themes and possibly some key questions to be covered, although their use may vary from interview to interview. This means that you may omit some questions in particular interviews, given a specific organisational context that is encountered in relation to the research topic. The order of questions may also be varied depending on the flow of the conversation. On the other hand, additional questions may be required to explore your research question and objectives given the nature of events within particular organisations. The nature of the questions and the ensuing discussion mean that data will be captured by audio-recording the conversation or perhaps note taking (Section 10.5). Apart from containing the list of themes and questions to be covered, the **interview schedule** for this type of interview will also be likely to contain some comments to open the discussion, a possible list of prompts to promote and further discussion, and some comments to close it. These are discussed in more detail later.

Unstructured interviews are informal. You would use these to explore in depth a general area in which you are interested. We therefore refer to these as 'in-depth interviews' in this chapter and elsewhere in this book. There is no predetermined list of questions to ask in this situation, although you need to have a clear idea about the aspect or aspects that you want to explore. The interviewee is given the opportunity to talk freely about events, behaviour and beliefs in relation to the topic area, so that this type of interaction is sometimes called non-directive. It has been labelled as an **informant interview** since it is the interviewee's perceptions that guide the conduct of the interview and the topics discussed. In comparison, a **respondent interview** is one where the interviewer exercises greater direction over the interview while allowing the interviewee's opinions to emerge as he or she responds to the questions of the researcher.

The context of the unstructured interview may also be important to consider. While unstructured interviews are informal, in some research designs they will be pre-arranged so that the interviewer and interviewee agree to meet in a particular place at the specific time for an agreed period. This suggests a formal arrangement to an informal process. In other research designs, such as those involving an Action Research or ethnographic strategy, 'interviews' may be more opportunistic as well as informal. In this way, the researcher may listen to talk, engage in talk and have informal conversations, as well as pre-arrange interviews. Where you use an Action Research or ethnographic research strategy, you should be able to benefit from this immersion in the research setting and ability to witness and participate in natural, authentic conversations.

We can also differentiate types of interview according to the number of participants. Interviews may be conducted on a one-to-one basis, between you and a single participant. Such interviews are most commonly conducted by meeting your participant 'face-to-face', but there may be some situations where you conduct an interview by telephone

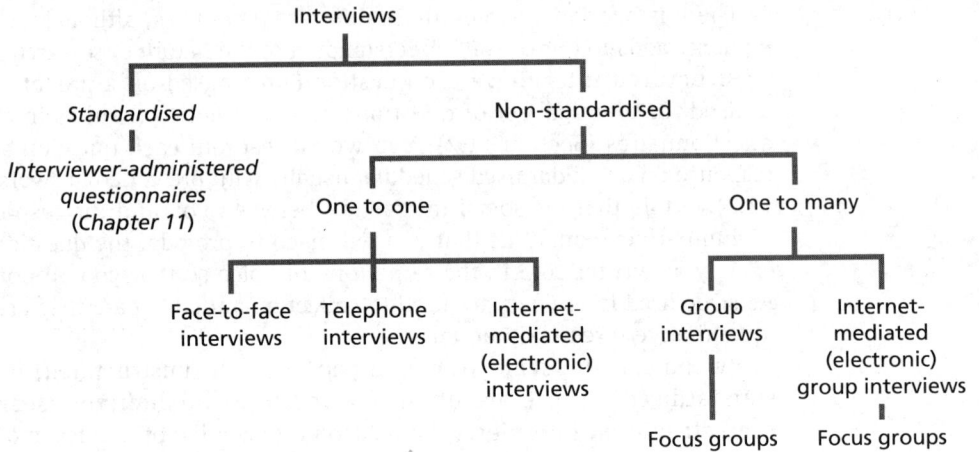

Figure 10.1 Forms of interview

or using the Internet. There may be other situations where you conduct a semi-structured or in-depth interview on a group basis, where you meet with a small number of participants to explore an aspect of your research through a group discussion that you facilitate. These forms of interview are summarised in Figure 10.1. The discussion throughout most of this chapter applies to each of these forms. However, the final two sections (10.8 and 10.9) include specific consideration of the issues and advantages related to the use of one-to-many group interviews and focus groups, and to the use of telephone and Internet-mediated interviews as an alternative to a 'face-to-face' meeting, respectively.

Links to the purpose of research and research strategy

Each form of interview outlined above has a distinct purpose. Structured, standardised interviews are normally used to gather data which will then be the subject of quantitative analysis (Chapter 12), for example as part of a survey strategy. Semi-structured and in-depth interviews are used to gather data which are normally analysed qualitatively (Chapter 13), for example as part of a case study or Grounded Theory strategy. These data are likely to be used not only to understand the 'what' and the 'how' but also to place more emphasis on 'why'.

In Chapter 5 we outlined how the purpose of your research may be classified as either exploratory, descriptive, explanatory or evaluative (Section 5.4). Different types of interview may be used to gather data for each kind of study:

- In an exploratory study, in-depth interviews can be very helpful to find out what is happening and to understand the context. Semi-structured interviews may also be used in an exploratory study. Both of these types of interview may provide important background or contextual material for your study. You will find it helpful to conduct exploratory, qualitative interviews where your research design adopts an inductive approach, such as in the development of grounded theory (Sections 4.3 and 5.5).
- In a descriptive study, structured interviews (Section 11.2) can be used as a means to identify general patterns. You may find it helpful to conduct structured interviews where your research design uses a deductive approach to test a theory, as the standardised nature of the data will make it easier to test statistical propositions or hypotheses (Chapter 12).

Table 10.1 Uses of different types of interview for each research purpose

	Exploratory	Descriptive	Explanatory	Evaluative
Structured		✓✓	✓	✓
Semi-structured	✓		✓✓	✓✓
Unstructured	✓✓			✓

✓✓ = more frequent, ✓ = less frequent

- In an explanatory study, semi-structured interviews may be used in order to understand the relationships between variables, such as those revealed from a descriptive study (Section 5.4). Structured interviews may also be used in relation to an explanatory study, in a statistical sense (Section 12.5). Research interviews used for an explanatory purpose may be useful in both inductive and deductive approaches because of the intention to explain why relationships exist (Section 2.4).
- In an evaluative study, you may find it useful to use one type of interview, or a combination of types, depending on the nature of your study. In many cases, semi-structured interviews may be used to understand the relationships between your evaluation or effectiveness criteria. Research interviews used for an evaluative purpose may be useful in either an inductive or deductive approach (Section 2.4).

This is summarised in Table 10.1.

Your research may incorporate more than one type of interview, as in multiple methods (Section 5.3). As part of a survey strategy, for example, you may decide to use in-depth or semi-structured interviews initially to help identify the questions that should be asked in a questionnaire completed as a structured interview. The data that you gather from such exploratory interviews will be used in the design of your structured interview. Alternatively, semi-structured interviews may be used as part of a mixed methods design to explore, explain or validate themes that have emerged from the use of a questionnaire (Teddlie and Tashakkori 2009). Different types of interview question may be also used within one interview. For example, one section of an interview may be composed of a set of questions with pre-coded responses, while another section may use semi-structured questions to explore responses.

We can therefore see that the various types of interview have a number of potentially valuable uses in terms of undertaking your research project. The key is to ensure consistency between your research question(s) and objectives, the strategy you will employ and the methods of data collection you will use.

10.3 When to use semi-structured and in-depth interviews 适用半结构化访谈和深度访谈的情形

There are many situations in which collecting data using a semi-structured or in-depth research interview may be advantageous. These situations can be grouped into four categories:

- the purpose of the research;
- the importance of establishing personal contact;
- the nature of the data collection questions;
- length of time required and completeness of the process.

We examine each of these in turn.

The purpose of the research

Where you are undertaking an exploratory study, or a study that includes an exploratory element, it is likely that you will include in-depth or semi-structured research interviews in your design. Similarly, an explanatory study is also likely to include interviews in order for the researcher to be able to infer causal relationships between variables (Sections 2.4 and 11.4). Where it is necessary for you to understand the reasons for the decisions that your research participants have taken, or to understand the reasons for their attitudes and opinions, you are likely to need to conduct an in-depth or semi-structured interview.

Semi-structured and in-depth interviews also provide you with the opportunity to 'probe' answers, where you want your interviewees to explain, or build on, their responses. This is important if, for example, you are adopting an interpretivist philosophy, where you will be concerned to understand the meanings that participants ascribe to various phenomena (Section 4.4). Interviewees may use words or ideas in a particular way, and the opportunity to probe these meanings will add significance and depth to the data you obtain. They may also lead the discussion into areas that you had not previously considered but which are significant for your understanding, and which help you to address your research question and objectives, or indeed help you formulate such a question. Interviews also afford each interviewee an opportunity to hear herself or himself 'thinking aloud' about things she or he may not have previously thought about. The result should be that you are able to collect a rich and detailed set of data. However, you need to be aware that the manner in which you interact with your interviewees and ask questions will impact on the data you collect.

The importance of establishing personal contact

We have found that managers are more likely to agree to be interviewed, rather than complete a questionnaire, especially where the interview topic is seen to be interesting and relevant to their current work. An interview provides them with an opportunity to reflect on events without needing to write anything down. This situation also provides the opportunity for interviewees to receive feedback and personal assurance about the way in which information will be used (Sections 6.2 and 6.5).

Potential research participants who receive a questionnaire via the Internet or through the post may be reluctant to complete it for a number of reasons. They may feel that it is not appropriate to provide sensitive and confidential information to someone they have never met. They may also not completely trust the way in which the information is to be used. They may be reluctant to spend time providing written explanatory answers, where these are requested, especially if the meaning of any question is not entirely clear. The use of personal interviews, where appropriate, may therefore achieve a higher response rate than using questionnaires (Sections 7.2 and 7.3). Where a questionnaire is received by a manager who is not inclined to complete it, it may also be passed to another person to complete, which will adversely affect your control over those whom you wish to answer your questions and also possibly the reliability of the data that you receive.

The nature of the data collection questions

An in-depth or semi-structured interview is likely to be the most advantageous approach to attempt to obtain data in the following circumstances:

- where there are a large number of questions to be answered;
- where the questions are either complex or open ended;
- where the order and logic of questioning may need to be varied (Box 10.1).

Box 10.1
Focus on student research

The need to vary the order and logic of questioning

Val undertook a series of semi-structured interviews into the approach used to manage public relations (PR) activities in 30 organisations. It soon became evident that it would not be meaningful to ask exactly the same questions in each organisation. For example, some organisations had centralised PR as part of the marketing function, whereas in other organisations it was devolved to individual business units. Another significant variable was associated with the public-relations styles adopted. Some organisations adopted a 'press agency' approach where the main focus was to get the organisation or product mentioned in the media as often as possible, the nature of the mention being of secondary importance. Others adopted a 'public information' approach where the main aim was to get media exposure for the organisation or product.

The impact of these and other variables meant that it was not sensible to ask exactly the same questions at each interview, even though many questions remained applicable in all cases and the underlying intention was to ensure consistency between interviews. It was not until each interview had started that Val was able to learn which of these different variables operated within the particular organisation. Fortunately, the flexibility offered by the use of semi-structured interviews enabled her to do this.

Length of time required and completeness of the process

Often the complexity of issues to be covered or their number and variety mean that an interview is the best or only means of collecting data. In our experience, where expectations have been established clearly about the length of time required and participants understand and agree with the objectives of the research interview, they have generally been willing to agree to be interviewed. Some negotiation is, in any case, possible and the interview can be arranged at a time when the interviewee will be under least pressure.

We have found that our participants tend to be generous with their time, and sometimes when interviews have been organised to start at mid-morning they will arrange for lunch, which can allow the discussion and exploration of issues to continue. However, for those of you who fancy a free lunch, we do not want to raise your expectations falsely, and the start time for an interview should not be set with this in mind!

Your aim will be to obtain data to enable you to answer all your research questions, allowing for the right of participants to decline to respond to any question you ask. Where you conduct the interaction skilfully an interview is more likely to achieve this than the use of a self-completed or interviewer-completed questionnaire. Where your participant does not provide an answer to a particular question or questions in an in-depth or semi-structured interview, you are likely to have some idea why a response was not provided. This may even lead you to modify the question or to compose another where this would be appropriate. Section 6.6 considers the ethical issues associated with seeking to obtain answers.

Situations are likely to occur where you will consider the choice between using research interviews and other qualitative methods such as observation (Chapter 9). In this regard, a distinction has been made between contrived and natural data. **Natural** or naturally occurring **data** are those observed from real conversations that

> ### Box 10.2
> ### Checklist
>
> **To help you decide whether to use in-depth or semi-structured interviews**
>
> ✔ Is your research exploratory or explanatory?
> ✔ Will it help to be able to probe interviewees' responses to build on or seek explanation of their answers and meanings?
>
> ✔ Will it help to seek personal contact in terms of gaining access to participants and their data?
> ✔ Are your data collection questions large in number, complex or open-ended?
> ✔ Will there be a need to vary the order and logic of questioning?
> ✔ Will the data collection process with each individual involve a relatively lengthy period?
> ✔ Will interviews allow you to reveal and explore social phenomena that you would not be able to observe in action?

take place in everyday, authentic situations. **Contrived data** are those that result from a researcher organising an experiment, interview or survey (Speer 2008). One type of data is not necessarily superior to the other, but where it is possible, data collected naturally may be more authentic and reliable. Speer (2008) recognises that for some research topics there are reasons why it is not possible to collect observed, natural data. These reasons relate to the taken-for-granted assumptions, sensitivity and hidden nature of some social phenomena (such as in personal relationships) that mean it is difficult to gain access to and observe these in action. Using interviews to explore such phenomena means that you are able to gain access to authentic accounts that you would not be able to observe in action. As a result, the distinction between natural and contrived data may be too rigid (Speer 2008). It should, however, help you to think about the nature of your research topic and then to consider how best to attempt to gain access to your informants' (Chapter 9), participants' or respondents' (Chapter 11) data.

Box 10.2 provides a checklist to help you in your deliberations about whether or not to use in-depth or semi-structured interviews.

10.4   Data quality issues associated with semi-structured and in-depth interviews

与半结构化访谈和深度访谈有关的数据质量问题

Data quality issues

Before discussing how to prepare for and conduct semi-structured or in-depth interviews we consider data quality issues associated with these types of research interview. This is because your preparation for and conduct of these interviews will be influenced by the need to ensure data quality. This was introduced in Section 5.8 and the issues we discuss here that impact on semi-structured and in-depth interviews are related to:

- reliability/dependability;
- forms of bias;
- cultural differences;
- generalisability/transferability;
- validity/credibility.

The lack of standardisation in semi-structured and in-depth interviews can lead to concerns about reliability/dependability (Section 5.8 and in particular Table 5.5). In relation to qualitative research, this is concerned with whether alternative researchers would reveal similar information. The concern about reliability/dependability in these types of interview is also related to issues of bias. There are three types of potential bias to consider. The first of these is related to **interviewer bias**. This is where the comments, tone or non-verbal behaviour of the interviewer creates bias in the way that interviewees respond to the questions being asked. This may be because you attempt to impose your own beliefs and frame of reference through the questions that you ask. It is also possible that you will demonstrate bias in the way you interpret responses. Where you are unable to gain interviewees' trust, or perhaps where your personal credibility is seen to be lacking, the value of the data given may also be limited, raising doubts about its validity and reliability.

Related to this is **interviewee** or **response bias**. This type of bias can be caused by interviewees' perceptions about the interviewer, or perceived interviewer bias. However, the cause of this type of bias may not be linked to perceptions of the interviewer. Taking part in an interview is an intrusive process. This is especially true in the case of in-depth or semi-structured interviews, where your aim will be to explore events or to seek explanations. An interviewee may, in principle, be willing to participate but still be sensitive to the unstructured exploration of certain themes. Interviewees may therefore choose not to reveal and discuss an aspect of a topic that you wish to explore, because this would lead to probing questions that would intrude on sensitive information that they do not wish, or are not empowered, to discuss with you. The outcome of this may be that the interviewee provides only a partial 'picture' of the situation that casts himself or herself in a 'socially desirable' role, or the organisation for which they work in a positive or even negative fashion.

Bias may also result from the nature of the individuals or organisational participants who agree to be interviewed (Box 10.3). This is called **participation bias**. The amount of time required for an interview may result in a reduction in willingness to take part by some. This may bias your sample from whom data are collected. This is an issue that you will need to consider carefully and attempt to overcome through the approach taken to sampling (Sections 7.2 and 7.3).

Further concerns may arise from cultural differences between the interviewer and intended interviewees. Gobo (2011) sees the research interview as the product of individualistic societies, which may not be so well suited to societies and participants with

Box 10.3
Focus on student research

Willingness (or otherwise) to be interviewed

Saffron's research project involved her interviewing people about their perceptions of the real benefits of different hair products. She decided that the best way to conduct these interviews was, with the permission of the owner, to interview customers at her local hairdresser. Saffron discovered that although some of the customers were willing to be interviewed, others were not. A minority of customers, often smartly dressed in business suits, refused outright, saying that they had insufficient time. In contrast, others, particularly pensioners, were happy to answer her questions in considerable detail and appeared to wish to prolong the interview.

a different cultural orientation. He argues that the research interview makes certain assumptions:

- that it is acceptable to discuss issues with outsiders;
- that issues may be considered public and able to be discussed rather than being kept private and restricted;
- that it is permissible for a person to hold independent views and to speak as an individual.

Gobo also refers to societies where there may be a tendency to respond to an interviewer's questions by only being positive or by agreeing.

The cultural differences that an interviewer has to cope with may be more subtle. Court and Abbas (2013) provide an account of a cross-cultural interview they conducted with two Israeli Druze women. One of the researchers is a Canadian woman, living in Israel, who speaks English and Hebrew; the other researcher is an Israeli Druze woman, who speaks Hebrew and Arabic. The interview they conducted yielded valuable data for their research, but their reflections about it reveal issues related to language and cultural nuances. Because one of the researchers shared a similar cultural background to that of the participants, she was able to interact with them and develop a rapport that helped to facilitate the interview to a greater extent than the other researcher. Cultural differences may affect what the interviewee is willing to say, how the researcher interprets the interviewee's words and meanings, or fails to understand these, and influence the questions that the interviewer asks. Although this research is not related to business and management, it emphasises how cultural differences can impact on the scope to collect data and the implications of operating as either a cultural insider or outsider.

An issue is often raised about the generalisability/transferability of findings from qualitative research interviews, although the validity/credibility of the data they produce is generally seen to be less of an issue (Section 5.8 and in particular Table 5.5). Generalisability/transferability refers to the extent to which the findings of a research study are applicable to other settings. This may be questioned in relation to the statistical generalisability of qualitative research studies where these are based on a small sample. However, this should not be interpreted as meaning that a qualitative study is intrinsically less valuable than a quantitative study. As we noted in Section 10.2, such studies are more likely to be used to explore and explain and provide insights that can be used to develop theory, rather than to provide statistical generalisations. Validity/credibility refers to the extent to which the researcher has gained access to a participant's knowledge and experience, and is able to infer meanings that the participant intends from the language used by that person. The scope to explore meanings during a semi-structured or in-depth interview may help to enhance the validity/credibility of the data collected, although forms of bias and cultural differences may impair this outcome.

Overcoming data quality issues

Reliability/dependability

One response to the issue of reliability/dependability (Section 5.8 and in particular Table 5.5) in relation to findings derived from using in-depth or semi-structured interviews is that these are not necessarily intended to be repeatable since they reflect reality at the time they were collected, in a situation which may be subject to change. The assumption behind this type of research is that the circumstances to be explored are complex and dynamic. The value of using in-depth or semi-structured interviews is derived from the flexibility that you may use to explore the complexity of the topic. Therefore, an attempt to ensure that qualitative, non-standardised research could be replicated by other researchers would not be realistic or feasible without undermining the strength of this type of research.

However, where you use this approach you should explain your research design, the reasons underpinning the choice of strategy and methods, and how the data were obtained. This will be referred to by others, to help understand the processes you used, and your research findings. The use of in-depth or semi-structured interviews should not lead to a lack of rigour in relation to the research process – rather there is a need to use a rigorous design and ensure your explanation of how the data were obtained and analysed provides sufficient detail to show your findings are dependable.

Interviewer and interviewee bias

Overcoming these forms of bias is related to the ways in which these types of interview are prepared for (Section 10.5 and Box 10.6) and conducted (Section 10.6 and Box 10.11).

Cultural reflexivity and participatory research

As we discussed earlier, where your research involves interviewing participants from a different culture, whether this is in a cross-national or multicultural setting, you will need to ensure that you minimise any form of bias or threat to reliability. Cultural reflexivity may be helpful in your preparation. As we noted in Section 2.1, the foundation of reflexivity involves reflecting critically on your role as researcher – for example, what motivates you to research a particular topic; why have you chosen your research strategy and methods to collect data; evaluating how can you conduct your research project in an unbiased and meaningful way; how you interact with your participants (Lincoln et al. 2011).

Cultural reflexivity will involve you reflecting on the nature of the relationship between you and your intended participants and how differing and similar cultural customs may affect your interactions (Court and Abbas 2013). Prior to your interviews, you may wish to visit a workplace and observe, listen or participate in informal conversations so that you become more familiar with the research setting. Such understandings will help you to develop rapport with those whom you wish to interview and to gain their acceptance.

Cultural reflexivity will also involve you considering how to engage your participants and involve them. This is likely to include evaluating how best to conduct interviews: whether to conduct these individually or on a group basis; choosing the most appropriate level of structure and formality to use; and whether to attempt to gather data in a single interview or in more than one to develop rapport and understanding. It may also be appropriate to use an informal conversational approach, rather than too many interviewer-led questions. A series of discussions may be helpful to develop rapport, understanding and to involve your participants in the process of interpreting, exploring, confirming and analysing data and meanings in a cultural context. Adopting a culturally reflexive approach may help to overcome cultural differences that affect what is discussed and not discussed, clarify what is important and what is not, and reveal what should be followed up and explored.

One way to achieve cultural contact is, where feasible, to engage in participatory forms of research. In Section 5.5 we outlined two such participatory strategies: ethnography and Action Research. Ethnography involves participation by a researcher in the research setting over time in order to begin to understand the context, develop rapport and be accepted into that community. Using this strategy to immerse yourself in a cultural context may help you to achieve greater acceptance and access to meanings, in comparison to the realist interviewer who seeks to rush in, collect some data and leave with whatever she or he expected to find, irrespective of the expectations of those being interviewed! Action research is an emergent and iterative process of inquiry designed to develop solutions to real organisational problems through a participative and collaborative approach (Section 5.5). Neither of these research strategies may be appropriate to your research project, although both suggest that participation in the research setting may help to alleviate cultural differences.

Generalisability/transferability

Earlier we stated that a concern may be raised about the generalisability of findings from qualitative research using only one case or a small number of cases. A number of different responses may be made in relation to this concern.

The first of these involves examining the nature of the single case or limited number of cases being used. Although you may be basing your research in a single case study, such as your employing organisation, within this case you may be planning to interview a wide cross-section of participants. This allows you to collect data from a representative sample of those who work in this setting. Alternatively, using a single case may also encompass a number of settings; where for example it involves a study in a large organisation with sites across the country, or even around the world. A well-planned and rigorous qualitative case study may therefore be just as likely to produce valuable findings.

A second response to questions of generalisability is based on the ability of qualitative research to be used to test existing theory, or for an emergent theory to be subsequently discussed in relation to a pre-existing theory. Where you are able to relate your research project to existing theory you will be in a position to demonstrate that your findings have a broader theoretical significance than the case or cases that form the basis of your work. It will be up to you to establish how the findings from your particular case or cases are related to existing theory in order to be able to demonstrate their broader significance. This should allow you to test the applicability of existing theory to the setting(s) that you are examining and where this is found wanting to suggest why. It will also allow theoretical propositions to be advanced that can then be tested in another context.

A third argument focuses on the transferability of a research design, using the definition we outlined of this concept in Table 5.5. In this table, transferability was defined as the need to provide a full description of the research questions, design, context, findings and resulting interpretations in the project report. This allows another researcher to design a similar research project to be used in a different, although suitable, research setting.

However, in seeking to counter arguments about the generalisability/transferability of qualitative research studies using semi-structured or in-depth interviews, it is important to recognise that such studies cannot be used to make statistical generalisations about an entire population (whatever this may be in the context of the research topic) where your data are from a small non-probability sample.

Validity/credibility

Semi-structured and in-depth interviews can achieve a high level of validity/credibility (Section 5.8 and in particular Table 5.5) where conducted carefully using clarifying questions, probing meanings and by exploring responses from a variety of angles. The use of questioning in such interviews is discussed in detail in Section 10.6. In Table 5.5 in Section 5.8 we outlined further ways in which credibility may be achieved through using qualitative interviews. Their use should help you to build trust and rapport, collect sufficient data and provide you with the opportunity to ask participants to check these data. Credibility may also be achieved by accounting for negative cases (those that are counter to other cases) during analysis in the explanations you develop and being reflective and reflexive about your research.

10.5 Preparing for semi-structured or in-depth interviews 准备半结构化访谈或深度访谈

Like all research methods, the key to a successful interview is careful preparation. When using in-depth or semi-structured interviews, the 'five Ps' will be useful to remember: prior planning prevents poor performance. In particular, we believe it is crucial that you plan precisely how you are going to demonstrate your competence and credibility to obtain the confidence of your interviewees.

In order to avoid data quality issues when you conduct in-depth or semi-structured interviews, we consider some key measures that your preparations will need to include. These are:

- Your level of knowledge.
- Developing interview themes and supplying information to the interviewee before the interview.
- The appropriateness of the intended interview location.

We discuss these in turn.

Your level of knowledge

You need to be knowledgeable about the research topic and organisational or situational context in which the interview is to take place. In addition to your literature review, a prior search in your university library (Sections 3.4 and 3.5) may reveal articles written by senior employees of the organisation that is participating in your research. There may also be other material about the organisation on the Internet, in the 'trade' press and the quality newspapers. This is likely to include company annual reports and other publications, as well as financial data relating to the organisation. The ability to draw on this type of information in the interview will help to demonstrate your credibility, allow you to assess the accuracy of responses and encourage the interviewee to offer a more detailed account of the topic under discussion. As you undertake later interviews, you will also be able to draw on the initial analysis that you make of data previously collected.

Successfully interviewing participants from different cultures requires some knowledge about those cultures. Without adequate preparation, there may be misinterpretation because of the cultural differences between the interviewee and the interviewer. An in-depth interview offers the opportunity to explore meanings, including those that may be culturally specific, but you will need to be aware of cultural differences and their implications (see our earlier discussion). Brinkmann and Kvale (2015) highlight some of the verbal and non-verbal cues that may have contrary or different meanings between cultures. For example, answering 'yes' to a question may indicate agreement in some cultures, but in others it may be a way of telling the interviewer that the question has been understood, or in others to recognise its importance. A nod of the head indicates agreement in some cultures but in others it may mean something else. Brinkmann and Kvale (2015) note the importance of being aware of social conventions in a culture in order to understand the way answers are constructed and also not to cause offence. Cultural differences exist not only between countries but between groups, social classes and organisations and some prior knowledge about those you wish to interview will invariably be helpful.

Developing interview themes and supplying information to the interviewee before the interview

Credibility may also be promoted through the supply of relevant information to participants before the interview. Providing participants with a list of the interview themes before the event, where this is appropriate, should help this. This list of themes (Box 10.4) may help to promote validity and reliability because it informs the interviewee about the information you are interested in and provides them with the opportunity to prepare for the interview by assembling supporting organisational documentation from their files. We can testify to this approach and the value of allowing participants to prepare themselves for the discussion in which they are to engage. Access to organisational documentation also allows for triangulation of the data provided (Sections 8.2 and 8.3). Our experience is that participants are generally willing to supply a photocopy or a PDF file of such material, although of course it will be necessary to conceal any confidential or personal details in the research report.

Interview themes may be derived from the literature that you read, the theories that you consider, your experience of a particular topic, common sense and discussions with co-workers, fellow students, tutors and research participants, or a combination of these approaches. You will need to have some idea of the theme or themes that you wish to discuss with your participants even if you intend to commence with exploratory, in-depth interviews as part of a Grounded Theory strategy to your research project (Section 5.5).

Without at least some focus, your interview will lack a sense of direction and purpose. You should therefore start with a set of themes that reflect the variables being studied, or at least one or more general questions related to your research topic that you could use to start your interview. These can be incorporated into your interview guide (Box 10.5). This lists topics that you intend to cover in the interview along with initial questions and

Box 10.4
Focus on student research

Developing interview themes

Karl was interested in understanding why some employees in his organisation used the IT Help Desk while others did not. This subject was felt to be important in relation to perceptions about service-level agreements, service relationships and service quality. He decided to provide his interviewees with a list of themes that he wished to explore during interviews. After some deliberation and reading of the

academic literature he came up with the following list of themes:

- the extent to which employees feel they know when and how to use the IT Help Desk;
- the nature of support employees feel they are receiving;
- the services employees feel the IT Help Desk should be providing;
- the nature of employees' knowledge of service-level agreements;
- the extent to which the IT Help Desk is meeting employees' needs.

He subsequently used this list of themes to develop his interview guide (Box 10.5).

Box 10.5
Focus on student research

Extract from an interview guide

Karl was interested in understanding why some employees in his organisation used the IT Help Desk while others did not. Using his interview themes (Box 10.4), he began to develop his guide:

Help Desk Support

- To what extent does the IT Help Desk meet your needs?

- *Probe*: In what ways? [ask for real-life examples]
- *Probe*: Can you give me an example (if possible) of when you received good support from the IT Help Desk?
- *Probe*: Can you give me an example (if possible) of when you received insufficient support from the IT Help Desk?

- Do you consider you have enough support from the IT Help Desk?

- *Probe*: How is this support provided (e.g. telephone, face-to-face)?
- *Probe*: What else (if anything) could usefully be done?

---

probes that may be used to follow up initial responses and obtain greater detail from your participants. When creating your guide, you need to try to ensure that the order of questions is likely to be logical to your participants and that the language you use will be comprehensible. Using your guide, you will be able to develop and/or explore research themes through the in-depth or semi-structured interviews that you conduct to see whether you can identify and test relationships between them (Chapter 13).

Appropriateness of the intended interview location

It is possible that the location where you conduct your interviews will influence the data you collect. As we discussed in Section 6.6, you should choose the location for your interviews with regard to your own personal safety. You should also think about the impact that the location may have upon your participants and the way they respond (Box 10.6). The location should be convenient for your participants, where they will feel comfortable and where the interview is unlikely to be disturbed. Your research interviews may be

Box 10.6
Focus on student research

Choosing an appropriate location

Anne was pleased that the manufacturing company in which she was undertaking her research had arranged for her to use a room in the Human Resources Department. The room contained a low table and chairs, and she had been provided with bottled water and glasses as well. However, after her third interview she was beginning to doubt her own interviewing skills. Her participants, the company's production line workers, seemed unwilling to be open in their responses. She began to wonder if something was wrong with the interview location and decided to ask the next participant about this. At the end of that interview she had her answer. Her participants were unhappy with the interview location. Prior to being interviewed by Anne, the only time they or their colleagues had visited the Human Resources Department was to receive a reprimand. The location was, therefore, inappropriate!

Box 10.7 Checklist

To help you prepare for your semi-structured or in-depth interview

✔ What level of knowledge about your research topic will be required in order to demonstrate your competence and credibility to gain the confidence of your interviewees?

✔ What level of knowledge about the research context will be required in order to demonstrate your competence and credibility to gain the confidence of your interviewees?

✔ What level of knowledge about the culture of your interviewees will be required in order to gain their confidence before they are willing to share data?

✔ What will be the broad focus of your in-depth interview, or what are the themes that you wish to explore or seek explanations for during a semi-structured interview?

✔ What type of information, if any, will it be useful to send to your interviewee prior to the interview?

✔ What did you agree to supply to your interviewee when you arranged the interview? Has this been supplied?

✔ Have you considered the impact that your interview location may have on participants' responses and on your own personal safety?

hosted by an organisation which has granted you access to undertake your research and you will be able to discuss these requirements about safety, convenience, neutrality of the space and not being overheard when talking normally, with the person who makes the arrangements for your interviews (Box 10.6).

You also need to choose a place that is quiet so that outside noise will not reduce the quality of your audio-recording of the interview. Each of us has experienced situations when conducting interviews where noise from outside the building or even from within it has been disruptive. In particular, Mark recalls an interview in a room where noise from building work outside meant that although he was able to hear the participant's responses clearly while the interview was taking place, much of the audio-recording of this interview was unintelligible due to the sound of a very loud pneumatic drill!

In many cases, the interview location will be arranged by those whom you interview. When you interview organisational participants such as managers in their offices, this has the advantage that they are able to find documents which support points they are making.

Box 10.7 provides a checklist of the key points considered in this section to help you to prepare for semi-structured or in-depth interviews.

10.6 Conducting semi-structured or in-depth interviews 实施半结构化访谈或深度访谈

This section is about actually conducting semi-structured or in-depth interviews. The aspects we discuss here are intended to avoid forms of bias that would affect the reliability and validity of the data produced. These aspects relate to the:

- appropriateness of your appearance at the interview;
- nature of your comments to open the interview;
- approach to questioning;
- appropriate use of different types of questions;

- nature and impact of your behaviour during the interview;
- demonstration of attentive listening skills;
- scope to summarise and test understanding;
- dealing with difficult participants;
- approach to recording data.

We discuss these in turn. Key points are summarised as a checklist at the end of this section (Box 10.12).

Appropriateness of your appearance at the interview

Your appearance may affect the perception of the interviewee. Where this has an adverse effect on your credibility in the view of interviewees, or results in a failure to gain their confidence, the resulting bias may affect the reliability of the information provided. Where appropriate you should consider wearing a similar style of clothing to those to be interviewed, although this may not always be appropriate. For example, your interviewees would not expect you to wear the same work wear that they need to put on to work on the production line. Essentially, this means that you will need to wear clothing that will be generally acceptable for the setting within which the interview is to occur (Box 10.8).

Nature of your comments to open the interview

Where the interviewee has not met you before, the first few minutes of conversation will have a significant impact on the outcome of the interview – again related to the issue of your credibility and the level of the interviewee's confidence. Often such interviews occur in a setting that is unfamiliar to you. Despite this, it is your responsibility to shape the start of the conversation. You will need to explain your research to the participant and, hopefully, gain consent (Section 6.6). As part of this you will need to establish your credibility and gain the interviewee's confidence. During these initial discussions we have found that the interviewee often has some uncertainties about sharing information,

Box 10.8
Focus on student research

Checking out the dress code

Mal arranged to visit the administration centre of a large insurance company on a Friday to conduct a group interview with staff drawn from one of its telephone sales divisions and two one-to-one interviews with senior managers. He felt that it was appropriate to wear fairly 'formal' clothes to match what he thought would be the dress code of the organisation. Indeed, for four days of the working week this assumption would have been appropriate.

However, the organisation had recently introduced the practice of not wearing such formal work clothes on Fridays. Thus he found himself the only one dressed formally in the organisation on the day of his visit. Taking lunch proved to be a memorable experience, as he mingled with everyone else dressed in jeans and tee shirts, etc. His 'mistake' proved to be an amusing opening at the start of each interview rather than a barrier to gaining access to participants' data. Indeed, it might not have been appropriate for him to match the 'dress-down' style of participants too closely. Nevertheless, it does provide a useful example of the way in which expectations about appearance are likely to be noticed.

and about the manner in which these data may be used. Alternatively, she or he may still need clarification about the exact nature of the data that you wish to obtain. We have found that a pre-prepared participant information sheet (Section 6.6, Box 6.15) and consent form (Box 6.16) are both extremely helpful in reducing such anxieties. There may also be a degree of curiosity on the part of the interviewee and probably a genuine level of interest in the research, related to the reason why the request to participate was accepted. This curiosity and interest will offer an opening for both parties to start a conversation, probably before the 'intended discussion' commences. You may find it appropriate to follow the initial discussion by demonstrating interest in the interviewee by asking about her or his role within the host organisation. However, you need to make sure that these opening moves to demonstrate credibility and friendliness, and to relax and develop a positive relationship, are not overstated, so that too much time is used and the interviewee starts to become bored or restive.

The start of the interview needs to be shaped by you. It is your opportunity to allay, wherever possible, the interviewee's uncertainties about providing data, establish the participant's rights and, based upon this, hopefully, obtain informed consent. Box 10.9 provides a structure that you can adapt for starting your interviews.

An assurance from you that confidential information is not being sought should make interviewees more relaxed and open about the data that they are willing to provide you. Combined with assurances about anonymity, this should increase the level of confidence in your trustworthiness and reduce the possibility of interviewee or response bias. You can also demonstrate your commitment to confidentiality by not naming other individuals or organisations that have participated in your research, or by talking about the data you obtained from them.

Box 10.9
Focus on student research

Opening a semi-structured interview

As part of her research project, Beth undertook a series of semi-structured interviews with freelance consultants working for a range of organisations. She covered the following points at the start of each interview:

- The participant was thanked for considering the request for access and for agreeing to the meeting.
- The purpose of the research and its progress to date were outlined briefly. As part of this, the participant was given an information sheet to keep.
- The previously agreed right to confidentiality and anonymity was reiterated by stating that nothing said by the participant would be attributed to

him/her without first seeking and obtaining permission.
- The participant's right not to answer any question was emphasised and that the interview would be stopped if the participant wished.
- The participant was told about the nature of the outputs to which the research was intended to lead and what would happen to the data collected during and after the project.
- The offer to provide a summary of the research findings to the interviewee was also restated and the participant was told when this would happen.
- The request to record the interview electronically was restated and, where agreed, this was used subsequently.
- Before the substantive discussion started, Beth again requested permission to undertake the interview, summarised the themes to be covered, confirmed the amount of time available and requested that the participant read and signed the informed consent form.

All of these points were dealt with within the first few minutes of the interview.

Approach to questioning

When conducted appropriately, your approach to questioning should reduce the scope for bias during the interview and increase the reliability of the information obtained. Your questions need to be phrased clearly, so that the interviewee can understand them, and you should ask them in a neutral tone of voice. The use of open questions should help to avoid bias. These can then be followed up by the use of appropriately worded probing questions. The use of these types of question will help you to explore the topic and to produce a fuller account. These types of questions are discussed more fully in the following sub-section.

Conversely, questions that seek to lead the interviewee or which indicate bias on your part should be avoided. Perceived interviewer bias may well lead to interviewee or response bias. Long questions or those that are really made up of two or more questions (known as double-barrel questions) should also be avoided if you are to obtain a response to each aspect that you are interested to explore.

Questions should also avoid too many theoretical concepts or jargon since your understanding of such terms may vary from that of your interviewees. Where theoretical concepts or specific terminology need to be used, you will have to ensure that both you and the interviewee have the same understanding (Box 10.10).

When asking questions it is important that, wherever possible, these are grounded in the real-life experiences of your participants rather than being discussed as abstract concepts. One approach to questioning which makes use of key participant experiences is the **critical incident technique**, in which participants are asked to describe in detail a critical incident or number of incidents that are relevant to the research question. A **critical incident** is defined as an activity or event where the consequences were so clear that the participant has a definite idea regarding the effects (Keaveney 1995).

It will also be important to consider when to ask sensitive questions. Leaving these until near the end of an interview will provide your participant with some time to build up trust and confidence in you and to allay any doubts about your intentions, as Box 10.11 illustrates. This will also affect the nature of the questions that you may ask during the early part of an interview, as you attempt to build trust and gain your participant's confidence.

Once this position of trust has been reached and you wish to ask potentially sensitive questions, the wording of these deserves very particular attention in order to avoid any negative inferences related to, for example, responsibility for failure or error. Care taken over the exploration of sensitive questions should help towards the compilation of a fuller and more reliable account.

Box 10.10
Focus on student research

(Mis)understanding terminology

Sven was conducting an interview with the European sales manager of a large multinational corporation. Throughout the interview the sales manager referred to the European Division. Sven assumed that the sales manager meant continental Europe. However, by chance, later questions revealed that, for this organisation, Europe extended into parts of Asia, including Turkey, the United Arab Emirates, Saudi Arabia, Kuwait and Israel. Until this point in the interview, Sven had assumed that these countries were the responsibility of another sales manager!

Box 10.11
Focus on student research

Establishing trust and asking sensitive questions

Sam recalls an occasion when her treatment by her participants altered as her group interview progressed. For the first hour of a two-hour interview it appeared to her that the participants were convinced that she was really there to sell them a consultancy service. When they accepted that she was not going to try to sell them something, the mood of the interview changed and they became much more relaxed and responsive to the questions that Sam wished to ask. It was at this point that she was able to ask and pursue more sensitive questions that could have led to the interview being terminated during the period when the participants mistrusted her motives.

Appropriate use of different types of questions

Formulating appropriate questions to explore areas in which you are interested is critical to achieving success in semi-structured or in-depth interviews. It is also important to word your questions in a factual way, avoiding emotional language. We now discuss the types of question that you can use during semi-structured and in-depth interviews:

Open questions

The use of **open questions** allows participants to define and describe a situation or event. An open question is designed to encourage the interviewee to provide an extensive and developmental answer, and can be used to reveal attitudes or obtain facts. It encourages the interviewee to reply as they wish. An open question is likely to start with, or include, one of the following words: 'what', 'how' or 'why'. Examples of open questions include:

'Why did the organisation introduce its marketing strategy?'
'What methods have been used to make employees redundant?'
'How has corporate strategy changed over the past five years?'

Probing questions

Probing questions are be used to explore responses further that are of significance to the research topic. They may be worded like open questions but request a particular focus or direction. Examples of this type of question include:

'How would you evaluate the success of this new marketing strategy?'
'Why did you choose a compulsory method to make redundancies?'
'What external factors caused the corporate strategy to change?'

These questions may be prefaced with, for example, 'That's interesting . . .' or 'Tell me more about. . .'.

Probing questions can also be used to seek an explanation where you do not understand the interviewee's meaning or where the response does not reveal the reasoning involved. Examples include:

'What do you mean by "bumping" as a means to help to secure volunteers for redundancy?'
'What is the relationship between the new statutory requirements that you referred to and the organisation's decision to set up its corporate affairs department?'

The use of reflection may also help you to probe a theme. This is where you will 'reflect' a statement made by the interviewee by paraphrasing their words. For example:

'Why don't you think that the employees understand the need for advertising?'

The intention will be to encourage exploration of the point made without offering a view or judgement on your part.

Where an open question does not reveal a relevant response, you may also probe further using a supplementary question that rephrases the original question.

Specific and closed questions

These types of question may be used as introductory questions when you commence questioning about a particular interview theme. Examples of this might be:

'Could you tell me about the change to the pricing policy' or
'Can you describe the production process?'

They can also be used to obtain specific information or to confirm a fact or opinion (Section 11.4):

'How many people responded to the customer survey?'
'Has the old Central Region been merged with the Southern Region?'
'Do you prefer the new training programme?'

Other means to further your questioning

There are a number of ways of prompting further answers to a question you have asked. These include:

- follow-up expressions, such as: 'Ah', 'Oh' or 'Um';
- short follow-up statements, such as: 'That's interesting' or 'Really!';
- short follow-up questions, such as: 'Will you please tell me more?', 'When did that happen?' or 'What happened then?';
- short reflective questions where you rephrase what you have just been told to reflect it back, such as: 'So that was when . . .?' or 'They felt the investment had been worthwhile?';
- interpretation and extension questions, where you seek to explore the implications of an answer, such as: 'Because they have diversified into Internet sales, does that mean that they are also going to build new distribution centres?';
- silence, where the participant is effectively invited to fill this by offering more information;
- using these devices in combination to explore a theme, but you will need to be very careful if you use this approach as it may be interpreted as being overbearing, stressful and confrontational. It will be more productive and ethical to maintain an even pace and respectful stance when asking questions.

Types of question to avoid

In phrasing questions, remember that you should avoid using leading or proposing types of question in order to control any bias that may result from their use (Section 11.4).

Nature and impact of your behaviour during the interview

Appropriate behaviour by the researcher should also reduce the scope for bias during the interview. Comments or non-verbal behaviour, such as gestures, which indicate any bias in your thinking, should be avoided. Rather, a neutral (but not an uninterested) response to the interviewee's answers should be used to ensure your own opinions do not bias responses. You should enjoy the interview opportunity, or at least appear to do so; any appearance of boredom on your part is hardly likely to encourage your interviewee!

Your posture and tone of voice may also encourage or inhibit the flow of the discussion. You should sit slightly inclined towards the interviewee and adopt an open posture, avoiding folded arms. This should provide a signal of attentiveness to your interviewee. Tone of voice can also provide a signal to the interviewee. You need to project interest and enthusiasm through your voice, avoiding any impression of anxiety, disbelief, astonishment or other negative signal.

Demonstration of attentive listening skills

The purpose of a semi-structured or in-depth interview will be to understand your participant's explanations and meanings. This type of interaction will not be typical of many of the conversations that you normally engage in, where those involved often compete to speak rather than concentrate on listening. You therefore need to recognise that different skills will be emphasised in this kind of interaction. Attentive listening will involve you attending to and being sensitive to your participants by spending the time needed to listen to them to build your understanding. You will need to hold back your own thoughts where these would compete with those of your participant(s), or stray from the theme being explored.

It will be necessary for you to explore and probe explanations and meanings, but you must also provide the interviewee with reasonable time to develop their responses, and you must avoid projecting your own views.

Scope to summarise and test understanding

You may test your understanding by summarising responses provided by the interviewee. This will allow your participant to tell you whether your summary is adequate and to add points to this to further or correct your understanding where appropriate. This can be a powerful tool for avoiding a biased or incomplete interpretation. It may also act as a means to explore and probe the interviewee's responses further.

In addition you may also ask the interviewee to read through the factual account that you produce of the interview (Section 5.8). Where the interviewee is prepared to undertake this, it will provide a further opportunity for you to test your understanding and for the interviewee to add any further points of relevance that may not previously have been apparent.

Dealing with difficult participants

Inevitably, during the course of your interviews you will meet some participants who are difficult to interview. In such circumstances it is imperative that you remain polite and do not show any irritation. Although it is impossible for us to highlight all the possible variations, the most common difficulties are summarised in Table 10.2, along with suggestions about how you might attempt to deal with them. However, while reading

Table 10.2 Difficult interview participants and suggestions on how to address them

Recognised difficulty	Suggestion
Participant appears willing only to give monosyllabic answers, these being little more than 'yes' or 'no'	Reasons for this are varied If it is due to limited time, or worries about anonymity, then this can be minimised by careful opening of the interview (Box 10.9) If the participant gives these answers despite such precautions, try phrasing your questions in as open a way as possible; also use long pauses to signify that you want to hear more
Participant repeatedly provides long answers which digress from the focus of your interview	Although some digression should be tolerated, as it can lead to aspects in which you are interested, you will need to impose more direction This must be done subtly so as not to cause offence, such as by referring back to an earlier relevant point and asking them to tell you more, or requesting that they pause so you can note down what they have just said
Participant starts interviewing you	This can suggest that you have created rapport. However, you need to stress that you are interested in their opinions and that, if they wish, they can ask you questions at the end
Participant is proud of their status relative to you and wants to show off their knowledge, criticising what you do	This is extremely difficult and at times like this you will have to listen attentively and be respectful Remember that you are also likely to be knowledgeable about the research topic, so be confident and prepared to justify your research and the research design you have chosen
Participant becomes noticeably upset during the interview and, perhaps, starts to cry	Another difficult one for you You need to give your participant time to answer your question and, in particular, do not do anything to suggest that you are feeling impatient If your participant starts crying or is obviously very distressed, it is probably a good idea to explain that the question does not have to be answered Do not end the interview straight away as this is likely to make the participant even more upset

Source: King (2004); authors' experiences

Table 10.2 will give you some ideas of what to do, the best advice we can give is to undertake practice interviews in which a colleague introduces one or more of these 'difficulties' and you have to deal with them!

Approach to recording data

Where possible we believe it is beneficial to audio-record an interview and also make notes as it progresses. Using both methods to record interview data has a number of advantages. Notes provide a backup if the audio-recording does not work. Making notes can help you to maintain your concentration, formulate points to summarise back to the interviewee to test your understanding and devise follow-up probing questions. Note taking demonstrates to your interviewee that her or his responses are important to you. It also allows you to record your own thoughts and any events that would not be evident from the audio-recording. For example, if you think there may be a relationship between two variables that you wish to explore later, if your interviewer uses a facial expression or provides another non-verbal cue, or if someone enters the room, you can make a note about each of these. Most people have their own means of making notes, which may range from an attempt to create a verbatim account to a diagrammatic style that records key words and phrases, perhaps using mind mapping (Section 2.3).

The task of note making in this situation will be a demanding one. As you seek to test your understanding of what your interviewee has told you, this will allow some time to complete your notes concurrently in relation to the particular aspect being discussed. Most interviewees recognise the demands of the task and act accordingly. For example, Adrian recalls one particular interviewee who paused at the end of the main part of each of his answers to allow notes of this to be completed before adding some supplementary data which could also be noted down. However, the actual interview is not the occasion to perfect your interviewing skills, and we advise you to practise in a simulated situation: for example, by watching an interview on television and attempting to produce a set of notes.

To optimise the value from the interview you should compile a full record of the interview, including contextual data. If you cannot do this immediately after the interview, this should be done as soon as possible. Where you do not do this, the detailed understanding of what was said may be lost as well as general points of value. There is also the possibility that you may mix up data from different interviews, where you carry out several of these within a short period of time and you do not complete a record of each one at the time it takes place. Either situation will clearly lead to an issue about the trustworthiness of any data. You therefore need to allocate time to complete a full set of notes soon after the event. In addition to your notes from the actual interview, you should also record the following **contextual data:**

- the location of the interview (e.g. the organisation, the place);
- the date and time;
- the setting of the interview (e.g. was the room quiet or noisy, could you be overheard, were you interrupted?);
- background information about the participant (e.g. role, post title, gender);
- your immediate impression of how well (or badly) the interview went (e.g. was the participant reticent, were there aspects about which you felt you did not obtain answers in sufficient depth?).

You may be wondering how, if you are recording both of these types of data, you can still ensure the anonymity of your participants where this has been promised. As we outlined in Section 6.6, the best course of action is to ensure that your data are completely and genuinely anonymised. To help to achieve this you should store the contextual data separately from your interview transcripts. We suggest that you should only be able to link these two sets of data by using a 'key', such as an impersonal code number. Where it is absolutely necessary to retain a 'key' that allows participants to be linked to their data using their real name, this 'key' should be kept securely and separately, not by those who control the data.

Audio-recording your data where permission is given, making notes, compiling a full record of the interview immediately or soon after it has occurred and producing a set of contextual data and related memos (Chapter 13) are all means to control bias and produce reliable data. Most interviewers audio-record their interviews, where permission is given. Audio-recording interviews has both advantages and disadvantages and these are summarised in Table 10.3.

Permission should always be sought to audio-record an interview. You should also explain why you believe it would be beneficial to use an audio-recorder and to offer guarantees about your participant's rights over its use. Where it is likely to have a detrimental effect, it is better not to use a recorder. However, most interviewees adapt quickly to the use of the recorder. It is more ethical to allow your interviewee to maintain

Table 10.3 Advantages and disadvantages of audio-recording the interview

Advantages	Disadvantages
Allows the interviewer to concentrate on questioning and listening	May adversely affect the relationship between interviewee and interviewer (possibility of 'focusing' on the audio-recorder rather than the interview process)
Allows questions formulated at an interview to be accurately recorded for use in later interviews where appropriate	May inhibit some interviewee responses and reduce reliability
Can re-listen to the interview, especially during data analysis	Possibility of a technical problem
Accurate and unbiased record provided	Time required to transcribe the audio-recording (Section 13.4)
Allows direct quotes to be used	
Permanent record for others to use	

Source: authors' experience

Box 10.12
Checklist

To help you conduct your semi-structured or in-depth interview

Appearance at the interview
✔ How will your appearance at the interview affect the willingness of the interviewee to share data?

Opening the interview
✔ How will you open the interview to gain the confidence of your interviewee?
✔ What will you tell your interviewee about yourself, the purpose of your research, its funding and your progress?
✔ What concerns, or need for clarification, may your interviewee have?
✔ How will you seek to overcome these concerns or provide this clarification?
✔ In particular, how do you intend to use the data to which you are given access, ensuring, where appropriate, its confidentiality and your interviewee's anonymity?
✔ What will you tell your interviewee about their right not to answer particular questions and to end the interview should they wish?
✔ How will you explain the structure of the interview?

Asking questions and behaviour during the interview
✔ How will you use appropriate language and tone of voice, and avoid jargon when asking questions or discussing themes?
✔ How will you word open questions appropriately to obtain relevant data?
✔ How will you word probing questions to build on, clarify or explain your interviewee's responses?
✔ How will you avoid asking leading questions that may introduce forms of bias?
✔ Have you devised an appropriate order for your questions to avoid asking sensitive questions too early where this may introduce interviewee bias?
✔ How will you maintain a check on the interview themes that you intend to cover and to steer the discussion where appropriate to raise and explore these aspects?
✔ How will you avoid overzealously asking questions and pressing your interviewee for a response where it should be clear that they do not wish to provide one?
✔ How will you avoid projecting your own views or feelings through your actions or comments?
✔ How might you identify actions and comments made by your interviewee that indicate an aspect of the discussion that should be explored in order to reveal the reason for the response?
✔ How will you listen attentively and demonstrate this to your interviewee?

Box 10.12
Checklist (*continued*)

To help you conduct your semi-structured or in-depth interview

✔ How will you summarise and test your understanding of the data that are shared with you in order to ensure accuracy in your interpretation?

✔ Where appropriate, how will you deal with difficult participants while remaining polite?

Recording data during the interview

✔ How will you record the data that are revealed to you during the interview? Where this involves using an audio-recorder, have you raised this as a request and provided a reason why it would help you to use this technique?

✔ How will you allow your interviewee to maintain control over the use of an audio-recorder, where used, if they wish to do this?

✔ Have you practised to ensure you can carry out a number of tasks at the same time, including listening, note taking and identifying where you need to probe further?

Closing the interview

✔ How will you draw the interview to a close within the agreed time limit and thank the interviewee for their time and the data they have shared with you?

control over the recorder so that if you ask a question that they are prepared to respond to, but only if their words are not audio-recorded, they have the option to switch it off (Section 6.6). It will inevitably be necessary to make notes in this situation.

10.7 Managing logistical and resource issues
管理逻辑和来源问题

Issues

Time

Interviewing is a time-consuming process. Where the purpose of the interview is to explore themes or to explain findings, the process may call for a fairly lengthy discussion. In such cases the time required to obtain data is unlikely to be less than one hour and could easily exceed this, perhaps taking two hours or longer. This may have an adverse impact on the number and representativeness of those who are willing to be interview participants, as we discussed earlier. Where managers or other potential participants receive frequent requests to participate in research projects, they will clearly need to consider how much of their time they may be willing to devote to such activities. It will therefore be important for you to establish credibility with, and to engender the interest of, potential interviewees.

Cost and other resources

Your decision to collect data through interviewing will have particular resource issues. Conducting interviews may become a costly process where it is necessary to travel to the location of participants, although this can be kept to a minimum by cluster sampling (Section 7.2) or using the Internet (Section 10.9). Interviews are almost certainly likely to be more expensive than using self-completed or telephone questionnaires to collect data. Choice of method should be determined primarily by the nature of the research question and objectives rather than by cost considerations. This highlights the need to examine the feasibility of the proposed question and research strategy in relation to resource constraints, including time available and expense, before proceeding to the collection of data.

Logistics

Where your research question and objectives require you to undertake semi-structured or in-depth interviews, you need to consider the logistics of scheduling interviews. Thought needs to be given to the number of interviews to be arranged within a given period, and to the time required to compose notes and/or transcribe audio-recordings of each one, and undertake an initial analysis of the data collected (Section 13.4).

Management

Time management

In the preceding sub-section, the issue of time required to collect data through interviewing was raised. You need to consider very carefully the amount of time that will be required to conduct an interview. In our experience, the time required to undertake qualitative research interviews is usually underestimated. The likely time required should be referred to clearly in any initial contact, and it may be better to suggest that interviews are envisaged to last up to, say, one, one and a half, or two hours, so that a willing participant sets aside sufficient time. Some negotiation is in any case possible with an interested participant who feels unable to agree to a request for, say, two hours but who is prepared to agree to a briefer meeting. The interview can also be arranged at a time when the interviewee will be under least pressure.

Interview scheduling

Another possible strategy is to arrange two or more shorter interviews in order to explore a topic thoroughly. This might have the added advantage of allowing participants to reflect on the themes raised and questions being asked, and therefore to provide a fuller account and more accurate set of data. In order to establish this option, it may be beneficial to arrange an initial meeting with a potential participant to discuss this request, where you will be able to establish your credibility. A series of exploratory interviews may then be agreed. Consideration also needs to be given to the number of interviews that may be undertaken in a given period. It is easy to overestimate what is practically possible (Box 10.13).

These are all factors that need to be considered in the scheduling of semi-structured and in-depth interviews. Where you are undertaking interviews at one establishment, it may be more practical to undertake a number of interviews in one day, although there is still a need to maintain concentration, make notes and write up information, and to conduct your initial analysis. Even in this situation, conducting more than three interviews per day is likely to be challenging.

Interview management

The nature of semi-structured or in-depth interviews also has implications for the management of the time available during the meeting. The use of open-ended questions and reliance on participant responses means that, while you must remain responsive to the objectives of the interview and the time constraint, interviewees need the opportunity to

Box 10.13
Focus on student research

Calculating the number of in-depth interviews to be undertaken in one day

Feroz arranged two interviews in a capital city during the course of a day, which involved travelling some miles across the city during the lunch hour. Two interviews appeared to be a reasonable target. However, a number of logistical issues were experienced even in relation to the plan to undertake two such interviews in one day. These issues included the following: the total travelling time to and from the city; the time to find the appropriate buildings; the transfer time during a busy period; the time to conduct the interviews; the need to maintain concentration, to probe responses, to make initial notes and then to write these up without too much time elapsing. Because of his experience, Feroz took a decision not to conduct more than one interview per day where significant travel was involved, even though this necessitated more journeys and greater expense.

provide full answers. You should avoid making frequent interruptions but will need to cover the themes and questions indicated and probe responses in the time available. The intensive nature of the discussion and the need to be clear about your understanding of what has been revealed means that time must be found to write up notes as soon as possible after an interview.

Recording and transcription

Where an audio-recorder has been used (Section 10.6), you will need to decide whether to work directly from the recording or to produce a transcription of all or parts of the recording. This decision will depend on your research strategy and the way in which you intend to analyse your qualitative data (Chapter 13). For example, using a Grounded Theory strategy (Sections 5.5 and 13.9) is likely to mean that you will need to transcribe the whole of each interview. Each hour of recording is likely to take at least seven hours to transcribe or to process ready for entry into computer-assisted qualitative data analysis software, unless you are a very competent audio-typist, or you know one who will undertake this task for you! Use of software to assist the transcription of audio-recordings may also be helpful.

In some cases it may not only be necessary to transcribe an audio-recording but also to translate it from the one language to another. Translations require care to ensure that the meanings contained in the original or source language are reproduced authentically in the translated language. We consider potential problems associated with translations in Section 11.4 and outline different translation techniques in Table 11.4, together with their respective advantages and disadvantages.

10.8   Group interviews and focus groups   分组访谈和焦点小组

Semi-structured and in-depth interviews may also be conducted on a group basis, where the interviewer asks questions to a group of participants. Figure 10.1 summarised forms of interview earlier in this chapter. A variety of terms are used interchangeably to describe group interviews, which are often assumed to have equivalent meanings (Boddy 2005). These include focus group, group interview, group discussion and various combinations of these words! In this section we use **group interview** as a general

Box 10.14
Focus on management research

Using group interviews in research about pay

Hakonen, Maaniemi and Hakanen (2011) undertook a study of perceptions about group-based pay published in *The International Journal of Human Resource Management*. Their data collection was based on the use of semi-structured group interviews. The three researchers conducted a total of 29 group interviews with 88 employees drawn from six public-sector organisations.

They report that each interview took 45 to 60 minutes to conduct. Each interview commenced with a short briefing about its purpose and to provide assurances about confidentiality. An interview guide was designed to conduct each interview. The use of the interview guide also helped to ensure some level of consistency between the conduct of different interviews, as each was conducted by either researcher working alone. The interview guide included a list of research themes and participants were encouraged to discuss these through the course of the interview. A particular focus for researcher intervention related to asking participants to provide reasons for their perceptions about the pay system.

Participants agreed for the interviews to be audio-recorded and these were then transcribed in their entirety before being checked and analysed.

term to describe all semi-structured and in-depth interviews conducted with two or more interviewees. In contrast, and as suggested by Figure 10.1, the term **focus group** is used to refer to those group interviews where the topic is defined clearly and precisely and there is a focus on enabling and recording interactive discussion between participants (Carson et al. 2001; Krueger and Casey 2009; Box 10.14).

Typically group interviews (and focus groups) involve between 4 and 12 participants, the precise number depending upon the nature of the participants, the topic matter and the skill of the interviewer. Inevitably, the more complex the subject matter the smaller the number of interviewees. Participants are normally chosen using non-probability sampling, often with a specific purpose in mind (Section 7.3), such as they are typical of the group being researched or they represent those who are critical to a particular operation. For many group interviews the underlying reason is that you believe you will learn a great deal from these specific individuals. Krueger and Casey (2009: 21) refer to such participants as being 'information rich'.

If you are thinking about using group interviews, or specifically focus groups, consideration of the following issues may help.

• Where your research project (or part of it) occurs within an organisation the request to participate in a group interview may be received by individuals as an instruction rather than allowing them a choice about whether to take part. This may be the case where an organisation is acting as a host for your research and the request is sent in the name of a manager, or because of your own position in the organisation. Where this is the case it is likely to lead to some level of non-attendance, or to unreliable data. In our experience, participants often welcome the chance to 'have their say'. However, where any request may be perceived as indicating lack of choice, to gain their confidence and participation you will need to exercise care over the wording to be used in the request that is sent to them to take part. You will also need to exercise similar care in your introduction to the group when the interview occurs in order to provide a clear assurance about confidentiality.

- Once your sample has been selected, participants should be grouped so as not to inhibit each individual's possible contribution. This may be related to lack of trust, to perceptions about status differences or because of the dominance of certain individuals. The nature and selection of each group will affect the first two elements. We would advise using a series of horizontal slices through an organisation so that, within each group, participants have a similar status and similar work experiences. (Using a vertical slice would introduce perceptions about status differences and variations in work experience.) In this way, group interviews can be conducted at a number of levels within an organisation. A reference may be made about the nature of the group to provide reassurance, and you may consider asking people to introduce themselves by their first name only without referring to their exact job.

- To realise the benefits of a group interview, it is important to encourage every person in a group to participate. This commences when you ask each person to introduce himself or herself. You may also need to encourage contributions by drawing group members into the discussion, particularly where some appear reluctant to take part. This needs to be managed sensitively and participation may increase naturally as group members become more familiar with each other. Occasions may occur during a group interview when participants talk over one another and you will need to manage the flow of contributions while ensuring that each participant has an opportunity to offer her or his contribution. Where one or two people dominate the discussion, you should seek to reduce their contributions by encouraging others. This may be attempted in a specific way:

  'What do you think, Yuksel?'
  'How does Emma's point relate to the one that you raised, Kristie?'

  A question posed more generally to other group members should also have the effect of inhibiting the contribution of a dominant member:

  'What do other people think about this?'
  'What do you think about Johan's suggestion?'

  The interviewer may also seek to manage the flow of the discussion through using non-verbal signals. You may try to reduce the contribution of a dominant member by temporarily minimising eye contact with him or her and draw others into the discussion by looking or gesturing in their direction. You will need to remain attentive throughout the interview, appearing friendly and relaxed in your approach but also purposeful and interested, encouraging each member to take part and providing opportunities to listen to and discuss contributions.

- You will need to ensure that participants understand each other's contributions and that you develop an accurate understanding of the points being made. Asking a participant to clarify the meaning of a particular contribution, where it has not been understood, and testing understanding through summarising should help to ensure this.

- You will need to consider the location and setting for a group interview. It is advisable to conduct the interview in a neutral setting rather than, say, in a manager's office, where participants may not feel relaxed. There should be no likelihood of interruption or being overheard. You should consider the layout of the seating in the room where the interview is to be held. Where possible, arrange the seating in a circular fashion so that everyone will be facing inward and so that they will be an equal distance from the central point of this circle.

- Finally, students often ask, 'When will I know that I have undertaken sufficient group interviews or focus groups?' Writing about focus groups, Krueger and Casey (2009) suggest that you should plan to undertake three or four group interviews with any one type of participant. If after the third or fourth group interview you are no longer receiving new information you will have reached **saturation**, in which case you will have heard the full range of ideas.

The demands of conducting all types of group interview, including focus groups, and the potential wealth of ideas that may flow from them mean that it is likely to be difficult to manage the process and note key points at the same time. We have managed to overcome this in two ways: by audio-recording group interviews or using two interviewers. Where two interviewers are used, one person facilitates the discussion and the other person makes notes. We would recommend that you use two interviewers, even if you are audio-recording the group interview, as it will allow one interviewer to concentrate fully on managing the process while the other ensures the data are recorded. Where you cannot audio-record the group interview, you will need to write up any notes immediately afterwards. As with one-to-one interviews, your research will benefit from the making of notes about the nature of the interactions that occur in the group interviews that you conduct. We would not advise you to undertake more than one group interview in a day on your own because of the danger of losing or confusing data.

Group interviews

In a group interview your role will be to ensure that all participants have the opportunity to state their points of view in answer to your questions, and to record the resulting data. This type of interview can range from being structured to unstructured, although it tends to be relatively unstructured and fairly free-flowing in terms of both breadth and depth of topics. The onus will be placed firmly on you to explain the interview's purpose, to encourage participants to relax, and to initiate, encourage and direct the discussion. The use of this method is likely to necessitate a balance between encouraging participants to provide answers to a particular question or questions that you introduce, and allowing them to range more freely in discussion where this may reveal data that provide you with important insights. Thus once you have opened the interview (Box 10.9) and the discussion is established, it will need to be managed carefully.

Group interactions may lead to a highly productive discussion as interviewees respond to your questions and evaluate points made by the group. However, as the opportunity to develop an individual level of rapport with each participant is less (compared with a one-to-one interview), there may also emerge a group effect where certain participants effectively try to dominate the interview while others may feel inhibited. This may result in some participants publicly agreeing with the views of others, while privately disagreeing. As a consequence a reported consensus may, in reality, be a view that nobody wholly endorses and nobody disagrees with (Stokes and Bergin 2006). You will therefore need to test the validity of emergent views by trying to encourage involvement of all group members and pursuing the interview's exploratory purpose through the use of open and probing questions. A high level of skill will be required in order for you to be able to conduct this type of discussion successfully, as well as to try to record its outcomes.

Despite this reference to the potential difficulties of using group interviews, there are distinct advantages arising from their use. Because of the presence of several participants, this type of situation allows a breadth of points of view to emerge and for the group to respond to these views. A dynamic group can generate or respond to a number of ideas and evaluate them, thus helping you to explore or explain concepts. You are also likely to benefit from the opportunity that this method provides in terms of allowing your participants to consider points raised by other group members and to challenge one another's views. In one-to-one interviews, discussion is of course limited to the interviewer and interviewee. Stokes and Bergin (2006) highlight that while group interviews, and in particular focus groups, are able to identify principal issues accurately, they are not able to provide the depth and detail in relation to specific issues that can be obtained from individual interviews.

The use of group interviews may also provide an efficient way for you to interview a larger number of individuals than would be possible through the use of one-to-one interview. Linked to this point, their use may allow you to adopt an interview-based strategy that can more easily be related to a representative sample, particularly where the research project is being conducted within a specific organisation or in relation to a clearly defined population. This may help to establish the credibility of this research where an attempt is made to overcome issues of bias associated with interviews in general and this type in particular.

Group interviews can also help to identify key themes that will be used to develop items that are included in a questionnaire. This particular use of group interviews may inform subsequent parts of your data collection, providing a clearer focus. For example, the initial use of group interviews can lead to a 'bottom-up' generation of concerns and issues, which subsequently inform a questionnaire's content.

Focus groups

Focus groups are well known because of the way they have been used by political parties to test voter reactions to particular policies and election strategies, and in market research to test reactions to products, as well as being used in academic research (Macnaghten and Myers 2007). A **focus group**, sometimes called a 'focus group interview', is a group interview that focuses upon a particular issue, product, service or topic by encouraging discussion among participants and the sharing of perceptions in an open and tolerant environment (Krueger and Casey 2009). Participant interaction is a key feature of focus group design, although this focus on enabling interactive discussion is used for two distinct purposes.

Positivist or critical realist researchers use the focus group to encourage interactions between participants as an effective means to articulate pre-held views about a particular issue or topic. The aim of using focus groups in this way is to reveal these pre-held views. Interpretivist researchers use focus groups as a means to construct meanings through social interactions and sense making about a topic. The aim of using focus groups for this purpose relates to the ability to analyse how participant interactions and group dynamics lead to the construction of shared meanings (Belzile and Oberg 2012).

If you are running a focus group, you will probably be referred to as the **moderator** or 'facilitator'. These labels emphasise the dual role of the person running the focus group, namely to:

* keep the group within the boundaries of the topic being discussed;
* generate interest in the topic and encourage discussion, while at the same time not leading the group towards certain opinions.

The purpose of a focus group is likely to affect the level of interviewer-led structure and intervention that is required. Focus groups used to reveal participants' views are likely to be associated with greater structure; those used to study how participants interact are likely to be associated with less structure. Participants are selected because they have certain characteristics in common that are relevant to the topic being discussed. Discussions may be conducted several times, with similar participants, to enable trends and patterns to be identified. The size of a focus group may vary according to the nature of the topic. A focus group designed to obtain views about a product is likely to be larger than one that explores a topic related to a more emotionally involved or sensitive construct, such as attitudes to performance-related pay or the way in which employees rate their treatment by management. You may also choose to design smaller groups as you seek to develop your competence in relation to the use of this interviewing technique to collect qualitative data.

电话和互联网访谈

10.9 Telephone and Internet-mediated interviews

Most semi-structured or in-depth interviews occur on a face-to-face basis. Qualitative interviews may also be conducted by telephone, using a voice/listening-only mode of interviewing (Box 10.15). Developments in video telephony are also opening up new possibilities to conduct interviews through use of a video calling service. This means that interviews may be conducted by mobile phone using a particular software application or electronically via the Internet. In the next sub-section, we discuss potential advantages and disadvantages of using telephone interviews. However, the research methods literature has not yet caught up with the use of video telephony as opposed to voice-only, traditional telephony, so you will need to evaluate your own experience of access to and use of video chat apps such as Skype™ or Facetime™ when you consider how you might seek to conduct qualitative interviews. In the following sub-section, we consider Internet-mediated interviewing.

Telephone interviews

Conducting semi-structured or in-depth interviews by telephone can offer advantages associated with access, speed and lower cost. In particular you may be able to interview participants with whom it would otherwise be impractical to do so due to the distance and prohibitive costs involved and time required. Even where 'long-distance' access is not an issue, conducting interviews by telephone may still offer advantages associated with speed of data collection and lower cost. In other words, this approach may be seen as more convenient.

There are, however, potential disadvantages to the use of telephone interviews to collect qualitative data. We have already discussed the importance of establishing personal contact in this type of interviewing. The intention of semi-structured or in-depth interviewing is to be able to explore participants' responses and meanings. This is likely to become more feasible once rapport and trust have been established. Establishing rapport and trust will be particularly important where you wish to conduct interviews that ask your participants to be reflective and to provide you with richly detailed and in-depth accounts. Conducting this type of exploratory discussion by telephone will be difficult if your participants are uncomfortable with this mode of interviewing. This may lead to issues of (reduced) reliability where your participants are reluctant to engage in this type of exploratory discussion by telephone, or even a refusal to take part.

In spite of this concern, researchers conducting semi-structured and in-depth qualitative interviews by telephone report successful outcomes. For example, Holt (2010) reports using telephone interviews to collect narrative accounts. These interviews produced a rich set of qualitative data, with each one lasting on average an hour. Trier-Bieniek (2012) conducted 39 telephone interviews to produce a rich set of qualitative data. The reported advantages of using telephone interviews in these research projects go beyond those related to access, speed and lower cost. Both Holt (2010) and Trier-Bieniek (2012) report that the fact that they did not meet their participants actually helped in terms of producing open and full accounts. There are a number of reasons for this outcome. The anonymity of a voice/listening-only mode of interviewing helped to reduce participants' inhibitions in providing accounts about very personal matters. This suggests that exploring sensitive issues by telephone interview may in some contexts be advantageous. The use of the telephone also facilitated participation, by allowing participants to chose a suitable time of day to be interviewed, to stop an interview in progress when this became unavoidable and to rearrange a time for it to continue, and to move around their environment when necessary to avoid being overheard. Participants also reported to Holt (2010) and Trier-Bieniek (2012) that they had enjoyed this mode of participation and many would not have found it so easy to take part in a face-to-face interview.

It is important to note that in both of these projects there were contextual factors which helped to facilitate the research. Both researchers found empathy with their participants and developed rapport with them; some participants expressed enjoyment and gratitude at being able to take part and for the opportunity to express their views. This indicates a positive outcome for researchers and participants but you may not be so fortunate in terms of your own research topic and intended participants. Choice of research method and participant consent will be contingent on a range of contextual factors related to your research.

There are also practical issues that need to be managed when using telephone interviews. These include your ability to control the pace of a telephone interview and to record data. Conducting an interview by telephone and taking notes is a difficult and demanding process. In addition, the normal visual cues that allow your participant to control the flow of the data that they share with you would be absent in a voice-only telephone interview. In this type of interview you lose the opportunity to witness the non-verbal behaviour of your participant, which may adversely affect your interpretation of how far to pursue a particular line of questioning. Your participant may be less willing to provide you with as much time to talk to them in comparison with a face-to-face interview. You may also encounter difficulties in developing more complex questions in comparison with a face-to-face interview situation (Box 10.15). Finally, attempting to gain access through a telephone call may lead to ethical issues (Section 6.6).

There are strategies that may help you to overcome some of these practical issues when you use telephone interviews. You can audio-record a (voice-only) telephone interview with your participant's consent. You will find it helpful to reflect on a telephone interview after it ends and make notes about it. Your reflections and notes may help you to improve your approach to your next telephone interview. You should also find it helpful to write a number of interview questions and to revise these to make sure they are clear and succinct before undertaking interviews (Box 10.15). You may also find it helpful to practise conducting a telephone interview (about another topic) with a friend.

As noted, developments in video telephony are opening up new possibilities to conduct interviews through use of a video calling service. Conducting an interview by mobile phone or another supported device may overcome some of the potential disadvantages of using voice-only telephony. Using this technology may help to build rapport and trust, while the ability for you and your participant to see each other and to interact visually should provide both of you with some contextual cues, even if these are limited by the screen frame. Using a screen-recording application with your participant's consent will provide you with a recording of the interview. You will need to ensure that you and your

Box 10.15
Focus on management research

Comparing the nature of spoken interactions in telephone interviews with those in face-to-face interviews

Irvine et al. (2012) compared the nature of spoken interactions in two sets of semi-structured, qualitative interviews: one set conducted by telephone and the other carried out face-to-face, in a study published in *Qualitative Research*. Both sets of interviews had originally been conducted by Irvine (2008) for a study on mental health and employment.

Six interviews had been conducted by telephone and five face-to-face. All 11 were conducted by the same researcher and carried out before the idea to compare them was devised, with choice of interview mode being determined by geographical distance rather than interviewee preference. The authors believe that these factors reduced any bias and threats to reliability in their findings.

The aim of the study was to evaluate the impact of interview mode on the nature of spoken interactions, based on actual data that had been transcribed systematically to facilitate detailed analysis. Their analysis revealed five areas where interactional differences were evident between interview modes (face-to-face versus telephone).

In face-to-face interviews, the researcher was more likely to interact with the interviewee during an answer, say by helping an interviewee find an appropriate word or by summarising the answer to show understanding. Possible explanations suggested for this may be because greater rapport was developed during face-to-face interviews, and because during telephone interviews the interviewer needed

to concentrate on listening given the absence of non-verbal prompts or signals.

Also in face-to-face interviews, the researcher used verbal acknowledgements (e.g. by saying 'Yeah', 'Ah', 'Oh', 'Um', etc.) to the interviewee more frequently than in telephone interviews. This is surprising because use of verbal acknowledgements may be expected to be more frequently used in telephone interviews to compensate for the lack of visual contact. Possible explanations suggested for this lesser frequency during telephone interviews may be because of the need to concentrate on listening and also because the researcher used the lack of visual contact to concentrate on taking notes.

In telephone interviews, interviewees were slightly more likely to ask the researcher to clarify or repeat her questions. This did not mean that interviewees experienced difficulty in their understanding; instead this may be explained by the quality of the phone connection, the effort and concentration required in a listening-only mode of interview and resulting fatigue, and the need for interview questions to be phrased clearly and succinctly.

Also in telephone interviews, interviewees were more likely to ask if their responses were adequate. Possible explanations suggested for this may be related to lack of visual cues and the reduced scope to discuss the purpose of the research at the start of the interview with regard to the lesser rapport developed in telephone interviews and greater level of task orientation in this interview mode.

Finally telephone interviews were shorter than face-to-face ones. Possible explanations suggested for this relate to lesser rapport developed and greater effort required, with the implication that telephone interviews may be less suitable for research studies that are designed to rely on richly detailed and in-depth accounts. However, Irvine et al. (2012) also note that this comparative study of interactional differences was small scale and that further research in this area would be beneficial.

participant both have access to a supported and compatible platform before considering using this technology.

Developments in technology therefore add to ways in which you may be able to conduct interviews. In addition to face-to-face interviews, you may consider using telephone interviews based on voice-only or video telephony. In the next sub-section we also consider choice of other types of electronic interview. In considering the choice open to you, you will need to focus on the preferences of your intended participants and the need to be guided by ethical principles. You will need to be aware of any cultural norms related to the nature and conduct of telephone conversations.

Internet-mediated interviewing

Interviews can be conducted using mobile and computing technologies via the Internet. These are collectively referred to as **electronic interviews**. A distinction is often made between electronic interviews conducted in real time (**synchronous**) and those not conducted in real time (**asynchronous**). An asynchronous electronic interview will be conducted through exchanges of text and can involve gaps in time between the interviewer asking a question and the participant providing an answer. In this way it is sometimes partly undertaken offline. Figure 10.2 shows the main ways in which electronic interviews are conducted: by email, instant messaging and web conferencing. The nature of these forms of electronic interview varies and each is associated with different advantages and disadvantages. Electronic interviews are being used in a wider range of applications (Box 10.16).

An email interview is generally described as an asynchronous form because of the nature of the technology used and because it is not necessary to ask questions and answer these sequentially without any time gaps. However, it may be possible to conduct an email interview in one period, where the interviewee responds immediately to each question and emails continue to be exchanged until the interviewer draws it to a close and thanks the interviewee for her/his participation. This may be after a pre-arranged period has been reached. We return to consider synchronous text-based interviewing later in this section.

An **email interview** therefore consists of a series of emails each containing a question or small number of questions and the replies to these. Although you can send one email containing a series of questions, this would really be an Internet questionnaire (Sections 11.2 and 11.5). After making contact and obtaining agreement to participate, you initially email a question or small number of questions, or introduce a topic to which the participant will (hopefully) reply. You then need to respond to each reply, asking further questions, raising points of clarification and pursuing ideas that are of further interest. Email interviews may last for some time where there is a delay between each question being asked and an answer being received. This may be advantageous in terms of allowing time for reflection on the part of the interviewer, in forming appropriate questions, and the participant, in terms of providing a considered response, but it may also mean that the interviewee may lose focus and interest so that the email interview ends without all questions being answered. Another advantage related to all forms of text-based electronic interview is that data are recorded as they are typed in, thereby removing problems associated with other forms of recording and transcription such as cost, accuracy and participants' apprehension.

An electronic interview conducted by text-based instant messaging is described as a synchronous form because the technology uses real-time transmission. However, there

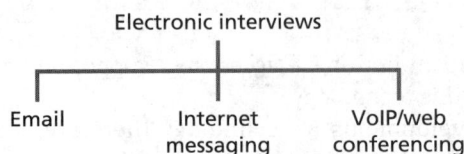

Electronic interviews

Email   Internet   VoIP/web
             messaging   conferencing

Figure 10.2 Forms of electronic interview

Box 10.16 Focus on research in the news

The avatar will see you now: interviewers go virtual

By Andrew Bounds

Jobseekers may no longer have to leave the comfort of home as a British software developer introduces interview by avatar.

Shortlister.com uses lifelike avatars to pose scripted questions over the Internet while candidates answer through their computer camera.

The system is believed to be the first in the world to use avatars to conduct interviews and is aimed at saving time and money for companies that recruit heavily, such as retailers and restaurants.

Shortlister.com was founded by David Dewey and is based at York St John University's creative incubator.

Mr Dewey said: "The advances in video conferencing and call technology in recent years have led to a dramatic increase in the use of video devices in every aspect of our lives, and recruiters are now taking advantage of these benefits."

Research by Shortlister.com shows that 58 per cent of working people between the ages of 18 and 50 in the UK now use video calling at work or home, and that figure rises to 64 per cent within the 18–24 age group.

"By using an avatar to conduct the interview, our software ensures that the process is professional and consistent while also enabling the recruiting company to hire higher-quality candidates as a result of using this innovative technology," said Mr Dewey.

"For candidates, it makes the experience as natural as possible, simulating interaction with a real person and allowing them to focus on effectively answering the interview questions and presenting themselves professionally."

He said it could reduce the average cost by almost half.

Shortlister.com also cuts out scheduling hassles and ensures consistency by asking all candidates the same set of questions, speeding up the screening process. The pre-recorded interviews can then be easily scored and shared with colleagues at a convenient time and every candidate can be notified after the interview as to whether or not they have been successful.

FT *Source:* Extracts from 'The avatar will see you now: interviewers go virtual', Andrew Bounds, *Financial Times*, 23 February 2014. Copyright © 2014 The Financial Times Ltd.

may be time gaps between the interviewer asking a question and the interviewee providing a response and this type of electronic interview may extend over several periods when both are online. Instant messaging originally developed as a synchronous text service. The technologies which support electronic communication have been advancing rapidly and as a result, instant messaging now supports synchronous text, visual and aural services. We consider electronic interviews using web conferencing later in this section.

Pearce et al. (2014) evaluate the use of electronic interviews using synchronous text-based instant messaging. They intentionally chose this means to conduct electronic interviews because of the sensitive nature of their research topic. They conclude that for research topics where the researcher wishes to ask personal or sensitive questions, the anonymity offered by the interviewer and interviewee typing synchronously to each other is likely to produce reliable and useful data. For these types of research topic the lack of face-to-face contact may prove to be an advantage rather than a disadvantage.

Electronic interviews featuring vision and sound may be conducted using a Voice over Internet Protocol (VoIP) or web conferencing service. There are a multitude of these types of service, providing proprietary software. Services such as Skype™ allow users to conduct electronic interviews in real time. In addition to one-to-one video facilities, this technology facilitates video-conferencing between several users. Skype™ also provides other facilities through which to conduct electronic interviews such as instant messaging. This type of software also facilitates file transfers. As with video telephony discussed earlier, software can be used to produce an audio-visual recording of the interview, providing that the research participant consents to this. Hanna (2012) provides a favourable evaluation of using Skype for research interviewing, referring to advantages associated with access, ability to interact visually, and those discussed earlier in relation to telephone interviews. Hanna also makes the point that use of such an interview mode allows both researcher and participant to remain in their own familiar and safe locations.

Using this technology has significant advantages where the population you wish to interview are geographically dispersed. Using this approach, you may be able to build up rapport with an interviewee during an online interview where you have carefully prepared for this, including sending pre-interview information to your participant, taking into account any cultural differences and practising with this technology. However, as you will remember from Sections 6.5 and 6.6, electronic interviews have their own set of ethical issues that you will need to consider.

10.10 Summary 小结

- The use of semi-structured and in-depth interviews should allow you to collect a rich and detailed set of data, although you will need to develop a sufficient level of competence to conduct these and to be able to gain access to the type of data associated with their use.
- Interviews can be differentiated according to the level of structure and standardisation adopted.
- Semi-structured and in-depth research interviews can be used to explore topics and explain findings.
- There are situations favouring semi-structured and in-depth interviews that will lead you to use either or both of these to collect data. Apart from the purpose of your research, these are related to the significance of establishing personal contact, the nature of your data collection questions, and the length of time required from those who provide data.
- Your research design may incorporate more than one type of interview.
- Semi-structured and in-depth interviews can be used in a variety of research strategies.
- Data quality issues related to reliability/dependability, forms of bias, cultural differences and generalisability/transferability may be overcome by considering why you have chosen to use interviews, recognising that all research methods have limitations and through careful preparation to conduct interviews to avoid bias that would threaten the reliability/dependability and validity/credibility of your data.
- The conduct of semi-structured and in-depth interviews will be affected by the appropriateness of the researcher's appearance, opening comments when the interview

commences, approach to questioning, appropriate use of different types of question, nature of the interviewer's behaviour during the interview, demonstration of attentive listening skills, scope to summarise and test understanding, ability to deal with difficult participants and ability to record data accurately and fully.

- Logistical and resource matters will need to be considered and managed when you use in-depth and semi-structured interviews.
- Apart from one-to-one interviews conducted on a face-to-face basis, you may consider conducting such interviews by telephone or electronically.
- You may consider using group interviews or focus group interviews. There may be particular advantages associated with group interviews, but these are considerably more difficult to manage than one-to-one interviews.

Self-check questions 自测题

Help with these questions is available at the end of the chapter.

10.1 What type of interview would you use in each of the following situations:
   a a market research project?
   b a research project seeking to understand whether attitudes to working from home have changed?
   c following the analysis of a questionnaire?

10.2 What are the advantages of using semi-structured and in-depth interviews?

10.3 During a presentation of your proposal to undertake a research project, which will be based on semi-structured or in-depth interviews, you feel that you have dealt well with the relationship between the purpose of the research and the proposed methodology when one of the panel leans forward and asks you to discuss the trustworthiness and usefulness of your work for other researchers. This is clearly a challenge to see whether you can defend such an approach. How do you respond?

10.4 Having quizzed you about the trustworthiness and usefulness of your work for other researchers, the panel member decides that one more testing question is in order. He explains that interviews are not an easy option. 'It is not an easier alternative for those who want to avoid statistics', he says. 'How can we be sure that you're competent to get involved in interview work, especially where the external credibility of this organisation may be affected by the impression that you create in the field?' How will you respond to this concern?

10.5 What are the key issues to consider when planning to use semi-structured or in-depth interviews?

10.6 What are the key areas of competence that you need to develop in order to conduct an interview successfully?

Review and discussion questions 复习与讨论题

10.7 Watch and, if possible, record a television interview such as one that is part of a chat show or a documentary. It does not matter if you record an interview of only 10 to 15 minutes' duration.
   a As you watch the interview, make notes about what the participant is telling the interviewer. After the interview, review your notes. How much of what was being said did you manage to record?

b If you were able to record the television interview, watch it again and compare your notes with what was actually said. What other information would you like to add to your notes?

c Either watch the interview again or another television interview that is part of a chat show or a documentary. This time pay careful attention to the questioning techniques used by the interviewer. How many of the different types of question discussed in Section 10.5 can you identify?

d How important do you think the non-verbal cues given by the interviewer and the interviewee are in understanding the meaning of what is being said?

10.8 With a friend, each decide on a topic about which you think it would be interesting to interview the other person. Separately develop your interview themes and prepare an interview guide for a semi-structured interview. At the same time, decide which one of the 'difficult' participants in Table 10.2 you would like to role-play when being interviewed.

a Conduct both interviews and, if possible, make a recording. If this is not possible either audio-record or ensure the interviewer takes notes.

b Watch each of the recordings – what aspects of your interviewing technique do you each need to improve?

c If you were not able to record the interview, how good a record of each interview do you consider the notes to be? How could you improve your interviewing technique further?

d As an interviewer, ask your friend an open question about the topic. As your friend answers the question, note down her/his answer. Summarise this answer back to your friend. Then ask your friend to assess whether you have summarised their answer accurately and understood what s/he meant.

10.9 Obtain a transcript of an interview that has already been undertaken. If your university subscribes to online newspapers such as ft.com, these are a good source of business-related transcripts. Alternatively, typing 'interview transcript' into a search engine such as Google or Bing will generate numerous possibilities on a vast range of topics!

a Examine the transcript, paying careful attention to the questioning techniques used by the interviewer. To what extent do you think that certain questions have led the interviewee to certain answers?

b Now look at the responses given by the interviewer. To what extent do you think these are the actual verbatim responses given by the interviewee? Why do you think this?

改进研究项目

Progressing your research project

在你的研究中使用半结构化访谈、深度访谈或分组访谈
Using semi-structured, in-depth or group interviews in your research

- Review your research question(s) and objectives. How appropriate would it be to use non-standardised (qualitative) interviews to collect data? Where it is appropriate, explain the relationship between your research question(s) and objectives, and the use of such interviews.

Where this type of interviewing is not appropriate, justify your decision.

- If you decide that semi-structured or in-depth interviews are appropriate, what practical problems do you foresee? How might you attempt to overcome these practical problems?

- Think about how your interviews are likely to be analysed before you conduct them. This will guide your preparation of the list of interview themes as well as the conduct of your subsequent interviews and data transcription (Chapter 13).

- What threats to the trustworthiness of the data collected are you likely to encounter? How might you overcome these?
- Draft a list of interview themes to be explored and compare these thoroughly with your research question(s) and objectives.
- Ask your project tutor to comment on your judgement about the use of non-standardised (qualitative) interviews, the issues and threats that you have identified, your suggestions to overcome these, and the fit between your interview themes and your research question(s) and objectives.
- Use the questions in Box 1.4 to guide your reflective diary entry.

Self-check answers   自测题答案

10.1 The type of interview that is likely to be used in each of these situations is as follows:

   a A standardised and structured interview where the aim is to develop response patterns from the views of people. The interview schedule might be designed to combine styles so that comments made by interviewees in relation to specific questions could also be recorded.

   b The situation outlined suggests an exploratory approach to research, and therefore an in-depth interview would be most appropriate.

   c The situation outlined here suggests that an explanatory approach is required in relation to the data collected, and in this case a semi-structured interview is likely to be appropriate.

10.2 Reasons that suggest the use of interviews include:

- the exploratory or explanatory nature of your research;
- situations where it will be significant to establish personal contact, in relation to interviewee sensitivity about the nature of the information to be provided and the use to be made of this;
- situations where the researcher needs to exercise control over the nature of those who will supply data;
- situations where there are a large number of questions to be answered;
- situations where questions are complex or open-ended;
- situations where the order and logic of questioning may need to be varied.

10.3 Certainly politely! Your response needs to show that you are aware of the issues relating to reliability/dependability, bias and generalisability/transferability that might arise. It would be useful to discuss how these might be overcome through the following: the design of the research; the keeping of records or a diary in relation to the processes and key incidents of the research project as well as the recording of data collected; attempts to control bias through the process of collecting data; the relationship of the research to theory.

10.4   Perhaps it will be wise to say that you understand his position. You realise that any approach to research calls for particular types of competence. Your previous answer touching on interviewee bias has highlighted the need to establish credibility and to gain the interviewee's confidence. While competence will need to be developed over a period of time, allowing for any classroom simulations and dry runs with colleagues, probably the best approach will be your level of preparation before embarking on interview work. This relates first to the nature of the approach made to those whom you would like to participate in the research project and the information supplied to them, second to your intellectual preparation related to the topic to be explored and the particular context of the organisations participating in the research, and third to your ability to conduct an interview. You also recognise that piloting the interview themes will be a crucial element in building your competence.

10.5   Key issues to consider include the following:
- planning to minimise the occurrence of forms of bias where these are within your control, related to interviewer bias, interviewee bias and sampling bias;
- considering your aim in requesting the research interview and how you can seek to prepare yourself in order to gain access to the data that you hope your participants will be able to share with you;
- devising interview themes that you wish to explore or seek explanations for during the interview;
- sending a list of your interview themes to your interviewee prior to the interview, where this is considered appropriate;
- requesting permission and providing a reason where you would like to use an audio-recorder during the interview;
- making sure that your level of preparation and knowledge (in relation to the research context and your research question and objectives) is satisfactory in order to establish your credibility when you meet your interviewee;
- considering how your intended appearance during the interview will affect the willingness of the interviewee to share data.

10.6   There are several areas where you need to develop and demonstrate competence in relation to the conduct of semi-structured and in-depth research interviews. These areas are:
- opening the interview;
- using appropriate language;
- questioning;
- listening;
- testing and summarising understanding;
- behavioural cues;
- recording data.

Get ahead using resources on the companion website at: **www.pearsoned.co.uk/saunders**.
- Improve your IBM SPSS Statistics and NVivo research analysis with practice tutorials.
- Save time researching on the Internet with the Smarter Online Searching Guide.
- Test your progress using self-assessment questions.
- Follow live links to useful websites.

Chapter 11

Collecting primary data using questionnaires 利用问卷收集原始数据

Learning outcomes 学习目标

By the end of this chapter you should:

- understand the advantages and disadvantages of questionnaires as a data collection method;
- be aware of a range of self-completed (Internet, postal, delivery and collection) and interviewer-completed (telephone, face-to-face) questionnaires;
- be aware of the possible need to combine data collection methods within a research project;
- be able to select and justify the use of appropriate questionnaire methods for a variety of research scenarios;
- be able to design, pilot and deliver a questionnaire to answer research questions and to meet objectives;
- be able to take appropriate action to enhance response rates and to ensure the validity and reliability of the data collected;
- be able to apply the knowledge, skills and understanding gained to your own research project.

11.1 Introduction 引 言

Within business and management research, the greatest use of questionnaires is made within the survey strategy (Section 5.5). However, both experiment and case study research strategies can make use of these methods. Although you probably have your own understanding of the term 'questionnaire', it is worth noting that there are a variety of definitions (Oppenheim 2000). Some people reserve it exclusively for questionnaires where the person answering the question actually records their own answers, when it is **self-completed**. Others use it as a more general term to include interviews in which the questions are asked either face-to-face or by telephone.

In this book we use **questionnaire** as a general term to include all methods of data collection in which each person is asked to respond to the same set of questions in a predetermined order (De Vaus 2014). An alternative term, which is also widely used, is **instrument** (Ekinci 2015). It therefore includes both face-to-face and telephone questionnaires as well as those in which the questions are answered without an interviewer being present, such as the Auchentoshan Distillery's Internet questionnaire. The range of data collection methods that fall under this broad heading, are outlined in the next section (11.2), along with their relative advantages and disadvantages.

The use of questionnaires is discussed in many research methods texts. These range from those that devote a few pages to it to those that specify precisely how you should construct and use them, such as Dillman et al.'s (2014) **tailored design method**. Perhaps not surprisingly,

Questionnaires are a part of our everyday lives. For modules in your course, your lecturers have probably asked you and your fellow students to complete module evaluation questionnaires, thereby collecting data on students' views. Similarly, when we visit a tourist attraction or have a meal in a restaurant there is often the opportunity to complete a comment card or visitor feedback form. Auchentoshan Whisky Distillery, one of Morrison Bowmore Distillers' three distilleries, is no exception. Visitors to the distillery can take a guided tour during which they see the complete single malt whisky production process, including the triple distillation process, usually only associated with Irish whiskey. They can also taste one of the range of Auchentoshan single malt whiskies. At the end of the tour visitors are asked by their tour guide if they would be willing to complete a one-page feedback form. It starts with a brief introduction emphasising the importance of visitors' opinions in helping the Distillery to improve:

Auchentoshan Distillery
Source: © Morrison Bowmore Distillers Ltd.

Here at Auchentoshan Distillery we are dedicated to the continual improvement of our products, services and to the company itself. To assist us in achieving this and to be in with a chance of winning a free bottle of our Single Malt Whisky, we would be grateful if you could tell us what you thought of your experience today– thank you.

This is followed by eight questions including:

Please score the following topics according to the ratings shown:

1. Distillery Tour & Shop	**Score**	**Ratings**
Welcome and friendliness of our staff.	☐	5 = Excellent
How informative was the tour?	☐	4 = Very Good
How interesting was the tour?	☐	3 = Good
The knowledge of the tour guide.	☐	2 = Fair
Our tour in comparison with any other distilleries you may have visited	☐	1 = Poor
Value for money.	☐	
Product range within the shop	☐	
What did you think of the DVD presentation?	☐	
Name of your tour guide:	☐	

4. Have you visited Auchentoshan Distillery before?   Yes ☐   No ☐

5. Would you recommend us to others or return in the future?   Yes ☐   No ☐

7. Comments/Improvements (please tell us what you thought or where we could improve).

Source: Extract from Auchentoshan questionnaire reproduced with permission of Morrison Bowmore Distillers Ltd

Details about the respondent including their name, country and email address are also collected, visitors being asked to tick a box ☑ if they are over 18 years of age, the legal drinking age in the United Kingdom. Anne Kinnes, the Visitor Centre Operations and Development Manager for Morrison Bowmore, said 'We are committed to offering world class service at all our visitors' centres and the most effective way for us to improve our service is to listen to our customers. One of the methods we use is the feedback form, by using the information we collect this enables us to make improvements to our visitor experience.' These data help the Auchentoshan Distillery maintain high levels of visitor satisfaction.

the questionnaire is one of the most widely used data collection methods within the survey strategy. Because each person (respondent) is asked to respond to the same set of questions, it provides an efficient way of collecting responses from a large sample prior to quantitative analysis (Chapter 12). However, before you decide to use a questionnaire we should like to include a note of caution. Many authors (for example, Bell and Waters 2014; Oppenheim 2000) argue that it is far harder to produce a good questionnaire than you might think. You need to ensure that it will collect the precise data that you require to answer your research question(s) and achieve your objectives. This is of paramount importance because, like the Auchentoshan Distillery, you are unlikely to have more than one opportunity to collect the data. In particular, you will be unable to go back to those individuals who choose to remain anonymous and collect additional data using another questionnaire. These, and other issues, are discussed in Section 11.3.

The design of your questionnaire will affect the response rate and the reliability and validity of the data you collect (Section 5.8). These, along with response rates, can be maximised by:

- careful design of individual questions;
- clear and pleasing visual presentation;
- lucid explanation of the purpose;
- pilot testing;
- carefully planned and executed delivery, and return of completed questionnaires.

Together these form Sections 11.4 and 11.5. In Section 11.4 we discuss designing your questionnaire. Delivery and return of the questionnaire is considered in Section 11.5 along with actions to help ensure high response rates.

11.2 An overview of questionnaires   问卷方法概述

When to use questionnaires

We have found that many people use a questionnaire to collect data without considering other methods such as examination of secondary sources (Chapter 8), observation (Chapter 9) and semi-structured or unstructured interviews (Chapter 10). Our advice is to evaluate all possible data collection methods and to choose those most appropriate to your research question(s) and objectives. Questionnaires are usually not particularly good for exploratory or other research that requires large numbers of open-ended questions (Sections 10.2 and 10.3). They work best with standardised questions that you can be confident will be interpreted the same way by all respondents (Robson 2011).

Questionnaires therefore tend to be used for descriptive or explanatory research. Descriptive research, such as that undertaken using attitude and opinion questionnaires and questionnaires of organisational practices, will enable you to identify and describe the variability in different phenomena. In contrast, explanatory or analytical research will enable you to examine and explain relationships between variables, in particular cause-and-effect relationships. These two purposes have different research design requirements (Gill and Johnson 2010), which we shall discuss later (Section 11.3).

Although questionnaires may be used as the only data collection method, it may be better to link them with other methods in a mixed or multiple method research design (Sections 5.3 and 5.5). For example, a questionnaire to discover customers' attitudes can be complemented by in-depth interviews to explore and understand these attitudes (Section 10.3).

Types of questionnaire

The design of a questionnaire differs according to how it is delivered, returned or collected and the amount of contact you have with the respondents (Figure 11.1). **Self-completed questionnaires** are usually completed by the respondents and are often referred to as surveys. Such questionnaires can be distributed to respondents through the Internet (**Internet questionnaire**), respondents either accessing the questionnaire through their web browser using a hyperlink (**Web questionnaire**) or directly via a QR (quick response) code scanned into their mobile device (**mobile questionnaire**). Alternatively the questionnaire can be posted to respondents who return them by post after completion (**postal** or **mail questionnaires**) or delivered by hand to each respondent and collected later (**delivery and collection questionnaires**). Responses to **interviewer-completed questionnaires** are recorded by the interviewer on the basis of each respondent's answers. Questionnaires undertaken using the telephone are known as **telephone questionnaires**. The final category, **face-to-face questionnaires**, refers to those questionnaires where interviewers physically meet respondents and ask the questions face-to-face. These are also known as **structured interviews** but differ from semi-structured and unstructured (in-depth) interviews (Section 10.2), as there is a defined schedule of questions from which interviewers should not deviate.

The choice of questionnaire

Your choice of questionnaire will be influenced by a variety of factors related to your research question(s) and objectives (Table 11.1), and in particular the:

- characteristics of the respondents from whom you wish to collect data;
- importance of reaching a particular person as respondent;
- importance of respondents' answers not being contaminated or distorted;
- size of sample you require for your analysis, taking into account the likely response rate;
- types of question you need to ask to collect your data;
- number of questions you need to ask to collect your data.

These factors will not apply equally to your choice of questionnaire, and for some research questions or objectives may not apply at all. The type of questionnaire you choose will dictate how sure you can be that the respondent is the person whom you

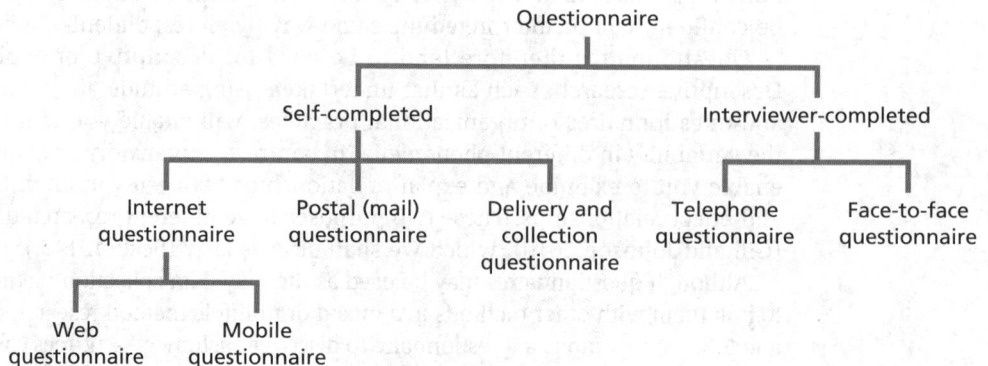

Figure 11.1 Types of questionnaire

Table 11.1 Main attributes of questionnaires

Attribute	Web and mobile	Postal	Delivery and collection	Telephone	Structured interview
Population's characteristics for which suitable	Individuals with access to the Internet, often contacted by email	Literate individuals who can be contacted by post; selected by name, household, organisation, etc.		Individuals who can be telephoned; selected by name, household, organisation, etc.	Any; selected by name, household, organisation, in the street etc.
Confidence that right person has responded	High with email	Low	Low but can be checked at collection	High	
Likelihood of contamination or distortion of respondent's answer	Low	May be contaminated by consultation with others		Occasionally distorted or invented by interviewer	Occasionally contaminated by consultation or distorted/invented by interviewer
Size of sample	Large, can be geographically dispersed		Dependent on number of field workers	Dependent on number of interviewers	
Likely response rate[a]	Variable to low, 30–50% reasonable for web within organisations, otherwise 10% or even lower	Variable, 30–50% reasonable		High, 50–70% reasonable	
Feasible length of questionnaire	Equivalent of 6–8 A4 pages, minimise scrolling down	6–8 A4 pages		Up to half an hour	Variable depending on location
Suitable types of question	Closed questions but not too complex; complicated sequencing fine if uses software; must be of interest to respondent	Closed questions but not too complex; simple sequencing only; must be of interest to respondent		Open and closed questions, including complicated questions; complicated sequencing feasible	
Time taken to complete collection	2–6 weeks from distribution (dependent on number of follow-ups)	4–8 weeks from posting (dependent on number of follow-ups)	Dependent on sample size, number of field workers, etc.	Dependent on sample size, number of interviewers, etc., but slower than self-completed for same sample size	
Main financial resource implications	Cost of online survey tool, purchase of list of respondents' email addresses	Outward and return postage, photocopying, clerical support, data entry	Field workers, travel, photocopying, clerical support, data entry	Interviewers, telephone calls, clerical support; photocopying and data entry if not using CATI[b]; survey tool if using CATI	Interviewers, travel, clerical support; photocopying and data entry if not using CAPI[c]; survey tool if using CAPI
Role of the interviewer/field worker	None		Delivery and collection of questionnaires; enhancing respondent participation	Enhancing respondent participation; guiding the respondent through the questionnaire and recording responses; answering respondents' questions	
Data input[d]	Automated	Closed questions can be designed so that responses may be entered using optical mark readers after questionnaire has been returned		Response to all questions entered at time of collection using CATI[c]	Response to all questions can be entered at time of collection using CAPI[d]

[a]Discussed in Chapter 7. [b]Computer-aided telephone interviewing. [c]Computer-aided personal interviewing. [d]Discussed in Section 12.2.

Sources: Authors' experience; Baruch and Holtom (2008); De Vaus (2014); Dillman et al. (2014); Oppenheim (2000)

wish to answer the questions and thus the reliability of responses (Table 11.1). Even if you address a postal questionnaire to a company manager by name, you have no way of ensuring that the manager will be the respondent. The manager's assistant or someone else could complete it! Internet questionnaires, delivered by an emailed hyperlink, offer greater control because most people read and respond to their own emails. With delivery and collection questionnaires, you can sometimes check who has answered the questions at collection. By contrast, interviewer-completed questionnaires enable you to ensure that the respondent is whom you want. This improves the reliability of your data. In addition, you can record some details about non-respondents, allowing you to give some assessment of the impact of bias caused by refusals.

Any contamination of respondents' answers will reduce your data's reliability (Table 11.1). Sometimes, if they have insufficient knowledge or experience, they may deliberately guess at the answer, a tendency known as **uninformed response**. This is particularly likely when the questionnaire has been incentivised (Section 11.5). Respondents to self-completed questionnaires are relatively unlikely to answer to please you or because they believe certain responses are more **socially desirable** (Dillman et al. 2014). They may, however, discuss their answers with others, thereby contaminating their response. Respondents to telephone questionnaires and structured interviews are more likely to answer to please due to their contact with you, although the impact of this can be minimised by good interviewing technique (Sections 10.5 and 10.6). Responses can also be contaminated or distorted when recorded. In extreme instances, interviewers may invent responses. For this reason, random checks of interviewers are often made by survey organisations. When writing your project report you will be expected to state your response rate (Section 7.2). When doing this you need to be careful not to make unsubstantiated claims if comparing with other surveys' response rates. While such comparisons place your survey's response rate in context, a higher than normal response rate does not prove that your findings are unbiased (Rogelberg and Stanton 2007). Similarly, a lower than normal response rate does not necessarily mean that responses are biased.

The type of questionnaire you choose will affect the number of people who respond (Section 7.2). Interviewer-completed questionnaires will usually have a higher response rate than self-completed questionnaires (Table 11.1). The size of your sample and the way in which it is selected will have implications for the confidence you can have in your data and the extent to which you can generalise (Section 7.2).

Longer questionnaires are best presented face-to-face like a structured interview. In addition, they can include more complicated questions than telephone questionnaires or self-completed questionnaires (Oppenheim 2000). The presence of an interviewer (or the use of an online survey tool) means that it is also easier to route different subgroups of respondents to answer different questions using a filter question (Section 11.4). The suitability of different types of question also differs between methods.

Your choice of questionnaire will also be affected by the resources you have available (Table 11.1), and in particular the:

- time available to complete the data collection;
- financial implications of data collection and entry;
- availability interviewers and field workers to assist;
- online survey tool.

The time needed for data collection increases markedly for delivery and collection questionnaires and structured interviews where the samples are geographically dispersed (Table 11.1). One way you can overcome this constraint is to select your sample using cluster sampling (Section 7.2). Unless you are using an Internet questionnaire, **computer-aided personal interviewing (CAPI)** or **computer-aided telephone interviewing (CATI)**, you will need to consider the costs of reproducing the questionnaire, clerical support and entering the data for computer analysis. For Internet questionnaires you will need to consider the availability (and often the cost) of obtaining lists of email addresses/telephone numbers and for postal and telephone questionnaires the cost estimates for postage and telephone calls. If you are working for an organisation, postage costs may be reduced by using *Freepost* for questionnaire return. This means that you pay only postage and a small handling charge for those questionnaires that are returned by post. However, the use of Freepost rather than a stamp may adversely affect your response rates (see Table 11.4 below).

Virtually all data collected by questionnaires will be analysed by computer. Many online survey tools (e.g. Qualtrics™, Snap Surveys™ and SurveyMonkey™) allow you to design your questionnaire, capture and automatically save the data, and either analyse the data within the survey tool or download it as a data file for external analysis (Box 11.1). For self-completed questionnaires and structured interviews, data capture is most straightforward for closed questions where respondents select their answer from a prescribed list. Such data will need subsequently to be coded, entered (typed) and saved in the analysis software for subsequent analysis (Section 12.2). Once this has been done

Box 11.1
Focus on student research

Ben's research project involved emailing a hyperlink to a Web questionnaire to small- and medium-sized enterprise owners to discover how they defined small business success. He designed his questionnaire using the online survey tool SurveyMonkey as this would either allow him to analyse his data within the survey tool or export his data to analysis software such as IBM SPSS Statistics, a spreadsheet or a database.

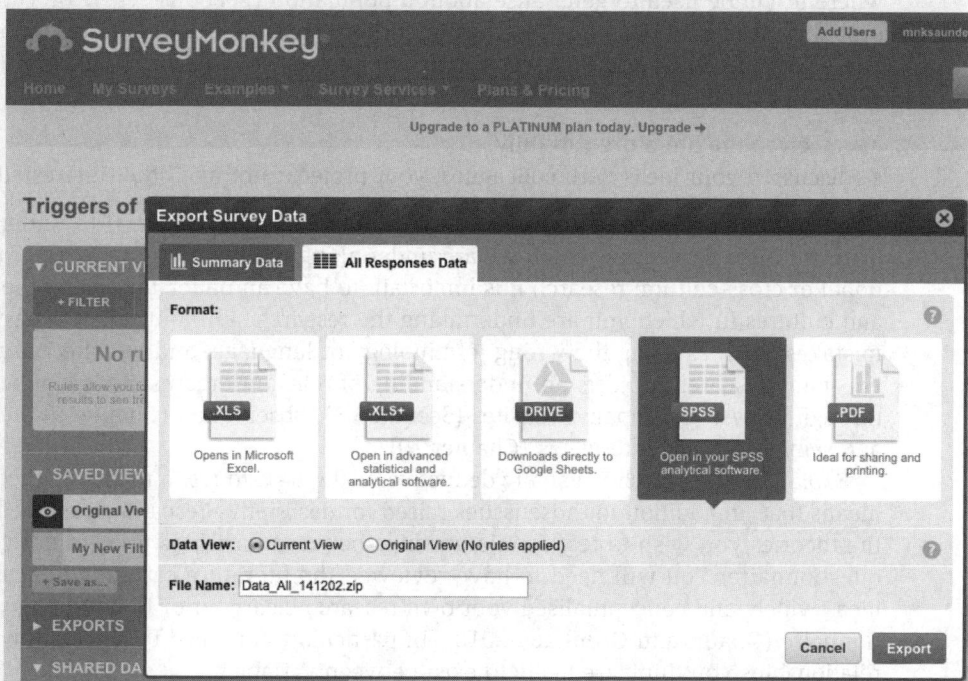

Source: Screenshot created by SurveyMonkey.com, LLC (2014) Palo Alto, Reproduced with permission

and the data checked, you will be able to explore and analyse your data far more quickly and thoroughly than by hand (Sections 12.3–12.5). As a rough rule, you should analyse questionnaire data by computer if they have been collected from 30 or more respondents.

In reality, you are almost certain to have to make compromises in your choice of questionnaire. These will be unique to your research as the decision about which questionnaire is most suitable cannot be answered in isolation from your research question(s) and objectives and the population or sample from which you are collecting data.

11.3 Deciding what data need to be collected

确定需要收集哪些数据

Research design requirements

Unlike in-depth and semi-structured interviews (Chapter 10), the questions you ask in questionnaires need to be defined precisely prior to data collection. Whereas you can prompt and explore issues further with in-depth and semi-structured interviews, this will not be possible using questionnaires. In addition, the questionnaire offers only one chance to collect the data as it is often difficult to identify respondents or to return to collect additional information. This means that the time you spend planning precisely what data you need to collect, how you intend to analyse them (Chapter 12) and designing your questionnaire to meet these requirements is crucial if you are to answer your research question(s) and meet your objectives.

For most business and management research the data you collect using questionnaires will be used for either descriptive or explanatory purposes. For questions where the main purpose is to describe the population's characteristics either at a fixed time or at a series of points over time to enable comparisons, you will normally need to deliver your questionnaire to a sample. The sample needs to be as representative and accurate as possible where it will be used to generalise about a population (Sections 7.1–7.3). You will also probably need to relate your findings to earlier research. It is therefore important that you select the appropriate characteristics to answer your research question(s) and to address your objectives. You will need to have:

- reviewed the literature carefully;
- discussed your ideas with colleagues, your project tutor and other interested parties.

For research involving organisations, we have found it essential to understand the organisational context in which we are undertaking the research. Similarly, for international or cross-cultural research it is important to have an understanding of the countries and cultures in which you are undertaking the research. Without this it is easy to make mistakes, such as using the wrong terminology or language, and to collect useless data. For many research projects an understanding of relevant organisations can be achieved through browsing company websites (Section 8.3), observation (Chapter 9) and in-depth and semi-structured interviews (Chapter 10).

Explanatory research is usually deductive, using data to test a theory or theories. This means that, in addition to those issues raised for descriptive research, you need to define the theories you wish to test as relationships between variables prior to designing your questionnaire. You will need to have reviewed the literature carefully, discussed your ideas widely and conceptualised your own research clearly prior to designing your questionnaire (Ghauri and Grønhaug 2010). In particular, you need to be clear about which relationships you think are likely to exist between variables:

- a **dependent variable** that changes in response to changes in other variables;
- an **independent variable** that causes changes in a dependent variable;

- a **mediating variable** that transmits the effect of an independent variable to a dependent variable;
- a **moderating variable** that affects the relationship between an independent variable and a dependent variable (Box 11.2 and Table 5.2).

As these relationships are likely to be tested through statistical analysis (Section 12.5) of the data collected by your questionnaire, you need to be clear about the detail in which they will be measured at the design stage. Where possible, you should ensure that measures are compatible with those used in other relevant research so that comparisons can be made (Section 12.2).

Types of data variable

Dillman et al. (2014) distinguishes between three types of data variable that can be collected through questionnaires:

- factual or demographic;
- attitudes and opinions;
- behaviours and events.

These distinctions are important as they relate to the ease of obtaining accurate data and influence the way your questions are worded (Box 11.3). **Factual** and **demographic variables** contain data that are readily available to the respondent and are likely, assuming the respondent is willing to disclose, to be accurate. These variables include characteristics such as age, gender, marital status, education, occupation and income. They are used to explore how attitudes and opinions, and behaviours and events, differ, as well as to check that the data collected are representative of the total population (Section 7.2). **Attitude** and **opinion variables** contain data that respondents may have needed to think about before answering. They are likely to be influenced by the context in which the question was asked; recording how respondents feel about something or what they think or believe is true or false. **Behaviour** and **event variables** are also likely to be influenced by context. They contain data about what people did (behaviours) or what happened (events) in the past, is happening now, or will happen in the future.

Box 11.2
Focus on student research

Defining theories in terms of relationships between variables

As part of her research, Marie-Claude wished to test the theory that the use of professional fundraisers in charitable fundraising altered the donations made by members of the public.

The relationship that she thought existed between these two variables was that the donations made were higher when professional fundraisers were used. The dependent variable was the value of donations received, and the independent variable was the use of professional fundraisers.

Marie-Claude thought that mediating factors such as the tactics devised by the professional fundraisers (such as media events and advertising) would transmit the effect of the use of professional fundraisers, acting as mediating variables. In contrast, factors such as public opinion about the cause the charity represented and potential donors' disposable income would act as moderating variables. Data were collected on each of these variables.

Box 11.3
Focus on student research

Opinion, behaviour and attribute questions

Sally was asked by her employer to undertake an anonymous survey of financial advisors' ethical values. In particular, her employer was interested in the advice given to clients. After some deliberation she came up with three questions that addressed the issue of putting clients' interests before their own:

2 How do you feel about the following statement? 'Financial advisors should place their clients' interest before their own.'

	strongly agree ❑
	mildly agree ❑
(please tick the appropriate box)	neither agree or disagree ❑
	mildly disagree ❑
	strongly disagree ❑

3 In general, do financial advisors place their clients' interests before their own?

	always yes ❑
	usually yes ❑
(please tick the appropriate box)	sometimes yes ❑
	seldom yes ❑
	never yes ❑

4 How often do you place your clients' interests before your own?

	81–100% of my time ❑
	61–80% of my time ❑
(please tick the appropriate box)	41–60% of my time ❑
	21–40% of my time ❑
	0–20% of my time ❑

Sally's choice of question or questions to include in her questionnaire was dependent on whether she needed to collect data on financial advisors' attitudes, opinions or behaviours. She designed question 2 to collect data on respondents' opinions about financial advisors placing their clients' interest before their own. This question asks respondents how they feel. In contrast question 3 asks respondents whether financial advisors in general place their clients' interests before their own. It is therefore concerned with their individual opinions regarding how financial advisors act.

Question 4 focuses on how often the respondents actually place their clients' interests before their own. Unlike the previous questions, it is concerned with their actual behaviour rather than their opinion.

To answer her research questions and to meet her objectives Sally also needed to collect data to explore how ethical values differed between subgroupings of financial advisors. One theory she had was that ethical values were related to age. To test this she needed to collect demographic data on respondents' ages. After some deliberation she came up with question 5:

5 How old are you?

	Less than 30 years ❑
	30 to less than 40 years ❑
(please tick the appropriate box)	40 to less than 50 years ❑
	50 to less than 60 years ❑
	60 years or over ❑

Ensuring that essential data are collected

A problem experienced by many students and organisations we work with is how to ensure that the data collected will enable the research question(s) to be answered and the objectives achieved. Although no method is infallible, one way is to create a **data requirements table** (Table 11.2). This summarises the outcome of a six-step process:

1 Decide whether the main outcome of your research is descriptive or explanatory.
2 Subdivide each research question or objective into more specific investigative questions about which you need to gather data, noting how it relates to theory and key concepts in the literature.
3 Repeat the second stage if you feel that the investigative questions are not sufficiently precise.
4 Keeping in mind relevant theory and key concepts in the literature, identify the variables about which you must collect data to answer each investigative question.
5 Establish the level of detail required from the data for each variable.
6 Develop measurement questions to capture the data at the level required for each variable.

Investigative questions are the questions that you need to answer in order to address satisfactorily each research question and to meet each objective (Bloomberg et al. 2014). They need to be generated with regard to your research question(s) and objectives. For some investigative questions you will need to subdivide your first attempt into more detailed investigative questions. For each you need to be clear whether you are interested in facts/demographics, attitudes/opinions or behaviours/events (discussed earlier), as what appears to be a need to collect one sort of variable frequently turns out to be a need for another. We have found theory and key concepts from the literature, discussions with interested parties and pilot studies to be of help here.

You should then identify the variables about which you need to collect data to answer each investigative question and to decide the level of detail at which these are measured. Again, the review of the literature and associated research can suggest possibilities. However, if you are unsure about the detail needed you should measure at a more precise level. Although this is more time consuming, it will give you flexibility in your analyses. In these you will be able to use computer software to group or combine data (Section 12.2).

Once your table is complete (Box 11.4), it must be checked to make sure that all data necessary to answer your investigative questions are included. When checking, you need

Table 11.2 Data requirements table

Research question/objective:

Type of research:

Investigative questions	Variable(s) required	Detail in which data measured	Relation to theory and key concepts in the literature	Check measurement question included in questionnaire ✓

Box 11.4
Focus on student research

Data requirements table

As part of his work placement Greg was asked to discover customer attitudes to the outside smoking area at restaurants and bars. Discussion with senior management and colleagues and reading relevant literature helped him to firm up his objective and investigative questions and the level of detail in which the data were measured. In addition he wanted to be able to compare his findings with earlier research by Louka et al. (2006) in the *Journal of Health Psychology* and Hyland et al. (2009) in the *European Journal of Public Health*.

A selection of his objectives is included in the extract from his table of data requirements:

• **Research question/objective:** To establish customers' attitudes to the outside smoking area at restaurants and bars				
• **Type of research:** Predominantly descriptive, although wish to examine differences between restaurants and bars, and between different groups of customers				
Investigative questions	**Variable(s) required**	**Detail in which data measured**	**Relation to theory and key concepts in literature**	**Check included in questionnaire ✓**
• Do customers feel that they should have an outside smoking area at restaurants and bars as a right? (opinion)	• Opinion of customer on restaurants and bars providing an outside smoking area as a right	• Feel . . . should be a right, should not be a right, no strong feelings [N.B. will need separate questions for restaurants and for bars]		
• Do customers feel that restaurants and bars should provide an outside smoking area for smokers? (opinion)	• Opinion of customer to the provision of an outside smoking area for smokers	• Feel . . . very strongly that it should, quite strongly that it should, no strong opinions, quite strongly that it should not, very strongly that it should not [N.B. will need separate questions for restaurants and for bars]		
• Do customers' opinions differ depending on. . .	• (Opinion of employee – outlined above)	• (Included above)		
• . . .whether or not a smoker? (behaviour)	• Smoker	• Smoker or non-smoker	• Hyland et al. (2009) define a smoker as person who has smoked within last month and smoked 100+ cigarettes in their lifetime	

Investigative questions	Variable(s) required	Detail in which data measured	Relation to theory and key concepts in literature	Check included in questionnaire ✓
• . . .nationality (factual)		• Country of origin	• Louka et al. (2006) highlights differences between nationalities	
• How representative are the responses of customers? (demographic)	• Gender of customer; Job	• (Included above) Male, female; Higher managerial and professional occupations, Lower managerial and professional occupations, Intermediate occupations, Small employers and own account workers, Lower supervisory and technical occupations, Semi-routine occupations, Routine occupations, Never worked and long-term unemployed	• Must be able to compare with Office for National Statistics (2005) Socio-Economic Classification	

to ensure that only data which are essential to answering your research question(s) and meeting your objectives are included. The final column is to remind you to check that your questionnaire actually includes a measurement question that collects the precise data required!

11.4 Designing the questionnaire 设计问卷

The internal validity and reliability of the data you collect and the response rate you achieve depend, to a large extent, on the design of your questions, the structure of your questionnaire and the rigour of your pilot testing (all discussed in this section). A valid questionnaire will enable accurate data that actually measure the concepts you are interested in to be collected, while one that is reliable will mean that these data are collected consistently. Foddy (1994: 17) discusses validity and reliability in terms of the questions and answers making sense. In particular, he emphasises that 'the question must be understood by the respondent in the way intended by the researcher and the answer given by the respondent must be understood by the researcher in the way intended by the respondent'. This means that there are at least four stages that must occur if the question is to be valid and reliable (Figure 11.2). It also means that the design stage is likely to involve you in substantial rewriting in order to ensure that the respondent decodes the question in the way you intended.

Researcher is clear
about data requirements
and designs the question

Researcher decodes
the answer in the
way the respondent
intended

Respondent decodes
the question as the
researcher intended

Respondent
answers the question

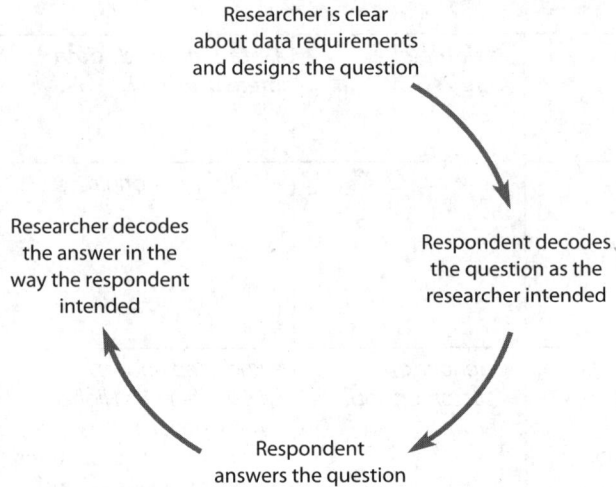

Figure 11.2 Stages that must occur if a question is to be valid and reliable

Source: Developed from Foddy (1994) *Constructing Questions for Interviews and Questionnaires.* Reproduced with permission from Cambridge University Press

Assessing validity

Internal validity in relation to questionnaires refers to the ability of your questionnaire to measure what you intend it to measure. It is sometimes termed **measurement validity** as it refers to concerns that what you find with your questionnaire actually represents the reality of what you are measuring. This presents you with a problem as, if you actually knew the reality of what you were measuring, there would be no point in designing your questionnaire and using it to collect data! Researchers get round this problem by looking for other relevant evidence that supports the answers found using the questionnaire, relevance being determined by the nature of their research question and their own judgement.

Often, when discussing the validity of a questionnaire, researchers refer to content validity, criterion-related validity and construct validity. **Content validity** refers to the extent to which the measurement device, in our case the questions in the questionnaire, provides adequate coverage of the investigative questions. Judgement of what is 'adequate coverage' can be made in a number of ways. One is through careful definition of the research through the literature reviewed and, where appropriate, prior discussion with others. Another is to use a panel of individuals to assess whether each question in the questionnaire is 'essential', 'useful but not essential' or 'not necessary'.

Criterion-related validity, sometimes known as **predictive validity**, is concerned with the ability of the measures (questions) to make accurate predictions. This means that if you are using the data collected by questions within your questionnaire to predict customers' future buying behaviours then a test of these questions' criterion-related validity will be the extent to which the responses actually predict these customers' buying behaviours. In assessing criterion-related validity, you will be comparing the data from your questionnaire with that specified in the criterion in some way. Often this is undertaken using statistical analysis such as correlation (Section 12.5).

Construct validity refers to the extent to which a set of questions (known individually as scale items, and discussed later in this section) actually measures the presence of the construct you intended them to measure. This term is normally used when referring to constructs such as attitude scales, customer loyalty and the like (Section 11.4) and can be thought of as answering the question: 'How well can I generalise from this set of questions to the construct?' Because validation of such constructs against existing data is difficult, other methods are used. Where different scales are used to measure the same construct, the overlap (or correlation) between these scales is known as **convergent validity**. In contrast, where different scales are used to measure theoretically distinct constructs, an absence of overlap (or correlation) between the scales means they are distinctive and have **discriminant validity**. These are discussed in more detail in a range of texts, including Bloomberg et al. (2014).

Testing for reliability

As we outlined earlier, reliability refers to consistency. Although for a questionnaire to be valid it must be reliable, this is not sufficient on its own. Respondents may consistently interpret a question in your questionnaire in one way, when you mean something else! As a consequence, although the question is reliable, this does not really matter as it has no internal validity and so will not enable your research question to be answered. Reliability is therefore concerned with the robustness of your questionnaire and, in particular, whether or not it will produce consistent findings at different times and under different conditions, such as with different samples or, in the case of an interviewer-completed questionnaire, with different interviewers.

Mitchell (1996) outlines three common approaches to assessing reliability, in addition to comparing the data collected with other data from a variety of sources. Although the analysis for each of these is undertaken after data collection, they need to be considered at the questionnaire design stage. They are:

- test re-test;
- internal consistency;
- alternative form.

Test re-test estimates of reliability are obtained by correlating data collected with those from the same questionnaire collected under as near equivalent conditions as possible. The questionnaire therefore needs to be delivered and completed twice by respondents. This may create problems, as it is often difficult to persuade respondents to answer the same questionnaire twice. In addition, the longer the time interval between the two questionnaires, the lower the likelihood that respondents will answer the same way. We therefore recommend that you use this method only as a supplement to other methods.

Internal consistency involves correlating the responses to questions in the questionnaire with each other. It thus measures the consistency of responses across a subgroup of the questions. There are a variety of methods for calculating internal consistency, of which one of the most frequently used is **Cronbach's alpha**. This statistic is usually used to measure the consistency of responses to a set of questions (scale items) that are combined as a scale (discussed later in this section) to measure a particular concept. It consists of an alpha coefficient with a value between 0 and 1. Values of 0.7 or above indicate that the questions combined in the scale are measuring the same thing. Further details of this and other approaches can be found in Mitchell (1996) and in books discussing more advanced statistics and analysis software such as Field (2013).

The final approach to testing for reliability outlined by Mitchell (1996) is 'alternative form'. This offers some sense of the reliability within your questionnaire through comparing responses to alternative forms of the same question or groups of questions.

Where questions are included for this purpose, usually in longer questionnaires, they are often called 'check questions'. However, it is often difficult to ensure that these questions are substantially equivalent. Respondents may suffer from fatigue owing to the need to increase the length of the questionnaire, and they may spot the similar question and just refer back to their previous answer! It is therefore advisable to use check questions sparingly.

Designing individual questions

The design of each question should be determined by the data you need to collect (Section 11.3). When designing individual questions researchers do one of three things (Bourque and Clark 1994):

- adopt questions used in other questionnaires;
- adapt questions used in other questionnaires;
- develop their own questions.

Adopting or adapting questions may be necessary if you wish to replicate, or to compare your findings with, another study. This can allow reliability to be assessed. It is also more efficient than developing your own questions, provided that you can still collect the data you need to answer your research question(s) and to meet your objectives. Some online survey tools include questions that you may use. Alternatively, you may find questions and coding schemes that you feel will meet your needs in existing questionnaires, journal articles or in Internet-based question banks, such as the UK Data Service's Variable and Question Bank (2014). This provides searchable access to over 450,000 questions, over 250,000 of which are closed questions, from a range of UK and cross-national surveys since the mid-1990s.

However, before you adopt questions, beware! There are a vast number of poor questions in circulation, so always assess each question carefully. In addition, you need to check whether they are under copyright. If they are, you need to obtain the author's permission to use them. Even where there is no formal copyright you should, where possible, contact the author and obtain permission. In your project report you should state where you obtained the questions and give credit to their author.

Initially, you need only consider the type, wording and length of individual questions rather than the order in which they will appear on the form. Clear wording of questions using terms that are likely to be familiar to, and understood by, respondents can improve the validity of the questionnaire. Shorter questions are easier to understand than longer ones and questions should, ideally, be no longer than 20 words, excluding possible answers (Sekeran and Bougie 2013). Most types of questionnaire include a combination of open and closed questions. **Open questions**, sometimes referred to as open-ended questions, allow respondents to give answers in their own way (Fink 2013). **Closed questions**, sometimes referred to as closed-ended questions (Fink 2013) or **forced-choice questions** (De Vaus 2014), provide a number of alternative answers from which the respondent is instructed to choose. Closed questions are usually quicker and easier to answer, as they require minimal writing. Responses are also easier to compare as they have been predetermined. However, if these responses cannot be easily interpreted then these benefits are, to say the least, marginal (Foddy 1994). Within this chapter we highlight six types of closed question that we discuss later:

- list, where the respondent is offered a list of items, any of which may be selected;
- category, where only one response can be selected from a given set of categories;

- ranking, where the respondent is asked to place something in order;
- rating, in which a rating device is used to record responses;
- quantity, to which the response is a number giving the amount;
- matrix, where responses to two or more questions can be recorded using the same grid.

As well as:

- creating scales to measure constructs by combining rating questions.

Prior to data analysis, you will need to group and code responses to each question. Detailed coding guidance is given in Section 12.2. You are strongly advised also to read this chapter prior to designing your questions.

Open questions

Open questions are used widely in in-depth and semi-structured interviews (Section 10.5). In questionnaires they are useful if you are unsure of the response, such as in exploratory research, when you require a detailed answer, when you want to find out what is uppermost in the respondent's mind or do not wish to list all possible answers. An example of an open question (from a self-completed questionnaire) is:

6 Please list up to three things you like about your job:

   1 ....

   2 ....

   3 ....

With open questions, the precise wording of the question and the amount of space partially determine the length and fullness of response. However, if you leave too much space the question becomes off-putting. Question 6 collects data about each respondent's opinion of what they like about their job. Thus if salary had been the reason uppermost in their mind this would probably have been recorded first. Unfortunately, when questionnaires are returned by large numbers of respondents, responses to open questions are extremely time consuming to code (Section 12.2). This may be compounded by illegible handwriting. For this reason, it is usually advisable to keep their use to a minimum.

List questions

List questions offer the respondent a list of responses from which she or he can choose either one or more responses. Such questions are useful when you need to be sure that the respondent has considered all possible responses. However, the list of responses must be defined clearly and meaningfully to the respondent. For structured interviews, it is often helpful to present the respondent with a prompt card listing all responses. The response categories you can use vary widely and include 'yes/no', 'agree/disagree' and 'applies/does not apply' along with 'don't know' or 'not sure'. If you intend to use what you hope is a complete list, you may wish to add a catch-all category of 'other'. This has been included in question 7, which collects data on respondents' religion. However, as you can read in Box 11.5, the use of 'other' can result in unforeseen responses, especially where the question is considered intrusive!

7 What is your religion?

Please tick ✓ the appropriate box.

Buddhist	❏	None	❏
Christian	❏	Other	❏
Hindu	❏		
Jewish	❏	(Please say:)	
Muslim	❏		
Sikh	❏		

Question 7 collects demographic data on religion, the respondent ticking (checking) the response that applies. In this list question, the common practice of not asking respondents to both check those that do apply and those which do not has been adopted. Consequently, respondents are not asked to indicate those religions to which they do not belong. If you choose to do this, beware: non-response could also indicate uncertainty, or for some questions that an item does not apply! It is also likely that respondents will not read the list from which they have to select appropriate responses so carefully (Dillman et al. 2014).

Box 11.5 Research in the news

Piety gives way to secularism and heavy metal worship

By Matthew Engel

It is not really appropriate for someone who filled in their 2011 census form with my niggardly gracelessness to start taking an interest now. Nonetheless, the census results announced this week about religious belief are very striking. They tell us a good deal about Britain's progression towards becoming a post religious country. They also tell us something about the way the British fill in forms.

The headline figures were that almost a quarter of the population of England and Wales, 14.1m people, said they had no religion, compared with just under 15 per cent in 2001. This fits with a corresponding fall in the number of declared Christians, from 71 per cent to 59 per cent. The statistics also provided a platform for the right wing press to go off on an anti-immigration riff since they showed a near doubling in the number of Muslims, which ought not to have taken anyone by surprise.

And there were all sorts of little snippets: Norwich and (less surprisingly) Brighton emerged as the most godless towns in the country, followed (very surprisingly) by some once chapel dominated areas of the

South Wales Valleys, all of them with more than 40 per cent saying "no religion". In Northern Ireland, the Protestants universally referred to as "the majority" have fallen below half and now lead the Catholics by only 48 per cent to 45 per cent, a finding with all kinds of political implications.

There was much enlightenment in the deepest recesses, too. The number of those calling themselves Jedi knights has halved, the best joke of the 2001 census having run out of steam, but at 176,000 they still outnumbered the 56,000 pagans, 39,000 spiritualists, 30,000 atheists (is that all?), 6,000 heavy metal worshippers (many of them in Norwich) and 2,500 Scientologists, and were not that far behind the 263,000 Jews...

When I put my religion on the census form, I was being bad tempered, resenting the impertinent question. I put myself down as a Myobist. But actually I have adopted, by accident, the sanest religion in the world. I hope the census checkers grasped that Myob was an acronym and remembered what MYOB stands for.

Category questions

In contrast, **category questions** are designed so that each respondent's answer can fit only one category. Such questions are particularly useful if you need to collect data about behaviour or attributes. The number of categories that you can include without affecting the accuracy of responses is dependent on the type of questionnaire. Self-completed questionnaires and telephone questionnaires should usually have no more than five response categories (Fink 2013). Structured interviews can have more categories provided that a *prompt card* is used (Box 11.6) or, as in question 8, the interviewer categorises the responses.

8　How often do you visit this shopping centre?

Interviewer: listen to the respondent's answer and tick ✓ as appropriate.

❏	First visit	2 or more times a week	❏
❏	Once a week	Less than once a week to fortnightly	❏
❏	Less than fortnightly to once a month	Less often	❏

You should arrange responses in a logical order so that it is easy to locate the response category that corresponds to each respondent's answer. Your categories should be mutually exclusive (not overlapping), and should cover all possible responses. The layout of your questionnaire should make it clear which boxes refer to which response category by placing them close to the appropriate text.

Ranking questions

A **ranking question** asks the respondent to place things in rank order. This means that you can discover their relative importance to the respondent. In question 9, taken from a Web questionnaire created in Qualtrics, the respondents are asked their opinions about the relative importance of a series of features when choosing a new car. The catch-all

---

9. Drag and drop the factors listed below so they are in order of importance to you in your choice of a new car.

Place the most important item at the top [1], the next second [2] and so on.

Boot size	1
Carbon dioxide (CO_2) emissions	2
Depreciation	3
Safety features	4
Fuel economy	5
Price	6
Driving enjoyment	7
Other	8

Source: This question was generated using Qualtrics software, Version 595160.546s of the Qualtrics Research Suite. Copyright © 2014 Qualtrics. Qualtrics and all other Qualtrics product or service names are registered trademarks or trademarks of Qualtrics, Provo, UT, USA. http://www.qualtrics.com. The authors are not affiliated to Qualtrics.

**Box 11.6
Focus on student
research**

**Use of a prompt card as part
of a structured interview**

As part of his interview schedule, Peter asked the following question:

Which of the following newspapers have you read
during the past month?

[Show respondent card 3 with the names of the
newspapers. Read out names of the newspapers
one at a time. Record their response with a ✓ in the
appropriate box].

	Read	Not read	Don't know
Daily Express	❑	❑	❑
Daily Mail	❑	❑	❑
The Daily Mirror	❑	❑	❑
Daily Star	❑	❑	❑
Financial Times	❑	❑	❑
The Guardian	❑	❑	❑
The Daily Telegraph	❑	❑	❑
The Independent	❑	❑	❑
The Sun	❑	❑	❑
The Times	❑	❑	❑

Peter gave card 3 to each respondent prior to
reading out newspaper names and collected the card
after the question had been completed.

DAILY EXPRESS
Daily Mail
DAILY Mirror
DAILY STAR
FINANCIAL TIMES
theguardian
The Daily Telegraph
THE INDEPENDENT
THE Sun
THE TIMES

3

feature of 'other' is included to allow respondents to add one other feature, a subsequent question asking them to describe this.

With such questions, you need to ensure that the instructions are clear and will be understood by the respondent. In general, respondents find that ranking more than seven items takes too much effort, reducing their motivation to complete the questionnaire, so you should keep your list to this length or shorter (Bloomberg et al. 2014). Respondents can rank accurately only when they can see or remember all items. This can be overcome with face-to-face questionnaires by using prompt cards on which you list all of the features to be ranked. However, telephone questionnaires should ask respondents to rank fewer items, as the respondent will need to rely on their memory.

Rating questions

Rating questions are often used to collect opinion data. They should not be confused with **scales** to measure concepts (discussed later in this section), which are a coherent set of questions or scale items that are regarded as indicators of a construct or concept (Bruner 2013). Rating questions most frequently use the **Likert-style rating** in which the respondent is asked how strongly she or he agrees or disagrees with a statement or series of statements, usually on a four-, five-, six- or seven-point rating scale (Box 11.7). Possible responses to rating questions should be presented in a straight line (such as in question 10) rather than in multiple lines or columns, as this is how respondents are most likely to process the data (Dillman et al. 2014). If you intend to use a series of

Box 11.7
Focus On
management
research

Tourists' perceptions of world heritage destinations

Paula Remoaldo and colleagues (2014) published findings from a study examining the profile, destination image and motivations of tourists' visiting the UNESCO world heritage site of Guimarães in Portugal in the *Journal of Tourism and Hospitality Research*.

Prior to designing their questionnaire, Remoaldo and colleagues conducted an in-depth interview with the Office for Tourism to obtain information about the attributes and motivations of tourists. Subsequently a self-administered questionnaire (in both English and Portuguese) was used in the two tourist offices in the City of Guimarães to collect data from the visitors.

The questionnaire comprised three parts. The first part collected data on the cities visited before the tourist arrived at Guimarães. The second part explored each respondent's opinion of the importance of 21 attributes of the city in attracting the tourist to Guimarães. These included monumental and artistic heritage, gastronomy, weather, safety, quality hotels and the like. For each attribute respondents indicated their level of agreement (or disagreement) regarding whether each of these attributes had been a factor in their choice of the city as a specific heritage destination. Agreement/disagreement was rated using a 5-point Likert-type scale comprising 'Completely disagree', 'Disagree', 'Neutral', 'Agree', 'Completely agree'. The third part of the questionnaire asked for demographic data such as gender, age and education.

Data were collected from respondents during three different periods: December (low season), April (middle season) and July and August (high season). A total of 300 questionnaires were filled in, of which 276 provided usable data. The findings suggested that many tourists were aware of the city's status as a world heritage site and that Guimarães' historical background and functionality as a city were the main factors in their choice of visiting the city.

statements, you should keep the same order of response categories to avoid confusing respondents (Dillman et al. 2014). You should include both positive and negative statements so as to ensure that the respondent reads each one carefully and thinks about which box to tick.

10 For the following statement please tick ✓ the box that matches your view most closely.

	Agree	Tend to agree	Tend to disagree	Disagree
I feel employees' views have influenced the decisions taken by management.	❑	❑	❑	❑

Question 10 has been taken from a delivery and collection questionnaire to employees in an organisation and is designed to collect opinion data. In this rating question, an even number of points (four) has been used to force the respondent to express their feelings towards the statement. By contrast, question 11, also from a delivery and collection questionnaire, contains an odd number (five) of points. This inclusion of a neutral point allows the respondent to 'sit on the fence' by ticking the middle 'not sure' category when considering an implicitly negative statement. The phrase 'not sure' is used here as it is less threatening to the respondent than admitting they do not know. This rating question is designed to collect data on employees' opinions of the situation now.

11 For the following statement please tick ✓ the box that matches your view most closely.

	Agree	Tend to agree	Not sure	Tend to disagree	Disagree
I believe there are 'them and us' barriers to communication in the company now.	❑	❑	❑	❑	❑

Both questions 10 and 11 are balanced rating scales as the possible answers are reflected around either an implicit (question 10) or an explicit (question 11) neutral point. The alternative is an unbalanced rating scale, such as question 12, which does not have a neutral point.

You can expand this form of rating question further to record finer shades of opinion, a variety of which are outlined in Table 11.3. However, respondents to telephone questionnaires find it difficult to distinguish between values when rating more than five points plus 'don't know'. In addition, there is little point in collecting data for seven or nine response categories, if these are subsequently combined in your analysis (Chapter 12). Colleagues and students often ask us how many points they should have on their rating scale. This is related to the likely measurement error. If you know that your respondents can only respond accurately to a three-point rating, then it is pointless to have a finer rating scale with more points!

In question 12 (created in Qualtrics) a respondent's opinion – how hot they usually like their curry – is captured on a 10-point numeric rating scale. In such rating questions it is important that the numbers reflect the answer of the respondent. Thus, 1 reflects a mild curry (korma) and 10 an extremely hot curry (phal), the number increasing as the temperature increases. Only these end categories (and sometimes the middle) are labelled and these are known as self-anchoring rating scales. The intermediate numbers are not labelled to maintain simplicity (Allreck and Settle 2004). As in this question,

Table 11.3 Response categories for different types of rating questions

Type of rating	Five categories	Seven categories
Agreement	Strongly agree	Strongly agree
	Agree	Agree/moderately agree/mostly agree*
	Neither agree nor disagree/not sure/uncertain*	Slightly agree
	Disagree	Neither agree nor disagree/not sure/uncertain*
	Strongly disagree	Slightly disagree
		Disagree/moderately disagree/mostly disagree*
		Strongly disagree
Amount	Far too much/nearly all/very large*	Far too much/nearly all/very large*
	Too much/more than half/large*	Too much/more than half/large*
	About right/about half/some*	Slightly too much/quite large*
	Too little/less than half/small*	About right/about half/some*
	Far too little/almost none/not at all*	Slightly too little/quite small*
		Too little/less than half/small*
		Far too little/almost none/not at all*
Frequency	All the time/always*	All the time/always*
	Frequently/very often/most of the time*	Almost all the time/almost always*
	Sometimes/about as often as not/about half the time*	Frequently/very often/most of the time*
	Rarely/seldom/less than half the time*	Sometimes/about as often as not/about half the time*
	Never/practically never*	Seldom
		Almost never/practically never*
		Never/not at all*
Likelihood	Very	Extremely
	Good	Very
	Reasonable	Moderately
	Slight/bit*	Quite/reasonable*
	None/not at all*	Somewhat
		Slight/bit*
		None/not at all*

*Response dependent on question.

Source: Developed from Tharenou et al. (2007) and authors' experience

12. On a scale of 10 to 1, where...

10 is a phal (extremely hot) curry
1 is a korma (mild) curry

How hot do you usually like your curry?

Source: This question was generated using Qualtrics software, Version 595160.546s of the Qualtrics Research Suite. Copyright © 2014 Qualtrics. Qualtrics and all other Qualtrics product or service names are registered trademarks or trademarks of Qualtrics, Provo, UT, USA. http://www.qualtrics.com. The authors are not affiliated to Qualtrics.

a graphic that alters as the slider is moved, can be used to reflect the rating scale visually and aid the respondent's interpretation. An additional category of 'not sure' or 'don't know' can be added and should be separated slightly from the rating scale.

Another variation is the **semantic differential rating question**. These are often used in consumer research to determine underlying attitudes. The respondent is asked to rate a single object or idea on a series of bipolar rating scales. Each bipolar scale is described by a pair of opposite adjectives (question 13), designed to anchor respondents' attitudes. For these rating scales, you should vary the position of positive and negative adjectives from left to right to reduce the tendency to read only the adjective on the left (Bloomberg et al. 2014).

13   On each of the lines below, place an x to show how you feel about the service you received at our restaurant.

Fast	_|_|_|_|_|_|_|_|_	Slow
Unfriendly	_|_|_|_|_|_|_|_|_	Friendly
Value for money	_|_|_|_|_|_|_|_|_	Overpriced

Quantity questions

The response to a **quantity question** is a number, which gives a factual amount of a characteristic. For this reason, such questions tend to be used to collect behaviour or attribute data. A common quantity question, which collects attribute data, is:

14   What is your year of birth?

(for example for 1994 write:) | 1 | 9 | 9 | 4 |

Because the response to this question data is coded by the respondent, the question can also be termed a **self-coded** question.

Matrix questions

A **matrix** or grid of questions enables you to record the responses to two or more similar questions at the same time. As can be seen from question 15, created in SurveyMonkey™, questions are listed down the left-hand side of the page, and responses listed across the top. The appropriate response to each question is then recorded in the cell where the row and column meet. Although using a matrix saves space, Dillman et al. (2014) suggests that respondents may have difficulties comprehending these designs and that they are a barrier to response.

15. The following items refer to your treatment by managers in general, who are responsible for making decisions in Anytown Manufacturing Company that affects your work. To what extent:	to a large extent	to a quite large extent	to some extent	to a quite small extent	to a small extent	not at all
a. do they treat you with dignity?	○	○	○	○	○	○
b. do they treat you with respect?	○	○	○	○	○	○
c. are they at least as honest with bad news as good news in their communications with you?	○	○	○	○	○	○

Source: Question layout created by SurveyMonkey.com, LLC (2014) Palo Alto, California. Reproduced with permission

Combining rating questions into scales

Rating questions have been combined into scales to measure a wide variety of concepts such as customer loyalty, service quality and job satisfaction. For each concept the resultant measure or **scale** is represented by a scale score created by combining the scores for each of the rating questions. Each rating question is often referred to as a **scale item**. In the case of a simple Likert-type scale, for example, the scale (or composite) score for each case would be calculated by adding together the scores of each of the rating questions (items) selected (De Vaus 2014). A detailed discussion of creating scales, including those by Likert and Guttman, can be found in DeVellis (2012). However, rather than developing your own scales, it often makes sense to use or adapt existing scales (Schrauf and Navarro 2005). Since scaling techniques were first used in the 1930s, literally thousands of scales have been developed to measure attitudes and personality dimensions and to assess skills and abilities. Details of an individual scale can often be found by following up references in an article reporting research that uses that scale. In addition, there are a wide variety of handbooks that list these scales (e.g. Bruner 2013). These scales can, as highlighted in Box 11.8, be used in your own research providing they:

- measure what you are interested in;
- have been empirically tested and validated;
- were designed for a reasonably similar group of respondents.

Box 11.8
Focus on student research

Using existing scales from the literature

When planning his questionnaire David, like most students, presumed he would need to design and develop his own measurement scale. However, after reading Schrauf and Navarro's (2005) paper on using existing scales, he realised that it would probably be possible to adopt an existing scale, which had been reported in the academic literature. As he pointed out to his project tutor, this was particularly fortunate because the process of scale development was hugely time consuming and could distract his attention from answering the actual research question.

In looking for a suitable published scale David asked himself a number of questions:

- Does the scale measure what I am interested in?
- Has the scale been empirically tested and validated?
- Was the scale designed for a similar group of respondents as my target population?

Fortunately, the answer to all these questions was 'yes'. David, therefore, emailed the scale's author to ask for formal permission.

It is worth remembering that you should only make amendments to the scale where absolutely necessary as significant changes could impact upon both the validity of the scale and, subsequently, your results! You also need to be aware that existing scales may be subject to copyright constraints. Even where there is no formal copyright, you should, where possible, contact the author and ask for permission. In your project report you should note where you obtained the scale and give credit to the author.

Question wording

The wording of each question will need careful consideration to ensure that the responses are valid – that is, measure what you think they do. Your questions will need to be checked within the context for which they were written rather than in abstract to ensure they are not misread and that they do not encourage a particular answer (Box 11.9). Given this, the checklist in Box 11.10 should help you to avoid the most obvious problems associated with wording that threaten the validity of responses.

Box 11.9 Focus on research in the news

Salmond's wording of vote on Scotland rejected

By Kiran Stacey and Mure Dickie

The Scottish government has accepted an amended referendum question for the 2014 vote on whether Scotland should end its three century old union with England. The UK independent Electoral Commission yesterday opposed the Scottish government's plan to ask voters "Do you agree that Scotland should be an independent country?" It said the use of "Do you agree" could encourage them to answer "yes".

The ruling was a rejection of the phrasing championed by Alex Salmond, Scotland's first minister. However, Nicola Sturgeon, the deputy first minister, said the Scottish government would accept the commission's suggestion that the referendum question read simply "Should Scotland be an independent country?"

Ms Sturgeon also accepted the commission's recommendation of campaign spending limits well above the levels proposed by the Scottish government. The commission's report put forward proposed spending limits for the two campaigns, suggesting that each of the lead campaigns should be allowed to spend £1.5m, double the £750,000 limit proposed by the Scottish government.

"I am also pleased with the spending limits proposed by the Electoral Commission they deliver a level playing field and will allow a fair and balanced debate on both sides," said Ms Sturgeon.

The Scottish government's immediate acceptance of the commission's advice avoids a potential dispute that could have been politically damaging to the ruling Scottish National party. The SNP welcomed the commission's call for the UK and Scottish governments to agree a "joint position" on what would happen in the event of a Yes or No vote.

FT *Source:* From 'Salmond's wording on vote for Scotland rejected', Kiran Stacey and Mure Dickie, *Financial Times*, 31 Jan 2013. Copyright © 2013 The Financial Times

Box 11.10
Checklist

Your question wording

✔ Does your question collect data at the right level of detail to answer your investigative question as specified in your data requirements table?

✔ Will respondents have the necessary knowledge to answer your question? A question on the implications of a piece of European Union legislation would yield meaningless answers from those who were unaware of that legislation.

✔ Does your question appear to talk down to respondents? It should not!

✔ Does your question challenge respondents' mental or technical abilities? Questions that do this are less likely to be answered.

✔ Are the words used in your question familiar to all respondents, and will all respondents understand them in the same way? In particular, you should use simple words and avoid jargon, abbreviations and colloquialisms.

✔ Are there any words that sound similar and might be confused with those used in your question? This is a particular problem with interviewer-completed questionnaires.

✔ Are there any words that look similar and might be confused if your question is read quickly? This is particularly important for self-completed questionnaires.

✔ Are there any words in your question that might cause offence? These might result in biased responses or a lower response rate.

✔ Can your question be shortened? Long questions are often difficult to understand, especially in interviewer-completed questionnaires, as the respondent needs to remember the whole question. Consequently, they often result in no response at all.

✔ Are you asking more than one question at the same time? The question 'How often do you visit your mother and father?' contains two separate questions, one about each parent, so responses would probably be impossible to interpret.

✔ Does your question include a negative or double negative? Questions that include the word 'not' are sometimes difficult to understand. The question 'Would you rather not use a non-medicated shampoo?' is far easier to understand when rephrased as: 'Would you rather use a medicated shampoo?'

✔ Is your question unambiguous? This can arise from poor sentence structure, using words with several different meanings or having an unclear investigative question. If you ask 'When did you leave school?' some respondents might state the year, others might give their age, while those still in education might give the time of day! Ambiguity can also occur in category questions. If you ask employers how many employees they have on their payroll and categorise their answers into three groups (up to 100, 100–250, 250 plus), they will not be clear which group to choose if they have 100 or 250 employees.

✔ Does your question imply that a certain answer is correct? If it does, the question is biased and will need to be reworded, such as with the question 'Many people believe that too little money is spent on our public Health Service. Do you believe this to be the case?' For this question, respondents are more likely to answer 'yes' to agree with and please the interviewer.

✔ Does your question prevent certain answers from being given? If it does, the question is biased and will need to be reworded. The question 'Is this the first time you have pretended to be sick?' implies that the respondent has pretended to be sick whether they answer yes or no!

✔ Is your question likely to embarrass the respondent? If it is, then you need either to reword it or to place it towards the end of the survey when you will, it is to be hoped, have gained the respondent's confidence. Questions on income can be asked as either precise amounts (more embarrassing), using a quantity question, or income bands (less embarrassing), using a category question. Questions on self-perceived shortcomings are unlikely to be answered.

✔ Have you incorporated advice appropriate for your type of questionnaire (such as the maximum number of categories) outlined in the earlier discussion of question types?

✔ Are answers to closed questions written so that at least one will apply to every respondent and so that each of the responses listed is mutually exclusive?

✔ Are the instructions on how to record each answer clear?

Translating questions into other languages

Translating questions and associated instructions into another language requires care if your translated or target questionnaire is to be decoded and answered by respondents in the way you intended. For international research this is extremely important if the questions are to have the same meaning to all respondents. For this reason Usunier (1998) suggests that when translating the source questionnaire attention should be paid to:

- **lexical meaning** – the precise meaning of individual words (e.g. the French word *chaud* can be translated into two concepts in English and German, 'warm' and 'hot');
- **idiomatic meaning** – the meanings of a group of words that are natural to a native speaker and not deducible from those of the individual words (e.g. the English expression for informal communication, 'grapevine', has a similar idiomatic meaning as the French expression *téléphone arabe*, meaning literally 'Arab telephone' and the German expression *Mundpropaganda*, meaning literally 'mouth propaganda');
- **experiential meaning** – the equivalence of meanings of words and sentences for people in their everyday experiences (e.g. terms that are familiar in the source questionnaire's context such as 'dual career household' may be unfamiliar in the target questionnaire's context);
- **grammar and syntax** – the correct use of language, including the ordering of words and phrases to create well-formed sentences (e.g. in Japanese the ordering is quite different from English or Dutch, as verbs are at the end of sentences).

Usunier (1998) outlines a number of techniques for translating your source questionnaire.

These, along with their advantages and disadvantages, are summarised in Table 11.4. In this table, the **source questionnaire** is the questionnaire that is to be translated, and the **target questionnaire** is the translated questionnaire. When writing your final project report, remember to include a copy of both the source and the target questionnaire as appendices. This will allow readers familiar with both languages to check that equivalent questions in both questionnaires have the same meaning.

Question coding

As you will be analysing your data by computer, question responses will need to be coded prior to entry. If you are using an online survey tool, this will be done automatically. The selected response to each closed question will either be given a numeric code or the selected answer recorded. For open questions the text entered by the respondent should be recorded verbatim. Responses automatically saved and can subsequently be exported as a data file in a variety of formats such as Excel™, IBM SPSS Statistics compatible or a comma-delimited file (Box 11.1).

For paper-based questionnaires you will need to allocate the codes yourself. For numerical responses, actual numbers can be used as codes. For other responses, you will need to design a coding scheme. Whenever possible, you should establish the coding scheme prior to collecting data and incorporate it into your questionnaire. This should take account of relevant existing coding schemes to enable comparisons with other data sets (Section 12.2).

For most closed questions codes are given to each response category. If you are using a paper questionnaire, these can be printed on the questionnaire, thereby **pre-coding** the question and removing the need to code after data collection. Two ways of doing this are illustrated by questions 16 and 17, which collect data on the respondents' opinions.

Table 11.4 Translation techniques for questionnaires

	Direct translation	Back-translation	Parallel translation	Mixed techniques
Approach	Source questionnaire to target questionnaire	Source questionnaire to target questionnaire to source questionnaire; comparison of two new source questionnaires; creation of final version	Source questionnaire to target questionnaire by two or more independent translators; comparison of two target questionnaires; creation of final version	Back-translation undertaken by two or more independent translators; comparison of two new source questionnaires; creation of final version
Advantages	Easy to implement, relatively inexpensive	Likely to discover most problems	Leads to good wording of target questionnaire	Ensures best match between source and target questionnaires
Disadvantages	Can lead to many discrepancies (including those relating to meaning) between source and target questionnaire	Requires two translators, one a native speaker of the source language, the other a native speaker of the target language	Cannot ensure that lexical, idiomatic and experiential meanings are kept in target questionnaire	Costly, requires two or more independent translators. Implies that the source questionnaire can also be changed

Source: Developed from Usunier (1998) 'Translation techniques for questionnaires' in International and Cross-Cultural Management Research. Copyright © 1998 Sage Publications, reprinted with permission

16	Is the service you receive? (Please circle O the number)	Excellent 5	Good 4	Reasonable 3	Poor 2	Awful 1
17	Is the service you receive? (Please tick ✓ the box)	Excellent $\square_5$	Good $\square_4$	Reasonable $\square_3$	Poor $\square_2$	Awful $\square_1$

The codes allocated to response categories will affect your analyses. In both questions 16 and 17 an ordered scale of numbers has been allocated to adjacent responses. This will make it far easier to aggregate responses using a computer (Section 12.2) to 'satisfactory' (5, 4 or 3) and 'unsatisfactory' (2 or 1). Consequently we recommend that when an online survey tool records responses to closed questions as text, these are re-coded to numerical values.

For open questions you will need to reserve space on your data collection form to code responses after data collection. Question 18 has been designed to collect attribute data in a sample survey of 5000 people. Theoretically there could be hundreds of possible responses, and so sufficient spaces are left in the 'For office use only' box.

18 What is your full job title?

....

For Office use only

□ □ □

Open questions, which generate lists of responses, are likely to require more complex coding using either the multiple-response or the multiple-dichotomy method. These are discussed in Section 12.2, and we recommend that you read this prior to designing your questions.

Constructing the questionnaire

The order and flow of questions

When constructing your questionnaire it is a good idea to spend time considering the order and flow of your questions. These should be logical to the respondent (and interviewer) rather than follow the order in your data requirements table (Table 11.2). They should take account of possible bias caused by the ordering of the questions. For example, a question asking a respondent to list the possible benefits of a new shopping centre could, if preceding a question about whether the respondent supports the proposed new shopping centre, bias respondents' answers in favour of the proposal.

To assist the flow of the questions it may be necessary to include **filter questions**. These identify those respondents for whom the following question or questions are not applicable, so they can skip those questions. You should beware of using more than two or three filter questions in paper-based self-completed questionnaires, as respondents tend to find having to skip questions annoying. More complex filter questions can be programmed using online survey tools and CAPI and CATI software so that skipped questions are never displayed on the screen and as a consequence never asked (Dillman et al. 2014). In such situations the respondent is unlikely to be aware of the questions that have been skipped. The following example uses the answer to question 19 to determine whether questions 20 to 24 will be answered. (Questions 19 and 20 both collect factual data.)

19   Are you currently registered as unemployed?   Yes   ☐₁

   If 'no' go to question 25   No   ☐₂

20   How long have you been registered as unemployed?   ☐☐ years   ☐☐ months

   (for example, for no years and six months write):   ☐ 0 years   ☐ 6 months

Where you need to introduce new topics, phrases such as 'the following questions refer to . . . or 'I am now going to ask you about . . .' are useful. And when wording your questions, you should remember the particular population for whom your questionnaire is designed. For interviewer-completed questionnaires, you will have to include instructions for the interviewer (Box 11.11). The checklist in Box 11.12 should help you to avoid the most obvious problems associated with question order and flow. For some questionnaires the advice contained may be contradictory. Where this is the case, you need to decide what is most important for your particular population.

The visual presentation of the questionnaire

Visual presentation is important for interviewer-completed, Internet and other self-completed questionnaires. Interviewer-completed questionnaires should be designed to make reading questions and filling in responses easy. The visual presentation of Internet and

Box 11.11
Focus on student research

Introducing a series of rating questions in a telephone questionnaire

As part of a telephone questionnaire, Stefan needed to collect data on respondents' opinions about motorway service stations. To do this he asked respondents to rate a series of statements using a Likert-type rating scale. These were recorded as a matrix. Because his survey was conducted by telephone the rating scale was restricted to four categories: strongly agree, agree, disagree, strongly disagree.

In order to make the questionnaire easy for the interviewer to follow, Stefan used italic script to highlight the interviewer's instructions and the words that the interviewer needed to read in bold. An extract is given below:

Now I'm going to read you several statements. Please tell me whether you strongly agree, agree, disagree or strongly disagree with each.

Interviewer: read out statements 21 to 30 one at a time and after each ask...

Do you strongly agree, agree, disagree or strongly disagree?

Record respondent's response with a tick ✓

	strongly agree	agree	disagree	strongly disagree
21 I think there should be a greater number of service stations on motorways	❑$_4$	❑$_3$	❑$_2$	❑$_1$

Box 11.12
Checklist

Your question order

✔ Are questions at the beginning of your questionnaire more straightforward and ones the respondent will enjoy answering? Questions about attributes and behaviours are usually more straightforward to answer than those collecting data on opinions.

✔ Are questions at the beginning of your questionnaire obviously relevant to the stated purpose of your questionnaire? For example, questions requesting contextual information may appear irrelevant.

✔ Are questions and topics that are more complex placed towards the middle of your questionnaire? By this stage most respondents should be undertaking the survey with confidence but should not yet be bored or tired.

✔ Are personal and sensitive questions towards the end of your questionnaire, and is their purpose clearly explained? On being asked these a respondent may refuse to answer; however, if they are at the end of an interviewer-completed questionnaire you will still have the rest of the data!

✔ Are filter questions and routing instructions easy to follow so that there is a clear route through the questionnaire?

✔ (For interviewer-completed questionnaires) Are instructions to the interviewer easy to follow?

✔ Are questions grouped into obvious sections that will make sense to the respondent?

✔ Have you re-examined the wording of each question and ensured it is consistent with its position in the questionnaire as well as with the data you require?

other self-completed questionnaires should, in addition, be attractive to encourage the respondent to fill it in and to return it, while not appearing too long. A two-column lay-out for a paper-based questionnaire (as in Case 11 at the end of this chapter) can look attractive without decreasing legibility (Ekinci 2015). For Internet questionnaires a single column is preferable while, due to the screen size, only one question per page is often preferable for mobile questionnaires (Dillman et al. 2014). However, where the choice is between an extra page (or screen) and a cramped questionnaire the former is likely to be more acceptable to respondents (Dillman et al. 2014). Online survey tools contain a series of style templates for typefaces, colours and page layout, which are helpful in pro-ducing a professional-looking questionnaire more quickly. For paper-based surveys, the use of colour will increase the printing costs. However, it is worth noting that the best way of obtaining valid responses to questions is to keep both the visual presentation of the questionnaire and the wording of each question simple (Dillman 2014).

Research findings on the extent to which the length of your questionnaire will affect your response rate are mixed (De Vaus 2014). There is a widespread view that longer question-naires will reduce response rates relative to shorter questionnaires (Edwards et al. 2002). However, a very short questionnaire may suggest that your research is insignificant and hence not worth bothering with. Conversely, a questionnaire that takes over an hour to complete might just be thrown away by the intended respondent. In general, we have found that a length of between four and eight A4 pages has been acceptable for within-organisation self-completed questionnaires. Telephone questionnaires of up to half an hour have caused few problems, whereas the acceptable length for structured interviews can vary from only a few minutes in the street to over two hours in a more comfortable environment (Section 10.6). Based on these experiences, we recommend you follow De Vaus' (2014) advice:

- Do not make the questionnaire longer than is really necessary to meet your research questions and objectives.
- Do not be too obsessed with the length of your questionnaire.

Remember you can reduce apparent length without reducing legibility by using matrix questions (discussed earlier) and, for paper questionnaires, presenting the questions in two columns. Box 11.13 discusses the impact on responses of delivering a questionnaire using the Internet rather than by mail and Box 11.14 summarises the most important layout issues as a checklist of common mistakes to avoid.

Explaining the purpose of the questionnaire

The covering letter or welcome screen

Most self-completed questionnaires are accompanied by a **covering letter**, email, text or SMS message, or have a welcome screen which explains the purpose of the survey. This is the first part of the questionnaire that a respondent should look at. Unfortunately, some of your sample will ignore it, while others use it to decide whether to answer the accompanying questionnaire.

Dillman et al. (2014) and others note the messages contained in a self-completed questionnaire's covering letter will affect the response rate. The results of Dillman et al.'s research, along with requirement of most ethics committees to stress that participation is voluntary, are summarised in the annotated letter (Figure 11.3).

For some research projects you may also send a letter prior to delivering your ques-tionnaire. This will be used by the respondent to decide whether to grant you access. Consequently, it is often the only opportunity you have to convince the respondent to participate in your research. Ways of ensuring this are discussed in Sections 6.2 to 6.4.

Box 11.13
Focus on management research

Comparing responses to Internet (Web) and postal (mail) questionnaires

Saunders' (2012) paper, 'Web versus mail: The influence of survey distribution mode on employees' response' in the journal *Field Methods*, uses an experimental design to examine implicitly the impact of distribution mode where employees are IT literate and already have access to the Internet as part of their everyday work.

Using an employee attitude survey distributed to a 50 per cent systematic sample of 3338 employees by mail, remaining employees receiving the survey via a web link (hyperlink), Saunders found, in contrast to many earlier studies, the return rate for the Web (49.1 per cent) was higher than that for mail (33.5 per cent). Although utility of web returns was reduced by a higher number of partial responses and abandonments (particularly for demographic questions), the rate for complete responses was still higher for the Web than for mail. Significant differences between web and mail responses were small other than those for open question: 'If there are any other areas or issues that concern you, please feel free to comment below . . .' Nearly 20 per cent of respondents provided written response to this question, there being no significant association between the distribution modes regarding whether or not a comment was provided, its tone or the topics covered. However, length of responses to this open question differed significantly, the mean length for web responses being twice that for mail distribution.

Drawing on his findings and the literature reviewed, Saunders offered a series of recommendations concerning the use of web surveys:

1 For research in organisations, the use of web-based questionnaires should be considered only where respondents are IT literate and have ready access to the Internet at work.

Partial response and, in particular, abandonment and complete non-response of demographic questions, prompted his second recommendation:

2 Web-based questionnaires should be designed to allow the impact of people not responding to be assessed.

As the literature reviewed had highlighted that the use of web questionnaires might influence responses where this is related to the survey topic, his third recommendation was:

3 Caution should be exercised regarding the inclusion of questions on topics related to the use of the Web or associated technologies.

Finally, based on the difference in length between responses to the Internet and mail delivered questionnaires he recommended:

4 Care should be taken when comparing or aggregating responses to open (write in) questions from web-based questionnaires with those from questionnaires delivered using other methods due to the impact of the technology on response length.

Introducing the questionnaire

At the start of your questionnaire you need to explain clearly and concisely why you want the respondent to complete the survey. Dillman et al. (2014) argue that, to achieve as high a response rate as possible, this should be done on the first page of the questionnaire in addition to the covering letter. He suggests that in addition to a summary of the main messages in the covering letter (Figure 11.3) you include:

• a clear unbiased banner or title, which conveys the topic of the questionnaire and makes it sound interesting;

Box 11.14
Checklist

Avoiding common mistakes in questionnaire layout

✔ (For self-completed questionnaires) Do questions appear well spaced on the page or screen? A cramped design will put the respondent off reading it and reduce the response rate. Unfortunately, a thick questionnaire is equally off-putting!

✔ (For paper-based self-completed questionnaires) Is the questionnaire going to be printed on good-quality paper? Poor-quality paper implies that the survey is not important.

✔ (For self-completed questionnaires) Is the questionnaire going to be printed or displayed on a warm pastel colour? Warm pastel shades, such as yellow and pink, generate slightly more responses than white (Edwards et al. 2002) or cool colours, such as green or blue. White is a good neutral colour but bright or fluorescent colours should be avoided.

✔ (For structured interviews) Will the questions and instructions be printed on one side of the paper only? An interviewer will find it difficult to read the questions on the back of pages if you are using a questionnaire attached to a clipboard!

✔ Is your questionnaire easy to read? Questionnaires should be typed in 12 point or 10 point using a plain font. Excessively long and unduly short lines reduce legibility. Similarly, respondents find CAPITALS, italics and shaded backgrounds more difficult to read. However, if used consistently, they can make completing the questionnaire easier.

✔ Have you ensured that the use of shading, colour, font sizes, spacing and the formatting of questions is consistent throughout the questionnaire?

✔ Is your questionnaire laid out in a format that respondents are accustomed to reading? Research has shown that many people skim-read questionnaires (Dillman et al. 2014). Instructions that can be read one line at a time from left to right moving down the page are, therefore, more likely to be followed correctly.

- a subtitle, which conveys the research nature of the topic (optional);
- a neutral graphic illustration or logo to add interest and to set the questionnaire apart (self-completed questionnaires).

This advice also applies to Internet questionnaires and is discussed later in this section. Interviewer-completed questionnaires will require this information to be phrased as a short introduction, given in the interviewer's own words to each respondent. A template for this (developed from De Vaus 2014), which the interviewer would paraphrase, is given in the next paragraph, while Box 11.15 provides an example from a self-completed questionnaire.

Good morning/afternoon/evening. My name is [your name] from [your organisation]. I am doing a research project to find out [brief description of purpose of the research]. Your telephone number was drawn from a random sample of [brief description of the total population]. The questions I should like to ask will take about [number] minutes. If you have any queries, I shall be happy to answer them. [Pause] Before I continue please can you confirm that this is [read out the telephone number] and that I am talking to [read out name/occupation/position in organisation to check that you have the right person]. Please can I confirm that you consent to answering the questions and ask you them now?

You will also need to have prepared answers to the more obvious questions that the respondent might ask you. These include the purpose of the survey, how you obtained the respondent's telephone number, who is conducting or sponsoring the survey, and why someone else should not answer the questions instead (Lavrakas 1993).

Banner: explains purpose clearly

Paper: good-quality, warm pastel colour or white

Letterhead: official; includes logo, address, telephone number and (if possible) email

Recipient's name: title, initial/forename (absence suggests impersonality)

Recipient's address: (absence suggests impersonality)

Date: in full

Salutation: title and name if possible

1st set of messages: what research is about, why it is useful

2nd set of messages: recipient's response valued, time needed

3rd set of messages: confidentiality and/or anonymity

4th set of messages: how results will be used, token reward for participation (if any)

Final set of messages: contact for queries, who to return to, date for return

Signature: by hand, in ink

Name: title, forename and surname

Closing remarks: thank recipient

Font size: 12 or 11 point

Length: one side maximum

Late Night Drinking
Your views on late night drinking in pubs and clubs

Anytown Business School

U*of*A

University of Anytown
Freepost 1234
Anytown
AN1 6RU

Email: kwhalley@anytown.ac.uk
Tel: 0123 4567890

Mr Bradley Oozer
17, Artois Court
Anytown
AN1 3CO

10 September 2015

Dear Mr Oozer,

This questionnaire is part of a research project to understand people's views about late night drinking in pubs and clubs. Your responses are important in enabling me to obtain as full an understanding as possible of this topical issue. However, your decision to take part is entirely voluntary.

If you do decide to take part, the questionnaire should take you about five minutes to complete. Please answer the questions in the spaces provided. If you wish to add further comments, please do. The information you provide will be treated in the strictest confidence. You will notice that you are not asked to include your name or address anywhere on the questionnaire.

The answers from your questionnaire and others will be used as the main data set for my research project for my degree in Business Studies at the University of Anytown.

I hope that you will find completing the questionnaire enjoyable. Please return the completed questionnaire to me, Kate Whalley, by 24 September 2015 in the enclosed Freepost envelope to the above address. If you have any questions or would like further information, please do not hesitate to telephone me on 0123 4567890 or email me at kwhalley@anytown.ac.uk.

Thank you for your help.

Kate Whalley

Ms Kate Whalley

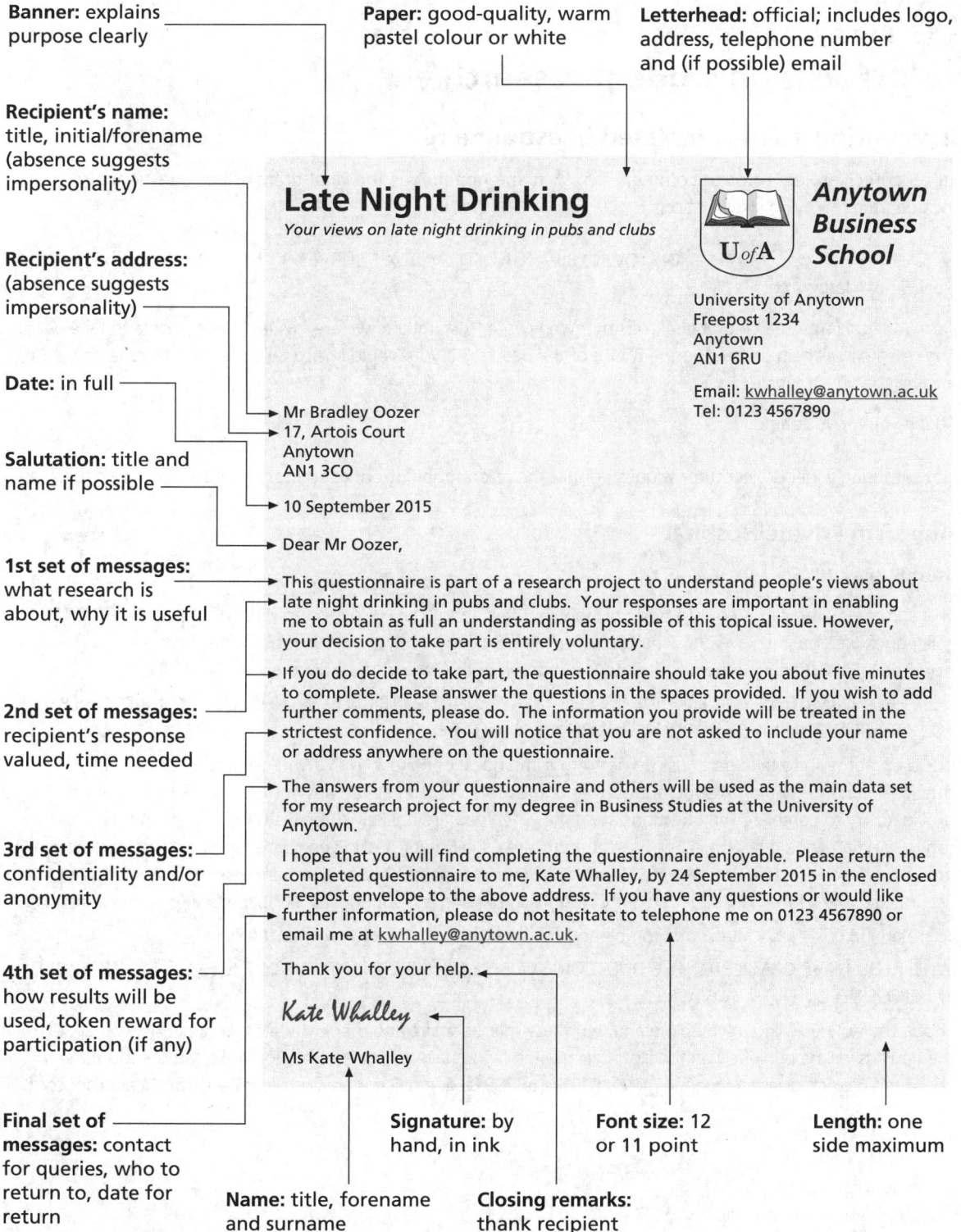

Figure 11.3 Structure of a covering letter or email

427

Box 11.15
Focus on student research

Introducing a self-completed questionnaire

Lil asked her project tutor to comment on what she hoped was the final draft of her questionnaire. This included the following introduction:

ANYTOWN PRIVATE HOSPITAL STAFF SURVEY

Dear Sir or Madam

I am undertaking research on behalf of Anytown Private Hospital and we are inviting some people to take part. The research will help us develop the future of the hospital. If you would like to take part in this research please answer the questionnaire.

Thank you for your time.

Not surprisingly, her project tutor suggested that she re-draft her introduction. Her revised introduction follows:

Anytown Private Hospital

Staff Survey 2015

This survey is being carried out to find out how you feel about the Hospital's policies to support colleagues like you in your work. Please answer the questions freely. You cannot be identified from the information you provide, and no information about individuals will be given to the Hospital.

ALL THE INFORMATION YOU PROVIDE WILL BE TREATED IN THE STRICTEST CONFIDENCE. YOUR DECISION TO PARTICIPATE IN THIS RESEARCH IS ENTIRELY VOLUNTARY.

If you do not wish to take part, just do not return the questionnaire to me. If you do decide to take part, the questionnaire should take you about five minutes to complete. Please answer the questions in the space provided. Try to complete the questions at a time when you are unlikely to be disturbed. Also, do not spend too long on any one question. Your first thoughts are usually your best! Even if you feel the items covered may not apply directly to your working life please do not ignore them. Your answers are essential in building an accurate picture of the issues that are important to improving our support for people working for this Hospital.

There are no costs associated with completing the questionnaire other than your time.

WHEN YOU HAVE COMPLETED THE QUESTIONNAIRE PLEASE RETURN IT TO US IN THE ENCLOSED FREEPOST ENVELOPE NO LATER THAN 6 APRIL.

I hope you will be willing to complete and return the questionnaire and thank you for your time. A summary of the findings will be published on the Hospital intranet. If you have any queries or would like further information about this project, please telephone me on 01234–5678910 or email me on l.woollons@anytownhealthcare.com.

Thank you for your help.

Lily Woollons

Lily Woollons
Human Resources Department
Anytown Private Hospital
Anytown AN99 9HS

Closing the questionnaire

At the end of your questionnaire you need to explain clearly what you want the respondent to do with their completed questionnaire. It is usual to start this section by thanking the respondent for completing the questionnaire, and restating the contact name, email address and telephone number for any queries they may have from the covering letter (Figure 11.3). You should restate details of the date by which you would like the questionnaire returned and how and where to return it. A template for this is given in the next paragraph:

> **Thank you for taking the time to complete this questionnaire. If you have any queries please do not hesitate to contact [your name] by telephoning [contact telephone number with answer machine/voice mail] or emailing [email address].**
>
> **Please return the completed questionnaire by [date] in the envelope provided to:**
>
> **[your name]**
>
> **[your address]**

Sometimes, as in Box 11.15, you may wish to make a summary of your research findings available. If you do make this offer, don't forget to actually provide the summary!

Pilot testing and assessing validity

Prior to using your questionnaire to collect data it should be pilot tested with respondents who are similar to those who will actually complete it. The purpose of the **pilot test** is to refine the questionnaire so that respondents will have no problems in answering the questions and there will be no problems in recording the data. In addition, it will enable you to obtain some assessment of the questions' validity and the likely reliability of the data that will be collected both for individual questions and, where appropriate, scales comprising a number of questions. Preliminary analysis using the pilot test data can be undertaken to ensure that the data collected will enable your investigative questions to be answered.

Initially you should ask an expert or group of experts to comment on the representativeness and suitability of your questions. As well as allowing suggestions to be made on the structure of your questionnaire, this will help establish content validity and enable you to make necessary amendments prior to pilot testing with a group as similar as possible to the final population in your sample. For any research project there is a temptation to skip the pilot testing. We would endorse Bell and Waters' (2014:167) advice, 'however pressed for time you are, do your best to give the questionnaire a trial run', as, without a trial run, you have no way of knowing whether your questionnaire will succeed.

The number of people with whom you pilot your questionnaire and the number of pilot tests you conduct are dependent on your research question(s), your objectives, the size of your research project, the time and money resources you have available, and how well you have initially designed your questionnaire. Very large surveys such as national censuses will have numerous field trials, starting with individual questions and working up to larger and more rigorous pilots of later drafts.

For smaller-scale surveys you are unlikely to have sufficient financial or time resources for large-scale field trials. However, it is still important that you pilot test your questionnaire. The number of people you choose should be sufficient to include any major variations in your population that you feel are likely to affect responses. For most student questionnaires this means that the minimum number for a pilot is 10 (Fink 2013), although for large surveys between 100 and 200 responses is usual (Dillman et al. 2014).

Occasionally you may be extremely pushed for time. In such instances it is better to pilot test the questionnaire using friends or family than not at all! This will provide you with at least some idea of your questionnaire's **face validity**: that is, whether the questionnaire appears to make sense.

As part of your pilot you should check each completed pilot questionnaire to ensure that respondents have had no problems understanding or answering questions and have followed all instructions correctly (Fink 2013). Their responses will provide you with an idea of the reliability and suitability of the questions. For self-completed questionnaires additional information about problems can be obtained by giving respondents a further short questionnaire. Bell and Waters (2014) suggest you should use this to find out:

- how long the questionnaire took to complete;
- the clarity of instructions;
- which, if any, questions were unclear or ambiguous;
- which, if any, questions the respondent felt uneasy about answering;
- whether in their opinion there were any major topic omissions;
- whether the layout was clear and attractive;
- any other comments.

Interviewer-completed questionnaires need to be tested with the respondents for all these points other than layout. One way of doing this is to form an assessment as each questionnaire progresses. Another is to interview any interviewers you are employing. However, you can also check by asking the respondent additional questions at the end of their interview. In addition, you will need to pilot test the questionnaire with interviewers to discover whether:

- there are any questions for which visual aids should have been provided;
- they have difficulty in finding their way through the questionnaire;
- they are recording answers correctly.

Once you have completed pilot testing you should write to these respondents thanking them for their help.

提交和收集问卷

11.5   Delivering and collecting the questionnaire

When your questionnaire is designed, pilot tested and amended and your sample selected, it can be used to collect data. Within business and management research reports, it is often not clear whether respondents felt compelled to respond to the questionnaire (Baruch and Holtom 2008). Respondents' feelings of compulsion are usually signified by stating the questionnaire was 'administered', whereas non-compulsion is signified by phrases such as 'invited to fill out a questionnaire voluntarily' or 'voluntary response'. In collecting data using your questionnaire it is important that you abide by your university's or professional body's code of ethics (Sections 6.5 and 6.6). Although, when a respondent answers questions and returns their questionnaire they are giving their implied consent, they have rights just like all research participants.

Inevitably you will need to gain access to your sample (Sections 6.2 to 6.4) and attempt to maximise the response rate. A large number of studies have been conducted to assess the impact of different strategies for increasing the response to postal questionnaires. Fortunately, the findings of these studies have been analysed and synthesised by Edwards et al. (2002) and, more recently, by Anseel et al. (2010). As you can

Table 11.5 Relative impact of strategies for raising postal questionnaire response rates

Strategy	Relative impact
Incentives	
Monetary incentive v. no incentive	Very high
Incentive sent with questionnaire v. incentive on questionnaire return	High
Non-monetary incentive v. no incentive	Low
Length	
Shorter questionnaire v. longer questionnaire	Very high
Appearance	
Brown envelope v. white envelope	High but variable
Coloured ink v. standard	Medium
Folder or booklet v. stapled pages	Low
More personalised (name, hand signature etc.) v. less personalised	Low
Coloured questionnaire v. white questionnaire	Very low
Identifying feature on the return v. none	Very low but variable
Delivery	
Recorded delivery v. standard delivery	Very high
Stamped return envelope v. business reply or franked	Medium
First class post outwards v. other class	Low
Sent to work address v. sent to home address	Low but variable
Pre-paid return v. not pre-paid	Low but variable
Commemorative stamp v. *ordinary stamp*	Low but variable
Stamped outward envelope v. franked	Negligible
Contact	
Pre-contact (advanced notice) v. no pre-contact	Medium
Follow-up v. no follow-up	Medium
Postal follow-up including questionnaire v. postal follow-up excluding questionnaire	Medium
Pre-contact by telephone v. *pre-contact by post*	Low
Mention of follow-up contact v. none	Negligible
Content	
More interesting/relevant v. less interesting/relevant topic	Very high
User-friendly language v. standard	Medium
Demographic and behaviour questions only v. demographic, behaviour and attitude questions	Medium
More relevant questions first v. other questions first	Low
Most general question first v. *last*	Low
Sensitive questions included v. *sensitive questions not included*	Very low
Demographic questions first v. other questions first	Negligible
'Don't know' boxes included v. not included	Negligible
Origin	
University sponsorship as a source v. other organisation	Medium
Sent by more senior or well-known person v. *less senior or less well-known*	Low but variable
Ethnically unidentifiable/white name v. other name	Low but variable

(continued)

Table 11.5 (*Continued*)

Strategy	Relative impact
Communication	
Explanation for not participating requested v. not requested	Medium
Anonymity stressed v. not mentioned	Medium
Choice to opt out from study offered v. *not given*	Low
Instructions given v. *not given*	Low but variable
Benefits to respondent stressed v. other benefits	Very low
Benefits to sponsor stressed v. other benefits	Negligible
Benefits to society stressed v. other benefits	Negligible
Response deadline given v. no deadline	Negligible

Note: Strategies in italics increase response rates relative to those in normal font
Source: Developed from Anseel et al. 2010; Edwards et al. 2002

see from Table 11.5, response rates can be improved by careful attention to a range of factors, including visual presentation, length, content, delivery methods and associated communication as well as being clearly worded. In addition, it must be remembered that organisations and individuals are increasingly being bombarded with requests to respond to questionnaires and so may be unwilling to answer your questionnaire. Which of these techniques you use to help to maximise responses will inevitably be dependent, at least in part, on the way in which your questionnaire is delivered. It is the processes associated with delivering each of the five types of questionnaire that we now consider.

Internet questionnaires

For both Web and mobile questionnaires, it is important to have a clear timetable that identifies the tasks that need to be done and the resources that will be needed. A good response is dependent on the recipient being motivated to answer the questionnaire and to send it back. Although the covering email or SMS message (Section 11.4) and visual appearance will help to ensure a high level of response, it must be remembered that, unlike paper questionnaires, the designer and respondent may see different images displayed on their screens. Alternative computer operating systems, Internet browsers and display screens can all result in the image being displayed differently, emphasising the need to ensure the questionnaire design is clear across all display media (Dillman et al. 2014).

Web and mobile questionnaires are usually delivered via a Web link. This normally uses email or a Web page to display the hyperlink (Web link) to the questionnaire and is dependent on having a list of addresses. If you are using the Internet for research, you should abide by the general operating guidelines or **netiquette**. This includes (Hewson et al. 2003):

- ensuring emails and postings to user groups are relevant and that you do not send junk emails (spam);
- remembering that invitations to participate sent to over 20 user groups at once are deemed as unacceptable by many net vigilantes and so you should not exceed this threshold;

- avoiding sending your email to multiple mailing lists as this is likely to result in individuals receiving multiple copies of your email (this is known as **cross-posting**);
- avoiding the use of email attachments as these can contain viruses.

For within-organisation research, questionnaires can be easily delivered as a hyperlink within an email to employees, provided all of the sample have access to it and use email. If you choose to use email with a direct hyperlink to the questionnaire, we suggest that you:

1 contact recipients by email and advise them to expect a questionnaire – a pre-survey contact (Section 6.3);

2 email the hyperlink to the questionnaire with a covering email. Where possible, the letter and questionnaire or hyperlink should be part of the email message rather than an attached file to avoid viruses. You should make sure that this will arrive when recipients are likely to be receptive. For most organisations Fridays and days surrounding major public holidays have been shown to be a poor time;

3 summarise the purpose of the research and include an explicit request for the respondent's consent in the welcome screen at the start of the questionnaire (Box 11.16);

4 email the first follow-up one week after emailing out the questionnaire to all recipients. This should thank early respondents and remind non-respondents to answer (a copy of the hyperlink should be included);

Box 11.16
Focus on student research

Request for respondent's consent in an Internet questionnaire

Lily had decided to collect her data using an Internet questionnaire. She emailed potential respondents explaining the purpose of her research and requesting their help. At the end of her email she included a hyperlink to the Internet questionnaire created in SurveyMonkey™.

The first page of Lily's Internet questionnaire included a summary of the main messages in her email. This was followed by a formal request to the respondent for their consent, which stressed that the decision to participate was entirely voluntary and that they could withdraw at any time:

Consent	○	Exit this survey

Thank you for your interest in my research. Before you participate, I need to make sure you know what my research is about, what your involvement will be and that you consent to take part.

By clicking the NEXT button to begin the online questionnaire I understand:

1. I am participating in a research study.

2. I have been given an explanation of the research I am about to participate in and I know what is involved in my participating.

3. My participation in this research is voluntary and that I am free to withdraw at any time without giving any reason.

4. My identity cannot be linked to my data and that all information I give remains anonymous.

5. I have been given the name and email address of the researcher, Lily Woollons (l.woollons@anytown.ac.uk) to contact if I have questions about this research.

Next

Source: Question layout created by SurveyMonkey.com, LLC (2014) Palo Alto, California. Reproduced with permission

Figure 11.4 QR Code linking directly to Mark's research methods publications that are available on academia.edu

5 email the second follow-up to people who have not responded after three weeks. This should include another covering letter and a copy of the hyperlink. The covering letter should be reworded to further emphasise the importance of completing the questionnaire;
6 also use a third follow-up if time allows or your response rate is low;
7 when the respondent completes the questionnaire, their responses will be saved automatically. However, you may need to select the online survey tool option that prevents multiple responses from one respondent.

Alternatively, the questionnaire can be advertised online or in printed media and potential respondents invited to access the questionnaire by clicking on a hyperlink or scanning a QR (quick response) code (Figure 11.4) using their mobile phone. Adopting either approach observes netiquette and means that respondents can remain anonymous. The stages involved are:

1 Ensure that a website has been set up that explains the purpose of the research and has the hyperlink to the questionnaire (this takes the place of the covering letter).
2 Advertise the research website widely using a range of media (for example, an email pre-survey contact or a banner advertisement on a page that is likely to be looked at by the target population) and highlight the closing date.
3 When respondents complete the questionnaire, their responses will be saved automatically. However, you may need to select the online survey tool option that prevents multiple responses from one respondent.

Response rates from web advertisements and QR codes are likely to be very low, and there are considerable problems of non-response bias as the respondent has to take extra steps to locate and complete the questionnaire. Consequently, it is likely to be very difficult to obtain a representative sample from which you might generalise. This is not to say that this approach should not be used as it can, for example, enable you to contact difficult-to-access groups. It all depends, as you would expect us to say, on your research question and objectives!

Postal questionnaires

For postal questionnaires, it is important to have a concise and clear covering letter and good visual presentation to help to ensure a high level of response. As with Internet questionnaires, a clear timetable and well-executed administration process are important (Box 11.17).

Box 11.17
Focus On management research

Questionnaire administration

Mark undertook an attitude survey of employees in a large organisation using a questionnaire. Within the organisation, 50 per cent of employees received a Web questionnaire by a hyperlink in an email, the remaining 50 per cent receiving a paper questionnaire by post.

General information regarding the forthcoming survey was provided to employees using the staff intranet, the normal method for such communications. Subsequently each employee received five personal contacts including the questionnaire:

- One week before the questionnaire was delivered a pre-survey notification letter, jointly from

the organisation's Chief Executive and Mark, was delivered in the same manner as the potential respondent would receive their questionnaire.
- Covering letter/email and questionnaire/hyperlink to Web questionnaire.
- Personal follow-up/reminder designed as an information sheet re-emphasising the deadline for returns at the end of that week.
- First general reminder (after the deadline for returns) posted on the staff intranet.
- Second general reminder (after the deadline for returns) posted on the staff intranet.

The following graph records the cumulative responses for both the Web and postal questionnaire, emphasising both the impact of deadlines, follow-up/reminders and the length of time required (over 7 weeks) to collect all the completed questionnaires.

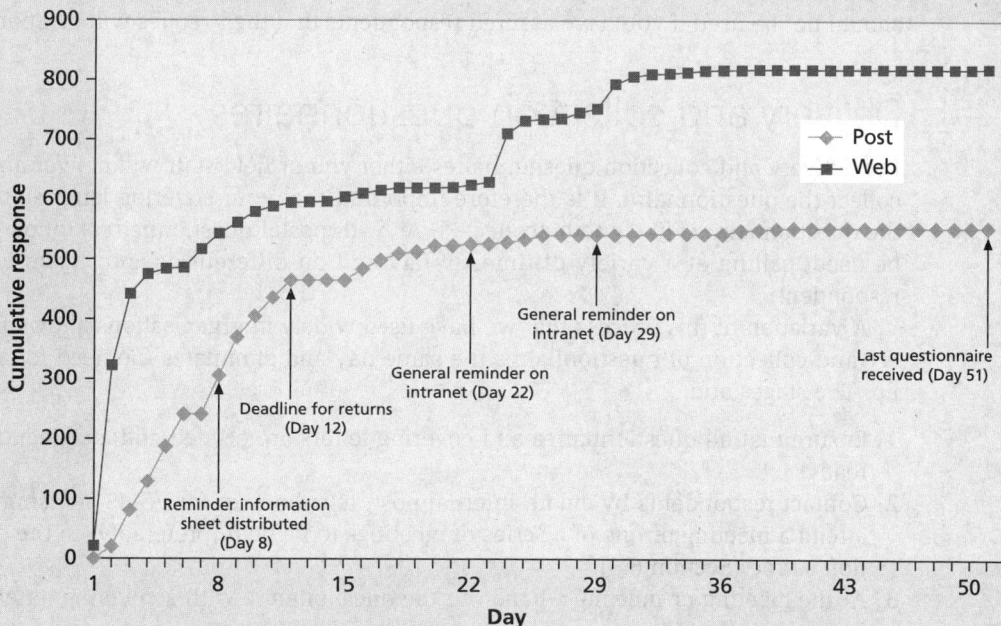

Cumulative questionnaires returned by Intranet and post

Source: Unpublished data; details of research from Saunders, 2012

Our advice for postal questionnaires (developed from De Vaus 2014) can be split into six stages:

1 Ensure that questionnaires and letters are printed, and envelopes addressed.
2 Contact recipients by post, telephone or email and advise them to expect a questionnaire – a pre-survey contact (Section 6.3). This stage is often omitted for cost reasons.
3 Post the survey with a covering letter and a return envelope. You should make sure that this will arrive when recipients are likely to be receptive. For most organisations Fridays and days surrounding major public holidays have been shown to be a poor time.
4 Post (or email) the first follow-up one week after posting out the survey to all recipients. For posted questionnaires this should take the form of a postcard designed to thank early respondents and to remind rather than to persuade non-respondents.
5 Post the second follow-up to people who have not responded after three weeks. This should contain another copy of the questionnaire, a new return envelope and a new covering letter. The covering letter should be reworded to emphasise further the importance of completing the questionnaire. For anonymous questionnaires a second follow-up will not be possible, as you should not be able to tell who has responded!
6 Also use a third follow-up if time allows or your response rate is low. For this it may be possible to use 'signed for' delivery (post), telephone calls or even call in person to emphasise the importance of responding.

Additionally, De Vaus (2014) advises placing a unique identification number on each questionnaire, which is recorded on your list of recipients. This makes it easy to check and follow up non-respondents and, according to Dillman et al. (2014) and Edwards et al. (2002), has little, if any, effect on response rates. However, identification numbers should not be used if you have assured respondents that their replies will be anonymous!

Delivery and collection questionnaires

For delivery and collection questionnaires either you or field staff will deliver and call to collect the questionnaire. It is therefore important that your covering letter states when the questionnaire is likely to be collected. As with postal questionnaires, follow-ups can be used, calling at a variety of times of day and on different days to try to catch the respondent.

A variation of this process that we have used widely in organisations allows for delivery and collection of questionnaires the same day and eliminates the need for a follow-up. The stages are:

1 Ensure that all questionnaires and covering letters are printed and a collection box is ready.
2 Contact respondents by email, internal post, telephone or text/SMS advising them to attend a meeting or one of a series of meetings to be held (preferably) in the organisation's time (Section 6.3).
3 At the meeting or meetings, hand out the questionnaire with a covering letter to each respondent.
4 Introduce the questionnaire, stress its anonymous or confidential nature and that participation is voluntary.
5 Ensure that respondents place their questionnaires in a collection box before they leave the meeting.

Although this adds to costs, as employees are completing the questionnaire in work time, response rates as high as 98 per cent are achievable!

Telephone questionnaires

The quality of data collected using telephone questionnaires will be affected by the researcher's competence to conduct interviews. This is discussed in Section 10.5. Once your sample has been selected, you need to:

1 ensure that all questionnaires are printed or, for CATI, that the survey tool has been programmed and tested;
2 where possible and resources allow, contact respondents by email, post or telephone advising them to expect a telephone call (Section 6.3);
3 telephone each respondent, recording the date and time of call and whether or not the questionnaire was completed. You should note any specific times that have been arranged for call-backs. For calls that were not successful you should note the reason, such as no reply or telephone disconnected;
4 for unsuccessful calls where there was no reply, try three more times, each at a different time and on a different day, and note the same information;
5 make call-back calls at the time arranged.

Face-to-face questionnaires

Conducting face-to-face questionnaires uses many of the skills required for in-depth and semi-structured interviews (Section 10.5). Issues such as interviewer appearance and preparedness are important and will affect the response rate (Section 10.4). However, once your sample has been selected you need to:

1 ensure that all questionnaires are printed or, for CAPI, that the survey tool has been programmed and tested;
2 contact respondents by email, post or telephone advising them to expect an interviewer to call within the next week. This stage is often omitted for cost reasons;
3 (for large-scale surveys) divide the sample into assignments that are of a manageable size (50–100) for one interviewer;
4 contact each respondent or potential respondent in person, recording the date and time of contact and whether or not the interview was completed. You should note down any specific times that have been arranged for return visits. For contacts that were not successful, you should note down the reason;
5 try unsuccessful contacts at least twice more, each at a different time and on a different day, and note down the same information;
6 visit respondents at the times arranged for return visits.

11.6 Summary 小 结

- Questionnaires collect data by asking people to respond to exactly the same set of questions. They are often used as part of a survey strategy to collect descriptive and explanatory data about facts/demographics, attitudes/opinions and behaviours/events. Data collected are normally analysed by computer.
- Your choice of questionnaire will be influenced by your research question(s) and objectives and the resources that you have available. The five main types are Internet, postal, delivery and collection, telephone and face-to-face (structured interview).
- Prior to designing a questionnaire, you must know precisely what data you need to collect to answer your research question(s) and to meet your objectives. One way of helping to ensure that you collect these data is to use a data requirements table.

- The validity and reliability of the data you collect and the response rate you achieve depend largely on the design of your questions, the structure of your questionnaire and the rigour of your pilot testing.
- When designing your questionnaire you should consider the wording of individual questions prior to the order in which they appear. Questions can be divided into open and closed. The six types of closed questions are list, category, ranking, rating, quantity and matrix.
- Responses for closed questions in Internet questionnaires are coded automatically within the online survey software. For other types of questionnaire closed questions should, wherever possible, be pre-coded on your questionnaire to facilitate data input and subsequent analyses.
- The order and flow of questions in the questionnaire should be logical to the respondent. This can be assisted by filter questions and linking phrases.
- The visual appearance of the questionnaire should be attractive, easy to read and the responses easy to fill in.
- Questionnaires must be introduced carefully to the respondent to ensure a high response rate. For self-completed questionnaires this should take the form of a covering letter or email or included in the welcome screen; for interviewer-completed questions it will be done by the interviewer.
- All questionnaires should be pilot tested prior to their delivery to assess the validity and likely reliability of the questions.
- Delivery of questionnaires needs to be appropriate to the type of questionnaire.

Self-check questions   自测题

11.1   In what circumstances would you choose to use a delivery and collection questionnaire rather than an Internet questionnaire? Give reasons for your answer.

11.2   The following questions have been taken from a questionnaire about flexibility of labour.

i   Do you agree or disagree with the use of nil hours contracts by employers? (Please tick appropriate box)

Strongly agree $\square_4$
Agree $\square_3$
Disagree $\square_2$
Strongly disagree $\square_1$

ii   Have you ever been employed on a nil hours contract? (Please tick appropriate box)

Yes $\square_1$
No $\square_2$
Not sure $\square_3$

iii   What is your marital status? (Please tick appropriate box)

Single $\square_1$
Married or living in long-term relationship $\square_2$
Widowed $\square_3$
Divorced $\square_4$
Other $\square_5$
.... ($\Leftarrow$ Please describe)

iv   Please describe what you think would be the main impact on employees of a nil hours contract.

For each question identify:
a the type of data variable for which data are being collected;
b the type of question.
You should give reasons for your answers.

11.3 You are undertaking research on the use of children's book clubs by householders within mainland Europe. As part of this, you have already undertaken in-depth interviews with households who belong and do not belong to children's book clubs. This, along with a literature review, has suggested a number of investigative questions from which you start to construct a table of data requirements.

    a For each investigative question listed, decide whether you will need to collect factual/demographic, attitude/opinion or behaviour/event data.

    b Complete the table of data requirements for each of the investigative questions already listed. (You may embellish the scenario to help in your choice of variables required and the detail in which the data will be measured as you feel necessary, but you do not have to explore the relation to theory and key concepts in the literature.)

Research question/objective: To establish mainland Europe's householders' opinions about children's book clubs				
Type of research: Predominantly descriptive, although wish to explain differences between householders				
Investigative questions	**Variable(s) required**	**Detail in which data measured**	**Relation to theory and key concepts in literature**	**Check included in questionnaire ✓**
A Do householders think that children's book clubs are a good or a bad idea?				
B What things do householders like most about children's book clubs?				
C Would householders be interested in an all-ages book club?				
D How much per year do households spend on children's books?				
E Do households' responses differ depending on (i) number of children? (ii) whether already members of a children's book club?				

11.4 Design pre-coded or self-coded questions to collect data for each of the investigative questions in Question 11.3. Note that you will need to answer self-check question 11.3 first (or use the answer at the end of this chapter).

11.5 What issues will you need to consider when translating your questionnaire?

11.6 You work for a major consumer research bureau that has been commissioned by 11 major UK companies to design, deliver and analyse the data collected from a telephone questionnaire. The purpose of this questionnaire is to describe and explain relationships between adult consumers' lifestyles, opinions and purchasing intentions. Write the introduction to this telephone questionnaire, to be read by an interviewer to each respondent. You may embellish the scenario and include any other relevant information you wish.

11.7 You have been asked by a well-known national charity 'Work for All' to carry out research into the effects of long-term unemployment throughout the UK. The charity intends to use the findings of this research as part of a major campaign to highlight public awareness about the effects of long-term unemployment. The charity has drawn up a list of names and postal addresses of people who are or were long-term unemployed with whom they have had contact over the past six months. Write a covering letter to accompany the postal questionnaire. You may embellish the scenario and include any other relevant information you wish.

11.8 You have been asked to give a presentation to a group of managers at an oil exploration company to gain access to undertake your research. As part of the presentation you outline your methodology, which includes piloting the questionnaire. In the ensuing question and answer session one of the managers asks you to justify the need for a pilot study, arguing that 'given the time constraints the pilot can be left out'. List the arguments that you would use to convince him that pilot testing is essential to your methodology'.

Review and discussion questions   复习与讨论题

11.9 If you wish for more help with designing questionnaires, visit the website www.statpac .com/surveys/ and download and work through the 'Survey Design Tutorial'.

11.10 Obtain a copy of a 'customer questionnaire' from a department store or restaurant. For each question on the questionnaire establish whether it is collecting factual/ demographic, attitude/opinion or behaviour/event data. Do you consider any of the questions are potentially misleading? If yes, how do you think the question could be improved? Discuss the answer to these questions in relation to your questionnaire with a friend.

11.11 Visit the website of an online survey tool provider. A selection of possible providers can be found by typing 'Internet questionnaire provider' or 'online survey provider' into the Google search engine. Use the online survey tool to design a simple questionnaire. To what extent does the questionnaire you have designed meet the requirements of the checklists in Boxes 11.10, 11.12 and 11.14?

11.12 Visit your university library or use the Internet to view a copy of a report for a recent national government survey in which you are interested. If you are using the Internet, the national government websites listed in Table 8.2 are a good place to start. Check the appendices in the report to see if a copy of the questionnaire used to collect the data is included. Of the types of question – open, list, category, ranking, rating, quantity and grid – which is most used and which is least frequently used? Note down any that may be of use to you in your research project.

改进研究项目

Progressing your research project

Using questionnaires in your research 在你的研究中使用问卷

- Return to your research question(s) and objectives. Decide on how appropriate it would be to use questionnaires as part of your research strategy. If you do decide that this is appropriate, note down the reasons why you think it will be sensible to collect at least some of your data in this way. If you decide that using a questionnaire is not appropriate, justify your decision.
- If you decide that using a questionnaire is appropriate, re-read Chapter 7 on sampling and, in conjunction with this chapter, decide which of the five types of questionnaire will be most appropriate. Note down your choice of questionnaire and the reasons for this choice.
- Construct a data requirements table and work out precisely what data you need to answer your investigative questions. Remember that you will need to relate your investigative questions and data requirements to both theory and key concepts in the literature you have reviewed and any preliminary research you have already undertaken.

- Design the separate questions to collect the data specified in your data requirements table. Wherever possible, try to use closed questions and to adhere to the suggestions in the question wording checklist. If you are intending to analyse your questionnaire by computer, read Section 12.2 and pre-code questions on the questionnaire whenever possible.
- Order your questions to make reading the questions and filling in the responses as logical as possible to the respondent. Wherever possible, try to adhere to the checklist for layout. Remember that interviewer-completed questionnaires will need instructions for the interviewer.
- Write the introduction to your questionnaire and, where appropriate, a covering letter.
- Pilot test your questionnaire with as similar a group as possible to the final group in your sample. Pay special attention to issues of validity and reliability.
- Deliver your questionnaire and remember to send out a follow-up survey to non-respondents whenever possible.
- Use the questions in Box 1.4 to guide your reflective diary entry

Self-check answers 自测题答案

11.1 When you:
- wanted to check that the person whom you wished to answer the questions had actually answered the questions;
- have sufficient resources to devote to delivery and collection and the geographical area over which the questionnaire is delivered is small;
- can use field workers to enhance response rates. Delivery and collection questionnaires have a moderately high response rate of between 30 and 50 per cent compared with approximately 10 per cent offered on average by an Internet questionnaire;
- are delivering a questionnaire to an organisation's employees and require a very high response rate. By delivering the questionnaire to groups of employees in work time and collecting it on completion, response rates of up to 98 per cent can be achieved.

11.2 a i Opinion data: the question is asking how the respondent feels about the use of nil hours contracts by employees.

    ii Behaviour data: the question is asking about the concrete experience of being employed on a nil hours contract.

    iii Demographic data: the question is asking about the respondent's characteristics.

    iv Opinion data: the question is asking the respondent what they think or believe would be the impact on employees.

  b i Rating question using a Likert-type scale in which the respondent is asked how strongly they agree or disagree with the statement.

    ii Category question in which the respondent's answer can fit only one answer.

    iii Category question as before.

    iv Open question in which the respondent can answer in their own way.

11.3 Although your answer is unlikely to be precisely the same, the completed table of data requirements below should enable you to check you are on the right lines.

Research question/objective: To establish householders' opinions about children's book clubs

Type of research: Predominantly descriptive, although wish to explain differences between householders

Investigative questions	Variable(s) required	Detail in which data measured	Relation to theory and key concepts in literature	Check included in questionnaire ☑
Do householders think that children's book clubs are a good or a bad idea? (opinion – this is because you are really asking how householders feel)	Opinion about children's book clubs	Very good idea, good idea, neither a good nor a bad idea, bad idea, very bad idea		
What things do householders like most about children's book clubs? (opinion)	What householders like about children's book clubs	Get them to rank the following things (generated from earlier in-depth interviews): monthly magazine, lower prices, credit, choice, special offers, shopping at home		
Would householders be interested in an all-ages book club? (behaviour)	Interest in a book club which was for both adults and children	Interested, not interested, may be interested		

(continued)

Investigative questions	Variable(s) required	Detail in which data measured	Relation to theory and key concepts in literature	Check included in questionnaire ☑
How much per year do households spend on children's books? (behaviour)	Amount spent on children's books by adults and children per year by household	(Answers to the nearest €) €0 to €10, €11 to €20, €21 to €30, €31 to €50, €51 to €100, over €100		
Do households' responses differ depending on: Number of children? (demographic) Whether already members of a children's book club? (behaviour)	Number of children aged under 16 Children's book club member	Actual number yes, no		

11.4 a Please complete the following statement by ticking the phrase that matches your feelings most closely . . .

I feel children's book clubs are . . . .

. . . a very good idea	❑5
. . . a good idea	❑4
. . . neither a good nor a bad idea	❑3
. . . a bad idea	❑2
. . . a very bad idea	❑1

b Please number each of the features of children's book clubs listed below in order of how much you like them. Number the most important 1, the next 2 and so on. The feature you like the least should be given the highest number.

Feature	How much liked
Monthly magazine	....
Lower prices	....
Credit	....
Choice	....
Special offers	....
Shopping at home	....

c Would you be interested in a book club that was for both adults and children?
(Please tick the appropriate box)

Yes	❑1
No	❑2
Not sure	❑3

d How much money is spent in total each year on children's books by all the adults and children living in your household?

(Please tick the appropriate box)   €0 to €10   ❏₁

€11 to €20   ❏₂

€21 to €30   ❏₃

€31 to €50   ❏₄

€51 to €100   ❏₅

Over €100   ❏₆

e i   How many children aged under 16 are living in your household?

☐   children

(for example, for 3 write:)   3   children

ii   Is any person living in your household a member of a children's book club?

(Please tick the appropriate box)   Yes   ❏₁

No   ❏₂

11.5 When translating your questionnaire you will need to ensure that:
- the precise meaning of individual words is kept (lexical equivalence);
- the meanings of groups of words and phrases that are natural to a native speaker but cannot be translated literally are kept (idiomatic equivalence);
- the correct grammar and syntax are used.

In addition, you should, if possible, use back-translation, parallel translation or mixed translation techniques to ensure that there are no differences between the source and the target questionnaire.

11.6 Although the precise wording of your answer is likely to differ, it would probably be something like this:

Good morning/afternoon/evening. My name is _____ from JJ Consumer Research. We are doing an important national survey covering lifestyles, opinions and likely future purchases of adult consumers. Your telephone number has been selected at random. The questions I need to ask you will take about 15 minutes. If you have any queries I shall be happy to answer them [pause]. Before I continue please can you confirm that this is [read out telephone number including dialling code] and that I am talking to a person aged 18 or over. Please can I confirm that you are willing to take part and ask you the first question now?

11.7 Although the precise wording of your answer is likely to differ, it would probably be something like the letter below.

Work for All

B&J Market Research Ltd
St Richard's House
Malvern
Worcestershire WR14 12Z
Phone 01684–56789101
Fax 01684–56789102

Respondent's name

Email andy@b&jmarketresearch.co.uk

Respondent's address

Today's date

Dear *title name*

Work for All is conducting research into the effects of long-term unemployment. This is an issue of great importance within the UK and yet little is currently known about the consequences.

You are one of a small number of people who are being asked to give your opinion on this issue. You were selected at random from Work for All's list of contacts. In order that the results will truly represent people who have experienced long-term unemployment, it is important that your questionnaire is completed and returned.

All the information you give us will be totally confidential. You will notice that your name and address do not appear on the questionnaire and that there is no identification number. The results of this research will be passed to Work for All, who will be mounting a major campaign in the New Year to highlight public awareness about the effects of long-term unemployment.

If you have any questions you wish to ask or there is anything you wish to discuss please do not hesitate to telephone me, or my assistant Benjamin Marks, on 01684–56789101 during the day. You can call me at home on 01234–123456789 evenings and weekends. Thank you for your help.

Yours sincerely

Andy Nother

Mr Andy Nother

Project Manager

11.8 Despite the time constraints, pilot testing is essential to your methodology for the following reasons:

- to find out how long the questionnaire takes to complete;
- to check that respondents understand and can follow the instructions on the questionnaire (including filter questions);
- to ensure that all respondents understand the wording of individual questions in the same way and that there are no unclear or ambiguous questions;

- to ensure that you have the same understanding of the wording of individual questions as the respondents;
- to check that respondents have no problems in answering questions; for example:
- all possible answers are covered in list questions;
- whether there are any questions that respondents feel uneasy about answering;
- to discover whether there are any major topic omissions;
- to provide an idea of the validity of the questions that are being asked;
- to provide an idea of the reliability of the questions by checking responses from individual respondents to similar questions;
- to check that the visual presentation is clear and attractive;
- to provide limited test data so you can check that the proposed analyses will work.

> Get ahead using resources on the companion website at: **www.pearsoned.co .uk/saunders**.
>
> - Improve your IBM SPSS Statistics and NVivo research analysis with practice tutorials.
> - Save time researching on the Internet with the Smarter Online Searching Guide.
> - Test your progress using self-assessment questions.
> - Follow live links to useful websites.

Chapter 12

Analysing quantitative data 分析定量数据

Learning outcomes 学习目标

By the end of this chapter, you should be able to:

- identify the main issues that you need to consider when preparing quantitative data for analysis and when analysing these data by computer;
- recognise different types of data and understand the implications of data type for subsequent analyses;
- create a data matrix and code data for analysis by computer;
- select the most appropriate tables and graphs to explore and illustrate different aspects of your data;
- select the most appropriate statistics to describe individual variables and to examine relationships between variables and trends in your data;
- interpret the tables, graphs and statistics that you use correctly.

12.1 Introduction 引 言

Quantitative data in a raw form, that is, before these data have been processed and analysed, convey very little meaning to most people. These data, therefore, need to be processed to make them useful, that is, to turn them into information. Quantitative analysis techniques such as tables, graphs and statistics allow us to do this, helping us to explore, present, describe and examine relationships and trends within our data.

Virtually any business and management research you undertake is likely to involve some numerical data or contain data that could usefully be quantified to help you answer your research question(s) and to meet your objectives. Quantitative data refer to all such primary and secondary data and can range from simple counts such as the frequency of occurrences to more complex data such as test scores, prices or rental costs. To be useful these data need to be analysed and interpreted. Quantitative analysis techniques assist you in this process. They range from creating simple tables or graphs that show the frequency of occurrence and using statistics such as indices to enable comparisons, through establishing statistical relationships between variables to complex statistical modelling.

Within quantitative analysis, calculations and chart drawing are undertaken using analysis software ranging from spreadsheets such as Excel™ to more advanced data management and statistical analysis software packages such as Minitab™, SAS™, IBM SPSS Statistics™ and Statview™. You might also use more specialised survey design and analysis packages such as Qualtrics™ or

The Big Mac Index is published biannually by *The Economist* to provide a simple way of measuring differences in purchasing power between currencies. The index provides an idea of the extent to which currency exchange rates actually result in goods costing the same in different countries. Obviously the index does not take into account that Big Mac hamburgers are not precisely the same in every country; nutritional values, weights and sizes often differ. Similarly it does not allow for prices within a country differing between McDonald's restaurants, McDonald's providing *The Economist* with a single price for each country. However, it does provide an indication of whether purchasing power parity exists between different currencies.

The Big Mac Index is calculated by first converting the country price of a Big Mac (in the local currency) to US dollars using the current exchange rate. Using Big Mac Index figures available on the Internet (bigmacindex.org 2014), the British price of a Big Mac was £2.89 in July 2014. Using the exchange rate at that time of £1 equals $1.69, this converts to $4.93. At this time, the price of a Big Mac in the USA was $4.80, only 13 cents less than was charged in Britain. This means theoretically you could buy a Big Mac in the USA for $4.80 and sell it in the USA for $4.93, a profit of 13 cents. Unlike most index numbers which use the value 100 to express parity, the difference between the country price and the USA price is expressed as a percentage in the Big Mac Index. Consequently, as the British price for a Big Mac was 13 cents more than the USA price, the value of the index was −1.7 per cent. This indicates that purchasing power of the British pound was very slightly less than the US dollar, suggesting the currencies were valued about the same. According to the July 2014 index, one of the currencies with the greatest difference in purchasing power to the US dollar was the Ukrainian hryvnia; a Big Mac cost the equivalent of $1.63, less than a third of the price in the USA (with a Big Mac index value of +195 per cent). This suggests the currency was overvalued. In contrast, the Norwegian kroner could be considered undervalued; a Big Mac costing the equivalent of $7.60, over one and a half times the price in the USA (with a Big Mac Index value of −38 per cent). Where there is a parity of purchasing power, the index value is zero. This allows for easy comparisons between countries.

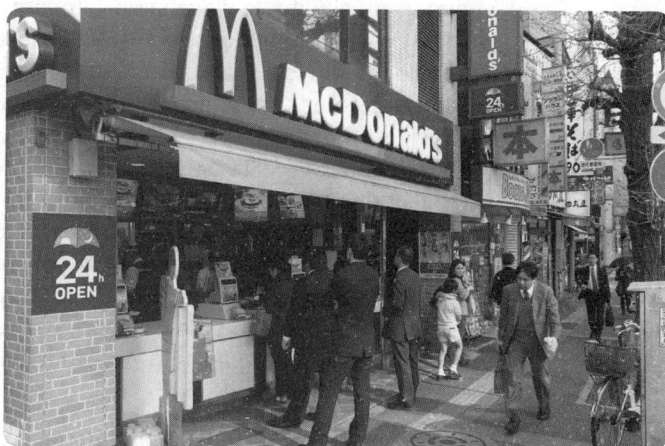

statistical shareware such as the R Project for Statistical Computing. However, while this means you do not have to be able to draw charts by hand or undertake calculations manually, if your analyses are to be straightforward and of any value you need to:

- have prepared your data with quantitative analyses in mind;
- be aware of and know when to use different graphing and statistical techniques.

This is not to say that there is only one possible technique for any analysis situation. As we will see, a range of factors need to be taken into account when selecting the most appropriate tables, graphs and statistics. Consequently, if you are unsure about which of these to use, you need to seek advice.

This chapter builds on the ideas outlined in earlier chapters about secondary data and primary data collection, including issues of sample size. It assumes that you will use a computer (with at least a spreadsheet) to undertake all but the simplest quantitative analyses. Although it does not focus on one particular piece of analysis software, you will notice in the Focus on student research boxes that many of the analyses were undertaken using widely available software such as Excel and IBM SPSS Statistics. If you wish to develop your skills in either of these software packages, self-teach packages are available via our companion website. In addition, there are numerous statistics books already published that concentrate on specific software packages. These include Dancey and Reidy (2011), Field (2013) or Pallant (2013) on IBM SPSS Statistics, Swift and Piff (2014) on IBM SPSS Statistics and Excel, and Scherbaum and Shockley (2015) on Excel. Likewise, this chapter does not attempt to provide an in-depth discussion of the wide range of graphical and statistical techniques available or to cover more complex statistical modelling, as these are already covered elsewhere (e.g. Dancey and Reidy 2011; Everitt and Dunn 2001; Hair et al. 2013; Hays 1994). Rather it discusses issues that need to be considered at the planning and analysis stages of your research project, and outlines analytical techniques that our students have found to be of most use. In particular, the chapter is concerned with:

- preparing, entering into a computer and checking your data (Section 12.2);
- selecting appropriate tables and graphs to explore and present your data (Section 12.3);
- selecting appropriate statistics to describe your data (Section 12.4);
- selecting appropriate statistics to examine relationships and trends in your data (Section 12.5).

准备、输入和检查数据

12.2   Preparing, entering and checking data

If you intend to undertake quantitative analysis we recommend that you consider the:

- number of cases of data, that is the sample size (already discussed in Section 7.2);
- type or types of data (scale of measurement);
- data layout and format required by the analysis software;
- impact of data coding on subsequent analyses (for different types of data);
- process of entering (or inputting) data;
- need to weight cases;
- process of checking the data for errors.

Ideally, all of these should be considered before obtaining your data. This is equally important for both primary and secondary data analysis, although you obviously have far greater control over the type, format and coding of primary data. We shall now consider each of these.

Types of data

Many business statistics textbooks classify quantitative data into *data types* using a hierarchy of measurement, often in ascending order of numerical precision (Berman Brown and Saunders 2008; Dancey and Reidy 2011). These different levels of numerical measurement dictate the range of techniques available to you for the presentation, summary and analysis of your data. They are discussed in more detail in subsequent sections of this chapter.

Quantitative data can be divided into two distinct groups: categorical and numerical (Figure 12.1). **Categorical data** refer to data whose values cannot be measured

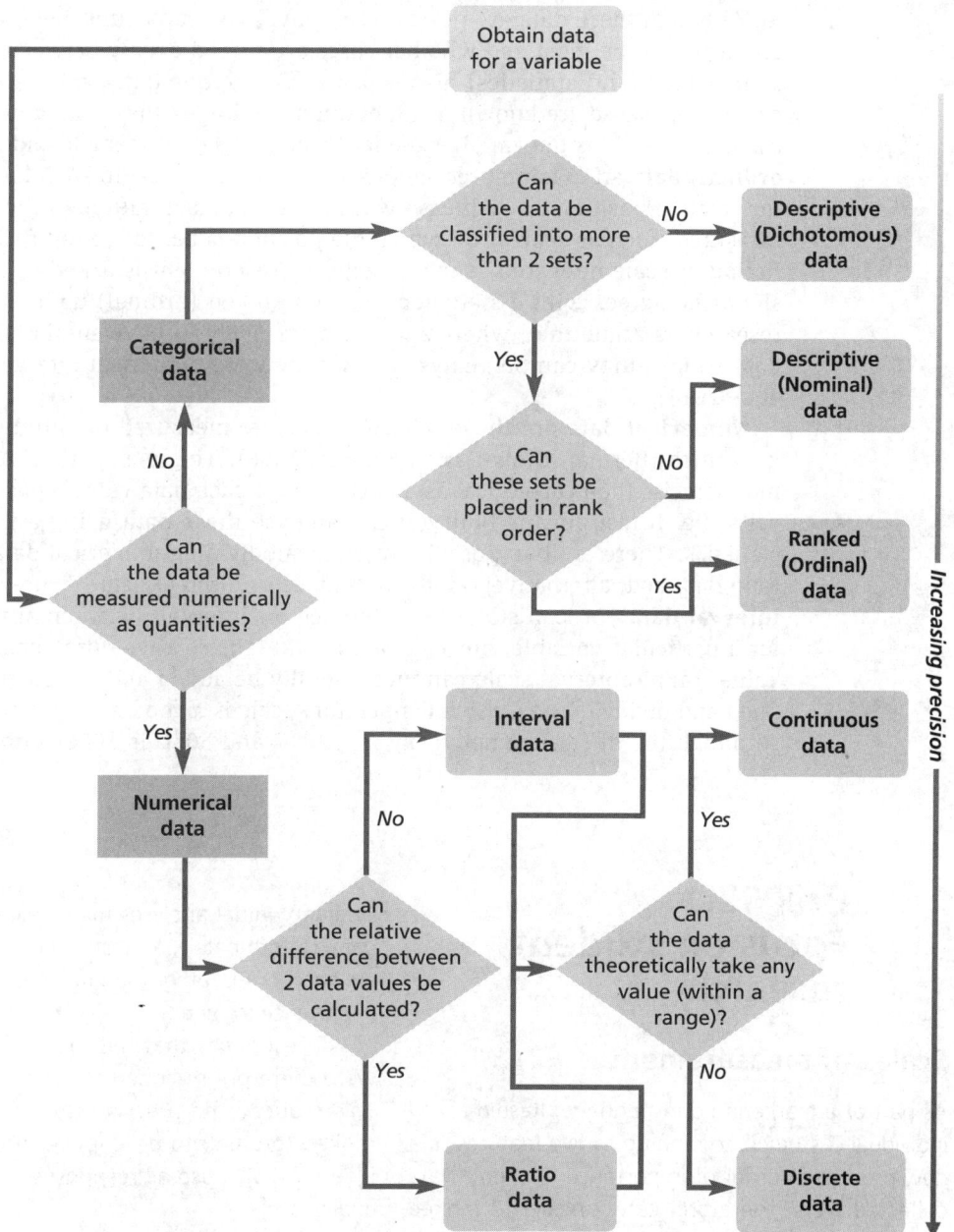

Figure 12.1 Defining the data type

numerically but can be either classified into sets (categories) according to the characteristics that identify or describe the variable or placed in rank order (Berman Brown and Saunders 2008). They can be further subdivided into descriptive and ranked. A car manufacturer might categorise the types of cars it produces as hatchback, saloon and estate. These are known as **descriptive data** or **nominal data** as it is impossible to define the category numerically or to rank it. Rather, these data simply count the number of occurrences in each category of a variable. For virtually all analyses the categories should be unambiguous and discrete; in other words, having one particular feature, such as a car being a hatchback, excludes all other features for that variable. This prevents questions arising regarding which category an individual case belongs to. Although these data are purely descriptive, you can count them to establish which category has the most and whether cases are spread evenly between categories. Some statisticians (and statistics) also separate descriptive data where there are only two categories. These are known as **dichotomous data**, as the variable is divided into two categories, such as the variable gender being divided into female and male. **Ranked** (or **ordinal**) **data** are a more precise form of categorical data. In such instances you know the relative position of each case within your data set, although the actual numerical measures (such as scores) on which the position is based are not recorded (Box 12.1). Rating or scale questions, such as where a respondent is asked to rate how strongly she or he agrees with a statement, collect ranked (ordinal) data. Despite this, some researchers argue that, where such data are likely to have similar size gaps between data values, they can be analysed as if they were numerical interval data (Blumberg et al. 2014).

Numerical data are those whose values are measured or counted numerically as quantities (Berman Brown and Saunders 2008). This means that numerical data are more precise than categorical as you can assign each data value a position on a numerical scale. It also means that you can analyse these data using a far wider range of statistics. There are two possible ways of subdividing numerical data: into interval or ratio data and, alternatively, into continuous or discrete data (Figure 12.1). If you have **interval data** you can state the difference or 'interval' between any two data values for a particular variable, but you cannot state the relative difference. This means that values on an interval scale can meaningfully be added and subtracted, but not multiplied and divided. The Celsius temperature scale is a good example of an interval scale. Although the difference between, say, $20°C$ and $30°C$ is $10°C$ it does not mean that

Box 12.1
Focus on student research

Scales of measurement

As part of a marketing questionnaire, Rashid asked individual customers to rank up to five features of a new product in order of importance to them. Data collected were, therefore, categorical and ranked (ordinal). Initial analyses made use of these ranked data. Unfortunately, a substantial minority of customers had ticked, rather than ranked, those features of importance to them.

All responses that had been ranked originally were therefore re-coded to 'of some importance'. This reduced the precision of measurement from ranked (ordinal) to descriptive (nominal) but enabled Rashid to use all responses in the subsequent analyses.

30°C is one and a half times as warm. This is because 0°C does not represent a true zero. When it is 0°C outside, there is still some warmth, rather than none at all! In contrast, for **ratio data**, you can also calculate the relative difference or ratio between any two data values for a variable. Consequently, if a multinational company makes a profit of $1,000,000,000 in one year and $2,000,000,000 the following year, we can say that profits have doubled.

Continuous data are those whose values can theoretically take any value (sometimes within a restricted range) provided that you can measure them accurately enough (Dancey and Reidy 2011). Data such as furnace temperature, delivery distance and length of service are therefore continuous data. **Discrete data** can, by contrast, be measured precisely. Each case takes one of a finite number of values from a scale that measures changes in discrete units. These data are often whole numbers (**integers**) such as the number of mobile telephones manufactured or customers served. However, in some instances (e.g. UK shoe size) discrete data will include non-integer values. Definitions of discrete and continuous data are, in reality, dependent on how your data values are measured. The number of customers served by a large organisation is strictly a discrete datum as you are unlikely to get a part customer! However, for a large organisation with many customers you might treat this as a continuous datum, as the discrete measuring units are exceedingly small compared with the total number being measured.

Understanding differences between types of data is extremely important when analysing your data quantitatively, for two reasons. Firstly, it is extremely easy with analysis software to generate statistics from your data that are inappropriate for the data type and are consequently of little value (Box 12.2). Secondly, as we will see in Sections 12.4 and 12.5, the more precise the scale of measurement, the greater the range of analytical techniques available to you. Data that have been collected and coded using a precise numerical scale of measurement can also be regrouped to a less precise level where they can also be analysed (Box 12.1). For example, a student's score in a test could be recorded as the actual mark (discrete data) or as the position in their class (ranked data). By contrast, less precise data cannot be made more precise. Therefore, if you are not sure about the scale of measurement you require, it is usually better to collect data at the highest level of precision possible and to regroup them if necessary.

Data layout

Some primary data collection methods, such as computer-aided personal interviewing (CAPI), computer-aided telephone interviewing (CATI) and Internet questionnaires, automatically enter and save data to a computer file at the time of collection, normally using predefined codes. These data can subsequently be exported in a range of formats to ensure they are compatible with different analysis software. Survey design and analysis software such as Qualtrics™ and SurveyMonkey™ goes one stage further and integrates the analysis software in the same package as the questionnaire design/data entry software (Qualtrics 2014; SurveyMonkey 2014). Alternatively, secondary data (Section 8.3) downloaded from the Internet can be saved to a file, removing the need for re-entering. For such data, it is often possible to specify a data layout compatible with your analysis software. For other data collection methods, you will have to prepare and enter your data for computer analysis. You therefore need to be clear about the precise data layout requirements of your analysis software.

Box 12.2
Focus on student research

The implications of data types for analysis

Pierre's research was concerned with customers' satisfaction for a small hotel group of six hotels. In collecting the data he had asked 760 customers to indicate the hotel at which they were staying when they completed their Internet questionnaires. When he downloaded his data, the Internet questionnaire software automatically allocated a numerical code to represent the hotel and named the variable. The codes allocated for the hotels were:

Hotel	Code
Amsterdam	1
Antwerp	2
Eindhoven	3
Nijmegen	4
Rotterdam	5
Tilburg	6

```
DESCRIPTIVES VARIABLES=Hotel
    /STATISTICS=MEAN STDDEV MIN MAX.
```

Descriptives

[DataSet1] /Users/marksaunders/Documents/SPSS/Pearson/RMB7/Box12.2.sav

Descriptive Statistics

	N	Minimum	Maximum	Mean	Std. Deviation
Hotel at which staying	760	1	6	3.74	1.256
Valid N (listwise)	760				

In his initial analysis, Pierre used the analysis software to calculate descriptive statistics for every data variable, including the variable 'Hotel'. These included the minimum value (the code for Amsterdam), the maximum value (the code for Tilburg), the mean and the standard deviation. Looking at his computer screen, Pierre noted that the mean (average) was 3.74 and the standard deviation was 1.256. He had forgotten that the data for this variable were categorical and, consequently, the descriptive statistics he had chosen were inappropriate.

Virtually all analysis software will accept your data if they are entered in table format. This table is called a **data matrix** (Table 12.1). Once data have been entered into your analysis software, it is usually possible to save them in a format that can be read by other software. Within a data matrix, each column usually represents a separate **variable** for which you have obtained data. Each matrix row contains the variables for an individual **case**, that is, an individual unit for which data have been obtained. If your data have been collected using a questionnaire, each row will contain the data from one completed questionnaire. Secondary data that have already been stored in a data file are almost always held as a large data matrix. For such data sets you usually select the subset of variables and cases you require and save these

Table 12.1 A simple data matrix

	Id	Variable 1	Variable 2	Variable 3	Variable 4
Case 1	1	27	1	2	1
Case 2	2	19	2	1	2
Case 3	3	24	2	3	1

as a separate matrix. If you are entering your own data, they are typed directly into your chosen analysis software one case (row) at a time using codes to record the data (Box 12.3). Larger data sets with more data variables and cases are recorded using larger data matrices. Although data matrices store data using one column for each variable, this may not be the same as one column for each question for data collected using surveys.

We strongly recommend that you save your data regularly as you are entering it, to minimise the chances of deleting it all by accident! In addition, you should save a backup or security copy on your MP3 player or other mass storage device, the cloud and email it to yourself.

Box 12.3
Focus on student research

An Excel data matrix

Lucy's data related to employees who were working or had worked for a large public-sector organisation. In her Excel spreadsheet, the first variable (id) was the *survey form identifier*. This meant that she could link data for each case (row) in her matrix to the survey form when checking for errors (discussed later). The second variable (age) contained

numerical data, the age of each respondent (case) at the time her questionnaire was administered. Subsequent variables contained the remaining data: the third (gender) recorded this dichotomous data using code 1 for male and 2 for female; the fourth (service) recorded numerical data about each case's length of service to the nearest year in the organisation. The final dichotomous variable (employed) recorded whether each respondent was (code 1) or was not (code 2) employed by the organisation at the time the data were collected. The codes used by Lucy, therefore, had different meanings for different variables.

If you intend to enter data into a spreadsheet, the first variable is in Column A, the second in Column B and so on. Each cell in the first row (1) should contain a short variable name to enable you to identify each variable. Subsequent rows (2 onwards) will each contain the data for one case (Box 12.3). Statistical analysis software follows the same logic, although the variable names are usually displayed 'above' the first row (Box 12.4).

Box 12.4
Focus on student research

Data coding

As part of a market research interview survey, Zack needed to discover which of four products (tomato ketchup, brown sauce, soy sauce, vinegar) had been purchased within the last month by consumers. He therefore needed to collect four data items from each respondent:

- Tomato ketchup purchased within   Yes/No
  the last month?
- Brown sauce purchased within   Yes/No
  the last month?
- Soy sauce purchased within   Yes/No
  the last month?
- Mayonnaise purchased within   Yes/No
  the last month?

Each of these data items is a separate variable. However, the data were collected using one question:

1 Which of the following items have you purchased within the last month?

Item	Purchased	Not purchased	Not sure
Tomato ketchup	$\square_1$	$\square_2$	$\square_3$
Brown sauce	$\square_1$	$\square_2$	$\square_3$
Soy sauce	$\square_1$	$\square_2$	$\square_3$
Mayonnaise	$\square_1$	$\square_2$	$\square_3$

The data Zack collected from each respondent formed four separate variables in the data matrix using numerical codes (1 = purchased, 2 = not purchased, 3 = not sure). This is known as multiple-dichotomy coding.

	tomato	brown	soy	mayonaise	like1	like2
1	1	1	1	2	23	31
2	2	2	2	3	12	15
3	1	2	3	1	23	12

Zack also included a question (question 2 below) that could theoretically have millions of possible responses for each of the 'things'. For such questions, the number that each respondent mentions may also vary. Our experience suggests that virtually all respondents will select five or fewer. Zack therefore left space to code up to five responses after data had been collected.

For office use only

2   List up to five things you like about tomato ketchup   ....   ☐ ☐ ☐ ☐
....   ☐ ☐ ☐ ☐
....   ☐ ☐ ☐ ☐
....   ☐ ☐ ☐ ☐
....   ☐ ☐ ☐ ☐

The **multiple-response method** of coding uses the same number of variables as the maximum number of different responses from any one case. For Question 2 these were named 'like1', 'like2', 'like3', 'like4' and 'like5' (Box 12.4). Each of these variables would use the same codes and could include any of the responses as a category. Statistical analysis software often contains special multiple-response procedures to analyse such data. The alternative, the **multiple-dichotomy method** of coding, uses a separate variable for each different answer (Box 12.4). For Question 2 (Box 12.4) a separate variable could have been used for each 'thing' listed: for example, flavour, consistency, bottle shape, smell, price and so on. You subsequently would code each variable as 'listed' or 'not listed' for each case. This makes it easy to calculate the number of responses for each 'thing' (De Vaus 2014).

Coding

All data types should, with few exceptions, be recorded using numerical codes. This enables you to enter the data quickly using the numeric keypad and with fewer errors. It also makes subsequent analyses, in particular those that require re-coding of data to create new variables, more straightforward. Unfortunately, meaningless analyses are also easier, such as calculating a mean (average) gender from codes 1 and 2, or the mean hotel location (Box 12.2)! A common exception to using a numerical code for categorical data is where a postcode or zip code is used as the code for a geographical reference. If you are using a spreadsheet, you will need to keep a list of codes for each variable. Statistical analysis software can store these so that each code is automatically labelled.

Coding numerical data

Actual numbers are often used as codes for numerical data, even though this level of precision may not be required. Once you have entered your data as a matrix, you can use analysis software to group or combine data to form additional variables with less detailed categories. This process is referred to as **re-coding**. For example, a Republic of Ireland employee's salary could be coded to the nearest euro and entered into the matrix as 53543 (numerical discrete data). Later, re-coding could be used to place it in a group of similar salaries, from €50,000 to €59,999 (categorical ranked data).

Coding categorical data

Codes are often applied to categorical data with little thought, although you can design a coding scheme that will make subsequent analyses far simpler. For many secondary data sources (such as government surveys), a suitable coding scheme will have already been devised when the data were first collected. However, for some secondary and all primary data you will need to decide on a coding scheme. Prior to this, you need to establish the highest level of precision required by your analyses (Figure 12.1).

Existing coding schemes can be used for many variables. These include industrial classification (Prosser 2009), occupation (Office for National Statistics nd a), social class and socioeconomic classification (Office for National Statistics nd b) and ethnic group (Office for National Statistics nd c) as well as social attitude variables (Park et al. 2013). Wherever possible, we recommend you use these as they:

- save time;
- are normally well tested;
- allow comparisons of your results with other (often larger) surveys.

Where possible these codes should be included on your data collection form or online survey software as **pre-set codes** provided that there are a limited number of categories (Section 11.4). Even if you decide not to use an existing coding scheme, perhaps because of a lack of detail, you should ensure that your codes are still compatible. This means that you will be able to compare your data with those already collected.

Coding at data collection usually occurs when there is a limited range of well-established categories into which the data can be placed. These are either included on your data collection form, the person filling in the form selecting the correct category, or can be undertaken automatically by your Internet questionnaire software.

Coding after data collection is necessary when you are unclear as to the likely responses or there are a large number of possible responses in the coding scheme. To ensure that the coding scheme captures the variety in responses (and that it will work!) it is better to wait until data from the first 50 to 100 cases are available and then develop the coding scheme. This is called the **codebook** (Box 12.5). As when designing your data collection method(s) (Chapters 8, 9, 10 and 11), it is essential to be clear about the intended analyses, in particular:

- the level of precision required;
- the coding schemes used by surveys with which comparisons are to be made.

To create your codebook for each variable you:

1 examine the data and establish broad groupings;
2 subdivide the broad groupings into increasingly specific subgroups dependent on your intended analyses;
3 allocate codes to all categories at the most precise level of detail required;
4 note the actual responses that are allocated to each category and produce a codebook;
5 ensure that those categories that may need to be aggregated are given adjacent codes to facilitate re-coding.

Coding missing data

Each variable for each case in your data set should have a code, even if no data have been collected. The choice of code is up to you, although some statistical analysis software has a code that is used by default. A missing data code is used to indicate why data are missing. Missing data are important as they may affect whether the data you have collected are representative of the population. If missing data follow some form of pattern, such as occurring for particular questions or for a subgroup of the population, then your results are unlikely to be representative of the population and so you should not ignore the fact they are missing. However, if data are missing at random, then it is unlikely that this will affect your results being representative of the

Box 12.5
Focus on student research

Creating a codebook, coding multiple responses and entering data

As part of his research project, Amil used a questionnaire to collect data from the customers of a local themed restaurant. The questionnaire included an open question which asked 'List up to three things you like about this restaurant'. The answers included over 50 different 'things' that the 186 customers responding liked about the restaurant, although the maximum number mentioned by any one customer was three.

Once data had been collected, Amil devised a hierarchical coding scheme based on what the customers liked about the restaurant. Codes were allocated to each 'thing' a customer liked, as shown in the extract below.

Codes were entered into three (the maximum number customers were asked to list) variables, like1, like2 and like3, in the data matrix using the multiple-response method for coding. This meant that any response could appear in any of the three variables. When there were fewer than three responses given, the code '.' was entered automatically by the software into empty cells in the remaining outlet variables, signifying missing data. The first customer in the extract below listed 'things' coded 11, 21 and 42, the next 3 and 21 and so on. No significance was attached to the order of variables to which responses were coded.

	numvisit	reason	like1	like2	like3	offer
1	3	14	11	21	42	.
2	5	12	3	21	.	2
3	6	22	32	11	38	1

Box 12.5
Focus on student research (*continued*)

Creating a codebook, coding multiple responses and entering data

Extract from coding scheme used to classify responses

Grouping	Subgrouping	Response	Code
Physical surroundings			1–9
		Decoration	1
		Use of colour	2
		Comfort of seating	3
Dining experience	*Menu*		10–19
		Choice	11
		Regularly changed	12
	Food		20–29
		Freshly prepared	21
		Organic	22
		Served at correct temperature	23
	Staff attitude		30–39
		Knowledgeable	31
		Greet by name	32
		Know what diners prefer	33
		Discreet	34
		Do not hassle	35
		Good service	36
		Friendly	37
		Have a sense of humour	38
	Drinks		40–49
		Value for money	41
		Good selection of wines	42
		Good selection of beers	43
		Served at correct temperature	44

The hierarchical coding scheme meant that individual responses could subsequently be re-coded into subgroupings and groupings such as those indicated earlier to facilitate a range of different analyses. These were undertaken using statistical analysis software.

population (Little and Rubin 2002). Four main reasons for missing data are identified by De Vaus (2014):

- The data were not required from the respondent, perhaps because of a skip generated by a filter question in a survey.
- The respondent refused to answer the question (a **non-response**).
- The respondent did not know the answer or did not have an opinion. Sometimes this is treated as implying an answer; on other occasions it is treated as missing data.
- The respondent may have missed a question by mistake, or the respondent's answer may be unclear.

In addition, it may be that:

- leaving part of a question in a survey blank implies an answer; in such cases the data are not classified as missing (Section 11.4).

Statistical analysis software often reserves a special code for missing data. Cases with missing data can then be excluded from subsequent analyses when necessary (Box 12.5). For some analyses it may be necessary to distinguish between reasons for missing data using different codes.

Entering and saving data

If you have downloaded secondary data as a file, or have used Internet questionnaire software, your data will already have been entered (input) and saved. However, often you will need to enter and save the data as a file on your computer. Although some data analysis software contains algorithms that check the data for obvious errors as it is entered, it is essential that you take considerable care to ensure that your data are entered correctly and save the file regularly. We have found it helpful to include the word data in the filename. When entering data the well-known maxim 'rubbish in, rubbish out' certainly applies! More sophisticated analysis software allows you to attach individual labels to each variable and the codes associated with each of them. If this is feasible, we strongly recommend that you do this. By ensuring the labels replicate the exact words used in the data collection, you will reduce the number of opportunities for misinterpretation when analysing your data. Taking this advice for the variable 'like1' in Box 12.5 would result in the variable label 'List up to three things you like about this restaurant', each value being labelled with the actual response in the coding scheme.

Checking for errors

No matter how carefully you code and subsequently enter data there will always be some errors. The main methods to check data for errors are as follows:

- Look for illegitimate codes. In any coding scheme, only certain numbers are allocated. Other numbers are, therefore, errors. Common errors are the inclusion of letters O and o instead of zero, letters l or I instead of 1, and number 7 instead of 1.
- Look for illogical relationships. For example, if a person is coded to the 'higher managerial occupations' socioeconomic classification category and she describes her work as 'manual', it is likely an error has occurred.
- Check that rules in filter questions are followed. Certain responses to filter questions (Section 11.4) mean that other variables should be coded as missing values. If this has not happened, there has been an error.

For each possible error, you need to discover whether it occurred at coding or data entry and then correct it. By giving each case a unique identifier (normally a number), it is possible to link the matrix to the original data. You must, however, remember to ensure the identifier is on the data collection form and entered along with the other data into the matrix.

Data checking is very time consuming and so is often not undertaken. Beware: not doing it is very dangerous and can result in incorrect results from which false conclusions are drawn!

Weighting cases

Most data you use will be a sample. For some forms of probability sampling, such as stratified random sampling (Section 7.2), you may have used a different sampling fraction for each stratum. Alternatively, you may have obtained a different response rate for each of the strata. To obtain an accurate overall picture you will need to take account of these differences in response rates between strata. A common method of achieving this is to use cases from those strata that have lower proportions of responses to represent more than one case in your analysis (Box 12.6). Most statistical analysis software allows you to do this by **weighting** cases. To weight the cases you:

1 Calculate the percentage of the population responding for each stratum.
2 Establish which stratum had the highest percentage of the population responding.
3 Calculate the weight for each stratum using the following formula:

$$\text{Weight} = \frac{\text{highest proportion of population responding for any stratum}}{\text{proportion of population responding in stratum for which calculating weight}}$$

(Note: if your calculations are correct this will always result in the weight for the stratum with the highest proportion of the population responding being 1.)

4 Apply the appropriate weight to each case.

Box 12.6
Focus on student research

Weighting cases

Doris had used stratified random sampling to select her sample. The percentage of each stratum's population that responded is given below:

- Upper stratum: 90%
- Lower stratum: 65%

To account for the differences in the response rates between strata she decided to weight the cases prior to analysis.

The weight for the upper stratum was: $\frac{90}{90} = 1$

This meant that each case in the upper stratum counted as 1 case in her analysis.

The weight for the lower stratum was: $\frac{90}{65} = 1.38$

This meant that each case in the lower stratum counted for 1.38 cases in her analysis.

Doris entered these as a separate variable in her data set and used the statistical analysis software to apply the weights.

Beware: many authors (for example, Hays 1994) question the validity of using statistics to make inferences from your sample if you have weighted cases.

12.3 Exploring and presenting data 挖掘和列示数据

Once your data have been entered and checked for errors, you are ready to start your analysis. We have found Tukey's (1977) **Exploratory Data Analysis (EDA)** approach useful in these initial stages. This approach emphasises the use of graphs to explore and understand your data. Although within data analysis the term graph has a specific meaning: '. . . a visual display that illustrates one or more relationships among numbers' (Kosslyn 2006: 4), it is often used interchangeably with the term 'chart'. Consequently, while some authors (and data analysis software) use the term bar graphs, others use the term bar charts. Even more confusingly, what are referred to as 'pie charts' are actually graphs! Tukey (1977) also emphasises the importance of using your data to guide your choice of analysis techniques. As you would expect, we believe that it is important to keep your research question(s) and objectives in mind when exploring your data. However, the Exploratory Data Analysis approach allows you flexibility to introduce previously unplanned analyses to respond to new findings. It therefore formalises the common practice of looking for other relationships in data, which your research was not initially designed to test. This should not be discounted, as it may suggest other fruitful avenues for analysis. In addition, computers make this relatively easy and quick.

Even at this stage it is important that you structure and label clearly each graph and table to avoid possible misinterpretation. Box 12.7 provides a summary checklist of the points to remember when designing a graph or table.

We have found it best to begin exploratory analysis by looking at individual variables and their components. The key aspects you may need to consider will be guided by your

Box 12.7 Checklist

Designing your graphs and tables

For both graphs and tables

✔ Does it have a brief but clear and descriptive title?

✔ Are the units of measurement used stated clearly?

✔ Are the sources of data used stated clearly?

✔ Are there notes to explain abbreviations and unusual terminology?

✔ Does it state the size of the sample on which the values in the table are based?

For graphs

✔ Does it have clear axis labels?

✔ Are bars and their components in the same logical sequence?

✔ Is more dense shading used for smaller areas?

✔ Have you avoided misrepresenting or distorting the data?

✔ Is a key or legend included (where necessary)?

For tables

✔ Does it have clear column and row headings?

✔ Are columns and rows in a logical sequence?

research question(s) and objectives, and are likely to include (Kosslyn 2006) for single variables:

- specific amounts represented by individual data values;
- relative amounts such as:
  - highest and lowest data values;
  - trends in data values;
  - proportions and percentages for data values;
  - distributions of data values.

Once you have explored these, you can then begin to compare variables and interdependences between variables, by (Kosslyn 2006):

- comparing intersections between the data values for two or more variables;
- comparing cumulative totals for data values and variables;
- looking for interdependences between cases for variables.

These are summarised in Table 12.2. Most analysis software contains procedures to create tables and graphs. Your choice will depend on those aspects of the data to which you wish to direct your readers' attention and the scale of measurement at which the data were recorded. This section is concerned only with tables and two-dimensional graphs, including pictograms, available on most spreadsheets (Table 12.2). Three-dimensional graphs are not discussed, as these can often mislead or hinder interpretation (Kosslyn 2006). Those tables and graphs most pertinent to your research question(s) and objectives will eventually appear in your research report to support your arguments. You should therefore save an electronic copy of all tables and graphs you create.

Exploring and presenting individual variables

To show specific amounts

The simplest way of summarising data for individual variables so that specific amount can be read is to use a **table** (**frequency distribution**). For categorical data, the table summarises the number of cases (frequency) in each category. For variables where there are likely to be a large number of categories (or values for numerical data), you will need to group the data into categories that reflect your research question(s) and objectives.

To show the highest and lowest values

Tables attach no visual significance to highest or lowest data values unless emphasised by alternative fonts. Graphs can provide visual clues, although both categorical and numerical data may need grouping. For categorical and discrete data, bar graphs and pictograms are both suitable. Generally, bar graphs provide a more accurate representation and should be used for research reports, whereas pictograms convey a general impression and can be used to gain an audience's attention. In a **bar graph**, also often known as **a bar chart**, the height or length of each bar represents the frequency of occurrence. Bars are separated by gaps, usually half the width of the bars. Bar graphs where the bars are vertical (as in Figure 12.2) are sometimes called bar or column charts. This bar graph emphasises that the European Union member state with the highest total carbon dioxide emissions in 2011 was Germany, while either Latvia, Luxembourg or Malta had the lowest total carbon dioxide emissions.

Table 12.2 Data presentation by data type: A summary

	Categorical		Numerical	
	Descriptive	**Ranked**	**Continuous**	**Discrete**
To show one variable so that any *specific amount* can be read easily	Table/frequency distribution (data often grouped)			
To show the relative amount for categories or values for one variable so that *highest* and *lowest* are clear	Bar graph/chart or pictogram (data may need grouping)		Histogram or frequency polygon (data must be grouped)	Bar graph/chart or pictogram (data may need grouping)
To show the *trend* for a variable		Line graph or bar graph/chart	Line graph or histogram	Line graph or bar graph/chart
To show the *proportion* or *percentage* of occurrences of categories or values for one variable	Pie chart or bar graph/chart (data may need grouping)		Histogram or pie chart (data must be grouped)	Pie chart or bar graph/chart (data may need grouping)
To show the *distribution* of values for one variable			Frequency polygon, histogram (data must be grouped) or box plot	Frequency polygon, bar graph/chart (data may need grouping) or box plot
To show the *interdependence* between two or more variables so that any *specific* amount can be read easily	Contingency table/cross-tabulation (data often grouped)			
To compare the relative amount for categories or values for two or more variables so that *highest* and *lowest* are clear	Multiple bar graph/chart (continuous data must be grouped, other data may need grouping)			
To compare the *proportions* or *percentages* of occurrences of categories or values for two or more variables	Comparative pie charts or percentage component bar graph/chart (continuous data must be grouped, other data may need grouping)			
To compare the *distribution* of values for two or more variables			Multiple box plot	
To compare the *trends* for two or more variables so that *intersections* are clear		Multiple line graph or multiple bar graph/chart		
To compare the frequency of occurrences of categories or values for two or more variables so that *cumulative totals* are clear	Stacked bar graph/chart (continuous data must be grouped, other data may need grouping)			
To compare the *proportions* and *cumulative totals* of occurrences of categories or values for two or more variables	Comparative proportional pie charts (continuous data must be grouped, other data may need grouping)			
To show the *interdependence* between cases for two variables		Scatter graph/scatter plot		

Source: © Mark Saunders, Philip Lewis and Adrian Thornhill 2015

Total carbon dioxide emissions in 2011 by European Union Member States
Source: Eurostat (2014) Environment and Energy Statistics

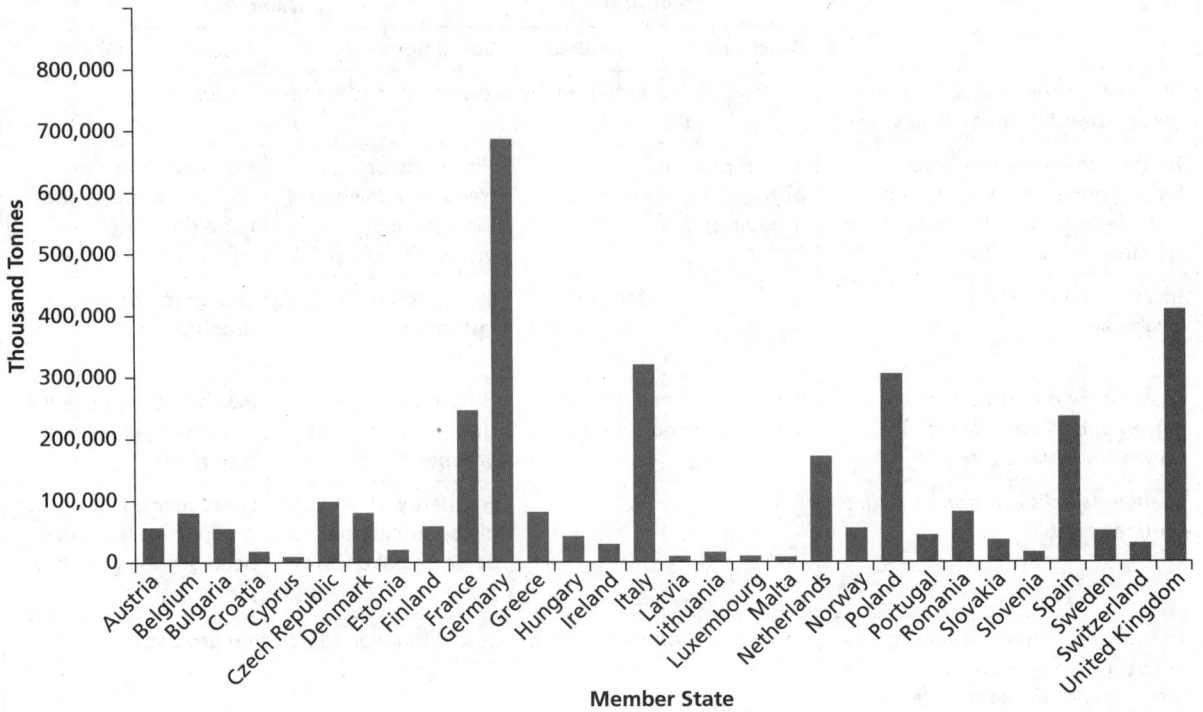

Figure 12.2 Bar graph
Source: Adapted from Eurostat (2014) © European Communities, 2014. Reproduced with permission

To emphasise the relative values represented by each of the bars in a bar graph, the bars may be reordered in either descending or ascending order of the frequency of occurrence represented by each bar (Figure 12.3). It is now from the order of the bars that Malta has the lowest greenhouse gas emissions.

Most researchers use a histogram to show highest and lowest values for continuous data. Prior to being drawn, data will often need to be grouped into class intervals. In a **histogram**, the area of each bar represents the frequency of occurrence and the continuous nature of the data is emphasised by the absence of gaps between the bars. For equal width class intervals, the height of your bar still represents the frequency of occurrences (Figure 12.4) and so the highest and lowest values are easy to distinguish. For histograms with unequal class interval widths, this is not the case. In Figure 12.4 the histogram emphasises that the highest number of Harley-Davidson motorcycles shipped worldwide was in 2006, and the lowest number in 2000.

Analysis software treats histograms for data of equal width class intervals as a variation of a bar chart. Unfortunately, few spreadsheets will cope automatically with the calculations required to draw histograms for unequal class intervals. Consequently, you may have to use a bar chart owing to the limitations of your analysis software.

In a **pictogram**, each bar is replaced by a picture or series of pictures chosen to represent the data. To illustrate the impact of doing this, we have used data of worldwide Harley-Davidson motorcycle shipments to generate both a histogram (Figure 12.4) and a pictogram

Total carbon dioxide emissions in 2011 by European Union Member States
Source: Eurostat (2014) Environment and Energy Statistics

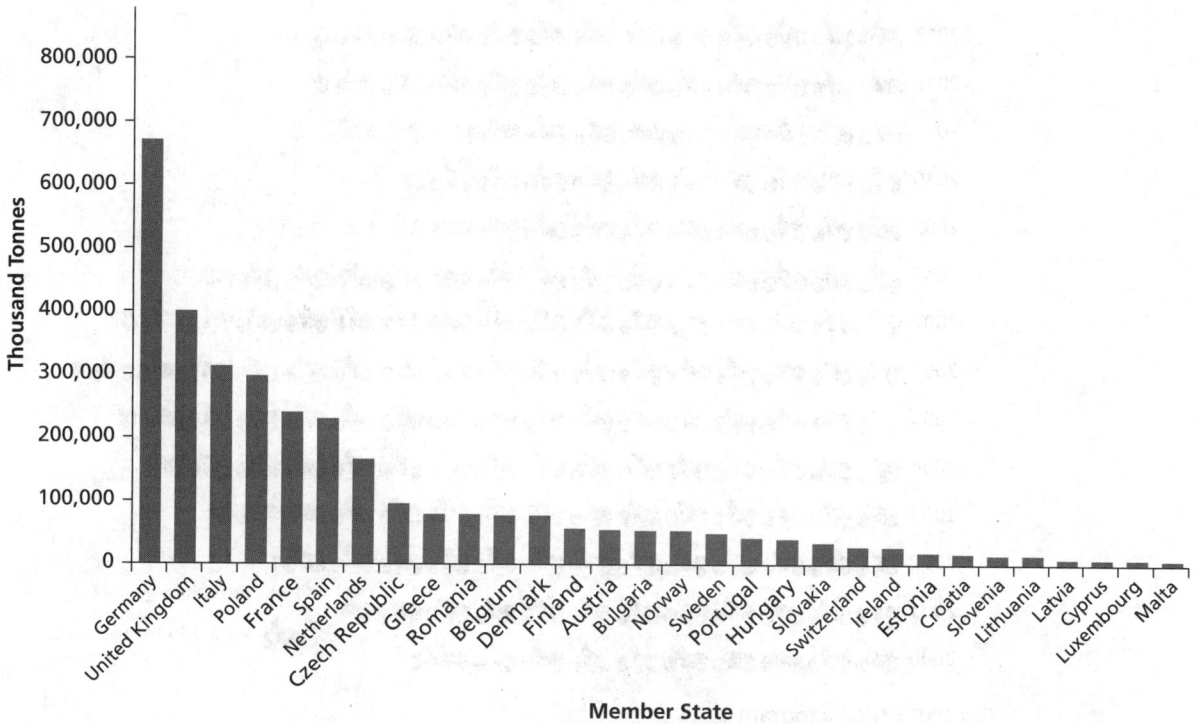

Figure 12.3 Bar graph (data reordered)
Source: Adapted from Eurostat (2014) © European Communities, 2014. Reproduced with permission

Worldwide Harley-Davidson motorcycle shipments 2000–2013
Source: Harley-Davidson Inc. (2014)

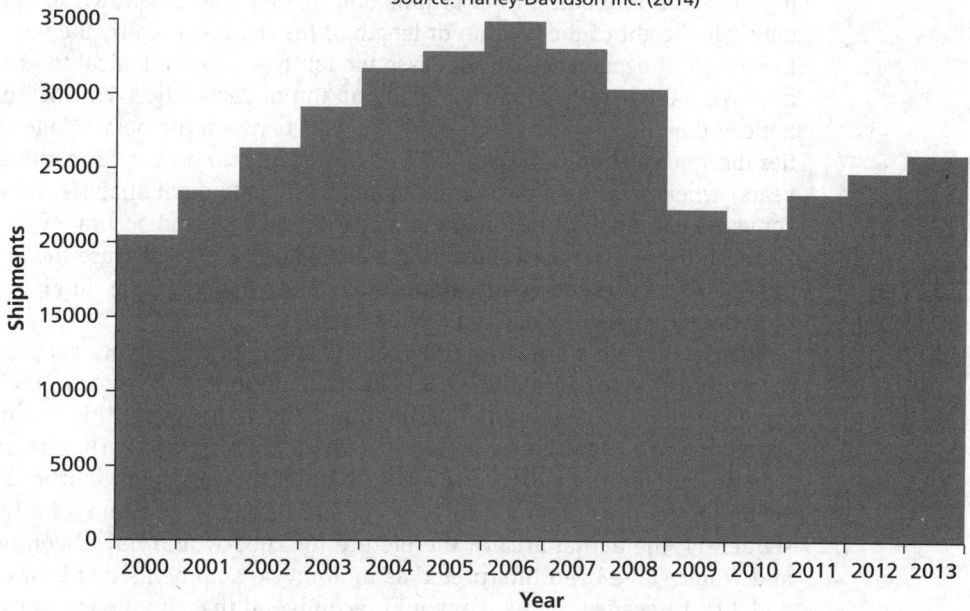

Figure 12.4 Histogram
Source: Adapted from Harley-Davidson Inc. (2014)

467

Worldwide Harley-Davidson motorcycle shipments 2000–2013
Sources: Harley-Davidson Inc. (2014)

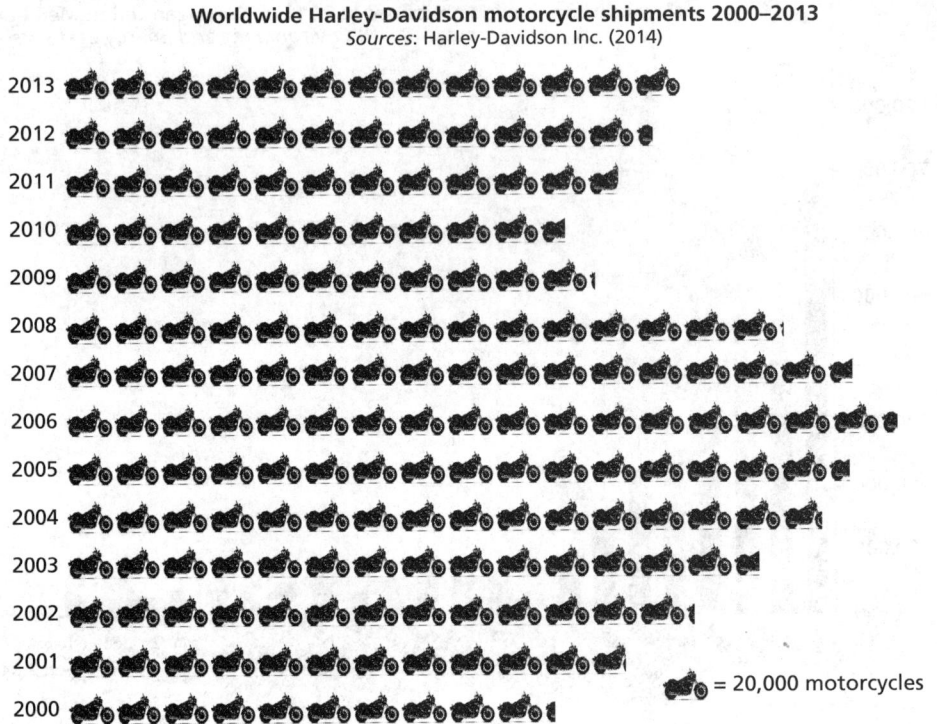

= 20,000 motorcycles

Figure 12.5 Pictogram
Source: Adapted from Harley-Davidson Inc. (2014)

(Figure 12.5). In the pictogram each picture represents 20,000 motorcycles. Pictures in pictograms can, like bars in bar graphs and histograms, be shown in columns or horizontally. The height of the column or length of the bar made up by the pictures represents the frequency of occurrence. In this case we felt it was more logical to group the pictures as a horizontal bar rather than vertically on top of each other. You will have probably also noticed that, in the pictogram, there are gaps between the bars. While this normally signifies discrete categories of data, it is also acceptable to do this for continuous data (such as years) when drawing a pictogram, to aid clarity. Although analysis software allows you to convert a bar graph or histogram to a pictogram easily and accurately, it is more difficult to establish the actual data values from a pictogram. This is because the number of units part of a picture represents is not immediately clear. For example, in Figure 12.5, how many motorcycles shipped would a rear wheel represent?

Pictograms have a further drawback, namely that it is very easy to misrepresent the data. Both Figures 12.4 and 12.5 show that shipments of Harley-Davidson motorcycles grew between 2006 and 2010. Using our analysis software, this could have been represented using a picture of a motorcycle in 2006 that was nearly one and a half times as long as the picture in 2010. However, in order to keep the proportions of the motorcycle accurate, the picture would have needed to be nearly one and a half times as tall. Consequently, the actual area of the picture for 2006 would have been over twice as great and would have been interpreted as motorcycle shipments being twice as large in 2006 and 2010! Because of this we would recommend that, if you are using a pictogram, you decide on a standard value for each picture and do not alter its size. In addition, you should include a key or note to indicate the value each picture represents.

Frequency polygons are used less often to illustrate limits. Most analysis software treats them as a version of a line graph (Figure 12.6) in which the lines are extended to meet the horizontal axis, provided that class widths are equal.

To show a trend

Trends can only be presented for variables containing numerical (and occasionally ranked) longitudinal data. The most suitable diagram for exploring the trend is a **line graph** (Kosslyn 2006) in which your data values for each time period are joined with a line to represent the trend (Figure 12.6). In Figure 12.6 the line graph reveals the rise and decline in the number of Harley-Davidson motorcycles shipped worldwide between 2000 and 2013. You can also use histograms (Figure 12.4) to show trends over continuous time periods and bar graphs (Figure 12.2) to show trends between discrete time periods. The trend can also be calculated using time-series analysis (Section 12.5).

To show proportions or percentages

Research has shown that the most frequently used diagram to emphasise the proportion or share of occurrences is the pie chart, although bar charts have been shown to give equally good results (Anderson et al. 2014). A **pie chart** is divided into proportional segments according to the share each has of the total value and the total value represented by the pie is noted (Box 12.8). For numerical and some categorical data you will need to group data prior to drawing the pie chart, as it is difficult to interpret pie charts with more than six segments (Keen 2010).

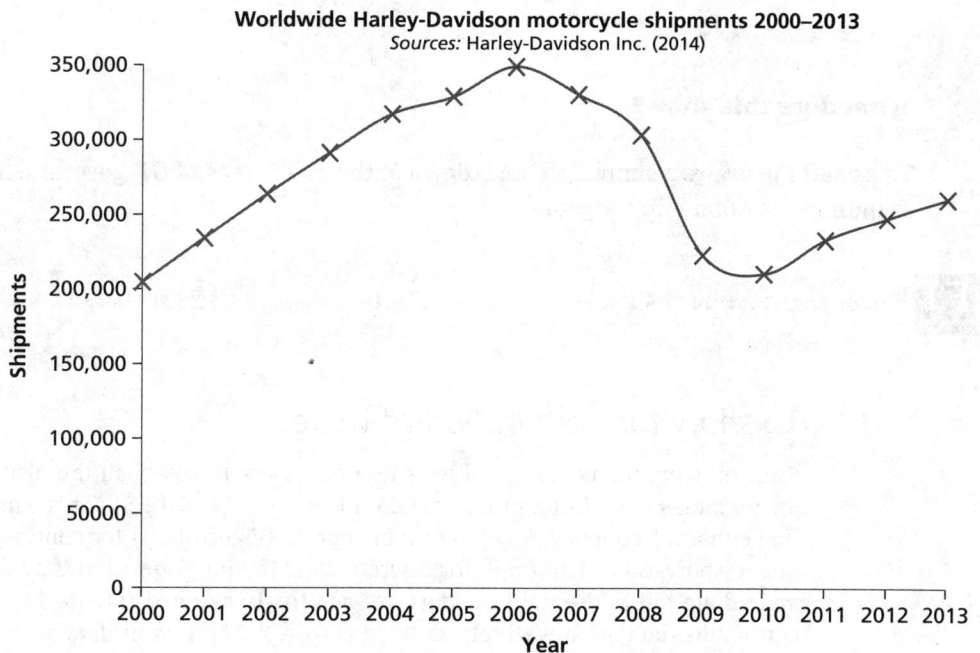

Figure 12.6 Line graph
Source: Adapted from Harley-Davidson Inc. (2014)

Box 12.8 Focus on research in the news

Pie chart

Chart that tells a story – tax summaries

Adam Palin   Author alerts ⌄

How your tax was (really) spent in 2013-14

% of total tax paid

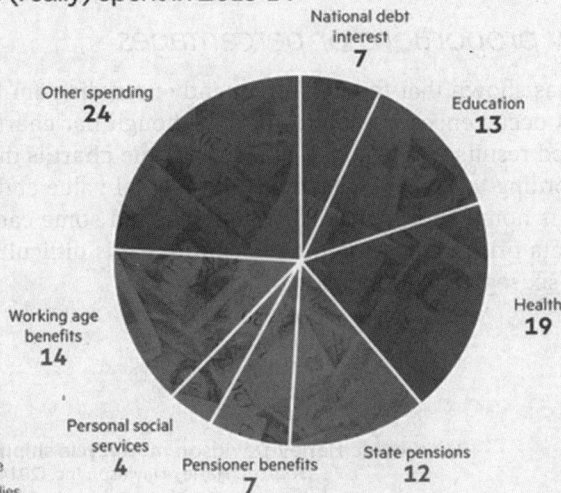

- National debt interest **7**
- Other spending **24**
- Education **13**
- Health **19**
- Working age benefits **14**
- State pensions **12**
- Personal social services **4**
- Pensioner benefits **7**

FT graphic Photo: Dreamstime
Source: Institute for Fiscal Studies

FT

What does this show?

This chart illustrates a simplified breakdown of the main areas of UK government spending – £686bn – in 2013-14.

To show the distribution of values

Prior to using many statistical tests it is necessary to establish the distribution of values for variables containing numerical data (Sections 12.4, 12.5). This can be seen by plotting either a frequency polygon or a histogram (Figure 12.4) for continuous data or a frequency polygon or bar graph for discrete data. If your graph shows a bunching to the left and a long tail to the right the data are **positively skewed** (Figure 12.7). If the converse is true, the data are **negatively skewed** (Figure 12.7). If your data are equally distributed either side of the highest frequency then they are **symmetrically distributed**. A special form of the symmetric distribution, in which the data can be plotted as a bell-shaped curve, is known as **normal distribution** (Figure 12.7).

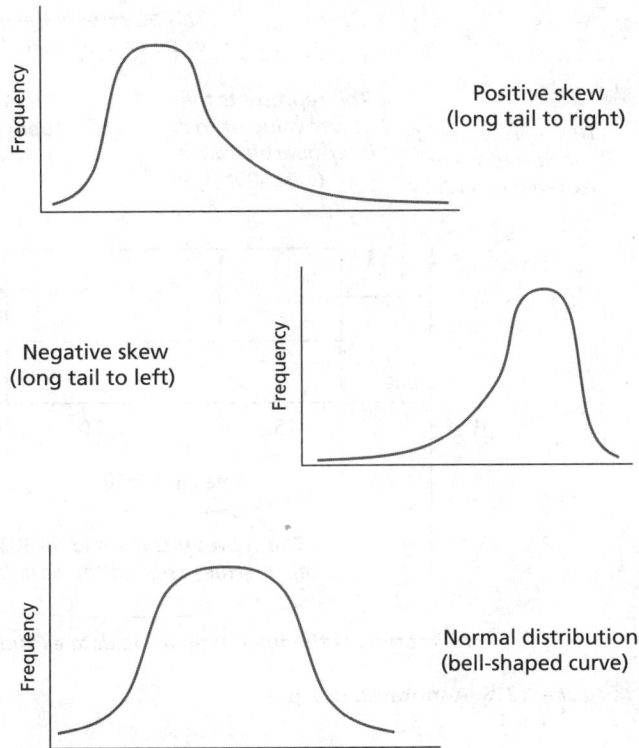

Figure 12.7 Distributions of values

The other indicator of the distribution's shape is **kurtosis** – the pointedness or flatness of the distribution compared with normal distribution. If a distribution is more pointed or peaked, it is said to be leptokurtic and the kurtosis value is positive. If a distribution is flatter, it is said to be platykurtic and the kurtosis value is negative. A distribution that is between the extremes of peakedness and flatness is said to be mesokurtic and has a kurtosis value of zero (Dancey and Reidy 2011).

An alternative often included in more advanced statistical analysis software is the **box plot** (Figure 12.8). This provides a pictorial representation of the distribution of the data for a variable. The plot shows where the middle value or median is, how this relates to the middle 50 per cent of the data or inter-quartile range, and highest and lowest values or *extremes* (Section 12.4). It also highlights outliers, those values that are very different from the data. In Figure 12.8 the two outliers might be due to mistakes in data entry. Alternatively, they may be correct and emphasise that sales for these two cases (93 and 88) are far higher. In this example we can see that the data values for the variable are positively skewed as there is a long tail to the right.

Comparing variables

To show interdependence and specific amounts

As with individual variables, the best method of showing interdependence between variables so that any specific amount can be discerned easily is a table. This is known as a

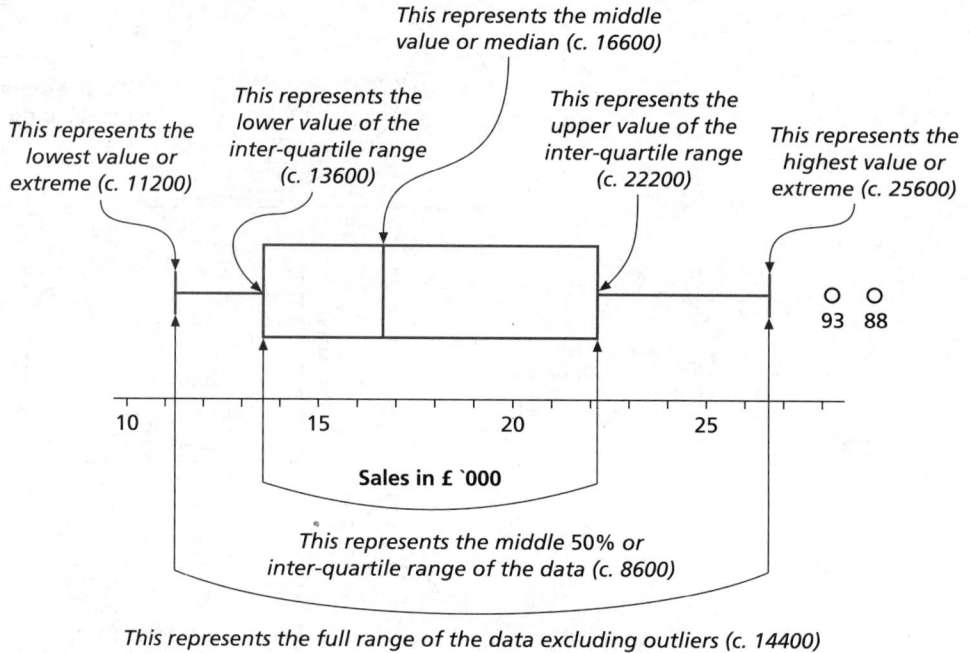

This represents the middle
value or median (c. 16600)

This represents the
lower value of the
inter-quartile range
(c. 13600)

This represents the
upper value of the
inter-quartile range
(c. 22200)

This represents the
lowest value or
extreme (c. 11200)

This represents the
highest value or
extreme (c. 25600)

93 88

10   15   20   25

Sales in £ `000

This represents the middle 50% or
inter-quartile range of the data (c. 8600)

This represents the full range of the data excluding outliers (c. 14400)

Figure 12.8 Annotated box plot

contingency table or as a **cross-tabulation** (Table 12.3). For variables where there are likely to be a large number of categories (or values for numerical data), you may need to group the data to prevent the table from becoming too large.

Most statistical analysis software allows you to add totals, and row and column percentages when designing your table. Statistical analyses such as chi square can also be undertaken at the same time (Section 12.5).

To compare the highest and lowest values

Comparisons of variables that emphasise the highest and lowest rather than precise values are best explored using a **multiple bar graph**, also known as a **multiple bar chart**

Table 12.3 Contingency table: Number of insurance claims by gender, 2015

Number of claims*	Male	Female	Total
0	10032	13478	23510
1	2156	1430	3586
2	120	25	145
3	13	4	17
Total	12321	14937	27258

*No clients had more than three claims
Source: PJ Insurance Services

Box 12.9
Focus on student research

Exploring and presenting data for individual variables

As part of audience research for his dissertation, Valentin asked people attending a play at a provincial theatre to complete a short questionnaire. This collected responses to 25 questions including:

3 How many plays (including this one) have you seen at this theatre in the past year?

11 This play is good value for money

strongly disagree $\square_1$ disagree $\square_2$
agree $\square_3$ strongly agree $\square_4$

24 How old are you?

Under 18 $\square_1$ 18 to 34 $\square_2$
35 to 64 $\square_3$ 65 and over $\square_4$

Exploratory analyses were undertaken using analysis software and diagrams and tables generated. For Question 3, which collected discrete data, the aspects that were most important were the distribution of values and the highest and lowest numbers of plays seen. A bar graph, therefore, was drawn:

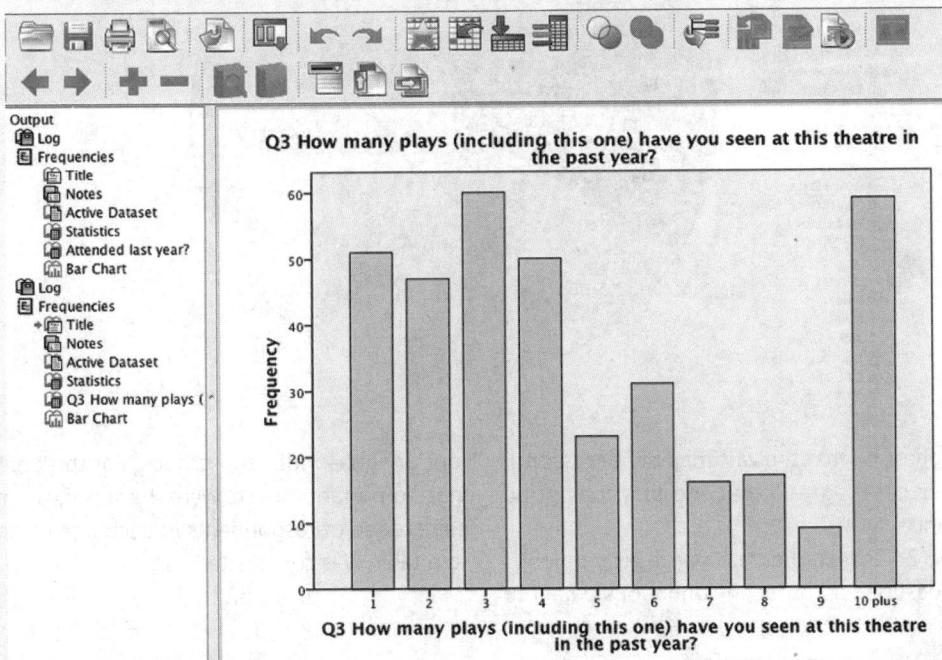

This emphasised that the most frequent number of plays seen by respondents was three and the least frequent number of plays seen by the respondents was either nine or probably some larger number. It also suggested that the distribution was positively skewed towards lower numbers of plays seen.

For Question 11 (categorical data), the most important aspect was the proportion of people agreeing and disagreeing with the statement. A pie chart was therefore drawn, although unfortunately the shadings were not similar for the two agree categories and for the two disagree categories.

Box 12.9
Focus on student research (continued)

Exploring and presenting data for individual variables

This emphasised that the vast majority of respondents (95 per cent) agreed that the play was good value for money.

Question 24 collected data on each respondent's age. This question had grouped continuous data into four unequal-width age groups. For this analysis, the most important aspects were the specific number and percentage of respondents in each age category and so a table was constructed.

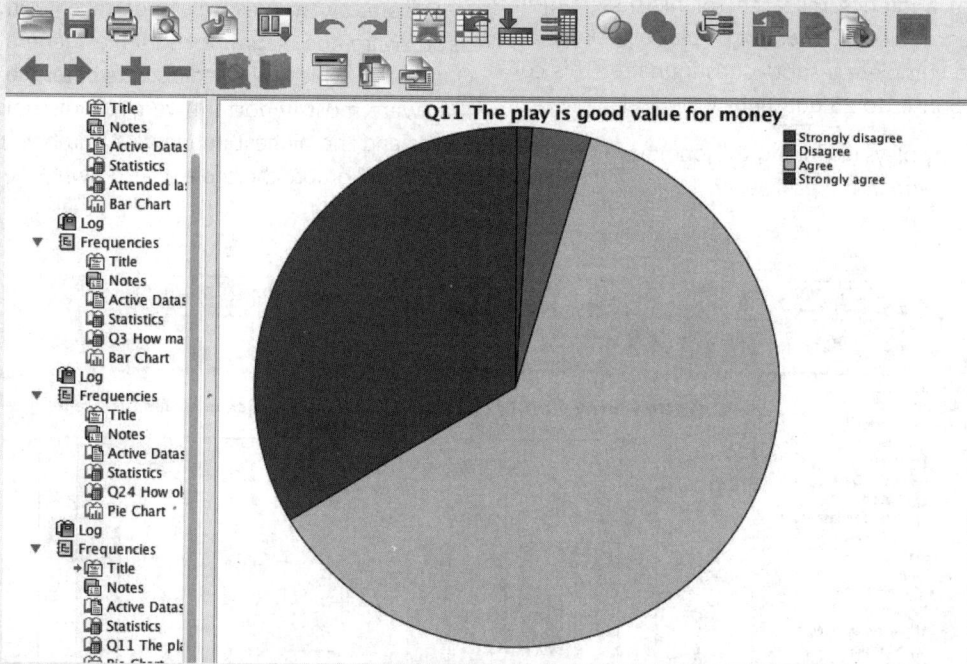

Q24 How old are you?

		Frequency	Percent	Valid Percent	Cumulative Percent
Valid	Under 18	30	4.4	4.4	4.4
	18 to 34	144	20.9	21.0	25.4
	35 to 64	366	53.2	53.4	78.8
	65 plus	145	21.1	21.2	100.0
	Total	685	99.6	100.0	
Missing	System	3	.4		
Total		688	100.0		

Number of insurance claims by gender, 2015
Source: PJ Insurance Services

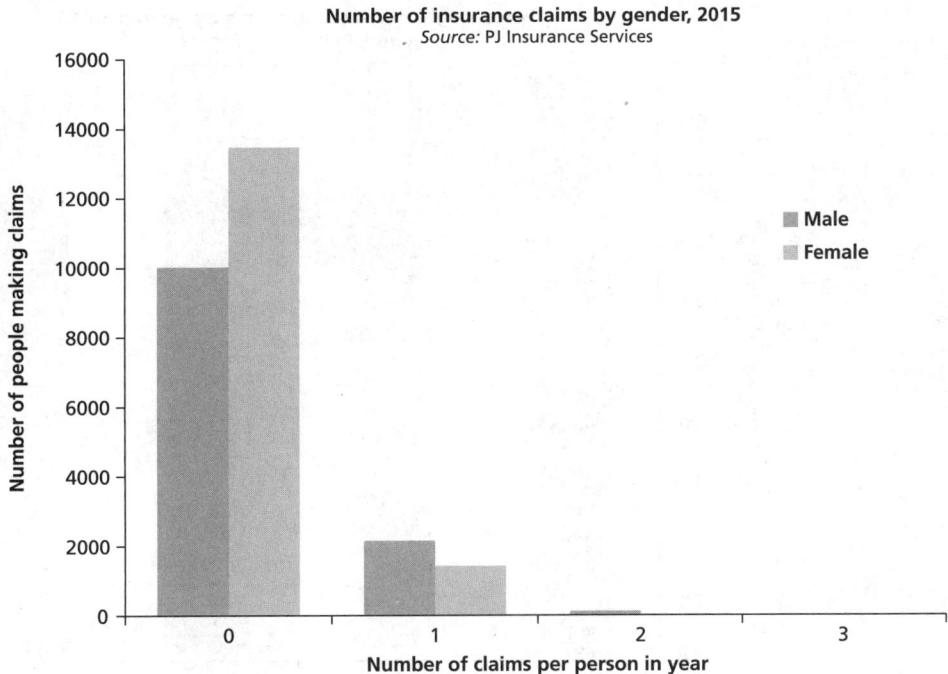

Figure 12.9 Multiple bar graph

(Kosslyn 2006), alternatively known as a **compound bar graph** or **compound bar chart**. As for a bar graph, continuous data – or data where there are many values or categories – need to be grouped. Within any multiple bar graph you are likely to find it easiest to compare between adjacent bars. The multiple bar graph (Figure 12.9) has therefore been drawn to emphasise comparisons between males and females rather than between numbers of claims.

To compare proportions or percentages

Comparison of proportions between variables uses either a **percentage component bar graph** (**percentage component bar chart** also known as a divided bar chart) or two or more pie charts. Either type of diagram can be used for all data types, provided that continuous data, and data where there are more than six values or categories, are grouped. Percentage component bar graphs are more straightforward to draw than comparative pie charts when using most spreadsheets. Within your percentage component bar graphs, comparisons will be easiest between adjacent bars. The chart in Figure 12.10 has been drawn to emphasise the proportions of males and females for each number of insurance claims in the year. Males and females, therefore, form a single bar.

To compare trends so the intersections are clear

The most suitable diagram to compare trends for two or more numerical (or occasionally ranked) variables is a **multiple line graph** where one line represents each variable

Percentage of insurance claims by gender, 2015
Source: PJ Insurance Services

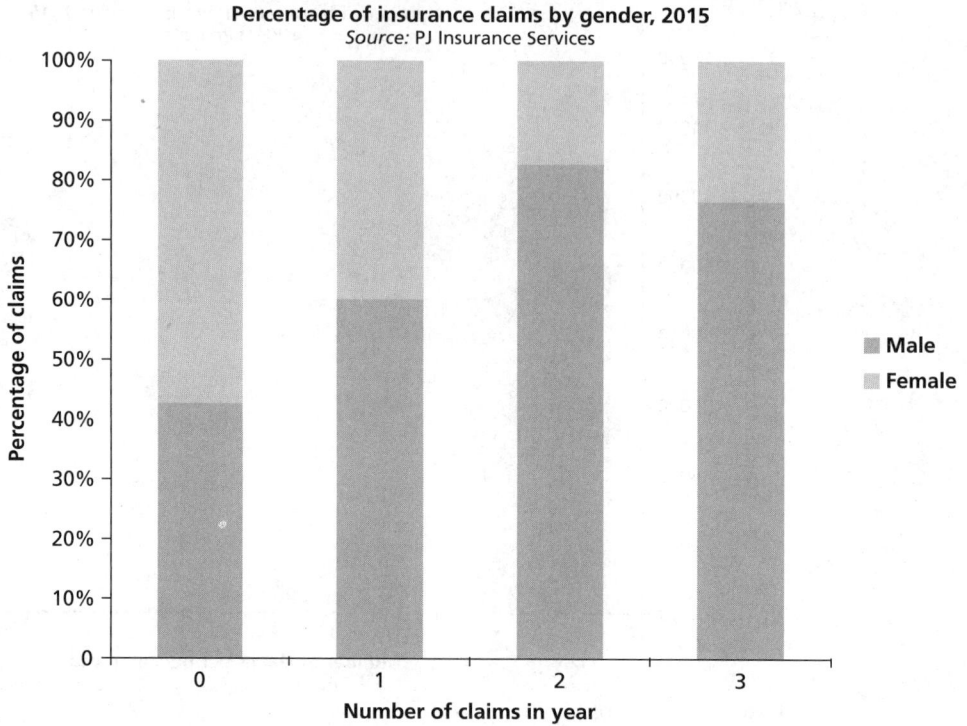

Figure 12.10 Percentage component bar graph

(Kosslyn 2006). You can also use multiple bar graphs (Box 12.10) in which bars for the same time period are placed adjacent to each other.

Conjunctions in trends – that is, where values for two or more variables intersect – are shown by the place where the lines on a multiple line graph cross.

Box 12.10
Focus on student research

Comparing variables

Francis was asked by his uncle, an independent ice cream manufacturer, to examine the records of monthly sales of ice cream for 2013 and 2014. In addition, his uncle had obtained longitudinal data on average (mean) daily hours of sunshine for each month for the same time period from their local weather station. Francis decided to explore data on sales of the three best-selling flavours (vanilla, strawberry and chocolate), paying particular attention to:

• comparative trends in sales;
• the relationship between sales and amount of sunshine.

To compare trends in sales between the three flavours he plotted a multiple line graph using a spreadsheet.

This indicated that sales for all flavours of ice cream were following a seasonal pattern but with an overall upward trend. It also showed that sales of vanilla ice cream were highest, and that those of chocolate had overtaken strawberry. The multiple line graph highlighted the intersection when sales of chocolate first exceeded strawberry, September 2014.

To show interdependence between sales and amount of sunshine Francis plotted scatter graphs for sales of each ice cream flavour against average (mean) daily hours of sunshine for each month. He plotted sales on the vertical axis, as he presumed that these were dependent on the amount of sunshine (see below).

Trends in sales of ice cream 2013–14

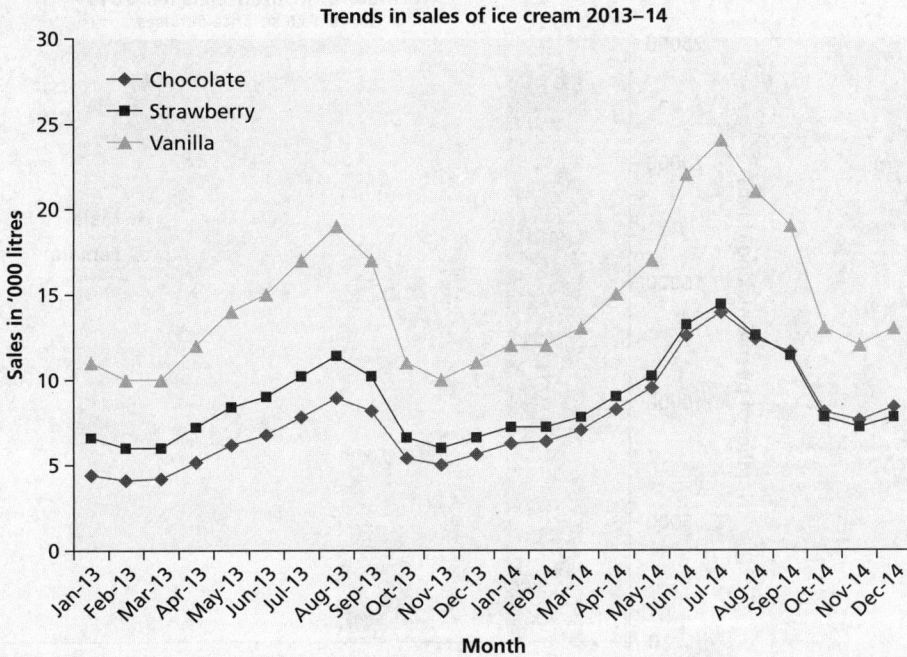

The scatter graph showed that there was a positive relationship between the amount of sunshine and sales of vanilla flavour ice cream. Subsequent scatter plots revealed similar relationships for strawberry and chocolate flavours.

Sales of vanilla ice cream and amount of sunshine 2013–14

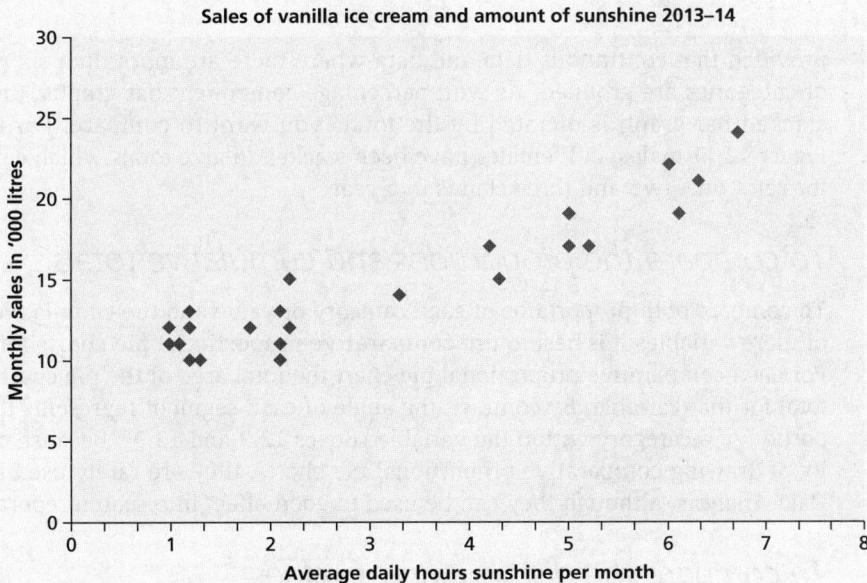

To compare the cumulative totals

Comparison of cumulative totals between variables uses a variation of the bar chart. A **stacked bar graph**, also known as a **stacked bar chart**, can be used for all data types

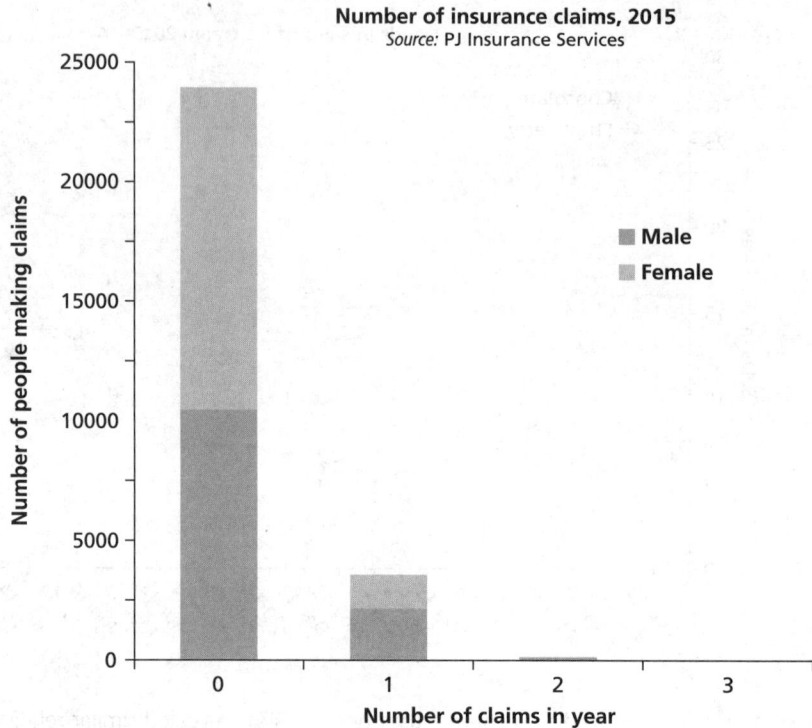

Figure 12.11 Stacked bar graph

provided that continuous data and data where there are more than six possible values or categories are grouped. As with percentage component bar graphs, the design of the stacked bar graph is dictated by the totals you want to compare. For this reason, in Figure 12.11 males and females have been stacked to give totals which can be compared for zero, one, two and three claims in a year.

To compare the proportions and cumulative totals

To compare both proportions of each category or value and the cumulative totals for two or more variables it is best to use **comparative proportional pie charts** for all data types. For each comparative proportional pie chart the total area of the pie chart represents the total for that variable. By contrast, the angle of each segment represents the relative proportion of a category within the variable (Boxes 12.8 and 12.9). Because of the complexity of drawing comparative proportional pie charts, they are rarely used for Exploratory Data Analysis, although they can be used to good effect in research reports.

To compare the distribution of values

Often it is useful to compare the distribution of values for two or more variables. Plotting multiple frequency polygons (Box 12.10) or bar graphs will enable you to compare distributions for up to three or four variables. After this your diagram is likely just to look a mess! An alternative is to use a diagram of multiple box plots, similar to the one in Figure 12.8. This provides a pictorial representation of the distribution of the data for the

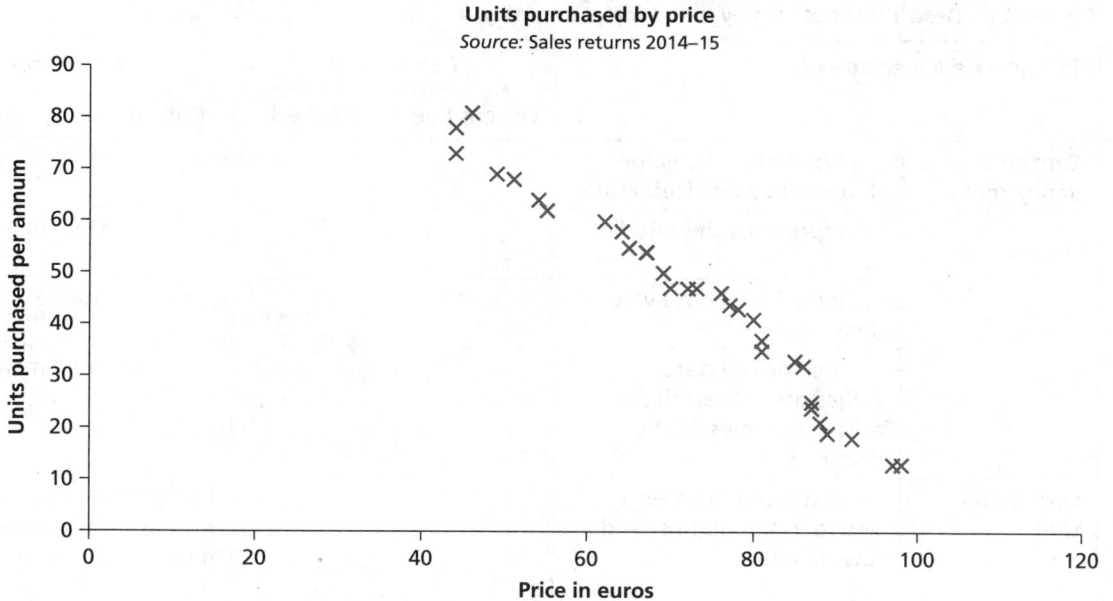

Figure 12.12 Scatter graph

variables in which you are interested. These plots can be compared and are interpreted in the same way as the single box plot.

To show the interdependence between cases for variables

You can explore possible interdependence between ranked and numerical data variables by plotting one variable against another. This is called a **scatter graph** (also known as a **scatter plot)**, and each cross (point) represents the values for one case (Figure 12.12). Convention dictates that you plot the **dependent variable** – that is, the variable that changes in response to changes in the other **(independent) variable** – against the vertical axis. The strength of the interdependence or relationship is indicated by the closeness of the points to an imaginary straight line. If as the values for one variable increase so do those for the other then you have a positive relationship. If as the values for one variable decrease those for the other variable increase then you have a negative relationship. Thus, in Figure 12.12 there is a negative relationship between the two variables. The strength of this relationship can be assessed statistically using techniques such as correlation or regression (Section 12.5).

12.4 Describing data using statistics 使用统计学描述数据

The Exploratory Data Analysis approach (Section 12.3) emphasised the use of diagrams to understand your data. **Descriptive statistics** enable you to describe (and compare) variables numerically. Your research question(s) and objectives, although limited by the type of data (Table 12.4), should guide your choice of statistics. Statistics to describe a variable focus on two aspects:

- the central tendency;
- the dispersion.

Table 12.4 Descriptive statistics by data type: a summary

To calculate a measure of:		Categorical		Numerical	
		Descriptive	Ranked	Continuous	Discrete
Central tendency that . . .	. . . represents the value that occurs most frequently	Mode			
	. . . represents the middle value			Median	
	. . . includes all data values (average)			Mean	
	. . . includes all data values other than those at the extremes of the distribution			Trimmed mean	
Dispersion that . . .	. . . states the difference between the highest and lowest values			Range (data need not be normally distributed but must be placed in rank order)	
	. . . states the difference within the middle 50% of values			Inter-quartile range (data need not be normally distributed but must be placed in rank order)	
	. . . states the difference within another fraction of the values			Deciles or percentiles (data need not be normally distributed but must be placed in rank order)	
	. . . describes the extent to which data values differ from the mean			Variance, or more usually, the standard deviation (data should be normally distributed)	
	. . . compares the extent to which data values differ from the mean between variables			Coefficient of variation (data should be normally distributed)	
	. . . allows the relative extent that data values differ to be compared			Index numbers	

Source: © Mark Saunders, Philip Lewis and Adrian Thornhill 2015

These are summarised in Table 12.4. Those most pertinent to your research question(s) and objectives will eventually be quoted in your project report as support for your arguments.

Describing the central tendency

When describing data for both samples and populations quantitatively it is usual to provide some general impression of values that could be seen as common, middling or average. These are termed measures of **central tendency** and are discussed in virtually all statistics textbooks. The three main ways of measuring the central tendency most used in business research are the:

- value that occurs most frequently (mode);
- middle value or mid-point after the data have been ranked (median);
- value, often known as the average, that includes all data values in its calculation (mean).

However, as we saw in Box 12.2, beware: if you have used numerical codes, most analysis software can calculate all three measures whether or not they are appropriate!

To represent the value that occurs most frequently

The **mode** is the value that occurs most frequently. For descriptive data, the mode is the only measure of central tendency that can be interpreted sensibly. You might read in a report that the most common (modal) colour of motor cars sold last year was silver, or that the two equally most popular makes of motorcycle in response to a questionnaire were Honda and Yamaha. In such cases where two categories occur equally most frequently, this is termed bi-modal. The mode can be calculated for variables where there are likely to be a large number of categories (or values for numerical data), although it may be less useful. One solution is to group the data into suitable categories and to quote the most frequently occurring or **modal group**.

To represent the middle value

If you have quantitative data it is also possible to calculate the middle or **median** value by ranking all the values in ascending order and finding the mid-point (or **50th percentile**) in the distribution. For variables that have an even number of data values the median will occur halfway between the two middle data values. The median has the advantage that it is not affected by extreme values in the distribution (Box 12.11).

To include all data values

The most frequently used measure of central tendency is the **mean** (average in everyday language), which includes all data values in its calculation. However, it is usually only possible to calculate a meaningful mean using numerical data.

The value of your mean is unduly influenced by extreme data values in skewed distributions (Section 12.3). In such distributions the mean tends to get drawn towards the long tail of extreme data values and may be less representative of the central tendency. For this and other reasons Anderson et al. (2014) suggest that the median may be a more useful descriptive statistic. Alternatively, where the mean is affected by extreme data values (outliers) these may be excluded and a **trimmed mean** calculated. This excludes a certain proportion (for example 5 per cent) of the data from both ends of the distribution, where the outliers are located. Because the mean is the building block for many of the statistical tests used to explore relationships (Section 12.5), it is usual to include it as at least one of the measures of central tendency for numerical data in your report. This is, of course, provided that it makes sense!

Describing the dispersion

As well as describing the central tendency for a variable, it is important to describe how the data values are dispersed around the central tendency. As you can see from

Box 12.11
Focus on student research

Measuring the central tendency

As part of her research project, Kylie had obtained secondary data from the service department of her organisation on the length of time for which their customers had held service contracts:

Length of time held contract	Number of customers
< 3 months	50
3 to < 6 months	44
6 months to < 1 year	71
1 to < 2 years	105
2 to < 3 years	74
3 to < 4 years	35
4 to < 5 years	27
5+ years	11

Her exploratory analysis revealed a positively skewed distribution (long tail to the right).

From the table, the largest single group of customers were those who had contracts for 1 to 2 years. This was the modal time period (most commonly occurring). However, the usefulness of this statistic is limited owing to the variety of class widths. By definition, half of the organisation's customers will have held contracts below the median time period (approximately 1 year 5 months) and half above it. As there are 11 customers who have held service contracts for over 5 years, the mean time period (approximately 1 year 9 months) is pulled towards longer times. This is represented by the skewed shape of the distribution.

Kylie needed to decide which of these measures of central tendency to include in her research report. As the mode made little sense she quoted the median and mean when interpreting her data:

The length of time for which customers have held service contracts is positively skewed. Although mean length of time is approximately 1 year 9 months, half of customers have held service contracts for less than 1 year 5 months (median). Grouping of these data means that it is not possible to calculate a meaningful mode.

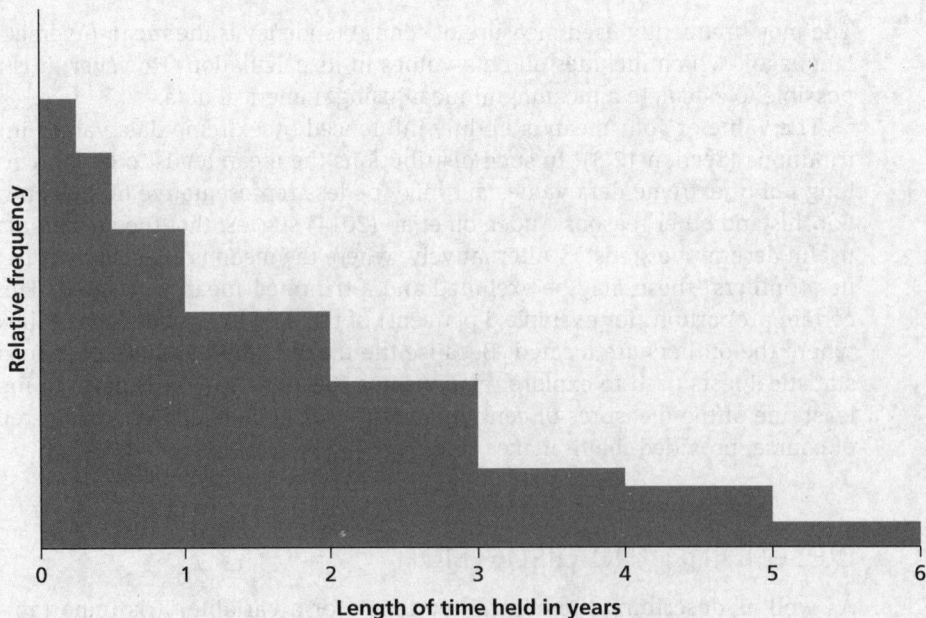

Length of time held in years

Table 12.4, this is only possible for numerical data. Two of the most frequently used ways of describing the dispersion are the:

- difference within the middle 50 per cent of values (inter-quartile range);
- extent to which values differ from the mean (standard deviation).

Although these **dispersion measures** are suitable only for numerical data, most statistical analysis software will also calculate them for categorical data if you have used numerical codes!

To state the difference between values

In order to get a quick impression of the distribution of data values for a variable you could simply calculate the difference between the lowest and the highest values – that is, the **range**. However, this statistic is rarely used in research reports as it represents only the extreme values.

A more frequently used statistic is the **inter-quartile range**. As we discussed earlier, the median divides the range into two. The range can be further divided into four equal sections called **quartiles**. The **lower quartile** is the value below which a quarter of your data values will fall; the **upper quartile** is the value above which a quarter of your data values will fall. As you would expect, the remaining half of your data values will fall between the lower and upper quartiles. The difference between the upper and lower quartiles is the inter-quartile range (Anderson et al. 2014). As a consequence, it is concerned only with the middle 50 per cent of data values and ignores extreme values.

You can also calculate the range for other fractions of a variable's distribution. One alternative is to divide your distribution using **percentiles**. These split your distribution into 100 equal parts. Obviously the lower quartile is the 25th percentile and the upper quartile the 75th percentile. However, you could calculate a range between the 10th and 90th percentiles so as to include 80 per cent of your data values. Another alternative is to divide the range into 10 equal parts called **deciles**.

To describe and compare the extent by which values differ from the mean

Conceptually and statistically in research it is important to look at the extent to which the data values for a variable are spread around their mean, as this is what you need to know to assess its usefulness as a typical value for the distribution. If your data values are all close to the mean, then the mean is more typical than if they vary widely. To describe the extent of spread of numerical data you use the **standard deviation**. If your data are a sample (Section 7.1), this is calculated using a slightly different formula than if your data are a population, although if your sample is larger than about 30 cases there is little difference in the two statistics.

You may need to compare the relative spread of data between distributions of different magnitudes (e.g. one may be measured in hundreds of tonnes, the other in billions of tonnes). To make a meaningful comparison you will need to take account of these different magnitudes. A common way of doing this is:

1 to divide the standard deviation by the mean;
2 then to multiply your answer by 100.

This results in a statistic called the **coefficient of variation** (Black 2009). The values of this statistic can then be compared. The distribution with the largest coefficient of variation has the largest relative spread of data (Box 12.12).

Box 12.12
Focus on student research

Describing variables and comparing their dispersion

Cathy was interested in the total value of transactions at the main and sub-branches of a major bank. The mean value of total transactions at the main branches was approximately five times as high as that for the sub-branches. This made it difficult to compare the relative spread in total value of transactions between the two types of branches. By calculating the coefficients of variation Cathy found that there was relatively more variation in the total value of transactions at the main branches than at the sub-branches. This is because the coefficient of variation for the main branches was larger (23.62) than the coefficient for the sub-branches (18.08).

	A	B	C	D
	Branch type	Mean total transaction value	Standard deviation	Coefficient of variation
1				
2	Main	£6,000,000	£1,417,000	23.62
3	Sub	£1,200,000	£217,000	18.08
4				

Alternatively, as discussed in the introduction in relation to the cost of Big Mac hamburgers in different countries, you may wish to compare the relative extent to which data values differ. One way of doing this is to use **index numbers** and consider the relative differences rather than actual data values. Such indices compare each data value against a base value that is normally given the value of 100, differences being calculated relative to this value. An index number greater than 100 represents a larger or higher data value relative to the base value and an index less than 100, a smaller or lower data value.

To calculate an index number for each case for a data variable you use the following formula:

$$\text{Index number for case} = \frac{\text{data value for case}}{\text{base data value}} \times 100$$

12.5   Examining relationships, differences and trends using statistics 使用统计学检验关系、差异和趋势

One of the questions you are most likely to ask in your analysis is: 'How does a variable relate to another variable?' In statistical analysis you answer this question by testing the likelihood of a relationship (or one more extreme) occurring by chance alone, if there really was no difference in the population from which the sample was drawn (Robson 2011). This process is known as significance or hypothesis testing as, in effect, you are comparing the data you have collected with what you would theoretically expect to happen. Significance testing can therefore be thought of as helping to rule out the possibility that your result could be due to random variation in your sample.

There are two main groups of statistical significance tests: non-parametric and parametric. **Non-parametric statistics** are designed to be used when your data are not normally distributed. Not surprisingly, this most often means they are used with categorical data. In contrast, **parametric statistics** are used with numerical data. Although parametric statistics are considered more powerful because they use numerical data, a number of assumptions about the actual data being used need to be satisfied if they are not to produce spurious results (Blumberg et al. 2014). These include:

- the data cases selected for the sample should be independent – in other words the selection of any one case for your sample should not affect the probability of any other case being included in the same sample;
- the data cases should be drawn from normally distributed populations (Section 12.3 and later in Section 12.5);
- the populations from which the data cases are drawn should have equal variances (don't worry, the term variance is explained later in Section 12.5);
- the data used should be numerical.

In addition, as we will discuss later, you need to ensure that your sample size is sufficiently large to meet the requirements of the statistic you are using (see also Section 7.2). If the assumptions are not satisfied, it is often still possible to use non-parametric statistics.

The way in which this significance is tested using both non-parametric and parametric statistics can be thought of as answering one from a series of questions, dependent on the data type:

- Is the independence or association statistically significant?
- Are the differences statistically significant?
- What is the strength of the relationship, and is it statistically significant?
- Are the predicted values statistically significant?

These are summarised in Table 12.5 along with statistics used to help examine trends.

Testing for normality

As we have already noted, parametric tests assume that the numerical data cases in your sample are drawn from normally distributed populations. This means that the data values for each quantitative variable should also be normally distributed, being clustered around the variable's mean in a symmetrical pattern forming a bell-shaped frequency distribution. Fortunately, it is relatively easy to check if data values for a particular variable are distributed normally, both using graphs and statistically.

In Section 12.3 we looked at a number of different types of graphs including histograms (Figure 12.4), box plots (Figure 12.8) and frequency polygons (Figure 12.13). All of these can be used to assess visually whether the data values for a particular numerical variable are clustered around the mean in a symmetrical pattern, and so normally distributed. For normally distributed data, the value of the mean, median and mode are also likely to be the same.

Table 12.5 Statistics to examine relationships, differences and trends by data type: A summary

	Categorical		Numerical	
	Descriptive	**Ranked**	**Continuous**	**Discrete**
To test normality of a distribution			Kolmogorov–Smirnov test, Shapiro–Wilk test	
To test whether two variables are independent	Chi square (data may need grouping)		Chi square if variable grouped into discrete classes	
To test whether two variables are associated	Cramer's V and Phi (both variables must be dichotomous)			
To test whether two groups (categories) are different		Kolmogorov–Smirnov (data may need grouping) or Mann–Whitney U test	Independent t-test or paired t-test (often used to test for changes over time) or Mann–Whitney U test (where data skewed or a small sample)	
To test whether three or more groups (categories) are different			Analysis of variance (ANOVA)	
To assess the strength of relationship between two variables		Spearman's rank correlation coefficient (Spearman's rho) or Kendall's rank order correlation coefficient (Kendall's tau)	Pearson's product moment correlation coefficient (PMCC)	
To assess the strength of a relationship between one dependent and one independent variable			Coefficient of determination	
To assess the strength of a relationship between one dependent and two or more independent variables			Coefficient of multiple determination	
To predict the value of a dependent variable from one or more independent variables			Regression equation	
To explore relative change (trend) over time			Index numbers	
To compare relative changes (trends) over time			Index numbers	
To determine the trend over time of a series of data			Time series: moving averages or regression equation (regression analysis)	

Source: © Mark Saunders, Philip Lewis and Adrian Thornhill 2015

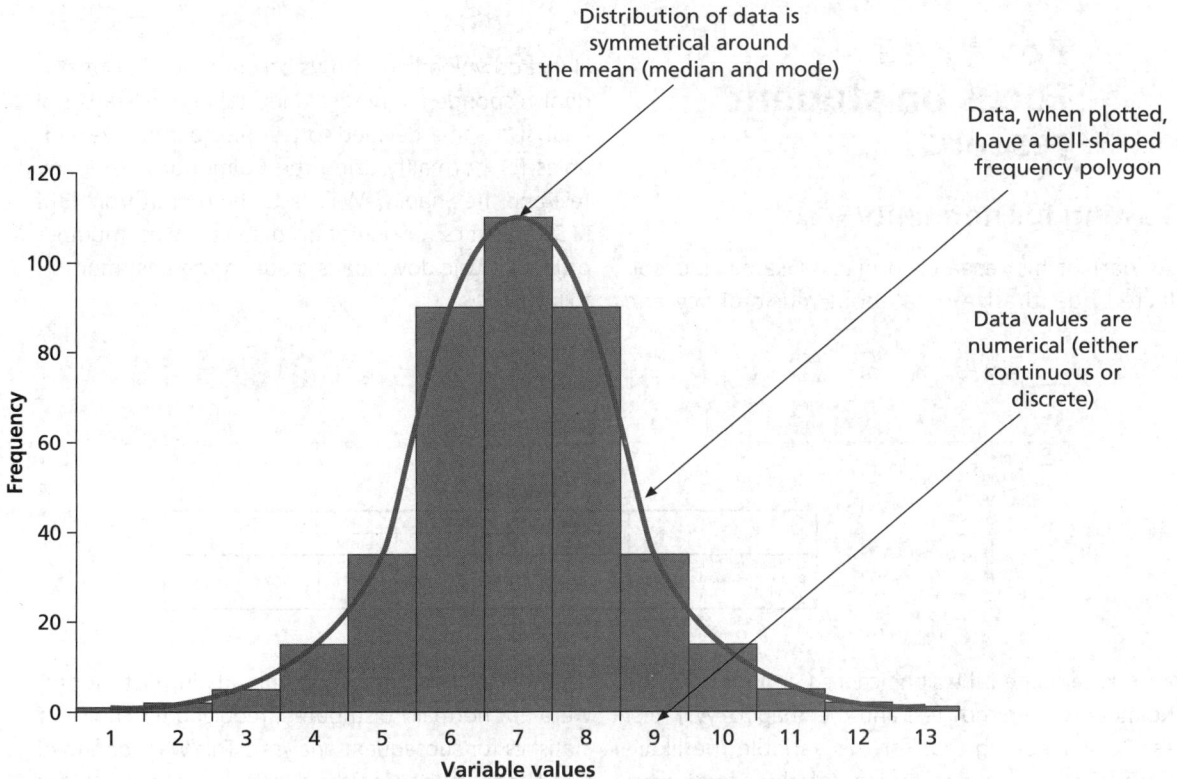

Figure 12.13 Annotated frequency polygon showing a normal distribution

Another way of testing for normality is to use statistics to establish whether the distribution as a whole for a variable differs significantly from a comparable normal distribution. Fortunately, this is relatively easy to do in statistical software such as IBM SPSS Statistics using the **Kolmogorov–Smirnov test** and the **Shapiro–Wilk test** (Box 12.13), as the software also calculates a comparable normal distribution automatically. For both these tests the calculation consists of the test statistic (labelled D and W respectively), the degrees of freedom[1] (df) and, based on this, the probability (p-value) that the data for your variable differ by chance from a comparable normal distribution for that variable. For either statistic, a probability of 0.05 means there is only a 5 per cent likelihood of the actual data distribution differing from a comparable normal distribution by chance alone. Therefore a probability of 0.05 or lower[2] for either statistic means that these data are not normally distributed. When interpreting probabilities from software packages, beware: owing to statistical rounding of numbers a probability of 0.000 does not mean zero, but that it is less than 0.001 (Box 12.13). If the probability

[1]Degrees of freedom are the number of values free to vary when computing a statistic. The number of degrees of freedom for a contingency table of at least 2 rows and 2 columns of data is calculated from: (number of rows in the table − 1) × (number of columns in the table − 1).

[2]A probability of 0.05 means that the probability of your test result or one more extreme occurring by chance alone, if there really was no difference, is 5 in 100, that is 1 in 20.

Box 12.13
Focus on student research

Testing for normality

As part of his research project, Osama had collected quantitative data about music piracy and illegal downloading of music from a number of student respondents. Before undertaking his statistical analysis Osama decided to test his quantitative variables for normality using the Kolmogorov–Smirnov test and the Shapiro–Wilk test. The output from IBM SPSS Statistics for one of his data variables, 'number of legal music downloads made in the past month', follows:

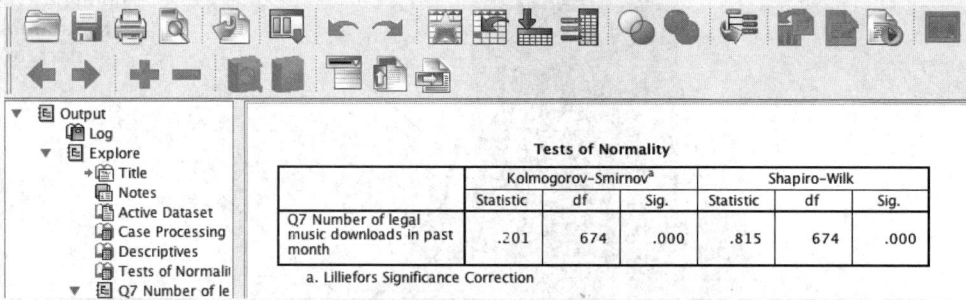

Tests of Normality

	Kolmogorov–Smirnov[a]			Shapiro–Wilk		
	Statistic	df	Sig.	Statistic	df	Sig.
Q7 Number of legal music downloads in past month	.201	674	.000	.815	674	.000

a. Lilliefors Significance Correction

This calculated the significance (Sig.) for both the Kolmogorov–Smirnov test and the Shapiro–Wilk test as '000', meaning that for this variable the likelihood of the actual distribution differing from a normal distribution occurring by chance alone was less than 0.001. Consequently the data values for variable 'Number of legal music downloads in past month' were not normally distributed, reducing his choice of statistics for subsequent analyses. This was confirmed by a bar chart showing the distribution of the data for the variable:

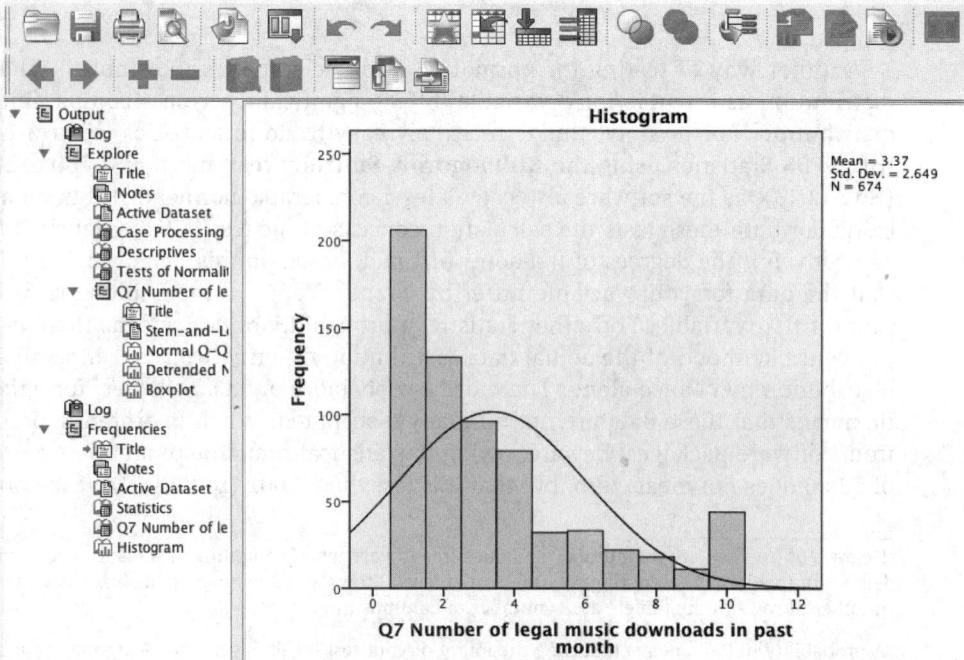

Histogram

Mean = 3.37
Std. Dev. = 2.649
N = 674

Q7 Number of legal music downloads in past month

Osama reported the outcome of this analysis in his project report, quoting the test statistics 'D' and 'W' and their associated degrees of freedom 'df' and probabilities 'p' in brackets:

Tests for normality revealed that data for the variable 'number of legal music downloads in the past month' were not normally distributed [$D = 0.201$, $df = 674$, $p < 0.001$; $W = 0.815$, $df = 674$, $p < 0.001$].

is greater than 0.05, then the data are considered to be normally distributed. However, you need to be careful. With very large samples it is easy to get significant differences between a sample variable and a comparable normal distribution when actual differences are quite small. For this reason it is often helpful to also use a graph to make an informed decision.

Testing for significant relationships and differences

Testing the probability of a pattern or hypothesis such as a relationship between variables occurring by chance alone is known as **significance testing** (Berman Brown and Saunders 2008). As part of your research project, you might have collected sample data to examine the relationship between two variables. Once you have entered data into the analysis software, chosen the statistic and clicked on the appropriate icon, an answer will appear as if by magic! With most statistical analysis software this consists of a test statistic, the degrees of freedom (df) and, based on these, the probability (p-value) of your test result or one more extreme occurring by chance alone. If the probability of your test statistic or one more extreme having occurred by chance alone is very low (usually $p < 0.05$ or lower[3]), then you have a statistically significant relationship. Statisticians refer to this as rejecting the null hypothesis and accepting the hypothesis, often abbreviating the terms null hypothesis to H_0 and hypothesis to H_1. Consequently, rejecting a null hypothesis will mean rejecting a testable statement something like 'there is no difference between . . .' and accepting a testable statement something like 'there is a difference between . . .'. If the probability of obtaining the test statistic or one more extreme by chance alone is higher than 0.05, then you conclude that the relationship is not statistically significant. Statisticians refer to this as failing to reject the null hypothesis. There may still be a relationship between the variables under such circumstances, but you cannot make the conclusion with any certainty. Remember, when interpreting probabilities from software packages, beware: owing to statistical rounding of numbers a probability of 0.000 does not mean zero, but that it is less than 0.001 (Box 12.14).

The hypothesis and null hypothesis we have just stated are often termed **non-directional**. This is because they refer to a difference rather than also including the nature of the difference. A **directional hypothesis** includes within the testable statement the direction of the difference, for example 'larger'. This is important when interpreting the probability of obtaining the test result, or one more extreme, by chance. Statistical software (Box 12.17) often states whether this probability is one-tailed or two-tailed. Where you have a directional hypothesis such as when the direction of the difference is larger, you should use the one-tailed probability. Where you have a non-directional hypothesis and are only interested in the difference you should use the two-tailed probability.

---

[3]A probability of 0.05 means that the probability of your test result or one more extreme occurring by chance alone, if there really was no difference in the population from which the sample was drawn (in other words if the null hypothesis was true), is 5 in 100, that is 1 in 20.

Despite our discussion of hypothesis testing, albeit briefly, it is worth mentioning that a great deal of quantitative analysis, when written up, does not specify actual hypotheses. Rather, the theoretical underpinnings of the research and the research questions provide the context within which the probability of relationships between variables occurring by chance alone is tested. Thus, although hypothesis testing has taken place, it is often only discussed in terms of statistical significance.

The statistical significance of the relationship indicated by a test statistic is determined in part by your sample size (Section 7.2). One consequence of this is that it is very difficult to obtain a significant test statistic with a small sample. Conversely, by increasing your sample size, less obvious relationships and differences will be found to be statistically significant until, with extremely large samples, almost any relationship or difference will be significant (Anderson 2003). This is inevitable as your sample is becoming closer in size to the population from which it was selected. You therefore need to remember that small populations can make statistical tests insensitive, while very large samples can make statistical tests overly sensitive. There are two consequences to this:

- If you expect a difference, relationship or association will be small, you need to have a larger sample size.
- If you have a large sample and the difference, relationship or association is significant, you need to assess the practical significance of this relationship by calculating an effect size index such as Cohen's d. An excellent discussion of these can be found in Ellis (2010).

Type I and Type II errors

Inevitably, errors can occur when making inferences from samples. Statisticians refer to these as Type I and Type II errors. Blumberg et al. (2014) use the analogy of legal decisions to explain Type I and Type II errors. In their analogy they equate a Type I error to a person who is innocent being unjustly convicted and a Type II error to a person who is guilty of a crime being unjustly acquitted. In business and management research we would say that an error made by wrongly rejecting a null hypothesis and therefore accepting the hypothesis is a **Type I error**. Type I errors might involve you concluding that two variables are related when they are not, or incorrectly concluding that a sample statistic exceeds the value that would be expected by chance alone. This means you are rejecting your null hypothesis when you should not. The term '**statistical significance**' discussed earlier therefore refers to the probability of making a Type I error. A **Type II error** involves the opposite occurring. In other words, you fail to reject your null hypothesis when it should be rejected. This means that Type II errors might involve you in concluding that two variables are not related when they are, or that a sample statistic does not exceed the value that would be expected by chance alone.

Given that a Type II error is the inverse of a Type I error, it follows that if we reduce our likelihood of making a Type I error by setting the significance level to 0.01 rather than 0.05, we increase our likelihood of making a Type II error by a corresponding amount. This is not an insurmountable problem, as researchers usually consider Type I errors more serious and prefer to take a small likelihood of saying something is true when it is not (Figure 12.14). It is therefore generally more important to minimise Type I than Type II errors.

To test whether two variables are independent or associated

Often descriptive or numerical data will be summarised as a two-way contingency table (such as Table 12.3). The **chi square test** enables you to find out how likely it is that

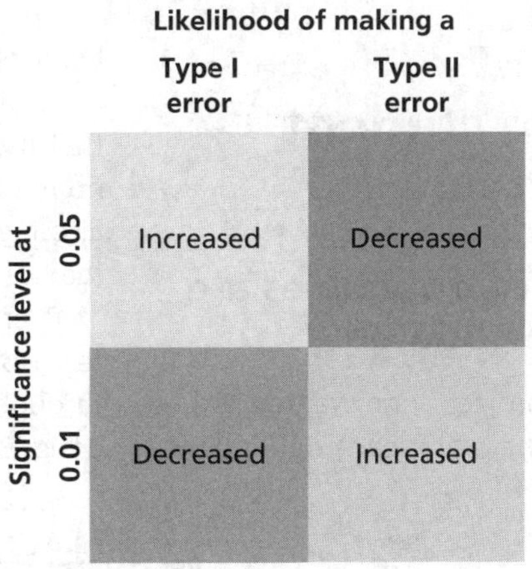

Figure 12.14 Type I and Type II errors

the two variables are independent. It is based on a comparison of the observed values in the table with what might be expected if the two distributions were entirely independent. Therefore you are assessing the likelihood of the data in your table, or data more extreme, occurring by chance alone by comparing it with what you would expect if the two variables were independent of each other. This could be phrased as the null hypothesis: 'there is no dependence . . .'.

The test relies on:

- the categories used in the contingency table being mutually exclusive, so that each observation falls into only one category or class interval;
- no more than 25 per cent of the cells in the table having expected values of less than 5. For contingency tables of two rows and two columns, no expected values of less than 10 are preferable (Dancey and Reidy 2011).

If the latter assumption is not met, the accepted solution is to combine rows and columns where this produces meaningful data.

The chi square (χ^2) test calculates the probability that the data in your table, or data more extreme, could occur by chance alone. Most statistical analysis software does this automatically. However, if you are using a spreadsheet you will usually need to look up the probability in a 'critical values of chi square' table using your calculated chi square value and the degrees of freedom.[4] There are numerous copies of this table online. A probability of 0.05 means that there is only a 5 per cent likelihood of the data in your table occurring by chance alone, and is termed statistically significant. Therefore, a probability of 0.05 or smaller means you can be at least 95 per cent certain that the dependence between your two variables represented by the data in the table could not have occurred by chance factors alone.

Some software packages, such as IBM SPSS Statistics, calculate the statistic **Cramer's V** alongside the chi square statistic (Box 12.14). If you include the value of Cramer's V in your research report, it is usual to do so in addition to the chi square statistic. Whereas

---

[4]Degrees of freedom are the number of values free to vary when computing a statistic. The number of degrees of freedom for a contingency table of at least two rows and two columns of data is calculated from (number of rows in the table − 1) × (number of columns in the table − 1).

Box 12.14
Focus on student research

Testing whether two variables are independent or associated

As part of his research project, John wanted to find out whether there was a significant dependence between salary grade of respondent and gender. Earlier analysis using IBM SPSS Statistics had indicated that there were 385 respondents in his sample with no missing data for either variable. However, it had also highlighted there were only 14 respondents in the five highest salary grades (GC01 to GC05).

Bearing in mind the assumptions of the chi square test, John decided to combine salary grades GC01 through GC05 to create a combined grade GC01–5 using IBM SPSS Statistics:

Grade (current) * *Gender Crosstabulation

Count

		*Gender		
		Male	Female	Total
Grade (current)	GC01–5	14	2	16
	GC06	19	4	23
	GC07	61	11	72
	GC08	65	25	90
	GC09	97	87	184
Total		256	129	385

He then used his analysis software to undertake a chi square test and calculate Cramer's V.

As can be seen, this resulted in an overall chi square value of 33.59 with 4 degrees of freedom (*df*).

Chi-Square Tests

	Value	df	Asymp. Sig. (2-sided)
Pearson Chi-Square	33.587[a]	4	.000
Likelihood Ratio	35.279	4	.000
N of Valid Cases	385		

a. 0 cells (0.0%) have expected count less than 5. The minimum expected count is 5.36.

Symmetric Measures

		Value	Approx. Sig.
Nominal by Nominal	Phi	.295	.000
	Cramer's V	.295	.000
N of Valid Cases		385	

The significance of .000 (Asymp. Sig. – two sided) meant that the probability of the values in his table occurring by chance alone was less than 0.001. He therefore concluded that the gender and grade were extremely unlikely to be independent and quoted the statistic in his project report:

$$[x^2 = 33.59, df = 4, p < 0.001]*$$

The Cramer's V value of .295, significant at the <.001 level (Approx. Sig.), showed that the association between gender and salary grade, although weak, was positive. This meant that men (coded 1 whereas females were coded 2) were more likely to be employed at higher salary grades GC01–5 (coded using lower numbers). John also quoted this statistic in his project report:

To explore this association further, John examined the cell values in relation to the row and column totals. Of males, 5 per cent were in higher salary grades (GC01–5) compared to less than 2 per cent of females. In contrast, only 38 per cent of males were in the lowest salary grade (GC09) compared with 67 per cent of females.

$$[V_c = 0.295, p < 0.001]$$

*You will have noticed that the computer printout in this box does not have a zero before the decimal point. This is because most software packages follow the North American convention, in contrast to the UK convention of placing a zero before the decimal point.

the chi square statistic gives the probability that data in a table, or data more extreme, could occur by chance alone, Cramer's V measures the association between the two variables within the table on a scale where 0 represents no association and 1 represents perfect association. Because the value of Cramer's V is always between 0 and 1, the relative strengths of significant associations between different pairs of variables can be compared.

An alternative statistic used to measure the association between two variables is **Phi**. This statistic measures the association on a scale between -1 (perfect negative association), through 0 (no association) to 1 (perfect association). However, unlike Cramer's V, using Phi to compare the relative strengths of significant associations between pairs of variables can be problematic. This is because, although values of Phi will only range between -1 and 1 when measuring the association between two dichotomous variables, they may exceed these extremes when measuring the association for categorical variables where at least one of these variables has more than two categories. For this reason, we recommend that you use Phi only when comparing pairs of dichotomous variables.

To test whether two groups are different

Ranked data

Sometimes it is necessary to see whether the distribution of an observed set of values for each category of a variable differs from a specified distribution other than the normal distribution, for example whether your sample differs from the population from which it was selected. The **Kolmogorov–Smirnov test** enables you to establish this for ranked data (Kanji 2006). It is based on a comparison of the cumulative proportions of the observed values in each category with the cumulative proportions in the same categories for the specified population. Therefore you are testing the likelihood of the distribution of your observed data differing from that of the specified population by chance alone.

The Kolmogorov–Smirnov test calculates a D statistic to work out the probability of the two distributions differing by chance alone. Although the test statistic is not often found in analysis software other than for comparisons with a normal distribution (discussed earlier), it is relatively straightforward to calculate using a spreadsheet (Box 12.15). A reasonably clear description of this can be found in Cohen and Holliday (1996). Once calculated, you will need to look up the significance of your D value in a 'critical values of D for the Kolmogorov–Smirnov test' table. A probability of 0.05 means that there is only a 5 per cent likelihood that the two distributions differ by chance alone, and is termed statistically significant. Therefore a probability of 0.05 or smaller means you can be at least 95 per cent certain that the difference between your two distributions cannot be explained by chance factors alone.

Numerical data

If a numerical variable can be divided into two distinct groups using a descriptive variable, you can assess the likelihood of these groups being different using an **independent**

Box 12.15
Focus on student research

Testing the representativeness of a sample

Benson's research question was, 'To what extent do the espoused values of an organisation match the underlying cultural assumptions?' As part of his research, he emailed a link to a Web questionnaire to the 150 employees in the organisation where he worked and 97 of these responded. The responses from each category of employee in terms of their seniority within the organisation's hierarchy were as shown in the spreadsheet below.

The maximum difference between his observed cumulative proportion (that for respondents) and his specified cumulative proportion (that for total employees) was 0.034. This was the value of his D statistic. Consulting a 'critical values of D for the Kolmogorov–Smirnov test' table online for a sample size of 97 revealed the probability that the two distributions did not differ by chance alone was less than 0.01, in other words, less than 1 per cent. He concluded that those employees who responded did not differ significantly from the total population in terms of their seniority within the organisation's hierarchy. This was stated in his research report:

Statistical analysis showed the sample selected did not differ significantly from all employees in terms of their seniority within the organisation's hierarchy [$D = .034$, $p = .014$].

	Arial	▼ 10 ▼	≡ ≡ ≡	abc ▼	Wrap Text ▼	General	▼		
Paste	B I U ◇ ▼ A ▼		≡ ≡ ≡ ≡ ≡	Merge ▼		🟡 ▼ % ❯	Conditional Formatting	Styles	

J14 | ⊗ ⊘ fx

	A	B	C	D	E	F	G	H
1			Shop floor workers	Technicians	Supervisors	Quality managers	Management team	Total
2	Respondents	Number	49	15	21	8	4	97
3		Cumulative proportion	0.505	0.660	0.876	0.959	1.000	
4	Total Employees	Number	73	31	24	17	5	150
5		Cumulative proportion	0.487	0.693	0.853	0.967	1.000	
6	Difference		0.018	0.034	0.023	0.008	0.000	
7								

groups *t*-test. This compares the difference in the means of the two groups using a measure of the spread of the scores. If the likelihood of any difference between these two groups occurring by chance alone is low, this will be represented by a large *t* statistic with a probability less than 0.05. This is termed statistically significant.

Alternatively, you might have numerical data for two variables that measure the same feature but under different conditions. Your research could focus on the effects of an intervention such as employee counselling. As a consequence, you would have pairs of data that measure work performance before and after counselling for each case. To assess the likelihood of any difference between your two variables (each half of the pair) occurring by chance alone, you would use a **paired *t*-test** (Box 12.16). Although the calculation of this is slightly different, your interpretation would be the same as for the independent groups *t*-test.

Although the *t*-test assumes that the data are normally distributed (discussed earlier and Section 12.3), this can be ignored without too many problems even with sample sizes of less than 30 (Hays 1994). The assumption that the data for the two groups have the same variance (standard deviation squared) can also be ignored provided that the two samples are of similar size (Hays 1994). If the data are skewed or the sample size is small, the most appropriate statistical test is the Mann–Whitney *U* Test. This test is the non-parametric equivalent of the independent groups *t*-test (Dancey and Reidy 2011). Consequently, if the likelihood of any difference between these two groups occurring by

---

Box 12.16
Focus on management research

Testing whether groups are different

Behavioural ethics research has traditionally viewed ethical decision making as rational and deliberate. However, more recently research has argued it comprises both conscious and subconscious components. Welsh and Ordóñez's (2014) article in the *Academy of Management Journal* explores the extent to which subconscious processes can influence ethical behaviour, particularly in relation to performance goals. Their research comprised three studies, including an experiment using 291 US residents recruited online using Amazon mTurk. These participants were randomly assigned to one of six conditions relating to all possible combinations of the subconscious and conscious components of their ethical standards. These were the two independent variables in the study:

- initial subconscious activation of ethical standards. Here participants were divided into three groups and primed by an exercise involving either (1) ethical, (2) unethical or (3) neutral sentences. These three groups were referred to as the three subconscious activation conditions ethical, unethical and neutral;

- subsequent conscious activation of ethical standards. Participants in each of the three subconscious groups were next divided into two groups and asked to complete either (1) a 1 neutral recall task or (2) a recall task designed to activate their moral standards. These two groups were referred to as the two conscious activation conditions, neutral and activated;

and one dependent variable:

- reported unethical behaviour, in which participants in each of the six groups read a scenario describing a manager who had an opportunity to behave unethically and indicate how likely they would be to behave unethically on a seven-point scale. This ranged from 1 = not likely to 7 = very likely.

Box 12.16
Focus on management research (*continued*)

Testing whether groups are different

Welsh and Ordóñez (2014) found that participants whose initial subconscious ethical standards had not been activated (the neutral subconscious activation condition) and who had also not subsequently had their ethical standards consciously activated (the neutral conscious activation condition) were significantly more likely to engage in unethical behaviour than those whose ethical standards had been activated. They reported these results in their article, quoting both the mean score for the likelihood of unethical behaviour and the value of the t-test for the neutral subconscious activation condition, writing (Welsh and Ordóñez 2014: 732): 'the mean unethical behaviour likelihood (3.59) was significantly higher than in the conscious activation condition (mean = 2.61, $t(95) = 2.18$, $p < 0.05$), the subconscious activation condition (mean = 2.84, $t(140) = 2.06$, $p < .05$), and the conscious-subconscious activation condition (mean = 2.84, $t(141) = 2.00$, $p < 0.05$)'. Based upon this they noted that subconscious priming produces unethical behaviour through the activation of moral standards.

chance alone is low, this will be represented by a large U statistic with a probability less than 0.05. This is termed statistically significant.

To test whether three or more groups are different

If a numerical variable is divided into three or more distinct groups using a descriptive variable, you can assess the likelihood of these groups being different occurring by chance alone by using **one-way analysis of variance** or one-way **ANOVA** (Table 12.5). As you can gather from its name, ANOVA analyses the **variance**, that is, the spread of data values, within and between groups of data by comparing means. The F ratio or F statistic represents these differences. If the likelihood of any difference between groups occurring by chance alone is low, this will be represented by a large F ratio with a probability of less than 0.05. This is termed statistically significant.

The following assumptions need to be met before using one-way ANOVA. More detailed discussion is available in Hays (1994) and Dancey and Reidy (2011).

- Each data value is independent and does not relate to any of the other data values. This means that you should not use one-way ANOVA where data values are related in some way, such as the same case being tested repeatedly.
- The data for each group are normally distributed (discussed earlier and Section 12.3). This assumption is not particularly important provided that the number of cases in each group is large (30 or more).
- The data for each group have the same variance (standard deviation squared). However, provided that the number of cases in the largest group is not more than 1.5 times that of the smallest group, this appears to have very little effect on the test results.

Assessing the strength of relationship

If your data set contains ranked or numerical data, it is likely that, as part of your Exploratory Data Analysis, you will already have plotted the relationship between cases for these ranked or numerical variables using a scatter graph (Figure 12.12). Such relationships might include those between weekly sales of a new product and those of a similar established product, or age of employees and their length of service with the company. These examples emphasise the fact that your data can contain two sorts of relationship:

- those where a change in one variable is accompanied by a change in another variable but it is not clear which variable caused the other to change, a **correlation**;
- those where a change in one or more (independent) variables causes a change in another (dependent) variable, a cause-and-effect relationship.

To assess the strength of relationship between pairs of variables

A **correlation coefficient** enables you to quantify the strength of the linear relationship between two ranked or numerical variables. This coefficient (usually represented by the letter r) can take on any value between $+1$ and -1 (Figure 12.15). A value of $+1$ represents a perfect **positive correlation**. This means that the two variables are precisely related and that as values of one variable increase, values of the other variable will increase. By contrast, a value of -1 represents a perfect **negative correlation**. Again, this means that the two variables are precisely related; however, as the values of one variable increase those of the other decrease. Correlation coefficients between $+1$ and -1 represent weaker positive and negative correlations, a value of 0 meaning the variables are perfectly independent. Within business research it is extremely unusual to obtain perfect correlations.

For data collected from a sample you will need to know the probability of your correlation coefficient having occurred by chance alone. Most analysis software calculates this probability automatically (Box 12.17). As outlined earlier, if this probability is very low (usually less than 0.05) then it is considered statistically significant. If the probability is greater than 0.05 then your relationship is usually considered not statistically significant.

If both your variables contain numerical data you should use **Pearson's product moment correlation coefficient** (PMCC) to assess the strength of relationship (Table 12.5). Where these data are from a sample then the sample should have been selected at random and the data should be normally distributed. However, if one or both of your variables contain ranked data you cannot use PMCC, but will need to use a correlation coefficient that is calculated using ranked data. Such rank correlation coefficients represent the degree of agreement between the two sets of rankings. Before calculating the rank correlation coefficient, you will need to ensure that the data for both variables are ranked. Where one of the variables is numerical this will necessitate converting these data to ranked data. Subsequently, you have a choice of rank correlation coefficients. The two used most widely in business and management research are

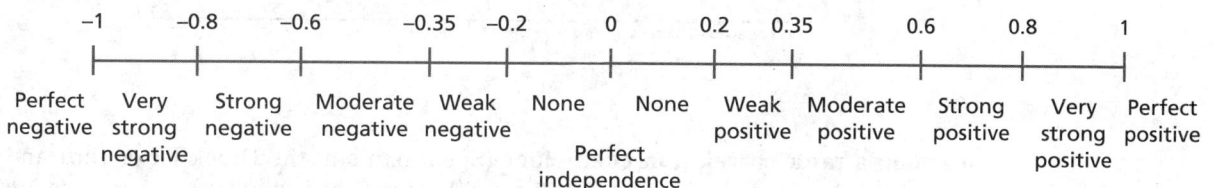

Figure 12.15 Values of the correlation coefficient
Sources: Developed from earlier editions; Hair et al. (2006)

Box 12.17
Focus on student research

Assessing the strength of relationship between pairs of variables

As part of his research project, Hassan obtained data from a company on the number of television advertisements, number of enquiries and number of sales of their product. These data were entered into the statistical analysis software. He wished to discover whether there were any relationships between the following pairs of these variables:

- number of television advertisements and number of enquiries;
- number of television advertisements and number of sales;
- number of enquiries and number of sales.

As the data were numerical, he used the statistical analysis software to calculate Pearson's product moment correlation coefficients for all pairs of variables. The output was a correlation matrix below.

Hassan's matrix is symmetrical because correlation implies only a relationship rather than a cause-and-effect relationship. The value in each cell of the matrix is the correlation coefficient. Thus, the correlation between the number of advertisements and the number of enquiries is 0.362. This coefficient shows that there is a weak to moderate positive relationship between the number of television advertisements and the number of enquiries. The (**) highlights that the probability of this correlation coefficient occurring by chance alone is less than or equal to 0.01 (1 per cent). This correlation coefficient is therefore statistically significant. A two-tailed significance for each correlation, rather than a one-tailed significance, is used as correlation does not test the direction of a relationship, just whether they are related.

Using the data in this matrix Hassan concluded that:

There is a statistically significant strong positive relationship between the number of enquiries and the number of sales ($r = .726$, $p < 0.001$) and a statistically significant but weak to moderate relationship between the number of television advertisements and the number of enquiries ($r = .362$, $p = 0.006$). However, there is no statistically significant relationship between the number of television advertisements and the number of sales ($r = .204$, $p = 0.131$).

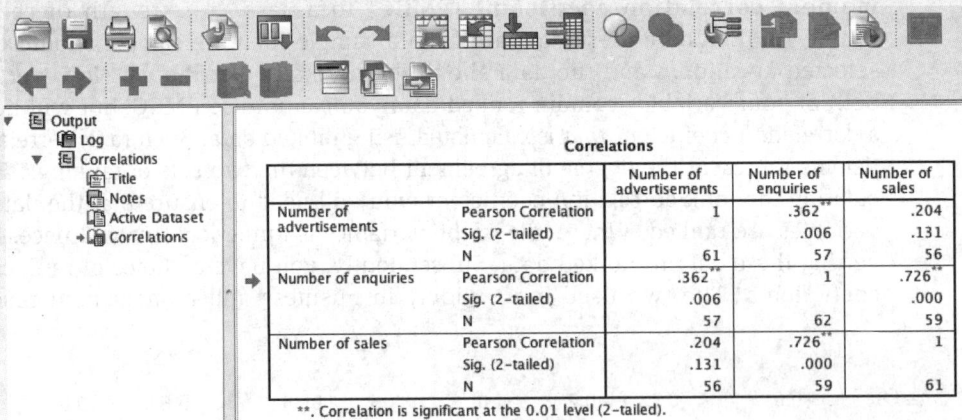

Correlations

		Number of advertisements	Number of enquiries	Number of sales
Number of advertisements	Pearson Correlation	1	.362**	.204
	Sig. (2–tailed)		.006	.131
	N	61	57	56
Number of enquiries	Pearson Correlation	.362**	1	.726**
	Sig. (2–tailed)	.006		.000
	N	57	62	59
Number of sales	Pearson Correlation	.204	.726**	1
	Sig. (2–tailed)	.131	.000	
	N	56	59	61

**. Correlation is significant at the 0.01 level (2–tailed).

Spearman's rank correlation coefficient (Spearman's ρ, the Greek letter rho) and **Kendall's rank correlation coefficient** (Kendall's τ, the Greek letter tau). Where data are being used from a sample, both these rank correlation coefficients assume that the sample is selected at random and the data are ranked (ordinal). Given this, it is not surprising that whenever you can use Spearman's rank correlation coefficient you can also use Kendall's rank correlation coefficient. However, if your data for a variable contain tied ranks, Kendall's rank correlation coefficient is generally considered to be the more appropriate of these coefficients to use. Although each of the correlation coefficients discussed uses a different formula in its calculation, the resulting coefficient is interpreted in the same way as PMCC.

To assess the strength of a cause-and-effect relationship between dependent and independent variables

In contrast to the correlation coefficient, the **coefficient of determination** enables you to assess the strength of relationship between a numerical dependent variable and one numerical independent variable and the **coefficient of multiple determination** enables you to assess the strength of relationship between a numerical dependent variable and two or more independent variables. Once again, where these data have been selected from a sample, the sample must have been selected at random. For a dependent variable and one (or perhaps two) independent variables you will have probably already plotted this relationship on a scatter graph. If you have more than two independent variables this is unlikely as it is very difficult to represent four or more scatter graph axes visually!

The coefficient of determination (represented by r^2) and the coefficient of multiple determination (represented by R^2) can both take on any value between 0 and $+1$. They measure the proportion of the variation in a dependent variable (amount of sales) that can be explained statistically by the independent variable (marketing expenditure) or variables (marketing expenditure, number of sales staff, etc.). This means that if all the variation in amount of sales can be explained by the marketing expenditure and the number of sales staff, the coefficient of multiple determination will be 1. If 50 per cent of the variation can be explained, the coefficient of multiple determination will be 0.5, and if none of the variation can be explained, the coefficient will be 0 (Box 12.18). Within our research we have rarely obtained a coefficient above 0.8.

For a dependent variable and two or more independent variables you will have probably already plotted this relationship on a scatter graph.

The process of calculating the coefficient of determination and regression equation using one independent variable is normally termed **regression analysis**. Calculating a coefficient of multiple determination and regression equation using two or more independent variables is termed **multiple regression analysis**. The calculations and interpretation required by multiple regression are relatively complicated, and we advise you to use

---

Box 12.18
Focus on student research

Assessing a cause-and-effect relationship

As part of her research project, Arethea wanted to assess the relationship between all the employees' annual salaries and the number of years each had been employed by an organisation. She believed that an employee's annual salary would be dependent on the number of years for which she or he had been employed (the independent variable). Arethea entered these data into her analysis software and calculated a coefficient of determination (r^2) of 0.37.

As she was using data for all employees of the firm (the total population) rather than a sample, the probability of her coefficient occurring by chance alone was 0. She therefore concluded that 37 per cent of the variation in current employees' salary could be explained by the number of years they had been employed by the organisation.

statistical analysis software and consult a detailed statistics textbook that also explains how to use the software, such as Field (2013). Most statistical analysis software will automatically calculate the significance of the coefficient of multiple determination for sample data. A very low significance value (usually less than 0.05) means that your coefficient is unlikely to have occurred by chance alone. A value greater than 0.05 means you can conclude that your coefficient of multiple determination could have occurred by chance alone.

To predict the value of a variable from one or more other variables

Regression analysis can also be used to predict the values of a dependent variable given the values of one or more independent variables by calculating a **regression equation** (Box 12.19). You may wish to predict the amount of sales for a specified marketing expenditure and number of sales staff. You would represent this as a regression equation:

$$AoS_i + \alpha + \beta_1 ME_i + \beta_2 NSS_i$$

where:
AoS is the amount of sales
ME is the marketing expenditure
NSS is the number of sales staff
α is the regression constant
β_1 and β_2 are the beta coefficients

This equation can be translated as stating:

$Amount\ of\ sales_i = value + (\beta_1 * Marketing\ expenditure_i) + (\beta_2 * Number\ of\ sales\ staff_i)$

Using regression analysis you would calculate the values of the constant coefficient α and the slope coefficients β_1 and β_2 from data you had already collected on amount of sales, marketing expenditure and number of sales staff. A specified marketing expenditure and number of sales staff could then be substituted into the regression equation to predict the amount of sales that would be generated. When calculating a regression equation you need to ensure the following assumptions are met:

- The relationship between dependent and independent variables is linear. **Linearity** refers to the degree to which the change in the dependent variable is related to the change in the independent variables. Linearity can easily be examined through residual plots (these are usually drawn by the analysis software). Two things may influence the linearity. First, individual cases with extreme values on one or more variables (outliers) may violate the assumption of linearity. It is, therefore, important to identify these outliers and, if appropriate, exclude them from the analysis. Second, the values for one or more variables may violate the assumption of linearity. For these variables the data values may need to be transformed. Techniques for this can be found in other, more specialised books on multivariate data analysis, for example Hair et al. (2013).
- The extent to which the data values for the dependent and independent variables have equal variances (this term was explained earlier in Section 12.4), also known as **homoscedasticity**. Again, analysis software usually contains statistical tests for equal variance. For example, the Levene test for homogeneity of variance measures the equality of variances for a single pair of variables. If **heteroscedasticity** (that is, unequal variances) exists, it may still be possible to carry out your analysis. Further details of this can again be found in more specialised books on multivariate analysis, such as Hair et al. (2013).
- Absence of correlation between two or more independent variables (**collinearity** or **multicollinearity**), as this makes it difficult to determine the separate effects of individual variables. The simplest diagnostic is to use the correlation coefficients, extreme

collinearity being represented by a correlation coefficient of 1. The rule of thumb is that the presence of high correlations (generally 0.90 and above) indicates substantial collinearity (Hair et al. 2013). Other common measures include the tolerance value and its inverse – the **variance inflation factor** (VIF). Hair et al. (2013) recommend that a very small tolerance value (0.10 or below) or a large VIF value (10 or above) indicates high collinearity.

- The data for the independent variables and dependent variable are normally distributed (discussed earlier in this section and Section 12.3).

The coefficient of determination, r^2 (discussed earlier), can be used as a measure of how good a predictor your regression equation is likely to be. If your equation is a perfect predictor then the coefficient of determination will be 1. If the equation can predict only 50 per cent of the variation, then the coefficient of determination will be 0.5, and if the equation predicts none of the variation, the coefficient will be 0. The coefficient of multiple

Box 12.19
Focus on student research

Forecasting the number of road injury accidents

As part of her research project, Nimmi had obtained data on the number of road injury accidents and the number of drivers breath tested for alcohol in 39 police force areas. In addition, she obtained data on the total population (in thousands) for each of these areas from the most recent census. Nimmi wished to find out if it was possible to predict the number of road injury accidents (RIA) in each police area (her dependent variable) using the number of drivers breath tested (BT) and the total population in thousands (POP) for each of the police force areas (independent variables). This she represented as an equation:

$$RIA_i + \alpha + \beta_1 BT_i + \beta_2 POP_i$$

Nimmi entered her data into the analysis software and undertook a multiple regression analysis. She scrolled down the output file and found the

Coefficients[a]

Model		Unstandardized Coefficients B	Unstandardized Coefficients Std. Error	Standardized Coefficients Beta	t	Sig.
1	(Constant)	−30.689	11.798		−2.601	.013
	Population of area in thousands	.127	.013	.803	9.632	.000
	Number of breath tests	.011	.005	.184	2.206	.034

a. Dependent Variable: Number of injury accidents

table headed 'Coefficients'. Nimmi substituted the 'unstandardized coefficients' into her regression equation (after rounding the values):

$$RIA_i = -30.689 + 0.011\ BT_i + 0.127\ POP_i$$

This meant she could now predict the number of road injury accidents for a police area of different populations for different numbers of drivers breath tested for alcohol. For example, the number of road injury accidents for an area of 500,000 population in which 10,000 drivers were breath tested for alcohol can now be estimated:

$-30.689 + (0.011 \times 10000) + (0.127 \times 500)$
$= -30.689 + 110 + 49 + 63.5$
$= 81.8$

Box 12.19
Focus on student
research (*continued*)

Forecasting the number of road injury accidents

In order to check the usefulness of these estimates, Nimmi scrolled back up her output and looked at the results of R^2, t-test and F-test:

The R^2 and adjusted R^2 values of 0.965 and 0.931 respectively both indicated that there was a high degree of goodness of fit of her regression

▼ ⊟ Output
  📖 Log
▼ ⊟ Regression
  📄 Title
  📄 Notes
  📄 Active Dataset
  📄 Variables Enterec
  📄 Model Summary
  📄 ANOVA
→📄 Coefficients

Model Summary

Model	R	R Square	Adjusted R Square	Std. Error of the Estimate
1	.965[a]	.931	.927	43.42389

a. Predictors: (Constant), Number of breath tests, Population of area in thousands

ANOVA[a]

Model		Sum of Squares	df	Mean Square	F	Sig.
1	Regression	909927.069	2	454963.535	241.279	.000[b]
	Residual	67882.828	36	1885.634		
	Total	977809.897	38			

a. Dependent Variable: Number of injury accidents
b. Predictors: (Constant), Number of breath tests, Population of area in thousands

model. It also meant that over 90 per cent of variance in the dependent variable (the number of road injury accidents) could be explained by the regression model. The F-test result was 241.279 with a significance ('Sig.') of .000. This meant that the probability of these results occurring by chance was less than 0.001. Therefore, a significant relationship was present between the number of road injury accidents in an area and the population of the area, and the number of drivers breath tested for alcohol.

The t-test results for the individual regression coefficients (shown in the first extract) for the two independent variables were 9.632 and 2.206. Once again, the probability of both these results occurring by chance was less than 0.05, being less than 0.001 for the independent variable population of area in thousands and 0.034 for the independent variable number of breath tests. This means that the regression coefficients for these variables were both statistically significant at the $p < 0.05$ level.

determination (R^2) indicates the degree of the goodness of fit for your estimated multiple regression equation. It can be interpreted as how good a predictor your multiple regression equation is likely to be. It represents the proportion of the variability in the dependent variable that can be explained by your multiple regression equation. This means that when multiplied by 100, the coefficient of multiple determination can be interpreted as the percentage of variation in the dependent variable that can be explained by the estimated regression equation. The adjusted R^2 statistic (which takes into account the number of independent variables in your regression equation) is preferred by some researchers as it helps avoid overestimating the impact of adding an independent variable on the amount of variability explained by the estimated regression equation.

The t-test and F-test are used to work out the probability of the relationship represented by your regression analysis having occurred by chance. In simple linear regression (with one independent and one dependent variable), the t-test and F-test will give you the same answer. However, in multiple regression, the t-test is used to find out the probability of the relationship between each of the individual independent variables and the dependent variable occurring by chance. In contrast, the F-test is used to find out the overall probability of the relationship between the dependent variable and all the independent variables occurring by chance. The t distribution table and the F distribution table are used to determine whether a t-test or an F-test is significant by comparing the results with the t distribution and F distribution respectively, given the degrees of freedom and the predefined significance level.

Examining trends

When examining longitudinal data the first thing we recommend you do is to draw a line graph to obtain a visual representation of the trend (Figure 12.6). Subsequent to this, statistical analyses can be undertaken. Three of the more common uses of such analyses are:

- to explore the trend or relative change for a single variable over time;
- to compare trends or the relative change for variables measured in different units or of different magnitudes;
- to determine the long-term trend and forecast future values for a variable.

These were summarised earlier in Table 12.5.

To explore the trend

To answer some research question(s) and meet some objectives you may need to explore the trend for one variable. One way of doing this is to use **index numbers** to compare the relative magnitude for each data value (case) over time rather than using the actual data value. Index numbers are also widely used in business publications and by organisations. Various share indices (Box 12.20), such as the *Financial Times* FTSE 100, and the UK's Consumer Prices Index are well-known examples.

Although such indices can involve quite complex calculations, they all compare change over time against a base period. The **base period** is normally given the value of 100 (or 1000 in the case of many share indices, including the FTSE 100), and change is calculated relative to this. Thus a value greater than 100 would represent an increase relative to the base period, and a value less than 100 a decrease.

To calculate simple index numbers for each case of a longitudinal variable you use the following formula:

$$\text{Data value for case index number of a case} = \frac{\text{data value for case}}{\text{data value for base period}} \times 100$$

Thus, if a company's sales were 125,000 units in 2014 (base period) and 150,000 units in 2015, the index number for 2014 would be 100 and for 2015 it would be 120.

To compare trends

To answer some other research question(s) and to meet the associated objectives you may need to compare trends between two or more variables measured in different units or at different magnitudes. For example, to compare changes in prices of fuel oil and coal over time is difficult as the prices are recorded for different units (litres and tonnes). One way of overcoming this is to use index numbers (Section 12.4) and compare the relative changes in the value of the index rather than actual figures. The index numbers for each variable are calculated in the same way as outlined earlier.

Box 12.20   Focus on research in the news

Global overview US: Advance continues as German data and M&A buoy sentiment

By Dave Shellock

Chinese equities respond positively to central bank interest rate cut and prospect of further easing in the pipeline. US stocks were heading for yet another record breaking session as a flurry of merger and acquisition activity and some encouraging German economic data added to the afterglow from Friday's bout of global central bank dovishness.

By midday in New York, the S&P 500 equity benchmark was up 0.2 per cent at 2,068, putting it on track for a third successive record close although it failed to break above Friday's intraday all time peak of 2,071.46.

The FTSE Eurofirst 300 pared its early advance but still ended 0.1 per cent higher at a two month peak. BT shares rose 3.7 per cent after the telecoms group confirmed talks to acquire mobile businesses of EE or Telefónica. Chinese equities got their first chance to respond to the unexpected cut in interest rates by the People's Bank of China as well as reports that further easing could be in the pipeline. The Shanghai Composite index rose 1.9 per cent to a three year high while, in Hong Kong, the Hang Seng China Enterprises Index of "H" shares climbed 3.8 per cent, its biggest one day gain in a year. Tokyo was closed for a holiday.

According to media reports, the central bank was ready to cut rates further to head off slowing inflation. "Needless to say anytime the market gets a

sense the Chinese government and central bank are poised to apply more muscle to stabilising and boosting growth you are going to see a strong rally in regional shares," said Adrian Miller at GMP Securities. Divyang Shah, a global strategist at IFR Markets, said further monetary stimulus in the form of rate and reserve ratio requirement cuts, and "smart" fiscal stimulus were likely in the first half of next year as policy makers deal with slower growth with greater urgency. "The shift from targeted easing should not be seen as a return to the old days of prizing growth above anything else the emphasis on reforms and responsible lending will remain in play," Mr Shah said. "Instead, officials are uneasy at the pace of structural reforms and want to slow things down a touch to keep growth from falling below 7 per cent."

Meanwhile, the outlook for the Eurozone economy, another thorny subject for the markets, appeared to improve as Germany's Ifo index of business confidence rose for the first time in seven months. November's reading came in at 103.2, up from 104.7, defying expectations for a fall.

"Finally, stabilisation," said Carsten Brzeski, an economist at ING. "In our view, the Ifo index is currently the best single leading indicator for the German economy. Therefore, today's Ifo reading gives clear comfort for our view of an accelerating economy in the final quarter of the year."

To determine the trend and forecasting

The trend can be estimated by drawing a freehand line through the data on a line graph. However, these data are often subject to variations such as seasonal fluctuations, and so this method is not very accurate. A straightforward way of overcoming this is to calculate a moving average for the time series of data values. Calculating a **moving average** involves replacing each value in the time series with the mean of that value and those values directly preceding and following it (Anderson et al. 2014). This smoothes out the variation in the data so that you can see the trend more clearly. The calculation of a moving average is relatively straightforward using either a spreadsheet or statistical analysis software.

Once the trend has been established, it is possible to forecast future values by continuing the trend forward for time periods for which data have not been collected. This involves calculating the **long-term trend** – that is, the amount by which values are changing in each time period after variations have been smoothed out. Once again, this is relatively straightforward to calculate using analysis software. Forecasting can also be undertaken using other statistical methods, including regression analysis.

If you are using regression for your time-series analysis, the **Durbin–Watson statistic** can be used to discover whether the value of your dependent variable at time t is related to its value at the previous time period, commonly referred to as $t - 1$. This situation, known as **autocorrelation** or **serial correlation**, is important as it means that the results of your regression analysis are less likely to be reliable. The Durbin–Watson statistic ranges in value from zero to 4. A value of 2 indicates no autocorrelation. A value towards zero indicates positive autocorrelation. Conversely, a value towards 4 indicates negative autocorrelation. More detailed discussion of the Durbin–Watson test can be found in other, more specialised books on multivariate data analysis, for example Hair et al. (2013).

12.6 Summary 小 结

- Data for quantitative analysis can be collected and subsequently coded at different scales of measurement. The data type (precision of measurement) will constrain the data presentation, summary and analysis techniques you can use.
- Data are entered for computer analysis as a data matrix in which each column usually represents a variable and each row a case. Your first variable should be a unique identifier to facilitate error checking.
- All data should, with few exceptions, be recorded using numerical codes to facilitate analyses.
- Where possible, you should use existing coding schemes to enable comparisons.
- For primary data you should include pre-set codes on the data collection form to minimise coding after collection. For variables where responses are not known, you will need to develop a codebook after data have been collected for the first 50 to 100 cases.
- You should enter codes for all data values, including missing data.
- Your data matrix must be checked for errors.
- Your initial analysis should explore data using both tables and graphs. Your choice of table or graph will be influenced by your research question(s) and objectives, the aspects of the data you wish to emphasise, and the measurement precision with which the data were recorded. This may involve using:
  - tables to show specific amounts;
  - bar graphs, multiple bar graphs, histograms and, occasionally, pictograms to show (and compare) highest and lowest amounts;
  - line graphs to show trends;
  - pie charts and percentage component bar graphs to show proportions or percentages;
  - box plots to show distributions;
  - multiple line graphs to compare trends and show intersections
  - scatter graphs to show interdependence between variables.
- Subsequent analyses will involve describing your data and exploring relationships using statistics and testing for significance. Your choice of statistics will be influenced by your research question(s) and objectives, your sample size the measurement precision at which the data

were recorded and whether the data are normally distributed. Your analysis may involve using statistics such as:

- the mean, median and mode to describe the central tendency;
- the inter-quartile range and the standard deviation to describe the dispersion;
- chi square to test whether two variables are independent;
- Cramer's V and Phi to test whether two variables are associated;
- Kolmogorov–Smirnov to test whether the values differ from a specified population;
- *t*-tests and ANOVA to test whether groups are different;
- correlation and regression to assess the strength of relationships between variables;
- regression analysis to predict values.
- Longitudinal data may necessitate selecting different statistical techniques such as:
  - index numbers to establish a trend or to compare trends between two or more variables measured in different units or at different magnitudes;
  - moving averages and regression analysis to determine the trend and forecast.

Self-check questions 自测题

Help with these questions is available at the end of the chapter.

12.1 The following secondary data have been obtained from the Park Trading Company's audited annual accounts:

Year end	Income	Expenditure
2007	11000000	9500000
2008	15200000	12900000
2009	17050000	14000000
2010	17900000	14900000
2011	19000000	16100000
2012	18700000	17200000
2013	17100000	18100000
2014	17700000	19500000
2015	19900000	20000000

  a Which are the variables and which are the cases?
  b Sketch a possible data matrix for these data for entering into a spreadsheet.

12.2 a How many variables will be generated from the following request?

Please tell me up to five things you like about this film.   For office use

....   ❏ ❏ ❏

....   ❏ ❏ ❏

....   ❏ ❏ ❏

....   ❏ ❏ ❏

....   ❏ ❏ ❏

  b How would you go about devising a coding scheme for these variables from a survey of 500 cinema patrons?

12.3 a Illustrate the data from the Park Trading Company's audited annual accounts (Question 12.1) to show trends in income and expenditure.

b What does your diagram emphasise?

c What diagram would you use to emphasise the years with the lowest and highest income?

12.4 As part of research into the impact of television advertising on donations by credit card to a major disaster appeal, data have been collected on the number of viewers reached and the number of donations each day for the past two weeks.

a Which diagram or diagrams would you use to explore these data?

b Give reasons for your choice.

12.5 a Which measures of central tendency and dispersion would you choose to describe the Park Trading Company's income (Question 12.1) over the period 2007–15?

b Give reasons for your choice.

12.6 A colleague has collected data from a sample of 74 students. He presents you with the following output from the statistical analysis software:

degree programme * quality of feedback from project tutor Crosstabulation

Count

		quality of feedback from project tutor				Total
		awful	poor	reasonable	good	
degree programme	BSc Management	1	2	11	21	35
	BSc International Management	0	2	6	13	21
	BSc Hospitality Management	0	1	4	4	9
	BSc Entrepreneurship and Small Business Management	0	1	2	6	9
Total		1	6	23	44	74

Chi-Square Tests

	Value	df	Asymp. Sig. (2-sided)
Pearson Chi-Square	2.845[a]	9	.970
Likelihood Ratio	3.228	9	.955
Linear-by-Linear Association	.000	1	.986
N of Valid Cases	74		

a. 10 cells (62.5%) have expected count less than 5. The minimum expected count is .12.

Explain what this tells you about students' opinions about feedback from their project tutor.

12.7 Briefly describe when you would use regression analysis and correlation analysis, using examples to illustrate your answer.

12.8 a Use an appropriate technique to compare the following data on share prices for two financial service companies over the past six months, using the period six months ago as the base period:

	EJ Investment Holdings	AE Financial Services
Price 6 months ago	€10	€587
Price 4 months ago	€12	€613
Price 2 months ago	€13	€658
Current price	€14	€690

b Which company's share prices have increased most in the last six months? (Note: you should quote relevant statistics to justify your answer.)

Review and discussion questions   复习与讨论题

12.9   Use a search engine to discover coding schemes that already exist for ethnic group, family expenditure, industry group, socio-economic class and the like. To do this you will probably find it best to type the phrase 'coding ethnic group' into the search box.

   a Discuss how credible you think each coding scheme is with a friend. To come to an agreed answer pay particular attention to:

   • the organisation (or person) that is responsible for the coding scheme;
   • any explanations regarding the coding scheme's design;
   • use of the coding scheme to date.

   b Widen your search to include coding schemes that may be of use for your research project. Make a note of the web address of any that are of interest.

12.10   With a friend, choose a large company in which you are interested. Obtain a copy of the annual report for this company. Examine the use of tables, graphs and charts in your chosen company's report.

   a To what extent does the use of graphs and charts in your chosen report follow the guidance summarised in Box 12.8 and Table 12.2?

   b Why do you think this is?

12.11   With a group of friends, each choose a different share price index. Well-known indices you might choose include the Nasdaq Composite Index, France's CAC 40, Germany's Dax, Hong Kong's Hang Seng Index (HSI), Japan's Nikkei Index, the UK's FTSE 100 and the USA's Dow Jones Industrial Average Index.

   a For each of the indices, find out how it is calculated and note down its daily values for a one-week period.

   b Compare your findings regarding the calculation of your chosen index with those for the indices chosen by your friends, noting down similarities and differences.

   c To what extent do the indices differ in the changes in share prices they show? Why do you think this is?

改进研究项目
Progressing your research project

定量分析你的数据
Analysing your data quantitatively

• Examine the technique(s) you are proposing to use to collect data to answer your research question. You need to decide whether you are collecting any data that could usefully be analysed quantitatively.

• If you decide that your data should be analysed quantitatively, you must ensure that the data collection methods you intend to use have been designed to make analysis by computer as straightforward as possible. In particular, you need to pay attention to the coding scheme for each variable and the layout of your data matrix.

• Once your data have been entered into a computer and the data set opened in your analysis software, you will need to explore and present them. Bearing your research question in mind, you should select the most appropriate diagrams and tables after considering the suitability of all possible techniques. Remember to label your diagrams clearly and to keep an electronic copy, as they may form part of your research report.

• Once you are familiar with your data, describe and explore relationships using those statistical techniques that best help you to answer your research questions and are suitable for the data type. Remember to keep an annotated copy of your analyses, as you will need to quote statistics to justify statements you make in the findings section of your research report.

• Use the questions in Box 1.4 to guide you in your reflective diary entry.

12.12 Find out whether your university provides you with access to IBM SPSS Statistics. If it does, visit this book's companion website and download the self-teach package and associated data sets. Work through this to explore the features of IBM SPSS Statistics.

Self-check answers   自测题答案

12.1 a The variables are 'income', 'expenditure' and 'year'. There is no real need for a separate case identifier as the variable 'year' can also fulfil this function. Each case (year) is represented by one row of data.

b When the data are entered into a spreadsheet the first column will be the case identifier, for these data the year. Income and expenditure should not be entered with the £ sign as this can be formatted subsequently using the spreadsheet:

	A	B	C
1	Year	Income (£)	Expenditure (£)
2	2007	11000000	9500000
3	2008	15200000	12900000
4	2009	17050000	14000000
5	2010	17900000	14900000
6	2011	19000000	16100000
7	2012	18700000	17200000
8	2013	17100000	18100000
9	2014	17700000	19500000
10	2015	19900000	20000000
11			

12.2 a There is no one correct answer to this question as the number of variables will depend on the method used to code these descriptive data. If you choose the multiple-response method, five variables will be generated. If the multiple-dichotomy method is used, the number of variables will depend on the number of different responses.

b Your first priority is to decide on the level of detail of your intended analyses. Your coding scheme should, if possible, be based on an existing coding scheme. If this is of insufficient detail then it should be designed to be compatible to allow comparisons. To design the coding scheme you need to take the responses from the first 50–100 cases and establish broad groupings. These can be subdivided into increasingly specific subgroups until the detail is sufficient for the intended analysis. Codes can then be allocated to these subgroups. If you ensure that similar responses receive adjacent codes, this will make any subsequent grouping easier. The actual responses that correspond to each code should be noted in a codebook. Codes should be allocated to data on the data collection form in the 'For office use' box. These codes need to include missing data, such as when four or fewer 'things' have been mentioned.

12.3 a Park Trading Company – Income and Expenditure 2007–15.

b Your diagram (it is hoped) emphasises the upward trends of expenditure and (to a lesser extent) income. It also highlights the conjunction where income falls below expenditure in 2013.

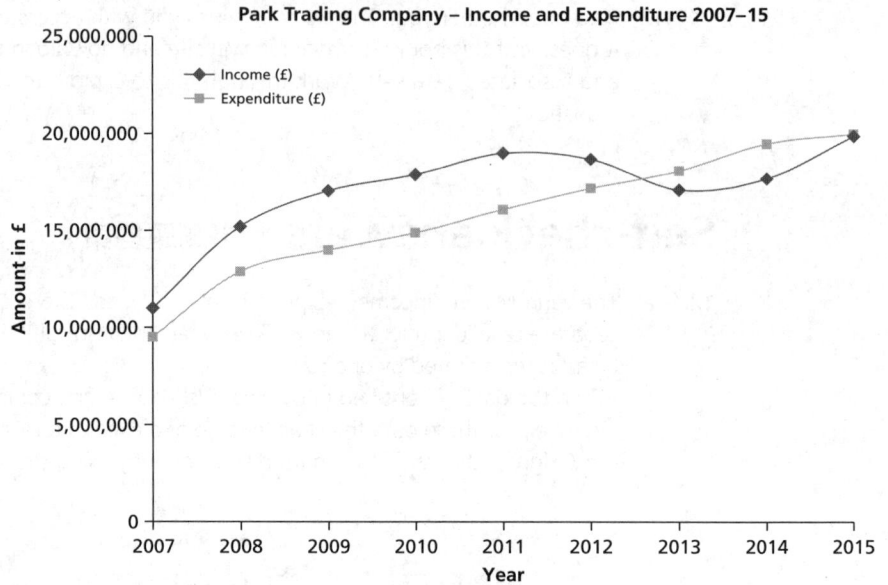

Park Trading Company – Income and Expenditure 2007–15

c To emphasise the years with the lowest and highest income, you would probably use a histogram because the data are continuous. A frequency polygon would also be suitable.

12.4 a You would probably use a scatter graph in which number of donations would be the dependent variable and number of viewers reached by the advertisement the independent variable.

b This would enable you to see whether there was any relationship between number of viewers reached and number of donations.

12.5 a The first thing you need to do is to establish the data type. As it is numerical, you could theoretically use all three measures of central tendency and both the standard deviation and inter-quartile range. However, you would probably calculate the mean and perhaps the median as measures of central tendency and the standard deviation and perhaps the inter-quartile range as measures of dispersion.

b The mean would be chosen because it includes all data values. The median might be chosen to represent the middle income over the 2007–15 period. The mode would be of little use for these data as each year has different income values.

   If you had chosen the mean you would probably choose the standard deviation, as this describes the dispersion of data values around the mean. The inter-quartile range is normally chosen where there are extreme data values that need to be ignored. This is not the case for these data.

12.6 The probability of a chi square value of 2.845 with 9 degrees of freedom occurring by chance alone for these data is 0.970. This means that statistically the interdependence between students' degree programmes and their opinion of the quality of feedback from project tutors is extremely likely to be explained by chance alone. In addition, the assumption of the chi square test that no more than 20 per cent of expected values should be less than 5 has not been satisfied.

   To explore this lack of interdependence further, you examine the cell values in relation to the row and column totals. For all programmes, over 80 per cent of respondents thought the quality of feedback from their project tutor was reasonable or good.

12.7 Your answer needs to emphasise that correlation analysis is used to establish whether a change in one variable is accompanied by a change in another. In contrast, regression analysis is used to establish whether a change in a dependent variable is caused by changes in one or more independent variables – in other words, a cause-and-effect relationship. Although it is impossible to list all the examples you might use to illustrate your answer, you should make sure that your examples for regression illustrate a dependent and one or more independent variables.

12.8 a These quantitative data are of different magnitudes. Therefore, the most appropriate technique to compare these data is index numbers. The index numbers for the two companies are:

	EJ Investment Holdings	AE Financial Services
Price 6 months ago	100	100.0
Price 4 months ago	120	104.4
Price 2 months ago	130	112.1
Current price	140	117.5

b The price of AE Financial Services' shares has increased by €103 compared with an increase of €4 for EJ Investment Holdings' share price. However, the proportional increase in prices has been greatest for EJ Investment Holdings. Using six months ago as the base period (with a base index number of 100), the index for EJ Investment Holdings' share price is now 140 while the index for AE Financial Services' share price is 117.5.

Get ahead using resources on the companion website at: **www.pearsoned.co.uk/ saunders**.

- Improve your IBM SPSS Statistics and NVivo research analysis with practice tutorials.
- Save time researching on the Internet with the Smarter Online Searching Guide.
- Test your progress using self-assessment questions.
- Follow live links to useful websites.

Chapter 13

Analysing qualitative data 分析定性数据

Learning outcomes 学习目标

By the end of this chapter you should be:

- able to understand the nature of qualitative data and appreciate the implications of this for their analysis;
- able to evaluate different approaches to analyse your qualitative data;
- able to identify the main issues that you need to consider when preparing your qualitative data for analysis including preparation to use computer-aided qualitative data analysis software (CAQDAS);
- able to transcribe a recorded interview or notes of an interview or observation and create a data file for analysis by computer;
- aware of different analytical aids to help you to analyse your qualitative data, including keeping a reflective or reflexive journal;
- able to select an appropriate analytical technique for your research project to undertake qualitative data analysis;
- able to identify the common functions of CAQDAS and describe the issues associated with its use.

13.1 Introduction 引 言

This chapter is designed to help you analyse qualitative data. The nature of qualitative data is discussed in Section 13.2. Following this we discuss two important aspects related to the nature of qualitative analysis in Section 13.3. The first of these relates to whether you approach your qualitative data analysis from a deductive or inductive perspective (Section 4.4). The second relates to the interactive nature of qualitative data collection and analysis. As you read through the sections of this chapter you will recognise the interrelated and interactive nature of qualitative data collection and analysis. Because of this it will be necessary to plan your qualitative research as an interconnected process where you collect and begin to analyse and interpret data as you undertake each interview or observation.

In Section 13.4 we discuss the preparation of your data for analysis and in Section 13.5 we outline a number of aids that will help you analyse these data and record your ideas about how to progress your research.

Sections 13.6–13.13 discuss different analytical techniques to analyse your qualitative data. These are Thematic Analysis (Section 13.6), Template Analysis (Section 13.7), Explanation Building and Testing (Section 13.8), Grounded Theory Method (Section 13.9), Narrative Analysis (Section 13.10), Discourse Analysis (Section 13.11), Content Analysis (Section 13.12) and Data Display and Analysis (Section 13.13).

Nearly all of us have, at some time in our lives, completed a jigsaw puzzle. As children we may have played with jigsaw puzzles and, as we grew older, those we were able to complete became more complex. In some ways, qualitative data analysis can be likened to the process of completing a jigsaw puzzle in which the pieces represent data. These pieces of data and the relationships between them help us as researchers to create a picture of what we think the data are telling us!

When trying to complete a jigsaw puzzle, most of us begin by looking at the picture on the lid of our puzzle's box. A puzzle for which there is no picture is usually more challenging as we have no idea how the pieces fit together or what the picture will be! Similarly, we may not be clear about how, or even if, the data we have collected can form a clear picture.

Perhaps you haven't tried to complete a jigsaw puzzle for many years but you might find the following useful as well as entertaining! Get a friend to give you the contents of a jigsaw in a bag without the box (since this normally shows the picture of what it is!). Turn all of the pieces picture side up. Think about how you will categorise these data that lie in front of you. What do they mean? You will be likely to group pieces with similar features such as those of a particular colour together. Normally you might then try to fit these similar pieces together to begin to reveal the picture that the fitted pieces are

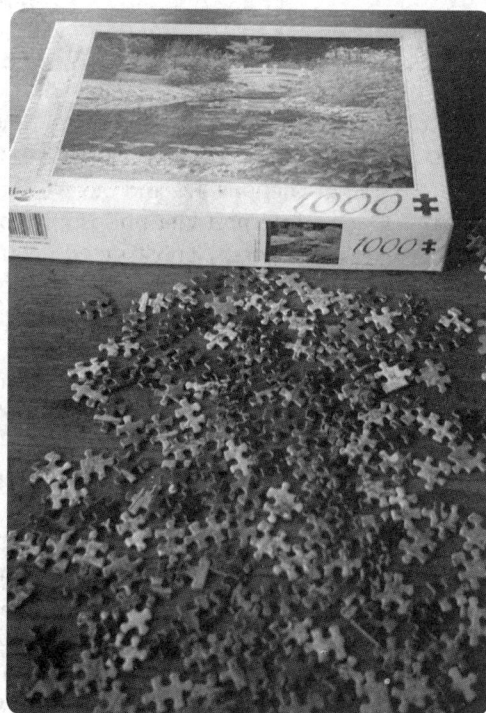

Source: © Mark Saunders, 2015

designed to show. Perhaps completing jigsaws reinforces a sense of there being an external reality 'out there', so all we need to do is reveal it! However, for many qualitative researchers, the picture that our pieces of data reveal will depend on the nature of our research question and the concepts we use to make sense of what we see!

A range of computer-aided qualitative data analysis software (CAQDAS) now exists, which we consider in Section 13.14. Consequently, although you need to understand which analytical technique, or combination of techniques, is suitable for the nature of your qualitative or mixed methods research project to be able to make an informed choice about how to analyse your data, it may no longer be necessary for you to undertake routine qualitative data management tasks manually, such as coding your data and sorting these into categories. However, we do not assume that use of CAQDAS is automatic, for two reasons. Firstly, you may not have access to CAQDAS, or at least to software that is suitable for the nature of your research project. Secondly, qualitative data analysis is, as we noted, an interactive and iterative process, a gradual process and a thoughtful and reflective rather than a mechanical process, so using CAQDAS isn't a quick fix. On the other hand, using CAQDAS helps the management and organisation of data, helping to facilitate analysis, where you are able to use a suitable program for your research project.

Consequently, although we make reference to, and include screenshots of, different software packages in some worked examples, these are used to illustrate generic issues associated with analysis rather than imply that you must use such software. If you wish to develop your skills in one of the more widely used CAQDAS packages, called NVivo™, a self-teach package is available via our companion website.

13.2 The nature of qualitative data 定性数据的性质

It is helpful to commence our discussion by understanding what we mean by qualitative data. Understanding **qualitative data** will help you to analyse these meaningfully. In Sections 4.2 and 5.3 we recognised that qualitative research is often associated with an interpretivist philosophy because researchers need to make sense of the subjective and socially constructed meanings expressed by those who take part in research about the phenomenon being studied. **Social constructionism** indicates that partially shared meanings and realities are dependent on people's interpretation of the events that occur around them. Since meanings in qualitative research depend on social interaction, qualitative data are likely to be more varied, elastic and complex than quantitative data. Analysis and understanding of these data therefore need to be sensitive to these characteristics to be meaningful.

Qualitative data are likely to be characterised by their richness and fullness, based on your opportunity to explore a subject in as real a manner as is possible. A contrast can thus be drawn between the 'thin' abstraction or description that principally results from quantitative data collection and the 'thick' or 'thorough' abstraction or description associated with qualitative data (Brekhus et al. 2005; Dey 1993).

A further way to understand qualitative data is to distinguish them from quantitative data. Table 13.1 highlights three distinct differences between quantitative and qualitative data.

In qualitative research, meanings are principally derived from words and images, not numbers. Since words and images may have multiple meanings as well as unclear meanings, it is necessary to explore and clarify these with great care. This indicates that the quality of qualitative research depends on the interaction between data collection and data analysis to allow meanings to be explored and clarified. This aspect permeates much of the discussion in this chapter.

The nature of qualitative data has further implications for their analysis. These non-standardised data will be likely to be large in volume and complex in nature. You will therefore be confronted by ether a mass of paper, still images, visual recordings or electronic files that you will need to explore, analyse, synthesise and transform in order to

Table 13.1 Distinctions between quantitative and qualitative data

Quantitative data	Qualitative data
Based on meanings derived from numbers	Based on meanings expressed through words (spoken and textual) and images
Collection results in numerical and standardised data	Collection results in non-standardised data requiring classification into categories
Analysis conducted through the use of diagrams and statistics	Analysis conducted through the use of conceptualisation

address your research objectives and answer your research question. In making use of many techniques discussed later, this will involve you in processes where you summarise some parts of your data to condense them, code and categorise data in order to group them according to themes that begin to make sense of these data, and then to link these categories and themes in ways that provide you with a structure or structures to answer your research question. Without undertaking one or more of these processes, the most that may result may be an impressionistic view of what these qualitative data mean.

While it might be possible to make some use of diagrams and statistics at this stage, such as the frequency of occurrence of certain categories of data (Sections 12.3, 12.4 and Section 13.6), the way in which you are likely to analyse the qualitative data that you collect is through the development of research-specific concepts that you may then link into a conceptual framework. This framework may be developed before, during or after your data collection and then refined as your research progresses. These analytical processes are discussed in much greater detail in Sections 13.6–13.13.

13.3 The nature of qualitative analysis 定性分析的性质

As we noted earlier, it is important to understand the nature of qualitative analysis before embarking on its use. In this section we consider two aspects related to the nature of qualitative analysis: your approach to analysis and the interactive nature of qualitative research.

Deciding on your approach to analysis

Research commences from either a deductive or an inductive approach (Section 4.4). Where you commence your research project using a deductive approach you will seek to use existing theory to shape the qualitative research process and aspects of data analysis. Where you commence your research project using an inductive approach you will seek to build up a theory that is adequately grounded in your data. In this section we discuss the difference between using theory at the start of your research to analyse qualitative data and commencing your research by collecting and exploring your data without a pre-determined theoretical or descriptive framework.

Using a deductive approach

Yin (2014) suggests that, where you have made use of existing theory to formulate your research question and objectives, you may also use the theoretical propositions that helped you do this as a means to devise a framework to help you to organise and direct

Box 13.1
Focus on student research

Incorporating an inductive approach

Phil commenced a research project by adopting a deductive approach, but found that the theoretical framework he adopted did not yield a sufficiently convincing answer to his research questions and objectives. He therefore decided to reanalyse his data inductively. This revealed themes that had not figured prominently in the deductive analysis. A combination of the two approaches generated a more convincing answer to Phil's research questions and objectives.

your data analysis. There is debate about this approach when applied to qualitative analysis because this theoretical framework may be too restrictive in relation to the issues revealed in the data and fail to allow the meanings expressed by research participants to be explored adequately. If this occurs when you use a theoretical framework to design and analyse your research, you will need to adapt your approach (Box 13.1).

Even though you may incorporate an inductive approach in your research, commencing your work from a theoretical perspective may have certain advantages. It will link your research into the existing body of knowledge in your subject area, help you to get started and provide you with an initial analytical framework.

To devise a theoretical or descriptive framework you need to identify the main variables, components, themes and issues in your research project and the predicted or presumed relationships between them. A descriptive framework will rely more on your prior experience and what you expect to occur, although it is of course possible to develop an explanatory framework based on a mixture of theory derived from the literature you used and your own expectations. You will use this framework as the means to start and direct the analysis of your data.

Using an inductive approach

The alternative to a deductive approach is to start to collect data and then explore them to see which themes or issues to follow up and concentrate on. An inductive approach may be a difficult strategy to follow and may not lead to success for someone who is an inexperienced researcher. This is likely to happen where you simply go ahead and collect data without examining them to assess which themes are emerging from the data as you progress. Where you commence your data collection with this type of approach – related initially to an exploratory purpose – you should analyse the data as you collect them and develop a conceptual framework to guide your subsequent work. This is also referred to as a grounded approach because of the nature of the theory or explanation that emerges as a result of the research process. In this approach:

- you do not commence such a study with a clearly defined theoretical framework;
- instead you identify relationships between your data and develop questions and hypotheses or research propositions to test these;
- theory emerges from the process of data collection, analysis and interpretation.

You will need to commence this approach with a clear research purpose and careful preparation before embarking on data collection and analysis. Researchers who use an inductive approach develop a competent level of knowledge about their research topic. Their research generally commences with a clearly defined research question and objectives, even though these may be amended by the data they subsequently collect.

Not using a predetermined theoretical framework in an inductive approach is related to the desire to avoid being sensitised by existing theoretical constructs. Instead, researchers using an inductive approach aim to search for and recognise meanings in the data and to understand the social context and perceptions of research participants. The use of an inductive approach should allow a good 'fit' to develop between the social reality of the research participants and the theory that emerges – it will be 'grounded' in that reality. You will need to compare your grounded theory with existing theory contained in the literature once you have developed this.

The use of an inductive approach may involve you in a lengthy period of concurrent data collection and analysis in order to research an issue or topic adequately or to derive a well-grounded theory. Corbin and Strauss (2008) suggest that this type of approach may take months to complete. This is an important consideration if, like many of our students, your research project is time-constrained by a submission date. It is also likely that this approach will combine some elements of a deductive approach as you develop theoretical propositions and then test their applicability through subsequent data collection and analysis (see the discussion of abduction in Section 4.4). Consequently, while you may commence with either an inductive or a deductive approach, in practice your research is likely to combine elements of both.

The interactive nature of the process

Data collection, data analysis and the development and verification of propositions are very much an interrelated and interactive set of processes in qualitative research. Analysis is undertaken during the collection of data as well as after it. This analysis helps to shape the direction of data collection, especially where you are following a more inductive, grounded approach. The research propositions that emerge from your data in an inductive approach or those you commenced with at the start of your data collection in a deductive approach will be tested as you compare them with the data in your study. The key point here is the relative flexibility that this type of process permits you.

The interactive nature of data collection and analysis allows you to recognise important themes, patterns and relationships as you collect data: in other words, to allow these to emerge from the process of data collection and analysis. As part of this you will need to re-categorise and re-code your existing data to see whether emergent themes, patterns and relationships are present in the cases where you have already collected data. You will also be able to adjust your future data collection to see whether related data exist in cases where you intend to conduct your research (Corbin and Strauss 2008).

The concurrent process of data collection and analysis also has implications for the way in which you manage your time and organise your data and related documentation. It will be necessary to arrange interviews or observations with enough space between them to allow yourself sufficient time to write up or word process a transcript or set of notes, and to analyse this before proceeding to your next data collection session (Section 10.6). Where you conduct a small number of interviews in one day, you will need time during the evening to undertake some initial analysis on these before carrying out further interviews. You may also be able to find a little time between interviews to carry out a cursory level of analysis. As part of this we have found it extremely helpful to listen to audio-recordings of interviews while travelling to and from the university.

There is a clear limit to the value of continuing to undertake interviews or observations without properly analysing these in this way. There is a danger of data overload where you continue to collect data without sufficiently analysing these. This will be associated with a lost opportunity to understand what your data reveal in relation to your research question and the directions that might be worth pursuing for your research. Important ideas that occur to you as you undertake an interview, conduct an observation, read a document, listen to an audio-recording, or view a set of images or a visual-recording may be lost if you do not record these because you are focused on collecting data without interacting with and analysing these.

13.4 Preparing your data for analysis 为分析准备数据

As we have seen in Chapters 5, 8, 9, 10 and 11, qualitative data can be generated in many forms. In Chapter 5, when we considered archival and documentary research, and Chapter 8, when we considered secondary data, we highlighted how documentary data were available in a range of written and non-written forms. In Chapter 9, we considered how observation may be video-recorded, in addition to being recorded using an observation schedule or by taking notes. Chapter 10 highlighted the role of audio or digital recording as well as note taking. Finally, Chapter 11, although focusing on collecting data that will be quantified, noted that open questions may be used to collect qualitative data from respondents, which are recorded in writing by either the respondent or an interviewer.

It is important to emphasise the importance of copying any recordings you make and transcribing both these and your notes to ensure data are not lost. In this section we focus upon the conversion of qualitative data from oral or handwritten form to word-processed text, as this is the way that you are most likely to use these in your analysis. As part of this, we discuss the general requirements of CAQDAS packages (see Section 13.14).

Transcribing qualitative data

In Chapter 10 we emphasised that, in qualitative research interviews, the interview is often audio-recorded and subsequently **transcribed**, that is, reproduced verbatim as a word-processed account. We also emphasised that, as an interviewer, you would be interested not only in what participants said, but in the way they said it as well. This means that the task of transcribing audio-recorded interviews is likely to be time-consuming as you will need not only to record exactly what was said and by whom, but also try to give an indication of the tone in which it was said and the participants' non-verbal communications. Without this additional contextual information, important incidents that affect the conduct of your interview or observation may be missed (e.g. see Boxes 10.12 and 13.4). You also need to ensure it can be linked to the contextual information that locates the interview (Section 10.4).

Even if you are a touch-typist, you will find the task of transcribing an audio-recording extremely time-consuming. Most research methods texts suggest that it takes a touch-typist between 6 and 10 hours to transcribe every hour of audio-recording. Consequently, it is helpful if your interviews are transcribed as soon as possible after they are undertaken in order to avoid a build-up of audio-recordings and associated transcription work. Fortunately, there are a number of possible ways of reducing the vast amount of personal time needed to transcribe interviews verbatim. These are summarised in Table 13.2 along with some of the associated potential problems. As you will see in Table 13.2, one problem, however you choose to transcribe the data, is making sure that the transcription is accurate by correcting any transcription errors. This process is known as data cleaning. Once this has been done, some researchers send a copy of the transcript to the participant for final checking. While this can be helpful for ensuring factual accuracy, we have found that interviewees often want to correct their own grammar and use of language as well! This is

Table 13.2 Alternative ways of reducing the time needed to transcribe audio-recordings

Alternative	Potential problems
Pay a touch-typist to transcribe your audio-recordings	• Expense of paying someone else • Important data such as pauses, coughs, sighs and the like may not be included • You will not be familiarising yourself with the data as you are not transcribing them yourself • The transcription will still require careful checking as errors can creep in
Borrow a transcription machine with a foot-operated play–pause–rewind–fast forward mechanism and software to control the audio speed	• Although this will allow you to control the audio-recorder more easily, the speed of transcription will still be dependent upon your typing ability • The transcription will still require careful checking • You may not be able to gain access to a transcription machine
'Dictate' your audio-recordings to your computer using voice-recognition software	• You will need to discover which voice-recognition software works best with your voice • You will also need to discover which voice-recognition software is suited to the needs of your research project • You will need to 'teach' the voice-recognition software to understand your voice • You will need to listen to and dictate the entire audio-recording • The transcription will still require careful checking as the software is not entirely accurate
Only transcribe those sections of each audio-recording that are pertinent to your research (**data sampling**)	• You will need to listen to the entire recording carefully first, at least twice • You may miss certain things, meaning you will have to go back to the audio-recording later • Those sections you transcribe will still require careful checking

because spoken and written language are very different. For this reason, you need to think carefully before offering to provide each interviewee with a full copy of their transcript.

Each interview you transcribe should be saved as a separate word-processed file. As part of this we recommend that you use a filename that maintains confidentiality and preserves anonymity but that you can easily recognise and which codifies important information. When doing this Mark always starts his transcription filenames with the interview number and saves the word-processed transcripts for each research project in a separate subdirectory. Subsequent parts of the filename provide more detail. Thus the file '26MPOrg1.docx' is the transcript of the **26**th interview, **M**ale, **P**rofessional, undertaken at **Org**anisation1. As some CAQDAS programs require filenames of eight or fewer characters, you may need to limit your filenames to this length.

When transcribing interviews and group interviews, you need to be able to distinguish between the interviewer and the participant or participants. This means you need to have clear speaker identifiers such as '17FA' for the 17th interviewee who is a female administrator. This tends to be more visible in the transcript if they are in capitals (Box 13.2). Similarly, you need to be able to distinguish between any topic headings you use, questions and responses. One way of doing this, dependent upon the precise requirements of

Box 13.2
Focus on student research

Extract from an interview transcript

Martin had decided to use the code IV to represent himself in the transcripts of his in-depth interviews and 01FS to represent his first interviewee, a female student. By using capital letters to identify both himself and the interviewee Martin could identify clearly where questions and responses started. In addition, it reduced the chance of a mistype in the transcription as identifiers were always a combination of

capital letters and numbers. Martin used transcription symbols such as '(.)' to represent a brief pause and '.hhh' to represent an in-breath. He also included brief comments relating to a respondent's actions in the interview transcript. These he enclosed with double parentheses (()). A brief extract from a transcript follows:

IV: So tell me, why do you use the Student Union Bar?

01FS: Well,.hhh (.), a lot of my friends go there for the final drink of the evening (.) there is an atmosphere and the drinks are cheap. I don't feel embarrassed to walk in on my own and there's always someone to talk to and scrounge a fag off ((laughs))

your CAQDAS, is to put topic headings in CAPITALS, questions in *italics* and responses in normal font. The most important thing is to be consistent within and across all your transcriptions. Some authors also recommend the use of specific transcription symbols to record intakes of breath, overlapping talk and changes in intonation. A useful list of transcription symbols is provided as an appendix by Silverman (2013).

In a transcription of a more structured interview, you also need to include the question number and the question in your transcription. For example, by including the question number 'Q27' at the start of the question you will be able to search for and find question 27 quickly. In addition, by having the full question in your transcript you will be far less likely to misinterpret the question your respondent is answering.

When transcribing audio-recordings or your own notes you need to plan in advance how you intend to analyse your transcriptions. If you only have access to a black and white printer, there is little point in using different coloured fonts to distinguish between participants in a group interview or to distinguish non-verbal responses such as nervous laughter in your transcripts as these will be difficult to discern when working from the paper copies. You also need to be careful about using these and other word-processing software features if you are going to analyse the data using CAQDAS. These programs often have precise file formats which can mean that word-processing software features such as *bold* and *italics* generated by your word-processing software will disappear when your data file is imported (Lewins and Silver 2009). For example, although you may transcribe your interviews using a word processor such as Microsoft Word, your chosen CAQDAS package may require this textual data to be saved as a text-only file (.txt) or using rich text format (.rtf), resulting in the loss of some of these features. These are summarised as a checklist in Box 13.3.

Using electronic textual data including scanned documents

For some forms of textual data such as, for example, email interviews (Section 10.9) or electronic versions of documents (Section 8.2), including organisational emails, blogs and web-based reports, your data may already be in electronic format. Although these data have already been captured electronically, you are still likely to need to spend some

Box 13.3
Checklist

Transcribing your interviews

✔ Have you thought about how you intend to analyse your data and made sure that your transcription will facilitate this?

✔ Have you chosen clear interviewer and respondent identifiers and used them consistently?

✔ Have you included the interview questions in full in your transcription?

✔ Have you saved your transcribed data using a separate file for each interview?

✔ Does your filename maintain confidentiality and preserve anonymity while still allowing you to recognise important information easily?

✔ Have you checked your transcript for accuracy and, where necessary, 'cleaned up' the data?

✔ (If you intend to use CAQDAS) Will the package you are going to use help you to manage and analyse your data effectively? In other words, will it do what you need it to do?

✔ (If you intend to use CAQDAS) Are your saved transcriptions compatible with the CAQDAS package you intend to use, so you will not lose any features from your word-processed document when you import the data?

✔ (If you intend to use CAQDAS) Have you checked your transcript for accuracy and 'cleaned up' the data prior to importing into your chosen CAQDAS package?

✔ Have you stored a separate backup or security copy of each data file on your USB mass storage device?

time preparing them for analysis. This is likely to involve you in ensuring that, where necessary, the data are:

- suitably anonymised, such as by using separate codes for yourself and different participants;
- appropriately stored for analysis, for example one file for each interview, each meeting's minutes or each organisational policy;
- free of typographical errors that you may have introduced, and, where these occurred, they have been 'cleaned up'.

Consequently, you are likely to find much of the checklist in Box 13.3 helpful. If you intend to use CAQDAS to help you to manage and analyse documents which are not available electronically, you will need to scan these into your word-processing software and ensure they are in a format compatible with your chosen CAQDAS.

13.5 Aids to help your analysis 有助于分析的辅助手段

In addition to transcribing your notes and audio or digital recordings, it will also help your analysis if you record contextual information about the interviews or observations that you conduct (Section 10.4). This will help you to recall the context and content of each interview or observation as well as informing your interpretation as you will be more likely to remember the precise circumstances of your data collection. Various researchers have suggested ways of recording information and developing reflective ideas to supplement your written-up notes or transcripts and your categorised data (e.g. Brinkmann and Kvale 2015; Gerstl-Pepin and Patrizio 2009). These include:

- interim or progress summaries;
- transcript summaries;
- document summaries;

- self-memos;
- a research notebook;
- a reflective diary or journal.

The way in which you use these analytical aids should be dependent on your preferred approach to recording your ideas and reflections, and the context of your research. You may, for example, develop a preference for using either interim summaries or self-memos or a research notebook. You may decide to use more than one of these aids. Where you produce transcripts of interviews or observations, it will be helpful to write a transcript summary for each one; similarly where you use documents, it will be helpful to write document summaries. Your university or awarding body may require you to keep a reflective diary, although you may also find it helpful to write interim summaries, self-memos or a research notebook to produce this. We recommend using these analytical aids to help you with your research project, although choice of which to use is partly a matter of personal preference.

Interim or progress summaries

As your analysis progresses you may wish to write an **interim summary** of your progress to date. You may decide to write an interim summary after each interview or observation, or after a set of related interviews or observations. Similarly, you may wish to write an interim summary after a period of using secondary data or conducting a search of the literature. In this way, you may write up a number of summaries that detail the development of your thoughts to aid your analysis and the direction of your data collection. Alternatively, your interim summary may become a unified working document that you modify and continue to refer to, as your research project progresses. The way in which you use this analytical aid should suit your preferred approach. An interim summary may include:

- what you have found so far;
- what level of confidence you have in your findings and explanations to date;
- what you need to do in order to improve the quality of your data and/or to seek to substantiate your apparent explanations, or to seek alternative explanations;
- how you will seek to achieve the needs identified by the interim analysis.

Transcript summaries

After you have written up your notes, or produced a transcript, of an interview or observation session, you can also produce a summary of the key points that have emerged from undertaking this activity. A **transcript summary** compresses long statements into briefer ones in which the main sense of what has been said or observed is rephrased in a few words. Through summarising you will become conversant with the principal themes that have emerged from each interview or observation. You may be able to identify apparent relationships between themes that you wish to note down so that you can return to these to seek to establish their validity. It will also be useful to make some comments about the person(s) you interviewed or observed, the setting in which this occurred and whether anything occurred during the interview or observation which might have affected the nature of the data that you collected (Box 13.4).

Once you have produced a summary of the key points that emerge from the interview or observation and its context, you should attach a copy to the file of your written-up notes or transcript for further reference.

Box 13.4
Focus on student research

Noting an event that affected the nature of data collection

Birjit was facilitating a focus group whose participants were the customers of a large department store. Approximately halfway through the allotted time, an additional participant joined the group. This person almost immediately took control of the discussion, two other participants appearing to become reticent and withdrawing from the group's discussion. Despite this, all Birjit's questions were answered fully and she felt the data she had obtained was valuable. However, she recorded the point at which the new participant joined the group in a post-transcript summary in case any divergence was apparent between the nature of the data in the two parts of the focus group.

Document summaries

Where you use any sort of documentation it is helpful to produce a **document summary**. A document summary may fulfil two purposes. It may be used to summarise and list the document's key points for your research. These points become part of your data set. Secondly, you may use it to describe the purpose of the document, how it relates to your work and why it is significant.

This type of summary is likely to be useful as you continue to conduct your analysis. You will be able to return to a document summary to look again at the data you drew from the document, to see how you coded and categorised these data, and to be able to re-read your notes about its relevance to your research. As a research project progresses, there is a likelihood that you will forgot some of your thoughts about your previous data collection and analysis, so that a document summary, like other analytical aids discussed in this sub-section, will act as a reminder of your earlier ideas.

Self-memos

Self-memos allow you to record ideas that occur to you about any aspect of your research, as you think of them. Where you omit to record any idea as it occurs to you it may well be forgotten. The occasions when you are likely to want to write a memo include:

- when you are writing up interview or observation notes, or producing a transcript of this event;
- when you are coding and categorising data;
- as you continue to categorise, analyse and interpret these data;
- when you are constructing a narrative;
- when you engage in writing your research project.

Most CAQDAS programs include some form of writing tool that allows you make notes, add comments or write self-memos as you are analysing your data (Lewins and Silver 2009). This facility is very helpful and, as your self-memos are automatically dated, you can also trace the development of your ideas.

Ideas may also occur as you engage in an interview or observation session. In this case you may record the idea very briefly as a margin note and write it as a memo to yourself after the event. Similarly, ideas may occur as you work through a documentary source.

It may be useful to carry a reporter's notebook or an e-notebook in order to be able to record your ideas, whenever and wherever they occur. When you are undertaking the production of notes, or a transcript, or any aspect of qualitative analysis, the notebook will be available for you to record your ideas.

Self-memos may vary in length from a few words to one or more pages. They can be written as simple notes – they do not need to be set out formally. It will be useful to date them and to provide cross-references to appropriate places in your written-up notes or transcripts, where appropriate. Alternatively, an idea that is not grounded in any data (which may nevertheless prove to be useful) should be recorded as such. Memos should be filed together, not with notes or transcripts, and may themselves be categorised where this will help you to undertake later stages of your qualitative analysis. Memos may also be updated as your research progresses, so that your bank of ideas continues to have currency and relevance.

Research notebook

An alternative approach to recording your ideas about your research is to keep a **research notebook**. You may of course keep such a notebook alongside the creation of self-memos. Its purpose will be similar to the creation of self-memos: to record your ideas and reflections, and to act as an aide-mémoire about your intentions for the direction of your research. Using a chronological format may help you to identify the development of certain ideas (such as data categories, propositions or hypotheses) and the way in which your research has progressed, as well as providing an approach that suits the way in which you like to think.

Reflective diary or journal

In Chapter 1 we recommended you also keep a reflective diary or journal. This is devoted to reflections about your experiences of undertaking research, what you have learnt from these experiences, how you will seek to apply this learning as your research progresses and what you will need to do to develop your competence to further your research. Universities generally require students to reflect on their research as part of their project reports to be able to evaluate their learning from the research process. In Section 1.5 we talked about keeping a reflective diary and provided you with a checklist (Box 1.4).

Reflection may occur in a number of ways. It may occur during an event, so that you reflect on your approach while you conducting an activity. This type of reflection may occur, for example, while you are interviewing or observing. Reflection may also occur after an activity has taken place so that you reflect on what occurred and how you might be able to do better next time. A more fundamental type of reflection, known as reflexivity, involves you in monitoring and reflecting on all aspects of the research project from initial ideas to submission of the project report (Section 2.1). It includes examining your reactions to what is being researched, the nature of your relationship with those who take part in the research and evaluating the way in which you interpret data to construct knowledge (Haynes 2012). Given its interpretivist nature, Finlay (2002: 211) says that reflexivity is 'now the defining feature of qualitative research'. Your reactions, your interactions with those taking part and your attitudes and beliefs may each impact on your interpretation of the data that are shared with you. Engaging in forms of reflexivity may enable you to develop greater insights as you explore and analyse these data. Developing a reflexive focus in your reflective diary may therefore prove to be a valuable aid to further your research (Section 1.5).

13.6 Thematic Analysis 主题分析

Introduction

We start by outlining **Thematic Analysis** as this is often thought of as a generic approach to analysing qualitative data. Braun and Clarke (2006: 78) refer to Thematic Analysis as a 'foundational method for qualitative analysis'. The process of Thematic Analysis is found in other approaches to qualitative analysis, albeit in more particularised ways, as we outline in the following sections. The essential purpose of this approach is to search for themes, or patterns, that occur across a data set (such as a series of interviews, observations, documents or websites being analysed). Thematic Analysis involves a researcher coding her or his qualitative data to identify themes or patterns for further analysis, related to his or her research question. We discuss procedures to undertake analysis in the next part of this section.

Thematic Analysis offers a systematic yet flexible and accessible approach to analyse qualitative data (Braun and Clarke 2006). It is systematic as it provides an orderly and logical way to analyse qualitative data. In this way, Thematic Analysis can be used to analyse large qualitative data sets, as well as smaller ones, leading to rich descriptions, explanations and theorising. Thematic Analysis can be used to help you:

1 comprehend often large and disparate amounts of qualitative data;
2 integrate related data drawn from different transcripts and notes;
3 identify key themes or patterns from a data set for further exploration;
4 produce a thematic description of these data; and/or
5 develop and test explanations and theories based on apparent thematic patterns or relationships;
6 draw and verify conclusions.

Thematic Analysis is flexible as it is not tied to a particular philosophical position. You may use Thematic Analysis irrespective of whether you are adopting an objectivist or subjectivist position (Chapter 4). Your assumptions will, however, affect how you use it to interpret your data (which is why you should be explicit about your philosophical assumptions and remain reflexive through your research project). You may use Thematic Analysis in a realist study that seeks to understand factors underpinning human attitudes and actions. You may also use Thematic Analysis in an interpretivist study to explore different interpretations of a phenomenon. The reason why you may use Thematic Analysis irrespective of your position relates to its development as a standalone analytical technique or process, rather than being part of a theoretically mounted methodological approach.

For the same reason, Thematic Analysis may be used irrespective of whether you adopt a deductive or inductive approach. In a deductive approach, the themes you wish to examine would be linked to existing theory. Your research question is also more likely to be firmly established and this and your research objectives may be used to derive themes to examine in your data. This may lead you to focus on parts of your data set rather than seek to analyse it all in an undiscriminating way. In an inductive approach, themes will be derived from the data. You will search for themes to explore related to your research interest but will not impose a framework of themes to examine your data set based on existing theory. Depending on which themes you decide to explore in an inductive approach, you may also modify your research question. Initially you will be likely to explore the whole data set looking for the occurrence and reoccurrence of themes. You may also use a combination of a deductive and inductive approach, commencing analysis with theoretically-derived themes which you then modify or add to as you explore your data set (Box 13.1).

The nature and flexibility of Thematic Analysis mean that it is fairly straightforward to use in comparison to some of the techniques discussed later. Where you use Thematic Analysis, your energy can be invested in making sure your analysis is rigorous, rather than spending lots of time checking you are applying a more particularised approach to qualitative analysis according to strict rules advocated for its use. In practice, your choice of analytical method will be influenced by the nature of your research question and philosophical position, approach and research strategy, although Thematic Analysis may offer you an effective technique to analyse your qualitative data set. We now outline the procedures used in Thematic Analysis.

Procedure

The following procedures provide a set of guidelines to undertake Thematic Analysis. In practice, these procedures do not occur in a simple linear progression. Instead they are often concurrent and recursive, involving you analysing data as you collect them and going back over earlier data and analysis as you refine the way in which you code and categorise newly collected data and search for analytical themes.

The procedures outlined here involve: becoming familiar with your data; coding your data; searching for themes and recognising relationships; refining themes and testing propositions. We now consider each of these.

Becoming familiar with your data

You will start to become familiar with your data as you produce transcripts of the interviews or observations you conduct. The act of transcribing a data item yourself, although laborious, allows you to develop familiarity. This should also prompt you to generate summaries, self-memos or entries in your notebook or diary that aid your analysis.

Familiarisation with your data involves a process of immersion that continues throughout your research project. You will need to read and re-read your data during your analysis. You will be interested to look for meanings, recurring themes and patterns in your data. Without familiarity, you will not be able to engage in the analytical procedures that follow. Producing transcripts and data familiarisation are therefore important elements in analysing data.

Coding your data

Coding is used to categorise data with similar meanings. **Coding** involves labelling each unit of data within a data item (such as a transcript or document) with a code that symbolises or summarises that extract's meaning. Your purpose in undertaking this process is to make each piece of data in which you are interested accessible for further analysis. Qualitative data sets are frequently large and their content complex. A qualitative data set may include references to actions, behaviours, beliefs, conditions, events, ideas, interactions, outcomes, policies, relationships, strategies, etc. Without coding these data you may struggle to comprehend all of the meanings in your data in which you are interested. Coding is therefore an important means to manage your data so that you may rearrange and retrieve it under relevant codes. It is also an important element in data analysis, as we discuss later.

A **code** is a single word or a short phrase, which may also be abbreviated in use (Box 13.5). A coded extract of data is referred to as a unit of data. A **unit of data** may be a number of words, a line of a transcript, a sentence, a number of sentences, a complete paragraph, other chunk of textual data, or visual image that is summed up by a particular code (Boxes 13.5 and 13.6). The exact size of a unit of data will be determined by its meaning. Some units of data will overlap and some with be coded using more than one code (Box 13.6).

Box 13.5
Focus on student research

Interview extract with categories attached

Adrian's research project was concerned with how human resource management professionals managed a downsizing process in their own organisations. He derived initial codes from existing theory in the academic literature and attached them to appropriate units of data in each transcript. His initial categories were hierarchical; the codes he used being shown in brackets:

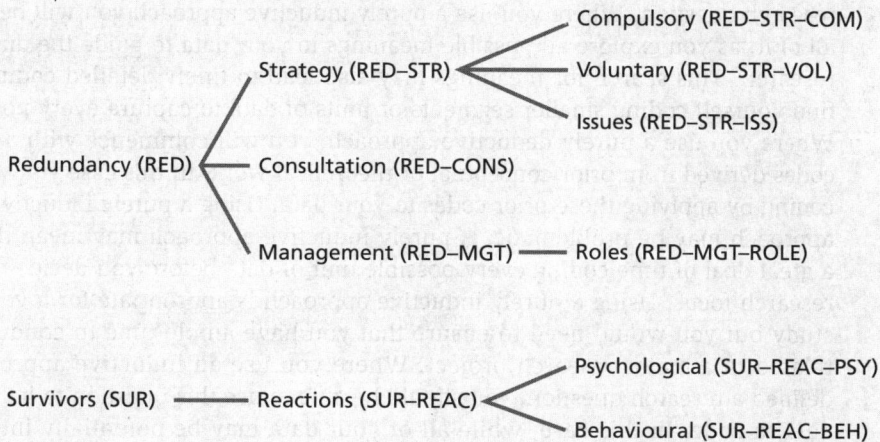

Redundancy (RED)
- Strategy (RED–STR)
  - Compulsory (RED–STR–COM)
  - Voluntary (RED–STR–VOL)
  - Issues (RED–STR–ISS)
- Consultation (RED–CONS)
- Management (RED–MGT)
  - Roles (RED–MGT–ROLE)

Survivors (SUR)
- Reactions (SUR–REAC)
  - Psychological (SUR–REAC–PSY)
  - Behavioural (SUR–REAC–BEH)

These were then attached to the interview transcript, using sentences as units of data. Like our jigsaw example at the start of this chapter, those units of data that were coded with more than one category suggested interrelationships:

RED–CONS	27MM The first stage is to find out what particular employees	1
	want for themselves and how they want this to happen. Staff are	2
	seen by their line manager and/or a member of personnel.	3
RED–MGT–ROLE	Employees might want to talk to someone from personnel rather	4
	than talk with their line manager – well, you know, for obvious	5
	reasons, at least as they see it – and this would be acceptable to the	6
RED–STR–VOL	organisation. This meeting provides them with the opportunity to	7
	opt for voluntary redundancy. We do not categorise employees	8
RED–STR–ISS	into anything like core or non-core, although we will tell a group	9
RED–CONS	of employees something like 'there are four of you in this	10
	particular function and we only need two of you, so you think	1
RED–CONS	about what should happen'. Sometimes when we attempt to give	2
	employees a choice about who might leave, they actually ask us to	3
	make the choice. This is one such situation where a compulsory	4
RED–STR–COM	selection will occur. We prefer to avoid this compulsory selection	5
SUR–REAC–PSY	because of the impact on those who survive – negative feelings,	6
	guilt and so on.	7

If you think that a new piece of data has a similar meaning to a previously coded unit of data, it should be labelled with the same code. If you think that a new piece of data does not have a similar meaning to a previously coded unit of data, you will need to devise a new code for it. Throughout the process of coding it will be important to keep a list of codes you are using and a working definition for each, to ensure consistency (Box 13.6).

At this point you may be asking two questions. How much of my data should I code – all or only some of it? Where should my codes come from? Both of these questions are related to your research approach and also to your research question – whether you are setting out to use an inductive or deductive approach and how well you have defined your research question. We now answer each of these questions in turn.

How much of your data you code will depend upon your research approach and research question. Where you use a purely inductive approach you will be likely to code all of it, as you explore all possible meanings in your data to guide the direction of your research. This search for meanings may also lead to finely detailed coding, where you find yourself coding smaller segments or units of data to capture every possible nuance. Where you use a purely deductive approach, you will commence with a framework of codes derived from prior conceptual or theoretical work. In this case you will commence coding by applying these prior codes to your data. Using a purely inductive or deductive approach may be problematic. A purely inductive approach may mean that you spend a great deal of time coding every possible unit of data before you decide on a particular research focus. Using a purely inductive approach is appropriate for a very exploratory study but you would need to ensure that you have ample time to conduct it, perhaps related to a major research project. Where you use an inductive approach and have defined a research question, you should be able to use this question to help select which data to code. In this case, while all of your data may be potentially interesting, your research question will help you focus on which data to code. Using a purely deductive approach may lead you to conclude that your list of prior codes is inadequate and that you need to devise other codes in order to be able to code your data adequately to begin to answer your research question and address your research objectives.

This discussion indicates where your codes may come from. There are three main sources of codes:

- They may be based on the actual terms used by your participants, recorded in your data. These are often referred to as 'in vivo' codes.
- They may be labels you develop which you think best describe a unit of data you wish to code.
- They may be derived from terms used in existing theory and the literature. These are often referred to as 'a priori' codes.

These sources of codes are shown in Figure 13.1 to illustrate their relationship.

Coding is a simple but versatile and valuable tool. The process of coding allows you to link units of data that refer to the same aspect or meaning, or to link aspects or meanings that you want to compare and contrast. It allows you to rearrange your original data into groupings for the next stage of analysis. Any unit of data may be coded with as many different codes as you think is appropriate, creating a web of connections to aid your analysis (Box 13.6). It is often important to understand the context of the data you are analysing. Where it is important to include some contextual background, you can code larger units of data such as whole paragraphs, as opposed to smaller units such as a few words or single sentences (Box 13.6). (Note in Box 13.6 that codes are referred to as categories. These terms are sometimes used interchangeably and sometimes to refer to different aspects of the analytical process – see the next sub-section.)

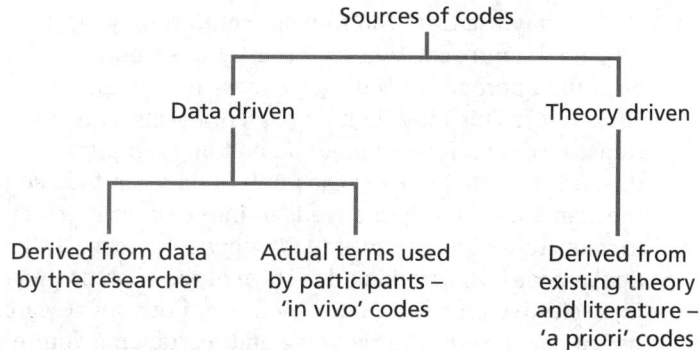

Figure 13.1 Sources and types of codes

Your approach to coding will be guided by the purpose of your research as expressed through your research question and objectives. Another researcher with different objectives to you may derive different codes from the same data. You will be likely to develop new codes as you conduct more interviews or observations and expand your data set. You will also be likely to gain new insights from existing codes that suggest new ones during the process of analysis. This will require you to re-read all of your earlier data transcripts to re-code them according to your current list of codes. This process is termed constant comparison and is undertaken to ensure consistency in the way you code and analyse your data set.

Your codes will show the occurrence or non-occurrence of a phenomenon and the strength of opinion in some instances. Some codes may attract large numbers of units of data. Some of these may prove to be too broad for further analysis without being subdivided. For example, Adrian undertook a research project where some codes had large amounts of data attached to them, while others attracted relatively small amounts of data. This led to the large codes being subdivided into further codes, which was helpful in pursuing the analysis (Box 13.5). Codes attracting small numbers of units of data may be merged with similar ones, or retained until later in the process of analysis in case they prove to be more important than they appear initially.

Box 13.6
Focus on management research

Assigning data to and developing categories

'After each interview, I transcribed the interview verbatim and filed its material according to the categorisation then in use. The material was typically in the form of paragraphs [that] were cross-classified to several categories. As I filed each statement, I compared it with previous statements in that category and kept running notes on the content of the category. The categories changed over time; some disappeared and were merged under more general titles. Some emerged out of previous categories that became too heterogeneous. Some categories became parts of matched pairs or triads in which any given comment would typically be filed in each constituent category. For example, comments [that] described instances of lax work or bad workmanship also typically mentioned abusive management. Similarly, statements that described devising one's own procedures also typically included statements of satisfaction with the autonomy that provided. This helped to reveal connections between categories.'

Source: Hodson (1991), cited in Erlandson *et al.* (1993: 119) *Journal of Contemporary Ethnography*. Copyright © 1991 by Sage Publications, Inc. Reprinted by permission

You may use CAQDAS to help you to code your data (Section 13.14) or you may use a manual approach. Where you use the second approach, you can label a unit of data with the appropriate code (or codes) in the margin of your transcript or set of notes (Box 13.6). This may then be copied, cut up and stuck onto a data card, or otherwise transferred, and filed so that you end up with piles of related units of data. When doing this, it is essential to label each unit of data carefully so that you know its precise source (Section 13.4). An alternative is to index codes by recording precisely where they occur in your transcripts or notes (e.g. interview 7, page 2, line 16) on cards headed with particular codes. Undertaking this stage of the analytic process means that you are engaging in a selective process, guided by the aim of your research and your research objectives, which has the effect of reducing and rearranging your data into a more manageable and comprehensible form.

One way of achieving this reduction and rearrangement of your data, depending on its suitability, is to use one or more of the analytical techniques described by Miles et al. (2014). These are considered later in Section 13.13.

Searching for themes and recognising relationships

This is seen as a distinct stage of analysis that follows coding, although in practice you will be searching for themes, patterns and relationships in your data as you collect and code them. Producing progress summaries, transcript summaries, document summaries, self-memos and/or entries in your research notebook and reflective diary will help you to record your ideas about possible themes, patterns and relationships in your data.

The search for themes fully begins when you have coded all of your data set. At this point you will have a long list of codes that you have created to make sense of and draw meaning from your data. Advice about the number of codes you might be working with at this point varies considerably. Some advice refers to working with up to 30 codes. Other advice refers to creating as many codes as you require to interpret every distinct meaning in your data. This may mean creating up to a couple of hundred codes, or possibly more. Our view is that data should not be forced into a particular number of codes. The number of codes you create will be related to the meanings you wish to explore in your data set, the nature of your research approach and the focus of your research question. However, where you find yourself creating very large numbers of codes you will need to evaluate whether your coding is too detailed or whether you are trying to analyse too much data for your project. Always refer back to your research question, research aim and research objectives to focus your approach to data analysis.

This stage of analysis involves you searching for patterns and relationships in your long list of codes to create a short list of themes that relate to your research question. A **theme** is a broad category incorporating several codes that appear to be related to one another and which indicates an idea that is important to your research question. A theme may also be a single code which indicates an idea that assumes general importance to your research question and is therefore elevated to become a theme. Searching for themes is part of the overall process of condensing your raw data, firstly by coding them and then grouping these coded data into analytic categories.

Searching for themes involves you making judgements about your data and immersing yourself in them. You will be looking to see how the codes you have created might fit together to allow you to further your analysis. As you search these codes, some initial questions you may ask include:

- What are the key concepts in these codes?
- What, if anything, seems to be recurring in these codes?
- What seems to be important, whether it recurs often or not?

- What patterns and/or trends are evident in the coded data?
- Which codes appear to be related?
- How do a particular set of codes appear to be related?

As you start to decide on themes to analyse your data further, some additional questions you may ask include:

- What is the essence of each apparent theme?
- How might themes be related to each other?
- Which themes appear to be main themes and which appear to be sub-themes (related to a main theme)?
- How may the relationship between themes be represented (as a hierarchy or a network) to produce a thematic map?
- Is there an overarching theme (or more than one) that unites your analysis?

You should not expect this process to be unproblematic. In attempting to achieve a thorough understanding of your data set, some further questions you may ask include:

- How well does this initial thematic map represent the relationships between themes?
- Which themes, if any, do not fit within this thematic representation?
- Does the way the data have been coded need to be revised; if so which data and how?
- Which themes need to be refined, discarded or newly introduced?
- How may the thematic representation be modified to represent my data better?

In the first set of questions, you begin to decide on themes to further your analysis. In the second set of questions, you begin to define your themes and the relationships between them (Box 13.5). Some themes will become main themes; some may become secondary-level themes, linked to a main theme; yet others may be tertiary-level themes, linked to a secondary-level theme. In the third set of questions, you evaluate your themes and the relationships between them. This will mean refining your themes and testing proposed relationships, as we discuss further in the next sub-section.

Refining themes and testing propositions

Refining themes and the relationships between them is likely to be an important part of your analytical process. The themes that you devise need to be part of a coherent set so that they provide you with a well-structured analytical framework to pursue your analysis. As you develop themes you should reorganise your coded data extracts under the relevant theme or sub-theme. This will help you to evaluate whether these coded data are meaningful to one another within their theme and whether (and how) themes are meaningful in relation to one another and in relation to your data set. This is likely to be a developmental process, as you re-read and reorganise your data. As you continue to examine your data set, the codes you have used and the themes you devise to organise your coded data to answer your research question, you will be likely to refine these themes.

You may decide that some of your initial themes should be combined to make a new theme while others should be separated into different themes. You may also decide that some of your initial themes should be discarded. Your decisions to make these changes will be based on re-reading the coded data that you have reorganised under each relevant theme. By reading the coded data attached to a possible theme, you will be able to evaluate whether these data support the continuation of the theme, or whether there is insufficient data to sustain it. This will allow you to decide whether these data are too dissimilar so that it should be separated into more than one theme. It will also allow you to decide whether two or more themes contain similar meanings and so should be collapsed into a single theme. As you refine your themes in this way you will also be able to revise the relationships between them.

Box 13.7
Focus on student research

Research propositions

During the process of qualitative data analysis a student evaluating the growth of online retailing formulated the following proposition:

Customers' willingness to trust online retailers depends on the ease of use of their website.

A student exploring mortgage borrowers' decision making drew up this proposition:

Potential mortgage borrowers' choice of lending institution is strongly affected by the level of customer service that they receive during the initial inquiry stage.

Another student investigating cause-related marketing formulated the following proposition:

Companies engaging in cause-related marketing are motivated principally by altruism.

A relationship is evident in each of these propositions. Each was tested using the data that had been collected.

As you seek to reveal patterns within your data and to recognise relationships between themes, you will be able to develop testable propositions (Box 13.7). The appearance of an apparent relationship or connection between themes will need to be tested if you are to be able to conclude that there is an actual relationship. However, while this is sometimes referred to as 'testing a hypothesis', it is not the same as the statistical hypothesis or significance testing we discussed in relation to quantitative analysis in Section 12.5.

It is important to test the propositions that emerge inductively from the data by seeking alternative explanations and negative examples that do not conform to the pattern or relationship being tested. Alternative explanations frequently exist, and only by testing the propositions that you identify will you be able to move towards formulating valid conclusions and an explanatory theory, even a simple one (Miles et al. 2014). Dey (1993: 48) points out that 'the association of one variable with another is not sufficient ground for inferring a causal or any other connection between them'. The existence of an intervening variable may offer a more valid explanation of an association that is apparent in your data (Box 13.8).

By rigorously testing your propositions against your data, looking for alternative explanations and seeking to explain why negative cases occur, you will be able to move towards the development of valid and well-grounded conclusions. The validity of your conclusions needs to be verified by their ability to withstand alternative explanations and the nature of negative cases. **Negative cases** are those that do not support your explanations and the induction of your grounded theory. Finding cases that do not fit with your analysis should be seen positively as these will help to refine your explanations and direct the selection of further cases to collect and analyse data.

This will help you to avoid interpretations that prove to be unreliable because you only notice evidence that supports your own opinions. It relates to our discussion of reflexivity in Section 13.5. As a researcher you need to recognise your own attitudes and beliefs about the topic being researched, perhaps by writing about these to make them explicit, in order to understand how this affects your judgement about what the research data might mean and to gain greater insights while analysing these data. Brinkmann and Kvale (2015: 278) refer to this process as seeking to achieve 'reflexive objectivity'.

Box 13.8
Focus on student research

The impact of an intervening variable

Kevin's research project involved looking at the use of subcontractors by an organisation. A relationship appeared to emerge between the total value of contracts a particular subcontractor had been awarded and the size of that contractor in terms of number of employees; in particular, those contractors with larger numbers of employees had a larger total value of contracts. This could have led Kevin to conclude that the value of work undertaken by a particular subcontractor was related to that organisation's size

and that, in particular, the organisation tended to use subcontractors with large numbers of employees.

Reality was not so simple. The organisation had originally used over 2500 subcontractors but had found this exceedingly difficult to manage. To address this issue the organisation had introduced a system of preferred contractors. All 2500 subcontractors had been graded according to the quality of their work, with those whose work had been consistently of high quality being awarded preferred contractor status. This meant that they were invited by the organisation Kevin was researching to tender for all relevant contracts. The intervening variable was therefore the introduction of preferred contractor status dependent upon the quality of work previously undertaken. The fact that the majority of these subcontractors also had relatively large numbers of employees was not the reason why the organisation had awarded them contracts.

Evaluation

Thematic Analysis offers a systematic approach to qualitative data analysis that is accessible and flexible. Compared to some qualitative approaches, it is not overly prescriptive about the application of its analytical procedures. As a generic approach to qualitative data analysis it is suitable to use with several qualitative research strategies, where you are not following a named version of a strategy that prescribes precise analytic procedures, as in Grounded Theory Method.

Thematic Analysis may be used to induce theory in a similar way to Grounded Theory Method, but without following its prescribed approach to coding (Section 13.9). It may also be used to produce descriptive or explanatory accounts that fall short of generating a grounded theory.

Thematic Analysis is more adaptable, so that if the research strategy you are using requires you to search for particular themes you may consider using it. The process of searching for themes is common to other analytical approaches, as we consider in the following sections of this chapter.

Thematic Analysis may also be used in relation to deductive and inductive research approaches. Using a purely deductive or inductive research approach may be problematic, affecting the scope of the analysis. Thematic Analysis allows the researcher to move between these approaches.

13.7 Template Analysis 模板分析

Introduction

Template Analysis is a type of Thematic Analysis, with a few key differences. In Thematic Analysis all data items (transcripts or other text) are coded first before the search for themes fully begins. In Template Analysis a researcher only codes a proportion of the data items before developing an initial list of codes and themes, known as a coding template (King 2012).

This **coding template** is the hierarchical list of codes and themes, which is used as the central analytical tool in Template Analysis. A researcher using Template Analysis will start by coding a sufficient part of their data to develop an initial coding template (Box 13.9). This may mean coding the first interview or observation transcript, or a number of these, in order to be able to develop a set of initial codes. These codes are then arranged and rearranged until a satisfactory initial template is developed. Subsequent transcripts are then coded using the codes in this initial template, which is modified as new data suggests deficiencies in the codes being used, leading eventually to the development of a final coding template. We provide further information on the procedures involved in this approach in the next sub-section.

Like Thematic Analysis, Template Analysis is a standalone analytical technique, rather than being part of a wider methodological approach. As a consequence it may be used irrespective of whether you are adopting an objectivist or subjectivist position or whether you adopt a deductive or inductive research approach (see Section 13.6, Introduction, for further explanation of this point). Template Analysis may commence with a number of a priori codes which are then supplemented by the use of in vivo codes, as we discussed earlier.

Procedure

The initial procedure of Template Analysis reflects that of Thematic Analysis. You will need to become familiar with the data you collect by transcribing this and reading it carefully. The initial transcript or transcripts will be coded as described in Section 13.6. Prior codes may be used where appropriate and these will be supplemented by the development of in vivo codes.

At an appropriate point in this process you reflect on the coding you have undertaken and begin to develop an initial coding template. The development of an initial coding template will be an exploratory process involving the arrangement and rearrangement of the codes you have used until you devise themes that appear to represent key ideas and relationships in your data. The resulting coding template will be able to show relationships between themes hierarchically and also laterally if you wish (King 2012).

Box 13.9 provides an example of an initial coding template, with a hierarchical relationship shown between the codes listed. In this example, three levels of codes or themes have been used. The highest level codes or themes are shown in capital letters (e.g. CONTEXTUAL FACTORS). The numbering system and placing of lower-level codes towards the right-hand side also helps to indicate the hierarchical relationships in this coding template. Codes are also grouped together in levels 2 and 3 to show how higher-order themes are constituted.

As data collection proceeds, your template will be subject to modification. The process of analysing interview transcripts or observation notes will lead to some of the codes being revised and even changes to their level or place in the template hierarchy. Where you consider introducing a new code or altering the level of an existing code in the template, you need to verify this action and explore its implications in relation to your previous coding activity. This is usually more straightforward using CAQDAS (Lewins and Silver 2009). As part of this, it is helpful to use self-memos to note the reasons for these changes.

King (2012) outlines five principal ways in which a template may be reorganised and revised:

- insertion of a new code into the hierarchy as the result of a relevant issue being identified through data collection for which there is no existing code;
- deletion of a code from the hierarchy if it is not needed;
- merging codes that were originally considered distinctive;
- altering the classification of codes/themes, so that some are promoted to a higher level in the coding template, while others may be demoted;
- changing the scope of a code. Inserted, deleted, merged and altered codes may have implications for other related codes. This may result in the need to move a code within the coding template, change its purpose or split it into two or more new codes.

Box 13.9
Focus on student research

Part of an initial template to analyse an advertising campaign's impact

Joss was asked to gather and analyse perceptions from a range of professionals in an organisation about a recent advertising campaign it had commissioned. Using her interview topic guide, she used the main questions to set higher-order codes or themes (shown in CAPITALS). Subsidiary questions and probes were used to generate lower-order codes, shown in lower case and italic script. An extract of her initial template follows:

1 CONTEXTUAL FACTORS
  1.1 Reasons for campaign
  1.2 Environment
    1.2.1 *Political*
    1.2.2 *Economic*
    1.2.3 *Socio-cultural*
    1.2.4 *Technological*
    1.2.5 *Legal*
  1.3 Nature of the product
    1.3.1 *Cost*
    1.3.2 *Features*
    1.3.3 *Target groups*
2 NATURE OF THE CAMPAIGN
  2.1 Media
  2.2 Coverage
3 AWARENESS BY TARGET GROUPS AND OTHERS
  3.1 Those in target groups
  3.2 Others

Box 13.10 shows how the codes in the initial coding template in Box 13.9 were altered as the process of data collection and analysis progressed. Several codes have been deleted and new ones inserted that better reflect the terms used in the data by participants. Some initial codes have been merged. For example, the original, second-level code, 'Reasons for campaign' has been merged with the first-level code 'Contextual factors' to form a new first-level code, 'Perceiving the need for the campaign'. The original second-level codes, 'Media' and 'Coverage' have both been reclassified to become first-level codes. As a result of this reclassification, the scope of these themes has been enlarged and new subsidiary codes created to encompass this.

The template may continue to be revised until all of the data collected have been coded and analysed carefully. It therefore serves as an analytical device through which to devise an initial conceptual framework, which is subsequently revised and then final-ised as a means to represent and explore key themes and relationships in your data. Using a template will also help you to select key themes to explore and to identify emergent issues that arise through the process of data collection and analysis that you may not have intended to focus on as you commenced your research project (King 2012).

Evaluation

Like Thematic Analysis, Template Analysis offers a systematic, flexible and accessible approach to analyse qualitative data. It adopts a higher level of structure earlier on than Thematic Analysis through the development of an initial coding template. This may be preferred by some who like the idea of developing a very structured approach to analys-ing their data early on. Others may prefer to code all of their data first before playing around with analytical structures.

The flexibility of developing a coding template early on and then revising this in rela-tion to each subsequent data item allows a researcher to undertake the stages of analysis (e.g. coding, devising and linking themes, exploring relationships, sense-making) in a more holistic way. However, some researchers may feel constrained by using a template

Box 13.10
Focus on student research

Part of a final template to analyse an advertising campaign's impact

As Joss continued to collect data she used her coding template to conduct analysis. The coding template was revised as these data were analysed. An extract of her final template follows:

1 PERCEIVING THE NEED FOR THE CAMPAIGN
  1.1 Market changes
    1.1.1 *Globalisation*
    1.1.2 *Competition*

    1.1.3 *Segmentation*
    1.1.4 *Technological convergence*
    1.1.5 *Compliance*
  1.2 Product promotion
    1.2.1 *Product awareness*
    1.2.2 *Product differentiation*
    1.2.3 *Product upgrades*
2 EVALUATING MEDIA
  2.1 Social media
  2.2 Television
  2.3 Radio
  2.4 Newspapers
3 EXPLORING COVERAGE
  3.1 National
  3.2 Regional/Local
  3.3 Market segments

while working though transcripts and may become too focused on applying the template to the data rather than using the data to develop the template (King 2012).

13.8 Explanation Building and Testing 解释的建立与验证

In this section we outline three techniques where the nature of reaching an explanation and theorising may be differentiated from both Thematic Analysis and Template Analysis. In these three techniques the emphasis is on building (or predicting) and testing an explanation. These techniques are Analytic Induction, Deductive Explanation Building and Pattern Matching. We discuss each of these in turn.

Analytic Induction

Introduction

Analytic Induction is an inductive version of Explanation Building. A key characteristic of this technique is that it uses an incremental approach to build and test an explanation or theory. **Analytic Induction** seeks to develop and test an explanation by intensively examining the phenomenon being explored through the successive selection of purposive cases. This means that the process of collecting and analysing data will be composed of a number of repeated steps to find a valid explanation of the phenomenon being studied. Johnson (2004: 165) defines Analytic Induction as 'the intensive examination of a strategically selected number of cases so as to empirically establish the causes of a specific phenomenon'. Analytic Induction emphasises a cycle of developing and testing propositions that are inductively grounded in participants' data rather than using existing knowledge and theory. Its analytical procedures are not highly developed or formalised. As a result, where you use Analytic Induction, you may also find the generic procedures outlined for Thematic Analysis in Section 13.6 helpful to guide your analysis within each case you examine.

Procedure

Data will need to be collected from an initial purposive case study, usually by conducting exploratory interviews or observations. These data should be analysed to devise codes and themes, and to recognise relationships between them to develop an initial definition of a proposition that seeks to explain the phenomenon being studied. This initial proposition is then tested through the purposive selection of a second, related case study (Section 7.3), involving further exploratory interviews or observations.

Given the loosely defined nature of this initial proposition, it is likely that it will either need to be redefined or that the scope of the phenomenon to be explained will need to be narrowed. Redefining the proposition leads to a third iteration or step in the Analytic Induction process, involving the purposive selection of a third case study to explore the phenomenon and test this redefined proposition. If at this stage your redefined proposition appears to explain the phenomenon, you may either cease data collection on the basis that you believe you have found a valid explanation or seek to test the explanation in other purposively selected cases to see whether it is still valid.

You will be likely to encounter one or more cases where your proposition is not adequate to explain the phenomenon you are studying. These are referred to as negative or deviant cases. When you encounter a negative case you will need to redefine the proposition you are testing and to test this in the context of another purposively selected case. This process may continue until a redefined proposition is generated that reasonably explains the phenomenon in relevant cases where you have collected and analysed data. In practice several redefinitions of the proposition may be necessary to develop a valid explanation of the phenomenon being studied.

Evaluation

As an inductive and incremental way of collecting and analysing data qualitatively this technique has the capability to lead to the development of well-grounded explanations. Analytic Induction encourages the collection of data that are thorough and rich by exploring the actions and meanings of those who participate in this process, through in-depth interviews or observation, or some combination of these methods.

However, like each of the techniques in this section, it should not be thought of as a quick or easy approach to conducting qualitative analysis. While it may lead to a well-grounded and unassailable explanation, where all negative cases are either accounted for by the final revised explanation or excluded by redefining the phenomenon being studied, this outcome is only likely to occur as the result of using this technique in a thorough and rigorous way. This will involve a search for cases that are related to the phenomenon being studied, the in-depth collection of data within each case and the rigorous analysis of these data to devise a final revised proposition that explains the phenomenon being studied throughout these cases.

Analytic Induction may be criticised because of issues about its limited representativeness and generalisability. Because the final explanation of the research phenomenon will be completely grounded in the cases that give rise to it, this explanation may be without the ability to predict what may be found in other cases, even those containing the same characteristics or conditions. This is similar to criticism which is often made about other inductive research.

Two points may be made in response to such criticism. First, this type of criticism misses the point of inductive research, which is to find explanations that are well grounded in the context being researched. These explanations will exhibit high levels of reliability and internal validity. Others may subsequently seek to test these explanations in other settings. Secondly, such criticism may also be made in relation to much survey research. While survey research will be representative of a wider population, the nature of that population may be restricted to a particular case or number of cases.

In relation to Analytic Induction, you will need to select your sample of cases with care to be able to demonstrate how they relate to the phenomenon you are studying. Selecting diverse cases related to the phenomenon being studied may also help to overcome issues related to theoretical generalisability. For example, if you were seeking to explain how small enterprises respond to regulatory change you could select a sample of cases (organisations) from different business sectors and in relation to a range of regulatory changes, where feasible.

Deductive Explanation Building

Introduction

This version of Explanation Building uses a deductive approach (Yin 2014). It involves an incremental attempt to build an explanation by testing and refining a predetermined theoretical proposition. As with Analytic Induction, the process of collecting and analysing data to understand the research topic or phenomenon will be composed of a number of repeated steps to find a valid explanation.

Procedure

This explanation-building procedure follows these steps (Yin 2014):

1 Devise a theoretically based proposition, which you will then seek to test.
2 Undertake data collection through an initial, purposive case study in order to be able to compare the findings from this in relation to your theoretically based proposition.
3 Where necessary, amend the theoretically based proposition in the light of the findings from the initial case study.
4 Select a further, purposive case study to undertake a further round of data collection in order to compare the findings from this in relation to the revised proposition.
5 Where necessary, further amend the revised proposition in the light of the findings from the second case study.
6 Undertake further iterations of this process until a satisfactory explanation is derived.

Evaluation

This technique and the one discussed next, Pattern Matching, use a deductive approach involving the testing of a theoretical proposition or prediction. Where you are able to utilise existing theory to produce such a proposition or prediction (as in Pattern Matching) this may make the process of explaining the phenomenon being studied less onerous than using Analytic Induction, although use of these techniques may be just as demanding. Given the commonality of using a deductive approach in both of these techniques, we evaluate them together after outlining Pattern Matching, next.

Pattern Matching

Introduction

Pattern Matching involves predicting a pattern of outcomes based on theoretical propositions to explain what you expect to find from analysing your data (Yin 2014). Using this approach, you will need to develop a conceptual or analytical framework, utilising existing theory, and then test the adequacy of the framework deductively as a means to explain your findings. If the pattern of your data matches that which has been predicted through the conceptual framework you will have found an explanation, where possible threats to the validity of your conclusions can be discounted. We discuss examples related to two uses of this procedure that depend on whether you are matching patterns for the dependent or for the independent variables.

Procedure

The first use is matching patterns for dependent variables arising from another, independent variable. For example, based on theoretical propositions drawn from appropriate literature you specify a number of related outcomes (dependent variables) that you expect to find as a result of the implementation of a particular change management programme (independent variable) in an organisation where you intend to undertake research. Having specified these expected outcomes, you then engage in the process of data collection and analysis. Where your predicted outcomes are found, it is likely that your theoretically based explanation is appropriate to explain your findings. If, however, you reveal one or more outcomes that have not been predicted by your explanation, you will need to seek an alternative one (Yin 2014).

The second use is matching patterns for variables that are independent of each other. In this case you would identify two or more alternative explanations to explain the pattern of outcomes that you expect to find (Box 13.11). As a consequence, only one of these predicted explanations may be valid. If one explanation is found to explain your findings then the others may be discarded. Where you find a match between one of these predicted explanations and the data you have collected and analysed, you will have evidence to suggest that this is indeed an explanation for your findings. Further evidence that this is a correct explanation will flow from finding the same pattern of outcomes in other similar cases (Yin 2014).

Evaluation

In relation to Pattern Matching and Explanation Building, you will still be able to follow the generic processes outlined earlier for analysing qualitative data (Section 13.6), with some modification. First, you will be in a position to commence your data collection with a well-defined research question and set of objectives, and a clear framework and propositions, derived from the theory that you have used. Second, with regard to sampling

Box 13.11
Focus on student research

Alternative predicted explanations

The objective of Linzi's research project was to explain why productivity had increased in a case study organisation even though a number of factors had been held constant (technology, numbers of staff employed, pay rates and bonuses, and the order book) during the period of the increase in productivity. She developed two alternative explanations based on different theoretical propositions to explain why this increase in productivity had occurred in the organisation. Her explanations were related to the following propositions:

1 the productivity increase is due to better management, which has been able to generate greater employee engagement, where this proposition is based on theory related to strategic human resource management;

2 the productivity increase is due to fears about change and uncertainty in the future, where this proposition is based on theory related to organisational behaviour and the management of change.

These propositions offered her two possible and exclusive reasons why the described phenomenon had occurred, so that where evidence could be found to support one of these, the other, which did not match her outcomes, could be discounted.

(Section 7.3), you will be in a position to identify the number and type of organisations to which you wish to gain access in order to undertake data collection. You should select sufficient cases to test the propositions that have been advanced and to answer your research question and meet your objectives. Third, the literature that you used and the theory within it should help to shape the data collection questions that you ask those who participate in your research project (Section 3.2). It is also to be expected that codes for analysis will emerge from the nature of your interview questions. Therefore you will be able to commence data collection with an initial set of codes derived from your theoretical propositions and conceptual framework, linked to your research question and objectives.

Of course, these codes will be subject to change (insertions, deletions and merging) depending on their appropriateness for the data that your participants provide. However, where your predicted theoretical explanations appear to fit the data being revealed, your predetermined codes may prove to be useful, subject to some revision and development.

Your use of this deductive approach will also provide you with key themes and patterns to search for in your data. For example, as you collect data and analyse these by attaching units of data to codes, and examine these for emergent patterns, your analysis will be guided by the theoretical propositions and explanations with which you commenced. Your propositions will still need to be tested with rigour – associated with the thoroughness with which you carry out this analytical process and by seeking negative examples and alternative explanations that do not conform to the pattern or association being tested for.

The use of predicted explanations should mean that the pathway to an answer to your research question and objectives is reasonably defined. The extent to which this is the case will depend on two factors:

- your level of thoroughness in using existing theory to define clearly the theoretical propositions and conceptual framework that will guide your research project;
- the appropriateness of these theoretical propositions and the conceptual framework for the data that you reveal.

The use of a deductive approach is underpinned by the need to specify theoretical propositions before the commencement of data collection and analysis. Even in Explanation Building, a theoretically based proposition is suggested initially, although this may be revised through the iterative stages of the process involved. The general processes outlined earlier for analysing qualitative data will be useful to you in carrying out these deductive analytical procedures. In particular, the stages of the process related to devising codes and identifying themes and patterns are likely to be more apparent, at least initially, because this approach is based on existing theory.

13.9 Grounded Theory Method 扎根理论法

Introduction

Grounded Theory Method is part of a wider methodological approach. We discussed Grounded Theory in Section 5.5. Grounded Theory is an emergent and systematic research strategy. It avoids using a priori codes (Section 13.6) derived from existing theory and commences inductively, by developing codes from the data. The development of an emergent idea or theory from these data informs the direction of a Grounded Theory study. Grounded Theory is seen as systematic, or even prescriptive, because it sets out a number of tenets or elements that should be followed. Its use in practice is criticised when researchers only implement some of these elements, not all (Box 5.9).

Grounded Theory is not as flexible as Thematic Analysis or Template Analysis. In Sections 13.6 and 13.7 we discussed how both Thematic Analysis and Template Analysis are not tied to a particular philosophical position or research approach. Both are standalone analytical techniques, rather than being part of a wider strategy. As a consequence, either may be used irrespective of whether you are adopting a realist or interpretivist position or whether you adopt a deductive or inductive research approach. Such flexibility offered by these analytical approaches may suit your choice of research strategy.

Alternatively, the existence and clarity of the elements and procedures developed for Grounded Theory may suit your approach. As a strategy and a method, Grounded Theory may provide you with a holistic approach to your research project that guides you from inception through the processes of data collection and analysis to completion.

We discussed the elements of Grounded Theory as a research strategy in Section 5.5. These include the early commencement of data collection, concurrent collection and analysis of data, development of codes from the data, and the use of constant comparison, self-memos, theoretical sampling, theoretical saturation and theoretical sensitivity, leading to the development of a theory that is grounded in the data. We suggest re-reading about these elements of Grounded Theory in Section 5.5 before reading further in this section.

Grounded Theory Method is associated with a number of defined procedures to collect and analyse data. An issue arises in that the exact nature of these procedures varies between sources that outline Grounded Theory Method (e.g. Bryant and Charmaz 2007; Charmaz 2006; Corbin and Strauss 2008; Glaser and Strauss 1967) and even between editions of the same book (Corbin and Strauss 2008; Strauss and Corbin 1998). For example, the Grounded Theory Method of Strauss and Corbin (1998) and Corbin and Strauss (2008) is highly structured and systematic, with set procedures to follow at each stage of analysis. However, between the two editions of this book, advice about some of these analytical procedures changed. In the Grounded Theory Method of Strauss and Corbin (1998) the disaggregation of data into units is called open coding, the process of recognising relationships between categories is referred to as axial coding, and the integration of categories around a core category to develop a grounded theory is labelled selective coding. In the 2008 edition, open coding and axial coding have been merged and selective coding has been relabelled as integration. Alternatively, the more flexible approach to Grounded Theory Method of Charmaz (2006) consists of two major phases of coding: initial coding and focused coding, while she also discusses and evaluates axial coding (Strauss and Corbin 1998) and the theoretical coding approach developed by Glaser (1978, 1998).

As an introduction to the analytical procedures associated with using Grounded Theory Method, we focus on those of Strauss and Corbin (1998) and Charmaz (2006) (Figure 13.2). Where you decide to use a Grounded Theory strategy (Section 5.5) you may find it useful to consult not only these two books but also the others to which we have referred. However, the key to the success of using Grounded Theory Method is choosing one approach to this method with which you are comfortable, undertaking this without too much adaptation, and to develop your appreciation of and skills in using this method (Kenealy 2012). We would advise you to discuss this choice with your project tutor.

Procedure

Because we outlined the elements of Grounded Theory in Section 5.5, we concentrate here on discussing the procedures used to code data. It is important, however, to recognise that all of these elements are used in combination throughout a Grounded Theory

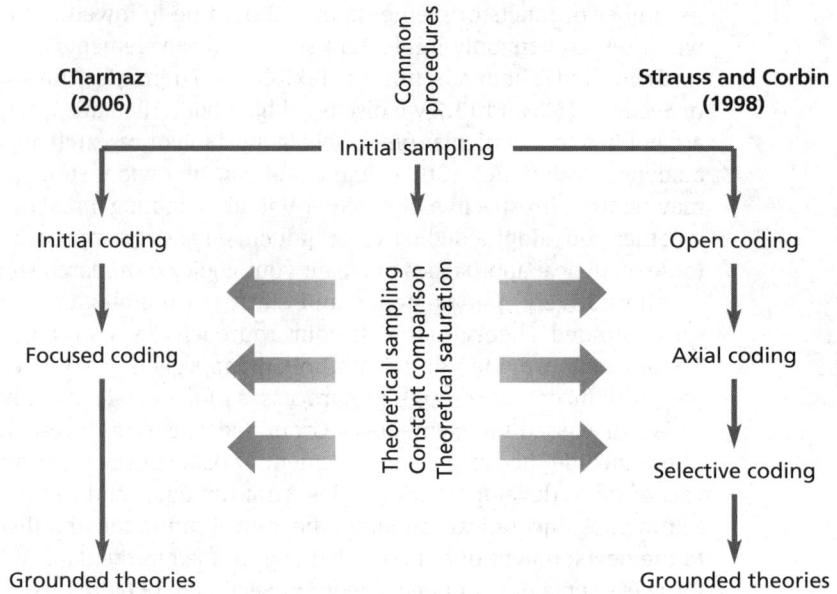

Figure 13.2 Comparing approaches to Grounded Theory Method
Source: © Mark Saunders, Philip Lewis and Adrian Thornhill 2015

study. Theoretical sampling (Section 7.3) is used to choose pertinent cases at each phase of data collection and analysis. An initial sample will be chosen that relates to your research question or topic. Each further case will be selected to explore analytical ideas and categories emerging from coding data in the previous case or cases. The purpose of this will be to further the development of your codes and analytical categories to be able to explore relationships between these to develop a grounded theory. Underpinning this is the process of constantly comparing the data being collected with the codes and categories being used, so as to aid the process of developing an emerging theory that will be thoroughly grounded in these data. Memo writing throughout your Grounded Theory study allows you to sum up, clarify and develop ideas that relate to the codes you develop, the categories you derive, the relationships between these, the emergence of theory and other aspects related to the conduct of your study. Theoretical sampling continues until theoretical saturation is reached. This will occur when data collection ceases to reveal new data that are relevant to a category, where the properties or dimensions of categories have become well developed and understood, and relationships between categories have been verified (Figure 13.2).

Having recognised the interrelated nature of the procedures of Grounded Theory Method we discuss coding and differences in approaches to this.

Initial coding or open coding

Initial coding or **open coding** is similar to the coding procedure outlined in Section 13.6. The data that you collect will be disaggregated into conceptual units and provided with a label. The same label or name will be given to similar units of data. However, because this research process commences without an explicit basis in existing theory, the result may be the creation of a multitude of conceptual labels related to the lower level of focus and structure with which you commence your research (Box 13.12). The emphasis in Grounded Theory Method is to derive meaning from the activities, subjects and settings being studied. In this way you will use in vivo codes (Section 13.6) to code your data.

Box 13.12
Focus on student research

Using open coding

James's research was concerned with the micro-strategising activities of individuals in small enterprises. He was particularly interested in how 'firm-level' strategy might evolve from 'day-to-day' mundane and routine activities. He undertook a series of semi-structured interviews with owner-managers of small enterprises. The audio-recordings of each interview were subsequently transcribed into a text file and imported into the CAQDAS package NVivo™. Open codes such as 'sharing knowledge' and 'formal strategy' and 'strategy as lived'

were then applied to each transcript as illustrated in the extract.

Based upon analysis using his codes James noticed that these small organisations all seemed to have at least one individual (Karen in the extract) who was performing at least some micro-strategising activities (indicated by her strategic vision 'concerning what we might do in the future'). He theorised that most small organisations performed at least some micro-strategising activities, although the accumulation of such actions into an explicit and disseminated strategy was not so prevalent. Taking the theoretical perspective of 'Strategy-as-Practice', James developed his analysis to argue that even those firms which did not believe they were indulging in strategic thinking were actually creating some of its precursors.

In Section 13.6 we stated that a unit of data might relate to a few words, a line, a sentence or number of sentences, or a paragraph. The need to understand meanings and to generate codes to encompass these in Grounded Theory Method is likely to lead you to conduct your early analysis by looking at smaller rather than larger units of data. The resulting multitude of code labels will therefore need to be compared and placed into broader, related groupings or categories. This will allow you to produce a more manageable and focused research project and to develop the analytical process. This is discussed in focused coding and axial coding.

Coding your data should lead you to identify analytical concepts and categories and help you to consider where data collection should be focused in the future (theoretical sampling). It may also help you to develop the focus of your research question. Using a Grounded Theory strategy may mean that your initial research question is broadly focused, although still within manageable exploratory confines. As you develop a narrower focus through this process, you will be able to refine and limit the scope of your research question.

Focused coding

In Charmaz's (2006) approach, **focused coding** involves deciding which of your initial codes to use to develop the analytic and explanatory focus of your coded data. This results in a smaller number of codes being attached to larger units of data and may be seen as serving the same purpose as searching for themes in Thematic Analysis (Section 13.6). Data from various initial codes are re-coded to a smaller number of more focused codes. During initial coding some of the codes you develop may appear to have greater analytic potential, to help you to explain your data and to develop a grounded theory related to you research question. Selecting these codes will lead you to work through all of your coded data again to see if they are suitable to begin to develop a more explanatory focus. Charmaz suggests that codes with the capability to become focused codes, and to able to categorise larger units of your data, are likely to be those that proved to be the most important or frequently used during initial coding. It is worth noting that codes which are frequently used during initial coding may not necessarily prove to have the greatest analytical potential, just as codes that become important may not have initially attracted large amounts of data.

Charmaz (2006) believes that progressing from initial coding to focused coding is unlikely to be a simple, linear process. Working out and working through which initial codes may be the best ones to use as focused codes may lead you to re-code your data and develop a new set of codes. If this occurs, do not despair: it will take time but it will allow you to get closer to and understand your data through the development of greater insight. Such reflection and re-working may occur irrespective of which qualitative analytic technique you choose. As you gain insights about what your data mean, you should use these insights to evaluate which codes will have the analytical capability to become focused codes to progress your analysis. These conceptually more useful focused codes should allow you to code and compare data across different interviews and observations. You will be able to develop your analysis by constantly comparing the codes you are using to categorise your data with the data you have collected, to gain further insights and work towards an emergent explanation of what your data mean to you.

Charmaz's (2006) approach to Grounded Theory Method may be seen as being less prescriptive than other approaches. She adopts a constructivist approach, which assumes that people construct their social realities, with both the participants' and the researcher's interpretations being socially constructed. Charmaz emphasises a Grounded

Theory Method that is interactive, flexible and less prescriptive. Analysis develops from constantly comparing data to codes and codes to data, codes with other codes, and data with other data to develop higher levels of abstraction rather than necessarily using axial coding or selective coding (discussed later). Analysis is shaped by the researcher's interaction with and interpretation of these constant comparisons. As a result, this approach to Grounded Theory Method does not follow the more tightly defined prescriptive procedures of other approaches.

For these reasons, Charmaz (2006) believes that axial coding (Strauss and Corbin 1998) may be too rigid for some Grounded Theory researchers. As we go on to describe, axial coding is a way of rearranging the data that were fragmented during open or initial coding into a new whole, based on a hierarchical structure. In some Grounded Theory Method prescriptions, this may involve identifying structural elements such as the situation involved, the issue at the centre of this situation, the interactions that took place and the outcomes or consequences of these actions to develop a hierarchical structure. Charmaz believes that this approach may be appropriate where you wish to use a prescribed analytical framework to develop your analysis. But she believes that some will find it to be too prescriptive and will prefer to use a simpler, more flexible approach. For these, axial coding as specified by Strauss and Corbin will not be useful. The use of initial coding and focused coding, combined with the use of theoretical sampling, constant comparison and theoretical saturation, will provide a more suitable and flexible approach (Figure 13.2). Where axial coding is still used in this more flexible Grounded Theory Method it is used in a less prescriptive and more flexible way.

We now describe Strauss and Corbin's (1998) approach to axial coding and the approach to selective coding of Strauss and Corbin (1998) and Corbin and Strauss (2008) (see also Figure 13.2).

Axial coding

Axial coding refers to the process of looking for relationships between the categories of data that have emerged from open coding. It indicates a process of theoretical development. As relationships between categories are recognised, they are rearranged into a hierarchical form, with the emergence of subcategories. The essence of this approach is to explore and explain a phenomenon (a subject of your research) by identifying what is happening and why, the environmental factors that affect this (such as economic, technological, political, legal, social and cultural), how it is being managed within the context being examined, and the outcomes of action that has been taken. Clearly, there will be a relationship between these aspects, or categories, and the purpose of your analysis will be to explain this.

Once these relationships have been recognised, you will then seek to verify them against actual data that you have collected. Strauss and Corbin (1998) recommend that you undertake this by formulating questions or statements, which can then be phrased as hypotheses, to test these apparent relationships. As you undertake this process you will be testing these hypotheses by looking for both supporting evidence and negative cases that demonstrate variations from these relationships.

Selective coding

Strauss and Corbin (1998) suggest that after a lengthy period of data collection, which may take several months, you will have developed a number of principal categories and related subcategories. The stage that follows is called **selective coding**. This is intended to identify one of these principal categories, which becomes known as the central or core category, in order to relate the other categories to this with the intention of integrating the research and developing a grounded theory (Corbin and Strauss 2008; Strauss and Corbin 1998). In the previous stage the emphasis was placed on recognising the relationships between categories and their subcategories. In this stage the emphasis is placed on recognising and developing the relationships between the principal categories that have emerged from this grounded approach in order to develop an explanatory theory.

Evaluation

A number of implications have emerged from this brief outline of the main procedures involved in the use of grounded theory. These may be summed up by saying that the use of Grounded Theory Method will involve you in processes that will be time-consuming, intensive and reflective.

Before you commit yourself to this method, you will need to consider the time that you have to conduct your research, the level of competence you will need, your access to data, and the logistical implications of immersing yourself in such an intensive approach to research. There may also be a concern that little of significance will emerge at the end of the research process, and this will be an important aspect for you to consider when determining the focus of your research if you use Grounded Theory Method.

Grounded Theory Method has the scope to provide you with a systematic analytical technique where you wish to use an emergent research approach that is part of a wider methodological strategy which you can follow to guide your research project from its inception, through the processes of data collection and analysis, to completion. The theory that you develop from using this approach should have the capacity to be well grounded in the meanings expressed by your participants and the context of the research setting. The successful application of this approach is likely to be related to making sure that you understand one or other of the published versions of Grounded Theory Method and your willingness to commit yourself to following its procedures.

13.10 Narrative Analysis 叙事分析

Introduction

We discussed Narrative Inquiry as a research strategy in Section 5.5. Our discussion here focuses on the different ways in which narrative data may be analysed. Narrative Analysis is not a specific analytical technique, such as Thematic Analysis or Template Analysis (discussed earlier). Nor is Narrative Analysis part of a wider methodological approach, as with Grounded Theory Method. Instead **Narrative Analysis** is a collection of analytical approaches to analyse different aspects of narrative. These may be combined in practice, depending on your research question and purpose, and the nature of your data.

What these analytical approaches have in common is the preservation of the data's narrative form. Unlike Thematic Analysis, Template Analysis or Grounded Theory Method, where original data are fragmented by coding and then assigned to analytical categories, narrative data are preserved and analysed as a whole unit or narrative sequence. Categories, themes and facets of content may still be identified and coded but this occurs from within a narrative. In Narrative Analysis it is important to preserve data within their narrated context to maintain the sequential and structural elements of each case.

While a narrative tends to be analysed as a whole, the nature of what constitutes a narrative varies considerably. Textual narratives may vary from a segment of text or speech to a whole life story provided by a narrator. Within this range of possibilities, analysis may focus on extracts from interview transcripts, which each provide a short narrative about a related topic or incident in which the researcher is interested. These extracts will tend to be short stories that have a clear purpose, encompassing a situation, an action and an outcome, expressed in a structure containing a beginning, middle and end. Analysis may also focus on passages of speech or dialogue, where the purpose is to analyse how the narrative is constructed. In terms of extended narratives, analysis may focus on narrated accounts of life stories or organisational events, where emphasis is likely to be placed on sequential and structural elements. Analysis may also involve a researcher constructing a narrative from fragments of data collected from multiple sources, such as different documents or research interviews. A narrative may also be constructed from other narratives to provide a unified account to further analysis, sometimes referred to as re-storying.

Narrative Analysis may use a deductive or inductive research approach. In thematic narrative analysis, prior theory can be used to develop codes and categories to help to analyse each narrative. Codes and categories may also be allowed to emerge inductively from each narrative. As in some other qualitative approaches, analysis of narratives may combine the use of deductive and inductive approaches.

Because Narrative Analysis is a collection of analytical approaches, with variations evident in each approach in terms of the way they have been used in practice by researchers, it is not sensible to describe a procedural outline as we have done in earlier sections. Instead, we briefly outline two approaches used in Narrative Analysis. These are Thematic Narrative Analysis and Structural Narrative Analysis (Maitlis 2012; Riessman, 2008).

Outline

Thematic Narrative Analysis

The purpose of **Thematic Narrative Analysis** is to identify analytical themes within narratives. This approach to Narrative Analysis focuses on the content of a narrative, rather than on the way in which it is structured. In this approach the emphasis is therefore on 'what' the narrative is about rather than 'how' it is constructed.

Thematic Narrative Analysis can be used to analyse an individual narrative or multiple, related narratives. In either approach, you will need to pay attention to the chronological sequence and contextual background of the themes you identify. Understanding sequence and context is important to be able to develop a rich and full explanation when analysing an individual narrative. Analysis of multiple narratives can commence by analysing each narrative separately or by working across all of the narratives at the same time, as we go on to describe. Multiple narratives will be related by a common focus, such as an organisational event, with each narrative provided by a different person involved in this. In analysing multiple narratives separately, the initial emphasis will be on the in-depth analysis of each narrative before then comparing and contrasting findings across them. The reason why you may wish to analyse multiple narratives individually will be to illustrate how variations in context affect the actions taken and outcomes recorded, or; to illustrate how differences in the actions taken and outcomes recorded may vary in spite of contextual similarities and to explain why (Box 13.13).

Analysis of multiple narratives can also commence by searching for themes across these narratives, rather than concentrating on the in-depth analysis of each narrative in turn in the dataset. This difference in emphasis may be more suitable where you

> ## Box 13.13
> ## Focus on management research
>
> ### Using Narrative Analysis to analyse acts of workplace courage
>
> In an article published in *Academy of Management Journal*, Koerner (2014) analysed narratives relating to acts of workplace courage. Koerner defines courage as acting intentionally in spite of the risks associated with undertaking such an act. From the literature about courage she identifies three essential elements of a courageous act: 'a morally worthy goal, intentional action and perceived risks, threats or obstacles' (Koerner 2014: 65). Data collection resulted in 89 narrative accounts of workplace courage.
>
> Koerner analysed these narratives using two complementary approaches. The first approach focused on the broad subject or storyline of each narrative, in order to be able to categorise (label) the act of courage told in the story. This involved analysing each narrative as a whole unit. The second approach focused on more detailed aspects of the content of the narratives, related to, for example, the occurrence of the three elements of a courageous act theorised in the literature. In this second approach the unit of
>
> analysis was a segment of data rather than the whole narrative. This second approach led to the text of each narrative being coded with a number of analytical categories.
>
> The first approach led to the development of five storyline categories, from which Koerner was able to develop a typology of acts of courage in the workplace. These five types are: endurance of a difficult situation to achieve a worthy goal; reaction to a difficult situation to overcome it; opposition to a more powerful individual to remedy a problem; creation of a solution to remedy a problem in spite of risks; failure to act courageously in the face of a problem. This allowed each of the 89 narratives to be categorised into one of these five types of workplace courage (or lack of it).
>
> The second approach led to the development of a number of categories to code data within and across these narratives, including how the three elements of a courageous act manifested themselves in each narrative. This approach allowed Koerner to analyse how these elements varied in relation to each type of courage. For example, narrators in her study associated enduring a difficult situation with the worthy goal of achieving an outcome, retaining a job or providing an income for families; whereas opposing a powerful person to remedy a problem was associated with the worthy goal of retaining integrity, being fair, or preventing harm.

commence your research approach deductively with a predetermined theoretical framework of analytical categories or themes for which to search. In this approach, you will be able to identify whether and which themes occur across the narratives in the dataset or parts of it, where variations occur and how contextual factors affect these. This should help you to develop an explanation that evaluates the application of prior theory to your data as well as being grounded in these data, while preserving the integrity of your narratives (Box 13.13).

Analysing narratives to identify themes while keeping each narrative intact can be achieved by adapting the method of coding we discussed earlier in this chapter. One adaptation you might use is to colour-code analytical themes in each narrative. By using a particular colour-code for a theme, you will be able to identify its occurrence across different narratives, without fragmenting these data. This simple procedure will allow you to compare different narrative accounts more easily as you read and reread each one. A further adaptation that you may find useful in order to keep your narratives intact is to make several copies of each set of narratives and to code a particular theme on one set of copies. A further tactic you may use is to read each narrative transcript several times to become familiar with its content to aid your analysis.

Structural Narrative Analysis

Structural Narrative Analysis analyses the way in which a narrative is constructed. This approach to Narrative Analysis examines use of language to understand how it affects a listener or an audience. In this approach the emphasis is therefore on 'how' the narrative is constructed and language is used rather than 'what' it is about.

While Thematic Narrative Analysis is likely to be easier to use and therefore to be used more often, the use of Structural Narrative Analysis is capable of adding a further level of insight when conducting Narrative Analysis. To use this approach you will need to develop some understanding of the socio-linguistic and cognitive theories that underpin it (see the discussion in Riessman 2008). These have led to methods to analyse the structures of spoken narratives. A key method to analyse the way narrative accounts are sequenced and structured is the technique developed by Labov and Waletzky (1967) and Labov (1972), which remains a standard approach today. In this approach a researcher analyses a narrative to look for the presence of six elements and the way these have been used. These are:

- an abstract (which states the point of the story);
- an orientation (which describes the situation including when and where it took place and who was involved);
- a complicating action (which describes the sequence of events including a critical point);
- an evaluation (where the narrator explains the meaning of the narrative);
- a resolution (how the issue is solved – the outcome); and
- a coda (which ends the narrative and relates it to the present).

This analytical structure provides a framework to evaluate narratives, since not every element may be present in a narrative and the nature and sequencing of these elements is likely to vary. It is, however, worth noting that the purpose of much of the research undertaken using this and other approaches to analyse the structure of narratives is not so much to form judgemental evaluations but to understand how people in different groups form narratives. This has been undertaken to fulfil different aims: sometimes to understand how acts of speech may lead to certain actions or to falsely negative perceptions; sometimes to change professional practice.

Where your research focuses on interactions between individuals or across those in different groups, where you have collected narrated accounts of these interactions, you may consider using Structural Narrative Analysis. This potentially encompasses a wide range of interactions; for example, between managers and other employees; across occupational groups; up and down organisational levels; across cultural and transnational boundaries, to understand the relationship between the way a narrative is constructed and the effect of this on the attitudes and subsequent actions of those who receive it. More generally, Structural Narrative Analysis may be suitable for you to analyse the narratives you collect through conducting interviews or recording naturally occurring conversations.

Evaluation

We noted that collecting data through narratives may be advantageous in certain circumstances (Section 5.5). These include research contexts where the experiences of your participants can best be understood by collecting and analysing these as complete stories or narrative sequences. The ways in which events in a narrative are linked, the actions that follow and their implications are more likely to be revealed by encouraging a participant to narrate his or her experiences than asking them to respond to a series of pre-formed questions. Narrative Analysis allows chronological connections and the sequencing of events as told by the narrator to be preserved, with the potential to enrich understanding and aid analysis.

A number of the research strategies outlined in Section 5.5 may lead to the use of Narrative Analysis, not just the use of Narrative Inquiry. Narrative research is a case-centred approach and you may find that use of an Action Research, Case Study, Documentary, Ethnographic or Grounded Theory research strategy will lead to the collection of narrative sequences that draw you towards the use of Narrative Analysis. In this way, your data collection may lead you to use Narrative Analysis as a complementary method to analyse some data that you judge are best analysed in their narrative form, or as your primary method of analysis, depending on your research question and purpose, and nature of your data. In analysing data in narrative form, Narrative Analysis offers you a choice of analytical approaches to suit the purpose of your research. These approaches may be used individually or in combination. Where they are combined in practice, your analysis is likely to be richer in terms of the insights you will be able to produce from your data.

13.11 Discourse Analysis 讨论分析

Introduction

'Discourse Analysis' is a term covering a variety of approaches that analyse the social effects of the use of language. In general terms 'discourse' refers to the spoken or written use of language, often referred to as talk or text. In Discourse Analysis, the emphasis is not on studying the way in which language is used for its own sake. Use of language is a key way in which people make sense of their social world. In this more specific sense, 'discourse' describes how language is used to shape this meaning-making process, to construct social reality. A **discourse** is therefore not just seen as neutrally reflecting social practice or relations but as constructing these (although the notion of 'constructing' is contentious and we return to it later). In this way, **Discourse Analysis** explores how discourses construct or constitute social reality and social relations through creating meanings and perceptions.

This conceptualisation allows the complexity and diversity of social practice and relations to be recognised through the existence of different, often competing and sometimes conflicting discourses. For example, different discourses construct perceptions about organisations and organisational relations. It also follows that language (discourse) can be used intentionally to attempt to create ideologically mounted positions, intended to be in the interests of those who produce and disseminate them. A unitarist view would emphasise the commonality of interest within an organisation (or society) and use some means (focusing on discourse) to persuade its members of this approach. By contrast, a pluralist view would see an organisation (or society) as a collection of competing interests. Even within the pluralist view, some discourses may be seen to dominate while others are marginalised.

Discourse Analysis involves studying textual sources or passages of naturally occurring talk. Textual sources may be organisational documents such as those outlined in the discussion of documentary research in Section 5.5. Discourse Analysis will often involve using multiple texts that are interrelated to understand the nature and development of a discourse. Phillips and Hardy (2002) point out that the (diffuse, interactional and often taken-for-granted) nature of a discourse means that although it cannot be explored comprehensively, by using a range of interrelated sources it should be possible to gain access to aspects of its formation, propagation and acceptance.

Transcripts of recordings of naturally occurring talk can also be used to explore a discourse. Such data may be collected through conducting and recording observation in an ethnographic study, or one incorporating ethnography (Section 5.5). As discourse occurs through naturally occurring talk, it is preferred to contrived talk through interviewing (Section 10.3) where the intervention of the researcher in asking questions, eliciting responses and analysing the data is likely to affect the authenticity of the discourse being analysed (Hepburn and Potter 2007). There may of course be a use for interview data in a subsequent, supplementary capacity.

To be able to explore the relationship between discourse and social reality also means placing emphasis on contextual and social theoretical aspects. The way in which a discourse emerges and constructs social reality through influencing social relations and practices is likely to be rooted in a particular period or event, such as the foundation of an organisation or an organisational change. Discourse Analysis may therefore require an understanding of historical context to be able to understand the ways in which discourse develops and constructs social practices. Using a range of texts may help to reveal this historical contextual development. Some approaches to Discourse Analysis also draw on existing theoretical perspectives to explore the nature of a discourse and to contextualise its impact on social practice and relations. We consider this further in the following sub-section.

Outline

Discourse Analysis encompasses a range of approaches and unlike some of the techniques we discussed earlier does not specify a particular set of procedures to conduct analysis. For this reason we briefly outline some of the approaches used in Discourse Analysis in this sub-section. Approaches to Discourse Analysis can be differentiated according to their focus and philosophical assumptions. The focus of Discourse Analysis ranges from 'finely-grained' analysis of text or talk to grand theoretical abstractions about the nature of social practice.

A finely grained approach focuses on the analysis (deconstruction) of an individual text, or of a transcript of 'talk' that occurred during a social interaction located within a particular situation. The purpose of this type of close reading of a text (or passage of talk) is to understand how the use of language indicates meaning and to categorise the nature of this discourse. Hyatt (2005, 2013) provides advice about conducting this type of analysis. His 'Critical Literacy Analysis' (2005) and 'Critical Policy Discourse Analysis' (2013) include a range of criteria for analysing text. Although these analyses are devised within the context of education, the generic analytical criteria they include are transferable or translatable to other contexts. If you are considering using Discourse Analysis you may find it useful to consult these articles.

Further (and complementary) approaches include interdiscursive and intertextual analyses. **Interdiscursivity** refers to the way one discourse is introduced into another discourse. For example, discourses and practices associated with the private sector have been introduced into the public sector in some societies to justify change. Box 13.14 provides an example of this in the context of the UK's National Health Service where the discourse of 'privatisation', value for money and income generation now sit alongside its traditional discourse of public service. **Intertextuality** refers to the way a text or texts overtly or covertly borrow from and are informed by other texts. Overt borrowing from another text is acknowledged through use of quotations and citations. Covert borrowing involves adopting ideas or ideological positions and arguments from other texts without overtly

> ## Box 13.14 Focus on research in the news
>
> # Health reform fails to lift private patient income
>
> **By Sarah Neville**
>
> The sums earned by the National Health Service from treating private patients have barely risen even though most foundation trust hospitals are struggling to make ends meet amid a historic budget squeeze.
>
> Rules introduced last year allowed a far higher percentage of turnover to be raised from non-NHS work, leading to warnings by critics of health service "privatisation".
>
> But research by the Foundation Trust Network (FTN), based on an analysis of hospital accounts, suggests some parts of the sector are finding it far easier than others to earn money in this way.
>
> Big, specialist hospitals such as Moorfields Eye Hospital and the Royal Marsden, both in London, can use their equipment, expertise and internationally known brands to attract private patients and pursue cash-generating research.
>
> Although district general hospitals have also entered into the non-NHS market, they must bear the costs of running a full range of services, including maternity and accident and emergency, for their local communities, making it harder for some to compete with independent providers able to focus on single specialities such as orthopaedics.
>
> Underlining the importance of developing non-NHS income for overstretched hospitals, Chris Hopson, chief executive of the FTN, said it was "a crucial revenue stream . . . in the current financially challenging climate".
>
> **FT** *Source:* Extract from 'Health reform fails to lift private patient income', Sarah Neville, Public Policy Editor (2014) *Financial Times*, 4 September. Copyright © The Financial Times Ltd

acknowledging this. The focus of these types of analysis in Discourse Analysis is to analyse how discourses and texts are used in the construction of other discourses and texts, to identify how discourses change and develop, and to understand how attempts are made to give credibility to such changes or developments. These approaches to analysis point to the importance of contextual knowledge, not only to understand how discourses develop and evolve, but also to appreciate the factors that bring about change – why change occurs. Using interdiscursive and intertextual analyses therefore involves using multiple texts.

Our discussion so far has emphasised the role of social constructionism in Discourse Analysis. By this we mean the assumption that the social world is socially constructed through discourse and that Discourse Analysis analyses how use of language constructs versions of social reality (including dominant, marginalised and competing discourses). However, the extent to which social reality is socially constructed is contested. To this end, Holstein and Gubrium (2011: 342) reflect a dictum of Karl Marx in saying 'that people actively construct their worlds but not completely on, or in, their own terms'. This points to the (ontological) distinction between objectivism and subjectivism we discussed in Section 4.2. According to realist philosophical positions, objective entities exist that are external to social actors, which impact on their social constructions. It is therefore important to understand external factors that affect human attitudes and actions, whether or not social actors are aware of these influences on the ways in which they make sense of their social world.

A methodological approach to Discourse Analysis based on a realist epistemological view exists in the form of **Critical Discourse Analysis** (e.g. Fairclough, 1992, 2010). Critical Discourse Analysis adopts a critical realist approach (Section 4.3), drawing a distinction between the natural world and the social world, with the implication that social actors' understanding of the latter is affected by the former and is not entirely socially constructed. Fairclough (2010: 4–5) captures this when he writes,

> The socially constructive effects of discourse are thus a central concern, but a distinction is drawn between construal and construction; the world is discursively construed (or represented) in many and various ways, but which construals come to have socially constructive effects depends upon a range of conditions which include for instance power relations but also properties of whatever parts or aspects of the world are being construed. We cannot transform the world in any old way we happen to construe it; the world is such that some transformations are possible and others are not. So CDA is a 'moderate' or 'contingent' form of social constructionism.

Critical Discourse Analysis examines relations between discourse and other objects in the world that are recognised as existing, including the exercise of power by those who control resources (power relations). In this approach, discourse is seen as being affected or conditioned by social reality, knowingly or unknowingly, as well as socially construing it. As a result it incorporates the need to not only analyse incidents of discourse (analysis of social interactions or text) but also to understand how wider discursive and social practices influence and are influenced by discourse. This approach, in which an incidence of discourse is 'simultaneously a piece of text, an instance of discursive practice, and an instance of social practice (Fairclough, 1992: 4), is outlined in Figure 13.3. This approach involves analysing discourse at the level of text or social inaction (discussed earlier in this sub-section), discursive practice (including the use of interdiscursive and intertextual analyses outlined earlier) and social practice (seen as requiring an interdisciplinary or transdisciplinary approach to analysis) in order to achieve an integrated and critical understanding.

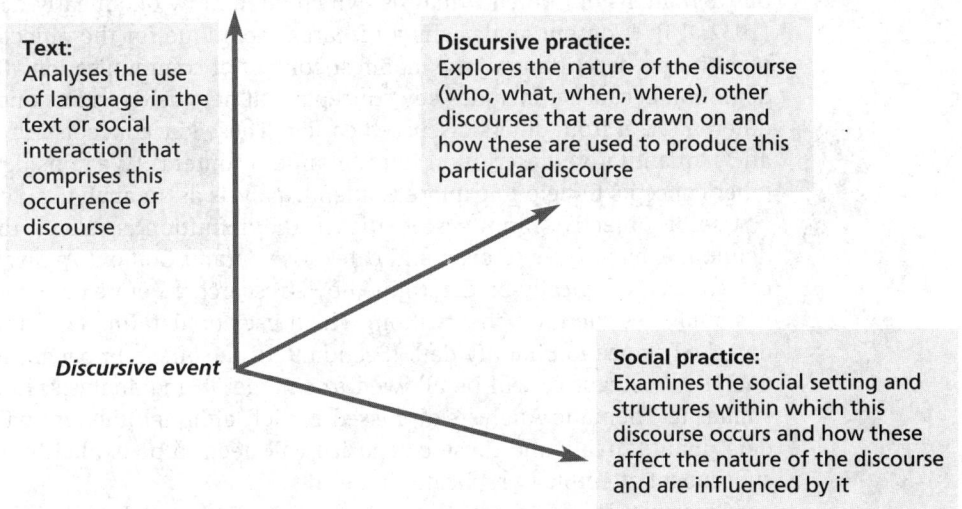

Text:
Analyses the use of language in the text or social interaction that comprises this occurrence of discourse

Discursive practice:
Explores the nature of the discourse (who, what, when, where), other discourses that are drawn on and how these are used to produce this particular discourse

Discursive event

Social practice:
Examines the social setting and structures within which this discourse occurs and how these affect the nature of the discourse and are influenced by it

Figure 13.3 A three-dimensional analytical framework for Critical Discourse Analysis
Source: Developed from Fairclough (1992)

Evaluation

Discourse Analysis potentially provides you with a valuable analytical approach where your research involves social action and interaction within a particular setting such as an organisation. This analytical approach may be appropriate where your research is focused on a topic such as organisational communication, culture, decision making, governance, power, practices, processes, relations or trust. It may be an approach that provides you with an insightful means to analyse data resulting from the use, for example, of an Action Research, documentary or ethnographic strategy where you have transcripts relating to the use of language in discourse.

Where you consider using this approach as you formulate your research design, you will need to develop some level of familiarity with and understanding of approaches to Discourse Analysis. In particular you will need to be able to articulate your approach to Discourse Analysis and say why it is suitable for your research. Discourse Analysis, like some other analytical approaches, has developed to suit a number of purposes, incorporating different philosophical and theoretical assumptions suitable for different types of data and using different methods. Discourse Analysis can be used as your primary analytical technique, depending on your research question, research design and nature of your data, or in support of other analytical techniques where appropriate. Discourse Analysis therefore offers a potentially valuable research approach but consideration about using this approach will benefit from adequate and early preparation!

13.12 Content Analysis and quantifying qualitative data 内容分析与量化定性数据

Introduction

Content Analysis is an analytical technique that codes and categorises qualitative data in order to analyse them quantitatively. Content Analysis has a long history that illustrates its use as an approach spanning qualitative and quantitative methods. There are numerous definitions of Content Analysis, which often draw on an early definition by Berelson (1952: 18): 'Content analysis is a research technique for the objective, systematic and quantitative description of the manifest content of communication.' This is an important definition because it includes key concepts that help us to understand this technique and differentiate it from others discussed earlier. These key concepts are 'objective', 'systematic', 'quantitative description' and 'manifest content'. We consider each of these and other concepts to help to explore Content Analysis as an analytical technique.

Use of 'objective' and 'systematic' in the definition is related to the importance of defining explicit rules to code and categorise data in Content Analysis. These codes and categories are typically predetermined by a researcher before data collection begins. This is similar to structured observation, which uses predetermined categories and adopts a detached stance to quantify data (Section 9.3). In some approaches to Content Analysis, analytical categories will be allowed to emerge during analysis, in a way that appears similar to Thematic Analysis discussed earlier, although the aim will still be to analyse data quantitatively and these categories will need to be explicitly reported to facilitate subsequent attempts to replicate the results.

'Objective' in the definition also extends to the researcher identifying 'factual' objects in the data and not relying on subjective judgement. These are objects which are seen as possessing an external reality to the researcher that do not rely on her or his interpretive opinion. Stress is laid on different researchers being able to replicate a Content Analysis by using explicit categories to produce an identical outcome. A research project may focus, for example, on attitudes towards an organisational policy and who holds these views. Content Analysis may be used to identify positive and negative attitudes towards the policy and who voices such views. Terms denoting negative or positive attitudes will be identified, typically being predetermined before analysis commences, so that the researcher, perhaps using an analytical software program (Section 13.14), is required to identify instances of these in the text or visual data being analysed. The researcher will also identify the characteristics of the holders of each of these attitudes – perhaps related to gender, age, occupation, work department and so forth. This example illustrates another aspect of Content Analysis, which stresses the importance of understanding the contextual use of the content being analysed (Krippendorff 2004).

'Systematic' in the definition also relates to the conduct of Content Analysis. Content Analysis should be conducted in a consistent, transparent and replicable way. This includes explicitly explaining how the data were categorised in a consistent and transparent way that can be understood and replicated by others (see next sub-section). Holsti (1969) advocates five general principles for the systematic development of analytical categories in Content Analysis. Categories should:

- link obviously to the scope and purpose of the research topic, not least so that the relationship of these categories to the research question(s) and objectives is evident (Section 2.4);
- be exhaustive so that every relevant unit of data may be placed into an analytical category;
- be mutually exclusive so that each unit of data may only be placed into one analytical category, rather than possibly fitting into more than one (this is different from the approach in qualitative analytical techniques discussed earlier);
- be independent so that units of data exhibiting related but not the same characteristics cannot be coded into the same category; and
- be developed from a single classification to avoid conceptual confusion.

'Quantitative description' in the definition makes apparent that the purpose of Content Analysis is to quantify and describe aspects of textual or visual data after coding and categorising them. These data are collected qualitatively (Section 13.2) or derived from existing, qualitative sources and then categorised in order to reduce them to a relatively small number of content categories for subsequent quantitative analysis. This analysis may vary from identifying frequencies to examining relationships between variables (Section 12.5). Using our earlier example about attitudes towards an organisational policy and who holds these views, the frequencies of different attitudes may be measured and the relative importance of negative or positive ones identified; it would also be possible to examine relationships between these different attitudes and the characteristics of those who hold them. Depending on the nature of the research question, research purpose and research strategy, Content Analysis may be used as either the main or secondary method to produce this type of data analysis.

'**Manifest content**' in the definition makes clear that Content Analysis is concerned with analysing what is apparent in the data. In Berelson's definition 'objective' and 'manifest content' are linked, and we noted earlier that 'objective' refers to the researcher identifying 'factual' objects in the data, not relying on subjective judgement. The most manifest way to achieve this is to use words or phrases that are physically present in a data set as the basis of a system of categories to analyse its content. Returning to our example about attitudes towards an organisational policy, the occurrence of positive words such as 'enthusiastic', 'involved', 'trust' and negative words such as 'concerned', 'distrust', 'sceptical' may be coded and their frequencies counted and analysed in the data. Analysing 'manifest content' should increase the chance that analysis is conducted in a consistent, transparent and replicable way, thereby improving reliability.

Content Analysis may involve analysing data for other than just 'manifest content'. Greater latitude is often required to infer meanings in the data and to categorise these. This goes beyond simply coding particular words or phrases in the data. Interpreting meanings in order to code units of data such as sentences or paragraphs is referred to as '**latent content**'. Coding 'latent content' may reduce reliability in comparison to 'manifest content'. In order to ensure consistency and transparency, it will be necessary to define the properties of the categories devised for such latent content very clearly.

Choosing to use Content Analysis will depend on the nature of your research data and your research question. Where you have collected a large amount of qualitative data, Content Analysis may be suitable to analyse and describe some of its content, depending on your research question. We considered the nature of research questions in Section 2.4. Content Analysis may be suitable to use in relation to descriptive types of 'what', 'when', 'where', 'who' and 'how' questions. For example, it may help you to analyse what is included in the content (and what is not included by omission); when and where an issue is evident in the content; who is included in the content; how much or how many of a variable occurs in the content; how much something changes and what trends or patterns are evident across comparable data sources. Using Content Analysis to address these descriptive types of question may partially help to answer a research question with a wider exploratory, explanatory or evaluative purpose. As we have noted in our example about attitudes towards an organisational policy, Content Analysis will also provide you with a means to quantify given variables in your data in order to be able to statistically analyse relationships between these variables (Section 12.5).

Content Analysis may be applied in a wide variety of contexts. It has been used to analyse the content of newspapers and other media, including radio and television programmes. It can be used to analyse textual material, such as documents, and audio-visual material, including online media. In an organisational context, it can be used in the analysis of a wide range of documents, including agendas and minutes of meetings, briefing papers, contracts, diaries, email, letters, memos, plans, policy statements, press releases, reports and strategy documents (Section 5.5). It may also be used to analyse textual material in corporate websites, social media websites and blog postings. In an organisational context, it can also be used in the analysis of a wide range of visual and audio sources including advertising posters, audio-visual corporate communications, digital recordings, promotional advertisements and recordings, and web images. In a broader context related to business and management it may be used to analyse other online material and government publications and reports. These potential sources of data to which Content Analysis may be applied have in common the fact that they existed before the research project was conducted – they were not created as data in response to a research project. This has a number of possible implications for the use of Content Analysis, which we consider later in our evaluation of this analytical technique.

Content Analysis may also be used to analyse the qualitative data you generate through conducting interviews or including open-ended questions in questionnaires, as we indicated in our example about attitudes towards an organisational policy. This would involve producing a transcript of each semi-structured or unstructured interview, or of the responses to open-ended questions included in questionnaires, in order to apply Content Analysis. Content Analysis may also be applied to data from conducting participant observation, where transcripts or recordings of these are available.

Procedure

Unlike the qualitative analytical techniques considered earlier, which tend to follow a concurrent and even recursive or circular approach to data sampling, collection and analysis, Content Analysis is more likely to follow a step-by-step or sequential process. For Content Analysis, this process involves sampling, devising analytical categories, defining the unit of analysis, conducting coding and undertaking quantitative analysis. We outline briefly each of these procedural steps.

Where you use existing textual or visual sources you may need to select a sample if the amount of material available is large, in order to conduct your research in a manageable way. Determining the amount of material that exists will depend on your research question and factors such as the existence of and access to suitable documents. Where it is necessary to select a sample, the sampling techniques discussed in Chapter 7 should be reviewed to guide your choice of a sampling method that is appropriate for the purpose of your research. You may find that there is a shortage of suitable material and we consider this possibility further in our evaluation of Content Analysis in the next sub-section.

Devising analytical categories is a critical part of using Content Analysis. The categories you devise signify the essence of what you wish to record and analyse. We noted five general principles for the systematic development of analytical categories earlier whereby they should link to the scope and purpose of the research topic, be exhaustive, mutually exclusive, independent and developed from a single classification. Where the categories you devise are not clearly defined and do not fulfil these principles, it is likely that the validity and reliability of your Content Analysis will be flawed.

You will also need to define the unit of analysis you intend to use to record content. This will be determined by your research question and purpose. The unit of analysis may focus on individual words, based on identifying and counting particular words in the content of your sample, as in our example about attitudes towards an organisational policy. The unit of analysis may be larger than the word, related to the occurrence of particular phrases or to sentences or paragraphs. Larger units (sentences or paragraphs) may be used where it is important to contextualise content in order to be able to categorise its meaning. The distinction we highlighted earlier between manifest content and latent content is likely to be evident in the size of the unit of analysis used. Manifest content is likely to be reflected in the use of the word or phrase as the unit of analysis and latent content is likely to be reflected in the use of larger units of analysis. The unit of analysis may also focus on the characteristics of those involved, as in our example where gender, age, occupation, work department were recorded. It may also focus on other characteristics of the content that are relevant to record and analyse in your research. The unit of analysis in visual materials varies from individual images to visual sequences.

Coding involves you working through your data to code units of these data according to the categories you have devised. This will provide you with the opportunity to test your system of categories, where this is predetermined, on a sample of your data and to modify it if necessary before applying it across all of your data. An important way for you to assess whether your system of categories is transparent and capable of being applied consistently by others is for you and a friend to code the same sample of data separately using this system of categories and then to compare your results. This is known as inter-rater reliability and may be assessed by measuring the extent to which two coders agree using a measure known as Cohen's Kappa (which may be calculated using IBM SPSS Statistics).

Where categories are derived from the data rather than being predetermined, you will need to 'immerse' yourself in the data set you have collected. Initially you will need to read through your data very carefully, highlighting or noting key aspects that relate to the purpose of your research and your anticipated use of this technique. As this process continues you will need to identify analytical categories, define these and ensure that they fulfil the general principles for their systematic development (e.g. be exhaustive, mutually exclusive). You may also test the system of categories you devise in this way with a friend to assess inter-rater reliability on a sample of the data before applying it across all of your data. Once you have coded and categorised your data you will be able to undertake quantitative analysis (Chapter 12).

Evaluation

Content Analysis potentially offers a number of advantages. It can provide a means to analyse large amounts of qualitative data where your aim is to describe these quantitatively. In addition to being able to count frequencies and examine relationships between variables in the data, use of this technique may also allow you to observe patterns, shifts and trends in documentary forms of data over time.

Combining Content Analysis and documentary research (Section 5.5) can provide you a means to undertake a longitudinal study (Section 5.6) relatively easily where this is appropriate to your research question and where suitable documentary sources are readily available. As we noted earlier, a wide range of documentary sources may be suitable, including those accessible online. Using pre-existing documentary or visual forms of data also has the advantage that their use is unobtrusive. This means that you can use these types of data without the creators of these documents being aware of their use. This avoids the possibility in face-to-face data collection of research participants reacting to the presence of the researcher affecting the reliability of the data being collected.

Content Analysis can also be used in combination with other qualitative analytical techniques discussed in this chapter. This allows Content Analysis to be used to support the exploratory and explanatory purposes of qualitative analytical techniques, by describing the quantitative aspects of qualitative data, where you are willing to analyse your data for each purpose.

While Content Analysis can be useful, it may also be problematic. Issues may arise when you seek to use Content Analysis in relation to documentary sources. In some situations, the documentary sources you wish to use for your data will be inaccessible, missing, incomplete, or unusable. This will mean that you will not be able to pursue your research unless you are able to source an alternative set of documentary sources. Even where you are able to pursue this research approach, some documents may be incomplete or unusable for your purpose and you will need to discard these. Because documentary sources have been created for another purpose, they may also prove to be partial and biased accounts. Consequently, while they are available to you to use, you will need to use these with care, in a qualified way, or to reject them, depending on the purpose of your research project.

Issues can also arise in relation to data you collect and your analysis of this. Earlier we discussed the need to devise analytical categories, define units of analysis and conduct coding systematically and objectively to ensure reliability. We discussed tactics related to inter-rater reliability. Coding all of your data consistently will also require you to exercise care, skill and concentration to avoid analytical 'drift', which will affect **intra-rater reliability** (which concerns the reliability of coding by a single researcher over time). We also noted the distinction earlier between manifest and latent forms of content. Coding latent content will necessitate a higher level of interpretation than that of manifest content, leading to a higher risk of making invalid inferences and producing unreliable results.

In analysing data, we noted that Content Analysis may be used to examine relationships between variables in the data. However, Content Analysis is not appropriate to assess causal relationships. In our earlier example about attitudes towards an organisational policy and who holds these views, we noted that it would be possible to examine relationships between different attitudes and the characteristics of those who hold them. However, it would not be possible to explain why particular groups tended to hold particular attitudes (e.g. those in particular occupational groups may hold much more positive attitudes to those in other groups). To understand why this would be the case requires in-depth analysis of the qualitative data that you have collected.

Box 13.15
Focus on student research

Using a data cloud to display the frequency of key terms

Luca undertook a research project evaluating types of pay structure. This involved him conducting interviews in organisations that each used a different pay structure. Luca wanted to understand the reasons why each had decided to adopt a particular structure and to evaluate perceptions about that structure's use in practice. He was interested to use different types of data analysis and this led him to code some of manifest content in his data to categorise key terms. To demonstrate the frequency of key terms used by his interview participants he thought it might be useful to produce a data cloud for each set of interviews exploring a particular pay structure. Since these data clouds would represent the actual terms used by his interview participants, they also helped Luca to demonstrate how he had derived the 'in vivo' codes he used in his Grounded Theory analytical approach. This data cloud represents the terms used by interview participants in an organisation that had implemented a Job Families pay structure:

This raises a general concern about the extent to which you should collect qualitative data in order to quantify them. As we have discussed, there are advantageous reasons why you may wish to code and categorise qualitative data in order to describe them quantitatively, but more generally there is limited purpose in collecting qualitative data if you intend to ignore the nature and value of these data by reducing most of them to a simplified form. In this way, Content Analysis may prove to be a main method when applied to documentary sources but a secondary method when applied to qualitative data you collect yourself (Box 13.15).

13.13 Data Display and Analysis 数据列示与分析

Introduction

The Data Display and Analysis approach is based on the work of Miles et al. (2014). For them, the process of analysis consists of three concurrent sub-processes:

- data condensation;
- data display;
- drawing and verifying conclusions.

We now outline each of these.

Procedural outline

As part of the process, **data condensation** includes summarising and simplifying the data collected and/or selectively focusing on some parts of this data. The aim of this process is to transform the data and to condense it. Miles et al. (2014) outline a number of methods for condensing data. These include the production of interview or observation summaries, document summaries, coding and categorising data and perhaps constructing a narrative.

Data display involves organising and assembling your data into summary diagrammatic or visual displays. Miles et al. (2014) describe a number of ways of displaying data, and refer to two main families of data display: matrices and networks. Matrices are generally tabular in form, with defined columns and rows, where data are entered selectively into the appropriate cells of such a matrix, to facilitate further data analysis (Box 13.16). A network is a collection of nodes or boxes that are joined or linked by lines, perhaps with arrows to indicate relationships. The boxes or nodes contain brief descriptions or labels to indicate variables or key points from the data.

Box 13.16
Focus on student research

Using CAQDAS to explore how key words are used in context

Marcus' research was concerned with how staff were responding to the managed changes in the organisation where he worked. He had collected his data using a Web questionnaire, which contained the open question: 'If there is anything further you would like to add in relation to the changes at OrgCo, please type your comment in the box'. Marcus downloaded the responses verbatim from the online survey tool as a data file and spellchecked

them, correcting words that had been misspelled or used American spellings to the English spelling. This ensured he would pick up all occurrences of particular words such as 'staff' or 'OrgCo', the pseudonym he used to anonymise the organisation. He then loaded the spellchecked data into Provalis Research's text analysis software WordStat. These were displayed in a tabular form. During the next stage of his analysis Marcus wanted to see which respondents had mentioned staff or staffing in their responses to the question and the context in which the words had been used. He therefore searched for the keyword 'staff' within his data.

Scanning the responses suggested that those respondents who had answered this question often appeared to talk about how staff were treated at OrgCo. Marcus decided to investigate further.

RECNO		KEYWORD		COLOUR
83	firectorate since latest re-organisation. Currently awaiting outcome of	staffing	review. Too many elements unknown to give more accurate opinions	Mail
87	I currently supervise 12 members of	staff	within a day service as part of a management team. I feel supported t	Mail
87	centre we will amalgamate with another service. Seven members of	staff	have reported concerns of bullying and harassment by a deputy mana	Mail
87	we will amalgamate with. One incident was witnessed by the whole	staff	team at a training day (40+ staff) and staff are saying they do not feel	Mail
87	ncident was witnessed by the whole staff team at a training day (40+	staff	) and staff are saying they do not feel they are able to make official co	Mail
87	is witnessed by the whole staff team at a training day (40+ staff) and	staff	are saying they do not feel they are able to make official complaints fo	Mail
89	Environmental services is in 'melt down' – still reducing	staff	, everyone left is severely overworked and the current policy is to cor	Mail
89	is severely overworked and the current policy is to continue reducing	staff	members. This is creating a very overwhelmed, over stressed workfo	Mail
96	he longer established managers/supervisors are not recognising their	staffs	skills/drive/ambition and do not encourage them to train or further their	Mail
100	xd of, is seemingly short sighted about an issue that so impacts on the	staff	's daily working life. Just one more point; it's a bit frustrating that Cou	Web
106	uncil is an excellent employer providing very good levels of support to	staff	in all aspects of their work.	Web
110	ll would like to see the issue resolved so that skilled and experienced	staff	can be retained. I am all in favour of sustainable transport but strong	Web

Recognising relationships and patterns in the data, as well as drawing conclusions and verifying these, is helped by the use of data displays. A display allows you to make comparisons between the elements of the data and to identify any relationships, key themes, patterns and trends that may be evident. These will be worthy of further exploration and analysis. In this way, the use of data displays can help you to interpret your data and to draw meaning from it.

Evaluation

Miles et al. (2014) believe there are a number of advantages associated with using forms of data display. Qualitative data collection tends to produce hours of audio-recorded interviews or extensive piles of notes. Once these have been transcribed or word processed, they are generally referred to as 'extended text'. Extended text is considered an unreduced form of display that is difficult to analyse because it is both extensive and poorly ordered. Based on the logic that 'you know what you display', the analysis of data and the drawing of conclusions from these will be helped by using matrices, networks or other visual forms to display reduced or selected data drawn from your extended text. These forms of display are relatively easy to generate, can be developed to fit your data specifically, and help you to develop your analytical thinking as you work through several iterations to develop a visual form that represents your data well.

Use of Data Display and Analysis can provide you with a set of procedures to analyse your qualitative data, or alternatively one or more of the techniques that Miles et al. (2014) outline can be useful as part of your approach to analysing this type of data. They describe the analysis of qualitative data as an interactive process, and in this sense their approach includes many aspects of analysis that complement the analytical techniques we discussed earlier. Their approach is a systematic and structured one, and they recognise that the procedures they outline are often associated with a fairly high level of formalisation. However, unlike grounded theory, the exact procedures to be followed within their framework of data reduction, display and conclusion drawing and verification are not specified. Miles et al. (2014) refer to their book as a 'sourcebook', and as such they offer a number of possible techniques that may be appropriate within your overall approach to analysis. If you intend to use their book we suggest you take care in identifying what is useful for you in the context of your own research question and objectives.

Data Display and Analysis is suited to an inductive strategy to analyse qualitative data, although it is also compatible with a deductive strategy. Miles et al.'s (2014) book is useful both for its overall discussion of the analysis of qualitative data and in relation to its many analytical tools.

13.14 **Using CAQDAS** 使用 CAQDAS

Introduction

CAQDAS (Computer Assisted Qualitative Data Analysis Software, sometimes abbreviated to QDAS) refers to programs containing a range of tools to facilitate the analysis of qualitative data. The use of CAQDAS offers a number of advantages in relation to the analytical procedures we have been discussing. In particular, when used systematically, it can aid continuity and increase both transparency and methodological rigour (Lewins and Silver 2009). These points were summarised by one of our students as 'it forces you to do your analysis properly!'

The literature that evaluates CAQDAS raises issues associated with its use. CAQDAS programs vary in relation to the type and style of facilities that they offer and, therefore, potentially in their usefulness for different analytic situations. Consequently, you need to develop some familiarity with a range of programs to be able to evaluate their applicability for the particular analyses you wish to undertake. However, attempting to use CAQDAS may be problematic if the program you wish to explore is not readily available, although it is worth noting that some programs that may be suitable for your purpose are available to download as freeware and software producers offer free downloads of trial versions. Lewins and Silver (2009: 1) summarise the problem you may experience in evaluating which programs to invest time in to explore their potential use in analysing the data you collect:

> It is not always easy to visualise exactly what a CAQDAS package offers when exploring it for the first time yourself. Equally when asking someone else for their opinion, it is not always easy to know which questions you should be asking. Most of the software packages we are aware of and discuss regularly are excellent products in several ways. Sometimes you choose a package that is already in situ and make good use of it – but if you have a choice about which software to purchase for your research project, you may be in some uncertainty about how to proceed.

Functions

Despite differences between CAQDAS programs, the basic ways in which they can facilitate your qualitative data analysis are similar. Lewins and Silver (2009) summarise these as:

- *Structure of work:* all data files can be stored in or linked through a project file created within the software, allowing access to all elements of the project.
- *Closeness to data and interactivity:* by bringing data files together rapid access to any aspect of these data will be facilitated, increasing closeness to and interactivity with the data.
- *Explore the data:* allows data to be explored prior to coding and text search tools enable individual, or collections of, words to be searched and retrieved within context.
- *Code and retrieve:* offers scope to devise a coding scheme that is appropriate to the research approach to generate codes and subsequently to be able to retrieve, reflect on, re-code and output data, and generate themes from initial coding.
- *Project management and data organisation:* provides the means to manage the research project throughout its progress by being able to import any relevant files that are supported by the software and organise the qualitative data collected to facilitate analysis.
- *Searching and interrogating:* facilitates searching and interrogating the data set for a range of purposes including exploring the content of the data, linking and grouping codes, conceptualising and mapping themes, developing relationships and representing explanations.
- *Writing memos, comments, notes, etc.:* allow thoughts about the data and the research process to be recorded systematically.
- *Output:* produces reports allowing you to view material in hard copy or to export it to other applications such as word-processing and spreadsheet programs, as well as producing tabular reports, charts and graphical representations.

What is not apparent from this list is that the functions contained in some CAQDAS packages are better at supporting certain types of qualitative data analysis procedures than others. A wide range of qualitative data exists and your research may involve collecting one particular type or some combination of these. Text makes up a major type of qualitative data but this comprises different types such as documents, narratives

Box 13.17
Checklist

Choosing a CAQDAS package

✔ How much data do you have that needs to be analysed qualitatively?

✔ How important are these qualitative data in relation to any other data you have collected for your research project and will you want to integrate any quantitative data into the qualitative software package you use?

✔ What type(s) of qualitative data do you need to analyse: audio, documentary, narratives, transcripts or visual?

✔ How much time do you have to learn how to use the package?

✔ What is the timeframe for your research project?

✔ How much support is available in your university to help you learn to use the package?

✔ What is the operating system of your computer?

✔ How much memory does your computer have?

✔ Do you want software that will allow you to take an inductive, deductive or combined approach to your analysis?

✔ Do you want a package that will help you manage your thinking and assist you in developing your own codes?

✔ Do you want a package that will allow you to explore the way language is used in your data?

✔ Do you want a package that allows you to display relationships within your data diagrammatically?

✔ Do you want a package that will allow you to quantitatively describe the content of your data?

and transcripts, affecting what you wish to achieve through analysis. Audio, still images and video sources are also important types of qualitative data. This means that you may need to experiment with more than one package before you find the CAQDAS that meets your needs. Your final choice of CAQDAS package will be dependent on a range of factors, including, not least, the relative benefits you will gain relative to the time you need to invest to learn a CAQDAS program. These factors are summarised in Box 13.17 as a checklist.

Where you decide to use a CAQDAS program and have selected a package, you will need to familiarise yourself with it before you start collecting your data. This will avoid the problem of trying to learn the features of the package at the same time as you analyse your data, although you will of course continue to learn about these as you conduct this analysis.

Exploring the latest versions of CAQDAS

Published information about CAQDAS programs is likely to become out of date fairly quickly. Fortunately, there is a wealth of up-to-date information available from the CAQDAS Networking Project's website hosted by the University of Surrey.[1] If you are considering using CAQDAS, we would strongly recommend a visit to this website which, in addition to a wealth of useful articles, also contains web links to commercial software producers' sites including downloadable demonstration versions of the software. We would also advise you to explore the Internet sites of CAQDAS producers to obtain details and demonstrations of the latest versions of these packages and the features that they offer. Some of those most widely used are listed in Table 13.3.

---

[1]The Internet address for the CAQDAS Networking Project is http://www.surrey.ac.uk/sociology/ research/researchcentres/caqdas/.

Table 13.3 Internet addresses for a range of selected CAQDAS developers

Name	Internet address	Brief comments
ATLAS.ti	http://www.atlasti.com	Windows and MAC versions. Versatile and flexible. Supports multimedia
Dedoose	http://www.dedoose.com	Windows and MAC versions. Web-based application for analysis of mixed methods data by members of a research team in different locations
HyperRESEARCH	http://www.researchware.com	Windows and MAC versions. Simple to use. Case-based structure. Supports multimedia
Leximancer	https://www.leximancer.com	Windows and MAC versions. Content analysis software with a wide range of applications
MAXQDA	http://www.maxqda.com	Windows and MAC versions. Intuitive and easy to use. Mixed methods features. Supports multimedia. Content analysis features with addition of MAXDictio in MAXQDAplus
QSR NVivo	http://www.qsrinternational.com	Windows and MAC versions. Versatile with large range of searching possibilities. Supports multimedia
QDA Miner	http://www.provalisresearch.com	Windows and MAC versions. Mixed methods analytical capabilities. Supportive functionality. Content analysis features with addition of WordStat
Qualrus	http://www.qualrus.com	Windows version. May also run on MAC OS using a Windows virtual machine according to the www.ideaworks website. Uses artificial intelligence to offer suggestive coding based on learning from coding trends. Supports multimedia
Transana	http://www.transana.org	Windows and MAC versions. Specifically designed for qualitative analysis of audio, still image and video data. Ability to synchronise multiple video streams during playback and to synchronise playback with transcripts

Sources: Developed from QUIC Working Paper software reviews available from the CAQDAS Networking Project website hosted by the University of Surrey and/or software producers' websites. Each comment in this table only provides a very brief indication and is not intended to promote or discourage the use of a particular software program, or to advocate the use of one program over other compatible programs. You are advised to evaluate the features and applications of current versions of CAQDAS at the time of your project in relation to the requirements of research.

13.15 Summary 小 结

- Qualitative data are rich and full textual and/or visual data. They may also be characterised as non-standardised and as non-numerical data.
- A qualitative approach involves commencing your research from a deductive or inductive perspective.

- Data collection, analysis and interpretation are very much an interrelated and interactive set of processes in qualitative research. Analysis occurs during the collection of data as well as after it.
- Qualitative data need to be carefully prepared for manual or computer-assisted analysis, usually involving transcription where the spoken word is involved.
- There are a number of aids that you might use to help you through the process of qualitative analysis, including: interim summaries, event summaries, document summaries, self-memos, maintaining a research notebook and keeping a reflective diary or reflexive journal.
- There are several different approaches to analyse your qualitative data. In this chapter we discuss Thematic Analysis; Template Analysis; Explanation Building and Testing; Grounded Theory Method; Narrative Analysis; Discourse Analysis; Content Analysis; and Data Display and Analysis.
- The use of computer-assisted qualitative data analysis software (CAQDAS) can help you during qualitative analysis with regard to project management and data organisation, keeping close to your data, exploration, coding and retrieval of your data, searching and interrogating to build propositions and theorise, and recording your thoughts systematically.

Self-check questions 自测题

Help with these questions is available at the end of the chapter.

13.1 Why do we describe qualitative analysis as an 'interactive process'?

13.2 Which sorts of data will you need to retain and file while you are undertaking qualitative research?

13.3 How would you differentiate between a deductive and an inductive analytical approach?

13.4 What are the main implications of using a deductive analytical approach for the way in which you conduct the process of qualitative analysis?

13.5 What are the main implications of using an inductive analytical approach for the way in which you conduct the process of qualitative analysis?

Review and discussion questions 复习与讨论题

13.6 With a friend, use the extract of the interview transcript in Case 10 (at the end of Chapter 10) to undertake the following tasks.
  a Using the aim of the focus group stated in Case 10, independently code the data in the extract.
  b Compare the results of your coding.
  c Identify where your coding is similar to and where it differs from that of your friend.
  d Where you identify differences in coding, discuss the assumptions you each made when you coded these data and why you made these.
  e By reflecting on your attempt at coding these data, which codes, if any, would you change and why?

13.7 Visit one of the CAQDAS websites listed in Table 13.3. Find and download a demonstration version of the CAQDAS package and explore its features. How useful do you think this will be for analysing your research data?

13.8 Find out whether your university provides you with access to the NVivo™ CAQDAS. If it does, visit this book's companion website and download the self-teach package and associated data sets. Work through this to explore the features of NVivo™.

改进研究项目
Progressing your research project

定性地分析数据
Analysing your data qualitatively

- Undertake and audio-record an initial semi-structured or in-depth interview related to your research project, transcribe this interview, and make a few copies of your transcript. Alternatively obtain a copy of a relevant document.
- Decide whether it is most appropriate to summarise, categorise or develop a narrative using your data in order to answer your research question.
- Where a summary is most appropriate develop this, ensuring you also include contextual data.
- Where a narrative is most appropriate, develop this paying particular attention to the temporal order and the organisational and social contexts.
- Where categorising is most appropriate and your research project is based on a deductive approach, develop a provisional set of categories and codes from your research question and objectives, conceptual framework, research themes and initial propositions. Produce a description of each of these categories. Evaluate these categories to see whether they appear to form a coherent set in relation to the aim of your research.
- Using one of your transcripts, attempt to allocate units of data to appropriate categories by using CAQDAS or writing their code labels alongside the text in the left-hand margin. Again, evaluate this provisional set of categories and codes and modify any that appear to be inappropriate.
- Where categorising is most appropriate and your research project is based on an inductive approach, work through one of the transcript copies and seek to identify categories related to your research purpose. Allocate units of data to appropriate categories by using CAQDAS or writing appropriate code labels for these categories alongside the text in the left-hand margin. List these categories and their labels and produce a description for each of the categories that you have devised.
- Once you have allocated units of data to the set of categories, use the CAQDAS program to organise your data by different categories. Alternatively, cut out the units of data related to different categories and transfer them to an appropriately labelled index card (reference to the interview, location of the text in the transcript and the date and so forth). Read through the units of data within each category.
- Analyse these data by asking questions such as: What are the points of interest that emerge within each category? How will you seek to follow these up during your next data collection session? How does the material that has been revealed through this interview relate to any theoretical explanation or initial propositions with which you commenced your data collection? Are any connections evident between the categories?
- Produce a summary of the interview and attach it to a copy of the transcript. Memo any ideas that you have and file these.
- Repeat the procedures for the remaining qualitative data as appropriate and revise your ideas as necessary.
- Use the questions in Box 1.4 to guide your reflective diary entry.

Self-check answers 自测题答案

13.1 There are a number of reasons why we may describe qualitative analysis as an 'interactive process'. Analysis needs to occur during the collection of data as well as after it. This helps to shape the direction of data collection, especially where you are following a grounded theory approach. The interactive nature of data collection and analysis allows you to recognise important themes, patterns and relationships as you collect data. As a result, you will be able to re-code and re-categorise your existing data to see whether emergent themes, patterns and relationships are present in the cases you have previously analysed. In addition, you will be able to adjust your future data collection approach to see whether they exist in cases where you intend to conduct your research.

13.2 You will generate three sorts of data that you will need to retain and file as the result of undertaking qualitative research.

The first of these may be referred to as raw data files. A wide range of files potentially fit within this category. These include audio-visual recordings, documents, images, original notes, written up notes and transcripts you make or collect. Electronic and word-processed versions of these files may be contained in a computer-based project file.

The second of these is analytical files containing your coded and categorised data. Alternatively, this may contain your summary or your narrative. These may also be contained in a computerised project file.

The third of these may be referred to as a supporting file, or indeed it may be different files, containing working papers, self-memos, interim reports and so forth. Again, these may also be contained in a computerised project file. You are well advised to keep all of this until the end of your research project.

Eventually you will create a fourth type of file – containing your finished work!

13.3 A *deductive* analytical approach is one where you will seek to use existing theory to shape the approach that you adopt to the qualitative research process and to aspects of data analysis. An *inductive* analytical approach is one where you will seek to build up a theory that is adequately grounded in a number of relevant cases. The design of qualitative research requires you to recognise this choice and to choose an appropriate approach to guide your research project.

13.4 There are a number of implications of using a deductive analytical approach for the way in which you conduct the process of qualitative analysis:

- You will be in a position to commence your data collection with a well-defined research question and objectives and a clear framework and propositions, derived from the theory that you will have used.
- With regard to sampling, you will be in a position to identify the number and type of organisations to which you wish to gain access in order to undertake data collection to answer your research question and meet your objectives.
- The use of literature and the theory within it will shape the data collection questions that you wish to ask those who participate in your research project.
- You will be able to commence data collection with an initial set of categories and codes derived from your theoretical propositions/hypotheses and conceptual framework linked to your research question and objectives.
- This approach will provide you with key themes and patterns to search for in your data, and your analysis will be guided by the theoretical propositions and explanations with which you commenced

13.5 The main implications of using an inductive analytical approach for the process of qualitative analysis are likely to be related to:

- managing and categorising a large number of code labels, which will probably emerge from the data that you collect;
- working with smaller rather than larger units of data;
- recognising significant themes and issues during early analysis to help you to consider where data collection should be focused in the future;
- recognising the relationships between categories and rearranging these into a hierarchical form, with the emergence of subcategories;
- seeking to verify apparent relationships against the actual data that you have collected;
- understanding how negative cases broaden (or threaten) your emerging explanation;
- recognising the relationships between the principal categories that have emerged from this grounded approach in order to develop an explanatory theory;
- being rigorous in your use of the procedures that are advocated in order to be able to produce a research report that contains findings that are sufficiently 'grounded' to substantiate the analysis or theory that you are seeking to advance.

Get ahead using resources on the companion website at: **www.pearsoned.co .uk/saunders**.

- Improve your IBM SPSS Statistics and NVivo research analysis with practice tutorials.
- Save time researching on the Internet with the Smarter Online Searching Guide.
- Test your progress using self-assessment questions.
- Follow live links to useful websites.

Chapter **14**

Writing and presenting your project report 撰写和演示项目报告

Learning outcomes 学习目标

By the end of this chapter you should be able to:

- view the writing of your project report as an exciting prospect;
- write in such a way that you can reflect on all you have learnt while conducting the research;
- write a final project report that presents an authoritative account of your research;
- adopt an appropriate structure and style for the final project report;
- differentiate between a project report and a consultancy report;
- ensure that your report meets the necessary assessment criteria;
- plan and design an oral presentation of your project report.

14.1 Introduction 引言

Some of you may view the process of writing your project report and presenting it orally as an exciting prospect. However, it is more likely that you will approach this stage of your research with some trepidation. This would be a great pity. We believe that writing about your work is the most effective way of clarifying your thoughts. Writing may be the time when we think most deeply. This suggests that writing should not be seen as the last stage of your research but, as we illustrated at the start of this book in Figure 1.2, thought of as something that is continuous throughout the research process. In this way your project report may be seen as something you develop throughout your research rather than leaving it until every other part has been completed.

Writing is a powerful way to learn. Most teachers will tell you that the best way to learn is to teach. This is because of the necessity to understand something thoroughly yourself before you can begin to explain it to others. This is the position you are in as the writer of your project report. You have to explain a highly complex set of ideas and findings to an audience that you must assume has little or no knowledge of your subject. There is another problem here, which has a parallel with teaching. Often, the more familiar you are with a subject, the more difficult it is to explain it to others with no knowledge of that subject. You will be so familiar with your research topic that, like the teacher, you will find it difficult to put yourself in the place of the

reader. The result of this is that you may fail to explain something that you assume the reader will know. Even worse, you may leave out important material that should be included.

However, why do most of us view writing with such concern? This may be because of our experience of writing. Many of us are afraid of exposing our efforts to an audience that we feel will be more likely to criticise than encourage. In our education much of our writing has been little more than rehashing the ideas of others. This has taught us to think of writing as a boring, repetitive process. Some of us are impatient. We are unwilling to devote the time and energy (and inevitable frustration) that is needed for writing.

This fear of criticism is captured perfectly by Richards (2007), who recites the story of being asked by the distinguished sociologist Howard Becker to adopt his method of sitting down and

If you have ever thought about visiting London, you will have a list of places that you would like to visit. One that is on many people's list is the Tower of London. This is a complex of historical buildings dating from the twelfth century, which has served a number of purposes, including being a royal palace and fortress. Parts of the Tower of London have also been a prison and visitors to the Tower see 'attractions' including Traitors' Gate, the Bloody Tower, Torture at the Tower and the Scaffold Site. During the reign of England's Tudor kings and queens, important prisoners were held in the Beauchamp Tower. In the Prisoners' Room on the first floor of this tower you will see an extraordinary collection of graffiti carved into its walls. Unlike much modern graffiti these are carefully preserved as an historical record of those who were imprisoned there. These political and religious prisoners carved not only their names but also statements about their situation and their innocence.

If they had been alive today these prisoners would have wanted to send emails, instant messages and tweets and to use a range of social media to bring attention to their plight and to represent their points of view. Increasingly our world is being connected through the use of these media, so that individuals can talk, share information and coordinate their activities. Even in the isolation of a prison in a tower our ancestors sought to express themselves through carving words in a wall. Today we have many more

The White Tower, Tower of London
Source: © Mark Saunders 2015

means to express ourselves by writing to others. The speed with which we can write and communicate with others means that we are likely to take writing for granted, without seeing this as something to be fearful about.

writing what came into her head about the research she had done without even consulting her notes. Her fears of producing poor-quality material, which would be derided by colleagues who saw her work, are described vividly. It is a fear most of us experience. Set against this, most of us write a lot more than we imagine. We all have thoughts that we want to express and the desire to write about these has always been common, as the opening vignette illustrates. This vignette should be interpreted as giving you the confidence to write, even when you do this for formal reasons, rather than being fearful about writing.

This chapter looks at a number of issues that may concern you as you write your report. As we have discussed, undertaking writing remains a concern for many of us. In this chapter we begin by looking at some general issues about undertaking writing (Section 14.2). Section 14.3 focuses on a key issue about your project report – how to structure it. This section recognises that your research approach and research strategy may affect the way in which you wish to structure your project report; it discusses alternative ways to do this. Section 14.4 also focuses on structure, related to composing a consultancy report for an organisational audience.

Structural issues continue to be important after you have devised an overall structure for your project report. In Section 14.5 we look at some ways in which you may make the content of your report clear and accessible to your readers. Also critical to your ability to produce a clear and accessible project report will be your writing style. In Section 14.6 we offer some ideas about how to develop an appropriate writing style for your project report. Underpinning your choice of structure, the way in which you compose the content of your report and the writing style you use will be your concern to meet the criteria established to assess your work. In Section 14.7 we consider some generic criteria that often inform the specific criteria set by examining institutions to assess project reports.

In addition many universities also require a reflective essay or statement as part of your project report. This can be developed from the entries you have made in your reflective diary throughout the research process when answering the questions in Box 1.4 (Section 1.5). We consider this in Section 14.8. For many of us the fear of making an oral presentation is even more daunting than writing. As we note in Section 14.9, some of this apprehension can be overcome by thorough preparation and this section examines the preparation and delivery of the oral presentation.

14.2 Undertaking writing 着手撰写

Writing may be approached as a continuous process throughout your research project. Before you commence your research, you will need to draft your research proposal. As you undertake your research you will be writing summaries, self-memos or entries in your research notebook and keeping a reflective diary, as we outlined in Sections 1.5 and 13.5. You may also be consulting literature related to your research topic and drafting an early version of your literature review, and then revising this as your research progresses.

Approaching the task of writing as a continual process throughout the research project may be helpful to you in different ways. It should help to progress the task of producing your project report, dissertation or thesis and avoid the perception that this is a monumental chore to be undertaken at the final stage of your project. It should also help to focus your thoughts and aid your analysis. We now consider some practical hints to assist you in undertaking your writing.

Create time for your writing

Writing is not an activity that can be allocated an odd half-hour whenever it is convenient. It requires sustained effort and concentration. Some people prefer to write all day until they drop from exhaustion! Others like to set a strict timetable where three or four hours à day are devoted to writing. You may find it helpful to set aside a particular period each day to write. Writing on successive days will also help to ensure the continuity of your ideas and avoid having to keep 'thinking your way back' into your research.

Write when your mind is fresh

Writing is a creative process so it is important to write at the time of day when your mind is at its freshest. All of us have jobs to do that require little or no creativity so arrange your day to do uncreative jobs when you are at your least mentally alert.

Find a regular writing place

Writing is often best undertaken in the same place. This may be because you are psychologically comfortable in a particular space. It may be for more practical reasons. If that space is your own room you will already be familiar with the need to make sure you do not disturb yourself or allow others to do this. Switching off all distractions such as your mobile phone, social media and television and putting a 'do not disturb' sign on the door may allow you to work undisturbed in your own room. However, if this doesn't work, you may be able to concentrate better if you find a neutral space, such as an area in your university's library, where you can write without your possessions or your friends being able to distract you! What is important is to know what distracts you and to remove those distractions.

Create a structure for your writing

Writing requires structure. Your research project is likely to be the largest piece of written work you undertake. We discuss ways in which you may create an overall structure to write up your research project in Section 14.3. You will also need to create a structure for each chapter.

Box 14.1
Focus on student research

Devising an outline structure

Andrea found the task of writing each part of her project report to be demanding. She started her literature review in the early stages of her research project. She felt that this early attempt lacked coherence and development. She returned to the planning phase of her literature review and mapped her ideas using some mind mapping software.

This process provided her with a number of discrete ideas from the literature related to her research question that she wanted to include in her review. She worked on the order of these ideas until they matched the flow of her research objectives. This provided her with an idea or ideas for each section of her review. She then devised headings for each section and for the various sub-sections. She now had the 'skeleton' or framework of her literature review. This provided Andrea with an outline structure to start to write her literature review and she now worked on each section in turn.

The wording of some these headings changed, as did the order of some of the subheadings. However, she found the creation of this type of outline structure or framework to be very helpful, both in terms of facilitating her writing and providing targets to complete, such as a section in a given period. She used the same approach to write each of the other parts of each project report.

It is important to think about what you want a chapter to contain before you attempt to write it. As you work though the materials you have assembled to write a chapter and jot down ideas that flow from this, you will start to work out how these ideas and materials may be grouped and how such groupings may be related to one another. Your purpose will be to create a sequential structure for the chapter you intend to write up.

Once you have a structure for the chapter composed of a number of sections and possibly sub-sections, you can start to write each section in turn. Even if you alter this structure or rearrange the order of the sections within it, you will have a framework to guide the writing of the chapter on which you are working (Box 14.1).

Set goals and achieve them

Writing may involve goal or target setting. You may decide to set yourself the goal to write a section of a chapter in a given period, or to target writing a number of words. This can be helpful where you have allocated yourself a certain amount of time to write the chapter on which you working, to be able to judge if you are 'on time'. However, it is important to be realistic about these goals. If you are too ambitious the quality of your work may suffer as you rush to meet your target.

Finish a writing session on a high point and provide a link to a new session

Writing is about ideas. Many writers prefer to get to the end of a section before they finish writing so that they do not lose any ideas they have developed during that session. This also allows them to tidy up one set of materials and to lay out the set for the next session of writing. The worst thing you can do is to leave a complex section half completed as it will be difficult to pick up your thoughts and ideas (Box 14.2).

Ensure you keep multiple copies of your work

Writing is time-consuming and enables you to develop your ideas and complete your analysis, so don't forget to keep multiple copies of your work in which you have invested so much effort (Box 14.3)!

Box 14.2
Focus on student research

Getting restarted

Veronika always tried to complete a section or sub-section within a writing session. This allowed her to concentrate on a set of ideas without interruption. When she did not have time to complete a section or sub-section, she made notes about her ideas to act as an aide-mémoire for her next writing session.

Veronika also found it useful to start a writing session by reading the section on which she had worked previously. Her mind was very 'clear' at the start of a new writing session and she was able to read and improve her previous work. This also had the benefit of refreshing her thoughts about what she had completed previously and directing her thoughts about what she wanted to achieve next.

Box 14.3
Focus on student research

'Help, I've lost my research project'

Ross had heard of cases where others hadn't been able to submit their assignments because of computer problems. He had always found his course demanding and wondered how he would cope if the same happened to him.

This made him determined to keep at least one backup copy of every document that he created or altered. It would be disastrous if he lost any of his files without these being backed up. He very carefully followed the same routine every time he worked on his project. At the end of every session working on his project, he backed up files he had worked on or new files he had created on to a USB mass storage device that he kept specifically for his research and on the cloud. On every Sunday afternoon he also emailed all of his project files to himself.

Some weeks into his project he encountered a problem with the Netbook that he used for all of his work. He took it along to the Students' Union, where there was an IT shop. They examined the machine and told Ross that his solid state drive had failed. Ross was annoyed and shocked by this. This was another expense for Ross to have the component replaced. This left him feeling pretty low. He was reassured, however, because his work had been carefully filed and fully backed up.

Get friends to read your work

Writing is creative and exciting, but checking our work is not. The importance of getting someone else to read through your material cannot be overemphasised. Your project tutor should not be the first person who reads your report, even in its draft form.

Ask a friend to be constructively critical. Your friend must be prepared to tell you about things in the text that are not easy to understand – to point out omissions, spelling, punctuation and grammatical errors. Overall, your friend must tell you whether the piece of writing makes sense and achieves its purpose.

This is not an easy process for you or your critical friend. Most of us are sensitive to criticism, particularly when the consequence of it is the necessity to do a lot more work. Many of us are also hesitant about giving criticism. However, if your project report does not communicate to the reader in the way it should, you will get it back for revision work in the long run. It is much better to try to ensure that this does not happen.

14.3 Structuring your project report 构造你的项目报告

Choosing a structure to write up your research project

There are different ways to structure a project report, dissertation or thesis. The way you write up your project report may follow the traditional structure or an alternative structure that better reflects your choice of research strategy. Whether you have a choice about how to structure your project report will depend on the requirements of your examining body. This may be something you can discuss with your research project tutors.

Charmaz (2006) refers to the traditional way to structure a project report as a 'logico-deductive' approach. In this way, the report's structure reflects the logic and linear nature of the process used to undertake a deductive approach (Figure 14.1).

There are two ways in which alternative structures vary from the traditional structure, related to the order and nature of the report's content. Firstly, in relation to order,

Abstract

Introduction

Literature review

Methodology/Method

Findings/Results

Discussion

Conclusion

References/Bibliography

Appendices

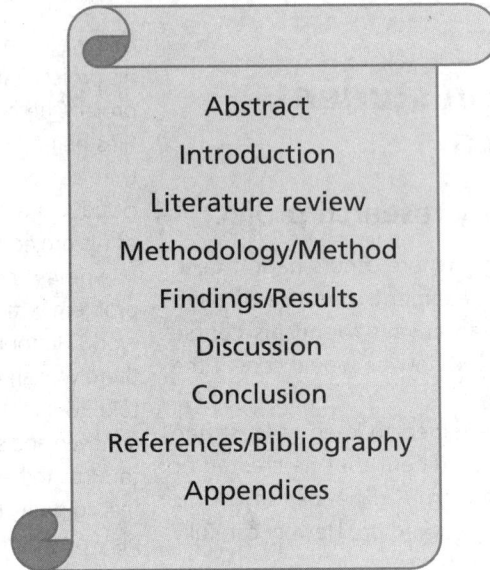

Figure 14.1 The traditional (logico-deductive) project report structure

content may be arranged differently, or in a more integrated way, to that of the traditional structure. For example, rather than placing the Literature Review immediately after the Introduction, as is the case in the traditional structure, it may be considered later in an alternative structure, or integrated throughout the report. Secondly, in relation to the nature of content, the material in the report will vary, perhaps so much so that the content of an alternative structure may seem, on face appearance, to bear little or limited resemblance to that of the traditional structure.

It would be unwise to suggest that a specific report structure should be used for a particular research strategy. Researchers using the same research strategy write up their work using different structures. They may choose to use the traditional structure (Figure 14.1), variations on this, or an alternative structure. However, inductive and abductive approaches are sometimes associated with alternative ways of presenting and structuring a project report. As you consider different ways to structure your project report, it is important to realise the structure you use will emphasise (or reflect) certain aspects of your research. Yin (2014) usefully summarises six underlying 'reporting approaches' in terms of what they emphasise or reflect. These are: linear-analytic; comparative; chronological; theory building; suspense; and unsequenced. We outline the first five before discussing the traditional and alternative ways to structure your research report.

Linear-analytic approach

In a linear-analytic approach a project report is structured to logically reflect the research process. The traditional way to structure a project report is essentially a linear-analytic approach. It is well suited to a deductive, theory-testing approach but is also adaptable to other research approaches.

Comparative approach

In a comparative approach the emphasis is placed on devising a structure that allows analytical comparisons to be made. Different types of comparisons may be made. In one type of comparative approach, the structure used will reflect the fact that the same set of data is analysed more than once using different analytical perspectives to allow the results of these analyses to then be compared. In another type of comparative approach, the structure will reflect the fact that different but related data sets are analysed so that the results of these may then be compared.

Chronological approach

In a chronological approach a structure is devised that allows the emphasis to be placed on the sequence of events evident in the data set. At its simplest, this is essentially an historical account, where it is important to use a structure that allows the data to be reported in a chronological way to understand how the order of events and contextual factors produce cause-and effect sequences.

Theory-building approach

In a theory-building approach a structure is devised that allows the emphasis to be placed on the emergence of data collection and analysis, the refinement of research ideas and the development of themes, relationships and explanations. Whereas the linear-analytic approach presents the research process in a logical, rational and 'sanitised' way, the theory-building approach is likely to present research as an emergent and messy process but which ultimately produces a convincing story and compelling theoretical explanation. This approach may resemble a chronological approach, albeit that it reports how a theory is developed rather than documenting the sequential development of explanations.

Suspense approach

In a suspense approach, the emphasis is placed on devising a structure that allows the reader to understand how an explanation has been built. Yin (2014) suggests that the explanation or answer to the research question is presented in the introduction. The structure of the project report is then devoted to exploring alternative explanations of the phenomenon being studied to be able to evaluate why the chosen explanation is the most convincing.

How might these underlying structural types affect your choice of report structure?

These reporting approaches should help you to evaluate what type of structure will best suit your project report. They should prompt you to ask yourself the following questions:

- How does my research design affect the way I might structure my project report?
- How does the way I analysed my data affect the way I might structure my project report?
- How does the purpose of my research affect the way I might structure my project report?

These and other questions you may wish to ask yourself will help you to evaluate these approaches to choosing a structure for your project report. They may also be used in combination and you may wish to devise a structure that incorporates elements from more than one approach.

Your answers to these questions may lead you adopt the traditional structure to write up your project report, or to seek to adapt this structure, or to use an alternative structure. Whichever structure you wish to adopt, you will first need to check that this will meet two requirements. Firstly, is it permissible? Will your awarding body allow you to use the structure you devise? You may be able to discuss this with your project tutor. Secondly, will it be clear to those who will read your project report, to allow them to understand what you have done, and will it allow you to show how you have sought to answer your research question. Where you are able to exercise some choice about how to structure your project report, you will need to think about this second requirement carefully to ensure that your proposed structure is fit for purpose.

Characteristics of the traditional structure

The traditional structure generally contains the following parts: Abstract; Introduction; Literature Review; Method; Findings/Results; Discussion; Conclusions; References; Appendices. Some of these parts are likely to be required irrespective of the structure you use to write up your project report. These include an Introduction and Conclusions, even if these are titled differently, as well as an Abstract, References and any appendices. The substantive parts in between these are likely to vary when you use an alternative structure in relation to an inductive research strategy such as Action Research, a Case Study, Ethnography, Grounded Theory or Narrative Inquiry, as we go on to discuss later.

Abstract

The **Abstract** is a short summary of the complete content of the project report. It often contains four short paragraphs with the answers to the following questions:

1 What were my research questions, and why were these important?
2 How did I go about answering the research questions?
3 What did I find out in response to my research questions?
4 What conclusions do I draw regarding my research questions?

A good Abstract should be short (generally between 300 and 500 words); self-contained; a reflection of the report's content; adequate to inform your reader about the report; objective, precise and easy to read.

The academic publisher, Emerald, gives advice to potential academic authors on how to compile an abstract. This is shown in Box 14.4. Although referring to academic journal articles (papers), it is useful to consider in terms of preparation of your research report. Writing a good abstract is difficult. The obvious thing to do is to write it after you have finished the report. We suggest that you draft it at the start of your writing so that you have got your storyline abundantly clear in your mind. You can then amend the draft when you have finished the report. Box 14.5 contains an example of a short abstract (200 words) by Mark, Graham Dietz and Adrian.

Introduction

The **Introduction** should give the reader a clear idea about the central issue of concern in your research and why you thought that this was worth studying. It should also include a full statement of your research question(s), research aim and research objectives. If your research is based in an organisation, we think that it is a good idea to include some details about the organisation, such as its history, size, products and services. This may be a general background to the more specific detail on the research setting you include in the method chapter.

It is also important to include a 'route map' to guide the reader through the rest of the report. This will give brief details of the content of each chapter and present an overview of how your storyline unfolds. You will probably find it helpful to write the Introduction

Box 14.4
Focus on management research

Advice on the preparation of an abstract for publication

Abstracts should contain no more than 250 words. Write concisely and clearly. The abstract should reflect only what appears in the original paper.

Purpose

What are the reason(s) for writing the paper or the aims of the research?

Design/methodology/approach

How are the objectives achieved? Include the main method(s) used for the research. What is the approach to the topic and what is the theoretical or subject scope of the paper?

Findings

What was found in the course of the work? This will refer to analysis, discussion or results.

Research limitations/implications (if applicable)

If research is reported on in the paper this section must be completed and should include suggestions for future research and any identified limitations in the research process.

Practical implications (if applicable)

What outcomes and implications for practice, applications and consequences are identified? How will the research impact on the business or enterprise? What changes to practice should be made as a result of this research? What is the commercial or economic impact? Not all papers will have practical implications.

Social implications (if applicable)

What will be the impact on society of this research? How will it influence public attitudes? How will it influence (corporate) social responsibility or environmental issues? How could it inform public or industry policy? How might it affect quality of life? Not all papers will have social implications.

Originality/value

What is new in the paper? State the value of the paper and to whom.

Source: Emerald Group Publishing (2014) 'How to... write an abstract'. From The Emerald website, www.emeraldgrouppublishing.com/authors/guides/write/abstracts.htm. Reproduced with permission.

after drafting the rest of your report to ensure that it accurately represents the report's content.

Literature Review

Chapter 3 deals in detail with the writing of a literature review. In the traditional, logico-deductive structure this is placed before the Method chapter. The main purpose of your Literature Review is to set your study within its wider, theoretical context so the reader understands how your study relates to the work that has already been done on your topic. The Literature Review will directly inform your research questions (see Box 14.6) and any specific hypotheses or propositions that your research is designed to test. These hypotheses or propositions will also suggest a particular research approach, strategy and data collection techniques.

The title of your literature review chapter should reflect the content of the chapter and we recommend that you do not call it simply 'Literature Review'. It may be that

Box 14.5
Focus on management research

Abstract from a refereed journal article

'This article provides an empirical test of whether trust and distrust can co-exist in the mind of an employee. Two interrelated questions are considered: firstly, whether trust and distrust judgements are 'symmetrical' or whether they can occur 'simultaneously' as separate constructs; and, secondly, whether trust and distrust judgements entail the same or conceptually different expectations as revealed in their expressions and anticipated manifestations. Using a concurrent mixed-method design incorporating a structured card sort and in-depth interviews, data were collected from 56 participants in two organizations. The card-sort findings offer little support for the co-existence of trust and distrust, but suggest they could be separate constructs. Interview data indicate that participants do perceive trust and distrust as entailing different sets of expectations and having different manifestations, providing some support for the 'separate constructs' thesis. We also find evidence of two new combinations of weak levels of trust and distrust not previously specified. The findings highlight how employees' trust and distrust judgements are shaped, in part, by managerial actions and policies relating to quality of communication and job security. They also emphasize how, when employees are distrustful, different practice interventions may be needed to reduce distrust from those used to build trust.'

Source: Mark N.K. Saunders, Graham Dietz and Adrian Thornhill, (2014) 'Trust and distrust: polar opposites, or independent but co-existing?', *Human Relations*, Vol. 67, No. 6, p. 639. Reproduced with permission.

Box 14.6
Focus on student research

Using the literature review to inform the research questions

Guiyan was a Chinese student studying for a master's degree. In her research dissertation she was interested to know whether Chinese managers would be able to conduct performance appraisal schemes effectively in China with Chinese employees. She was aware that there were certain aspects of Chinese culture that would make this difficult. Guiyan studied two bodies of literature: one relating to the managerial skills of performance appraisal, and a second concerned with the effects of Chinese culture on the ways in which Chinese managers manage their employees.

She presented both in a literature review chapter. She structured her chapter around three questions:

1 What are the key skills needed by managers to conduct performance appraisal effectively?
2 What are the most important aspects of Chinese culture which impact upon on the ways in which Chinese managers manage their employees?
3 To what extent will the aspects of Chinese culture, explained in the answer to Question 2, affect the ability of Chinese managers to conduct performance appraisal effectively?

From this, Guiyan developed a theoretical proposition that supported her initial idea that certain aspects of Chinese culture would make the conduct of performance appraisal by Chinese managers with Chinese employees difficult. She was then ready to move on to her method chapter, which was an explanation of the way in which she would test her theoretical proposition.

your literature is reviewed in more than one chapter. This may be the case, for example, where you were using more than one body of literature in your research.

Method

This should be a detailed and transparent chapter giving the reader sufficient information to understand why you chose the method you used, to assess the reliability and validity of the procedures you used, and to evaluate the trustworthiness of your findings. Box 14.7 provides a checklist of the points you should include in the Method chapter.

Findings/Results

This provides you with the opportunity to report your results and is probably the most straightforward part of your report to write. In a quantitative study you will include the results of your statistical analyses and use tables and graphs to illustrate your findings (do not put these in the appendices if they are important to your argument). In a qualitative study you will include the results of your qualitative analysis. You may also

---

Box 14.7 Checklist

Points to include in your method chapter

Setting
- What was the research setting?
- Why did you choose that particular setting?
- When was the research carried out?

Sample selection and research informants/participants/respondents
- How were those who took part selected and why?
- How many took part and why?
- What were their characteristics and how do they relate to the research question?
- What were the characteristics of those who refused to take part?

Data collection materials and practice
- Which existing questions/scales/interview or observation schedules/questionnaires were used and why?
- How were purpose-made instruments developed and why?
- How were these used to collect data: (1) what instructions were given to those from

whom data were collected; (2) how many questionnaires were delivered or interviews/observations conducted and why; (3) how long did each questionnaire/interview/observation take to complete?

Data analysis procedures
- How were the resulting data analysed?
- Have you ensured that procedures (including statistical techniques) were applied correctly and, where appropriate, assumptions satisfied?

Reliability and validity
- Have you explained how you sought to ensure internal reliability and provided an adequate account of your method to facilitate external reliability?
- Have you assessed the validity of the measures you used in the research?
- Have you assessed the internal validity of your results?
- Have you assessed the external validity/generalisability of your findings?
- Have you recognised the limitations of your research?

Ethical concerns
- Which ethical issues were raised by the study, and how were these addressed?

consider including illustrative quotations as a way to convey the richness of such data and to convey with penetrating simplicity a difficult concept you wish to explain. The Findings/Results may be composed of more than one chapter. The question you should ask yourself is: 'Is more than one chapter necessary to communicate my findings/results clearly?'

There are two important points to bear in mind when writing about your findings. The first is to stress that the purpose is to present the results of your data analysis. It is normally not appropriate in this chapter to discuss these results. This is the purpose of the Discussion and Conclusions chapters. Many of us become confused about the difference between findings and discussion. One way of overcoming any confusion is to draw up a table with two columns. The first should be headed 'What I found out' and the second 'What judgements I have formed on the basis of what I found out'. The first list will be based on your data analysis (e.g. 66 per cent of responding customers indicated they preferred to receive email messages rather than mail shots) and therefore the content of your Findings/Results. The second list will be your judgements based on what you found out (e.g. it appears that electronic forms of communication are preferred to traditional) and therefore the content of your Discussion chapter.

The second point links to the first. Drawing up a table will lead you to a consideration of the way in which you present your findings. The purpose of your project report is to communicate the answer to your research question in as clear a manner as possible to your readers. Therefore you should structure your findings in a clear, logical and easily understood manner. There are many ways of doing this. One of the simplest is to return to the research objectives and let these dictate the order in which you present your findings. Alternatively, you may prefer to report your findings thematically. You could present the themes in descending order of importance. Whichever method you choose should be obvious to the reader. As with the Literature Review, the chapter(s) devoted to results should be titled in an interesting way that reflects the content of findings.

The clarity of your findings should be such that they may find their way into a news report similar to that in Box 14.8.

Discussion

Findings presented without thought run the risk of your reader asking 'so what?': what meaning do these findings have for me?; for my organisation?; for professional practice?; for the development of theory? So the main focus of the Discussion is to interpret the results you presented in the previous chapter. You should state the relation of the findings to the research questions or objectives discussed in the Introduction. In addition, the Discussion should discuss the implications of your research for the relevant theories which you detailed in your Literature Review. It is usual to discuss the strengths, weaknesses and limitations of your study. However, it is not a good idea to be too modest here and draw attention to aspects of your research which you may consider to be a limitation but that the reader is unlikely to notice!

The Discussion is where you have the opportunity to shine. It will show the degree of insight that you exhibit in reaching your conclusions. However, it is the part of the report that most of us find difficult. It is the second major opportunity in the research process to demonstrate real originality of thought (the first time being at the stage where you choose the research topic). Because of that, we urge you to pay due attention to the Discussion. Crucially, here you are making judgements rather than reporting results, so this is where your maturity of understanding can shine through.

Box 14.8 Focus on research in the news

High pay does not equal high quality

By Ruth Sullivan

The argument that higher pay leads to the selection of better senior executives is a familiar one, particularly for shareholders contesting dizzyingly high bonuses at this season's annual general board meetings.

However, two academics, Philippe Jacquart, assistant professor of leadership at French business school EMLyon, and Scott Armstrong, professor of marketing at Wharton at the University of Pennsylvania, argue in a paper to be published this autumn that high pay not only fails to promote better performance but can harm productivity.

"There is no evidence that massive financial incentives attract the best talent," says Mr Jacquart, who believes the "job itself should be sufficient motivation". Not only are financial incentives unnecessary but they can be counterproductive. "Financial incentives fill up your entire thinking space, preventing you from focusing on other things or being open to ideas," he argues.

Although excessive pay may lure candidates to a particular job, there is no guarantee the most talented person will get it. Mr Jacquard believes the recruitment process itself is flawed, often undermining the incentives of high financial reward.

"Recruiters [the board of directors] are not good at hiring because they cannot work out who are the best candidates, as many biases come into play," he argues.

These include too much emphasis on past performance, personal recommendations and the use of unstructured interviewing techniques where candidates are asked different questions, making meaningful comparisons difficult.

Mr Jacquart suggests radical solutions are called for, such as abandoning current high incentive remuneration practices and reducing senior executive pay across industries, not just in the banking sector.

Closing the pay ratio gap would be a good starting place, he says. "The gap between the highest and lowest paid employees is ever widening," he adds.

If several companies agreed to lower remuneration packages, proving over a few years it was not harmful to business, then it would bring about change, he argues. But he believes it will take a large shareholder to drive such reform.

FT *Source:* Extracts from 'High pay does not equal high quality', Ruth Sullivan (2013) *Financial* Times, 20 May. Copyright © 2013 The Financial Times Ltd.

Conclusions

This chapter should not be used to present any new material and should be a conclusion to the whole project (not just the research findings). Check your Conclusions using the questions in Box 14.9.

You may find that the clearest way to present your Conclusions is to follow a similar structure to the one used in your Findings/Results. If that structure reflects the research objectives then it should make certain that your conclusions would address them. Drawing up a matrix similar to that in Figure 14.2 may help you in structuring your Findings/Results and Conclusions. The result should be a clear statement of conclusions drawn similar to that shown in Box 14.9.

An alternative approach to the matrix is to draw a 'mind map' (see Section 2.3), which places the findings randomly on a blank page and links conclusions to these findings by way of lines and arrows. For some of you this may be a more creative approach, which enables you to associate groups of findings with conclusions and vice versa.

Box 14.9 Checklist

Do your conclusions answer these questions?

- ✔ Did the research project meet your aim or answer your research question(s)?
- ✔ Did the research project meet your research objectives?
- ✔ What are the main findings of the research?
- ✔ Are there any recommendations for future action based on the conclusions you have drawn?
- ✔ Do you have any overall conclusions on the research process itself?
- ✔ Where should further research be focused? (Typically this will consider two points: firstly, new areas of investigation implied by developments in your project, and secondly, parts of your work which were not completed due to time constraints and/or problems encountered.)

Answering the research question(s), meeting the objectives and, if appropriate, supporting or refuting the research hypotheses or propositions is the main purpose of the Conclusions. This is where you will consider the findings presented in the previous chapter. You should also return to your literature review and ask yourself 'What do my conclusions add to the understanding of the topic displayed in the literature?'

It may be that there are practical implications of your findings. In a management report this would normally form the content of a chapter specifically devoted to recommendations. We suggest that you check your assessment criteria carefully to establish whether this is expected. In the reports that students are required to prepare on some professional courses this is an important requirement. For some academic degree programmes it is not required.

Even if you do not specify any practical implications of your research you may comment in the Conclusions chapter on what your research implies for any future research. This is a logical extension of a section in the Conclusions that should be devoted to the limitations of your research. These limitations may be about the size of sample, the snapshot nature of the research, or the restriction to one geographical area of an organisation. Virtually all research has its limitations. This section should not be seen as a confession of your weaknesses, but as a mature reflection on the degree to which your findings and conclusions can be said to be generalisable.

Research questions	Results (what factual information did I discover in relation to the specific research questions?)	Conclusions (what judgements can I make about the results in relation to the specific research questions?)
What are the operational differences between different shifts in the production plant?	Cases of indiscipline in the last six months have been twice as frequent on the night shift as on the day shift	The night shift indiscipline problems may be due to the reluctance of operators to work on this shift

Figure 14.2 Using a matrix in the planning of the content for the results and conclusions chapters

References

A range of conventions are used to reference other writers' material that you have cited in your text. (Appendix 1 illustrates three of the most popular of these, the Harvard, footnotes and American Psychological Association (APA) systems.) However, we suggest that you check your project assessment criteria to establish the system that is required for your project report, as many universities require their own variation of these systems.

It is a good idea to start your references section at the beginning of the writing process and add to it as you go along. It will be a tedious and time-consuming task if left until you have completed the main body of the text. If you do leave it until the end, the time spent on compiling the reference section is time that would have been better spent on checking and amending your report.

At the start of your report you must acknowledge all those who have contributed to your research (including your project tutor!). In addition, you should ensure that you have cited in your reference section all those sources to which you have referred in the text. In order to avoid charges of plagiarism you should also ensure that all data and material taken verbatim (that is copied exactly) from another person's published or unpublished written or electronic work is explicitly identified and referenced to its author (see Neville 2010 and Section 3.9) giving the page numbers(s) of the copied material if possible. This also extends to work which is referred to in the written work of others. Even if this work is not quoted verbatim, the originator should be cited in your references. If you are in any doubt about this it is important that you consult your university's guidelines on how to ensure that you do not plagiarise. The proliferation of online material now is such that all academic institutions are very mindful of plagiarism and will almost certainly check your work carefully.

Appendices

In general, **appendices** should be kept to the minimum. If the material in an appendix is crucial to your reader's understanding, then it should be included in the main body of your report. If, on the other hand, the material is 'interesting to know' rather than 'essential to know' then it should be in the appendices.

Often students feel tempted to include appendices to 'pad out' a project report. Resist this temptation. Your readers will not be reading your report for relaxation. They will be pressed for time and will probably not look at your appendices. Your project report will stand or fall on the quality of the main text.

However, your appendices should include a blank copy of your questionnaire, interview or observation schedule. Where these have been conducted in a language different from that in which you write your submitted project report you will need to submit both this version and the translation.

Recommendations

You may have wondered why we make little reference to recommendations in the report structure. In the typical management report or consultancy report (discussed later) this may be the most important section. The hard-pressed executive reading your report may turn to your recommendations first to see what action needs to be taken to tackle the issue.

Whether you include a recommendation section depends on the objectives of your research. If you are doing exploratory research you may well write recommendations, among which will be suggestions for the pursuit of further research. However, if your research is designed to explain or describe, recommendations are less likely. For example, the research question 'Why do small engineering companies in the UK reinvest less of their profits in their businesses than their German counterparts?' may imply clear points for action.

However, strictly speaking, recommendations are outside the scope of the research question, which is to discover 'Why?' not 'What can be done about it?' The message is clear. If you want your research to change the situation that you are researching, then include the need to develop recommendations in your research objectives.

Characteristics of alternative structures

Our purpose in this section is to consider how your choice of an inductive or abductive research strategy may affect the way in which you structure your project report. It is not to suggest that there is a specific way to structure your report when you use a particular strategy. Instead we look at the implications of using different strategies for structuring your project report, dissertation or thesis. The strategies whose implications we consider are Action Research, Case Study, Ethnography, Grounded Theory and Narrative Research. The implications of using these strategies may affect the structure of a project report, dissertation or thesis in one of two ways. It may lead you to use a report structure that is different to the traditional one or to use a report form that appears to be the same as or similar to the traditional structure, but where some sections within it are constructed differently. This is particularly likely to be the case with regard to the main body of the report (i.e. the 'Literature Review', 'Method' and 'Findings' in the traditional structure), as we outline in the sub-sections that follow.

You may be reading this at the time you are writing up your project report, dissertation or thesis. You may initially decide to read only the sub-section that relates to your research strategy. If so, we would advise you instead to read all of the following sub-sections. In writing this material, we found that it didn't really make sense to construct a single section offering ideas about alternative reporting structures for inductive and abductive research approaches. There are two related reasons for this. First, there are clear differences between research strategies that use an inductive or abductive approach, with different implications for reporting structures. Second, literature has developed for each research strategy about how to write up such a study. While our decision results in some repetition or patterning across these sub-sections, we advise you to read through all of these as there may be ideas that are relevant and helpful to you in a sub-section that does not relate to your choice of research strategy.

Action Research

Action Research is very different to traditional, deductive research (Section 5.5). This is likely to have implications for the way you structure your Action Research project report. Given that the traditional structure is suited to reporting a logico-deductive approach, where prior theory is used to determine research hypotheses or propositions, which are then tested before being analysed and reported in a linear manner, there must be doubts whether this type of structure will be adequate to present the complexity of, and learning from, an Action Research project.

In Section 5.5 we outlined how Action Research is both emergent and iterative. It commences in a specific context, guided by an initial research question and works through several stages or cycles. Each cycle of the research involves a process of diagnosing or constructing issues, planning action, taking action and evaluating action. Learning from each cycle may lead to the focus of the question changing as the research develops. Your Action Research is likely to involve at least three such cycles. In this way, Action Research differs from other research strategies because of its explicit focus on action related to multiple stages of research. Your task in writing up this research will therefore be to devise a structure that allows you to report and evaluate this process without losing any of its richness and emergent character.

While your report will contain an Introduction and a Method (Box 14.7), the construction of these and subsequent sections will be affected by your choice of an Action Research strategy. Those who read your report will be interested to know about the context within which this Action Research project occurred and to understand why this strategy was chosen. In this way, you need to explain the setting within which this research occurs and to justify why this strategy was the most appropriate one to use. This will help to establish the credibility of using this research approach and help your readers make sense of what is to follow. Explaining about context may mean that you dedicate a chapter to this in your report, or you may decide to incorporate discussion of context within another chapter. Justifying your choice of an Action Research strategy and establishing the credibility of this approach will become an important part of the Method. Action Research is a participative form of research (Section 5.5) and this aspect is also relevant to consider in both your discussion of the context and method.

In our discussion of the traditional structure we noted the role of the Literature Review. In writing up deductive research the Literature Review is placed logically after the Introduction and before the Method. Theory in the existing literature is used to help to devise the research hypotheses or propositions that are subsequently tested in this approach. In an inductive or abductive approach, literature plays a different role. In Action Research, as in the other inductive or abductive approaches discussed in this section, different strands of literature become relevant at different points in this type of emergent research process. In your report you may initially wish to use literature for the following reasons. As part of your discussion of the context of your project you may wish to begin to locate your study within existing knowledge by referring to published studies that relate to your research. This may help to establish the reason for undertaking your project and why you chose to use Action Research. You will also use literature about the theory and practice of Action Research in your Method to demonstrate your understanding of this research strategy. However, unless you are obliged to include a unified Literature Review early on in your report structure, it is likely that you will need to introduce further strands of literature later in your report, as you interpret and discuss the themes which emerge from your Action Research. We return to this later in this sub-section.

The emergent nature of Action Research involving multiple stages of research is likely to mean it is inappropriate to present one section of 'findings' as is the case in the traditional structure. An alternative approach is likely to be required to present the main body of an Action Research project report. Coghlan and Brannick (2014) refer to the need to tell the story of an Action Research project. They suggest that this part of your report may first present an account of each of the Action Research cycles in your project. This will mean following a chronological approach. The purpose of this will be to provide a clear outline of the research process and its principal events. At the end of each section or chapter describing a particular cycle or stage of your Action Research, they suggest including a section of interpretation that seeks to make sense of these events and starts to theorise about them. Coghlan and Brannick (2014) state that it is important to separate description from sense-making in order to provide clarity and to help to establish the rigour and credibility of your research. While stressing the importance of separating description from sense-making, they also advise that it is important to locate the section of interpretation at the end of, or close to, the description of those events, to help readers understand the direction and flow of your work.

Following this part of the report, Coghlan and Brannick (2014) suggest the inclusion of a chapter that allows your interpretations to be drawn together into a general discussion, to allow you to make sense of the project as a whole. It will be at this stage that you will need to return to the literature to understand how your attempts to theorise about its outcomes relate to prior theory. As this is an emergent process it will be more authentic to introduce and discuss new strands of literature, which only become obvious to consult after undertaking Action Research, rather than attempting to hide this by producing a unified literature review that is placed early in the report to imply that all literature was consulted before research commenced! Your purpose in using this literature will be to say how your Action Research links to existing knowledge, how it may be applied in other contexts and possibly how it contributes to Action Research theory and practice. The latter part of your report is also likely to include your personal reflections about having participated in an Action Research project and an account of your learning from this experience, such as questioning your assumptions and developing skills related to participation and process (Section 14.8).

Case Study

When considering how to structure a report based on case study research, you will need to reflect on how you used this research strategy. First, was the purpose of your case study research designed to be descriptive, exploratory, explanatory or evaluative? Second, was your case study research based on a deductive, inductive or abductive approach? Third, was your case study research based on a single case or multiple cases? Fourth, did you analyse your case study or studies holistically, as whole units, or did you analyse separate analytical units within each case, such as different groups of staff or functions within a case study organisation? The purpose, nature and analysis of, and approach to, case study research is likely to affect the way in which you wish to structure your project report.

Where the purpose of your case study research is descriptive and explanatory, and you use a deductive approach, it may be appropriate to use the traditional report structure described earlier. Where the purpose of your case study research is exploratory (at least initially) and you use an inductive approach, it may be more appropriate to use an alternative structure for your project report. An alternative structure may be particularly relevant where your case study strategy incorporates Action Research, Ethnographic Research, a Theory-Building Approach or Narrative Research.

Two points are relevant here in relation to the report structure. The first relates to being able to express the reality of your research process and the way in which you analysed your data. Using an inductive or abductive approach (Section 4.4) means that the conduct of your research will follow an emergent and incremental direction. In some case-based analytical approaches you will preserve the emergent and incremental nature of your research process. This will be the case when you use Analytic Induction. Analytic Induction involves successively selecting cases to be able to develop and test an explanation related to the phenomenon being studied (Section 13.8). Where you use an analytical approach that preserves the incremental nature of your research process, you may find it helpful to devise a report structure that allows you to emphasise the chronology of your research and findings, so that those who read your work can understand what you did and make a judgement about the quality of your research and conclusions. In some other inductive or abductive research methods, such as Thematic Analysis,

Template Analysis and Grounded Theory Method, the emergent and incremental nature of the research process tends to be subsumed during analysis. While data are collected incrementally in these strategies, the nature of analysis means that these data are merged into the categories and themes being used to analyse them. In this approach you will probably find it helpful to devise a structure that allows you to report your research in a way that emphasises themes or theory building.

The second point relates to the place of literature and the role of theory. In an inductive research approach it is likely that the emergence of themes during data analysis will lead you to consult new strands of literature. You will be seeking to make sense of your data and relate it to existing literature. This involves a different way of working to that implied by the traditional report structure, where the Literature Review is placed after the Introduction and before the Method because in a deductive approach the theory in literature is used to construct the research hypotheses or propositions that are subsequently tested. An inductive research approach has implications for the place of literature and it may be helpful to include more than one review of literature in your report structure where you use an inductive or abductive research approach. This may take the form of a review of the initial literature you consulted before embarking on data collection and analysis, and a later, subsequent review of literature you consulted to help to make sense of the themes that emerged from your data. It will also be important to demonstrate how your use of literature has allowed you to relate your emergent theory to existing theory. This will allow you to explain how your findings contribute to knowledge about your research subject. This suggests that it will be important to explain how you used literature throughout your research when you use an inductive or abductive approach and the structure of your report will need to reflect this.

The inclusion of a single case or multiple cases and the way in which this case or these cases are analysed will also affect the way in which you structure your project report. A traditional report structure may best suit a single case analysed as a whole unit. A case study strategy using a single case which requires embedded analytical units within it to be analysed separately, or one that includes multiple cases, suggests using a reporting structure that allows these different analytical units or cases to be compared. This may lead to the inclusion of separate chapters or sections in your report to describe the results from, or story of, each case or analytical unit. It will also be likely to necessitate the inclusion of a chapter that compares the results or stories from each case or analytical unit. Alternatively, you may choose a structure where the emphasis is placed on theory building using a cross-case analysis. In this type of report structure, each case or analytical unit is only considered in relation to the other cases or analytical units being reported and is not described and discussed separately (Yin 2014).

The structure you use will also require description of the context of the case study or case studies in your research. This contextualisation will not only describe the characteristics of the case or cases but also establish its or their importance. It will be important to establish whether and how the case or cases you selected for your research are critical, extreme, typical or unique (Chapter 7.3). Where you use multiple cases it will also be important to establish whether the cases you included in your research have comparative power because they represent the same contextual variables (e.g. three marketing departments in the same industry), a similar contextual variable under different conditions (e.g. four finance departments in different industries), or different contextual variables under similar conditions (e.g. a small, medium and large enterprise operating in the same industry). However, while case study research requires a structure that permits the context of the case study to be described and its analytical importance to be established, it will be important to make sure that the structure you choose maintains an appropriate balance between description, analysis and interpretation.

Ethnography

As we noted in Section 5.5, ethnography literally means a written account of a people or group. In this way ethnography is best seen as the product of research (Watson 2011). Many ethnographies published in academic journals broadly reflect the structural outline of the traditional structure (i.e. they include an introductory section, review of contextual literature, method, main section, discussion and conclusions). However, a closer reading of ethnography reveals that its content and the conventions used to write it are different to those in a typical deductive research report. Watson (2011: 205–6) defines ethnography as a 'style of social science writing which draws upon the writer's close observation of and involvement with people in a particular social setting and relates the words spoken and the practices observed or experienced to the overall cultural framework within which they occurred'.

Van Maanen (2011a) also emphasises the textual nature of ethnography and the role of writing style in its composition, although he sees it as being composed of several styles. These styles result from the ways in which different characteristics of ethnographic research come together in practice. These characteristics include:

- the philosophical position of the research (e.g. critical realist or interpretivist);
- the relative emphasis on description, interpretation and theoretical development in the ethnography;
- whether the author of an ethnography writes herself or himself into the text (using the first person, 'I' or 'me');
- the inclusion or exclusion of reflexivity in an ethnography;
- the way in which participants or informants are referred to and their 'voice' is expressed in the ethnography (e.g. directly by quoting them or indirectly through the author's version of events); and
- the ways in which language and imagery are used in an ethnography (e.g. using 'thick' descriptions, metaphors, tropes, illustrative examples and dramatic representations).

The purpose and nature of ethnographic research will affect how these characteristics join together, with implications for the way in which ethnography is written and also for the way it is structured.

In an influential work, recently republished and updated, Van Maanen (2011b) discusses several styles of writing ethnography. We outline some of these here (Table 14.1). These descriptions are necessarily very brief. Our purpose in outlining them is not to suggest that a particular style is associated with a specific way of structuring an ethnographic report. Rather it is to recognise that each style will have implications for the content and therefore the structure of the resulting ethnography. Where you are going to write an ethnographic report we would recommend you to read Van Maanen (2011b). We also refer you to the earlier discussion of ethnography in Section 5.5.

Grounded Theory

It is possible to write up a Grounded Theory research project using the traditional structure, described earlier. However, use of this traditional structure flags up a number of issues. We briefly examine these in turn. In a Grounded Theory study, the research

Table 14.1 Categories of ethnographic writing

Account	Description
Realist	In a realist account the researcher does not write her/himself into the text and uses a detached documentary style where emphasis is placed on reporting in detail the actions and viewpoints of those being observed. The author uses his/her authorial position to interpret the data and to theorise about their meanings. 'Facts' are presented by the researcher to support her/his interpretation
Confessional	In a confessional account much greater emphasis is placed on the role of the researcher and how the research was conducted. It uses a highly personalised style of writing. When this style is used in a complete ethnography, the content will therefore reflect not only cultural descriptions but also the researcher's reflections about being there as witness or participant. This may also be embedded in another style of ethnography as an account of the methods used or as a reflective appendix
Critical	In a critical approach fieldwork is intentionally conducted within a culture affected by particular political, economic, social or technological factors, allowing the effects of these to be studied on those affected. This account commences from a theoretical framework (often a radical one) and the report will place as much emphasis on theory and theorising about the meanings in the data, as on reporting ethnographic details
Formal	In a formal account the purpose is to develop or test a theory. It places emphasis on theoretical considerations and de-emphasises description and contextualisation in the resulting ethnographic account
Structural	This is a development from and merger of critical and formal accounts with an emphasis on analysis and conceptualisation, focusing on a cultural process and incorporating first-person reporting. The resulting account blends observational reporting and theoretical explanations
Post-structural	A post-structural approach is based on a social constructionist perspective emphasising multiple interpretations. This type of account stresses uncertainty about what can be known and is inevitably inconclusive
Advocacy	In an advocacy approach fieldwork is focused on a particular issue or cause, on which the researcher takes a stance, putting forward this point of view clearly in the account produced. This is therefore one of those accounts of an ethnography that is unlikely to be appropriate for you to use, not least because theory is only likely to be used in a partial way where it supports the stance being advocated

Source: Developed from Van Maanen (2011b) with additional comments by the authors

question is likely to be subject to refinement, initially being broad or fuzzy and later becoming much more focused. The initial literature consulted is unlikely to be the only literature used and will not be used to develop research hypotheses or propositions, as is the case in a deductive research approach. Initial literature will instead be used to contextualise the research and perhaps to identify weaknesses in existing knowledge about the topic. New strands of literature will subsequently be consulted to understand how the grounded theory fits within existing theoretical perspectives. The method will also be likely to develop incrementally as the research progresses, so it may also be difficult to produce a unified draft of this that implies it was a predetermined and straightforward process. Writing up 'findings' will not simply be a case of reporting the equivalent of the results from statistical analyses and displaying these, as is the case in a quantitatively based research report. The focus of a Grounded Theory study should do exactly what it says: devise a theory grounded in the data. The 'findings' therefore need to go further than simply saying what was 'found'. The report needs to demonstrate not only what the grounded theory is but also how it was developed in order to produce a convincing explanation. Subsequently, the discussion needs to consider the relationship of this grounded theory to existing theory and how it contributes to the generation or refinement of knowledge. This raises an issue about how the continued use of literature should be reviewed in a Grounded Theory study. In summary, the concern about using the traditional structure to report a Grounded Theory study is that its incremental, iterative and emergent nature will be lost by being rearranged and 'cleaned up' to fit a logico-deductive form! This may mean that a theory is proposed without being demonstrably grounded in the data and analytical processes that gave rise to it.

A Grounded Theory report should seek to preserve 'the form and content of the analytic work' that leads to it (Charmaz 2006: 151). The purpose of a Grounded Theory project is to build theory and this analytical approach needs to be emphasised through the structure of the report. In order to preserve the form and content of the process and to emphasis its analytical nature it may therefore be useful to incorporate a chronological approach into the structure of your Grounded Theory project report. Where your research follows the Grounded Theory Method of Strauss and Corbin (1998), for example, you can adopt a report structure that allows you to outline the relationships you developed between categories during axial coding and then how you integrated these categories during selective coding. By also exploring the circumstances when these relationships appear to make sense and those when they do not, you should be able to demonstrate how and why you developed your grounded theory to produce a convincing explanation about the conditions under which it applies and those when it does not.

In a deductive research approach you develop a theoretical framework which you then test. In a Grounded Theory approach your theoretical framework is developed from the data you collect and analyse. The structure of your report will need to allow you to demonstrate how you developed your theoretical framework. The process of writing your report is also likely to allow you to continue to develop your analysis. You may not fully appreciate the analytical potential of your data until you start to write about them! For these reasons, you should find it helpful to devise a structure that preserves the analytical processes you have been engaged in, continues to encourage the development of your analysis, emphasises how it developed and evaluates it with the intention of demonstrating to your readers that your grounded theory is convincing.

Such a structure should allow you to describe the development of your analysis and grounded theory before outlining how you returned to the literature to review theoretical perspectives that relate to your grounded theory. Where you have no choice but to use the traditional structure, you may nevertheless be creative in the way you use the standard elements of this approach (e.g. Introduction, Literature Review, Method, Findings/Results and Discussion) to ensure that your Grounded Theory project report emphasises the required qualities of being analytical, developmental and theoretical.

Narrative

Writing up a Narrative Research project may take a number of forms. Unless a particular form such as the traditional structure is prescribed, you may find that you are advised to reflect on how you might write up your study rather than being told how to do this. This is because the reporting of Narrative Research lends itself to structural experimentation. How you structure your Narrative Research project report may be influenced by the following factors:

- your purpose in using a narrative approach;
- the nature of the narratives you collect; and
- the type of Narrative Analysis you undertake.

We discuss these and consider how they may affect report structure.

In general, the use of a narrative strategy will have implications for report structure. As we noted in Section 5.5, this research strategy preserves chronological connections and the sequencing of events. It enables events, the activities that compose these and their consequences to be analysed as a whole. It is associated with 'thick descriptions' of contextual detail and social relations.

More specifically, basing your Narrative Research strategy on one participant, a few participants or many participants will each be likely to affect the way in which you wish to structure your report. Your research may be based, for example, on the narrated account of one entrepreneur. In this case your structure will need to include a description of this person and a rationale for choosing her or him as your research participant. Your structure may then adopt either a chronological, event-based or thematic approach, emphasising the way this life story develops, or focusing on key events or particular themes drawn from the narrated account. Your structure may need to accommodate lengthy quotations from your participant. You will also need to interpret how this narrated account relates to wider contextual factors and to include a theoretical evaluation that draws on relevant literature.

Your research may instead be based on narrative accounts from, say, three or four participants. This choice will necessitate including a description of these participants, the context within which they operate and a rationale for choosing them. You may then decide to devote a section to each of these narrated accounts followed by a discussion that draws them together and relates themes from these accounts to relevant theories in the literature. Alternatively, you may decide to use a structure that presents a cross-narrative analysis. In this approach you would focus on key events or themes drawn from across these narrated accounts. This is likely to involve a comparative approach, which emphasises perceptions about the same event as seen from different perspectives. This approach may involve devoting a section to each theme or event you consider within which you incorporate description, interpretation and theoretical evaluation.

These examples also illustrate how the nature of the narratives you collect may affect the structure of a project report. A contrast may be drawn between extended narratives, such as those we have just considered, and short narratives, which comprise storied segments of text you collect from conducting interviews or observations. The structure of a project report is likely to be shaped around the use of an extended narrative or narratives. A narrative structure provided by the sole narrator or by a small number of narrators may influence not only the analysis of the data provided but also the form that the report adopts. This relationship is less likely where you are dealing with a larger number of short narratives, if only because there will be many more options available to you in terms of how you seek to combine and present these narratives and the data they contain. In this case, the role of the researcher as analyst and presenter is likely to be more dominant in terms of shaping the structure of the project report.

The type of Narrative Analysis you undertake may also affect the structure you devise for your project report. In Section 13.10, we discussed two analytical approaches: Thematic Narrative Analysis and Structural Narrative Analysis. The themes you derive during Thematic Narrative Analysis may provide you with a means to structure the sections of your project report that present your analysis and discussion. Where you undertake Structural Narrative Analysis you will be interested in the way a narrative or dialogue is constructed, to examine how use of language affects others or influences the course of an interaction. This research approach may be based on prior theory, so it may be appropriate to use a traditional (logico-deductive) report structure. In any case, it is likely that you will use examples of dialogue in your analysis and theoretical evaluation, so you will need to devise a structure to accommodate the reporting of these.

A final note about the length of the project report

You will probably have guidelines on the number of words your project report should contain. Do stick to these. However interesting your report, your tutors will have others to read, so they will not thank you for exceeding the limit. Reports that exceed the word limit are usually excessively verbose. It is more difficult to be succinct. Do not fall into the trap of writing a long report because you did not have the time to write a shorter one.

为不同的读者写报告

14.4   Writing reports for different audiences

In the previous section we discussed different ways to structure your project report. This may mean using the traditional structure for your report, or using a different structure that allows you to tell the story more clearly about the way in which you conducted your research and developed a theory. This section considers the situation that some of you may face, which is the need to write two reports about your research, each of which may require a different structure! Many researchers of management topics face the dilemma of having to write for more than one audience. In addition to the academic audience, who will mark and grade your report for a degree or a diploma, it may be necessary to prepare a report for the management of your employing or host organisation, who will be interested in the practical benefit of your research findings.

The academic report will usually be much longer and contain contextual description that the organisational audience does not require. Similarly, those managers reading the report will probably be less interested in the literature review and the development of theory than the academic audience. They will, however, be interested in recommendations for future action and these will need to be written into the organisational version.

Fortunately, word processors make the job of compiling more than one report relatively easy. Some careful cutting and pasting along with subsequent careful proofreading will be necessary. However, what should always be kept in mind is the audience that each specific report is addressing. Take care not to fall between two stools. Each report will need to be structured so that its content and style are suitable for its respective audience. Having discussed structures for academic project reports earlier, in the next sub-section we include a brief discussion on structuring and writing consultancy reports.

The consultancy report

You will need to consider a number of key questions as you plan a consultancy report. These include:

- Who will read your consultancy report?
- What information and level of detail will they expect?
- How will they expect the report to be presented?
- How much knowledge will they already have?
- For what purpose will the report be used?
- What key messages and recommendations do you want to impart?

As with your academic project report structure, you will have a choice about how to present this consultancy report. A simplified version of the traditional structure may be appropriate, such as:

- Executive summary;
- Introduction;
- Background and method
- Results/Findings;
- Recommendations;
- References;
- Appendices.

Irrespective of the structure you use, you should avoid presenting a partial point of view and selecting only those data that support it. Where the analysis of your data lead to a complex situation suggesting alternative courses of action, you will need to devise a structure that allows you to convey these messages to the organisational audience who will read your report. Writing a consultancy report does not mean that you should produce an inferior account of your research. We recall occasions when we have presented consultancy reports to various management teams: in these situations you can always expect to be asked a range of astute and relevant questions!

Decisions about what to include in (and, just as importantly, to exclude from) the report requires care. Only information that is essential to management should go in the main body of the report; any information that is 'important' or 'of interest' should be relegated to appendices. Your readers may be short of time and want only essential detail. That said, the management reader will be interested in the background to the project and in how you carried out the research. You may therefore expect to be questioned about your research methods. But the key purpose of the report is often to provide management with clear justified recommendations. Recommendations equate with action, and managers are paid to act! As with the academic report, division of the report content into logical sections with clear subheadings will lead management through the report and show them where to find specific topics.

The Executive Summary is likely to be the part of the report on which managers will concentrate. It is important that it can stand alone and that it contains real information, including hard facts and figures. If your report includes recommendations, the executive summary should make it clear what these are and include their implications, values and costs. As with the abstract, the executive summary should be short (no more than two pages) and designed to get your main message across.

One final point may be made about the writing style of the consultancy report. The reader will not appreciate long words, complicated language, 'management speak' or a multitude of acronyms and abbreviations. If it is necessary to use complex technical terms, make sure you provide a glossary as an appendix.

As well as composing two written reports you may have to present one or both of these orally. In the final section (14.9), we turn our attention to their oral presentation.

14.5 Making the report's content clear and accessible 使报告的内容清晰可读

The discussion in the previous two sections focused on devising an overall structure for your report or reports. In this section we make some general comments about the content of your report, irrespective of the structure you devise for it. These comments focus on the importance of choosing a title, making sure you tell a clear story throughout your report and using simple devices to make sure that your readers are able to get all of the information out of your report that they need.

Choosing a title

A good title is one that has the minimum possible number of words while describing the content of the report accurately (Day and Gastel 2011). Try choosing a title and then ask a colleague who knows your subject what they think the title describes. If their description matches your content then stick with your title.

Tell a clear story

Be prepared for your project tutor to ask you 'What's your main storyline?' Your storyline (your central argument or thesis) should be clear, simple and straightforward. It should be so clear that you can stop the next person you see walking towards you and tell that person what your project report's storyline is and he or she will say 'Yes, I understand that'. This is where writing the abstract helps. It forces you to think clearly about the storyline because you have to summarise it in so few words.

Another way of checking to see whether your storyline is clear is to 'reason backwards'. An example of this is a project report that ends in clear conclusions. Start by explaining your conclusions to a tutor. This invites the question from that tutor: 'On what basis do you draw these conclusions?' Here your answer is, of course, on the findings that you established. The next question asked by the tutor is: 'How did you arrive at these findings?' in response to which you explain your method. The tutor may counter by asking you why she should take any notice of your findings. The response to this is that you took care to design a research strategy that would lead to valid and reliable findings. Moreover, that research strategy is based on a clear research question and objectives and a detailed review of the relevant literature. Such 'reasoning backwards' is a useful check to see not only whether your storyline is clear but also that it stands up to logical analysis.

Helping the reader to get all the information out that they need
Dividing your work

One of us once received the first draft of a 20,000-word project report that had virtually no divisions except the chapters. It was like looking at a road map that did not include any road numbers or towns. It was just as difficult to find your way around that report as it would be to journey between two cities using a townless road map. The content of the project report seemed fine. However, it was hard to be sure about this because it was so difficult to spot any gaps in the ground it covered. What were needed were some signposts and some town names. Do not think about how you can put in all your information. Instead, concentrate on helping the reader to get all the information out (Box 14.10).

The message is simple. Divide your work in such a way that it is easy for readers to find their way round it and for them always to be clear where they are, where they have come from, and where they are going. To do this you may find it helpful to return to the matrix idea in Figure 14.2. You will see that each column of the matrix represents the broad content of a chapter. The cells indicate the way in which the chapters may be divided. Each division may have a subdivision.

We hope you have noticed that we have employed a similar system in this book. Each chapter section is identified by a heading made up of large, bold characters. The subheadings use slightly smaller, bold lettering, and further divisions of the content of a sub-section are denoted by bold, italicised characters. There are various textual and numerical ways of organising and signposting text. It is not important which way you do this as long as your approach is consistent and it helps the reader around the report and matches the ways specified by your examining institution.

Previewing and summarising chapters

A further way in which you can signpost your work is to 'top and tail' each chapter. This is to include a few words at the beginning of the chapter that provide a description of how the chapter is to contribute to answering the research question, the methods used in this part of the study, and the points that are covered. At the end of each chapter it

Box 14.10 Focus on management research

Developing a storyline

The article by Palmer (2013) published in the *California Management Review* that we featured in the opening vignette in Chapter 6 provides an example of writing that demonstrates a very clear storyline. Palmer's subject is wrongdoing in organisations – unethical behaviour that can be costly in a number of ways. People are offended by such behaviour and may act by taking their custom elsewhere. It may also have adverse consequences for individuals in the organisation who are implicated in unethical behaviour. Having introduced

common perceptions about organisational wrong-doing and its possible implications, Palmer's article is structured into four sections, each containing a key part of the storyline.

Section 1

Here Palmer outlines the dominant view of organisational wrongdoing: that it is atypical, citing four commonly held reasons for this view.

Sections 2 & 3

Here Palmer reviews new research that believes unethical behaviour in organisations may be more common and normal than we might think, outlining four reasons for this emerging view.

Section 4

Here Palmer discusses a number of implications for managers.

is useful if the reader has a brief summary of the content of the chapter and a very brief indication of how this content links to the following chapter. This may seem like repetition. However, it helps the reader on her or his journey through your report and ensures that you, the writer, are on the correct road.

Tables and graphics

Your reader will find your project report more accessible and easier to read if you present some of your data and ideas in tables and graphics. It is not only numerical data that can be presented in tables. You can also present ideas that can be easily compared. Table 13.1 is an example of this.

Do not be tempted to put your tables in the appendices. They will probably be some of your most important data. Include them and comment on them in the text. Your commentary should note the significance of the data in the tables. It should not simply describe the table's contents.

Section 12.3, and in particular Box 12.8, provides details on the design and presentation of tables and diagrams. A final note of caution should be sounded. To avoid confusing your reader, do make sure that, wherever possible, you have introduced the table or diagram before it appears in the text.

形成恰当的写作风格

14.6 Developing an appropriate writing style

Much of your concern in writing your project report will be about what you write. In this section of the chapter we ask you to think about the way you write. Your writing style is just as important as the structure and content of your report. That said, it is often observed that good writing cannot substitute for flawed thinking (Phillips and Pugh 2010). In fact, the clearer the writing the more flawed thinking is exposed. However, poor writing can spoil the effect of good-quality thought.

Clarity and simplicity

> The . . . lack of ready intelligibility [in scholarly writing], I believe, usually has little or nothing to do with the complexity of the subject matter, and nothing at all to do with profundity of thought. It has to do almost entirely with certain confusions of the academic writer about his own status . . . To overcome the academic prose you first of all have to overcome the academic pose.
>
> Wright Mills (1970: 239–40)

Each Christmas, Mark accompanies his Christmas cards with a family newsletter. It is written in a simple, direct and friendly manner that is easy and enjoyable to read. Few of the project reports we read are written in such a simple, direct manner. They are more elaborate in their explanation: they use difficult words where Mark's family newsletter would use simple ones. They adopt the academic pose.

Phil tells a story that reinforces the point made by Wright Mills in the above quotation. He was asked by a student to comment on her thesis in progress, which was about the impact of a particular job advertising strategy. He thought that it was written in an over-elaborate and 'academic' way. After many suggestions for amendments Phil came across a sentence that explained that the strategy his student was studying 'was characterised by factors congruent with the results of a lifestyle analysis of the target market'. Phil thought that this was too wordy. He suggested making it simpler. His student examined the sentence at length and declared she could see no way of improving it. Phil thought that it could say 'it was a strategy that matched the lifestyles of those at whom it was aimed'. His student protested. She agreed it was shorter and clearer but protested that it was less 'academic'. We think that clarity and simplicity are more important than wishing to appear 'academic'. Your project report is a piece of communication in the same way as Mark's Christmas newsletter.

Phillips and Pugh (2010) advise that you should aim to provide readers with a report that they cannot put down until 2.00 a.m. or later for fear of spoiling the flow. (If you are reading this chapter at 2.30 a.m. we have succeeded!)

Write simple sentences

A common source of lack of clarity is the confusing sentence (see Box 14.11). This is often because it is too long. A simple rule to adopt is: one idea – one sentence. Try reading your work out loud. If your sentences are too long, you will run out of breath!

Avoid jargon

Jargon should not be confused with technical terminology. Some technical terms are unavoidable. To assist your reader, it is best to put a glossary of such terms in the appendices. However, do not assume that your reader will have such a full knowledge as you of the subject and, in particular, the context. Here, and in all cases, try to put yourself in the position of the reader. Phil makes this point to students who use organisations as

Box 14.11
Focus on student research

Writing clearer sentences

Consider the following sentence:

While it is true to say that researchers have illusions of academic grandeur when they sit down to write their project report, and who can blame them because they have had to demonstrate skill and resilience to get to this point in their studies, they nonetheless must consider that writing a project report is an exercise in communication, and nobody likes reading a lot of ideas that are expressed in such a confusing and pretentious way that nobody can understand them, let alone the poor tutor who has to plough through it all to try and make some sense of it.

There appear to be at least six separate ideas in this sentence. It contains 101 words (when marking, we sometimes come across sentences with over 150!).

In addition, it contains a common way of introducing multiple ideas into a sentence: the embedded clause. In the sentence above the embedded clause is '. . ., and who can blame them because they have had to demonstrate skill and resilience to get to this point in their studies, . . .' The give-away is the first word in the sentence: 'While'. This invites an embedded clause. The point here is that potentially rich ideas get buried in the literary undergrowth. Dig them up and replant them. Let them flourish in a sentence of their own.

The sentence needs to be clearer and simpler. However, it should not lose any of its meaning. Halving the number of words and dividing up the sentence into smaller, clearer sentences results in the following:

Researchers have illusions of academic grandeur when they write their project report. This is understandable. They have demonstrated skill and resilience to reach this point in their studies. However, writing a project report is an exercise in communication. Nobody likes confusing and pretentious writing that is difficult to understand. Pity the tutor who has to make sense of it.

vehicles to write assignments. He asks them to 'mark' past (anonymous) assignments. They are usually horrified at the assumptions that their fellow students make about the tutor's prior knowledge of the organisation.

What can be avoided is the sort of jargon that *The Free Dictionary* (2014) defines as 'gibberish' and 'debased language'. You will know the sort of phrases: 'ongoing situation'; 'going down the route of'; 'at the end of the day'; 'the bottom line'; 'at this moment in time'. It is not just that they are ugly but they are not clear and simple. For example, 'now' is much clearer and simpler than 'at this moment in time'.

Beware of using large numbers of quotations from the literature

We believe that quotations from the literature should be used infrequently in your project report. Occasionally we receive draft projects that consist of little more than a series of quotations from books and journal articles that a student has linked together with a few sentences of her or his own. This tells us very little about the student's understanding of the concepts within the quotations. All it shows is that he or she has looked at the book or journal article and, it is hoped, can acknowledge sources correctly! In addition, by using quotations in this way the student's line of argument tends to become disjointed and less easy to follow. It is therefore usually better to explain other people's ideas in your own words.

That is not to say that you should never use quotations. As you have seen, we have used direct quotations from other people's work in this book. Rather we would advise you to use them sparingly to create maximum impact in supporting your storyline.

Check your spelling and grammar

Spelling is still a problem for many of us, in spite of spellcheckers. A spellchecker will not correct your 'moral' when you wished to say 'morale' or sort out when you should write 'practise' rather than 'practice'. This is where the friend who is reading your draft can help, provided that friend is a competent speller. Tutors tend to be more patient with errors of this kind than those that reflect carelessness. However, the point remains that spelling errors detract from the quality of your presentation and the authority of your ideas.

Avoiding common grammatical errors

Grammatical errors threaten the credibility of our writing. In Table 14.2 we outline 10 of the most common errors, most of which, with some careful checking, can be avoided. It is not our intention here to conduct an English grammar lesson. Some of the common errors in Table 14.2 are self-explanatory.

You may argue that the **split infinitive** is not often thought of as an error these days. However, 'to boldly go' ahead with your project report ignoring this rule risks irritating your reader – something you can ill afford to do. You want the reader to concentrate on your ideas.

Day's 'dangling participle' warning is amusingly illustrated by the draft questionnaire shown to us by a student. This asked for 'the amount of people you employ in your organisation, broken down by sex'. The tutor had written: 'We haven't got people in that category: they've not got the energy when they work here!'

Some of the more obvious grammatical errors you can spot by reading your text aloud to yourself. You need not know the grammatical rules; they often just sound wrong.

Table 14.2 Ten common grammatical errors

Often we write	The correct way is
Each pronoun should agree with their antecedent	Each pronoun should agree with its antecedent
Just between you and I, case is important	Just between you and me, case is important
A preposition is a poor word to end a sentence with	A preposition is a poor word with which to end a sentence
Verbs has to agree with their subject	Verbs have to agree with their subject
Do not use no double negatives	Do not use double negatives
Remember to never split an infinitive	Remember never to split an infinitive
When dangling, do not use participles	Do not use dangling participles
Avoid clichés like the plague	To avoid clichés like the plague!
Do not write a run-on sentence it is difficult when you have got to punctuate it so it makes sense when the reader reads what you wrote	Do not write a run-on sentence. It is difficult to punctuate it so that it makes sense to the reader
The data is included in this section	The data are included in this section

Source: Developed from Day (1998: 160)

Person, tense and gender

Traditionally, academic writing has been dry and unexciting. This is partly because the convention has been to write impersonally, in the past **tense** and in the **passive voice** (e.g. 'interviews were conducted following the analysis of questionnaires').

The writer was expected to be distanced from the text. This convention is no longer as strong. It is now a matter of preferred style rather than rules. The research approach and strategy that informs your methods may dictate your choice of **personal pronoun**. We noted earlier that one feature of positivism is that 'the researcher is independent of, and neither affects nor is affected by, the subject of the research', so that an impersonal style is appropriate. (By contrast, Section 9.2 notes that the participant observer 'participates in the daily life of people under study'.) The researcher is an intrinsic part of the research process. Use of the first person seems more logical here. However, style is important. Use of the term 'the author' sounds too impersonal and stilted. In contrast, excessive use of 'I' and 'we' may raise questions in your readers' minds about your ability to stand outside your data and to be objective.

Day (1998) identifies rules for the correct use of tense. He suggests that you should normally use the present tense when referring to previously published work (e.g. Day identifies . . .) and the past tense when referring to your present results (e.g. I found that . . .)'. Although he notes exceptions to this rule, it serves as a useful guide.

Day and Gastel (2011) and Becker (2007) both stridently attack the passive voice (it was found that) and champion the use of the **active voice** (I found that). Certainly, it is clearer, shorter and unambiguous. It is a good idea to check with your project tutor here which is most likely to be acceptable.

Finally, a note about the use of language that assumes the gender of a classification of people. The most obvious example of these is the constant reference to managers as 'he'. Not only is this inaccurate in organisations, it also gives offence to many people of both sexes. Those offended will probably include your readers! It is simple enough to avoid (e.g. 'I propose to interview each executive unless he refuses' becomes 'I propose to interview each executive unless I receive a refusal') but often less easy to spot. The further reading section in the first draft of this chapter referred to Becker as a 'master craftsman'. These notes on language and gender prompted us to change it to 'an expert in the field'. Appendix 4 gives more detailed guidance on the use of non-discriminatory language.

It is a good idea to be aware of any specific discriminatory or potentially insulting concepts, terms and expressions which may be used in your research due to the particular context of the research (e.g. the industry or organisation in which you work). If your work has an international dimension, it is also a good idea to be aware of any country-specific or national guidelines on the non-discriminatory use of language.

Preserving anonymity

You may have given those people (and the organisations) from whom you collected data an undertaking that you would not disclose their identity in anything you write. In this case you will need to conceal their identities in your project report. The usual way of doing this is to invent pseudonyms for organisations and not to name individual participants. This should not detract from the impact of your report.

Similarly, your sponsoring organisation(s) may have requested sight of your report before it is submitted. Should there be misgivings about the content of the report you should be able to alleviate these by the use of pseudonyms. This is usually a better option than significant text changes.

The need for continual revision

Phil asked a group of undergraduate students how many of them wrote more than one draft of their assignment papers. He did not expect that many would reply that they did. What he did not predict was that many of them had not even thought this was necessary. Submitting the first attempt is due partly to the heavy assessment loads on many courses, which means that students are constantly having to 'keep up with the clock'. On part-time courses, students these days have so many demands in their daily work that writing an assignment just once is all that is possible. This is the way most of us learnt to write at school. The work is usually seen only by the teacher. The arrangement is a private one.

However, project reports are different. They will be seen by an audience much wider than one tutor. They will usually be lodged in the library to be read by succeeding students. You will be judged on the quality of your work. For that reason we urge you most strongly to polish your work with successive drafts until you are happy that you can do no better (Box 14.12).

Having been through this checklist you may decide to make minor alterations to your text. On the other hand you may rewrite sections or move sections within chapters to other chapters. Keep asking yourself 'How can I make the reader's task easier?'

After each successive draft do leave enough time for your thoughts to mature. It is amazing how something you wrote a few days before will now make no sense to you. However, you will also be impressed with the clarity and insight of some passages.

Having completed a second draft you may now feel confident enough to give it to your colleague or friend to read. Ask your reader to use the checklist in Box 14.12 to which you can add specific points that you feel are important (e.g. are my arguments well reasoned?).

Box 14.12
Checklist

To evaluate each draft of your project report

✔ Is there a clear structure?
✔ Is there a clear storyline?
✔ Does your abstract reflect the whole content of the report accurately?
✔ Does your introduction state the research question(s) and objectives clearly?
✔ Does your literature review inform the later content of the report?
✔ Are your methods clearly explained?
✔ Have you made a clear distinction between findings and conclusions in the relevant chapters?

✔ Have you checked all your references and presented these in the required manner?
✔ Is there any text material that should be in the appendices or vice versa?
✔ Does your title reflect accurately your content?
✔ Have you divided up your text throughout with suitable headings?
✔ Does each chapter have a preview and a summary?
✔ Are you happy that your writing is clear, simple and direct?
✔ Have you eliminated all jargon?
✔ Have you eliminated all unnecessary quotations?
✔ Have you checked spelling and grammar?
✔ Have you checked for assumptions about gender?
✔ Is your report in a format that will be acceptable to the assessing body?
✔ Would you be proud of your project if it was placed in the university's library as it is now?

14.7 Meeting the assessment criteria 满足评估标准

Your readers will assess your work against the assessment criteria that apply to your research programme. It is therefore essential that you familiarise yourself with these criteria. More generally, Bloom's (1971) taxonomy (or classification) of educational objectives will help you understand the standard that your project report needs to meet. At the lower levels of this taxonomy project reports should show knowledge and comprehension of the topic covered. At the intermediate levels they should contain evidence of application and analysis. Application is thought of as the ability to apply certain principles and rules in particular situations. Your method section should be the principal vehicle for demonstrating application. Analysis may be illustrated by your ability to break down your data and to clarify the nature of the component parts and the relationship between them. Whatever your assessment criteria, it is certain that you will be expected to demonstrate your ability at these lower and intermediate levels.

The higher levels of this taxonomy are synthesis and evaluation. **Synthesis** is the process of putting together or assembling various elements so as to create a new statement or conclusion. The emphasis put on conclusions and, in particular, on the development of a storyline in your project report suggests that we feel that you should be showing evidence of synthesis. **Evaluation** is the process of judging materials or methods in terms of their accuracy and internal consistency or by comparing them against external criteria. You have the chance to show this ability in the literature review and in the awareness of the limitations of your own research (see Section 14.3). Each of these levels of educational objectives should be demonstrated in your project report.

In addition to meeting these, you will also need to make sure that you meet any other assessment criteria. You will need to make sure that your project is correctly formatted, does not exceed the maximum permitted length and contains all of the elements specified for inclusion. A final, more holistic consideration that many of our students find useful is to ask yourself whether you would be proud for your project to be placed in the university's library as it is now. If your honest answer is 'no, not yet' you will have more work to do! Conversely, you will need to submit by the due date and so you will need to make sure that you do not keep polishing one part to the exclusion of completing the whole project. You will therefore need to manage your time carefully in terms of drafting the whole and then refining each part.

撰写一个反思性章节
14.8   Writing a reflective essay or section

As we discussed in earlier chapters, being reflective and reflexive is integral to some research strategies, or particular variants of these. This is particular true of interpretive research strategies. For example, in Section 5.5 we outlined Interpretive Ethnography as an approach in which the researcher engages in continuous reflexivity. Conducting research in a reflective and reflexive way is also important in Action Research and Grounded Theory strategies. This approach involves the researcher writing himself or herself into the research by writing in the first person. Of course, not all research strategies encourage reflection and reflexivity during the research process. Neither do they encourage writing in the first person; instead they use an impersonal approach to report the research. This is often true of deductive, survey research. If being reflective and reflexive has not been integral to your research strategy, you will still be familiar with this approach if you have kept a reflective diary or journal throughout your research project. This will be very helpful in writing a reflective essay about your research, or a reflective section in your project report.

As we noted in Section 1.5, many universities require a reflective essay or section to be included in the assessment of a research project, sometimes as an appendix in the report. In Section 1.5 we discussed how reflection is a key part of learning. Your reflections about your research should be recorded throughout this process in your reflective diary or journal (Section 13.5). This will enable you to record your progress in a continuous cycle of experience, reflection, evaluation and revised practice. Your reflective diary or journal will help you to improve your practice as your research progresses and then provide you with the source material to write your reflective essay or section. It will of course be important to make regular entries in your research diary or journal and we have encouraged you to do this as you work through the 'Progressing your research project' section included in each chapter.

Questions that you may ask yourself to help you write your reflective essay or section include:

- Which aspects of my research project went well?
- Why do I think these aspects of my research project went well?
- What are my key learning points from these aspects?
- Which aspects of my research project did not go so well?
- Why do I think these aspects of my research project did not go so well?
- What are my key learning points from these aspects?
- What adjustments did I make to my research practice as a result of this learning?
- How well did these adjustments work in practice?
- What further adjustments did I make, or could I have made, to my research practice and why?
- How would I summarise my learning from my research project and what skills have I developed?
- How has my learning from this experience influenced what I would do in the event of another research project: what would I do the same and what would I do differently, and why?

You should be able to highlight material in your reflective diary or journal to help you to answer these questions to write your reflective essay or section. Where you have used a research strategy that incorporates a reflective and reflexive approach and written this into your project report you should also be able to draw on this material to answer these questions to produce a reflective overview. As your reflective essay or section is a personal account of your experiences, practice and learning, it will be appropriate to write this in the first person, using 'I' and 'my': such as 'my experience', 'what did I learn' and 'what I did differently'.

14.9 Oral presentation of the report 口头报告

Many students, particularly on professional courses, have to present their project report orally as part of the assessment process. The skills required here are quite different from those involved with writing. We discuss them here under three headings: planning and preparing; the use of visual aids; and presenting.

Planning and preparing

We make no apology for starting this section with the trainer's proverb: 'Failing to prepare is preparing to fail.' Your assessors will forgive any inadequacies that stem from inexperience, but they will be much less forgiving of students who have paid little attention to preparation. You can be sure of one thing about insufficient preparation: it shows, particularly to the experienced tutor.

All presentations should have clear aims and objectives. This is not the place to analyse the difference between these. Suffice to say that your aim should be to give the audience members an overview of your report in such a way that it will capture their interest. Keep it clear and simple. By achieving this you will meet the most basic assessment criterion: that some time later the tutor in the audience can remember clearly your main project storyline. Your objectives are more specific. They should start you thinking about the interests of your audience. These should be phrased in terms of what it is you want your audience members to be able to do after your presentation. Since your presentation will usually be confined to the imparting of knowledge, it is sufficient to phrase your objectives in terms of the audience members being able, for example, to define, describe, explain or clarify. It is a good idea to share the objectives with your audience members so they know about the journey on which they are being taken (Box 14.13).

Setting clear objectives for your presentation leads you neatly to deciding the content. This should be straightforward because your abstract should serve as your guide to the content. After all, the purpose of the abstract is to give the reader a brief overview of the report, which is precisely the same purpose as the presentation. How much detail you go into on each point will be determined largely by the time at your disposal. But the audience member who wants more detail can always ask you to elaborate, or read it in the report.

The final point to note here is to think about the general approach you will adopt in delivering your presentation. It is a good idea to involve the audience members rather than simply tell them what it is you want them to know. Thirty minutes of you talking at the audience members can seem like an age, for you and sometimes for them! Inviting them to ask questions throughout the presentation is a good way of ensuring that the talk is not all in one direction. Rarely will tutors miss the opportunity of asking you

Box 14.13
Focus on student research

Presenting the objectives for a project

Phil created the following slides in Microsoft Power-Point as part of a lecture on project presentation. This allowed him to produce various designs of slide to meet his purpose, examples of which are shown in the following versions:

Version 1: Standard PowerPoint slide

> # Objectives for a presentation
>
> - To describe the purpose of the research project
> - To explain the context in which the research project research was set
> - To identify the research strategy adopted and the reasons for its choice
> - To list the main findings, conclusions and recommendations flowing from the research
> - *N.B. Detail related to the specific project may be added*

Version 2: PowerPoint slide using design template

> # Objectives for a presentation
>
> - To describe the purpose of the research project
> - To explain the context in which the research project research was set
> - To identify the research strategy adopted and the reasons for its choice
> - To list the main findings, conclusions and recommendations flowing from the research
> - *N.B. Detail related to the specific project may be added*

Version 3: PowerPoint slide using more colour

Objectives for a presentation

- To describe the purpose of the research project

- To explain the context in which the research project research was set

- To identify the research strategy adopted and the reasons for its choice

- To list the main findings, conclusions and recommendations flowing from the research

- *N.B. Detail related to the specific project may be added*

Version 4: PowerPoint slide with photograph inserted

OBJECTIVES FOR A PRESENTATION

- To describe the purpose of the research project

- To explain the context in which the research project research was set

- To identify the research strategy adopted and the reasons for its choice

- To list the main findings, conclusions and recommendations flowing from the research

N.B. Detail related to the specific project may be added

Version 5: PowerPoint slide with space for audience to add notes

OBJECTIVES FOR A PRESENTATION

- To describe the purpose of the research project

- To explain the context in which the research project research was set

- To identify the research strategy adopted and the reasons for its choice

- To list the main findings, conclusions and recommendations flowing from the research

N.B. Detail related to the specific project may be added

to 'dig a little deeper' to test your understanding, so don't worry that no questions will arise. However, you must be careful to ensure that you do not let questions and answers run away with time. The more you open up your presentation to debate, the less control you have of time. In general we do not think it is a good idea to attempt to emulate tutors and turn your presentation into a teaching session. We have seen students set the audience mini-exercises to get them involved, but often these tend to fall flat. Play to your strengths and enjoy the opportunity to share your detailed knowledge with an interested audience.

Using visual aids

Now another proverb: 'I hear and I forget, I see and I remember' (Rawlins 1999: 37). The use of **visual aids** will do more than enhance the understanding of your audience. It will help you to look better prepared and therefore more professional. It is unlikely that you will have the time in your presentation to incorporate visual aids such as videoclips, and often your subject matter will not lend itself to their use. So we shall confine our discussion here to using slides with a digital video projector and using the whiteboard.

A simple set of slides will perform the same function as a set of notes, in that it will ensure that you do not forget key points, and will help you to keep your presentation on track. You will know the material so well that a key point noted on the overhead will be enough to trigger your thought process and focus the attention of the audience. Key points will also ensure that you are not tempted to read a script for your presentation, something that will not sustain the attention of your audience for very long.

The use of Microsoft PowerPoint™ has revolutionised the preparation of overhead presentation slides and handouts (Box 14.13). It is now easy to produce a highly professional presentation, using slides which can include simple illustrations to reinforce a point or add a little humour. Virtually all organisations have digital video projectors to project the slides directly from a computer, which adds to the degree of professionalism. This allows you electronically to reveal each point as you talk about it while concealing forthcoming points. PowerPoint also allows you to print miniature versions of your slides as a handout or note pages (Box 14.13, version 5), which is a very useful aide-mémoire for the audience.

You may want to supplement your pre-prepared slides with the use of the whiteboard. This may be useful for explaining points in relation to questions you receive. A word of warning here: ensure that you use dry markers that can be wiped from the board. A vain attempt to erase the results of a permanent pen in front of your audience will do nothing to enhance your confidence. Ensuring that you have dry wipe markers (use only black and blue pens – red and green are too faint), and checking computers and projectors before the presentation, serve to emphasise the need for careful preparation.

Making the presentation

The first thing to say here is: don't worry about nerves. You may expect to be a little nervous as you commence your presentation and your audience may also expect this. The best way to minimise nervousness is to have prepared your presentation carefully and to have practised it beforehand.

Be positive about your presentation and your report. Trial your presentation in front of a friend to ensure that it flows logically and smoothly. You also need to ensure that you can deliver it in the allotted time. In our experience most students put too much material in their presentations, although they worry beforehand that they have not got enough.

It is important that your presentation has a clear structure. We can do no better than repeat the words of a famous evangelist: when asked how he held the attention of his audience, he replied 'First I tell them what I'm going to say, then I say it, then I tell them what I've said' (Parry 1991: 17). Parry (1991) notes that audiences like to know where they are going, they like to know how they are progressing on the journey and they like to know when they have arrived.

Finally some practical points that will help:

- Think about whether you would prefer to sit or stand at the presentation. The former may be better to foster debate, the latter is likely to give you a sense of 'control' (Rawlins 1999). Which one you choose may depend upon the circumstances of the presentation, including the approach you wish to adopt, the room layout, the equipment you are using and your preferred style.
- Consider how you will deal with difficult questions. Try to anticipate these and how you would answer them, so that you can deal with them confidently during the presentation.
- Avoid jargon.
- Check the room before the presentation to ensure you have everything you need, you are happy and familiar with the layout, and all your equipment is working.

14.10 **Summary** 小 结

- Writing is a powerful way of clarifying your thinking.
- Writing is a creative process, which needs the right conditions if it is to produce successful results.
- Your project report should have a clear structure that enables you to develop a clear storyline.
- The structure you use should be suitable for the nature of your research strategy.
- The structure you use should also be suitable for the report's audience. This audience may be an academic one or an organisational one, as in the case of a consultancy report.
- Your report should be laid out in such a way that your reader finds all the information readily accessible.
- You should try to develop a clear, simple writing style that will make reading the report an easy and enjoyable experience.
- Spelling and grammatical errors should be avoided.
- Do not think of your first draft as your last. Be prepared to rewrite your report several times until you think it is the best you can do.
- Failing to prepare for your presentation is preparing to fail.
- Visual aids will enhance the understanding of your audience and lend your presentation professionalism.
- Remember: tell them what you're going to say, say it, then tell them what you've said.

Self-check questions   自测题

Help with these questions is available at the end of the chapter.

14.1 Your project tutor has returned your draft project report with the suggestion that you make a clearer distinction between your results and your conclusions. How will you go about this?

14.2 Why is it considered good practice to acknowledge the limitations of your research in the project report?

14.3 Look again at the quote from Wright Mills cited early in Section 14.5. Rewrite this so that his idea is communicated to the reader in the clearest way possible.

14.4 There are other problems that must be avoided when repositioning sections of your report in the redrafting processes. What are they?

14.5 Your friend or colleague is concerned about preparing her or his project presentation. What advice will you give to help him or her prepare this presentation?

Review and discussion questions   复习与讨论题

14.6 Draft a plan for your project report, show it to your friends and compare your plan with those they have drafted. Explain the reason for any differences between your plan and those of your friends.

14.7 Look through several of the refereed academic journals that relate to your subject area. Choose an article that is based upon some primary research and note the structure of the article. Decide whether you agree with the way in which the author has structured the article and think of ways in which you may have done this differently.

14.8 Share pieces of your writing with a group of your friends. Look at the example in Box 14.11 and subject all the pieces to the 'write clearer sentences' test.

改进研究项目
Progressing your research project

Writing your project report   撰写你的项目报告

- Where you have a choice about how to structure your report, use the discussion in Section 14.3 to help you to devise a report structure that will be suitable for the research approach and research strategy you used, to allow you to tell a clear story about your project. Where you do not have a choice about how to structure your report but you feel that the given format is inappropriate for your approach and strategy, consider how you may present your research within this structure to tell a clear story about

your project. Discuss this with your project tutor and ensure that the structure you use meets the expectations of your examiners.

- As you draft each part of your project report, continue to review your work to ensure that the content is clear and accessible and your writing style is appropriate. Be prepared to read your draft material very carefully and repeatedly in order to seek to improve its clarity and style. Where possible, re-read and amend drafts of a section or chapter when your mind is fresh.

- The structure you devise, related to your research approach and research strategy, will have implications for the way in which you discuss the role of literature, theory, methods, findings and conclusions in your project report. As you produce your draft, continue to evaluate how well these elements fit together without overlapping (see next point) in your report. Where the story of your research is not clear, you will need to continue to re-draft the report.

- As the draft of your report develops, ensure that you distinguish between describing events, outlining methods, reporting findings, and interpreting and theorising about what you found. This will be important irrespective of the structure you use so that your readers may distinguish between these elements in your work. Where you use an alternative structure and wish to include more than one of these elements in the same chapter, you will need to distinguish between these by, for example, using different sections with unmistakable headings.
- Give your report the 'reader-friendly' test to ensure that your style is easy to read, and the content is clear and free from avoidable errors.
- Use the questions in Box 1.4 to guide your reflective diary entry.

Self-check answers   自测题答案

14.1 This is easier said than done. Start by going through your results chapter, continually asking yourself 'Did I find this out?' You will probably weed out a lot of things that you have thought about that are related to points you found out. These belong in the conclusions (or discussion) chapter.

Now turn to the conclusions chapter, asking yourself the question: 'Is this a reflection of what I found out?' If the points are a repeat of what you covered in your findings section, then cut them out and make sure you write reflections on the findings.

14.2 It will demonstrate good practice in two respects. First, it will demonstrate that you have evaluated your research design. Second, it will help you to evaluate how you would alter this design if you were going to repeat your research, or if you were going to undertake further research. Remember that there is no perfect research design.

14.3 Academic writing is often difficult to understand. This is not usually because the subject matter is complex or the thoughts profound. It is because the writer thinks it necessary to write in an 'academic' way.

14.4 The 'road map' you announced in the introduction may not now be correct. The previews and summaries at the beginning and end of the relevant chapters may need changing. A more serious potential problem is that the storyline may be altered. This should not be the case. Nonetheless, it would important to re-read the whole report to ensure that any repositioning does not alter its sense of coherence.

14.5 You may emphasise the general point that preparation is very important, not least because this will help to overcome any nervousness that your friend will feel when he or she makes the presentation. You may also emphasise that she or he should think about the audience and what is it that he or she will want to tell them. You may tell her or him to make sure that the presentation has clear objectives and that it should be kept simple so that there is no danger of overloading the audience with too much information in a short period. This will mean telling the audience what they need to know and eliminating other information. You may also tell him or her that using visual aids will be important but that these should support the key points you wish to make and not be used to show off your technical skills as this may only serve to annoy or confuse your audience. Clear visual aids will also be helpful to your friend in delivering her or his presentation. You may also advise your friend to practise his or her presentation, to invite members of the audience to ask some questions during the actual performance to help to engage them but to remain mindful of the time allowed to complete it.

Get ahead using resources on the companion website at: **www.pearsoned.co .uk/saunders**.

- Improve your IBM SPSS Statistics and NVivo research analysis with practice tutorials.
- Save time researching on the Internet with the Smarter Online Searching Guide.
- Test your progress using self-assessment questions.
- Follow live links to useful websites.

Bibliography 参考书目

A

Access to Research (2014) *Access to Research*. Available at http://www.accesstoresearch.org.uk/ [Accessed 2 May 2014].

Allreck, P.L. and Settle, R.B. (2004) *The Survey Research Handbook* (3rd edn) New York: McGraw-Hill.

Alvesson, M. and Sandberg, J. (2011) 'Generating research questions through problematization', *Academy of Management Review*, Vol. 36, No. 2, pp. 247–71.

Alvesson, M. and Sköldberg, K. (2000) *Reflexive Methodology: New Vistas for Qualitative Research*. London: Sage.

American Association for Public Opinion Research (2011) *Standard Definitions: Final Dispositions of Case Codes and Outcome Rates for Surveys* (7th edn). Lenexa, KA: AAPOR. Available at https://www.aapor.org//AM/Template.cfm?Section=Home [Accessed 14 April 2014].

Anderson, D.R., Sweeney, D.J., Williams, T.A., Freeman, J. and Shoesmith, E. (2014) *Statistics for Business and Economics* (3rd edn). Andover: Cengage Learning.

Anderson, T.W. (2003) *An Introduction to Multivariate Statistical Analysis*. New York: John Wiley.

Angrosino, M. and Rosenberg, J. (2011) 'Observations on observation: Continuities and challenges', in N.K. Denzin and Y.S. Lincoln (eds) *The Sage Handbook of Qualitative Research* (4th edn). London: Sage, pp. 467–78.

Anseel, F., Lievens, F., Schollaert, E. and Choragwicka, B. (2010) 'Response rates in organizational science, 1995–2008: A meta-analytic review and guidelines for survey researchers', *Journal of Business Psychology*, Vol. 25, pp. 335–49.

Ataullah, A., Davidson, I., Le, H. and Wood, G. (2014) 'Corporate diversification, information asymmetry and insider trading', *British Journal of Management*, Vol. 25, pp. 228–51.

B

Bakardjieva, M. and Feenberg, A. (2000) 'Involving the virtual subject', *Ethics and Information Technology*, Vol. 2, pp. 233–40.

Bansal, P. and Corley, K. (2011) 'The coming of age for qualitative research: Embracing the diversity of qualitative methods', *Academy of Management Review*, Vol. 54, No. 2, pp. 233–7.

Barnett, V. (2002) *Sample Survey Principles and Methods* (3rd edn). Chichester: Wiley.

Baruch, Y. and Holtom, B.C. (2008) 'Survey response rate levels and trends in organizational research', *Human Relations*, Vol. 61, pp. 1139–60.

Basil, M. (2011) 'Use of photography and video in observational research', *Qualitative Market Research: An International Journal*, Vol. 14, No. 3, pp. 246–57.

BBC College of Journalism (2014) *Interviewing*. Available at http://www.bbc.co.uk/academy/journalism/skills/interviewing [Accessed 8 May 2014].

Becker, H. (2007) *Writing for Social Scientists* (2nd edn). Chicago, IL: University of Chicago Press.

Becker, H.S. (1998) *Tricks of the Trade: How to Think About Your Research While You're Doing It*. Chicago, IL: Chicago University Press.

Bell, E. and Bryman, A. (2007) 'The ethics of management research: An exploratory content analysis', *British Journal of Management*, Vol. 18, No. 1, pp. 63–77.

Bell, J. and Waters, S. (2014) *Doing Your Research Project* (6th edn). Maidenhead: Open University Press.

Belzile, J.A. and Oberg, G. (2012) 'Where to begin? Grappling with how to use participant interaction in focus group design', *Qualitative Research*, Vol. 12, No. 4, pp. 459–72.

Berelson, B. (1952) *Content Analysis in Communication Research*. Glencoe, IL: Free Press.

Berman Brown, R. and Saunders, M. (2008) *Dealing with Statistics: What You Need to Know*. Maidenhead: McGraw-Hill/Open University Press.

Berry, D. (2004) 'Internet research: Privacy, ethics and alienation: An open source approach', *Internet Research*, Vol. 14, No. 4, pp. 323–32.

Bhaskar R. (1978) *A Realist Theory of Science*. Hassocks: Harvester Press.

Bhaskar, R. (1989) *Reclaiming Reality: A Critical Introduction to Contemporary Philosophy*. London: Verso.

Bidlake, S. (2011) 'Outdoor hall of fame contest opens', *Campaign,* 10 February. Available at http://www.campaignlive.co.uk/news/1054277/Outdoor-Hall-Fame-contest-opens/ [Accessed 14 April 2014].

Bigmacindex.org (2014) *Big Mac Index 2014: Historical Data from the BIG Mac Index*. Available at http://bigmacindex.org/ [Accessed 17 November 2014].

Birnbaum, M.H. (2004) 'Human research and data collection via the internet', *Annual Review of Psychology*, Vol. 55, pp. 803–32.

Black, K. (2009) *Business Statistics* (6th edn). Hoboken, NJ: Wiley.

Blaikie, N. (2010) *Designing Social Research* (2nd edn). Cambridge: Polity.

Bloom, B. (ed.) (1971) *Taxonomy of Educational Objectives: Cognitive Domain*. New York: McKay.

Bloomberg, B., Cooper, D.R. and Schindler, P.S. (2014) *Business Research Methods* (4th edn). Boston, MA and Burr Ridge, IL: McGraw-Hill.

Boddy, C. (2005) 'A rose by any other name may smell as sweet but "group discussion" is not another name for "focus group" nor should it be', *Qualitative Market Research*, Vol. 8, No. 3, pp. 248–55.

Bolino, M.C., Turnley, W.H. and Bloodgood, J.M. (2002) 'Citizenship behaviour and the creation of social capital in organizations', *Academy of Management Review*, Vol. 27, No. 4, pp. 505–22.

Bourque, L.B. and Clark, V.A. (1994) 'Processing data: The survey example', in M.S. Lewis-Beck (ed.) *Research Practice*. London: Sage, pp. 1–88.

Boyde, E. (2013) 'A degree of relevance for the 21st century?', *Financial Times*, 15 July, 2013.

Bradley, N. (1999) 'Sampling for Internet surveys: An examination of respondent selection', *Journal of the Market Research Society*, Vol. 41, No. 4, pp. 387–95.

Bradley, N. (2013) *Marketing Research: Tools and Techniques* (3rd edn). Oxford: Oxford University Press.

Brannan, M.J. and Oultram, T. (2012) 'Participant observation', in G. Symon and C. Cassell (eds) *Qualitative Organisational Research Core Methods and Current Challenges*. London: Sage, pp. 296–313.

Brannick, T. and Coghlan, D. (2007) 'In defense of being native: The case for insider academic research', *Organizational Research Methods*, Vol. 10, No. 1, pp. 59–74.

Braun, V. and Clarke, V. (2006) 'Using thematic analysis in psychology', *Qualitative Research in Psychology*, Vol. 3, No. 2, pp. 77–101.

Brekhus, W.H., Galliher, J.F. and Gubrium, J.F. (2005) 'The need for thin description', *Qualitative Inquiry*, Vol. 11, No. 6, pp. 861–79.

Bresnen, M. and Burrell, G. (2012) 'Journals à la mode? Twenty years of living alongside Mode 2 and the new production of knowledge', *Organization,* Vol. 20, No. 1, pp. 25–37

Brinkmann, S. and Kvale, S. (2015) *InterViews: Learning the Craft of Qualitative Research Interviewing* (3rd edn). London: Sage.

British Psychological Society (2009) *Code of Ethics and Conduct*. Leicester: British Psychological Society.

Available at http://www.bps.org.uk/system/files/documents/code_of_ethics_and_conduct.pdf [Accessed 24 March 2014].

British Psychological Society (2013) *Ethics Guidelines for Inter-mediated Research*. INF206/1.2013 Leicester: British Psychological Society. Available at http://www.bps.org.uk/publications/policy-and-guidelines/research-guidelines-policy-documents/research-guidelines-poli [Accessed 24 March 2014].

British Sociological Association (2002) *Statement of Ethical Practice*. Available at http://www.britsoc.co.uk/media/27107/StatementofEthicalPractice.pdf [Accessed 24 March 2014].

Bruner, G.C. (2013).*Marketing Scales Handbook: The Top 20 Multi Item Measure Used in Consumer Research*. Fort Worth, TX: GBII productions.

Bryant, A. and Charmaz, K. (2007) *The Sage Handbook of Grounded Theory*. London: Sage.

Bryman, A. (1988) *Quantity and Quality in Social Research*. London: Unwin Hyman.

Bryman, A. (1989) *Research Methods and Organisation Studies*. London: Unwin Hyman.

Bryman, A. (2006) 'Integrating quantitative and qualitative research: How is it done?', *Qualitative Research*, Vol. 6, No. 1, pp. 97–113.

Buchanan, D.A. (2012) 'Case studies in organizational research', in G. Symon and C. Cassell (eds) *Qualitative Organisational Research Core Methods and Current Challenges*. London: Sage, pp. 351–70.

Buchanan, D., Boddy, D. and McCalman, J. (2013) 'Getting in, getting on, getting out and getting back', in A. Bryman (ed.) *Doing Research in Organisations*. London: Routledge Library Edition, pp. 53–67.

Bulmer, M., Sturgis, P.J. and Allum, N. (2009) 'Editors' introduction', in M. Bulmer, P.J. Sturgis and N. Allum (eds) *Secondary Analysis of Survey Data*. Los Angeles: Sage, pp. xviii–xxvi.

Burrell, G. and Morgan, G. (1979) *Sociological Paradigms and Organisational Analysis*. London: Heinemann.

Buzan, T. (2011) *Buzan's Study Skills: Mind Maps, Memory Techniques, Speed Reading and More*. London: BBC.

C

Calás, M. and Smircich, L. (1997) *Postmodern Management Theory*. Aldershot: Ashgate/Dartmouth.

Carroll, L. (1989) *Alice's Adventures in Wonderland*. London: Hutchinson.

Carson, D., Gilmore, A., Perry, C. and Grønhaug, K. (2001) *Qualitative Marketing Research*. London: Sage.

Cassell, C. and Lee, B. (eds) (2011a) *Challenges and Controversies in Management Research*. New York: Routledge.

Cassell, C. and Lee, B. (2011b) 'Introduction: Key debates, challenges and controversies in management research', in C. Cassell and B. Lee (eds) *Challenges and Controversies in Management Research*. New York: Routledge, pp. 1–16.

Cayla, J. and Arnould, E. (2013) 'Ethnographic stories for market learning', *Journal of Marketing*, Vol. 77, July, pp. 1–16.

Charmaz, K. (2006) *Constructing Grounded Theory*. London, Sage.

Charmaz, K. (2011) 'Grounded theory methods in social justice research', in N.K. Denzin and Y.S. Lincoln (eds) *The Sage Handbook of Qualitative Research* (4th edn). London: Sage, pp. 359–80.

Chartered Institute of Library and Information Professionals (2014) *Libraries and Information Services in the United Kingdom and Republic of Ireland 2013–14* (38th edn). London: Facet Publishing.

Chase, S.E. (2011) 'Narrative inquiry: Still a field in the making', in N.K. Denzin and Y.S. Lincoln (eds) *The Sage Handbook of Qualitative Research* (4th edn). London: Sage, pp. 421–34.

Chaudhury, M.M. and Harrigan, P. (2014) 'CRM to social CRM: The integration of new technologies into customer relationship management', *Journal of Strategic Marketing,* Vol. 22, No. 2, pp. 149–76.

Chia, R. (2003) 'Organization theory as a postmodern science', in H. Tsoukas and C. Knudsen (eds) *The Oxford Handbook of Organization Theory: Meta-Theoretical Perspectives*. Oxford: Oxford University Press, pp. 113–40.

Choi, J.N. (2009) 'Collective dynamics of citizenship behaviour: What group characteristics promote group-level helping?', *Journal of Management Studies*, Vol. 46, No. 8, pp. 1396–420.

CIPD (2012) *Employee Communication Factsheet*. London: Chartered Institute of Personnel and Development.

Clough, P. and Nutbrown, C. (2012) *A Student's Guide to Methodology* (3rd edn). London: Sage.

Coffey, A. and Atkinson, P. (1996) *Making Sense of Qualitative Data*. London: Sage.

Coghlan, D. (2011) 'Action research: Exploring perspectives on a philosophy of practical knowing', *The Academy of Management Annals*, Vol. 5, No. 1, pp. 53–87.

Coghlan, D. and Brannick, T. (2014) *Doing Action Research in Your Own Organisation* (4th edn). London: Sage.

Cohen, L. and Holliday, M. (1996) *Practical Statistics for Students*. London: Paul Chapman.

Colquitt, J.A. (2013) 'Crafting references in AMJ submissions', *Academy of Management Journal*, Vol. 56, No. 5, pp. 1221–4.

Cook, T.D. and Campbell, D.T. (1979) *Quasi-experimentation: Design and Analysis Issues for Field Settings*. Chicago, IL: Rand McNally.

Corbin, J. and Strauss, A. (2008) *Basics of Qualitative Research* (3rd edn). Thousand Oaks, CA: Sage.

Corley, K.G. and Gioia, D.A. (2011) 'Building theory about theory building: What constitutes a theoretical contribution?', *Academy of Management Review*, Vol. 36, No. 1, pp. 12–32.

Court, D. and Abbas, R. (2013) 'Whose interview is it, anyway? Methodological and ethical challenges of insider-outsider research, multiple languages, and dual-researcher cooperation', *Qualitative Inquiry*, Vol. 19, No. 6, pp. 480–8.

Cowton, C.J. (1998) 'The use of secondary data in business ethics research', *Journal of Business Ethics*, Vol. 17, No. 4, pp. 423–34.

Creswell, J.W. (2009) 'Mapping the field of mixed methods research', *Journal of Mixed Methods Research*, Vol. 3, No. 2, pp. 95–108.

Creswell, J.W. (2013) *Qualitative Inquiry and Research Design: Choosing among Five Approaches* (3rd edn). Thousand Oaks, CA: Sage.

Creswell, J.W. and Plano Clark, V.L. (2011) *Designing and Conducting Mixed Methods Research* (2nd edn). Thousand Oaks, CA: Sage.

Crotty, M. (1998) *The Foundations of Social Research*. London: Sage.

Cunliffe, A.L. (2003) 'Reflexive inquiry in organizational research: Questions and possibilities', *Human Relations*, Vol. 56, pp. 983–1003.

Cunliffe, A.L. (2010) 'Retelling tales of the field: In search of organisational ethnography 20 years on', *Organizational Research Methods*, Vol. 13, No. 2, pp. 224–39.

Czarniawska, B. (1997) *Narrating the Organization: Dramas of Institutional Identity*. Chicago, IL: University of Chicago Press.

D

Dale, A., Arber, S. and Procter, M. (1988) *Doing Secondary Research*. London: Unwin Hyman.

Dancey, C.P. and Reidy, J. (2011) *Statistics Without Maths for Psychology: Using SPSS for Windows* (5th edn). Harlow: Prentice Hall.

Daneshkhu, S. and Consumer Industries Editor (2013) 'Emerging markets shoppers turn to web for deals', *Financial Times*, 13 October.

Davis, A., Hirsch, D. and Padley, M. (2014) *A minimum income standard for the UK in 2014. A Joseph Rowntree Foundation Report*. Available at http://www.jrf.org.uk/sites/files/jrf/Minimum-income-standards-2014-FULL.pdf [Accessed 11 December 2014].

Day, R. (1998) *How to Write and Publish a Scientific Paper* (5th edn). Phoenix, AZ: Oryx Press.

Day, R. and Gastel, B. (2011) *How to Write and Publish a Scientific Paper* (7th edn). Oxford: Greenwood.

De Cock, C. and Land, C. (2006) 'Organization/Literature: Exploring the seam', *Organization Studies*, Vol. 27, pp. 517–35.

De Vaus, D.A. (2014) *Surveys in Social Research* (6th edn). Abingdon: Routledge.

Dees, R. (2003) *Writing the Modern Research Paper* (4th edn). Boston, MA: Allyn and Bacon.

Dekas, K.H., Bauer, T.N., Welle, B., Kurkoski, J. and Sullivan, S. (2013) 'Organizational citizenship behavior, version 2.0: A review and qualitative investigation of OCBs for knowledge workers at Google and beyond', *Academy of Management Perspectives*, Vol. 27, No. 3, pp. 219 – 37.

Delamont, S. (2007) 'Ethnography and participant observation', in C. Seale, G. Gobo, J.F. Gubrium and D. Silverman (eds) *Qualitative Research Practice*. London: Sage, pp. 205–17.

Delbridge, R. and Kirkpatrick, I. (1994) 'Theory and practice of participant observation', in V. Wass and P. Wells (eds) *Principles and Practice in Business and Management Research*. Aldershot: Dartmouth, pp. 35–62.

DeMers, J. (2014) 'The top ten benefits of social media marketing'. Available at http://www.forbes.com/sites/jaysondemers/2014/08/11/the-top-10-benefits-of-social-media-marketing/ [Accessed 10 December 2014].

Denscombe, M. (2007) *The Good Research Guide* (3rd edn). Buckingham: Open University Press.

Denyer, D. and Tranfield, D. (2009) 'Producing a systematic review', in D.A. Buchanan and A. Bryman (eds) *The Sage Handbook of Organisational Research Methods*. London: Sage, pp. 671–89.

Denzin, N.K. (2001) 'The reflexive interview and a performative social science', *Qualitative Research*, Vol. 1, No. 1, pp. 23–46.

Denzin, N.K. (2012) 'Triangulation 2.0', *Journal of Mixed Methods Research*, Vol. 6, No. 2, pp. 80–8.

Denzin, N.K. and Lincoln, Y.S. (2005) *The Sage Handbook of Qualitative Research* (3rd edn). London: Sage.

Denzin, N.K. and Lincoln, Y.S. (2011) 'Introduction: The discipline and practice of qualitative research', in N.K. Denzin and Y.S. Lincoln (eds) *The Sage Handbook of Qualitative Research* (4th edn). London: Sage, pp. 1–19.

Department for Business, Innovation and Skills (2013) *Workplace employment relations study (WERS)*. Available at https://www.gov.uk/government/collections/workplace-employment-relations-study-wers [Accessed 10 March 2014].

Derrida, J. (1976) *Of Grammatology*. Baltimore: Johns Hopkins University Press.

DeVellis, R.F. (2012) *Scale Development: Theory and Applications* (3rd edn). Los Angeles: Sage.

Dey, I. (1993) *Qualitative Data Analysis*. London: Routledge.

Dillman, D.A., Smyth, J.D. and Christian, J.M. (2014) *Internet, Phone, Mail and Mixed Mode Surveys: The Tailored Design Method* (4th edn). Hoboken, NJ: Wiley.

Ditton, J. (1977) *Part-Time Crime: An Ethnography of Fiddling and Pilferage*. London: Macmillan.

Dochartaigh, N.O. (2007) *Internet Research Skills: How to Do Your Literature Search and Find Research Information Online*. London: Sage.

Dubois, A. and Gadde, L-E. (2002) 'Systematic combining: An abductive approach to case research', *Journal of Business Research*, Vol. 55, pp. 553–60.

Dye, J. (2013) *Understanding the Information Needs of Postgraduate Taught Students and How These Can Be Met*. London: HEFCE.

E

Easterby-Smith, M., Thorpe, R., Jackson, P. and Lowe, A. (2012) *Management Research* (4th edn). London: Sage.

Eden, C. and Huxham, C. (1996) 'Action research for management research', *British Journal of Management*, Vol. 7, No. 1, pp. 75–86.

Edwards, P., Roberts, I., Clarke, M., Di Giuseppe, C., Pratap, S., Wentz, R. and Kwan, I. (2002) 'Increasing response rates to postal questionnaires: Systematic review', *British Medical Journal*, No. 324, May, pp. 1183–91.

Edwards, T., Tregaskis, O., Edwards, P., Ferner, A., Marginson, A. with Arrowsmith, J., Adam, D., Meyer, M. and Budjanovcanin, A. (2007) 'Charting the contours of multinationals in Britain: Methodological challenges arising in survey-based research', *Warwick Papers in Industrial Relations*, No. 86. Available at http://www.cbs.dk/files/cbs.dk/charting_the_contours_of_multinationals_in_britain.pdf [Accessed 14 April 2014].

Eisenhardt, K.M. (1989) 'Building theories from case study research', *Academy of Management Review*, Vol. 14, No. 4, pp. 532–50.

Eisenhardt, K.M. and Graebner, M.E. (2007) 'Theory building from cases: Opportunities and challenges', *Academy of Management Journal*, Vol. 50, No. 1, pp. 25–32.

Ekinci, Y. (2015) *Designing Research Questionnaires for Business and Management Students*. London: Sage.

Elkjaer, B. and Simpson, B. (2011) 'Pragmatism: A lived and living philosophy. What can it offer to contemporary organization theory?' in H. Tsoukas and R. Chia (eds) *Philosophy and Organization Theory*. Bradford: Emerald Publishing Ltd, pp. 55–84.

Ellis, P. (2010) *The Essential Guide to Effect Sizes*. Cambridge: Cambridge University Press.

Elsbach, K.D., Cable, D.M. and Sherman, J.W. (2010) 'How passive "face time" affects perceptions of employees: Evidence of spontaneous trait inference', *Human Relations*, Vol. 63, No. 6, pp. 735–60.

Emerald Group Publishing (2014) How to . . . write an abstract. Available at http://www.emeraldgrouppublishing.com/authors/guides/write/abstracts.htm [Accessed 16 December 2014].

Erlandson, D.A., Harris, E.L., Skipper, B.L. and Allen, S.D. (1993) *Doing Naturalistic Inquiry*. Newbury Park, CA: Sage.

European Commission (2014) *European Union Labour Force Survey (EU LFS)*. Available at http://epp.eurostat.ec.europa.eu/portal/page/portal/microdata/lfs [Accessed 27 November 2014].

Eurostat (2011) Definitions of Employment and Unemployment. Available at http://epp.eurostat.ec.europa.eu/cache/ITY_SDDS/Annexes/hrst_st_esms_an8.pdf [Accessed 12 December 2013].

Eurostat (2012) Statistics Database. Available at http://epp.eurostat.ec.europa.eu/portal/page/portal/statistics/search_database [Accessed 8 March 2014].

Eurostat (2014) Environment and energy statistics – air emissions accounts by industry and households (NACE Rev. 2) carbon dioxide. Available at http://appsso.eurostat.ec.europa.eu/nui/show.do?dataset=env_ac_ainah_r2&lang=en [Accessed 17 November 2014].

Eurostat (2014) *Europe in Figures: Eurostat Yearbook 2014*. Available at http://epp.eurostat.ec.europa.eu/statistics_explained/index.php/Europe_in_figures_-_Eurostat_yearbook [Accessed 9 December 2014].

Eurostat (2014) *Eurostat Home Page*. Available at http://epp.eurostat.ec.europa.eu/portal/page/portal/eurostat/home/ [Accessed 9 December 2014].

Eurostat (2015) Eurostat: Your Key to European Statistics. Available at http://ec.europa.eu/eurostat/web/main [Accessed 10 March 2015].

Everitt, B.S. and Dunn, G. (2001) *Applied Multivariate Data Analysis* (2nd edn). London: Arnold.

Eysenbach, G. and Till, J.E. (2001) 'Ethical issues in qualitative research on internet communities', *British Medical Journal*, Vol. 323, pp. 1103–5.

F

Fairclough, N. (1992) *Discourse and Social Change*. Cambridge: Polity Press.

Fairclough, N. (2010) *Critical Discourse Analysis: The Critical Study of Language* (2nd edn). Harlow: Pearson Education.

Farey-Jones, D. (2011) '"Hello Boys" voted greatest poster ever created', *Campaign,* 31 March Available at http://www.campaignlive.co.uk/news/1063405/Hello-Boys-voted-greatest-poster-ever-created/ [Accessed 14 April 2014].

Farh, J.L., Earley, P.C. and Lin, S.C. (1997) 'Impetus for action: A cultural analysis of justice and organizational citizenship behaviour in Chinese society', *Administrative Science Quarterly*, Vol. 42, No. 3, pp. 421–44.

Festing, M. (2012) 'Strategic human resource management in Germany: Evidence of convergence to the U.S. model, the European model, or a distinctive national model?', *Academy of Management Perspectives*, Vol. 26, No. 2, pp. 37–54.

Festinger, L. (1957) *A Theory of Cognitive Dissonance*. Stanford, CA: Stanford University Press.

Field, A. (2013) *Discovering Statistics Using SPSS* (4th edn). London: Sage.

Fink, A. (2013) *How to Conduct Surveys* (5th edn). Thousand Oaks, CA: Sage.

Finlay, L. (2002). 'Negotiating the swamp: The opportunity and challenge of reflexivity in research practice', *Qualitative Research*, Vol. 2, No. 2, pp. 209–30.

Fisher, C. (2010) *Researching and Writing a Dissertation for Business Students* (3rd edn). Harlow: Financial Times Prentice Hall.

Fleetwood, S. (2005) 'Ontology in organization and management studies: A critical realist perspective', *Organization*, Vol. 12, pp. 197–222.

Flyvberg, B. (2011) 'Case study', in N.K. Denzin and Y.S. Lincoln (eds) *The Sage Handbook of Qualitative Research* (4th edn). London: Sage, pp. 301–16.

Foddy, W. (1994) *Constructing Questions for Interviews and Questionnaires*. Cambridge: Cambridge University Press.

Foucault, M. (1991) *Discipline and Punish: The Birth of Prison*. London: Penguin Books.

Fournier, V. and Grey, C. (2000) 'At the critical moment: Conditions and prospects for critical management studies', *Human Relations*, Vol. 53, pp. 7–32.

Fukami, C. (2007) 'The third road', *Journal of Management Education*, Vol. 31, pp. 358–64.

G

Gabriel, Y, Gray, D.E. and Goregaokar, H. (2013) 'Job loss and its aftermath among managers and professionals: Wounded, fragmented and flexible', *Work, Employment & Society*, Vol. 27, pp. 56–72.

Gabriel, Y. and Griffiths, D.S. (2004) 'Stories in organizational research', in C. Cassell and G. Symon (eds) *Essential Guide to Qualitative Methods in Organizational Research*. London: Sage, pp. 114–26.

Geertz, C. (1988) *Works and Lives: The Anthropologist as Author*. Stanford, CA: Stanford University Press.

George, G., Haas, M.R. and Pentland, S. (2014) 'Big data and management', *Academy of Management Journal*, Vol. 57, No. 2, pp. 321–6.

Gerstl-Pepin, C. and Patrizio, K. (2009) 'Learning from Dumbledore's Pensieve: Metaphor as an aid in teaching reflexivity in qualitative research', *Qualitative Research*, Vol. 9, No. 3, pp. 299–308.

Ghauri, P. and Grønhaug, K. (2010) *Research Methods in Business Studies: A Practical Guide* (4th edn). Harlow: Financial Times Prentice Hall.

Gibb, F. (1995) 'Consumer group accuses lawyers of shoddy service', *The Times*, 5 October.

Gibbons, M.L., Limoges, H., Nowotny, S., Schwartman, P., Scott, P. and Trow, M. (1994) *The New Production of Knowledge: The Dynamics of Science and Research in Contemporary Societies*. London: Sage.

Gill, J. and Johnson, P. (2010) *Research Methods for Managers* (4th edn). London: Sage.

Ginsberg, J., Mohebbi, M.H., Patel, R.S., Bramer, L., Smolinski, M.S. and Brilliant, L. (2009) 'Detecting influenza epidemics using search engine query data', *Nature*, No. 457, pp. 1012–14.

Glaser, B.G. (1978) *Theoretical Sensitivity: Advances in the Methodology of Grounded Theory*. Mill Valley, CA: Sociology Press.

Glaser, B. and Strauss, A. (1967) *The Discovery of Grounded Theory*. Chicago, IL: Aldine.

Glaser, B.G. (1998) *Doing Grounded Theory: Issues and Discussions*. Mill Valley, CA: Sociology Press.

Glaser, B.G. (1992) *Basics of Grounded Theory*. Mill Valley, CA: Sociology Press.

Gobo, G. (2011) 'Glocalizing methodology? The encounter between local methodologies', *International Journal of Social Research Methodology*, Vol. 14, No. 6, pp. 417–37.

Google (2014) *Google Flu Trends: How Does It Work?* Available at: http://www.google.org/flutrends/about/how.html [Accessed 20 November 2014].

Gouldner, A.W. (1970) *The Coming Crisis of Western Sociology*. New York: Basic Books.

Greene, J.C. (2007) *Mixed Methods in Social Inquiry*. San Francisco, CA: Jossey-Bass.

Greene, J.C., Caracelli, V.J. and Graham, W.F. (1989) 'Towards a conceptual framework for mixed-method evaluation designs', *Educational Evaluation and Policy Analysis*, Vol. 11, No. 3, pp. 255–74.

Greenwood, D.J. and Levin, M. (2007) *Introduction to Action Research* (2nd edn). London: Sage.

Groves, R.M. and Peytcheva, E. (2008) 'The impact of non-response rates on nonresponse bias', *Public Opinion Quarterly,* Vol. 72, No. 2, pp. 167–89.

Guba, E.G. and Lincoln, Y.S. (1989) *Fourth Generation Evaluation*. Newbury Park, CA: Sage.

Guest, G., Bunce, A. and Johnson, L. (2006) 'How many interviews are enough? An experiment with data saturation and validity', *Field Methods*, Vol. 18, No. 1, pp. 59–82.

Gummesson, E. (2000) *Qualitative Methods in Management Research* (2nd edn). Thousand Oaks, CA: Sage.

H

Hair, J.F., Black, B., Babin, B., Anderson, R.E. and Tatham, R.L. (2013) *Multivariate Data Analysis* (7th edn). Harlow: Pearson.

Hair, J.F., Celsi, J.W., Money, A.H., Samouel, P. and Page, M.J. (2011) *Essentials of Business Research Methods* (2nd edn). Armonk, NY: M.E. Sharpe.

Hakim, C. (1982) *Secondary Analysis in Social Research*. London: Allen & Unwin.

Hakim, C. (2000) *Research Design: Successful Designs for Social and Economic Research* (2nd edn). London: Routledge.

Hakonen, A., Maaniemi, J. and Hakanen, J.J. (2011) 'Why is group-based pay perceived as meaningful, meaningless or negative? Exploring the meanings of pay suggested by reflection theory', *The International Journal of Human Resource Management*, Vol. 22, No. 10, pp. 2245–61.

Hanna, P. (2012) 'Using internet technologies (such as Skype) as a research medium: A research note', *Qualitative Research*, Vol. 12, No. 2, pp. 239–42.

Harley-Davidson Inc. (2014) *Harley-Davidson Inc. Investor Relations: Motorcycle Shipments*. Available at http://investor.harley-davidson.com/phoenix.zhtml?c=87981&p=irol-shipments [Accessed 10 September 2014].

Hart, C. (1998) *Doing a Literature Review*. London: Sage.

Harvard Library (2013) *Interrogating texts: 6 reading habits to develop in your first year at Harvard*. Available at: http://guides.library.harvard.edu/friendly.php?s=sixreadinghabits&gid=4877 [Accessed 21 March 2014].

Haynes, K. (2012) 'Reflexivity in qualitative research', in C. Cassell and B. Lee (eds) *Challenges and Controversies in Management Research*. New York: Routledge, pp. 72–89.

Hays, W.L. (1994) *Statistics* (4th edn). London: Holt-Saunders.

Healey, M.J. (1991) 'Obtaining information from businesses', in M.J. Healey (ed.) *Economic Activity and Land Use*. Harlow: Longman, pp. 193–251.

Health Research Authority (2013) *Defining Research*. London: Health Research Authority.

Hedrick, T.E., Bickmann, L. and Rog, D.J. (1993) *Applied Research Design*. Newbury Park, CA: Sage.

Hein, W., O'Donohoe, S. and Ryan, A. (2011) 'Mobile phones as an extension of the participant observer's self', *Qualitative Market Research: An International Journal*, Vol. 14, No. 3, pp. 258–73.

Henry, G.T. (1990) *Practical Sampling*. Newbury Park, CA: Sage.

Hepburn, A. and Potter, J. (2007) 'Discourse analytic practice', in C. Seale, G. Gobo, J. F. Gubrium and D. Silverman (eds) *Qualitative Research Practice*. London: Sage.

Herndon, T., Ash, M. and Pollin, R. (2013) 'Does high public debt consistently stifle economic growth? A critique of Reinhart and Rogoff', *Cambridge Journal of Economics*. DOI:10.1093/cje/bet075 [Accessed 21 March 2014].

Heron, J. (1996) *Co-operative Inquiry: Research into the Human Condition*. London: Sage.

Hewson, C., Yule, P., Laurent, D. and Vogel, C. (2003) *Internet Research Methods: A Practical Guide for the Social and Behavioural Sciences*. London: Sage.

Heyl, B.S. (2005) 'Ethnographic interviewing', in P. Atkinson, A. Coffey, S. Delamont, J. Lofland and L. Lofland (eds) *Handbook of Ethnography*. Thousand Oaks, CA: Sage, pp. 369–83.

Hitt, M.A.S. and Greer, C.R. (2012) 'The value of research and its evaluation in business schools: Killing the goose that laid the golden egg?', *Journal of Management Inquiry,* Vol. 21, No. 2, pp. 236–40.

Hodgkinson, G.P. and Rousseau, D. (2009) 'Bridging the rigour–relevance gap in management research. It's already happening!', *Journal of Management Studies*, Vol. 46, No. 3, pp. 534–46.

Hodgkinson, G.P. and Starkey, K. (2011) 'Not simply returning to the same answer over and over again: Reframing relevance', *British Journal of Management,* Vol. 22, pp. 355–69.

Hodgkinson, G.P., Herriot, P. and Anderson, N. (2001) 'Re-aligning the stakeholders in management research: Lessons from industrial, work and organizational psychology', *British Journal of Management*, Vol. 12, Special Issue, pp. 41–8.

Hodson, R. (1991) 'The active worker: Compliance and autonomy at the workplace', *Journal of Contemporary Ethnography*, Vol. 20, No. 1, pp. 47–8.

Holstein, J.A. and Gubrium, J.F. (2011) 'The constructionist analytics of interpretive practice', in N.K. Denzin and Y.S. Lincoln (eds) *The Sage Handbook of Qualitative Research*. London: Sage.

Holsti, O.R. (1969) *Content Analysis for the Social Sciences and Humanities*. Reading, MA: Addison-Wesley.

Holt, A. (2010) 'Using the telephone for narrative interviewing: A research note', *Qualitative Research*, Vol. 10, No. 1, pp. 113–21.

Hookway, N. (2008) 'Entering the blogosphere: Some strategies for using blogs in social research', *Qualitative Research*, Vol. 8, No. 1, pp. 91–113.

Huff, A.S. and Huff, J.O. (2001) 'Re-focusing the business school agenda', *British Journal of Management*, Vol. 12, Special Issue, pp. 49–54.

Hui, C., Lee, C. and Rousseau, D.M. (2004) 'Psychological contract and organizational citizenship behaviour in China: Generalizability and Instrumentality', *Journal of Applied Psychology*, Vol. 89, No. 2, pp. 311–21.

Hyatt, D. (2005) 'A critical literacy frame for UK secondary education contexts', *English in Education*, Vol. 39, No. 1, pp. 43–59.

Hyatt, D. (2013) 'The critical policy discourse analysis frame: Helping doctoral students engage with the educational policy analysis', *Teaching in Higher Education*, Vol. 18, No. 8, pp. 833–45.

I

Idea Works (2012) *Methodologist's toolchest ex-sample*. Available at http://www.ideaworks.com/mt/exsample.html [Accessed 12 April 2014].

IJMR (2007) 'Special Issue on Ethnography', *International Journal of Market Research*, Vol. 49, No. 6, pp. 681–778.

Irvine, A. (2008) *Managing Mental Health and Employment*. Department for Work and Pensions Research Report No. 537, Leeds: Corporate Document Services.

Irvine, A., Drew, P. and Sainsbury, R. (2012) '"Am I not answering your questions properly?' Clarification, adequacy and responsiveness in semi-structured telephone and face-to-face interviews', *Qualitative Research*, Vol. 13, No. 1, pp. 87–106.

J

Jacobs, E. (2013) 'Business life – working lives – close observers of consumers', *Financial Times*, 20 September.

Jankowicz, A.D. (2005) *Business Research Projects* (4th edn). London: Thomson Learning.

Jarzabkowski, P., LeBaron, C., Phillips, K. and Pratt, M. (2014) 'Call for papers; Feature topic: Video-based research methods', *Organizational Research Methods*, Vol. 17, No. 1, pp. 3–4.

Jenkins, M.F., Zapf, D., Winefield, H. and Sarris, A. (2012) 'Bullying allegations from the accused bully's perspective', *British Journal of Management*, Vol. 23, No. 4, pp. 489–501.

Johnson, J.M. (1975) *Doing Field Research*. New York: Free Press.

Johnson, P. (2004) 'Analytic induction', in G. Symon and C. Cassell (eds) *Essential Guide to Qualitative Methods and Analysis in Organizational Research*. London: Sage, pp. 165–79.

Johnson, P. and Clark, M. (2006) 'Editors' introduction: Mapping the terrain: An overview of business and management research methodologies', in P. Johnson and M. Clark (eds) *Business and Management Research Methodologies*. London: Sage, pp. xxv–lv.

K

Kanji, G.K. (2006) *100 Statistical Tests* (3rd edn). London: Sage.

Kaufman, B.E. (2012) 'Strategic human resource management research in the United States: A failing grade after 30 years', *Academy of Management Perspectives*, Vol. 26, No. 2, pp. 12–36.

Kavanagh, M.J., Thite, M. and Johnson, R.D. (eds) (2012) *Human Resource Information Systems: Basics, Applications, and Future Directions* (3rd edn) Thousand Oaks, CA: Sage.

Keaveney, S.M. (1995) 'Customer switching behaviour in service industries: An exploratory study', *Journal of Marketing*, Vol. 59, No. 2, pp. 71–82.

Keen, K.J. (2010) *Graphics for Statistics and Data Analysis with R*. Boca Raton, FL: Chapman and Hall.

Kelemen, M. and Rumens, N. (2008) *An Introduction to Critical Management Research*. London: Sage.

Kelly, G.A. (1955) *The Psychology of Personal Constructs*. New York: Norton.

Kenealy, G.J.J. (2012) 'Grounded theory: A theory building approach', in G. Symon and C. Cassell (eds) *Qualitative Organisational Research Core Methods and Current Challenges*. London: Sage, pp. 408–25.

Kervin, J.B. (1999). *Methods for Business Research* (2nd edn). New York: HarperCollins.

Ketokivi, M. and Mantere, S. (2010) 'Two strategies for inductive reasoning in organizational research', *Academy of Management Review*, Vol. 35, No. 2, pp. 315–33.

Kilduff, M. and Mehra, A. (1997) 'Postmodernism and organizational research', *The Academy of Management Review*, Vol. 22, pp. 453–81.

King, N. (2004) 'Using interviews in qualitative research', in C. Cassell and G. Symon (eds) *Essential Guide to Qualitative Methods in Organizational Research*. London: Sage, pp. 11–22.

King, N. (2012) 'Doing template analysis', in G. Symon and C. Cassell (eds) *Qualitative Organizational Research: Core Methods and Current Challenges*. London: Sage.

Knoblauch, H. (2012) 'Introduction to the special issue of *Qualitative Research*: Video-analysis and videography', *Qualitative Research*, Vol. 12, No. 3, pp. 251–4.

Knudsen, C. (2003) 'Pluralism, scientific progress, and the structure of organization theory', in H. Tsoukas and C. Knudsen (eds) *The Oxford Handbook of Organization Theory: Meta-Theoretical Perspectives*. Oxford: Oxford University Press, pp. 262–86.

Koerner, M.M. (2014) 'Courage as identity work: Accounts of workplace courage', *Academy of Management Journal*, Vol. 57, No. 1, pp. 63–93.

Kosslyn, S.M. (2006) *Graph Design for the Eye and Mind*. New York: Oxford University Press.

Kozinets, R.V. (2006) 'Netography 2.0', in R.W. Belk (ed.) *Handbook of Qualitative Research Methods in Marketing*. Cheltenham: Edward Elgar Publishing, pp. 129–42.

Krippendorff, K. (2004) *Content Analysis: An Introduction to its Methodology* (2nd edn). Thousand Oaks, CA: Sage.

Krueger, R.A. and Casey, M.A. (2009) *Focus Groups: A Practical Guide for Applied Research* (4th edn). Thousand Oaks, CA: Sage.

Kumra, S. and Vinnicombe, S. (2010) 'Impressing for success: A gendered analysis of a key social capital accumulation strategy', *Gender, Work and Organization*, Vol. 17, No. 5, pp. 521–46.

L

Labov, W. (1972) *Language in the Inner City: Studies in the Black English Vernacular*. Philadelphia: University of Pennsylvania Press.

Labov, W. and Waletzky, J. (1967) 'Narrative analysis: Oral versions of personal experience', in J. Helm (ed.) *Essays on the Verbal and Visual Arts*. Seattle, WA: University of Washington Press.

Lavrakas, P.J. (1993) *Telephone Survey Methods: Sampling, Selection and Supervision*. Newbury Park, CA: Sage.

Lazer, D.R., Kennedy, G., King, A. and Vespignani, A. (2014) 'The parable of Google Flu: Traps in big data analysis', *Science*, Vol. 343, No. 6176, pp. 1203–5.

LeCompte, M.D. and Goetz, J.P. (1982) 'Problems of reliability and validity in ethnographic research', *Review of Educational Research*, Vol. 52, No. 1, pp. 31–60.

Lee, B. (2012) 'Using documents in organizational research', in G. Symon and C. Cassell (eds) *Qualitative Organisational Research Core Methods and Current Challenges*. London: Sage, pp. 389–407.

Lee, R.M. (2000) *Doing Research on Sensitive Topics*. London: Sage.

Lee, R.M. and Fielding, N. (1996) 'Qualitative data analysis: Representations of a technology', *Sociological Research Online*, Vol. 1, No. 4. Available at socresonline.org.uk/1/4/16.html [Accessed 11 October 2011].

Lenth, R.V. (2001) 'Some practical guidelines for effective sample size determination', *The American Statistician*, Vol. 55, No. 3, pp. 187–93.

Lewins, A. and Silver, C. (2009) 'Choosing a CAQDAS package – 6th edition', CAQDAS Networking Project Working Paper. Available at http://www.surrey.ac.uk/sociology/research/researchcentres/caqdas/files/2009ChoosingaCAQDASPackage.pdf [Accessed 30 June 2014].

Liang, X., Marler, J.H. and Cui, Z. (2012) 'Strategic human resource management in China: East meets West', *Academy of Management Perspectives*, Vol. 26, No. 2, pp. 55–70.

Lincoln, Y.S. and Guba, E.G. (1985) *Naturalistic Inquiry*. Beverly Hills, CA: Sage.

Lincoln, Y.S., Lynham, S.A. and Guba, E.G. (2011) 'Paradigmatic controversies, contradictions, and emerging confluences, revisited', in N.K. Denzin and Y.S. Lincoln (eds) *The Sage Handbook of Qualitative Research* (4th edn). London: Sage, pp. 97–128.

Little, R. and Rubin, D. (2002) *Statistical Analysis with Missing Data* (2nd edn). New York: John Wiley.

Luff, P. and Heath, C. (2012) 'Some "technical challenges" of video analysis: Social actions, objects, material realities and the problems of perspective', *Qualitative Research*, Vol. 12, No. 3, pp. 255–79.

M

Macdonald, S. and Kam, J. (2007) 'Ring a ring o' roses: Quality journals and gamesmanship in management studies', *Journal of Management Studies*, Vol. 44, pp. 640–55.

Macnaghten, P. and Myers, G. (2007) 'Focus groups', in C. Seale, G. Gobo, J.F. Gubrium and D. Silverman (eds) *Qualitative Research Practice*. London: Sage, pp. 65–79.

Madge, C. (2010) *Online Research Ethics*. Available at http://www.restore.ac.uk/orm/ethics/ethprint3.pdf [Accessed 25 March 2014]

Maitlis, S. (2012) 'Narrative analysis', in G. Symon and C. Cassell (eds) *Qualitative Organisational Research Core Methods and Current Challenges*. London: Sage, pp. 492–511.

Manyika, J., Chui, M., Brown, B., Bughir, J., Dobbs, R., Roxburgh, C. and Byers, A.H. (2011) *Big Data: The Next Frontier for Innovation, Competition, and Productivity*. Lexington, KY: McKinsey & Co.

Marchington, M. and Wilkinson, A. (2012) *Human Resource Management at Work* (5th edn). London: Chartered Institute of Personnel and Development.

Marler, J.H. (2012) 'Strategic human resource management in context: A historical and global perspective', *Academy of Management Perspectives*, Vol. 26, No. 2, pp. 6–11.

Marshall, C. and Rossman, G.B. (2011) *Designing Qualitative Research* (5th edn). Thousand Oaks, CA: Sage.

Martí, I. and Fernández, P. (2013) 'The institutional work of oppression and resistance: Learning from the Holocaust', *Organization Studies*, Vol. 34, pp. 1195–223.

McAreavey, R. and Muir, J. (2011) 'Research ethics committees: Values and power in higher education', *International Journal of Social Research Methodology*, Vol. 14, No. 5, pp. 391–405.

McDonald, S. (2005) 'Studying actions in context: A qualitative shadowing method for organisational research', *Qualitative Research*, Vol. 5, No. 4, pp. 455–73.

McNeill, P. (2005) *Research Methods* (3rd edn). London: Routledge.

Mellors-Bourne, R., Hooley, T. and Marriott, J. (2014). *Understanding How People Choose to Pursue Taught Postgraduate Study*. London: HEFCE.

Miles, M.B., Huberman, A.M. and Saldana, J. (2014) *Qualitative Data Analysis: A Methods Sourcebook* (3rd edn). London: Sage.

MindGenius (2014) *MindGenius Homepage*. Available at http://www.mindgenius.com/default.aspx [Accessed 1 April 2014].

Mingers, J. (2000) 'What is it to be critical? Teaching a critical approach to management undergraduates', *Management Learning*, Vol. 31, No. 2, pp. 219–37.

Mintzberg, H. (1973) *The Nature of Managerial Work*. New York: Harper& Row.

Mitchell, V. (1996) 'Assessing the reliability and validity of questionnaires: An empirical example', *Journal of Applied Management Studies*, Vol. 5, No. 2, pp. 199–207.

Moher, D., Liberati, A., Tetzlaff, J. and Altman, D.G. (2009) 'Preferred reporting for systematic reviews and meta-analyses: The PRISMA statement', *British Medical Journal (BMJ)*, No. 338, b2535. Available at www.bmj.com/content/339/bmj.b2535.full?view=long&pmid=19622551 [Accessed 27 March 2011].

Molina-Azorin, J.F. (2011) 'The use and added value of mixed methods in management research', *Journal of Mixed Methods Research*, Vol. 5, No. 1, pp. 7–24.

Molina-Azorin, J.F. (2012) 'Mixed methods research in strategic management: Impact and applications', *Organizational Research Methods*, Vol. 15, No. 1, pp. 33–56.

Monahan, T. and Fisher, J.A. (2010) 'Benefits of "observer effects": Lessons from the field', *Qualitative Research*, Vol. 10, No. 3, pp. 357–76.

Morgan, G. (1986) *Images of Organization*. London: Sage.

Mueller, S., Volery, T. and von Siemens, B. (2012) 'What do entrepreneurs actually do? An observational study of entrepreneurs' everyday behavior in the start-up and growth stage', *Entrepreneurship Theory and Practice*, Vol. 36, No. 5, pp. 995–1017.

Musson, G. (2004) 'Life histories', in C. Cassell and G. Symon (eds) *Essential Guide to Qualitative Methods in Organizational Research*. London: Sage, pp. 34–46.

N

Naipaul, V.S. (1989) *A Turn in the South*. London: Penguin.

Nastasi, B.K., Hitchcock, J.H. and Brown, L.M. (2010) 'An inclusive framework for conceptualising mixed methods typologies', in A. Tashakkori and C. Teddlie (eds) *The Sage Handbook of Mixed Methods in Social and Behavioural Research* (2nd edn). Thousand Oaks, CA: Sage.

Neuman, W.L. (2014) *Social Research Methods* (7th edn). Harlow: Pearson.

Neville, C. (2010) *The Complete Guide to Referencing and Avoiding Plagiarism* (2nd edn). Maidenhead: Open University Press/McGraw-Hill.

Niglas, K. (2010) 'The multidimensional model of research methodology: An integrated set of continua', in A. Tashakkori and C. Teddlie (eds) *The Sage Handbook of Mixed Methods in Social and Behavioural Research*. Thousand Oaks, CA: Sage, pp. 215–36.

Nijmeijer, K.J., Fabbricotti, I.N. and Huijsman, R. (2014) 'Making franchising work: A framework based on a Systematic Review', *International Journal of Management Reviews*, Vol. 16, No. 1, pp. 62–73.

O

Office for National Statistics (2005) *The National Statistics Socio-economic Classification User Manual*. Basingstoke: Palgrave Macmillan.

Office for National Statistics (2013) *General Lifestyle Survey 2011*. Available at http://www.ons.gov.uk/ons/rel/ghs/general-lifestyle-survey/2011/index.html [Accessed 7 December 2014.

Office for National Statistics (2014a) *Census History*. http://www.ons.gov.uk/ons/guide-method/census/2011/how-our-census-works/about-censuses/census-history/index.html [Accessed 8 December 2014].

Office for National Statistics (2014b) *Family Spending 2014 Edition*. Available at ww.ons.gov.uk/ons/rel/family-spending/family-spending/2014-edition/index.html [Accessed 5 December 2014].

Office for National Statistics (2014c) *200 Years of the Census*. Available at http://www.ons.gov.uk/ons/guide-method/census/2011/how-our-census-works/about-censuses/census-history/200-years-of-the-census/census-1911–2001/index.html [Accessed 10 March 2015].

Office for National Statistics (no date a) *Standard Occupation Classification 2010 (SOC2010)*. Available at http://www.ons.gov.uk/ons/guide-method/classifications/current-standard-classifications/soc2010/index.html [Accessed 27 November 2014].

Office for National Statistics (no date b) *The National Statistics Socio-economic Classification (NS-SEC rebased on the SOC2010)*. Available at http://www.ons.gov.uk/ons/guide-method/classifications/current-standard-classifications/soc2010/soc2010-volume-3-ns-sec-rebased-on-soc2010-user-manual/index.html [Accessed 27 November 2014].

Office for National Statistics (no date c) *Ethnic Group* Available at http://www.ons.gov.uk/ons/guide-method/measuring-equality/equality/ethnic-nat-identity-religion/ethnic-group/index.html [Accessed 27 November 2014].

Ogbonna, E. and Harris, L.C. (2014) 'Organizational cultural perpetuation: A case study of an English Premier League football club', *British Journal of Management*, Vol. 25, No. 4, pp. 667–86.

Okumus, F., Altinay, L. and Roper, A. (2007) 'Gaining access for research: Reflections from experience', *Annals of Tourism Research*, Vol. 34, No. 1, pp. 7–26.

Oppenheim, A.N. (2000) *Questionnaire Design, Interviewing and Attitude Measurement* (new edn). London: Continuum International.

Organ, D.W. (1988) *Organizational Citizenship Behaviour: The Good Soldier Syndrome*. Lexington, MA: Lexington Books.

Organ, D.W. (1997) 'Organizational citizenship behaviour: It's construct cleanup time', *Human Performance*, Vol. 10, No. 2, pp. 85–97.

Organ, D.W., Podsakoff, P.M. and MacKenzie, S.B. (2006) *Organizational Citizenship Behaviour: Its Nature, Antecedents, and Consequences*. Thousand Oaks, CA: Sage.

P

Paechter, C. (2013) 'Researching sensitive issues online: Implications of a hybrid insider/outsider position in a retrospective ethnographic study', *Qualitative Research*, Vol. 13, No. 1, pp. 71–86.

Pallant, J. (2013) *SPSS Survival Manual: A Step-by-Step Guide to Data Analysis Using IBM SPSS* (5th edn). Maidenhead: McGraw-Hill.

Palmer, D.A. (2013) 'The new perspective on organizational wrongdoing', *California Management Review*, Vol. 56, No. 1, pp. 5–23.

Pandza, K. and Thorpe, R. (2010) 'Management as design, but what kind of design? An appraisal of the design science analogy for management', *British Journal of Management*, Vol. 21, No. 2, pp. 171–86.

Paraskevas, A. and Saunders, M.N.K. (2012) 'Beyond consensus: An alternative use of Delphi enquiry in hospitality research', *International Journal of Contemporary Hospitality Management*, Vol. 24, No. 6, pp. 907–24.

Park, A., Bryson, C., Clery, E., Curtice, J. and Phillips, M. (2013) *British Social Attitudes: The 30th Report*. London: NatCen Social Research. Available at http://www.bsa-30.natcen.ac.uk/media/37580/bsa30_full_report_final.pdf [Accessed 27 November 2014].

Park, C. (2003) 'In other (people's) words: Plagiarism by university students – literature and lessons', *Assessment and Evaluation in Higher Education*, Vol. 28, No. 5, pp. 471–88.

Parker, M. (2002) *Against Management*. Cambridge: Polity Press.

Parry, H. (1991) *Successful Business Presentations*. Kingston-upon-Thames: Croner.

Patton, M.Q. (2002) *Qualitative Research and Evaluation Methods* (3rd edn). Thousand Oaks, CA: Sage.

Pearce, G., Thogersen-Ntoumani, C. and Duda, J.L. (2014) 'The development of synchronous text-based instant messaging as an online interviewing tool', *International Journal of Social Research Methodology*, Vol. 17, No. 6, pp. 677–92.

Petticrew, M. and Roberts, H. (2006) *Systematic Review in the Social Sciences: A Practical Guide*. Malden, MA: Blackwell.

Phillips, E.M. and Pugh, D.S. (2010) *How to Get a PhD* (5th edn). Maidenhead: Open University Press/McGraw-Hill.

Phillips, N. and Hardy, C. (2002) *Discourse Analysis: Investigating Processes of Social Construction*. London: Sage.

Plankey-Videla, N. (2012) 'Informed consent as process: Problematizing informed consent in organizational ethnographics', *Qualitative Sociology*, Vol. 35, pp. 1–21.

Podsakoff, N.P., Whiting, S. W., Podsakoff, P.M. and Blume, B.D. (2009) 'Individual and organizational level consequences of organizational citizenship behaviors: A meta-analysis', *Journal of Applied Psychology*, Vol. 94, No. 1, pp. 122–41.

Podsakoff, P.M., MacKenzie, S.B., Moorman, R.H. and Fetter, R. (1990) 'Transformational leader behaviours and their effects on followers' trust in leader, satisfaction, and organizational citizenship behaviors', *Leadership Quarterly*, No. 1, pp. 107–42.

Post-it (2014) *About Post-it*. Available at http://solutions.3m.co.uk/wps/portal/3M/en_GB/PostIt-EU-Global/PostIt/About-Post-it/ [Accessed 11 December 2014].

Powney, J. and Watts, M. (1987) *Interviewing in Educational Research*. London: Routledge and Kegan Paul.

Prior, D.D. and Miller, L.M. (2012) 'Webethnography: Towards a typology for quality in research design', *International Journal of Market Research*, Vol. 54, No. 4, pp. 503–20.

Prior, L. (2007) 'Documents', in C. Seale, G. Gobo, J. F. Gubrium and D. Silverman (eds) *Qualitative Research Practice*. London: Sage, pp. 345–60.

Prosser, L. (2009) *Office for National Statistics UK Standard Industrial Classification of Activities 2007 (SIC 2007)*. Basingstoke: Palgrave Macmillan. Available at http://www.ons.gov.uk/ons/guide-method/classifications/current-standard-classifications/standard-industrial-classification/index.html [Accessed 27 November 2014].

Q

Qualtrics (2014) *Qualtrics Research Suite: Sophisticated Online Surveys Made Simple*. Available at http://www.qualtrics.com/research-suite/ [Accessed 17 November 2014]

R

Raimond, P. (1993) *Management Projects*. London: Chapman & Hall.

Rawlins, K. (1999) *Presentation and Communication Skills: A Handbook for Practitioners*. London: Emap Healthcare Ltd.

Reason, P. (2006) 'Choice and quality in action research practice', *Journal of Management Inquiry*, Vol. 15, No. 2, pp. 187–202.

Reason, P. and Bradbury, H. (2008) *Handbook of Action Research* (2nd edn). London: Sage.

Reed, M. (2005) 'Reflections on the "realist turn" in organization and management studies', *Journal of Management Studies*, Vol. 42, pp. 1621–44.

Reichertz, J. (2007) 'Abduction: The logic of discovery of grounded theory', in A. Bryant and K. Charmaz (eds) *The Sage Handbook of Grounded Theory*. London: Sage.

Reichman, C.S. (1962) *Use and Abuse of Statistics*. New York: Oxford University Press.

Reinhart, C. and Rogoff, K. (2010) 'Growth in a time of debt', *American Economic Review*, Vol. 100, No. 2, pp. 573–8.

Remoaldo, P.C., Ribeiro, J.C., Vareiro, L. and Santos, J.F. (2014) 'Tourists' perceptions of world heritage destinations: The case of Guimarães (Portugal)', *Tourism and Hospitality Research*, Vol. 14, No. 4, pp. 206–18.

Richards, P. (2007) 'Risk', in H. Becker (ed.) *Writing for Social Scientists* (2nd edn). Chicago, IL: University of Chicago Press.

Ridder, H-G., Hoon, C., and McCandless Baluch, A. (2014) 'Entering a dialogue: Positioning case study findings towards theory', *British Journal of Management*, Vol. 25, No. 2, pp. 373–87.

Ridenour, C.S. and Newman, I. (2008) *Mixed Methods Research: Exploring the Interactive Continuum*. Carbondale, IL: South Illinois University Press.

Riessman, C.K. (2008) *Narrative Methods for the Human Sciences*. London: Sage.

Robson, C. (2011) *Real World Research: A Resource for Users of Social Research Methods in Applied Settings* (3rd edn). Chichester: John Wiley.

Rogelberg, S.G. and Stanton, J.M. (2007) 'Introduction: Understanding and dealing with organizational survey non-response', *Organizational Research Methods*, Vol. 10, No. 2, pp. 195–209.

Rogers, C.R. (1961) *On Becoming a Person*. London: Constable.

Rousseau, D. (2006). 'Is there such a thing as "evidence-based management"?', *Academy of Management Review,* Vol. 31, No. 2, pp. 256–69.

S

Saunders, M.N.K. (2011) 'The management researcher as practitioner', in B. Lee and C. Cassell (eds) *Challenges and Controversies in Management Research.* New York: Routledge, pp. 243–57.

Saunders, M.N.K. (2012) 'Choosing research participants', in G. Symons and C. Cassell (eds) *The Practice of Qualitative Organizational Research: Core Methods and Current Challenges.* London: Sage, pp. 37–55.

Saunders, M.N.K. (2012) 'Web versus mail: The influence of survey distribution mode on employees' response', *Field Methods*, Vol. 24, No. 1, pp. 56–73.

Saunders, M.N.K., Dietz, G. and Thornhill, A. (2014) 'Trust and distrust: Polar opposites, or independent but co-existing?', *Human Relations*, Vol. 67, No. 6, pp. 639–65.

Saunders, M.N.K. and Lewis, P. (1997) 'Great ideas and blind alleys? A review of the literature on starting research', *Management Learning*, Vol. 28, No. 3, pp. 283–99.

Schein, E. (1999) *Process Consultation Revisited: Building the Helping Relationship*. Reading, MA: Addison-Wesley.

Schoneboom, A. (2011) 'Workblogging in a Facebook age', *Work, Employment and Society*, Vol. 25, No. 1, pp. 132–40.

Schrauf, R.W. and Navarro, E. (2005) 'Using existing tests and scales in the field', *Field Methods*, Vol. 17, No. 4, pp. 373–93.

Sekaran, U. and Bougie, R. (2013) *Research Methods for Business: A Skill-Building Approach* (6th edn). Chichester: John Wiley.

Shani, A.B. and Pasmore, W.A. (1985) 'Organization inquiry: Towards a new model of the action research process', in D.D. Warrick (ed.) *Contemporary Organization Development*. Glenview, IL: Scott Foresman, pp. 438–48.

Shellenbarger, S. (2013) 'Tactics to spark creativity', *Wall Street Journal*, 5–7 April, p. 29.

Sherbaum, C. and Shockley, K. (2015) *Analysing Quantitative Data for Business and Management Students*. London: Sage.

Silverman, D. (2013) *A Very Short, Fairly Interesting and Reasonably Cheap Book about Qualitative Research* (2nd edn.) London: Sage.

SimpleMind (2014) *SimpleMind Homepage*. Available at http://www.simpleapps.eu/simplemind/ [Accessed 1 April 2014]

Smith, C.A., Organ, D.W., and Near, J.P. (1983) 'Organizational citizenship behavior: Its nature and antecedents', *Journal of Applied Psychology*, Vol. 68, No. 4, pp. 653–63.

Smith, E. (2006) *Using Secondary Data in Educational and Social Research*. Maidenhead: Open University Press.

Snap Surveys (2014) *Snap Surveys. Software Solutions Services*. Available at www.snapsurveys.com [Accessed 4 December 2014].

Social Research Association (2001) *A Code of Practice for the Safety of Social Researchers*. Available at http://the-sra.org.uk/sra_resources/safety-code/ [Accessed 25 March 2014].

Sonnenshein, S., DeCelles, K. and Dutton, J.E. (2014) 'It's not easy being green: The role of self evaluations in explaining the support of environmental issues', *Academy of Management Journal,* Vol. 57, No. 1, pp. 7–37.

Spano, R. (2005) 'Potential sources of observer bias in police observational data', *Social Science Research*, Vol. 34, pp. 591–617.

Speer, S.A. (2008) 'Natural and contrived data', in P. Alasuutari, L. Bickman, and J. Brannen (eds) *The Sage Handbook of Social Research Methods*. London: Sage, pp. 290–312.

Spence, M., Gherib, J.B.B. and Biwolé, V.O. (2011) 'Sustainable development: Is entrepreneurial will enough?', *Journal of Business Ethics,* Vol. 99, No. 3, pp. 335–67.

Stake, R.E. (2005) 'Qualitative case studies', in N.K. Denzin and Y.S. Lincoln (eds) *The Sage Handbook of Qualitative Research* (3rd edn). London: Sage, pp. 443–65.

Starbuck, W. (2003) 'The origins of organization theory', in H. Tsoukas and C. Knudsen (eds) *The Oxford Handbook of Organization Theory: Meta-Theoretical Perspectives*. Oxford: Oxford University Press.

Starkey, K. and Madan, P. (2001) 'Bridging the relevance gap: Aligning stakeholders in the future of management research', *British Journal of Management*, Vol. 12, Special Issue, pp. 3–26.

Starr, R. and Fernandez, K. (2007) 'The mindcam methodology: Perceiving through the native's eye', *Qualitative Market Research*, Vol. 10, No. 2, pp. 168–82.

Stationery Office, *The (1998) Data Protection Act 1998*. London: The Stationery Office.

Stewart, D.W. and Kamins, M.A. (1993) *Secondary Research: Information Sources and Methods* (2nd edn). Newbury Park: CA, Sage.

Stieger, S. and Goritz, A.S. (2006) 'Using instant messaging for internet-based interviews', *CyberPsychology and Behavior*, Vol. 9, No. 5, pp. 552–9.

Stokes, D. and Bergin, R. (2006) 'Methodology or "methodolatry"? An evaluation of focus groups and depth interviews', *Qualitative Market Research*, Vol. 9, No. 1, pp. 26–37.

Strauss, A. and Corbin, J. (1998) *Basics of Qualitative Research* (2nd edn). Thousand Oaks, CA: Sage.

Suddaby, R. (2006) 'From the editors: What grounded theory is not', *Academy of Management Journal*, Vol. 49, No. 4, pp. 633–42.

SurveyMonkey (2014) *SurveyMonkey*. Available at www.surveymonkey.com [Accessed 5 December 2014].

Sutton, R. and Staw, B. (1995) 'What theory is not', *Administrative Science Quarterly*, Vol. 40, No. 3, pp. 371–84.

Swift, L. and Piff, S. (2014) *Quantitative Methods for Business, Management and Finance* (4th edn) Basingstoke: Palgrave Macmillan.

T

Tang, J., Crossan, M. and Rowe, W.G. (2011) 'Dominant CEO, deviant strategy, and extreme performance: The moderating role of a powerful board', *Journal of Management Studies*, Vol. 48, No. 7, pp. 1479–503.

Tashakkori, A. and Teddlie, C. (eds) (2010) *The Sage Handbook of Mixed Methods in Social and Behavioural Research* (2nd edn). Thousand Oaks, CA: Sage.

Teddlie, C. and Tashakkori, A. (2009) *Foundations of Mixed Methods Research: Integrating Quantitative and Qualitative Approaches in the Social and Behavioural Sciences*. Thousand Oaks, CA: Sage.

Teddlie, C. and Tashakkori, A. (2011) 'Mixed methods research: Contemporary issues in an emerging field', in N.K. Denzin and Y.S. Lincoln (eds) *The Sage Handbook of Qualitative Research* (4th edn). London: Sage, pp. 285–99.

Tedlock, B. (2005) 'The observation of participation and the emergence of public ethnography', in N.K. Denzin and Y.S. Lincoln (eds) *The Sage Handbook of Qualitative Research* (3rd edn). London: Sage.

Tennant, J. (2013) *The Economist Numbers Guide: The Essentials of Business Numeracy* (6th edn). [Kindle e-book] London: Profile Books.

Tharenou, P., Donohue, R. and Cooper, B. (2007) *Management Research Methods*. Melbourne: Cambridge University Press.

The Free Dictionary (2014) 'Gibberish'. Available at http://www.thefreedictionary.com/gibberish [Accessed 15 December 2014].

Thomas, J. (1996) 'Introduction: A debate about the ethics of fair practices for collecting social science data in cyberspace', *The Information Society*, Vol. 12, No. 2, pp. 107–17.

Thomas, R. and Hardy, C. (2011) Reframing resistance to organizational change. *Scandinavian Journal of Management*, Vol. 27, pp. 322–31.

Tietze, S. (2012) 'Researching your own organization', in G. Symon and C. Cassell (eds) *Qualitative Organisational Research Core Methods and Current Challenges*. London: Sage, pp. 53–71.

Titscher, S., Meyer, M., Wodak, R. and Vetter, E. (2000) *Methods of Text and Discourse Analysis*. London: Sage, pp. 467–82.

Townley, B. (1994) *Reframing Human Resource Management: Power, Ethics and the Subject at Work*. London: Sage.

Tranfield, D. and Denyer, D. (2004) 'Linking theory to practice: A grand challenge for management research in the 21st century?', *Organization Management Journal*, Vol. 1, No. 1, pp. 10–14.

Tranfield, D. and Starkey, K. (1998) 'The nature, social organization and promotion of management research: Towards policy', *British Journal of Management*, Vol. 9, pp. 341–53.

Tranfield, D., Denyer, D. and Smart, P. (2003) 'Towards a methodology for developing evidence-informed management knowledge by means of systematic review', *British Journal of Management*, Vol. 14, No. 3, pp. 207–22.

Trier-Bieniek, A. (2012) 'Framing the telephone interview as a participant-centred tool for qualitative research: A methodological discussion', *Qualitative Research*, Vol. 12, No. 6, pp. 630–44.

Tucker, C. and Lepkowski, J.M. (2008) 'Telephone survey methods: Adapting to change', in J.M. Lepkowski, C. Tucker, J.M. Brick, E.D. De Leeuw, L. Japec, P.J. Lavrakas, M.W. Link and R.L. Sangster (eds) *Advances in Telephone Survey Methodology*. Hoboken, NJ: Wiley, pp. 3–28.

Tukey, J.W. (1977) *Exploratory Data Analysis*. Reading, MA: Addison-Wesley.

U

UK Data Archive (2011) *Managing and Sharing Data: Best Practice for Researchers* (3rd edn). Available at http://www.data-archive.ac.uk/media/2894/managingsharing.pdf [Accessed 26 March 2014].

UK Data Archive (2014) *Create and Manage Data – Anonymisation*. Available at http://www.data-archive.ac.uk/create-manage/consent-ethics/anonymisation [Accessed 26 March 2014].

UK Data Archive (2014) *UK Data Archive*. Available at www.data-archive.ac.uk/ [Accessed 12 October 2014].

UK Data Service (2014) *Variable and Question Bank*. Available at: http://discover.ukdataservice.ac.uk/variables [Accessed 27 November 2014].

University of Southern California (2014) *Organising your Social Sciences Research Paper*. Available at http://libguides.usc.edu/content.php?pid=83009&sid=615851 [Accessed 20 March 2014].

Usunier, J.-C. (1998) *International and Cross-Cultural Management Research*. London: Sage.

V

Van Aken, J.E. (2005) 'Management research as a design science: Articulating the research products of Mode 2 knowledge production in management', *British Journal of Management*, Vol. 16, No. 1, pp. 19–36.

Van Maanen, J. (2011a) 'Ethnography as work: Some rules of engagement', *Journal of Management Studies*, Vol. 48, No. 1, pp. 218–34.

Van Maanen, J. (2011b) *Tales of the Field: On Writing Ethnography* (2nd edn). London: University of Chicago Press.

Van Maanen, J., Sørensen, J.B. and Mitchell, T.R. (2007) 'The interplay between theory and method', *Academy of Management Review*, Vol. 32, No. 4, pp. 1145–54.

Vartanian, T.P. (2011) *Secondary Data Analysis*. Oxford: Oxford University Press.

Verisign Inc. (2014) *The Domain Name Industry Brief*, Vol. 11, No. 3. Available at http://www.verisigninc.com/assets/domain-name-report-december2014.pdf [Accessed 9 December 2014].

W

Waddington, D. (2004) 'Participant observation', in C. Cassell and G. Symon (eds) *Essential Guide to Qualitative Methods in Organizational Research*. London: Sage, pp. 154–64.

Wallace, M. and Wray, A. (2011) *Critical Reading and Writing for Postgraduates* (2nd edn). London: Sage.

Walliman, N. (2011) *Your Research Project: A Step by Step Guide for the First-Time Researcher* (3rd edn). London: Sage.

Waskul, D. and Douglass, M. (1996) 'Considering the electronic participant: Some polemical observations on the ethics of on-line research', *The Information Society*, Vol. 12, No. 2, pp. 129–39.

Watson, T.J. (2011) 'Ethnography, Reality, and truth: The vital need for studies of "how things work" in organizations and management', *Journal of Management Studies*, Vol. 48, No. 1, pp. 202–17.

Webspiration (2014) *Webspiration pro Homepage*. Available at http://www.webspirationpro.com/home [Accessed 1 April 2014].

Wells, P. (1994) 'Ethics in business and management research', in V.J. Wass and P.E. Wells (eds) *Principles and Practice in Business and Management Research*. Aldershot: Dartmouth, pp. 277–97.

Welsh, D.T. and Ordóñez, L.D. (2014) 'Conscience without cognition: The effects of subconscious priming on ethical behaviour', *Academy of Management Journal*, Vol. 57, No. 3, pp. 723–42.

Wensley, R. (2011) 'Seeking relevance in management research', in C. Cassell and B. Lee (eds) *Challenges and Controversies in Management Research*. New York: Routledge, pp. 258–74.

Wernicke, I.H. (2014) 'Quality of official statistics data on the economy', *Journal of Finance, Accounting and Management*, Vol. 5, No. 2, pp. 77–93.

Whetten, D. (1989) 'What constitutes a theoretical contribution?', *Academy of Management Review*, Vol. 14, No. 4, pp. 490–5.

Whyte, W.F. (1993) *Street Corner Society: The Social Structure of an Italian Slum* (4th edn). Chicago, IL: University of Chicago Press.

Wikipedia (2014) *Wikipedia:About*. Available at http://en.wikipedia.org/wiki/About_Wikipedia [Accessed 1 April 2014].

Willimack, D.K., Nichols, E. and Sudman, S. (2002) 'Understanding unit and item nonresponse in business surveys', in D.A. Dillman, J.L. Eltringe, J.L. Groves and R.J.A. Little (eds) *Survey Nonresponse*. New York: Wiley Interscience, pp. 213–27.

Witmer, D.F., Colman, R.W. and Katzman, S.L. (1999) 'From paper and pen to screen and keyboard: Towards a methodology for survey research on the Internet', in S. Jones (ed.) *Doing Internet Research*. Thousand Oaks, CA: Sage, pp. 145–62.

Wolf, A. (2007) 'People have a tendency to assume that quantitative data must be out there on the web waiting to be found', *The Times Higher Education Supplement*, 12 Oc. Available at http://www.timeshighereducation.co.uk/news/alison-wolf/310797.article [Accessed 3 December 2014].

Wright Mills, C. (1970) 'On intellectual craftsmanship', in C. Wright Mills, *The Sociological Imagination*. London: Pelican.

Y

Yin, R.K. (2014) *Case Study Research: Design and Method* (5th edn). London: Sage.

Z

Zigterman, B (2013) The 10 worst video game consoles of all time. Available at http://bgr.com/2013/12/16/video-game-consoles-the-top-10-worst/ [Accessed 20 July 2014].

Appendix 1 Systems of referencing
附录 1　引用体系

Preferred styles of referencing differ both between universities and between departments within universities. Even styles that are in wide use such as 'Harvard' vary in how they are used in practice by different institutions. When this is combined with the reality that some lecturers apply an adopted style strictly, while others are more lenient, it emphasises the need for you to use the precise style prescribed in your assessment criteria. Within business and management, two author–date referencing systems predominate, the Harvard style and the American Psychological Association (APA) style, both of which are author–date systems. The alternative, numeric systems, is used far less widely.

Six points are important when referencing:

- Full credit must be given to the author or originator (the person or organisation taking main responsibility for the source) when quoting or citing others' work.
- Adequate information must be provided in the reference to enable that work to be located.
- References must be consistent, complete and accurate.
- References must be recorded using precisely the style required by your university and are often part of the marking criteria.
- Wherever you directly quote an author you should use 'quotation marks' to show this and also record the precise location (normally page number).
- If you fail to reference fully, you are likely to be accused of plagiarism (Section 3.9).

As you will see later in this appendix, when referring to an electronic document, principally a journal article, accessed online, it is becoming more usual to include that document's DOI (digital object identifier) as part of the reference. The DOI provides a permanent and unique identifier for that document. Where there is no DOI, it is usual to include the document's URL (uniform resource locator – usually its web address). As the URL is not permanent, the date when it was accessed is also included in the reference.

Author–date systems

The Harvard style

Referencing in the text

The Harvard style is an *author–date system*, a variation of which we use in this book. It appears to have its origins in a referencing practice developed by a professor of anatomy at Harvard University (Neville 2010) and usually uses the author's or originator's name and year of publication to identify cited documents within the text. All references are listed alphabetically at the end of the text. Common institutional variations within the Harvard style which are applied consistently include (Neville 2010):

- Where there are more than two authors, the names of the second and subsequent authors may or may not be replaced in the text by *et al.* This phrase may be in italics and is usually followed by a full stop to signify it is an abbreviation of et alia.
- Name(s) of authors or originators may or may not be in UPPER CASE in the list of references.
- The year of publication may or may not be enclosed in (brackets) in the list of references.
- Capitalisation of words in the title is usually kept to a minimum rather than being used for Many of the Words in the Title.
- The title of the publication may be in *italics* or may be underlined in the list of references.

The style for referencing work in the text and in the list of references or bibliography is outlined in Table A1.1, additional conventions for referencing in the text being given in Table A1.2.

Table A1.1 Conventions when using the Harvard style to reference

To cite	In the text		In the list of references/bibliography	
	General format	**Example**	**General format**	**Example**
Books				
Book (first edition)	*1 author:* (Family name year)	*1 author:* (Silverman 2007)	Family name, Initials. (year). *Title*. Place of publication: Publisher.	Silverman, D. (2007). *A Very Short, Fairly Interesting and Reasonably Cheap Book about Qualitative Research*. London: Sage.
	2 or 3 authors: (Family name, Family name and Family name year)	*2 or 3 authors:* (Berman Brown and Saunders 2008)	Family name, Initials. and Family name, Initials. (year). *Title*. Place of publication: Publisher.	Berman Brown, R. and Saunders, M. (2008). *Dealing with Statistics: What You Need to Know*. Maidenhead: Open University Press.
	4+ authors: (Family name et al. year)	4+ *authors:* (Millmore et al. 2010)	Family name, Initials., Family name, Initials. and Family name, Initials [can be discretionary to include more than first author] (year). *Title*. Place of publication: Publisher.	Millmore, M., Lewis, P., Saunders, M., Thornhill, A. and Morrow, T. (2007). *Strategic Human Resource Management: Contemporary Issues*. Harlow: FT Prentice Hall.
Book (other than first edition)	*As for 'Book (first edition)'*	(Anderson et al. 2014)	Family name, Initials. and Family name, Initials. (year). *Title*. (# edn). Place of publication: Publisher.	Anderson, D.L., Sweeney, D.J., Williams, T.A., Freeman, J. and Shoesmith, E. (2014). *Statistics for Business and Economics*. (3rd edn). Andover: Cengage Learning EMA.

(Continued)

629

Table A1.1 (*Continued*)

To cite	In the text		In the list of references/bibliography	
	General format	**Example**	**General format**	**Example**
Book (edited)	*As for* 'Book (first edition)'	(Saunders et al. 2010)	Family name, Initials. and Family name, Initials. (eds.) (year). *Title*. Place of publication: Publisher.	Saunders, M.N.K, Skinner, D., Gillespie, N., Dietz, G. and Lewicki, R.J. (eds.) (2010). *Organizational Trust: A Cultural Perspective*. Cambridge: Cambridge University Press.
Book (not in English language)	*As for* 'Book (first edition)'	(Fontaine et al. 2010)	Family name, Initials. and Family name, Initials. (year). *Title* [English translation of title]. Place of publication: Publisher.	Fontaine, C., Salti, S. and Thivard, T. (2010). *100 CV et lettres de motivation* [100 CV and cover letters]. Paris: Studyrama.
Book (translated into English)	*As for* 'Book (first edition)'	(Hugo 2003)	Family name, Initials. and Family name, Initials. (year). *Title*. (Initials of translator. Family name of translator. Trans). Place of publication: Publisher. (Original work published year).	Hugo, V. (2003). *Les Miserables*. (N. Denny. Trans.). London: Penguin. (Original work published 1862).
Republished book	*As for* 'Book (first edition)'	(Marshall 1981)	Family name, Initials. and Family name, Initials. (year). *Title*. Place of publication: Publisher (originally published by Publisher year).	Marshall, J.D. (1981). *Furness and the Industrial Revolution*. Beckermont: Michael Moon (originally published by Barrow Town Council 1958).
E-book	*As for* 'Book (first edition)'	(Saunders 2013)	Family name, Initials. (year). *Title*. [name of e-book reader]. Place of publication: Publisher.	Saunders, J.J. (2013). *The Holocaust: History in an Hour* [Kindle e-book]. London: William Collins.
Online book	*As for* 'Book (first edition)' or 'Edited book'	(Sungsoo 2013)	Family name, Initials. and Family name, Initials. (year). *Title*. (# edn) Place of publication: Publisher. [Accessed day month year from Database name].	Sungsoo, P. (ed.) (2013). *Benchmarks in Hospitality and Tourism*. New York: Routledge. [Accessed 6 Apr. 2014 from MyLibrary.com]
Chapters in books				
Chapter in a book	*As for* 'Book (first edition)'	(Robson 2011)	Family name, Initials. and Family name, Initials. (year). *Title*. Place of publication: Publisher. Chapter #.	Robson, C. (2011). *Real World Research*. (3rd edn). Oxford: Blackwell. Chapter 3.

To cite	In the text		In the list of references/bibliography	
	General format	**Example**	**General format**	**Example**
Chapter in an edited book containing a collection of articles (sometimes called a reader)	(Chapter author family name year)	(King 2012)	Family name, Initials. (year). Chapter title. In Initials. Family name and Initials. Family name (eds) *Title*. Place of publication: Publisher. pp. ###–###.	King, N. (2012). Doing template analysis. In G. Symon and C. Cassell (eds) *Qualitative Organizational Research*. London: Sage. pp. 426–50.
Chapter in an online book	(Chapter author family name year)	(Roper 2007)	Chapter author family name, Initials. (year). Chapter title. In Initials. Family name and Initials. Family name (eds) *Title*. Place of publication: Publisher. pp. ###–###. [Accessed day month year from Database name].	Roper, A. (2007). The international marketing management decisions of UK ski tour operators. In M. Saunders, P. Lewis and A. Thornhill. *Research Methods for Business Students*. (4th edn) Harlow: FT Prentice Hall. pp. 158–9. [Accessed 6 Apr. 2014 from MyLibrary.com]
Dictionaries and other reference books				
. . . where author known	*As for* 'Book (first edition)'	(Vogt and Johnson 2011)	Family name, Initials. (year). *Title*. (# edn). Place of Publication: Publisher. pp. ###–###.	Vogt, W.P. and Johnson, R.B. (2011). *Dictionary of Statistics and Methodology: A Nontechnical Guide for the Social Sciences*. (4th edn). Thousand Oaks, CA: Sage. pp. 31–2.
. . . where no author or editor	(*Publication title* year)	(*The right word at the right time* 1985)	*Publication title*. (year). (# edn). Place of Publication: Publisher. pp. ###–###.	*The right word at the right time*. (1985). Pleasantville, NY: Readers Digest Association. pp. 563–4.
. . . where editor known and author for particular entry	(Entry author family name data)	(Watson 2008)	Entry author family name, Initials. (year). Entry title. In Initials. Family name and Initials. Family name (eds) *Title*. Place of publication: Publisher. pp. ###–###.	Watson, T. (2008). Field research. In R. Thorpe and R. Holt (eds) *The SAGE Dictionary of Qualitative Management Research*. London: Sage. pp. 99–100.
. . . where accessed online and is no author or editor	(*Publication title* year)	(*Encyclopaedia Britannica Online* 2014)	*Publication title*. (year). Available at http://www.remainderoffullInternet address/ [Accessed day month year].	*Encyclopaedia Britannica. Online*. (2014). Available at http://www.britannica.com/ [Accessed 4 Mar. 2014].

(*Continued*)

Table A1.1 (*Continued*)

To cite	In the text		In the list of references/bibliography	
	General format	**Example**	**General format**	**Example**
. . . where accessed online and no author or editor for a particular entry	(*Publication title* year)	(*Encyclopaedia Britannica Online* 2014)	*Publication title.* (year). Title of entry. Available at http://www .remainderoffullInternet address/ [Accessed day month year].	*Encyclopaedia Britannica Online.* (2014). Definition of 'Marketing'. Available at http://www.britannica.com/ EBchecked/topic/365730/ marketing [Accessed 4 Mar. 2014].
Reports				
Report	*As for* 'Book (first edition)'	(Gray et al. 2012)	Family name, Initials. and Family name, Initials. (year). *Title.* Place of publication: Publisher.	Gray, D.E., Saunders M.N.K. and Goregaokar, H. (2012). *Success in Challenging Times: Key Lessons for UK SMEs.* London: Kingston Smith LLP.
Report (no named author)	(Originator name *or Publication title* year)	(Mintel Marketing Intelligence 2008)	Originator name *or* Publication title. (year). *Title.* Place of publication: Publisher.	Mintel Marketing Intelligence. (1998). *Designerwear: Mintel marketing intelligence report.* London: Mintel International Group Ltd.
Organisation's annual report	*As for* 'Book (first edition)'	(Tesco Plc 2013)	Organisation name. (year). *Title.* Place of publication: as author.	Tesco Plc. (2013). *Working to make what matters better, together: Annual report 2013.* Cheshunt: as author.
Online report	*As for* 'Book (first edition)'	(Thorlby et al. 2014)	Family name, Initials. and Family name, Initials. (year). *Title of report.* Available at http://www. remainderoffullInternet address/ [Accessed day month year].	Thorlby, R., Smith, J., Williams, S. and Dayan, M. (2014). *The Francis Report: One year on.* Available at: http://www.nuffieldtrust. org.uk/sites/files/nuffield/ publication/140206_the_ francis_inquiry.pdf. [Accessed 20 Mar. 2014].
Online report (no named author)	(Originator name *or Publication title* year)	(Mintel 2013)	Originator name. (year). *Title of report.* Available at http://www. remainderoffullInternet address/ [Accessed day month year].	Mintel (2013) – *Online Retailing in China – May 2013.* Available at: http:// academic.mintel.com/ display/642908/#atom0 [Accessed 3 Oct. 2013].
Government and governmental bodies' publications				
Parliamentary papers including acts and bills	(Country of origin year)	(United Kingdom 2013)	Country of origin. (year). *Title.* Place of publication: Publisher.	United Kingdom. (2013). *The Financial Services (Banking Reform) Act.* London: TSO (The Stationery Office).

To cite	In the text		In the list of references/bibliography	
	General format	**Example**	**General format**	**Example**
Parliamentary debates (Hansard)	(Country Parliament year)	(United Kingdom Parliament 2013)	Country Parliament. House of Commons (HC) or House of Lords (HL) Deb. day month year. Command paper #.	United Kingdom Parliament HC Deb. 20 November 2013. Command paper 8655.
Other	*As for* 'Book (first edition)'	(Francis 2013)	*As for* 'Book (first edition)'	Francis, R. (2013). *Report of the Mid Staffordshire NHS Foundation Trust Public Inquiry: Executive Summary*. London: The Stationery Office.
Other (no named author or editor)	(Department name *or* Committee name year)	(United Nations 2013)	Department name or Committee name. (year). *Title*. Place of publication: Publisher.	United Nations. (2013). *The Millennium Development Goals Report 2013*. New York: United Nations.
Other (online)	(Family name year)	(Browne and Alstrup 2006)	Family name, Initials. and Family name, Initials. (year). *Title of report*. Available at http://www.remainderoffull Internetaddress/ [Accessed day month year].	Browne, L. and Alstrup, P. (Eds.) (2006). *What exactly is the Labour Force Survey?* Available at http://www.statistics.gov.uk/downloads/_theme_labour/_What_exactly_is_LFS1.pdf [Accessed 25 Dec. 2007].
Other (no named author or editor; online)	(Department name *or* Committee name year)	(Department for Business Innovation and Skills 2014)	Department name or Committee name. (year). *Title*. Available at http://www.remainderoffull Internetaddress/ [Accessed day month year].	Department for Business Innovation and Skills. (2014). *Women on Boards: Voluntary Code for Executive Search firms*. Available at: https://www.gov.uk/government/uploads/system/uploads/attachment_data/file/286342/bis-14–640-women-on-boards-voluntary-code-for-executive-search-firms-taking-the-next-step-march-2014.pdf [Accessed 20 Mar. 2014].
Journal articles				
Journal article (print form or facsimile of print form accessed via full text database)	*As for* 'Book (first edition)'	(Rojon et al. 2011)	Family name, Initials. and Family name, Initials. (year). Title of article. *Journal name*. Vol. ##, No. ##, pp. ###–####.	Rojon, C., McDowall, A. and Saunders, M.N.K. (2011). On the Experience of Conducting a Systematic Review in Industrial, Work and Organizational Psychology: Yes, It Is Worthwhile. *Journal of Personnel Psychology*. Vol. 10, No. 3, pp. 133–8.

(Continued)

Table A1.1 (*Continued*)

To cite	In the text		In the list of references/bibliography	
	General format	Example	General format	Example
Journal article (facsimile of print form, where full text database details required by University)	*As for* 'Book (first edition)'	(Rojon et al., 2011)	Family name, Initials. and Family name, Initials. (year). Title of article. *Journal name*. Vol. ##, No. ##, pp. ###–####. [Accessed day month year from Database name].	Rojon, C., McDowall, A. and Saunders, M.N.K. (2011). On the Experience of Conducting a Systematic Review in Industrial, Work and Organizational Psychology: Yes, It Is Worthwhile. *Journal of Personnel Psychology*. Vol. 10, No. 3, pp. 133–8. [Accessed 6 Apr. 2010 from PsycARTICLES].
Journal article which is forthcoming but published online, prior to appearing in the journal; available in facsimile form	*As for* 'Book (first edition)'	(Saunders and Rojon 2014)	Family name, Initials. and Family name, Initials. (year). Title of article, *Journal name*. Available at full doi *or* Internet address [Accessed day month year].	Saunders, M.N.K. and Rojon, C. (2014) There's no madness in my method: explaining how your coaching research findings are built on firm foundations. *Coaching: An International Journal of Theory, Research and Practice.* Available at DOI: 10.1080/ 17521882.2014.889185 [Accessed 6 Mar. 2014].
Journal article only published online, which is not published in print or facsimile form	*As for* 'Journal article made available by the publisher in advance online . . .'	(Yang and Banamah 2013)	*As for* 'Journal article made available by the publisher in advance online . . .'	Yang, K. and Banamah, A. (2013). Quota Sampling as an Alternative to Probability Sampling? An Experimental Study. *Sociological Research Online*. Vol. 18, No. 4. Available at http://www. socresonline.org.uk/19/1/29. html [Accessed 4 Mar. 2014].
Magazine articles				
Magazine article	*As for* 'Book (first edition)'	(Saunders 2004)	Family name, Initials. and Family name, Initials. (year). Title of article. *Magazine name*. Vol. ##, No. ## (*or* Issue *or* day *and/or* month), pp. ###–###.	Saunders, M. (2004). Land of the long white cloud. *HOG News UK*. Issue 23, Oct. pp. 24–6.
Magazine article (no named author)	(Originator name *or Publication name* year)	(*People Management* 2014)	Originator name *or* Publication *name*. (year). Title of article. *Magazine name*. Vol. ##, No. ## (*or* Issue *or* day *and/or* month), pp. ###–###.	People Management. (2014). Efficiency rule was misused. *People Management*. Mar. p. 17.

To cite	In the text		In the list of references/bibliography	
	General format	**Example**	**General format**	**Example**
News articles including newspapers and online news				
Newspaper article	*As for* 'Book (first edition)'	(Frean 2014)	Family name, Initials. and Family name, Initials. Title of article. *Newspaper name*, day month year, p. ###.	Frean, A. Credit Suisse bankers 'assisted tax evasion'. *The Times*. 27 Feb. 2014, p. 35.
Newspaper article (no named author)	(*Newspaper name* year)	(*The Times* 2014)	*Newspaper name*. Title of article, day month year, p. ##.	*The Times*. Budweiser's early win, 27 Feb. 2014, p. 33.
Newspaper article (published online)	*As for* other News articles	(Rankin 2014)	Family name, Initials. and Family name, Initials. Title of article. *Newspaper name*, day month year. Available at http://www. full-Internetaddress/ [Accessed day month year].	Rankin J. Record number of women make 28th annual Forbes' billionaires list. *The Guardian*. 4 Mar. 2014. Available at http://www.theguardian. com/business/2014/mar/03/ record-number-women- forbes-28th-billionaires-list. html?src=linkedin [Accessed 4 Mar. 2014].
Newspaper article (from electronic database)	*As for* other News articles	(Anderson 2009)	Family name, Initials. and Family name, Initials. Title of article. *Newspaper name*, day month year, p. ### (if known). [Accessed day month year from Database name].	Anderson, L. How to choose a Business School. *Financial Times*, 23 Jan. 2009. [Accessed 20 Mar. 2010 from ft.com].
News article (from news web site)	*As for* other News articles	(Gordon 2014)	Family name, Initials. and Family name, Initials. Title of article. *News web site*, day month year. Available at http://www.full- Internetaddress/ [Accessed day month year].	Gordon, O. Keeping crowdsourcing honest. Can we trust the reviews? BBC News, 14 Feb. 2014. Available at: http://www.bbc.co.uk/ news/technology-26182642 [Accessed 4 Mar. 2014].
CD-ROMS				
CD-ROM	*As for* 'Book (first edition)'	(Friedman et al. 2007)	Family name, Initials. and family name, initials. (year). *Title of CD-ROM*. [CD-ROM]. Place of publication: Publisher.	Friedman, M., Friedman, R. and Adams, J. (2007). *Free to chase*. [CD-ROM]. Ashland, OR: Blackstone Audiobooks.
CD-ROM (no named author)	(*CD-ROM title* year)	(*Encarta 2006 Encyclopaedia* 2005)	*Title of CD-ROM*. (year). [CD-ROM]. Place of publication: Publisher.	*Encarta 2006 Encyclopaedia*. (2005). [CD-ROM]. Redmond, WA: Microsoft.

(Continued)

Table A1.1 (*Continued*)

To cite	In the text		In the list of references/bibliography	
	General format	**Example**	**General format**	**Example**
Brochures and Media/Press releases				
Brochure	(Originator name *or* Brochure title year)	(BMW AG 2013)	Originator name *or* Brochure title. (year). *Title*. Place of publication: as author.	BMW AG. (2013). *Mini Hatch. Mini Convertible. Mini Clubman*. Munich: as author.
Media/press releases	(Originator name *or Release title* year).	(BBC 2014)	Originator name *or Release title*. (year). *Title*. Place of publication: as author.	BBC. (2014). *BBC Trust approves proposals for BBC store*. London: as author.
Online/websites				
Internet site or specific site pages	(Source organisation year)	(European Commission 2014)	Source organisation. (year). *Title of site or page within site*. Available at http://www.remainderoffull Internetaddress/ [Accessed day month year].	European Commission. (2014). *Eurostat – structural indicators*. Available at http://epp.eurostat.ec.europa.eu/portal/page/portal/structural_indicators/introduction [Accessed 5 Mar. 2014].
Blogs (weblogs), web forums, Wikis				
Blogs (weblogs)	(Owners family name year of posting)	(Kitces 2014)	Owner's family name, Owner's Initials. (year of posting). Specific subject. *Title of blog*. Day Month Year (of posting). [Blog] Available at http://www.remainderoffull Internetaddress/ [Accessed day month year].	Kitces, M. (2014). Best practice in client communication for financial advisors *Nerd's Eye View*. 3 Mar. 2014. [Blog] Available at http://www.kitces.com/blog/weekend-reading-for-financial-planners-mar-1–2/ [Accessed 7 Mar. 2014].
Web forums (Usenet groups, bulletin boards etc.)	(Author's family name year of posting)	(Manchip 2013)	Authors family name, Authors initials. (year of posting). Title of posting. *Name of forum*. Posted day month year (of posting). *Name of forum*. Posted day month year (of posting). [Web forum]. Available at http://www.remainderoffull Internetaddress/ [Accessed day month year].	Manchip, S. (2013). Physical accessibility. *Access to transport for people with physical disabilities web forum*. Posted 5 Jun. 2013. [Web forum] Available at http://www.parliament.uk/business/committees/committees-a-z/commons-select/transport-committee/inquiries/parliament-2010/disabled-access-to-transport/web-forum/physical-accessibility/ [Accessed 9 Mar. 2014].

To cite	In the text		In the list of references/bibliography	
	General format	**Example**	**General format**	**Example**
Wiki	(Originator name or *Wiki title* year of posting)	(Microformats Wiki 2014)	Originator name or *Wiki title*. *Title of Wiki*. Day Month Year (of posting). [Wiki article]. Available at http://www.remainderoffull Internetaddress/ [Accessed day month year].	Microfromats Wiki. *Chat: brainstorming*. 5 Mar. 2014. [Wiki article] Available at http://microformats.org/wiki/chat-brainstorming [Accessed 9 Mar. 2014].
Discussion list email (where email sender known)	(Author's family name year of posting)	(Cox 2013)	Sender's Family name, Sender's Initials. (year of posting). Re. Subject of discussion. Posted day month year. Sender's email address (see note below). [Accessed day month year].	Cox, F. (2013). Census 2011 link to longitudinal studies. Posted 10 Feb. 2013. fion . . . @mail.com [Accessed 19 Mar. 2014].
Letters and personal emails				
Letter	(Sender's family name year)	(Saunders 2014)	Sender's family name, Sender's Initials. (year). Unpublished letter to Recipient's Initials. Recipient's Family name re. Subject matter, day, month, year.	Saunders, J.J. (2014). Unpublished letter to M.N.K. Saunders re. Holocaust, 10 Sept. 2014.
Personal email	(Sender's family name year)	(Harrison 2013)	Sender's family name, Sender's initials. (year). Email to recipient's initials. recipient's family name re. Subject matter, day month year.	Harrison, D. (2013). Email to M.N.K. Saunders re. Reviewers' feedback, 27 Nov. 2013.
Online images and diagrams				
Online image or diagram	*As for* 'Book (first edition)'	(Gilroy 1936)	Author's name, Author's initials. (year of production if available). *Title of image or diagram*. Format, name and place of source if available. Available at http://www.remainderoffull Internetaddress/ [Accessed day month year].	Gilroy, J. (1936). *Lovely day for a Guinness*. Advertising poster, Guinness Webstore. Available at http://www.guinnesswebstore.com/imagesEdp/p82866b.jpg [Accessed 23 Mar. 2014].

(Continued)

Table A1.1 (*Continued*)

To cite	In the text		In the list of references/bibliography	
	General format	**Example**	**General format**	**Example**
Online image or diagram (no named author)	(*Diagram or image title* year)	*Iron Maiden, A matter of life and death* 2006)	*Title of image or diagram.* (year of production if available). Format, name and place of source if available. Available at http://www.remainderoffull Internetaddress/ [Accessed day month year].	*Iron Maiden, A matter of life and death.* (2006). Tour poster, Starstore.com. Available at http://www.starstore.com/acatalog/Starstore_Catalogue_IRON_MAIDEN_POSTERS__IRON_MAIDEN_POSTER_1815.html [Accessed 20 Mar. 2014].
Conference papers				
Conference paper published as part of proceedings	*As for* 'Book (first edition)'	(Saunders 2009)	Family name, Initials. and Family name, Initials. (year). Title of paper. In Initials. Family name and Initials. Family name (eds) *Title.* Place of publication: Publisher. pp. ###–###.	Saunders, M.N.K. (2009). A real world comparison of responses to distributing questionnaire surveys by mail and web. In J. Azzopardi (Ed.) *Proceedings of the 8th European Conference on Research Methods in Business and Management.* Reading: ACI, pp. 323–30.
Unpublished conference paper	*As for* 'Book (first edition)'	(Saunders et al. 2010)	Family name, Initials. and Family name, Initials. (year). *Title of paper.* Unpublished paper presented at 'Conference name'. Location of conference, day month year.	Saunders, M.N.K., Slack, R. and Bowen, D. (2010). *Location, the development of swift trust and learning: insights from two doctoral summer schools.* Unpublished paper presented at the 'EIASM 5th Workshop on Trust Within and Between Organizations'. Madrid, 28–29 January 2010.
Film, Video, TV, Radio, Downloads				
Television or radio programme	(*Television or radio programme title* year)	(*Today Programme* 2014)	*Programme title.* (year of production). Transmitting organisation and nature of transmission, day month year of transmission.	*The Today Programme.* (2014). British Broadcasting Corporation Radio broadcast, 11 Apr. 2014.
Television or radio programme that is part of a series	(*Television or radio programme series title* year)	(*Money Programme* 2011)	*Series title.* (year of production). Episode. episode title. Transmitting organisation and nature of transmission, day month year of transmission.	*The Money Programme.* (2011). Episode. BP $30 Billion Blowout. British Broadcasting Corporation Television broadcast, 3 Mar. 2011.

To cite	In the text		In the list of references/bibliography	
	General format	**Example**	**General format**	**Example**
Commercial DVD	(DVD title year)	(*Bruce Springsteen live in New York City* 2003)	*DVD title*. (Year of production). [DVD]. Place of publication: Publisher.	*Bruce Springsteen live in New York City* (2003). [DVD]. New York: Sony.
Commercial DVD that is part of a series	(DVD series title year)	(*The Office complete series 1 and 2 and the Christmas specials* 2005)	*DVD series title* (Year of production) Episode. Episode title. [DVD]. Place of publication: Publisher.	*The Office complete series 1 and 2 and the Christmas specials*. (2005). Episode. Series 1 Christmas Special. [DVD]. London: British Broadcasting Corporation.
Video download (e.g. YouTube)	(Company name *or* Family name year)	(Miller 2008)	Company name *or* Family name, Initials. (year). Title of audio download. *YouTube*. Available at http://www.remainderoffull Internetaddress/ [Accessed day month year].	Miller, L. (2008). Harvard style referencing made easy. *YouTube*. Available at http://www.youtube.com/watch?v=RH1lzyn7Exc [Accessed 5 Mar. 2014].
Audio CD	(Family name *or* Artist *or* Group year)	(Goldratt 2005)	Family name, Initials. *or* Artist. *or* Group. (year). *Title of CD*. [Audio CD]. Place of Publication: Publisher.	Goldratt, E.M. (2005). *Beyond the goal*. [Audio CD]. Buffalo NY: Goldratt's Marketing Group.
Audio download (e.g. Podcast)	(Company name *or* Family name year)	(Friedman 2014)	Company name *or* Family name, Initials. (year). Title of audio download. *Title of series* ### [Audio podcast] Available at http://www.remainderoffull Internetaddress/ [Accessed day month year].	Friedman, S.D. (2014). Is work family conflict reaching a tipping point? *Harvard Business IdeaCast 394*. [Audio podcast] Available at https://itunes.apple.com/gb/podcast/hbr-ideacast/id152022135?mt=2 [Accessed 9 May 2014].
Course materials and online teaching materials from virtual learning environments (VLEs)				
Lecture*	(Lecturer family name year)	(Saunders 2013)	Lecturer family name, Initials. (year). *Lecture on title of lecture*. Module title. Year (if appropriate) and course title. Place of lecture: Institution. Day month year.	Saunders, M.N.K. (2013). *Lecture on Using Secondary Data*. Research Methods (MANM169). MSc International Business Management. Guildford: University of Surrey. 17 Oct. 2013.
Module and course notes*	*As for* 'Book (first edition)'	(Bell 2013)	Lecturer family name, Initials. (year). *Title of material*. Module title (if appropriate). Level (if appropriate) and course title. Institution, Department or School.	Bell, J. (2013). *Postgraduate dissertation handbook 2013–14*. MSc Management. University of Surrey, Faculty of Business Economics and Law.

(*Continued*)

Table A1.1 (*Continued*)

To cite	In the text		In the list of references/bibliography	
	General format	**Example**	**General format**	**Example**
Materials available on a VLE*	(Author family name year)	(Saunders 2014)	Author family name, Initials. (year of production). *Title of material* [nature of material]. Module title (if appropriate). Level (if appropriate) and course title. Institution *name of VLE* [online]. Available at http://www.remainderoffull Internetaddress/ [Accessed day month year].	Saunders, MNK. (2014). *New developments in trust, distrust and the management of change* [PowerPoint slides]. New Directions in Management Research (MANM295). Integrated PhD. University of Surrey *SurreyLearn* [online]. Available at surreylearn.surrey.ac.uk/ d2l/home/102366 [Accessed 10 Mar. 2014].

Notes: Where date is not known or unclear, follow conventions outlined towards the end of Table A1.2.
Email addresses should not be included except when they are in the public domain. Even where this is the case, permission should be obtained or the email address replaced by '. . .' after the fourth character, for example: 'abcd . . . @isp.ac.uk'.
*Be warned, most lecturers consider citing of lectures as 'lazy' scholarship.

Table A1.2 Additional conventions when using the Harvard style to reference in the text

To refer to	Use the general format	For example
Work by different authors generally	(Family name year, Family name year) in alphabetical order	(Cassell 2014, Dillman 2009, Robson 2011)
Different authors with the same family name	(Family name Initial year)	(Smith J. 2008)
Different works by the same author	(Family name year, year) in ascending year order	(Saunders 2012, 2013)
Different works by the same author from the same year	(Family name year letter), make sure the letter is consistent throughout	(Tosey 2014a)
An author referred to by another author where the original has not been read (*secondary reference*)*	(Family name year, cited by Family name year)	(Cassell 2012, cited by Lanham-New 2014)
A work for which the year of publication cannot be identified	(Family name or Originator name nd), where 'nd' means no data	(Woollons nd)
	(Family name or Originator name c. year) where 'c.' means circa	(Hattersley c. 2004)
A direct quotation	(Family name or Originator name year, p. ###) where 'p.' means 'page' and ### is the page in the original publication on which the quotation appears	"A card sort offers the simplest form of sorting technique" (Saunders 2012, p. 112)

*For secondary references, whilst many universities only require you to give details of the source you looked at in your list of references, you may also be required the reference for the original source in your list of references.

Referencing in the list of references or bibliography

In the list of references or bibliography all the sources are listed alphabetically in one list by the originator or author's family name, and all authors' family names and initials are normally listed in full. If there is more than one work by the same author or originator, these are listed chronologically. A style for referencing work in the list of references or bibliography is outlined in Table A1.1. While it would be impossible for us to include an example of every type of reference you might need to include, the information contained in this table should enable you to work out the required format for all your references. If there are any about which you are unsure, Colin Neville's (2010) book *The Complete Guide to Referencing and Avoiding Plagiarism* is one of the most comprehensive sources we have found.

For copies of journal articles from printed journals that you have obtained electronically online it is usually acceptable to reference these using exactly the same format as printed journal articles (Table A1.1), provided that you have obtained and read a facsimile (exact) copy of the article. Facsimile copies of journal articles have precisely the same format as the printed version, including page numbering, tables and diagrams, other than for the copy, which is published 'online first'. **Online first** refers to forthcoming articles that have been published online, prior to them appearing in journals. They therefore do not have a volume or part number, and the page numbering will not be the same as the final copy. When referencing an 'online first' copy in the list of references, you should always include the DOI. A facsimile copy usually obtained by downloading the article as a pdf file that can be read on the screen and printed using Adobe Acrobat Reader.

Finally, remember to include a, b, c etc. immediately after the year when you are referencing different publications by the same author from the same year. Do not forget to ensure that these are consistent with the letters used for the references in the main text.

The American Psychological Association (APA) style

The *American Psychological Association style* or *APA style* is a variation on the author–date system. Like the Harvard style it dates from the 1930s and 1940s, and has been updated subsequently. The latest updates are outlined in the latest edition of the American Psychological Association's (2009) *Concise Rules of the APA Style*, which is likely to be available for reference in your university's library.

Relatively small but significant differences exist between the Harvard and APA styles, and many authors adopt a combination of the two styles. The key differences are outlined in Table A1.3.

Numeric systems

Referencing in the text

When using a numeric system such as the Vancouver style, references within the project report are shown by a number that is either bracketed or in superscript. This number refers directly to the list of references at the end of the text, and it means it is not necessary for you to include the authors' names or year of publication:

'Research[1] indicates that . . .'

---

[1] Ritzer, G. *The McDonaldization of Society*. (6th edn). Thousand Oaks, CA: Sage, Pine Forge Press, 2011.

Table A1.3 Key differences between Harvard and APA styles of referencing

Harvard style	APA style	Comment
Referencing in the text		
(Lewis 2001)	(Lewis, 2001)	Note punctuation
(McDowall and Saunders 2010)	(McDowall & Saunders, 2011)	'&' not 'and'
(Altinay et al. 2014)	(Altinay, Saunders & Wang, 2014)	For first occurrence if three to five authors
(Millmore et al. 2007)	(Millmore et al., 2007)	For first occurrence if six or more authors; note punctuation and use of italics
(Tosey et al. 2012)	(Tosey et al., 2012)	For subsequent occurrences of two or more authors; note punctuation and use of italics
Referencing in the list of references or bibliography		
Berman Brown, R. and Saunders, M. (2008). *Dealing with Statistics: What You Need to Know.* Maidenhead: Open University Press.	Berman Brown, R. & Saunders, M. (2008). *Dealing with Statistics: What You Need to Know.* Maidenhead: Open University Press.	Note: use of 'and' and '&'
Varadarajan, P.R. (2003). Musings on relevance and rigour of scholarly research in marketing. *Journal of the Academy of Marketing Science*. Vol. 31, No. 4, pp. 368–76. [Accessed 6 Apr. 2010 from Business Source Complete].	Varadarajan, P.R. (2003). Musings on relevance and rigour of scholarly research in marketing. *Journal of the Academy of Marketing Science*. 31 (4): 368–376. doi: 10.1177/0092070303258240	Note: Volume, part number and page numbers; DOI (digital object identifier) number given in APA. Name of database not given in APA if DOI number given; Date accessed site not included in APA.

Referencing in the list of references

The list of references in numeric systems is sequential, referencing items in the order they are referred to in your project report. This means that they are unlikely to be in alphabetical order. When using the numeric system you need to ensure that:

- The layout of individual references is that prescribed by the style you have adopted. This is likely to differ from both the Harvard and APA styles (Table A1.3) and will be dependent upon precisely which style has been adopted. The reference to Ritzer's book in the previous sub-section (indicated by the number and the associated endnote at the end of this appendix) follows the Vancouver style. Further details of this and other numeric styles can be found in Neville's (2010) book.
- The items referred to include only those you have cited in your report. They should therefore be headed 'References' rather than 'Bibliography'.
- Only one number is used for each item, except where you refer to the same item more than once but need to refer to different pages. In such instances you use standard bibliographic abbreviations to save repeating the reference in full (Table A1.4).

Table A1.4 Bibliographic abbreviations

Abbreviation	Explanation	For example
Op. cit. (opere citato)	Meaning 'in the work cited'. This refers to a work previously referenced, and so you must give the author and year and, if necessary, the page number	Robson (2011) *op. cit.* pp. 23–4.
Loc. cit. (loco citato)	Meaning 'in the place cited'. This refers to the same page of a work previously referenced, and so you must give the author and year	Robson (2011) *loc. cit.*
Ibid. (ibidem)	Meaning 'the same work given immediately before'. This refers to the work referenced immediately before, and replaces all details of the previous reference other than a page number if necessary	*Ibid*. p. 59.

References

American Psychological Association (2009) *Concise Rules of the APA Style*. Washington, DC: American Psychological Association.

Neville, C. (2010) *The Complete Guide to Referencing and Avoiding Plagiarism* (2nd edn). Maidenhead: Open University Press.

Further reading

American Psychological Association (2009) *Concise Rules of the APA Style*. Washington, DC: American Psychological Association. The most recent version of this manual contains full details of how to use this form of the author–date system of referencing as well as how to lay out tables, figures, equations and other statistical data. It also provides guidance on grammar and writing.

Neville, C. (2010) *The Complete Guide to Referencing and Avoiding Plagiarism* (2nd edn). Maidenhead: Open University Press. This fully revised edition provides a comprehensive, up-to-date discussion of the layout required for a multitude of information sources including online. It includes guidance on the Harvard, American Psychological Association, numerical and other referencing styles as well as chapters on plagiarism and answering frequently asked questions.

Taylor & Francis (nd) *Taylor & Francis Reference Style APA Quick Guide*. Available at www.tandf.co.uk/journals/authors/style/quickref/tf_A.pdf [Accessed 27 November 2013]. This document provides an excellent one-page guide to using the American Psychological Association author–date system as well as a direct link to a document providing full details of this style including how to cite references in the text.

University of New South Wales (2009) *Harvard Referencing Electronic Sources*. Available at www.lc.unsw.edu.au/onlib/pdf/elect_ref.pdf [Accessed 27 November 2013]. This document provides an excellent guide to referencing electronic sources and has useful 'troubleshooting' and 'frequently asked questions' sections.

Appendix 2 Calculating the minimum sample size 附录 2 计算最小样本规模

In some situations, such as experimental research, it is necessary for you to calculate the precise minimum sample size you require. This calculation assumes that data will be collected from all cases in the sample and is based on:

- how confident you need to be that the estimate is accurate (the level of confidence in the estimate);
- how accurate the estimate needs to be (the margin of error that can be tolerated);
- the proportion of responses you expect to have some particular attribute.

Provided that you know the level of confidence and the margin of error, it is relatively easy to estimate the proportion of responses you expect to have a particular attribute. To do this, ideally you need to collect a pilot sample of about 30 observations and from this to infer the likely proportion for your main survey. It is therefore important that the pilot sample uses the same methods as your main survey. Alternatively, you might have undertaken a very similar survey and so already have a reasonable idea of the likely proportion. If you do not, then you need either to make an informed guess or to assume that 50 per cent of the sample will have the specified attribute – the worst scenario. Most surveys will involve collecting data on more than one attribute. It is argued by De Vaus (2014) that for such multi-purpose surveys you should determine the sample size on the basis of those variables in the sample that are likely to have the greatest variability.

Once you have all the information you substitute it into the formula,

$$n = \rho\% \times q\% \times \left[\frac{z}{e\%}\right]^2$$

where

n is the minimum sample size required

$\rho\%$ is the percentage belonging to the specified category

$q\%$ is the percentage not belonging to the specified category

z is the z value corresponding to the level of confidence required (see Table A2.1)

$e\%$ is the margin of error required.

Table A2.1 Levels of confidence and associated z values

Level of confidence	z value
90% certain	1.65
95% certain	1.96
99% certain	2.57

Box A2.1
Focus on student research

Calculating the minimum sample size

To answer a research question Jon needed to estimate the proportion of a total population of 4000 restaurant customers who had visited that restaurant at least five times in the past year. Based on his reading of the research methods literature he decided that he needed to be 95 per cent certain that his 'estimate' was accurate (the level of confidence in the estimate); this corresponded to a z score of 1.96 (Table A2.1). Based on his reading he also decided that his 'estimate' needed to be accurate to within plus or minus 5 per cent of the true percentage (the margin of error that can be tolerated).

In order to calculate the minimum sample size, Jon still needed to estimate the proportion of respondents who had visited the restaurant at least five times in the past year. From his pilot survey he discovered that 12 out of the 30 restaurant customers had visited the restaurant at least five times in the past year – in other words, that 40 per cent belonged to this

specified category. This meant that 60 per cent did not.

Jon substituted these figures into the formula:

$$n = 40 \times 60 \times \left(\frac{1.96}{5}\right)^2$$
$$= 2400 \times (0.392)^2$$
$$= 2400 \times 0.154$$
$$= 369.6$$

His minimum sample size, therefore, was 370 returns.

As the total population of restaurant customers was 4000, Jon could now calculate the adjusted minimum sample size:

$$n' = \frac{369.6}{1 + \left(\frac{369.6}{4000}\right)}$$
$$= \frac{369.6}{1 + 0.092}$$
$$= \frac{369.6}{1.092}$$
$$= 338.46$$

Because of the small total population, Jon needed a minimum sample size of only 339. However, this assumed he had a response rate of 100 per cent

Where your population is less than 10,000, a smaller sample size can be used without affecting the accuracy. This is called the *adjusted minimum sample size* (Box A2.1). It is calculated using the following formula:

$$n' = \frac{n}{1 + \left(\frac{n}{N}\right)}$$

where
n' is the adjusted minimum sample size
n is the minimum sample size (as calculated above)
N is the total population.

Reference

De Vaus, D.A. (2014) *Surveys in Social Research* (6th edn). London: Routledge.

Appendix 3 Random sampling numbers
附录 3　随机抽样数

78 41	11 62	72 18	66 69	58 71	31 90	51 36	78 09	41 00
70 50	58 19	68 26	75 69	04 00	25 29	16 72	35 73	55 85
32 78	14 47	01 55	10 91	83 21	13 32	59 53	03 38	79 32
71 60	20 53	86 78	50 57	42 30	73 48	68 09	16 35	21 87
35 30	15 57	99 96	33 25	56 43	65 67	51 45	37 99	54 89
09 08	05 41	66 54	01 49	97 34	38 85	85 23	34 62	60 58
02 59	34 51	98 71	31 54	28 85	23 84	49 07	33 71	17 88
20 13	44 15	22 95	98 97	60 02	85 07	17 57	20 51	01 67
36 26	70 11	63 81	27 31	79 71	08 11	87 74	85 53	86 78
00 30	62 19	81 68	86 10	65 61	62 22	17 22	96 83	56 37
38 41	14 59	53 03	52 86	21 88	55 87	85 59	14 90	74 87
18 89	40 84	71 04	09 82	54 44	94 23	83 89	04 59	38 29
34 38	85 56	80 74	22 31	26 39	65 63	12 38	45 75	30 35
55 90	21 71	17 88	20 08	57 64	17 93	22 34	00 55	09 78
81 43	53 96	96 88	36 86	04 33	31 40	18 71	06 00	51 45
59 69	13 03	38 31	77 08	71 20	23 28	92 43	92 63	21 74
60 24	47 44	73 93	64 37	64 97	19 82	27 59	24 20	00 04
17 04	93 46	05 70	20 95	42 25	33 95	78 80	07 57	86 58
09 55	42 30	27 05	27 93	78 10	69 11	29 56	29 79	28 66
46 69	28 64	81 02	41 89	12 03	31 20	25 16	79 93	28 22
28 94	00 91	16 15	35 12	68 93	23 71	11 55	64 56	76 95
59 10	06 29	83 84	03 68	97 65	59 21	58 54	61 59	30 54
41 04	70 71	05 56	76 66	57 86	29 30	11 31	56 76	24 13
09 81	81 80	73 10	10 23	26 29	61 15	50 00	76 37	60 16
91 55	76 68	06 82	05 33	06 75	92 35	82 21	78 15	19 43
82 69	36 73	58 69	10 92	31 14	21 08	13 78	56 53	97 77
03 59	65 34	32 06	63 43	38 04	65 30	32 82	57 05	33 95
03 96	30 87	81 54	69 39	95 69	95 69	89 33	78 90	30 07
39 91	27 38	20 90	41 10	10 80	59 68	93 10	85 25	59 25
89 93	92 10	59 40	26 14	27 47	39 51	46 70	86 85	76 02
99 16	73 21	39 05	03 36	87 58	18 52	61 61	02 92	07 24
93 13	20 70	42 59	77 69	35 59	71 80	61 95	82 96	48 84
47 32	87 68	97 86	28 51	61 21	33 02	79 65	59 49	89 93
09 75	58 00	72 49	36 58	19 45	30 61	87 74	43 01	93 91
63 24	15 65	02 05	32 92	45 61	35 43	67 64	94 45	95 66
33 58	69 42	25 71	74 31	88 80	04 50	22 60	72 01	27 88
23 25	22 78	24 88	68 48	83 60	53 59	73 73	82 43	82 66
07 17	77 20	79 37	50 08	29 79	55 13	51 90	36 77	68 69
16 07	31 84	57 22	29 54	35 14	22 22	22 60	72 15	40 90
67 90	79 28	62 83	44 96	87 70	40 64	27 22	60 19	52 54
79 52	74 68	69 74	31 75	80 59	29 28	21 69	15 97	35 88
69 44	31 09	16 38	92 82	12 25	10 57	81 32	76 71	31 61
09 47	57 04	54 00	78 75	91 99	26 20	36 19	53 29	11 55
74 78	09 25	95 80	25 72	88 85	76 02	29 89	70 78	93 84

Source: From Morris, C. (2012) *Quantitative Approaches in Business Studies* (8th edn). Reproduced by permission of Pearson Education Ltd

Reference

Morris, C. (2012) *Quantitative Approaches in Business Studies* (8th edn). Harlow: Pearson.

Appendix 4 Guidelines for non-discriminatory language

附录 4　非歧视语言指南

Writing in a non-discriminatory manner is important in all areas of business and management. For example, in Section 14.5 we noted how the use of language that assumes the gender of a group of people, such as referring to a clerical assistant as 'she', not only is inaccurate but also gives offence to people of both sexes. Similar care needs to be exercised when using other gender-based terms, referring to people from different ethnic groups, and people with disabilities. Without this, the language used may reinforce beliefs and prejudices, as well as being oppressive, offensive, unfair and incorrect. The impact of this is summarised clearly by Bill Bryson (1995: 425) in his book *Made in America*, when he observes: 'at the root of the bias-free language movement lies a commendable sentiment: to make language less wounding or demeaning to those whose sex, race, physical condition or circumstances leave them vulnerable to the raw power of words'.

Therefore, although the task of ensuring that the language you use is non-discriminatory may at first seem difficult, it is important that you do so. Some universities have developed their own guidelines, which are available via their intranet or the Internet. However, if your university has not developed its own guidelines, we hope those in this appendix will help you to ensure that your language is not discriminatory.

Guidelines for gender

When referring to both sexes, it is inappropriate to use the terms 'men' or 'women' and their gender-based equivalents; in other words, do not use gender-specific terms generically. Some of the more common gender-neutral alternatives are listed in Table A4.1.

Guidelines for ethnicity

Attention needs to be paid when referring to different ethnic groups. This is especially important where the term used refers to a number of ethnic groups. For example, the term 'Asian' includes a number of diverse ethnic groups that can be recognised with the terms 'Asian peoples' or 'Asian communities'. Similarly, the diversity of people represented by the term 'Black' can be recognised by referring to 'Black peoples' or 'Black communities'. Where possible, the individual groups within these communities should be identified separately.

'Black' is used as a term to include people who are discriminated against due to the colour of their skin. It is often used to refer to people of Caribbean, South Asian and African descent. 'African-Caribbean' has replaced the term 'Afro-Caribbean' and is used to describe Caribbean people who are of African descent. Increasingly, there is a view that hyphenated terms such as 'Afro-Caribbean', 'Black-British' or 'African-American' should not be used. Rather terms such as 'African Caribbean', 'Black British' or 'African American'

Table A4.1 Gender-specific terms and gender-neutral alternatives

Gender-specific term	Gender-neutral alternative
chairman	chair, chairperson
Dear Sir	Dear Sir/Madam
disseminate	broadcast, inform, publicise
forefathers	ancestors
foreman	supervisor
layman	lay person
man	person
man hours	work hours
mankind	humanity, humankind, people
man-made	manufactured, synthetic
manning	resourcing, staffing
manpower	human resources, labour, staff, workforce
master copy	original, top copy
masterful	domineering, very skillful
policewoman/policeman	police officer
rights of man	people's/citizens' rights, rights of the individual
seminal	classical, formative
women	people
working man/working woman	worker, working people

Source: Developed from British Psychological Society (2004); British Sociological Association (2004a)

should be used to refer to second or subsequent generations who, although born in the country, often wish to retain their origins.

If you are unsure of the term to use, then ask someone from the appropriate community for the most acceptable current term.

Guidelines for disability

Disability is also an area where terminology is constantly changing as people voice their own preferences. Despite this, general guidelines can be offered:

- Do not use medical terms as these emphasise the condition rather than the person.
- Where it is necessary to refer to a person's medical condition, make the person explicit (see Table A4.2).
- Where referring to historical and some contemporary common terms, place speech marks around the term.

There are non-disablist alternatives for the more common disablist terms. These are summarised in Table A4.2. However, if you are unsure of the term to use, ask someone from the appropriate group for the most acceptable current term.

Table A4.2 Disablist terms and non-disablist alternatives

Disablist term	Non-disablist alternative
the blind	blind and partially sighted people, visually impaired people
cripple	mobility impaired person
the deaf	deaf or hard of hearing people
the disabled, the handicapped, invalid	disabled people, people with disabilities, employees with disabilities
dumb, mute	person with a speech impairment
epileptic, epileptics	person who has epilepsy
handicap	disability
mentally handicapped	person with a learning difficulty or learning disability
mentally ill, mental patient	mental health service user
patient	person
spastic	person who has cerebral palsy
wheelchair-bound	wheelchair user
victim of, afflicted by, suffering from, crippled by	person who has, person with

Source: Adapted from British Sociological Association (2004b)

References

British Psychological Society (1988) 'Guidelines for the use of non-sexist language', *The Psychologist*, Vol. 1, No. 2, pp. 53–4.

British Psychological Society (2004) *Style Guide*. Available at http://www.bps.org.uk/sites/default/files/images/bps_style_guide.pdf [Accessed 10 March 2015].

British Sociological Association (2004a) *Language and the BSA: Sex and Gender*. Available at www.britsoc.co.uk/equality/ [Accessed 4 April 2014].

British Sociological Association (2004b) *Language and the BSA: Non-Disablist*. Available at www.britsoc.co.uk/equality/ [Accessed 4 April 2014].

British Sociological Association (2005) *Language and the BSA: Ethnicity and Race*. Available at www.britsoc.co.uk/equality/ [Accessed 4 April 2014].

Bryson, B. (1995) *Made in America*. London: Minerva.

Glossary
术语表

50th percentile The middle value when all the values of a variable are arranged in rank order; usually known as the median.

A

abductive approach Approach to theory development involving the collection of data to explore a phenomenon, identify themes and explain patterns, to generate a new – or modify an existing – theory which is subsequently tested.

abstract (1) Summary, usually of an article or book, which also contains sufficient information for the original to be located. (2) Summary of the complete content of the project report.

access (1) The process involved in gaining entry into an organisation to undertake research. (2) The situation where a research participant is willing to share data with a researcher. *See also* cognitive access, continuing access, physical access.

Action Research Research strategy concerned with the management of a change and involving close collaboration between practitioners and researchers. The results flowing from Action Research should also inform other contexts.

active response rate The total number of responses divided by the total number in the sample after ineligible and unreachable respondents have been excluded. *See* ineligible respondent, unreachable respondent. *See also* break off, complete response, complete refusal, partial response total response rate.

active voice The voice in which the action of the verb is attributed to the person. For example, '*I* conducted interviews'.

ad hoc survey A general term normally used to describe the collection of data that only occurs once due to the specificity of focus. Although the term is normally interpreted as referring to questionnaires, it also includes other techniques such as structured observation and structured interviews. *See also* survey.

alpha coefficient *see* Cronbach's alpha.

alternative hypothesis Testable proposition stating that there is a difference or relationship between two or more variables. Often referred to as H_a. *See also* hypothesis, null hypothesis.

analysis The ability to break down data and to clarify the nature of the component parts and the relationship between them.

analysis of variance Statistical test to determine the probability (likelihood) that the values of a numerical data variable for three or more independent samples or groups are different. The test assesses the likelihood of any difference between these groups occurring by chance alone.

analytic induction Analysis of qualitative data that involves the iterative examination of a number of strategically selected cases to identify the cause of a particular phenomenon.

anonymity (1) The process of concealing the identity of participants in all documents resulting from the research. (2) The promise that even the researcher will not be able to identify by whom responses are made.

ANOVA *see* analysis of variance.

appendix A supplement to the project report. It should not normally include material that is essential for the understanding of the report itself, but additional relevant material in which the reader may be interested.

application The ability to apply certain principles and rules in particular situations.

applied research Research of direct and immediate relevance to practitioners that addresses issues they see as important and is presented in ways they can understand and act upon.

archival research Research strategy that analyses administrative records and documents as principal sources of data because they are products of day-to-day activities.

asynchronous Not undertaken in real time, working offline.

attitude variable Variable that records data about what respondents feel about something.

autocorrelation The extent to which the value of a variable at a particular time (t) is related to its value at the previous time period ($t-1$).

availability sampling *see* convenience sampling.

axial coding The process of recognising relationships between categories in grounded theory.

axiology A branch of philosophy concerned with the role of values and ethics within the research process.

B

bar graph/chart Graph for showing frequency distributions for a categorical or grouped discrete data variable, which highlights the highest and lowest values.

base period The period against which index numbers are calculated to facilitate comparisons of trends or changes over time. *See also* index number.

basic research Research undertaken purely to understand processes and their outcomes, predominantly in universities as a result of an academic agenda, for which the key consumer is the academic community.

behaviour variable Variable that records data about behaviours, what people did in the past, do now or will do in the future.

beneficence Actions designed to promote beneficial effects. *See also* code of ethics.

between-subjects design Experimental design allowing a comparison of results to be made between an experimental group and a control group. *See also* experiment, within-subjects design.

bibliographic details The information needed to enable readers to find original items consulted or used for a research project. These normally include the author, date of publication, title of article, title of book or journal.

bibliography Alphabetical list of the bibliographic details for all relevant items consulted and used, including those items not referred to directly in the text. The university will specify the format of these.

big data Extremely large and complex (socio-economic) data sets that are analysed by powerful computer techniques to reveal patterns and trends.

blog A personal online journal on which an individual or group of individuals record opinions, information and the like on a regular basis for public consumption. Most blogs are interactive allowing visitors to leave comments. 'Blog' is an abbreviation of 'weblog'.

Boolean logic System by which the variety of items found in a search based on logical propositions that can be either true or false can be combined, limited or widened.

box plot Diagram that provides a pictorial representation of the distribution of the data for a variable and statistics such as median, inter-quartile range, and the highest and lowest values.

brainstorming Technique that can be used to generate and refine research ideas. It is best undertaken with a group of people.

break off The level of response to questionnaires or structured interviews in which less than 50% of all questions answered other than by a refusal or no answer. Break off therefore includes complete refusal.

broker *see* gatekeeper.

C

CAQDAS Computer-Aided Qualitative Data Analysis Software.

case (1) Individual element or group member within a sample or population such as an employee. (2) Individual unit for which data have been collected.

case study Research strategy that involves the empirical investigation of a particular contemporary phenomenon within its real-life context, using multiple sources of evidence.

categorical data Data whose values cannot be measured numerically but can either be classified into sets (categories) or placed in rank order.

categorising The process of developing categories and subsequently attaching these categories to meaningful units of data. *See also* unitising, units of data.

category question Closed question in which the respondent is offered a set of mutually exclusive categories and instructed to select one.

causality Relationship between cause and effect. Everything that happens will have a cause, while each action will cause an effect.

causal relationship Relationship between two or more variables in which the change (effect) in one variable is caused by the other variable(s).

census The collection and analysis of data from every possible case or group member in a population.

central limit theorem The larger the absolute size of a sample, the more closely its distribution will be to the normal distribution. *See* normal distribution.

central tendency measure The generic term for statistics that can be used to provide an impression of those values for a variable that are common, middling or average.

chat room An online forum operating in synchronous mode. *See also* synchronous.

chi square test Statistical test to determine the probability (likelihood) that two categorical data variables are independent. A common use is to discover whether there are statistically significant associations between the observed frequencies and the expected frequencies of two variables presented in a cross-tabulation.

classic experiment Experiment in which two groups are established and members assigned at random to each. *See also* experiment, experimental group.

closed question Question that provides a number of alternative answers from which the respondent is instructed to choose.

cluster sampling Probability sampling procedure in which the population is divided into discrete groups or clusters prior to sampling. A random sample (systematic or simple) of these clusters is then drawn.

code (1) A single word or short phrase, sometimes abbreviated, used to label a unit of data. (2) a number or word used to represent a response by a respondent or participant. *See also* coding, codebook, coding template unit of data.

code of ethics Statement of principles and procedures for the design and conduct of research. *See also* privacy, research ethics, research ethics committee.

codebook Complete list of all the codes used to code data variables.

coding The process of labelling of data using a code that symbolises or summarises the meaning of that data. *See also* axial coding, categorising, data code, focused coding, initial coding, open coding, selective coding, unitizing, unit of data.

coding template An hierarchical list of codes and themes, which is used as the central analytical tool in Template Analysis. *See also* Template Analysis.

coefficient of determination Number between 0 and 1 that enables the strength of the relationship between a numerical dependent variable and a numerical independent variable to be assessed. The coefficient represents the proportion of the variation in the dependent variable that can be explained statistically by the independent variable. A value of 1 means that all the variation in the dependent variable can be explained statistically by the independent variable. A value of 0 means that none of the variation in the dependent variable can be explained by the independent variable. *See also* regression analysis.

coefficient of multiple determination Number between 0 and 1 that enables the strength of the relationship between a numerical dependent variable and two or more numerical independent variables to be assessed. The coefficient represents the proportion of the variation in the dependent variable that can be explained statistically by the independent variables. A value of 1 means that all the variation in the dependent variable can be explained statistically by the independent variables. A value of 0 means that none of the variation in the dependent variable can be explained by the independent variables. *See also* multiple regression analysis.

coefficient of variation Statistic that compares the extent of spread of data values around the mean between two or more variables containing numerical data.

cognitive access The process of gaining access to data from intended participants. This involves participants agreeing to be interviewed or observed, within agreed limits. *See also* informed consent.

cohort study Study that collects data from the same cases over time using a series of 'snapshots'.

collinearity The extent to which two or more independent variables are correlated with each other. Also termed multicollinearity.

comparative proportional pie chart Diagram for comparing both proportions and totals for all types of data variables.

compiled data Data that have been processed, such as through some form of selection or summarising.

complete observer Observational role in which the researcher does not reveal the purpose of the research activity to those being observed. However, unlike the complete participant role, the researcher does not take part in the activities of the group being studied.

complete participant Observational role in which the researcher attempts to become a member of the group in which research is being conducted. The true purpose of the research is not revealed to the group members.

complete refusal The level of response to questionnaires or structured interviews in which none of the questions are answered.

complete response The level of response to questionnaires or structured interviews in which over 80% of all questions answered other than by a refusal or no answer.

computer-aided personal interviewing (CAPI) Type of interviewing in which the interviewer reads questions from a computer screen and enters the respondent's answers directly into the computer.

computer-aided telephone interviewing (CATI) Type of telephone interviewing in which the interviewer reads questions from a computer screen and enters the respondent's answers directly into the computer.

conclusion The section of the project report in which judgements are made rather than just facts reported. New material is not normally introduced in the conclusion.

concurrent embedded design Mixed-methods research design where the collection of either quantitative or qualitative data is embedded within the collection of the other. *See also* concurrent mixed-methods research, embedded mixed methods research.

concurrent mixed-methods research Research using both quantitative and qualitative methods that are conducted concurrently during a single phase of data collection and analysis. *See also* concurrent embedded design, concurrent triangulation design, mixed methods research, single-phase research design.

concurrent triangulation design Mixed-methods research design where quantitative and qualitative data are collected in the same phase so that these data can be compared to see where they converge or diverge in relation to addressing your research question. *See also* concurrent mixed methods research.

confidentiality (1) Concern relating to the right of access to the data provided by the participants and, in particular the need to keep these data secret or private.(2)Promise made by the researcher not to reveal the identity of participants or present findings in a way that enables participants to be identified.

confounding variables Extraneous but difficult to observe or measure variables than can potentially undermine the inferences drawn about the relationship between the independent variable and the dependent variable. *See also* control variables, experiment.

consent *see* implied consent, informed consent.

consent form Written agreement, signed by both parties in which the participant agrees to take part in the research and gives her or his permission for data to be used in specified ways.

constant comparison Process of constantly comparing data to analytical categories and vice versa, as well comparing data with other data and each category with other categories, to develop higher level categories and further your analysis towards the emergence of a grounded theory. *See also* inductive approach; Grounded Theory Method.

construct validity Extent to which your measurement questions actually measure the presence of those constructs you intended them to measure. *See also* convergent validity, discriminant validity.

consultancy report *see* management report.

Content Analysis An analytical technique that codes and categorises qualitative data in order to analyse them quantitatively.

content validity *see* face validity.

contextual data Additional data recorded when collecting primary or secondary data that reveals background information about the setting and the data collection process.

contingency table Technique for summarising data from two or more variables so that specific values can be read.

continuing access Gaining agreed research access to an organisation on an incremental basis.

continuous data Data whose values can theoretically take any value (sometimes within a restricted range) provided they can be measured with sufficient accuracy.

contrived data Data that result from a researcher organising an experiment, interview or survey. *See also* natural data.

control group Group in an experiment that, for the sake of comparison, does not receive the intervention in which you are interested. *See also* experiment, experimental group.

control variables Unwanted but measurable variables that need to be kept constant to avoid them influencing the effect of the independent variable on the dependent variable. *See also* confounding variables, experiment.

controlled index language The terms and phrases used by databases to index items within the database. If search terms do not match the controlled index language, the search is likely to be unsuccessful.

convenience sampling Non-probability haphazard sampling procedure in which cases are selected only on the basis that they are easiest to obtain. *See also* haphazard sampling, non-probability sampling.

convergent validity The overlap (or correlation) between two different scales that have been used to measure the same construct.

correlation The extent to which two variables are related to each other. *See also* correlation coefficient, negative correlation, positive correlation.

correlation coefficient Number between -1 and $+1$ representing the strength of the relationship between two ranked or numerical variables. A value of $+1$ represents a perfect positive correlation. A value of -1 represents a perfect negative correlation. Correlation coefficients between $+1$ and -1 represent weaker positive and negative correlations, a value of 0 meaning the variables are perfectly independent. *See also* negative correlation, Pearson's product moment correlation coefficient, positive correlation, Spearman's rank correlation coefficient.

coverage The extent to which a data set covers the population it is intended to cover.

covering letter Letter accompanying a questionnaire, which explains the purpose of the survey. *See also* introductory letter.

covert research Research undertaken where those being researched are not aware of this fact.

Cramer's V Statistical test to measure the association between two variables within a table on a scale where 0 represents no association and 1 represents perfect association. Because the value of Cramer's V is always between 0 and 1, the relative strengths of significant associations between different pairs of variables can be compared.

creative thinking technique One of a number of techniques for generating and refining research ideas based on non-rational criteria. These may be, for example, biased heavily in favour of the individual's preferences or the spontaneous ideas of the individual or others. *See also* brainstorming, Delphi technique, relevance tree.

criterion-related validity Ability of a statistical test to make accurate predictions.

critical case sampling A purposive sampling method which focuses on selecting those cases on the basis of making a point dramatically or because they are important. *See also* purposive sampling.

Critical Discourse Analysis Discourse Analysis that adopts a critical realist philosophy. *See also* Discourse Analysis.

critical ethnography Ethnographic strategy that questions the status quo and often adopts an advocacy role to bring about change. *See also* ethnography, interpretive ethnography, realist ethnography.

critical incidence technique A technique in which respondents are asked to describe in detail a critical incident or number of incidents that is key to the research question. *See also* critical incident.

critical incident An activity or event where the consequences were so clear that the respondent has a definite idea regarding its effects.

critical (literature) review Detailed and justified analysis and commentary of the merits and faults of the literature within a chosen area, which demonstrates familiarity with what is already known about your research topic.

critical realism The philosophical stance that what we experience are some of the manifestations of the things in the real world, rather than the actual things. *See also* direct realism, realism.

Cronbach's alpha Statistic used to measure the consistency of responses across a set of questions (scale items) designed together to measure a particular concept (scale). It consists of an alpha coefficient with a value between 0 and 1. Values of 0.7 or above suggest that the questions in the scale are measuring the same thing. *See also* scale item, scale.

cross-posting Receipt by individuals of multiple copies of an email, often due to the use of multiple mailing lists on which that individual appears.

cross-sectional research The study of a particular phenomenon (or phenomena) at a particular time, i.e. a 'snapshot'.

cross-tabulation *see* contingency table.

D

data Facts, opinions and statistics that have been collected together and recorded for reference or for analysis.

data display and analysis A process for the collection and analysis of qualitative data that involves three concurrent subprocesses of data reduction, data display, and drawing and verifying conclusions.

data matrix The table format in which data are usually entered into analysis software consisting of rows (cases) and columns (variables).

data reduction Condensing data by summarising or simplifying these as a means to analyse them. *See also* data display and analysis.

data requirements table A table designed to ensure that, when completed, the data collected will enable the research question(s) to be answered and the objectives achieved.

data sampling The process of only transcribing those sections of an audio-recording that are pertinent to your research, having listened to it repeatedly beforehand.

data saturation The stage when any additional data collected provides few, if any, new insights.

debriefing Providing research participants with a retrospective explanation about a research project and its purpose where covert observation has occurred.

deception Deceiving participants about the nature, purpose or use of research by the researcher(s). *See also* informed consent, research ethics.

decile One of 10 sections when data are ranked and divided into 10 groups of equal size.

deductive approach Approach to theory development involving the testing of a theoretical proposition by the employment of a research strategy specifically designed for the purpose of its testing.

deliberate distortion Form of bias that occurs when data are recorded inaccurately on purpose. It is most common for secondary data sources such as organisational records.

delivery and collection questionnaire Data collection technique in which the questionnaire is delivered to each respondent. She or he then reads and answers the same set of questions in a predetermined order without an interviewer being present before the completed questionnaire is collected.

Delphi technique Technique using a group of people who are either involved or interested in the research topic to generate and select a more specific research idea.

demographic variable Variable that records data about characteristics.

deontological view View that the ends served by research can never justify research which is unethical.

dependent variable Variable that changes in response to changes in other variables.

descriptive data Data whose values cannot be measured numerically but can be distinguished by classifying into sets (categories).

descriptive observation Observation where the researcher concentrates on observing the physical setting, the key participants and their activities, particular events and their sequence and the attendant processes and emotions involved.

descriptive research Research for which the purpose is to produce an accurate representation of persons, events or situations.

descriptive statistics Generic term for statistics that can be used to describe variables.

descripto-explanatory study A study whose purpose is both descriptive and explanatory where, usually, description is the precursor to explanation.

deviant sampling see extreme case sampling.

dichotomous data Descriptive data that are grouped into two categories. See also descriptive data.

direct realism The philosophical stance that what you see is what you get: what we experience through our senses portrays the world accurately. See also critical realism, realism.

directional hypothesis Testable statement of the direction of the association, difference or relationship between two or more variables. See also alternative hypothesis, hypothesis, null hypothesis.

directional null hypothesis Testable statement that there is no directional association, difference or relationship between two or more variables. See also alternative hypothesis, directional hypothesis, null hypothesis.

discourse Term used in discourse analysis to describe how language is used to shape meanings and give rise to social practices and relations. See also discourse analysis.

discourse analysis General term covering a variety of approaches to the analysis of language in its own right. It explores how language constructs and simultaneously reproduces and/or changes the social world rather than using it as a means to reveal the social world as a phenomenon.

discrete data Data whose values are measured in discrete units and therefore can take only one of a finite number of values from a scale that measures changes in this way.

discussion The section of the project report in which the wider implications of the findings (and conclusions) are considered.

dispersion measures Generic term for statistics that can be used to provide an impression of how the values for a variable are dispersed around the central tendency.

dissertation The usual name for research projects undertaken as part of undergraduate and taught master's degrees. Dissertations are usually written for an academic audience.

divergent validity The absence of overlap (or correlation) between different scales used to measure theoretically distinct constructs. See also construct validity.

document secondary data Data that, unlike the spoken word endure physically (including digitally) as evidence allowing them to be transposed across both time and space and reanalysed for a purpose different to that for which they were originally collected.

document summary Type of summary used an analytical aid. See also interim summary; transcript summary.

DOI Digital object identifier name used to uniquely identify an electronic document such as a specific journal article stored in an online database.

double-phase research design Research involving two phases of data collection and analysis. See also sequential mixed methods research.

Durbin–Watson statistic Statistical test to measure the extent to which the value of a dependent variable at time t is related to its value at the previous time period, $t-1$ (autocorrelation). The statistic ranges in value from zero to 4. A value of 2 indicates no autocorrelation. A value of towards zero indicates positive autocorrelation. A value towards 4 indicates negative autocorrelation. See also autocorrelation.

E

ecological validity A type of external validity referring to the extent to which findings can be generalised from one group to another. See also external validity.

effect size index A measure of the practical significance of a statistically significant difference, association or relationship. The statistic is normally used when the data sample is large.

electronic interview An Internet- or intranet-mediated interview conducted through either a chat room, Internet forum, web conferencing or email. See also email interview, chat room, Internet forum.

electronic questionnaire An Internet- or intranet-mediated questionnaire. See also Internet-mediated questionnaire, intranet-mediated questionnaire.

element Individual case or group member within a sample or population such as an employee.

email interview A series of emails each containing a small number of questions rather than one email containing a series of questions.

embedded mixed-methods research Use of quantitative and qualitative methods in research design where use of one is embedded within the other. *See also* concurrent embedded design, concurrent mixed methods research.

epistemological relativism Subjectivist approach to knowledge that recognises knowledge is historically situated and that social facts are social constructions agreed on by people rather than existing independently.

epistemology A branch of philosophy concerned with assumptions about knowledge, what constitutes acceptable, valid and legitimate knowledge, and how we can communicate knowledge to others.

ethics *see* research ethics, research ethics committees, code of ethics.

ethnography Research strategy that focuses upon describing and interpreting the social world throughfirst-hand field study.

evaluation The process of judging materials or methods in terms of internal accuracy and consistency or by comparison with external criteria.

event variable Variable that records data about events, what happened in the past, now or will happen in the future.

existing contacts Colleagues, friends, relatives or fellow students who may agree to become research informants, participants or respondents.

experiential data Data about the researcher's perceptions and feelings as the research develops.

experiential meaning The equivalence of meaning of a word or sentence for different people in their everyday experiences.

experiment Research strategy whose purpose is to study the probability of a change in an independent variable causing a change in another, dependent variable. Involves the definition of null and alternative hypotheses; random allocation of participants to either an experimental group(s) or a control group; manipulation of the independent variable; measurement of changes in the dependent variable and; control of other variables. *See also* between-subjects design, control group, experimental group, quasi-experiment.

experimental group Group in an experiment that receives the intervention in which you are interested. *See also* control group, experiment.

explanation building Deductive process for analysing qualitative data that involves the iterative examination of a number of strategically selected cases to test a theoretical proposition.

explanatory research Research that focuses on studying a situation or a problem in order to explain the relationships between variables.

exploratory data analysis (EDA) Approach to data analysis that emphasises the use of diagrams to explore and understand the data.

exploratory study Research that aims to seek new insights into phenomena, to ask questions, and to assess the phenomena in a new light.

external researcher Researcher who wishes to gain access to an organisation for which she or he does not work. *See also* access, internal researcher.

external validity The extent to which the research results from a particular study are generalisable to all relevant contexts.

extreme case sampling A purposive sampling method which focuses on unusual or special cases. *See also* purposive sampling.

F

face validity Agreement that a question, scale, or measure appears logically to reflect accurately what it was intended to measure.

factual variable Variable that records factual data.

feasibility [of access] Being able to negotiate access to conduct research.

filter question Closed question that identifies those respondents for whom the following question or questions are not applicable, enabling them to skip these questions.

focus group Group interview, composed of a small number of participants, facilitated by a 'moderator', in which the topic is defined clearly and precisely and there is a focus on enabling and recording interactive discussion between participants. *See also* group interview.

focused coding Analysis or reanalysis of data to identify which of the initial codes may be used as higher level codes to categorise larger units of data to further the analysis towards the emergence of a grounded theory.

focused interview Interviewer exercises direction over the interview while allowing the interviewee's opinions to emerge as he or she responds to the questions of the researcher.

focused observation Phase in an observation study when the researcher focuses her or his observations on particular events or interactions between key informants.

follow-up Contact made with respondents to thank them for completing and returning a survey and to remind non-respondents to complete and return their surveys.

forced-choice question *see* closed question.

forum *see* Internet forum.

frequency distribution Table for summarising data from one variable so that specific values can be read.

full-text online database Online database that indexes and provides a summary and full text of articles from a range of journals. Sometimes includes books, chapters from books, reports, theses and conference papers.

fully integrated mixed-methods research Use of both quantitative and qualitative methods throughout the research. *See also* partially integrated mixed methods research.

functionalist paradigm Paradigm concerned with rational explanations and developing sets of recommendations within the current structures such as why a particular organisational problem is occurring in terms of the functions they perform.

fundamental research *see* basic research.

G

Gantt chart Chart that provides a simple visual representation of the tasks or activities that make up a project, each being plotted against a time line.

gatekeeper The person, often in an organisation, who controls research access.

general focus research question Question that flows from the research idea and may lead to several more detailed questions or the definition of research objectives.

generalisability The extent to which the findings of a research study are applicable to other settings.

generalisation The making of more widely applicable propositions based upon the process of deduction from specific cases.

Goldilocks test A test to decide whether research questions are either too big, too small, too hot or just right. Those that are too big probably demand too many resources. Questions that are too small are likely to be of insufficient substance, while those that are too hot may be so because of sensitivities that may be aroused as a result of doing the research.

grammatical error Error of grammar that detracts from the authority of the project report.

graph A visual display that illustrates the values of one variable or the relationship between two or more variables.

grey literature *see* primary literature.

grounded theory (1) Including both Grounded Theory Methodology and Grounded Theory Method. **(2)** Theory that is grounded or developed using an inductive approach. *See also* Grounded Theory Methodology, Grounded Theory Method, inductive approach.

Grounded Theory (Methodology) Research strategy in which theory is developed from data collected by a series of observations or interviews principally involving an inductive approach. *See also* deductive approach, Grounded Theory Method, inductive approach.

Grounded Theory Method Data collection techniques and analytic procedures used in a Grounded Theory research strategy to derive meaning from the subjects and settings being studied. *See also* Grounded Theory (Methodology).

group interview General term to describe all non-standardised interviews conducted with two or more people.

H

habituation Situation where, in observation studies, the subjects being observed become familiar with the process of observation so that they take it for granted. This is an attempt to overcome 'observer effect' or reactivity.

haphazard sampling Non-probability sampling procedure in which cases are selected without any obvious principles of organisation. *See also* convenience sampling, non-probability sampling.

hermeneutics Strand of interpretivism that focuses on the study of cultural artefacts such as texts, symbols, stories, images. *See also* intepretivism.

heterogeneous sampling A purposive sampling method which focuses on obtaining the maximum variation in the cases selected. *See also* purposive sampling.

heteroscedasticity Extent to which the data values for the dependent and independent variables have unequal variances. *See also* variance.

histogram Diagram for showing frequency distributions for a grouped continuous data variable in which the area of each bar represents the frequency of occurrence.

homogeneous sampling A purposive sampling method which focuses on selecting cases from one particular subgroup in which all the members are similar. *See also* purposive sampling.

homoscedasticity Extent to which the data values for the dependent and independent variables have equal variances. *See also* variance.

hybrid access Use of both traditional access and Internet-mediated access to conduct research.

hypothesis (1) Testable statement that there is an association, difference or relationship between two or more variables. Often referred to as H_1. *See also* alternative hypothesis, directional hypothesis, null hypothesis. **(2)** Testable proposition about the relationship between two or more events or concepts.

I

idiomatic meaning The meaning ascribed to a group of words that are natural to a native speaker, but which is not deducible from the individual words.

incommensurability The assertion that the radical humanist, radical structuralist, interpretive and functionalist paradigms contain mutually incompatible assumptions and therefore cannot be combined. *See also* functionalist paradigm, interpretive paradigm, radical humanist paradigm, radical structuralist paradigm.

independent groups *t*-test Statistical test to determine the probability (likelihood) that the values of a numerical data variable for two independent samples or groups are different. The test assesses the likelihood of any difference between these two groups occurring by chance alone.

independent measures Use of more than one experimental group in an experiment where more than one intervention or manipulation is to be tested and measured. *See also* experiment.

independent variable Variable that causes changes to a dependent variable or variables.

in-depth interview *See* unstructured interview.

index number Summary data value calculated from a base period for numerical variables, to facilitate comparisons of trends or changes over time. *See also* base period.

inductive approach Approach to theory development involving the development of a theory as a result of the observation of empirical data.

ineligible respondent Respondent selected for a sample who does not meet the requirements of the research.

inference, statistical *see* statistical inference.

inferred consent Informants, participants or respondents may or may not fully understand the implications of taking part but their consent to participate, is inferred from their participating in the research. The researcher assumes that data may be recorded, analysed, used, stored or reported as she or he wishes without clarifying such issues with those who take part. *See also* informed consent.

informant error Errors that occur when informants are observed in situations that are inconsistent with their normal behaviour patterns, leading to atypical responses. *See also* informants.

informant interview Interview guided by the perceptions of the interviewee.

informant verification Form of triangulation in which the researcher presents written accounts of, for example, interview notes to informants for them to verify the content. *See also* triangulation.

informants Those who agree to be observed in participant observation or structured observation studies.

informed consent Position achieved when intended participants are fully informed about the nature, purpose and use of research to be undertaken and their role within it, and where their consent to participate, if provided, is freely given. *See also* deception, implied consent.

initial coding *see* open coding.

initial sample Purposively selected initial case from which to collect and analyse data used in Grounded Theory. *See also* Grounded Theory Method.

instrument *See* questionnaire.

integer A whole number.

interdiscursivity The way one discourse is introduced into another discourse within discourse analysis. *See also* discourse analysis.

inter-library loan System for borrowing a book or obtaining a copy of a journal article from another library.

interim summary Type of summary used to outline progress and to aid analysis. *See also* document summary; transcript summary.

internal researcher Person who conducts research within an organisation for which they work. *See also* cognitive access, external researcher.

internal validity Extent to which findings can be attributed to interventions rather than any flaws in your research design. *See also* measurement validity.

Internet forum Commonly referred to as web forums, message boards, discussion boards, discussion forums, discussion groups and bulletin boards. Usually only deal with one topic and discourage personal exchanges.

Internet-mediated access Use of Internet technologies to gain virtual access to conduct research.

Internet-mediated observation Adaptation of traditional observation from oral/visual/near to textual/digital/virtual to allow researchers purely to observe or participate with members of an online community to collect data.

Internet questionnaire Data collection technique in which the questionnaire is delivered online to each respondent. She or he then reads and answers the same set of questions in a predetermined order without an interviewer being present before returning it electronically. *See also* Web questionnaire, mobile questionnaire.

interpretive ethnography Ethnographic strategy stressing subjectivity, reflection and identifying multiple meanings. *See also* ethnography, critical ethnography, realist ethnography.

interpretive paradigm Paradigm concerned with he way humans attempt to make sense of the world around them; for example, understanding the fundamental meanings attached to organisational life.

interpretivism Philosophical stance that advocates humans are different from physical phenomena because they create meanings. Argues that argues that human beings and their social worlds cannot be studied in the same way as physical phenomena due to the need to take account of complexity.

inter-quartile range The difference between the upper and lower quartiles, representing the middle 50% of the data when the data values for a variable have been ranked.

inter-rater reliability The extent which two coders agree when coding the same set of data.

intertextuality The way a text or texts overtly or covertly borrow from and are informed by other texts within Discourse Analysis. *See also* Discourse Analysis.

interval data Numerical data for which the difference or 'interval' between any two data values for a particular variable can be stated, but for which the relative difference can not be stated. *See also* numerical data.

interview schedule *see* structured interview.

interviewee bias Attempt by an interviewee to construct an account that hides some data or when she or he presents herself or himself in a socially desirable role or situation.

interviewer bias Attempt by an interviewer to introduce bias during the conduct of an interview, or where the appearance or behaviour of the interviewer has the effect of introducing bias in the interviewee's responses.

interviewer-completed questionnaire Data collection technique in which an interviewer reads the same set of questions to the respondent in a predetermined order and records his or her responses. *See also* structured interview, telephone questionnaire.

intranet-mediated access Use of an intranet within an organisation to gain access to conduct research.

intra-rater reliability Reliability of coding by a single coder over time.

Introduction The opening to the project report, which gives the reader a clear idea of the central issue of concern of the research, states the research question(s) and research objectives, and explains the research context and the structure of the project report.

introductory letter Request for research access, addressed to an intended participant or organisational broker/gatekeeper, stating the purpose of the research, the nature of the help being sought, and the requirements of agreeing to participate. *See also* covering letter, gatekeeper.

intrusive research methods Methods that involve direct access to participants, including qualitative interviewing, observation, longitudinal research based on these methods and phenomenologically based approaches to research. *See also* access, cognitive access.

investigative question One of a number of questions that need to be answered in order to address satisfactorily each research question and meet each objective.

'in vivo' codes Names or labels for codes based on actual terms used by those who take part in research.

J

journal *see* professional journal, refereed academic journal.

judgemental sampling *see* purposive sampling.

K

Kendall's rank correlation coefficient Statistical test that assesses the strength of the relationship between two ranked data variables, especially where the data for a variable contain tied ranks. For data collected from a sample, there is also a need to calculate the probability of the correlation coefficient having occurred by chance alone.

key word Basic term selected from the controlled index language specified by the online database to describe the research question(s) and objectives to search the tertiary literature.

Kolmogorov–Smirnov test Statistical test to determine the probability (likelihood) that an observed set of values for each category of a variable differs from a specified distribution. Common uses are to discover whether a data variable's distribution differs significantly from a normal distribution, or an alternative distribution such as that of the population from which it was selected.

kurtosis The pointedness or flatness of a distribution's shape compared with the normal distribution. If a distribution is pointier or peaked, it is leptokurtic and the kurtosis value is positive. If a distribution is flatter, it is platykurtic and the kurtosis value is negative. *See also* normal distribution.

L

latent content Meanings in the data that are not manifest and so need to be interpreted or inferred. *See also* Content Analysis, manifest content.

law of large numbers Samples of larger absolute size are more likely to be representative of the population from which they are drawn than smaller samples and, in particular, the mean (average) calculated for the sample is more likely to equal the mean for the population, providing the samples are not biased.

level of access The nature and depth of access to participants required and achieved. *See also* cognitive access, continuing access, physical access.

lexical meaning The precise meaning of an individual word.

Likert-style rating question Rating question that allows the respondent to indicate how strongly she or he agrees or disagrees with a statement.

linearity Degree to which change in a dependent variable is related to change in one or more independent variables. *See also* dependent variable, independent variable

line graph Diagram for showing trends in longitudinal data for a variable.

list question Closed question, in which the respondent is offered a list of items and instructed to select those that are appropriate.

literal replication Replication of findings across selected multiple case studies in a case study strategy. *See also* case study, theoretical replication.

literature review *see* critical (literature) review.

logical reasoning Process used in theory development to explain why relationships may exist based on what is already known.

longitudinal study The study of a particular phenomenon (or phenomena) over an extended period of time.

long-term trend The overall direction of movement of numerical data values for a single variable after variations have been smoothed out. *See also* moving average.

lower quartile The value below which a quarter of the data values lie when the data values for a variable have been ranked.

M

mail questionnaire *see* postal questionnaire.

management report Abbreviated version of the project report, usually written for a practitioner audience. Normally includes a brief account of objectives, method, findings, conclusions and recommendations.

manifest content Content that is apparent in the data. *See also* Content Analysis, latent content.

Mann–Whitney *U* test Statistical test to determine the probability (likelihood) that the values of a ordinal data variable for two independent samples or groups are different. The test assesses the likelihood of any difference between these two groups occurring by chance alone and is often used when the assumptions of the independent samples *t*-test are not met.

matched pair analysis Used in an experimental design to match participants in an experimental group with those in a control group before conducting the experiment where random assignment is not possible. *See also* quasi-experiment.

matrix question Series of two or more closed questions in which each respondent's answers are recorded using the same grid.

maximum variation sampling *see* heterogeneous sampling.

mean The average value calculated by adding up the values of each case for a variable and dividing by the total number of cases.

measurement validity The extent to which a scale or measuring instrument measures what it is intended to measure. *See also* internal validity.

median The middle value when all the values of a variable are arranged in rank order; sometimes known as the 50th percentile.

mediating variable A variable that transmits the effect of an independent variable to a dependent variable. *See also* dependent variable, independent variable.

member validation Process of allowing participants to comment on and correct data to validate these.

memo writing Key element used in Grounded Theory Method during the collection, analysis and interpretation of data, which helps to facilitate and link these stages of research and aid the development of a grounded theory. May also be used in other research strategies.

method The techniques and procedures used to obtain and analyse research data, including for example questionnaires, observation, interviews, and statistical and non-statistical techniques.

methodology The theory of how research should be undertaken, including the theoretical and philosophical assumptions upon which research is based and the implications of these for the method or methods adopted.

minimal interaction Process in which the observer tries as much as possible to 'melt into the background', having as little interaction as possible with the subjects of the observation. This is an attempt to overcome observer effect. *See also* observer effect.

mixed methods research Use of both quantitative and qualitative data collection techniques and analysis procedures either at the same time (concurrent) or one after the other (sequential).

mixed-model research Combination of quantitative and qualitative data collection techniques and analysis procedures as well as combining quantitative and qualitative approaches in other phases of the research such as research question generation.

mobile questionnaire Data collection technique in which the questionnaire is delivered electronically to each respondent's mobile telephone. She or he then reads and answers the same set of questions in a predetermined order without an interviewer being present before returning it electronically. *See also* online questionnaire.

modal group The most frequently occurring category for data that have been grouped.

mode The value of a variable that occurs most frequently.

Mode 0 knowledge creation Research based on power and patronage, these being particularly visible in the close relationships between sponsor and researcher.

Mode 1 knowledge creation Research of a fundamental rather than applied nature, in which the questions are set and solved by academic interests with little, if any, focus on exploitation of research by practitioners.

Mode 2 knowledge creation Research of an applied nature, governed by the world of practice and highlighting the importance of collaboration both with and between practitioners.

Mode 3 knowledge creation Research growing out of Mode 1 and Mode 2 whose purpose is 'to assure survival and promote the common good at various levels of social aggregation' (Huff and Huff 2001:S53).

moderating variable A variable that affects the relationship between an independent variable and a dependent variable. *See also* dependent variable, independent variable.

moderator Facilitator of focus group interviews. *See also* focus group, group interview.

mono method Use of a single data collection technique and corresponding analysis procedure or procedures.

moving average Statistical method of smoothing out variations in numerical data recorded for a single variable over time to enable the long-term trend to be seen more clearly. *See also* long-term trend.

multicollinearity *see* collinearity.

multi-method Use of more than one data collection technique and corresponding analysis procedure or procedures.

multi-method qualitative study Use of more than one qualitative data collection technique and corresponding qualitative analysis procedure or procedures.

multi-method quantitative study Use of more than one quantitative data collection technique and corresponding quantitative analysis procedure or procedures.

multi-phase research design Research involving more than two phases of data collection and analysis. *See also* sequential mixed methods research.

multiple bar graph/chart Diagram for comparing frequency distributions for categorical or grouped discrete or continuous data variables, which highlights the highest and lowest values.

multiple-dichotomy method Method of data coding using a separate variable for each possible response to an open question or an item in a list question. *See also* list question, open question.

multiple line graph Diagram for comparing trends over time between numerical data variables.

multiple methods Use of more than one data collection technique and analysis procedure or procedures. *See also* mixed methods.

multiple regression analysis The process of calculating a coefficient of multiple determination and regression equation using two or more independent variables and one dependent variable. For data collected from a sample, there is also a need to calculate the probability of the regression coefficient having occurred by chance alone. *See also* multiple regression coefficient, regression analysis, regression equation.

multiple-response method Method of data coding using the same number of variables as the maximum number of responses to an open question or a list question by any one case. *See also* list question, open question.

multiple-source secondary data Secondary data created by combining two or more different data sets prior to the data being accessed for the research. These data sets can be based entirely on documentary or on survey data, or can be an amalgam of the two.

multi-stage sampling Probability sampling procedure that is a development of cluster sampling. It involves taking a series of cluster samples, each of which uses random sampling (systematic, stratified or simple).

N

narrative A personal account that interprets an event or series of events, which is significant for the narrator and which convey meaning to the researcher, and which are narrated in a sequenced way. *See also* narrative inquiry.

Narrative Analysis The collection and analysis of qualitative data that preserves the integrity and narrative value of data collected, thereby avoiding their fragmentation.

narrative inquiry Qualitative research strategy to collect the experiences of participants as whole accounts or narratives, or which attempts to reconstruct such experiences into narratives. *See also* narrative.

natural data Data that are recorded from real conversations that take place in everyday, authentic situations. *See also* contrived data.

naturalistic Adopting an ethnographic strategy in which the researcher researches the phenomenon within the context in which it occurs.

negative cases Cases that do not support emergent explanations, but which help the refining of these explanations and direct the selection of further cases to collect data.

negative correlation Relationship between two variables for which, as the values of one variable increase, the values of the other variable decrease. *See also* correlation coefficient.

negative skew Distribution of numerical data for a variable in which the majority of the data are found bunched to the right, with a long tail to the left.

netiquette General operating guidelines for using the Internet, including not sending junk emails.

new contacts People approached to become research informants, participants or respondents previously unknown to the researcher.

nominal data *see* descriptive data.

nominalism Ontological position that asserts that the order and structures of social phenomena (and the phenomena themselves) are created by social actors through use of language, conceptual categories, perceptions and consequent actions.

non-maleficence Avoidance of harm.

non-parametric statistic Statistic designed to be used when data are not normally distributed. Often used with categorical data. *See also* categorical data.

non-probability sampling Selection of sampling techniques in which the chance or probability of each case being selected is not known.

non-random sampling *See* non-probability sampling.

non-response When the respondent refuses to take part in the research or answer a question.

non-response bias Bias in findings caused by respondent refusing to take part in the research or answer a question.

non-standardised interview *See* semi-structured interview, unstructured interview.

normal distribution Special form of the symmetric distribution in which the numerical data for a variable can be plotted as a bell-shaped curve.

notebook of ideas Books or equivalent for noting down any interesting research ideas as you think of them.

null hypothesis Testable statement stating that there is no association, difference or relationship between two or more variables. Often referred to as H_0. *See also* alternative hypothesis, directional null hypothesis, hypothesis.

numeric rating question Rating question that uses numbers as response options to identify and record the respondent's response. The end response options, and sometimes the middle, are labelled.

numerical data Data whose values can be measured numerically as quantities.

O

objectivism An ontological position that incorporates the assumptions of the natural sciences arguing that social reality is external external to, and independent of, social actors concerned with their existence. *See also* ontology, subjectivism.

objectivity Avoidance of (conscious) bias and subjective selection during the conduct and reporting of research. In some research philosophies the researcher will consider that interpretation is likely to be related to a set of values and therefore will attempt to recognise and explore this.

observation The systematic observing, recording, description, analysis and interpretation of people's behaviour. *See also* participant observation, structured observation.

observer as participant Observational role in which the researcher observes activities without taking part in those activities in the same way as the 'real' research subjects. The researcher's identity as a researcher and research purpose is clear to all concerned. *See also* participant as observer.

observer bias This may occur when observers give inaccurate responses in order to distort the results of the research.

observer drift Occurs when the observer starts to redefine the way in which similar observations are interpreted leading to inconsistency.

observer effect The impact of being observed on how people act. *See also* habituation, reactivity.

observer error Systematic errors made by observers, as a result of tiredness, for example.

one stage cluster sampling *see* cluster sampling.

one-way analysis of variance *see* analysis of variance.

online first The publication of forthcoming articles online, prior to them appearing in a journal.

online form (questionnaire) *See* Internet questionnaire.

online questionnaire *See* Internet questionnaire.

ontology Branch of philosophy concerned with assumptions about the nature of reality or being. *See also* axiology, epistemology.

open coding The process of disaggregating data into units in grounded theory.

open question Question allowing respondents to give answers in their own way.

operationalisation The translation of concepts into tangible indicators of their existence.

opinion variable Variable that records what respondents believe about something, what they think is true or false.

ordinal data *see* ranked data.

outlier A case or unit of analysis that has extreme values for a variable which may distort the interpretation of data or make a statistic misleading.

P

paired *t*-test Statistical test to determine the probability (likelihood) that the values of two (a pair of) numerical data variables collected for the same cases are different. The test assesses the likelihood of any difference between two variables (each half of the pair) occurring by chance alone.

paradigm A set of basic and taken-for-granted assumptions which underwrite the frame of reference, mode of theorising and ways of working in which a group operates.

parametric statistic Statistic designed to be used when data are normally distributed. Used with numerical data. *See also* numerical data.

partial response The level of response to questionnaires or structured interviews in which 50% to 80% of all questions are answered other than by a refusal or no answer.

partially integrated mixed-methods research Use of both quantitative and qualitative methods at only one stage or at particular stages of the research. *See also* fully integrated mixed methods research.

participant The person who answers the questions, usually in an interview or group interview.

participant as observer Observational role in which the researcher takes part in and observes activities in the same way as the 'real' research subjects. The researcher's identity as a researcher and research purpose is clear to all concerned. *See also* observer as participant.

participation bias Type of bias resulting from the nature of the individuals or organisational participants who agree to take part in a research study.

participant information sheet Document providing information required by gatekeepers and intended participants in order for informed consent to be given.

participant observation Observation in which the researcher attempts to participate fully in the lives and activities of the research subjects and thus becomes a member of the subjects' group(s), organisation(s) or community. *See also* complete observer, complete participant, observer as participant, participant as observer.

participant researcher *see* internal researcher.

participant validation *see* member validation.

passive voice The voice in which the subject of the sentence undergoes the action of the verb: for example, 'interviews were conducted'.

pattern matching Analysis of qualitative data involving the prediction of a pattern of outcomes based on theoretical propositions to seek to explain a set of findings.

Pearson's product moment correlation coefficient Statistical test that assesses the strength of the relationship between two numerical data variables. For data collected from a sample there is also a need to calculate the probability of the correlation coefficient having occurred by chance alone.

percentage component bar graph/chart Diagram for comparing proportions for all types of data variables.

percentile One of 100 sections when data are ranked and divided into 100 groups of equal size.

personal data Category of data, defined in law, relating to identified or identifiable persons. *See also* sensitive personal data.

personal entry Situation where the researcher needs to conduct research within an organisation, rather than rely on the use and completion of self-administered, postal questionnaires or the use of publicly available secondary data. *See* access.

personal pronoun One of the pronouns used to refer to people: I, me, you, he, she, we, us, they, him, her, them.

phenomenology Strand of interpretivism that focuses on participants' lived experience, that is the participants' recollections and interpretations of those experiences, being particularly concerned with generating meanings and gaining insights into those phenomena. *See also* interpretivism.

Phi Statistic to measure association between two variables using a scale between −1 (perfect negative association), through 0 (no association) to +1 (perfect association).

physical access The initial level of gaining access to an organisation to conduct research. *See also* cognitive access, continuing access, gatekeeper.

pictogram Diagram in which a picture or series of pictures are used to represent the data proportionally.

pie chart Diagram frequently used for showing proportions for a categorical data or a grouped continuous or discrete data variable.

pilot test Small-scale study to test a questionnaire, interview checklist or observation schedule, to minimise the likelihood of respondents having problems in answering the questions and of data recording problems as well as to allow some assessment of the questions' validity and the reliability of the data that will be collected.

plagiarism Presenting work or ideas as if they are your own when in reality they are the work or ideas of someone else, and failing to acknowledge the original source.

population The complete set of cases or group members. *See also* research population.

positive correlation Relationship between two variables for which, as the value of one variable increases, the values of the other variable also increase. *See also* correlation coefficient.

positive skew Distribution of numerical data for a variable in which the majority of the data are found bunched to the left, with a long tail to the right.

positivism The philosophical stance of the natural scientist entailing working with an observable social reality to produce law-like generalisations The emphasis is on highly structured methodology to facilitate replication.

postal questionnaire Data collection technique in which the questionnaire is delivered by post to each respondent. She or he then reads and answers the same set of questions in a predetermined order without an interviewer being present before returning it by post.

postmodernism Philosophical stance emphasising the role of language and power-relations that seeks to question accepted ways of thinking and give voice to alternative marginalised views.

post-test Outcome measurement for the dependent variable in an experiment. *See also* pre-test.

PowerPoint™ Microsoft computer package that allows the presenter to design overhead slides using text, pictures, photographs etc., which lend a professional appearance.

practitioner-researcher Role occupied by a researcher when she or he is conducting research in an organisation, often her or his own, while fulfilling her or his normal working role.

pragmatism Philosophical stance that argues that concepts are only relevant where they support action. It considers research starts with a problem, and aims to contribute practical solutions that inform future practice. Pragmatists research may vary considerably in terms of how objectivist or subjectivist it is. *See also* objectivist, subjectivist.

pre-coding The process of incorporating coding schemes in questions prior to a questionnaire's administration.

predictive validity *see* criterion-related validity.

preliminary inquiry The process by which a research idea is refined in order to turn it into a research project. This may be simply a review of the relevant literature

preliminary search This way of searching the literature may be a useful way of generating research ideas. It

may be based, for example, on lecture notes or course textbooks.

pre-set codes Codes established prior to data collection and often included as part of the data collection form.

pre-survey contact Contact made with a respondent to advise them of a forthcoming survey in which she or he will be asked to take part.

pre-test Baseline measurement for the dependent variable in an experiment. *See also* post-test.

primary data Data collected specifically for the research project being undertaken.

primary literature The first occurrence of a piece of work, including published sources such as government white papers and planning documents and unpublished manuscript sources such as letters, memos and committee minutes.

primary observation Observation where the researcher notes what happened or what was said at the time. This is often done by keeping a research diary.

privacy Primary ethical concern relating to the rights of individuals not to participate in research and to their treatment where they agree to participate. *See also* research ethics, informed consent.

probability sampling Selection of sampling techniques in which the chance, or probability, of each case being selected from the population is known and is not zero.

probing questions Questions used to explore further responses that are of significance to the research topic.

professional journal Journal produced by a professional organisation for its members, often containing articles of a practical nature related to professional needs. Articles in professional journals are usually not refereed.

project report The term used in this book to refer generally to dissertations, theses and management reports. *See also* dissertation, management report, thesis.

pure research *see* basic research.

purposive sampling Non-probability sampling procedure in which the judgement of the researcher is used to select the cases that make up the sample. This can be done on the basis of extreme cases, heterogeneity (maximum variation), homogeneity (maximum similarity), critical cases, theoretical cases or typical cases.

Q

qualitative data Non-numerical data or data that have not been quantified.

qualitative interview Collective term for semi-structured and unstructured interviews aimed at generating qualitative data.

qualitise Conversion of quantitative data into narrative that can be analysed qualitatively.

quantifiable data *see* numerical data.

quantitative data Numerical data or data that have been quantified.

quantitise Conversion of qualitative data into numerical codes that can be analysed statistically.

quantity question Closed question in which the respondent's answer is recorded as a number giving the amount.

quartile One of four sections when data are ranked and divided into four groups of equal size. *See also* lower quartile, upper quartile.

quasi-experiment Experimental design using an experimental group and a control group but where experimental participants cannot be assigned randomly to each group. *See also* matched pair analysis.

questionnaire General term including all data collection techniques in which each person is asked to respond to the same set of questions in a predetermined order. *See also* delivery and collection questionnaire, interviewer-administered questionnaire, online questionnaire, postal questionnaire, self-administered questionnaire.

quota sampling Non-probability sampling procedure that ensures that the sample represents certain characteristics of the population chosen by the researcher.

R

r^2 **value** *See* coefficient of determination.

R^2 **value** *See* coefficient of multiple determination.

radical change perspective A perspective which fundamentally question the way things are done in organisations, and, through research, offers insights that would help to change the organisational and social worlds.

radical humanist paradigm Paradigm concerned with changing the status quo, focusing on issues of power and politics, domination and oppression and emphasising the importance of social construction, language, processes, and instability of structures and meanings.

radical structuralist paradigm Paradigm concerned with achieving fundamental change based upon an analysis of phenomena such as structural power relationships and patterns of conflict.

random sampling *see* simple random sampling.

range The difference between the highest and the lowest values for a variable.

ranked data Data whose values cannot be measured numerically but which can be placed in a definite order (rank).

ranking question Closed question in which the respondent is offered a list of items and instructed to place them in rank order.

rating question Closed question in which a scaling device is used to record the respondent's response. *See also* Likert-type rating question, numeric rating question, semantic differential rating question.

ratio data Numerical data for which both the difference or 'interval' and relative difference between any two data values for a particular variable can be stated. *See also* numerical data.

rational thinking technique One of a number of techniques for generating and refining research ideas based on a systematic approach such as searching the literature or examining past projects.

raw data Data for which little, if any, data processing has taken place.

reactivity Reaction by research participants to any research intervention that affects data reliability. *See also* habituation, observer effect.

realism The epistemological position that objects exist independently of our knowledge of their existence. *See also* critical realism, direct realism.

realist ethnography Ethnographic strategy stressing objectivity, factual reporting and identifying 'true' meanings. *See also* ethnography, critical ethnography, interpretive ethnography.

re-coding The process of grouping or combining a variable's codes to form a new variable, usually with less detailed categories.

reductionism The idea that problems as a whole are better understood if they are reduced to the simplest possible elements.

refereed academic journal Journal in which the articles have been evaluated by academic peers prior to publication to assess their quality and suitability. Not all academic journals are refereed.

references, list of Bibliographic details of all items referred to directly in the text. The university will specify the format required.

reflection Process of observing your own research practice and examining the way you do things.

reflective diary Diary in which the researcher notes down what has happened and lessons learnt during the research process. *See also* research notebook.

reflexivity Self-examination, evaluation and interpretation of your attitudes and beliefs, reactions to data and findings, and interactions with those who take part in the research and acknowledgement of the way these affect both the processes and outcomes of the research.

regression analysis The process of calculating a regression coefficient and regression equation using one independent variable and one dependent variable. For data collected from a sample, there is also a need to calculate the probability of the regression coefficient having occurred by chance alone. *See also* multiple regression analysis, coefficient of determination, r^2 value, regression equation.

regression equation Equation used to predict the values of a dependent variable given the values of one or more independent variables. The associated coefficient of determination provides an indication of how good a predictor the regression equation is likely to be. *See* coefficient of determination.

regulation perspective A perspective concerned primarily with the need for the regulation of societies and human behavior. It seeks to explain the way in which organisational affairs are regulated and offer suggestions as to how they may be improved within the framework of the way things are done at present.

relevance tree Technique for generating research topics that starts with a broad concept from which further (usually more specific) topics are generated. Each of these topics forms a separate branch, from which further sub-branches that are more detailed can be generated.

reliability The extent to which data collection technique or techniques will yield consistent findings, similar observations would be made or conclusions reached by other researchers or there is transparency in how sense was made from the raw data.

repeated measures *see* within-subjects design.

representative sample Sample that represents exactly the population from which it is drawn.

representative sampling *see* probability sampling.

research The systematic collection and interpretation of information with a clear purpose, to find things out. *See also* applied research, basic research.

research approach General term for inductive, deductive or abductive research approach. *See also* abductive approach, deductive approach, inductive approach.

research design Framework for the collection and analysis of data to answer research question and meet research objectives providing reasoned justification for choice of data sources, collection methods and analysis techniques.

research ethics The standards of the researcher's behaviour in relation to the rights of those who become the subject of a research project, or who are affected by it. *See also* code of ethics, privacy, research ethics committee.

research ethics committee Learned committee established to produce a code of research ethics, examine and approve or veto research proposals and advise in relation to the ethical dilemmas facing researchers during the conduct and reporting of research projects. *See also* code of ethics.

research idea Initial idea that may be worked up into a research project.

research interview Purposeful conversation between two or more people requiring the interviewer to establish rapport, to ask concise and unambiguous questions and to listen attentively.

research notebook Notebook in which the researcher records chronologically aspects of their research project such as useful articles they have read, notes of discussions with their project supervisor etc. and their emergent thoughts about all aspects of their research. Can be used as an analytical aid. Can incorporate a reflective diary. *See also* reflective diary; self-memo.

research objectives Clear, specific statements that identify what the researcher wishes to accomplish as a result of doing the research.

research philosophy Overarching term relating to a system of beliefs and assumptions about the development of knowledge and the nature of that knowledge in relation to research.

research proposal Structured plan of a research project, occasionally referred to as a protocol or outline.

research question The key question that the research process will address, or one of the key questions that it will address. The research question is generally the precursor of research objectives.

research strategy General plan of how the researcher will go about answering the research question(s).

respondent The person who answers the questions usually on a questionnaire. *See also* participant.

response bias *see* interviewee bias.

response rate The total number of responses divided by the total number in the sample after ineligible respondents have been excluded. *See* ineligible respondent. *See also* active response rate, break off, complete refusal, complete response, partial response.

review article Article, normally published in a refereed academic journal, that contains both a considered review of the state of knowledge in a given topic area and pointers towards areas where further research needs to be undertaken. *See also* refereed academic journal.

review question Specific question you ask of the material you are reading, which is linked either directly or indirectly to your research question. *See also* research question.

S

sample Subgroup or part of a larger population.

sampling fraction The proportion of the total population selected for a probability sample.

sampling frame The complete list of all the cases in the population, from which a probability sample is drawn.

saturation *see* data saturation.

scale Measure of a concept, such as customer loyalty or organisational commitment, created by combining scores to a number of rating questions.

scale item Rating question used in combination with other rating questions to create a scale. *See* rating question, scale.

scale question *see* rating question.

scatter graph Diagram for showing the relationship between two numerical or ranked data variables.

scatter plot *see* scatter graph.

scientific research Research that involves the systematic observation of and experiment with phenomena.

scoping study Preliminary exploratory study undertaken as part of Systematic Review to establish whether Systematic Reviews have already been published and determine the focus of the literature search. *See also* Systematic Review.

search engine Automated software that searches an index of documents on the Internet using key words and Boolean logic.

search string Combination of key words or search terms used in searching online databases.

search term Basic terms that describes your research question(s) and objectives, and is be used to search the tertiary literature.

secondary data Data that were originally collected for some other purpose. They can be can be further analysed to provide additional or different knowledge, interpretations or conclusions. *See also* document secondary data, multiple source secondary data, survey-based secondary data.

secondary literature Subsequent publication of primary literature such as books and journals.

secondary observation Statement made by an observer of what happened or was said. By necessity this involves that observer's interpretations.

selective coding The process of integrating categories to produce theory in grounded theory.

self-coded question Question each respondent codes her or himself as part of the process of recording their answer.

self-completed questionnaire Data collection technique in which each respondent reads and answers the same set of questions in a predetermined order without an interviewer being present.

self-memo Way of recording own ideas about research as they occur, which may then be used as an analytical aid. *See also* research notebook.

self-selection sampling Non-probability sampling procedure in which the case, usually an individual, is allowed to identify their desire to be part of the sample.

semantic differential rating question Rating question that allows the respondent to indicate his or her attitude to a concept defined by opposite adjectives or phrases.

semi-structured interview Wide-ranging category of interview in which the interviewer commences with a set of interview themes but is prepared to vary the order in which questions are asked and to ask new questions in the context of the research situation.

sensitive personal data Category of data, defined in law, that refers to certain specified characteristics or beliefs relating to identified or identifiable persons.

sensitivity Level of concern on the part of a potential host organisation, informant, participant or respondent about the nature of a research project and use of data that will affect willingness to cooperate.

sequential explanatory design Mixed methods research design where initial phase of quantitative data collection is followed by second phase of explanatory qualitative data collection. *See also* sequential mixed methods research.

sequential exploratory design Mixed methods research design where initial phase of exploratory qualitative data collection is followed by second phase of quantitative data collection. *See also* sequential mixed methods research.

sequential mixed-methods research Research using both quantitative and qualitative methods that are conducted in more than one phase of data collection and analysis. *See also* double-phase research design, multi-phase research design, sequential explanatory design, sequential exploratory design.

sequential multi-phase design Mixed methods research design involving multiple phases of data collection and analysis.

serial correlation *see* autocorrelation.

shadowing Process that the researcher would follow in order to gain a better understanding of the research context. This might involve following employees who are likely to be important in the research.

Shapiro–Wilk test Statistical test to determine the probability (likelihood) that an observed set of values for each category of a variable differs from a specified distribution.

signficance testing Testing the probability of a pattern such as a relationship between two variables occurring by chance alone if the null hypothesis were true.

simple random sampling Probability sampling procedure that ensures each case in the population has an equal chance of being included in the sample.

single-phase research design Research involving one phase of data collection and analysis. *See also* concurrent mixed methods research. *See also* concurrent mixed methods research.

snowball sampling Non-probability sampling procedure in which subsequent respondents are obtained from information provided by initial respondents.

social constructionism Ontological position that asserts that reality is constructed through social interaction in which social actors create partially shared meanings and realities, in other words it is socially constructed.

social norm The type of behaviour that a person ought to adopt in a particular situation.

socially desirable response Answer given by a respondent due to her or his desire, either conscious or unconscious, to gain prestige or appear in a different social role.

source questionnaire The questionnaire that is to be translated from another language when translating a questionnaire.

Spearman's rank correlation coefficient Statistical test that assesses the strength of the relationship between two ranked data variables. For data collected from a sample, there is also a need to calculate the probability of the correlation coefficient having occurred by chance alone.

split infinitive Phrase consisting of an infinitive with an adverb inserted between 'to' and the verb: for example, 'to readily agree'.

stacked bar graph/chart Diagram for comparing totals and subtotals for all types of data variable.

standard deviation Statistic that describes the extent of spread of data values around the mean for a variable containing numerical data.

statistical inference The process of coming to conclusions about the population on the basis of data describing a sample drawn from that population.

statistical significance The likelihood of the pattern that is observed (or one more extreme) occurring by chance alone, if there really was no difference in the population from that which the sample was drawn.

storyline The way in which the reader is led through the research project to the main conclusion or the answer to the research question. The storyline is, in effect, a clear theme that runs through the whole of the project report to convey a coherent and consistent message.

stratified random sampling Probability sampling procedure in which the population is divided into two or more relevant strata and a random sample (systematic or simple) is drawn from each of the strata.

structural narrative analysis Narrative Analysis that focuses on the way a narrative is constructed. *See also* Narrative Analysis.

structured interview Data collection technique in which an interviewer physically meets the respondent, reads them the same set of questions in a predetermined order, and records his or her response to each.

structured methodology Data collection methods that are easily replicated (such as the use of an observation schedule or questionnaire) to ensure high reliability.

structured observation Observation method using a high level of predetermined structure, often used to quantify observed behaviours. *See also* participant observation.

subject directory Hierarchically organised index categorised into broad topics, which, as it has been compiled by people, is likely to have its content partly censored and evaluated.

subject or participant bias Bias that may occur when research subjects are giving inaccurate responses in order to distort the results of the research.

subjectivism Ontological position that incorporates assumptions of the Arts and Humanities and asserts that social reality is made from the perceptions and consequent actions of social actors (people). *See also* ontology, objectivism.

sufficiency [of access] Being able to negotiate adequate access to conduct research.

survey Research strategy that involves the structured collection of data from a sizeable population. Although the term 'survey' is often used to describe the collection of data using questionnaires, it includes other techniques such as structured observation and structured interviews.

survey-based secondary data Data collected by surveys, such as by questionnaire, which have already been analysed for their original purpose.

symbolic interactionism Strand of interpretivism derived from pragmatist thinking that sees meaning as something that emerges out of interactions between people. It focuses on the observation and analysis of social interaction such as conversations, meetings and teamwork. *See also* interpretivism, pragmatism.

symmetric distribution Description of the distribution of data for a variable in which the data are distributed equally either side of the highest frequency.

symmetry of potential outcomes Situation in which the results of the research will be of similar value whatever they are.

synchronous Undertaken in real time, occurring at the same time.

synthesis Process of arranging and assembling various elements so as to make a new statement, or conclusion.

systematic random sampling Probability sampling procedure in which the initial sampling point is selected at random, and then the cases are selected at regular intervals.

Systematic Review A process for reviewing the literature using a comprehensive pre-planned strategy to locate existing literature, evaluate the contribution, analyse and synthesise the findings and report the evidence to allow conclusions to be reached about what is known and, also, what is not known.

systematic sampling *see* systematic random sampling.

T

table Technique for summarising data from one or more variables so that specific values can be read. *See also* contingency table, frequency distribution.

tailored design method Approach to designing questionnaires specifying precisely how to construct and use them; previously referred to as the 'total design method'.

target population Complete set of cases or group members that is the actual focus of the research inquiry, and from which a sample may be drawn.

target questionnaire The translated questionnaire when translating from a source questionnaire.

teleological view View that the ends served by research justify the means. Consequently, the benefits of research findings are weighed against the costs of acting unethically.

telephone questionnaire Data collection technique in which an interviewer contacts the respondent and administers the questionnaire using a telephone. The interviewer reads the same set of questions to the respondent in a predetermined order and records his or her responses.

Template Analysis Analysis of qualitative data that involves creating and developing a hierarchical template of data codes or categories representing themes revealed in the data collected and the relationships between these.

tense The form taken by the verb to indicate the time of the action (i.e. past, present or future).

tertiary literature source Source designed to help locate primary and secondary literature, such as an index, abstract, encyclopaedia or bibliography.

Thematic Analysis A technique used to analyse qualitative data that involves the search for themes, or patterns, occurring across a data set.

thematic narrative analysis Narrative Analysis that focuses on the thematic content of a narrative, rather than on the way in which it is structured. *See also* Narrative Analysis.

theme A broad category incorporating several codes that appear to be related to one another and which indicates an idea that is important to your research question.

theoretical replication Realisation or replication of predicted theoretical outcomes in selected case studies in a case study strategy. *See also* case study, literal replication.

theoretical sampling A purposive sampling method particularly associated with Grounded Theory which focuses on the needs of the emerging theory and the evolving story line, participants being chosen purposively to inform this.

theoretical saturation Procedure used in Grounded Theory Method and reached when data collection ceases to reveal new data that are relevant to a category, where categories have become well developed and understood and relationships between categories have been verified. *See also* Grounded Theory Method.

theoretical sensitivity Sensitivity to meanings in the data and using *in vivo* and researcher generated codes to guide theorising activity, rather than being sensitised by concepts in existing theory.

theory Formulation regarding the cause and effect relationships between two or more variables, which may or may not have been tested.

thesis The usual name for research project reports undertaken for Master of Philosophy (MPhil) and Doctor of Philosophy (PhD) degrees, written for an academic audience.

time error Error, usually associated with structured observations, where the time at which the observation is being conducted provides data that are untypical of the time period in which the event(s) being studied would normally occur.

time series Set of numerical data values recorded for a single variable over time usually at regular intervals. *See also* moving average.

total response rate The total number of responses divided by the total number in the sample after ineligible respondents have been excluded. *See* ineligible respondent. *See also* active response rate, break off, complete response, complete refusal, partial response.

trade journal Journal produced by a trade organisation for its members, often containing articles of a practical nature related to the trade's needs. Articles in trade journals are usually not refereed.

traditional access Use of face-to-face interactions, correspondence for postal questionnaires, 'phone conversations or visits to data archives to conduct research.

transcript The written record of what a participant (or respondent) said in response to a question, or what participants (or respondents) said to one another in conversation, in their own words.

transcript summary Type of summary produced following the transcription of an interview or observation and used as an analytical aid. *See also* document summary; interim summary.

triangulation The use of two or more independent sources of data or data-collection methods within one study in order to help ensure that the data are telling you what you think they are telling you.

trimmed mean A mean calculated after extreme values (known as outliers) have been excluded.

t-**test** *see* independent groups *t*-test, paired *t*-test.

Type I error Error made by wrongly coming to the decision that something is true when in reality it is not.

Type II error Error made by wrongly coming to the decision that something is not true when in reality it is.

type of access Way used to gaining access to conduct research. *See also* Internet-mediated access, intranet-mediated access, hybrid access, traditional access.

typical case sampling A purposive sampling method which focuses on selecting cases on the basis that they are typical or illustrative. *See also* purposive sampling.

U

uninformed response Tendency for a respondent to deliberately guess where they have sufficient knowledge or experience to answer a question.

unitising data The process of attaching relevant 'bits' or 'chunks' of your data to the appropriate category or categories that you have devised.

unit of data A number of words, a line of a transcript, a sentence, a number of sentences, a complete paragraph, or some other single chunk of textual data or visual image that will be coded. See *also* code, coding.

unreachable respondent Respondent selected for a sample who cannot be located or who cannot be contacted.

unstructured interview Loosely structured and informally conducted interview that may commence with one or more themes to explore with participants but without a predetermined list of questions to work through. *See also* informant interview.

upper quartile The value above which a quarter of the data values lie when the data values for a variable have been ranked.

URL Uniform resource locator specifying where a known resource can be found.

V

validity (1) The extent to which data collection method or methods accurately measure what they were intended to measure. (2) The extent to which research findings are really about what they profess to be about. *See also* construct validity, criterion related validity, ecological validity, face validity, internal validity, measurement validity, predictive validity.

variable Individual element or attribute upon which data have been collected.

variance Statistic that measures the spread of data values; a measure of dispersion. The smaller the variance, the closer individual data values are to the mean. The value of the variance is the square of the standard deviation. *See also* dispersion measures, standard deviation.

variance inflation factor (VIF) Statistic used to measure collinearity *see* collinearity.

videography (1) the process of recording moving images onto electronic media; (2) the ethnographic analysis of recorded video sequences.

VIF *see* variance inflation factor.

virtual access The initial level of gaining access to online communities to conduct research. *See also* cognitive access, continuing access, gatekeeper.

visual aid Item such as an overhead projector slide, whiteboard, video recording or handout that is designed to enhance professional presentation and the learning of the audience.

W

web log *see* blog.

Web questionnaire Data collection technique in which the questionnaire is delivered electronically to each respondent's email address. She or he then reads and answers the same set of questions in a predetermined order without an interviewer being present before returning it electronically. *See also* online questionnaire.

weighting The process by which data values are adjusted to reflect differences in the proportion of the population that each case represents.

within-subjects design Experimental design using only a single group where every participant is exposed to the planned intervention or series of interventions. *See also* experiment, between-subjects design.